For the professor

- **Teaching Resources** provide material contributed by professors throughout the world–including teaching tips, techniques, academic papers, and sample syllabi–and **Talk to the Team**, a moderated faculty chat room.
- **Online Faculty Support** includes downloadable supplements, additional cases, articles, links, and suggested answers to Current Events Activities.
- **What's New** gives you one-click access to all newly posted PHLIP resources.

For the student

- **Talk to the Tutor** schedules virtual office hours that allow students to post questions from any supported discipline and receive responses from the dedicated PHLIP/CW faculty team.
- **Writing Resource Center** provides an online writing center that supplies links to online directories, thesauruses, writing tutors, style and grammar guides, and additional tools.
- **Career Center** helps students access career information, view sample résumés, even apply for jobs online.
- **Study Tips** provides an area where students can learn to develop better study skills.

ONLINE LEARNING SOLUTIONS
IN BLACKBOARD, WEBCT, AND PEARSON COURSECOMPASS

STANDARD COURSES
(Free with New Text Purchase) Standard courses include traditional online course features:

• Online Testing	• Multiple-Section Chat Rooms
• Course Management and Page Tracking	• Bulletin Board Conferencing
• Gradebook	• Syllabus and Calendar Functions
• Course Information	• E-mail Capability

WWW.PRENHALL.COM/HORNGREN

INTRODUCTION TO MANAGEMENT ACCOUNTING

Charles T. Horngren Series in Accounting
Charles T. Horngren, Consulting Editor

Auditing: An Integrated Approach, 8/E
Arens/Loebbecke

Financial Statement Analysis, 2/E
Foster

Governmental and Nonprofit Accounting: Theory & Practice, 6/E
Freeman/Shoulders

Financial Accounting, 4/E
Harrison/Horngren

Cases in Financial Reporting, 3/E
Hirst/McAnally

Cost Accounting: A Managerial Emphasis, 10/E
Horngren/Foster/Datar

Accounting, 5/E
Horngren/Harrison/Bamber

Introduction to Financial Accounting, 8/E
Horngren/Sundem/Elliott

Introduction to Management Accounting, 12/E
Horngren/Sundem/Stratton

INTRODUCTION TO MANAGEMENT ACCOUNTING

Twelfth Edition

CHARLES T. HORNGREN
Stanford University

GARY L. SUNDEM
University of Washington—Seattle

WILLIAM O. STRATTON
Pepperdine University

PRENTICE HALL, *Upper Saddle River, New Jersey 07458*

Library of Congress Cataloging-in-Publication Data

Horngren, Charles T., 1926–
    Introduction to management accounting/Charles T. Horngren, Gary L. Sundem,
William O. Stratton.—13th ed.
        p. cm.
    Includes index.
    ISBN 0-13-032373-X
    1. Managerial accounting. I. Sundem, Gary L. II. Stratton, William O. III. Title.

HF5635 .H814 2002
658.15'11—dc21

2001036121

Executive Editor: Deborah Hoffman
Editor-in-Chief: P. J. Boardman
Senior Editorial Assistant: Jane Avery
Associate Editor: Kathryn Sheehan
Media Project Manager: Nancy Welcher
Executive Marketing Manager: Beth Toland
Marketing Assistant: Brian Rappelfeld
Managing Editor (Production): Cynthia Regan
Production Editor: Michael Reynolds
Production Assistant: Dianne Falcone
Permissions Supervisor: Suzanne Grappi
Associate Director, Manufacturing: Vincent Scelta
Production Manager: Arnold Vila
Accounting Hotline Customer Service Representative: Walter Mendez
Design Manager: Patricia Smythe
Interior Design/Cover Design/Photo Montage: Michael J. Fruhbeis
Photo Credits: David R. Frazier/*Photo Researchers Inc.;* Randy Wells/*Stone;* Siegfried
Layda/*Stone;* Brad Rickerby/*Stone;* Jeremy Woodhouse/*Photodisc;* Mark Segal/*Stone;*
Corbis Digital Stock
Associate Director, Multimedia Production: Karen Goldsmith
Manager, Multimedia Production: Christy Mahon
Print Production Liaison: Ashley Scattergood
Composition: Progressive Information Technologies
Full-Service Project Management: Progressive Publishing Alternatives
Printer/Binder: R. R. Donnelley, Willard
Cover Printer: Phoenix Color

Credits and acknowledgments borrowed from other sources and reproduced, with permission, in this textbook appear on appropriate page within text or on page P1.

10 9 8 7 6 5 4 3
ISBN 0-13-032373-X

Charles T. Horngren (center) is the Edmund W. Littlefield Professor of Accounting, Emeritus, at Stanford University. A graduate of Marquette University, he received his MBA from Harvard University and his Ph.D. from the University of Chicago. He is also the recipient of honorary doctorates from Marquette University and DePaul University.

A Certified Public Accountant, Horngren served on the Accounting Principles Board for six years, the Financial Accounting Standards Board Advisory Council for five years, and the Council of the American Institute of Certified Public Accountants for three years. For six years, he served as a trustee of the Financial Accounting Foundation, which oversees the Financial Accounting Standards Board and the Government Accounting Standards Board.

Horngren is a member of the Accounting Hall of Fame.

A member of the American Accounting Association, Horngren has been its President and its Director of Research. He received its first annual Outstanding Accounting Educator Award.

The California Certified Public Accountants Foundation gave Horngren its Faculty Excellence Award and its Distinguished Professor Award. He is the first person to have received both awards.

The American Institute of Certified Public Accountants presented its first Outstanding Educator Award to Horngren.

Horngren was named Accountant of the Year, Education, by the national professional accounting fraternity, Beta Alpha Psi.

Professor Horngren is also a member of the Institute of Management Accountants, where he has received its Distinguished Service Award. He was a member of the Institute's Board of Regents, which administers the Certified Management Accountant examinations.

Horngren is the author of other accounting books published by Prentice-Hall: *Cost Accounting: A Managerial Emphasis,* Tenth Edition, 2000 (with George Foster and Srikant Datar); *Introduction to Financial Accounting,* Eighth Edition, 2002 (with Gary L. Sundem and John A. Elliott); *Accounting,* Fifth Edition, 2002 (with Walter T. Harrison, Jr., and Linda Bamber); and *Financial Accounting,* Fourth Edition, 2001 (with Walter T. Harrison, Jr.).

Horngren is the Consulting Editor for the Charles T. Horngren Series in Accounting.

Gary L. Sundem (left) is the Julius A. Roller Professor of Accounting and Associate Dean at the University of Washington, Seattle. He received his B.A. degree from Carleton College and his MBA and Ph.D. degrees from Stanford University.

Professor Sundem was the 1992–93 President of the American Accounting Association. He was Executive Director of the Accounting Education Change Commission, 1989–91, and served as Editor of *The Accounting Review,* 1982–86.

A member of the Institute of Management Accountants, Sundem is past president of the Seattle chapter. He has served on IMA's national Board of Directors, and chaired its Academic Relations and Professional Development Committees.

Professor Sundem has numerous publications in accounting and finance journals including *Issues in Accounting Education, The Accounting Review, Journal of Accounting Research,* and *The Journal of Finance.* He was selected as the Outstanding Accounting Educator by the American Accounting Association in 1998 and by the Washington Society of CPAs in 1987. He has made more than 200 presentations at universities in the United States and abroad.

William O. Stratton (right) is Professor of Accounting at Pepperdine University. He received B.S. degrees from Florida State University and Pennsylvania State University, his MBA from Boston University, and his Ph.D. from the Claremont Graduate University.

A Certified Management Accountant, Stratton has lectured extensively at management accounting conferences in North America, South America, and Europe. He has developed and delivered professional workshops on activity-based management and performance achievement to manufacturing and service organizations throughout the United States and South America. In 1993, Professor Stratton was awarded the Boeing Competition prize for classroom innovation.

Stratton has numerous publications in accounting and international business journals including *Management Accounting, Decision Sciences, IIE Transactions,* and *Synergie.*

BRIEF CONTENTS

PART FIVE   BASIC FINANCIAL ACCOUNTING

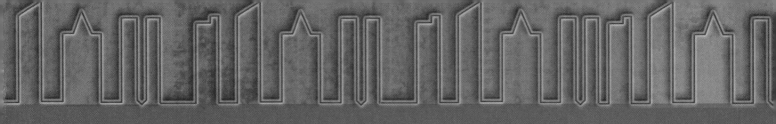

CONTENTS

PART TWO   ACCOUNTING FOR PLANNING AND CONTROL

PART THREE   CAPITAL BUDGETING

PART FOUR   PRODUCT COSTING

PART FIVE   BASIC FINANCIAL ACCOUNTING

PREFACE

"Managers have to understand how their decisions affect costs if they want to make good decisions."

Introduction to Management Accounting, 12/E, takes the view that managers make important economic decisions. We want students to view management accounting as an essential tool that enhances managers' abilities to make good economic decisions. *IMA,* 12/E, describes the concepts and techniques that managers and accountants use to produce information for decision making. Because understanding concepts is more important than memorizing techniques, this book introduces the concepts together with the techniques. From the first chapter, students are encouraged to think about why techniques are used, not to blindly apply the techniques. We hope that students will thus be able to learn both the *theory* and *practice* of management accounting. Understanding today's accounting practice, though, goes beyond mere concepts and techniques. To illustrate real-world practice and to highlight how management accounting helps managers understand the potential impacts of their decisions, the concepts and techniques in this book are presented in the context of real decisions. Two of the authors were members of the Accounting Education Change Commission (AECC) and recommendations of the AECC have been implemented throughout the text.

This book attempts a balanced, flexible approach. It deals as much with nonprofit, retail, wholesale, selling, and administrative situations as it does with manufacturing. It focuses broadly on planning and control decisions, not on product costing for inventory valuation and income determination.

OUR PHILOSOPHY

Introduce the simple concepts and principles early, revisit them at more complex levels as students gain understanding, and provide appropriate real-company examples at every stage.

Just as management accounting builds on financial accounting, the concepts within management accounting build on one another as they are used to facilitate managerial decision making. Once students have fully grasped the more basic concepts, they can then build on what they have learned and progress on to more complex topics. Students begin their understanding of managerial decision making by asking, "How will my decisions affect the costs and revenues of the organization?" and then progress to more complex questions: What is the most appropriate cost management system for the company? What products should we produce? What do our budget variances mean? As students absorb the simpler concepts and techniques of management accounting and move on to the more complex, they will become more comfortable with, and more adept at, using those concepts and techniques to make business decisions.

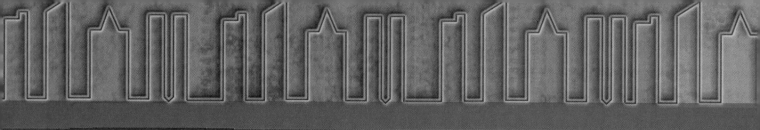

Our goals have been to choose relevant subject matter and to present it clearly and accessibly, using many examples drawn from actual companies. *IMA*, 12/E, stresses the understanding of concepts, yet makes them concrete with numerous illustrations.

WHO SHOULD USE THIS BOOK?

Introduction to Management Accounting, 12/E, is primarily for students who have had one or two terms of basic accounting. It is also appropriate for continuing educational programs of varying lengths in which the students have had no formal training in accounting. The four financial accounting chapters (Chapters 16–19) make the book especially appropriate for short courses introducing managers to accounting because both financial and management accounting can be presented from a user's perspective without requiring two textbooks.

This text is oriented to managers who use management accounting reports, not accountants. Managers should understand the basics of management accounting, and this book shows how management accounting will be useful to them. However, *IMA*, 12/E, also pays ample attention to the needs of potential accountants and provides them with an understanding of how the reports they produce will be used by decision makers. In focusing on accounting within the context of the overall managerial function, this text covers important topics that all business students should study and demonstrates how accounting bolsters and fits into the broader scheme of today's business environment.

NEW AND RETAINED FEATURES

- **NEW and revised Chapter Opening Vignettes with "On Location!" Videos.** Chapter openers help students understand accounting's role in current business practice. "On Location!" video segments, specially produced for this text, reinforce and expand upon chapter openers. New segments include Three Dog Bakery, Nantucket Nectars, Oracle, and Teva Sandals.
- **NEW "Take 5's".** Study Breaks appear throughout each chapter and encourage students to stop and think about material just read. Answers immediately follow.
- **NEW Cognitive Exercises.** Based on focus group feedback, short cognitive exercises serve as critical-thinking "warm-ups" to more complex case material.
- **NEW and revised Business First Boxes.** Provide insights into operations at well-known domestic and international companies, including technology and e-Commerce companies.
- *Introduction to Financial Accounting* 8/e and its companion text, *Introduction to Management Accounting* 12/e, provide a seamless presentation for any first year accounting course. Please ask your Prentice Hall representative about cost-saving discounts when you adopt and package both books together.

ONLINE AND TECHNOLOGY SOLUTIONS

- **myPHLIP** offers FREE one-click, personalized access to free Web resources for faculty and students. Resources include chapter-by-chapter current events, Internet resources and hotlinks, online study guide, online tutor, and much more! Go to www.prenhall.com/myphlip and register today.

- **NEW Online courses** available in WebCT, Blackboard, and Pearson CourseCompass, Prentice Hall's nationally hosted solution.
- **NEW Student CD-ROM** contains tutorial software, Spreadsheet Templates, and PowerPoints.
- **NEW Instructor Resource CD-ROM** contains all print and technology supplements so that instructors can provide seamless classroom presentations.
- **NEW Mastering Accounting CD-ROM**
  Allows students to watch professionally written, acted, and filmed videos about a fictional Internet start-up company to see how accounting concepts are related to workplace events and challenges.

UPDATED MATERIAL INCLUDES:

- Expanded discussion of ABC and ABM in chapter 4, including both two-stage and multi-stage ABC. New structure introduced to describe traditional and ABC systems.
- Complete revision of "Opportunity, Outlay, and Differential Costs" in chapter 6.
- Expanded discussion of Balanced Scorecard in chapter 9 with emphasis on the importance of intellectual capital and learning as a driver of competitiveness. Includes new illustration using General Electric.
- Expanded discussion of economic value added (EVA) in chapter 10, with real world company illustrations, and end-of-chapter exercises and problems.
- Chapter 12 uses new illustrations to present general guidelines for allocation, step-down allocation methods for service departments, joint-cost allocation, two-stage ABC allocation, and multi-stage ABC allocation.
- New structure in chapter 14 compares job-order and process costing and applies material to Planters Specialty Peanut Company.

SUPPLEMENTS FOR INSTRUCTORS

NEW INSTRUCTOR RESOURCE CD-ROM (SEE DESCRIPTION UNDER "ONLINE AND TECHNOLOGY SOLUTIONS")

INSTRUCTOR'S RESOURCE MANUAL BY SCOTT YETMAR (DRAKE UNIVERISITY) Contains chapter overviews, chapter outlines organized by objectives, teaching tips, chapter quiz, transparency masters derived from textbook exhibits, and suggested readings each chapter of the text.

SOLUTIONS MANUAL AND SOLUTIONS TRANSPARENCIES BY TEXT AUTHORS Special thanks to Robert Bauman, Allan Hancock College, and to Rosalie C. Hallbauer, Florida International University, for their technical reviews.

TEST ITEM FILE BY ANNE WESSLEY   The Test Item File includes multiple choice, true/false, exercises, comprehensive problems, short answer problems, critical thinking essay questions, etc. Each test item is tied to the corresponding learning objective, has an assigned difficulty level, and provides a page reference.

PRENTICE HALL WINDOWS CUSTOM TEST MANAGER, BY ENGINEERING SOFTWARE ASSOCIATES (ESA), INC.   This easy-to-use computerized testing program can create exams, evaluate, and track student results. The PH Test Manager also provides on-line testing capabilities. You may ***call 1-800-550-1701, our Test Paper Preparation Center,*** to have a hardcopy of your custom test created to suit your classroom needs.

ON LOCATION! CUSTOM VIDEO LIBRARY BY BEVERLY AMER (NORTHERN ARIZONA UNIVERSITY)   Highlighted companies include Three Dog Bakery, Nantucket Nectars, Oracle, Teva Sport Sandals, Dell, etc. A Video Guide in the Instructor's Resource Manual helps integrate the videos into your classroom lectures.

SUPPLEMENTS FOR STUDENTS

STUDY GUIDE BY FRANK SELTO (UNIVERSITY OF COLORADO AT BOULDER)
For each chapter of the text, the study guide contains a chapter overview, a detailed chapter review including study tips, self-test questions and demonstration problems with worked-out solutions. Special thanks to Mary Sheets, University of Central Oklahoma, for technical assistance.

STUDENT RESOURCE CD-ROM   All student software programs, from Power-Points to ReEnforcer, tutorial available on one CD-ROM.

ADDITIONAL RESOURCES

New WALL STREET JOURNAL offer: 10 weeks for $10.00 net with new student texts.

ACTIVITIES IN MANAGEMENT ACCOUNTING BY MARTHA DORAN

Free eBIZ FOR ACCOUNTING booklet may be packaged with new student texts.

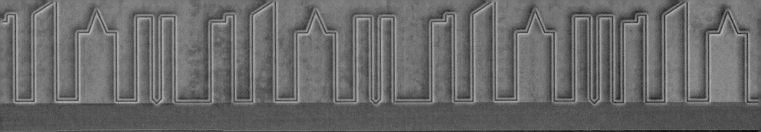

ACKNOWLEDGMENTS

We have received ideas, assistance, miscellaneous critiques, and assorted assignment material in conversations and by mail from many students, professors, and business leaders. Each has our gratitude, but the complete list is too long to enumerate here.

Steven V. Campbell, University of Alaska-Anchorage
C. Douglas Cloud, Pepperdine University
Kenneth P. Couvillion, San Joaquin Delta College
Susan Cox, University of South Florida
Kreag Danvers, Indiana University of Pennsylvania
Cindy K. Harris, Ursinus College
Leon Korte, University of South Dakota
Julie A. Lockhart, Western Washington University
Cheryl E. Mitchem, Virginia State University
Shirish B. Seth, California State University-Fullerton
Donald R. Simons, University of Wisconsin-Oshkosh
Kim B. Tan, California State University-Stanislaus
James E. Williamson, San Diego State University
Peter Woodlock, Youngstown State University

The Chapters 4 and 12 illustrations of activity-based costing and the Chapter 9 illustration of a management control system are based (in part) on cases developed by Hyperion Solutions. Derek Sandison of Hyperion Solutions provided useful suggestions for these illustrations.

Kim Sawers provided help in proofing.

And, finally our thanks to P.J. Boardman, Deborah Hoffman, Jane Avery, Beth Toland, Vincent Scelta, Richard Bretan, Pat Smythe, Kathryn Sheehan, Brian Rappelfeld, Arnold Vila, Michael Reynolds, Michael Fruhbeis, Christy Mahon, Nancy Welcher, and Walter Mendez at Prentice Hall.

Comments from readers are welcome.

Charles T. Horngren
Gary L. Sundem
William O. Stratton

1

MANAGERIAL ACCOUNTING & THE BUSINESS ORGANIZATION

Managers at companies work closely with accountants. The accounting system crunches the numbers that these managers need for daily decision making.

www.prenhall.com/horngren

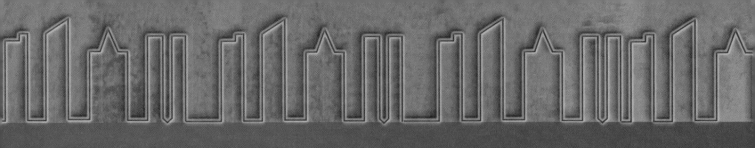

Learning Objectives

When you have finished studying this chapter, you should be able to

1. Describe the major users of accounting information.

2. Explain the cost-benefit and behavioral issues involved in designing an accounting system.

3. Explain the role of budgets and performance reports in planning and control.

4. Discuss the role accountants play in the company's value chain functions.

5. Contrast the functions of controllers and treasurers.

6. Identify current trends in management accounting.

7. Explain a management accountant's ethical responsibilities.

8. **Understand how managerial accounting is used in companies.***

The Internet is hot, hot, hot! One recent study revealed that the Internet economy grew to more than $525 billion in 2000, and now directly supports 2.5 million workers. Businesses are scrambling to establish virtual stores. Educational institutions now offer virtual degrees and certifications. And with the click of a mouse, in an instant anyone can find music, e-mail, news articles, and more! Soon we'll be able to access the Internet wherever and whenever we want, for any purpose at all. There's no question that this economy is unlike any we've ever seen. Yet it couldn't exist without the services and products of companies like Cisco Systems.

Cisco is the worldwide leader in networking for the Internet. The company's router products connect people, computers, and computer networks around the globe and help form the infrastructure for the Internet. Cisco shipped its first products in 1986 and has seen its annual revenues explode to over $12 billion in the most recent fiscal year. Last year alone the company acquired 15 smaller firms to fuel its growth and today shows no sign of slowing down. How does Cisco keep track of it all? Accounting systems do the heavy job of "crunching" all the transaction details, yet there are analysts, accountants, and staff operating those systems each day. Managers at all levels rely on the information those systems provide for daily decision making, budgeting, and planning. And since Cisco is a publicly held company, the accounting systems and employees must be prepared to generate financial reports quickly and accurately for use by external decision makers around the globe.

---

* The last learning objective in each chapter is an overall objective. It stresses the importance of understanding the material covered throughout the chapter; therefore, it is not identified at a specific point in the text.

As you embark on your journey into the world of managerial accounting, you'll discover what it takes for a company like Cisco to be able to manage its financial activities and make decisions with ease. And keep this in mind: Every business that's part of the Internet economy has traveled the same path, and manages the same set of accounting information.

Just as the case at Cisco, managerial accounting can help managers in all types of organizations answer vital questions. Consider questions raised in the following situations:

- Boeing engineers have prepared manufacturing specifications for a new airplane, the 747-X. There are three possible ways to organize the assembly of the plane. Which is the most cost-effective approach?

- A product manager at Kellogg's is designing a new marketing plan for Frosted Flakes. Market research predicts that distributing free samples in the mail will increase annual sales by 4%. How will the cost of the free samples (including the cost of distributing them) compare with the profits from the added sales?

- University National Bank offers free checking to customers who keep a minimum balance of $600 in their account. How much does it cost the bank to provide this free service?

- Kitsap County Special Olympics holds a series of athletic events for disabled youth. How much money must be raised in the group's annual fund drive to support its planned activities?

- Chez Bonaparte is a dinner-only restaurant located in a middle-class neighborhood. The proprietor is considering opening for lunch. To be competitive, the average lunch must be priced about $7, and about 40 patrons can be served. Can the restaurant produce a lunch that meets its quality standards at an average cost of less than $7?

- The Monroe County School District is negotiating with the teachers' union. Among the issues are teachers' salaries, class size, and number of extracurricular activities offered. The union and the district have both made several proposals. How much will each of the various proposals cost? If class size were to increase by one student per class, what would be the added cost, and would these costs differ for elementary, junior high, and high school levels?

In answering these and a wide variety of other questions, managers turn to management accountants for information. In this chapter, we consider the purposes and roles of accounting and accountants in different types of organizations as well as some of the trends and challenges faced by accountants today.

ACCOUNTING AND DECISION MAKING

The basic purpose of accounting information is helping someone make decisions. That someone may be a company president, a production manager, a hospital or school administrator, an investor—the list could go on and on. Regardless of who is making the decision, the understanding of accounting information allows for a more informed, and better, decision.

USERS OF ACCOUNTING INFORMATION

In general, users of accounting information fall into three categories.

1. Internal managers who use the information for short-term planning and controlling routine operations.
2. Internal managers who use the information for making nonroutine decisions (for example, investing in equipment, pricing products and services, choosing which products to emphasize or de-emphasize) and formulating overall policies and long-range plans.
3. External parties, such as investors and government authorities, who use the information for making decisions about the company.

Both internal parties (managers) and external parties use accounting information, but the ways in which they use it differ. The types of accounting information they demand may also differ. Management accounting refers to accounting information developed for managers within an organization. In other words, **management accounting** is the process of identifying, measuring, accumulating, analyzing, preparing, interpreting, and communicating information that helps managers fulfill organizational objectives. In contrast, **financial accounting** refers to accounting information developed for the use of external parties such as stockholders, suppliers, banks, and government regulatory agencies.[1] The major differences between management accounting and financial accounting are listed in Exhibit 1-1. Despite these differences, most organizations prefer a general-purpose accounting system that meets the needs of all three types of users.

What are the needs or uses? Good accounting information helps an organization achieve its goals and objectives by helping to answer three types of questions.

1. *Scorecard questions:* Am I doing well or poorly? **Scorekeeping** is the accumulation and classification of data. This aspect of accounting enables both internal and external parties to evaluate organizational performance.
2. *Attention-directing questions:* Which problems should I look into? **Attention directing** means reporting and interpreting information that helps managers to focus on operating problems, imperfections, inefficiencies, and opportunities. Attention directing is commonly associated with current planning and control, and with the analysis and investigation of recurring routine internal accounting reports.
3. *Problem-solving questions:* Of the several ways of doing a job, which is the best? The **problem-solving** aspect of accounting quantifies the likely results of possible courses of action and often recommends the best course to follow.

The scorecard and attention-directing uses of information are closely related. The same information may serve a scorecard function for a manager and an attention-directing function for the manager's superior. For example, many accounting systems provide performance reports in which actual results of decisions and activities are compared with previously determined plans. By pinpointing where actual results differ from plans, such performance reports can show managers how they are doing and show the managers' superiors where to take action.

In contrast, problem-solving information may be used in long-range planning and in making special, nonrecurring decisions, such as whether to make or buy parts, replace equipment, or add or drop a product. These decisions often require expert advice from specialists such as industrial engineers, budgetary accountants, and statisticians.

---

[1] *For a book-length presentation of the subject, see Charles T. Horngren, Gary L. Sundem, and John A. Elliott, Introduction to Financial Accounting (Upper Saddle River, NJ: Prentice Hall, 2001), the companion to this textbook.*

Objective 1
Describe the major users of accounting information.

management accounting The process of identifying, measuring, accumulating, analyzing, preparing, interpreting, and communicating information that helps managers fulfill organizational objectives.

financial accounting The field of accounting that develops information for external decision makers such as stockholders, suppliers, banks, and government regulatory agencies.

scorekeeping The accumulation and classification of data.

attention directing Reporting and interpreting information that helps managers to focus on operating problems, imperfections, inefficiencies, and opportunities.

problem solving The aspect of accounting that quantifies the likely results of possible courses of action and often recommends the best course of action to follow.

Exhibit 1-1

Distinctions Between Management Accounting and Financial Accounting

	Management Accounting	Financial Accounting
Primary users	Organization managers at various levels.	Outside parties such as investors and government agencies but also organization managers.
Freedom of choice	No constraints other than costs in relation to benefits of improved management decisions.	Constrained by generally accepted accounting principles (GAAP).
Behavioral implications	Concern about how measurements and reports will influence managers' daily behavior.	Concern about how to measure and communicate economic phenomena. Behavioral considerations are secondary, although executive compensation based on reported results may have behavioral impacts.
Time focus	Future orientation: formal use of budgets as well as historical records, Example: 20X2 budget versus 20X2 actual performance.	Past orientation: historical evaluation. Example: 20X2 actual performance versus 20X1 actual performance.
Time span	Flexible, varying from hourly to 10 to 15 years.	Less flexible; usually 1 year or 1 quarter.
Reports	Detailed reports: concern about details of parts of the entity, products, departments, territories, etc.	Summary reports: concern primarily with entity as a whole.
Delineation of activities	Field is less sharply defined. Heavier use of economics, decision sciences, and behavioral sciences.	Field is more sharply defined. Lighter use of related disciplines.

ACCOUNTING SYSTEMS

accounting system A formal mechanism for gathering, organizing, and communicating information about an organization's activities.

An **accounting system** is a formal mechanism for gathering, organizing, and communicating information about an organization's activities. Using one accounting system for both financial and management purposes sometimes creates problems. External forces (for example, income tax authorities and regulatory bodies such as the U.S. Securities and Exchange Commission and the California Health Facility Commission) often limit management's choices of accounting methods for external reports. Many organizations develop systems primarily to satisfy legal requirements imposed by external parties. These systems often neglect the needs of internal users.

generally accepted accounting principles (GAAP) Broad concepts or guidelines and detailed practices, including all conventions, rules, and procedures, that together make up accepted accounting practice at a given time.

Consider the annual financial reports by public corporations. These reports must adhere to a set of standards known as **generally accepted accounting principles (GAAP).** GAAP includes broad concepts or guidelines and detailed practices, including all conventions, rules, and procedures, that together make up accepted accounting practice at a given time. However, internal accounting reports need not be restricted by GAAP. For instance, GAAP requires that organizations account for their assets (economic resources) according to their historical cost. For its own management purposes, however, an organization can account for its economic resources on the basis of their current values, as measured by estimates of replacement costs. No outside agency can prohibit such accounting. Managers can create whatever kind of internal accounting system they want—provided they are willing to pay the cost of developing and operating the system.

Of course, satisfying internal demands for information (as well as external demands) means that organizations may have to keep more than one set of records. At least in the United States, there is nothing immoral or unethical about having simultaneous sets of books—but they are expensive. Because external financial reports are required by authorities, many organizations do not choose to invest in a separate system for internal management purposes. Managers are thus forced to use information designed to meet external users' needs instead of information designed for their specific decisions.

EFFECTS OF GOVERNMENT REGULATION

Even when management is willing to pay for a separate internal accounting system, that system may be affected by government regulation. The reason is that government agencies have legal power to order into evidence any internal document that they deem necessary.

Universities and defense contractors, for example, must allocate costs to government contracts in specified ways or risk government's refusal to pay. For example, in a widely publicized case in the early 1990s, Stanford University and several other prominent universities were denied reimbursement for certain costs that the government deemed inappropriate.

The **Foreign Corrupt Practices Act** is a U.S. law forbidding bribery and other corrupt practices. This law also requires that accounting records be maintained in reasonable detail and accuracy, and that an appropriate system of internal accounting controls be maintained. The title is misleading because the act's provisions apply to all publicly held companies, even if they conduct no business outside the United States.

The greatest impact of the act on accounting systems stems from the requirement that management must document the adequacy of internal accounting controls. As a result, many companies have greatly increased their internal auditing staffs and have elevated the status of such staffs. Often the internal audit staff reports directly to the president, sometimes even to the board of directors.

Internal auditors help review and evaluate systems to help minimize errors, fraud, and waste. More important, many internal auditing staffs have a primary responsibility for conducting management audits. A **management audit** is a review to determine whether the policies and procedures specified by top management have been implemented. Management audits are not confined to profit-seeking organizations. The General Accounting Office (GAO) of the U.S. government conducts these audits on a massive scale. Most states also have audit agencies that audit departments of state government. Some also audit municipalities and other local government organizations.

The overall impact of government regulation is very controversial. Many managers insist that the extra costs of compliance far exceed any possible benefits. One benefit, however, is that operating managers, now more than ever, must become more intimately familiar with their accounting systems. The resulting changes in the systems sometimes provide stronger controls and more informative reports.

Foreign Corrupt Practices Act U.S. law forbidding bribery and other corrupt practices, and requiring that accounting records be maintained in reasonable detail and accuracy, and that an appropriate system of internal accounting controls be maintained.

management audit A review to determine whether the policies and procedures specified by top management have been implemented.

The scorekeeping, attention-directing, and problem-solving duties of the accountant are described in this chapter. The accountant's usefulness to management is said to be directly influenced by how good an attention director and problem solver he or she is. We can evaluate this contention by specifically relating the accountant's duties to the duties of operating management. Operating managers may have to be good scorekeepers, but their major duties are to concentrate on the day-to-day problems that need the most attention, to make longer-range plans, and to arrive at special decisions. Accordingly, because managers are concerned mainly with attention directing and problem solving, they will obtain the most benefit from the alert internal accountant who is a useful attention director and problem solver.

MANAGEMENT ACCOUNTING IN SERVICE AND NONPROFIT ORGANIZATIONS

The basic ideas of management accounting were developed in manufacturing organizations. These ideas, however, have evolved so that they apply to all types of organizations including service organizations. Service organizations, for our purposes, are all organizations other than manufacturers, wholesalers, and retailers. That is, they are organizations that do not make or sell tangible goods. Public accounting firms, law firms, management consultants, real estate firms, transportation companies, banks, insurance companies, and hotels are profit-seeking service organizations.

Almost all nonprofit organizations, such as hospitals, schools, libraries, museums, and government agencies, are also service organizations. Managers and accountants in nonprofit organizations have much in common with their counterparts in profit-seeking organizations. There is money to be raised and spent. There are budgets to be prepared and control systems to be designed and implemented. There is an obligation to use resources wisely. If used intelligently, accounting contributes to efficient operations and helps nonprofit organizations achieve their objectives.

The characteristics of both profit-seeking and nonprofit service organizations include the following:

1. *Labor is intensive:* The highest proportion of expenses in schools and law firms are wages, salaries, and payroll-related costs, not the costs relating to the use of machinery, equipment, and physical facilities.

2. *Output is usually difficult to define:* The output of a university might be defined as the number of degrees granted, but many critics would maintain that the real output is "what is contained in the students' brains." Therefore, measuring output is often considered impossible.

3. *Major inputs and outputs cannot be stored:* An empty airline seat cannot be saved for a later flight, and a hotel's available labor force and rooms are either used or unused as each day occurs.

Simplicity is the watchword for installation of systems in service industries and nonprofit organizations. In fact, many professionals such as physicians, professors, or government officials resist even filling out a time card. In fact, simplicity is a fine watchword for the design of any accounting system. Complexity tends to generate costs of gathering and interpreting data that often exceed prospective benefits. Concern for simplicity is sometimes expressed as KISS (which means "keep it simple, stupid," or, better yet, "keep it simple for success").

COST-BENEFIT AND BEHAVIORAL CONSIDERATIONS

In addition to simplicity, managers should keep two other ideas in mind when designing accounting systems: (1) cost-benefit balances and (2) behavioral implications.

cost-benefit balance
Weighing estimated costs against probable benefits, the primary consideration in choosing among accounting systems and methods.

The **cost-benefit balance**—weighing estimated costs against probable benefits—is the primary consideration in choosing among accounting systems and methods. Therefore, we will refer again and again to cost-benefit considerations throughout this book. For now, consider accounting systems to be economic goods—like office supplies or labor—available at various costs. Which system does a manager want to buy? A simple file drawer for amassing receipts and canceled checks? An elaborate budgeting system based on computerized models of the organization and its subunits? Or something in between?

The answer depends on the buyer's perceptions of the expected benefits in relation to the costs. For example, a hospital administrator may consider installing a ConTrol®-computerized system made by Advanced Medical Systems for controlling hospital operations.

Users of such a system need only enter a piece of information once and the system automatically incorporates it into *budgeting, purchasing, and payables records*. Such a system is highly efficient and is subject to few errors, but it costs $300,000. Is the ConTrol® system a good buy? That depends on its expected benefit. If its value to the hospital is greater than $300,000, then it is a good buy. If not, the administrator should consider another accounting system.

Objective 2
Explain the cost-benefit and behavioral issues involved in designing an accounting system.

The value of a loaf of bread may exceed a cost of $0.50 a loaf, but it may not exceed a cost of $5 per loaf. Similarly, a particular accounting system may be a wise investment if its cost is sufficiently small. Like a consumer who switches from bread to potatoes if the cost of bread is too high, managers seek other sources of information if accounting systems are too expensive. In many organizations it may be more economical to gather some kinds of data by one-shot special efforts than by a ponderous system that repetitively gathers rarely used data.

In addition to the costs and benefits of an accounting system, the buyer of such a system should also consider **behavioral implications,** that is, the system's effect on the behavior (decisions) of managers. The system must provide accurate, timely budgets and performance reports in a form useful to managers. If managers do not use accounting reports, the reports create no benefits.

behavioral implications The accounting system's effect on the behavior (decisions) of managers.

Management accounting reports affect employees' feelings and behavior. Consider a performance report that is used to evaluate the operations under the responsibility of a particular manager. If the report unfairly attributes excessive costs to the operation, the manager may lose confidence in the system and not let it influence future decisions. In contrast, a system that managers believe in and trust can be a major influence on their decisions and actions.

In a nutshell, management accounting can best be understood as a balance between costs and benefits of accounting information coupled with an awareness of the importance of behavioral effects. Even more than financial accounting, management accounting spills over into related disciplines, such as economics, the decision sciences, and the behavioral sciences.

THE MANAGEMENT PROCESS AND ACCOUNTING

Regardless of the type of organization, managers benefit when accounting provides information that helps them plan and control the organization's operations.

THE NATURE OF PLANNING AND CONTROLLING

The management process is a series of activities in a cycle of planning and control. **Decision making**—the purposeful choice from among a set of alternative courses of action designed to achieve some objective—is the core of the management process. Decisions range from the routine (making daily production schedules) to the nonroutine (launching a new product line).

decision making The purposeful choice from among a set of alternative courses of action designed to achieve some objective.

Decisions within an organization are often divided into two types: (1) planning decisions and (2) control decisions. In practice, planning and control are so intertwined that it seems artificial to separate them. In studying management, however, it is useful to concentrate on either the planning phase or the control phase to simplify the analysis.

The left side of Exhibit 1-2 demonstrates the planning and control cycle of current operations for The Chop House restaurant in Colorado Springs. Planning (the top box) refers to setting objectives and outlining how they will be attained. Thus, planning provides the answers to two questions: What is desired? When and how is it to be accomplished? For The Chop House, management desires to improve profitability. This will be accomplished by adding new entrees and improving advertising. In contrast, controlling (the box labeled "Actions" and "Evaluation") refers to implementing plans and using

Objective 3
Explain the role of budgets and performance reports in planning and control.

Exhibit 1-2

The Chop House Restaurant. Accounting Framework for Planning and Control

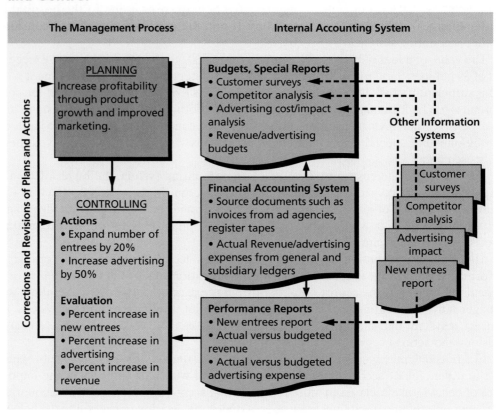

feedback to attain objectives. The Chop House will expand its menu offerings and expand advertising. The effectiveness of these actions will be evaluated based on selected performance measures such as the percent increase in new entrees. Feedback is crucial to the cycle of planning and control. Planning determines action, action generates feedback, and feedback influences further planning and actions. Timely, systematic reports provided by the internal accounting system are the chief source of useful feedback. None of this cycle would be possible without accounting.

MANAGEMENT BY EXCEPTION

The right side of Exhibit 1-2 shows that accounting formalizes plans by expressing them as budgets. A **budget** is a quantitative expression of a plan of action. The Chop House would express its plan for product growth and improved marketing through revenue and advertising budgets. Budgets are also an aid to coordinating and implementing plans. Budgets are the chief devices for compelling and disciplining management planning. Without budgets, planning may not get the front-and-center focus that it usually deserves.

The financial accounting system supports both planning and controlling and is a key source for **performance reports.** The accounting system records, measures, and classifies actions to produce performance reports. Accounting formalizes control as performance reports (the last box), which provide feedback by comparing results with plans and by highlighting **variances,** which are deviations from plans. For example, managers of The Chop House restaurant would evaluate the effectiveness of its advertising plan by comparing the percent increase in revenue to the percent increase in advertising. Based on their evaluation, managers at The Chop House would make corrections and revisions to their plans.

budget A quantitative expression of a plan of action, and an aid to coordinating and implementing the plan.

performance reports Feedback provided by comparing results with plans and by highlighting variances.

variances Deviations from plans.

Exhibit 1-3
Performance Report

	Budgeted Amounts	Actual Amounts	Deviations or Variances	Explanation
Revenue from fees	xxx	xxx	xx	—
Various expenses	xxx	xxx	xx	—
Net income	xxx	xxx	xx	—

Exhibit 1-3 shows a simple performance report for a law firm. Performance reports are used to judge decisions and the productivity of organizational units and managers. By comparing actual results to budgets, performance reports motivate managers to achieve the budgeted objectives.

Performance reports spur investigation of exceptions—items for which actual amounts differ significantly from budgeted amounts. Operations are then made to conform with the plans, or the plans are revised. This is often called **management by exception,** which means concentrating on areas that deviate from the plan and ignoring areas that are presumed to be running smoothly. Thus, the management-by-exception approach frees managers from needless concern with those phases of operations that are adhering to plans. However, well-conceived plans should incorporate enough discretion or flexibility so that the manager may feel free to pursue any unforeseen opportunities. In other words, control should not be a straightjacket. When unfolding events call for actions not specifically authorized in the plan, managers should be able to take these actions.

management by exception Concentrating on areas that deviate from the plan and ignoring areas that are presumed to be running smoothly.

ILLUSTRATION OF BUDGETS AND PERFORMANCE REPORTS

Suppose the Casaverde Company manufactures and sells electric fans. Consider the department that assembles the fans. Workers assemble the parts and install the motor largely by hand. They then inspect each fan before transferring it to the packaging and shipping department. The present sales forecast has led managers to plan a production schedule of 10,000 fans for the coming month. The assembly department budget in Exhibit 1-4 shows cost classifications.

The operating plan for the department, in the form of a department budget for the coming month, is prepared in conferences attended by the department manager, the manager's supervisor, and an accountant. They scrutinize each of the costs subject to the manager's control. They often use the average amount of the cost for the past few months as a

Exhibit 1-4
Casaverde Company
Assembly Department Budget for the Month Ended March 31, 20X1

Production activity	10,000 fans
Material (detailed by type: metal stampings, motors, and so on)	$ 68,000
Assembly labor (detailed by job classification, number of workers, and so on)	43,000
Other labor (managers, inspectors)	12,000
Utilities, maintenance, and so on	7,500
Supplies (small tools, lubricants, and so on)	2,500
Total	$133,000

Exhibit 1-5

Casaverde Company
Assembly Department Performance Report for the Month Ended March 31, 20X2

	Budget	Actual	Variance
Production activity in units	10,000	9,860	140 U
Material (detailed by type: metal stampings, motors, and so on)	$ 68,000	$ 69,000	$1,000 U
Assembly labor (detailed by job classification, number of workers, and so on)	43,000	44,300	1,300 U
Other labor (managers, inspectors)	12,000	11,200	800 F
Utilities, maintenance, and so on	7,500	7,400	100 F
Supplies (small tools, lubricants, and so on)	2,500	2,600	100 U
Total	$133,000	$134,500	$ 1,500 U

U = Unfavorable—actual exceeds budget
F = Favorable—actual is less than budget

guide, especially if past performance has been good. However, the budget is a forecast of costs for the projected level of production activity. Hence, conference members must predict each cost in light of trends, price changes, alterations in product mix and characteristics, production methods, and changes in the level of production activity from month to month. Only then can they formulate the budget that becomes the manager's target for the month.

As actual factory costs are incurred, Casaverde's accounting system collects them and classifies them by department. At the end of the month (or weekly, or even daily, for such key items as materials or assembly labor), the accounting department prepares an assembly department performance report. Exhibit 1-5 is a simplified report. In practice, this report may be very detailed and contain explanations of variances from the budget.

Department heads and their superiors use the performance report to help appraise how effectively and efficiently the department is operating. Their focus is on the variances—the deviations from the budget. Casaverde's assembly department performance report (Exhibit 1-5) shows that although the department produced 140 fewer fans than planned, material costs were $1,000 over budget, and assembly labor was $1,300 over budget. By investigating such variances, managers may find better ways of doing things.

Notice that although budgets aid planning and performance reports aid control, it is not accountants but other managers and their subordinates who evaluate accounting reports and actually plan and control operations. Accounting assists the managerial planning and control functions by providing prompt measurements of actions and by systematically pinpointing trouble spots.

PLANNING AND CONTROL FOR PRODUCT LIFE CYCLES AND THE VALUE CHAIN

product life cycle The various stages through which a product passes, from conception and development through introduction into the market through maturation and, finally, withdrawal from the market.

Many management decisions relate to a single good or service, or to a group of related products. To effectively plan for and control production of such goods or services, accountants and other managers must consider the product's life cycle. **Product life cycle** refers to the various stages through which a product passes, from conception and development through introduction into the market through maturation and, finally, withdrawal from the market. At each stage, managers face differing costs and potential returns. Exhibit 1-6 shows a typical product life cycle.

Product life cycles range from a few months (for fashion clothing or faddish toys) to many years (for automobiles or refrigerators). Some products, such as many computer software packages, have long development stages and relatively short market lives. Others, such as Boeing 777 airplanes, have market lives many times longer than their development stage.

Exhibit 1-6
Typical Product Life Cycle

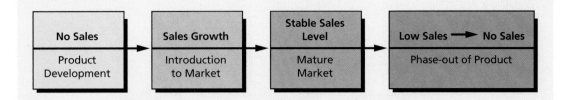

In the planning process, managers must recognize revenues and costs over the entire life cycle—however long or short. Accounting needs to track actual costs and revenues throughout the life cycle, too. Periodic comparisons between planned costs and revenues and actual costs and revenues allow managers to assess the current profitability of a product, determine its current product life-cycle stage, and make any needed changes in strategy.

For example, suppose a pharmaceutical company is developing a new drug to reduce high blood pressure. The budget for the product should plan for costs without revenues in the product development stage. Most of the revenues come in the introduction and mature-market stages, and a pricing strategy should recognize the need for revenues to cover both development and phase-out costs as well as the direct costs of producing the drug. During phase-out, costs of producing the drug must be balanced with both the revenue generated and the need to keep the drug on the market for those who have come to rely on it.

THE VALUE CHAIN

How does a company actually create the goods or services that it sells? Whether we are making donuts in a shopping mall or making $50 million airplanes, all organizations try to create goods or services that are valued by their customers. The **value chain** is the set of business functions that add value to the products or services of an organization. These functions are as follows:

value chain The set of business functions that add value to the products or services of an organization.

- *Research and development*—the generation of, and experimentation with, ideas related to new products, services, or processes.
- *Design of products, services, or processes*—the detailed design and engineering of products.
- *Production*—the coordination and assembly of resources to produce a product or deliver a service.
- *Marketing*—the manner by which individuals or groups learn about the value and features of products or services (for example, advertising).
- *Distribution*—the mechanism by which a company delivers products or services to the customer.
- *Customer service*—the support activities provided to the customer.
- *Support functions*—the support activities provided to other internal business functions (for example, management information systems, accounting)

Exhibit 1-7 shows these business functions. Not all of these functions are of equal importance to the success of a company. Senior management must decide which of these functions enables the company to gain and maintain a competitive edge. For example, Dell Computers (see Chapter 12 for a more detailed company profile) considers the design function a critical success factor. The features designed into Dell's computers create higher quality. In addition, the design of efficient processes used to make and deliver computers lowers costs and speeds up delivery to its customers. Of course, Dell also performs the other value chain functions, but it concentrates on being the best process designer in the computer market.

Exhibit 1-7
The Value Chain of Business Functions

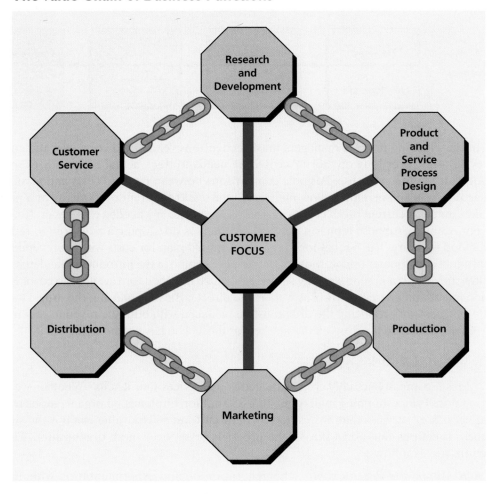

Support activities such as management information systems and accounting are not shown. These activities support all other value chain functions.

Objective 4
Discuss the role accountants play in the company's value chain functions.

Accountants play a key role in all value-chain functions. Providing estimated revenue and cost data during the research and development and design stages (especially the design stage) of the value chain enables managers and engineers to reduce the life-cycle costs of products or services more than in any other value-chain function. Using computer-based planning software, accountants can give managers rapid feedback on ideas for cost reductions long before the company must make a commitment to purchase expensive equipment. Then, during the production stage, accountants help track the effects of continuous improvement programs. Accountants also play a central role in cost planning and control through the use of budgets and performance reporting, as described in the previous section. Marketing decisions have a significant impact on sales but the cost of promotional programs is also significant. Accountants analyze the trade-off between increased costs and revenues. Distributing products or services to customers is a complex function. Should a company sell its products directly to a chain of retail stores, or should it sell to a wholesaler? What transportation system should be used—trucks or trains? What are the costs of each alternative? Finally, accountants provide cost data for customer service activities, such as warranty and repair costs and the costs of goods returned. As you can see, cost management is very important throughout the value chain.

Note that customer focus is at the center of Exhibit 1-7. Successful businesses never lose sight of the importance of maintaining a focus on the needs of its customers. For example, consider the comments of the following business leaders.

> *Customers, by the choices they make, grant companies a future or con-demn them to extinction. We will continuously strive to achieve total customer satisfaction. . . . We will seek to truly understand the com-plexity of our customers' needs, not push our own ideas or technology.*

> *Philip Condit, Chairman and Chief Executive Officer, Boeing Company*

> *Improving comparable sales in the competitive U.S. market means selling more food. So, our emphasis is on increasing customer visits. In the U.S., we'll do that by concentrating on our customers: re-energizing and focusing our marketing efforts, being aggressive in providing maximum price value, continuing to improve service in our restaurants and enhancing food taste.*

> *Mike Conley, Executive Vice President and Chief Financial Officer, McDonald's Corporation*

The value chain and the concepts of adding value and focusing on the customer are extremely important to companies, and they are becoming more so every day. Accountants must focus on the values created compared to the costs incurred in each link of the value chain. Therefore, we will return to the value chain and use it as a focus for dis-cussion throughout the book.

Starbucks Coffee Company is the leading roaster and retailer of specialty coffee in North America, with annual sales revenue of more than $1.5 billion. For each of the following activities, indicate the value chain function that is being performed.

1. Process engineers investigate methods to reduce the time to roast coffee beans and to better preserve their flavor.
2. A direct-to-your-home mail-order system is established to sell custom coffees.
3. Arabica coffee beans are purchased and transported to company processing plants.
4. Focus groups investigate the feasibility of a new line of Frappuccino drinks.
5. A hot line is established for mail-order customers to call with comments on the quality and speed of delivery.
6. Each company-owned retail store provides information to customers about the processes used to make its coffee products.

ANSWERS

1. Design. Both the design of products and, as here, design of production processes are part of the design function.
2. Distribution. This provides an additional way to deliver products to customers.
3. Production. The purchase price of beans and transportation (or freight-in) costs are part of product costs incurred during the production function.
4. Research and development. These costs (mostly wages) are incurred prior to manage-ment's final decision to design and produce a new product.
5. Customer service. These costs include all expenditures made after the product has been delivered to the customer; in this case, Starbucks obtains feedback on the quality and speed of delivery.
6. Marketing. These costs are for activities that enhance the existing or potential customers' awareness and opinion of the product.

ACCOUNTING'S POSITION IN THE ORGANIZATION

To assist other managers in the decision making vital to an organization's success, most companies (and many nonprofit organizations and government agencies) employ a variety of accounting personnel with various types of authority and responsibility.

LINE AND STAFF AUTHORITY

line authority Authority exerted downward over subordinates.

staff authority Authority to advise but not command. It may be exerted downward, laterally, or upward.

The organization chart in Exhibit 1-8 shows how a typical manufacturing company divides responsibilities. Notice the distinction between line and staff authority. **Line authority** is authority exerted downward over subordinates. **Staff authority** is authority to advise but not command. It may be exerted downward, laterally, or upward.

Most organizations specify certain activities as their basic mission. Most missions involve the production and sale of goods or services. All subunits of the organization that are directly responsible for conducting these basic activities are called line departments. The others are called staff departments because their principal task is to support or service the line departments. Thus, staff activities are indirectly related to the basic activities of the organization. Exhibit 1-8 shows a series of factory-service departments that perform staff functions supporting the line functions carried on by the production departments.

Exhibit 1-8

Partial Organization Chart of a Manufacturing Company

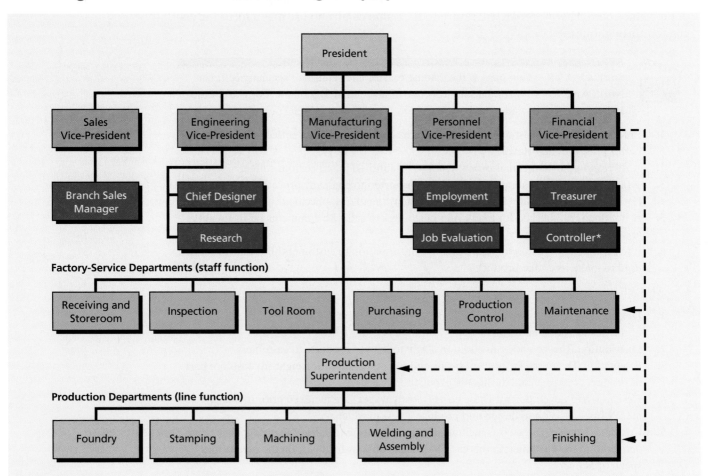

---

* *For detailed organization of a controller's department, see Exhibit 1-9. Dashed line represents staff authority of the finance staff to advise those in manufacturing operations.*

Exhibit 1-9

Organization Chart of a Controller's Department

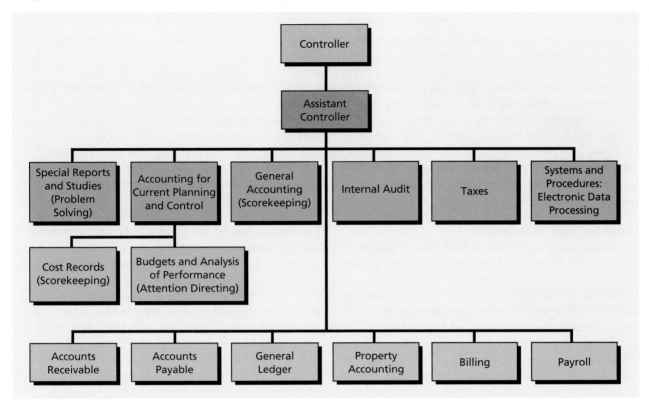

The top accounting officer of an organization is often called the **controller** or, especially in a government organization, a **comptroller**. This executive, like virtually everyone in an accounting function, fills a staff role, whereas sales and production executives and their subordinates fill line roles. The accounting department does not exercise direct authority over line departments. Rather, the accounting department provides other managers with specialized services, including advice and help in budgeting, analyzing variances, pricing, and making special decisions.

Exhibit 1-9 shows how a controller's department may be organized. In particular, note the distinctions among the scorekeeping, attention-directing, and problem-solving roles of various personnel. Unless some internal accountants are given the last two roles as their primary responsibilities, the scorekeeping tasks tend to dominate and the system becomes less responsive to management's decision making.

controller (comptroller)
The top accounting officer of an organization. The term *comptroller* is used primarily in government organizations.

THE CONTROLLER

The controller position varies in stature and duties from company to company. In some firms, the controller is confined to compiling data, primarily for external reporting purposes. In others, such as General Electric, the controller is a key executive who aids managerial planning and control throughout the company's subdivisions. In most firms, controllers have a status somewhere between these two extremes. For example, their opinions on the tax implications of certain management decisions may be carefully weighed, yet their opinions on other aspects of these decisions may not be sought. In many organizations (such as the Marmon Group companies), controllers have a growing role as internal "consultants," helping managers gather relevant information for their decisions.

The Marmon Group, Inc., embodies nearly all of the reasons why management accounting is a vital and growing function in today's leading companies. The Marmon Group, Inc., headquartered in Chicago, is an international association of more than 100 manufacturing, distribution, and service companies with annual revenues in excess of $6 billion. Because operations are spread out in more than 40 different countries with thousands of diverse products and services (such as worker's gloves, water coolers, railroad tank cars, medical products, and credit services for banks), managers at Marmon make extensive use of management accounting information to make important decisions.

What exactly is the role of management accountants at Marmon? According to Jim Smith, Marmon's Director of Cost Management, "The role of the management accountant is changing dramatically in most of our companies." In the past, Marmon's management accountants were basically clerical workers who spent most of their time analyzing monthly cost variances. Now, however, Marmon's management accountants work closely with operating and sales managers, providing cost information in a format that makes sense to those managers. Says Smith, "In the past few years the management accountant has become much more of a financial and business strategy adviser to senior management. Operating and sales managers are demanding meaningful cost information, and management accountants are helping them see how their actions affect costs and the bottom line."

Management accountants have become more important to Marmon, according to Smith, because recessions and foreign competition over the past 10 years have awakened the understanding in most managers that costs must be managed. Knowing what a product truly costs or the cost of servicing a particular customer has become essential to Marmon's profitability.

"To help manage costs," says Smith, "accountants and managers are shying away from using one cost, often the cost used for financial reporting purposes, as the only important cost." Instead, they are now using costs calculated for the decision at hand. "Depending on the decision, any of the cost methods described in *Introduction to Management Accounting* are relevant." According to Smith, this is a very positive change, "since it allows and, in fact, requires the management accountant to understand all of the functions in a business and how each one adds value to the product or service."

Source: Discussions with James Smith.

Although controllers (or comptrollers) have a staff role, they are generally empowered by the firm's president to approve, install, and oversee the organization's accounting system to ensure uniform accounting and reporting methods. In theory, the controller proposes these systems and methods to the president, who approves and orders compliance with them on the part of line personnel (thus preserving the "staff" advisory role of accounting). In practice, however, controllers usually directly specify how production records should be kept or how time records should be completed. The controller holds delegated authority from top-line management over such matters.

In theory, then, controllers have no line authority except over the accounting department. Yet, by reporting and interpreting relevant data, controllers do exert a force or influence that leads management toward logical decisions that are consistent with the organization's objectives.

DISTINCTIONS BETWEEN CONTROLLER AND TREASURER

Objective 5
Contrast the functions of controllers and treasurers.

Many people confuse the offices of controller and treasurer. The Financial Executives Institute, an association of corporate treasurers and controllers, distinguishes their functions as follows:

CONTROLLERSHIP	TREASURERSHIP
1. Planning for control	1. Provision of capital
2. Reporting and interpreting	2. Investor relations

3. Evaluating and consulting
4. Tax administration
5. Government reporting
6. Protection of assets
7. Economic appraisal

3. Short-term financing
4. Banking and custody
5. Credits and collections
6. Investments
7. Risk management (insurance)

Management accounting is the primary means of implementing the first three functions of controllership.

The treasurer is concerned mainly with the company's financial matters, the controller with operating matters. The exact division of accounting and financial duties varies from company to company. In a small organization, the same person might be both treasurer and controller.

SUMMARY PROBLEM FOR YOUR REVIEW

PROBLEM

Using the organization charts in this chapter (Exhibits 1-8 and 1-9), answer the following questions:

1. Which of the following have line authority over the machining manager: maintenance manager, manufacturing vice-president, production superintendent, purchasing agent, scorekeeper, personnel vice-president, president, chief budgetary accountant, chief internal auditor?

2. What is the general role of service departments in an organization? How are they distinguished from operating or production departments?

3. Does the controller have line or staff authority over the cost accountants? Over the accounts receivable clerks?

4. What is probably the major duty (scorekeeping, attention directing, or problem solving) of the following:

Payroll clerk
Accounts receivable clerk
Cost record clerk
Head of general accounting
Head of taxes
Budgetary accountant

Cost analyst
Head of internal auditing
Head of special reports and studies
Head of accounting for planning
    and control
Controller

SOLUTION

1. The only executives having line authority over the machining manager are the president, the manufacturing vice-president, and the production superintendent.

2. A typical company's major purpose is to produce and sell goods or services. Unless a department is directly concerned with producing or selling, it is called a service or staff department. Service departments exist only to help the production and sales departments with their major tasks: the efficient production and sale of goods or services.

3. The controller has line authority over all members of his or her own department, all those shown in the controller's organization chart (Exhibit 1-9).

4. The major duty of the first five—through the head of taxes—is typically scorekeeping. Attention directing is probably the major duty of the next three. Problem solving is probably the primary duty of the head of special reports and

studies. The head of accounting for planning and control and the controller should be concerned with all three duties: scorekeeping, attention directing, and problem solving. However, there is a perpetual danger that day-to-day pressures will emphasize scorekeeping. Therefore, accountants and managers should make sure that attention directing and problem solving are also stressed. Otherwise, the major management benefits of an accounting system may be lost.

CAREER OPPORTUNITIES IN MANAGEMENT ACCOUNTING

The many types and levels of accounting personnel found in the typical organization mean that there are broad opportunities awaiting those who master the accounting discipline.

CERTIFIED MANAGEMENT ACCOUNTANT

Certified Public Accountant (CPA) In the United States, an accountant earns this designation by a combination of education, qualifying experience, and the passing of a two-day written national examination.

Certified Management Accountant (CMA) The management accountant's counterpart to the CPA.

Institute of Management Accountants (IMA) The largest U.S. professional organization of accountants whose major interest is management accounting.

When accounting is mentioned, most people think first of independent auditors who reassure the public about the reliability of the financial information supplied by company managers. These external auditors are called certified public accountants in the United States and chartered accountants in many other English-speaking nations. In the United States, an accountant earns the designation of **Certified Public Accountant (CPA)** by a combination of education, qualifying experience, and the passing of a two-day written national examination. The major U.S. professional association in the private sector that regulates the quality of outside auditors is the American Institute of Certified Public Accountants (AICPA).

In recent years, increased interest in and demand for management accounting has led to the development of the **Certified Management Accountant (CMA)** designation, the internal accountant's counterpart to the CPA. The **Institute of Management Accountants (IMA)** oversees the CMA program and is the largest U.S. professional organization of accountants whose major interest is management accounting.

The highlight of the CMA program is a two-day qualifying examination in four parts: (1) economics, finance, and management; (2) financial accounting and reporting; (3) management reporting, analysis, and behavioral issues; and (4) decision analysis and information systems.[2] The CMA designation is recognized as the management accounting equivalent of the CPA.

Recent studies by the IMA have shown that finance and management accounting positions in industry are very closely related. In response, the IMA developed the Certified in Financial Management (CFM) designation. The CFM examination requires three of the same parts as the CMA, with financial accounting and reporting replaced by corporate financial management.

TRAINING FOR TOP MANAGEMENT POSITIONS

In addition to preparing you for a position in an accounting department, studying accounting—and working as a management accountant—can prepare you for the very highest levels of management. Accounting deals with all facets of an organization, no matter how complex, so it provides an excellent opportunity to gain broad knowledge. Accounting must embrace all management functions, including purchasing, manufacturing, wholesaling, retailing, and a variety of marketing and transportation activities. Senior

---

[2] *Information can be obtained from the IMA, 10 Paragon Drive, Montvale, NJ 07645, or log on to www.imanet.org.*

accountants or controllers in a corporation are sometimes picked as production or marketing executives. Why? Because they may have impressed other executives as having acquired general management skills. A number of recent surveys have indicated that more chief executive officers began their careers in an accounting position than in any other area, including marketing, production, and engineering.

For example, former controllers have risen to the top of such mammoth companies as Pepsico and Pfizer. According to *Business Week*, controllers

> *are now getting involved with the operating side of the company, where they give advice and influence production, marketing, and investment decisions as well as corporate planning. Moreover, many controllers who have not made it to the top have won ready access to top management. . . . Probably the main reason the controller is getting the ear of top management these days is that he or she is virtually the only person familiar with all the working parts of the company.*

ADAPTATION TO CHANGE

The growing interest in management accounting also stems from its ability to help managers adapt to change. The one constant in the world of business is change. Today's economic decisions differ from those of 10 years ago. As decisions change, demands for information change. Accountants must adapt their systems to the changes in management practices and technology. A system that produces valuable information in one setting may be valueless in another.

Accountants have not always been responsive to the need to change. A decade ago many managers complained about the irrelevance of accounting information. Why? Because their decision environment had changed but accounting systems had not. However, most progressive companies have now changed their accounting systems to recognize the realities of today's complex, technical, and global business environment. Instead of being irrelevant, accountants in such companies are adding more value than ever. For example, *Management Accounting* reported on a Champion International Corporation paper mill that made major changes in its accounting system. By working with managers to produce the information considered relevant for their decisions, accountants became regarded as "business partners." Previously, managers had considered accountants to be a "financial police department." Instead of merely pointing out problems, the accountants became part of the solution. In essence, management accountants today are internal consultants rather than merely preparers of reports.

CURRENT TRENDS

Three major factors are causing changes in management accounting today:

> **Objective 6**
> Identify current trends in management accounting.

1. Shift from a manufacturing-based to a service-based economy
2. Increased global competition
3. Advances in technology, including e-commerce

Each of these factors will affect your study of management accounting.

The service sector now accounts for almost 80% of the employment in the United States. Service industries are becoming increasingly competitive, and their use of accounting information is growing. Basic accounting principles are applied to service organizations throughout this book.

Global competition has increased in recent years as many international barriers to trade, such as tariffs and duties, have been lowered. In addition, there has been a

One of the early adopters of e-commerce is Boeing Company. In 1996, Boeing launched its "Boeing PART Page," providing airlines and maintenance organizations with a direct link to a half million different types of spare parts stored in Boeing distribution centers. By the end of 1999, the web site processed more than 18,000 transactions each day. Almost 85% of all Boeing's spare parts are ordered electronically. According to Tom DiMarco, director of spares systems at Boeing, "In retrospect, it was one of the best steps we've ever taken. It saves time, simplifies business processes for our customers, reduces paperwork, and has improved the productivity of our work force."

In early 2000, Boeing announced the formation of the Global Trading Exchange, an e-commerce alliance with other key businesses in the aerospace and defense industry, with the goal to create a single e-commerce site for the entire industry. According to Harry Stonecipher, President and Chief Operating Officer, "Transactions, from order placement to shipping and billing, can be completed electronically, reducing transaction costs significantly."

In another business environment, Champion Exposition Services, a $55 million company, provides national trade show and convention decorating services. Champion uses e-commerce to speed up the order-taking process. Salespeople take orders, invoice customers, and receive payments in real time. The company expects to double its growth and increase accounting department productivity by 50% as a result of using B2C (business to consumer) e-commerce.

Sources: News releases, The Boeing Company, January 20, 1999 and March 28, 2000; "Is E-Business for You?" *Strategic Finance*, March 1999, pp. 74–77.

---

worldwide trend toward deregulation. The result has been a shift in the balance of economic power in the world. Nowhere has this been more evident than in the United States. To regain their competitive edge, many U.S. companies are redesigning their accounting systems to provide more accurate and timely information about the cost of activities, products, or services. To be competitive, managers must understand the effects of their decisions on costs, and accountants must help managers predict such effects.

By far the most dominant influence on management accounting over the past decade has been technological change. This change has affected both the production and the use of accounting information. The increasing capabilities and decreasing cost of computers, especially personal computers (PCs), has changed how accountants gather, store, manipulate, and report data. Most accounting systems, even small ones, are automated. In addition, in many cases computers enable managers to access data directly and to generate their own reports and analyses. By using spreadsheet software and graphics packages, managers can use accounting information directly in their decision process. Thus, today all managers need a better understanding of accounting information than they may have needed in the past. In addition, accountants need to create databases that can be readily understood by managers.

One of the most rapidly growing uses of technology is **electronic commerce** or **e-commerce**—conducting business on-line. This includes buying and selling products and services with digital cash. Terms used to describe various types of e-commerce include business-to-business transactions **(B2B)** and business-to-consumer transactions **(B2C)**. Various studies indicate that the impact of e-commerce on our economy will continue to grow. One survey predicts that in the United States alone, B2B and B2C transactions will reach more than $3,200 billion in revenue by the year 2004.

One type of B2B transaction that has received much attention is **e-procurement**—buying manufacturing or operating inputs electronically. According to one survey, companies that are early adopters of e-procurement for purchasing have realized a 5 to 10% reduction in prices for goods and services through improved controls. In addition, the

electronic commerce (e-commerce) Conducting business on-line.

B2B Electronic commerce from one business to another business.

B2C Electronic commerce from a business to customer.

e-procurement Buying manufacturing or operating inputs electronically.

costs of ordering can be reduced by as much as 70%. Manually processing purchase orders can take days or weeks because of the time it takes exchanging paper work and communicating with suppliers. It is not unusual for the labor-intensive process of handling a purchase order to cost more than $100 to $200. Multiply this by thousands of purchase orders processed by companies and the costs are significant. In e-procurement, employees make purchases using a shopping cart–style browser. Company purchasing agents and operating managers can pick and choose in real-time, and the transaction is completed. An e-procurement purchase can take as little as a day from the time a request is made to the receipt of the goods.

Technological change has had a dramatic effect on the manufacturing environment for many companies, in turn changing in how accounting information is used. Manufacturing processes are increasingly automated, making extensive use of robots and other computer-controlled equipment and less use of human labor for direct production activities. Many early accounting systems were designed primarily to measure and report the cost of labor. Why? Because human labor was the largest cost in the production of many products and services. Clearly, such systems are not appropriate in automated environments. Accountants in such settings have had to change their systems to produce information for decisions about how to acquire and use materials and automated equipment efficiently.

JUST-IN-TIME PHILOSOPHY AND COMPUTER-INTEGRATED MANUFACTURING

Changes in technology have produced changes in management philosophy. The most important recent change leading to increased efficiency in U.S. factories has been the adoption of a **just-in-time (JIT) philosophy.** The essence of the philosophy is to eliminate waste. Managers try to (1) reduce the time that products spend in the production process and (2) eliminate the time that products spend on activities that do not add value (such as inspection and waiting time).

Process time can be reduced by redesigning and simplifying the production process. Companies can use computer-aided design (CAD) to design products that can be manufactured efficiently. Even small changes in design often lead to large manufacturing cost savings. Companies can also use computer-aided manufacturing (CAM), in which computers direct and control production equipment. CAM often leads to a smoother, more efficient flow of production with fewer delays.

Systems that use CAD and CAM together with robots and computer-controlled machines are called **computer-integrated manufacturing (CIM) systems.** Companies that install a full CIM system use very little labor. Robots and computer-controlled machines perform the routine jobs that were previously accomplished by assembly-line workers. In addition, well-designed systems provide great flexibility because design changes require alterations only in computer programs, not retraining of an entire workforce.

Time spent on activities that do not add value to the product can be eliminated or reduced by focusing on quality, improving plant layout, and cross-training workers. Achieving zero production defects ("doing it right the first time") reduces inspection time and eliminates rework time. One midwestern factory saved production time by redesigning its plant layout so that the distance products traveled from one operation to the next during production was reduced from 1,384 feet to 350 feet. Another company reduced setup time on a machine from 45 minutes to 1 minute by storing the required tools nearby and training the machine operator to do the setup. A British company reduced the time to manufacture a vacuum pump from 3 weeks to 6 minutes by switching from long assembly lines to manufacturing cells that accomplish the entire process in quick succession.

just-in-time (JIT) philosophy A philosophy to eliminate waste by reducing the time products spend in the production process and eliminating the time products spend on activities that do not add value.

computer-integrated manufacturing (CIM) systems Systems that use computer-aided design and computer-aided manufacturing, together with robots and computer-controlled machines.

Originally, JIT referred only to an inventory system that minimized inventories by arranging for materials and subcomponents to arrive just as they were needed and for goods to be made just in time to be shipped to customers—no sooner and no later. But JIT has become the cornerstone of a broad management philosophy. It originated in Japanese companies such as Toyota and Kawasaki, and now has been adopted by many large U.S. companies including Hewlett-Packard, Goodyear, General Motors, Intel, and Xerox. Many small firms have also embraced JIT. One of the advantages of an e-procurement purchasing system described earlier is the reduced level of inventory when the time required to purchase materials and supplies is substantially reduced. Thus, e-commerce is an important element of a JIT system.

IMPLICATIONS FOR THE STUDY OF MANAGEMENT ACCOUNTING

As you read the remainder of this book, remember that accounting systems change as the world changes. The techniques presented in this book are being applied in real organizations today. Tomorrow, however, everything may be different. To adapt to changes, you must understand *why* the techniques are being used, not just *how* they are used. We urge you to resist the temptation simply to memorize rules and techniques. Instead, develop your understanding of the underlying concepts and principles. These will continue to be useful in developing and understanding new techniques for changing environments.

IMPORTANCE OF ETHICAL CONDUCT

Although accounting systems may change, the need for accountants to adhere to high ethical standards of professional conduct has never been greater.

STANDARDS OF ETHICAL CONDUCT

Standards of Ethical Conduct for Practitioners of Management Accounting and Financial Management Codes of conduct developed by the Institute of Management Accountants; these codes include competence, confidentiality, integrity, and objectivity.

Public opinion surveys consistently rank accountants high in terms of their professional ethics. CPAs and CMAs adhere to codes of conduct regarding competence, confidentiality, integrity, and objectivity. Exhibit 1-10 contains the **Standards of Ethical Conduct for Practitioners of Management Accounting and Financial Management** developed by the IMA. Professional accounting organizations have procedures for reviewing alleged behavior not consistent with the standards.

Preparing objective, accurate external and internal financial reports is primarily the responsibility of line managers. However, management accountants are also responsible for the reports. Ensuring that accounting systems, procedures, and compilations are reliable and free of manipulation is the responsibility of every accountant.

ETHICAL DILEMMAS

What makes an action by an accountant unethical? An unethical act is one that violates the ethical standards of the profession. The standards, however, leave much room for individual interpretation and judgment.

When one action is clearly unethical and another alternative is clearly ethical, managers and accountants should have no difficulty choosing between them. Unfortunately, most ethical dilemmas are not that clear-cut. The most difficult ethical situations arise when there is strong pressure to take an action that is borderline or when two ethical standards conflict.

Suppose you are an accountant who has been asked to supply the company's banker with a profit forecast for the coming year. A badly needed bank loan rides on the prediction. The company president is absolutely convinced that profits will be at least $500,000. Anything less than that and the loan is not likely to be approved.

Exhibit 1-10

Standards of Ethical Conduct for Practitioners of Management Accounting and Financial Management

Objective 7
Explain a management
accountant's ethical
responsibilities.

Practitioners of management accounting and financial management have an obligation to the public, their profession, the organization they serve, and themselves to maintain the highest standards of ethical conduct. In recognition of this obligation, the Institute of Management Accountants has promulgated the following standards of ethical conduct for practitioners of management accounting and financial management. Adherence to these standards, both professionally and internationally, is integral to achieving the *Objectives of Management Accounting*. Practitioners of management accounting and financial management shall not commit acts contrary to these standards nor shall they condone the commission of such acts by others within their organizations.

Competence

Practitioners of management accounting and financial management have a responsibility to

- Maintain an appropriate level of professional competence by ongoing development of their knowledge and skills.
- Perform their professional duties in accordance with relevant laws, regulations, and technical standards.
- Prepare complete and clear reports and recommendations after appropriate analyses of relevant and reliable information.

Confidentiality

Practitioners of management accounting and financial management have a responsibility to

- Refrain from disclosing confidential information acquired in the course of their work except when authorized, unless legally obligated to do so.
- Inform subordinates as appropriate regarding the confidentiality of information acquired in the course of their work and monitor their activities to assure the maintenance of that confidentiality.
- Refrain from using or appearing to use confidential information acquired in the course of their work for unethical or illegal advantage either personally or through third parties.

Integrity

Practitioners of management accounting and financial management have a responsibility to

- Avoid actual or apparent conflicts of interest and advise all appropriate parties of any potential conflict.
- Refrain from engaging in any activity that would prejudice their ability to carry out their duties ethically.
- Refuse any gift, favor, or hospitality that would influence or would appear to influence their actions.
- Refrain from either actively or passively subverting the attainment of the organization's legitimate and ethical objectives.
- Recognize and communicate professional limitations or other constraints that would preclude responsible judgment or successful performance of an activity.
- Communicate unfavorable as well as favorable information and professional judgments or opinions.
- Refrain from engaging in or supporting any activity that would discredit the profession.

Objectivity

Practitioners of management accounting and financial management have a responsibility to

- Communicate information fairly and objectively.
- Disclose fully all relevant information that could reasonably be expected to influence an intended user's understanding of the reports, comments, and recommendations presented.

(continued)

Exhibit 1-10 (Continued)

Standards of Ethical Conduct for Practitioners of Management Accounting and Financial Management

---

Resolution of Ethical Conflict

In applying the standards of ethical conduct, practitioners of management accounting and financial management may encounter problems in identifying unethical behavior or in resolving an ethical conflict. When faced with significant ethical issues, practitioners of management accounting and financial management should follow the established policies of the organization bearing on the resolution of such conflict. If these policies do not resolve the ethical conflict, such practitioners should consider the following courses of action.

- Discuss such problems with the immediate superior except when it appears that the superior is involved, in which case the problem should be presented initially to the next higher managerial level. If a satisfactory resolution cannot be achieved when the problem is initially presented, submit the issues to the next higher managerial level. If the immediate superior is the chief executive officer, or equivalent, the acceptable reviewing authority may be a group such as the audit committee, executive committee, board of directors, board of trustees, or owners. Contact with levels above the immediate superior should be initiated only with the superior's knowledge, assuming the superior is not involved. Except where legally prescribed, communication of such problems to authorities or individuals not employed or engaged by the organization is not considered appropriate.

- Clarify relevant ethical issues by confidential discussion with an objective advisor (for example, IMA Ethics Counseling service) to obtain a better understanding of possible courses of action. Consult your own attorney as to legal obligations and rights concerning the ethical conflict.

- If the ethical conflict still exists after exhausting all levels of internal review, there may be no other recourse on significant matters than to resign from the organization and to submit an informative memorandum to an appropriate representative of the organization. After resignation, depending on the nature of the ethical conflict, it may also be appropriate to notify other parties.

Source: Institute of Management Accountants, Ethical Standards, www.imanet.org.

Your analysis shows that if the planned introduction of a new product goes extraordinarily well, profits will exceed $500,000. The most likely outcome, however, is for a modestly successful introduction and a $100,000 profit. If the product fails, the company stands to lose $600,000. Without the loan, the new product cannot be taken to the market, and there is no way the company can avoid a loss for the year. Bankruptcy is even a possibility.

What forecast would you make? There is no easy answer. A forecast of less than $500,000 seems to guarantee financial problems, perhaps even bankruptcy. Stockholders, management, employees, suppliers, and customers may all be hurt. But a forecast of $500,000 may not be fair and objective. The bank may be misled by it. Still, the president apparently thinks a $500,000 forecast is reasonable, and you know that there is some chance it will be achieved. Perhaps the potential benefit to the company of an overly optimistic forecast is greater than the possible cost to the bank.

There is no right answer to this dilemma. The important point is to recognize the ethical dimensions and weigh them when forming your judgment.

The tone set by top management can have a great influence on managers' ethics. Complete integrity and outspoken support for ethical standards by senior managers is the

The importance of ethics to management accountants was emphasized when *Management Accounting*, the former journal of the Institute of Management Accountants, put out a special issue on ethics in June 1990. Two thrusts run through the articles in the issue: (1) Business schools must make students aware of the ethical dimension of the decisions they will face in the business world, and (2) business firms must recognize that establishing standards of ethical conduct for their employees is important to financial success. Further emphasizing the importance of ethics to accounting is the existence of a journal devoted completely to such ethical issues—*Research in Accounting Ethics*. A recent article in that journal pointed out that adhering to ethical standards creates economic advantages for companies; it is not simply an altruistic objective.

Companies also recognize that ethics create value. Roger B. Smith, former Chairman and Chief Executive Officer of General Motors, stated that "ethical practice is, quite simply, good business." Since 1977, GM has had a formal policy on personal integrity. But GM recognizes that making ethical decisions is not always easy. Because the world is complex, there are often competing obligations to shareholders, customers, suppliers, fellow managers, society, and self and family. As Smith says, "It is easy to do what is right; it is hard to know what is right." A basic rule used by GM is that employees "should never do anything [they] would be ashamed to explain to [their] families or be afraid to see on the front page of the local newspaper."

General Motors is not alone in promoting ethical conduct. Over half of the large companies in the United States have a "Corporate Code of Conduct." These codes provide support to employees who feel pressured to make decisions they believe to be unethical. They also provide training in the types of behavior expected of employees.

Sources: Adapted from Roger B. Smith, "Ethics in Business: An Essential Element of Success," *Management Accounting*, Special Issue on Ethics in Corporate America, June 1990, p. 50; Robert B. Sweeney and Howard L. Siers, "Ethics in America," *Management Accounting*, Special Issue on Ethics in Corporate America, June 1990, pp. 34–40; and Gary L. Sundem, and Andrew C. Wicks, "Ethics, Economics, and Information," *Research in Accounting Ethics*, Volume 6 (2000), pp. 205–220.

single greatest motivator of ethical behavior throughout an organization. In the final analysis, however, ethical standards are personal and depend on the values of the individual.

SUMMARY PROBLEM FOR YOUR REVIEW

PROBLEM

Yang Electronics Company (YEC) developed a high-speed, low-cost copying machine. It marketed the machine primarily for home use. However, as YEC customers learned how easy and inexpensive it was to make copies with the YEC machine, its use by small businesses grew. Sales soared as some businesses ordered large numbers of the copiers. However, the heavier use by these companies caused breakdowns in a certain component of the equipment. The copiers were warranted for two years, regardless of the amount of usage. Consequently, YEC experienced high costs for replacing the damaged components.

As the quarterly meeting of the Board of Directors of YEC approached, Mark Chua, Assistant Controller, was asked to prepare a report on the situation. Unfortunately, it was hard to predict the exact effects. However, it seemed that many business customers were starting to switch to more expensive copiers sold by competitors. And it was clear that the increased maintenance costs would significantly affect YEC's profitability. Mark summarized the situation as best he could for the Board.

Alice Martinez, the controller of YEC, was concerned about the impact of the report on the Board. She does not disagree with the analysis, but thinks it makes management look bad and might even lead the Board to discontinue the product. She is convinced from conversations with the head of engineering that the copier can be slightly redesigned to meet the needs of high-volume users, so discontinuing it may pass up a potentially profitable opportunity.

Martinez called Chua into her office and asked him to delete the part of his report dealing with the component failures. She said it was all right to mention this orally to the Board, noting that engineering is nearing a solution to the problem. However, Chua feels strongly that such a revision in his report would mislead the Board about a potentially significant negative impact on the company's earnings.

Explain why Martinez's request to Chua is unethical. How should Chua resolve this situation?

SOLUTION

According to the Standards of Ethical Conduct for Practitioners of Management Accounting and Financial Management in Exhibit 1-10, Martinez's request violates requirements for competence, integrity, and objectivity. It violates competence because she is asking Chua to prepare a report that is not complete and clear, one that omits potentially relevant information. Therefore, the Board will not have all the information it should to make a decision about the component failure problem.

The request violates the integrity requirement because the revised report may subvert the attainment of the organization's objectives to achieve Martinez's objectives. Management accountants are specifically responsible for communicating unfavorable as well as favorable information.

Finally, the revised report would not be objective. It would not disclose all relevant information that could be expected to influence the Board's understanding of operations and therefore their decisions.

Chua's responsibility is to discuss this issue with increasingly higher levels of authority within YEC. First, he should let Martinez know about his misgivings. Possibly the issue can be resolved by her withdrawing the request. If not, he should inform her that he intends to take up the matter with her superior and then continue up to higher levels of authority, even to the Board, if necessary, until the issue is resolved. So that Chua does not violate the standard of confidentiality, he should not discuss the matter with persons outside of YEC.

Highlights to Remember

Describe the major users of accounting information. Accounting information is useful to internal managers for making short-term planning and control decisions, for making nonroutine decisions, and for formulating overall policies and long-range plans. Using accounting information, managers answer scorekeeping, attention-directing, and problem-solving questions.

Explain the cost-benefit and behavioral issues involved in designing an accounting system. Management accounting information systems are designed for the benefit of managers. These systems should be judged by a cost-benefit criterion—the benefits of better decisions should exceed the cost of the system. The benefit of a system will be affected by behavioral factors—how the system affects managers and their decisions.

Explain the role of budgets and performance reports in planning and control. Budgets and performance reports are essential tools for planning and control. Budgets result from the planning process and are a means of translating the organization's goals into action. A performance report compares actual results to the budget. Managers use these reports to monitor, evaluate, and reward performance and thus exercise control.

Discuss the role accountants play in the company's value chain functions. Accountants play a key role in planning and control. Throughout the company's value chain, accountants gather and report cost and revenue information for decision makers.

Contrast the functions of controllers and treasurers. Accountants are staff employees who provide information and advice for line managers. The head of accounting is often called the controller. Unlike the treasurer, who is concerned mainly with financial matters, the controller measures and reports on operating performance.

Identify current trends in management accounting. The future worth of an accounting system and accountants themselves will be affected by how easily and well they can adapt to change. Current trends affecting accounting systems include growth in the service sector of the economy, increased global competition, and advances in technology, including e-commerce.

Explain a management accountant's ethical responsibilities. Both external and internal accountants are expected to adhere to standards of ethical conduct. Many ethical dilemmas, however, require value judgments, not the simple application of standards.

Understand how managerial accounting is used in companies. Management accounting plays a vital role in the achievement of company goals and objectives. Management accounting information is used across the entire value chain of activities as well as throughout the life cycle of products and services. In today's modern business environment, management accountants are playing an increasingly vital role because the need for accounting information to support decision making is greater than ever before.

Accounting Vocabulary

Vocabulary is an essential and often troublesome phase of the learning process. A fuzzy understanding of terms hampers the learning of concepts and the ability to solve accounting problems.

Before proceeding to the assignment material or to the next chapter, be sure you understand the words and terms listed below. Their meaning is explained in the chapter and in the glossary at the end of this book.

accounting system, p. 6
attention directing, p. 5
B2B, p. 22
B2C, p. 22
behavioral implications, p. 9
budget, p. 10
Certified Management
  Accountant (CMA), p. 20
Certified Public Accountant
  (CPA), p. 20
comptroller, p. 17
computer-integrated manufacturing (CIM) systems, p. 23
controller, p. 17
cost-benefit balance, p. 8

decision making, p. 9
electronic commerce, p. 22
e-commerce, p. 22
e-procurement, p. 22
financial accounting, p. 5
Foreign Corrupt Practices Act,
  p. 7
generally accepted accounting
  principles (GAAP), p. 6
Institute of Management
  Accountants (IMA), p. 20
just-in-time (JIT) philosophy,
  p. 23
line authority, p. 16
management accounting, p. 5

management audit, p. 7
management by exception,
  p. 11
performance reports, p. 10
problem solving, p. 5
product life cycle, p. 12
scorekeeping, p. 5
staff authority, p. 16
Standards of Ethical Conduct
  for Practitioners of
  Management Accounting and
  Financial Management, p. 24
variances, p. 10
value chain, p. 13

Fundamental Assignment Material

The assignment material for each chapter is divided into two groups: fundamental and additional. The fundamental assignment material consists of two sets of parallel problems that convey the essential concepts and techniques of the chapter. The additional assignment material consists of questions, cognitive exercises, exercises, problems, cases, a collaborative exercise, and an Internet exercise that cover the chapter in more detail.

1-A1 Scorekeeping, Attention Directing, and Problem Solving

For each of the following activities, identify the function that the accountant is performing—scorekeeping, attention directing, or problem solving—and explain why it fits that category.

1. Analyzing, for an Alcoa production superintendent, the impact on costs of some new drill presses.
2. Preparing a scrap report for the finishing department of a Nissan parts factory.
3. Preparing the budget for the maintenance department of Providence Hospital.
4. Interpreting why a Springfield foundry did not adhere to its production schedule.
5. Explaining the stamping department's performance report.
6. Preparing a monthly statement of European sales for the General Motors marketing vice-president.
7. Preparing, for the manager of production control of an Inland Steel plant, a cost comparison of two computerized manufacturing control systems.
8. Interpreting variances on the Harvard University purchasing department's performance report.
9. Analyzing, for a Honda international manufacturing manager, the desirability of having some auto parts made in Korea.
10. Preparing a schedule of depreciation for forklift trucks in the receiving department of a General Electric factory in Scotland.

1-A2 Management by Exception

Beta Alpha Psi, the accounting honorary fraternity, held a homecoming party. The fraternity expected attendance of 80 persons and prepared the following budget.

Room rental	$ 150
Food	800
Entertainment	600
Decorations	220
Total	$1,770

After all bills for the party were paid, the total cost came to $1,948, or $178 over budget. Details are $150 for room rental; $1,008 for food; $600 for entertainment; and $190 for decorations. Ninety-five persons attended the party.

Required

1. Prepare a performance report for the party that shows how actual costs differed from the budget. That is, include in your report the budgeted amounts, actual amounts, and variances.
2. Suppose the fraternity uses a management-by-exception rule. Which costs deserve further examination? Why?

1-A3 Accounting's Position in the Organization: Line and Staff Functions

1. Of the following, who has line authority over a cost record clerk: budgetary accountant, head of accounting for current planning and control, head of general accounting, controller, storekeeper, production superintendent, manufacturing vice-president, president, production control chief?
2. Of the following, who has line authority over an assembler: stamping manager, assembly manager, production superintendent, production control chief, storekeeper, manufacturing vice-president, engineering vice-president, president, controller, budgetary accountant, cost record clerk?

1-B1   Scorekeeping, Attention Directing, and Problem Solving

For each of the following activities, identify the function the accountant is performing—scorekeeping, attention directing, or problem solving. Explain each of your answers.

1. Daily recording of material purchase vouchers.
2. Analyzing the costs of acquiring and using each of two alternate types of welding equipment.
3. Preparing a report of overtime labor costs by production departments.
4. Posting daily cash collections to customers' accounts.
5. Estimating the costs of moving corporate headquarters to another city.
6. Interpreting increases in nursing costs per patient-day in a hospital.
7. Analyzing deviations from the budget of the factory maintenance department.
8. Assisting in a study by the manufacturing vice-president to determine whether to buy certain parts needed in large quantities for manufacturing products or to acquire facilities for manufacturing these parts.
9. Allocating factory service department costs to production departments.
10. Recording overtime hours of the product finishing department.
11. Compiling data for a report showing the ratio of advertising expenses to sales for each branch store.
12. Investigating reasons for increased returns and allowances for drugs purchased by a hospital.
13. Preparing a schedule of fuel costs by months and government departments.
14. Estimating the operating costs and outputs that could be expected for each of two large metal-stamping machines offered for sale by different manufacturers. Only one of these machines is to be acquired by your company.
15. Computing and recording end-of-year adjustments for expired fire insurance on the factory warehouse for materials.

1-B2   Management by Exception

The Makah Indian tribe sells fireworks for the 5 weeks preceding the Fourth of July. The tribe's stand at the corner of Highway 104 and Eagle Drive was the largest, with budgeted sales for 20X1 of $70,000. Expected expenses were as follows.

Cost of fireworks	$ 30,000
Labor cost	15,000
Other costs	8,000
Total costs	$53,000

Actual sales were $69,860, almost equal to the budget. The tribe spent $34,000 for fireworks, $13,000 for labor, and $8,020 for other costs.

Required

1. Compute budgeted profit and actual profit.
2. Prepare a performance report to help identify those costs that were significantly different from the budget.
3. Suppose the tribe uses a management-by-exception rule. What costs deserve further explanation? Why?

1-B3   Accounting's Position in the Organization: Controller and Treasurer

For each of the following activities, indicate whether it is most likely to be performed by the controller or by the treasurer. Explain each answer.

1. Prepare credit checks on customers.
2. Help managers prepare budgets.
3. Advise which alternative action is least costly.
4. Prepare divisional financial statements.
5. Arrange short-term financing.
6. Prepare tax returns.
7. Arrange insurance coverage.
8. Meet with financial analysts from Wall Street.

Additional Assignment Material

QUESTIONS

1-1. Who uses information from an accounting system?

1-2. "The emphases of financial accounting and management accounting differ." Explain.

1-3. "The field is less sharply defined. There is heavier use of economics, decision sciences, and behavioral sciences." Identify the branch of accounting described in the quotation.

1-4. Distinguish among scorekeeping, attention directing, and problem solving.

1-5. "Additional government regulation assists the development of management accounting systems." Do you agree? Explain.

1-6. "The Foreign Corrupt Practices Act applies to bribes paid outside the United States." Do you agree? Explain.

1-7. Give three examples of service organizations. What distinguishes them from other types of organizations?

1-8. What two major considerations affect all accounting systems? Explain each.

1-9. "The accounting system is intertwined with operating management. Business operations would be in a hopeless tangle without the paperwork that is so often regarded with disdain." Do you agree? Explain, giving examples.

1-10. Distinguish among a budget, a performance report, and a variance.

1-11. "Management by exception means abdicating management responsibility for planning and control." Do you agree? Explain.

1-12. "Good accounting provides automatic control of operations." Do you agree? Explain.

1-13. Why are accountants concerned about product life cycle?

1-14. Name the six primary business functions that make up the value chain. (Do not include the support activities.)

1-15. "Accountants in every company should measure and report on every function in the company's value chain." Do you agree? Explain.

1-16. Distinguish between line authority and staff authority.

1-17. Does every company have both a controller and a treasurer? Explain

1-18. "The controller does control in a special sense." Explain.

1-19. Describe the contents of the qualifying examination for becoming a CMA.

1-20. How are changes in technology affecting management accounting?

1-21. What is e-commerce?

1-22. What is the essence of the JIT philosophy?

1-23. "We can certainly improve our cash flow position by switching to a JIT system." Do you agree? Explain why or why not.

1-24. Briefly describe how a change in a plant's layout can make its operation more efficient.

1-25. Standards of ethical conduct for management accountants have been divided into four major responsibilities. Describe each of the four in 20 words or less.

1-26. "Why are there ethical dilemmas? I thought accountants had standards that specified what is ethical behavior." Discuss this quote.

COGNITIVE EXERCISES

1-27 Finance and Management Accounting
Often there is confusion between the roles played by the controller and treasurer in an organization. In fact, in many small companies, a single person performs activities related to both functions.

Distinguish between the controller and the treasurer functions by listing typical activities that are associated with each.

1-28 Marketing and Management Accounting
Each of the following activities is performed by a cross-functional team of managers including the management accountant. However, depending on the nature of the decision to be made, one functional area will take the leadership role. Which of these activities is primarily a marketing decision? What would the management accountant contribute to each of the marketing decisions?

1. Ford Motor Company must decide whether to buy a part for one of its cars or to make the part at one of its plants.
2. Boeing Company must decide the price for spare parts it sells over the Internet using its Spare Parts Web site.
3. Penrose Hospital must decide how to finance the purchase of expensive new medical analysis equipment.
4. Amazon.com must forecast the impact on video sales of a new advertising program.
5. Sparta Foods, Inc., a regional market leader in the production and distribution of tortillas to retail and food service industries, must decide whether to accept a special order for tortilla chips by a large national retail chain.
6. Target Stores, Inc., must decide whether to close one of its retail stores that is operating at a loss.

1-29 Production and Management Accounting

Each of the following activities is performed by a cross-functional team of managers, including the management accountant. However, depending on the nature of the decision to be made, one functional area will take the leadership role. Which of these activities is primarily a production decision? What would the management accountant contribute to each of the production decisions?

1. Ford Motor Company must decide whether to buy a part for one of its cars or to make the part at one of its plants.
2. Boeing Company must decide the price for spare parts it sells over the Internet using its Spare Parts Web site.
3. Penrose Hospital must decide how to finance the purchase of expensive new medical analysis equipment.
4. Amazon.com must forecast the impact on video sales of a new advertising program.
5. Sparta Foods, Inc., a regional market leader in the production and distribution of tortillas to retail and food service industries, must decide whether to accept a special order for tortilla chips by a large national retail chain.
6. Kmart must evaluate its overall vision and strategic goals in the light of competitive pressures from Target, Sears, and Wal-Mart.
7. Dell Computers must decide whether to spend money on training workers to perform setups and changeovers faster. This will free up capacity to be used to make more computers without purchasing more equipment.
8. General Motors must decide whether to keep or replace four-year-old equipment used in one of its Saturn plants.

EXERCISES

1-30 Planning and Control, Management by Exception

Study Exhibit 1-2 and the illustration of The Chop House restaurant. For 20X1 the restaurant budgeted revenue of $220,000, a 10% increase over the current revenue of $200,000. The actions listed in Exhibit 1-2 resulted in 6 budgeted entire additions and a total advertising budget of $15,000. Actual results were

New entrees added	7
Advertising	$ 16,000
Revenues	$230,000

Required

1. Prepare a performance report using the format of Exhibit 1-3.
2. Net income results were not available until several months after the plan was implemented. The net income results were disappointing to management because profits actually declined even though revenues increased. List some factors that may not have been considered when the restaurant's plan was formulated.

1-31 Management Accounting and Financial Accounting

Consider the following short descriptions. Indicate whether each description more closely relates to a major feature of financial accounting or management accounting.

1. Provides internal consulting advice to managers
2. Has less flexibility
3. Has a future orientation
4. Is characterized by detailed reports
5. Field is more sharply defined
6. Is constrained by generally accepted accounting principles
7. Behavioral impact is secondary

1-32 Line Versus Staff and Value Chain Responsibility

For each of the following, indicate whether the employee has line or staff responsibility and which value chain business function is most closely related to activities performed by the employee.

1. Production superintendent
2. Cost accountant
3. Market research analyst
4. District sales manager
5. Head of the legal department
6. President

1-33 Organization Chart

Draw an organization chart for a single-factory company with the following personnel. Which represent factory-service departments? Production departments?

Personnel vice-president
Maintenance manager
Sales vice-president
Production control chief
Production planning chief
Assembly manager
Purchasing agent
Secretary and treasurer
President

Punch press manager
Vice-president and controller
Scorekeeper
Drill press manager
Production superintendent
Chairman of the board
Engineering vice-president
Manufacturing vice-president

1-34 Objectives of Management Accounting

The Institute of Management Accountants (IMA) is composed of about 70,000 members. The IMA "Objectives of Management Accounting" states, "The management accountant participates, as part of management, in assuring that the organization operates as a unified whole in its long-run, intermediate, and short-run best interests."

Required

Based on your reading in this chapter, prepare a 100-word description of the principal ways that accountants participate in managing an entity.

1-35 Cost/Benefit of the Ethical Environment

A poor ethical environment results in costs to the company. Examples include the cost of internal theft and the cost of absenteeism. On the other hand, a good ethical environment creates benefits. Examples include reduced risk of legal fines and sanctions and improved employee morale and productivity.

Required

List several additional costs of a poor ethical environment and benefits of a good ethical environment.

1-36 Ethics Early Warning Signs

The following statements are early warning signs of ethical conflict.

- "I don't care how you do it, just get it done!"
- "No one will ever know . . ."

Required

List several other statements that are early warning signs of ethical conflict.

PROBLEMS

1-37 Management and Financial Accounting

Judy Burkett, an able mechanical engineer, was informed that she would be promoted to assistant factory manager. Judy was pleased but uncomfortable. In particular, she knew little about accounting. She had taken one course in financial accounting.

Judy planned to enroll in a management accounting course as soon as possible. Meanwhile, she asked Burt Greenspan, a cost accountant, to state three or four of the principal distinctions between financial and management accounting.

Required

Prepare Burt's written response to Judy.

1-38 Use of Accounting Information in Hospitals

Most revenues of U.S. hospitals are not derived directly from patients. Instead, revenues come through third parties such as insurance companies and government agencies. Until the 1980s, these payments generally reimbursed the hospital's costs of serving patients. Such payments, however, are now generally flat fees for specified services. For example, the hospital might receive $5,000 for an appendectomy or $25,000 for heart surgery—no more, no less.

How might the method of payment change the demand for accounting information in hospitals? Relate your answer to the decisions of top management.

Required

1-39 Costs and Benefits

Marks & Spencer, a huge retailer in the United Kingdom, was troubled by its paper bureaucracy. Looked at in isolation, each form seemed reasonable, but overall a researcher reported that there was substantial effort in each department to verify the information. Basically, the effort seemed out of proportion to any value received, and, eventually, many of the documents were simplified or eliminated.

Describe the rationale that should govern systems design.

Required

1-40 Importance of Accounting

A news story reported

> *A veteran manager of Rockwell's automotive operations, recalls that when he sat in on meetings at Rockwell's North American Aircraft Operations 20 years ago, "there'd be sixty or seventy guys talking technical problems, with never a word on profits." Such inattention to financial management helped Rockwell lose the F-15 fighter to McDonnell Douglas, Pentagon sources say. The manager brought in profit-oriented executives, and he has now transformed North American's staff meetings to the point that "you seldom hear talk of technical problems any more," he says. "It's all financial."*

What is your reaction to the manager's comments? Are his comments related to management accounting?

Required

1-41 Changes in Accounting Systems

In the early 1990s, the Boeing Company undertook a large-scale study of its accounting system. The study led to several significant changes. None of these changes was required for reporting to external parties. Management thought, however, that the new system gave more accurate costs of the airplanes and other products produced.

1. Boeing had been a very successful company using its old accounting system. What might have motivated it to change the system?
2. When Boeing changed its system, what criteria might its managers have used to decide whether to invest in the new system?
3. Is changing to a system that provides more accurate product costs always a good strategy? Why or why not?

Required

1-42 Value Chain

Nike is an Oregon-based company that focuses on the design, development, and worldwide marketing of high-quality footwear, apparel, equipment, and accessory products. Nike is the largest seller of athletic footwear and athletic apparel in the world. The company sells its products to approximately 19,700 retail accounts in the United States and through a mix of independent distributors, licensees, and subsidiaries in approximately 110 countries around the world. Virtually all of the company's products are manufactured by independent contractors. Most footwear products are produced outside the United States, while apparel products are produced both in the United States and abroad.

1. Identify one decision that Nike managers make in each of the six value chain functions.
2. For each decision in requirement 1, identify one piece of accounting information that would aid the manager's decision.

Required

1-43 Role of Controller

Juanita Palencia, newly hired controller of Braxton Industries, had been lured away from a competitor to revitalize the controller's department. Her first day on the job proved to be an eye-opener. One of her first interviews was with Bill Belton, Production Supervisor in the Cleveland factory. Belton commented, "I really don't want to talk to anyone from the controller's office. The only time we see those accountants is when our costs go over their budget. They wave what they call a 'performance report,' but it's actually just a bunch of numbers they make up. It has nothing to do with what happens on the shop floor. Besides, my men can't afford the time to fill out all the paperwork those accountants want, so I just plug in some numbers and send it back. Now, if you'll let me get back to important matters. . . ." Palencia left quickly, but she was already planning for her next visit with Belton.

Required

1. Identify some of the problems in the relationship between the controller's department and the production departments (assuming that the Cleveland factory is representative of the production departments).
2. What should Juanita Palencia do next?

1-44 Ethical Issues

Suppose you are controller of a medium-size oil exploration company in west Texas. You adhere to the standards of ethical conduct for management accountants. How would those standards affect your behavior in each of the following situations?

1. Late one Friday afternoon you receive a geologist's report on a newly purchased property. It indicates a much higher probability of oil than had previously been expected. You are the only one to read the report that day. At a party on Saturday night, a friend asks about the prospects for the property.
2. An oil industry stock analyst invites you and your spouse to spend a week in Hawaii free of charge. All she wants in return is to be the first to know about any financial information your company is about to announce to the public.
3. It is time to make a forecast of the company's annual earnings. You know that some additional losses will be recognized before the final statements are prepared. The company's president has asked you to ignore these losses in making your prediction because a lower-than-expected earnings forecast could adversely affect the chances of obtaining a loan that is being negotiated and that will be completed before actual earnings are announced.
4. You do not know whether a particular expense is deductible for income tax purposes. You are debating whether to research the tax laws or simply to assume that the item is deductible. After all, if you are not audited, no one will ever know the difference. If you are audited, you can plead ignorance of the law.

1-45 The Accountant's Role in an Organization

Marmon Company is a collection of more than 100 different operating companies with revenues of more than $6 billion. Its member companies manufacture such diverse products as copper tubing, water purification products, railroad tank cars, and store fixtures, and they provide services such as credit information for banks.

The boxed example on page 18 described the role of accountants in Marmon. Others have described accountants as "internal consultants." Refer to the discussion of Marmon on page 18. Discuss how accountants at Marmon can act as internal consultants. What kind of background and knowledge would an accountant require to be an effective internal consultant?

CASES

1-46 Line and Staff Authority (CMA adapted)

Electronic Equipment Leasing Company (EEL) leases office equipment to a variety of customers. The company's organization chart follows.

The four positions highlighted in the chart are described below.

- J. P. Shores, Assistant Controller–Special Projects. Shores works on projects assigned to him by the controller. The most recent project was to design a new accounts payable system.

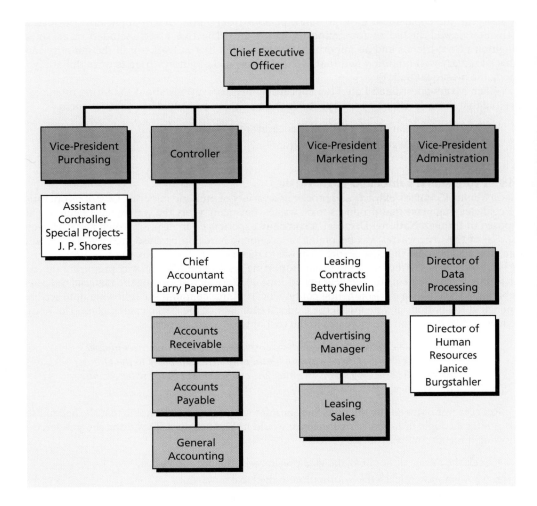

- Betty Shevlin, Leasing Contracts Manager. Shevlin coordinates and implements leasing transactions. Her department handles all transactions after the sales department gets a signed contract. This includes requisitioning equipment from the purchasing department, maintaining appropriate insurance, delivering equipment, issuing billing statements, and seeking renewal of leases.
- Larry Paperman, Chief Accountant. Paperman supervises all the accounting functions. He produces reports for the four supervisors in the functional areas.
- Janice Burgstahler, Director of Human Resources. Burgstahler works with all departments of EEL in hiring personnel. Her department advertises all positions and screens candidates, but the individual departments conduct interviews and make hiring decisions. Burgstahler also coordinates employee evaluations and administers the company's salary schedule and fringe benefit program.

Required

1. Distinguish between line and staff positions in an organization and discuss why conflicts might arise between line and staff managers.
2. For each of the four managers described, identify whether their position is a line or staff position and explain why you classified it that way. Also, indicate any potential conflicts that might arise with other managers in the organization.

1-47   Ethics and Accounting Personnel

Red Ball Beverage Company has an equal opportunity employment policy. This policy has the full support of the company's president, Beverly Chiapello, and is included in all advertisements for open positions.

Hiring in the accounting department is done by the controller, D. W. "Butch" Laughton. The assistant controller, Jack Myers, also interviews candidates, but Laughton's makes all decisions. In the last year, the department hired five new persons from a pool of 175 applicants. Thirteen had been interviewed, including four minority candidates. The five hired included three sons of Laughton's close friends and no minorities. Myers had felt that at least two of the minority candidates were very well qualified and that the three sons of Laughton's friends were definitely not among the most qualified.

When Myers questioned Laughton concerning his reservations about the hiring practices, he was told that these decisions were Laughton's and not his, so he should not question them.

Required

1. Explain why Laughton's hiring practices were probably unethical.
2. What should Myers do about this situation?

1-48 Professional Ethics and Toxic Waste

Yukon Mining Company extracts and processes a variety of ores and minerals. One of its operations is a coal cleaning plant that produces toxic wastes. For many years the wastes have been properly disposed of through National Disposal, a company experienced in disposing such items. However, disposal of the toxic wastes was becoming an economic hardship because increasing government regulations had caused the cost of such disposal to quadruple in the last six years.

Rebecca Long, Director of Financial Reporting for Yukon Mining, was preparing the company's financial statements for the year ended June 30, 2001. In researching the material needed for preparing a footnote on environmental contingencies, Rebecca found the following note scribbled in pencil at the bottom of a memo to the General Manager of the coal cleaning plant. The body of the memo gave details on the increases in the cost of toxic waste disposals:

> *Ralph———— We've got to keep these costs down or we won't meet budget. Can we mix more of these wastes with the shipments of refuse to the Oak Hill landfill? Nobody seems to notice the coal-cleaning fluids when we mix it in well.*

Rebecca was bothered by the note. She considered ignoring it, pretending that she had not seen it. But after a couple of hours, her conscience would not let her do it. Therefore, she pondered the following three alternative courses of action.

- Seek the advice of her boss, the vice-president of finance for Yukon.
- Anonymously release the information to the local newspaper.
- Give the information to an outside member of the board of directors of Yukon whom she knew because he lived in her neighborhood.

Required

1. Discuss why Rebecca Long has an ethical responsibility to take some action about her suspicion of illegal dumping of toxic wastes.
2. For each of the three alternative courses of action, explain whether the action is appropriate.
3. Assume that Rebecca sought the advice of the vice-president of finance and discovered that he both knew about and approved of the dumping of toxic wastes. What steps should she take to resolve the conflict in this situation?

COLLABORATIVE LEARNING EXERCISE

1-49 The Future Management Accountant

Form groups of four to six students each. Half of each group should read the first of the following articles and half should read the second article. (Alternatively, this exercise can be done with the class as a whole, with half of the class reading each article.)

- Kulesza, C., and G. Siegel, "It's Not Your Father's Management Accounting," *Management Accounting,* May 1997, pp. 56–59.
- Russell, K., G. Siegel, and C. Kulesza, "Counting More, Counting Less: Transformations in the Management Accounting Profession," *Strategic Finance,* September 1999, pp. 39–44.

Required

1. Individually, write down the three most important lessons you learned from the article you read.
2. As a group, list all the lessons identified in requirement 1. Combine those that are essentially the same.

3. Prioritize the list you developed in requirement 2 in terms of their importance to one considering a career in management accounting.

4. Discuss whether this exercise has changed your impression of management accounting and, if so, how your impression has changed.

INTERNET EXERCISE

www.prenhall.com/horngren

1-50 Institute of Management Accountants

Chapter one discussed managerial accounting and ethics. The Institute of Management Accountants (IMA) is a major professional organization that is geared toward managerial accounting and finance. The IMA has local chapters throughout the United States and international chapters. The IMA is also very concerned about ethics. Log on to http://www.imanet.org, the Web site for the IMA.

1. Click on "About IMA." What is the IMA devoted to?

2. Follow the link that shows the Mission Statement for the IMA. What is the mission of the IMA?

3. One of the stated missions of IMA is to help its members' professional development through education. Click on the Education link. What options does the IMA provide to help educate the members?

4. Using the menu return to "About IMA" then on the side bar, click on the "Ethics Center" link. What type of services are provided by the Ethics Center?

5. Click on the Ethics Center Resource and Articles link. What are some of the resource links that are provided through this site?

6. The IMA is made up of local chapters where members can interact with other management accountants. Click on the Chapters and Councils link to see if there is a chapter in your state. List the chapters in your state. Does the chapter closest to your school have a Web site? You may wish to contact the chapter to find out about student involvement and scholarships.

Go to the "Managerial Accounting and Cost Analysis" episode on the *Mastering Accounting* CD-ROM for an interactive, video-enhanced exercise that focuses on CanGo's need for standardized accounting reports as it prepares for an IPO.

chapter 2

INTRODUCTION TO COST BEHAVIOR AND COST-VOLUME RELATIONSHIPS

Boeing's 767-400 ER has earned passenger ratings as one of the most preferred airplanes in every class of service. One reason is that 87% of the seats are next to a window or on the aisle. Delivery of the first 767-400 ER to launch customer Delta Airlines was made in 2000.

www.prenhall.com/horngren

Learning Objectives

When you have finished studying this chapter, you should be able to

1. Explain how cost drivers affect cost behavior.

2. Show how changes in cost-driver activity levels affect variable and fixed costs.

3. Calculate break-even sales volume in total dollars and total units.

4. Create a cost-volume-profit graph and understand the assumptions behind it.

5. Calculate sales volume in total dollars and total units to reach a target profit.

6. Differentiate between contribution margin and gross margin.

7. Explain the effects of sales mix on profits (Appendix 2A).

8. Compute cost-volume-profit relationships on an after-tax basis (Appendix 2B).

9. **Understand how cost behavior and cost-volume-profit analysis are used by managers.**

In 1915, William Boeing, a Seattle timberman, assembled his first airplane in a boathouse. Today, the Boeing Company produces more than 50 jetliners each month and has annual revenues of more than $60 billion. The company has two-thirds of the world's market share in airplane sales, but that could change as the competition steps up to meet growing demand. Over the next two decades, the airline industry will need 16,000 new airplanes worth over $1 trillion. How will Boeing maintain its competitive edge and profitability? With increased competition, Boeing knows that profits can be improved more by controlling (reducing) costs than by increasing prices to customers. So, should it build bigger airplanes or more of the existing size but with improvements in features and efficiencies that will lower customers' costs? Which alternative has lower costs for Boeing and its customers? To answer these questions, Boeing had to understand its own costs as well as the costs of its customers. The real question is what do its customers value in return for a price tag of $50+ million per airplane?

A case in point is the Boeing 747-X. Nearly a decade ago, the company began its research and development program for this huge 500-passenger airplane. An important part of its research was the assessment of its customers' costs—both of operating their existing fleet of planes and of the reduced costs of the new 747-X planes. It formed a working group with 19 airline customers (for example, United and American Airlines, and British Airways) to look at their requirements in the 500+-seat market. After four years of research, the company had completed the design of the new airplane and was faced with the final decision to launch. A decision to launch would involve a huge immediate investment in costly plant and equipment resources. To pay for these assets and make a profit, it had to be confident that its customers would demand the new plane.

The key question was whether customers wanted the latest, largest, and most costly airplane or one with the highest value. Despite the years of development activities, Boeing decided not to proceed with the 747-X. According to Philip Condit, Chairman and Chief Executive Officer, "The prospective market for airplanes with over 500 seats was limited. We were at last in a position of balancing the significant cost of the program against the limited size of the market." Most of the company's customers needed more airplanes for the expected increase in the number of nonstop routes. In short, customers said, "We would rather have two new 250-seat airplanes that are more cost efficient than one 500-seat super airplane." So the 747-X program was stopped. Instead, the company is concentrating on upgrading its existing aircraft. For example, Boeing's new model of the existing 747 will offer 16% more seats and up to 10% lower "seat-mile" costs.

Managers need to understand costs. How are the costs and revenues of an airline affected when one more passenger is added at the last moment, or when one more flight is added to the schedule? How should the budget request by the Arizona Department of Motor Vehicles be affected by the predicted increase in the state's population? These questions are really different forms of one common question: What will happen to financial results if a specified level of activity or volume changes?

Although financial results are based on revenues and costs, we will focus primarily on costs in this chapter. After all, as we saw in the case of Boeing, companies usually have more control over their costs than they do over their revenues. In fact, one of the main goals of management accounting is controlling (and reducing) costs. But managers cannot control costs unless they understand **cost behavior**—how costs are related to and affected by the activities of the organization.

cost behavior How costs are related to and affected by the activities of an organization.

ACTIVITIES, COSTS, AND COST DRIVERS

Objective 1
Explain how cost drivers affect cost behavior.

Different types of costs behave in different ways. Consider Boeing Company's costs of an existing plant that makes 737 business jets. The cost of materials such as electrical wire, seats, and aluminum increase as the number of airplanes manufactured increases. But the cost of the plant and salaries of key managers stay the same regardless of the number of airplanes made. Associating cost behavior with units of product produced gives us an overall view of how costs behave, but it does little to help managers control costs on a day-to-day basis.

On a day-to-day basis, managers focus their efforts on managing the activities required to make products or deliver services—not on the products and services themselves. A production manager needs to know how routine activities such as machine maintenance and repairs affect costs. So, because understanding costs is so important for cost control, associating costs with activities is a key. For example, one of the activities performed at Boeing's plant is receiving parts to be installed on the airplane. Receiving managers need to know how their activities affect costs. Costs such as depreciation of the equipment used to move parts from one location in the plant to another do not change when receiving activity increases or decreases. However, costs such as fuel for the same moving equipment do change with activity changes. Actually, we should say that activities such as receiving require resources such as moving equipment and fuel and that these resources cost money.

Exhibit 2-1

Examples of Value Chain Functions, Costs, and Cost Drivers

Value Chain Function and Example Costs	Example Cost Drivers
Research and development	
• Salaries of marketing research personnel, costs of market surveys	Number of new product proposals
• Salaries of product and process engineers	Complexity of proposed products
Design of products, services, and processes	
• Salaries of product and process engineers	Number of engineering hours
• Cost of computer-aided design equipment, cost to develop prototype of product for testing	Number of parts per product
Production	
• Labor wages	Labor hours
• Supervisory salaries	Number of people supervised
• Maintenance wages	Number of mechanic hours
• Depreciation of plant and machinery, supplies	Number of machine hours
• Energy	Kilowatt hours
Marketing	
• Cost of advertisements	Number of advertisements
• Salaries of marketing personnel, travel costs, entertainment costs	Sales dollars
Distribution	
• Wages of shipping personnel	Labor hours
• Transportation costs including depreciation of vehicles and fuel	Weight of items delivered
Customer service	
• Salaries of service personnel	Hours spent servicing products
• Costs of supplies, travel	Number of service calls

But how exactly do accountants relate activities to resource costs in a way that makes cost control possible? Accountants first identify the activities in their organization and determine measures of output for each activity. They then relate each output measure to the resources that are necessary to produce it. Any output measure that causes costs (that is, causes the use of costly resources) is called a **cost driver.** In our receiving example, the cost driver or output measure of receiving activity could be "number of parts received" or "weight of parts received." The receiving manager can easily understand how an increase in the number of parts received or the weight of parts received can increase or "drive" the use (and therefore cost) of fuel and moving equipment.

An organization has many cost drivers across its value chain. Exhibit 2-1 lists examples of costs and potential cost drivers for each of the value chain functions. How well the accountant does at identifying the most appropriate cost drivers determines how well managers understand cost behavior and how well costs are controlled.

cost driver Any output measure that causes costs (that is, causes the use of costly resources).

COMPARISON OF VARIABLE AND FIXED COSTS

A key to understanding cost behavior is distinguishing variable costs from fixed costs. Costs are classified as variable or fixed depending on how much they change as the level of a particular cost driver changes. A **variable cost** is a cost that changes in direct proportion to changes in the cost driver level. In contrast, a **fixed cost** is not immediately affected by changes in the cost-driver level. Suppose units of production is the cost driver of interest. A 10% increase in the units of production would produce a 10% increase in variable costs. However, the fixed costs would remain unchanged.

variable cost A cost that changes in direct proportion to changes in the cost driver level.

fixed cost A cost that is not immediately affected by changes in the cost driver level.

Exhibit 2-2
Variable-Cost Behavior

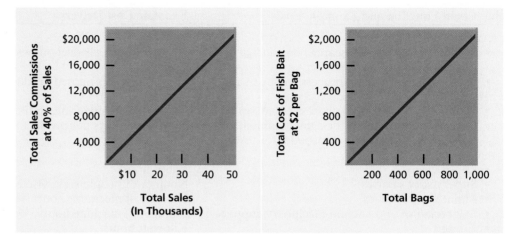

Consider some variable costs. Suppose Watkins Products pays its door-to-door sales personnel a 40% straight commission on sales. The total cost of sales commissions to Watkins is 40% of sales dollars—a variable cost with respect to sales revenues. Or suppose Dan's Bait Shop buys bags of fish bait for $2 each. The total cost of fish bait is $2 times the number of bags purchased—a variable cost with respect to units (number of bags) purchased. Notice that variable costs do not change per unit, but that the total costs change in direct proportion to the cost-driver activity. Exhibit 2-2 shows these relationships between cost and cost-driver activity graphically.

Now consider a fixed cost. Suppose Sony rents a factory to produce picture tubes for color television sets for $500,000 per year. The total cost of $500,000 is not affected by the number of picture tubes produced. The unit cost of rent applicable to each tube, however, does depend on the total number of tubes produced. If 100,000 tubes are produced, the unit cost will be $500,000 ÷ 100,000 = $5. If 50,000 tubes are produced, the unit cost will be $500,000 ÷ 50,000 = $10. Therefore, a fixed cost does not change in total, but it becomes progressively smaller on a per-unit basis as the volume increases.

Note carefully from these examples that the "variable" or "fixed" characteristic of a cost relates to its total dollar amount and not to its per-unit amount. The following table summarizes these relationships.

<table>
<tr><td></td><td colspan="2" style="text-align:center">If Cost-Driver Activity Level Increases
(or Decreases)</td></tr>
<tr><td>Type of Cost</td><td>Total Cost</td><td>Cost Per Unit*</td></tr>
<tr><td>Fixed costs</td><td>No change</td><td>Decrease (or increase)</td></tr>
<tr><td>Variable costs</td><td>Increase (or decrease)</td><td>No change</td></tr>
</table>

* Per unit of activity volume, for example, product units, passenger-miles, sales dollars.

Objective 2
Show how changes in cost-driver activity levels affect variable and fixed costs.

When analyzing costs, two rules of thumb are useful:

1. Think of fixed costs as a total. Total fixed costs remain unchanged regardless of changes in cost-driver activity.
2. Think of variable costs on a per-unit basis. The per-unit variable cost remains unchanged regardless of changes in cost-driver activity.

A key to understanding cost behavior is distinguishing between variable and fixed costs. Test your understanding by answering the following questions.

1. Kilowatt hours used is a cost driver for power cost. Is power cost a variable or a fixed cost?
2. Square feet occupied is a cost driver for occupancy costs such as building depreciation and insurance. Is occupancy cost variable or fixed?

ANSWERS

The best way to determine whether the cost of a resource is fixed or variable is to ask the question, "If the level of the cost driver changes, what will happen to the cost?" If kilowatt hours increases (decreases), then the cost of power will also increase (decrease). Thus, power cost is variable. If the square feet occupied by a particular unit in an organization increases (decreases), the building depreciation and insurance on the building will not change. Thus, building occupancy costs such as depreciation and insurance are fixed costs.

RELEVANT RANGE

Although we have just described fixed costs as unchanging regardless of changes in the given cost driver, this rule of thumb holds true only within reasonable limits. For example, rent costs, which are generally fixed, will rise if increased production requires a larger or additional building—or if the landlord just decides to raise the rent. Conversely, rent costs may go down if decreased production causes the company to move to a smaller plant. The **relevant range** is the limit of cost-driver activity level within which a specific relationship between costs and the cost driver is valid. Even within the relevant range, though, a fixed cost remains fixed only over a given period of time—usually the budget period. Fixed costs may change from budget year to budget year solely because of changes in insurance and property tax rates, executive salary levels, or rent levels. But these items are unlikely to change within a given year.

> **relevant range** The limit of cost-driver activity level within which a specific relationship between costs and the cost driver is valid.

For example, suppose that a General Electric plant has a relevant range of between 40,000 and 85,000 cases of lightbulbs per month and that total monthly fixed costs within the relevant range are $100,000. Within the relevant range, fixed costs will remain the same. If production falls below 40,000 cases, changes in personnel and salaries would slash fixed costs to $60,000. If operations rise above 85,000 cases, increases in personnel and salaries would boost fixed costs to $115,000.

These assumptions—a given period and a given activity range—are shown graphically at the top of Exhibit 2-3. It is highly unusual, however, for monthly operations to be outside the relevant range. Therefore, the three-level refinement at the top of Exhibit 2-3 is usually not graphed. Instead, a single horizontal line is typically extended through the plotted activity levels, as at the bottom of the exhibit. Often a dashed line is used outside the relevant range.

The basic idea of a relevant range also applies to variable costs. That is, outside a relevant range, some variable costs, such as fuel consumed, may behave differently per unit of cost-driver activity. For example, the variable cost of a canning machine at Del Monte might be $5 for every hour it is used, assuming that it will be used between 30 and 50 hours each week. However, if it is used for more than 50 hours a week, the added wear and tear might increase variable costs to $6 for those hours beyond 50.

DIFFERENCES IN CLASSIFYING COSTS

As you may suspect, it is often difficult to classify a cost as exactly variable or exactly fixed. Many complications arise including the possibility of costs behaving in some

Exhibit 2-3

Fixed Costs and Relevant Range

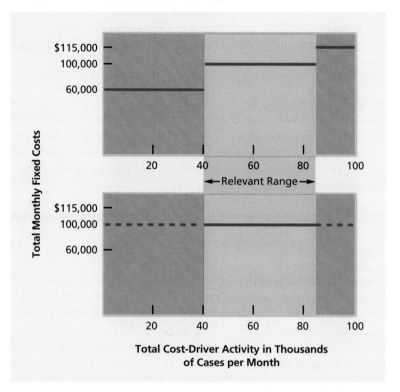

nonlinear way (not producing a straight line graph). For example, as tax preparers learn to process the new year's tax forms, their productivity rises. This means that total costs may actually behave as in Panel A that follows, not as in Panel B.

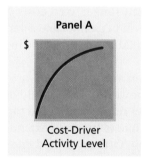

Panel A

$

Cost-Driver
Activity Level

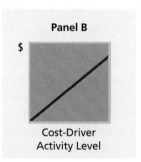

Panel B

$

Cost-Driver
Activity Level

Moreover, costs may simultaneously be affected by more than one cost driver. For example, the costs of shipping labor may be affected by both the weight and the number of units handled. We shall investigate various facets of this problem in succeeding chapters; for now, we shall assume that any cost may be classified as either variable or fixed. We assume also that a given variable cost is associated with only one volume-related cost driver and that relationship is linear.

Classifying costs as fixed or variable depends on the decision situation. More costs are fixed and fewer are variable when decisions involve very short time spans and very small changes in activity level. Suppose a United Airlines plane with several empty seats will depart from its gate in two minutes. A potential passenger is running down a corridor bearing a transferable ticket from a competing airline. Unless the airplane is held for an extra 30 seconds, the passenger will miss the departure and will not switch to United for the planned trip. What are the variable costs to United of delaying the departure and placing one more passenger in an otherwise empty seat? Variable costs (for example, one more meal) are negligible. Virtually all the costs in that decision situation are fixed (for example, maintenance crew salaries). Now in contrast, suppose United's decision is whether to add another flight, acquire another gate, add another city to its routes, or acquire another airplane. Many more costs would be regarded as variable and fewer as fixed. For example, in the case of adding a flight, the salaries of the maintenance crew would now be variable.

This example underscores the importance of how the decision situation affects the analysis of cost behavior. Whether costs are really "fixed" depends heavily on the relevant range, the length of the planning period in question, and the specific decision situation.

COST-VOLUME-PROFIT ANALYSIS

Managers often classify costs as fixed or variable when making decisions that affect the volume of output. The managers want to know how such decisions will affect costs and revenues. They realize that many factors in addition to the volume of output will affect costs. Yet, a useful starting point in their decision process is to specify the relationship between the volume of output and costs and revenues.

The managers of profit-seeking organizations usually study the effects of output volume on revenue (sales), expenses (costs), and net income (net profit). This study is commonly called **cost-volume-profit (CVP) analysis.** The managers of nonprofit organizations also benefit from the study of CVP relationships. Why? No organization has unlimited resources, and knowledge of how costs fluctuate as volume changes helps managers to understand how to control costs. For example, administrators of nonprofit hospitals are constantly concerned about the behavior of costs as the volume of patients fluctuates.

To apply CVP analysis, managers usually resort to some simplifying assumptions. The major simplification is to classify costs as either variable or fixed with respect to a single measure of the volume of output activity. This chapter focuses on such a simplified relationship.

cost-volume-profit (CVP) analysis The study of the effects of output volume on revenue (sales), expenses (costs), and net income (net profit).

CVP Scenario

Amy Winston, the manager of food services for Middletown Community College, is trying to decide whether to rent a line of snack vending machines. Although individual snack items have various acquisition costs and selling prices, Winston has decided that an average selling price of 50¢ per unit and an average acquisition cost of 40¢ per unit will suffice for purposes of this analysis. She predicts the following revenue and expense relationships.

	Per Unit	Percentage of Sales
Selling price	$ .50	100%
Variable cost of each item	.40	80
Selling price less variable cost	$ .10	20%
Monthly fixed expenses		
Rent	$1,000	
Wages for replenishing and servicing	4,500	
Other fixed expenses	500	
Total fixed expenses per month	$6,000	

We will now use these data in examining several applications of CVP analysis.

Increased worldwide competition in the automobile industry has made many companies acutely aware of their break-even points. In the early 1990s most auto companies were losing money. With dim prospects for large increases in volume of sales, the companies would be profitable only if they could decrease their break-even points. That is exactly what most companies did.

Break-even points vary greatly for different auto companies. The larger companies have high fixed costs and therefore must achieve higher sales to break even. For example, Chrysler reduced its break-even point from 1.9 million to 1.6 million vehicles from the late 1980s to 1993. Still, the reduction of 16% in the break-even point is less than that achieved by some competitors.

Saab, a Swedish company, has focused on bringing down the number of production hours per car. In the mid-1990s, Saab reduced production hours from 120 hours to 45 hours. This decreased the break-even volume from 125,000 vehicles to 83,000.

The assembly operations for Jaguar, located 100 miles north of London, have had a dual focus: quality and production time. Quality improvements were expected to increase sales, and this appears to be working. Warranty costs in the United States alone are down 60% and sales are up. Production improvements were intended to reduce the break-even volume. During the early 1990s, Jaguar had cut the time required to build a car by 54%. This cut the break-even point from between 50,000 and 60,000 vehicles to 30,000 per year.

In 1993, Volkswagen's variable costs of making a car were actually higher than its average price. As stated by VW's Chairman, Ferdinand Piech, "The more cars we sold, the more money we would lose." But VW lowered its breakeven by redesigning its cars and improving production processes.

It is clear that break-even volumes differ greatly among automobile companies. Rolls-Royce can generate a profit at a sales level of 1,300 vehicles, but Saab, Jaguar, Volkswagen, and Chrysler would go out of business at that volume. Similarly, Chrysler could not survive selling at volumes that are highly profitable to Saab and Jaguar. Each company must compute its own break-even volume based on its own fixed and variable costs. If a company's sales fall below its break-even point, either it must find a way to get more sales or it must restructure its production operations to reduce its break-even point.

Sources: Adapted from Paul A. Eisenstein, "Jaguar Ledgers to Feature Black, Not Red, Ink Next Year," *Washington Times,* September 16, 1994, p. D3; Mary Beth Vander Schaaf, "Saab Counts on V-6 to Boost 9000," *Automotive News,* September 26, 1994, p. 37; "GM's Saab Unit Climbs Back into Black," *Investor's Business Daily,* September 27, 1994, p. A4; James Bennet, "Chrysler Chief's World View: Place to Sell, Not Build, Cars," *New York Times,* September 30, 1994, p. D1; Christopher Jensen, "Jaguar's Renaissance: Ford Helps Its British Acquisition Make Quality Job One," *Plain Dealer,* October 9, 1994, p. 1H; Paul Eisenstein, "VW Can Afford Expansion," *Automotive Industries,* October 1, 1998.

BREAK-EVEN POINT — CONTRIBUTION-MARGIN AND EQUATION TECHNIQUES

break-even point The level of sales at which revenue equals expenses and net income is zero.

The most basic CVP analysis computes the monthly break-even point in number of units and in dollar sales. The **break-even point** is the level of sales at which revenue equals expenses and net income is zero. The business press frequently refers to break-even points. For example, a news story on hotel occupancy rates in San Francisco stated that "seventy percent [occupancy] is considered a break-even for hoteliers." Another news story stated that "the Big Three auto makers have slashed their sales break-even point in North America from 12.2 million cars and trucks to only 9.1 million this year." Finally, an article on Outboard Marine Corporation reported that, as a result of restructuring, the company's "break-even point will be $250 million lower than it was in 1993."

The study of cost-volume-profit relationships is often called break-even analysis. This term is misleading, because finding the break-even point is often just the first step in a planning decision. Managers usually concentrate on how the decision will affect sales, costs, and net income.

One direct use of the break-even point, however, is to assess possible risks. By comparing planned sales with the break-even point, managers can determine a margin of safety:

$$\text{Margin of Safety} = \text{Planned Unit Sales} - \text{Break-Even Unit Sales}$$

The **margin of safety** shows how far sales can fall below the planned level before losses occur.

There are two basic techniques for computing a break-even point: contribution margin and equation.

Contribution-Margin Technique.   Consider the following commonsense arithmetic approach. Every unit sold generates a **contribution margin** or **marginal income,** which is the unit sales price minus the variable cost per unit. For the vending machine snack items, the contribution margin per unit is $.10:

Unit sales price	$.50
Unit variable cost	.40
Unit contribution margin	$.10

When is the break-even point reached? When enough units have been sold to generate a total contribution margin (total number of units sold × contribution margin per unit) equal to the total fixed costs. Divide the $6,000 in fixed costs by the $.10 unit contribution margin. The number of units that must be sold to break even is $6,000 ÷ $.10 = 60,000 units. The sales revenue at the break-even point is 60,000 units × $.50 per unit, or $30,000.

Objective 3
Calculate break-even sales volume in total dollars and total units.

Think about the contribution margin of the snack items. Each unit purchased and sold generates extra revenue of $.50 and extra cost of $.40. Fixed costs are unaffected. If zero units were sold, a loss equal to the fixed cost of $6,000 would be incurred. Each unit reduces the loss by $.10 until sales reach the break-even point of 60,000 units. After that point, each unit adds (or contributes) $.10 to profit.

The condensed income statement at the break-even point is

	Total	Per Unit	Percentage
Units	60,000		
Sales	$30,000	$.50	100%
Variable costs	24,000	.40	80
Contribution margin*	$ 6,000	$.10	20%
Fixed costs	6,000		
Net income	$ 0		

* Sales less variable costs.

Sometimes the unit price and unit variable costs of a product are not known. This situation is common at companies that sell more than one product because no single price or variable cost applies to all products. For example, a grocery store sells hundreds of products at many different prices. A break-even point in overall units sold by the store would not be meaningful. In such cases, you can use total sales and total variable costs to calculate variable costs as a percentage of each sales dollar.

Consider our vending machine example:

Sales price	100%
Variable expenses as a percentage of dollar sales	80
Contribution-margin percentage	20%

Therefore, 20% of each sales dollar is available for the recovery of fixed expenses and the making of net income: $6,000 ÷ .20 = $30,000 sales are needed to break even. The contribution-margin percentage is based on dollar sales and is often expressed as a ratio (.20 instead of 20%). Using the contribution-margin percentage, you can compute the break-even volume in dollar sales without determining the break-even point in units.

Equation Technique. The equation technique is the most general form of analysis, the one that may be adapted to any conceivable cost-volume-profit situation. You are familiar with a typical income statement. Any income statement can be expressed in equation form, or as a mathematical model, as follows:

$$\text{sales} - \text{variable expenses} - \text{fixed expenses} = \text{net income} \tag{1}$$

That is,

$$\begin{pmatrix} \text{unit} & \text{number} \\ \text{sales} \times & \text{of} \\ \text{price} & \text{units} \end{pmatrix} - \begin{pmatrix} \text{unit} & \text{number} \\ \text{variable} \times & \text{of} \\ \text{cost} & \text{units} \end{pmatrix} - \begin{matrix} \text{fixed} \\ \text{expenses} \end{matrix} = \begin{matrix} \text{net} \\ \text{income} \end{matrix}$$

At the break-even point net income is zero:

$$\text{sales} - \text{variable expenses} - \text{fixed expenses} = 0$$

Let N = number of units to be sold to break even. Then, for the vending machine example,

$$\$.50N - \$.40N - \$6,000 = 0$$
$$\$.10N = \$6,000$$
$$N = \$6,000 \div \$.10$$
$$N = 60,000 \text{ units}$$

Total sales in the equation is a price-times-quantity relationship, which was expressed in our example as $.50N. To find the dollar sales, multiply 60,000 units by $.50, which would yield the break-even dollar sales of $30,000.

You can also solve the equation for sales dollars without computing the unit break-even point by using the relationship of variable costs and profits as a percentage of sales:

$$\text{variable-cost ratio or percentage} = \frac{\text{variable cost per unit}}{\text{sales price per unit}}$$
$$= \frac{\$.40}{\$.50}$$
$$= .80 \text{ or } 80\%$$

Let S = sales in dollars needed to break even. Then

$$S - .80S - \$6,000 = 0$$
$$.20S = \$6,000$$
$$S = \$6,000 \div .20$$
$$S = \$30,000$$

Relationship between the Two Techniques. You may have noticed that the contribution-margin technique is merely a shortcut version of the equation technique. Look at the last three lines in the two solutions given for equation 1. They read

Break-Even Volume	
Units	*Dollars*
$\$.10N = \$6,000$	$.20S = \$6,000$
$N = \dfrac{\$6,000}{\$.10}$	$S = \dfrac{\$6,000}{.20}$
$N = 60,000$ units	$S = \$30,000$

From these equations, we can derive the following general shortcut formulas:

$$\text{break-even volume in units} = \frac{\text{fixed expenses}}{\text{contribution margin per unit}} \qquad (2)$$

$$\text{break-even volume in dollars} = \frac{\text{fixed expenses}}{\text{contribution-margin ratio}} \qquad (3)$$

Which should you use, the equation or the contribution-margin technique? Use either. Both yield the same results, so the choice is a matter of personal preference or convenience in a particular case.

Using short-cut formulas (2) and (3), answer the following questions. Remember that the contribution margin per unit equals the sales price per unit minus the variable costs per unit.

1. What would be the effect on the unit and dollar break-even level if fixed costs increase (and there are no other changes)?
2. What would be the effect on the unit and dollar break-even level if variable cost per unit decreases (and there are no other changes)?
3. What would be the effect on the unit and dollar break-even level if sales volume increases (and there are no other changes)?

ANSWERS

1. The break-even level in both units and sales dollars would increase if fixed costs increase.
2. The break-even level in both units and sales dollars would decrease if variable costs decrease.
3. Think before answering this question. The *actual (or even planned)* volume of sales in units has nothing to do with determining the break-even point. This is why unit volume does not appear in either equation (2) or (3).

Break-Even Point — Graphical Techniques. Exhibit 2-4 is a graph of the cost-volume-profit relationship in our vending machine example. Study the graph as you read the procedure for constructing it.

Objective 4
Create a cost-volume-profit graph and understand the assumptions behind it.

1. Draw the axes. The horizontal axis is the sales volume, and the vertical axis is dollars of cost and revenue.
2. Plot sales volume. Select a convenient sales volume, say, 100,000 units, and plot point A for total sales dollars at that volume: $100,000 \times \$.50 = \$50,000$. Draw the revenue (that is, sales) line from point A to the origin, point 0.
3. Plot fixed expenses. Draw the line showing the $6,000 fixed portion of expenses. It should be a horizontal line intersecting the vertical axis at $6,000, point B.

Exhibit 2-4

Cost-Volume-Profit Graph

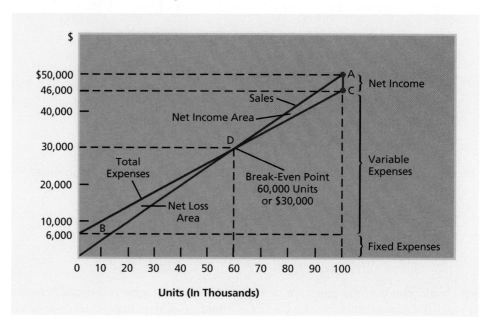

4. Plot variable expenses. Determine the variable portion of expenses at a convenient level of activity: 100,000 units × $.40 = $40,000. Add this to the fixed expenses: $40,000 + $6,000 = $46,000. Plot point C for 100,000 units and $46,000. Then draw a line between this point and point B. This is the total expenses line.

5. Locate the break-even point. The break-even point is where the total expenses line crosses the sales line, 60,000 units or $30,000, namely, where total sales revenues exactly equal total costs, point D.

The break-even point is only one part of this cost-volume-profit graph. The graph also shows the profit or loss at any rate of activity. At any given volume, the vertical distance between the sales line and the total expenses line measures the net income or net loss.

Managers often use break-even graphs because these graphs show potential profits over a wide range of volume more easily than numerical exhibits. Whether graphs or other presentations are used depends largely on management's preference.

Note that the concept of relevant range applies to the entire break-even graph. Almost all break-even graphs show revenue and cost lines extending back to the vertical axis as shown in Exhibit 2-5(A). This approach is misleading because the relationships depicted in such graphs are valid only within the relevant range that underlies the construction of the graph. Exhibit 2-5(B), a modification of the conventional break-even graph, partially demonstrates the multitude of assumptions that must be made in constructing the typical break-even graph. Some of these assumptions follow.

1. Expenses may be classified into variable and fixed categories. Total variable expenses vary directly with activity level. Total fixed expenses do not change with activity level.

2. The behavior of revenues and expenses is accurately portrayed and is linear over the relevant range. The principal differences between the accountant's break-even chart and the economist's are that (1) the accountant's sales line is drawn on the assumption that selling prices do not change with production or sales, and the economist assumes that reduced selling prices are normally associated with

Exhibit 2-5

Conventional and Modified Break-Even Graphs

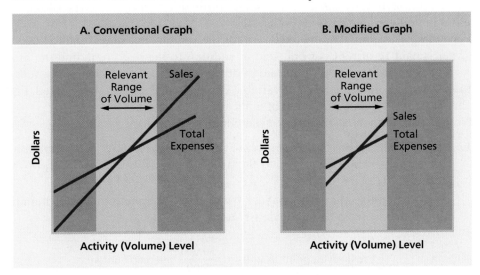

increased sales volume; and (2) the accountant usually assumes a constant variable expense per unit, and the economist assumes that variable expense per unit changes with production levels. Within the relevant range, the accountant's and the economist's sales and expense lines are usually close to one another, although the lines may diverge greatly outside the range.

3. Efficiency and productivity will be unchanged.

4. Sales mix will be constant. The **sales mix** is the relative proportions or combinations of quantities of products that constitute total sales. (See Appendix 2A for more on sales mixes.)

5. The difference in inventory level at the beginning and at the end of a period is insignificant. (The impact of inventory changes on CVP analysis is discussed in Chapter 15.)

> **sales mix** The relative proportions or combinations of quantities of products that constitute total sales.

Changes in Fixed Expenses. Changes in fixed expenses cause changes in the break-even point. For example, if the $1,000 monthly rent of the vending machines were doubled, what would be the monthly break-even point in number of units and dollar sales?

The fixed expenses would increase from $6,000 to $7,000, so

$$\frac{\text{break-even volume}}{\text{in units}} = \frac{\text{fixed expenses}}{\text{contribution margin per unit}} = \frac{\$7,000}{\$.10} = 70,000 \text{ units}$$

$$\frac{\text{break-even volume}}{\text{in dollars}} = \frac{\text{fixed expenses}}{\text{contribution margin ratio}} = \frac{\$7,000}{20} = 35,000$$

Note that a one-sixth increase in fixed expenses altered the break-even point by one-sixth: from 60,000 to 70,000 units and from $30,000 to $35,000. This type of relationship always exists between fixed expenses and the break-even point if everything else remains constant.

Companies frequently lower their break-even points by reducing their total fixed costs. For example, closing or selling factories decreases property taxes, insurance, depreciation, and managers' salaries.

Changes in Contribution Margin per Unit. Changes in variable costs also cause the break-even point to shift. Companies can reduce their break-even points by increasing their contribution margins per unit of product through either increases in sales prices or decreases in unit variable costs, or both.

For example, assume that the fixed rent for the vending machines is still $1,000. (1) If the owner is paid 1¢ of rent per unit sold in addition to the fixed rent, find the monthly break-even point in number of units and in dollar sales. (2) If the selling price falls from 50¢ to 45¢ per unit, and the original variable expenses per unit are unchanged, find the monthly break-even point in number of units and in dollar sales.

Here's what happens to the break-even point:

1. The variable expenses would increase from 40¢ to 41¢, the unit contribution margin would decline from 10¢ to 9¢, and the contribution-margin ratio would become .18 ($.09 ÷ $.50).

   The original fixed expenses of $6,000 would stay the same, but the denominators would change from those previously used. Thus,

$$\text{break-even point in units} = \frac{\$6,000}{\$.09} = 66,667 \text{ units}$$

$$\text{break-even point in dollars} = \frac{\$6,000}{.18} = \$33,333$$

2. If the selling price fell from 50¢ to 45¢, and the original variable expenses were unchanged, the unit contribution would be reduced from 10¢ to 5¢ (that is, 45¢ − 40¢), and the break-even point would soar to 120,000 units ($6,000 ÷ $.05). The break-even point in dollars would also change because the selling price and contribution-margin ratio change. The contribution-margin ratio would be .1111 ($.05 ÷ $.45). The break-even point, in dollars, would be $54,000 (120,000 units × $.45) or, using the formula:

$$\text{break-even point in dollars} = \frac{\$6,000}{.1111} = \$54,000$$

TARGET NET PROFIT AND AN INCREMENTAL APPROACH

Managers can also use CVP analysis to determine the total sales, in units and dollars, needed to reach a target profit. For example, in our snack vending example, suppose Winston considers $480 per month the minimum acceptable net income. How many units will have to be sold to justify the adoption of the vending machine plan? How does this figure "translate" into dollar sales?

The method for computing desired or target sales volume in units to meet the desired or target net income is the same as was used in our earlier break-even computations. Now the targets, however, are expressed in the equations:

Objective 5
Calculate sales volume in total dollars and total units to reach a target profit.

$$\text{target sales} - \text{variable expenses} - \text{fixed expenses} = \text{target net income} \qquad (4)$$

or

$$\text{target sales volume in units} = \frac{\text{fixed expenses} + \text{target net income}}{\text{contribution margin per unit}}$$

$$= \frac{\$6,000 + \$480}{\$.10} = 64,800 \text{ units} \qquad (5)$$

Another way of getting the same answer is to use your knowledge of the break-even point and adopt an incremental approach. The phrase **incremental effect** is widely used in accounting. It refers to the change in total results (such as revenue, expenses, or income) under a new condition in comparison with some given or known condition.

In this case, the given condition is the 60,000-unit break-even point. All expenses would be recovered at that volume. Therefore the change or increment in net income for every unit beyond 60,000 would be equal to the contribution margin of $.50 − $.40 = $.10. If $480 were the target net profit, $480 ÷ $.10 would show that the target volume must exceed the break-even volume by 4,800 units; it would therefore be 60,000 + 4,800 = 64,800 units.

To find the answer in terms of dollar sales, multiply 64,800 units by $.50 or use the formula:

$$\text{target sales volume in dollars} = \frac{\text{fixed expenses + target net income}}{\text{contribution-margin ratio}} \quad (6)$$

$$= \frac{\$6,000 + \$480}{.20} = \$32,400$$

To solve directly for sales dollars with the alternative incremental approach, we would start at the break-even point in dollar sales of $30,000. Every sales dollar beyond that point contributes $.20 to net profit. Divide $480 by .20. Dollar sales must exceed the break-even volume by $2,400 to produce a net profit of $480. Thus the total dollar sales would be $30,000 + $2,400 = $32,400.

The following table summarizes these computations:

	Break-Even Point	Increment	New Condition
Volume in units	60,000	4,800	64,800
Sales	$30,000	$2,400	$32,400
Variable expenses	24,000	1,920	25,920
Contribution margin	$ 6,000	$ 480	$ 6,480
Fixed expenses	6,000	—	6,000
Net income	$ 0	$ 480	$ 480

MULTIPLE CHANGES IN KEY FACTORS

So far, we have seen only changes in one CVP factor at a time. In the real world, managers often must make decisions about the probable effects of multiple factor changes. For instance, suppose that after the vending machines have been in place a while, Winston is considering locking them from 6:00 P.M. to 6:00 A.M., which she estimates will save $820 in wages monthly. However, the cutback from 24-hour service would hurt volume substantially because many nighttime employees use the machines. Should the machines remain available 24 hours per day? Assume that monthly sales would decline by 10,000 units from current sales. We will perform the analysis assuming two different levels of current sales volume: (1) 62,000 units and (2) 90,000 units. Consider two approaches. One approach is to construct and solve equations for conditions that prevail under each alternative and select the volume level that yields the highest net income.

Regardless of the current volume level, be it 62,000 or 90,000 units, if we accept the prediction that sales will decline by 10,000 units as accurate, the closing from 6:00 P.M. to 6:00 A.M. will decrease net income by $180.

	Decline from 62,000 to 52,000 Units		Decline from 90,000 to 80,000 Units	
Units	62,000	52,000	90,000	80,000
Sales	$31,000	$26,000	$45,000	$40,000
Variable expenses	24,800	20,800	36,000	32,000
Contribution margin	$ 6,200	$ 5,200	$ 9,000	$ 8,000
Fixed expenses	6,000	5,180	6,000	5,180
Net income	$ 200	$ 20	$ 3,000	$ 2,820
Change in net income	($180)		($180)	

A second approach—an incremental approach—is quicker and simpler. Simplicity is important to managers because it keeps the analysis from being cluttered by irrelevant and potentially confusing data.

What does the insightful manager see in this situation? First, whether 62,000 or 90,000 units are being sold is irrelevant to the decision at hand. The issue is the decline in volume, which would be 10,000 units in either case. The essence of this decision is whether the prospective savings in fixed costs exceed the prospective loss in total contribution-margin dollars.

Lost total contribution margin, 10,000 units @ .10	$1,000
Savings in fixed expenses	820
Prospective decline in net income	$ 180

Locking the vending machines from 6:00 P.M. to 6:00 A.M. would cause a $180 decrease in monthly net income. Whichever way you analyze it, locking the machines is not a sound financial decision.

CVP ANALYSIS IN THE COMPUTER AGE

As we have seen, cost-volume-profit analysis is based on a mathematical model, the following equation.

$$\text{sales} - \text{variable expenses} - \text{fixed expenses} = \text{net income}$$

The CVP model is widely used as a planning model. Managers in a variety of organizations use a personal computer and a CVP modeling program to study combinations of changes in selling prices, unit variable costs, fixed costs, and desired profits. Many non-profit organizations also use computerized CVP modeling. For example, some private universities have models that help measure how decisions such as raising tuition, adding programs, and closing dormitories during winter holidays will affect financial results. The computer quickly calculates the results of changes and can display them both numerically and graphically.

Exhibit 2-6 is a sample spreadsheet that shows what the sales level would have to be at three different fixed expense levels and three different variable expense levels to reach three different income levels. The computer calculates the 27 different sales levels rapidly and without error. Managers can insert any numbers they want for fixed expenses (column A), variable expense percentage (column B), target net income (row 3 of columns C, D, and E), or combinations thereof, and the computer will compute the required sales level.

In addition to speed and convenience, computers allow a more sophisticated approach to CVP analysis than the one illustrated in this chapter. The assumptions listed

Exhibit 2-6

Spreadsheet Analysis of CVP Relationships

	A	B	C	D	E
				Sales Required to Earn	
1					
2	Fixed	Variable		Annual Net Income of	
3	Expenses	Expense %	$ 2,000	$ 4,000	$ 6,000
4					
5	$4,000	0.40	$10,000*	$13,333	$16,667
6	$4,000	0.44	$10,714*	$14,286	$17,857
7	$4,000	0.48	$11,538*	$15,385	$19,231
8	$6,000	0.40	$13,333	$16,667	$20,000
9	$6,000	0.44	$14,286	$17,857	$21,429
10	$6,000	0.48	$15,385	$19,231	$23,077
11	$8,000	0.40	$16,667	$20,000	$23,333
12	$8,000	0.44	$17,857	$21,429	$25,000
13	$8,000	0.48	$19,231	$23,077	$26,923
15					
16	*(A5 + C3)/(1 − B5) = ($4,000 + $2,000)/(1 − $.40) = $10,000				
17	(A6 + C3)/(1 − B6) = ($4,000 + $2,000)/(1 − $.44) = $10,714				
18	(A7 + C3)/(1 − B7) = ($4,000 + $2,000)/(1 − $.48) = $11,538				
19					

on pages 52–53 are necessary to simplify the analysis enough for most managers to construct a CVP model by hand. Computer analysts, however, can construct a model that does not require all the simplifications. Computer models can include multiple cost drivers, nonlinear relationships between costs and cost drivers, varying sales mixes, and analyses that need not be restricted to a relevant range.

Use of computer models is a cost-benefit issue. Sometimes the costs of modeling are exceeded by the value of better decisions made using the models. However, the reliability of these models depends on the accuracy of their underlying assumptions about how revenues and costs will actually be affected. Moreover, in small organizations, simplified CVP models often are accurate enough that more sophisticated modeling is unwarranted.

ADDITIONAL USES OF COST-VOLUME ANALYSIS

BEST COST STRUCTURE

Analyzing cost-volume-profit relationships is an important management responsibility. Managers usually try to find the most profitable cost structure—the combination of variable- and fixed-cost factors. For example, purchasing automated machinery may raise fixed costs but reduce labor cost per unit. Conversely, it may be wise to reduce fixed costs to obtain a more favorable combination. Thus, direct selling by a salaried sales force (a fixed cost) may be replaced by the use of salespeople who are compensated via sales commissions (variable costs).

Generally, companies that spend heavily for advertising are willing to do so because they have high contribution-margin percentages (e.g., airlines, cigarette, and cosmetic companies). Conversely, companies with low contribution-margin percentages usually spend less for advertising and promotion (e.g., manufacturers of industrial equipment). As a result, two companies with the same unit sales volumes at the same unit prices could have different attitudes toward risking an advertising outlay. Assume the following:

	Perfume Company	Janitorial Service Company
Unit sales volume	100,000 bottles	100,000 square feet
Dollar sales at $20 per unit	$2,000,000	$2,000,000
Variable costs	200,000	1,700,000
Contribution margin	$1,800,000	$ 300,000
Contribution-margin percentage	90%	15%

Suppose each company wants to increase sales volume by 10%:

	Perfume Company	Janitorial Service Company
Increase in sales volume, 10,000 × $20	$200,000	$200,000
Increase in contribution margin, 90%, 15%	180,000	30,000

The perfume company would be inclined to increase advertising considerably to boost the contribution margin by $180,000. In contrast, the janitorial service company would be foolhardy to spend large amounts to increase the contribution margin by $30,000.

Note that when the contribution margin as a percentage of sales is low, great increases in volume are necessary before significant increases in net profits can occur. On the other hand, as sales exceed the break-even point, a high contribution-margin percentage increases profits faster than does a small contribution-margin percentage.

OPERATING LEVERAGE

operating leverage A firm's ratio of fixed to variable costs.

In addition to weighing the varied effects of changes in fixed and variable costs, managers need to consider their firm's ratio of fixed to variable costs, called **operating leverage**. In highly leveraged companies—those with high fixed costs and low variable costs—small changes in sales volume result in large changes in net income. Companies with less leverage (that is, lower fixed costs and higher variable costs) are not affected as much by changes in sales volume.

Exhibit 2-7 shows cost behavior relationships at two firms, one highly leveraged and one with low leverage. The firm with higher leverage has fixed costs of $14,000 and variable cost per unit of $.10. The firm with lower leverage has fixed costs of only $2,000 but variable costs of $.25 per unit. Expected sales at both companies are 80,000 units at $.30 per unit. At this sales level, both firms would have net incomes of $2,000. If sales fall short of 80,000 units, profits drop most sharply for the highly leveraged business. If sales exceed 80,000 units, however, profits increase most sharply for the highly leveraged concern.

The highly leveraged alternative is more risky. Why? Because it provides the highest possible net income and the highest possible losses. In other words, net income is highly variable, depending on the actual level of sales. The low-leverage alternative is less risky because variations in sales lead to only small variability in net income. At sales of 90,000 units, net income is $4,000 for the higher-leveraged firm but only $2,500 for the lower-leveraged firm. At sales of 70,000 units, however, the higher-leveraged firm has zero profits, compared to $1,500 for the lower-leveraged firm.

CONTRIBUTION MARGIN AND GROSS MARGIN

variable-cost ratio (variable-cost percentage) All variable costs divided by sales.

Contribution margin may be expressed as a total absolute amount, a unit absolute amount, a ratio, and a percentage. The **variable-cost ratio** or **variable-cost percentage** is defined as all variable costs divided by sales. Thus a contribution-margin ratio of 20% means that the variable-cost ratio is 80%.

Exhibit 2-7

High versus Low Leverage

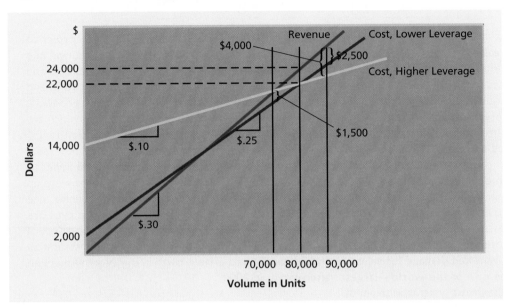

Too often people confuse the terms *contribution margin* and *gross margin*. **Gross margin** (which is also called gross profit) is the excess of sales over the **cost of goods sold** (that is, the cost of the merchandise that is acquired or manufactured and then sold). It is a widely used concept, particularly in the retailing industry.

Compare the gross margin with the contribution margin:

gross margin = sales price − cost of goods sold

contribution margin = sales price − all variable expenses

The following comparisons from our vending machine illustration show the similarities and differences between the contribution margin and the gross margin in a retail store:

Sales	$.50
Variable costs: acquisition cost of unit sold	.40
Contribution margin and gross margin are equal	$.10

Thus the original data resulted in no difference between the measure of contribution margin and gross margin. There would be a difference between the two, however, if the firm had to pay additional rent of 1¢ per unit sold:

	Contribution Margin	Gross Margin
Sales	$.50	$ .50
Acquisition cost of unit sold	$.40	.40
Variable rent	.01	
Total variable expense	.41	
Contribution margin	$.09	
Gross margin		$.10

gross margin (gross profit) The excess of sales over the total cost of goods sold.

cost of goods sold The cost of the merchandise that is acquired or manufactured and resold.

Objective 6
Differentiate between contribution margin and gross margin.

One way that companies cope with hard economic times is to lower their break-even point. *Business Week* suggested that investors look for such firms "because efficiency gains at companies that have pared fixed costs as well as variable ones should be deep and lasting."

Why is lowering the break-even point important? Because a company that maintains its profitability in times of low sales is poised to take off when the economy improves. Baldwin, the piano maker, actually improved its profits in a time of decreasing sales by successfully cutting costs—especially fixed costs. If it maintains its new cost structure as sales rebound, profits will soar. Lowering fixed costs is especially important because these costs will not necessarily increase as production increases to meet renewed demand for sales.

Tenneco Automotive is one of the world's largest makers of ride-control and exhaust systems, with annual revenues of more than $3 billion (1999). In early 1999, Tenneco announced weak earnings in its automotive aftermarket business. But Chairman and CEO Dana Mead predicted that its profitability would improve and

its break-even point would be lower. How? According to Mead, the company is rationalizing manufacturing and distribution capacity (in other words, selling excess and idle plants and equipment), reducing head count, and introducing new high contribution margin products. "The steps we have taken in the aftermarket, which are lowering our break-even point, should position us for the aftermarket rebound," Mead said.

Did Tenneco's strategy work? In April 2000, Tenneco announced that its first-quarter 2000 revenues were up 2% over 1999. According to David Gabriel, senior vice president, "We slashed our break-even point by more than 25% in the last 12 months. The combination of sharper marketing focus, new products, and cost control should continue to drive growth in our North American aftermarket in 2000."

Sources: Adapted from "Lots of Companies Are Lean, But Which Are Mean?" *Business Week*, February 3, 1992, p. 84; News Releases, Tenneco Automotive, Inc., January 5, 1999 and April 27, 2000.

As the preceding tabulation indicates, contribution margin and gross margin are not the same concepts. Contribution margin focuses on sales in relation to all variable costs, whereas gross margin focuses on sales in relation to cost of goods sold. For example, consider MascoTech, a Detroit-based auto parts supplier. A newspaper article reported that MascoTech's "gross profit margin on sales is about 21% today, but for each additional sales dollar the contribution margin is more like 30%."

NONPROFIT APPLICATION

Consider how cost-volume-profit relationships apply to nonprofit organizations. Suppose a city has a $100,000 lump-sum budget appropriation to conduct a counseling program for drug addicts. The variable costs for drug prescriptions are $400 per patient per year. Fixed costs are $60,000 in the relevant range of 50 to 150 patients. If all of the budget appropriation is spent, how many patients can be served in a year?

We can use the break-even equation to solve the problem. Let N be the number of patients.

$$\text{revenue} - \text{variable expenses} - \text{fixed expenses} = 0 \text{ if budget is completely spent}$$
$$\$100,000 \text{ lump sum} - \$400N - \$60,000 = 0$$
$$\$400N = \$100,000 - \$60,000$$
$$N = \$40,000 \div \$400$$
$$N = 100 \text{ patients}$$

Suppose the total budget appropriation for the following year is cut by 10%. Fixed costs will be unaffected, but service will decline.

$$\text{revenue} - \text{variable expenses} - \text{fixed expenses} = 0$$
$$\$90{,}000 - \$400N - \$60{,}000 = 0$$
$$\$400N = \$90{,}000 - \$60{,}000$$
$$N = \$30{,}000 \div \$400$$
$$N = 75 \text{ patients}$$

The percentage reduction in service is more than the 10% reduction in the budget. Unless the city restructures its operations, the service volume must be reduced 25% (from 100 to 75 patients) to stay within budget. Note that lump-sum revenue is a horizontal line on the graph:

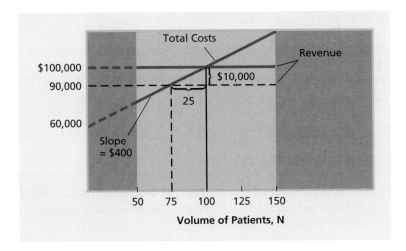

SUMMARY PROBLEM FOR YOUR REVIEW

PROBLEM

The budgeted income statement of Port Williams Gift Shop is summarized as follows.

Net revenue	$800,000
Less: expenses, including $400,000 of fixed expenses	880,000
Net loss	$(80,000)

The manager believes that an increase of $200,000 on advertising outlays will increase sales substantially.

1. At what sales volume will the store break even after spending $200,000 on advertising?
2. What sales volume will result in a net profit of $40,000 after spending the 200,000 on advertising?

SOLUTION

1. Note that all data are expressed in dollars. No unit data are given. Most companies have many products, so the overall break-even analysis deals with dollar sales, not units. The variable expenses are $880,000 − $400,000 = $480,000. The variable-expense ratio is $480,000 ÷ $800,000 = .60. Therefore the contribution-margin ratio is .40. Let S = break-even sales in dollars. Then

$$S - \text{variable expenses} - \text{fixed expenses} = \text{net profit}$$

$$S - .60S - (\$400,000 + \$200,000) = 0$$

$$.40S = \$600,000$$

$$S = \frac{\$600,000}{.40} = \frac{\text{fixed expenses}}{\text{contribution-margin ratio}}$$

$$S = \$1,500,000$$

2. $$\text{required sales} = \frac{\text{fixed expenses} + \text{target net profit}}{\text{contribution-margin ratio}}$$

$$\text{required sales} = \frac{\$600,000 + \$40,000}{.40} = \frac{\$640,000}{.40}$$

$$\text{required sales} = \$1,600,000$$

Alternatively, we can use an incremental approach and reason that all dollar sales beyond the $1.5 million break-even point will result in a 40% contribution to net profit. Divide $40,000 by .40. Sales must therefore be $100,000 beyond the $1.5 million break-even point to produce a net profit of $40,000.

Highlights to Remember

Explain how cost drivers affect cost behavior. A cost driver is an output measure that causes the use of costly resources. When the level of an activity changes, the level of the cost driver or output measure will also change, causing changes in costs.

Show how changes in cost-driver activity levels affect variable and fixed costs. Different types of costs behave in different ways. If the costs of the resources used changes in proportion to changes in the cost driver level, the resource is a variable-cost resource (its costs are variable). If the cost of the resource used does not change because of cost driver level changes, the resource is a fixed-cost resource (its costs are fixed).

Calculate break-even sales volume in total dollars and total units. CVP analysis (sometimes called break-even analysis) can be approached graphically or with equations. To calculate the break-even point in total units, divide the fixed costs by the unit contribution margin. To calculate the break-even point in total dollars (sales dollars), divide the fixed costs by the contribution-margin ratio.

Create a cost-volume-profit graph and understand the assumptions behind it. A cost-volume-profit graph can be created by drawing revenue and total cost lines as functions of the cost-driver level. Be sure to recognize the limitations of CVP analysis and that it assumes constant efficiency, sales mix, and inventory levels.

Calculate sales volume in total dollars and total units to reach a target profit. Managers use CVP analysis to compute the sales needed to achieve a target profit or to examine the effects on profit of changes in factors such as fixed costs, variable costs, or cost driver volume.

Differentiate between contribution margin and gross margin. The contribution margin—the difference between sales price and variable costs—is an important concept. Do not confuse it with gross margin, the difference between sales price and cost of goods sold.

Understand how cost behavior and CVP analysis are used by managers. Understanding cost behavior patterns and cost-volume-profit (CVP) relationships can help guide a manager's decisions. Because one of the main goals of management accounting is controlling and reducing costs, understanding cost behavior is vital to the manager's decision-making role. CVP analysis is a technique that is used often by management accountants both to gain an understanding of the cost and profit structure in a company and to explain it to other managers.

Appendix 2A: Sales-Mix Analysis

Objective 7
Explain the effects of sales mix on profits.

To emphasize fundamental ideas, the cost-volume-profit analysis in this chapter has focused on a single product. Nearly all companies, however, sell more than one product. Sales mix is defined as the relative proportions or combinations of quantities of products that comprise total sales. If the proportions of the mix change, the cost-volume-profit relationships also change.

Suppose Ramos Company has two products, wallets (W) and key cases (K). The income budget follows.

	Wallets (W)	Key Cases (K)	Total
Sales in units	300,000	75,000	375,000
Sales @ $8 and $5	$2,400,000	$375,000	$2,775,000
Variable expenses @ $7 and $3	2,100,000	225,000	2,325,000
Contribution margins @ $1 and $2	$ 300,000	$150,000	$ 450,000
Fixed expenses			180,000
Net income			$ 270,000

For simplicity, ignore income taxes. What would be the break-even point? The typical answer assumes a constant mix of 4 units of W for every unit of K. Therefore, let K = number of units of product K to break even, and 4K = number of units of product W to break even:

$$\text{sales} - \text{variable expenses} - \text{fixed expenses} = \text{zero net income}$$

$$[\$8(4K) + \$5(K)] - [\$7(4K) + \$3(K)] - \$180,000 = 0$$

$$\$32K + \$5K - \$28K - \$3K - \$180,000 = 0$$

$$\$6K = \$180,000$$

$$K = 30,000$$

$$4K = 120,000 = W$$

The break-even point is 30,000K + 120,000W = 150,000 units.

This is the only break-even point for a sales mix of four wallets for every key case. Clearly, however, there are other break-even points for other sales mixes. For instance, suppose only key cases were sold, fixed expenses being unchanged.

$$\text{break-even point} = \frac{\text{fixed expenses}}{\text{contribution margin per unit}}$$

$$= \frac{\$180,000}{\$2}$$

$$= 90,000 \text{ key cases}$$

If only wallets were sold:

$$\text{break-even point} = \frac{\$180,000}{\$1}$$

$$= 180,000 \text{ wallets}$$

Managers are not interested in the break-even point for its own sake. Instead, they want to know how changes in a planned sales mix will affect net income. When the sales mix changes, the break-even point and the expected net income at various sales levels are altered. For example, suppose overall actual total sales were equal to the budget of 375,000 units. However, only 50,000 key cases were sold.

	Wallets (W)	Key Cases (K)	Total
Sales in units	325,000	50,000	375,000
Sales @ $8 and $5	$2,600,000	$250,000	$2,850,000
Variable expenses @ $7 and $3	2,275,000	150,000	2,425,000
Contribution margins @ $1 and $2	$ 325,000	$100,000	$ 425,000
Fixed expenses			180,000
Net income			$ 245,000

The change in sales mix has resulted in a $245,000 actual net income rather than the $270,000 budgeted net income, an unfavorable difference of $25,000. The budgeted and actual sales in number of units were identical, but the proportion of sales of the product bearing the higher unit contribution margin declined.

Managers usually want to maximize the sales of all their products. Faced with limited resources and time, however, executives prefer to generate the most profitable sales mix achievable. For example, consider a recent annual report of Deere & Co., a manufacturer of farm equipment: "The increase in the ratio of cost of goods sold to net sales resulted from higher production costs [and] a less favorable mix of products sold."

Profitability of a given product helps guide executives who must decide to emphasize or de-emphasize particular products. For example, given limited production facilities or limited time of sales personnel, should we emphasize wallets or key cases? These decisions may be affected by other factors beyond the contribution margin per unit of product. Chapter 5 explores some of these factors, including the importance of the amount of profit per unit of time rather than per unit of product.

Appendix 2B: Impact of Income Taxes

Objective 8
Compute cost-volume-profit relationships on an after-tax basis.

Thus far we have (as so many people would like to) ignored income taxes. In most nations, however, private enterprises are subject to income taxes. Reconsider the vending machine example in this chapter. As part of our CVP analysis, we discussed the sales necessary to achieve a target income before income taxes of $480. If an income tax were levied at 40%, the new result would be

Income before income tax	$480	100%
Income tax	192	40
Net income	$288	60%

Note that

net income = income before income taxes − .40 (income before income taxes)

net income = .60 (income before income taxes)

$$\text{income before income taxes} = \frac{\text{net income}}{.60}$$

or

$$\text{target income before income taxes} = \frac{\text{target after-tax net income}}{1 - \text{tax rate}}$$

$$\text{target income before income taxes} = \frac{\$288}{1 - .40} = \frac{\$288}{.60} = \$480$$

Suppose the target net income after taxes was $288. The only change in the general equation approach would be on the right-hand side of the following equation:

$$\text{target sales} - \text{variable expenses} - \text{fixed expenses} = \frac{\text{target after-tax net income}}{1 - \text{tax rate}}$$

Thus, letting N be the number of units to be sold at $.50 each with a variable cost of $.40 each and total fixed costs of $6,000,

$$\$.50N - \$.40N - \$6,000 = \frac{\$288}{1 - .4}$$

$$\$.10N = \$6,000 + \frac{\$288}{.6}$$

$$\$.06N = \$3,600 + \$288 = 3,888$$

$$N = \$3,888 \div \$.06 = 64,800 \text{ units}$$

Sales of 64,800 units produce an after-tax profit of $288 as shown here and a before-tax profit of $480 as shown in the chapter.

Suppose the target net income after taxes was $480. The volume needed would rise to 68,000 units, as follows:

$$\$.50N - \$.40N - \$6,000 = \frac{\$480}{1 - .4}$$

$$\$.10N = \$6,000 + \frac{\$480}{.6}$$

$$\$.06N = \$3,600 + \$480 = \$4,080$$

$$N = \$4,080 \div \$.06 = 68,000 \text{ units}$$

As a shortcut to computing the effects of volume on the change in after-tax income, use the formula

$$\begin{pmatrix} \text{change} \\ \text{in net} \\ \text{income} \end{pmatrix} = \begin{pmatrix} \text{change in volume} \\ \text{in units} \end{pmatrix} \times \begin{pmatrix} \text{contribution margin} \\ \text{per unit} \end{pmatrix} \times (1 - \text{tax rate})$$

In our example, suppose operations were at a level of 64,800 units and $288 after-tax net income. The manager is wondering how much after-tax net income would increase if sales become 68,000 units.

$$\text{change in net income} = (68,000 - 64,800) \times \$.10 \times (1 - .4)$$

$$= 3,200 \times \$.10 \times .60 = 3,200 \times \$.06$$

$$= \$192$$

In brief, each unit beyond the break-even point adds to after-tax net profit at the unit contribution margin multiplied by (1 − income tax rate).

Throughout our illustration, the break-even point itself does not change. Why? Because there is no income tax at a level of zero profits.

Accounting Vocabulary

break-even point, p. 48
contribution margin, p. 49
cost behavior, p. 42
cost driver, p. 43

cost of goods sold, p. 59
cost-volume-profit (CVP)
 analysis, p. 47
fixed cost, p. 43

gross margin, p. 59
gross profit, p. 59
incremental effect, p. 55
marginal income, p. 49

Fundamental Assignment Material

2-A1   Cost-Volume-Profits and Vending Machines

Delgado Food Services Company operates and services soft drink vending machines located in restaurants, gas stations, and factories in four southeastern states. The machines are rented from the manufacturer. In addition, Delgado must rent the space occupied by its machines. The following expense and revenue relationships pertain to a contemplated expansion program of 40 machines.

Fixed monthly expenses follow.

Machine rental: 40 machines @ $43.50	$1,740
Space rental: 40 locations @ $28.80	1,152
Part-time wages to service the additional 40 machines	1,908
Other fixed costs	200
Total monthly fixed costs	$5,000

Other data follow.

	Per Unit	Per $100 of Sales
Selling price	$1.00	100%
Cost of snack	.80	80
Contribution margin	$ .20	20%

Required

These questions relate to the above data unless otherwise noted. Consider each question independently.

1. What is the monthly break-even point in number of units? In dollar sales?
2. If 36,000 units were sold, what would be the company's net income?
3. If the space rental cost were doubled, what would be the monthly break-even point in number of units? In dollar sales?
4. If, in addition to the fixed rent, Delgado Food Services Company paid the vending machine manufacturer 2¢ per unit sold, what would be the monthly break-even point in number of units? In dollar sales? Refer to the original data.
5. If, in addition to the fixed rent, Delgado paid the machine manufacturer 4¢ for each unit sold in excess of the break-even point, what would the new net income be if 36,000 units were sold? Refer to the original data.

2-A2   Exercises in Cost-Volume-Profit Relationships

The Global United Moving Company specializes in hauling heavy goods over long distances. The company's revenues and expenses depend on revenue miles, a measure that combines both weights and mileage. Summarized budget data for next year are based on predicted total revenue miles of 800,000.

	Per Revenue Mile
Average selling price (revenue)	$1.50
Average variable expenses	1.30
Fixed expenses, $110,000	

1. Compute the budgeted net income. Ignore income taxes.

2. Management is trying to decide how various possible conditions or decisions might affect net income. Compute the new net income for each of the following changes. Consider each case independently.

   a. A 10% increase in revenue miles

   b. A 10% increase in sales price

   c. A 10% increase in variable expenses

   d. A 10% increase in fixed expenses

   e. An average decrease in selling price of 3¢ per revenue mile and a 5% increase in revenue miles. Refer to the original data

   f. An average increase in selling price of 5¢ and a 10% decrease in revenue miles

   g. A 10% increase in fixed expenses in the form of more advertising and a 5% increase in revenue miles

2-B1 Basic CVP Exercises

Each problem is unrelated to the others.

1. Given: Selling price per unit, $20; total fixed expenses, $5,000; variable expenses per unit, $15. Find break-even sales in units.

2. Given: Sales, $40,000; variable expenses, $30,000; fixed expenses, $7,500; net income, $2,500. Find break-even sales.

3. Given: Selling price per unit, $30; total fixed expenses, $33,000; variable expenses per unit, $14. Find total sales in units to achieve a profit of $7,000, assuming no change in selling price.

4. Given: Sales, $50,000; variable expenses, $20,000; fixed expenses, $20,000; net income, $10,000. Assume no change in selling price; find net income if activity volume increases 10%.

5. Given: Selling price per unit, $40; total fixed expenses, $80,000; variable expenses per unit, $30. Assume that variable expenses are reduced by 20% per unit, and the total fixed expenses are increased by 10%. Find the sales in units to achieve a profit of $20,000, assuming no change in selling price.

2-B2 Basic CVP Analysis

Peter Landis opened Peter's Corner, a small day care facility, just over two years ago. After a rocky start, Peter's Corner has been thriving. Landis is now preparing a budget for November 20X2.

Monthly fixed costs for Peter's Corner are

Rent	$ 800
Salaries	1,400
Other fixed costs	100
Total fixed costs	$2,300

The salary is for Ann Penilla, the only employee, who works with Peter in caring for the children. Landis does not pay himself a salary, but he receives the excess of revenues over costs each month.

The cost driver for variable costs is "child-days." One child-day is one day in day care for one child, and the variable cost is $10 per child-day. The facility is open from 6:00 A.M. to 6:00 P.M. weekdays (that is, Monday through Friday), and there are 22 weekdays in November 20X2. An average day has 8 children attending Peter's Corner. State law prohibits Peter's Corner from having more than 14 children, a limit it has never reached. Landis charges $30 per day per child, regardless of how long the child is at the facility.

1. Suppose attendance for November 20X2 is equal to the average, resulting in 22 × 8 = 176 child-days. What amount will Landis have left after paying all his expenses?

2. Suppose both costs and attendance are difficult to predict. Compute the amount Landis will have left after paying all his expenses for each of the following situations. Consider each case independently.

a. Average attendance is 9 children per day instead of 8, generating 198 child-days.

b. Variable costs increase to $11 per child-day.

c. Rent is increased by $200 per month.

d. Landis spends $300 on advertising (a fixed cost) in November, which increases average daily attendance to 9.5 children.

e. Landis begins charging $33 per day on November 1, and average daily attendance slips to 7 children.

Additional Assignment Material

QUESTIONS

2-1. "Cost behavior is simply identification of cost drivers and their relationships to costs." Comment.

2-2. Give two rules of thumb to use when analyzing cost behavior.

2-3. Give three examples of variable costs and of fixed costs.

2-4. "Fixed costs decline as volume increases." Do you agree? Explain.

2-5. "It is confusing to think of fixed costs on a per-unit basis." Do you agree? Why or why not?

2-6. "All costs are either fixed or variable. The only difficulty in cost analysis is determining which of the two categories each cost belongs to." Do you agree? Explain.

2-7. "The relevant range pertains to fixed costs, not variable costs." Do you agree? Explain.

2-8. Identify the major simplifying assumption that underlies CVP analysis.

2-9. "Classification of costs into variable and fixed categories depends on the decision situation." Explain.

2-10. "Contribution margin is the excess of sales over fixed costs." Do you agree? Explain.

2-11. Why is "break-even analysis" a misnomer?

2-12. "Companies in the same industry generally have about the same break-even point." Do you agree? Explain.

2-13. "It is essential to choose the right CVP technique— equation, contribution margin, or graphical. If you pick the wrong one, your analysis will be faulty." Do you agree? Explain.

2-14. Describe three ways of lowering a break-even point.

2-15. "Incremental analysis is quicker, but it has no other advantage over an analysis of all costs and revenues associated with each alternative." Do you agree? Why or why not?

2-16. "CVP analysis is a common management use of personal computers." Do you agree? Explain.

2-17. Explain operating leverage and why a highly leveraged company is risky.

2-18. "The contribution margin and gross margin are always equal." Do you agree? Explain.

2-19. "CVP relationships are unimportant in nonprofit organizations." Do you agree? Explain.

2-20. "Two products were sold. Total budgeted sales and actual total sales in number of units were identical to the units budgeted. Actual unit variable costs and sales prices were the same as budgeted. Actual contribution margin was lower than budgeted." What could be the reason for the lower contribution margin?

2-21. Given a target after-tax net income, present the CVP formula for computing the required income before income taxes.

2-22. Present the CVP formula for computing the effects of a change in volume on after-tax income.

2-23. "As I understand it, costs such as the salary of the vice president of transportation operations are variable because the more traffic you handle, the less your unit cost. In contrast, costs such as fuel are fixed because each ton-mile should entail consumption of the same amount of fuel and hence bear the same unit cost." Do you agree? Explain.

COGNITIVE EXERCISES

2-24 Marketing Function of Value Chain and Cost Behavior
Refer to Exhibit 2-1. For the two examples of marketing costs given in Exhibit 2-1, describe their cost behavior in relation to the cost driver listed.

2-25 Production Function of Value Chain and Cost Behavior
Refer to Exhibit 2-1. For the labor wages and depreciation of plant and machinery examples of production costs given in Exhibit 2-1, describe their cost behavior in relation to the cost driver listed.

2-26 Tenneco Automotive's Value Chain
Refer to the Business First box "Lowering the Break-Even Point" on page 60. Tenneco's senior vice president listed the key elements of the company's strategy, stating, "We are gaining momentum

and transforming our North American aftermarket business with new products, new technology, new positioning strategies, and new pricing." For each of these elements of Tenneco's aftermarket business strategy, list the value chain function that is most applicable.

EXERCISES

2-27 Identifying Cost Drivers
The following list identifies several potential cost drivers for a manufacturing company that makes eight products. The company uses a just-in-time (JIT) production system so finished product is stored for a very limited time. The eight products vary substantially in size from small (plastic casings for pens) to large (plastic casings for truck instrument panels).

- Number of setups
- Setup time
- Square feet
- Cubic feet
- Cubic feet weeks

For each situation described below (activity and related resource), identify the best cost driver from the list and briefly justify your choice.

Required

1. To produce a product, production mechanics must set up machinery. It takes about the same time to set up for a production run regardless of the product being produced. What is the best cost driver for mechanic wages?

2. Instead of the situation described in 1, what driver should be used for mechanic wages if it takes longer to set up for complex products such as the instrument panel casings than for simple products such as pen casings?

3. What driver should be used for warehouse occupancy costs (depreciation and insurance)? The warehouse is used to store finished product.

4. What driver should be used for the warehouse occupancy costs if a JIT system is not used (that is, the company maintains inventories), and upon inspection, one of the products had a thick layer of dust on it.

2-28 Basic Review Exercises
Fill in the blanks for each of the following independent cases (ignore income taxes):

	Sales	Variable Expenses	Contribution Margin	Fixed Expenses	Net Income
1.	$900,000	$500,000	$ —	$350,000	$ —
2.	800,000	—	350,000	—	80,000
3.	—	600,000	340,000	250,000	—

2-29 Basic Review Exercises
Fill in the blanks for each of the following independent cases:

Case	(a) Selling Price per Unit	(b) Variable Cost per Unit	(c) Total Units Sold	(d) Total Contribution Margin	(e) Total Fixed Costs	(f) Net Income
1.	$25	$—	120,000	$720,000	$640,000	$ —
2.	10	6	100,000	—	320,000	—
3.	20	15	—	100,000	—	15,000
4.	30	20	70,000	—	—	12,000
5.	—	9	80,000	160,000	110,000	—

2-30 Basic Cost-Volume-Profit Graph

Refer to Exercise 2-29. Construct a cost-volume-profit graph for Case 2 that depicts the total revenue, total variable cost, total fixed cost, and total cost lines. Estimate the break-even point in total units sold and the net income for 100,000 units sold.

2-31 Basic Cost-Volume-Profit Graph

Refer to Exercise 2-29. Construct a cost-volume-profit graph for Case 4 that depicts the total revenue, total variable cost, total fixed cost, and total cost lines. Estimate the break-even point in total units sold and the net income (loss) for 50,000 units sold.

2-32 Hospital Costs and Pricing

St. Vincent Hospital has overall variable costs of 30% of total revenue and fixed costs of $42 million per year.

Required

1. Compute the break-even point expressed in total revenue.
2. A patient-day is often used to measure the volume of a hospital. Suppose there are to be 50,000 patient-days next year. Compute the average daily revenue per patient necessary to break even.

2-33 Motel Rentals

Suppose a Motel 6 ("We'll leave the light on for you") has annual fixed costs applicable to its rooms of $3.2 million for its 400-room motel, average daily room rents of $50, and average variable costs of $10 for each room rented. It operates 365 days per year.

Required

1. How much net income on rooms will be generated (a) if the motel is completely full throughout the entire year and (b) if the motel is half full?
2. Compute the break-even point in number of rooms rented. What percentage occupancy for the year is needed to break even?

2-34 Variable Cost to Break Even

General Mills makes Wheaties, Cheerios, Betty Crocker cake mixes, and many other food products. Suppose the product manager of a new General Mills cereal has determined that the appropriate wholesale price for a carton of the cereal is $48. Fixed costs of the production and marketing of the cereal is $15 million.

Required

1. The product manager estimates that she can sell 800,000 cartons at the $48 price. What is the largest variable cost per carton that can be paid and still achieve a profit of $1 million?
2. Suppose the variable cost is $30 per carton. What profit (or loss) would be expected?

2-35 Basic Relationships, Hotel

The Pippin Blazer Hotel in Portland has 400 rooms, with a fixed cost of $350,000 per month during the busy season. Room rates average $62 per day with variable costs of $12 per rented room per day. Assume a 30-day month.

Required

1. How many rooms must be occupied per day to break even?
2. How many rooms must be occupied per month to make a monthly profit of $100,000?
3. Assume that the Pippin Blazer Hotel has these average contribution margins per month from use of space in its hotel:

Leased shops in hotel	$60,000
Meals served, conventions	30,000
Dining room and coffee shop	30,000
Bar and cocktail lounge	20,000

Fixed costs for the total hotel are $350,000 per month. Variable costs are $12 per day per rented room. The hotel has 400 rooms and averages 80% occupancy per day. What average rate per day must the hotel charge to make a profit of $100,000 per month?

2-36 Sales-Mix Analysis

Study Appendix 2A. Nakata Farms produces strawberries and raspberries. Annual fixed costs are $14,400. The cost driver for variable costs is pints of fruit produced. The variable cost is $.65 per pint of strawberries and $.85 per pint of raspberries. Strawberries sell for $1.00 per pint, raspberries for $1.35 per pint. Two pints of strawberries are produced for every pint of raspberries.

Required

1. Compute the number of pints of strawberries and the number of pints of raspberries produced and sold at the break-even point.
2. Suppose only strawberries are produced and sold. Compute the break-even point in pints.
3. Suppose only raspberries are produced and sold. Compute the break-even point in pints.

2-37 Income Taxes

Review the illustration in Appendix 2B. Suppose the income tax rate were 20% instead of 40%. How many units would have to be sold to achieve a target after-tax net income of (1) $288 and (2) $480? Show your computations.

2-38 Income Taxes and Cost-Volume-Profit Analysis

Study Appendix 2B. Suppose Manriquez Construction Company has a 40% income tax rate, a contribution-margin ratio of 30%, and fixed costs of $440,000. What sales volume is necessary to achieve an after-tax income of $42,000?

PROBLEMS

2-39 Fixed Costs and Relevant Range

Boulder Systems Group (BSG) has a substantial year-to-year fluctuation in billings to clients. Top management has the following policy regarding the employment of key professional personnel:

If Gross Annual Billings Are	Number of Persons to be Employed	Key Professional Annual Salaries and Related Expenses
$2,000,000 or less	10	$1,000,000
$2,000,001–2,400,000	11	$1,100,000
$2,400,001–2,800,000	12	$1,200,000

Top management believes that a minimum of 10 individuals should be retained for a year or more even if billings drop drastically below $2 million.

For the past five years, gross annual billings for BSG have fluctuated between $2,020,000 and $2,380,000. Expectations for next year are that gross billings will be between $2,100,000 and $2,300,000. What amounts should be budgeted for key professional personnel? Graph the relationships on an annual basis, using the two approaches illustrated in Exhibit 2-3. Indicate the relevant range on each graph. You need not use graph paper; simply approximate the graphical relationships.

2-40 Movie Manager

Malia Mertz is the manager of Stanford's traditional Sunday Flicks. Each Sunday a film has two showings. The admission price is deliberately set at a very low $2. A maximum of 500 tickets is sold for each showing. The rental of the auditorium is $220 and labor is $290, including $60 for Mertz. Mertz must pay the film distributor a guarantee, ranging from $200 to $600, or 50% of gross admission receipts, whichever is higher.

Before and during the show, refreshments are sold; these sales average 12% of gross admission receipts and yield a contribution margin of 40%.

Required

1. On June 3, Mertz screened *Pokémon: The First Movie*. The film grossed $1,500. The guarantee to the distributor was $500, or 50% of gross admission receipts, whichever is higher. What operating income was produced for the Students' Association, which sponsored the showings?

2. Recompute the results if the film grossed $900.

3. The "four-wall" concept is increasingly being adopted by movie producers. In this plan, the movie's producer pays a fixed rental to the theater owner for, say, a week's showing of a movie. As a theater owner, how would you evaluate a "four-wall" offer?

2-41 Promotion of a Rock Concert

NLR Productions, Ltd., is promoting a rock concert in London. The bands will receive a flat fee of £8 million in cash. The concert will be shown worldwide on closed-circuit television. NLR will collect 100% of the receipts and will return 30% to the individual local closed-circuit theater managers. NLR expects to sell 1.1 million seats at a net average price of £13 each. NLR will also receive £300,000 from the London arena (which has sold out its 19,500 seats, ranging from £150 for box seats to £20 for general admission, for a gross revenue of £1.25 million); NLR will not share the £300,000 with the local promoters.

Required

1. The general manager of NLR Productions is trying to decide what amount to spend for advertising. What is the most NLR could spend and still break even on overall operations, assuming sales of 1.1 million tickets?

2. If NLR desired an operating income of £500,000, how many seats would have to be sold? Assume that the average price was £13 and the total fixed costs (including £1,000,000 in advertising) were £9 million.

2-42 Basic Relationships, Restaurant

Genevieve Giraud owns and operates a restaurant. Her fixed costs are $21,000 per month. She serves luncheons and dinners. The average total bill (excluding tax and tip) is $18 per customer. Giraud's present variable costs average $9.60 per meal.

Required

1. How many meals must be served to attain a profit before taxes of $8,400 per month?

2. What is the break-even point in number of meals served per month?

3. Giraud's rent and other fixed costs rise to a total of $29,925 per month and variable costs also rise to $11.50 per meal. If Giraud increases her average price to $22, how many meals must be served to make $8,400 profit per month?

4. Assume the same situation described in 3. Giraud's accountant tells her she may lose 10% of her customers if she increases her prices. If this should happen, what would be Giraud's profit per month? Assume that the restaurant had been serving 3,500 customers per month.

5. Assume the same situation described in 3. To help offset the anticipated 10% loss of customers, Giraud hires a pianist to perform for four hours each night for $2,000 per month. Assume that this would increase the total monthly meals from 3,150 to 3,450. Would Giraud's total profit change? By how much?

2-43 Changing Fixed Costs to Variable Costs at Blockbuster Video

According to an article in *Business Week* (March 8, 1999, p. 64), when John F. Antioco took charge of Blockbuster Video in July 1997, he changed the company's strategy. Traditionally, Blockbuster had bought videotapes for an average cost of about $70 each, planning to rent them out often enough to make a profit. Mr. Antioco replaced this strategy with one that allows Blockbuster to purchase videos for an average of $5 per tape and pay the studio 40% of any rental fee received for the tape. With this arrangement, Blockbuster could afford to stock more copies of each tape and guarantee customers that the tape they want will be in stock—or the rental is free. Suppose that Blockbuster rents videotapes for $2.00 a day. Assume that operating costs are all fixed.

Required

1. Under the traditional strategy, how many days must each tape be rented before Blockbuster will break even on the tape?

2. Under the new strategy, how many days must each tape be rented before Blockbuster will break even on the tape?

3. Suppose a copy of *Titanic* was rented for 50 days. What profit would Blockbuster make on rentals of the tape (considering only the direct costs of the tape, not the costs of operating the rental store) under the traditional strategy? Under the new strategy?

4. Suppose a copy of *You've Got Mail* was rented only 5 days. What profit would Blockbuster make on rentals of the tape (considering only the direct costs of the tape, not the costs of operating the rental store) under the traditional strategy? Under the new strategy?

5. Comment on how the new arrangement affects the risks Blockbuster accepts when purchasing an additional copy of a particular videotape.

2-44 Cost-Volume-Profit Analysis, Barbering

Andre's Hair Styling in Singapore has five barbers. (Andre is not one of them.) Each barber is paid $9.90 per hour and works a 40-hour week and a 50-week year, regardless of the number of haircuts. Rent and other fixed expenses are $1,750 per month. Assume that the only service performed is the giving of haircuts, the unit price of which is $12.

Required

1. Find the contribution margin per haircut. Assume that the barbers' compensation is a fixed cost.
2. Determine the annual break-even point, in number of haircuts.
3. What will be the operating income if 20,000 haircuts are performed?
4. Suppose Andre revises the compensation method. The barbers will receive $4 per hour plus $6 for each haircut. What is the new contribution margin per haircut? What is the annual break-even point (in number of haircuts)?
5. Ignore requirements 3 and 4 and assume that the barbers cease to be paid by the hour but receive $7 for each haircut. What is the new contribution margin per haircut? The annual break-even point (in number of haircuts)?
6. Refer to requirement 5. What would be the operating income if 20,000 haircuts are performed? Compare your answer with the answer in requirement 3.
7. Refer to requirement 5. If 20,000 haircuts are performed, at what rate of commission would Andre earn the same operating income as he earned in requirement 3?

2-45 CVP and Financial Statements

ConAgra, Inc., is an Omaha-based company that produces food products under brand names such as Healthy Choice, Armour, and Banquet. The company's 2000 income statement showed the following (in millions):

Net sales	$25,386
Costs of goods sold	21,206
Selling, administrative, and general expense	2,888
Interest expense	303
Income before income tax and non-recurring charges	$ 989

Suppose that the cost of goods sold is the only variable cost; selling, administrative, general, and interest expenses are fixed with respect to sales.

Assume that ConAgra had a 10% increase in sales in 2001 and that there was no change in costs except for increases associated with the higher volume of sales. Compute the predicted 2001 operating profit for ConAgra and the percentage increase in operating profit. Explain why the percentage increase in profit differs from the percentage increase in sales.

2-46 Bingo and Leverage

A California law permits bingo games when offered by specified nonprofit institutions, including churches. Reverend Wilbur Means, the pastor of a new parish in Orange County, is investigating the desirability of conducting weekly bingo nights. The parish has no hall, but a local hotel would be willing to commit its hall for a lump-sum rental of $600 per night. The rent would include cleaning, setting up and taking down the tables and chairs, and so on.

Required

1. A local printer would provide bingo cards in return for free advertising. Local merchants would donate door prizes. The services of clerks, callers, security force, and others would be donated by volunteers. Admission would be $3 per person, entitling the player to one card; extra cards would be $1.50 each. Many persons buy extra cards, so there would be an average of four cards played per person. What is the maximum in total cash prizes that the church may award and still break even if 200 persons attend each weekly session?

2. Suppose the total cash prizes are $900. What will be the church's operating income if 100 persons attend? If 200 persons attend? If 300 persons attend? Briefly explain the effects of the cost behavior on income.

3. After operating for 10 months, Reverend Means is thinking of negotiating a different rental arrangement but keeping the prize money unchanged at $900. Suppose the rent is $200 weekly plus $2 per person. Compute the operating income for attendance of 100, 200, and 300 persons, respectively. Explain why the results differ from those in requirement 2.

2-47 Adding a Product

Andy's Ale House, a pub located near State University, serves as a gathering place for the university's more social scholars. Andy sells beer on draft and all brands of bottled beer at a contribution margin of 60¢ a beer.

Andy is considering also selling hamburgers during selected hours. His reasons are twofold. First, sandwiches would attract daytime customers. A hamburger and a beer are a quick lunch. Second, he has to meet competition from other local bars, some of which provide more extensive menus.

Andy analyzed the costs as follows:

	Per Month			Per Hamburger
Monthly fixed expenses		Variable expenses		
Wages of part-time cook	$1,200	Rolls		$.12
Other	360	Meat @ $2.80 per pound		
Total	$1,560	(7 hamburgers per pound)		.40
		Other		.18
		Total		$.70

Andy planned a selling price of $1.10 per hamburger to lure many customers. For all questions, assume a 30-day month.

Required

1. What are the monthly and daily break-even points, in number of hamburgers?
2. What are the monthly and daily break-even points, in dollar sales?
3. At the end of two months, Andy finds he has sold 3,600 hamburgers. What is the operating profit per month on hamburgers?
4. Andy thinks that at least 60 extra beers are sold per day because he has these hamburgers available. This means that 60 extra people come to the bar or that 60 buy an extra beer because they are attracted by the hamburgers. How does this affect Andy's monthly operating income?
5. Refer to requirement 3. How many extra beers would have to be sold per day so that the overall effects of the hamburger sales on monthly operating income would be zero?

2-48 Cost-Volume-Profit Relationships and a Dog Track

The Miami Kennel Club is a dog-racing track. Its revenue is derived mainly from attendance and a fixed percentage of the parimutuel betting. Its expenses for a 90-day season are as follows:

Wages of cashiers and ticket takers	$150,000
Commissioner's salary	20,000
Maintenance (repairs, etc.)	20,000
Utilities	30,000
Other expenses (depreciation, insurance, advertising, etc.)	100,000
Purses: total prizes paid to winning racers	810,000

The track made a contract with PK, Inc., to park the cars. PK charged the track $4.80 per car. A survey revealed that on the average three persons arrived in each car and that half the attendees arrived by private automobiles. The others arrived by taxi and public buses.

The track's sources of revenue are

Rights for concession and vending	$50,000
Admission charge (deliberately low)	$1 per person
Percentage of bets placed	10%

Assume that each person bets $25 a night.

Required

1. **a.** How many persons have to be admitted for the track to break even for the season?

   b. If the desired operating profit for the year is $270,000, how many people would have to attend?

2. If a policy of free admission brought a 20% increase in attendance, what would be the new level of operating profit? Assume that the previous level of attendance was 600,000 people.

3. If the purses were doubled in an attempt to attract better dogs and thus increase attendance, what would be the new break-even point? Refer to the original data and assume that each person bets $25 a night.

2-49 Traveling Expenses

Yukio Nomo is a traveling inspector for the State Treasurer's Office. He uses his own car, and the agency reimburses him at 23¢ per mile. Yukio Nomo claims he needs 27¢ per mile just to break even.

Marilyn McDyess, the district manager, looks into the matter and compiles the following information about Nomo's expenses:

Oil change every 3,000 miles	$ 30
Maintenance (other than oil) every 6,000 miles	240
Yearly insurance	700
Auto cost $13,500 with an average cash trade-in value of $6,000; has a useful life of three years.	
Gasoline is approximately $1.70 per gallon and Nomo averages 17 miles per gallon.	

When Nomo is on the road, he averages 120 miles a day. McDyess knows that Nomo does not work Saturdays or Sundays, has 10 working days vacation and 6 holidays, and spends approximately 15 working days in the office.

Required

1. How many miles per year would Nomo have to travel to break even at the current rate of reimbursement?

2. What would be an equitable mileage rate?

2-50 Government Organization

A social welfare agency has a government budget appropriation for 20X2 of $900,000. The agency's major mission is to help disabled persons who are unable to hold jobs. On the average, the agency supplements each person's other income by $5,000 annually. The agency's fixed costs are $290,000. There are no other costs.

Required

1. How many disabled persons were helped during 20X2?

2. For 20X3, the agency's budget appropriation has been reduced by 15%. If the agency continues the same level of monetary support per person, how many disabled persons will be helped in 20X3? Compute the percentage decline in the number of persons helped.

3. Assume a budget reduction of 15%, as in requirement 2. The manager of the agency has discretion as to how much to supplement each disabled person's income. She does not want to reduce the number of persons served. On the average, what is the amount of the supplement that can be given to each person? Compute the percentage decline in the annual supplement.

2-51 Airline CVP

Airline companies regularly provide operating statistics with their financial statements. In 1996 Continental Airlines reported that it had approximately 61,000 million seat-miles available, of which 68.1% were filled. (A seat-mile is one seat traveling one mile. For example, if an airplane with 100 seats traveled 400 miles, capacity would have been $100 \times 400 = 40,000$ seat miles.) The average revenue was $.1310 per revenue-passenger-mile, where a revenue-passenger-mile is one seat occupied by a passenger traveling one mile. In 1995, approximately the same number of seat-miles were available, but only 65.6% of them were filled at an average revenue of $.1251 per filled seat-mile. Continental calls the percentage of seat-miles available that are filled with passengers their load factor.

Required

1. Compute Continental's passenger revenue for 1996 and 1995.
2. Assume that Continental's variable costs were $.05 per revenue-passenger-mile in both 1995 and 1996 and that fixed costs are $3,000 million per year each year.
   a. Compute Continental's break-even point at the 1995 level of revenue per passenger mile. Express it in both revenue-passenger-miles and as a load factor (that is, as a percentage of available capacity used).
   b. Compute Continental's break-even point at the 1996 level of revenue per passenger mile. Express it in both revenue-passenger-miles and as a load factor (that is, as a percentage of available capacity used).
3. Suppose Continental maintained the same level of seat-miles available in 1997, had revenue of $.13 per revenue-passenger-mile, and maintained the same level of fixed and variable costs as in the previous two years. Compute the load factor necessary to achieve an operating income of $400 million.

2-52 Gross Margin and Contribution Margin

Eastman Kodak Company produces and sells cameras, film, and other imaging products. A condensed 2000 income statement follows (in millions):

Sales	$13,994
Costs of goods sold	8,019
Gross margin	5,975
Other operating expenses	3,761
Operating income	$ 2,214

Assume that $1,800 million of the cost of goods sold is a fixed cost representing depreciation and other production costs that do not change with the volume of production. In addition, $3,000 million of the other operating expenses is fixed.

Required

1. Compute the total contribution margin for 2000 and the contribution margin percentage. Explain why the contribution margin differs from the gross margin.
2. Suppose that sales for Eastman Kodak were predicted to increase by 10% in 2001 and that the cost behavior was expected to continue in 2001 as it did in 2000. Compute the predicted operating income for 2001. By what percentage did this predicted 2001 operating income exceed the 2000 operating income?
3. What assumptions were necessary to compute the predicted 2001 operating income in requirement 2?

2-53 Choosing Equipment for Different Volumes

(CMA, adapted.) Multiplex Cinema owns and operates a nationwide chain of movie theaters. The 500 properties in the Multiplex chain vary from low-volume, small-town, single-screen theaters to high-volume, big-city, multiscreen theaters.

The management is considering installing machines that will make popcorn on the premises. These machines would allow the theaters to sell popcorn that would be freshly popped daily rather than the prepopped corn that is currently purchased in large bags. This proposed feature would be properly advertised and is intended to increase patronage at the company's theaters.

The machines can be purchased in several different sizes. The annual rental costs and operating costs vary with the size of the machines. The machine capacities and costs are as follows:

	Popper Model		
	E5	*R12*	*S30*
Annual capacity	50,000 boxes	120,000 boxes	300,000 boxes
Costs			
Annual machine rental	$8,000	$11,200	$20,200
Popcorn cost per box	.14	.14	.14
Cost of each box	.09	.09	.09
Other variable costs per box	.22	.14	.05

Required

1. Calculate the volume level in boxes at which the E5 and R12 poppers would earn the same operating profit (loss).
2. The management can estimate the number of boxes to be sold at each of its theaters. Present a decision rule that would enable Multiplex management to select the most profitable machine without having to make a separate cost calculation for each theater. That is, at what anticipated range of unit sales should the E5 model be used? The R12 model? The S30 model?
3. Could the management use the average number of boxes sold per seat for the entire chain and the capacity of each theater to develop this decision rule? Explain your answer.

2-54 Boeing Break-Even

Boeing is the largest commercial airplane manufacturer in the world. In 1996 it began development of the 757-300, a 240-passenger plane with a range up to 4,010 miles. First deliveries took place in 1999, at a price of about $70 million per plane.

Assume that Boeing's annual fixed costs for the 757-300 are $950 million, and its variable cost per airplane is $45 million.

Required

1. Compute Boeing's break-even point in number of 757-300 airplanes and in dollars of sales.
2. Suppose Boeing plans to sell forty-two 757-300 airplanes in 2002. Compute Boeing's projected operating profit.
3. Suppose Boeing increased its fixed costs by $84 million and reduced variable costs per airplane by $2 million. Compute its operating profit if forty-two 757-300 airplanes are sold. Compute the break-even point. Comment on your results.
4. Ignore requirement 3. Suppose fixed costs do not change but variable costs increase by 10% before deliveries of 757-300 airplanes begin in 2002. Compute the new break-even point. What strategies might Boeing use to help assure profitable operations in light of increases in variable cost?

2-55 Sales-Mix Analysis

Study Appendix 2A. The New England Catering Company specializes in preparing tasty main courses that are frozen and shipped to the finer restaurants in the Boston area. When a diner orders the item, the restaurant heats and serves it. The budget data for 20X2 are

	Product	
	Chicken Cordon Bleu	*Veal Marsala*
Selling price to restaurants	$7	$9
Variable expenses	4	5
Contribution margin	$3	$4
Number of units	250,000	125,000

The items are prepared in the same kitchens, delivered in the same trucks, and so forth. Therefore, the fixed costs of $1,320,000 are unaffected by the specific products.

Required

1. Compute the planned net income for 20X2.
2. Compute the break-even point in units, assuming that the planned sales mix is maintained.
3. Compute the break-even point in units if only veal were sold and if only chicken were sold.
4. Suppose 99,000 units of veal and 297,000 units of chicken were sold. Compute the net income. Compute the new break-even point if these relationships persisted in 20X2. What is the major lesson of this problem?

2-56 Hospital Patient Mix

Study Appendix 2A. Hospitals measure their volume in terms of patient-days, which are defined as the number of patients multiplied by the number of days that the patients are hospitalized. Suppose a large hospital has fixed costs of $48 million per year and variable costs of $600 per patient-day. Daily revenues vary among classes of patients. For simplicity, assume that there are two classes: (1) self-pay patients (S) who pay an average of $1,000 per day and (2) non–self-pay patients (G) who are the responsibility of insurance companies and government agencies and who pay an average of $800 per day. Twenty percent of the patients are self-pay.

Required

1. Compute the break-even point in patient-days, assuming that the planned mix of patients is maintained.
2. Suppose that 200,000 patient-days were achieved but that 25% of the patient-days were self-pay (instead of 20%). Compute the net income. Compute the break-even point.

2-57 Income Taxes on Hotels

Study Appendix 2B. The All Seasons Hotel in downtown Denver has annual fixed costs applicable to rooms of $10 million for its 600-room hotel, average daily room rates of $105, and average variable costs of $25 for each room rented. It operates 365 days per year. The hotel is subject to an income tax rate of 40%.

Required

1. How many rooms must the hotel rent to earn a net income after taxes of $720,000? Of $360,000?
2. Compute the break-even point in number of rooms rented. What percentage occupancy for the year is needed to break even?
3. Assume that the volume level of rooms sold is 150,000. The manager is wondering how much income could be generated by adding sales of 15,000 rooms. Compute the additional net income after taxes.

2-58 Tax Effects, Multiple Choice

Study Appendix 2B. Raprock Company is a wholesaler of compact disks. The projected after-tax net income for the current year is $120,000, based on a sales volume of 200,000 CDs. Raprock has been selling the CDs at $16 each. The variable costs consist of the $10 unit purchase price and a handling cost of $2 per unit. Raprock's annual fixed costs are $600,000, and Raprock is subject to a 40% income tax rate.

Management is planning for the coming year when it expects that the unit purchase price will increase 30%.

1. Raprock Company's break-even point for the current year is (a) 150,000 units, (b) 100,000 units, (c) 50,000 units, (d) 60,000 units, and (e) some amount other than those given.
2. An increase of 10% in projected unit sales volume for the current year would result in an increased after-tax income for the current year of (a) $80,000, (b) $32,000, (c) $12,000, (d) $48,000, and (e) some amount other than those given.
3. The volume of sales in dollars that Raprock Company must achieve in the coming year to maintain the same after-tax net income as projected for the current year if unit selling price remains at $16 is (a) $12,800,000, (b) $14,400,000, (c) $11,520,000, (d) $32,000,000, or (e) some amount other than those given.
4. To cover a 30% increase in the unit purchase price for the coming year and still maintain the current contribution-margin ratio, Raprock Company must establish a selling price per unit for the coming year of (a) $19.60, (b) $20.00, (c) $20.80, (d) $19.00, or (e) some amount other than those given.

CASES

2-59 Hospital Costs

Metropolitan City Hospital is unionized. In 20X1 nurses received an average annual salary of $45,000. The hospital administrator is considering how the contract with nurses should be changed for 20X2. In turn, the charging of nursing costs to each department might also be changed.

Each department is accountable for its financial performance. Revenues and expenses are allocated to departments. Consider the expenses of the obstetrics department in 20X1.

Variable expenses (based on 20X1 patient-days) are

Meals	$ 510,000
Laundry	260,000
Laboratory	900,000
Pharmacy	800,000
Maintenance	150,000
Other	530,000
Total	$3,150,000

Fixed expenses (based on number of beds) are

Rent	$3,000,000
General administrative services	2,200,000
Janitorial	200,000
Maintenance	150,000
Other	350,000
Total	$5,900,000

Nurses are assigned to departments on the basis of annual patient-days as follows:

Volume Level in Patient-Days	Number of Nurses
10,000–12,000	30
12,000–16,000	35

Total patient-days are the number of patients multiplied by the number of days they are hospitalized. Each department is charged for the salaries of the nurses assigned to it.

During 20X1 the obstetrics department had a capacity of 60 beds, billed each patient an average of $800 per day, and had revenues of $12 million.

Required

1. Compute the 20X1 volume of activity in patient-days.
2. Compute the 20X1 patient-days that would have been necessary for the obstetrics department to recoup all fixed expenses except nursing expenses.
3. Compute the 20X1 patient-days that would have been necessary for the obstetrics department to break even including nurses' salaries as a fixed cost.
4. Suppose obstetrics must pay $200 per patient-day for nursing services. This plan would replace the two-level fixed-cost system employed in 20X1. Compute what the break-even point in patient-days would have been in 20X1 under this plan.

2-60 CVP and Prediction of Income

According to an article in *Business Week*, T. J. Izzo had a great idea after a bad back almost forced him to give up golf. His problem was carrying a golf bag, not swinging a club. So he designed a harnesslike golf bag strap that distributes the weight equally on both shoulders. In April 1991 he formed Izzo Systems, Inc. In 1993 Izzo made operating income of $12,000 on revenue of $1 million from selling 75,000 straps. In 1994 Izzo expected to sell 92,000 straps for $1.7 million.

Required

1. Suppose that variable costs per strap are $10. Compute total fixed and total variable costs for 1993.

2. Suppose the cost behavior in 1994 was the same as in 1993. Estimate Izzo's operating income for 1994 (a) with sales at the predicted 92,000 straps, (b) with unit sales 10% above the predicted level, and (c) with unit sales 10% below the predicted level.

3. Explain why the predicted 1994 operating income was so much greater than the 1993 operating income.

2-61   CVP in a Modern Manufacturing Environment

A division of Hewlett-Packard Company changed its production operations from one where a large labor force assembled electronic components to an automated production facility dominated by computer-controlled robots. The change was necessary because of fierce competitive pressures. Improvements in quality, reliability, and flexibility of production schedules were necessary just to match the competition. As a result of the change, variable costs fell and fixed costs increased, as shown in the following assumed budgets:

	Old Production Operation	New Production Operation
Unit variable cost		
Material	$ .88	$ .88
Labor	1.22	.22
Total per unit	$ 2.10	$ 1.10
Monthly fixed costs		
Rent and depreciation	$450,000	$ 875,000
Supervisory labor	85,000	175,000
Other	50,000	90,000
Total per month	$585,000	$1,140,000

Expected volume is 600,000 units per month, with each unit selling for $3.10. Capacity is 800,000 units.

Required

1. Compute the budgeted profit at the expected volume of 600,000 units under both the old and the new production environments.

2. Compute the budgeted break-even point under both the old and the new production environments.

3. Discuss the effect on profits if volume falls to 500,000 units under both the old and the new production environments.

4. Discuss the effect on profits if volume increases to 700,000 units under both the old and the new production environments.

5. Comment on the riskiness of the new operation versus the old operation.

2-62   Multiproduct Break-Even in a Restaurant

Study Appendix 2A. An article in Washington Business included an income statement for La Brasserie, a French restaurant in Washington, D.C. A simplified version of the statement follows:

Revenues	$2,098,400
Cost of sales, all variable	1,246,500
Gross profit	851,900
Operating expenses	
Variable	222,380
Fixed	170,700
Administrative expenses, all fixed	451,500
Net income	$ 7,320

The average dinner tab at La Brasserie is $40, and the average lunch tab is $20. Assume that the variable cost of preparing and serving dinner is also twice that of a lunch. The restaurant serves twice as many lunches as dinners. Assume that the restaurant is open 305 days a year.

Required

1. Compute the daily break-even volume in lunches and dinners for La Brasserie. Compare this to the actual volume reflected in the income statement.

2. Suppose that an extra annual advertising expenditure of $15,000 would increase the average daily volume by three dinners and six lunches, and that there is plenty of capacity to accommodate the extra business. Prepare an analysis for the management of La Brasserie explaining whether this would be desirable.

3. La Brasserie uses only premium food, and the cost of food makes up 25% of the restaurant's total variable costs. Use of average rather than premium ingredients could cut the food cost by 20%. Assume that La Brasserie uses average-quality ingredients and does not change its prices. How much of a drop-off in volume could it endure and still maintain the same net income? What factors in addition to revenue and costs would influence the decision about the quality of food to use?

2-63 Effects of Changes in Costs, Including Tax Effects

Study Appendix 2B. Pacific Fish Company is a wholesale distributor of salmon. The company services grocery stores in the Chicago area.

Small but steady growth in sales has been achieved by Pacific Fish over the past few years while salmon prices have been increasing. The company is formulating its plans for the coming fiscal year. Presented below are the data used to project the current year's after-tax net income of $138,000.

Average selling price per pound	$	5.00
Average variable costs per pound		
Cost of salmon	$	2.50
Shipping expenses		.50
Total	$	3.00
Annual fixed costs		
Selling	$	200,000
Administrative		350,000
Total	$	550,000
Expected annual sales volume (390,000 pounds)		$1,950,000
Tax rate		40%

Fishing companies have announced that they will increase prices of their products an average of 15% in the coming year, owing mainly to increases in labor costs. Pacific Fish Company expects that all other costs will remain at the same rates or levels as in the current year.

1. What is Pacific Fish Company's break-even point in pounds of salmon for the current year?

2. What selling price per pound must Pacific Fish Company charge to cover the 15% increase in the cost of salmon and still maintain the current contribution-margin ratio?

3. What volume of sales in dollars must the Pacific Fish Company achieve in the coming year to maintain the same net income after taxes as projected for the current year if the selling price of salmon remains at $5 per pound and the cost of salmon increases 15%?

4. What strategies might Pacific Fish Company use to maintain the same net income after taxes as projected for the current year?

COLLABORATIVE LEARNING EXERCISE

2-64 CVP for a Small Business

Form a group of two to six students. Each group should select a very simple business, one with a single product or one with approximately the same contribution margin percentage for all products. Some possibilities are

A child's lemonade stand

A retail video rental store

An espresso cart

A retail store selling compact disks

An athletic shoe store

A cookie stand in a mall

However, you are encouraged to use your imagination rather than just select one of these examples.

The following tasks might be split up among the group members.

1. Make a list of all fixed costs associated with running the business you selected. Estimate the amount of each fixed cost per month (or per day or per year, if one of them is more appropriate for your business).

2. Make a list of all variable costs associated with making or obtaining the product or service your company is selling. Estimate the cost per unit for each variable cost.

3. Given the fixed and variable costs you have identified, compute the break-even point for your business in either units or dollar sales.

4. Assess the prospects of your business making a profit.

www.prenhall.com/horngren

INTERNET EXERCISE

2-65 Cost Behavior at Southwest Airlines

It is critical that managers understand how costs and revenues behave. One company that is affected by changes in costs and may not have the capability to rapidly change revenues because of competition is Southwest Airlines. Let's take a closer look at SWA and it's costs and revenues. Log on to SWA's Web site at http://www.iflyswa.com. This Web site serves many purposes for the airline, such as providing flight schedules, making reservations and selling tickets and displaying vacation and airfare specials.

1. Click on the reservations icon. How many cities does SWA serve? What is the closest city served by SWA to your current location? Click on that city as the departure city and then select any city you like for the arrival city. Now select a date about a month from now for leaving and one for returning. Click to continue to the next screen. What type of fares are available? Why do you think that there are different types of fares offered? Click on one of the fare types captions to see if any restrictions are placed on this fare. If there are any restrictions, what purpose do they serve?

2. Return to the reservations screen and select a departure date that is less than a week away. What type of fare choices are available now? Are the rates the same as those that you found for a trip more than a month away? Why do you think that the choices remaining are for the most part the higher priced ones? Is there any advantage to the fare(s) still available? Who is the most likely user of a ticket purchased at the last minute?

3. Now that you have looked at the revenue side, let's focus on the expense side. Individuals on the same flight may pay different prices for the ticket. Do you think that the cost of flying a passenger differs due to the price that they pay for the ticket? Why or why not?

4. Return to the homepage for SWA. Now let's take a look at the costs that SWA actually incurs. Click on the "About SWA" icon and then click on "Investor Relations." Click on the "Annual reports" icon and then select the most recent annual report. Open the annual report using Adobe Acrobat Reader. When you have located the annual report, notice the summary information that the company has provided in the "Consolidated Highlights" section. What format does it use to report revenues? What is the format that it uses to report expenses? Are these two measures the same? Can comparisons be made between the two measures?

5. Now go to the Financial Review section by clicking on the "Financial Review" bookmark on the left panel of the display. Look at the table that summarizes "Operating Expenses per ASM". Do any of these expense categories appear to contain mostly fixed costs? Why do you think that the expense(s) is fixed? Which appear to be variable in nature? Do you think that using the ASM for the cost driver is a proper reflection of the nature of the expense?

Go to the "Cost-Volume-Profit Analysis" episode on the *Mastering Accounting* CD-ROM for an interactive, video-enhanced exercise showing CanGo managers' use of reports that predict outcomes based on estimates of cost and revenue to help make a new venture decision.

3

MEASUREMENT OF COST BEHAVIOR

An America West flight on final approach to San Diego's airport. America West serves the low cost—full service market at more than 144 destinations in the United States, Canada, and Mexico. Understanding the company's costs is an important factor in the company's competitive strategy.

www.prenhall.com/horngren

Learning Objectives

When you have finished studying this chapter, you should be able to

1. Explain step- and mixed-cost behavior.

2. Explain management influences on cost behavior.

3. Measure and mathematically express cost functions and use them to predict costs.

4. Describe the importance of activity analysis for measuring cost functions.

5. Measure cost behavior using the account analysis, high-low, visual-fit, and least-squares regression methods.

6. **Understand the relationship between management decision making and cost behavior.**

With annual revenues of more than $2 billion, America West is the ninth-largest U.S. commercial airline. The company focuses on the low-cost, full-service market with primary operations (hubs) in Phoenix, Las Vegas, and Columbus, Ohio. America West rode a booming economy to increased revenues in the late 1990s. As a result, management decided to expand by introducing service to new destinations including Acapulco, Miami, and Detroit, and by adding more daily flights to existing markets including Las Vegas, Mexico City, and Boston. To accomplish this, the company had to expand its labor force, add new aircraft, and spend more than $40 million on new technology.

Management at America West did not take lightly the decision to invest large amounts of money in aircraft and equipment. They knew that their decision would have a significant influence on costs and thus profits for many years. They also knew that most of the costs would be fixed but the revenues would fluctuate with the economy. When the economy is bad, revenues may not cover these costs.

How does an airline protect itself against losses when the economy turns down? According to Richard Goodmanson, President and Chief Executive Officer of America West, "management has a goal to have from 5% to 10% of the fleet of aircraft leased and thus subject to annual renewal. This enhances the company's ability to decrease capacity (and related costs) in the event of an industry downturn." This example illustrates that understanding how costs behave, as well as how managers' decisions can influence costs, helped the airline improve its cost control.

Chapter 2 demonstrated the importance of understanding the cost structure of an organization and the relationships between an organization's activities and its costs, revenues, and profits. This chapter focuses on **measurement of cost behavior,** which means understanding and quantifying how activities of an organization affect levels of costs. Recall that activities use resources and these resources have costs. We measure the relationship between activity and cost using output measures called cost drivers. Understanding relationships between costs and their cost drivers allows managers in all types of organizations—profit-seeking, nonprofit, and government—to

- Evaluate new manufacturing methods or service practices (Chapter 4)
- Make proper short-run marketing decisions (Chapter 5)
- Make short-run production decisions (Chapter 6)
- Plan or budget the effects of future activities (Chapters 7 and 8)
- Design effective management control systems (Chapters 9 and 10)
- Make proper long-run decisions (Chapter 11)
- Design accurate and useful product costing systems (Chapters 12 to 15)

As you can see, understanding cost behavior is fundamental to management accounting. There are numerous real-world cases in which managers have made very poor decisions to drop product lines, close manufacturing plants, or bid too high or too low on jobs because they had erroneous cost behavior information. This chapter, therefore, deserves careful study.

COST DRIVERS AND COST BEHAVIOR

linear-cost behavior Activity that can be graphed with a straight line because costs are assumed to be either fixed or variable.

Accountants and managers often assume that cost behavior is linear over some relevant range of activity levels or cost-driver levels. **Linear-cost behavior** can be graphed with a straight line because each cost is assumed to be either fixed or variable. Recall that the relevant range specifies the limits of cost-driver activity within which a specific relationship between a cost and its cost driver will be valid. Managers usually define the relevant range based on their previous experience with different levels of activity and cost.

Many activities can influence costs. However, in this chapter we focus on those costs for which the volume of a product produced or service provided is the primary driver. These costs are easy to identify with, or trace to, products or services. Examples of volume-driven costs include the costs of printing labor, paper, ink, and binding to produce all the copies of this textbook. The number of copies printed obviously affects the total printing labor, paper, ink, and binding costs. Equally important, we could relatively easily trace the use of these resources to the copies of the text printed. Schedules, payroll records, and other documents show how much of each was used to produce the copies of this text.

Other costs are more affected by activities not directly related to volume and often have multiple cost drivers. Such costs are not easy to identify with or trace to outputs. Examples of costs that are difficult to trace include the wages and salaries of the editorial staff of the publisher of this textbook. These editorial personnel produce many different textbooks, and it would be very difficult to determine exactly what portion of their costs went into a specific book, such as *Introduction to Management Accounting*.

Understanding and measuring costs that are difficult to trace to outputs can be especially challenging. In practice, many organizations use a linear relationship with a single cost driver to describe each cost even though many have multiple causes. This approach is easier and less expensive than using nonlinear relationships or multiple cost drivers. Careful use of linear-cost behavior with a single cost driver often provides cost

Exhibit 3-1

Linear-Cost Behavior

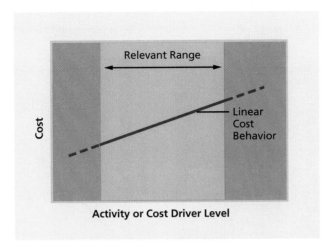

estimates that are accurate enough for most decisions. Linear-cost behavior with a single cost driver may seem at odds with reality and economic theory, but the added benefit of understanding "true" cost behavior may be less than the cost of determining "true" cost behavior.

For ease of communication and understanding, accountants usually describe cost behavior in visual or graphical terms. Exhibit 3-1 shows linear-cost behavior, the relevant range, and an activity or cost driver. Note the similarity to the CVP charts of Chapter 2.

STEP- AND MIXED-COST BEHAVIOR PATTERNS

Chapter 2 described two patterns of cost behavior: variable costs and fixed costs. Recall that a purely variable cost changes in proportion to changes in its cost driver's activity, while a purely fixed cost is not affected by the cost-driver level. In addition to these pure versions of cost, two additional types of costs combine characteristics of both fixed- and variable-cost behavior. These are step costs and mixed costs.

Step Costs. **Step costs** change abruptly at intervals of activity because the resources and their costs are only available in indivisible chunks. If the individual chunks of cost are relatively large and apply to a specific, broad range of activity, the cost is considered a fixed cost over that range of activity. An example is in panel A of Exhibit 3-2, which shows the cost of leasing oil and gas drilling equipment. When oil and gas exploration activity reaches a certain level in a given region, an entire additional rig must be leased. One level of oil and gas rig leasing, however, will support all volumes of exploration activity within a relevant range of drilling. Within each relevant range, this step cost behaves as a fixed cost. The total step cost at a level of activity is the amount of fixed cost appropriate for the range containing that activity level.

In contrast, accountants often describe step costs as variable when the individual chunks of costs are relatively small and apply to a narrow range of activity. Panel B of Exhibit 3-2 shows the wage cost of cashiers at a supermarket. Suppose one cashier can serve an average of 20 shoppers per hour and that within the relevant range of shopping activity, the number of shoppers can range from 40 per hour to 440 per hour. The corresponding number of cashiers would range between two and 22. Because the steps are relatively small, this step cost behaves much like a variable cost and could be used as such for planning with little loss of accuracy.

Objective 1
Explain step- and mixed-cost behavior.

step costs Costs that change abruptly at intervals of activity because the resources and their costs come in indivisible chunks.

Exhibit 3-2
Step-Cost Behavior

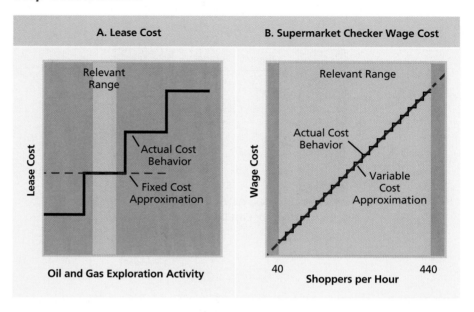

A. Lease Cost	B. Supermarket Checker Wage Cost

mixed costs Costs that contain elements of both fixed- and variable-cost behavior.

Mixed Costs. **Mixed costs** contain elements of both fixed- and variable-cost behavior. The fixed element is determined for a single planned range of activity level. The variable-cost element of the mixed cost is a purely variable cost that varies proportionately with activity within the single relevant range. In a mixed cost, the variable cost is incurred in addition to the fixed cost: The total mixed cost is the sum of the fixed cost plus the variable cost. You might think of the fixed cost as the cost of having available the capacity necessary to operate at any volume within the relevant range and the variable cost as the additional cost of using that capacity to produce ouputs.

Many costs are mixed costs. For example, consider the monthly facilities maintenance department cost of the Parkview Medical Center, shown in Exhibit 3-3. Salaries of the maintenance personnel and costs of equipment are fixed at $10,000 per month. In

Exhibit 3-3
Mixed-Cost Behavior

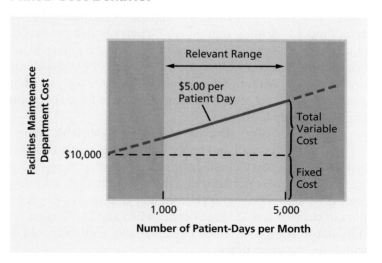

addition, cleaning supplies and repair materials may vary at a rate of $5 per patient-day[1] delivered by the hospital.

The chief administrator at Parkview Medical Center used knowledge of the facilities maintenance department cost behavior to

1. Plan costs: In May the hospital expected to service 4,000 patient-days. May's predicted facilities maintenance department costs are $10,000 fixed plus the variable cost of $20,000 (4,000 patient-days times $5 per patient-day) for a total of $30,000.

2. Provide feedback to managers: In May the actual facilities maintenance costs were $34,000 in a month when 4,000 patient-days were serviced as planned. The administrator wanted to know why the hospital overspent by $4,000 ($34,000 less the planned $30,000) so that managers could take corrective action.

3. Make decisions about the most efficient use of resources: For example, managers might weigh the long-run tradeoffs of increased fixed costs of highly automated floor cleaning equipment against the variable costs of extra hours needed to clean floors manually.

MANAGEMENT INFLUENCE ON COST BEHAVIOR

In addition to measuring and evaluating current cost behavior, managers can influence cost behavior through decisions about such factors as product or service attributes, capacity, technology, and policies to create incentives to control costs.

Objective 2
Explain management influences on cost behavior.

PRODUCT AND SERVICE DECISIONS AND THE VALUE CHAIN

Throughout the value chain, managers influence cost behavior. This influence occurs through their choices of process and product design, quality levels, product features, distribution channels, and so on. Each of these decisions contributes to the organization's performance and should be made in a cost-benefit framework. For example, Hertz, the car rental company, would add a feature to its services only if the cost of the feature (for example, free mileage) could be justified (more than recovered in profit from increased business).

CAPACITY DECISIONS

Strategic decisions about the scale and scope of an organization's activities generally result in fixed levels of capacity costs. **Capacity costs** are the fixed costs of being able to achieve a desired level of production or to provide a desired level of service while maintaining product or service attributes, such as quality. Companies in industries with long-term variations in demand must be careful when making capacity decisions. Fixed capacity costs cannot be recovered when demand falls during an economic downturn. Consider the dilemma facing Ford. In the mid-1980s, Ford was operating at full capacity. To meet demand, workers were on overtime and Ford even contracted with Mazda to produce some of its Probe cars. Ford had to choose either to build new plants and assembly lines or to continue to pay premiums for overtime and outside production. Building new plants would enable Ford to produce cars at lower cost, but the fixed capacity costs could not be reduced if production volumes were to fall. Overtime and outsourcing production to Mazda were expensive, but Ford could eliminate these variable costs during any business downturn when it did not need the extra cars. What did Ford do? According to executives at Ford, "We know in 1986 and 1987 we lost some sales. We could have probably had a higher market share. But we felt it was worth it to keep our costs under

capacity costs The fixed costs of being able to achieve a desired level of production or to provide a desired level of service while maintaining product or service attributes, such as quality.

---

[1] *A patient-day is one patient spending one day in the hospital. One patient spending five days in the hospital is five patient-days of service.*

control. . . . Sooner or later there's going to be a downturn and we'll be running down days and short weeks even with the capacity we have." Ford's decision to limit its fixed costs even in the face of higher variable costs helped the company to endure the business downturn in the early 1990s. Ford was better able to reduce its costs as demand for autos fell. Again, in the economic boom of the late 1990s, Ford faced the same strategic decision concerning scale and scope of operations.

COMMITTED FIXED COSTS

committed fixed costs
Costs arising from the possession of facilities, equipment, and a basic organization: large, indivisible chunks of cost that the organization is obligated to incur or usually would not consider avoiding.

Even if, like Ford, a company has chosen to minimize fixed capacity costs, every organization has some costs to which it is committed, perhaps for quite a few years. **Committed fixed costs** usually arise from the possession of facilities, equipment, and a basic organization. These are large, indivisible chunks of cost that the organization is obligated to incur or usually would not consider eliminating. Committed fixed costs include mortgage or lease payments, interest payments on long-term debt, property taxes, insurance, and salaries of key personnel. Only major changes in the philosophy, scale, or scope of operations could change these committed fixed costs in future periods. Recall the example of the facilities maintenance department for the Parkview Medical Center. The capacity of the facilities maintenance department was a management decision, and in this case the decision determined the magnitude of the equipment cost. Suppose Parkview Medical Center were to increase permanently its patient-days per month beyond the relevant range of 5,000 patient-days. Because more capacity would be needed, the committed equipment cost would rise to a new level per month.

DISCRETIONARY FIXED COSTS

discretionary fixed costs
Costs determined by management as part of the periodic planning process in order to meet the organization's goals. They have no obvious relationship with levels of capacity or output activity.

Some costs are fixed at certain levels only because management decided that these levels of cost should be incurred to meet the organization's goals. These **discretionary fixed costs** have no obvious relationship to levels of capacity or output activity but are determined as part of the periodic planning process. Each planning period, management will determine how much to spend on discretionary items such as advertising and promotion costs, public relations, research and development costs, charitable donations, employee training programs, and purchased management consulting services. These costs then become fixed until the next planning period.

Unlike committed fixed costs, managers can alter discretionary fixed costs easily—up or down—even within a budget period, if they decide that different levels of spending are desirable. Conceivably, managers could reduce such discretionary costs almost entirely for a given year in dire times, whereas they could not reduce committed costs. Discretionary fixed costs may be essential to the long-run achievement of the organization's goals, but managers can vary spending levels broadly in the short run.

Consider Marietta Corporation, which is experiencing financial difficulties. Sales for its major products are down, and Marietta's management is considering cutting back on costs temporarily. Marietta's management must determine which of the following fixed costs can be reduced or eliminated and how much money each would save:

Fixed Costs	Planned Amounts
Advertising and promotion	$ 30,000
Depreciation	400,000
Employee training	100,000
Management salaries	800,000
Mortgage payment	250,000
Property taxes	600,000
Research and development	1,500,000
Total	$3,680,000

Can Marietta reduce or eliminate any of these fixed costs? The answer depends on Marietta's long-run outlook. Marietta could reduce costs but also greatly reduce its ability to compete in the future if it cuts carelessly. Rearranging these costs by categories of committed and discretionary costs yields the following analysis:

Fixed Costs	Planned Amounts
Committed	
Depreciation	$ 400,000
Mortgage payment	250,000
Property taxes	600,000
Total committed	$1,250,000
Discretionary (potential savings)	
Advertising and promotion	$ 30,000
Employee training	100,000
Management salaries	800,000
Research and development	1,500,000
Total discretionary	$2,430,000
Total committed and discretionary	$3,680,000

Eliminating all discretionary fixed costs would save Marietta $2,430,000 per year. However, Marietta would be unwise to cut all discretionary costs completely. This would severely impair the company's long-run prospects. Nevertheless, distinguishing committed and discretionary fixed costs would be the company's first step to identifying where costs could be reduced.

Consider the difference between committed and discretionary fixed costs. Committed costs limit management's flexibility, while discretionary costs preserve flexibility. Are all fixed costs either committed or discretionary?

ANSWER

No. These are two ends of a spectrum. Most fixed costs have characteristics of both committed and discretionary costs. However, it is helpful to try to classify costs as committed or discretionary, because it forces managers to think about how much influence they might have over the cost if they want to change it.

TECHNOLOGY DECISIONS

One of the most critical decisions that managers make is the type of technology that the organization will use to produce its products or deliver its services. Choice of technology (for example, labor-intensive versus robotic manufacturing, traditional banking services versus automated tellers, or e-commerce versus in-store or mail-order sales) positions the organization to meet its current goals and to respond to changes in the environment (for example, changes in customer needs or actions by competitors). The use of high technology methods rather than labor usually means a much greater fixed-cost component to the total cost. This type of cost behavior creates greater risks for companies with wide variations in demand.

COST-CONTROL INCENTIVES

Finally, the incentives that management creates for employees can affect future costs. Managers use their knowledge of cost behavior to set cost expectations, and employees may receive compensation or other rewards that are tied to meeting these expectations. For example, the administrator of Parkview Medical Center gave the supervisor of the facilities maintenance department a favorable evaluation if the supervisor maintained quality of service and kept department costs below the expected amount for the actual level of patient-days. This feedback motivated the supervisor to watch department costs carefully and to find ways to reduce costs without reducing quality of service.

COST FUNCTIONS

cost measurement
Estimating or predicting costs as a function of appropriate cost drivers.

The decision making, planning, and controlling activities of management accounting require accurate and useful estimates of future fixed and variable costs. The first step in estimating or predicting costs is **cost measurement** or measuring cost behavior as a function of appropriate cost drivers. The second step is to use these cost measures to estimate future costs at expected, future levels of cost-driver activity.

Objective 3
Measure and mathematically express cost functions and use them to predict costs.

FORM OF COST FUNCTIONS

cost function An algebraic equation used by managers to describe the relationship between a cost and its cost driver(s).

To describe the relationship between a cost and its cost driver(s), managers often use an algebraic equation called a **cost function.** When there is only one cost driver, the cost function is similar to the algebraic CVP relationships discussed in Chapter 2. Consider the mixed cost graphed in Exhibit 3-3 on page 88, the facilities maintenance department cost:

$$\begin{array}{l} \text{Monthly facilities} \\ \text{maintenance} \\ \text{department costs} \end{array} = \begin{array}{l} \text{Monthly fixed} \\ \text{maintenance cost} \end{array} + \begin{array}{l} \text{Monthly variable} \\ \text{maintenance cost} \end{array}$$

$$= \begin{array}{l} \text{Monthly fixed} \\ \text{maintenance cost} \end{array} + \left(\begin{array}{l} \text{Variable cost per} \\ \text{patient-day} \end{array} \times \begin{array}{l} \text{Number of patient-} \\ \text{days in the month} \end{array} \right)$$

Let

Y = monthly facilities maintenance department cost

F = monthly fixed maintenance cost

V = variable cost per patient-day

X = cost-driver activity in number of patient-days per month

We can rewrite the mixed-cost function as

$$Y = F + VX \text{ or}$$

$$Y = \$10,000 + \$5.00X$$

This mixed-cost function has the familiar form of a straight line—it is called a linear-cost function. When graphing a cost function, F is the intercept, the point on the vertical axis where the cost function begins. In Exhibit 3-3, the intercept is the $10,000 fixed cost per month. V, the variable cost per unit of activity, is the slope of the cost function. In Exhibit 3-3, the cost function slopes upward at the rate of $5 for each additional patient-day.

CRITERIA FOR CHOOSING FUNCTIONS

Managers should apply two principles to obtain accurate and useful cost functions: *plausibility* and *reliability*.

1. The cost function must be plausible or believable. Personal observation of costs and activities, when it is possible, provides the best evidence of a plausible relationship between a cost and its driver. Some cost relationships, by nature, are not directly observable, so the cost analyst must be confident that the proposed relationship is sound. Many costs may move together with a number of cost drivers, but no cause-and-effect relationships may exist. A cause-and-effect relationship (that is, X causes Y) is desirable for cost functions to be accurate and useful.

2. In addition to being plausible, a cost function's estimates of costs at actual levels of activity must reliably conform with actually observed costs. Reliability can be assessed in terms of "goodness of fit"—how well the cost function explains past cost behavior. If the fit is good and conditions do not change, the cost function should be a reliable predictor of future costs.

Note especially that managers use these criteria together in choosing a cost function. Each is a check on the other. Knowledge of operations and how costs are recorded is helpful in choosing a plausible and reliable cost function that links cause and effect. For example, maintenance is often performed when output is low, because that is when machines can be taken out of service. Lower output does not cause increased maintenance costs, however, nor does increased output cause lower maintenance costs. A more plausible explanation is that over a longer period increased output causes higher maintenance costs, but daily or weekly recording of maintenance costs and outputs may make it appear otherwise. Understanding the nature of maintenance costs should lead to a reliable, long-run cost function.

A cost function is a mathematical expression of the components of a particular cost. However, an intuitive understanding of cost functions is just as important as being able to write the mathematical formula. For example, what does it mean when a cost function is linear?

ANSWER

It means that there are two parts to the cost. One part is fixed—that is, it's independent of the cost driver. The other part varies in proportion to the cost driver. That is, if the cost driver increases by $X\%$, this part of the cost also increases by $X\%$.

CHOICE OF COST DRIVERS: ACTIVITY ANALYSIS

How do managers choose reliable and plausible cost functions? Well, you cannot have a good cost function without knowing the right cost drivers, so choosing a cost function starts with choosing cost drivers. Managers use **activity analysis** to identify appropriate cost drivers and their effects on the costs of making a product or providing a service. The final product or service may have a number of cost drivers because a number of separate activities may be involved. The greatest benefit of activity analysis is that it directs management accountants to the appropriate cost drivers for each cost.

Activity analysis is especially important for measuring and predicting costs for which cost drivers are not obvious. **Cost prediction** applies cost measures to expected future activity levels to forecast future costs. Earlier in this chapter we said that a cost is fixed or

activity analysis The process of identifying appropriate cost drivers and their effects on the costs of making a product or providing a service.

cost prediction The application of cost measures to expected future activity levels to forecast future costs.

Objective 4
Describe the
importance of activity
analysis for measuring
cost functions.

variable with respect to a specific cost driver. A cost that appears fixed in relation to one cost driver could in fact be variable in relation to another cost driver. For example, suppose the Jupiter automobile plant uses automated painting equipment. The cost of adjusting this equipment may be fixed with respect to the total number of automobiles produced. That is, there is no clear cost relationship between these support costs and the number of automobiles produced. This same cost may vary greatly, however, with the number of different colors and types of finishes of automobiles produced. Activity analysis examines various potential cost drivers for plausibility and reliability. As always, the expected benefits of improved decision making from using more accurate cost behavior should exceed the expected costs of the cost-driver search.

Identifying the appropriate cost drivers is the most critical aspect of any method for measuring cost behavior. For many years, most organizations used only one cost driver: the amount of labor used. In essence, they assumed that the only activity affecting costs was the use of labor. In the past decade, however, we have learned that previously "hidden" activities greatly influence costs. Often, analysts in both manufacturing and service companies find that activities related to the complexity of performing tasks affect costs more directly than do labor usage or other cost drivers that are related to the volume of output activity.

Consider Northwestern Computers, which makes two products for personal computers: a plug-in music board (Mozart-Plus) and a hard-disk drive (Powerdrive). When most of the work on Northwestern's products was done by hand, most costs, other than the cost of materials, were related to (driven by) labor cost. The use of computer-controlled assembly equipment, however, has increased the costs of support activities and has reduced labor cost. Labor cost is now only 5% of the total costs at Northwestern. Furthermore, activity analysis has shown that most of today's support costs are driven by the number of components added to products (a measure of product complexity), not by labor cost. Mozart-Plus has five component parts, and Powerdrive has nine.

On average, support costs are twice as much as labor costs. Suppose Northwestern wants to predict how much support cost is incurred in producing one Mozart-Plus and how much for one Powerdrive. Using the old cost driver, labor cost, the prediction of support costs would be

	Mozart-Plus	**Powerdrive**
Labor cost	$ 8.50	$130.00
Support cost:		
2 × Direct labor cost	$17.00	$260.00

Using the more appropriate cost driver, the number of components added to products, the predicted support costs are

	Mozart-Plus	**Powerdrive**
Support cost		
at $20 per component		
$20 × 5 components	$100.00	
$20 × 9 components		$180.00
Difference in predicted support cost	$ 83.00	$ 80.00
	higher	lower

By using an appropriate cost driver, Northwestern can predict its support costs much more accurately. Managers will make better decisions with this more accurate information. For example, prices charged for products can be more closely related to the costs of production.

Manufacturing companies were the first organizations to use activity analysis. However, its use has spread to many service industries and nonprofit organizations. A recent article described how the Hospice of Central Kentucky (HCK) undertook an activity analysis to better understand its costs.

HCK is a Medicare/Medicaid–certified program providing medical care to the terminally ill in ten counties in central Kentucky. In addition to seeing to the medical needs of its patients, HCK has social workers, home health aides, volunteers, and chaplains. It also provides an 18-month bereavement program for families of patients.

Many of HCK's costs were directly patient related, and understanding these costs posed no problems. However, support costs were large, and HCK had little information about what caused these costs. Before undertaking an activity analysis, HCK simply assumed that the patient-day was the only cost driver for all support costs. Support costs were computed as $35.53 per patient-day.

Because HCK felt the squeeze of increasing costs and constant reimbursements from HMOs and insurance companies, management at HCK wanted better cost information to make various decisions. To do this, the organization undertook an activity analysis to determine the appropriate cost drivers for support costs. This consisted of two basic tasks: (1) Identify the activities being performed and (2) select a cost driver for each activity.

To identify the activities and the costs related to each activity, HCK formed a cross-functional team. Identifying the activities takes a thorough understanding of all the operations of the hospice, so a team of only finance or accounting professionals would not be knowledgeable

enough for this task. The team included the director of operations, the bereavement coordinator, the billing coordinator, a nurse, and a representative of the community service program. Among them they knew all aspects of the hospice's operations.

The team identified 14 activities. The next step was to select a cost driver for each activity. Some of the activities and their related cost drivers are

Activity	Cost Driver
Referral	Number of (indexed) referrals
Admission	Number of admissions
Bereavement	Number of deaths
Accounting/Finance	Number of (indexed) patient days
Billing	Number of billings
Volunteer services	Number of volunteers

Using the cost information from the activity analysis, management was able to learn how much each different activity costs and could recognize that patients that required use of expensive activities were more expensive to treat. Management could then try to reduce the costs of activities that were not worth the amount being spent for them, and they could better negotiate contracts so that HMOs and insurance companies would provide more support for patients that required the most expensive activities.

Source: Adapted from Sidney J. Baxendale and Victoria Dornbusch, "Activity-Based Costing for a Hospice," *Strategic Finance,* March 2000, pp. 65–70.

METHODS OF MEASURING COST FUNCTIONS

After determining the most plausible drivers behind different costs, managers can choose from a broad selection of methods of approximating cost functions. Methods include (1) engineering analysis, (2) account analysis, (3) high-low analysis, (4) visual-fit analysis, and (5) least-squares regression analysis. These methods are not mutually exclusive; managers frequently use two or more together to avoid major errors in measuring cost behavior. The first two methods may rely only on logical analysis, whereas the last three involve analysis of past costs.

ENGINEERING ANALYSIS

The first method, **engineering analysis,** measures cost behavior according to what costs should be, not by what costs have been. It entails a systematic review of materials, supplies, labor, support services, and facilities needed for products and services. Analysts can

engineering analysis The systematic review of materials, supplies, labor, support services, and facilities needed for products and services; measuring cost behavior according to what costs should be, not by what costs have been.

even use engineering analysis successfully for new products and services, as long as the organization has had experience with similar costs. Why? Because measures can be based on information from personnel who are directly involved with the product or service. In addition to actual experience, analysts learn about new costs from experiments with prototypes, accounting and industrial engineering literature, the experience of competitors, and the advice of management consultants. From this information, cost analysts determine what future costs should be. If the cost analysts are experienced and understand the activities of the organization, then their engineering cost predictions may be quite reliable and useful for decision making. The disadvantages of engineering cost analysis are that the efforts are costly and often not timely.

Weyerhauser Company, producer of wood products, used engineering analysis to determine the cost functions for its 14 corporate service departments. These cost functions are used to measure the cost of corporate services used by three main business groups. For example, accounts payable costs for each division are a function of three cost drivers: the number of hours spent on each division, number of documents, and number of invoices. This approach to measuring cost behavior also could be used by nearly any service organization.

At Parkview Medical Center, introduced earlier, an assistant to the hospital administrator interviewed facilities maintenance personnel and observed their activities on several random days for a month. From these data, the assistant confirmed that the most plausible cost driver for facilities maintenance cost is the number of patient-days. The assistant also estimated from current department salaries and equipment charges that monthly fixed costs approximated $10,000 per month. From interviews and supplies usage during the month that the assistant observed, the assistant estimated that variable costs are $5 per patient-day. The assistant gave this information to the hospital administrator but cautioned that the cost measures may be wrong because

1. The month observed may be abnormal.
2. The facilities maintenance personnel may have altered their normal work habits because the assistant was observing them.
3. The facilities maintenance personnel may not have told the complete truth about their activities because of their concerns about the use of the information they revealed.

However, if we assume the observed and estimated information is correct, facilities maintenance cost in any month could be predicted by first forecasting that month's expected patient-days and then entering that figure into the following algebraic, mixed-cost function:

$$Y = \$10,000 \text{ per month} + (\$5 \times \text{patient-days})$$

For example, if the administrator expects 4,000 patient-days next month, facilities maintenance costs are predicted to be

$$Y = \$10,000 + (\$5 \times 4,000 \text{ patient-days}) = \underline{\$30,000}$$

ACCOUNT ANALYSIS

account analysis Selecting a plausible cost driver and classifying each account as a variable cost or as a fixed cost.

In contrast to engineering analysis, users of **account analysis** look to the accounting system for information about cost behavior. The simplest method of account analysis selects a plausible cost driver and classifies each account as a variable or fixed cost with respect to the cost driver. The cost analyst then looks at each cost account balance and estimates either the variable cost per unit of cost-driver activity or the periodic fixed cost.

To illustrate this approach to account analysis, let's return to the facilities maintenance department at Parkview Medical Center and analyze costs for the month of January. Recall that the most plausible driver for these costs is the number of patient-days serviced per month. The table below shows costs recorded in a month with 3,700 patient-days:

Objective 5
Measure cost behavior using the account analysis, high-low, visual-fit, and least-squares regression methods.

Monthly Cost	January Amount
Supervisor's salary and benefits	$ 3,800
Hourly workers' wages and benefits	14,674
Equipment depreciation and rentals	5,873
Equipment repairs	5,604
Cleaning supplies	7,472
Total facilities maintenance cost	$37,423

Next, the analyst determines which costs may be fixed and which may be variable. Assume that the analyst has made the following judgments:

Monthly Cost	January Amount	Fixed	Variable
Supervisor's salary and benefits	$ 3,800	$3,800	
Hourly workers' wages and benefits	14,674		$14,674
Equipment depreciation and rentals	5,873	5,873	
Equipment repairs	5,604		5,604
Cleaning supplies	7,472		7,472
Total facilities maintenance costs	$37,423	$9,673	$27,750

Measuring total facilities maintenance cost behavior, then, requires only simple arithmetic. Add all the fixed costs to get the total fixed cost per month. Divide the total variable costs by the units of cost-driver activity to get the variable cost per unit of cost driver.

$$\text{Fixed cost per month} = \underline{\$9,673}$$

$$\text{Variable cost per patient-day} = \$27,750 \div 3,700 \text{ patient-days}$$
$$= \underline{\$7.50 \text{ per patient-day}}$$

The algebraic, mixed-cost function, measured by account analysis, is

$$Y = \$9,673 \text{ per month} + (\$7.50 \times \text{patient-days})$$

Account-analysis methods are less expensive to conduct than engineering analyses, but they require recording of relevant cost accounts and cost drivers. In addition, account analysis, like engineering analysis, is subjective because the analyst decides whether each cost is variable or fixed based on his or her own judgment.

SUMMARY PROBLEM FOR YOUR REVIEW

PROBLEM

The Reliable Insurance Company processes a variety of insurance claims for losses, accidents, thefts, and so on. Account analysis using one cost driver has estimated the variable cost of processing each claim at 0.5% (.005) of the dollar value of the claim. This estimate seemed reasonable because higher claims often involve more analysis before settlement. To control processing costs better, however, Reliable Insurance conducted an activity analysis of claims processing. The analysis suggested that there are three main cost drivers and that behavior for automobile accident claims are

0.2% of Reliable Insurance policyholders' property claims

+ 0.6% of other parties' property claims

+ 0.8% of total personal injury claims

Data from two recent automobile accident claims follow:

	Automobile Claim No. 607788	Automobile Claim No. 607991
Policyholder claim	$ 4,500	$23,600
Other party claim	0	3,400
Personal injury claim	12,400	0
Total claim amount	$16,900	$27,000

Required

1. Estimate the cost of processing each claim using data from (a) the single-cost-driver analysis and (b) the three-cost-driver analysis.

2. How would you recommend that Reliable Insurance estimate the cost of processing claims?

SOLUTION

1.

	Automobile Claim No. 607788		Automobile Claim No. 607991	
	Claim Amount	*Processing Cost*	*Claim Amount*	*Processing Cost*
Using single-cost-driver analysis				
Total claim amount	$16,900		$27,000	
Estimated processing cost at 0.5%		$ 84.50		$135.00
Using three-cost-driver analysis				
Policyholder claim	$ 4,500		$23,600	
Estimated processing cost at 0.2%		$ 9.00		$ 47.20
Other party claim	0		3,400	
Estimated processing cost at 0.6%		0		20.40
Personal injury claim	12,400		0	
Estimated processing cost at 0.8%		99.20		0
Total estimated processing cost		$108.20		$ 67.60

2. The three-cost-driver analysis estimates of processing costs are considerably different from those using a single cost driver. If the activity analyses are reliable, then automobile claims that include personal injury losses are more costly to process than property damage claims. If these estimates are relatively inexpensive to keep current and to use, then it seems reasonable to adopt the three-cost-driver approach. Reliable Insurance will have more accurate cost estimates and will be better able to plan its claims processing activities. Reliable

Insurance processes many different types of claims, however. Extending activity analysis to identify multiple cost drivers for all types of claims would result in a complicated system for predicting costs—much more complex (and costly) than simply using the total dollar value of claims. Whether to undertake an activity analysis for all types of policies depends on cost-benefit considerations. Managers can address such considerations by first adopting activity analysis for one type of claim and assessing the usefulness and cost of the more accurate information.

HIGH-LOW, VISUAL-FIT, AND LEAST-SQUARES METHODS

When enough cost data are available, we can use historical data to measure the cost function mathematically. Three popular methods that use such data are the high-low, visual-fit, and least-squares methods. All three of these methods are more objective than the engineering-analysis method because each is based on hard evidence as well as on judgment. They also can be more objective than is account analysis because they use more than one period's cost and activity information. Account analysis and especially engineering analysis will probably remain primary methods of measuring cost behavior because the above three methods require more past cost data. Products, services, technologies, and organizations are changing rapidly in response to increased global competition. In some cases, by the time enough historical data are collected to support these analyses, the data are obsolete—the organization has changed, the production process has changed, or the product has changed. The cost analyst must be careful that the historical data are from a past environment that still closely resembles the future environment for which costs are being predicted. Another concern is that historical data may hide past inefficiencies that could be reduced if they are identified.

Data for Illustration. In discussing the high-low, visual-fit, and least-squares regression methods, we will continue to use the Parkview Medical Center's facilities maintenance department costs. The following table shows monthly data collected on facilities maintenance department costs and on the number of patient-days serviced over the past year:

Facilities Maintenance Department Data

Month	Facilities Maintenance Department Cost (Y)	Number of Patient-Days (X)
January	$37,000	3,700
February	23,000	1,600
March	37,000	4,100
April	47,000	4,900
May	33,000	3,300
June	39,000	4,400
July	32,000	3,500
August	33,000	4,000
September	17,000	1,200
October	18,000	1,300
November	22,000	1,800
December	20,000	1,600

High-Low Method. When sufficient cost data are available, the cost analyst may use historical data to measure the cost function mathematically. The simplest of the three

Exhibit 3-4
High-Low Method

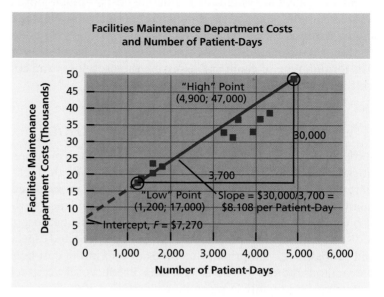

Facilities Maintenance Department Costs and Number of Patient-Days

high-low method   A simple method for measuring a linear-cost function from past cost data, focusing on the highest-activity and lowest-activity points and fitting a line through these two points.

methods to measure a linear-cost function from past cost data is the **high-low method** shown in Exhibit 3-4.

The first step in the high-low method is to plot the historical data points on a graph. This visual display helps the analyst see whether there are obvious errors in the data. Even though many points are plotted, the focus of the high-low method is normally on the highest- and lowest-activity points. However, if one of these points is an "outlier" that seems in error or nonrepresentative of normal operations, we will need to use the next-highest or next-lowest activity point. For example, you should not use a point from a period with abnormally low activity caused by a labor strike or fire. Why? Because that point is not representative of a normal relationship between the cost and the cost driver.

After selecting the representative high and low points, we can draw a line between them, extending the line to the vertical (Y) axis of the graph. Note that this extension in Exhibit 3-4 is a dashed line as a reminder that costs may not be linear outside the range of activity for which we have data (the relevant range). Also, managers usually are concerned with how costs behave within the relevant range, not with how they behave either at zero activity or at impossibly high activity levels. Measurements of costs within the relevant range probably are not reliable measures or predictors of costs outside the relevant range.

The point at which the line intersects the Y-axis is the intercept, F, or estimate of fixed cost. The slope of the line measures the variable cost, V, per patient-day. The clearest way to measure the intercept and slope with the high-low method is to use algebra:

Month	Facilities Maintenance Department Cost (Y)	Number of Patient-Days (X)
High: April	$47,000	4,900
Low: September	17,000	1,200
Difference	$30,000	$3,700

Variable cost per patient-day,

$$V = \frac{\text{change in costs}}{\text{change in activity}} = \frac{\$47,000 - \$17,000}{4,900 - 1,200 \text{ patient-days}}$$

$$V = \frac{\$30,000}{3,700} = \underline{\$8.1081} \text{ per patient-day}$$

Fixed cost per month, F = Total mixed cost less total variable cost

at X (high): $F = \$47,000 - (\$8.1081 \times 4,900 \text{ patient-days})$

$= \$47,000 - \$39,730$

$= \underline{\$7,270} \text{ per month}$

at X (low): $F = \$17,000 - (\$8.1081 \times 1,200 \text{ patient-days})$

$= \$17,000 - \$9,730$

$= \underline{\$7,270} \text{ per month}$

Therefore, the facilities maintenance department cost function, measured by the high-low method, is

$$Y = \$7,270 \text{ per month} + (\$8.1081 \times \text{patient-days})$$

The high-low method is easy to use and illustrates mathematically how a change in a cost driver can change total cost. The cost function that resulted in this case is plausible. Before the widespread availability of computers, managers often used the high-low method to measure a cost function quickly. Today, however, the high-low method is not used as often because of its unreliability and because it makes inefficient use of information, using only two periods' cost experience, regardless of how many relevant data points have been collected.

SUMMARY PROBLEM FOR YOUR REVIEW

PROBLEM

The Reetz Company has its own photocopying department. Reetz's photocopying costs include costs of copy machines, operators, paper, toner, utilities, and so on. We have the following cost and activity data.

Month	Total Photocopying Cost	Number of Copies
1	$25,000	320,000
2	29,000	390,000
3	24,000	300,000
4	23,000	310,000
5	28,000	400,000

1. Use the high-low method to measure the cost behavior of the photocopy department in formula form.
2. What are the benefits and disadvantages of using the high-low method for measuring cost behavior?

SOLUTION

1. The lowest and highest activity levels are in months 3 (300,000 copies) and 5 (400,000 copies).

$$\text{Variable cost per copy} = \frac{\text{change in cost}}{\text{change in activity}} = \frac{\$28,000 - \$24,000}{400,000 - 300,000}$$

$$= \frac{\$4,000}{100,000} = \underline{\$0.04} \text{ per copy}$$

Fixed cost per month = total cost less variable cost

at 400,000 copies: $28,000 − ($0.04 × 400,000) = $12,000 per month

at 300,000 copies: $24,000 − ($0.04 × 300,000) = $12,000 per month

Therefore, the photocopy cost function is

Y (total cost) = $12,000 per month + $0.04 × number of copies

2. The benefits of using the high-low method are
   - The method is easy to use.
   - Not many data are needed.

   The disadvantages of using the high-low method are:
   - The choice of the high and low points is subjective.
   - The method does not use all available data.
   - The method may not be reliable.

visual-fit method A method in which the cost analyst visually fits a straight line through a plot of all the available data.

Visual-Fit Method. Because it uses all the available data instead of just two points, the **visual-fit method** is more reliable than is the high-low method. In the visual-fit method, we draw a straight line through a plot of *all* the available data, using judgment to fit the line as close as possible to all the plotted points. If the cost function for the data is linear, it is possible to draw a straight line through the scattered points that comes reasonably close to most of them and thus captures the general tendency of the data. We can extend that line back until it intersects the vertical axis of the graph.

Exhibit 3-5 shows this method applied to the facilities maintenance department cost data for the past 12 months. By measuring where the line intersects the cost axis, we can estimate the monthly fixed cost—in this case, about $10,000 per month. To find the variable cost per patient-day, select any activity level (say, 1,000 patient-days) and find the total cost at that activity level ($17,000). Then divide the variable cost (which is total cost less fixed cost) by the units of activity.

Variable cost per patient-day = ($17,000 − $10,000) ÷ 1,000 patient-days

= $7 per patient-day

The linear-cost function measured by the visual-fit method is

Y = $10,000 per month + ($7 × patient-days)

Although the visual-fit method uses all the data, the placement of the line and the measurement of the fixed and variable costs are subjective. This subjectivity is the main reason that the visual-fit method is now often replaced by least-squares regression analysis.

Exhibit 3-5

Visual-Fit Method

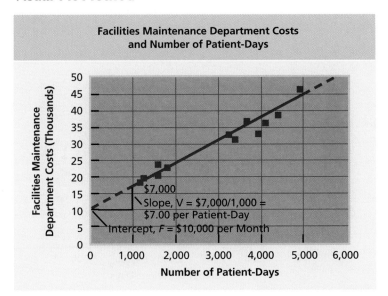

Facilities Maintenance Department Costs and Number of Patient-Days

Least-Squares Regression Method. **Least-squares regression** (or simply **regression analysis**) measures a cost function more objectively (with statistics rather than human eyesight) than does the visual-fit method. Least-squares regression analysis uses statistics to fit a cost function to all the historical data. Regression analysis that uses one cost driver to measure a cost function is called simple regression. The use of multiple cost drivers for a single cost is called multiple regression. We will discuss only simple regression analysis in this section of the chapter. Appendix 3 presents some statistical properties of regression and shows how to use computer regression software.

Regression analysis measures cost behavior more reliably than other cost measurement methods. In addition, regression analysis yields important statistical information about the reliability of cost estimates, so analysts can assess confidence in the cost measures and select the best cost driver. One such measure of reliability, or goodness of fit, is the **coefficient of determination, R^2** (or R-squared), which measures how much of the fluctuation of a cost is explained by changes in the cost driver. Appendix 3 explains R^2 and discusses how to use it to select the best cost driver.

Exhibit 3-6 shows the linear, mixed-cost function for facilities maintenance costs as measured by simple regression analysis. The fixed-cost measure is $9,329 per month. The variable-cost measure is $6.951 per patient-day. The linear-cost function is

Facilities maintenance department cost = $9,329 per month + $6.951 per patient-day

or

$$Y = \$9,329 + \$6.951 \times \text{patient-days}$$

Compare the cost measures produced by each of the five approaches:

Method	Fixed Cost per Month	Variable Cost per Patient-Day
Engineering analysis	$10,000	$5.000
Account analysis	9,673	7.500
High-low	7,270	8.108
Visual-fit	10,000	7.000
Regression	9,329	6.951

least-squares regression (regression analysis) Measuring a cost function objectively by using statistics to fit a cost function to all the data.

coefficient of determination (R^2) A measurement of how much of the fluctuation of a cost is explained by changes in the cost driver.

Exhibit 3-6
Least-Squares Regression Method

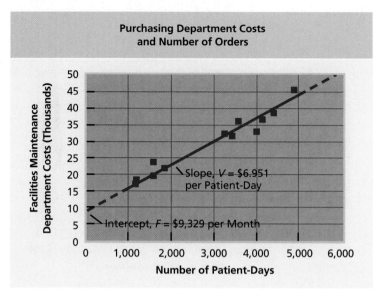

To see the differences in results between methods, we will use account-analysis and regression-analysis measures to predict total facilities maintenance department costs at 1,000 and 5,000 patient-days, the approximate limits of the relevant range:

	Account Analysis	Regression Analysis	Difference
1,000 patient-days:			
Fixed cost	$ 9,673	$ 9,329	$ 344
Variable costs			
$7.500 × 1,000	7,500		
$6.951 × 1,000		6,951	549
Predicted total cost	$17,173	$16,280	$ 893
5,000 patient-days:			
Fixed cost	$ 9,673	$ 9,329	$ 344
Variable costs			
$7.500 × 5,000	37,500		
$6.951 × 5,000		34,755	2,745
Predicted total cost	$47,173	$44,084	$3,089

At lower levels of patient-day activity the difference between cost predictions is small. At higher levels of patient-day activity, however, the account-analysis cost function predicts much higher costs. The difference between the predicted total costs is due primarily to the higher variable cost per patient-day (approximately $0.55 more) measured by account analysis. Because of their grounding in statistical analysis, the regression-cost measures are probably more reliable than are the other methods. Managers would thus have more confidence in cost predictions from the regression-cost function.

Highlights to Remember

Explain step- and mixed-cost behavior. Cost behavior refers to how costs change as levels of an organization's activities change. Costs can behave as fixed, variable, step, or

Consider how Hewlett-Packard (HP), the computer manufacturer, measured cost behavior as part of its companywide implementation of a new cost accounting system. HP used detailed engineering analysis to revise its accounting system at many of its manufacturing sites. The old cost system at HP used labor cost as the cost driver for all nonmaterial costs, regardless of the actual cost drivers. On average, labor costs were only 2% of total costs, so it was unlikely that they were the major cause of most other costs. The result of using labor cost was significant cost distortion—products with higher labor costs were overcosted whereas products with lower labor costs were undercosted. Managers did not have confidence in the product cost predictions using this labor-based system.

Cost analysts spent several years talking with managers and engineers and carefully observing facilities maintenance, manufacturing support, and other activities to identify more appropriate cost drivers and their relationships to cost behavior.

At HP's Surface Mount Center at Boise, the ABC system has been fully operational since early in 1993. This facility manufactures about 50 different electronic circuit boards for internal customers within HP. The selection of cost drivers at the Center resulted from an "intense analysis of the production process and cost behavior patterns by the accounting, production, and engineering staffs." This combination of account analysis and engineering analysis resulted in 10 different cost drivers.

One interesting aspect of the new cost accounting system is the continuous involvement of managers and engineers in improving the system. "An almost daily dialogue goes on among production, engineering, and the accountants about how the new cost system could be improved to reflect product costs more accurately."

A series of simple linear regressions between overhead dollars and cost-driver volumes was conducted to test the statistical validity of the cost drivers. For example, one of the regressions was "all automatic placement overhead costs" versus the cost-driver "number of automatic placements," which had a coefficient of determination (R^2) of 92%. Another regression measured the relationship between "material procurement overhead costs" and the cost-driver "number of distinct parts" and had an R^2 of 91%. The regression analyses tended to confirm that the cost drivers selected indeed were correlated with overhead costs.

Source: Adapted from Mike Merz and Arlene Hardy, "ABC Puts Accountants on Design Team at HP," *Management Accounting*, September 1993, pp. 22–27.

---

mixed costs. Step and mixed costs both combine aspects of variable and fixed cost behavior. Step costs form graphs that look like steps. Costs will remain fixed within a given range of activity or cost-driver level, but then will rise or fall abruptly when activity or cost-driver level is outside this range. Mixed costs involve a fixed element and a variable element of cost behavior. Unlike step costs, mixed costs usually have only one range of activity or cost driver.

Explain management influences on cost behavior. Managers can affect the costs and cost behavior patterns of their companies through the decisions they make. Decisions on product and service features, capacity, technology, and cost-control incentives, for example, can all affect cost behavior.

Measure and mathematically express cost functions and use them to predict costs. The first step in estimating or predicting costs is measuring cost behavior. This is done by finding a cost function. This is an algebraic equation that describes the relationship between a cost and its cost driver(s). To be useful for decision-making purposes, cost functions should be plausible and reliable.

Describe the importance of activity analysis for measuring cost functions. Activity analysis is the process of identifying the best cost drivers to use for cost estimation and prediction.

Measure cost behavior using the account analysis, high-low, visual-fit, and least-squares regression methods. Once cost drivers have been identified, one of several methods can be used to determine the cost function. Account analysis involves examining all accounts in terms of an appropriate cost driver and classifying each account as either fixed or variable with respect to the driver. The variable cost is then unitized and added to the total fixed cost to provide a working cost function. The high-low, visual-fit, and least-squares methods all use historical costs to determine cost functions. Of these three methods, high-low is the easiest, although least-squares is the most reliable.

Understand the relationship between management decision making and cost behavior. One of the key responsibilities of managers is making the best decisions possible for the organization. Understanding cost behavior provides managers with valuable insights about how costs will respond to managers' decisions as well as to outside influences. In today's highly competitive business environment, successful cost management is a key to profitability. So, it follows that a solid understanding of how costs behave is a prerequisite to effective decision making.

Appendix 3: Use and Interpretation of Least-Squares Regression

Regression analysis of historical cost data can be accomplished with no more than a simple calculator. It would be unusual, however, to find cost analysts doing regression analysis by hand—computers are much faster and less prone to error. Therefore, we focus on using a computer to perform regression analysis and on interpretation of the results.

This appendix should not be considered a substitute for a good statistics class. More properly, this appendix should be seen as a motivator for studying statistics so that analysts can provide and managers can interpret top-quality cost estimates.

Assume that there are two potential cost drivers for the costs of the facilities maintenance department in Parkview Medical Center: (1) number of patient-days and (2) total value of hospital room charges. Regression analysis helps to determine which activity is the better cost driver. Exhibit 3-7 shows the past 12 months' cost and cost-driver data for the facilities maintenance department.

Exhibit 3-7

Facilities Maintenance Department Data

Month	Facilities Maintenance Cost (Y)	Number of Patient-Days (X_1)	Value of Room Charges (X_2)
January	$37,000	3,700	$2,183,000
February	23,000	1,600	2,735,000
March	37,000	4,100	2,966,000
April	47,000	4,900	2,846,000
May	33,000	3,300	2,967,000
June	39,000	4,400	2,980,000
July	32,000	3,500	3,023,000
August	33,000	4,000	2,352,000
September	17,000	1,200	1,825,000
October	18,000	1,300	1,515,000
November	22,000	1,800	1,547,000
December	20,000	1,600	2,117,000

Most spreadsheet software available for PCs offers basic regression analysis in the Data Analysis or Tools commands. We will use these spreadsheet commands to illustrate regression analysis because many readers will be familiar already with spreadsheet software.

ENTERING DATA

First create a spreadsheet with the historical cost data in rows and columns. Each row should be data from one period. Each column should be a cost category or a cost driver. For ease of analysis, all the potential cost drivers should be in adjacent columns. Each row and column should be complete (no missing data) and without errors.

PLOTTING DATA

There are two main reasons why the first step in regression analysis should be to plot the cost against each of the potential cost drivers: (1) Plots may show obvious nonlinear trends in the data; if so, linear regression analysis may not be appropriate for the entire range of the data. (2) Plots help identify outliers—costs that are in error or are otherwise obviously inappropriate. There is little agreement about what to do with any outliers that are not the result of data-entry errors or nonrepresentative cost and activity levels (e.g., periods of labor strikes, natural catastrophes). After all, if the data are not in error and are representative, the process that is being studied generated them. Even so, some analysts recommend removing outliers from the data set. Leaving these outliers in the data makes regression analysis statistically less appealing, because data far removed from the rest of the data set will not fit the line well. The most conservative action is to leave all data in the data set unless uncorrectable errors are detected or unless the data are known to be not representative of the process.

Plotting with spreadsheets uses Graph commands on the columns of cost and cost-driver data. These Graph commands typically offer many optional graph types (such as bar charts and pie charts), but the most useful plot for regression analysis usually is called the *XY* graph. This graph is the type shown earlier in this chapter—the *X*-axis is the cost driver, and the *Y*-axis is the cost. The *XY* graph should be displayed without lines drawn between the data points (called data symbols)—an optional command. (Consult your spreadsheet manual for details, because each spreadsheet program is different.)

REGRESSION OUTPUT

The regression output is generated by commands that are unique to each software package but they identify the cost to be explained ("dependent variable") and the cost driver(s) ("independent variable[s]").

Producing regression output with spreadsheets is simple: Just select the Regression command, specify (or Highlight) the *X*-dimension[s] (the cost driver[s]), and specify the *Y*-dimension or "series" (the cost). Next specify a blank area on the spreadsheet where the output will be displayed, and select Go. Below is a regression analysis of facilities maintenance department costs using one of the two possible cost drivers, number of patient-days, X_1. Note that this output can be modified somewhat by the analyst, and the values in the output can be used elsewhere in the spreadsheet.

Facilities Maintenance Department Cost Explained by Number of Patient-Days

Regression Output	
Constant	9,329
Standard error of *Y* estimate	2,146
R^2	0.955
No. of observations	12
Degrees of freedom	10
X coefficient(s)	6.951
Standard error of coefficient(s)	0.479

INTERPRETATION OF REGRESSION OUTPUT

The fixed-cost measure is labeled "constant" or "intercept" and is $9,329 per month. The variable cost measure is labeled "*X* coefficient(s)" (or something similar in other spreadsheets) and is $6.951 per patient-day. The linear cost function (after rounding) is

$$Y = \$9,329 \text{ per month} + (\$6.951 \times \text{patient-days})$$

Typically, the computer output gives a number of statistical measures that indicate how well each cost driver explains the cost and how reliable the cost predictions are likely to be. A full explanation of the output is beyond the scope of this text. One of the most important statistics, the coefficient of determination, or R^2, is very important to assessing the goodness of fit of the cost function to the actual cost data.

What the visual-fit method tried to do with eyesight, regression analysis has accomplished more reliably. In general, the better a cost driver is at explaining a cost, the closer the data points will lie to the line, and the higher will be the R^2, which varies between 0 and 1. An R^2 of 0 would mean that the cost driver does not explain variability in the cost data, whereas an R^2 of 1 would mean that the cost driver explains the variability perfectly. The R^2 of the relationship measured with number of patient-days as the cost driver is 0.955, which is quite high. This value indicates that number of patient-days explains facilities maintenance department cost extremely well and can be interpreted as meaning that number of patient-days explains 95.5% of the past fluctuation in facilities maintenance department cost.

In contrast, performing a regression analysis on the relationship between facilities maintenance department cost and value of hospital room charges produces the following results:

Facilities Maintenance Department Cost Explained by Value of Hospital Room Charges

Regression Output	
Constant	$924
Standard error of *Y* estimate	$7,045
R^2	0.511
No. of observations	12
Degrees of freedom	10
X coefficient(s)	0.012
Standard error of coefficient(s)	0.004

The R^2 value, 0.511, indicates that the cost function using value of hospital room charges does not fit facilities maintenance department cost as well as the cost function using number of patient-days.

To use the information generated by regression analysis fully, an analyst must understand the meaning of the statistics and must be able to determine whether the statistical assumptions of regression are satisfied by the cost data. Indeed, one of the major reasons why cost analysts study statistics is to understand the assumptions of regression analysis better. With this understanding, analysts can provide their organizations with top-quality estimates of cost behavior.

SUMMARY PROBLEM FOR YOUR REVIEW

PROBLEM

Comtell, Inc., makes computer peripherals (disk drives, tape drives, and printers). Until recently, production scheduling and control (PSC) costs were predicted to vary in proportion to labor costs according to the following cost function:

$$\text{PSC costs} = 200\% \text{ of labor}$$

or

$$Y = 2 \times \text{labor cost}$$

Because PSC costs have been growing at the same time that labor cost has been shrinking, Comtell is concerned that its cost estimates are neither plausible nor reliable. Comtell's controller has just completed activity analysis to determine the most appropriate drivers of PSC costs. She obtained two cost functions using different cost drivers:

$$Y = 2 \times \text{labor cost}$$

$$R^2 = 0.233$$

and

$$Y = \$10,000/\text{month} + (11 \times \text{number of components used})$$

$$R^2 = 0.782$$

1. What would be good tests of which cost function better predicts PSC costs?
2. During a subsequent month, labor costs were $12,000 and 2,000 product components were used. Actual PSC costs were $31,460. Using each of the preceding cost functions, prepare reports that show predicted and actual PSC costs, and the difference or variance between the two.
3. What is the meaning and importance of each cost variance?

SOLUTION

1. A statistical test of which function better explains past PSC costs compares the R^2 of each function. The second function, based on the number of components used, has a considerably higher R^2, so it better explains the past PSC costs. If the

environment is essentially unchanged in the future, the second function probably will predict future PSC costs better than the first, too.

A useful predictive test would be to compare the cost predictions of each cost function with actual costs for several months that were not used to measure the cost functions. The function that more closely predicted actual costs is probably the more reliablefunction.

2. Note that more actual cost data would be desirable for a better test, but the procedure would be the same.

PSC cost predicted on a labor-cost basis follows:

Predicted Cost	Actual Cost	Variance
2 × $12,000 = $24,000	$31,460	$7,460 underestimate

PSC cost predicted on a component basis follows:

Predicted Cost	Actual Cost	Variance
$10,000 + ($11 × 2,000) = $32,000	$31,460	$540 overestimate

3. The cost function that relies on labor cost underestimated PSC cost by $7,460. The cost function that uses the number of components closely predicted actual PSC costs (off by $540). Planning and control decisions would have been based on more accurate information using this prediction than using the labor cost-based prediction. An issue is whether the benefits of collecting data on the number of components used exceeded the added cost of so doing.

Accounting Vocabulary

account analysis, p. 96
activity analysis, p. 93
capacity costs, p. 89
coefficient of determination
  (R^2), p. 103
committed fixed costs, p. 90
cost function, p. 92

cost measurement, p. 92
cost prediction, p. 93
discretionary fixed costs, p. 90
engineering analysis, p. 95
high-low method, p. 100
least-squares regression, p. 103
linear-cost behavior, p. 86

measurement of cost behavior,
  p. 86
mixed costs, p. 88
regression analysis, p. 103
step costs, p. 87
visual-fit method, p. 102

Fundamental Assignment Material

3-A1 Types of Cost Behavior
Identify the following planned costs as (a) purely variable costs, (b) discretionary fixed costs, (c) committed fixed costs, (d) mixed costs, or (e) step costs. For purely variable costs and mixed costs, indicate the most likely cost driver.

1. Straight-line depreciation on desks in the office of an attorney.
2. Sales commissions based on revenue dollars. Payments to be made to advertising salespersons employed by radio station WCCO, Minneapolis.
3. Jet fuel costs of Southwest Airlines.
4. Total costs of renting trucks by the city of Nashville. Charge is a lump sum of $300 per month plus $.20 per mile.

5. Total repairs and maintenance of a university classroom building.
6. Advertising costs, a lump sum planned by ABC, Inc.
7. Rental payment by the Internal Revenue Service on a five-year lease for office space in a private office building.
8. Advertising allowance granted to wholesalers by 7-Up Bottling on a per-case basis.
9. Compensation of lawyers employed internally by Microsoft.
10. Crew supervisor in a Lands' End, Inc., mail-order house. A new supervisor is added for every 12 workers employed.
11. Public relations employee compensation to be paid by Microsoft.

3-A2 Activity Analysis

Ackerloff Signs makes customized wooden signs for businesses and residences. These signs are made of wood, which the owner glues and carves by hand or with power tools. After carving the signs, she paints them or applies a natural finish. She has a good sense of her labor and materials cost behavior, but she is concerned that she does not have good measures of other support costs. Currently, she predicts support costs to be 60% of the cost of materials. Close investigation of the business reveals that $40 times the number of power tool operations is a more plausible and reliable support cost relationship.

Consider estimated support costs of the following two signs that Ackerloff Signs is making:

	SIGN A	SIGN B
Materials cost	$300	$150
Number of power tool operations	2	6
Support cost	?	?

Required

1. Prepare a report showing the support costs of both signs using each cost driver and showing the differences between the two.
2. What advice would you give Ackerloff Signs about predicting support costs?

3-A3 Division of Mixed Costs into Variable and Fixed Components

Martina Evert, President of Evert Tool Co., has asked for information about the cost behavior of manufacturing support costs. Specifically, she wants to know how much support cost is fixed and how much is variable. The following data are the only records available:

Month	Machine Hours	Support Costs
May	850	$ 9,000
June	1,300	12,500
July	1,000	7,900
August	1,250	11,400
September	1,750	13,500

Required

1. Find monthly fixed support cost and the variable support cost per machine hour by the high-low method.
2. A least-squares regression analysis gave the following output:

$$\text{Regression equation: } Y = \$3,355 + \$6.10X$$

What recommendations would you give the president based on these analyses?

3-B1 Identifying Cost Behavior Patterns

At a seminar, a cost accountant spoke on identification of different kinds of cost behavior. Tammy Li, a hospital administrator who heard the lecture, identified several hospital costs of concern to her. After her classification, Li presented you with the following list of costs and asked you to (1) classify their behavior as one of the following: variable, step, mixed, discretionary fixed, committed fixed, and (2) to identify a likely cost driver for each variable or mixed cost.

1. Nursing supervisors' salaries (a supervisor is needed for each 45 nursing personnel)
2. Straight-line depreciation of operating room equipment
3. Costs of services of Andersen Hospital Consulting
4. Training costs of an administrative resident
5. Operating costs of x-ray equipment ($95,000 a year plus $3 per film)
6. Health insurance for all full-time employees
7. Costs incurred by Dr. Rath in cancer research
8. Repairs made on hospital furniture

3-B2   Activity Analysis

Boise Technology, an Idaho manufacturer of printed circuit boards, has always estimated the production cost of its circuits boards with a 100% "markup" over its material costs to cover its manufacturing support costs (which include labor). An activity analysis suggests that support costs are driven primarily by the number of manual operations performed on each board, estimated at $4 per manual operation. Compute the estimated support costs of two typical circuit boards below using the traditional markup and the activity analysis results:

	Board BT1	Board BT2
Material cost	$30.00	$55.00
Manual operations	16	6

Why are the cost estimates different?

3-B3   Division of Mixed Costs into Variable and Fixed Components

The president and the controller of Acapulco Transformer Company (Mexico) have agreed that refinement of the company's cost measurements will aid planning and control decisions. They have asked you to measure the function for mixed-cost behavior of repairs and maintenance from the following sparse data. Currency is the Mexican peso ($).

Monthly Activity in Machine Hours	Monthly Repair and Maintenance Cost
8,000	$200,000,000
12,000	$260,000,000

Additional Assignment Material

QUESTIONS

3-1. What is a cost driver? Give three examples of costs and their possible cost drivers.

3-2. Explain linear-cost behavior.

3-3. "Step costs can be fixed or variable depending on your perspective." Explain.

3-4. Explain how mixed costs are related to both fixed and variable costs.

3-5. How do management's product and service choices affect cost behavior?

3-6. Why are fixed costs also called capacity costs?

3-7. How do committed fixed costs differ from discretionary fixed costs?

3-8. Why are committed fixed costs the most difficult of the fixed costs to change?

3-9. What are the primary determinants of the level of committed costs? Discretionary costs?

3-10. "Planning is far more important than day-to-day control of discretionary costs." Do you agree? Explain.

3-11. How can a company's choice of technology affect its costs?

3-12. Explain the use of incentives to control cost.

3-13. What are the benefits of using "cost functions" to describe cost behavior?

3-14. Explain "plausibility" and "reliability" of cost functions. Which is preferred? Explain.

3-15. What is activity analysis?

3-16. What is engineering analysis? Account analysis?

3-17. Describe the methods for measuring cost functions using past cost data.

3-18. How could account analysis be combined with engineering analysis?

3-19. Explain the strengths and weaknesses of the high-low and visual-fit methods.

3-20. Why is regression analysis usually preferred to the high-low method?

3-21. "You never know how good your fixed- and variable-cost measures are if you use account analysis or if you visually fit a line on a data plot. That's why I like least-squares regression analysis." Explain.

3-22. (Appendix 3) Why should an analyst always plot cost data in addition to applying least-squares regression analysis?

3-23. (Appendix 3) What can we learn from R^2, the coefficient of determination?

3-24. At a conference, a consultant stated, "Before you can control, you must measure." An executive complained, "Why bother to measure when work rules and guaranteed employment provisions in labor contracts prevent discharging workers, using part-time employees, and using overtime?" Evaluate these comments. Summarize your personal attitudes toward the usefulness of engineering analysis.

COGNITIVE EXERCISES

3-25 Mixed Costs and the Sales Force
Wysocki Company pays its sales force a fixed salary plus a 5% commission on all sales. Explain why sales force costs would be considered a mixed cost.

3-26 Committed and Discretionary Fixed Costs in Manufacturing
Among the fixed costs of Howarth Company are depreciation and research and development (R&D). Using these two costs as examples, explain the difference between committed and discretionary fixed costs.

3-27 Cost Functions and Decision Making
Why is it important that decision makers in a corporation know the cost function for producing the companies' products?

3-28 Statistical Analysis and Cost Functions
What advantages does using regression analysis have over the visual-fit method for determining cost functions?

EXERCISES

3-29 Step Costs
Which of the following are step costs? Why?

a. Rent on a warehouse that is large enough for all anticipated orders.

b. Teachers for a private elementary school. One teacher is needed for each 15 students.

c. Sheet steel for a producer of machine parts. Steel is purchased in carload shipments, where each carload contains enough steel for 1,000 parts.

3-30 Mixed Costs
The following cost function is a mixed cost. Explain why it is a mixed cost and not a fixed, variable, or step cost.

$$\text{Total cost} = \$5,000 + \$45 \times \text{units produced}$$

3-31 Various Cost-Behavior Patterns

In practice, there is often a tendency to simplify approximations of cost-behavior patterns, even though the "true" underlying behavior is not simple. Choose from the accompanying graphs A through H the one that matches the numbered items. Indicate by letter which graph best fits each of the situations described. Next to each number-letter pair, identify a likely cost driver for that cost.

The vertical axes of the graphs represent total dollars of costs incurred, and the horizontal axes represent levels of cost driver activity during a particular time period. The graphs may be used more than once.

1. Cost of machining labor that tends to decrease as workers gain experience
2. Price of an increasingly scarce raw material as the quantity used increases
3. Guaranteed annual wage plan, whereby workers get paid for 40 hours of work per week even at zero or low levels of production that require working only a few hours weekly
4. Water bill, which entails a flat fee for the first 10,000 gallons used and then an increasing unit cost for every additional 10,000 gallons used
5. Availability of quantity discounts, where the cost per unit falls as each price break is reached
6. Depreciation of office equipment
7. Cost of sheet steel for a manufacturer of farm implements
8. Salaries of supervisors, where one supervisor is added for every 12 phone solicitors
9. Natural gas bill consisting of a fixed component, plus a constant variable cost per thousand cubic feet after a specified number of cubic feet are used

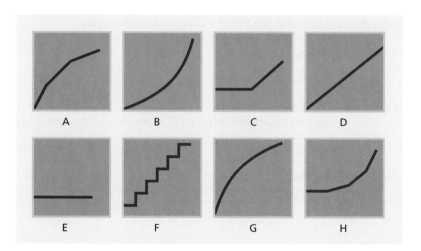

3-32 Predicting Costs

Given the following four cost behaviors and expected levels of cost-driver activity, predict total costs:

1. Fuel costs of driving vehicles, $0.20 per mile, driven 17,000 miles per month
2. Equipment rental cost, $6,000 per piece of equipment per month for seven pieces for three months
3. Ambulance and EMT personnel cost for a soccer tournament, $1,200 for each 250 tournament participants; the tournament is expecting 2,400 participants
4. Purchasing department cost, $7,500 per month plus $4 per material order processed at 4,000 orders in one month

3-33 Identifying Discretionary and Committed Fixed Costs

Identify and compute total discretionary fixed and total committed fixed costs from the following list prepared by the accounting supervisor for Pacioli Building Supply, Inc.:

Advertising	$19,000
Depreciation	47,000
Company health insurance	15,000
Management salaries	85,000
Payment on long-term debt	50,000
Property tax	32,000
Grounds maintenance	9,000
Office remodeling	21,000
Research and development	36,000

3-34 Cost Effects of Technology

Sports Equipment, Inc., an outdoor sports retailer, is planning to add a Web site for on-line sales. The estimated costs of two alternative approaches are as follows:

	Alternative 1	Alternative 2
Annual fixed cost	$200,000	$400,000
Variable cost per order	$7	$3
Expected number of orders	70,000	70,000

Required

At the expected level of orders, which online approach has the lower cost? What is the indifference level of orders, or the "break-even" level of orders? What is the meaning of this level of orders?

3-35 Mixed Cost, Choosing Cost Drivers, High-Low and Visual-Fit Methods

Peoria Implements Company produces farm implements. Peoria is in the process of measuring its manufacturing costs and is particularly interested in the costs of the manufacturing maintenance activity, since maintenance is a significant mixed cost. Activity analysis indicates that maintenance activity consists primarily of maintenance labor setting up machines using certain supplies. A setup consists of preparing the necessary machines for a particular production run of a product. During setup, machines must still be running, which consumes energy. Thus the costs associated with maintenance include labor, supplies, and energy. Unfortunately, Peoria's cost accounting system does not trace these costs to maintenance activity separately. Peoria employs two full-time maintenance mechanics to perform maintenance. The annual salary of a maintenance mechanic is $25,000 and is considered a fixed cost. Two plausible cost drivers have been suggested: units produced and number of setups.

Data had been collected for the past 12 months and a plot made for the cost driver—units of production. The maintenance cost figures collected include estimates for labor, supplies, and energy. Cory Fielder, Controller at Peoria, recently attended an activity-based costing seminar where he learned that some types of activities are performed each time a batch of goods is processed rather than each time a unit is produced. Based on this concept, he has gathered data on the number of setups performed over the past 12 months. The plots of monthly maintenance costs versus the two potential cost drivers follow on page 116.

Required

1. Find monthly fixed maintenance cost and the variable maintenance cost per driver unit using the visual-fit method based on each potential cost driver. Explain how you treated the April data.
2. Find monthly fixed maintenance cost and the variable maintenance cost per driver unit using the high-low method based on each potential cost driver.
3. Which cost driver best meets the criteria for choosing cost functions? Explain.

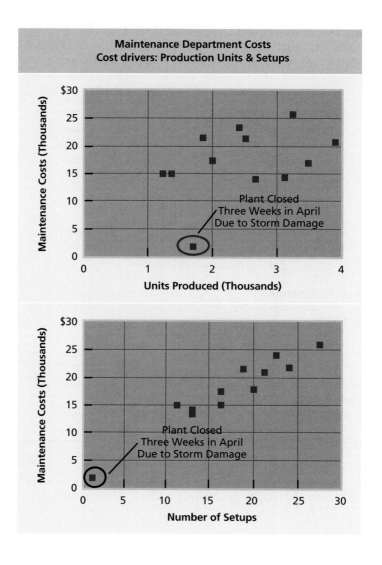

3-36   Account Analysis

Custom Computers, Inc., is a company started by two engineering students to assemble and market personal computers to faculty and students. The company operates out of the garage of one of the students' homes. From the following costs of a recent month, compute the total cost function and total cost for the month.

- Telephone   \$ 50, fixed
- Utilities   280: fixed, 25% attributable to the garage, 75% to the house
- Advertising   75, fixed
- Insurance   60, fixed
- Materials   7,500, variable, for five computers
- Labor   1,800: \$1,300 fixed plus \$500 for hourly help for assembling five computers

3-37   Linear Cost Functions

Let Y = total costs, X_1 = production volume, and X_2 = number of setups. Which of the following are linear cost functions? Which are mixed cost functions?

  a. $Y = \$1,500$
  b. $Y = \$8X_1$
  c. $Y = \$5,000 + \$4X_1$

d. $Y = \$4,000 + \$6X_1 + \$30X_2$
e. $Y = \$9,000 + \$3(X_1 \times X_2)$
f. $Y = \$8,500 + \$1.50X_1{}^2$

3-38 High-Low Method

Manchester Foundry produced 45,000 tons in March at a cost of £1,150,000. In April, the foundry produced 35,000 tons at a cost of £950,000. Using only these two data points, determine the cost function for Manchester.

3-39 Economic Plausibility of Regression Analysis Results

The head of the Warehousing Division of Northwest Food Distributors was concerned about some cost behavior information given to him by the new assistant controller, who was hired because of his recent training in cost analysis. His first assignment was to apply regression analysis to various costs in the department. One of the results was presented as follows:

"A regression on monthly data was run to explain building maintenance cost as a function of direct labor hours as the cost driver. The results are

$$Y = \$7,810 - \$.47X$$

I suggest that we use the building as intensively as possible to keep the maintenance costs down."

The department head was puzzled. How could increased use cause decreased maintenance cost? Explain this counterintuitive result to the department head. What step(s) did the assistant controller probably omit in applying and interpreting the regression analysis?

PROBLEMS

3-40 Controlling Risk, Capacity Decisions, Technology Decisions

Consider the previous discussion of Ford Motor on page 89 of the text. Ford had been outsourcing production to Mazda and using overtime for as much as 20% of production—Ford's plants and assembly lines were running at 100% of capacity and demand was sufficient for an additional 20%. Ford had considered building new highly automated assembly lines and plants to earn more profits since overtime premiums and outsourcing were costly. However, the investment in high technology and capacity expansion was rejected.

Assume that all material and labor costs are variable with respect to the level of production and that all other costs are fixed. Consider one of Ford's plants that makes Probes. The cost to convert the plant to use fully automated assembly lines is $20 million. The resulting labor costs would be significantly reduced. The costs, in millions of dollars, of the build option and the outsource/overtime option are given in the table below.

	Build Option		
Percent of capacity	60	100	120
Material costs	$18	$30	$36
Labor costs	6	10	12
Other costs	40	40	40
Total costs	$64	$80	$88

	Outsource/Overtime Option		
Percent of capacity	60	100	120
Material costs	$18	$30	$ 36
Labor costs	18	30	44
Other costs	20	20	20
Total costs	$56	$80	$100

1. Prepare a line graph showing total costs for the two options: (1) build new assembly lines, and (2) continue to use overtime and outsource production of Probes. Give an explanation of the cost behavior of the two options.

2. Which option enables Ford management to control risk better? Explain. Assess the cost-benefit trade-offs associated with each option.

3. A solid understanding of cost behavior is an important prerequisite to effective managerial control of costs. Suppose you are an executive at Ford and currently the production (and sales) level is approaching the 100% level of capacity and the economy is expected to remain strong for at least 1 year. While sales and profits are good now, you are aware of the cyclical nature of the automobile business. Would you recommend committing Ford to building automated assembly lines in order to service potential near-term increases in demand or would you recommend against building, looking to the likely future downturn in business? Discuss your reasoning.

3-41 Step Costs

Algona Beach Jail requires a staff of at least one guard for every four prisoners. The jail will hold 48 prisoners. Algona Beach attracts numerous tourists and transients in the spring and summer. However, the town is rather sedate in the fall and winter. The fall–winter population of the jail is generally between 12 and 16 prisoners. The numbers in the spring and summer can fluctuate from 12 to 48, depending on the weather, among other factors (including phases of the moon, according to some longtime residents).

Algona Beach has four permanent guards hired on a year-round basis at an annual salary of $36,000 each. When additional guards are needed, they are hired on a weekly basis at a rate of $600 per week. (For simplicity, assume that each month has exactly four weeks.)

1. Prepare a graph with the weekly planned cost of jail guards on the vertical axis and the number of prisoners on the horizontal axis.

2. What would be the budgeted amount for jail guards for the month of January? Would this be a fixed or variable cost?

3. Suppose the jail population of each of the four weeks in July was 25, 38, 26, and 43, respectively. The actual amount paid for jail guards in July was $19,800. Prepare a report comparing the actual amount paid for jail guards with the amount that would be expected with efficient scheduling and hiring.

4. Suppose Algona Beach treated jail-guard salaries for nonpermanent guards as a variable expense of $150 per week per prisoner. This variable cost was applied to the number of prisoners in excess of 16. Therefore, the weekly cost function was

$$\text{Weekly jail-guard cost} = \$3,000 + \$150 \times (\text{total prisoners} - 16)$$

Explain how this cost function was determined.

5. Prepare a report similar to that in requirement 3 except that the cost function in requirement 4 should be used to calculate the expected amount of jail-guard salaries. Which report, this one or the one in requirement 3, is more accurate? Is accuracy the only concern?

3-42 Government Service Cost Analysis

Auditors for the Internal Revenue Service scrutinize income tax returns after they have been pre-screened with the help of computer tests for normal ranges of deductions claimed by taxpayers. The IRS uses an expected cost of $7 per tax return, based on measurement studies that allow 20 minutes per return. Each agent has a workweek of five days of eight hours per day. Twenty auditors are employed at a salary of $830 each per week.

The audit supervisor has the following data regarding performance for the most recent 4-week period, when 8,000 returns were processed:

Actual Cost of Auditors	Expected Cost for Processing Returns	Difference or Variance
$66,400	?	?

1. Compute the planned cost and the variance.
2. The supervisor believes that audit work should be conducted more productively and that superfluous personnel should be transferred to field audits. If the foregoing data are representative, how many auditors should be transferred?
3. List some possible reasons for the variance.
4. Describe some alternative cost drivers for processing income tax returns.

3-43 Cost Analysis at America West

America West is the nation's ninth-largest commercial air carrier, with hubs in Phoenix, Las Vegas, and Columbus, Ohio. Listed below are some of the costs incurred by America West. For each cost, select an appropriate cost driver and indicate whether the cost is likely to be fixed, variable, or mixed in relation to your cost driver.

a. Airplane fuel
b. Flight attendants' salaries
c. Baggage handlers' salaries
d. In-flight meals
e. Pilots' salaries
f. Airplane depreciation
g. Advertising

3-44 Separation of Drug Testing Laboratory Mixed Costs into Variable and Fixed Components

A staff meeting has been called at SportsLab, Inc., a drug-testing facility retained by several professional and college sports leagues and associations. The Chief of Testing, Dr. Hyde, has demanded an across-the-board increase in prices for a particular test because of the increased testing and precision that is now required.

The administrator of the laboratory has asked you to measure the mixed-cost behavior of this particular testing department and to prepare a short report she can present to Dr. Hyde. Consider the following limited data:

	Average Test Procedures per Month	Average Monthly Cost of Test Procedures
Monthly averages, 20X4	500	$ 60,000
Monthly averages, 20X5	600	70,000
Monthly averages, 20X6	700	144,000

3-45 University Cost Behavior

Lakeview School, a private high school, is preparing a planned income statement for the coming academic year ending August 31, 20X2. Tuition revenues for the past two years ending August 31 were 20X1: $820,000, and 20X0: $870,000. Total expenses for 20X1 were $810,000 and in 20X0 were $830,000. No tuition rate changes occurred in 20X0 or 20X1, nor are any expected to occur in 20X2. Tuition revenue is expected to be $810,000 for 20X2. What net income should be planned for 20X2, assuming that the implied cost behavior remains unchanged?

3-46 Activity Analysis

Omaha Software develops and markets computer software for the agriculture industry. Because support costs are a large portion of the cost of software development, the Director of Cost Operations of Omaha, Melody Atkinson, is especially concerned with understanding the effects of support cost behavior. Atkinson has completed a preliminary activity analysis of one of Omaha's primary software products: FertiMix (software to manage fertilizer mixing). This product is a software template that is customized for specific customers, who are charged for the basic product plus customizing costs. The activity analysis is based on the number of customized lines of FertiMix code. Currently, support cost estimates are based on a fixed rate of 50% of the basic cost. Data are shown for two recent customers:

	Customer	
	Greencity Plants	*Beautiful Blooms*
Basic cost of FertiMix	$13,000	$13,000
Lines of customized code	490	180
Estimated cost per line of customized code	$22	$22

Required

1. Compute the support cost of customizing FertiMix for each customer using each cost-estimating approach.

2. If the activity analysis is reliable, what are the pros and cons of adopting it for all of Omaha's software products?

3-47 High-Low, Regression Analysis

On November 15, 2001, Sheila Lambright, a newly-hired cost analyst at Lightbody Company, was asked to predict overhead costs for the company's operations in 2002, when 510 units are expected to be produced. She collected the following quarterly data:

Quarter	Production in Units	Overhead Costs
1/98	76	$ 721
2/98	79	715
3/98	72	655
4/98	136	1,131
1/99	125	1,001
2/99	128	1,111
3/99	125	1,119
4/99	133	1,042
1/00	124	997
2/00	129	1,066
3/00	115	996
4/00	84	957
1/01	84	835
2/01	122	1,050
3/01	90	991

Required

1. Using the high-low method to estimate costs, prepare a prediction of overhead costs for 2002.

2. Sheila ran a regression analysis using the data she collected. The result was

$$Y = \$337 + \$5.75X$$

Using this cost function, predict costs for 2002.

3. Which prediction do you prefer? Why?

3-48 Interpretation of Regression Analysis

Study Appendix 3. The Tent Division of Arizona Outdoor Equipment Company has had difficulty controlling its use of supplies. The company has traditionally regarded supplies as a purely variable cost. Nearly every time production was above average, however, the division spent less than predicted for supplies; when production was below average, the division spent more than predicted. This pattern suggested to Yuki Li, the new controller, that part of the supplies cost was probably not related to production volume, or was fixed.

She decided to use regression analysis to explore this issue. After consulting with production personnel, she considered two cost drivers for supplies cost: (1) number of tents produced, and (2) square feet of material used. She obtained the following results based on monthly data.

| | Cost Driver | |
	Number of Tents	Square Feet of Material Used
Constant	2,300	1,900
Variable coefficient	.033	.072
R^2	.220	.686

Required

1. Which is the preferred cost function? Explain.
2. What percentage of the fluctuation of supplies cost depends on square feet of materials? Do fluctuations in supplies cost depend on anything other than square feet of materials? What proportion of the fluctuations is not explained by square feet of materials?

3-49 Regression Analysis

Study Appendix 3. Limand Company, a manufacturer of fine china and stoneware, is troubled by fluctuations in productivity and wants to compute how manufacturing support costs are related to the various sizes of batches of output. The following data show the results of a random sample of 10 batches of one pattern of stoneware:

Sample	Batch Size, X	Support Costs, Y
1	15	$180
2	12	140
3	20	230
4	17	190
5	12	160
6	25	300
7	22	270
8	9	110
9	18	240
10	30	320

Required

1. Plot support costs, Y, versus batch size, X.
2. Using regression analysis, measure the cost function of support costs and batch size.
3. Predict the support costs for a batch size of 25.
4. Using the high-low method, repeat requirements 2 and 3. Should the manager use the high-low or regression method? Explain.

3-50 Choice of Cost Driver

Study Appendix 3. Rico Consequa, the Director of Cost Operations of Micro Devices, wishes to develop an accurate cost function to explain and predict support costs in the company's printed circuit board assembly operation. Mr. Consequa is concerned that the cost function that he currently uses—based on direct labor costs—is not accurate enough for proper planning and control of support costs. Mr. Consequa directed one of his financial analysts to obtain a random sample of 25 weeks of support costs and three possible cost drivers in the circuit-board assembly department: direct labor hours, number of boards assembled, and average cycle time of boards assembled. (Average cycle time is the average time between start and certified completion—after quality testing—of boards assembled during a week.) Much of the effort in this assembly operation is devoted to testing for quality and reworking defective boards, all of which increase the average cycle time in any period. Therefore, Mr. Consequa believes that average cycle time will be the best support cost driver. Mr. Consequa wants his analyst to use regression analysis to demonstrate which cost driver best explains support costs.

Week	Circuit Board Assembly Support Costs Y	Direct Labor Hours X_1	Number of Boards Completed X_2	Average Cycle Time (Hours) X_3
1	$66,402	7,619	2,983	186.44
2	56,943	7,678	2,830	139.14
3	60,337	7,816	2,413	151.13
4	50,096	7,659	2,221	138.30
5	64,241	7,646	2,701	158.63
6	60,846	7,765	2,656	148.71
7	43,119	7,685	2,495	105.85
8	63,412	7,962	2,128	174.02
9	59,283	7,793	2,127	155.30
10	60,070	7,732	2,127	162.20
11	53,345	7,771	2,338	142.97
12	65,027	7,842	2,685	176.08
13	58,220	7,940	2,602	150.19
14	65,406	7,750	2,029	194.06
15	35,268	7,954	2,136	100.51
16	46,394	7,768	2,046	137.47
17	71,877	7,764	2,786	197.44
18	61,903	7,635	2,822	164.69
19	50,009	7,849	2,178	141.95
20	49,327	7,869	2,244	123.37
21	44,703	7,576	2,195	128.25
22	45,582	7,557	2,370	106.16
23	43,818	7,569	2,016	131.41
24	62,122	7,672	2,515	154.88
25	52,403	7,653	2,942	140.07

Required

1. Plot support costs, Y, versus each of the possible cost drivers, X_1, X_2, and X_3.
2. Use regression analysis to measure cost functions using each of the cost drivers.
3. According to the criteria of plausibility and reliability, which is the best cost driver for support costs in the circuit board assembly department?
4. Interpret the economic meaning of the best cost function.

3-51 Use of Cost Functions for Pricing

Study Appendix 3. Read the previous problem. If you worked this problem, use your measured cost functions. If you did not work the previous problem, assume the following measured cost functions:

$$Y = \$9,000/\text{week} + (\$6 \times \text{direct labor hours}); R^2 = .10$$

$$Y = \$20,000/\text{week} + (\$14 \times \text{number of boards completed}); R^2 = .40$$

$$Y = \$5,000/\text{week} + (\$350 \times \text{average cycle time}); R^2 = .80$$

Required

1. Which of the support cost functions would you expect to be the most reliable for explaining and predicting support costs? Why?
2. Assume that Micro Devices prices its products by adding a percentage markup to its product costs. Product costs include assembly labor, components, and support costs. Using each of the cost functions, compute the circuit board portion of the support cost of an order that used the following resources:

   a. Effectively used the capacity of the assembly department for three weeks
   b. Assembly labor hours: 20,000
   c. Number of boards: 6,000
   d. Average cycle time: 180 hours

3. Which cost would you recommend that Micro Devices use? Why?
4. Assume that the market for this product is extremely cost competitive. What do you think of Micro Devices's pricing method?

3-52 Review of Chapters 2 and 3

Madison Musical Education Company (MME) provides instrumental music education to children of all ages. Payment for services comes from two sources: (1) a contract with Country Day School to provide private music lessons for up to 150 band students a year (where a year is nine months of education) for a fixed fee of $150,000, and (2) payment from individuals at a rate of $100 per month for nine months of education each year. In 2000, MME made a profit of $5,000 on revenues of $295,000:

Revenues		
Country Day School contract	$150,000	
Private students	145,000	
Total revenues		$295,000
Expenses:		
Administrative staff	$ 75,000	
Teaching staff	81,000	
Facilities	93,500	
Supplies	40,500	
Total expenses		290,000
Profit		$ 5,000

MME conducted an activity analysis and found that teaching staff wages and supplies costs are variable with respect to student-months. (A student-month is one student educated for one month.) Administrative staff and facilities costs are fixed within the range of 2,000 to 3,000 student-months. At volumes between 3,000 and 3,500 student-months, an additional facilities charge of $8,000 would be incurred. During the last year, a total of 2,700 student-months of education were provided, 1,450 of which were for private students and 1,250 of which were offered under the contract with Country Day School.

Required

1. Compute the following using cost information from year 2000 operations:
   Fixed cost per year
   Variable cost per student-month
2. Suppose that in 2001 Country Day School decreased its use of MME to 120 students (that is, 1,080 student-months). The fixed contract price of $150,000 was still paid. If everything else stayed as it was in 2000, what profit or loss would be made in 2001?

3. Suppose that at the beginning of 2001 Country Day School decided not to renew its contract with MME and the management of MME decided to try to maintain business as usual with only private students. How many students (each signing up for 9 months) would MME require to continue to make a profit of $5,000 per year?

CASES

3-53 Government Health Cost Behavior

Dr. Stephanie White, the Chief Administrator of Uptown Clinic, a community mental health agency, is concerned about the dilemma of coping with reduced budgets next year and into the foreseeable future, but increasing demand for services. In order to plan for reduced budgets, she first must identify where costs can be cut or reduced and still keep the agency functioning. Below are some data from the past year.

Program Area	Costs
Administration	
Salaries	
Administrator	$60,000
Assistant	35,000
Two secretaries	42,000
Supplies	35,000
Advertising and promotion	9,000
Professional meetings, dues, and literature	14,000
Purchased services	
Accounting and billing	15,000
Custodial and maintenance	13,000
Security	12,000
Consulting	10,000
Community mental health services	
Salaries (two social workers)	46,000
Transportation	10,000
Outpatient mental health treatment	
Salaries	
Psychiatrist	86,000
Two social workers	70,000

Required

1. Identify which costs you think are likely to be discretionary or committed costs.

2. One possibility is to eliminate all discretionary costs. How much would be saved? What do you think of this recommendation?

3. How would you advise Dr. White to prepare for reduced budgets?

3-54 Activity Analysis

The costs of the Systems Support (SS) department (and other service departments) of Clark Paper Products, Inc., have always been charged to the three business divisions (Forest Management, Lumber Products, and Paper Products) based on the number of employees in each division. This measure is easy to obtain and update, and until recently none of the divisions had complained about the charges. The Paper Products division has recently automated many of its operations and has reduced the number of its employees. At the same time, however, to monitor its new process, Paper Products has increased its requests for various reports provided by the SS department. The other divisions have begun to complain that they are being charged more than their fair share of SS department costs. Based on activity analysis of possible cost drivers, cost analysts have suggested using the number of reports prepared as a means of charging for SS costs and have gathered the following information:

	Forest Management	Lumber Products	Paper Products
2000 Number of employees	762	457	502
2000 Number of reports	410	445	377
2000 SS Costs: $300,000			
2001 Number of employees	751	413	131
2001 Number of reports	412	432	712
2001 SS Costs: $385,000			

Required

1. Discuss the plausibility and probable reliability of each of the cost drivers—number of employees or number of reports.
2. What are the 2000 and 2001 SS costs per unit of cost driver for each division using each cost driver? Do the Forest Management and Lumber Products divisions have legitimate complaints? Explain.
3. What are the incentives that are implied by each cost driver?
4. Which cost driver should Clark Paper Products use to charge its divisions for SS services? For other services? Why?

3-55 Identifying Relevant Data

eComp.com manufactures palm-size portable computers. Because these very small computers compete with larger portable computers that have more functions and flexibility, understanding and using cost behavior is very critical to eComp.com's profitability. eComp.com's Controller, Kelly Hudson, has kept meticulous files on various cost categories and possible cost drivers for most of the important functions and activities of eComp.com. Because most of the manufacturing at eComp.com is automated, labor cost is relatively fixed. Other support costs comprise most of eComp.com's costs. Partial data that Hudson has collected over the past 25 weeks on one of these support costs, logistics operations (materials purchasing, receiving, warehousing, and shipping), follow:

Week	Logistics Costs, Y	Number of Orders, X
1	$23,907	1,357
2	18,265	1,077
3	24,208	1,383
4	23,578	1,486
5	22,211	1,292
6	22,862	1,425
7	23,303	1,306
8	24,507	1,373
9	17,878	1,031
10	18,306	1,020
11	20,807	1,097
12	19,707	1,069
13	23,020	1,444
14	20,407	733
15	20,370	413
16	20,678	633
17	21,145	711
18	20,775	228
19	20,532	488
20	20,659	655
21	20,430	722
22	20,713	373
23	20,256	391
24	21,196	734
25	20,406	256

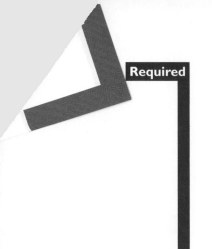

1. Plot logistics cost, Y, versus number of orders, X. What cost behavior is evident? What do you think happened in week 14?

2. What is your recommendation to Kelly Hudson regarding the relevance of the past 25 weeks of logistics cost and number of orders for measuring logistics cost behavior?

3. Hudson remarks that one of the improvements that eComp.com has made in the past several months was to negotiate just-in-time deliveries from its suppliers. This was made possible by substituting an automated ordering system for the previous manual (labor-intensive) system. Although fixed costs increased, the variable cost of placing an order was expected to drop greatly. Do the data support this expectation? Do you believe that the change to the automated ordering system was justified? Why or why not?

COLLABORATIVE LEARNING EXERCISE

3-56 Cost-Behavior Examples

Select about 10 students to participate in a "cost-behavior bee." The game proceeds like a spelling bee—when a participant is unable to come up with a correct answer, he or she is eliminated from the game. The last one in the game is the winner.

The object of the game is to identify a type of cost that fits a particular cost-behavior pattern. The first player rolls a die.[1] If a 1 or 6 comes up, the die passes to the next player (and the roller makes it to the next round). If a 2, 3, 4, or 5 come up, the player has to identify one of the following types of costs:

If a 2 is rolled, identify a variable cost.
If a 3 is rolled, identify a fixed cost.
If a 4 is rolled, identify a mixed cost.
If a 5 is rolled, identify a step cost.

A scribe should label four columns on the board, one for each type of cost, and list the costs that are mentioned for each category. Once a particular cost has been used, it cannot be used again.

Each player has a time limit of 10 seconds to produce an example. (For a tougher game, make the time limit five seconds.) The instructor is the referee, judging if a particular example is acceptable. It is legitimate for the referee to ask a player to explain why he or she thinks the cost mentioned fits the category before making a judgment.

After each player has had a turn, a second round begins with the remaining players taking a turn in the same order as in the first round. The game continues through additional rounds until all but one player has failed to give an acceptable answer within the time limit. The remaining player is the winner.

INTERNET EXERCISE

www.prenhall.com/horngren

3-57 Cost Behavior at Southwest Airlines

In this exercise we will look at some costs and see if we can determine to some extent the type of behavior associated with those costs. While firms are concerned about trying to label costs as either variable or fixed to help in planning, very few costs are completely variable or fixed. The information provided by firms to external users also often precludes a user from determining specifics about the cost behaviors—they don't want to give the competitors too much information!

Log on to the Southwest Airlines Web site at http://www.iflyswa.com. Once you get to the site, click on the information icon "About SWA," and then click on "Investor Relations." This will take you to the site where you can then access the financial information.

1. Click on the "Annual Reports" icon and then select the most recent annual report. Looking at the table of contents, find the page where the ten-year summary starts. On what page is this located? Go to this section of the report. What type of information do you find there?

---

[1] *Instead of rolling a die, players could draw one of the four cost categories out of a hat (or similar container) or from a deck of four 3 × 5 cards. This eliminates the chance element that can let some players proceed to a later round without having to give an example of a particular cost behavior. However, the chance element can add to the enjoyment of the game*

2. When you look at the operating revenue information, what do you see? Look at the information provided concerning operating expenses. Is it categorized in the same manner as the revenues? If the information is not in the same categories, why do you think Southwest did not match it up in the same manner?

3. Now look at the section on consolidated operating statistics. Southwest measures activity in Revenue Passenger Miles (RPMs) and capacity in Available Seat Miles (ASMs). Which of these is larger? How are the RPM and ASM determined? Is it possible for the two numbers to be the same? What information is provided for each of these items in the consolidated operating statistics section?

4. Compute the total operating expense per RPM.

5. Using data from the most recent year and three years earlier, use the high-low method to compute the variable operating expense per RPM. Compare the total operating expense per RPM and the variable expense per RPM. Is this relationship what you expected? Why or why not?

6. Airlines are often considered to be high-fixed-cost companies. Is this consistent with your findings in requirement 5? Explain why the high-low method over this time might overestimate the amount of variable costs.

4

COST MANAGEMENT SYSTEMS AND ACTIVITY-BASED COSTING

AT&T Wireless Services customers can use their cell phones in more than 5,500 locations across the United States and Canada, as well as in Europe, Asia, and Australia. People are able to call you nearly anywhere on Earth by dialing your local wireless number.

www.prenhall.com/horngren

Learning Objectives

When you have finished studying this chapter, you should be able to

1. Describe the purposes of cost management systems.

2. Explain the relationship between cost, cost objective, cost accumulation, and cost allocation.

3. Distinguish between direct, indirect, and unallocated costs.

4. Explain how the financial statements of merchandisers and manufacturers differ because of the types of goods they sell.

5. Understand the main differences between traditional and activity-based costing systems and why ABC systems provide value to managers.

6. Identify the steps involved in the design and implementation of an activity-based costing system.

7. Use activity-based cost information to improve the operations of an organization.

8. **Understand management accounting's role in a company's improvement efforts across the value chain.**

A recent survey asked 1,000 adults for their two choices of a "really good company." The company named the most was AT&T. Chances are, AT&T has reached out and touched you. With 90 million customers, it has annual revenues of more than $53 billion and net income exceeding $6 billion.

There is a communications revolution taking place on a global scale. Today, we communicate using wireless cell phones and computer on-line services in addition to the traditional telephone. How does AT&T, a company that has been synonymous with communications for more than 100 years, ensure that it remains competitive? Certainly AT&T has the people, technology, brand, market presence, and financial resources to get the job done—but it takes more. Like any other company, AT&T's managers, from top executives to local service managers, must understand their customers and their costs. This understanding is a common theme for all successful businesses.

Consider AT&T's Business Communication Services unit (BCS). With annual revenue of more than $16 billion, BCS is responsible for domestic and international voice and data communications services. To keep the unit's competitive edge, management began using a new cost accounting system in the mid-1990s. Accountants and managers designed the new costing system "to help operating managers gain a better understanding of the costs of each kind of service (product)." The old cost system gathered financial data used primarily by top management and accountants. The new cost system measures the key business processes in the BCS and the activities that the unit performs to support its various services.

One example of the results obtained using the new cost system is in the billing center. The BCS team computed the cost of investigating incorrect bills, a cost that was previously unknown. The cost was so high that BCS managers started a cost reduction effort. The result was an annual cost savings of about $500,000. The new cost system was an effective management tool for all operating managers, not just accountants.

COST MANAGEMENT SYSTEMS

Objective 1
Describe the purposes of cost management systems.

cost management system (CMS) Identifies how management's decisions affect costs, by first measuring the resources used in performing the organization's activities and then assessing the effects on costs of changes in those activities.

To support managers' decisions better, accountants go beyond simply determining the cost of products and services. They develop cost management systems. A **cost management system (CMS)** is a collection of tools and techniques that identifies how management's decisions affect costs. To do so, the CMS first measures the costs of resources used in performing the organization's activities and then assesses the effects on costs of changes in those activities. The primary purposes of a cost management system are to provide

1. aggregate measures of inventory value and cost of goods manufactured for external reporting to investors, creditors, and other external stakeholders,
2. cost information for strategic management decisions, and
3. cost information for operational control.

External users of cost information, such as investors and creditors, need aggregate measures of inventory value and the cost of goods sold. They do not need accurate cost information on individual products or services. It is the second and third purposes of a CMS that generate the need for more elaborate tools and techniques. Internal managers need accurate and timely cost information for strategic reasons, such as deciding on the optimal product and customer mix, choosing the value chain functions to be outsourced, and making investment decisions. For these decisions, managers want to know the costs of individual products, services, and customers. The assessment of process improvement efforts and other operational cost control programs also requires accurate and timely feedback on costs.

We have described many CMS tools and techniques throughout this text. An example is the contribution margin technique and cost-volume-profit analysis. This chapter focuses on two other important techniques—activity-based costing and activity-based management. But perhaps the most fundamental tool that supports all cost management systems is the cost accounting system.

Cost Accounting Systems

cost accounting That part of the cost management system that measures costs for the purposes of management decision making and financial reporting.

All kinds of organizations—manufacturing firms, service companies, and nonprofit organizations—need some form of **cost accounting,** that part of the cost management system that measures costs for the purposes of management decision making and financial reporting. Because it is the most general case, embracing production as well as all other value chain functions, we will focus on cost accounting in a manufacturing setting. Remember, though, that you can apply this framework to any organization.

Managers rely on accountants to design a cost accounting system that measures costs to meet each of the three purposes of a CMS. Consider the following commentaries on the modern role of management accountants.

We (cost accountants) had to understand what the numbers mean, relate the numbers to business activity, and recommend alternative courses of action. Finally, we had to evaluate alternatives and make decisions to maximize business efficiency.

—South Central Bell

Because the ABC (Activity-Based Costing) system now mirrors the manufacturing process, the engineers and production staff believe the cost data produced by the accounting system. Engineering and production regularly ask accounting to help find the product design combination that will optimize costs. . . . The accountants now participate in product design decisions. They help engineering and production understand how costs behave. . . . The ABC system makes the professional lives of the accountants more rewarding.

—Hewlett-Packard Company

Cost-management systems have three primary purposes. For each of the decisions listed below, indicate the purpose of the CMS being applied.

1. A production manager wants to know the cost of performing a setup for a production run in order to compare to a target cost established as part of a process improvement program.
2. Top management wants to identify the profitability of several product lines to establish the optimum product mix.
3. Financial managers want to know the manufactured cost of inventory to appear on the balance sheet of the annual report.

ANSWERS

The purposes of a CMS are to provide measurements of cost for external financial reporting, internal strategic decisions, and internal operational cost control. The production manager evaluates the operating cost of the setup process to evaluate a process improvement program. This is part of the operational control purpose of the CMS. Identifying the profitability of a company's various products and deciding on an optimal product mix is an example of the strategic purpose of the CMS. Measuring the cost of goods manufactured and determining how much of this cost is reported as inventory on the balance sheet is the external financial reporting purpose of the CMS.

The cost accounting system typically includes two processes.

1. **Cost accumulation:** Collecting costs by some "natural" classification such as materials or labor or by activities performed such as order processing or machine processing.
2. **Cost allocation:** Tracing and reassigning costs to one or more cost objectives such as activities, processes, departments, customers, or products.

Exhibit 4-1 illustrates these processes. First, the system collects the costs of all raw materials. Then it allocates these costs to the departments that use the materials and further to the specific items made by these departments. The total raw materials cost of a particular product is the sum of the raw materials costs allocated to it in the various departments.

Before describing the types of cost accounting (or simply costing) systems, we need to develop an understanding of the various costs terms that are commonly used in practice.

Objective 2
Explain the relationship between cost, cost objective, cost accumulation, and cost allocation.

cost accumulation
Collecting costs by some natural classification such as materials, labor, or activities performed.

cost allocation Tracing and reassigning costs to one or more cost objectives such as activities, departments, customers, or products.

Exhibit 4-1

Cost Accumulation and Allocation

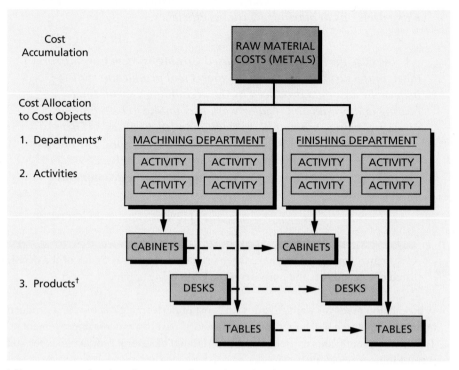

* Purpose: to evaluate performance of manufacturing departments.

† Purpose: to obtain costs of various products for valuing inventory, determining income, and judging product profitability.

DIFFERENT COSTS FOR DIFFERENT DECISIONS

To make intelligent decisions, managers want reliable measurements. Cost accounting systems that do not provide reliable information do not help managers make decisions. In fact, without reliable cost information, many decisions can be downright harmful. For example, an extremely large U.S. grocery chain, A&P, ran into profit difficulties and began retrenching by closing many stores. Management's lack of adequate cost information about individual store operations made the closing program a hit-or-miss affair. A news story reported the following:

> *Because of the absence of detailed profit-and-loss statements, and a cost-allocation system that did not reflect true costs, A&P's strategists could not be sure whether an individual store was really unprofitable. For example, distribution costs were shared equally among all the stores in a marketing area without regard to such factors as a store's distance from the warehouse. Says one close observer of the company: "When they wanted to close a store, they had to wing it. They could not make rational decisions, because they did not have a fact basis."*

We can classify and report costs in many ways—far too many for us to cover in a single chapter. We have already seen costs classified by their behavior—fixed, variable, step, and mixed. This section concentrates on the big picture of how accounting systems accumulate, classify, and report manufacturing costs.

COST OBJECTIVES

As stated by Jim Smith, former Director of Cost Management for The Marmon Group, "Depending on the decision, any of the cost classifications described in this book are relevant." A **cost** is a sacrifice or giving up of resources for a particular purpose. We generally measure costs by the monetary units (for example, dollars, yen, or euros) that must be paid for goods and services. Systems initially record costs in elementary form (for example, repairs or advertising). Then they group (classify) costs in different ways to help managers make decisions, such as evaluating subordinates and subunits of the organization, expanding or deleting products or territories, and replacing equipment.

To aid decisions, managers want to know the cost of something. We call this "something" a **cost objective** or **cost object,** defined as anything for which decision makers desire a separate measurement of costs. Examples of cost objectives include departments, products, territories, miles driven, bricks laid, patients seen, tax bills sent, checks processed, student hours taught, and library books shelved.

DIRECT, INDIRECT, AND UNALLOCATED COSTS

A major feature of costs in both manufacturing and nonmanufacturing activities is whether the costs have a direct or an indirect relationship to a particular cost objective or whether it is so difficult to determine a relationship that the costs are unallocated. Accountants can identify **direct costs** specifically and exclusively with a given cost objective in an economically feasible way. **Indirect costs** cannot be identified specifically and exclusively with a given cost objective in an economically feasible way. However, we can often identify plausible and reliable output measures (cost drivers) that can be used to allocate these indirect costs among cost objects. An example of an indirect cost is the depreciation on machinery that is used to produce many different products. Systems may allocate this indirect cost to products based on the output measure "machine hours." If making product A requires twice as many machine hours as making product B, then we allocate twice as much machine depreciation expense to A. Finally, there are some costs in many companies for which we can identify no relationship to a cost objective. These are **unallocated costs.** Examples of unallocated costs might include research and development, process design, legal, accounting, information services, and executive salaries. Keep in mind, though, that an unallocated cost for one company may be an indirect or even a direct cost for another. Why? Because businesses vary considerably in their value chains. For some businesses, the design function is a critical part of their success and therefore they are willing to spend the time and effort to deploy sophisticated systems to allocate or even directly trace such costs.

Consider the income statement in Exhibit 4-2. It represents a typical manufacturing company that makes products A, B, and C. Each item in the total column of the income statement represents accumulated totals for all products sold for an entire reporting period. How would we "unbundle" these totals to find the proper amounts for individual products A, B, and C?

First, note that all cost items except administrative salaries and other administrative expenses are either directly traced or allocated to individual products. Consider cost of goods sold. Most companies find that it is fairly easy to trace material costs to individual products. However, other manufacturing costs, even labor, are more difficult to trace and are normally allocated. It is not unusual for the amount of indirect manufacturing costs to be a large component of total company costs. As a result, many companies develop sophisticated cost allocation systems for these indirect costs. The complexity of cost allocation depends on the complexity of the associated production system. Let's assume that the use of machine hours to allocate the indirect manufacturing costs gives a reasonable degree of costing accuracy. Then, managers responsible for products A, B, and C would be satisfied that the cost of goods sold and gross profit amounts shown are fair. This is why most

cost A sacrifice or giving up of resources for a particular purpose, frequently measured by the monetary units that must be paid for goods and services.

cost objective (cost object) Anything for which a separate measurement of costs is desired. Examples include departments, products, activities, and territories.

Objective 3
Distinguish between direct, indirect, and unallocated costs.

direct costs Costs that can be identified specifically and exclusively with a given cost objective in an economically feasible way.

indirect costs Costs that cannot be identified specifically and exclusively with a given cost objective in an economically feasible way.

unallocated costs Costs for which we can identify no relationship to a cost objective.

Exhibit 4-2
Direct, Indirect, and Unallocated Costs in the Income Statement

	Total	Products A	B	C	Cost Type, Costing Method
Sales	$4,700	$2,800	$1,000	$ 900	
Cost of Goods Sold:					
Direct Material	1,200	500	300	400	Direct, Direct Trace
Indirect Manufacturing	1,100	450	300	350	Indirect, Allocation (machine hours)
Cost of Goods Sold	2,300	950	600	750	
Gross Profit	2,400	1,850	400	150	
Selling and Administrative Expenses:					
Commissions	470	280	100	90	Direct, Direct Trace
Distribution to warehouses	300	120	80	100	Indirect, Allocation (weight)
Total Selling and Administrative Expenses	770	400	180	190	
Operating Income (loss)	1,630	$1,450	$ 220	$ (40)	
Unallocated Expenses:					
Administrative Salaries	400				Unallocated
Other Administrative Expenses	600				Unallocated
Total Unallocated Expenses	1,000				
Income Before Tax	$ 630				

companies focus on gross profit as a key measure of individual product profitability. In our example, managers are also satisfied that commission expenses and expenses for distribution to warehouses can be allocated in a fair manner. So, while the managers of product C may not be happy with the reported operating loss of $40, they would feel that it is a reasonable measure of profitability.

We could find no reasonable means to allocate administrative salaries or other administrative expenses. So these expenses remain unallocated. Why not simply allocate the administrative salaries and other administrative expenses to the products by some simple method such as "percent of total revenue generated?" Because managers want allocations to be a fair measure of the costs incurred on their behalf. If we cannot find such a measure, companies often choose not to allocate.

Whenever it is economically feasible, managers prefer to classify costs as direct rather than indirect. In this way, managers have greater confidence in the reported costs of products, services, or other cost objectives. Economically feasible means cost effective, in the sense that managers do not want cost accounting to be too expensive in relation to expected benefits. For example, it may be economically feasible to trace the exact cost of steel and fabric (direct cost) to a specific lot of desk chairs, but it may be economically infeasible to trace the exact cost of rivets or thread (indirect costs) to the chairs.

Other factors also influence whether we consider a cost direct, indirect, or unallocated. The key is the particular cost objective. For example, consider a supervisor's salary in the maintenance department of a telephone company. If the cost objective is the department, the supervisor's salary is a direct cost. In contrast, if the cost objective is a service (the "product" of the company) such as a telephone call, the supervisor's salary is an indirect cost. In general, many more costs are direct when a department is the cost objective than when a service (a telephone call) or a physical product (a razor blade) is the cost objective.

Frequently managers want to know both the costs of running departments and the costs of products, services, activities, or resources. Companies inevitably allocate costs to more than one cost objective. Thus, a particular cost may simultaneously be direct and indirect. As you have just seen, a supervisor's salary can be both direct (with respect to his or her department) and indirect (with respect to the department's individual products or services).

CATEGORIES OF MANUFACTURING COSTS

Any raw material, labor, or other input used by any organization could, in theory, be a direct or indirect cost, depending on the cost objective. In manufacturing operations, which transform materials into other goods through the use of labor and factory facilities, products are frequently the cost objective. Manufacturing operations, though, have their own way of classifying costs. Manufacturing companies classify costs that they wish to allocate to products as either (1) direct material, (2) direct labor, and (3) indirect manufacturing.

1. **Direct-material costs** include the acquisition costs of all materials that a company identifies as a part of the manufactured goods and that it can trace to the manufactured goods in an economically feasible way. Examples are iron castings, lumber, aluminum sheets, and subassemblies. Direct materials often do not include minor items such as tacks or glue because the costs of tracing these items are greater than the possible benefits of having more precise product costs. Such items are usually called supplies or indirect materials, which are classified as a part of indirect manufacturing costs described in this list.

2. **Direct-labor costs** include the wages of all labor that a company can trace specifically and exclusively to the manufactured goods in an economically feasible way. Examples are the wages of machine operators and assemblers. In highly automated factories with a flexible workforce, there may be no direct labor costs. Why? Because workers spend time on numerous products, which makes it economically infeasible to physically trace any labor cost directly to specific products.

3. **Indirect manufacturing costs (or factory overhead)** include all costs associated with the manufacturing process that a company cannot trace to the manufactured goods in an economically feasible way. Other terms used to describe this category are **factory burden** and **manufacturing overhead.** Because each of these terms is used often in practice, we will use them interchangeably throughout this textbook. Many labor costs, such as that of janitors, forklift truck operators, plant guards, and storeroom clerks, are considered to be indirect labor because it is impossible or economically infeasible to trace such activity to specific products. Other examples are power, supplies, indirect labor, supervisory salaries, property taxes, rent, insurance, and depreciation.

direct-material costs The acquisition costs of all materials that are physically identified as a part of the manufactured goods and that may be traced to the manufactured goods in an economically feasible way.

direct-labor costs The wages of all labor that can be traced specifically and exclusively to the manufactured goods in an economically feasible way.

indirect manufacturing costs (factory burden, factory overhead, manufacturing overhead) All costs other than direct material or direct labor that are associated with the manufacturing process.

The application of computer technology has allowed modern cost systems to physically trace many previously indirect overhead costs to products in an economically feasible manner. For example, meters wired to computers can monitor the electricity used to produce each product, and costs of setting up a batch production run can be traced to the items produced in the run. In general, the more overhead costs that we can trace directly to products, the more accurate the product cost.

In addition to direct-material, direct-labor, and indirect manufacturing costs, all manufacturing companies also incur costs associated with the other value chain functions (research and development, design, marketing, distribution, and customer service). Accounting information systems accumulate these costs by departments such as R&D, advertising, and sales. Most firms' financial statements report these costs as selling and administrative expenses. In short, these costs do not become a part of the reported inventory cost of the manufactured products.

PRODUCT COSTS AND PERIOD COSTS

Regardless of the type of cost accounting system used for internal decision making purposes, the resulting costs appear in a company's financial statements for external financial reporting purposes. Costs appear on both the income statement, as cost of goods sold, and the balance sheet, as inventory amounts. When preparing both income statements and balance sheets, accountants frequently distinguish between product costs and period

product costs Costs identified with goods produced or purchased for resale.

period costs Costs that are deducted as expenses during the current period without going through an inventory stage.

costs. **Product costs** are costs identified with goods produced or purchased for resale. Product costs first become part of the inventory on hand. These product costs (inventoriable costs) become expenses (in the form of cost of goods sold) only when the company sells the inventory. In contrast, **period costs** become expenses during the current period without going through an inventory stage.

For example, look at the top half of Exhibit 4-3. A merchandising company (retailer or wholesaler) acquires goods for resale without changing their basic form. The only product cost is the purchase cost of the merchandise. The company holds unsold goods as merchandise inventory and shows their costs as an asset on a balance sheet. As the goods are sold, their costs become expenses in the form of "cost of goods sold."

A merchandising company also has a variety of selling and administrative expenses. These costs are period costs because they are deducted from revenue as expenses without ever being regarded as a part of inventory.

The bottom half of Exhibit 4-3 illustrates product and period costs in a manufacturing company. Note that the company transforms direct materials into salable items with the help of direct labor and indirect manufacturing. All these costs are product costs that are shown as inventory until the goods are sold. As in merchandising accounting, the selling and administrative expenses are period costs, not product costs.

Be sure you are clear on the differences between merchandising accounting and manufacturing accounting for such costs as insurance, depreciation, and wages. In merchandising accounting, all such items are period costs (expenses of the current period). In manufacturing accounting, many of these items are related to production activities and thus, as indirect manufacturing, are product costs (become expenses in the form of cost of goods sold as the inventory is sold).

In both merchandising and manufacturing accounting, selling and general administrative costs are period costs. Thus the inventory cost of a manufactured product excludes sales salaries, sales commissions, advertising, legal, public relations, and the president's salary. Manufacturing overhead is normally regarded as a part of finished-goods inventory cost, whereas selling expenses and general administrative expenses are not.

Confirm your understanding of the classification of manufacturing costs. Classify each of the following as *direct* or *indirect* with respect to traceability to product and as *variable* or *fixed* with respect to whether the costs fluctuates in total as volume of production changes over wide ranges.

1. The cost of components that are assembled into a final product.
2. The cost of supplies consumed when maintenance is performed on machines.
3. The cost of training mechanics who service processing machinery.
4. The cost of machine operators who work on only one product.

ANSWERS

The cost of components used in products is almost always directly traceable and is a variable cost. As volume changes over a wide range, the amount of supplies consumed for maintenance will also change so this cost is variable. However, there usually would not be an economically feasible way to trace these costs to individual products, so these costs would be indirect and allocated (normally the cost driver would be machine hours). Training costs for mechanics would not vary as a function of volume of production assuming that no new products would be made and that no new mechanics would be hired. Training costs are indirect assuming that the training cannot be associated with only one product. The wages of machine operators who work on only one product can be easily traced to the product. These wages would not vary over wide ranges of volume and this would be a fixed cost. We should note that if volume increases rapidly in a short time frame, it is often necessary to work overtime. In this case, the overtime portion of operator wages would be a variable cost.

Exhibit 4-3

Relationships of Product Costs and Period Costs

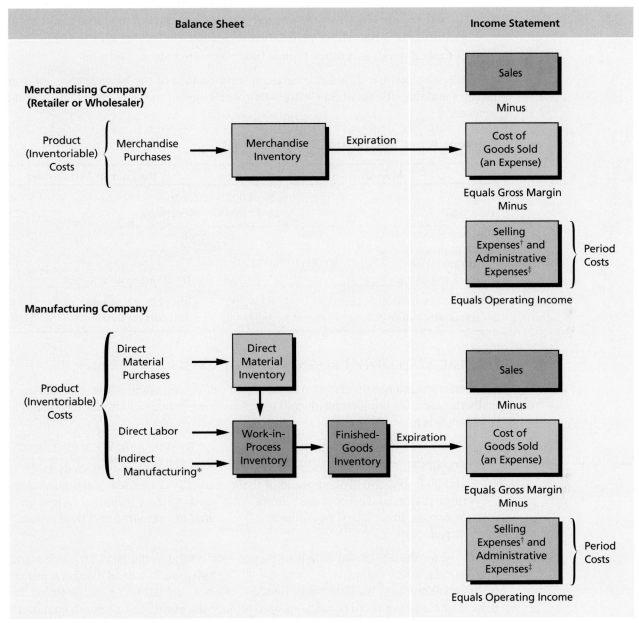

* Examples: indirect labor, factory supplies, insurance, and depreciation on plant.
† Examples: insurance on salespersons' cars, depreciation on salespersons' cars, salespersons' salaries.
‡ Examples: insurance on corporate headquarters building, depreciation on office equipment, clerical salaries.

Note particularly that when insurance and depreciation relate to the manufacturing function, they are inventoriable, but when they relate to selling and administration, they are not inventoriable.

BALANCE SHEET PRESENTATION OF COSTS

Examining both halves of Exhibit 4-3 together, you can see that the balance sheets of manufacturers and merchandisers differ with respect to inventories. The merchandiser's inventory account is supplanted in a manufacturing concern by three inventory classes that help managers trace all product costs through the production process to the time of sales. These classes are

Objective 4
Explain how the financial statements of merchandisers and manufacturers differ because of the types of goods they sell.

- Direct-material inventory: Material on hand and awaiting use in the production process.
- Work-in-process inventory: Goods undergoing the production process but not yet fully completed. Costs include appropriate amounts of the three major manufacturing costs (direct material, direct labor, and indirect manufacturing).
- Finished-goods inventory: Goods fully completed but not yet sold.

The only essential difference between the structure of the balance sheet of a manufacturer and that of a retailer or wholesaler would appear in their respective current asset sections:

Current Asset Sections of Balance Sheets

Manufacturer			Retailer or Wholesaler	
Cash		$ 4,000	Cash	$ 4,000
Receivables		25,000	Receivables	25,000
Finished goods	$32,000			
Work in process	22,000			
Direct material	23,000			
Total inventories		77,000	Merchandise inventories	77,000
Other current assets		1,000	Other current assets	1,000
Total current assets		$107,000	Total current assets	$107,000

INCOME STATEMENT PRESENTATION OF COSTS

In income statements, the detailed reporting of selling and administrative expenses is typically the same for manufacturing and merchandising organizations, but the cost of goods sold is different.

MANUFACTURER	RETAILER OR WHOLESALER
Manufacturing cost of goods produced and then sold, usually composed of the three major categories of cost: direct materials, direct labor, and indirect manufacturing.	Merchandise cost of goods sold, usually composed of the purchase cost of items, including freight in, that are acquired and then resold.

Consider the additional details as they are presented in the model income statement of a manufacturing company in Exhibit 4-4. The $40 million cost of goods manufactured includes subdivisions for direct materials, direct labor, and indirect manufacturing. In contrast, a wholesale or retail company would replace the entire cost-of-goods-manufactured section with a single line, cost of goods purchased.

Accountants and managers often use the terms *costs* and *expenses* loosely. Expenses denote all costs deducted from (matched against) revenue in a given period. On the other hand, costs is a much broader term and is used to describe both an asset (the cost of inventory) and an expense (the cost of goods sold). Thus manufacturing costs become an expense on an income statement (in the form of cost of goods sold) via the multistep inventory procedure shown earlier in Exhibit 4-3. In contrast, selling and general administrative costs become expenses immediately as they are incurred.

ACTIVITY-BASED COSTING

In the 1990s, many companies in the United States, struggling to keep up with competitors from Japan, Germany, and other countries, adopted new management philosophies and

Exhibit 4-4

Model Income Statement, Manufacturing Company

Sales (8,000,000 units @ $10)			$80,000,000
Cost of goods manufactured and sold			
Beginning finished-goods inventory		$ –0–	
Cost of goods manufactured			
Direct materials used	$20,000,000		
Direct labor	12,000,000		
Indirect manufacturing	8,000,000	40,000,000	
Cost of goods available for sale		$40,000,000	
Ending finished-goods inventory,			
2,000,000 units @ $4		8,000,000	
Cost of goods sold (an expense)			32,000,000
Gross margin or gross profit			$48,000,000
Less: other expenses			
Selling costs (an expense)		$30,000,000	
General and administrative costs			
(an expense)		8,000,000	38,000,000
Operating income*			$10,000,000

* Also net income in this example because other expenses such as interest and income taxes are ignored here for simplicity.

developed new production technologies. In many cases, these changes prompted corresponding changes in cost management systems.

For example, Borg-Warner's Automotive Chain Systems Operation transformed its manufacturing operation to a just-in-time manufacturing system with work cells. This change in the way manufacturing was done at Borg-Warner made the existing cost accounting system obsolete. A new cost accounting system coupled with the new production systems "improved the overall reporting, controls, and efficiency dramatically."[1]

In the past, almost all companies used **traditional costing systems**—those that do not accumulate or report costs of activities or processes. Traditional costing systems work well with fairly simple production and operating systems. In the 1990s, however, many businesses did what Borg-Warner did and changed their operating systems in response to a more complex business environment. This led to a need for new and improved cost accounting systems. The most significant improvement in cost accounting system design has been activity-based costing (ABC). Let's take a look at how ABC differs from traditional costing.

traditional costing systems One that does not accumulate or report costs of activities or processes.

Objective 5
Understand the main differences between traditional and activity-based costing systems and why ABC systems provide value to managers.

ACTIVITY-BASED COSTING AND TRADITIONAL COSTING COMPARED

The primary focus of the changes in operations and accounting has been an increased attention to the cost of the activities undertaken to research, design, produce, sell, and deliver a company's products or services (that is, the entire value chain of business functions). Managers have always focused their attention on operating activities, but, until recently, companies seldom directly measured the costs of these activities. **Activity-based costing (ABC) systems** first accumulate indirect costs for each of the activities of the area being costed (an area can be a plant, department, value chain function, or the entire organization). Then they assign the costs of activities to the products, services, or other cost objects that required that activity. One of the most important differences between traditional and activity-based costing systems is the extent of allocation. Traditional systems generally allocate only

activity-based costing (ABC) systems A system that first accumulates overhead costs for each of the activities of the area being costed, and then assigns the costs of activities to the products, services, or other cost objects that require that activity.

---

[1] A. Phillips and Don Collins, "How Borg-Warner Made the Transition from Pile Accounting to JIT," Management Accounting, October 1990, pp. 32–35.

In a recent survey, companies that use ABC were asked to indicate how many managers routinely used the ABC system. The vast majority, 62%, indicated that from 10 to 24 managers used ABC; 23% of the companies reported that between 25 and 99 managers used ABC information. Why do managers use ABC? The most frequent applications are for product and service costing, process and activity analysis, and performance measurement. These are the primary purposes of strategic decision making and operational control that we discussed at the beginning of this chapter.

A specific example of the use of ABC is Blue Cross and Blue Shield of Florida (BCBSF). BCBSF's major customers include local groups (persons in companies with headquarters in Florida), direct pay (individuals), national and corporate accounts (persons in companies with headquarters outside Florida), and government programs (persons 65 years or older with Medicare benefits). During the early 1990s, BCBSF faced increased competition for its healthcare products and services. But its cost management system did not adequately meet the needs of managers.

The primary goal of BCBSF's management was to develop a new cost management system that would help identify opportunities for increased operating control and cost reduction in administrative expenses. Administrative expenses are all the costs of doing business other than claims payments. In 1996 they were $588 million or 20% of total revenue. The company goal was to reduce administrative costs from 20% of revenue to less than 10%. The cost-management-system technique BCBSF used was an ABC system. This new cost accounting system provided more accurate and timely measurements of

1. customer and product profitability—a strategic purpose,

2. activities that provided the most value to managers and customers—an operational control purpose—and

3. costs of nonvalue-added activities–an operational control purpose.

Sources: Mohan Nair, "Activity-Based Costing: Who's Using It and Why?" *Management Accounting Quarterly,* Spring 2000, pp. 29–33; K. Thurston, D. Keleman, and J. MacArthur, "Cost for Pricing at Blue Cross Blue Shield of Florida," *Management Accounting Quarterly,* Spring 2000, pp. 4–13.

production costs to the products. They normally do not allocate the costs of other value chain functions. Activity-based costing systems often expand allocation of costs beyond production to processes such as order processing, design, marketing, and customer service. As a result, ABC systems are more complex but promise more accurate costs to aid decision makers.

Exhibit 4-5 contrasts the traditional costing system with the two major types of ABC systems. In the traditional costing system shown in Panel A, the portion of total indirect resource costs allocated to a product depends on the proportion of total direct-labor-hours (or other volume-based cost driver such as machine hours or units produced) consumed in making the product. Note that traditional systems often use only one cost driver. Also, traditional systems do not attempt to identify, accumulate, or report costs by activities performed. When does a traditional costing system work best? When there is a plausible and reliable relationship between the single cost driver and *all* the indirect resource costs being allocated and when the cost of providing activity-cost information exceeds the benefits of this information. In today's complex business environments, this is rare.

For example, consider a company that makes just two products—(1) plastic casings for pens and (2) plastic casings for cell phones. Pen casings have a very simple design and thus require a very simple production process. The company produces them in very high volumes, using 90% of its direct labor time and machine processing time. Pen casings are made for general use and rarely will require special customer support or engineering work. This means that the indirect costs of customer support and engineering of the pen casings will be very small.

Exhibit 4-5

Comparison of Traditional, Two-Stage ABC, and Multistage ABC Systems

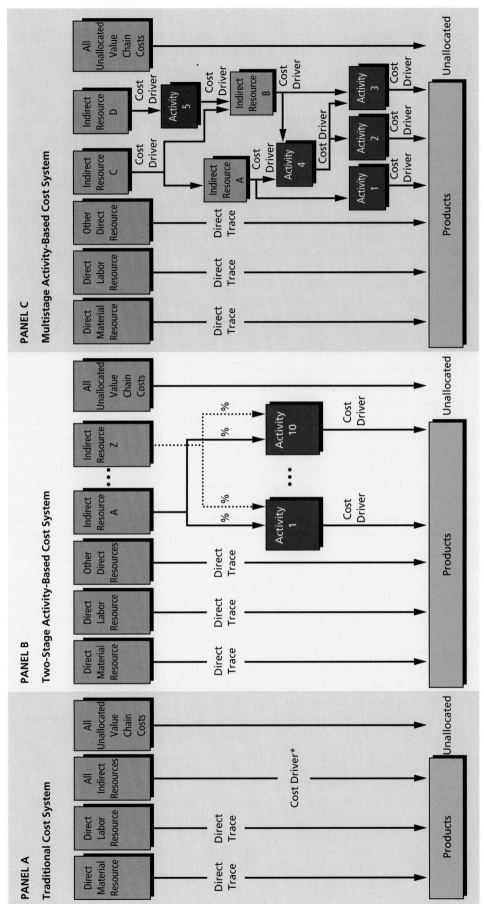

* Direct-labor-hours or other volume-based cost driver such as machine hours or units produced.

On the other hand, cell-phone casings have a much more complex design, and the company produces them in small volumes, accounting for only 10% of its direct labor and machine processing time. Customers (mainly telecommunications companies such as AT&T) who buy cell-phone casings have specific design requirements that cause much engineering work. So, common sense tells us that we *should* allocate most of the costs of engineering to the cell-phone casings. But suppose that we are using the traditional cost system depicted in Panel A of Exhibit 4-5. We would allocate all indirect costs using a volume-based cost driver such as the direct labor time that is spent making the products. Thus, we would allocate only 10% of the engineering costs to the cell-phone casings. This simply does not make sense. A much better cost driver of engineering cost would be "number of customer-generated engineering changes" or "number of distinct parts." If, for example, pen casings have only 5 distinct parts compared to 20 for cell-phone casings, then we would allocate 80% of the engineering activity costs to cell-phone casings rather than only 10% based on the traditional system. In general, the more complex the business environment, the less accurate is a traditional system. Accountants design ABC systems to deal with business complexity.

Just as there are many variations in the design of traditional costing systems, there are also many variations of ABC systems. Exhibit 4-5, Panel B depicts a two-stage ABC system. Compare Panel A to Panel B. During the development of an ABC system, managers often discover ways to trace previously indirect costs to cost objects. For example, an entire production line may be dedicated to produce only one product. This would enable a company to trace directly to the product, costs such as supervision that were previously indirect costs. In a **two-stage ABC system,** there are two stages of allocation to get from the original resource cost to the final product or service cost. The first stage allocates resource costs to activity-cost pools. A **cost pool** is a group of individual costs that is allocated to cost objectives using a single cost driver. The second stage is allocating activity costs to the products or services. In two-stage ABC systems, the first-stage cost drivers are usually percentages. For example, suppose the indirect resource A in Panel B of Exhibit 4-5 was supervisors. We would allocate the cost (salaries) to several activity-cost pools, one for each activity performed by supervisors, based on the percent of effort expended by the supervisors in support of each activity. We would base the second-stage allocation to products or services on the cost driver associated with the particular activity.

Two-stage ABC systems are the simplest ABC systems. They have a financial accounting flavor because the general ledger is at the heart of all the cost data used. It is not necessary to limit the number of stages of allocation to two. In fact, many organizations (such as FedEx, Boeing, and the United States Department of Labor) prefer to design **multistage ABC systems** (shown in Exhibit 4-5, Panel C) with more than two stages of allocations and cost drivers other than percentages. For example, activities two and three in Panel C may be processing customer returns and customer inquiries, respectively. Both of these activities may generate the need for correspondence activity (activity 4). The interrelationship between these three activities is shown by linking activities 2 and 3 to activity 4. In a two-stage ABC system all three activities would be shown but the interrelationship would not be determined.

The focus of multistage ABC is to first understand how a business actually operates by constructing an operations map similar to the one shown in Panel C of Exhibit 4-5. Then determine the financial and operational data needed. There is a distinctive operational flavor to multistage ABC systems because much of the required data comes from operational data sources, not just the general ledger. Many companies such as Pillsbury and AT&T began their use of ABC by using the two-stage approach. However, they later converted to the multistage approach because of its focus on operations and its tendency to enhance operating managers' understanding the business. Managers that use these more complex ABC systems believe that their additional complexity yields more accurate

two-stage ABC system A costing system with two stages of allocation to get from the original cost to the final product or service cost. The first stage allocates resource costs to activity-cost pools. The second stage allocates activity costs to products or services.

cost pool A group of individual costs that is allocated to cost objectives using a single cost driver.

multistage ABC systems Costing systems with more than two stages of allocations and cost drivers other than percentages.

costs and a deeper understanding of operations. A deeper understanding of the business leads to better ideas for process improvement. Process improvements, in turn, lead to more satisfied customers and a competitive edge.

We will illustrate the more general multistage ABC systems. Simple, two-stage ABC systems are simply a special case of the general multistage systems. However, before our detailed illustration of a multistage ABC system, let's explore the central concepts that give multistage ABC systems so much value to managers.

RELATIONSHIP BETWEEN ACTIVITIES, RESOURCES, COSTS, AND COST DRIVERS

Understanding the relationships between activities, resources, resource costs, and cost drivers is the key to understanding ABC and how ABC facilitates managers' understanding of operations. To gain more insight into how an ABC system actually works, we will look at one of the products produced by Woodland Park Company, a manufacturer of plastic components used in commercial trucks and buses.

One of the components Woodland Park makes, 102Z, is a plastic dashboard casing for the control panel of large trucks. Making 102Z requires resin material (directly traced) and several activities such as production scheduling, set-up, molding machine processing, assembly, inspection, packaging, and shipping. We will focus on the set-up and molding machine processing activities. The indirect resources required by these activities include an injection-molding machine, operating labor, and electrical energy. Exhibit 4-6 shows the relationships between the set-up and processing activities and the resources used. Look at the cost objective "Truck Dashboard Casing" in Exhibit 4-6. It takes 15 minutes of machine time to process each casing. This is shown by the activity-consumption rate $r_2 = 0.25$ machine hours per casing. Similarly, r_1 gives the consumption rate for set-up activity. Each production run produces 100 casings and requires one setup ($r_1 = 0.01$). Each casing requires 0.6 pounds of resin material. Therefore, the annual demand for 800 casings requires a total of 8 setups ($800 \times .01$), 200 processing hours ($800 \times .25$) and 480 pounds of resin (800×0.6).

A similar interpretation can be made for the activities. For example, each hour of machine processing activity requires (consumes) one molding machine hour, three operator labor hours, and 0.3 kilowatt hours of energy. We can see that the cost drivers are a measure of the activity level (setups and processing hours) and the amount of resources used (machine hours, labor hours, and kilowatt hours) to produce casings. The activity-consumption rates (the r's on each activity in Exhibit 4-6) give the rates at which the activity uses resources for each cost-driver unit of the activity.

We earlier defined cost drivers as factors that affect costs. So, how do the cost drivers affect the costs of the three resources? Energy cost varies directly with changes in the processing activity because the power company charges Woodland Park based on the kilowatt hours used. One additional processing hour will require .3 additional kilowatt hours that will increase energy cost by $0.90 ($3.00 \times .3$). Thus, energy is a variable-cost resource, and it is easy to see that processing hours and kilowatt hours are factors that affect energy costs.

However, the costs of the machine and labor resources are fixed with respect to changes (within the relevant range) in the cost drivers. One additional processing hour requires one additional machine hour and three labor hours, but the costs of the machine (depreciation) and labor (wages) resources do not change as long as machine time and labor time are available. Have we violated our definition of cost driver? Not really. If the number of processing hours increases enough, the required machine hours or labor hours will exceed the capacities of the machine and labor. Management will then decide whether to purchase more machines or to hire additional maintenance mechanics. This is

Exhibit 4-6

Relation Between Cost Objects, Activities, and Resources in an ABC System

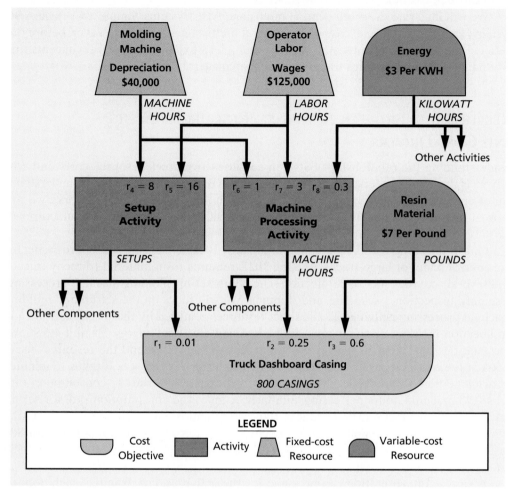

why costs of fixed-cost resources do not change *automatically* when cost drivers change—it involves a management decision. However, if cost drivers truly affect costs, good managers will eventually adjust the resource usage as the level of activity changes.

Why do managers prefer ABC systems to traditional costing systems? One key advantage of an ABC system is its capability to support cost control—the operational control purpose. The managers at Woodland Park Company now have cost and operational information that they can use to manage operations more effectively. For example, the costs of setups and machine processing that were not known (invisible) under the traditional system are now visible and thus more controllable. In addition, operational information about the relationships between activities and resources is now available.

For example, suppose that Woodland Park can increase its sales of truck casings to an annual total of 900 but does not have the machine time available for the extra 100 casings. It would require an additional 25 hours of processing time to meet this new demand. It is believed that by using special quick-change dies, the set-up time can be reduced by 75%. Will this process improvement save enough time to produce the extra 100 casings? The new consumption rate for machine time, r_4, is 2 hours. So the total machine time consumed during setups will be 18 hours (900 casings × 0.01 setups per casing × 2 machine hours per setup) compared to the current 64 hours (800 × 0.01 × 8). Thus, the time savings of 46 hours is more than enough to produce the extra 100 casings. Another advantage of the ABC system is its costing accuracy. Whereas the traditional system allocated all

Activity-Based Costing at Hewlett-Packard

The Roseville Network Division (RND) of Hewlett-Packard was one of the first groups to use activity-based costing. The producer of computer-networking devices referred to its system as "cost-driver accounting." Because RND's products were increasing in number and decreasing in length of product life, the design of new products and their production processes was especially important to the division's success. But the old accounting system did not produce information helpful in comparing the production costs of different designs.

RND's new system focused on the costs of each production process—essentially, the different activities of the division. The system evolved from one with only two cost drivers—direct-labor hours and number of insertions—to one with the following nine cost drivers:

1. Number of axial insertions
2. Number of radial insertions
3. Number of DIP insertions
4. Number of manual insertions
5. Number of test hours
6. Number of solder joints
7. Number of boards
8. Number of parts
9. Number of slots

The increase in the number of cost drivers came about as accountants and managers developed a better understanding of the economics of the design and production process. By knowing the costs of the various activities, product designers could develop designs that would minimize costs for a given level of functionality and reliability.

Recognizing the average product life cycle of 24 months, RND built its cost system around its strategy to keep product lines as up-to-date as possible. RND also recognized a trade-off between accuracy and complexity. The initial two-cost-driver system was simple, but not accurate enough. But with the current nine cost drivers, concern grows that adding more cost drivers may make the system too complex—that is, make its costs greater than its benefits.

Engineering managers at RND were pleased with the activity-based costing system. It greatly influenced the design of new products. For example, once it became clear that manual insertion was three times as expensive as automatic insertion, designs could be modified to include more automatic insertions. The system clearly had the desired effect of influencing the behavior of product designers.

Source: Adapted from R. Cooper and P. B. B. Turney, "Internally Forced Activity-Based Cost Systems," in R. S. Kaplan, ed., *Measures for Manufacturing Excellence* (Boston, MA: Harvard Business School Press, 1990).

indirect overhead costs using just one cost driver, the ABC system uses many cost drivers. The managers chose each of these cost drivers based on the cause-and-effect relationship between the level of product being made and the level of activity (machine processing, assembly, and so on).

SUMMARY PROBLEM FOR YOUR REVIEW

PROBLEM

Last year, TCY Company's demand for product H17 was 14,000 units. At a recent meeting, the sales manager asked the controller about the expected cost for the sales order activity for the current year. A new ABC system had been installed, and the controller had provided the sketch of the order processing activity to the sales manager. The sales manager wanted to know how the order processing activity affects costs. The average sales order is for 20 units. The order processing activity, shown in Exhibit 4-7, requires a computer, processing labor, and telecommunications. The computer is leased at a cost of

Exhibit 4-7

Relation Between Cost Object, Activities, and Resources in an ABC System

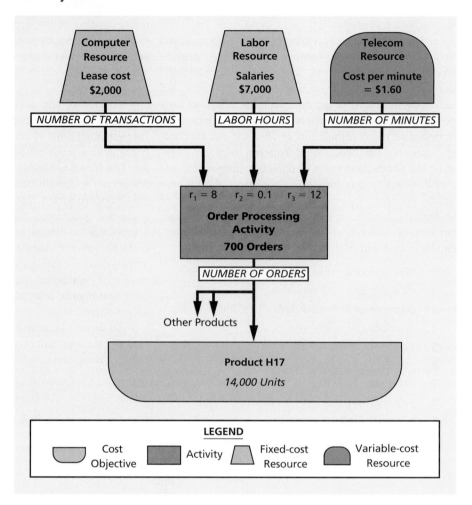

$2,000 per period. Salaries are $7,000, and telecommunications charges are $1.60 per minute.

1. How many labor hours does it take to process each order? How much telecommunications time does each order take?

2. What is the total cost formula for the order processing activity? What is the total and unit cost for demand of 14,000 units?

3. The sales manager calculated the cost per order to be $32.06, based on last year's demand of 14,000 units of H17. Because he believed that this year's demand for H17 may be only 12,000 units, he then calculated the total cost of processing 600 orders as $19,236 = (600 × $32.06). Comment on the validity of the sales manager's analysis.

SOLUTION

1. It takes 0.1 hours or 6 minutes of labor time and 12 minutes of telecommunication time to process an order.

2. The total cost formula for order processing activity is

Total cost = Fixed Costs + Variable Costs

= Lease Cost + Labor Cost + Telecommunications cost/minute

$\times$ minutes/order $\times$ number of orders

= \$2,000 + \$7,000 + \$1.60 $\times$ 12 $\times$ Number of Orders

= \$9,000 + \$19.20 $\times$ Number of Orders

For 14,000 units, there will be 700 orders processed (14,000 ÷ 20 units per order). The total cost to process these orders is \$9,000 + (\$19.20 × 700) = \$22,440 and the unit cost is \$1.60 (\$22,440 ÷ 14,000).

3. The sales manager has fallen into the trap of ignoring cost behavior. His calculation assumes that unit fixed costs will not change with changes in demand or the cost driver. Assuming that 600 orders (and 12,000 units) is within the relevant range, the correct prediction of total cost for a demand of 12,000 units is \$9,000 + \$19.20 × 600 = \$20,520, and the new cost per order is \$20,520 ÷ 600 = \$34.20.

This problem illustrates why it is important to take cost behavior into consideration when using any costing system for planning purposes.

ILLUSTRATION OF ACTIVITY-BASED COSTING[2]

Consider the Billing Department at Portland Power Company (PPC), an electric utility. The Billing Department (BD) at PPC provides account inquiry and bill-printing services for two major classes of customers—residential and commercial. Currently, the BD services 120,000 residential and 20,000 commercial customer accounts.

Two factors are having a significant impact on PPC's profitability. First, deregulation of the power industry has led to increased competition and lower rates, so PPC must find ways of reducing its operating costs. Second, the demand for power in PPC's area will increase with the addition of several large housing developments and a super shopping mall. The marketing department estimates that residential demand will increase by almost 50% and commercial demand will increase by 10% during the next year. Since the BD is currently operating at full capacity, it needs to find ways to create capacity to service the expected increase in demand. A local service bureau has offered to take over the BD functions at an attractive lower cost (compared to the current cost) and proposes to provide all the functions of the BD at \$3.50 per residential account and \$8.50 per commercial account. We can see that PPC's managers are faced with both strategic and operational decisions. To make informed decisions, PPC's managers need accurate estimates of its own cost per residential account and cost per commercial account.

Exhibit 4-8 depicts the residential and commercial customer classes (cost objects) and the resources used to support the BD. The costs associated with the BD are all indirect—they cannot be identified specifically and exclusively with either customer class in an economically feasible way. The BD uses a traditional costing system that allocates all indirect support costs based on the number of account inquiries of the two customer classes. Exhibit 4-8 shows that the cost of the resources used in the BD last month was \$565,340. This costing system is very simple. All costs are "bundled" together and then allocated based on the number of inquiries received from each customer class. BD received 23,000 account inquiries during the month, so the cost per inquiry was \$565,340 ÷ 23,000 = \$24.58. There were 18,000 residential account inquiries, 78.26% of the total. Thus, residential accounts were charged with 78.26% of the support costs, while

[2] Much of the discussion in this section is based on an illustration used in "Implementing Activity-Based Costing—The Model Approach," a workshop sponsored by the Institute of Management Accountants and Hyperion Solutions Corporation.

Exhibit 4-8

Current (Traditional) Costing System: Portland Power Company—Billing Department

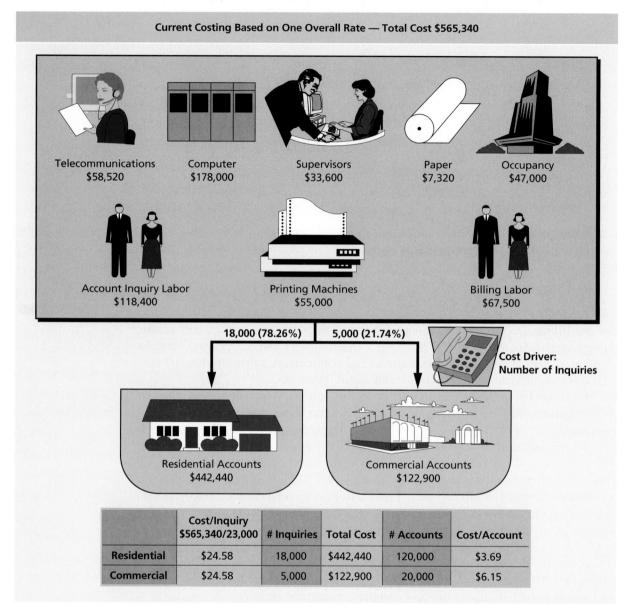

Current Costing Based on One Overall Rate — Total Cost $565,340

Telecommunications $58,520

Computer $178,000

Supervisors $33,600

Paper $7,320

Occupancy $47,000

Account Inquiry Labor $118,400

Printing Machines $55,000

Billing Labor $67,500

18,000 (78.26%)　　5,000 (21.74%)

Cost Driver: Number of Inquiries

Residential Accounts $442,440

Commercial Accounts $122,900

	Cost/Inquiry $565,340/23,000	# Inquiries	Total Cost	# Accounts	Cost/Account
Residential	$24.58	18,000	$442,440	120,000	$3.69
Commercial	$24.58	5,000	$122,900	20,000	$6.15

commercial accounts were charged with 21.74%. The resulting cost per account is $3.69 and $6.15 for residential and commercial accounts, respectively. Suppose you were the BD manager and you knew that billing labor spent much time verifying the accuracy of commercial bills and no time verifying residential bills because only commercial bills were verified! Yet the BD allocated 78.26% of the costs of this work to residential customers. Does this make any sense to you?

Based on the costs provided by the traditional cost system, the BD management would be motivated to accept the service bureau's proposal to service all residential accounts because of the apparent savings of $.19 ($3.69 − $3.50) per account. The BD would continue to service its commercial accounts because its costs are $2.35 ($8.50 − $6.15) less than the service bureau's bid. However, management believed that the actual consumption of support resources was much greater than 21.74% for commercial accounts because of their complexity. For example, in addition to the verification work mentioned in the previous paragraph, commercial accounts average 50 lines (or two pages) per bill compared with only 12 lines (or one page) for residential accounts.

Management was also concerned about activities such as correspondence (and its supporting labor) resulting from customer inquiries because these activities are costly but do not add value to PPC's services from the customer's perspective. Management wanted a more thorough understanding of key BD activities, their interrelationships, and their costs before making important decisions that would impact PPC's profitability. The company decided to perform a study of the BD using activity-based costing. The following is a description of the study and its results.

A team of managers from the BD and the chief financial officer from PPC performed the activity-based-costing study. The team followed a four-step procedure to conduct the study.

Step 1: *Determine the project scope, cost objectives, key activities, resources, and related cost drivers.* Management had set the objective for the study—(1) determine the BD cost per account for each customer class in order to support the strategic decision regarding outsourcing accounts to the local service bureau, and (2) develop a costing system that enhances the manager's understanding of key BD activities to support operational cost control. The team decided to implement a multistage ABC system because they wanted to focus on understanding the interrelationships between resources and activities. The team identified the following activities and related cost drivers for the BD through interviews with appropriate personnel.

Objective 6
Identify the steps involved in the design and implementation of an activity-based costing system.

Activity	Cost Driver
Account billing	Number of lines
Bill verification	Number of accounts
Account inquiry	Number of labor hours
Correspondence	Number of letters

The three key BD activities are account billing, bill verification, and account inquiry. The correspondence activity and resources shown in Exhibit 4-8 support these major activities.

Step 2: *Develop a process-based map representing the flow of activities, resources, and their interrelationships.* An important phase of any activity-based analysis is identifying the interrelationships between key activities and the resources consumed. This is typically done by interviewing key personnel. Once the team identified linkages between activities and resources it was able to draw a process map (Exhibit 4-9) that provides a visual representation of the operations of the BD. The management team first focused on understanding business processes. Costs were not considered until Step 3, after the key interrelationships of the business were understood.

Consider residential accounts. As shown in Exhibit 4-9, two key activities support these accounts: account inquiry and account billing. Account inquiry activity consumes account inquiry labor time. Account inquiry laborers, in turn, use telecommunication and computer resources, occupy space, and are supervised. Correspondence activity is sometimes necessary as a result of inquiries (an example of an activity generating the need for another activity). This activity requires account inquiry laborers and supervisors who review and sign letters. Billing laborers using printing machines perform the account billing activity. The printing machines occupy space and require paper and computer resources. Billing laborers also occupy space, use telecommunications, and are supervised. The team determined the costs of each of the resources consumed during Step 3—data collection.

Exhibit 4-9

Process Map of Billing Department Activities

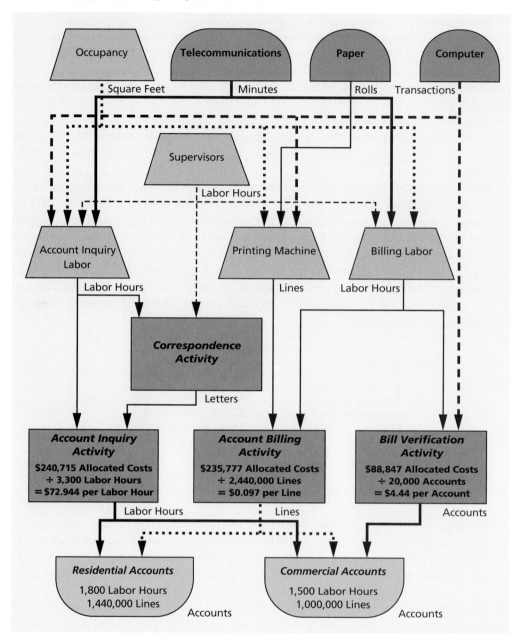

Step 3: *Collect relevant data concerning costs and the physical flow of the cost-driver units among resources and activities.* Using the process map as a guide, BD accountants collected the required cost and operational data by further interviews with relevant personnel. Sources of data include the accounting records, special studies, and sometimes "best estimates of managers."

Exhibit 4-10 is a graphical representation of some of the data collected for the bill verification activity identified in Step 1. Data collected included total costs for fixed-cost resources occupancy, supervisors, and billing labor and cost per cost-driver unit for variable costs telecommunications and computer. Additional data include capacity for the

Exhibit 4-10

ABC System: Portland Power Company—Billing Department

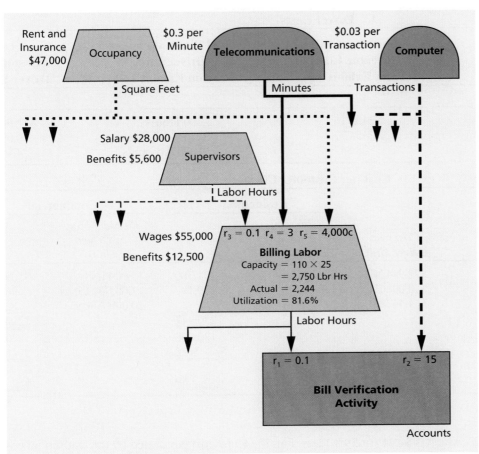

billing labor resource and resource consumption rates ($r_1, r_2 \ldots r_5$). The bill verification activity requires 6 minutes of billing labor per account verified ($r_1 = 0.1$ Labor Hours per Account) and takes 15 computer transactions per account verified ($r_2 = 15$ Transactions per Account). The team asked supervisors how they spend their time. They spend about 6 minutes each hour supervising billing labor (so $r_3 = 0.1$ supervisory Labor Hours per billing Labor Hour). Billing labor uses 3 minutes of telecommunication each hour (r_4) and occupies 4,000 square feet of building space (r_5). The team used a similar approach to collect data for the remaining activities. This is a key difference between a two-stage and multistage ABC system. In two-stage, we would have the supervisor estimate the percentage of time spent on each activity. In multistage ABC, we estimate the input and output relationships between the activities and resources consumed.

Step 4: Calculate and interpret the new activity-based information. After all required financial and operational data have been collected, new activity-based information can be calculated. The total traceable costs for the three primary activities and the physical flow of cost driver units is shown in Exhibit 4-11. Notice that the total traceable costs of $240,716 + $235,777 + $88,847 = $565,340 in Exhibit 4-11 equals the total indirect costs in Exhibit 4-8. We can determine the activity-based cost per account for each customer class from the data in Step 3. Exhibit 4-11 shows the computations.

Examine the last two items in Exhibit 4-11. Notice that traditional costing overcosted the high-volume residential accounts and substantially undercosted the low-volume, complex commercial accounts. The cost per account for residential accounts using ABC is

Exhibit 4-11

Key Results of Activity-Based Costing Study

Driver Costs			
	Traceable Costs (From Exhibit 4-9)	Total Physical Flow of Driver Units (From Exhibit 4-9)	Cost per Driver Unit
Activity (Driver Units)	*(1)*	*(2)*	*(1) ÷ (2)*
Account inquiry (labor hours)	$240,716	3,300 Hours	$72.94424
Account billing (lines)	235,777	2,440,000 Lines	0.09663
Bill verification (accounts)	88,847	20,000 Accounts	4.44235

Cost per Customer Class					
		Residential		Commercial	
	Cost per Driver Unit	*Physical Flow of Driver Units*	*Cost*	*Physical Flow of Driver Units*	*Cost*
Account inquiry	$72.94424	1,800 Hrs.	$ 131,300	1,500 Hrs.	$109,416
Account billing	$ 0.09663	1,440,000 Lines	139,147	1,000,000 Lines	96,630
Bill verification	$ 4.44235			20,000 Accts.	88,847
Total cost			$ 270,447		$294,893
Number of accounts			120,000		20,000
Cost per account			$ 2.25		$ 14.74
Cost per account, traditional system from Exhibit 4-8			$ 3.69		$ 6.15

$2.25, which is $1.44 (or 39%) less than the $3.69 cost generated by the traditional costing system. The cost per account for commercial accounts is $14.74, which is $8.59 (or 140%) more than the $6.15 cost from the traditional costing system. The analysis confirmed management's belief that traditional costing was undercosting commercial accounts. PPC's management now has more accurate cost information for planning and decision-making purposes. We will return to the BD a bit later, but for now, think about what decision you would favor regarding the service bureau's proposal.

These results are common when companies perform activity-based costing studies—high-volume cost objects with simple processes are overcosted when a traditional system uses only one volume-based cost driver. In the BD, this volume-based cost driver was the number of inquiries. Which system makes more sense—the traditional allocation system that "spreads" all support costs to customer classes based solely on the number of inquiries, or the activity-based costing system that identifies key activities and assigns costs based on the consumption of units of cost drivers for each key activity? For PPC, the probable benefits of the new activity-based costing system appear to outweigh the costs of implementing and maintaining the new cost system. However, managers must assess the cost-benefit balance on a case-by-case basis.

SUMMARY OF ACTIVITY-BASED COSTING

Activity-based costing systems can turn many indirect costs into direct costs, costs identified specifically with given cost objectives. ABC systems also turn unallocated costs from nonproduction functions of the value chain into indirect (allocated) costs. Appropriate selection of activities and cost drivers allows managers to trace many manufacturing indirect costs to cost objectives just as specifically as they have traced direct-material costs. Because activity-based costing systems classify more costs as direct than do traditional systems and because cost drivers have a stronger causal relationship between activities and resources, managers have greater confidence in the accuracy of the costs of products and services reported by activity-based costing systems.

Activity-based costing systems are more complex and costly than traditional systems, so not all companies use them. But more and more organizations in both manufacturing and nonmanufacturing industries are adopting activity-based costing systems for a variety of reasons:

- Fierce competitive pressure has resulted in shrinking profit margins. Companies may know their overall margin, but they often do not believe in the accuracy of the margins for individual products or services. Some are winners and some are losers—but which ones? Accurate costs are essential for answering this question.
- Business complexity has increased, which results in greater diversity in the types of products and services as well as customer classes. Therefore, the consumption of a company's shared resources also varies substantially across products and customers.
- New production techniques have increased the proportion of indirect costs—that is, indirect costs are far more important in today's world-class manufacturing environment than they have been in the past. In many industries direct labor is being replaced by automated equipment. Indirect costs are sometimes more than 50% of total cost.
- The rapid pace of technological change has shortened product life cycles. Hence, companies do not have time to make price or cost adjustments once costing errors are discovered.
- The costs associated with bad decisions that result from inaccurate cost determinations are substantial (for example, bids lost due to overcosted products, hidden losses from undercosted products, failure to detect activities that are not cost effective, etc.). Companies with accurate costs have a huge advantage over those with inaccurate costs.
- Computer technology has reduced the costs of developing and operating cost systems that track many activities.

ACTIVITY-BASED MANAGEMENT

Recall that managers' day-to-day focus is on managing activities, not costs. So, because ABC systems also focus on activities, they are a very useful tool in cost management systems. Using an activity-based costing system as a tool to aid strategic decision making and to improve operational control of an organization is **activity-based management (ABM).** In the broadest terms, activity-based management aims to improve the value received by customers and to improve profits by identifying opportunities for improvements in strategy and operations.

One of the most useful applications of ABM is distinguishing between value-added costs and non-value-added costs. A **value-added cost** is the cost of an activity that cannot be eliminated without affecting a product's value to the customer. Value-added costs are necessary (as long as the activity that drives such costs is performed efficiently). In contrast, companies try to minimize **non-value-added costs,** costs that can be eliminated without affecting a product's value to the customer. Activities such as handling and storing inventories, transporting partly finished products from one part of the plant to another, and changing the setup of production-line operations to produce a different model of the product are all non-value-adding activities that can be reduced, if not eliminated, by careful redesign of the plant layout and the production process.

activity-based management (ABM) Using an activity-based costing system to improve the operations of an organization.

value-added cost The necessary cost of an activity that cannot be eliminated without affecting a product's value to the customer.

non-value-added costs Costs that can be eliminated without affecting a product's value to the customer.

Another ABC-related technique that has gained popularity is **benchmarking,** the continuous process of measuring products, services, and activities against the best levels of performance. Benchmarking is a tool to help an organization measure its competitive posture. Benchmarks may be obtained within the organization or may be external from competing organizations or from other organizations having similar processes. Many consulting firms now maintain data bases of benchmarks and provide benchmarking services. Companies must exercise caution when benchmarking is used. Why? Because both financial and operational benchmarks can vary significantly depending on the scope of the ABC system. A company that implements two-stage ABC should not compare its costs per driver units to a benchmark from a company that uses a multistage ABC system. Even so, many companies have found value in the benchmarking process.

BUSINESS FIRST

Identifying Activities, Resources, and Cost Drivers in the Health Care Industry

Arkansas Blue Cross Blue Shield (ABCBS) is the largest health insurer in the state of Arkansas with annual revenues of more than $450 million. Recently, ABCBS implemented activity-based management (ABM). ABM uses activity-based information in the decision-making process. The identification of key activities, resources, and cost drivers was one of the early steps performed.

- A pilot study was performed on one area of the firm—information management. The criteria for selection of a pilot area included significant costs, the possibility of improving the existing cost-allocation system, access to data, and a receptive staff.

- The cost objectives were defined—the internal customers of information management.

- Activities, resources, and cost drivers were identified based on meetings with managers. Examples of key activities are Production (job scheduling, production control), Electronic Media Claims Processing, Printing, and Mail Processing. Resources include Systems Programmers, Mail Labor, Print Labor, Tape Labor, Data Base Administrators, 3080 CPU, 3090 CPU, LSM (robotic cartridge system), DASD (hard disk storage), and Telecommunications. Cost drivers included CPU minutes, single-density volumes (DASD), number of tape and cartridge mounts (LSM), number of jobs, and number of CRTs (telecommunications).

- Once the key activities, resources, and drivers were identified, a process map of the operations of the information management function

was developed by the project team. This map reflected the flow of activities and resources in support of the cost centers. The map also identified the data that needed to be collected to complete the study. The form of the process map is similar to Exhibit 4-9.

- Once the ABC model was built and validated, the results were interpreted and recommendations for improvement were made.

As a result of the ABC study, the following actions were taken by management:

- A separate utility meter was placed in the computer room.
- CRT purchases are now charged directly to the user. Maintenance costs for CRTs are now assigned based on CRT count.
- Three new cost centers were created: EMC Systems, Change Control, and Production Control.
- CPU was upgraded.

ABCBS is now in the process of expanding the new ABM system corporatewide to include purchasing, actuarial, advertising, and claims processing. The company is also using the new ABM system for activity-based budgeting.

Source: Adapted from "Implementing Activity-Based Costing—The Model Approach," Institute of Management Accountants and Hyperion Solutions Corporation, Orlando, November 1994.

STRATEGIC DECISIONS, OPERATIONAL COST CONTROL, AND ABM

Let us return now to the Portland Power Company to see how the billing department could use the ABC system to improve its strategic decisions and operational cost control. Recall that the BD needed to find a way to increase its capacity to handle more accounts due to an expected large increase in demand from a new housing development and a shopping center. A strategic action was proposed—outsource certain customer accounts to a local service bureau. BD managers were also interested (as always is the case) in reducing the operating costs of the department while not impairing the quality of the service it provided to its customers. To do so, they used the ABC information from Exhibit 4-11 to identify non-value-added activities that had significant costs. Account inquiry and bill verification activities are non-value-added and costly, so management asked for ideas for cost reductions. The new information provided by the ABC system generated the following ideas for improvement.

Objective 7
Use activity-based cost information to improve the operations of an organization.

- Use the service bureau for commercial accounts because of the significant cost savings. From Exhibit 4-11, the service bureau's bid is $8.50 per account compared to the BD's activity-based cost of $14.74, a difference of more than $6 per account! The freed-up capacity can be used to meet the expected increase in residential demand. Bill verification, a non-value-added activity, would also be eliminated because only commercial bills are verified.

- Exhibit 4-11 indicates that account inquiry activity is very costly, accounting for a significant portion of total BD costs. One idea is to make bills more descriptive in order to reduce the number of inquiries. Doing so would add lines to each bill, resulting in higher billing activity costs, but the number of inquiries would be reduced, thus reducing a significant non-value-added cost. Whether this idea would result in a net cost reduction needs to be evaluated by the accountants and managers with the help of the new ABC system.

SUMMARY PROBLEM FOR YOUR REVIEW

PROBLEM

Consider the portion of BD's process map shown in Exhibit 4-12. It shows the printing machine along with supporting resources, costs, and resource consumption rates. The printing machines occupy 7,000 square feet of space. The space used does not change when the number of printed lines changes, so this is a constant rate (thus the "c" in the rate 7,000c). This means the allocation of rent and insurance costs to the machinery resource is held constant at $17,315.79 (7,000/19,000 × $47,000) regardless of the number of lines printed. Each roll of paper is enough to print 100,000 lines, so the consumption rate is 0.00001 roll per line. Finally, there are two computer transactions performed for each line that is printed.

Required

1. Give the total cost function for the printing machines resource and determine the total cost based on the current number of lines printed. Explain why it is not necessary to know the consumption rate for the computer resource by the bill verification activity to determine the total cost function.

2. One idea for process improvement is to add additional lines to commercial bills and thus reduce the number of commercial account inquiries. Management estimates that adding eight lines to each commercial bill will result in an 80% reduction in inquiries. An analysis of the improvement indicates that the reduction in inquiries will save $28,000. Now management needs to determine the incremental costs due to additional lines. Determine whether this idea for process improvement will generate net savings or net incremental costs for PPC.

Exhibit 4-12

PPC's Printing Machines Resources

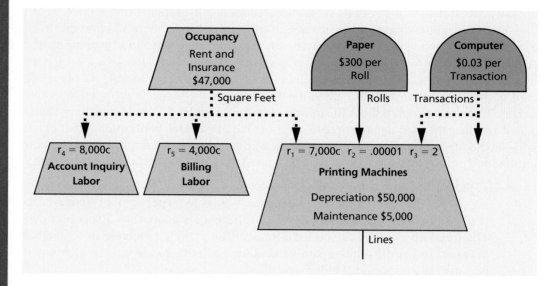

SOLUTION

1. The total cost function is given by

   Total Cost = ($50,000 + $5,000 + $17,315.79) + ($300 per Roll × .00001 Rolls per Line × Number of Lines) + ($.03 per transaction × 2 transactions per Line × Number of Lines)

   = $72,315.79 + .063 × Number of Lines

   The current number of lines is 2,440,000 so the total cost of printing machine resources equals 72,315.79 + .063 × 2,440,000 = $226,035.79. It is not necessary to know the computer resource consumption rate by the bill verification activity because the computer resource is a variable-cost resource. The output measure for any variable-cost resource is truly a cost driver. Compare this to the output measure for a fixed-cost resource such as occupancy. We need to know all of the consumption rates for fixed-cost resources because the cost allocation depends on the distribution of the output measure (square feet) among consuming activities or resources.

2. From Exhibit 4-12, incremental costs will be the variable costs of paper and computer charges. What would be the additional cost if eight lines were added to each commercial bill? The total cost function tells us that the fixed costs (depreciation, maintenance, and occupancy) would not change. Only variable resource costs would increase. There are 20,000 commercial accounts so there would be an additional 20,000 × 8 or 160,000 lines. Thus the incremental cost would be

   $.063 × 160,000 = $10,080

   The process improvement will yield an estimated net savings of $28,000 − $10,080 = $17,920. It is this kind of "what-if" analysis that leads to improved processes and more satisfied customers. PPC has met its goal of enhancing managers' understanding of operations and generating process improvement ideas (the operational cost control purpose of the cost-management system).

HIGHLIGHTS TO REMEMBER

Describe the purposes of cost management systems. Cost management systems provide cost information for external financial reporting, for strategic decision making, and for operational cost control.

Explain the relationship between cost, cost objective, cost accumulation, and cost allocation. Cost accounting systems provide cost information about various types of objectives—products, customers, activities, and so on. To do this, a system first accumulates resource costs by natural classifications such as materials, labor, and energy. Then it assigns these costs to cost objectives, either tracing them directly or assigning them indirectly through allocation.

Distinguish between direct, indirect, and unallocated costs. Direct costs can be identified specifically and exclusively with a cost object in an economically feasible way. When this is not possible, accountants may allocate costs to cost objectives using a cost driver. Such costs are called indirect costs. The greater the proportion of direct costs, the greater the accuracy of the cost system. When the proportion of indirect costs is significant, care must be taken to find the most appropriate cost drivers. Some costs are unallocated because no plausible and reliable relationship can be determined between resource costs and cost objectives.

Explain how the financial statements of merchandisers and manufacturers differ because of the types of goods they sell. The primary difference between the financial statements of a merchandiser and a manufacturer is the reporting of inventories. A merchandiser has only one type of inventory whereas a manufacturer has three types of inventory—raw materials, work-in-process, and finished goods.

Understand the main differences between traditional and activity-based costing systems and why ABC systems provide value to managers. Traditional systems usually allocate only the indirect costs of the production function. ABC systems allocate many (and sometimes all) of the value chain functions. Traditional costing accumulates costs using categories such as direct material, direct labor, and production overhead. ABC systems accumulate costs by activities required to produce a product or service. The key value of ABC systems is in their increased costing accuracy and better information provided that can lead to process improvements.

Identify the steps involved in the design and implementation of an activity-based costing system. Designing and implementing an activity-based costing system involves four steps. First, managers determine the cost objectives, key activities, and resources used, and they identify cost drivers (output measures) for each resource and activity. Second, they draw a process-based map that represents the flow of activities and resources that support the cost objects. The third step is collecting cost and operating data. The last step is to calculate and interpret the new activity-based information. Often, this last step requires the use of a computer due to the complexity of many ABC systems.

Use activity-based cost information to improve the operations of an organization. Using ABC information to improve operations is called activity-based management. One of the key advantages of an activity-based costing system is its capability to aid managers in decision making. ABC provides costs of value-added versus non-value-added activities. ABC also improves managers' understanding of how operations are performed. Managers can focus their attention on process improvements that reduce or eliminate non-value-added activities.

Understand cost accounting's role in a company's improvement efforts across the value chain. A good cost accounting system is critical to all value chain functions from research and development through customer service. Without accurate and timely cost information, decision making is poor at best. In today's complex business environment, the need for good cost information is critical to the success of the business. Improvements in the design of cost accounting systems through activity-based costing have expanded the role of the cost accountant to a position of strategic importance.

Accounting Vocabulary

activity-based costing (ABC)
  systems, p. 139
activity-based management
  (ABM), p. 153
benchmarking, p. 154
cost, p. 133
cost accounting, p. 130
cost accumulation, p. 131
cost allocation, p. 131
cost management system, p. 130
cost object, p. 133

cost objective, p. 133
cost pool, p. 142
direct costs, p. 133
direct-labor costs, p. 135
direct-material costs, p. 135
factory burden, p. 135
factory overhead, p. 135
indirect costs, p. 133
indirect manufacturing costs,
  p. 135
manufacturing overhead, p. 135

multistage ABC system, p. 142
non-value-added costs, p. 153
period costs, p. 136
product costs, p. 136
traditional costing systems,
  p. 139
two-stage ABC system, p. 142
unallocated costs, p. 133
value-added cost, p. 153

Fundamental Assignment Material

4-A1   Direct, Indirect, and Unallocated Costs

Listed below are several activities and related costs that have been observed at Wardy Company, a manufacturing company. The company makes a variety of products and currently uses a traditional costing system that allocates only production overhead based on direct labor hours. It is implementing a multistage ABC system for the design, production, and distribution functions of its value chain. You have been asked to complete the table below by indicating for each activity whether the related cost is direct, indirect, or unallocated. For each indirect cost, indicate *one* appropriate cost driver (more than one cost driver may be appropriate). The first two items have been completed for you.

Activity	Related Cost	Traditional	Multistage ABC
Supervising production	Supervisor salaries	Indirect (direct labor hours)	Indirect (people supervised)
Designing a prototype for new product	Depreciation of computers	Unallocated	Indirect (number of parts)
Setting up for a production run	Mechanic wages		
Purchasing materials and parts to be used in products	Materials and parts cost		
Shipping sold products to customers (distributors)	Fuel used on company's fleet of trucks		
Market research study conducted by marketing staff to assess demand for potential new product	Salaries of market research staff		
Production scheduling	Salaries of production scheduling managers		
Purchasing materials and parts to be used in products	Salaries of purchasing agents		
Order processing of customer orders	Salaries of order processing staff		
Preparing cost analyses	Cost accountant salary		
Designing a new product	Salaries of design engineers that are fully dedicated to this new product		
Managing overall operations of company	Salary of executive		

4-A2   Activities, Resources, Cost Drivers, and the Banking Industry

Best Bank is a branch of an established banking corporation. It is a retail branch located in a residential area and it services mostly individuals and local businesses. Best Bank's four main services are transaction processing (withdrawals, checks, currency exchange), loans, simple investments (individual clients), and complex investments (portfolios of large businesses).

To support these activities, Best Bank employs 10 front-office staff, 12 back-office staff dealing with loan applications and investments, and 2 people to consult with customers and manage complex portfolio investments. A team of 3 supervisors manages the overall operations of the bank.

As part of Best Bank's implementation of activity-based costing, it needed to identify activities, resources, and cost drivers. The following table summarizes the cost drivers Best Bank has chosen for its activities and resources.

	Cost Driver
1	Number of Investments
2	Number of Applications
3	Number of Loans
4	Number of Person Hours
5	Number of Minutes
6	Number of Computer Transactions
7	Number of Square Feet
8	Number of Loan Inquiries
9	Number of Transactions
10	Number of Schedules
11	Number of Securities

For each brief description below, indicate whether it is an activity or a resource (A or R). For each activity or resource choose the most appropriate cost driver from the list above and indicate for each resource whether it is a fixed-cost (F) or variable-cost resource (V). The first two items are completed as a guide.

Required

a. External service bureau providing customer credit checks for loan applications (R; Number of Loan Inquiries; V)

b. Maintenance of building, insurance, and so on (R; Number of Square Feet; F)

c. Staff for front-line customer service

d. Preparing investment documents for customers

e. Research to evaluate a loan application

f. Overtime by back-office staff

g. Telephones/facsimile

h. Staff for service and background research

i. Establish customer collateral for approved loans

j. External computing services

k. Development of repayment schedules

l. Staff for consulting with customers and arranging the portfolios

4-A3 Cost Allocation, Activity-Based Costing, and Activity-Based Management

Reliable Machining Products (RMP) is a discrete automotive component supplier. RMP has been approached by Chrysler with a proposal to significantly increase production of Part T151A to a total annual quantity of 100,000. Chrysler believes that by increasing the volume of production of Part T151A, RMP should realize the benefits of economies of scale and hence should accept a lower price than the current $6.20 per unit. Currently, RMP's gross margin on Part T151A is 3.2%, computed as follows.

	Total	Per Unit (÷ 100,000)
Direct materials	$150,000	$1.50
Indirect manufacturing (300% × direct materials)	$450,000	4.50
Total cost	$600,000	$6.00
Sales price		6.20
Gross margin		$ .20
Gross margin percentage		3.2%

Part T151A seems to be a marginal profit product. If additional volume of production of Part T151A is to be added, RMP management believes that the sales price must be increased, not reduced as requested by Chrysler. The management of RMP sees this quoting situation as an excellent opportunity to examine the effectiveness of their traditional costing system versus an activity-based costing system. RMP decided to implement a two-stage ABC system. A team consisting of accounting and engineering analysts has developed a process-based map. Exhibit 4-13 shows the second stage allocations from this map. Data have been collected and entered on the map. For example, the total annual cost for the quality assurance activity is estimated to be $800,000 and the total quantity of the cost driver "number of pieces scrapped" is estimated to be 10,000. Thus, the cost per piece scrapped is $80. Activity-consumption rates have also been entered on the map. The consumption rate for the production activity is 0.005 machine hours per unit of T151A produced.

Exhibit 4-13

Reliable Machining Product's ABC System

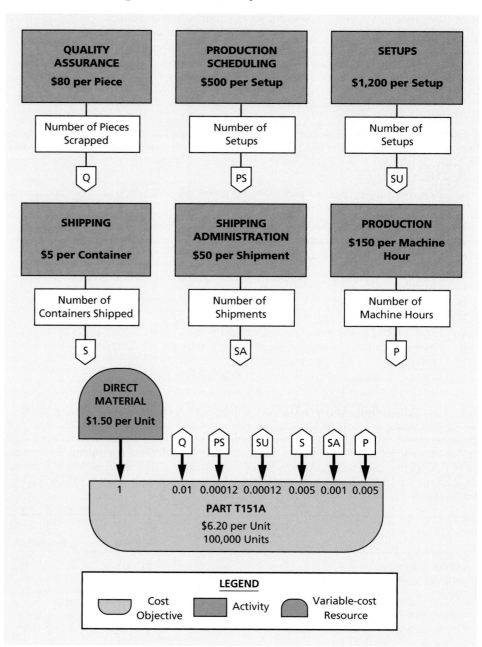

1. Prepare a schedule calculating the unit cost and gross margin percentage of Part T151A using the activity-based costing approach.
2. Based on the ABC results, what course of action would you recommend regarding the proposal by Chrysler? List the benefits and costs associated with implementing an activity-based-costing system at RMP.

4-B1 Direct, Indirect, and Unallocated Costs

Listed below are several activities and related costs that have been observed at Henderson Company, a manufacturing company. The company makes a variety of products and currently uses a traditional costing system that allocates only production overhead based on direct labor hours. It is implementing a multistage ABC system for the design, production, and customer service functions of its value chain. You have been asked to complete the table below by indicating for each activity whether the related cost is direct, indirect, or unallocated. For each indirect cost, indicate *one* appropriate cost driver (more than one cost driver may be appropriate).

Activity	Related Cost	Traditional	Multistage ABC
Supervising production	Supervisor salaries	Indirect (direct labor hours)	Indirect (people supervised)
Designing a prototype for a new product	Depreciation of computers	Unallocated	Indirect (number of parts)
Setting up for a production run	Depreciation of production processing machinery that must remain idle during set-up activity		
Purchasing materials and parts to be used in products	Materials and parts cost		
Shipping sold products to customers (distributors)	Fuel used on company's fleet of trucks		
Market research study conducted by marketing staff to assess demand for potential new product	Salaries of market research staff		
Moving partially completed products from processing to assembly area	Salaries of forklift operators		
Purchasing materials and parts to be used in products	Travel costs to interview potential vendors		
Customer inquiry	Telecommunication costs		
Preparing cost analyses	Cost accountant salary		
Designing a new product	Salaries of design engineers that are fully dedicated to this new product		
President delivering a speech to a trade conference	Travel and entertainment costs at conference		

4-B2 Process Improvement and Multistage ABC Systems

Refer to Exhibit 4-10 and the illustration of Portland Power Company in the text. Management wants to reduce activities that do not add value for the customer. One idea is to reduce the verification of commercial bills by verifying only 20% of bills (at random) and by verifying only certain parts of each bill. Verifying only part of each bill will reduce the billing labor time from 6 minutes to only 3 minutes per bill (account). Management believes that this procedure would not result in any increase in the number of inquiries and that bill accuracy would be unchanged. PPC's labor agreement specifies that whenever labor utilization falls below 70%, the company may lay off workers. Currently, billing labor utilization is at 81.6% consisting of 244 hours for actual billing and 2,000 hours for verification activity. Wages and benefits are $2,200 and $500 per month per billing laborer. Each laborer is available for 110 hours a month. Currently, there are 25 billing laborers. Because of the negative impact on employee moral from layoffs, management is hesitant to implement any layoffs unless the cost savings are significant.

a. Explain why it is not necessary to know the relationships between other resources and activities not shown in Exhibit 4-10 in order to determine the incremental billing labor cost savings from the process improvement.

b. Why is "minutes" a true cost driver for telecommunication costs whereas supervisor "labor hours" is not a true cost driver of supervisor costs?

c. Determine the billing labor cost savings from this process improvement. What other potential cost savings may result? What action would you recommend?

4-B3 Activity-Based Costing in an Electronics Company

The cordless phone manufacturing division of a Denver-based consumer electronics company uses activity-based accounting. For simplicity, assume that its accountants have identified only the following three activities and related cost drivers for indirect manufacturing costs.

Activity	Cost Driver
Materials handling	Direct-materials cost
Engineering	Engineering change notices
Power	Kilowatt hours

Three types of cordless phones are produced: SA2, SA5, and SA9. Direct costs and cost-driver activity for each product for a recent month are as follows:

	SA2	SA5	SA9
Direct-materials cost	$25,000	$ 50,000	$125,000
Direct-labor cost	$ 4,000	$ 1,000	$ 3,000
Kilowatt hours	50,000	200,000	150,000
Engineering change notices	13	5	2

Indirect manufacturing cost for the month was

Materials handling	$ 8,000
Engineering	20,000
Power	16,000
Total indirect manufacturing cost	$44,000

1. Compute the indirect manufacturing cost allocated to each product with the activity-based accounting system.

2. Suppose all indirect manufacturing costs had been allocated to products in proportion to their direct-labor costs. Compute the indirect manufacturing allocated to each product.

3. In which product costs, those in requirement 1 or those in requirement 2, do you have the most confidence? Why?

Additional Assignment Material

QUESTIONS

4-1. Define a cost management system and give its three purposes.

4-2. What is the major purpose of detailed cost-accounting systems?

4-3. Name four cost objectives or cost objects.

4-4. "Departments are not cost objects or objects of costing." Do you agree? Explain.

4-5. Distinguish between direct, indirect, and unallocated costs.

4-6. "The same cost can be direct and indirect." Do you agree? Explain.

4-7. "Economic feasibility is an important guideline in designing cost-accounting systems." Do you agree? Explain.

4-8. How does the idea of economic feasibility relate to the distinction between direct and indirect costs?

4-9. "The typical traditional accounting system does not allocate costs associated with value chain functions other than production to units produced." Do you agree? Explain.

4-10. "It is better not to allocate these costs than to use a cost driver that does not make any sense." Do you agree? Explain.

4-11. Production maintenance, sales commissions, and process design costs are part of a company's costs. Identify which of these costs are *most likely* direct, indirect, and unallocated.

4-12. "For a furniture manufacturer, glue or tacks become an integral part of the finished product, so they would be direct material." Do you agree? Explain.

4-13. "Depreciation is an expense for financial statement purposes." Do you agree? Explain.

4-14. Distinguish between "costs" and "expenses."

4-15. "Unexpired costs are always inventory costs." Do you agree? Explain.

4-16. Why is there no direct-labor inventory account on a manufacturing company's balance sheet?

4-17. Distinguish between manufacturing and merchandising companies.

4-18. Refer to Exhibit 4-5, panel C. Cost drivers for resources A, B, C, and D are sometimes called resource cost drivers, whereas cost drivers for activities 1 to 5 are called activity cost drivers. Explain.

4-19. Refer to Exhibit 4-6. Suppose Woodland Park Company has two plants—the Salem plant and the Youngstown plant. The Youngstown plant produces only three components that are very similar in material and production requirements. The Salem plant makes a wide variety of parts. Which type of costing system would you recommend for each plant (traditional or ABC)? Explain.

4-20. Distinguish between two-stage and multistage ABC systems.

4-21. We refer to resources as variable-cost or fixed-cost resources. Why do we not specify the cost behavior of activities?

4-22. Name four steps in the design and implementation of an activity-based costing system.

4-23. In Exhibits 4-10 and 4-12, the r's represent resource- and activity-consumption rates. Why are these rates important to managers looking for ideas for process improvements?

4-24. Explain the difference between resource-consumption rates and cost per driver unit.

4-25. Why are more and more organizations adopting activity-based costing systems?

4-26. Explain how the layout of a plant's production equipment can reduce non-value-added costs.

4-27. Contrast activity-based costing (ABC) with activity-based management (ABM).

4-28. Why do managers want to distinguish between value-added activities and non-value-added activities?

4-29. What is benchmarking?

4-30. Why should caution be exercised when comparing company performance to benchmarks?

COGNITIVE EXERCISES

4-31 Marketing and Capacity Planning

A company has just completed its marketing plan for the coming year and the management accountant has input the increases in sales volume into the process model. The result is that several key resource capacities have been exceeded. What are the three alternative courses of action to solve this dilemma?

4-32 ABC and ABM Compared

During seminars on activity-based management, participants often ask the difference between ABC and ABM. Explain briefly.

4-33 ABC and Cost Management Systems

Cost management systems have three primary purposes. Two of these are providing information for strategic and operational purposes. Activity-based costing systems are often adopted to increase the accuracy of cost information used by managers for strategic and operational decisions. Suppose a company produces only one product. This means that 100% of its costs are direct with respect to the product cost objective. The accurate product unit cost is simply all costs incurred divided by the total units produced. Why would this company be interested in an ABC system?

EXERCISES

4-34 Classification of Manufacturing Costs

Classify each of the following as direct or indirect (*D* or *I*) with respect to traceability to product and as variable or fixed (*V* or *F*) with respect to whether the cost fluctuates in total as activity or volume changes over wide ranges of activity. You will have two answers, *D* or *I* and *V* or *F*, for each of the 10 items.

1. Supervisor training program
2. Abrasives (e.g., sandpaper)

3. Cutting bits in a machinery department
4. Food for a factory cafeteria
5. Factory rent
6. Salary of a factory storeroom clerk
7. Workers' compensation insurance in a factory
8. Cement for a road builder
9. Steel scrap for a blast furnace
10. Paper towels for a factory washroom

4-35 Variable Costs and Fixed Costs; Manufacturing and Other Costs

For each of the numbered items, choose the appropriate classifications for a manufacturing company. If in doubt about whether the cost behavior is basically variable or fixed, decide on the basis of whether the total cost will fluctuate substantially over a wide range of volume. Most items have two answers among the following possibilities with respect to the cost of a particular job.

    a.   Selling cost
    b.   Manufacturing costs, direct
    c.   Manufacturing costs, indirect
    d.   General and administrative cost
    e.   Fixed cost
    f.   Variable cost
    g.   Other (specify)

Sample answers:

Direct material	b, f
President's salary	d, e
Bond interest expense	e, g (financial expense)

Items for your consideration:

1. Factory power for machines
2. Salespersons' commissions
3. Salespersons' salaries
4. Welding supplies
5. Fire loss
6. Sandpaper
7. Supervisory salaries, production control
8. Supervisory salaries, assembly department
9. Supervisory salaries, factory storeroom
10. Company picnic costs
11. Overtime premium, punch press
12. Idle time, assembly
13. Freight out
14. Property taxes
15. Paint for finished products
16. Heat and air conditioning, factory
17. Material-handling labor, punch press
18. Straight-line depreciation, salespersons' automobiles

4-36 Two-Stage Activity-Based Costing, Banking

Better Bank is an established banking corporation. Its Colorado City location is a retail branch in a rapidly growing residential area. It services individuals and local businesses. To support its services, the branch employs 14 tellers, 3 retail sales managers (RSMs), and the branch managing officer. The branch services about 2,900 customers. Each of the 30 branches of Better Bank is implementing ABC in order to improve its profitability. About half of the branches are implementing two-stage ABC systems and the other half are implementing multistage ABC systems.

Better Bank's branch managing officers have been given the responsibility to implement activity-based costing. The two-stage ABC system is less expensive and can be implemented faster than multistage ABC systems. However, multistage ABC systems provide more operational information and higher levels of cost accuracy. The managing officer at the Colorado City branch decided to implement the two-stage ABC system. Exhibit 4-14, Panel A, depicts the two-stage ABC system.

The Colorado City branch has the following cost data for the last year:

Teller wages	$ 350,000
RSM salaries and benefits	210,000
Managing officer salary and benefits	95,000
Other bank costs	435,000
Total	$1,090,000

The "other bank costs" include depreciation on the facility including furniture, building, equipment, insurance, rentals of computers, contracted computer services, telecommunications, and utilities. These costs cannot be directly or indirectly related to routine bank activities such as processing new accounts or processing deposits or withdrawals and thus are unallocated. There are no costs that can be traced directly to customers so the Colorado City branch has just two types of costs—indirect and unallocated. All employees have been interviewed as part of the ABC study. For example, tellers were asked how they spent their time. They indicated that they spent most of their time (65%) processing deposits and withdrawals. They also estimated that they spent about 5% of their time processing new accounts and about 25% of their time processing other transactions. The remaining 5% of their time was spent on all other banking activities. Three major activities were identified. The results of the interviews appear below.

Internal Activity Analysis					
	Process New Accounts	Process Deposits and Withdrawals	Process Other Transactions	All Other Banking Activities	Total
Teller wages	5%	65%	25%	5%	100%
Retail sales manager salary	5%	25%	25%	45%	100%
Managing officer salary	0%	5%	25%	70%	100%

Required

Determine the total traceable cost of the three major activities conducted at the Colorado City branch of Better Bank. Use Exhibit 4-14, Panel A, as a guide. (Note that this represents the first stage in the two-stage ABC method.)

4-37 Two-Stage Activity-Based Costing, Banking, Benchmarking. (This exercise is a continuation of Exercise 4-36 and should be assigned only if Exercise 4-36 is also assigned.)
A part of the activity analysis conducted at the Colorado City branch of Better Bank was identifying potential cost drivers for each major activity. The following cost drivers were chosen because they were both plausible, reliable, and data were available.

Activity	Cost Driver	Annual Flow of Cost Driver
Process new accounts	Number of new accounts	415
Process deposits and withdrawals	Number of deposits and withdrawals	150,500
Process other transactions	Number of other transactions	41,000

Of the 2,900 customers of the branch, only 400 are local businesses. The business customer class generated 40 new accounts, 88,000 deposits and withdrawals, and 26,000 other transactions.

The ABC implementation of ABC at all branches of Better Bank provided sufficient data for internal benchmarking. The following are the lowest activity costs among all branches.

Exhibit 4-14
Comparison of Two-Stage ABC and Process-Based Costing at the Colorado City Branch of Better Bank

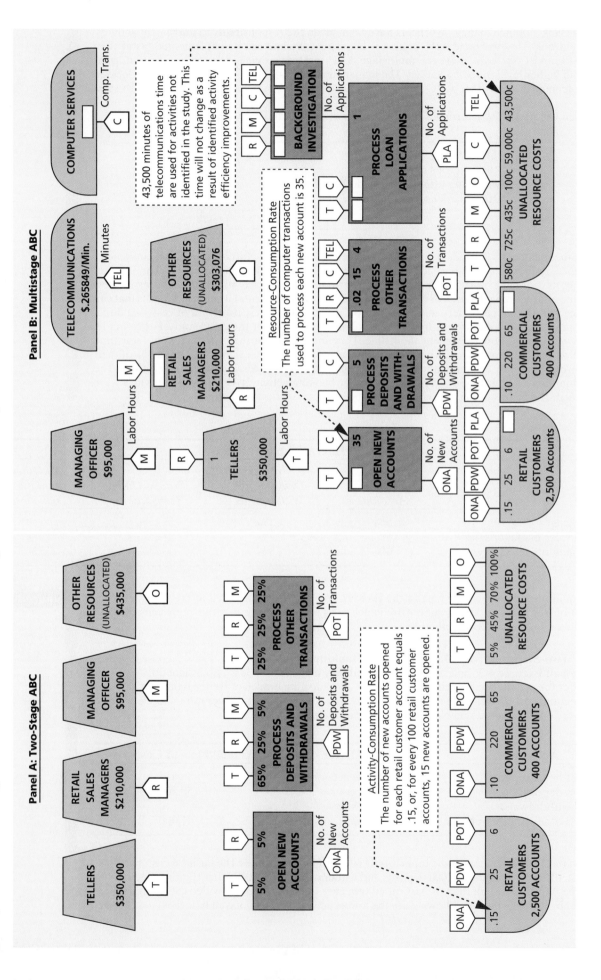

Activity	Lowest Activity Cost per Driver Unit
Open new accounts	$51.67 per new account
Process deposits and withdrawals	$.75 per deposit or withdrawal
Process other transactions	$3.55 per transaction

Customer Class	Lowest Customer Cost per Account
Retail	$ 68
Commercial	$580

Required

1. Determine the allocated (indirect) cost per account for retail and commercial accounts. Use Exhibit 4-14, Panel A, as a guide.
2. Under what conditions would benchmarking between the Colorado City branch of Better Bank and the other branches be inappropriate?
3. What do the results of the ABC study suggest?

4-38   Value-Added Analysis in a Service Company

Refer to the Portland Power Company illustration and Exhibit 4-9 on page 150.

Some companies that perform value-added cost analysis subdivide non-value-added activities into two categories—essential and discretionary. An example of an essential but non-value-added activity is setting up the company's computer system for a billing run. An example of a discretionary non-value-added activity is monitoring telephone inquiries. Most non-value-added discretionary activities should be eliminated. Non-value-added essential activities are reduced through continuous improvement efforts. For each resource and activity listed below, indicate whether it is value-added (VA), non-value-added essential (NVA-E), or non-value-added discretionary (NVA-D). Also indicate appropriate managerial actions to control costs for each type of resource and activity based on its classification.

Resource or Activity
Telecommunications
Paper
Computer
Supervisors
Account inquiry activity
Billing labor

4-39   Cost Allocation and Activity-Based Costing

Refer to the Portland Power Company illustration and Exhibit 4-9 on page 150. The data used in the BD study are averages for each customer class. Based on the study results, the company conducted a thorough investigation of all commercial customers that received correspondence. On average, these accounts consumed 7 minutes of inquiry labor time and had 75 lines on the electric bill. What was the cost per account to service this customer class? (Assume that commercial accounts are verified only one time.)

PROBLEMS

4-40   Cost Accumulation and Allocation

Hwang Manufacturing Company has two departments, machining and finishing. For a given period, the following costs were incurred by the company as a whole: direct material, $130,000; direct labor, $75,000; and indirect manufacturing, $80,000. The grand total costs were $285,000.

The machining department incurred 70% of the direct-material costs, but only 33-1/3% of the direct-labor costs. As is commonplace, indirect manufacturing incurred by each department was allocated to products in proportion to the direct-labor costs of products within the departments.

Three products were produced.

Product	Direct Material	Direct Labor
X-1	40%	30%
Y-1	30%	30%
Z-1	30%	40%
Total for the machining department	100%	100%
X-1	$33\frac{1}{3}$%	40%
Y-1	$33\frac{1}{3}$%	40%
Z-1	$33\frac{1}{3}$%	20%
Total added by finishing department	100%	100%

The indirect manufacturing incurred by the machining department and allocated to all products therein amounted to machining, $38,000 and finishing, $42,000.

Required

1. Compute the total costs incurred by the machining department and added by the finishing department.
2. Compute the total costs of each product that would be shown as finished-goods inventory if all the products were transferred to finished stock on completion. (There were no beginning inventories.)

4-41 Two-Stage Activity-Based Costing at Portland Power Company

Refer to the chapter illustration of the Portland Power Company's billing department. Suppose that instead of the multistage ABC system, the billing department has decided to implement a two-stage activity-based costing system to determine activity costs and customer costs. Exhibit 4-15 depicts this system. One of the key differences between two-stage and multistage ABC systems is in data collection. In two-stage systems, emphasis is on financial data taken from the general ledger. Subaccounts, such as supervisory salary expense, are the basis for stage one. The supervisor would be interviewed to determine the percentage of time he or she spent on various activities. Then these percentages would be multiplied by the account balance from the general ledger. This process is repeated for every expense account in the ledger. In a multistage (process-based) ABC system, the emphasis is on collecting operating data that reflect economic and physical relationships between cost objects, activities, and resources. As a result, financial data may come from various sources other than the general ledger. For example, cost rates for variable-cost resources are not found in the ledger. Rather than percentages of time spent on activities, the multistage system uses activity- and resource-consumption rates that reflect input-output relationships. These rates are more familiar to operating managers and thus help managers understand how their work relates to costs.

Required

a. Note that the data shown in Exhibit 4-15 are incomplete. Complete the diagram in Exhibit 4-15 by determining the missing data.
b. Calculate the cost per account for residential and commercial customers.
c. Based on this new ABC information, what recommendation would you make to BD management concerning outsourcing to the local service bureau?
d. Prepare a table or chart that contrasts the residential cost per account to the commercial cost per account using the traditional, two-stage, and multistage ABC systems. Comment on the results, indicating which system gives a greater level of accuracy and more information for management planning and control purposes.

4-42 Activity-Based Costing and Activity-Based Management, Automotive Supplier

Reliable Machining Products (RMP) is an automotive component supplier. RMP has been approached by General Motors to consider expanding its production of part H707 to a total annual quantity of 2,000 units. This part is a low-volume, complex product with a high gross margin that is based on a proposed (quoted) unit sales price of $7.50. RMP uses a traditional costing system that allocates indirect manufacturing costs based on direct-labor costs. The rate currently used to allocate indirect manufacturing costs is 400% of direct-labor cost. This rate is based on the $3,300,000 annual factory overhead divided by $825,000 annual direct-labor cost. To produce 2,000 units of H707 requires $5,000 of direct materials and $1,000 of direct labor. The unit cost and gross margin percentage for part H707 based on the traditional cost system are computed as follows.

Exhibit 4-15

Two-Stage Cost Allocation for Billing Department Operations

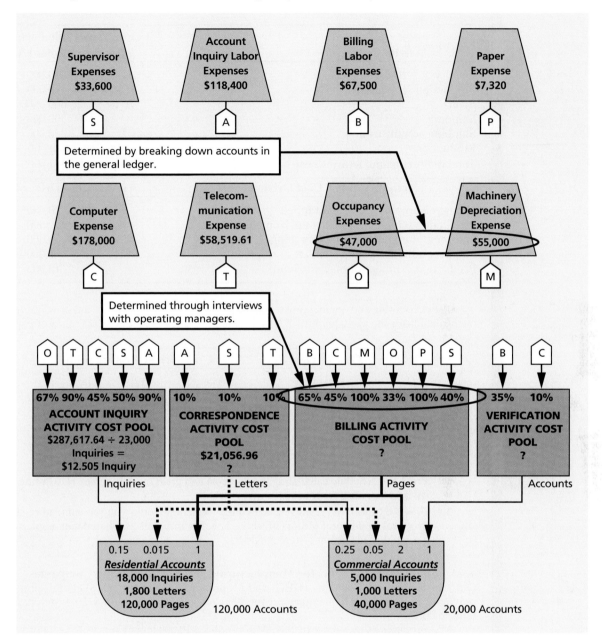

	Total	Per Unit (42,000)
Direct material	$ 5,000	$2.50
Direct labor	1,000	.50
Indirect manufacturing: (400% × direct labor)	4,000	2.00
Total cost	$10,000	$5.00
Sales price quoted		7.50
Gross margin		$2.50
Gross margin percentage		33.3%

The management of RMP decided to examine the effectiveness of their traditional costing system versus an activity-based costing system. The following data have been collected by a team consisting of accounting and engineering analysts:

Activity Center	Traceable Factory Overhead Costs (Annual)
Quality	$ 800,000
Production scheduling	50,000
Setup	600,000
Shipping	300,000
Shipping administration	50,000
Production	1,500,000
Total indirect manufacturing cost	$3,300,000

Activity Center: Cost Drivers	Annual Cost-Driver Quantity
Quality: Number of pieces scrapped	10,000
Production scheduling and set up: Number of setups	500
Shipping: Number of containers shipped	60,000
Shipping administration: Number of shipments	1,000
Production: Number of machine hours	10,000

The accounting and engineering team has performed activity analysis and provides the following estimates for the total quantity of cost drivers to be used to produce 2,000 units of part H707:

Cost Driver	Cost-Driver Consumption
Pieces scrapped	120
Setups	4
Containers shipped	10
Shipments	5
Machine hours	15

Required

1. Prepare a schedule calculating the unit cost and gross margin of part H707 using the activity-based costing approach.

2. Based on the ABC results, which course of action would you recommend regarding the proposal by General Motors? List the benefits and costs associated with implementing an activity-based costing system at RMP.

4-43 Financial Statements for Manufacturing and Merchandising Companies

Outdoor Equipment Company (OEC) and Mountain Supplies, Inc., (MSI) both sell tents. OEC purchases its tents from a manufacturer for $90 each and sells them for $120. It purchased 10,000 tents in 20X1.

MSI produces its own tents. In 20X1 MSI produced 10,000 tents. Costs were as follows.

Direct materials purchased		$535,000
Direct materials used		$520,000
Direct labor		260,000
Indirect manufacturing:		
Depreciation	$40,000	
Indirect labor	50,000	
Other	30,000	120,000
Total cost of production		$900,000

Assume that MSI had no beginning inventory of direct materials. There was no beginning inventory of finished tents, but ending inventory consisted of 1,000 finished tents. Ending work-in-process inventory was negligible.

Each company sold 9,000 tents for $1,080,000 in 20X1 and incurred the following selling and administrative costs.

Sales salaries and commissions	$ 90,000
Depreciation on retail store	30,000
Advertising	20,000
Other	10,000
Total selling and administrative cost	$150,000

Required

1. Prepare the inventories section of the balance sheet for December 31, 20X1, for OEC.
2. Prepare the inventories section of the balance sheet for December 31, 20X1, for MSI.
3. Using Exhibit 4-4 on page 139 as a model, prepare an income statement for the year 20X1 for OEC.
4. Using Exhibit 4-4 on page 139 as a model, prepare an income statement for the year 20X1 for MSI.
5. Summarize the differences between the financial statements of OEC, a merchandiser, and MSI, a manufacturer.

4-44 Distribution Company, Activity-Based Management, Capacity Planning

Southeast Distributors is in the business of distributing a variety of products to different classifications of customers from small corner grocery stores to large mega stores. There are 16 activities in the company's ABC system. Some of these activities are processing orders, receiving, warehousing, unpacking and stacking, picking, unstacking and packing, repackaging in boxes, repackaging in cartons, shipping, and returns processing. The company's activity-based model computes the profitability of its major customer types. The process map has 91 symbols and 200 financial categories. The figure below shows a small portion of this map, the order-processing (OP) department (8 symbols) for the month of April. The department performs three primary activities—regular order processing, returns processing, and order changes. Costs shown are the resource costs to be allocated to the department. Department total costs are to be allocated to departmental activities based on the number of OP documents processed. Note that each type of document (order changes, returns, and orders) takes about the same amount of work to process (hence the consumption rates are all 1).

Southeast Distributors receives telephone orders for cases of different products from the various customer types. In some situations, the customer prior to shipment can change orders. Orders are handled by the order desk staff and subsequently processed by invoicing and collections staff. Resources used by the department include computers, invoicing and collections staff, order desk staff, and telecommunications. The average total cost incurred for each OP document processed is $28.1364 based on April data.

April Data

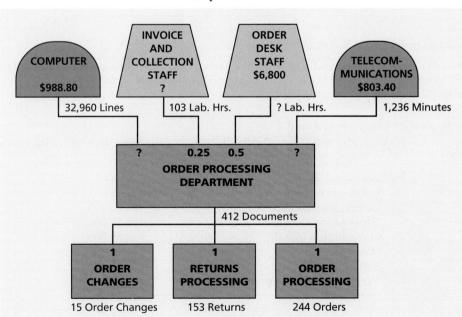

a. What is the resource-consumption rate for the computer and variable telecommunication resources?

b. What is the total cost of the invoicing and collections staff that supports the department?

c. How many labor hours of order desk staff support the department activities?

d. What is the activity-based cost of the three primary activities in the order processing department?

e. There is one person in the invoice and collection staff and two people in the order desk staff. Up until now, all staff worked an average of 135 hours each month. However, a new collective bargaining agreement lowers the number of available labor hours to 120 hours per month. April is a slow month for Southeast. The heaviest sales come in November when there are 19 order changes, 190 returns, and 300 orders. With the new union agreement, will the company be able to meet the processing needs in November? Explain.

f. Assume that one or more of the staff labor pools will not be able to meet the demand for processing in November. What alternative courses of action can management take?

4-45 Library Research in Activity-Based Costing or Activity-Based Management

Select an article from *Strategic Finance* (formerly *Management Accounting*), *Management Accounting Quarterly,* or *Journal of Cost Management* (available in most libraries) that describes a particular company's application of either (1) an activity-based costing system, or (2) activity-based management. Prepare a summary of 300 words or less that includes the following:

- Name of the company (if given)
- Industry of the company
- Description of the particular application
- Assessment of the benefits the company received from the application
- Any difficulties encountered in implementation

4-46 Review of Chapters 2, 3, and 4

The Gomez Hosiery Company provides you with the following miscellaneous data regarding operations in 20X1.

Gross profit	$ 20,000
Net loss	(5,000)
Sales	100,000
Direct material used	35,000
Direct labor	25,000
Fixed manufacturing overhead	15,000
Fixed selling and administrative expenses	10,000

There are no beginning or ending inventories.

Compute (1) variable selling and administrative expenses, (2) contribution margin in dollars, (3) variable manufacturing overhead, (4) break-even point in sales dollars, and (5) manufacturing cost of goods sold.

4-47 Review of Chapters 2, 3, and 4

Stephenson Corporation provides you with the following miscellaneous data regarding operations for 20X1.

Break-even point (in sales dollars)	$ 66,667
Direct material used	24,000
Gross profit	25,000
Contribution margin	30,000
Direct labor	28,000
Sales	100,000
Variable manufacturing overhead	5,000

There are no beginning or ending inventories.

Compute (1) the fixed manufacturing overhead, (2) variable selling and administrative expenses, and (3) fixed selling and administrative expenses.

Required

4-48 Review of Chapters 2, 3, and 4

U. Grant Company manufactured and sold 1,000 sabres during November. Selected data for this month follow.

Sales	$100,000
Direct materials used	21,000
Direct labor	16,000
Variable manufacturing overhead	13,000
Fixed manufacturing overhead	14,000
Variable selling and administrative expenses	?
Fixed selling and administrative expenses	?
Contribution margin	40,000
Operating income	22,000

There were no beginning or ending inventories.

1. What were the variable selling and administrative expenses for November?
2. What were the fixed selling and administrative expenses for November?
3. What was the cost of goods sold during November?
4. Without prejudice to your earlier answers, assume that the fixed selling and administrative expenses for November amounted to $14,000.

   a. What was the break-even point in units for November?
   b. How many units must be sold to earn a target operating income of $12,000?
   c. What would the selling price per unit have to be if the company wanted to earn an operating income of $17,000 on the sale of 900 units?

CASES

4-49 Identifying Activities, Resources, and Cost Drivers in Manufacturing

(D. Sandison) Extrusion Plastics is a multinational, diversified organization. One of its manufacturing divisions, Northeast Plastics Division, has become less profitable due to increased competition. The division produces three major lines of plastic products within its single plant. Product Line A is high-volume, simple pieces produced in large batches. Product Line B is medium-volume, more complex pieces. Product Line C is low-volume, small-order, highly complex pieces.

Currently, the division allocates indirect manufacturing costs based on direct labor. The vice president of manufacturing is uncomfortable using the traditional cost figures. He thinks the company is underpricing the more complex products. He decides to conduct an activity-based costing analysis of the business.

Interviews were conducted with the key managers in order to identify activities, resources, cost drivers, and their interrelationships.

Interviewee: Production Manager

Q1: What activities are carried out in your area?

A1: All products are manufactured using three similar, complex, and expensive molding machines. Each molding machine can be used in the production of the three product lines. Each setup takes about the same time irrespective of the product.

Q2: Who works in your area?

A2: Last year, we employed thirty machine operators, two maintenance mechanics, and two supervisors.

Q3: How are the operators used in the molding process?

A3: It requires nine operators to support a machine during the actual production process.

Q4: What do the maintenance mechanics do?

A4: Their primary function is to perform machine setups. However, they were also required to provide machine maintenance during the molding process.

Q5: Where do the supervisors spend their time?

A5: They provide supervision for the machine operators and the maintenance mechanics. For the most part, the supervisors appear to spend the same amount of time with each of the employees that they supervise.

Q6: What other resources are used to support manufacturing?

A6: The molding machines use energy during the molding process and during the setups. We put meters on the molding machines to get a better understanding of their energy consumption. We discovered that for each hour that a machine ran, it used 6.3 kilowatts of energy. The machines also require consumable shop supplies (e.g., lubricants, hoses, and so on). We have found a direct correlation between the amount of supplies used and the actual processing time.

Q7: How is the building used, and what costs are associated with it?

A7: We have a 100,000-square-foot building. The total rent and insurance costs for the year were $675,000. These costs are allocated to production, sales, and administration based on square footage.

Required

1. Identify the activities, resources, and cost drivers for the division.
2. For each resource identified in requirement 1, indicate its cost behavior with respect to the activities it supports (assume a planning period of 1 month).

4-50 Multistage Activity-Based Costing, Customer Costing, Benchmarking, Banking

Refer to Exercises 4-33 and 4-34. Independent of your answer to Exercise 4-34, assume that the results of the ABC study are as shown below.

Activity	Lowest Activity Cost per Driver Unit	Colorado City Branch Cost per Driver Unit
Process new accounts	$55.67 per new account	$67
Process deposits and withdrawals	$1.45 per deposit or withdrawal	$ 1.96
Process other transactions	$3.55 per transaction	$ 3.99

Customer Class	Lowest Customer Cost per Account	Colorado City Branch Cost per Account
Retail	$ 68	$ 83
Business	$580	$696

The branch managing officer at the Colorado City branch of Better Bank is concerned that branch costs are high compared to the benchmarks within the Better Bank system. In particular, she is not sure how to proceed with a process improvement program because there is insufficient operational data resulting from the study.

For example, although she knows that the cost of the activity "processing deposits and withdrawals" is clearly too high (reflecting operational inefficiencies) compared to the benchmark, she has no operational information from which to begin. When she asked the RSMs to suggest ideas for improvement, their typical response was, "These percentages do not help us any. We need more information, like the time it takes tellers to process deposits and withdrawals and how much supervision is needed for this process." Managers also noted that the unallocated costs amounted to over half of the total branch costs. So the branch managing officer decided to refine the two-stage ABC by implementing multistage ABC.

In order to convert the two-stage ABC to a multistage ABC model the following had to be done.

- For each activity in the two-stage model, determine if other activities are required. This is done through more extensive interviews and data analysis. Typically, the more in-depth analysis yields additional activities and more resources can be allocated.
- For each resource, determine a cost driver and cost behavior.
- For activities and related resources, determine the resource consumption rates. Replace the percentages in the two-stage model with these rates.

The result was a complete process map for the operations of the Colorado City branch. This map was the document used to enter the model into a computer program. The process map is shown in Exhibit 4-14, Panel B, on page 166. Key results of the interviews, data analysis, and computer analysis are given on the next page.

1. Collaboration with other branches that were implementing multistage ABC as well as further interviews with branch managers resulted in two additional activities being identified that could be allocated: processing loans and the background investigation (credit and employment history). The cost driver for both these activities is number of loan applications.

2. Two variable-cost resources were also identified: telecommunications and computers. The cost driver for telecommunications is minutes and the cost driver for computer services is on-line "computer transactions." The cost data for each of these variable-cost resources were specified on a "per cost-driver unit" basis and it is assumed that these rates would apply across the relevant range of activity. The resulting unallocated resource costs were reduced from $435,000 to $303,076.

3. Manuscript of interviews with assistant operations managers:

Q1: Can you identify other activities beyond those in the first ABC study that use up significant amounts of resources?

A1: *Yes, although we do not process many loan applications compared to deposits and withdrawals, when we do process them, it takes lots of time. Last year, we had 250 retail loan applications and 100 commercial applications. Tellers process applications and RSMs do a lot of loan research. We use the computers and are on the phone a lot of the time. Even the branch manager reviews each application.*

Q2: Can you estimate, in terms of labor hours, how tellers spend their time on the four activities?

A2: *It takes about one and one-half labor hours for tellers to process a new account. Our records show that on average it takes about 3 minutes to process a deposit or withdrawal and about 9 minutes to process the other transactions. That is why I mentioned the loans. Each loan application takes about 20 to 30 minutes. I would estimate that 24 minutes would be a good average.*

Q3: How many computer transactions and how much phone time did you say it takes to process loans?

A3: *Based on our records, tellers use the computer about 15 minutes and make about 38 computer transactions for each loan application. RSMs use the computer 10 minutes and make about 45 computer transactions for analysis and review. Tellers do not use the phone but between the assistant manager and branch manager, I would say that about 35 minutes of phone time is used for background investigation on each application.*

Q4: Do you lease computer time or own your computers?

A4: *We lease computers as well as an on-line computer service. We are charged by the number of on-line computer transactions we make and the current rate is $.05 per computer transaction. For example, it may take 15 to 20 transactions to process a deposit for an account but most of these will be off-line. There would be only 4 to 6 transactions made on-line for a deposit. The financial services firm we use has a new software program for processing deposits and withdrawals and an excellent training program. However, we have not purchased this program nor have we used their training. Last year the total cost of computer time was $73,503.75 and our records show that we were billed for 1,470,075 computer transactions.*

Q5: You mentioned that both RSMs and the managing officer were involved with loan applications. Can you specify how much time they spend?

A5: *Yes, most of the work in doing loan research is done by the RSMs. They spend close to two hours investigating each loan. In fact, the average last year was 1.75 hours per application. The final approval of a loan is made by the managing officer after her review. This takes about a half hour per application.*

Q6: You mentioned her review. Did you mean her review of the assistant managers' work or her separate analysis?

A6: *What I mean is her separate analysis takes 30 minutes. She also supervises all of their work. I would estimate that she spends about 9 minutes each hour with the RSMs.*

4. For those branches that implemented multistage ABC, much more benchmarking data were generated than for the two-stage method due to the operational focus. The following is benchmark data for those activities and resources where significant differences existed between the Colorado City branch and the best practices in the Better Bank system.

Selected Operational Benchmarks for Better Bank System

Activity and Related Resource	Benchmark
Processing new accounts—labor time	1 hour per new account
Processing deposits and withdrawals—labor time	2 minutes per deposit or withdrawal
Processing loan applications—labor time	15 minutes per application
Processing loan applications—computer	22 computer transactions per application
Background investigations—analysis time (RSMs)	1 hour per application
Background investigations—telecommunications time	20 minutes per application
Processing other transactions—labor time	6 minutes per transaction
Processing other transactions—computer	9 computer transactions per transaction

Selected Financial Benchmarks for Better Bank System

Processing cost per new account	$35
Processing cost per deposit or withdrawal	$.85
Processing cost of other transactions (per transaction)	$6.25
Processing cost of a loan application	$153
Cost per retail customer	$75
Cost per commercial customer	$ 830

5. Once the operational and financial data was collected and input into a computer program, the traceable costs for each of the four primary activities was calculated.

Activity	Traceable Cost
Open new accounts	$ 19,572
Process deposits and withdrawals	$265,442
Process other transactions	$317,680
Process loan applications	$ 65,975

Required

1. Refer to Exhibit 4-14, Panel B. Complete the business process map for the Colorado City branch by determining the missing data (13 data items depicted by ☐). Use the interview information.

2. Determine the activity cost per driver unit for each of the four primary activities.

3. Determine the cost per account for both retail and commercial customers.

4. What does your analysis suggest about the operations at the Colorado City branch?

5. The branch manager has decided to implement a process improvement program. The program has two components: (1) teller efficiency improvement including their use of computers (the use of computers for processing other transactions is entirely by tellers) and (2) RSM efficiency improvement including their use of telecommunications for researching loans. The goal of the program is to attain benchmark efficiency levels. The teller efficiency component would involve RSMs spending more time to train tellers. This additional time would add 3 minutes each hour to the existing time RSMs spend supervising tellers. The RSM component would involve self-improvement and the adoption of credit scoring. In credit scoring, a point system is used to evaluate the risk of applicants. If the applicant's initial score is higher than a specified cutoff, then the RSM automatically approves the loan without any background investigation. The managing officer needs an analysis of the expected cost savings associated with each program. It was assumed that efficiency improvements in activities (processing deposits and withdrawals, and so on) did not have an impact on unallocated resources. For example, the teller labor hours that are associated with unallocated resources (580) remained unchanged.

Cost savings from lower levels of teller labor or assistant managers will be realized through attrition rather than layoffs. Currently, there are 14 tellers who are available for 1,500 hours each year. Management has set a policy that efficiency gains in labor will not result in any layoffs but that through attrition, the number of tellers will be reduced by the full time equivalent positions saved [that is, (savings in hours)/1,500 rounded down].

A partially completed analysis is presented in Exhibit 4-16. Complete this analysis by doing the teller labor analysis section and determining the total expected cost savings.

4-51 Library Research and AT&T Corporation

AT&T Corporation was highlighted on page 129. AT&T used the same approach (multistage ABC) as our chapter example, Portland Power Company, to implement activity-based management. In

Exhibit 4-16
Benchmark Program Cost Analysis for the Colorado City Branch of Better Bank

	OPEN NEW ACCOUNTS	PROCESS DEPOSITS AND WITHDRAWALS	PROCESS OTHER TRANSACTIONS	PROCESS LOAN APPLICATIONS	BACKGROUND INVESTIGATIONS	SUPERVISION OF TELLERS	TOTAL
TELLER LABOR ANALYSIS							
Current resource consumption (hours): Current rate × Current flow							
Benchmark resource consumption (hours): Benchmark rate × Current flow							
Teller labor time savings (hours)							
Teller labor cost savings							(1)
RETAIL SALES MANAGER LABOR ANALYSIS							
Current resource consumption (hours): Current rate × Current flow						1.75 × 350 = 612.5	0.10 × 15,017.5 = 1,501.75	
Benchmark resource consumption (hours): Benchmark rate × Current flow						1.0 × 350 = 350.0	0.15 × 10,199.16 = 1,529.87	
RSM time savings (hours)						262.5	(28.1)	234.4
RSM cost savings								$-0- (2)*
COMPUTER RESOURCE ANALYSIS							
Current resource consumption (computer transactions):			15 × 41,000 = 615,000	15 × 350 = 5,250			
Benchmark resource consumption:			9 × 41,000 = 369,000	22 × 350 = 7,700			
Computer time savings (minutes)			246,000	5,600			251,600
Computer cost savings (251,600 × $0.05)							$12,580 (3)
TELECOMMUNICATIONS RESOURCE ANALYSIS							
Current resource consumption (minutes):					35 × 350 = 12,250		
Benchmark resource consumption (minutes):					20 × 350 = 7,000		
Telecommunications time savings (minutes)					5,250		5,250
Telecommunications time savings 5,250 × $.2649							$1,391 (4)
TOTAL COST SAVINGS (1) + (2) + (3) + (4)							?

* Assuming that no retail sales managers would be laid off.

fact, AT&T first tried the two-stage ABC approach but was not happy with it. A detailed description of AT&T's experience with ABM is given in the article "Activity-Based Management at AT&T" by T. Hobdy, J. Thomson, and P. Sharman, *Management Accounting* (April 1994).

Compare the approach to designing and implementing an ABC and ABM system described in the text (Portland Power Company) to that used by AT&T by answering the following questions.

1. At AT&T, how were "some billing costs" allocated to different customer classes (invoice types) prior to implementing the process modeling approach to ABC?

2. At AT&T, what business unit was selected for the pilot ABC project and what were the overall goals of the pilot study from the managers' perspective?

3. For AT&T, give examples of cost objects, activities, resources, and cost drivers.

4. For AT&T, "the cost of service support to these individual customers was determined by identifying activity and driver consumption characteristics." For Portland Power's billing activity, describe what is meant by the cost consumption characteristics for the labor resource.

5. Exhibit 4-12 on page 156 shows the operations of the billing department at Portland Power Company. AT&T used a similar flowchart. What function did it perform for AT&T?

6. At AT&T, "each cost object was costed by multiplying the quantity of driver units of each activity consumed by the cost per driver unit." Using the data from Exhibit 4-12, explain how this method applies to Portland Power Company for the residential customer class.

7. At AT&T, the ABC study revealed that "25% of total center costs were assignable to message investigation (account inquiry and correspondence)." For Portland Power Company, what is the percent of total billing department costs assigned to account inquiry investigation?

8. What process improvements were implemented at AT&T for the message investigation activity?

COLLABORATIVE LEARNING EXERCISE

4-52   Internet Research, ABC, and ABM

Form groups of three to five people each. Each member of the group should pick one of the following industries.

- Manufacturing
- Insurance
- Health care
- Government
- Service

Each person should explore the Internet for an example of a company that implemented activity-based costing and activity-based management. To do this, go to the following Web site—www.Hyperion.com—and choose one company from the industry chosen. Prepare and give a briefing for your group. Do this by completing the following.

1. Describe the company and its business.

2. What was the scope of the ABC/ABM project?

3. What were the goals for the ABC/ABM project?

4. Summarize the results of the project.

After each person has briefed the group on his or her company, discuss within your group the commonalities between the ABC/ABM applications.

INTERNET EXERCISE

www.prenhall.com/horngren

4-53   Vermont Teddy Bear Factory

Costs are very important to any manager. Managers focus on trying to keep costs as low as possible. There are many ways to report costs such as the total amount that is often seen on the income statement to an individual cost for a particular component part.

1. Go to the home page of Vermont Teddy Bear Factory—a small firm that manufacturers and sells teddy bears. The Web address is http://www.vermontteddybear.com. When you

click onto the Web site, what does it suggest that you should do? What is the current headline offering on the site?

2. Click to learn more about what a Bear-Gram gift is. What is a Bear-Gram gift? What does the gift contain?

3. What is unique about a Vermont Teddy Bear? What color can a teddy bear be? Can you choose what type of outfit you would like your bear to be sporting? What do you notice about the accessories?

4. Now take a tour of the factory. Click on "Online Factory Tour" in the QUICK LINKS section. What bear can we "see" being born online? Take the online tour. List several activities shown in the tour. What are some resources that are consumed by these activities? For one of the activities you listed give at least one fixed-cost and one variable-cost resource. Suggest a cost driver for one of the activities you listed.

5. Do you think that the Vermont Teddy Bear factory would be a good candidate for using activity-based costing? Why or why not?

6. Look at the section "About Us." Find the most recent annual report. What information can you find about the types of inventory accounts that the company has? Where did you find this information. What was the value of the inventory accounts for the past year? Is this amount increasing or decreasing?

7. Would you say the firm is a manufacturer or merchandiser based on the financial statements? Does the income statement provided give you a clue as to the type of firm this is? Why or why not? In the chapter we discussed the differences in the financial statements for a manufacturer and a merchandiser—do these differences really show up in the annual report?

RELEVANT INFORMATION AND DECISION MAKING: MARKETING DECISIONS

The Grand Canyon Railway offers classic train rides to the southern rim of the Grand Canyon. The train departs from the railway's Williams, Arizona, depot for the 65-mile trip.

www.prenhall.com/horngren

Learning Objectives

When you have finished studying this chapter, you should be able to

1. Discriminate between relevant and irrelevant information for making decisions.

2. Use the decision process to make business decisions.

3. Decide to accept or reject a special order using the contribution margin technique.

4. Decide to add or delete a product line using relevant information.

5. Compute a measure of product profitability when production is constrained by a scarce resource.

6. Discuss the factors that influence pricing decisions in practice.

7. Compute a target sales price by various approaches, and compare the advantages and disadvantages of these approaches.

8. Use target costing to decide whether to add a new product.

9. **Understand how relevant information is used when making marketing decisions.**

While you are on vacation, the last thing you want to worry about is transportation. For visitors to Grand Canyon National Park, The Grand Canyon Railway provides a relaxing alternative to driving to the canyon. Why drive when you can sit back and enjoy the scenery across 65 miles of beautiful Arizona countryside from the comfort of a fully reconditioned steam engine? Strolling musicians serenade you, and western characters stage attacks and holdups that offer a glimpse into what train travel might have been like for old-west loggers, miners, and ranchers at the turn of the century. The Grand Canyon Railway thus offers a ride not only to the canyon itself but into the past as well.

Of course, rides into the past aren't exactly cheap. Tracks for the narrow-gauge train as well as the authentic steam engines and passenger cars cost an awful lot to buy new or to recondition. The company spent upwards of $20 million before opening. Recovering that initial investment while earning a profit is not easy. According to the company controller, Kevin Call, "Pricing is really the key in running a successful operation."

The railway offers five different classes of service, and choosing the pricing on each one determines the profit and return on investment the company's going to make. To set prices, management uses the contribution margin technique introduced in Chapter 2. Among the influences on pricing discussed in the chapter, costs and customer demands are the most important to the railway. The prices charged must not only ensure a reasonable profit but also must be attractive to the customer.

Costs are important in the marketing decisions of many types of companies. What price should a Safeway store charge for a pound of hamburger? What should Boeing charge for a 777 airplane? Should a clothing manufacturer accept a special discount order from Wal-Mart? Should an appliance manufacturer add a new product, say, an automatic bread maker, to its product line? Or should an existing product be dropped? Marketing managers rely on accounting information to answer these questions and make important decisions on a daily basis. Without accounting information, it would be impossible for a firm to determine a marketing strategy. However, not all accounting information applies to each type of decision. In this chapter, we'll focus on identifying relevant information for marketing decisions. The ability to separate relevant from irrelevant information is often the difference between success and failure in modern business.[1]

THE CONCEPT OF RELEVANCE

Objective 1
Discriminate between relevant and irrelevant information for making decisions.

What information is relevant? That depends on the decision being made. Decision making essentially involves choosing among several courses of action. The available actions are determined by an often time-consuming formal or informal search and screening process, perhaps carried on by a company team that includes engineers, accountants, and operating executives. Accountants have an important role in the decision-making process, not as decision makers but as collectors and reporters of relevant information. (Although many managers want the accountant to recommend the proper decision, the final choice always rests with the operating executive.) The accountant's role in decision making is primarily that of a technical expert on financial analysis who helps managers focus on the relevant information that will lead to the best decision.

RELEVANCE DEFINED

Making business decisions requires managers to compare two or more alternative courses of action. Accountants should use two criteria to determine if information is relevant: (1) It must be an expected future revenue or cost, and (2) it must have an element of difference among the alternatives. **Relevant information** is the predicted future costs and revenues that will differ among the alternatives.

relevant information The predicted future costs and revenues that will differ among alternative courses of action.

Note that relevant information is a prediction of the future, not a summary of the past. Historical (past) data have no direct bearing on a decision. Such data can have an indirect bearing on a decision because they may help in predicting the future. But past figures, in themselves, are irrelevant to the decision itself. Why? Because the decision cannot affect past data. Decisions affect the future. Nothing can alter what has already happened.

Of the expected future data, only those that will differ from alternative to alternative are relevant to the decision. Any item that will remain the same regardless of the alternative selected is irrelevant. For instance, if a department manager's salary will be the same regardless of the products stocked, the salary is irrelevant to the selection of products.

EXAMPLES OF RELEVANCE

The following examples will help you clarify the sharp distinctions needed to discriminate between relevant and irrelevant information.

---

[1] *Throughout this and the next chapter, to concentrate on the fundamental ideas, we shall ignore the time value of money and income taxes (discussed in Chapter 11).*

Suppose you always buy gasoline from either of two nearby gasoline stations. Yesterday you noticed that one station was selling gasoline at $1.50 per gallon. The other was selling it at $1.40. Your automobile needs gasoline, and in making your choice of stations, you assume that these prices have not changed. The relevant costs are $1.50 and $1.40, the expected future costs that will differ between the alternatives. You use your past experience (that is, what you observed yesterday) for predicting today's price. Note that the relevant cost is not what you paid in the past, or what you observed yesterday, but what you expect to pay when you drive in to get gasoline. This cost meets our two criteria: (1) It is the expected future cost, and (2) it differs between the alternatives.

You may also plan to have your car lubricated. The recent price at each station was $12, and this is what you anticipate paying. This expected future cost is irrelevant because it will be the same under either alternative. It does not meet our second criterion.

On a business level, consider the following decision. A manufacturer is thinking of using aluminum instead of copper in making a line of ashtrays. The cost of direct material will decrease from 30¢ to 20¢ per ashtray.

The cost of copper used for this comparison probably came from historical cost records on the amount paid most recently for copper, but the relevant cost in the foregoing analysis is the expected future cost of copper compared with the expected future cost of aluminum.

The direct-labor cost will continue to be 70¢ per unit regardless of the material used. It is irrelevant because our second criterion—an element of difference between the alternatives—is not met.

	Aluminum	Copper	Difference
Direct material	$.20	$.30	$.10
Direct labor	.70	.70	—

Therefore we can safely exclude direct labor from the comparison of alternatives.

Exhibit 5-1 illustrates this simple decision, and it serves to show the appropriate framework for more complex decisions. Box 1(A) represents historical data from the accounting system. Box 1(B) represents other data, such as price indices or industry statistics, gathered from outside the accounting system. Regardless of their source, the data in step 1 help the formulation of predictions in step 2. (Remember that although historical data may act as a guide to predicting, they are irrelevant to the decision itself.)

In step 3 these predictions become inputs to the decision model. A **decision model** is any method used for making a choice. Such models sometimes require elaborate quantitative procedures, such as a petroleum refinery's mathematical method for choosing what products to manufacture for any given day or week. A decision model, however, may also be simple. It may be confined to a single comparison of costs for choosing between two materials. In this example our decision model is to compare the predicted unit costs and select the alternative with the lesser cost.

We will be referring to Exhibit 5-1 frequently because it illustrates the main concept in this chapter. In fact, this decision process applies to all business decisions, no matter how simple or complicated they may be. By using this process you will be able to focus squarely on the relevant information—the predicted future differences between alternatives—in any decision. In the rest of this chapter, we will use this decision process to apply the concept of relevance to several specific marketing decisions.

ACCURACY AND RELEVANCE

In the best of all possible worlds, information used for decision making would be perfectly relevant and accurate. However, in reality, such information is often too difficult or too costly to obtain. Accountants are thus forced to trade off relevance versus accuracy.

Exhibit 5-1
Decision Process and Role of Information

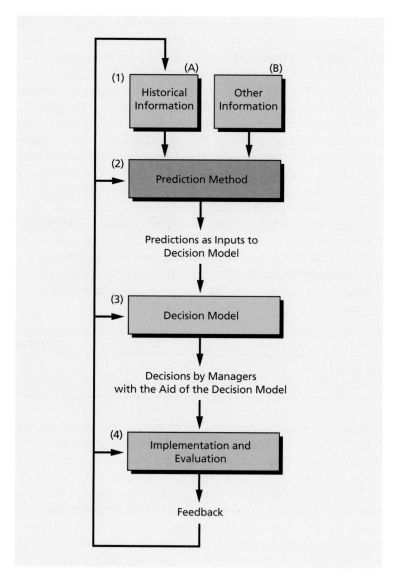

Precise but irrelevant information is worthless for decision making. For example, a university president's salary may be $140,000 per year, to the penny, but may have no bearing on the question of whether to buy or rent data processing equipment. However, imprecise but relevant information can be useful. For example, sales predictions for a new product may be subject to error, but they still are helpful to the decision of whether to manufacture the product. Of course, relevant information must be reasonably accurate but not precisely so.

The degree to which information is relevant or precise often depends on the degree to which it is qualitative or quantitative. Qualitative aspects are those for which measurement in dollars and cents is difficult and imprecise; quantitative aspects are those for which measurement is easy and precise. Accountants, statisticians, and mathematicians try to express as many decision factors as feasible in quantitative terms, because this approach reduces the number of qualitative factors to be judged. Just as we noted that relevance is more crucial than precision in decision making, so a qualitative aspect may easily carry more weight than a measurable (quantitative) financial impact in many decisions. For example, the extreme opposition of a militant union to new labor-saving machinery may cause a manager not to install such machinery even if it would save money. Alternatively, to avoid a long-range dependence on a particular supplier, a company may pass up the opportunity to purchase a component from the supplier at a price below the cost of producing it themselves.

Similarly, managers sometimes introduce new technology (for example, advanced computer systems or automated equipment) even though the expected quantitative results seem unattractive. Managers defend such decisions on the grounds that failure to keep abreast of new technology will surely bring unfavorable financial results sooner or later.

THE SPECIAL SALES ORDER

The first decision for which we examine relevant information is the special sales order.

ILLUSTRATIVE EXAMPLE

In our illustration we'll focus on the Cordell Company. Suppose Cordell makes and sells 1 million units of product, such as some automobile replacement part. The manufacturing cost of goods made is $30,000,000. The unit manufacturing cost of the product is $30,000,000 ÷ 1,000,000, or $30 per unit. Suppose a mail-order house near year-end offered Cordell $26 per unit for a 100,000-unit special order that (1) would not affect Cordell's regular business in any way, (2) would not raise any antitrust issues concerning price discrimination, (3) would not affect total fixed costs, (4) would not require any additional variable selling and administrative expenses, and (5) would use some otherwise idle manufacturing capacity. Should Cordell accept the order? Perhaps we should state the question more sharply: What is the difference in the short-run financial results between not accepting and accepting? As usual, the key question is, What are the differences between alternatives? Exhibit 5-2 presents the income statement (without the special order) of the Cordell Company, using the contribution margin technique.

CORRECT ANALYSIS — FOCUS ON RELEVANT INFORMATION AND COST BEHAVIOR

The correct analysis focuses on determining relevant information and cost behavior. It employs the contribution margin technique. As Exhibit 5-3 shows, this particular order affects only variable manufacturing costs, at a rate of $24 per unit. All other variable costs

Objective 3
Decide to accept or reject a special order using the contribution margin technique.

Exhibit 5-2

Cordell Company
Contribution Form of the Income Statement
For the Year Ended December 31, 20X1 (thousands of dollars)

Contribution Form		
Sales		$40,000
Less: variable expenses		
Manufacturing	$24,000	
Selling and administrative	2,200	26,200
Contribution margin		$13,800
Less: fixed expenses		
Manufacturing	$ 6,000	
Selling and administrative	5,800	11,800
Operating income		$ 2,000

Exhibit 5-3

Cordell Company

Comparative Predicted Income Statements, Contribution Margin Technique for Year Ended December 31, 20X1

	Without Special Order, 1,000,000 Units	Effect of Special Order 100,000 Units Total	Per Unit	With Special Order, 1,100,000 Units
Sales	$40,000,000	$2,600,000	$26	$42,600,000
Less: variable expenses				
Manufacturing	$24,000,000	$2,400,000	$24	$26,400,000
Selling and administrative	2,200,000	—	—	2,200,000
Total variable expenses	$26,200,000	$2,400,000	$24	$28,600,000
Contribution margin	$13,800,000	$ 200,000	$ 2	$14,000,000
Less: fixed expenses				
Manufacturing	$ 6,000,000	—	—	$ 6,000,000
Selling and administrative	5,800,000	—	—	5,800,000
Total fixed expenses	$11,800,000	—	—	$11,800,000
Operating income	$ 2,000,000	$ 200,000	$ 2	$ 2,200,000

and all fixed costs are unaffected and thus irrelevant, so a manager may safely ignore them in making this special-order decision. Note how the contribution margin technique's distinction between variable- and fixed-cost behavior patterns aids the necessary cost analysis. Total short-run income will increase by $200,000 if Cordell accepts the order—despite the fact that the unit selling price of $26 is less than the total unit manufacturing cost of $30. Why did we include fixed costs in Exhibit 5-3? After all, they are irrelevant. They were included because management wants to know the difference in short-run financial results between not accepting and accepting the special order. The analysis could have ended with the contribution margin line but we wanted to show how the difference would effect the "bottom line"—operating income. There will be occasions when irrelevant data will be included in the accountant's presentation of analysis. Why? To suit the preferences of managers who will use the information for decision making.

INCORRECT ANALYSIS — MISUSE OF UNIT COST

Faulty cost analysis sometimes occurs because of misinterpreting unit fixed costs. For instance, Cordell's managers might erroneously use the $30 per-unit total manufacturing cost to make the following prediction for the year:

Incorrect Analysis	Without Special Order 1,000,000 Units	Incorrect Effect of Special Order 100,000 Units	With Special Order 1,100,000 Units
Sales	$40,000,000	$2,600,000	$42,600,000
Less: manufacturing cost of goods sold @ $30	30,000,000	3,000,000	33,000,000
Gross margin	10,000,000	(400,000)	9,600,000
Selling and administrative expenses	8,000,000	—	8,000,000
Operating income	$ 2,000,000	$ (400,000)	$ 1,600,000

The incorrect prediction of a $3 million increase in costs results from multiplying 100,000 units by $30. Of course, the fallacy in this approach is that it treats a fixed cost (fixed manufacturing cost) as if it were variable. Avoid the assumption that unit costs may be used indiscriminately as a basis for predicting how total costs will behave. Unit costs are useful for predicting variable costs but often misleading when used to predict fixed costs.

CONFUSION OF VARIABLE AND FIXED COSTS

Consider the relationship between total fixed manufacturing costs and a fixed manufacturing cost per unit of product:

$$\text{fixed cost per unit of product} = \frac{\text{total fixed manufacturing costs}}{\text{some selected volume level as the denominator}}$$

$$= \frac{\$6,000,000}{1,000,000 \text{ units}} = \$6 \text{ per unit}$$

As noted in Chapter 2, the typical cost accounting system serves two purposes simultaneously: planning and control and product costing. The total fixed cost for budgetary planning and control purposes can be graphed as a lump sum:

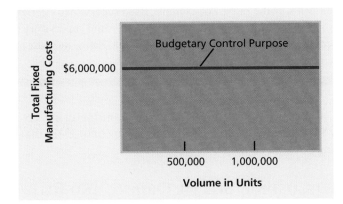

For product-costing purposes, however, using the total unit manufacturing cost implies that these fixed costs have a variable-cost behavior pattern:

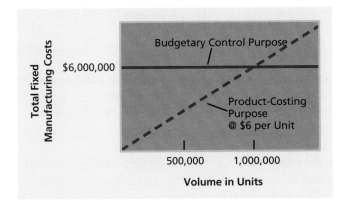

The addition of 100,000 units will not add any total fixed costs as long as total output is within the relevant range. The incorrect analysis, however, includes 100,000 × $6 = $600,000 of fixed cost in the predictions of increases in total costs.

We have presented two key lessons so far in this chapter: relevant information and misuse of unit costs. We cannot stress enough how important it is to clearly understand the definition and concept of relevant information. It is also important to understand why the use of unit fixed costs can lead to an incorrect analysis.

Consider the case where management of a company that makes small appliances is deciding whether to accept or reject a special order for 1,000 units. (Assume there is sufficient capacity available for the order.)

1. Which of the following costs are relevant: (a) parts for the order, (b) supervisor's salary, (c) assembly equipment depreciation, and (d) power to operate the assembly equipment?

2. Suppose the total unit manufacturing cost for the 1,000 units is $100 per unit. We determined this amount by dividing the total cost by 1,000 units. If the customer decided to double the order to 2,000 units, which unit costs listed in question 1 would change? Would the total cost of the order double?

ANSWERS

1. Relevant costs and revenues are predicted future costs and revenues that differ among alternative courses of action. In this case, the cost of parts and power would increase if management accepts the order, and thus they are relevant.

2. Fixed costs per unit will decrease if the customer doubles the order, whereas the variable cost per unit will stay the same. For example, fixed supervisory salaries will be divided by 2,000 units instead of only 1,000 units, and hence per-unit supervisory cost will decrease. The parts cost per unit would stay the same as would the power cost per unit. So, the total unit cost would fall, and the total cost of the order would not double.

In short, we should compute the increase in manufacturing costs by multiplying 1,000,000 units by $24, not by $30. The $30 includes a $6 component that will not affect the total manufacturing costs as volume changes.

ACTIVITY-BASED COSTING, SPECIAL ORDERS, AND RELEVANT COSTS

To identify relevant costs affected by a special order (or by other special decisions), more and more firms are going a step beyond simply identifying fixed and variable costs. As pointed out in Chapters 3 and 4, many different activities are associated with a company's operations. Businesses that have identified all their significant activities and related cost drivers can produce more detailed relevant information to predict the effects of special orders more accurately.

Suppose the Cordell Company examined its $24 million of variable manufacturing costs very closely and identified two significant activities and related cost drivers: $18 million of processing activity that varies directly with units produced at a rate of $18 per unit and $6 million of set-up activity that varies with the number of production setups. Normally, for processing 1,000,000 units, Cordell has 500 setups at a cost of $12,000 per setup, with an average of 2,000 units processed for each setup. Additional sales generally require a proportional increase in the number of setups.

Now suppose the special order is for 100,000 units that vary only slightly in production specifications. Instead of the normal 50 setups, Cordell will need only 5 setups. So processing 100,000 units will take $1,860,000 of additional variable manufacturing cost:

Additional unit-based variable manufacturing cost, 100,000 × $18	$1,800,000
Additional setup-based variable manufacturing cost, 5 × $12,000	60,000
Total additional variable manufacturing cost	$1,860,000

Instead of the original estimate of 100,000 × $24 = $2,400,000 additional variable manufacturing cost, the special order will cost only $1,860,000, or $540,000 less than the original estimate. Therefore, activity-based costing (ABC) allows managers to realize that the special order is $540,000 more profitable than predicted from the simple, unit-based assessment of variable manufacturing cost.

A special order may also be more costly than predicted by a simple fixed- and variable-cost analysis. Suppose the 100,000-unit special order called for a variety of models and colors delivered at various times, so that 100 setups are required. The variable cost of the special order would be $3.0 million.

Additional unit-based variable cost, 100,000 × $18	$1,800,000
Additional setup-based variable cost, 100 × $12,000	1,200,000
Total additional variable cost	$3,000,000

SUMMARY PROBLEM FOR YOUR REVIEW

PROBLEM

1. Return to the basic illustration in Exhibit 5-3. Suppose the Cordell Company received a special order for 100,000 units that had the following terms: Selling price would be $27.00 instead of $26.00, but a manufacturer's agent who had obtained the potential order would have to be paid a flat fee of $80,000 if the order is accepted. Should the special order be accepted?

2. What if the order was for 250,000 units at a selling price of $23.00 and there was no $80,000 agent's fee? Some managers have been known to argue for acceptance of such an order as follows: "Of course, we will lose $1.00 each on the variable manufacturing costs, but we will gain $1.20 per unit by spreading our fixed manufacturing costs over 1.25 million units instead of 1 million units. Consequently, we should take the offer because it represents an advantage of $.20 per unit."

Old fixed manufacturing cost per unit, $6,000,000 ÷ 1,000,000	$6.00
New fixed manufacturing cost per unit, $6,000,000 ÷ 1,250,000	4.80
"Saving" in fixed manufacturing cost per unit	$1.20
Loss on variable manufacturing cost per unit, $23.00 − $24.00	1.00
Net saving per unit in manufacturing cost	$ .20

Explain why this is faulty thinking.

SOLUTION

1. Focus on relevant information—the differences in revenues and costs. In this problem, in addition to the difference in variable costs, there is a difference in fixed costs between the two alternatives.

Additional revenue, 100,000 units @ $27.00 per unit	$2,700,000
Less additional costs	
Variable costs, 100,000 units @ $24 per unit	2,400,000
Fixed costs, agent's fee	80,000
Increase in operating income from special order	$ 220,000

So, from a strictly financial perspective, the special order should be accepted.

2. The faulty thinking comes from attributing a "savings" to the decrease in unit fixed costs. Regardless of how we "unitize" the fixed manufacturing costs or "spread" them over the units produced, the special order will not change the total of $6 million. Remember that we have a negative contribution margin of $1.00 per unit on this special order. Thus, there is no way we can cover any amount of fixed costs! Fixed costs are not relevant to this decision.

DELETION OR ADDITION OF PRODUCTS, SERVICES, OR DEPARTMENTS

Objective 4
Decide to add or delete a product line using relevant information.

Relevant information also plays an important role in decisions about adding or deleting products, services, or departments.

AVOIDABLE AND UNAVOIDABLE COSTS

Often existing businesses will want to expand or contract their operations to improve profitability. How can a manufacturer decide whether to add or to drop products? The same way a retailer decides whether to add or to drop departments: by examining all the relevant cost and revenue information. For example, consider a discount department store that has three major departments: groceries, general merchandise, and drugs. Management is considering dropping the grocery department, which has consistently shown an operating loss. The following table reports the store's present annual operating income (in thousands of dollars).

			Departments	
	Total	Groceries	General Merchandise	Drugs
Sales	$1,900	$1,000	$800	$100
Variable cost of goods sold and expenses*	1,420	800	560	60
Contribution margin	$ 480 (25%)	$ 200 (20%)	$240 (30%)	$ 40 (40%)
Fixed expenses (salaries, depreciation, insurance, property taxes, and so on):				
Avoidable	$ 265	$ 150	$100	$ 15
Unavoidable	180	60	100	20
Total fixed expenses	$ 445	$ 210	$200	$ 35
Operating income	$ 35	$ (10)	$ 40	$ 5

*Examples of variable expenses include paper shopping bags and sales commissions.

avoidable costs Costs that will not continue if an ongoing operation is changed or deleted.

unavoidable costs Costs that continue even if an operation is halted.

common costs Those costs of facilities and services that are shared by users.

Notice that the fixed expenses are divided into two categories, avoidable and unavoidable. **Avoidable costs**—costs that will not continue if an ongoing operation is changed or deleted—are relevant. In our example, avoidable costs include department salaries and other costs that could be eliminated by not operating the specific department. **Unavoidable costs**—costs that continue even if an operation is halted—are not relevant in our example because they are not affected by a decision to delete the department. Unavoidable costs include many **common costs,** which are those costs of facilities and services that are shared by users.[2] For example, store depreciation, heating, air

---

[2] *The concept of avoidable cost is used by government regulators as well as business executives. For example, Amtrak divides its costs into avoidable—costs that "would cease if the route were eliminated"—and fixed—costs that would "remain relatively constant if a single route were discontinued." The U.S. Interstate Commerce Commission then considers the avoidable costs when considering approval of a railroad's request to abandon a route. Similarly, the Canadian government looks at the avoidable cost when determining the amount of subsidy to give to the country's passenger rail system. The* Montreal Gazette *reported that revenues covered only 35% of the "$7 million in avoidable costs (costs that wouldn't exist if the train disappeared tomorrow—things like staff salaries, food, fuel, and upkeep of train stations)."*

conditioning, and general management expenses are costs of shared resources used by all departments. For our example, assume first that the only alternatives to be considered are dropping or continuing the grocery department, which shows a loss of $10,000. Assume further that the total assets invested would be unaffected by the decision. The vacated space would be idle, and the unavoidable costs would continue. Which alternative would you recommend? An analysis (in thousands of dollars) follows.

	Store as a Whole		
		Effect of	
	Total Before	Dropping	Total After
	Change	Groceries	Change
Income Statements	(a)	(b)	(a) − (b)
Sales	$1,900	$1,000	$900
Variable expenses	1,420	800	620
Contribution margin	$ 480	$ 200	$280
Avoidable fixed expenses	265	150	115
Profit contribution to common space and other unavoidable costs	$ 215	$ 50	$165
Common space and other unavoidable costs	180	—	180
Operating income	$ 35	$ 50	$ (15)

The preceding analysis shows that matters would be worse, rather than better, if the store drops the groceries department and leaves the vacated facilities idle. In short, as the income statement shows, groceries bring in a contribution margin of $200,000, which is $50,000 more than the $150,000 fixed expenses that would be saved by closing the grocery department. The grocery department showed a loss in the first income statement because of the unavoidable fixed costs charged to it.

Of course, most companies do not like having space left idle, so perhaps the preceding example was a bit too basic. Assume now that the store could use the space made available by the dropping of groceries to expand the general merchandise department. The space would be occupied by merchandise that would increase sales by $500,000, generate a 30% contribution-margin percentage, and have avoidable fixed costs of $70,000. The $80,000 increase in operating income of general merchandise more than offsets the $50,000 decline from eliminating groceries, providing an overall increase in operating income of $65,000 − $35,000 = $30,000.

	Effects of Changes			
	Total		Expand	Total
	Before	Drop	General	After
	Change	Groceries	Merchandise	Changes
(In thousands of dollars)	(a)	(b)	(c)	(a) − (b) + (c)
Sales	$1,900	$1,000	$500	$1,400
Variable expenses	1,420	800	350	970
Contribution margin	$ 480	$ 200	$150	$ 430
Avoidable fixed expenses	265	150	70	185
Contribution to common space and other unavoidable costs	$ 215	$ 50	$ 80	$ 245
Common space and other unavoidable costs*	180	—	—	180
Operating income	$ 35	$ 50	$ 80	$ 65

*Includes the $60,000 of former grocery fixed costs, which were allocations of unavoidable common costs that will continue regardless of how the space is occupied.

The purpose in deciding whether to add or drop new products, services, or departments is to obtain the greatest contribution possible to pay unavoidable costs. The unavoidable costs will remain the same regardless of any decision, so the key is picking the alternative that will contribute the most toward paying off these costs. The following analysis illustrates this concept for our example.

	Profit Contribution of Given Space (in thousands of dollars)		
	Groceries	Expansion of General Merchandise	Difference
Sales	$1,000	$500	$500 U
Variable expenses	800	350	450 F
Contribution margin	$ 200	$150	$ 50 U
Avoidable fixed expenses	150	70	80 F
Contribution to common space and other unavoidable costs	$ 50	$ 80	$ 30 F

F = Favorable difference resulting from replacing groceries with general merchandise.
U = Unfavorable difference.

In our example, the general merchandise will not achieve the dollar sales volume that groceries will, but the higher contribution margin percentage and the lower wage costs (mostly because of the diminished need for stocking and checkout clerks) combine to produce a more favorable bottom line.

This example illustrates that relevant costs are not always variable. In the special order decision, the relevant costs were the variable costs, which might have led you to believe that you should always ignore fixed costs and focus only on variable costs. However, the key to decision making is not relying on a hard and fast rule about what to ignore and what not to ignore. Rather, you need to analyze all pertinent cost and revenue data to determine what is and what is not relevant. In this case, the relevant costs included the fixed avoidable costs.

When managers face a decision about whether to add or delete a product, service, or department, it is useful to classify the associated fixed costs as avoidable or unavoidable. Indicate whether the following fixed costs are typically avoidable or unavoidable if a company deletes a product. Assume that the company produces many products in a single plant.

1. Depreciation on equipment used to produce the product. The equipment will be sold if the product is discontinued.
2. Salary of the plant manager.
3. Depreciation on the plant building.
4. Advertising costs for the product. Specific ads are placed just for this product.

ANSWER
Items (1) and (4) are avoidable fixed costs. The salary of the plant manager will usually be unchanged if the company discontinues only one product. Thus, it is unavoidable. The same is true for the plant depreciation. Hence, it is also an unavoidable cost.

OPTIMAL USE OF LIMITED RESOURCES

When a plant that makes more than one product is operating at capacity, managers often must decide which orders to accept. The contribution margin technique also applies here, because the product to be emphasized or the order to be accepted is the one that makes the biggest total profit contribution per unit of the limiting factor. A **limiting factor** or **scarce resource** restricts or constrains the production or sale of a product or service. Limiting factors include labor hours and machine hours that limit production (and hence sales) in manufacturing firms, and square feet of floor space or cubic meters of display space that limit sales in department stores.

limiting factor (scarce resource) The item that restricts or constrains the production or sale of a product or service.

The contribution margin technique must be used wisely. Managers sometimes mistakenly favor those products with the biggest contribution margin or gross margin per sales dollar, without regard to scarce resources.

Assume that a company has two products: a plain cellular phone and a fancier cellular phone with many special features. Unit data follow:

Objective 5
Compute a measure of product profitability when production is constrained by a scarce resource.

	Plain Phone	Fancy Phone
Selling price	$80	$120
Variable costs	64	84
Contribution margin	$16	$ 36
Contribution margin ratio	20%	30%

Which product is more profitable? On which should the firm spend its resources? The correct answer is, It depends. If sales are restricted by demand for only a limited number of phones, fancy phones are more profitable. Why? Because sale of a plain phone adds $16 to profit; sale of a fancy phone adds $36. Thus, if the limiting factor is units of sales, the more profitable product is the one with the higher contribution per unit.

Now suppose annual demand for phones of both types is more than the company can produce in the next year. Productive capacity is the limiting factor because only 10,000 hours of capacity are available. If plant workers can make either three plain phones or one fancy phone in one hour, the plain phone is more profitable. Why? Because it contributes more profit per hour of capacity.

	Plain Phone	Fancy Phone
1. Units per hour	3	1
2. Contribution margin per unit	$16	$36
Contribution margin per hour (1) × (2)	$48	$36
Total contribution for 10,000 hours	$480,000	$360,000

As we said earlier, the criterion for maximizing profits when one factor limits sales is to obtain the greatest possible contribution to profit for each unit of the limiting factor. However, the product that is most profitable when one particular factor limits sales may be the least profitable if a different factor restricts sales.

In retail sales, the limiting resource is often floor space. Thus, retail stores must focus either on products taking up less space or on using the space for shorter periods of time — greater **inventory turnover** (number of times the average inventory is sold per year). Consider an example of two department stores. The conventional gross profit percentage (gross profit ÷ selling price) is an insufficient clue to profitability because, as we said, profits depend on the space occupied and the inventory turnover. Discount department stores such as Wal-Mart, Target, and Kmart have succeeded while using lower markups than traditional department stores because they have been able to increase turnover and thus increase the contribution to profit per unit of space. Exhibit 5-4 illustrates the same

inventory turnover The number of times the average inventory is sold per year.

Exhibit 5-4

Effect of Turnover on Profit

	Regular Department Store	Discount Department Store
Retail price	$4.00	$3.50
Cost of merchandise and other variable costs	3.00	3.00
Contribution to profit per unit	$1.00 (25%)	$ .50 (14%)
Units sold per year	10,000	22,000
Total contribution to profit, assuming the same space allotment in both stores	$10,000	$11,000

product, taking up the same amount of space, in each of two stores. The contribution margins per unit and per sales dollar are less in the discount store, but faster turnover makes the same product a more profitable use of space in the discount store. In general, retail companies seek faster inventory turnover. A survey of retail shoe stores showed that those with above-average financial performance had an inventory turnover of 2.6 times per year compared to an industry average of 2.0.

PRICING DECISIONS

One of the major decisions managers face is pricing. Actually, pricing can take many forms. Among the many pricing decisions to be made are

1. Setting the price of a new or refined product
2. Setting the price of products sold under private labels
3. Responding to a new price of a competitor
4. Pricing bids in both sealed and open bidding situations

Pricing decisions are so important, in fact, that we will spend the rest of the chapter discussing the many aspects of pricing. Let us now take a look at some of the basic concepts behind pricing.

THE CONCEPT OF PRICING

perfect competition A market in which a firm can sell as much of a product as it can produce, all at a single market price.

Pricing decisions depend on the characteristics of the market a firm faces. In **perfect competition,** all competing firms sell the same type of product at the same price. Thus, a firm can sell as much of a product as it can produce, all at a single market price. If it charges more, no customer will buy. If it charges less, it sacrifices profits. Therefore, every firm in such a market will charge the market price, and the only decision for managers is how much to produce.

marginal cost The additional cost resulting from producing and selling one additional unit.

Although costs do not directly influence prices in perfect competition, they do affect the production decision. Consider the marginal cost curve in Exhibit 5-5. The **marginal cost** is the additional cost resulting from producing and selling one additional unit. The marginal cost often decreases as production increases up to a point because of efficiencies created by larger amounts. At some point, however, marginal costs begin to rise with increases in production because facilities begin to be overcrowded or overused, resulting in inefficiencies.

marginal revenue The additional revenue resulting from the sale of an additional unit.

Exhibit 5-5 also includes a marginal revenue curve. The **marginal revenue** is the additional revenue resulting from the sale of an additional unit. In perfect competition, the marginal revenue curve is a horizontal line equal to the price per unit at all volumes of sales.

Exhibit 5-5
Marginal Revenue and Cost in Perfect Competition

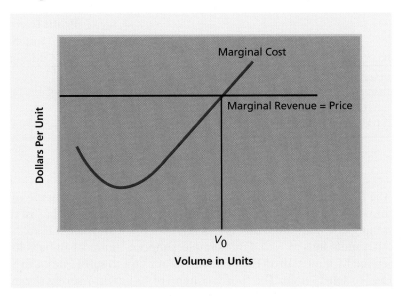

As long as the marginal cost is less than the marginal revenue (price), additional production and sales are profitable. When marginal cost exceeds price, however, the firm loses money on each additional unit. Therefore, the profit-maximizing volume is the quantity at which marginal cost equals price. In Exhibit 5-5, the firm should produce V_0 units. Producing fewer units passes up profitable opportunities, and producing more units reduces profit because each additional unit costs more to produce than it generates in revenue.

In **imperfect competition,** the price a firm charges for a unit will influence the quantity of units it sells. At some point, the firm must reduce prices to generate additional sales. Exhibit 5-6 contains a demand curve (also called the average revenue curve) for

imperfect competition A market in which the price a firm charges for a unit will influence the quantity of units it sells.

Exhibit 5-6
Marginal Revenue and Cost in Imperfect Competition

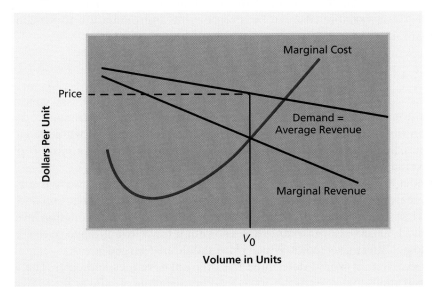

Exhibit 5-7

Profit Maximization in Imperfect Competition

Units Sold	Price per Unit	Total Revenue	Marginal Revenue	Marginal Cost	Profit from Production and Sale of Additional Unit
10	$50	10 × $50 = $500			
11	49	11 × 49 = 539	$539 − $500 = $39	$35	$39 − $35 = $4
12	48	12 × 48 = 576	576 − 539 = 37	36	37 − 36 = 1
13	47	13 × 47 = 611	611 − 576 = 35	37	35 − 37 = (2)

imperfect competition that shows the volume of sales at each possible price. To sell additional units, the firm must reduce the price of all units sold. Therefore, the marginal revenue curve, also shown in Exhibit 5-6, is below the demand curve. That is, the marginal revenue for selling one additional unit is less than the price at which it is sold because the price of all other units falls as well. For example, suppose 10 units can be sold for $50 per unit. However, the firm must drop the price to $49 per unit to sell 11 units, to $48 to sell 12 units, and to $47 to sell 13 units. The fourth column of Exhibit 5-7 shows the marginal revenue for units 11 through 13. Notice that the marginal revenue decreases as volume increases.

price elasticity The effect of price changes on sales volume.

To estimate marginal revenue, managers must predict the effect of price changes on sales volume, which is called **price elasticity.** If small price increases cause large volume declines, demand is highly elastic. If prices have little or no effect on volume, demand is highly inelastic.

For the marginal costs shown in the fifth column of Exhibit 5-7, the optimal production and sales level would be 12 units. The last column of that exhibit illustrates that the 11th unit adds $4 to profit, and the 12th adds $1, but production and sale of the 13th unit would decrease profit by $2. In general, firms should produce and sell units until the marginal revenue equals the marginal cost, represented by volume V_0 in Exhibit 5-6. The optimal price charged will be the amount that creates a demand for V_0 units.

Notice that the marginal cost is relevant for pricing decisions. In managerial accounting, marginal cost is essentially the variable cost. What is the major difference between marginal cost and variable cost? Variable cost is assumed to be constant within a relevant range of volume, whereas marginal cost may change with each unit produced. Within large ranges of production volume, however, changes in marginal cost are often small. Therefore, using variable cost can be a reasonable approximation to marginal cost in many situations.

PRICING AND ACCOUNTING

Objective 6
Discuss the factors that influence pricing decisions in practice.

Accountants seldom compute marginal revenue curves and marginal cost curves. Instead, they use estimates based on judgment to predict the effects of additional production and sales on profits. In addition, they examine selected volumes, not the whole range of possible volumes. Such simplifications are justified because the cost of a more sophisticated analysis would exceed the benefits.

Consider a division of General Electric (GE) that makes microwave ovens. Suppose market researchers estimate that GE can sell 700,000 ovens at $200 per unit and 1,000,000 ovens at $180. The variable cost of production is $130 per unit at production levels of both 700,000 and 1,000,000. Both volumes are also within the relevant range so that changes in volume do not affect fixed costs. Which price should be charged?

GE's accountant would determine the relevant revenues and costs. The additional revenue and additional costs of the 300,000 additional units of sales at the $180 prices are:

Additional revenue: (1,000,000 × \$180) − (700,000 × \$200) =	\$40,000,000
Additional costs: 300,000 × \$130 =	39,000,000
Additional profit:	\$ 1,000,000

Alternatively, the accountant could compare the total contribution for each alternative:

Contribution at \$180: (\$180 − \$130) × 1,000,000 =	\$50,000,000
Contribution at \$200: (\$200 − \$130) × 700,000 =	49,000,000
Difference:	\$ 1,000,000

Notice that comparing the total contributions is essentially the same as computing the additional revenues and costs—both use the same relevant information. Further, both approaches correctly ignore fixed costs, which are unaffected by this pricing decision.

GENERAL INFLUENCES ON PRICING IN PRACTICE

Several factors interact to shape the market in which managers make pricing decisions. Legal requirements, competitors' actions, and customer demands all influence pricing.

LEGAL REQUIREMENTS

Pricing decisions must be made within constraints imposed by U.S. and international laws. These laws often protect consumers, but they also help protect other companies from predatory and discriminatory pricing.

Predatory pricing involves setting prices so low that they drive competitors out of the market. The predatory pricer then has no significant competition and can raise prices dramatically. For example, Wal-Mart has been accused of predatory pricing—selling at low cost to drive out local competitors. However, in a 4-to-3 vote, the court ruled in favor of Wal-Mart. U.S. courts have generally ruled that pricing is predatory only if companies set prices below their average variable cost and actually lose money in order to drive their competitors out of business.

Discriminatory pricing is charging different prices to different customers for the same product or service. For example, a large group of retail druggists and big drugstore chains sued several large drug companies, alleging that their practice of allowing discounts to mail-order drug companies, health maintenance organizations, and other managed-care entities constitutes discriminatory pricing. The discounts were as large as 40%. However, pricing is not discriminatory if it reflects a cost differential incurred in providing the good or service. A tentative settlement to the \$600 million class action suit was reached, but it did not require the drug companies to alter their pricing practices.

predatory pricing
Establishing prices so low that competitors are driven out of the market. The predatory pricer then has no significant competition and can raise prices dramatically.

discriminatory pricing
Charging different prices to different customers for the same product or service.

COMPETITORS' ACTIONS

Competitors usually react to the price changes of their rivals. Many companies will gather information regarding a rival's capacity, technology, and operating policies. In this way, managers make more informed predictions of competitors' reactions to a company's prices. The study of game theory, for which two economists won the 1994 Nobel Prize, focuses on predicting and reacting to competitors' actions.

Tinkering with prices is often most heavily affected by the price setter's expectations of competitors' reactions and of the overall effects on the total industry demand for the good or service in question. For example, an airline might cut prices even if it expects price cuts from its rivals, hoping that total customer demand for the tickets of all airlines will increase sufficiently to offset the reduction in the price per ticket.

Competition is becoming increasingly international. Overcapacity in some countries often causes aggressive pricing policies, particularly for a company's exported goods.

CUSTOMER DEMANDS

More than ever before, managers are recognizing the needs of customers. Pricing is no exception. If customers believe a price is too high, they may turn to other sources for the product or service, substitute a different product, or decide to produce the item themselves.

ROLE OF COSTS IN PRICING DECISIONS

The influence of accounting on pricing is through costs. The exact role costs play in pricing decisions depends on both the market conditions and the company's approach to pricing. Two pricing approaches used by companies are cost-plus pricing and target costing.

COST-PLUS PRICING

markup The amount by which price exceeds cost.

Many managers say that they set prices by "cost-plus" pricing. For example, Grand Canyon Railway sets its prices by computing an average cost and then adding a desired **markup** (that is, the amount by which price exceeds cost) that will generate a target return on investment. The key, however, is the "plus" in cost plus. Instead of being a fixed markup, the "plus" will usually depend on both costs and the demands of customers. For example, the railway has a standard (rack rate) price that does not change during the year, but the company does offer discounts during the slow winter season.

Prices are most directly related to costs in industries where revenue is based on cost reimbursement. Cost-reimbursement contracts generally specify how costs should be measured and what costs are allowable. For example, only coach-class (not first-class) fares are reimbursable for business air travel on government projects, such as defense contracts.

Ultimately, though, the market sets prices. Why? Because the price as set by a cost-plus formula is inevitably adjusted "in light of market conditions." The maximum price a company can charge is the one that does not drive the customer away. The minimum price might be considered to be zero (for example, companies may give out free samples to gain entry into a market). A more practical guide is that, in the short run, the minimum price to be quoted, subject to consideration of long-run effects, should be equal to the costs that may be avoided by not landing the order—often all variable costs of producing, selling, and distributing the good or service. In the long run, the price must be high enough to cover all costs, including fixed costs.

COST BASES FOR COST-PLUS PRICING

Objective 7
Compute a target sales price by various approaches, and compare the advantages and disadvantages of these approaches.

Cost plus is often the basis for target prices. The size of the "plus" depends on target (desired) operating incomes. Target prices can be based on a host of different markups that are in turn based on a host of different definitions of cost. Thus, there are many ways to arrive at the same target price.

Exhibit 5-8 displays the relationships of costs to target selling prices, assuming a target operating income of $1 million. The percentages there represent four popular markup

Exhibit 5-8

Relationships of Costs to Same Target Selling Prices

		Alternative Markup Percentages to Achieve Same Target Sales Prices	
Target sales price	$20.00		
Variable cost:			
(1) Manufacturing	$12.00	($20.00 − $12.00) ÷ $12.00 = 66.67%	
Selling and administrative*	1.10		
(2) Unit variable costs	$13.10	($20.00 − $13.10) ÷ $13.10 = 52.67%	
Fixed costs:			
Manufacturing†	$ 3.00		
Selling and administrative	2.90		
Unit fixed costs	$ 5.90		
(3) Full costs	$19.00	($20.00 − $19.00) ÷ $19.00 = 5.26%	
Target operating income	$ 1.00		

*Selling and administrative costs include costs of value chain functions other than production.
†(4) A frequently used formula is based on total manufacturing costs: [$20.00 − ($12.00 + $3.00)] ÷ $15.00 = 33.33%

formulas for pricing: (1) as a percentage of variable manufacturing costs, (2) as a percentage of total variable costs, (3) as a percentage of full costs, and (4) as a percentage to total manufacturing cost.

Note particularly that **full cost** or **fully allocated cost** means the total of all manufacturing costs plus the total of all selling and administrative costs. As noted in earlier chapters, we use "selling and administrative" to include value chain functions other than production. Of course, the percentages differ. For instance, the markup on variable manufacturing costs is 66.67%, and on full costs it is only 5.26%. Regardless of the formula used, the pricing decision maker will be led toward the same target price. For a volume of 1 million units, assume that the target selling price is $20 per unit. If the decision maker is unable to obtain such a price consistently, the company will not achieve its $1 million operating income objective.

We have seen that prices can be based on various types of cost information, from variable manufacturing costs to full costs. Each of these costs can be relevant to the pricing decision. Each approach has advantages and disadvantages.

full cost (fully allocated cost) The total of all manufacturing costs plus the total of all selling and administrative costs.

ADVANTAGES OF CONTRIBUTION MARGIN APPROACH IN COST-PLUS PRICING

Prices based on variable costs represent a contribution approach to pricing. When used intelligently, the contribution margin approach has some advantages over the total-manufacturing-cost and full-cost approaches, because the latter two often fail to highlight different cost behavior patterns.

Obviously, the contribution margin approach offers more detailed information because it displays variable- and fixed-cost behavior patterns separately. Because the contribution margin approach is sensitive to cost-volume-profit relationships, it is a helpful basis for developing pricing formulas. As a result, this approach allows managers to prepare price schedules at different volume levels.

The correct analysis in Exhibit 5-9 shows how changes in volume affect operating income. The contribution margin approach helps managers with pricing decisions by readily displaying the interrelationships among variable costs, fixed costs, and potential changes in selling prices.

In contrast, target pricing with full costing presumes a given volume level. When volume changes, the unit cost used at the original planned volume may mislead managers.

Exhibit 5-9

Analyses of Effects of Changes in Volume on Operating Income

	Correct Analysis			Incorrect Analysis		
Volume in units	900,000	1,000,000	1,100,000	900,000	1,000,000	1,100,000
Sales @ $20.00	$18,000,000	$20,000,000	$22,000,000	$18,000,000	$20,000,000	$22,000,000
Unit variable costs @ $13.10*	11,790,000	13,100,000	14,410,000			
Contribution margin	6,210,000	6,900,000	7,590,000			
Fixed costs†	5,900,000	5,900,000	5,900,000			
Full costs @ $19.00*				17,100,000	19,000,000	20,900,000
Operating income	$ 310,000	$ 1,000,000	$ 1,690,000	$ 900,000	$ 1,000,000	$ 1,100,000

* From Exhibit 5-8.

† Fixed manufacturing costs $3,000,000
  Fixed selling and administrative costs   2,900,000
  Total fixed costs $5,900,000

Managers sometimes erroneously assume that the change in total costs may be computed by multiplying any change in volume by the full unit cost.

The incorrect analysis in Exhibit 5-9 shows how managers may be misled if they use the $19 full cost per unit to predict effects of volume changes on operating income. Suppose a manager uses the $19 figure to predict an operating income of $900,000 if the company sells 900,000 instead of 1,000,000 units. If actual operating income is $310,000 instead, as the correct analysis predicts, that manager may be stunned—and possibly looking for a new job.

The contribution margin approach also offers insight into the short-run versus long-run effects of cutting prices on special orders. For example, assume the same cost behavior patterns as in the Cordell Company example in Exhibit 5-3 (page 186). The 100,000-unit order added $200,000 to operating income at a selling price of $26, which was $14 below the target selling price of $40 and $4 below the total manufacturing cost of $30. Given all the stated assumptions, accepting the order appeared to be the better choice. As you saw earlier, the contribution margin approach generated the most relevant information. Consider the contribution and total-manufacturing-cost approaches.

	Contribution Margin Technique	Total Manufacturing-Cost Approach
Sales, 100,000 units @ $26	$2,600,000	$2,600,000
Variable manufacturing costs @ $24	2,400,000	
Total manufacturing costs @ $30		3,000,000
Apparent change in operating income	$ 200,000	($ 400,000)

Under the total-manufacturing-cost approach, the offer is definitely unattractive because the price of $26 is $4 below total manufacturing costs.

Under the contribution margin approach, the decision maker sees a short-run advantage of $200,000 from accepting the offer. Fixed costs will be unaffected by whatever decision is made and operating income will increase by $200,000. Still, there often are long-run effects to consider. Will acceptance of the offer undermine the long-run price structure? In other words, is the short-run advantage of $200,000 more than offset by highly probable long-run financial disadvantages? The decision maker may think so and may reject the offer. But—and this is important—by doing so the decision maker is, in effect, forgoing $200,000 now to protect certain long-run market advantages. Generally, the decision maker can assess problems of this sort by asking whether the probability of long-run benefits is worth an "investment" equal to the forgone contribution margin ($200,000 in this case). Under full-cost approaches, the decision maker must ordinarily conduct a special study to find the immediate effects. Under the contribution margin approach, the manager has a system that will routinely and more surely provide such information.

ADVANTAGES OF TOTAL-MANUFACTURING-COST AND FULL-COST APPROACHES IN COST-PLUS PRICING

Frequently, managers do not employ a contribution margin approach because they fear that variable costs will be substituted indiscriminately for full costs and will therefore lead to suicidal price cutting. This problem should not arise if the data are used wisely. However, if top managers perceive a pronounced danger of underpricing when variable-cost data are revealed, they may justifiably prefer a total-manufacturing-cost or full-cost approach for guiding pricing decisions.

Actually, total manufacturing costs or full costs are far more widely used in practice than is the contribution margin approach. Why? In addition to the reasons already mentioned, managers have cited the following reasons:

1. In the long run, all costs must be recovered to stay in business. Sooner or later fixed costs do indeed fluctuate as volume changes. Therefore it is prudent to assume that all costs are variable (even if some are fixed in the short run).

2. Computing target prices based on cost plus may indicate what competitors might charge, especially if they have approximately the same level of efficiency as you and also aim at recovering all costs in the long run.

3. Total-manufacturing-cost or full-cost formula pricing meets the cost-benefit test. It is too expensive to conduct individual cost-volume tests for the many products (sometimes thousands) that a company offers.

4. There is much uncertainty about the shape of the demand curves and the correct price-output decisions. Total-manufacturing-cost or full-cost pricing copes with this uncertainty by not encouraging managers to take too much marginal business.

5. Total-manufacturing-cost or full-cost pricing tends to promote price stability. Managers prefer price stability because it eases their professional lives, primarily because planning is more dependable.

6. Total-manufacturing-cost or full-cost pricing provides the most defensible basis for justifying prices to all interested parties including government antitrust investigators.

7. Total-manufacturing-cost or full-cost pricing provides convenient reference (target) points to simplify hundreds or thousands of pricing decisions.

USING MULTIPLE APPROACHES

To say that either a contribution margin approach or a total-manufacturing-cost or full-cost approach provides the "best" guide to pricing decisions is a dangerous oversimplification of one of the most perplexing problems in business. Lack of understanding and judgment can lead to unprofitable pricing regardless of the kind of cost data available or cost accounting system used.

Basically, no single method of pricing is always best. An interview study of executives reported that companies often use both full-cost and variable-cost information in pricing decisions.

The history of accounting reveals that most companies' systems have gathered costs via some form of full-manufacturing-cost system because this is what is required for financial reporting. In recent years, when systems have changed, variable costs and fixed costs were often identified. But managers have regarded this change as an addition to the existing full-manufacturing-cost system. That is, many managers insist on having information regarding both variable costs per unit and the allocated fixed costs per unit before setting selling prices. If the accounting system routinely gathers data regarding both variable and fixed costs, such data can readily be provided. However, most total-manufacturing-cost systems in practice do not organize their data collection to distinguish between variable and fixed costs. As a result, special studies or educated guessing must be used to designate costs as variable or fixed.

Managers are especially reluctant to focus on variable costs and ignore allocated fixed costs when their performance evaluations, and possibly their bonuses, are based on income shown in published financial statements. Why? Because such statements are based on full costing, and thus allocations of fixed costs affect reported income.

FORMATS FOR PRICING

Exhibit 5-8 showed how to compute alternative general markup percentages that would produce the same selling prices if used day after day. In practice, the format and arithmetic of quote sheets, job proposals, or similar records vary considerably.

Exhibit 5-10 is from an actual quote sheet used by the manager of a small job shop that bids on welding machinery orders in a highly competitive industry. The Exhibit 5-10 approach is a tool for informed pricing decisions. Notice that the maximum price is not a matter of cost at all. It is what you think you can obtain. The minimum price is the total variable cost.

Of course, the manager will rarely bid the minimum price. Businesses do need to make a profit. Still, the manager wants to know the effect of a job on the company's total variable costs. Occasionally, a company will bid near that minimum price to establish a presence in new markets or with a new customer.

Note that Exhibit 5-10 classifies costs specifically for the pricing task. Pricing decisions may be made by more than one person. The accountant's responsibility is to prepare an understandable format that involves a minimum of computations. Exhibit 5-10 combines direct labor and variable manufacturing overhead. All fixed costs, whether manufacturing, selling, or administrative, are lumped together and applied to the job using a single fixed-overhead rate per direct-labor-hour. Obviously, if more accuracy is desired, many more detailed cost items and overhead rates could be formulated. To obtain the desired accuracy, many companies are turning to activity-based costing.

Some managers, particularly in construction and in service industries such as auto repair, compile separate categories of costs of (1) direct materials, parts, and supplies and (2) direct labor. These managers then use different markup rates for each category. They use these rates to provide enough revenue to cover both indirect and unallocated costs

Exhibit 5-10
Quote Sheet for Pricing

Direct materials, at cost	$25,000
Direct labor and variable manufacturing overhead,	
600 direct-labor-hours × $30	18,000
Sales commission (varies with job)	2,000
Total variable costs—minimum price[*]	45,000
Add fixed costs allocated to job, 600 direct-labor-hours × $20	12,000
Total costs	57,000
Add desired markup	30,000
Selling price—maximum price that you think you can obtain[*]	$87,000

[*]This sheet shows two prices, maximum and minimum. Any amount you can get above the minimum price is a contribution margin.

and operating profit. For example, an automobile repair shop might have the following format for each job:

	Billed to Customers
Auto parts ($200 cost plus 40% markup)	$280
Direct labor (Cost is $20 per hour. Bill at 300% to recover indirect and unallocated costs and provide for operating profit. Billing rate is $20 × 300% = $60 per hour. Total billed for 10 hours is $60 × 10 = $600)	600
Total billed to customer	$880

Another example is an Italian printing company in Milan that wants to price its jobs so that each one generates a margin of 28% of revenues—14% to cover selling and administrative expenses and 14% for profit. To achieve this margin, the manager uses a pricing formula of 140% times predicted materials cost plus 25,000 Italian lira (abbreviated Lit) per hour of production time. The latter covers labor and overhead costs of Lit 18,000 per hour. For a product with Lit 400,000 of materials cost and 30 hours of production time, the price would be Lit 1,310,000:

	Cost	Price	Profit
Materials	Lit 400,000	Lit 560,000	Lit 160,000
Labor and overhead	540,000	750,000	210,000
Total	Lit 940,000	Lit 1,310,000	Lit 370,000

The profit of Lit 370,000 is approximately 40% of the cost of Lit 940,000 and 28% of the price of Lit 1,310,000.

Thus there are numerous ways to compute selling prices. However, some general words of caution are appropriate here. Managers are better able to understand their options and the effects of their decisions on profits if they know their costs. That is, it is more informative to pinpoint costs first, before adding markups, than to have a variety of markups already embedded in the "costs" used as guides for setting selling prices. For example, if materials cost $1,000, they should be shown on a price quotation guide at $1,000, not at, say, a marked-up $1,400 because that is what the seller hopes to get.

TARGET COSTING

Consider the situation when a company is deciding whether to develop and market a new product. In evaluating the feasibility of the new product, management must determine both the price it can charge and the expected cost. As we have seen, both the market conditions and actions of management can affect the price and the cost of the new product. The degree to which management actions can affect price and cost determines the most effective approach to use for pricing and cost management purposes. Companies use cost-plus pricing for products where management actions (for example, advertising) can influence the market price. Although cost management is important in this case, there is a strong focus on marketing and the revenue side of the profit equation.

But what if the market conditions are such that management cannot influence prices? If a company is to achieve management's desired profit, it must focus on the product's cost. What management needs is an effective tool to reduce costs without reducing value to the customer. A growing number of companies faced with this situation are adopting target costing. **Target costing** is a cost management tool for making cost reduction a key focus throughout the life of a product. A desired, or target, cost is set before creating or

target costing A cost management tool for making cost a key focus throughout the life of a product.

even designing the product. The target cost is based on the product's predicted price and the company's desired profit. Managers must then try to reduce and control costs so that the product's cost does not exceed its target cost. Target costing is most effective at reducing costs during the product design phase when the vast majority of costs are committed. For example, the costs of resources such as new machinery, materials, parts, and even future refinements are largely determined by the design of the product and the associated production processes. It is not easy to reduce these costs once production begins. So, the emphasis of target costing is on proactive, up-front planning throughout every activity of the new product development process.

TARGET COSTING AND NEW PRODUCT DEVELOPMENT

Exhibit 5-11 shows the target costing process for a new product. Based on the existing technology and related cost structure, the product has three parts, requires direct labor, and has four types of indirect costs. The first step in the target costing process is the determination of market price. The market sets this price. Management sets the gross margin for the new product. The difference between the gross margin and the market price is the target cost for the new product. The company determines the existing cost structure for the product by building up costs on an individual component level. This product has two components. Component 1 consists of parts A and B. Component 2 is part C. Both components and the final assembly use direct labor. Finally, the activities necessary to plan and process the product create indirect costs.

Marketing might appear to have a limited role in target costing because the price is set by competitive market conditions. Actually, market research from the marketing

Exhibit 5-11

The Target Costing Process

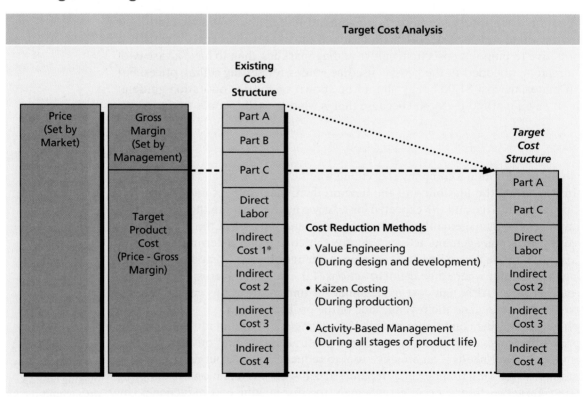

*Each indirect cost is associated with an indirect activity. Indirect Cost 1 was eliminated in the cost reduction process.

department at the beginning of the target costing activity guides the whole product development process by supplying information on customer demands and requirements. In fact, one of the key characteristics of successful target costing is a strong emphasis on understanding customer demands.

In the example in Exhibit 5-11, the existing cost is too large to generate the desired profit. Does this mean that the new product is not feasible? Not necessarily. A cross-functional team consisting of engineers, sales personnel, key suppliers, and accountants now must determine if cost reductions can be implemented that will reduce the costs enough to meet the target cost.

In the example in Exhibit 5-11, in the target cost structure, the company reduced the cost of parts by changing the design of the product so that part C could be used in place of part B. The company also asked suppliers of parts A and C to reduce their costs. Design and process engineers were also able to eliminate the activity that generated the first type of indirect cost. These cost reductions resulted from **value engineering**—a cost-reduction technique, used primarily during the design stage, that uses information about all value chain functions to satisfy customer needs while reducing costs. In total, the planned cost reductions were adequate to reduce costs to the target. However, not all the reductions in cost take place before production begins. **Kaizen costing** is the Japanese term for continuous improvement during manufacturing. How is kaizen costing applied? A company establishes kaizen goals each year as part of the planning process. Examples include the continual reduction in setup times and processing times due to employee experience. In total, target costing during design and kaizen costing during manufacturing enables the achievement of the target cost over the product's life.

Underlying these cost-reduction methods is the need for accurate cost information. Activity-based costing provides this information. Companies can then use activity-based management (ABM) to identify and eliminate non-value-added activities, waste, and their related costs. ABM is applied throughout both the design and manufacturing stages of the product's life.

value engineering A cost-reduction technique, used primarily during design, that uses information about all value chain functions to satisfy customer needs while reducing costs.

kaizen costing The Japanese term for continuous improvement during manufacturing.

ILLUSTRATION OF TARGET COSTING

Consider the target-costing system used by ITT Automotive—one of the world's largest automotive suppliers. The company designs, develops, and manufactures a broad range of products, including brake systems, electric motors, and lamps. Also, the company is the worldwide market leader in anti-lock braking systems (ABS), producing 20,000 such systems a day. Because these ABS are computerized, ITT Automotive actually ships 30% more computers daily than does Compaq!

What pricing approach does ITT Automotive use for the ABS? The pricing process starts when one of ITT's customers, say, Mercedes-Benz, sends an invitation to bid. The market for brake systems is so competitive that very little variance exists in the prices companies can ask (bid). ITT then forms a target-costing group that is charged with determining whether the price and costs allow for enough of a profit margin. This group is made up of engineers, cost accountants, and sales personnel. Factors considered in determining the feasibility of earning the desired target profit margin include competitor pricing, inflation rates, interest rates, and potential cost reductions during both the design (target costing) and production stages (kaizen costing) of the ABS product life. ITT purchases many of the component parts that make up the ABS. Thus, the target-costing group works closely with suppliers. After making product and process design improvements and receiving commitments from suppliers, the company has the cost information needed for deciding the price for the bid.

The target-costing system has worked well at ITT Automotive. The company's bid for the ABS resulted in Mercedes-Benz U.S. International selecting ITT Automotive as the developer and supplier of ABS for the automaker's M-Class All-Activity Vehicle.

TARGET COSTING AND COST-PLUS PRICING COMPARED

Objective 8
Use target costing to decide whether to add a new product.

Successful companies understand the market in which they operate and use the most appropriate pricing approach. To see how target costing and cost-plus pricing can lead to different decisions, suppose that ITT Automotive receives an invitation to bid from Ford on the ABS to be used in a new model car.

Assume the following data apply:

- The specifications contained in Ford's invitation lead to an estimated current manufacturing cost (component parts, direct labor, and manufacturing overhead) of $154.
- ITT Automotive had a desired gross margin rate of 30% on sales, which means that actual cost should make up 70% of the price.
- Highly competitive market conditions exist and have established a sales price of $200 per unit.

BUSINESS FIRST
Target Costing, ABC, and the Role of Management Accounting

Many companies use target costing together with an activity-based costing (ABC) system. Target costing requires a company to first determine what a customer will pay for a product and then work backwards to design the product and production process that will generate a desired level of profit. ABC provides data on the costs of the various activities needed to produce the product. Knowing the costs of activities allows product and production process designers to predict the effects of their designs on the product's cost. Target costing essentially takes activity-based costs and uses them for strategic product decisions.

For example, Culp, Inc., a North Carolina textile manufacturer, uses target costing and ABC to elevate cost management into one of the most strategically important areas of the firm. Culp found that 80% of its product costs are predetermined at the design stage, but earlier cost control efforts had focused only on the other 20%. By shifting cost management efforts to the design stage and getting accurate costs of the various activities involved in production, cost management at Culp evolved into a process of cutting costs when a product is being designed, not identifying costs that are out of line after the production is complete.

A basic goal of target costing is to reduce costs before they occur. After all, once a company has incurred costs, they cannot be changed. Such a strategy is especially important when product life cycles are short. Because most product life cycles are shrinking, use of target costing is expanding. Target costing focuses on reducing costs in the product design and development

stages—when costs can really be affected. For example, target costing heavily influenced DaimlerChrysler's design of the low-priced Neon, and Procter & Gamble's CEO credits target costing for helping eliminate costs that could cause managers to price products too high for the market. "The design process is where you can truly leverage (reduce) your costs," according to Ron Gallaway, CFO of Micrus Semiconductors.

What role does management accounting play in target costing? At Micrus, management accountants are responsible for setting final targets for all components and processes. One survey reports that 86% of companies using target costing take data directly from their cost systems to estimate product costs during product design. At Eastman Kodak, management accountants are a vital part of the cross-functional team that implements target costing. This team includes design and manufacturing engineers, procurement, and marketing, as well as management accounting. Peter Zampino, director of research at the Consortium for Advanced Manufacturing–International, agrees: "It's like anything else; if finance doesn't bless the numbers, they won't have the credibility throughout the organization."

Sources: Adapted from R. Banham, "Off Target," *CFO*, May 2000; J. Bohn, "Chrysler Cuts Costs by Nurturing Links with Suppliers," *Automotive Age*, January 17, 1994, p. 18; G. Boer and J. Ettlie, "Target Costing Can Boost Your Bottom Line," *Strategic Finance*, July 1999, pp. 49–52; J. Brausch, "Target Costing for Profit Enhancement," *Management Accounting*, November 1994, pp. 45–49; G. Hoffman, "Future Vision," *Grocery Marketing*, March 1994, p. 6.

If cost-plus pricing were used to bid on the ABS, the bid price would be $154 ÷ .7 = $220. Ford would most likely reject this bid because the market price is only $200. ITT Automotive's pricing approach would lead to a lost opportunity.

Suppose that managers at ITT Automotive recognize that the market conditions dictate a set price of $200. If a target-costing system were used, what would the pricing decision be? The target cost is $140 (that is, $200 × .7), so a required cost reduction of $14 per unit is necessary. The target-costing group would work with product and process engineers and suppliers to determine if the average unit cost could be reduced by $14 over the product's life. Note that it is not necessary to get costs down to the $140 target cost before production begins. The initial unit cost will likely be higher, say, $145. Continuous improvement over the product's life will result in the final $5 of cost reductions. If the managers receive commitments for cost reductions, they will decide to bid $200 per unit. Note that if ITT Automotive accepts the bid, it must carry through with its focus on cost management throughout the life of the product.

Target costing originated in Japan and is a common practice there. However, a growing number of companies now use it worldwide, including DaimlerChrysler, Boeing, Eastman Kodak, Honda of America, Mercedes-Benz, Proctor & Gamble, Caterpillar, and ITT Automotive. Even some hospitals use target costing.

Why the increasing popularity of target costing? With increased global competition in many industries, companies are more and more limited in influencing market prices. Cost management then becomes the key to profitability. Target costing forces managers to focus on costs to achieve the desired profits.

SUMMARY PROBLEM FOR YOUR REVIEW

PROBLEM

Custom Graphics is a Chicago printing company that bids on a wide variety of design and printing jobs. The owner of the company, Janet Solomon, prepares the bids for most jobs. Her cost budget for 20X1 follows.

Materials		$ 350,000
Labor		250,000
Overhead		
Variable	$300,000	
Fixed	150,000	450,000
Total production cost of jobs		1,050,000
Selling and administrative expenses*		
Variable	$ 75,000	
Fixed	125,000	200,000
Total costs		$ 1,250,000

*These expenses include costs of all value chain functions other than production.

Solomon has a target profit of $250,000 for 20X1.

Compute the average target markup percentage for setting prices as a percentage of

Required

1. Materials plus labor
2. Variable production cost of jobs (assume labor is a variable-cost resource)
3. Total production cost of jobs
4. All variable costs
5. All costs

SOLUTION

The purpose of this problem is to emphasize that many different approaches to pricing might be used that, properly employed, would achieve the same target selling prices. To achieve $250,000 of profit, the desired revenue for 20X1 is $1,250,000 + $250,000 = $1,500,000. The target markup percentages are

1. Percent of materials and labor $= \dfrac{(\$1,500,000 - \$600,000)}{(\$600,000)} = 150\%$

2. Percent of variable production costs of jobs $= \dfrac{(\$1,500,000 - \$900,000)}{(\$900,000)} = 66.7\%$

3. Percent of total production cost of jobs $= \dfrac{(\$1,500,000 - \$1,050,000)}{(\$1,050,000)} = 42.9\%$

4. Percent of all variable costs $= \dfrac{(\$1,500,000 - \$975,000)}{(\$975,000)} = 53.8\%$

5. Percent of all costs $= \dfrac{(\$1,500,000 - \$1,250,000)}{(\$1,250,000)} = 20\%$

Highlights to Remember

Discriminate between relevant and irrelevant information for making decisions. To be relevant to a particular decision, a cost (or revenue) must meet two criteria: (1) It must be an expected future cost (or revenue), and (2) it must have an element of difference among the alternative courses of action.

Use the decision process to make business decisions. All managers make business decisions based on some decision process. The best processes help decision making by focusing the manager's attention on relevant information.

Decide to accept or reject a special order using the contribution margin technique. Decisions to accept or reject a special sales order should use the contribution margin technique and focus on the additional revenues and additional costs of the order.

Decide to add or delete a product line using relevant information. Relevant information also plays an important role in decisions about adding or deleting products, services, or departments. Decisions on whether to delete a department or product line require analysis of the revenues forgone and the costs saved from the deletion.

Compute a measure of product profitability when production is constrained by a scarce resource. When production is constrained by a limiting resource, the key to obtaining the maximum profit from a given capacity is to obtain the greatest possible contribution to profit per unit of the limiting or scarce resource.

Discuss the factors that influence pricing decisions in practice. Market conditions, the law, customers, competitors, and costs influence pricing decisions. The degree that management actions can affect price and cost determines the most effective approach to use for pricing and cost management purposes.

Compute a target sales price by various approaches, and compare the advantages and disadvantages of these approaches. Companies use cost-plus pricing for products when management actions can influence the market price. They can add profit markups to a variety of cost bases including variable manufacturing costs, all variable costs, full manufacturing costs, or all costs. The contribution margin approach to pricing has the advantage of providing detailed cost behavior information that is consistent with cost-volume-profit analysis.

Use target costing to decide whether to add a new product. When market conditions are such that management cannot influence prices, companies must focus on cost control and reduction. They use target costing primarily for new products, especially during the design phase of the value chain. They deduct a desired target margin from the market-established price to determine the target cost. Cost management then focuses on controlling and reducing costs over the product's life cycle.

Understand how relevant information is used when making marketing decisions. Accountants and managers must have a thorough understanding of relevant information, especially costs, when making marketing decisions. Each of the marketing-related decision situations discussed in this chapter (special sales order; adding or deleting a product, service, or department; product emphasis when resources constrain capacity; and pricing) involve determining revenue and cost information that is relevant. The accountant's role in decision making is primarily that of a technical expert on both financial and managerial analyses. The accountant's responsibility is to help the manager use relevant data as guidance for decisions.

Accounting Vocabulary

avoidable costs, p. 190

common costs, p. 190

decision model, p. 183

discriminatory pricing, p. 197

full cost, p. 199

fully allocated cost, p. 199

imperfect competition, p. 195

inventory turnover, p. 193

kaizen costing, p. 205

limiting factor, p. 193

marginal cost, p. 194

marginal revenue, p. 194

markup, p. 198

perfect competition, p. 194

predatory pricing, p. 197

price elasticity, p. 196

relevant information, p. 182

scarce resource, p. 193

target costing, p. 203

unavoidable costs, p. 190

value engineering, p. 205

Fundamental Assignment Material

5-A1 Special Order

Consider the following details of the income statement of the Manteray Pen Company (MPC) for the year ended December 31, 20X1.

Sales	$10,000,000
Less cost of goods sold	6,000,000
Gross margin or gross profit	$ 4,000,000
Less selling and administrative expenses	3,300,000
Operating income	$ 700,000

MPC's fixed manufacturing costs were $2.4 million and its fixed selling and administrative costs were $2.5 million. Sales commissions of 3% of sales are included in selling and administrative expenses.

The division had sold 2 million pens. Near the end of the year, Pizza Hut offered to buy 150,000 pens on a special order. To fill the order, a special Pizza Hut logo would have to be added to each pen. Pizza Hut intended to use the pens in special promotions in an eastern city during early 20X2.

Even though MPC had some idle plant capacity, the president rejected the Pizza Hut offer of $660,000 for the 150,000 pens. He said

> *The Pizza Hut offer is too low. We'd avoid paying sales commissions, but we'd have to incur an extra cost of $.20 per pen to add the logo. If MPC sells below its regular selling prices, it will begin a chain reaction of competitors' price cutting and of customers wanting special deals. I believe in pricing at no lower than 8% above our full costs of $9,300,000 ÷ 2,000,000 units = $4.65 per unit plus the extra $.20 per pen less the savings in commissions.*

Required

1. Using the contribution margin technique, prepare an analysis similar to that in Exhibit 5-3, page 186. Use four columns: without the special order, the effect of the special order (total and per unit), and totals with the special order.
2. By what percentage would operating income increase or decrease if the order had been accepted? Do you agree with the president's decision? Why?

5-A2 Choice of Products

The Skill Craft Appliance Company has two products: a plain mixer and a fancy mixer. The plain mixer sells for $64 and has a variable cost of $48. The fancy mixer sells for $100 and has a variable cost of $70.

Required

1. Compute contribution margins and contribution-margin ratios for plain and fancy mixers.
2. The demand is for more units than the company can produce. There are only 20,000 machine-hours of manufacturing capacity available. Two plain mixers can be produced in the same average time (1 hour) needed to produce one fancy mixer. Compute the total contribution margin for 20,000 hours for plain mixers only and for fancy mixers only.
3. Use two or three sentences to state the major lesson of this problem.

5-A3 Formulas for Pricing

Randy Azarski, a building contractor, constructs houses in tracts, often building as many as 20 homes simultaneously. Azarski has budgeted costs for an expected number of houses in 20X2 as follows.

Direct materials	$3,500,000
Direct labor	1,000,000
Job construction overhead	1,500,000
Cost of jobs	$6,000,000
Selling and administrative costs	1,500,000
Total costs	$7,500,000

The job construction overhead includes approximately $600,000 of fixed costs, such as the salaries of supervisors and depreciation on equipment. The selling and administrative costs include $300,000 of variable costs, such as sales commissions and bonuses that depend fundamentally on overall profitability.

Azarski wants an operating income of $1.5 million for 20X2.

Required

Compute the average target markup percentage for setting prices as a percentage of

1. Direct materials plus direct labor
2. The full "cost of jobs"
3. The variable "cost of jobs"
4. The full "cost of jobs" plus selling and administrative costs
5. The variable "cost of jobs" plus variable selling and administrative costs

5-B1 Special Order, Terminology, and Unit Costs

Following is the income statement of Danube Company, a manufacturer of men's blue jeans:

Danube Company
Income Statement for the Year Ended December 31, 20X0

	Total	Per Unit
Sales	$40,000,000	$20.00
Less cost of goods sold	24,000,000	12.00
Gross margin	$16,000,000	$ 8.00
Less selling and administrative expenses	15,000,000	7.50
Operating income	$ 1,000,000	$ .50

Danube had manufactured 2 million pairs of jeans, which had been sold to various clothing wholesalers and department stores. At the start of 20X1, the president, Rosie Valenzuela, died from a stroke. Her son, Ricardo, became the new president. Ricardo had worked for 15 years in the marketing phases of the business. He knew very little about accounting and manufacturing, which were his mother's strengths. Ricardo has several questions for you including inquiries regarding the pricing of special orders.

Required

1. To prepare better answers, you decide to recast the income statement in contribution form. Variable manufacturing cost was $19 million. Variable selling and administrative expenses, which were mostly sales commissions, shipping expenses, and advertising allowances paid to customers based on units sold, were $9 million.

2. Ricardo asks, "I can't understand financial statements until I know the meaning of various terms. In scanning my mother's assorted notes, I found the following pertaining to both total and unit costs: full manufacturing cost, variable cost, full cost, fully allocated cost, gross margin, and contribution margin. Using our data for 20X0, please give me a list of these costs, their total amounts, and their per-unit amounts."

3. "Near the end of 20X0, I brought in a special order from Costco for 100,000 jeans at $17 each. I said I'd accept a flat $20,000 sales commission instead of the usual 6% of selling price, but my mother refused the order. She usually upheld a relatively rigid pricing policy, saying that it was bad business to accept orders that did not at least generate full manufacturing cost plus 80% of full manufacturing cost.

   "That policy bothered me. We had idle capacity. The way I figured, our manufacturing costs would go up by 100,000 × $12 = $1,200,000, but our selling and administrative expenses would go up by only $20,000. That would mean additional operating income of 100,000 × ($17 − $12) minus $20,000, or $500,000 minus $20,000, or $480,000. That's too much money to give up just to maintain a general pricing policy. Was my analysis of the impact on operating income correct? If not, please show me the correct additional operating income."

4. After receiving the explanations offered in requirements 2 and 3, Ricardo said, "Forget that I had the Costco order. I had an even bigger order from Lands' End. It was for 500,000 units and would have filled the plant completely. I told my mother I'd settle for no commission. There would have been no selling and administrative costs whatsoever because Lands' End would pay for the shipping and would not get any advertising allowances.

   "Lands' End offered $9.20 per unit. Our fixed manufacturing costs would have been spread over 2.5 million instead of 2 million units. Wouldn't it have been advantageous to accept the offer? Our old fixed manufacturing costs were $2.50 per unit. The added volume would reduce that cost more than our loss on our variable costs per unit.

   "Am I correct? What would have been the impact on total operating income if we had accepted the order?"

5-B2 Unit Costs and Capacity

Fargo Manufacturing Company produces two industrial solvents for which the following data have been tabulated. Fixed manufacturing cost is applied to products at a rate of $1.00 per machine hour.

Per Unit	XY-7	BD-4
Selling price	$6.00	$4.00
Variable manufacturing costs	3.00	1.50
Fixed manufacturing cost	.80	.20
Variable selling cost	2.00	2.00

The sales manager has had a $160,000 increase in her budget allotment for advertising and wants to apply the money on the most profitable product. The solvents are not substitutes for one another in the eyes of the company's customers.

Required

1. How many machine-hours does it take to produce one XY-7? To produce one BD-4? (*Hint:* Focus on applied fixed manufacturing cost.)

2. Suppose Fargo has only 100,000 machine-hours that can be made available to produce XY-7 and BD-4. If the potential increase in sales units for either product resulting from advertising is far in excess of these production capabilities, which product should be produced and advertised and what is the estimated increase in contribution margin earned?

5-B3 Dropping a Product Line

Hambley's Toy Store is on Regent Street in London. It has a magic department near the main door. Suppose that management is considering dropping the magic department, which has consistently shown an operating loss. The predicted income statements, in thousands of pounds (£), follow (for ease of analysis, only three product lines are shown):

	Total	General Merchandise	Electronic Products	Magic Department
Sales	£6,000	£5,000	£400	£600
Variable expenses	4,090	3,500	200	390
Contribution margin	£1,910 (32%)	£1,500 (30%)	£200 (50%)	£210 (35%)
Fixed expenses (compensation, depreciation, property taxes, insurance, etc.)	1,110	750	50	310
Operating income	£ 800	£ 750	£150	£(100)

The £310,000 of magic department fixed expenses include the compensation of employees of £100,000. These employees will be released if the magic department is abandoned. All of the magic department's equipment is fully depreciated, so none of the £310,000 pertains to such items. Furthermore, disposal values of equipment will be exactly offset by the costs of removal and remodeling.

If the magic department is dropped, the manager will use the vacated space for either more general merchandise or more electronic products. The expansion of general merchandise would not entail hiring any additional salaried help, but more electronic products would require an additional person at an annual cost of £25,000. The manager thinks that sales of general merchandise would increase by £300,000; electronic products, by £200,000. The manager's modest predictions are partially based on the fact that she thinks the magic department has helped lure customers to the store and thus improved overall sales. If the magic department is closed, that lure would be gone.

Required

Should the magic department be closed? Explain, showing computations.

Additional Assignment Material

QUESTIONS

5-1. "The distinction between precision and relevance should be kept in mind." Explain.

5-2. Distinguish between the quantitative and qualitative aspects of decisions.

5-3. Describe the accountant's role in decision making.

5-4. "Any future cost is relevant." Do you agree? Explain.

5-5. Why are historical or past data irrelevant to special decisions?

5-6. Describe the role of past or historical costs in the decision process. That is, how do these costs relate to the prediction method and the decision model?

5-7. "There is a commonality of approach to various special decisions." Explain.

5-8. "In relevant-cost analysis, beware of unit costs." Explain.

5-9. "The key to decisions to delete a product or department is identifying avoidable costs." Do you agree? Explain.

5-10. "Avoidable costs are variable costs." Do you agree? Explain.

5-11. Give four examples of limiting or scarce factors.

5-12. Why are customers one of the factors influencing pricing decisions?

5-13. What is target cost per unit?

5-14. What is value engineering?

5-15. What is kaizen costing?

5-16. "In target costing, prices determine costs rather than vice versa." Explain.

5-17. If a target-costing system is used and the existing cost cannot be reduced to the target cost through cost reductions, management should discontinue producing and selling the product. Do you agree? Explain.

5-18. "Basing pricing on only the variable costs of a job results in suicidal underpricing." Do you agree? Why?

5-19. Provide three examples of pricing decisions other than the special order.

5-20. List three popular markup formulas for pricing.

5-21. Describe two long-run effects that may lead to managers rejecting opportunities to cut prices and obtain increases in short-run profits.

5-22. Give two reasons why full costs are far more widely used than variable costs for guiding pricing.

5-23. Why do most executives use both full-cost and variable-cost information for pricing decisions?

COGNITIVE EXERCISES

5-24 Fixed Costs and the Sales Function
Many sales managers have a good intuitive understanding of costs, but they often are imprecise in how they describe the costs. For example, one manager said the following: "Increasing sales will decrease fixed costs because it spreads them over more units." Do you agree? Explain.

5-25 The Economics of the Pricing Decision
Economic theory states that managers should set price equal to marginal cost in perfect competition. Accountants use variable cost to approximate marginal costs. Compare and contrast marginal cost and variable cost, and explain whether using variable costs as an approximation for marginal cost is appropriate for making pricing decisions.

5-26 Pricing Decisions and the Law
Managers should base pricing decisions on both cost and market factors. In addition, they must also consider legal issues. Describe the influence that the law has on pricing decisions.

5-27 Target Costing and the Value Chain
According to Keith Hallin, senior manager of finance for decision support initiatives at Boeing Commercial Airplane Group, reaching target costs is a challenge for the company's entire value chain. Explain how managers of the various value chain functions at Boeing might be involved in the target costing process.

EXERCISES

5-28 Pinpointing Relevant Costs
Today you are planning to see a motion picture and you can attend either of two theaters. You have only a small budget for entertainment, so prices are important. You have attended both theaters recently. One charged $6 for admission; the other charged $7. You habitually buy popcorn in the theater—each theater charges $2. The motion pictures now being shown are equally attractive to you, but you are virtually certain that you will never see the picture that you reject today.

Identify the relevant costs. Explain your answer.

5-29 Information and Decisions
Suppose the historical costs for the manufacture of a calculator by Texas Instruments were as follows: direct materials, $4.60 per unit; direct labor, $3.00 per unit. Management is trying to decide whether to replace some materials with different materials. The replacement should cut material costs by 5% per unit. However, direct-labor time will increase by 5% per unit. Moreover, direct-labor rates will be affected by a recent 10% wage increase.

Prepare an exhibit like Exhibit 5-1 (p. 184), showing where and how the data about direct material and direct labor fit in the decision process.

Required

5-30 Identification of Relevant Costs
Paul and Paula Petroceli were trying to decide whether to go to the symphony or to the baseball game. They already have two nonrefundable tickets to "Pops Night at the Symphony" that cost $40 each. This is the only concert of the season they considered attending because it is the only one with the type of music they enjoy. The baseball game is the last one of the season, and it will decide the league championship. They can purchase tickets for $20 each.

The Petrocelis will drive 50 miles round-trip to either event. Variable costs for operating their auto are $.14 per mile, and fixed costs average $.13 per mile for the 18,000 miles they drive annually. Parking at the symphony is free, but it costs $6 at the baseball game.

To attend either event, Paul and Paula will hire a baby-sitter at $4 per hour. They expect to be gone 5 hours to attend the baseball game but only 4 hours to attend the symphony.

Compare the cost of attending the baseball game with the cost of attending the symphony. Focus on relevant costs. Compute the difference in cost, and indicate which alternative is more costly to the Petrocelis.

Required

5-31 Special-Order Decision
Belltown Athletic Supply (BAS) makes game jerseys for athletic teams. The F.C. Kitsap soccer club has offered to buy 100 jerseys for the teams in its league for $15 per jersey. The team price for such

CHAPTER 5 RELEVANT INFORMATION AND DECISION MAKING: MARKETING DECISIONS **213** jerseys normally is $18, an 80% markup over BAS's purchase price of $10 per jersey. BAS adds a name and number to each jersey at a variable cost of $2 per jersey. The annual fixed cost of equipment used in the printing process is $6,000, and other fixed costs allocated to jerseys are $2,000. BAS makes about 2,000 jerseys per year, so the fixed cost is $4 per jersey. The equipment is used only for printing jerseys and stands idle 75% of the usable time.

The manager of BAS turned down the offer, saying, "If we sell at $15 and our cost is $16, we lose money on each jersey we sell. We would like to help your league, but we can't afford to lose money on the sale."

Required

1. Compute the amount by which the operating income of BAS would change if the F.C. Kitsap's offer were accepted.

2. Suppose you were the manager of BAS. Would you accept the offer? In addition to considering the quantitative impact computed in requirement 1, list two qualitative considerations that would influence your decision—one qualitative factor supporting acceptance of the offer and one supporting rejection.

5-32 Unit Costs and Total Costs

You are a CPA who belongs to a downtown luncheon club. Annual dues are $120. You use the club solely for lunches, which cost $6 each. You have not used the club much in recent years and you are wondering whether to continue your membership.

Required

1. You are confronted with a variable-cost plus a fixed-cost behavior pattern. Plot each on a graph, where the vertical axis is total cost and the horizontal axis is annual volume in number of lunches. Also plot a third graph that combines the previous two graphs.

2. What is the cost per lunch if you pay for your own lunch once a year? Twelve times a year? Two hundred times a year?

3. Suppose the average price of lunches elsewhere is $10. (a) How many lunches must you have at the luncheon club so that the total costs of the lunches would be the same regardless of where you ate for that number of lunches? (b) Suppose you ate 250 lunches a year at the club. How much would you save in relation to the total costs of eating elsewhere?

5-33 Advertising Expenditures and Nonprofit Organizations

Many colleges and universities have been extensively advertising their services. For example, a university in Philadelphia used a biplane to pull a sign promoting its evening program, and one in Mississippi designed bumper stickers and slogans as well as innovative programs.

Suppose Wilton College charges a comprehensive annual fee of $14,000 for tuition, room, and board, and it has capacity for 2,500 students. The admissions department predicts enrollment of 2,000 students for 20X1. Costs per student for the 20X1 academic year are

	Variable	Fixed	Total
Educational programs	$4,000	$4,200	$8,200
Room	1,300	2,200	3,500
Board	2,600	600	3,200
	$7,900	$7,000*	$14,900

*Based on 2,000 to 2,500 students for the year.

The assistant director of admissions has proposed a two-month advertising campaign, however, using radio and television advertisements together with an extensive direct mailing of brochures.

Required

1. Suppose the advertising campaign will cost $1.83 million. What is the minimum number of additional students the campaign must attract to make the campaign break even?

2. Suppose the admissions department predicts that the campaign will attract 350 additional students. What is the most Wilton should pay for the campaign and still break even?

3. Suppose a three-month (instead of two-month) campaign will attract 450 instead of 350 additional students. What is the most Wilton should pay for the one-month extension of the campaign and still break even?

5-34 Variety of Cost Terms
Consider the following data.

Variable selling and administrative costs per unit	$ 4.00
Total fixed selling and administrative costs	$2,900,000
Total fixed manufacturing costs	$3,000,000
Variable manufacturing costs per unit	$ 9.00
Units produced and sold	500,000

Required

1. Compute the following per unit of product: (a) total variable costs, (b) full manufacturing, (c) full cost.
2. Give a synonym for full cost.

5-35 Profit per Unit of Space

1. Several successful chains of warehouse stores such as Costco and Sam's Club have merchandising policies that differ considerably from those of traditional department stores. Name some characteristics of these warehouse stores that have contributed to their success.
2. Food chains such as Safeway have typically regarded approximately 20% of selling price as an average target gross profit on canned goods and similar grocery items. What are the limitations of such an approach? Be specific.

5-36 Deletion of Product Line
Zurich American School is an international private elementary school. In addition to regular classes, after-school care is provided between 3:00 P.M. and 6:00 P.M. at SF 12 per child per hour. Financial results for the after-school care for a representative month are

Revenue, 600 hours @ SF 12 per hour		SF 7,200
Less		
Teacher salaries	SF 5,200	
Supplies	800	
Depreciation	1,300	
Sanitary engineering	100	
Other fixed costs	200	7,600
Operating income (loss)		SF (400)

The director of Zurich American School is considering discontinuing the after-school care services because it is not fair to the other students to subsidize the after-school care program. He thinks that eliminating the program will free up SF 400 a month to support regular classes.

Required

1. Compute the financial impact on Zurich American School from discontinuing the after-school care program.
2. List three qualitative factors that would influence your decision.

5-37 Acceptance of Low Bid
The Velasquez Company, a maker of a variety of metal and plastic products, is in the midst of a business downturn and is saddled with many idle facilities. Columbia Health Care has approached Velasquez to produce 300,000 nonslide serving trays. Columbia will pay $1.30 each.

Velasquez predicts that its variable costs will be $1.40 each. Its fixed costs, which had been averaging $1 per unit on a variety of other products, will now be spread over twice as much volume, however. The president commented, "Sure we'll lose $.10 each on the variable costs, but we'll gain $.50 per unit by spreading our fixed costs. Therefore, we should take the offer, because it represents an advantage of $.40 per unit."

Required

Suppose the regular business had a current volume of 300,000 units, sales of $600,000, variable costs of $420,000, and fixed costs of $300,000. Do you agree with the president? Why?

5-38 Pricing by Auto Dealer
Many automobile dealers have an operating pattern similar to that of Austin Motors, a dealer in Texas. Each month, Austin initially aims at a unit volume quota that approximates a break-even point. Until the break-even point is reached, Austin has a policy of relatively lofty pricing, whereby

the "minimum deal" must contain a sufficiently high markup to ensure a contribution to profit of no less than $400. After the break-even point is attained, Austin tends to quote lower prices for the remainder of the month.

Required

What is your opinion of this policy? As a prospective customer, how would you react to this policy?

5-39 Pricing to Maximize Contribution

Reynolds Company produces and sells picture frames. One particular frame for 8 × 10 photos was an instant success in the market, but recently competitors have come out with comparable frames. Reynolds has been charging $12 wholesale for the frames, and sales have fallen from 10,000 units last year to 7,000 units this year. The product manager in charge of this frame is considering lowering the price to $10 per frame. He believes sales will rebound to 10,000 units at the lower price, but they will fall to 6,000 units at the $12 price. The unit variable cost of producing and selling the frames is $6, and $40,000 of fixed cost is assigned to the frames.

Required

1. Assuming that the only prices under consideration are $10 and $12 per frame, which price will lead to the largest profit for Reynolds? Explain why.
2. What subjective considerations might affect your pricing decision?

5-40 Target Selling Prices

Consider the following data from Blackmar Company's budgeted income statement (in thousands of dollars).

Target sales	$60,000
Variable costs	
Manufacturing	30,000
Selling and administrative	6,000
Total variable costs	36,000
Fixed costs	
Manufacturing	8,000
Selling and administrative	6,000
Total fixed costs	14,000
Total of all costs	50,000
Operating income	$10,000

Required

Compute the following markup formulas that would be used for obtaining the same target sales as a percentage of (1) total variable costs, (2) full costs, (3) variable manufacturing costs.

5-41 Competitive Bids

Rimmer, Coles, and Diaz, a CPA firm, is preparing to bid for a consulting job. Although Alice Rimmer will use her judgment about the market in finalizing the bid, she has asked you to prepare a cost analysis to help in the bidding. You have estimated the costs for the consulting job to be

Materials and supplies, at cost	$ 30,000
Hourly pay for consultants, 2,000 hours @ $35 per hour	70,000
Fringe benefits for consultants, 2,000 hours @ $12 per hour	24,000
Total variable costs	124,000
Fixed costs allocated to the job	
Based on labor, 2,000 hours @ $10 per hour	20,000
Based on materials and supplies, 80% of 30,000	24,000
Total cost	$168,000

Of the $44,000 allocated fixed costs, $35,000 will be incurred even if the job is not undertaken.

Alice normally bids jobs at the sum of (1) 150% of the estimated materials and supplies cost and (2) $80 per estimated labor hour.

Required

1. Prepare a bid using the normal formula.
2. Prepare a minimum bid equal to the additional costs expected to be incurred to complete the job.
3. Prepare a bid that will cover full costs plus a markup for profit equal to 20% of full cost.

5-42 Target Costing

Quality Corporation believes that there is a market for a portable electronic toothbrush that can be easily carried by business travelers. Quality's market research department has surveyed the features and prices of electronic brushes currently on the market. Based on this research, Quality believes that $65 would be about the right price. At this price, marketing believes that about 80,000 new portable brushes can be sold annually. It will cost about $1,000,000 to design and develop the portable brush. Quality has a target profit of 20% of sales.

Required

Determine the total and unit target cost to manufacture, sell, distribute, and service each portable brush.

5-43 Target Costing

Best Cost Corporation has an aggressive R&D program and uses target costing to aid in the final decision to release new products to production. A new product is being evaluated. Market research has surveyed the potential market for this product and believes that its unique features will generate a total demand of 50,000 units at an average price of $230. Design and production engineering departments have performed a value analysis of the product and have determined that the total cost for the various value-chain functions using the existing process technology are as follows:

VALUE CHAIN FUNCTION	TOTAL COST OVER PRODUCT LIFE
Research and Development	$ 1,500,000
Design	750,000
Manufacturing	5,000,000
Marketing	800,000
Distribution	1,400,000
Customer Service	750,000
Total Cost over Product Life	$10,200,000

Management has a target profit percentage of 20% of sales. Production engineering indicates that new process technology can reduce the manufacturing cost by 40%, but it will cost $1,000,000.

Required

1. Assuming the existing process technology is used, should the new product be released to production? Explain.

2. Assuming the new process technology is purchased, should the new product be released to production? Explain.

PROBLEMS

5-44 Pricing, Ethics, and the Law

Great Lakes Pharmaceuticals, Inc. (GLPI), produces both prescription and over-the-counter medications. In January GLPI introduced a new prescription drug, Capestan, to relieve the pain of arthritis. The company spent more than $50 million over the last five years developing the drug, and advertising alone during the first year of introduction will exceed $10 million. Production cost for a bottle of 100 tablets is approximately $12. Sales in the first three years are predicted to be 500,000, 750,000, and 1,000,000 bottles, respectively. To achieve these sales, GLPI plans to distribute the medicine through three sources: directly to physicians, through hospital pharmacies, and through retail pharmacies. Initially, the bottles will be given free to physicians to give to patients, hospital pharmacies will pay $25 per bottle, and retail pharmacies will pay $40 per bottle. In the second and third year, the company plans to phase out the free distributions to physicians and move all other customers toward a $50-per-bottle sales price.

Required

Comment on the pricing and promotion policies of GLPI. Pay particular attention to the legal and ethical issues involved.

5-45 Pricing and Contribution Margin Technique

The Concord Trucking Company has the following operating results to date for 20X1:

Operating revenues	$100,000,000
Operating costs	80,000,000
Operating income	$ 20,000,000

A large Boston manufacturer has inquired about whether Concord would be interested in trucking a large order of its parts to Atlanta. Steve Minkler, Operations Manager, investigated the situation and estimated that the "fully allocated" costs of servicing the order would be $40,000. Using his general pricing formula, he quoted a price of $50,000. The manufacturer replied, "We'll give you $37,000, take it or leave it. If you do not want our business, we'll truck it ourselves or go elsewhere."

A cost analyst had recently been conducting studies of how Concord's operating costs tended to behave. She found that $64 million of the $80 million could be characterized as variable costs. Minkler discussed the matter with her and decided that this order would probably generate cost behavior little different from Concord's general operations.

Required

1. Using a contribution margin technique, prepare an analysis for Concord.
2. Should Concord accept the order? Explain.

5-46 Cost Analysis and Pricing

The budget for the Oxford University Printing Company for 20X2 follows:

Sales		£1,100,000
Direct material	£280,000	
Direct labor	320,000	
Overhead	400,000	1,000,000
Net income		£ 100,000

The company typically uses a so-called cost-plus pricing system. Direct-material and direct-labor costs are computed, overhead is added at a rate of 125% of direct labor, and 10% of the total cost is added to obtain the selling price.

Edith Smythe, the sales manager, has placed a £22,000 bid on a particularly large order with a cost of £5,600 direct material and £6,400 direct labor. The customer informs her that she can have the business for £19,800, take it or leave it. If Smythe accepts the order, total sales for 20X2 will be £1,119,800.

Smythe refuses the order, saying, "I sell on a cost-plus basis. It is bad policy to accept orders at below cost. I would lose £200 on the job."

The company's annual fixed overhead is £160,000.

Required

1. What would net income have been with the order? Without the order? Show your computations.
2. Give a short description of a contribution margin technique to pricing that Smythe might follow. Include a stipulation of the pricing formula that Smythe should routinely use if she hopes to obtain a target net income of £100,000.

5-47 Pricing of Education

You are the director of continuing education programs for a state university. Courses for executives are especially popular, and you have developed an extensive menu of one-day and two-day courses that are presented in various locations throughout the state. The performance of these courses for the current fiscal year, excluding the final course, which is scheduled for the next Saturday, is

Tuition revenue	$2,000,000
Costs of courses	800,000
Contribution margin	1,200,000
General administrative expenses	400,000
Operating income	$ 800,000

The costs of the courses include fees for instructors, rentals of classrooms, advertising, and any other items, such as travel, that can be easily and exclusively identified as being caused by a particular course.

The general administrative expenses include your salary, your secretary's compensation, and related expenses, such as a lump-sum payment to the university's central offices as a share of university overhead.

The enrollment for your final course of the year is 30 students, who have paid $200 each. Two days before the course is to begin, a city manager telephones your office. "Do you offer discounts to nonprofit institutions?" he asks. "If so, we'll send 10 managers. But our budget will not justify our spending more than $100 per person." The extra cost of including these 10 managers would entail lunches at $20 each and course materials at $40 each.

Required

1. Prepare a tabulation of the performance for the full year including the final course. Assume that the costs of the final course for the 30 enrollees' instruction, travel, advertising, rental of hotel classroom, lunches, and course materials would be $4,000. Show a tabulation in four columns: before final course, final course with 30 registrants, effect of 10 more registrants, and grand totals.

2. What major considerations would probably influence the pricing policies for these courses? For setting regular university tuition in private universities?

5-48 Videotape Sales and Rental Markets

Is it more profitable to sell your product for $50 or $15? This is a difficult question for many movie studio executives. Consider a movie that cost $60 million to produce and required another $40 million to promote. After its theater release, the studio must determine whether to sell videotapes directly to the public at a wholesale price of about $15 per tape or to sell to video rental store distributors for about $50 per tape. The distributors will then sell to about 14,000 video rental stores in the United States.

Assume that the variable cost to produce and ship one video tape is $2.00.

Required

1. Suppose each video rental store would purchase 10 tapes of this movie. How many tapes would need to be sold directly to customers to make direct sales a more profitable option than sales to video store distributors?

2. How does the cost of producing and promoting the movie affect this decision?

3. Walt Disney Co. elected to sell *The Lion King* directly to consumers, and it sold 30 million copies at an average price of $15.50 per tape. How many tapes would each video rental store have to purchase to provide Disney as much profit as the company received from direct sales? Assume that Disney would receive $50 per tape from the distributors.

5-49 Use of Passenger Jets

In a recent year Continental Air Lines, Inc., filled about 50% of the available seats on its flights, a record about 15 percentage points below the national average.

Continental could have eliminated about 4% of its runs and raised its average load considerably. The improved load factor would have reduced profits, however. Give reasons for or against this elimination. What factors should influence an airline's scheduling policies?

When you answer this question, suppose that Continental had a basic package of 3,000 flights per month, with an average of 100 seats available per flight. Also suppose that 52% of the seats were filled at an average ticket price of $200 per flight. Variable costs are about 70% of revenue.

Continental also had a marginal package of 120 flights per month, with an average of 100 seats available per flight. Suppose that only 20% of the seats were filled at an average ticket price of $100 per flight. Variable costs are about 50% of this revenue. Prepare a tabulation of the basic package, marginal package, and total package, showing percentage of seats filled, revenue, variable expenses, and contribution margin.

5-50 Effects of Volume on Operating Income

The Brownell Division of Victoria Sports Company manufactures boomerangs, which are sold to wholesalers and retailers. The division manager has set a target of 250,000 boomerangs for next month's production and sales. The manager, however, has prepared an analysis of the effects on operating income of deviations from the target:

Volume in units	200,000	250,000	300,000
Sales @ $3.00	$600,000	$750,000	$900,000
Full costs @ $2.50	500,000	625,000	750,000
Operating income	$100,000	$125,000	$150,000

The costs have the following characteristics. Variable manufacturing costs are $1.00 per boomerang; variable selling costs are $.20 per boomerang. Fixed manufacturing costs per month are $275,000; fixed selling and administrative costs, $50,000.

Required

1. Prepare a correct analysis of the changes in volume on operating income. Prepare a tabulated set of income statements at levels of 200,000, 250,000, and 300,000 boomerangs. Also show percentages of operating income in relation to sales.

2. Compare your tabulation with the manager's tabulation. Why is the manager's tabulation incorrect?

5-51 Pricing at The Grand Canyon Railway

Suppose a tour guide approached the general manager of The Grand Canyon Railway with a proposal to offer a special guided tour to the agent's clients. The tour would occur 20 times each summer and be part of a larger itinerary that the agent is putting together. The agent presented two options: (1) a special 65-mile tour with the agent's 30 clients as the only passengers on the train, or (2) adding a car to an existing train to accommodate the 30 clients on an already scheduled 65-mile tour.

Under either option Grand Canyon would hire a tour guide for $150 for the trip. Grand Canyon has extra cars in its switching yard, and it would cost $40 to move a car to the main track and hook it up. The extra fuel cost to pull one extra car is $.20 per mile. To run an engine and a passenger car on the trip would cost $2.20 per mile, and an engineer would be paid $400 for the trip.

Depreciation on passenger cars is $5,000 per year, and depreciation on engines is $20,000 per year. Each passenger car and each engine travels about 50,000 miles a year. They are replaced every 8 years.

The agent offered to pay $30 per passenger for the special tour and $15 per passenger for simply adding an extra car.

Required

1. Which of the two options is more profitable to Grand Canyon? Comment on which costs are irrelevant to this decision.

2. Should Grand Canyon accept the proposal for the option you found best in requirement 1? Comment on what costs are relevant for this decision but not for the decision in requirement 1.

5-52 Pricing of Special Order

The Drosselmeier Corporation, located in Munich, makes Christmas nutcrackers and has an annual plant capacity of 2,400 product units. Its predicted operating results (in German marks) for the year are:

Production and sales of 2,000 units, total sales	DM 180,000
Manufacturing costs	
Fixed (total)	60,000
Variable (per unit)	26
Selling and administrative expenses	
Fixed (total)	30,000
Variable (per unit)	10

Required

Compute the following, ignoring income taxes:

1. If the company accepts a special order for 300 units at a selling price of DM 40 each, how would the total predicted net income for the year be affected, assuming no effect on regular sales at regular prices?

2. Without decreasing its total net income, what is the lowest unit price for which the Drosselmeier Corporation could sell an additional 100 units not subject to any variable selling and administrative expenses, assuming no effect on regular sales at regular prices?

3. List the numbers given in the problem that are irrelevant (not relevant) in solving requirement 2.

4. Compute the expected annual net income (with no special orders) if plant capacity can be doubled by adding additional facilities at a cost of DM 500,000. Assume that these facilities have an estimated life of five years with no residual scrap value, and that the current unit selling price can be maintained for all sales. Total sales are expected to equal the new plant capacity each year. No changes are expected in variable costs per unit or in total fixed costs except for depreciation.

5-53 Pricing and Confusing Variable and Fixed Costs

Goldwyn Electronics had a fixed factory overhead budget for 20X1 of $10 million. The company planned to make and sell 2 million units of a particular communications device. All variable manufacturing costs per unit were $10. The budgeted income statement contained the following:

Sales	$40,000,000
Manufacturing cost of goods sold	30,000,000
Gross margin	10,000,000
Deduct selling and administrative expenses	4,000,000
Operating income	$ 6,000,000

For simplicity, assume that the actual variable costs per unit and the total fixed costs were exactly as budgeted.

Required

1. Compute Goldwyn's budgeted fixed factory overhead per unit.
2. Near the end of 20X1, a large computer manufacturer offered to buy 100,000 units for $1.2 million on a one-time special order. The president of Goldwyn stated, "The offer is a bad deal. It's foolish to sell below full manufacturing costs per unit. I realize that this order will have only a modest effect on selling and administrative costs. They will increase by a $10,000 fee paid to our sales agent." Compute the effect on operating income if the offer is accepted.
3. What factors should the president of Goldwyn consider before finally deciding whether to accept the offer?
4. Suppose the original budget for fixed manufacturing costs was $10 million, but budgeted units of product were 1 million. How would your answers to requirements 1 and 2 change? Be specific.

5-54 Demand Analysis

Ross Manufacturing Limited produces and sells one product, a three-foot Canadian flag. During 20X1, the company manufactured and sold 50,000 flags at $24 each. Existing production capacity is 60,000 flags per year.

In formulating the 20X2 budget, management is faced with a number of decisions concerning product pricing and output. The following information is available:

1. A market survey shows that the sales volume depends on the selling price. For each $1 drop in selling price, sales volume would increase by 10,000 flags.
2. The company's expected cost structure for 20X2 is as follows.
   a. Fixed cost (regardless of production or sales activities), $360,000
   b. Variable costs per flag (including production, selling, and administrative expenses), $15
3. To increase annual capacity from the present 60,000 to 90,000 flags, additional investment for plant, building, equipment, and the like of $200,000 would be necessary. The estimated average life of the additional investment would be 10 years, so the fixed costs would increase by an average of $20,000 per year. (Expansion of less than 30,000 additional units of capacity would cost only slightly less than $200,000.)

Required

Indicate, with reasons, what the level of production and the selling price should be for the coming year. Also indicate whether the company should approve the plant expansion. Show your calculations. Ignore income tax considerations and the time value of money.

5-55 Choice of Products

Florida Fashions sells both designer and moderately priced women's wear in Tampa. Profits have been volatile. Top management is trying to decide which product line to drop. Accountants have reported the following data:

	Per Item	
	Designer	*Moderately Priced*
Average selling price	$240	$140
Average variable expenses	120	75
Average contribution margin	$120	$ 65
Average contribution-margin percentage	50%	46%

The store has 8,000 square feet of floor space. If moderately priced goods are sold exclusively, 400 items can be displayed. If designer goods are sold exclusively, only 300 items can be displayed. Moreover, the rate of sale (turnover) of the designer items will be two-thirds the rate of moderately priced goods.

1. Prepare an analysis to show which product to drop.
2. What other considerations might affect your decision in requirement 1?

5-56 Analysis of Unit Costs

Sunlight Company manufactures small appliances such as electric can openers, toasters, food mixers, and irons. The peak season is at hand, and the president is trying to decide whether to produce more of the company's standard line of can openers or its premium line that includes a built-in knife sharpener, a better finish, and a higher-quality motor. The unit data follow:

	Product	
	Standard	*Premium*
Selling price	$26	$34
Direct material	$ 8	$12
Direct labor	2	1
Variable factory overhead	2	3
Fixed factory overhead	6	9
Total cost of goods sold	$18	$25
Gross profit per unit	$ 8	$ 9

The sales outlook is very encouraging. The plant could operate at full capacity by producing either product or both products. Both the standard and the premium products are processed through the same departments. Selling and administrative costs will not be affected by this decision, so they may be ignored.

Many of the parts are produced on automatic machinery. The factory overhead is allocated to products by developing separate rates per machine-hour for variable and fixed overhead. For example, the total fixed overhead is divided by the total machine-hours to get a rate per hour. Thus the amount of overhead allocated to products is dependent on the number of machine-hours used by the product. It takes one hour of machine time to produce one unit of the standard product.

Direct labor may not be proportionate with overhead because many workers operate two or more machines simultaneously.

Which product should be produced? If more than one should be produced, indicate the proportions of each. Show computations. Explain your answers briefly.

5-57 Use of Available Facilities

The Oahu Audio Company manufactures electronic subcomponents that can be sold directly or can be processed further into "plug-in" assemblies for a variety of intricate electronic equipment. The entire output of subcomponents can be sold at a market price of $2.20 per unit. The plug-in assemblies have been generating a sales price of $5.70 for three years, but the price has recently fallen to $5.30 on assorted orders.

Janet Oh, the vice president of marketing, has analyzed the markets and the costs. She thinks that production of plug-in assemblies should be dropped whenever the price falls below $4.70 per unit. However, at the current price of $5.30, the total available capacity should currently be devoted to producing plug-in assemblies. She has cited the data in Exhibit 5-12.

Direct-materials and direct-labor costs are variable. The total overhead is fixed; it is allocated to units produced by predicting the total overhead for the coming year and dividing this total by the total hours of capacity available.

The total hours of capacity available are 600,000. It takes 1 hour to make 60 subcomponents and 2 hours of additional processing and testing to make 60 plug-in assemblies.

1. If the price of plug-in assemblies for the coming year is to be $5.30, should sales of sub-components be dropped and all facilities devoted to the production of plug-in assemblies? Show computations.
2. Prepare a report for the vice president of marketing to show the lowest possible price for plug-in assemblies that would be acceptable.
3. Suppose 40% of the manufacturing overhead is variable with respect to processing and testing time. Repeat requirements 1 and 2. Do your answers change? If so, how?

5-58 Target Costing

Knoxville Electrical, Inc., makes small electric motors for a variety of home appliances. Knoxville sells the motors to appliance makers, who assemble and sell the appliances to retail outlets. Although Knoxville makes dozens of different motors, it does not currently make one to be used in garage-door openers. The company's market research department has discovered a market for such a motor.

Exhibit 5-12

Oahu Audio Company

Product Profitability Data

	Subcomponents	
Selling price, after deducting relevant selling costs		$2.20
Direct materials	$1.10	
Direct labor	.30	
Manufacturing overhead	.60	
Cost per unit		2.00
Operating profit		$ .20

	Plug-In Assemblies	
Selling price, after deducting relevant selling costs		$5.30
Transferred-in variable cost for subcomponents	$1.40	
Additional direct materials	1.45	
Direct labor	.45	
Manufacturing overhead	1.20*	
Cost per unit		4.50
Operating profit		$ .80

*For additional processing to make and test plug-in assemblies.

The market research department has indicated that a motor for garage-door openers would likely sell for $23. A similar motor currently being produced has the following manufacturing costs:

Direct materials	$12.00
Direct labor	5.00
Overhead	8.00
Total	$25.00

Knoxville desires a gross margin of 15% of the manufacturing cost.

Required

1. Suppose Knoxville used cost-plus pricing, setting the price 15% above the manufacturing cost. What price would be charged for the motor? Would you produce such a motor if you were a manager at Knoxville? Explain.

2. Suppose Knoxville uses target costing. What price would the company charge for a garage-door-opener motor? What is the highest acceptable manufacturing cost for which Knoxville would be willing to produce the motor?

3. As a user of target costing, what steps would Knoxville managers take to try to make production of this product feasible?

5-59 Target Costing Over Product Life Cycle

Southeast Equipment, Inc., makes a variety of motor-driven products for homes and small businesses. The market research department recently identified power lawn mowers as a potentially lucrative market. As a first entry into this market, Southeast is considering a riding lawn mower that is smaller and less expensive than those of most of the competition. Market research indicates that such a lawn mower would sell for about $995 at retail and $800 wholesale. At that price, Southeast expects life cycle sales as follows:

20X1	1,000
20X2	5,000
20X3	10,000
20X4	10,000
20X5	8,000
20X6	6,000
20X7	4,000

The production department has estimated that the variable cost of production will be $475 per lawn mower, and annual fixed costs will be $900,000 per year for each of the 7 years. Variable selling costs will be $25 per lawn mower and fixed selling costs will be $50,000 per year. In addition, the product development department estimates that $5 million of development costs will be necessary to design the lawn mower and the production process for it.

Required

1. Compute the expected profit over the entire product life cycle of the proposed riding lawn mower.
2. Suppose Southeast expects pretax profits equal to 10% of sales on new products. Would the company undertake production and selling of the riding lawn mower?
3. Southeast Equipment uses a target costing approach to new products. What steps would management take to try to make a profitable product of the riding lawn mower?

CASES

5-60 Use of Capacity

St. Tropez S. A. manufactures several different styles of jewelry cases in southern France. Management estimates that during the second quarter of 20X1 the company will be operating at 80% of normal capacity. Because the company desires a higher utilization of plant capacity, it will consider a special order.

St. Tropez has received special-order inquiries from two companies. The first is from Lyon, Inc., which would like to market a jewelry case similar to one of St. Tropez's cases. The Lyon jewelry case would be marketed under Lyon's own label. Lyon, Inc., has offered St. Tropez FF 67.5 per jewelry case for 20,000 cases to be shipped by July 1, 20X1. The cost data for the St. Tropez jewelry case, which would be similar to the specifications of the Lyon special order, are as follows:

Regular selling price per unit	FF 100
Costs per unit:	
Raw materials	FF 35
Direct labor, .5 hour @ FF 60	30
Overhead, .25 machine hour @ FF 40	10
Total costs	FF 75

According to the specifications provided by Lyon, Inc., the special-order case requires less expensive raw materials, which will cost only FF 32.5 per case. Management has estimated that the remaining costs, labor time, and machine time will be the same as those for the St. Tropez jewelry case.

The second special order was submitted by the Avignon Co. for 7,500 jewelry cases at FF 85 per case. These cases would be marketed under the Avignon label and would have to be shipped by July 1, 20X1. The Avignon jewelry case is different from any jewelry case in the St. Tropez line. Its estimated per-unit costs are as follows:

Raw materials	FF 42.5
Direct labor, .5 hour @ FF 60	30
Overhead, .5 machine hour @ FF 40	20
Total costs	FF 92.5

In addition, St. Tropez will incur FF 15,000 in additional setup costs and will have to purchase a FF 25,000 special device to manufacture these cases; this device will be discarded once the special order is completed.

The St. Tropez manufacturing capabilities are limited by the total machine-hours available. The plant capacity under normal operations is 90,000 machine-hours per year, or 7,500 machine-hours per month. The budgeted fixed overhead for 20X1 amounts to FF 2.16 million, or FF 24 per hour. All manufacturing overhead costs are applied to production on the basis of machine-hours at FF 40 per hour.

St. Tropez will have the entire second quarter to work on the special orders. Management does not expect any repeat sales to be generated from either special order. Company practice precludes St. Tropez from subcontracting any portion of an order when special orders are not expected to generate repeat sales.

Required

Should St. Tropez accept either special order? Justify your answer and show your calculations. (*Hint:* Distinguish between variable and fixed overhead.)

COLLABORATIVE LEARNING EXERCISE

5-61 Understanding Pricing Decisions

Form teams of three to six students. Each team should contact and meet with a manager responsible for pricing in a company in your area. This could be a product manager or brand manager for a large company or a vice president of marketing or sales for a smaller company.

Explore with the manager how his or her company sets prices. Among the questions you might ask are

- How do costs influence your prices? Do you set prices by adding a markup to costs? If so, what measure of costs do you use? How do you determine the appropriate markup?
- How do you adjust prices to meet market competition? How do you measure the effects of price on sales level?
- Do you use target costing? That is, do you find out what a product will sell for and then try to design the product and production process to make a desired profit on the product?
- What is your goal in setting prices? Do you try to maximize revenue, market penetration, contribution margin, gross margin, or some combination of these, or do you have other goals when setting prices?

After each team has its interview, it would be desirable, if time permits, to get together as a class and share your findings. How many different pricing policies did the groups find? Can you explain why policies differ across companies? Are there characteristics of different industries or different management philosophies that explain the different pricing policies?

INTERNET EXERCISE

5-62 Marketing Decisions at Colgate-Palmolive

Managers need information of all types in order to make decisions. Many marketing decisions are strategic—such as setting pricing policies and deciding to add or delete product lines (or even entire business segments). Managers rely on multiple sources to help locate relevant information to support these decisions. Managers must know how to use the information that is available and what weight to assign to the information that is deemed to be useful.

www.prenhall.com/horngren

A firm is not going to give us detailed information about its marketing strategy on its Web site. However, we can view a firm's Web site to look at some of the relevant information that managers might use to help make marketing decisions. Let's look at the Colgate-Palmolive Company to see what information on the site would be relevant for some marketing decisions.

1. Go to the home page of Colgate-Palmolive at http://www.colgatepalmolive.com. Notice that Colgate has a moving heading line—that means that by moving across the heading the user can see snapshots about different topics the firm wants to highlight. Move your cursor to the heading that says "For Investors." Click on "For Investors" and then on the most recent annual report and then on the "Management Letter." In this section, Colgate shares its worldwide strategy. What types of marketing decisions that are discussed in Chapter 5 are part of Colgate's strategy? What does this strategy reveal about the need for relevant information?

2. One area that many companies identify as a key component to strategy is new product development. Visit the Press Room where Colgate highlights its newest products. Based on the information in the press room, when was the last new product news release made? What product was released? Is this a "new" product or is it simply a variation of an existing product?

3. Now look at the products that the firm manufacturers. What format is offered for learning about the products that the firm offers? Look at the laundry products for the North America region. How many detergents does the firm offer? From looking at the information provided, can you tell what is different about the products? Does the Web site provide any information on how or when to use the products? If you had a particular type of stain, would the information provided on the Web site help determine which detergent was best for this problem? Would you want to make a decision about the "best" detergent for a problem, based on the information found on the Web site? Why or why not?

4. The company indicates three other ways that it plans to meet its worldwide strategy. Let's look at the most recent annual report and see how the firm did in each of those areas. Can you tell from a look at the income statement if each of those target areas was addressed? Can any of the areas be identified from financial statement footnotes? Does this appear to be in keeping with the strategy? Is there any information you are unable to determine for the strategy? Is the company improving profitability?

RELEVANT INFORMATION AND DECISION MAKING: PRODUCTION DECISIONS

When you relax with a bottle of Nantucket Nectars juice, you do not consider the various costs that go into producing, selling, and distributing the bottle. But these costs are very important to the managers at Nantucket Nectars.

www.prenhall.com/horngren

Learning Objectives

When you have finished studying this chapter, you should be able to

1. Use opportunity cost to analyze the income effects of a given alternative.

2. Decide whether to make or to buy certain parts or products.

3. Decide whether a joint product should be processed beyond the split-off point.

4. Identify irrelevant information in disposal of obsolete inventory and equipment replacement decisions.

5. Explain how unit costs can be misleading.

6. Discuss how performance measures can affect decision making.

7. Construct absorption and contribution format income statements and identify which is better for decision making.

8. **Understand the relationship between accounting information and decisions in the production stage of the value chain.**

Starting a beverage business can be a complex maze of decisions. Tom First and Tom Scott should know. After graduating from college, they operated a two-person boat service business off Nantucket Island, provisioning and cleaning yachts during the summer. In 1989, the inspiration for a juice drink made with fresh peaches hit. After a bit of experimentation, the self-proclaimed "juice guys" began bottling and selling their nectar drink from their boat. That first summer, they sold 2,000 bottles at $1.00 each. Today, Nantucket Nectars makes 48 different juice blends and sells millions of cases each year. Sales for 2000 topped $60 million.

Getting to this point, however, has been anything *but* smooth sailing. Their early attempts to sell juice to retailers failed. Profits were nonexistent. They sold half the business to an equity partner for $500,000 to venture into distribution, but ended up losing $1 million the first year. Employees stole caseloads of merchandise from the warehouse. And there have been inevitable product disappointments, such as bayberry tea. But the juice guys are quick learners. They got out of distribution, changed their marketing approach, and stopped the flow of red ink.

As the company has grown, it has tackled important production-related decisions. For example, should they build and operate their own bottling facilities? What criteria should be used for developing new products? What's the best approach for tracking and analyzing the growing volume of production, distribution, and sales data?

After examining the cost of building and operating bottling plants, Nantucket Nectars chose to contract with existing beverage co-packers in Rhode Island, Nevada, Florida,

Pennsylvania, and Maryland. This approach gives the company broader distribution options without the capital expenditure and overhead of multiple plants. Its managers scrutinize unit costs associated with new product ideas emerging from the test kitchen to be sure margins are on target. And they meticulously track every detail—from production costs to marketing promotions—through a new computerized Enterprise Resource Planning (ERP) information system from Oracle.

Throughout it all, the juice guys never wavered in their determination to produce a top-quality product and satisfy customers. They readily admit they both failed their first accounting course in college, but they have come to appreciate its relevance in decision making as they've weathered stormy periods and sailed smooth seas.

As with Nantucket Nectars, managers in other companies must make similar production-related decisions. Should Toyota make the tires it mounts on its cars, or should it buy them from suppliers? Should General Mills sell the flour it mills, or should it use the flour to make more breakfast cereal? Should Delta Airlines add routes to use idle airplanes, or should it sell the planes? These decisions all require a good deal of accounting information. But what information will be relevant to each decision? In Chapter 5, we identified relevant information for decisions in the marketing function of the value chain. We now need to determine relevance in the production function. The basic framework for identifying relevant information remains the same for production as it was for marketing. We are still looking only for future costs that differ among alternatives. However, we now expand our analysis by introducing the concepts of opportunity and differential costs.

OPPORTUNITY, OUTLAY, AND DIFFERENTIAL COSTS

differential cost (revenue)
The difference in total cost (revenue) between two alternatives.

Management decision making involves the comparison of two or more alternative courses of action. (Of course, if there were only one alternative, no decision would be necessary.) Suppose a manager has only two alternatives to compare. The key to determining the financial difference between the alternatives is to identify the *differential* costs and revenues. **Differential cost (revenue)** is the difference in total cost (revenue) between two alternatives. For example, consider the decision about which of two machines to purchase. Both machines perform the same function. The differential cost is the difference in the price paid for the machines plus the difference in the costs of operating the machines.

incremental cost Another term for differential cost when one alternative includes all the costs of the other plus some additional costs.

If one alternative includes all the costs of the other plus some additional costs, we often use the term **incremental cost** instead of differential cost. For instance, the incremental costs of increasing production from 1,000 automobiles to 1,200 automobiles per week would be the costs of producing the additional 200 automobiles each week. In the reverse situation, the decline in costs caused by reducing production from 1,200 to 1,000 automobiles per week would be called the *differential* or *incremental savings*.

When there are more than two alternative courses of action, managers often compare one particular action against the entire set of alternatives. For example, General Mills might consider introducing a new cereal, Frosted Rice Flakes. There are many alternatives to introducing Frosted Rice Flakes, including introducing other new cereals, expanding production of existing cereals, or producing noncereal products. Computing the differential costs and revenues for Frosted Rice Flakes with every alternative would be cumbersome. Thus, the General Mills managers might use a different approach.

Introducing Frosted Rice Flakes would entail two types of costs: **outlay costs,** which require a future cash disbursement, and opportunity costs. An **opportunity cost** is the maximum available contribution to profit foregone (or passed up) by using limited resources for a particular purpose. Opportunity costs apply to resources that are already owned or for which the company already has a commitment to purchase. The decision regarding Frosted Rice Flakes will not affect whether the company acquires these resources, only how it uses them. The opportunity cost of such resources depends on the potential uses for the resources, not on the amount paid for them. Why? Because the decision about Frosted Rice Flakes will not affect the amount paid. However, the decision to use the resources to produce Frosted Rice Flakes precludes using them for other alternatives. The amount that would have been gained if the resources had been used in their best alternative use (that is, the best use other than using them to produce Frosted Rice Flakes) becomes the opportunity cost of the resources.

Suppose General Mills has a machine for which it paid $100,000. The machine can be used to produce Frosted Rice Flakes or to increase the production of Wheaties. The contribution margin from the additional Wheaties produced would be $60,000. In addition, the machine could be sold for $50,000. The opportunity cost of the machine when analyzing the Frosted Rice Flakes alternative is $60,000, the larger of the $50,000 or $60,000, the two possible gains that could be achieved using the machine in its alternative uses. The $100,000 paid for the machine is irrelevant.

Now suppose that General Mills will sell the Frosted Rice Flakes for $500,000, and the production and marketing costs (outlay costs), excluding the cost of the machine, are $400,000. The net financial benefit from the Frosted Rice Flakes is $40,000.

Revenues		$500,000
Costs:		
Outlay costs	$400,000	
Opportunity costs	60,000	
Total cost		460,000
Net financial benefit		$ 40,000

General Mills will gain $40,000 more financial benefit using the machine to make Frosted Rice Flakes than it would make using it for the next most profitable alternative.

When considering only two alternatives, a manager might use straightforward differential analysis or an opportunity cost analysis. The two approaches are equivalent. To see this, consider Maria Morales, a certified public accountant employed by a large accounting firm for $60,000 per year. She is considering an alternative use of her time, her most valuable resource. The alternative is to have her own independent accounting practice. A straightforward differential analysis follows.

	Alternatives Under Consideration		
	Remain an Employee	*Open an Independent Practice*	**Difference**
Revenues	$60,000	$200,000	$140,000
Outlay costs (operating expenses)	—	120,000	120,000
Income effects per year	$60,000	$ 80,000	$ 20,000

Maria has revenues of $200,000—quite a bit more than she would have made as an employee of the large firm. However, she also had to pay $120,000 to rent office space,

outlay cost A cost that requires a future cash disbursement.

opportunity cost The maximum available contribution to profit foregone (or passed up) by using limited resources for a particular purpose.

Objective 1
Use opportunity cost to analyze the income effects of a given alternative.

lease equipment, buy advertising, and cover other out-of-pocket expenses. The $80,000 of operating income is $20,000 more than her salary with the firm.

Now if we look in isolation at the alternative of operating an independent practice, essentially comparing it to all alternative uses of Maria's time (which in this case is simply the alternative of working for the large firm), we must consider another cost. Had Maria remained an employee, she would have made $60,000. By starting her own company, Maria will forego this profit. Thus, the $60,000 is an opportunity cost of starting her own business:

		Alternative Chosen: Independent Practice
Revenue		$200,000
Expenses		
Outlay costs (operating expenses)	$120,000	
Opportunity cost of employee salary	60,000	180,000
Income effects per year		$ 20,000

Ponder the two preceding tabulations. Each produces the correct key difference between alternatives, $20,000. The first tabulation does not mention opportunity cost because the economic impacts (in the form of revenues and outlay costs) are individually measured for each of the alternatives (two in this case). We did not exclude either alternative from consideration. The second tabulation mentions opportunity cost because we included the $60,000 annual economic impact of the best excluded alternative as a cost of the chosen alternative. The failure to recognize opportunity cost in the second tabulation will misstate the difference between alternatives.

The major message here is straightforward: Do not overlook opportunity costs. Consider a homeowner who has made the final payment on a home mortgage. While celebrating, the owner says, "It's a wonderful feeling to know that future occupancy is free of any interest cost!" Many owners have similar thoughts. Why? Because no future outlay costs for interest are required. Nevertheless, there is an opportunity cost of continuing to live in the home. After all, an alternative would be to sell the home, place the proceeds in some other investment, and rent an apartment. The owner forgoes the interest in the other investment, so this foregone interest income becomes an opportunity cost of home ownership.

Consider how difficult it is to estimate opportunity costs. There is no sale or purchase to establish an appropriate cost. Further, the opportunity cost depends on the alternatives that are available at a point in time. The same alternatives may not be available at a different time. For example, excess capacity in September does not mean that there will also be excess capacity in October. How might a manager at Mattel, the toy company, estimate the opportunity cost of excess warehouse space in January?

ANSWER

The Mattel manager would know that excess warehouse space is a seasonal phenomenon. There is unlikely to be excess space late in the year as Christmas approaches. Therefore, he or she would look for temporary alternatives, ones that use the space for only a few months. After identifying alternatives, the manager would estimate the value of each. Because most of the alternatives are ones that are never undertaken, estimating their values is a subjective process. The highest valued alternative would establish the opportunity cost of the space.

Managers often must decide whether to produce a product or service within the firm or purchase it from an outside supplier. They apply relevant cost analysis to a variety of such make-or-buy decisions, including:

- Boeing must decide whether to buy or make many of the tools used in assembling 777 airplanes.
- IBM must decide whether to develop its own operating system for a new computer or to buy it from a software vendor.

BASIC MAKE-OR-BUY AND IDLE FACILITIES

A basic make-or-buy question is whether a company should make its own parts to be used in its products or buy them from vendors. Sometimes the answer to this question is based on qualitative factors. For example, some manufacturers always make parts because they want to control quality. Alternatively, some companies always purchase parts to protect long-run relationships with their suppliers. These companies may deliberately buy from vendors even during slack times to avoid difficulties in obtaining needed parts during boom times, when there may well be shortages of materials and workers, but no shortage of sales orders.

What quantitative factors are relevant to the decision of whether to make or buy? The answer, again, depends on the situation. A key factor is whether there are idle facilities. Many companies make parts only when their facilities cannot be used to better advantage.

Assume that the following costs are reported:

General Electric Company
Cost of Making Part No. 900

	Total Cost for 20,000 Units	Cost per Unit
Direct material	$ 20,000	$ 1
Direct labor	80,000	4
Variable factory overhead	40,000	2
Fixed factory overhead	80,000	4
Total costs	$220,000	$11

Another manufacturer offers to sell General Electric (GE) the same part for $10. Should GE make or buy the part?

Although the $11 unit cost shown seemingly indicates that the company should buy, the answer is rarely so obvious. The essential question is the difference in expected future costs between the alternatives. If the $4 fixed overhead per unit consists of costs that will continue regardless of the decision, the entire $4 becomes irrelevant. Examples of such costs include depreciation, property taxes, insurance, and allocated executive salaries.

Again, are only the variable costs relevant? No. Perhaps $20,000 of the fixed costs will be eliminated if the parts are bought instead of made. For example, a supervisor with a $20,000 salary might be released. In other words, fixed costs that may be avoided in the future are relevant.

For the moment, suppose the capacity now used to make parts will become idle if the parts are purchased and the $20,000 supervisor's salary is the only fixed cost that would be eliminated. The relevant computations follow.

	Make		Buy	
	Total	*Per Unit*	*Total*	*Per Unit*
Purchase cost			$200,000	$10
Direct material	$ 20,000	$1		
Direct labor	80,000	4		
Variable factory overhead	40,000	2		
Fixed factory overhead that can be avoided by not making (supervisor's salary)	20,000*	1*	0	0
Total relevant costs	$160,000	$8	$200,000	$10
Difference in favor of making	$ 40,000	$2		

* Note that unavoidable fixed costs of $80,000 − $20,000 = $60,000 are irrelevant. Thus the irrelevant costs per unit are $4 − $1 = $3.

The key to make-or-buy decisions is identifying the additional costs for making (or the costs avoided by buying) a part or subcomponent. Activity analysis, described in Chapter 3, helps identify these costs. Production of a product requires a set of activities. A company with accurate measurements of the costs of its various activities can better estimate the additional costs incurred to produce an item. GE's activities for production of part number 900 were measured by two cost drivers, units of production of $8 per unit and supervision at a $20,000 fixed cost. Sometimes identification and measurement of additional cost drivers, especially nonvolume-related cost drivers, can improve the predictions of the additional cost to produce a part or subcomponent.

MAKE OR BUY AND THE USE OF FACILITIES

Make-or-buy decisions are rarely as simple as the one in our GE example. As we said earlier, the use of facilities is a key to the make-or-buy decision. For simplicity, we assumed that the GE facilities would remain idle if the company chose to buy the product. This means that the opportunity cost of the facilities is zero. Of course, in most cases companies will not leave their facilities idle. Instead, they will often put idle facilities to some other use, and we must consider the financial outcomes of these uses when choosing to make or buy. The value received from the best of these alternative uses is an opportunity cost for the internal production of the parts or subcomponents.

Suppose the released facilities in our example can be used advantageously in some other manufacturing activity (to produce a contribution to profits of, say, $55,000) or can be rented out (say, for $35,000). We now have four alternatives to consider (figures are in thousands):

	Make	**Buy and Leave Facilities Idle**	**Buy and Rent Out Facilities**	**Buy and Use Facilities for Other Products**
Rent revenue	$ —	$ —	$ 35	$ —
Contribution from other products	—	—	—	55
Obtaining of parts	(160)	(200)	(200)	(200)
Net relevant costs	$(160)	$(200)	$(165)	$(145)

The final column indicates that buying the parts and using the vacated facilities for the production of other products would yield the lowest net costs in this case. Using opportunity

Make-or-buy decisions apply to services as well as to products. Companies are increasingly deciding to hire service firms to handle some of their internal operations, an option called outsourcing. According to The Outsourcing Institute, outsourcing is "the strategic use of outside resources to perform activities traditionally handled by internal staff and resources."

Outsourcing has been used for many business functions. The most common items to outsource, ranked by the total percent of outsourcing expenditures, are

Information technology	30%
Human resources	16%
Marketing and sales	14%
Finance	11%
Administration	9%
All others	20%

Although companies can outsource many functions, most of the recent growth in outsourcing has been driven by the Internet. During the 1990s, many companies installed Enterprise Resource Planning (ERP) systems to handle all their computing needs. However, by the beginning of the twenty-first century many companies were realizing that the huge investments necessitated by ERP systems may not be needed. The required services could be purchased over the Internet without investing in the systems' purchase and development costs. The formerly expensive process of communication with the service providers had become essentially free via the Internet. A new group of computing service providers—called Application Service Providers (ASP)—arose to provide outsourcing opportunities for a variety of computing applications.

A prime example of using an ASP is Owens Corning's outsourcing of its travel and expense (T&E) reporting system. By hiring VIN.net International, a specialist in automated expense management, Owens Corning has a state-of-the-art T&E system without a huge up-front investment. The Owens Corning employees can focus on their mission-critical activities, without worrying about a peripheral management function such as T&E management.

The company most identified with outsourcing is Sun Microsystems. Long before most companies seriously considered outsourcing large parts of their operations, Sun outsourced everything except its core technologies. Sun focuses on hardware and software design and outsources nearly everything else. Its employees do not actually produce any of the products that bear the company's name.

The driving forces behind most outsourcing decisions are access to technology and cost savings. As the complexity of data processing and especially networking has grown, companies have found it harder and harder to keep current with the technology. Instead of investing huge sums in personnel and equipment and diverting attention from the value-added activities of their own businesses, many firms have found outsourcing financially attractive. The big stumbling block to outsourcing has been subjective factors, such as control. To make outsourcing attractive, the services must be reliable, be available when needed, and be flexible enough to adapt to changing conditions. Companies that have successful outsourcing arrangements have been careful to include the subjective factors in their decisions.

Outsourcing has become so profitable that 77% of Fortune 500 companies outsource some aspect of their business support services. The total value of outsourcing contracts in the United States is more than $10 billion. An association, The Outsourcing Institute, was formed to provide "objective, independent information on the strategic use of outside resources." The institute regularly sponsors a special advertising section in *Fortune* magazine.

Sources: Adapted from T. Kearney, "Why Outsourcing Is In," *Strategic Finance*, January 2000, pp. 34–38; R. E. Drtina, "The Outsourcing Decision," *Management Accounting*, March, 1994, pp. 56–62; and The Outsourcing Institute, *How and Why to Outsource* (http://www.outsourcing.com/howandwhy/index.htm).

costs, the cost to make the parts is $215,000, which is $15,000 higher than the cost of purchasing them.

Cost to Make Parts or Subcomponents (in thousands)	
Outlay cost	$160
Opportunity cost	55
Total cost	$215

The opportunity cost is the $55,000 that is passed up when the facilities cannot be used to make other products.

In sum, the make-or-buy decision should focus on relevant costs in a particular decision situation. In all cases, companies should relate make-or-buy decisions to the long-run policies for the use of capacity.

To illustrate, suppose a company uses its facilities, on average, 80% of the time. However, because of seasonal changes in the demand for its product, the actual demand for the facilities varies from 60% in the off season to over 100% in the peak season. During the off season, the company may decide to perform special projects for other manufacturers (on a subcontract). There is profit on these projects but not enough to justify expanding the capacity of the facilities. The company will use facilities for these projects only when their opportunity cost is close to zero, that is, when there are no other profitable uses for the facilities. In contrast, during the peak season, the company meets the high volume by purchasing some parts. Again, the cost of purchased parts is higher than the cost to make them in the company's own facilities if there were idle capacity, but purchasing the parts is less costly than buying the facilities to produce them.

SUMMARY PROBLEM FOR YOUR REVIEW

PROBLEM

Exhibit 6-1 contains data for the Block Company for the year just ended. The company makes industrial power drills. Exhibit 6-1 shows the costs of the plastic housing separately from the costs of the electrical and mechanical components.

1. During the year, a prospective customer in an unrelated market offered $82,000 for 1,000 drills. The drills would be in addition to the 100,000 units sold. The regular sales commission rate would have been paid. The president rejected the order because "it was below our costs of $97 per unit." What would operating income have been if the order had been accepted?

Exhibit 6-1

Block Company Cost of Industrial Drills

	A	**B**	**A + B**
	*Electrical and Mechanical Components**	*Plastic Housing*	*Industrial Drills*
Sales: 100,000 units, @ $100			$10,000,000
Variable costs			
Direct material	$4,400,000	$ 500,000	$ 4,900,000
Direct labor	400,000	300,000	700,000
Variable factory overhead	100,000	200,000	300,000
Other variable costs	100,000	—	100,000
Sales commissions, @ 10% of sales	1,000,000	—	1,000,000
Total variable costs	$6,000,000	$1,000,000	$ 7,000,000
Contribution margin			$ 3,000,000
Total fixed costs	$2,220,000	$ 480,000	$ 2,700,000
Operating income			$ 300,000

* Not including the costs of plastic housing (column B).

2. A supplier offered to manufacture the year's supply of 100,000 plastic housings for $13.50 each. What would be the effect on operating income if the Block Company purchased rather than made the housings? Assume that $350,000 of the fixed costs assigned to housings would have been avoided if the housings were purchased.

3. The company could have purchased the housings for $13.50 each and used the vacated space for the manufacture of a deluxe version of its drill. Assume that 20,000 deluxe units could have been made (and sold in addition to the 100,000 regular units) at a unit variable cost of $90, exclusive of housings and exclusive of the 10% sales commission. The 20,000 extra plastic housings could also be purchased for $13.50 each. The sales price would have been $130. All the fixed costs pertaining to the plastic housings would have continued, because these costs related primarily to the manufacturing facilities used. What would operating income have been if Block had bought the housings and made and sold the deluxe units?

Solution

1. The costs of filling the special order follow:

Direct material	$49,000
Direct labor	7,000
Variable factory overhead	3,000
Other variable costs	1,000
Sales commission @ 10% of $82,000	8,200
Total variable costs	$68,200
Selling price	82,000
Contribution margin	$13,800

Operating income would have been $300,000 + $13,800, or $313,800, if the order had been accepted. In a sense, the decision to reject the offer implies that the Block Company is willing to invest $13,800 in immediate gains foregone (an opportunity cost) in order to preserve the long-run selling price structure.

2. Assuming that $350,000 of the fixed costs could have been avoided by not making the housings and that the other fixed costs would have continued, the alternatives can be summarized as follows.

	Make	Buy
Purchase cost		$1,350,000
Variable costs	$1,000,000	
Avoidable fixed costs	350,000	
Total relevant costs	$1,350,000	$1,350,000

If the facilities used for plastic housings became idle, the Block Company would be indifferent whether to make or buy. Operating income would be unaffected.

3. The effect of purchasing the plastic housings and using the vacated facilities for the manufacture of a deluxe version of its drill is

Sales would increase by 20,000 units, @ $130		$2,600,000
Variable costs exclusive of parts would increase by		
20,000 units, @ $90	$1,800,000	
Plus: sales commission, 10% of $2,600,000	260,000	$2,060,000
Contribution margin on 20,000 units		$ 540,000
Housings: 120,000 rather than 100,000 would		
be needed		
Buy 120,000 @ $13.50	$1,620,000	
Make 100,000 @ $10 (only the variable costs		
are relevant)	1,000,000	
Excess cost of outside purchase		620,000
Fixed costs, unchanged		—
Disadvantage of making deluxe units		$ 80,000

Operating income would decline to $220,000 ($300,000 − $80,000). The deluxe units bring in a contribution margin of $540,000, but the additional costs of buying rather than making housings is $620,000, leading to a net disadvantage of $80,000.

JOINT PRODUCT COSTS

NATURE OF JOINT PRODUCTS

joint products Two or more manufactured products that (1) have relatively significant sales values and (2) are not separately identifiable as individual products until their split-off point.

split-off point The juncture of manufacturing where the joint products become individually identifiable.

separable costs Any cost beyond the split-off point.

joint costs The costs of manufacturing joint products prior to the split-off point.

When two or more manufactured products (1) have relatively significant sales values and (2) are not separately identifiable as individual products until their split-off point, they are called **joint products.** The **split-off point** is that juncture of manufacturing where the joint products become individually identifiable. Any costs beyond that stage are called **separable costs** because they are not part of the joint process and can be exclusively identified with individual products. The costs of manufacturing joint products prior to the split-off point are called **joint costs.** Examples of joint products include chemicals, lumber, flour, and the products of petroleum refining and meat packing. A meat-packing company cannot kill a sirloin steak; it has to slaughter a steer, which supplies various cuts of dressed meat, hides, and trimmings.

To illustrate joint costs, suppose Dow Chemical Company produces two chemical products, X and Y, as a result of a particular joint process. The joint processing cost is $100,000. This includes raw material costs and the cost of processing to the point where X and Y go their separate ways. Both products are sold to the petroleum industry to be used as ingredients of gasoline. The relationships follow:

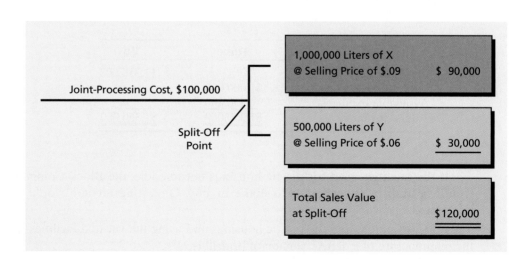

Exhibit 6-2

Illustration of Sell or Process Further

	Sell at Split-Off as Y	Process Further and Sell as YA	Difference
Revenues	$30,000	$80,000	$50,000
Separable costs beyond split-off @ $.08	—	40,000	40,000
Income effects	$30,000	$40,000	$10,000

SELL OR PROCESS FURTHER

Managers frequently face decisions of whether to sell joint products at the split-off point or to process some or all products further. Suppose the 500,000 liters of Y can be processed further and sold to the plastics industry as product YA, an ingredient for plastic sheeting. The additional processing cost would be $.08 per liter for manufacturing and distribution, a total of $40,000 for 500,000 liters. The net sales price of YA would be $.16 per liter, a total of $80,000.

Product X cannot be processed further and will be sold at the split-off point, but management is undecided about Product Y. Should Y be sold or should it be processed into YA? To answer this question we need to find the relevant costs involved. Because the joint costs must be incurred to reach the split-off point, they might seem relevant. However, they cannot affect anything beyond the split-off point. Therefore, they do not differ between alternatives and are completely irrelevant to the question of whether to sell or process further. The only approach that will yield valid results is to concentrate on the separable costs and revenue beyond split-off, as shown in Exhibit 6-2.

This analysis shows that it would be $10,000 more profitable to process Y beyond split-off than to sell Y at split-off. Briefly, it is profitable to extend processing or to incur additional distribution costs on a joint product if the additional revenue exceeds the additional expenses.

Exhibit 6-3 illustrates another way to compare the alternatives of (1) selling Y at the split-off point and (2) processing Y beyond split-off. It includes the joint costs, which are the same for each alternative and therefore do not affect the difference.

The allocation of joint costs would not affect the decision, as Exhibit 6-3 demonstrates. The joint costs are not allocated in the exhibit, but no matter how they might be allocated, the total income effects would be unchanged. Additional coverage of joint costs and inventory valuation can be found in Chapter 12.

> **Objective 3**
> Decide whether a joint product should be processed beyond the split-off point.

Exhibit 6-3

Sell or Process Further Analysis—Firm as a Whole

	(1) Alternative One			(2) Alternative Two			(3)
	X	Y	Total	X	YA	Total	Differential Effects
Revenues	$90,000	$30,000	$120,000	$90,000	$80,000	$170,000	$50,000
Joint costs			$100,000			$100,000	—
Separable costs			—		40,000	40,000	40,000
Total costs			$100,000			$140,000	
Income effects			$ 20,000			$ 30,000	$10,000

IRRELEVANCE OF PAST COSTS

The ability to recognize and thereby ignore irrelevant costs is sometimes just as important to decision makers as identifying relevant costs. How do we know that past costs, although sometimes predictors, are irrelevant in decision making? Consider such past costs as obsolete inventory and the book value of old equipment to see why they are irrelevant to decisions.

OBSOLETE INVENTORY

Objective 4
Identify irrelevant information in disposal of obsolete inventory and equipment replacement decisions.

Suppose General Dynamics has 100 obsolete aircraft parts in its inventory. The original manufacturing cost of these parts was $100,000. General Dynamics can (1) remachine the parts for $30,000 and then sell them for $50,000 or (2) scrap them for $5,000. Which should it do?

This is an unfortunate situation, yet the $100,000 past cost is irrelevant to the decision to remachine or scrap. The only relevant factors are the expected future revenues and costs:

	Remachine	Scrap	Difference
Expected future revenue	$ 50,000	$ 5,000	$45,000
Expected future costs	30,000	—	30,000
Relevant excess of revenue over costs	$ 20,000	$ 5,000	$15,000
Accumulated historical inventory cost*	100,000	100,000	—
Net overall loss on project	$(80,000)	$(95,000)	$15,000

* Irrelevant because it is unaffected by the decision.

As you can see from the fourth line of the preceding table, we can completely ignore the $100,000 historical cost and still arrive at the $15,000 difference, the key figure in the analysis.

BOOK VALUE OF OLD EQUIPMENT

depreciation The periodic cost of equipment that is spread over (or charged to) the future periods in which the equipment is expected to be used.

book value (net book value) The original cost of equipment less accumulated depreciation, which is the summation of depreciation charged to past periods.

Like obsolete parts, the book value of equipment is not a relevant consideration in deciding whether to replace the equipment. Why? Because it is a past cost, not a future cost. When equipment is purchased, its cost is spread over (or charged to) the future periods in which the equipment is expected to be used. This periodic cost is called **depreciation.** The equipment's **book value** (or **net book value**) is the original cost less accumulated depreciation. Accumulated depreciation is the sum of all depreciation charged to past periods. For example, suppose a $10,000 machine with a 10-year life span has depreciation of $1,000 per year. At the end of six years, accumulated depreciation is 6 × $1,000 = $6,000, and the book value is $10,000 − $6,000 = $4,000.

Consider the following data for a decision whether to replace an old machine:

	Old Machine	Replacement Machine
Original cost	$10,000	$8,000
Useful life in years	10	4
Current age in years	6	0
Useful life remaining in years	4	4
Accumulated depreciation	$ 6,000	0
Book value	$ 4,000	Not acquired yet
Disposal value (in cash) now	$ 2,500	Not acquired yet
Disposal value in 4 years	0	0
Annual cash operating costs (maintenance, power, repairs, coolants, and so on)	$ 5,000	$3,000

We have been asked to prepare a comparative analysis of the two alternatives. Before proceeding, consider some important concepts. The most widely misunderstood facet of replacement decision making is the role of the book value of the old equipment in the decision. The book value, in this context, is sometimes called a **sunk cost,** which is really just another term for historical or past cost, a cost that has already been incurred and, therefore, is irrelevant to the decision-making process. At one time or another, we all try to soothe the wounded pride arising from having made a bad purchase decision by using an item instead of replacing it. It is a serious mistake to think, however, that a current or future action can influence the long-run impact of a past outlay. All past costs are down the drain. Nothing can change what has already happened.

sunk cost A cost that has already been incurred and, therefore, is irrelevant to the decision-making process.

The irrelevance of past costs for decisions does not mean that knowledge of past costs is useless. Often managers use past costs to help predict future costs. In addition, past costs affect future payments for income taxes (as explained in Chapter 11). However, the past cost itself is not relevant. The only relevant cost is the predicted future cost.

In deciding whether to replace or keep existing equipment, we must consider the relevance of four commonly encountered items:[1]

- *Book value of old equipment:* Irrelevant, because it is a past (historical) cost. Therefore, depreciation on old equipment is irrelevant.
- *Disposal value of old equipment:* Relevant (ordinarily), because it is an expected future inflow that usually differs among alternatives.
- *Gain or loss on disposal:* This is the difference between book value and disposal value. It is therefore a meaningless combination of irrelevant and relevant items. The combination form, loss (or gain) on disposal, blurs the distinction between the irrelevant book value and the relevant disposal value. Consequently, it is best to think of each separately.
- *Cost of new equipment:* Relevant, because it is an expected future outflow that will differ among alternatives. Therefore, depreciation on new equipment is relevant.

Exhibit 6-4 shows the relevance of these items in our example. Book value of old equipment is irrelevant regardless of the decision-making technique used. The "difference" column in Exhibit 6-4 shows that the $4,000 book value of the old equipment does not differ between alternatives. It should be completely ignored for decision-making purposes. The difference is merely one of timing. The amount written off is still $4,000, regardless of any available alternative. The $4,000 appears on the income statement either as a $4,000 deduction from the $2,500 cash proceeds received to obtain a $1,500 loss on disposal in the first year or as $1,000 of depreciation in each of 4 years. But how it appears is irrelevant to the replacement decision. In contrast, the $2,000 annual depreciation on the new equipment is relevant because the total $8,000 depreciation is a future cost that may be avoided by not replacing. The three relevant items—operating costs, disposal value, and acquisition cost—give replacement a net advantage of $2,500.

EXAMINATION OF ALTERNATIVES OVER THE LONG RUN

Exhibit 6-4 is the first example that looks beyond one year. Examining the alternatives over the equipment's entire life ensures that peculiar nonrecurring items (such as loss on disposal) will not obstruct the long-run view vital to many managerial decisions.[2]

---

[1] *For simplicity, we ignore income tax considerations and the effects of the interest value of money in this chapter. Book value is irrelevant even if income taxes are considered, however, because the relevant item is then the tax cash flow, not the book value. The book value is essential information for predicting the amount and timing of future tax cash flows, but, by itself, the book value is irrelevant. For elaboration, see Chapter 11.*

[2] *A more complete analysis that includes the timing of revenues and costs appears in Chapter 11.*

Exhibit 6-4

Cost Comparison—Replacement of Equipment Including Relevant and Irrelevant Items

	Four Years Together		
	Keep	*Replace*	*Difference*
Cash operating costs	$20,000	$12,000	$ 8,000
Old equipment (book value)			
Periodic write-off as depreciation	4,000	—	
or			—
Lump-sum write-off		4,000*	
Disposal value	—	−2,500*	2,500
New machine			
Acquisition cost	—	8,000 †	−8,000
Total costs	$24,000	$21,500	$ 2,500

The advantage of replacement is $2,500 for the four years together.

* In a formal income statement, these two items would be combined as "loss on disposal" of $4,000 − $2,500 = $1,500.

† In a formal income statement, written off as straight-line depreciation of $8,000 ÷ 4 = $2,000 for each of four years.

Exhibit 6-5 concentrates on relevant items only: the cash operating costs, the disposal value of the old equipment, and the depreciation on the new equipment. To demonstrate that the amount of the old equipment's book value will not affect the answer, suppose the book value of the old equipment is $500,000 rather than $4,000. Your final answer will not change. The cumulative advantage of replacement is still $2,500. (If you are in doubt, rework this example, using $500,000 as the book value.)

It is sometimes difficult to accept the proposition that past or sunk costs are irrelevant to decisions. Consider the ticket you have to a major football game in December. After getting the ticket you learn that the game will be on television, and you really prefer to watch the game in the comfort of your warm home. Does your decision about attending the game or watching it on TV depend on whether you were given the ticket for free or paid $80 for it?

ANSWER

The amount paid, whether it be $0, $80, or $1,000, should make no difference to the decision. You have the ticket, and you have paid for it. That cannot be changed. If you really prefer to watch the game on TV, it may have been a bad decision to pay $80 for a ticket. But you cannot erase that bad decision. All you can do is choose the future action that has most value to you. You should not suffer through a less pleasant experience just because you paid $80 for the ticket.

Exhibit 6-5

Cost Comparison—Replacement of Equipment, Relevant Items Only

	Four Years Together		
	Keep	*Replace*	*Difference*
Cash operating costs	$20,000	$12,000	$ 8,000
Disposal value of old machine	—	−2,500	2,500
New machine, acquisition cost	—	8,000	−8,000
Total relevant costs	$20,000	$17,500	$ 2,500

It is easy to agree that—in theory—sunk costs should be ignored when making decisions. But in practice sunk costs often influence important decisions, especially when a decision maker doesn't want to admit that a previous decision to invest funds was a bad decision.

Consider two examples from the *St. Louis Post Dispatch*: (1) Larry O. Welch, the air force chief of staff, was quoted as saying that "the B-2 already is into production; cancel it and the $17 billion front end investment is lost." (2) Les Aspin, chairman of the House Armed Services Committee, was quoted as stating that "with $17 billion already invested in it, the B-2 is too costly to cancel."

The $17 billion already invested in the B-2 is a sunk cost. It is "lost" regardless of whether production of the B-2 is canceled or not. And whether B-2 production is too costly to continue depends only on the future costs necessary to complete production compared to the value of the completed B-2s. The $17 billion was relevant when the original decision to begin development of the B-2 was made, but now that the money has been spent, it is no longer relevant. No decision can affect it.

Why would intelligent leaders consider the $17 billion relevant to the decision on continuing production of the B-2? Probably because it is difficult to admit that

no benefit would be derived from the $17 billion investment. Those who favor canceling production of the B-2 would consider the outcome of the original investment decision to be unfavorable. With perfect hindsight, they believe the investment should not have been made. It is human nature to find unpleasant the task of admitting that $17 billion was wasted. Yet, it is more important to avoid throwing good money after bad—that is, if the value of the B-2 is not at least equal to the future investment in it, production should be terminated, regardless of the amount spent to date.

Failure to ignore sunk costs is not unique to the U.S. government. In reference to Russia's store of bomb-grade plutonium, the country's Minister of Atomic Energy stated, "We have spent too much money making this material to just mix it with radioactive wastes and bury it." Burying the plutonium may or may not be the best decision, but the amount already spent is not relevant to the decision.

Sources: Adapted from J. Berg, J. Dickhaut, and C. Kanodia, "The Role of Private Information in the Sunk Cost Phenomenon," unpublished paper, November 12, 1991; M. Wald and M. Gordon, "Russia Treasures Plutonium, But U.S. Wants to Destroy It," *New York Times*, August 19, 1994, p. A1.

IRRELEVANCE OF FUTURE COSTS THAT WILL NOT DIFFER

In addition to past costs, some future costs may be irrelevant because they will be the same under all feasible alternatives. These, too, may be safely ignored for a particular decision. The salaries of many members of top management are examples of expected future costs that will be unaffected by the decision at hand.

Other irrelevant future costs include fixed costs that will be unchanged by such considerations as whether machine X or machine Y is selected. However, it is not merely a case of saying that fixed costs are irrelevant and variable costs are relevant. Variable costs can be irrelevant, and fixed costs can be relevant. For instance, sales commissions might be paid on an order regardless of whether the order was filled from plant G or plant H. Variable costs are irrelevant whenever they do not differ among the alternatives at hand, and fixed costs are relevant whenever they differ between the alternatives at hand.

BEWARE OF UNIT COSTS

The pricing illustration in Chapter 5 showed that unit costs should be analyzed with care in decision making. There are two major ways to go wrong: (1) the inclusion of irrelevant costs, such as the $3 allocation of unavoidable fixed costs in the General Electric make-or-buy example (p. 231) that would result in a unit cost of $11 instead of the relevant

Objective 5
Explain how unit costs can be misleading.

unit cost of $8, and (2) comparisons of unit costs not computed on the same volume basis, as the following example demonstrates. Machinery sales personnel, for example, often brag about the low unit costs of using the new machines. Sometimes they neglect to point out that the unit costs are based on outputs far in excess of the volume of activity of their prospective customer. Assume that a new $100,000 machine with a five-year lifespan can produce 100,000 units a year at a variable cost of $1 per unit, as opposed to a variable cost per unit of $1.50 with an old machine. A sales representative claims that the new machine will reduce cost by $.30 per unit. Is the new machine a worthwhile acquisition?

The new machine is attractive at first glance. If the customer's expected volume is 100,000 units, unit-cost comparisons are valid, provided that new depreciation is also considered. Assume that the disposal value of the old equipment is zero. Because depreciation is an allocation of historical cost, the depreciation on the old machine is irrelevant. In contrast, the depreciation on the new machine is relevant because the new machine entails a future cost that can be avoided by not acquiring it.

	Old Machine	New Machine
Units	100,000	100,000
Variable costs	$150,000	$100,000
Straight-line depreciation	—	20,000
Total relevant costs	$150,000	$120,000
Unit relevant costs	$ 1.50	$ 1.20

Apparently, the sales representative is correct. However, if the customer's expected volume is only 30,000 units per year, the unit costs change in favor of the old machine.

	Old Machine	New Machine
Units	30,000	30,000
Variable costs	$45,000	$30,000
Straight-line depreciation	—	20,000
Total relevant costs	$45,000	$50,000
Unit relevant costs	$ 1.50	$1.6667

Generally, be wary of unit fixed costs. Use total costs rather than unit costs. Then, if desired, the totals may be unitized.

CONFLICTS BETWEEN DECISION MAKING AND PERFORMANCE EVALUATION

You should now know how to make good decisions based on relevant data. However, knowing how to make these decisions and actually making them are two different things. Managers might be tempted to make decisions they know are poor if the performance measures in place will reward them for those decisions. To motivate managers to make optimal decisions, methods of evaluating the performance of managers should be consistent with the decision analysis.

Objective 6
Discuss how performance measures can affect decision making.

Consider the replacement decision shown in Exhibit 6-5 on page 240, where replacing the machine had a $2,500 advantage over keeping it. To motivate managers to make the right choice, the method used to evaluate performance should be consistent with the decision model—that is, it should show better performance when managers replace the machine than when they keep it. Because performance is often measured by accounting income, consider the accounting income in the first year after replacement compared with that in years 2, 3, and 4.

	Year 1		Years 2, 3, and 4	
	Keep	*Replace*	*Keep*	*Replace*
Cash operating costs	$5,000	$3,000	$5,000	$3,000
Depreciation	1,000	2,000	1,000	2,000
Loss on disposal ($4,000 − $2,500)	—	1,500	—	—
Total charges against revenue	$6,000	$6,500	$6,000	$5,000

If the machine is kept rather than replaced, first-year costs will be $6,500 − $6,000 = $500 lower, and first-year income will be $500 higher. Because managers naturally want to make decisions that maximize the measure of their performance, they may be inclined to keep the machine. This is an example of a conflict between the analysis for decision making and the method used to evaluate performance.

The conflict is especially severe if managers are transferred often from one position to another. Why? Because the $500 first-year advantage for keeping will be offset by a $1,000 annual advantage of replacing in years 2 to 4. (Note that the net difference of $2,500 in favor of replacement over the four years together is the same as in Exhibit 6-5.) A manager who moves to a new position after the first year, however, bears the entire loss on disposal without reaping the benefits of lower operating costs in years 2 to 4.

The decision to replace a machine earlier than planned also reveals that the original decision to purchase the machine may have been flawed. The old machine was bought six years ago for $10,000. Its expected lifespan was 10 years. However, if a better machine is now available, then the useful life of the old machine was really six years, not 10. This feedback on the actual life of the old machine has two possible effects, the first good and the second bad. First, managers might learn from the earlier mistake. If the useful life of the old machine was overestimated, how believable is the prediction that the new machine will have a four-year lifespan? Feedback can help avoid repeating past mistakes. Second, another mistake might be made to cover up the earlier one. A "loss on disposal" could alert superiors to the incorrect economic-life prediction used in the earlier decision. By avoiding replacement, the $4,000 remaining book value is spread over the future as "depreciation," a more appealing term than "loss on disposal." The superiors may never find out about the incorrect prediction of economic life. The accounting income approach to performance evaluation mixes the financial effects of various decisions, hiding both the earlier misestimation of useful life and the current failure to replace.

The conflict between decision making and performance evaluation is a widespread problem in practice. Unfortunately, there are no easy solutions. In theory, accountants could evaluate performance in a manner consistent with decision making. In our equipment example, this would mean predicting year-by-year income effects over the planning horizon of four years, noting that the first year would be poor, and evaluating actual performance against the predictions.

The trouble is that evaluating performance, decision by decision, is a costly procedure. Therefore, aggregate measures are used. For example, an income statement shows the results of many decisions, not just the single decision of buying a machine. Consequently, in many cases like our equipment example, managers may be most heavily influenced by the first-year effects on the income statement. Thus managers refrain from taking the longer view that would benefit the company.

Exhibit 6-6

Samson Company

Schedules of Indirect Manufacturing Costs for the Year Ended December 31, 2001 (thousands of dollars)

Schedule 1: Variable Costs		
Supplies (lubricants, expendable tools, coolants, sandpaper)	$ 150	
Material-handling labor (forklift operators)	700	
Repairs	100	
Power	50	$1,000

Schedule 2: Fixed Costs		
Managers' salaries	$ 200	
Employee training	90	
Factory picnic and holiday party	10	
Supervisory salaries	700	
Depreciation, plant and equipment	1,800	
Property taxes	150	
Insurance	50	3,000
Total indirect manufacturing costs		$4,000

HOW INCOME STATEMENTS INFLUENCE DECISION MAKING

When executives use income statements to evaluate performance, managers need to know how their decisions will affect income as reported on the statements. Some income statements track fixed and variable costs using the contribution approach, whereas others adopt the absorption approach used in reporting to external parties. To highlight the different effects of these approaches, we will assume that in 2001 the Samson Company has direct-material costs of $7 million and direct-labor costs of $4 million. Assume also that the company incurred the indirect manufacturing costs illustrated in Exhibit 6-6 and the selling and administrative expenses illustrated in Exhibit 6-7. Total sales were $20 million. Finally, assume that the units produced are equal to the units sold. That is, there is no change in inventory levels. (In this way, we avoid some complications that are unnecessary and unimportant at this stage.[3])

Note that Exhibits 6-6 and 6-7 subdivide costs as variable or fixed. Many companies do not make such subdivisions in their income statements. Furthermore, when such subdivisions are made, sometimes arbitrary decisions are necessary about whether a given cost is variable, fixed, or partially fixed (for example, repairs). Nevertheless, to align income statements with the information that should be used in decision making, many companies are attempting to report the extent to which their costs are approximately variable or fixed.

Objective 7
Construct absorption and contribution format income statements and identify which is better for decision making.

ABSORPTION APPROACH

absorption approach A costing approach that considers all factory overhead (both variable and fixed) to be product (inventoriable) costs that become an expense in the form of manufacturing cost of goods sold only as sales occur.

Exhibit 6-8 presents Samson's income statement using the **absorption approach** (absorption costing), the approach used by companies for external financial reporting. Firms that take this approach consider all indirect manufacturing (both variable and fixed) to be product (inventoriable) costs that become an expense in the form of manufacturing cost of goods sold only as sales occur.

Note in Exhibit 6-8 that gross profit or gross margin is the difference between sales and the manufacturing cost of goods sold. Note too that the primary classifications of

---

[3] *These complexities are discussed in Chapters 14 and 15.*

Exhibit 6-7

Samson Company

Schedules of Selling and Administrative Expenses

For the Year Ended December 31, 2001 (thousands of dollars)

Schedule 3: Selling Expenses		
Variable		
Sales commissions	$ 700	
Shipping expenses for products sold	300	$1,000
Fixed		
Advertising	$ 700	
Sales salaries	1,000	
Other	300	2,000
Total selling expenses		$3,000

Schedule 4: Administrative Expenses		
Variable		
Some clerical wages	$ 80	
Computer time rented	20	$ 100
Fixed		
Office salaries	$ 100	
Other salaries	200	
Depreciation on office facilities	100	
Public-accounting fees	40	
Legal fees	100	
Other	360	900
Total administrative expenses		$1,000

costs on the income statement are by three major management functions: manufacturing, selling, and administrative.

CONTRIBUTION APPROACH

In contrast, Exhibit 6-9 presents Samson's income statement using the **contribution approach** (variable costing or direct costing). The contribution approach is not allowed for external financial reporting. However, many companies use this approach for internal

contribution approach
A method of internal (management accounting) reporting that emphasizes the distinction between variable and fixed costs for the purpose of better decision making.

Exhibit 6-8

Samson Company

Absorption Income Statement

For the Year Ended December 31, 2001 (thousands of dollars)

Sales		$20,000
Less: Manufacturing costs of goods sold		
Direct material	$7,000	
Direct labor	4,000	
Indirect manufacturing (Schedules 1 plus 2)*	4,000	15,000
Gross margin or gross profit		$ 5,000
Selling expenses (Schedule 3)	$3,000	
Administrative expenses (Schedule 4)	1,000	
Total selling and administrative expenses		4,000
Operating income		$ 1,000

* Note: Schedules 1 and 2 are in Exhibit 4-6. Schedules 3 and 4 are in Exhibit 4-7.

Exhibit 6-9

Samson Company

Contribution Income Statement

For the Year Ended December 31, 2001 (thousands of dollars)

Sales		$20,000
Less: Variable expenses		
Direct material	$ 7,000	
Direct labor	4,000	
Variable indirect manufacturing costs (Schedule 1)*	1,000	
Total variable manufacturing cost of goods sold	$12,000	
Variable selling expenses (Schedule 3)	1,000	
Variable administrative expenses (Schedule 4)	100	
Total variable expenses		13,100
Contribution margin		$ 6,900
Less: fixed expenses		
Manufacturing (Schedule 2)	$ 3,000	
Selling (Schedule 3)	2,000	
Administrative (Schedule 4)	900	5,900
Operating income		$ 1,000

* Note: Schedules 1 and 2 are in Exhibit 6-6. Schedules 3 and 4 are in Exhibit 6-7.

(management accounting) purposes and an absorption format for external purposes, because they expect the benefits of making better decisions to exceed the extra costs of using different reporting systems simultaneously.

For decision purposes, the major difference between the contribution approach and the absorption approach is that the former emphasizes the distinction between variable and fixed costs. Its primary classifications of costs are by variable- and fixed-cost behavior patterns, not by business functions.

The contribution income statement provides a contribution margin, which is computed after deducting from revenue all variable costs including variable selling and administrative costs. This approach makes it easier to understand the impact of changes in sales demand on operating income. It also dovetails neatly with the cost-volume-profit (CVP) analysis illustrated in Chapter 2 and the decision analyses in this chapter and the preceding one.

A major benefit of the contribution approach is that it stresses the role of fixed costs in operating income. Before a company can earn income, it first must recoup the fixed costs it has incurred for manufacturing and other value chain functions. This highlighting of total fixed costs focuses management attention on fixed-cost behavior and control in making both short-run and long-run plans. Remember that advocates of the contribution approach do not maintain that fixed costs are unimportant or irrelevant. They do stress, however, that the distinctions between behaviors of variable and fixed costs are crucial for certain decisions.

The difference between the gross margin (from the absorption approach) and the contribution margin (from the contribution approach) is striking in manufacturing companies. Why? Because fixed manufacturing costs are regarded as a part of cost of goods sold in an absorption–costing system, and these fixed costs reduce the gross margin accordingly. However, fixed manufacturing costs do not reduce the contribution margin, which is affected solely by revenues and variable costs.

COMPARING CONTRIBUTION AND ABSORPTION APPROACHES

In essence, the contribution approach deducts variable costs from sales to compute a contribution margin and then deducts fixed costs to measure profit. This is generally consistent with analyses used to make decisions. In contrast, the absorption approach deducts manufacturing costs from sales to compute a gross margin and then deducts nonmanufacturing costs to measure profit. This format is less helpful for decision making. Consider the following four-way breakdown of costs.

	Manufacturing Costs	Nonmanufacturing costs
Variable costs	A. Variable manufacturing costs	B. Variable nonmanufacturing costs
Fixed costs	C. Fixed manufacturing costs	D. Fixed nonmanufacturing costs

Contribution and absorption income statements would look as follows.

Contribution income statement	Absorption income statement
Sales	Sales
Less: A + B	Less: A + C
Contribution margin	Gross margin
Less: C + D	Less: B + D
Profit	Profit

SUMMARY PROBLEM FOR YOUR REVIEW

PROBLEM

1. Review the illustrations in Exhibits 6-6 through 6-9. Suppose that all variable costs fluctuate in direct proportion to units produced and sold, and that all fixed costs are unaffected over a wide range of production and sales. What would operating income have been if sales (at normal selling prices) had been $20.9 million instead of $20.0 million? Which statement, the absorption income statement or the contribution income statement, did you use as a framework for your answer? Why?

2. Suppose employee training (Exhibit 6-6) was regarded as a variable rather than a fixed cost at a rate of $90,000 ÷ 1,000,000 units, or $.09 per unit. How would your answer in requirement 1 change?

SOLUTION

1. Operating income would increase from $1,000,000 to $1,310,500, computed as follows.

Increase in revenue	$ 900,000
Increase in total contribution margin:	
Contribution-margin ratio in contribution income statement	
(Exhibit 6-9) is $6,900,000 ÷ $20,000,000 = .345	
Ratio times revenue increase is .345 × $900,000	$ 310,500
Increase in fixed expenses	0
Operating income before increase	$1,000,000
New operating income	$1,310,500

Computations are easily made by using data from the contribution income statement. In contrast, the traditional absorption-costing income statement must be analyzed and divided into variable and fixed categories before the effect on operating income can be estimated.

2. The original contribution-margin ratio would be lower because the variable costs would be higher by $.09 per unit: ($6,900,000 − $90,000) ÷ $20,000,000 = .3405.

	Given Level	Higher Level	Difference
Revenue	$20,000,000	$20,900,000	$900,000
Variable expense ($13,100,000 + $90,000)	13,190,000	13,783,550*	593,550
Contribution margin at .3405	$ 6,810,000	$ 7,116,450	$306,450
Fixed expenses ($5,900,000 − $90,000)	5,810,000	5,810,000	—
Operating income	$ 1,000,000	$ 1,306,450	$306,450

* $20,900,000 − $7,116,450 or (1 − .3405) × $20,900,000

Highlights to Remember

Use opportunity cost to analyze the income effects of a given alternative. Opportunity costs should always be considered when deciding on the use of limited resources. The opportunity cost of a course of action is the maximum profit foregone from other alternative actions. Decision makers may fail to consider opportunity costs because they are not reported in the financial accounting system.

Decide whether to make or to buy certain parts or products. One of the most important production decisions is the make-or-buy decision. Should a company make its own parts or products or should it buy them from outside sources? Both qualitative and quantitative factors affect this decision. In applying relevant cost analysis to a make-or-buy situation, a key factor to consider is the use of facilities.

Decide whether a joint product should be processed beyond the split-off point. Another typical production situation is deciding whether to process further a joint product or sell it at the split-off point. The relevant information for this decision includes the costs that differ beyond the split-off point. Joint costs that occur before split-off are irrelevant.

Identify irrelevant information in disposal of obsolete inventory and equipment replacement decisions. In certain production decisions, it is important to recognize and identify irrelevant costs. In the decision to dispose of obsolete inventory, the original cost of the inventory is irrelevant because the resources used to buy or produce the inventory cannot be restored. The book value of old equipment is also irrelevant to the equipment replacement decision. This sunk cost is a past or historical cost that has already been incurred.

Explain how unit costs can be misleading. Unit fixed costs can be misleading because of the differences in the assumed level of volume on which they are based. The more units a company makes, the lower the unit fixed cost will be. If a salesperson assumes 100,000 units will be produced and only 30,000 are actually made, the unit costs will be understated. You can avoid being misled by unit costs by always using total fixed costs.

Discuss how performance measures can affect decision making. If companies evaluate managers using performance measures that are not in line with relevant decision criteria, there could be a conflict of interest. Managers often make decisions based on how the decision affects their performance measures. Thus, performance measures work best when they are consistent with the long-term good of the company.

Construct absorption and contribution format income statements and identify which is better for decision making. The major difference between the absorption and contribution formats for the income statement is that the contribution format focuses on cost behavior (fixed and variable), whereas the absorption format reports costs by business functions. The contribution approach makes it easier for managers to evaluate the affects of changes in demand on income and thus it is better for decision making.

Understand the relationship between accounting information and decisions in the production stage of the value chain. In the production stage of the value chain, managers make decisions about product mix, production equipment, labor, and all other factors that affect the creation of goods and services. Managers need timely and relevant accounting information to make these decisions on an objective, quantifiable basis. The accounting information used must be relevant to the decision at hand, so accountants must take extra care in determining which factors affect future costs that differ between alternatives.

Accounting Vocabulary

absorption approach, p. 244
book value, p. 238
contribution approach, p. 245
depreciation, p. 238
differential cost, p. 228

incremental cost, p. 228
joint costs, p. 236
joint products, p. 236
net book value, p. 238
opportunity cost, p. 229

outlay cost, p. 229
revenue, p. 228
separable costs, p. 236
split-off point, p. 236
sunk cost, p. 239

Fundamental Assignment Material

6-A1   Make or Buy

Sunshine State Fruit Company sells premium-quality oranges and other citrus fruits by mail order. Protecting the fruit during shipping is important, so the company has designed and produces shipping boxes. The annual cost of 80,000 boxes is

Materials	$120,000
Labor	20,000
Overhead	
Variable	16,000
Fixed	60,000
Total	$216,000

Therefore, the cost per box averages $2.70.

   Suppose Weyerhauser submits a bid to supply Sunshine State with boxes for $2.35 per box. Sunshine State must give Weyerhauser the box design specifications, and the boxes will be made according to those specs.

Required

1.   How much, if any, would Sunshine State save by buying the boxes from Weyerhauser?
2.   What subjective factors should affect Sunshine State's decision whether to make or buy the boxes?
3.   Suppose all the fixed costs represent depreciation on equipment that was purchased for $600,000 and is just about at the end of its 10-year life. New replacement equipment will cost $1 million and is also expected to last 10 years. In this case, how much, if any, would Sunshine State save by buying the boxes from Weyerhauser?

6-A2   Joint Products: Sell or Process Further

The Karlsson Chemical Company produced three joint products at a joint cost of $120,000. These products were processed further and sold as follows.

Chemical Product	Sales	Additional Processing Costs
A	$230,000	$190,000
B	330,000	300,000
C	175,000	100,000

   The company has had an opportunity to sell at split-off directly to other processors. If that alternative had been selected, sales would have been A, $54,000; B, $28,000; and C, $54,000.

The company expects to operate at the same level of production and sales in the forthcoming year.

Required Consider all the available information, and assume that all costs incurred after split-off are variable.

1. Could the company increase operating income by altering its processing decisions? If so, what would be the expected overall operating income?

2. Which products should be processed further and which should be sold at split-off?

6-A3 Role of Old Equipment Replacement

On January 2, 2001, the Huang Company installed a brand-new $93,000 special molding machine for producing a new product. The product and the machine have an expected life of three years. The machine's expected disposal value at the end of three years is zero.

On January 3, 2001, Kang Lee, a star salesperson for a machine tool manufacturer, tells Mr. Huang, "I wish I had known earlier of your purchase plans. I can supply you with a technically superior machine for $102,000. The machine you just purchased can be sold for $17,000. I guarantee that our machine will save $35,000 per year in cash operating costs, although it too will have no disposal value at the end of three years."

Huang examines some technical data. Although he has confidence in Lee's claims, Huang contends, "I'm locked in now. My alternatives are clear: (a) Disposal will result in a loss, (b) keeping and using the 'old' equipment avoids such a loss. I have brains enough to avoid a loss when my other alternative is recognizing a loss. We've got to use that equipment until we get our money out of it."

The annual operating costs of the old machine are expected to be $60,000, exclusive of depreciation. Sales, all in cash, will be $915,000 per year. Other annual cash expenses will be $810,000 regardless of this decision. Assume that the equipment in question is the company's only fixed asset.

Required Ignore income taxes and the time value of money.

1. Prepare statements of cash receipts and disbursements as they would appear in each of the next three years under both alternatives. What is the total cumulative increase or decrease in cash for the three years?

2. Prepare income statements as they would appear in each of the next three years under both alternatives. Assume straight-line depreciation. What is the cumulative increase or decrease in net income for the three years?

3. Assume that the cost of the "old" equipment was $1 million rather than $93,000. Would the net difference computed in requirements 1 and 2 change? Explain.

4. As Kang Lee, reply to Mr. Huang's contentions.

5. What are the irrelevant items in each of your presentations for requirements 1 and 2? Why are they irrelevant?

6-A4 Straightforward Income Statements

The O'Sullivan Company had the following manufacturing data for the year 2001 (in thousands of dollars).

Beginning and ending inventories	None
Direct material used	$400
Direct labor	330
Supplies	20
Utilities—variable portion	40
Utilities—fixed portion	12
Indirect labor—variable portion	90
Indirect labor—fixed portion	40
Depreciation	110
Property taxes	20
Supervisory salaries	50

Selling expenses were $300,000 (including $60,000 that were variable) and general administrative expenses were $144,000 (including $24,000 that were variable). Sales were $1.85 million.

Direct labor and supplies are regarded as variable costs.

Required 1. Prepare two income statements, one using the contribution approach and one using the absorption approach.

2. Suppose that all variable costs fluctuate directly in proportion to sales and that fixed costs are unaffected over a very wide range of sales. What would operating income have been if sales had been $2.05 million instead of $1.85 million? Which income statement did you use to help obtain your answer? Why?

6-B1 Make or Buy

Suppose a BMW executive in Germany is trying to decide whether the company should continue to manufacture an engine component or purchase it from Frankfort Corporation for 52 euros (EUR) each. Demand for the coming year is expected to be the same as for the current year, 200,000 units. Data for the current year follow:

Direct material	EUR 5,000,000
Direct labor	1,900,000
Factory overhead, variable	1,100,000
Factory overhead, fixed	2,500,000
Total costs	EUR 10,500,000

If BMW makes the components, the unit costs of direct material will increase 10%.

If BMW buys the components, 40% of the fixed costs will be avoided. The other 60% will continue regardless of whether the components are manufactured or purchased. Assume that variable overhead varies with output volume.

Required

1. Tabulate a comparison of the make-or-buy alternatives. Show totals and amounts per unit. Compute the numerical difference between making and buying. Assume that the capacity now used to make the components will become idle if the components are purchased.
2. Assume also that the BMW capacity in question can be rented to a local electronics firm for EUR 1,250,000 for the coming year. Tabulate a comparison of the net relevant costs of the three alternatives: make, buy and leave capacity idle, buy and rent. Which is the most favorable alternative? By how much in total?

6-B2 Sell or Process Further

ConAgra, Inc., produces meat products with brand names such as Swift, Armour, and Butterball. Suppose one of the company's plants processes beef cattle into various products. For simplicity, assume that there are only three products: steak, hamburger, and hides, and that the average steer costs $750. The three products emerge from a process that costs $150 per steer to run, and output from one steer can be sold for the following net amounts.

Steak (100 pounds)	$ 400
Hamburger (500 pounds)	600
Hide (120 pounds)	100
Total	$1,100

Assume that each of these three products can be sold immediately or processed further in another ConAgra plant. The steak can be the main course in frozen dinners sold under the Healthy Choice label. The vegetables and desserts in the 400 dinners produced from the 100 pounds of steak would cost $120, and production, sales, and other costs for the 400 meals would total $350. Each meal would be sold wholesale for $2.15.

The hamburger could be made into frozen Salisbury steak patties sold under the Armour label. The only additional cost would be a $200 processing cost for the 500 pounds of hamburger. Frozen Salisbury steaks sell wholesale for $1.70 per pound.

The hide can be sold before or after tanning. The cost of tanning one hide is $80, and a tanned hide can be sold for $175.

Required

1. Compute the total profit if all three products are sold at the split-off point.
2. Compute the total profit if all three products are processed further before being sold.
3. Which products should be sold at the split-off point? Which should be processed further?
4. Compute the total profit if your plan in requirement 3 is followed.

6-B3 Replacing Old Equipment

Consider these data regarding Hardin County's photocopying requirements:

	Old Equipment	Proposed Replacement Equipment
Useful life, in years	5	3
Current age, in years	2	0
Useful life remaining, in years	3	3
Original cost	$30,000	$15,000
Accumulated depreciation	12,000	0
Book value	18,000	Not acquired yet
Disposal value (in cash) now	3,000	Not acquired yet
Disposal value in 2 years	0	0
Annual cash operating costs for power, maintenance, toner, and supplies	14,000	7,500

The county administrator is trying to decide whether to replace the old equipment. Because of rapid changes in technology, she expects the replacement equipment to have only a three-year useful life. Ignore the effects of taxes.

Required

1. Tabulate a cost comparison that includes both relevant and irrelevant items for the next three years together. (*Hint*: See Exhibit 6-4, page 240.)

2. Tabulate a cost comparison of all relevant items for the next three years together. Which tabulation is clearer, this one or the one in requirement 1? (*Hint*: See Exhibit 6-5, page 240.)

3. Prepare a simple "shortcut" or direct analysis to support your choice of alternatives.

6-B4 Decision and Performance Models

Refer to the preceding problem.

1. Suppose the "decision model" favored by top management consisted of a comparison of a three-year accumulation of cash under each alternative. As the manager of office operations, which alternative would you choose? Why?

2. Suppose the "performance evaluation model" emphasized the minimization of overall costs of photocopying operations for the first year. Which alternative would you choose?

6-B5 Contribution and Absorption Income Statements

The following information is taken from the records of the Manitoba Manufacturing Company for the year ending December 31, 2001. There were no beginning or ending inventories.

Sales	$10,000,000	Long-term rent, factory	$150,000
Sales commissions	500,000	Factory superintendent's salary	30,000
Advertising	200,000	Supervisors' salaries	100,000
Shipping expenses	300,000	Direct material used	4,000,000
Administrative executive salaries	100,000	Direct labor	2,000,000
Administrative clerical salaries (variable)	400,000	Cutting bits used	60,000
Fire insurance on factory equipment	2,000	Factory methods research	40,000
Property taxes on factory equipment	10,000	Abrasives for machining	100,000
		Indirect labor	800,000
		Depreciation on equipment	300,000

Required

1. Prepare a contribution income statement and an absorption income statement. If you are in doubt about any cost behavior pattern, decide on the basis of whether the total cost in question will fluctuate substantially over a wide range of volume. Prepare a separate

supporting schedule of indirect manufacturing costs subdivided between variable and fixed costs.

2. Suppose that all variable costs fluctuate directly in proportion to sales, and that fixed costs are unaffected over a wide range of sales. What would operating income have been if sales had been $10.5 million instead of $10 million? Which income statement did you use to help get your answer? Why?

Additional Assignment Material

QUESTIONS

6-1. Distinguish between an opportunity cost and an outlay cost.

6-2. "I had a chance to rent my summer home for two weeks for $800. But I chose to have it idle. I didn't want strangers living in my summer house." What term in this chapter describes the $800? Why?

6-3. "Accountants do not ordinarily record opportunity costs in the formal accounting records." Why?

6-4. Distinguish between an incremental cost and a differential cost.

6-5. "Incremental cost is the addition to costs from the manufacture of one unit." Do you agree? Explain.

6-6. "The differential costs or incremental costs of increasing production from 1,000 automobiles to 1,200 automobiles per week would be the additional costs of producing the additional 200 automobiles." If production were reduced from 1,200 to 1,000 automobiles per week, what would the decline in costs be called?

6-7. "Qualitative factors generally favor making over buying a component." Do you agree? Explain.

6-8. "Choices are often mislabeled as simply make or buy." Do you agree? Explain.

6-9. What is the split-off point and why is it important in analyzing joint costs?

6-10. "No technique used to assign the joint cost to individual products should be used for management decisions regarding whether a product should be sold at the split-off point or processed further." Do you agree? Explain.

6-11. "Inventory that was purchased for $5,000 should not be sold for less than $5,000 because such a sale would result in a loss." Do you agree? Explain.

6-12. "Recovering sunk costs is a major objective when replacing equipment." Do you agree? Explain.

6-13. "Past costs are indeed relevant in most instances because they provide the point of departure for the entire decision process." Do you agree? Why?

6-14. Which of the following items are relevant to replacement decisions? Explain.
   a. Book value of old equipment
   b. Disposal value of old equipment
   c. Cost of new equipment

6-15. "Some expected future costs may be irrelevant." Do you agree? Explain.

6-16. "Variable costs are irrelevant whenever they do not differ among the alternatives at hand." Do you agree? Explain.

6-17. There are two major reasons why unit costs should be analyzed with care in decision making. What are they?

6-18. "Machinery sales personnel sometimes erroneously brag about the low unit costs of using their machines." Identify one source of an error concerning the estimation of unit costs.

6-19. Give an example of a situation in which the performance evaluation model is not consistent with the decision model.

6-20. "Evaluating performance, decision by decision, is costly. Aggregate measures, such as the income statement, are frequently used." How might the wide use of income statements affect managers' decisions about buying equipment?

6-21. What is the advantage of the contribution approach as compared with the absorption approach?

6-22. "The primary classifications of costs are by variable- and fixed-cost behavior patterns, not by business functions." Name three commonly used terms that describe this type of income statement.

COGNITIVE EXERCISES

6-23 Measurement of Opportunity Cost
"Accountants cannot measure opportunity cost. Only managers have the knowledge to measure it." Do you agree with this statement? Why or why not?

6-24 Outsourcing Decisions
Decisions on whether to outsource services such a payroll accounting and systems development are much like make-or-buy decisions. What cost factors should influence the decision on whether to outsource payroll functions?

6-25 Historical Costs and Inventory Decisions
Explain why it is sometimes best to sell inventory for less than the amount paid for it.

6-26 Income Statements and Sales Managers

Suppose Chee Wong is in charge of selling Frosted Flakes for Kellogg's. What type of income statement, absorption or contribution, would Wong find most useful for his decisions? Why?

EXERCISES

6-27 Opportunity Costs

Valerie Monroe is an attorney employed by a large law firm at $85,000 per year. She is considering whether to become a sole practitioner, which would probably generate annually $320,000 in operating revenues and $220,000 in operating expenses.

Required

1. Present two tabulations of the annual income effects of these alternatives. The second tabulation should include the opportunity cost of Monroe's compensation as an employee.
2. Suppose Monroe prefers less risk and chooses to stay an employee. Show a tabulation of the income effects of rejecting the opportunity of independent practice.

6-28 Opportunity Cost of Home Ownership

Jaime Fernandez has just made the final payment on his mortgage. He could continue to live in the home; cash expenses for repairs and maintenance (after any tax effects) would be $500 monthly. Alternatively, he could sell the home for $200,000 (net of taxes), invest the proceeds in 6% municipal tax-free bonds, and rent an apartment for $10,000 annually. The landlord would then pay for repairs and maintenance.

Required

Prepare two analyses of Fernandez's alternatives, one showing no explicit opportunity cost and the second showing the explicit opportunity cost of the decision to hold the present home.

6-29 Hospital Opportunity Cost

An administrator at Sacred Heart Hospital is considering how to use some space made available when the outpatient clinic moved to a new building. She has narrowed her choices, as follows:

a. Use the space to expand laboratory testing. Expected future annual revenue would be $320,000; future costs, $290,000.
b. Use the space to expand the eye clinic. Expected future annual revenue would be $500,000; future costs, $480,000.
c. The gift shop is rented by an independent retailer who wants to expand into the vacated space. The retailer has offered $11,000 for the yearly rental of the space. All operating expenses will be borne by the retailer.

The administrator's planning horizon is unsettled. However, she has decided that the yearly data given will suffice for guiding her decision.

Required

Tabulate the total relevant data regarding the decision alternatives. Omit the concept of opportunity cost in one tabulation, but use the concept in a second tabulation. As the administrator, which tabulation would you prefer if you could receive only one?

6-30 Make or Buy

Assume that a division of Bose makes an electronic component for its speakers. Its manufacturing process for the component is a highly automated part of a just-in-time production system. All labor is considered to be an overhead cost, and all overhead is regarded as fixed with respect to output volume. Production costs for 100,000 units of the component are as follows:

Direct materials		$300,000
Factory overhead		
Indirect labor	$80,000	
Supplies	30,000	
Allocated occupancy cost	40,000	150,000
Total cost		$450,000

A small, local company has offered to supply the components at a price of $3.35 each. If the division discontinued its production of the component, it would save two-thirds of the supplies cost and $30,000 of indirect labor cost. All other overhead costs would continue.

The division manager recently attended a seminar on cost behavior and learned about fixed and variable costs. He wants to continue to make the component because the variable cost of $3.00 is below the $3.35 bid.

Required

1. Compute the relevant cost of (a) making and (b) purchasing the component. Which alternative is less costly and by how much?
2. What qualitative factors might influence the decision about whether to make or to buy the component?

6-31   Sell or Process Further

A Chevron petrochemical factory produces two products, A and B, as a result of a particular joint process. Both products are sold to manufacturers as ingredients for assorted chemical products.

Product A sells at split-off for $.25 per gallon; B, for $.30 per gallon. Data for April follow:

Joint processing cost	$1,600,000
Gallons produced and sold	
A	4,000,000
B	2,500,000

Suppose that in April the 2,500,000 gallons of B could have been processed further into Super B at an additional cost of $225,000. The Super B output would be sold for $.38 per gallon. Product A would be sold at split-off in any event.

Should B have been processed further in April and sold as Super B? Show computations.

Required

6-32   Joint Products, Multiple Choice

From a particular joint process, McClung Company produces three products, A, B, and C. Each product may be sold at the point of split-off or processed further. Additional processing requires no special facilities, and production costs of further processing are entirely variable and traceable to the products involved. In 20X0 all three products were processed beyond split-off. Joint production costs for the year were $72,000. Sales values and costs needed to evaluate McClung's 20X0 production policy follow:

			Additional Costs and Sales Values if Processed Further	
Product	Units Produced	Net Realizable Values (Sales Values) at Split-Off	Sales Values	Added Costs
A	6,000	$25,000	$42,000	$9,000
B	4,000	41,000	45,000	7,000
C	2,000	24,000	32,000	8,000

Answer the following multiple-choice questions:

Required

1. For units of C, the unit production cost most relevant to a sell-or-process-further decision is (a) $4, (b) $12, (c) $5, (d) $9.
2. To maximize profits, McClung should subject the following products to additional processing (a) C only, (b) A, B, and C, (c) B and C only, (d) A only.

6-33   Obsolete Inventory

The local bookstore bought more "Far Side" calendars than it could sell. It was nearly June and 200 calendars remained in stock. The store paid $4.50 each for the calendars and normally sold them for $8.95. Since February, they had been on sale for $6.00, and two weeks ago the price was dropped to $5.00. Still, few calendars were being sold. The bookstore manager thought it was no longer worthwhile using shelf space for the calendars.

The proprietor of Birmingham Collectibles offered to buy all 200 calendars for $240. He intended to store them a few years and then sell them as novelty items.

The bookstore manager was not sure she wanted to sell for $1.20 calendars that cost $4.50. The only alternative, however, was to scrap them because the publisher would not take them back.

Required

1. Compute the difference in profit between accepting the $240 offer and scrapping the calendars.
2. Describe how the $4.50 × 200 = $900 paid for the calendars affects your decision.

6-34 Replacement of Old Equipment

Three years ago the Heathrow TCBY bought a frozen yogurt machine for £8,000. A salesman has just suggested to the TCBY manager that she replace the machine with a new, £12,500 machine. The manager has gathered the following data:

	Old Machine	New Machine
Original cost	£8,000	£12,500
Useful life in years	8	5
Current age in years	3	0
Useful life remaining in years	5	5
Accumulated depreciation	£3,000	Not acquired yet
Book value	£5,000	Not acquired yet
Disposal value (in cash) now	£2,000	Not acquired yet
Disposal value in 5 years	0	0
Annual cash operating cost	£4,500	£ 2,000

Required

1. Compute the difference in total costs over the next five years under both alternatives, that is, keeping the original machine or replacing it with the new machine. Ignore taxes.
2. Suppose the Heathrow TCBY manager replaces the original machine. Compute the "loss on disposal" of the original machine. How does this amount affect your computation in requirement 1? Explain.

6-35 Unit Costs

K.C. Lim Company produces and sells a product that has variable costs of $9 per unit and fixed costs of $100,000 per year.

Required

1. Compute the unit cost at a production and sales level of 10,000 units per year.
2. Compute the unit cost at a production and sales level of 20,000 units per year.
3. Which of these unit costs is most accurate? Explain.

6-36 Relevant Investment

Roberta Alsdorf had obtained a new truck with a list price, including options, of $22,000. The dealer had given her a "generous trade-in allowance" of $5,500 on her old truck that had a wholesale price of $3,000. Sales tax was $1,260.

The annual cash operating costs of the old truck were $4,200. The new truck was expected to reduce these costs by one-third, to $2,800 per year.

Required

Compute the amount of the original investment in the new truck. Explain your reasoning.

6-37 Weak Division

Winnetka Electronics Company paid $8 million in cash four years ago to acquire a company that manufactures CD-ROM drives. This company has been operated as a division of Winnetka and has lost $500,000 each year since its acquisition.

The minimum desired return for this division is that, when a new product is fully developed, it should return a net profit of $500,000 per year for the foreseeable future.

Recently the IBM Corporation offered to purchase the division from Winnetka for $5 million. The president of Winnetka commented, "I've got an investment of $10 million to recoup ($8 million plus losses of $500,000 for each of four years). I have finally got this situation turned around, so I oppose selling the division now."

Prepare a response to the president's remarks. Indicate how to make this decision. Be as specific as possible.

6-38 Opportunity Cost

Rosiland Volkert, M.D., is a psychiatrist who is in heavy demand. Even though she has raised her fees considerably during the past five years, Dr. Volkert still cannot accommodate all the patients who wish to see her.

Volkert has conducted six hours of appointments a day, six days a week, for 48 weeks a year. Her fee averages $150 per hour.

Her variable costs are negligible and may be ignored for decision purposes. Ignore income taxes.

Required

1. Volkert is weary of working a six-day week. She is considering taking every other Saturday off. What would be her annual income (a) if she worked every Saturday and (b) if she worked every other Saturday?
2. What would be her opportunity cost for the year of not working every other Saturday?
3. Assume that Dr. Volkert has definitely decided to take every other Saturday off. She loves to repair her sports car by doing the work herself. If she works on her car during half a Saturday when she otherwise would not see patients, what is her opportunity cost?

6-39 Straightforward Absorption Statement

The Winthrop Company had the following data (in thousands) for a given period.

Sales	$690
Direct materials	210
Direct labor	150
Indirect manufacturing costs	170
Selling and administrative expenses	150

There were no beginning or ending inventories. Compute the (1) manufacturing cost of goods sold, (2) gross profit, (3) operating income, and (4) conversion cost (total manufacturing cost less materials cost).

6-40 Straightforward Contribution Income Statement

Ono Ltd. had the following data (in millions of yen) for a given period:

Sales	¥780
Direct materials	290
Direct labor	140
Variable factory overhead	60
Variable selling and administrative expenses	100
Fixed factory overhead	120
Fixed selling and administrative expenses	45

There were no beginning or ending inventories. Compute the (1) variable manufacturing cost of goods sold, (2) contribution margin, and (3) operating income.

6-41 Straightforward Absorption and Contribution Statement

Azteca Company had the following data (in millions) for a recent period. Fill in the blanks. There were no beginning or ending inventories.

a.	Sales	$940
b.	Direct materials used	350
c.	Direct labor	210
	Indirect manufacturing costs:	
d.	Variable	100
e.	Fixed	50
f.	Variable manufacturing cost of goods sold	_____
g.	Manufacturing cost of goods sold	_____
	Selling and administrative expenses:	
h.	Variable	90
i.	Fixed	80
j.	Gross profit	_____
k.	Contribution margin	_____

6-42 Absorption Statement

Pretoria Jewelry had the following data (in thousands of South African Rands) for a given period. Assume there are no inventories. Fill in the blanks.

Sales	R____
Direct materials	370
Direct labor	____
Indirect manufacturing	____
Manufacturing cost of goods sold	780
Gross margin	120
Selling and administrative expenses	____
Operating income	30
Prime cost (direct materials + direct labor)	600

6-43 Contribution Income Statement

Malcheski Company had the following data (in thousands) for a given period. Assume there are no inventories.

Direct labor	$170
Direct materials	210
Variable indirect manufacturing	110
Contribution margin	210
Fixed selling and administrative expenses	100
Operating income	20
Sales	980

Required

Compute the (1) variable manufacturing cost of goods sold, (2) variable selling and administrative expenses, and (3) fixed indirect manufacturing costs.

PROBLEMS

6-44 Hotel Rooms and Opportunity Costs

The Hilton Hotels Corporation operates many hotels throughout the world. Suppose one of its Chicago hotels is facing difficult times because of the opening of several new competing hotels.

To accommodate its flight personnel, American Airlines has offered Hilton a contract for the coming year that provides a rate of $50 per night per room for a minimum of 50 rooms for 365 nights. This contract would assure Hilton of selling 50 rooms of space nightly, even if some of the rooms are vacant on some nights.

The Hilton manager has mixed feelings about the contract. On several peak nights during the year, the hotel could sell the same space for $100 per room.

Required

1. Suppose the Hilton manager signs the contract. What is the opportunity cost of the 50 rooms on October 20, the night of a big convention of retailers when every nearby hotel room is occupied? What is the opportunity cost on December 28, when only 10 of these rooms would be expected to be rented at an average rate of $90?

2. If the year-round rate per room averaged $90, what percentage of occupancy of the 50 rooms in question would have to be rented to make Hilton indifferent about accepting the offer?

6-45 Extension of Preceding Problem

Assume the same facts as in the preceding problem. However, also assume that the variable costs per room per day are $10.

Required

1. Suppose the best estimate is a 53% general occupancy rate for the 50 rooms at an average $90 room rate for the next year. Should Hilton accept the contract?

2. What percentage of occupancy of the 50 rooms in question would make Hilton indifferent about accepting the offer?

6-46 Make or Buy

Eaton Corporation, based in Cleveland, is a global manufacturer of highly engineered products that serve industrial, vehicle, construction, commercial, aerospace, and semiconductor markets. It frequently subcontracts work to other manufacturers, depending on whether Eaton's facilities are fully occupied. Suppose Eaton is about to make some final decisions regarding the use of its manufacturing facilities for the coming year.

The following are the costs of making part ML7X, a key component of an emissions control system:

	Total Cost for 50,000 Units	Cost per Unit
Direct material	$ 400,000	$ 8
Direct labor	300,000	6
Variable factory overhead	150,000	3
Fixed factory overhead	300,000	6
Total manufacturing costs	$1,150,000	$23

Another manufacturer has offered to sell the same part to Eaton for $20 each. The fixed overhead consists of depreciation, property taxes, insurance, and supervisory salaries. All the fixed overhead would continue if Eaton bought the component except that the cost of $100,000 pertaining to some supervisory and custodial personnel could be avoided.

Required

1. Assume that the capacity now used to make parts will become idle if the parts are purchased. Should Eaton buy or make the parts? Show computations.

2. Assume that the capacity now used to make parts will either (a) be rented to a nearby manufacturer for $65,000 for the year or (b) be used to make oil filters that will yield a profit contribution of $200,000. Should Eaton buy or make part ML7X? Show computations.

6-47 Relevant-Cost Analysis

Following are the unit costs of making and selling a single product at a normal level of 5,000 units per month and a current unit selling price of $90:

Manufacturing costs	
Direct material	$35
Direct labor	12
Variable overhead	8
Fixed overhead (total for the year, $300,000)	5
Selling and administrative expenses	
Variable	15
Fixed (total for the year, $480,000)	8

Required

Consider each requirement separately. Label all computations, and present your solutions in a form that will be comprehensible to the company president.

1. This product is usually sold at a rate of 60,000 units per year. It is predicted that a rise in price to $97 will decrease volume by 10%. How much may advertising be increased under this plan without having annual operating income fall below the current level?

2. The company has received a proposal from an outside supplier to make and ship this item directly to the company's customers as sales orders are forwarded. Variable selling and administrative costs would fall 40%. If the supplier's proposal is accepted, the company will use its own plant to produce a new product. The new product would be sold through manufacturer's agents at a 10% commission based on a selling price of $40 each. The cost characteristics of this product, based on predicted yearly normal volume, are as follows:

	Per Unit
Direct material	$ 6
Direct labor	12
Variable overhead	8
Fixed overhead	6
Manufacturing costs	$32
Selling and administrative expenses	
Variable (commission)	10% of selling price
Fixed	$ 2

What is the maximum price per unit that the company can afford to pay to the supplier for sub-contracting production of the entire old product? Assume the following:

- Total fixed factory overhead and total fixed selling expenses will not change if the new product line is added.
- The supplier's proposal will not be considered unless the present annual net income can be maintained.
- Selling price of the old product will remain unchanged.
- All $300,000 of fixed manufacturing overhead will be assigned to the new product.

6-48 Hotel Pricing and Use of Capacity

A growing corporation in a large city has offered a 200-room Holiday Inn a one-year contract to rent 40 rooms at reduced rates of $50 per room instead of the regular rate of $85 per room. The corporation will sign the contract for 365-day occupancy because its visiting manufacturing and marketing personnel are virtually certain to use all the space each night.

Each room occupied has a variable cost of $12 per night (for cleaning, laundry, lost linens, and extra electricity).

The motel manager expects an 85% occupancy rate for the year, so she is reluctant to sign the contract. If the contract is signed, the occupancy rate on the remaining 160 rooms will be 95%.

Required

1. Compute the total contribution margin for the year with and without the contract. Is the contract profitable to Holiday Inn?
2. Compute the lowest room rate that the motel should accept on the contract so that the total contribution margin would be the same with or without the contract.

6-49 Special Air Fares

The manager of operations of Alaska Airlines is trying to decide whether to adopt a new discount fare. Focus on one 134-seat 737 airplane now operating at a 56% load factor. That is, on the average the airplane has $.56 \times 134 = 75$ passengers. The regular fares produce an average revenue of 12¢ per passenger mile.

Suppose an average 40% fare discount (which is subject to restrictions regarding time of departure and length of stay) will produce three new additional passengers. Also suppose that three of the previously committed passengers accept the restrictions and switch to the discount fare from the regular fare.

Required

1. Compute the total revenue per airplane mile with and without the discount fares.
2. Suppose the maximum allowed allocation to new discount fares is 50 seats. These will be filled. As before, some previously committed passengers will accept the restrictions and switch to the discount fare from the regular fare. How many will have to switch so that the total revenue per mile will be the same either with or without the discount plan?

6-50 Joint Costs and Incremental Analysis

Mario of Milan, a high-fashion women's dress manufacturer, is planning to market a new cocktail dress for the coming season. Mario of Milan supplies retailers in Europe and the United States.

Four yards of material are required to lay out the dress pattern. Some material remains after cutting, which can be sold as remnants. The leftover material could also be used to manufacture a matching cape and handbag. However, if the leftover material is to be used for the cape and handbag, more care will be required in the cutting, which will increase the cutting costs.

The company expects to sell 1,250 dresses if no matching cape or handbag is available. Market research reveals that dress sales will be 20% higher if a matching cape and handbag are available. The market research indicates that the cape and handbag will not be sold individually, but only as accessories with the dress. The various combinations of dresses, capes, and handbags that are expected to be sold by retailers are as follows:

	Percent of Total
Complete sets of dress, cape, and handbag	70%
Dress and cape	6%
Dress and handbag	15%
Dress only	9%
Total	100%

The material used in the dress costs EUR 80 a yard, or EUR 320 for each dress. The cost of cutting the dress if the cape and handbag are not manufactured is estimated at EUR 100 a dress, and the resulting remnants can be sold for EUR 25 for each dress cut out. If the cape and handbag are to be manufactured, the cutting costs will be increased by EUR 36 per dress. There will be no salable remnants if the capes and handbags are manufactured in the quantities estimated. The selling prices and the costs to complete the three items once they are cut are as follows:

	Selling Price per Unit	Unit Cost to Complete (Excludes Cost of Material and Cutting Operation)
Dress	EUR 1,050	EUR 400
Cape	140	100
Handbag	50	30

Required

1. Calculate the incremental profit or loss to Mario of Milan from manufacturing the capes and handbags in conjunction with the dresses.
2. Identify any nonquantitative factors that could influence the company's management in its decision to manufacture the capes and handbags that match the dress.

6-51 Relevant Cost

Debraceny Company's unit costs of manufacturing and selling a given item at the planned activity level of 10,000 units per month are

Manufacturing costs	
Direct materials	$4.20
Direct labor	.60
Variable overhead	.70
Fixed overhead	.80
Selling expenses	
Variable	3.00
Fixed	1.10

Ignore income taxes in all requirements. These four parts have no connection with each other.

Required

1. Compute the planned annual operating income at a selling price of $12 per unit.
2. Compute the expected annual operating income if the volume can be increased by 20% when the selling price is reduced to $11. Assume the implied cost behavior patterns are correct.
3. The company desires to seek an order for 5,000 units from a foreign customer. The variable selling expenses for the order will be 40% less than usual, but the fixed costs for obtaining the order will be $6,000. Domestic sales will not be affected. Compute the minimum break-even price per unit to be considered.
4. The company has an inventory of 2,000 units of this item left over from last year's model. These must be sold through regular channels at reduced prices. The inventory will be valueless unless sold this way. What unit cost is relevant for establishing the minimum selling price of these 2,000 units?

6-52 New Machine

A new $300,000 machine is expected to have a five-year life and a terminal value of zero. It can produce 40,000 units a year at a variable cost of $4 per unit. The variable cost is $6 per unit with an old machine, which has a book value of $150,000. It is being depreciated on a straight-line basis at $30,000 per year. It too is expected to have a terminal value of zero. Its current disposal value is also zero because it is highly specialized equipment.

The salesman of the new machine prepared the following comparison:

	New Machine	Old Machine
Units	40,000	40,000
Variable costs	$160,000	$240,000
Straight-line depreciation	60,000	30,000
Total cost	$220,000	$270,000
Unit cost	$ 5.50	$ 6.75

He said, "The new machine is obviously a worthwhile acquisition. You will save $1.25 for every unit you produce."

Required

1. Do you agree with the salesman's analysis? If not, how would you change it? Be specific. Ignore taxes.
2. Prepare an analysis of total and unit differential costs if the annual volume is 20,000 units.
3. At what annual volume would both the old and new machines have the same total relevant costs?

6-53 Conceptual Approach

A large automobile-parts plant was constructed four years ago in a Pennsylvania city served by two railroads. The PC Railroad purchased 40 specialized 60-foot freight cars as a direct result of the additional traffic generated by the new plant. The investment was based on an estimated useful life of 20 years.

Now the competing railroad has offered to service the plant with new 86-foot freight cars, which would enable more efficient shipping operations at the plant. The automobile-parts company has threatened to switch carriers unless PC Railroad buys 10 new 86-foot freight cars.

The PC marketing management wants to buy the new cars, but PC operating management says, "The new investment is undesirable. It really consists of the new outlay plus the loss on the old freight cars. The old cars must be written down to a low salvage value if they cannot be used as originally intended."

Required

Evaluate the comments. What is the correct conceptual approach to the quantitative analysis in this decision?

6-54 Book Value of Old Equipment

Consider the following data:

	Old Equipment	Proposed New Equipment
Original cost	$24,000	$12,000
Useful life in years	8	3
Current age in years	5	0
Useful life remaining in years	3	3
Accumulated depreciation	$15,000	0
Book value	9,000	*
Disposal value (in cash) now	3,000	*
Annual cash operating costs (maintenance, power, repairs, lubricants, etc.)	$12,000	$ 8,000

* Not acquired yet.

1. Prepare a cost comparison of all relevant items for the next three years together. Ignore taxes.

2. Prepare a cost comparison that includes both relevant and irrelevant items. (See Exhibit 6-4, p. 240.)

3. Prepare a comparative statement of the total charges against revenue for the first year. Would the manager be inclined to buy the new equipment? Explain.

6-55 Decision and Performance Models

Refer to problem 6-A3.

1. Suppose the "decision model" favored by top management consisted of a comparison of a three-year accumulation of wealth under each alternative. Which alternative would you choose? Why? (Accumulation of wealth means cumulative increase in cash.)

2. Suppose the "performance evaluation model" emphasized the net income of a subunit (such as a division) each year rather than considering each project, one by one. Which alternative would you expect a manager to choose? Why?

3. Suppose the same quantitative data existed, but the "enterprise" was a city and the "machine" was a computer in the treasurer's department. Would your answers to the first two parts change? Why?

6-56 Review of Relevant Costs

The *New York Times* reported that Neil Simon planned to open his play, *London Suite,* off-Broadway. Why? For financial reasons. Producer Emanuel Azenberg predicted the following costs before the play even opened:

	On Broadway	Off-Broadway
Sets, costumes, lights	$ 357,000	$ 87,000
Loading in (building set, etc.)	175,000	8,000
Rehearsal salaries	102,000	63,000
Director and designer fees	126,000	61,000
Advertising	300,000	121,000
Administration	235,000	100,000
Total	$1,295,000	$440,000

Broadway ticket prices average $55, and theaters can seat about 1,000 persons per show. Off-Broadway prices average only $40, and the theaters seat only 500. Normally plays run eight times a week, both on and off Broadway. Weekly operating expenses off Broadway average $82,000; they average an extra $124,000 on Broadway for a weekly total of $206,000.

1. Suppose 400 persons attended each show, whether on or off Broadway. Compare the weekly financial results from a Broadway production to one produced off Broadway.

2. Suppose attendance averaged 75% of capacity, whether on or off Broadway. Compare the weekly financial results from a Broadway production to one produced off Broadway.

3. Compute the attendance per show required just to cover weekly expenses (a) on Broadway and (b) off Broadway.

4. Suppose average attendance on Broadway was 600 per show and off Broadway was 400. Compute the total net profit for a 26-week run (a) on Broadway and (b) off Broadway. Be sure to include the pre-opening costs.

5. Repeat requirement 4 for a 100-week run.

6. Using attendance figures from requirements 4 and 5, compute (a) the number of weeks a Broadway production must run before it breaks even, and (b) the number of weeks an off-Broadway production must run before it breaks even.

7. Using attendance figures from requirements 4 and 5, determine how long a play must run before the profit from a Broadway production exceeds that from an off-Broadway production.

8. If you were Neil Simon, would you prefer *London Suite* to play on Broadway or off Broadway? Explain.

6-57 Make or Buy, Opportunity Costs, and Ethics

Camden Food Products, Inc., produces a wide variety of food and related products. The company's tomato canning operation relies partly on tomatoes grown on Camden's own farms and partly on tomatoes bought from other growers.

Camden's tomato farm is on the edge of Sharpestown, a fast-growing, medium-sized city. It produces 8 million pounds of tomatoes a year and employs 55 persons. The annual costs of tomatoes grown on this farm are

Variable production costs	$ 600,000
Fixed production costs	1,200,000
Shipping costs (all variable)	200,000
Total costs	$2,000,000

Fixed production costs include depreciation on machinery and equipment, but not on land because land should not be depreciated. Camden owns the land, which was purchased for $600,000 many years ago. A recent appraisal placed the value of the land at $15 million because it is a prime site for an industrial park and shopping center.

Camden could purchase all the tomatoes it needs on the market for $.25 per pound delivered to its factory. If it did this, it would sell the farmland and shut down the operations in Sharpestown. If the farm were sold, $300,000 of the annual fixed costs would be saved. Camden can invest excess cash and earn an annual rate of 8%.

Required

1. How much does it cost Camden annually for the land used by the tomato farm?
2. How much would Camden save annually if it closed the tomato farm? Is this more or less than would be paid to purchase the tomatoes on the market?
3. What ethical issues are involved with the decision to shut down the tomato farm?

6-58 Irrelevance of Past Costs at Starbucks

Starbucks purchases and roasts high-quality whole-bean coffees, its hallmark, and sells them, along with other coffee-related products, primarily through its company-operated retail stores.

Suppose that the quality-control manager at Starbucks discovered a 1,000-pound batch of roasted beans that did not meet the company's quality standards. Company policy would not allow such beans to be sold with the Starbucks name on it. However, it could be reprocessed, at which time it could be sold by Starbucks' retail stores, or it could be sold as-is on the wholesale coffee-bean market.

Assume that the beans were initially purchased for $2,000, and the total cost of roasting the batch was $1,500, including $500 of variable cost and $1,000 of fixed costs (primarily depreciation on the equipment).

The wholesale price at which Starbucks could sell the beans was $2.65 per pound. Purchasers would pay the shipping costs from the Starbucks plant to their warehouse.

If the beans were reprocessed, the processing cost would be $600 because the beans would not require as much processing as new beans. All $600 would be additional costs, that is, costs that would not be incurred without the reprocessing. The beans would be sold to the retail stores for $3.70 per pound, and Starbucks would have to pay an average of $.20 per pound to ship the beans to the stores.

Required

1. Should Starbucks sell the beans on the market as-is for $2.65 per pound, or should the company reprocess the beans and sell them through its own retail stores? Why?
2. Compute the amount of extra profit Starbucks earns from the alternative you selected in requirement 1 compared to what it would earn from the other alternative.
3. What cost numbers in the problem were irrelevant to your analysis? Explain why they were irrelevant.

CASES

6-59 Make or Buy

The Minnetonka Corporation, which produces and sells to wholesalers a highly successful line of water skis, has decided to diversify to stabilize sales throughout the year. The company is considering the production of cross-country skis.

After considerable research, a cross-country ski line has been developed. Because of the conservative nature of the company management, however, Minnetonka's president has decided to introduce only one type of the new skis for this coming winter. If the product is a success, further expansion in future years will be initiated.

The ski selected is a mass-market ski with a special binding. It will be sold to wholesalers for $80 per pair. Because of available capacity, no additional fixed charges will be incurred to produce the skis. A $100,000 fixed charge will be absorbed by the skis, however, to allocate a fair share of the company's present fixed costs to the new product.

Using the estimated sales and production of 10,000 pair of skis as the expected volume, the accounting department has developed the following costs per pair of skis and bindings:

Direct labor	$35
Direct material	30
Total overhead	15
Total	$80

Minnetonka has approached a subcontractor to discuss the possibility of purchasing the bindings. The purchase price of the bindings from the subcontractor would be $5.25 per binding, or $10.50 per pair. If the Minnetonka Corporation accepts the purchase proposal, it is predicted that direct-labor and variable-overhead costs would be reduced by 10% and direct-material costs would be reduced by 20%.

Required

1. Should the Minnetonka Corporation make or buy the bindings? Show calculations to support your answer.

2. What would be the maximum purchase price acceptable to the Minnetonka Corporation for the bindings? Support your answer with an appropriate explanation.

3. Instead of sales of 10,000 pair of skis, revised estimates show sales volume at 12,500 pair. At this new volume, additional equipment, at an annual rental of $10,000, must be acquired to manufacture the bindings. This incremental cost would be the only additional fixed cost required even if sales increased to 30,000 pair. (The 30,000 level is the goal for the third year of production.) Under these circumstances, should the Minnetonka Corporation make or buy the bindings? Show calculations to support your answer.

4. The company has the option of making and buying at the same time. What would be your answer to requirement 3 if this alternative were considered? Show calculations to support your answer.

5. What nonquantifiable factors should the Minnetonka Corporation consider in determining whether they should make or buy the bindings?

6-60 Make or Buy

The Rohr Company's old equipment for making subassemblies is worn out. The company is considering two courses of action: (a) completely replacing the old equipment with new equipment or (b) buying subassemblies from a reliable outside supplier, who has quoted a unit price of $1 on a seven-year contract for a minimum of 50,000 units per year.

Production was 60,000 units in each of the past two years. Future needs for the next seven years are not expected to fluctuate beyond 50,000 to 70,000 units per year. Cost records for the past two years reveal the following unit costs of manufacturing the subassembly:

Direct material	$ .30
Direct labor	.35
Variable overhead	.10
Fixed overhead (including $.10 depreciation and	
$.10 for direct departmental fixed overhead)	.25
	$1.00

The new equipment will cost $188,000 cash, will last seven years, and will have a disposal value of $20,000. The current disposal value of the old equipment is $10,000.

The sales representative for the new equipment has summarized her position as follows: The increase in machine speeds will reduce direct labor and variable overhead by 35¢ per unit. Consider last year's experience of one of your major competitors with identical equipment. They produced 100,000 units under operating conditions very comparable to yours and showed the following unit costs.

Direct material	$.30
Direct labor	.05
Variable overhead	.05
Fixed overhead, including depreciation of $.24	.40
Total	$.80

Required

For purposes of this case, assume that any idle facilities cannot be put to alternative use. Also assume that 5¢ of the old Rohr unit cost is allocated fixed overhead that will be unaffected by the decision.

1. The president asks you to compare the alternatives on a total-annual-cost basis and on a per-unit basis for annual needs of 60,000 units. Which alternative seems more attractive?
2. Would your answer to requirement 1 change if the needs were 50,000 units? 70,000 units? At what volume level would Rohr be indifferent between making and buying subassemblies? Show your computations.
3. What factors, other than the preceding ones, should the accountant bring to the attention of management to assist them in making their decision? Include the considerations that might be applied to the outside supplier.

6-61 Analysis with Contribution Income Statement

The following data have been condensed from Avignon Corporation's report of 2001 operations (in millions of Euros [EUR]):

	Variable	**Fixed**	**Total**
Manufacturing cost of goods sold	EUR 400	EUR 180	EUR 580
Selling and administrative expenses	140	60	200
Sales			900

Required

1. Prepare the 2001 income statement in contribution form, ignoring income taxes.
2. Avignon's operations have been fairly stable from year to year. In planning for the future, top management is considering several options for changing the annual pattern of operations. You are asked to perform an analysis of their estimated effects. Use your contribution income statement as a framework to compute the estimated operating income (in millions) under each of the following separate and unrelated assumptions.
   a. Assume that a 10% reduction in selling prices would cause a 30% increase in the physical volume of goods manufactured and sold.
   b. Assume that an annual expenditure of EUR 30 million for a special sales promotion campaign would enable the company to increase its physical volume by 10% with no change in selling prices.
   c. Assume that a basic redesign of manufacturing operations would increase annual fixed manufacturing costs by EUR 80 million and decrease variable manufacturing costs by 15% per product unit, but with no effect on physical volume or selling prices.
   d. Assume that a basic redesign of selling and administrative operations would double the annual fixed expenses for selling and administration and increase the variable expenses for selling and administration by 25% per product unit, but would also increase physical volume by 20%. Selling prices would be increased by 5%.
   e. Would you prefer to use the absorption form of income statement for the preceding analyses? Explain.
3. Discuss the desirability of alternatives a through d in requirement 2. If only one alternative could be selected, which would you choose? Explain.

COLLABORATIVE LEARNING EXERCISE

6-62 Outsourcing

A popular term for make-or-buy decisions is *outsourcing* decisions. There are many examples of outsourcing, from Nike's outsourcing of nearly all its production activities to small firms' outsourcing of their payroll activities. Especially popular outsourcing activities are warehousing and computer systems.

The purpose of this exercise is to share information on different types of outsourcing decisions. It can be done in small groups or as an entire class. Each student should pick an article from the literature that tells about a particular company's outsourcing decision. There are many such articles: a recent electronic search of the business literature turned up more than 4,000 articles. An easy way to find such an article is to search an electronic database of business literature. Magazines that have had outsourcing articles include *Fortune, Forbes, Business Week,* and *Management Accounting.* Many business sections of newspapers also have published such articles. The *Wall Street Journal* usually has a couple of articles on outsourcing each month.

Required

1. List as many details about the outsourcing decision as you can. Include the type of activity that is being outsourced, the size of the outsourcing, and the type of company providing the outsourcing service.

2. Explain why the company decided to outsource the activity. If reasons are not given in the article, prepare a list of reasons that you think influenced the decision.

3. What disadvantages are there to outsourcing the activity?

4. Be prepared to make a 3- to-5-minute presentation to the rest of the group or to the class covering your answers to requirements 1, 2, and 3.

INTERNET EXERCISE

6-63 Green Mountain Coffee Company

How do firms determine what type of information is useful for a given decision? Is it possible for firms to have too much information? While a look at a firm's Internet site provides us with lots of information, not all of it is necessarily useful for a particular decision. Let's look at the Green Mountain Coffee Company and see what information on the site would be useful for some specific decisions.

www.prenhall.com/horngren

1. Go to the home page of Green Mountain Coffee Roasters at http://www.greenmountaincoffee.com. What are the major topics on which a user can click and be taken to a page with more detailed information? Would you likely find the same type of information if you clicked on the links to anyone of these? Why do you suppose Green Mountain Coffee chose those particular subtopics for its home page?

2. Where would you look on the site if you wanted to know more about Green Mountain Coffee's financial information? Did the company make a profit for the last year? What was the major expense that the firm encountered? Did the firm pay any dividends last year? If you were interested in an income-producing stock, would you want to invest in Green Mountain Coffee Roasters?

3. Which link would you want to use if you wanted to gain knowledge concerning differences in coffees? Click on this link now. This page has additional links about coffee. Which one(s) of the links are likely to provide information to help learn about differences in coffees? Click on one of the links you just identified. What type of information about coffee differences does it provide? Did your link provide any information concerning costs as being a difference? Do you think that this would be a difference between coffees?

4. The site provides extensive information about Social Responsibility. What areas in particular does the firm highlight? Is this information useful in helping determine if the company's coffee products taste good? What about the quality of the product? Would this information be useful to a potential investor in Green Mountain Coffee's common stock?

Go to the "Special Decisions—Make or Buy" episode on the *Mastering Accounting* CD-ROM for an interactive, video-enhanced exercise that focuses on the need for CanGo's managers to understand the benefits and costs directly related to a project so CanGo can plan correctly for the holiday season rush.

THE MASTER BUDGET

This entrance to a Ritz-Carlton hotel projects its image of quality. High quality is expensive, and Ritz-Carlton managers must assess the planned expenditures for quality-enhancing features versus the added revenues these features will bring.

www.prenhall.com/horngren

Learning Objectives

When you have finished studying this chapter, you should be able to

1. *Explain the major features and advantages of a master budget.*

2. *Follow the principal steps in preparing a master budget.*

3. *Prepare the operating budget and the supporting schedules.*

4. *Prepare the financial budget.*

5. *Understand the difficulties of sales forecasting.*

6. *Anticipate possible human relations problems caused by budgets.*

7. *Use a spreadsheet to develop a budget (Appendix 7).*

8. **Understand the importance of budgeting to managers.**

If you have ever traveled, you will know that there is a big difference between staying in a cheap motel and staying in a five-star, world-class hotel. You can think of the difference as that of riding in an old Ford Pinto versus riding in a Rolls-Royce. The first takes care of your basic needs, but the second surrounds you in comfort and luxury, catering to your every whim. The experience of staying in a luxurious hotel can simply take your breath away. No one knows that better than the managers of the Ritz-Carlton chain of hotels. After all, the word *ritzy*, which means glamorous and luxurious, is actually derived from the name of the Ritz Hotel. Thanks to fierce competition in the industry, though, Ritz-Carlton managers have their share of challenges in running successful hotels.

What does it take to run a world-class hotel successfully? Good location, exquisite food, luxury, personalized service, and quality are essential ingredients. But you might be surprised to learn that, at the Ritz-Carlton hotels, the budgeting process is also a key to success. According to Ralph Vick, General Manager of the Phoenix Ritz-Carlton, "Budgets are crucial to the ultimate financial success of our hotels." Why are budgets so important? Mainly because they serve as a road map toward achieving goals. Budgets are a manager's tool to understand, plan, and control operations, and Ritz-Carlton wants to give its managers the best tools possible. As a result, the company takes the budgeting process very seriously.

At the Ritz-Carlton hotels, all employees, from the hotel manager, to the controller, to the newest housekeeper, are involved in the budgeting process. Working in teams, they set budget targets for the expenses they can control. These target figures help not only in planning, but also in controlling and evaluating employee performance. Actual results are compared with previously budgeted target figures, and workers are evaluated based on the differences. Even nonfinancial measures of performance are important. Ritz-Carlton managers use nonfinancial measures of quality and customer satisfaction in addition to financial reports to evaluate and reward employees.

Planning is the key to good management. This statement is certainly true for Ritz-Carlton, and it is also true for other types of business organizations—small family-owned companies, large corporations, government agencies, and nonprofit organizations—as well as for individuals. For example, most successful students who earn good grades, finance their education, and finish their degrees on time do so because they plan their time, their work, and their recreation. These students are budgeting their scarce resources to make the best use of their time, money, and energy. Similarly, business owners and managers need to budget their resources—which includes everything from raw materials to human resources to facilities—to make the best and most profitable use of what they have to work with. Budgeting can cover such diverse issues as how much time to spend sanding a piece of wood to how much money the company will allot to research and development in the coming year. Company budgets always aim to squeeze the most out of available resources.

In this chapter we will look at the uses and benefits of budgets and consider the construction of the master budget.

BUDGETS AND THE ORGANIZATION

Most people associate the word *budget* with limitations on spending. For example, governments often approve spending budgets for their various agencies. Then they expect the agencies to keep their expenditures within the limits prescribed by the budget. In contrast, most business organizations use budgets to focus attention on company operations and finances, not just to limit spending. Budgets highlight potential problems and advantages early, allowing managers to take steps to avoid these problems or use the advantages wisely.

A budget is a tool that helps managers in both their planning and control functions. Interestingly, budgets help managers with their control function not only by looking forward but also by looking backward. Budgets, of course, deal with what managers plan for the future. However, they also can be used to evaluate what happened in the past. Budgets can be used as a benchmark that allows managers to compare actual performance with estimated or desired performance. Keeping score is an American tradition, whether on the football field or in the boardroom, and budgets provide the standards for evaluating and "scoring" the company "players."

Recent surveys show just how valuable budgets can be. Study after study has shown the budget to be the most widely used and highest rated tool for cost reduction and control. Advocates of budgeting go so far as to claim that the process of budgeting forces a manager to become a better administrator and puts planning in the forefront of the manager's mind. Actually, many seemingly healthy businesses have died because managers failed to draw up, monitor, and adjust budgets to changing conditions.

ADVANTAGES OF BUDGETS

A budget is a formal business plan. All managers do some kind of planning. Sometimes plans are unwritten. Such plans might work in a small organization, but as an organization grows, informal, seat-of-the-pants planning is not enough. A more formal plan—a budgetary system—becomes a necessity.

Skeptical managers have claimed, "I face too many uncertainties and complications to make budgeting worthwhile for me." Be wary of such claims. Planning and budgeting are especially important in uncertain environments. A budget allows systematic rather than chaotic reaction to change. For example, the Natural Resources Group of W.R. Grace & Co. greatly reduced its planned expansion in reaction to a worldwide abundance of oil and gas. A top executive, quoted in the company's annual report, stated that "management used the business planning process to adjust to changes in operating conditions."

Three major benefits of budgeting are as follows.

1. Budgeting compels managers to think ahead by formalizing their responsibilities for planning.

2. Budgeting provides definite expectations that are the best framework for judging subsequent performance.

3. Budgeting aids managers in coordinating their efforts, so that the plans of an organization's subunits meet the objectives of the organization as a whole.

Let's look more closely at each of these benefits.

FORMALIZATION OF PLANNING

Budgeting forces managers to think ahead—to anticipate and prepare for changing conditions. The budgeting process makes planning an explicit management responsibility. Too often, managers operate on a day-to-day basis, extinguishing one business brush fire after another. They simply have "no time" for any tough-minded thinking beyond the next day's problems. Planning takes a back seat to or is actually obliterated by daily pressures.

The trouble with the day-to-day approach to managing an organization is that objectives are never crystallized. Managers react to current events rather than planning for the future. To prepare a budget, a manager should set goals and objectives and establish policies to aid their achievement. The objectives are the destination points, and budgets are the road maps guiding us to those destinations. Without goals and objectives, company operations lack direction, problems are not foreseen, and results are difficult to interpret afterward.

FRAMEWORK FOR JUDGING PERFORMANCE

Budgeted goals and performance are generally a better basis for judging actual results than is past performance. The news that a company had sales of $100 million this year, as compared with $80 million the previous year, may or may not indicate that the company has been effective and has met company objectives. Perhaps sales should have been $110 million this year. The major drawback of using historical results for judging current performance is that inefficiencies may be concealed in the past performance. Changes in economic conditions, technology, personnel, competition, and so forth also limit the usefulness of comparisons with the past.

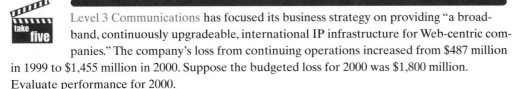

Level 3 Communications has focused its business strategy on providing "a broadband, continuously upgradeable, international IP infrastructure for Web-centric companies." The company's loss from continuing operations increased from $487 million in 1999 to $1,455 million in 2000. Suppose the budgeted loss for 2000 was $1,800 million. Evaluate performance for 2000.

ANSWER

Comparing Level 3's performance in 2000 to that in 1999 makes it appear that performance slipped because the loss was $968 larger in 2000 than it was in 1999. However, the loss was $345 less than budgeted, showing that the company did better than expected. During this period Level 3 was implementing a major shift in strategy to recognize the new Internet economy. The company stated that it is "well ahead of our original plans to position ourselves as the leading provider of broadband infrastructure services." Comparing actual results to plans gives a better picture of how well Level 3 is meeting its plans than would a comparison to past results.

COMMUNICATION AND COORDINATION

Budgets tell employees what is expected of them. Nobody likes to drift along, not knowing what the boss expects or hopes to achieve. A good budget process communicates both from the top down and from the bottom up. Top management makes clear the goals and objectives of the organization in its budgetary directives. Employees and lower-level managers then inform higher-level managers how they plan to achieve the goals and objectives.

Budgets also help managers coordinate objectives. For example, a budget forces purchasing personnel to integrate their plans with production requirements, while production managers use the sales budget and delivery schedule to help them anticipate and plan for the employees and physical facilities they will need. Similarly, financial officers use the sales budget, purchasing requirements, and so forth to anticipate the company's need for cash. Thus the budgetary process forces managers to visualize the relationship of their department's activities to those of other departments and the company as a whole.

TYPES OF BUDGETS

There are several different types of budgets used by businesses. The most forward-looking budget is the **strategic plan,** which sets the overall goals and objectives of the organization. Some business analysts won't classify the strategic plan as an actual budget, though, because it does not deal with a specific time frame, and it does not produce forecasted financial statements. In any case, the strategic plan leads to **long-range planning,** which produces forecasted financial statements for five- to ten-year periods. The financial statements are estimates of what management would like to see in the company's future financial statements. Decisions made during long-range planning include addition or deletion of product lines, design and location of new plants, acquisitions of buildings and equipment, and other long-term commitments. Long-range plans are coordinated with **capital budgets,** which detail the planned expenditures for facilities, equipment, new products, and other long-term investments.

Long-range plans and budgets give the company direction and goals for the future, while short-term plans and budgets guide day-to-day operations. Managers who pay attention only to short-term budgets will quickly lose sight of long-term goals. Similarly, managers who pay attention only to the long-term budget could wind up mismanaging day-to-day operations. There has to be a happy medium that allows managers to pay attention to their short-term budgets while still keeping an eye on long-term plans. Enter the master budget. The **master budget** is an extensive analysis of the first year of the long-range plan. A master budget summarizes the planned activities of all subunits of an organization—sales, production, distribution, and finance. The master budget quantifies targets for sales, cost-driver activity, purchases, production, net income, cash position, and any other objective that management specifies. It expresses these amounts in the form of forecasted financial statements and supporting operating schedules. These supporting schedules provide the information that is too highly detailed to appear in the actual financial statements. Thus, the master budget is a periodic business plan that includes a coordinated set of detailed operating schedules and financial statements. It includes forecasts of sales, expenses, cash receipts and disbursements, and balance sheets. Master budgets (also called pro forma statements, another term for forecasted financial statements) might consist of 12 monthly budgets for the year or perhaps monthly budgets for only the first quarter and quarterly budgets for the three remaining quarters. In the process of preparing the master budget, managers make many important decisions about how to best deploy the organization's resources.

Continuous budgets or rolling budgets are a very common form of master budgets that simply add a month in the future as the month just ended is dropped. Budgeting thus becomes an ongoing instead of periodic process. Continuous budgets force managers to

Margin glossary

strategic plan A plan that sets the overall goals and objectives of the organization.

long-range planning Producing forecasted financial statements for five- to ten-year periods.

capital budget A budget that details the planned expenditures for facilities, equipment, new products, and other long-term investments.

Objective 1
Explain the major features and advantages of a master budget.

master budget A budget that summarizes the planned activities of all subunits of an organization.

continuous budget (rolling budget) A common form of master budget that adds a month in the future as the month just ended is dropped.

always think about the next 12 months, not just the remaining months in a fixed budgeting cycle. As they add a new twelfth month to a continuous budget, managers may update the other 11 months as well. Then they can compare actual monthly results with both the original plan and the most recently revised plan.

COMPONENTS OF MASTER BUDGET

The terms used to describe specific budget schedules vary from organization to organization. However, most master budgets have common elements. The usual master budget for a nonmanufacturing company has the following components:

A. Operating budget

    1. Sales budget (and other cost-driver budgets as necessary)

    2. Purchases budget

    3. Cost-of-goods-sold budget

    4. Operating expenses budget

    5. Budgeted income statement

B. Financial budget

    1. Capital budget

    2. Cash budget

    3. Budgeted balance sheet

Exhibit 7-1 shows the relationships among the various parts of a master budget for a nonmanufacturing company. In addition to these categories, manufacturing companies that maintain inventories prepare ending inventory budgets and additional budgets for each type of resource activity (such as labor, materials, and factory overhead).

The two major parts of a master budget are the operating budget and the financial budget. The **operating budget** focuses on the income statement and its supporting schedules. Although sometimes called the profit plan, an operating budget may show a budgeted loss, or may even be used to budget expenses in an organization or agency with no sales revenues. In contrast, the **financial budget** focuses on the effects that the operating budget and other plans (such as capital budgets and repayments of debt) will have on cash.

In addition to the master budget, there are countless forms of special budgets and related reports. For example, a report might detail goals and objectives for improvements in quality or customer satisfaction during the budget period.

operating budget (profit plan) A major part of a master budget that focuses on the income statement and its supporting schedules.

financial budget The part of a master budget that focuses on the effects that the operating budget and other plans (such as capital budgets and repayments of debt) will have on cash.

PREPARING THE MASTER BUDGET

Let's return to Exhibit 7-1 and trace the preparation of the master budget components. Follow each step carefully and completely. Although the process may seem largely mechanical, remember that the master-budgeting process generates key decisions regarding all aspects of the company's value chain. Therefore, the first draft of the budget leads to decisions that prompt subsequent drafts before a final budget is chosen.

THE COOKING HUT

To illustrate the budgeting process we will use as an example the Cooking Hut Company (CHC), a local retailer of a wide variety of kitchen and dining room items such as coffeemakers, silverware, and table linens. The company rents a retail store in a midsize community near Denver. CHC's management prepares a continuous budget to aid

Exhibit 7-1

Preparation of Master Budget for Nonmanufacturing Company

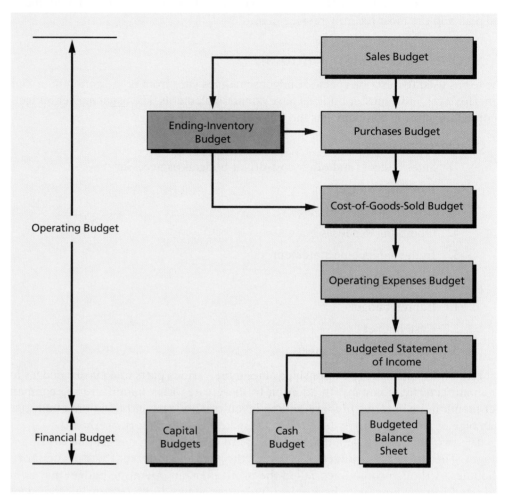

financial and operating decisions. For simplicity in this illustration, the planning horizon is only four months, April through July. In the past, sales have increased during this season. However, the company's collections have always lagged well behind its sales. As a result, the company has often found itself pressed to come up with the cash for purchases, employee wages, and other operating outlays. To help meet this cash squeeze, CHC has used short-term loans from local banks, paying them back when cash comes in. CHC plans to keep on using this system.

Exhibit 7-2 is the closing balance sheet for the fiscal year ending March 31, 20X1. Sales in March were $40,000. Monthly sales are forecasted as follows:

April	$50,000
May	$80,000
June	$60,000
July	$50,000
August	$40,000

Management expects future sales collections to follow past experience: customers pay 60% of the sales in cash and 40% on credit. All credit accounts are collected in the month following the sales. The $16,000 of accounts receivable on March 31 represents

Exhibit 7-2

The Cooking Hut Company
Balance Sheet March 31, 20X1

Assets

Current assets		
Cash	$10,000	
Accounts receivable, net (.4 × March sales of $40,000)	16,000	
Merchandise inventory, $20,000 + 7 (.8 × April sales of $50,000)	48,000	
Unexpired insurance	1,800	$ 75,800
Plant assets		
Equipment, fixtures, and other	$37,000	
Accumulated depreciation	12,800	24,200
Total assets		$100,000

Liabilities and Owners' Equity

Current liabilities		
Accounts payable (.5 × March purchases of $33,600)	$16,800	
Accrued wages and commissions payable ($1,250 + $3,000)	4,250	$ 21,050
Owners' equity		78,950
Total liabilities and owners' equity		$100,000

credit sales made in March (40% of $40,000). Uncollectible accounts are negligible and thus ignored. For simplicity's sake, we will ignore all local, state, and federal taxes for this illustration.

Because deliveries from suppliers and customer demands are uncertain, at the end of each month CHC wants to have on hand a basic inventory of items valued at $20,000 plus 80% of the expected cost of goods sold for the following month. The cost of merchandise sold averages 70% of sales. Therefore, the inventory on March 31 is $20,000 + .7(.8 × April sales of $50,000) = $20,000 + $28,000 = $48,000. The purchase terms available to CHC are net, 30 days. CHC pays for each month's purchases as follows: 50% during that month and 50% during the next month. Therefore, the accounts payable balance on March 31 is 50% of March's purchases, or $33,600 × .5 = $16,800.

CHC pays wages and commissions semimonthly, half a month after they are earned. They are divided into two portions: monthly fixed wages of $2,500 and commissions, equal to 15% of sales, which we will assume are uniform throughout each month. Therefore, the March 31 balance of accrued wages and commissions payable is (.5 × $2,500) + .5(.15 × $40,000) = $1,250 + $3,000 = $4,250. CHC will pay this $4,250 on April 15.

In addition to buying new fixtures for $3,000 cash in April, CHC's other monthly expenses are as follows.

Miscellaneous expenses	5% of sales, paid as incurred
Rent	$2,000, paid as incurred
Insurance	$200 expiration per month
Depreciation, including new fixtures	$500 per month

The company wants a minimum of $10,000 as a cash balance at the end of each month. To keep this simple, we will assume that CHC can borrow or repay loans in multiples of $1,000. Management plans to borrow no more cash than necessary and to

Photon Technology International, Inc., manufactures electro-optical instruments used for medical research and diagnostic procedures. Sales in 2000 were just over $7 million. Its products are state-of-the-art, but until the early 1990s, Photon did not have a formal budgeting procedure. Like many small, fast-growing companies, budgeting was not a priority. But as sales approached $5 million and the company found itself on the verge of financial failure, a budget became essential. Collection of sales from customers was slow, research and development outlays were high, and Photon was fast running out of cash.

Photon hired a professional financial manager who instituted a budget process that links cash flow, intensive high-technology research and development, customer training and education, and on-site product customization. Coordination of all of these factors is absolutely critical in this new, high-technology firm. This budget process develops three "what-if" scenarios: (1) a best-case budget where everything goes as hoped, (2) a worst-case budget that predicts just the opposite, and (3) a most-likely-case budget where each budget forecast (sales, sales collections, cost-driver activity, cost behavior, and so on) is examined and set at a realistic level. This budget process allows Photon to anticipate cash flow problems before they threaten the company's survival and to communicate critical resource needs within the company. Photon believes that implementing a formal budget process was a critical step in its transition from a start-up to a maturing company.

Source: Adapted from Charles L. Grant, "High-Tech Budgeting," *Management Accounting*, May 1991, pp. 30–31 and *Photon Technology International 2000 Annual Report.*

repay as promptly as possible. Assume that borrowing occurs at the beginning and repayment at the end of the months in question. Interest is paid, under the terms of this credit arrangement, when the related loan is repaid. The interest rate is 12% per year.

STEPS IN PREPARING THE MASTER BUDGET

Objective 2
Follow the principal steps in preparing a master budget.

The principal steps in preparing the master budget are

Basic Data

1. Using the data given, prepare the following detailed schedules for each of the months of the planning horizon:
   a. Sales budget
   b. Cash collections from customers
   c. Purchases budget
   d. Disbursements for purchases
   e. Operating expense budget
   f. Disbursements for operating expenses

Operating Budget

2. Using these schedules, prepare a budgeted income statement for the 4 months ending July 31, 20X1 (Exhibit 7-3).

Financial Budget

3. Using the data given and the supporting schedules, prepare the following forecasted financial statements:
   a. Capital budget
   b. Cash budget, including details of borrowings, repayments, and interest for each month of the planning horizon (Exhibit 7-4)
   c. Budgeted balance sheet as of July 31, 20X1 (Exhibit 7-5)

Exhibit 7-3

The Cooking Hut Company

Budgeted Income Statement for Four Months Ending July 31, 20X1

		Data	Source of Data
Sales		$240,000	Schedule a
Cost of goods sold		168,000	Schedule c
Gross margin		$ 72,000	
Operation expenses:			
Wages and commissions	$46,000		Schedule e
Rent	8,000		Schedule e
Miscellaneous	12,000		Schedule e
Insurance	800		Schedule e
Depreciation	2,000	68,800	Schedule e
Income from operations		$ 3,200	
Interest expense		440	Exhibit 7-4
Net income		$ 2,760	

Organizations with effective budget systems have specific guidelines for the steps and timing of budget preparation. Although the details differ, the guidelines invariably include the preceding steps. As we follow these steps to prepare CHC's master budget, be sure that you understand the source of each figure in each schedule and budget.

Exhibit 7-4

The Cooking Hut Company

Cash Budget for Four Months Ending July 31, 20X1

	April	May	June	July
Beginning cash balance	$ 10,000	$10,550	$ 10,980	$10,080
Minimum cash balance desired	10,000	10,000	10,000	10,000
Available cash balance (x)	$ 0	$ 550	$ 980	$ 80
Cash receipts and disbursements:				
Collections from customers (Schedule b*)	$ 46,000	$68,000	$ 68,000	$54,000
Payments for merchandise (Schedule d)	(42,700)	(48,300)	(40,600)	(32,900)
Payments for operating expenses (Schedule f)	(13,750)	(18,250)	(18,000)	(15,250)
Purchase of new fixtures (given)	(3,000)			
Net cash receipts and disbursements (y)	$(13,450)	$ 1,450	$ 9,400	$ 5,850
Excess (deficiency) of cash				
before financing ($x + y$)	$(13,450)	$ 2,000	$ 10,380	$ 5,930
Financing				
Borrowing (at beginning of month)	$ 14,000†			
Repayments (at end of month)	—	$(1,000)	$(10,000)	$ (3,000)
Interest (at 12% per year‡)	—	(20)	(300)	(120)
Total cash increase (decrease) from				
financing (z)	$ 14,000	$(1,020)	$(10,300)	$(3,120)
Ending cash balance (beginning balance + y + z)	$ 10,550	$10,980	$ 10,080	$12,810

* Letters are keyed to the explanation in the text.
† Borrowing and repayment of principal are made in multiples of $1,000, at an interest rate of 12% per year.
‡ Interest computations: .12 × $1,000 × 2/12; .12 × $10,000 × 3/12; .12 × $3,000 × 4/12.

Exhibit 7-5

The Cooking Hut Company

Budgeted Balance Sheet July 31, 20X1

Assets		
Current assets		
Cash (Exhibit 7-4)	$ 12,810	
Accounts receivable, net (.4 × July sales of $50,000, Schedule a)	20,000	
Merchandise inventory (Schedule c)	42,400	
Unexpired insurance ($1,800 − $800)	1,000	$ 76,210
Plant assets		
Equipment, fixtures, and other ($37,000 + $3,000 fixtures)	$ 40,000	
Accumulated depreciation ($12,800 + $2,000 depreciation expense)	(14,800)	25,200
Total assets		$101,410

Liabilities and Owners' Equity		
Current liabilities		
Accounts payable (.5 × July purchases of $29,400, Schedule c)	$ 14,700	
Accrued wages and commissions payable (.5 × $10,000, Schedule e)	5,000	$ 19,700
Owners' equity ($78,950 + $2,760 net income)		81,710
Total liabilities and owners' equity		$101,410

Note: Beginning balances are used as a start for the computations of unexpired insurance, plant, and owners' equity.

STEP 1: PREPARING BASIC DATA

Objective 3
Prepare the operating budget and the supporting schedules.

Step 1a: Sales Budget. The sales budget (Schedule a in the following table) is the starting point for budgeting for CHC because inventory levels, purchases, and operating expenses are geared to the expected level of sales. Accurate sales forecasting is essential to effective budgeting. (Sales forecasting is considered in a later section of this chapter.) March sales are included in Schedule a because they affect cash collections in April. Trace the final column in Schedule a to the first row of Exhibit 7-3. In nonprofit organizations, forecasts of revenue or some level of services are also the focal points for budgeting. Examples are patient revenues and government reimbursement expected by hospitals and donations expected by churches. If no revenues are generated, as in the case of municipal fire protection, a desired level of service is predetermined.

Step 1b: Cash Collections from Customers. It is easiest to prepare Schedule b, cash collections, at the same time that we prepare the sales budget. Cash collections from customers include the current month's cash sales plus the previous month's credit sales. We will use total collections in preparing the cash budget—see Exhibit 7-4.

	March	April	May	June	July	April–July Total
Schedule a: Sales Budget						
Credit sales, 40%	$16,000	$20,000	$32,000	$24,000	$20,000	
Plus cash sales, 60%	24,000	30,000	48,000	36,000	30,000	
Total sales	$40,000	$50,000	$80,000	$60,000	$50,000	$240,000

Schedule b: Cash Collections

Cash sales this month	$30,000	$48,000	$36,000	$30,000
Plus 100% of last month's credit sales	16,000	20,000	32,000	24,000
Total collections	$46,000	$68,000	$68,000	$54,000

Step 1c: Purchases Budget. After budgeting sales and cash collections, we prepare the purchases budget (Schedule c). The total merchandise needed will be the sum of the desired ending inventory plus the amount needed to fulfill budgeted sales demand. The total need will be partially met by the beginning inventory; the remainder must come from planned purchases. These purchases are computed as follows:

$$\text{budgeted purchases} = \text{desired ending inventory}$$
$$+ \text{cost of goods sold} - \text{beginning inventory}$$

Trace the total purchases figure in the final column of Schedule c to the second row of Exhibit 7-3.

	March	April	May	June	July	April–July Total
Schedule c: Purchases Budget						
Desired ending inventory	$48,000*	$64,800	$ 53,600	$48,000	$42,400	
Plus cost of goods sold†	28,000	35,000	56,000	42,000	35,000	$168,000
Total needed	$76,000	$99,800	$109,600	$90,000	$77,400	
Less beginning inventory	42,400‡	48,000	64,800	53,600	48,000	
Purchases	$33,600	$51,800	$ 44,800	$36,400	$29,400	
Schedule d: Disbursements for Purchases						
50% of last month's purchases		$16,800	$ 25,900	$22,400	$18,200	
Plus 50% of this month's purchases		25,900	22,400	18,200	14,700	
Disbursements for purchases		$42,700	$ 48,300	$40,600	$32,900	

* $20,000 + (.8 × April cost of goods sold) = $20,000 + .8($35,000) = $48,000.
† .7 × March sales of $40,000 = $28,000; .7 × April sales of $50,000 = $35,000, and so on.
‡ $20,000 + (.8 × March cost of goods sold of $28,000) = $20,000 + $22,400 = $42,400.

Step 1d: Disbursements for Purchases. We next use the purchases budget to develop Schedule d, disbursements for purchases. In our example, disbursements include 50% of the current month's purchases and 50% of the previous month's purchases. We will use total disbursements in preparing the cash budget, Exhibit 7-4.

Step 1e: Operating Expense Budget. The budgeting of operating expenses depends on several factors. Month-to-month changes in sales volume and other cost-driver activities directly influence many operating expenses. Examples of expenses driven by sales volume include sales commissions and many delivery expenses. Other expenses, such as rent, insurance, depreciation, and salaries, are not influenced by sales within appropriate relevant ranges, and we regard them as fixed. Trace the total operating expenses in the final column of Schedule e, which summarizes these expenses, to the budgeted income statement, Exhibit 7-3.

	March	April	May	June	July	April–July Total
Schedule e: Operating Expense Budget						
Wages (fixed)	$2,500	$ 2,500	$ 2,500	$ 2,500	$ 2,500	
Commissions (15% of current month's sales)	6,000	7,500	12,000	9,000	7,500	
Total wages and commissions	$8,500	$10,000	$14,500	$11,500	$10,000	$46,000
Miscellaneous expenses (5% of current sales)		2,500	4,000	3,000	2,500	12,000
Rent (fixed)		2,000	2,000	2,000	2,000	8,000
Insurance (fixed)		200	200	200	200	800
Depreciation (fixed)		500	500	500	500	2,000
Total operating expenses		$15,200	$21,200	$17,200	$15,200	$68,800

Step 1f: Disbursements for Operating Expenses. Disbursements for operating expenses are based on the operating expense budget. Disbursements include 50% of last month's and this month's wages and commissions, and miscellaneous and rent expenses. We will use the total of these disbursements in preparing the cash budget, Exhibit 7-4.

	March	April	May	June	July	April–July Total
Schedule f: Disbursements for Operating Expenses						
Wages and commissions:						
50% of last month's expenses		$ 4,250	$ 5,000	$ 7,250	$ 5,750	
50% of this month's expenses		5,000	7,250	5,750	5,000	
Total wages and commissions		$ 9,250	$12,250	$13,000	$10,750	
Miscellaneous expenses		2,500	4,000	3,000	2,500	
Rent		2,000	2,000	2,000	2,000	
Total disbursements		$13,750	$18,250	$18,000	$15,250	

STEP 2: PREPARING THE OPERATING BUDGET

Steps 1a, 1c, and 1e provide enough information to construct a budgeted income statement from operations (Exhibit 7-3). The income statement will be complete after addition of the interest expense, which we can compute only after the cash budget has been prepared. Budgeted income from operations is often a benchmark for judging management performance.

STEP 3: PREPARATION OF FINANCIAL BUDGET

Objective 4
Prepare the financial budget.

The second major part of the master budget is the financial budget, which consists of the capital budget, cash budget, and ending balance sheet. This chapter focuses on the cash budget and the ending balance sheet. Chapter 11 discusses the capital budget. In our illustration, the $3,000 purchase of new fixtures would be included in the capital budget.

cash budget A statement of planned cash receipts and disbursements.

Step 3b: Cash Budget. The **cash budget** is a statement of planned cash receipts and disbursements. The cash budget is heavily affected by the level of operations summarized in the budgeted income statement. The cash budget has the following major sections, where the letters w, x, y, and z refer to the lines in Exhibit 7-4 that summarize the effects of that section:

- The available cash balance (x) equals the beginning cash balance less the minimum cash balance desired.

- Cash receipts and disbursements (y):

  1. Cash receipts depend on collections from customers' accounts receivable, cash sales, and on other operating cash income sources such as interest received on notes receivable. Trace total collections from Schedule b to Exhibit 7-4.

  2. Disbursements for purchases depend on the credit terms extended by suppliers and the bill-paying habits of the buyer. Trace payments for merchandise from Schedule d to Exhibit 7-4.

  3. Payroll depends on wage, salary, and commission terms and on payroll dates. Trace wages and commissions from Schedule f to Exhibit 7-4.

  4. Some costs and expenses depend on contractual terms for installment payments, mortgage payments, rents, leases, and miscellaneous items. Trace disbursements for operating expenses from Schedule f to Exhibit 7-4.

  5. Other disbursements include outlays for fixed assets, long-term investments, dividends, and the like. An example is the $3,000 expenditure for new fixtures.

- The cash needed from (or used for) financing (z) depend on the total available cash balance, x in Exhibit 7-4, and the net cash receipts and disbursements, y. If cash available plus net cash receipts less disbursements is negative, borrowing is necessary—Exhibit 7-4 shows that CHC will borrow $14,000 in April to cover the planned deficiency. If it is positive, loans may be repaid—$1,000, $10,000, and $3,000 are repaid in May, June, and July, respectively. The pertinent outlays for interest expenses are usually contained in this section of the cash budget. Trace the calculated interest expense to Exhibit 7-3, which then will be complete.

- The ending cash balance is the beginning cash balance + y + z. Financing, z, has either a positive (borrowing) or a negative (repayment) effect on the cash balance. The illustrative cash budget shows the pattern of short-term, "self-liquidating" financing. Seasonal peaks often result in heavy drains on cash—for merchandise purchases and operating expenses—before the company makes sales and collects cash from customers. The resulting loan is "self-liquidating"—that is, the company uses borrowed money to acquire merchandise for sale, and uses the proceeds from sales to repay the loan. This "working capital cycle" moves from cash to inventory to receivables and back to cash.

Cash budgets help management to avoid having unnecessary idle cash, on the one hand, and unnecessary cash deficiencies, on the other. A well-managed financing program keeps cash balances from becoming too large or too small.

Step 3c: Budgeted Balance Sheet. The final step in preparing the master budget is to construct the budgeted balance sheet (Exhibit 7-5) that projects each balance sheet item in accordance with the business plan as expressed in the previous schedules. Specifically, the beginning balances at March 31 would be increased or decreased in light of the expected cash receipts and cash disbursements in Exhibit 7-4 and in light of the effects of noncash items appearing on the income statement in Exhibit 7-3. For example, unexpired insurance would decrease from its balance of $1,800 on March 31 to $1,000 on July 31, even though it is a noncash item.

When the complete master budget is formulated, management can consider all the major financial statements as a basis for changing the course of events. For example, the initial formulation of the financial statements may prompt management to try new sales strategies to generate more demand. Alternatively, management may explore the

The last decade has seen a flurry of entrepreneurial activities. Start-up companies in a variety of high-tech industries have mushroomed into multibillion dollar companies. Consider InfoSpace, Inc., as an example. Naveen Jain, chairman and chief strategist, founded InfoSpace in April 1996 after leaving Microsoft. Jain took InfoSpace public in December 1998. By March 2000 the market value of InfoSpace stock was $30 billion. Jain's vision for InfoSpace is grand: "When the history of the impending [information] revolution is written, one name will be credited for helping map its route, and powering its progress, InfoSpace."

How do start-up companies get started? An essential component in securing initial funding for a start-up is the development of a business plan. The federal government's Small Business Administration recommends a business plan with three sections:

1. The Business—Includes a description of the business, a marketing plan, an assessment of the competition, a listing of operating procedures, and a roster of personnel.

2. Financial Data—Includes the following items.

   Loan applications

   Capital equipment and supply list

   Balance sheet

   Break-even analysis

   Pro-forma income projections (profit and loss statements)
   Three-year summary
   Detail by month, first year
   Detail by quarters, second and third years
   Assumptions upon which projections were based

   Pro-forma cash flow

3. Supporting Documents—Includes a variety of legal documents and information about the principals involved, suppliers, customers, etc.

Financial data are an important part of a business plan, the centerpiece of which is the budget. Without a well-developed budget, companies such as InfoSpace would not be able to raise the capital needed to start and expand their businesses. The pro-forma income projections and pro-forma cash flow, essentially a budgeted income statement and budgeted cash flow statement, are essential to predicting the future prospects of any business. They are especially critical to assessing the prospects of a new company that has little history to analyze.

The importance of a budget to a start-up company was emphasized by Jim Rowan, former senior vice president of Sun America, Inc., who left to form a new company, EncrypTix. He raised $36 million in investment funding to spin EncrypTix off from Stamps.com. The company focuses on Internet delivery and storage of tickets, coupons, and vouchers. Rowan stated, "The key thing for a start-up is to develop a budget and put it like a stake in the ground, so you can measure against it. It's not a ceiling, it's not carved in stone, but you have to have something that's a benchmark."

Budgeting is not often the most exciting task for entrepreneurs. However, lack of a credible budget is one of the main reasons venture capitalists will refuse funding for start-up companies. Further, it is one of the main causes of failure of the companies themselves. Anyone wanting to be an entrepreneur would be well advised to study budgeting and learn how it can be a powerful tool both for managing the company and for promoting the company to potential investors.

Sources: Adapted from Small Business Administration, *The Business Plan: Roadmap to Success* (http://www.sba.gov/starting/indexbusplans.html), *InfoSpace 2000 Annual Report* (http://www.infospace.com/about/annual_report/html/home.htm), and K. Klein, "Budgeting Helps Secure Longevity," *Los Angeles Times* (Aug. 2, 2000), p. C6.

effects of various adjustments in the timing of receipts and disbursements. The large cash deficiency in April, for example, may lead to an emphasis on cash sales or an attempt to speed up collection of accounts receivable. In any event, the first draft of the master budget is rarely the final draft. As it is reworked, the budgeting process becomes an integral part of the management process itself—budgeting is planning and communicating.

How does the operating budget differ from the financial budget?

ANSWER

The operating budget focuses on the income statement, which is prepared using accrual accounting. It measures revenues and expenses. In contrast, the financial budget focuses primarily on cash flow. It measures the receipts and disbursements of cash. The operating budget is a better measure of overall performance, but the financial budget is essential to plan for cash needs. A lack of cash rather than poor operating performance often gets companies into trouble.

DIFFICULTIES OF SALES FORECASTING

Objective 5
Understand the difficulties of sales forecasting.

As you saw in the CHC example, the sales budget is the foundation of the entire master budget. The accuracy of estimated purchases budgets, production schedules, and costs depends on the detail and accuracy (in dollars, units, and mix) of the budgeted sales. At the Ritz-Carlton hotels, the process of developing the sales budget involves forecasting levels of room occupancy, group events, banquets, and other activities. Upper management initially sets the costs of these activities. Then, employee teams in each department provide ideas for improvements (cost reductions). Managers prepare monthly departmental budgets based on the annual master budget.

As we stated earlier, and as you might have noticed from Ritz-Carlton's budgeting practices, the sales budget depends entirely on sales forecasts. Although *sales budget* and *sales forecast* sound as if they might be the same thing, be aware that a forecast and a budget are not necessarily identical. A **sales forecast** is a prediction of sales under a given set of conditions. A **sales budget** is the result of decisions to create the conditions that will generate a desired level of sales. For example, you may have forecasts of sales at various levels of advertising. The forecast for the one level you decide to implement becomes the budget.

sales forecast A prediction of sales under a given set of conditions.

sales budget The result of decisions to create conditions that will generate a desired level of sales.

Sales forecasts are usually prepared under the direction of the top sales executive. Important factors considered by sales forecasters include the following.

1. *Past patterns of sales*: Past experience combined with detailed past sales by product line, geographical region, and type of customer can help predict future sales.

2. *Estimates made by the sales force*: A company's sales force is often the best source of information about the desires and plans of customers.

3. *General economic conditions*: Predictions for many economic indicators, such as gross domestic product and industrial production indexes (local and foreign), are published regularly. Knowledge of how sales relate to these indicators can aid sales forecasting.

4. *Competitors' actions*: Sales depend on the strength and actions of competitors. To forecast sales, a company should consider the likely strategies and reactions of competitors, such as changes in their prices, product quality, or services.

5. *Changes in the firm's prices*: Sales can be increased by decreasing prices and vice versa. A company should consider the effects of price changes on customer demand (see Chapter 5).

6. *Changes in product mix*: Changing the mix of products often can affect not only sales levels but also overall contribution margin. Identifying the most profitable products and devising methods to increase their sales is a key part of successful management.

7. *Market research studies*: Some companies hire market experts to gather information about market conditions and customer preferences. Such information is useful to managers making sales forecasts and product mix decisions.

8. *Advertising and sales promotion plans*: Advertising and other promotional costs affect sales levels. A sales forecast should be based on anticipated effects of promotional activities.

Sales forecasting usually combines various techniques. In addition to the opinions of the sales staff, statistical analysis of correlations between sales and economic indicators (prepared by economists and members of the market research staff) provide valuable help. The opinions of line management also heavily influence the final sales forecasts. Ultimately, no matter how many technical experts are used in forecasting, the sales budget is the responsibility of line management.

Sales forecasting is still somewhat mystical, but its procedures are becoming more formalized and are being reviewed more seriously because of the intensity of global competitive pressures. Although this book does not include a detailed discussion of the preparation of the sales budget, the importance of an accurate sales forecast cannot be overstressed.

Interestingly, governments and other nonprofit organizations also face a problem similar to sales forecasting. For example, the budget for city revenues may depend on a variety of factors, such as predicted property taxes, traffic fines, parking fees, license fees, and city income taxes. In turn, property taxes depend on the extent of new construction and, in most localities, general increases in real estate values. Thus, a municipal budget may require forecasting that is just as sophisticated as that required by a private firm.

GETTING EMPLOYEES TO ACCEPT THE BUDGET

Objective 6
Anticipate possible human relations problems caused by budgets.

No matter how accurate sales forecasts are, if budgets are to benefit an organization, they need the support of all the firm's employees. The attitude of top management will heavily influence lower-level workers' and managers' attitudes toward budgets. Even with the support of top management, however, budgets—and the managers who implement them—can run into opposition.

Managers often compare actual results with budgets in evaluating subordinates. Few individuals are immediately ecstatic about techniques used to check their performance. Lower-level managers sometimes regard budgets as embodiments of restrictive, negative top-management attitudes. Accountants reinforce this view if they use a budget only to point out managers' failings. Such negative attitudes are even greater when the budget's primary purpose is to limit spending. For example, budgets are generally unpopular in government agencies where their only use is to request and authorize funding. To avoid negative attitudes toward budgets, accountants and top management must demonstrate how budgets can help each manager and employee achieve better results. Only then will the budgets become a positive aid in motivating employees at all levels to work toward goals, set objectives, measure results accurately, and direct attention to the areas that need investigation.

Another serious human relations problem that can negate the benefits of budgeting arises if budgets stress one set of performance goals but employees and managers are rewarded for different performance measures. For example, a budget may concentrate on current costs of production, but managers and employees may be rewarded on quality of production (defect rate) and on timely delivery of products to customers (percent on time). These measures of performance could be in direct conflict.

The overriding importance of the human aspects of budgeting cannot be overemphasized. Too often, top management and accountants are overly concerned with the mechanics of budgets, ignoring the fact that the effectiveness of any budgeting system depends directly on whether the affected managers and employees understand and accept the budget. Budgets created with the active participation of all affected employees are generally more effective than budgets imposed on subordinates. This involvement is usually called **participative budgeting.**

For example, Ritz-Carlton's budgeting system includes all hotel employees and is thus a participative system. In fact, employee "buy-in" to the budget is so important at Ritz-Carlton that self-directed employee teams at all levels of the company have the authority to change operations based on budgets as they see fit.

participative budgeting
Budgets formulated with the active participation of all affected employees.

FINANCIAL PLANNING MODELS

Because a well-made budget considers all aspects of the company (the entire value chain), it serves as an effective model for decision making. For example, managers can use the master budget to predict how various decisions might affect the company in both the long run and the short run. Using the master budget in this way is a step-by-step process in which tentative plans are revised as managers exchange views on various aspects of expected activities.

Today, most large companies have developed **financial planning models,** mathematical models of the master budget that can react to any set of assumptions about sales, costs, product mix, and so on. For instance, Dow Chemical's model uses 140 separate, constantly revised cost inputs that are based on several different cost drivers.

financial planning models
Mathematical models of the master budget that can react to any set of assumptions about sales, costs, or product mix.

By mathematically describing the relationships among all the operating and financial activities covered in the master budget and among the other major internal and external factors that can affect the results of management decisions, financial planning models allow managers to assess the predicted impacts of various alternatives before final decisions are selected. For example, a manager might want to predict the consequences of changing the mix of products offered for sale to emphasize several products with the highest prospects for growth. A financial planning model would provide operational and financial budgets well into the future under alternative assumptions about the product mix, sales levels, production constraints, quality levels, scheduling, and so on. Most importantly, managers can get answers to "what if" questions, such as "What if sales are 10% below forecasts? What if material prices increase 8% instead of 4% as expected? What if the new union contract grants a 6% raise in consideration for productivity improvements?"

Financial planning models have shortened managers' reaction times dramatically. A revised plan for a large company that took many accountants many days to prepare by hand can be prepared in minutes. For example, Public Service Electric & Gas, a New Jersey utility company, can run its total master budget several times a day, if necessary.

Warning: The use of spreadsheet software on personal computers has put financial planning models within reach of even the smallest organizations. The ready access to powerful modeling, however, does not guarantee plausible or reliable results. Financial planning models are only as good as the assumptions and the inputs used to build and manipulate them—what computer specialists call GIGO (garbage in, garbage out). Nearly every chief financial officer has a horror story to tell about following bad advice from a faulty financial planning model.

Activity-based costing (ABC) is growing in popularity. However, companies do not realize the real benefits of ABC until they totally integrate it into their budgeting system. Often accountants "own" the costing system of a company, but the budgeting system belongs to managers. To use an activity-based framework for budgeting means that all managers must focus on managing activities. They must prepare their budgets using the same framework used by the ABC system. For example, in 1997 and 1998 Dow Chemical integrated its new ABC system with its budgeting process. To be successful, this required a massive training effort attended by "controllers, accountants, work process subject matter experts, cost center owners, business manufacturing leaders, and site general managers." With budgets consistent with cost reports, Dow gained much benefit from its activity-based budgeting system.

To see how activity-based budgeting helps a company, let's compare methods using a company's purchasing department as an example. The purchasing department's previous-year results might appear as follows, based on a traditional view of costs:

Purchasing Department	
Salaries	$200,000
Benefits	75,000
Supplies	30,000
Travel	10,000
Total	$315,000

If management wants to reduce costs by 10% overall ($31,500) using the traditional view of costs, purchasing may simply reduce each cost category by 10%. This method of cost reduction is sometimes referred to as "slash and burn." However, it is the managers who often wind up getting burned by this technique. For example, at Borg-Warner Automotive, virtually all managers expressed dissatisfaction with the budgeting process. Each year managers made cost estimates as part of the annual budgeting procedure. But because the company used a slash-and-burn cost-cutting technique, these

budgets were "almost surely" returned with a directive to cut costs across the board. Managers got so frustrated that they started overestimating costs to compensate for the cuts they knew were coming.

Using activity-based cost information, the purchasing department's budget might appear as follows:

Purchasing Department	
Activity	
Certify 10 new vendors	$ 65,450
Issue 450 purchase orders	184,640
Issue 275 releases	64,910
Total	$315,000

Activity-based budgeting links financial data with the activity that consumed the related resource. Instead of using the slash-and-burn method, the department now targets specific activities that can be reduced without hurting its overall effectiveness. For example, the department may be able to reduce the number of vendor certifications to five. Assuming that vendor certification costs are variable with respect to the number of vendors, this would reduce certification costs by $5 \times (\$65,450 \div 10)$ or $32,725, enabling the department to meet or exceed its budget target.

Many companies that implement activity-based costing primarily for product costing purposes realize many more benefits after implementation. For example, a snack-food processor used one financial planning model for activity-based product costing purposes but, after implementing the model, the company now uses it for budgeting, manpower projections, new pricing strategies, and product rationalization.

Sources: Adapted from "Implementing Activity-Based Costing: The Model Approach," Institute of Management Accounting and Sapling Corporation, November 1994; G. Hanks, M. Fried, and J. Huber, "Shifting Gears at Borg-Warner Automotive," *Management Accounting*, February 1994, pp. 25–29, and J. Damitio, G. Hayes, and P. Kintzele, "Integrating ANC and ABM at Dow Chemical," *Management Accounting Quarterly*, Winter 2000, pp. 22–26.

SUMMARY PROBLEM FOR YOUR REVIEW

Do not attempt to solve this problem until you understand every step in this chapter's CHC example.

PROBLEM

The Country Store is a retail outlet for a variety of hardware and housewares. The owner of the Country Store is eager to prepare a budget for the next quarter, which is typically quite busy. She is most concerned with her cash position because she expects that she will have to borrow to finance purchases in anticipation of sales. She has gathered all the data necessary to prepare the simplified budget shown in Exhibit 7-6. In addition, she will purchase equipment in April for $19,750 cash and pay dividends of $4,000 in June. Review the structure of the example in the chapter and then prepare the Country Store's master budget for the months of April, May, and June. The solution follows after the budget data. Note that there are a few minor differences between this example and the one in the chapter. These are identified in Exhibit 7-6 and in the solution. The primary difference is in the payment of interest on borrowing. Borrowing occurs at the end of a month when cash is needed. Repayments (if appropriate) occur at the end of a month when cash is available. Interest also is paid in cash at the end of the month at an annual rate of 12% on the amount of note payable outstanding during that month.

Exhibit 7-6

The Country Store
Budget Data

Balance Sheet as of March 31, 20X1		Budgeted Sales:	
Assets		March (actual)	$60,000
Cash	$ 9,000	April	70,000
Accounts receivable	48,000	May	85,000
Inventory	12,600	June	90,000
Plant and equipment (net)	200,000	July	50,000
Total assets	$269,600		
		Other data:	
Liabilities and equities		Required minimum cash balance	$ 8,000
Interest payable	0	Sales mix, cash/credit	
Note payable	0	Cash sales	20%
Accounts payable	18,300	Credit sales (collected the	
Capital stock	180,000	following month)	80%
Retained earnings	71,300	Gross profit rate	40%
Total liabilities and equities	$269,600	Loan interest rate	
		(interest paid in cash monthly)	12%
Budgeted expenses (per month)		Inventory paid for in	
Wages and salaries	$ 7,500	Month purchased	50%
Freight out as a percent of sales	6%	Month after purchase	50%
Advertising	$ 6,000		
Depreciation	$ 2,000		
Other expense as a percent of sales	4%		
Minimum inventory policy as a percent			
of next month's cost of goods sold	30%		

SOLUTION

Schedule a: Sales budget

	April	May	June	Total
Credit sales, 80%	$56,000	$68,000	$72,000	$196,000
Cash sales, 20%	14,000	17,000	18,000	49,000
Total sales	$70,000	$85,000	$90,000	$245,000

Schedule b: Cash collections

	April	May	June	Total
Cash sales	$14,000	$17,000	$18,000	$ 49,000
Collections from prior month	48,000	56,000	68,000	172,000
Total collections	$62,000	$73,000	$86,000	$221,000

Schedule c: Purchases budget

	April	May	June	Total
Desired ending inventory	$15,300	$16,200	$ 9,000	$ 40,500
Plus cost of goods sold	42,000	51,000	54,000	147,000
Total needed	$57,300	$67,200	$63,000	$187,500
Less beginning inventory	12,600	15,300	16,200	44,100
Total purchases	$44,700	$51,900	$46,800	$143,400

Schedule d: Cash disbursements for purchases

	April	May	June	Total
For March*	$18,300			$ 18,300
For April	22,350	$22,350		44,700
For May		25,950	$25,950	51,900
For June			23,400	23,400
Total disbursements	$40,650	$48,300	$49,350	$138,300

*The amount payable on the March 31, 20X1, balance sheet.

Schedules e and f: Operating expenses and disbursements for expenses (except interest)

	April	May	June	Total
Cash expenses:				
Salaries & wages	$ 7,500	$ 7,500	$ 7,500	$22,500
Freight-out	4,200	5,100	5,400	14,700
Advertising	6,000	6,000	6,000	18,000
Other expenses	2,800	3,400	3,600	9,800
Total disbursements for expenses	$20,500	$22,000	$22,500	$65,000
Noncash expenses:				
Depreciation	2,000	2,000	2,000	6,000
Total expenses	$22,500	$24,000	$24,500	$71,000

The Country Store
Cash Budget
April–June, 20X1

	April	May	June
Beginning cash balance	$ 9,000	$ 8,000	$ 8,000
Minimum cash balance desired	8,000	8,000	8,000
Available cash balance	1,000	0	0
Cash receipts and disbursements:			
Collections from customers	62,000	73,000	86,000
Inventory purchases	(40,650)	(48,300)	(49,350)
Operating expenses	(20,500)	(22,000)	(22,500)
Equipment purchases	(19,750)	0	0
Dividends	0	0	(4,000)
Interest*	0	(179)	(154)
Net cash receipts and disbursements	(18,900)	2,521	9,996
Excess (deficiency) of cash			
before financing	$(17,900)	$ 2,521	$ 9,996
Financing:			
Borrowing†	$ 17,900	$ 0	$ 0
Repayments	0	(2,521)	(9,996)
Total cash from financing	17,900	(2,521)	(9,996)
Ending cash balance	$ 8,000	$ 8,000	$ 8,000

*In this example interest is paid on the loan amounts outstanding during the month: May: $(.12 \div 12) \times (\$17,900) = \$179$; June: $(.12 \div 12) \times (\$17,900 - \$2,521) = \$154$.

†In this example, borrowings are at the end of the month in the amounts needed. Repayments also are made at the end of the month as excess cash permits.

The Country Store
Budgeted Income Statement
April–June, 20X1

	April	May	June	April–June Total
Sales	$70,000	$85,000	$90,000	$245,000
Cost of goods sold	42,000	51,000	54,000	147,000
Gross margin	28,000	34,000	36,000	98,000
Operating expenses				
Salaries and wages	7,500	7,500	7,500	22,500
Freight-out	4,200	5,100	5,400	14,700
Advertising	6,000	6,000	6,000	18,000
Other	2,800	3,400	3,600	9,800
Interest*	—	179	154	333
Depreciation	2,000	2,000	2,000	6,000
Total operating				
expense	$22,500	$24,179	$24,654	$ 71,333
Net operating income	$ 5,500	$ 9,821	$11,346	$ 26,667

*Note that interest expense is the monthly interest rate times the borrowed amount held for the month: May $(.12 \div 12) \times \$17,900 = \$179$; June: $(.12 \div 12) \times \$15,379 = \$154$.

The Country Store
Budgeted Balance Sheets as of the Ends of April–June, 20X1

Assets	April	May	June*
Current assets			
Cash	$ 8,000	$ 8,000	$ 8,000
Accounts receivable	56,000	68,000	72,000
Inventory	15,300	16,200	9,000
Total current assets	79,300	92,200	89,000
Plant, less accumulated depreciation†	217,750	215,750	213,750
Total assets	$297,050	$307,950	$302,750

Liabilities and Equities			
Liabilities			
Accounts payable	$ 22,350	$ 25,950	$ 23,400
Notes payable	17,900	15,379	5,383
Total liabilities	40,250	41,329	28,783
Stockholders' equity			
Capital stock	180,000	180,000	180,000
Retained earnings	76,800	86,621	93,967
Total equities	256,800	266,621	273,967
Total liabilities and equities	$297,050	$307,950	$302,750

*The June 30, 20X1 balance sheet is the ending balance sheet for the quarter.

†$200,000 + $19,750 − $2,000 = $217,750.

Highlights to Remember

Explain the major features and advantages of a master budget. A budget expresses, in quantitative terms, an organization's objectives and possible steps for achieving them. Thus, a budget is a tool that helps managers in both their planning and control functions. The two major parts of a master budget are the operating budget and the financial budget. Advantages of budgets include formalization of planning, providing a framework for judging performance, and aiding managers in coordinating their efforts.

Follow the principal steps in preparing a master budget. Master budgets typically cover relatively short periods—usually one month to one year. The steps involved in preparing the master budget vary across organizations but follow the general outline given on page 276. Invariably, the first step is to forecast sales or service levels. The next step should be to forecast cost-driver activity levels, given expected sales and service. Using these forecasts and knowledge of cost behavior, collection patterns, and so on, managers can prepare the operating and financing budgets.

Prepare the operating budget and the supporting schedules. The operating budget is the income statement for the budget period. Managers prepare it using the following supporting schedules: sales budget, purchases budget, and operating expenses.

Prepare the financial budget. The second major part of the master budget is the financial budget. The financial budget consists of a cash budget, capital budget, and a budgeted balance sheet. Managers prepare the cash budget from the following supporting schedules: cash collections, disbursements for purchases, and disbursements for operating expenses.

Understand the difficulties of sales forecasting. Sales forecasting combines various techniques as well as opinions of sales staff and management. Sales forecasters must consider many factors such as past patterns of sales, economic conditions, and competitors' actions. Sales forecasting is difficult because of its complexity and the rapid changes in the business environment in which most companies operate.

Anticipate possible human relations problems caused by budgets. The success of a budget depends heavily on employee reaction to it. Negative attitudes toward budgets usually prevent realization of many of the potential benefits. Such attitudes are usually caused by managers who use budgets to force behavior or to punish employees or who use budgets only to limit spending. Budgets generally are more useful when they are formulated with the willing participation of all affected parties.

Understand the importance of budgeting to managers. The budgetary process compels managers to think and to prepare for changing conditions. Budgets are aids in planning, communicating, setting standards of performance, motivating personnel toward goals, measuring results, and directing attention to problem areas that need investigation.

Appendix 7: Use of Spreadsheets for Budgeting

Objective 7
Use a spreadsheet to develop a budget.

Spreadsheet software for personal computers is an extremely powerful and flexible tool for budgeting. An obvious advantage of the spreadsheet is that arithmetic errors are virtually nonexistent. The real value of spreadsheets, however, is that they can be used to make a mathematical model (a financial planning model) of the organization. This model can be used repeatedly at a very low cost and can be altered to reflect possible changes in expected sales, cost drivers, cost functions, and so on. The objective of this appendix is to illustrate sensitivity analysis, one aspect of the power and flexibility of spreadsheet software that has made this software an indispensable budgeting tool.

Recall the chapter's CHC example. Suppose CHC has prepared its master budget using spreadsheet software. To simplify making changes to the budget, the relevant forecasts and other budgeting details have been placed in Exhibit 7-7. Note that for simplification, only the data necessary for the purchases budget have been shown here. The full master budget would require a larger table with all the data given in the chapter.

A spreadsheet consists of a grid where every "cell" falls in one row and one column. We label each cell with its column (a letter) and its row (a number). For example, the beginning inventory for the budget period is in "D4," which is shown as $48,000.

By referencing the budget data's cell addresses, you can generate the purchases budget (Exhibit 7-8) within the same spreadsheet by entering formulas instead of

Exhibit 7-7

The Cooking Hut Company
Budget Data (Column and row labels are given by the spreadsheet)

	A	B	C	D	E	F	G
1	Budget data						
2	Sales forecasts		Other information				
3							
4	March (actual)	$40,000	Beginning inventory	$48,000			
5	April	50,000	Desired ending inventory: Base amount	$20,000			
6	May	80,000	Plus percent of next				
7	June	60,000	month's cost of				
8	July	50,000	goods sold	80%			
9	August	40,000	Cost of goods sold				
10			as percent of sales	70%			

Exhibit 7-8

The Cooking Hut Company

Purchases Budget Formulas

	A	B	C	D	E	F	G
11	Schedule c						
12	Purchases budget			April	May	June	July
13	Desired ending inventory			=D5 + D8* (D10*B6)	=D5 + D8* (D10*B7)	=D5 + D8* (D10*B8)	=D5 + D8* (D10*B9)
14	Plus cost of goods sold			=D10*B5	=D10*B6	=D10*B7	=D10*B8
15							
16	Total needed			=D13 + D14	=E13 + E14	=F13 + F14	=G13 + G14
17	Less beginning inventory			=D4	=D13	=E13	=F13
18							
19	Purchases			=D16 − D17	=E16 − E17	=F16 − F17	=G16 − G17
20							

numbers into the schedule. Consider Exhibit 7-8. Instead of typing $48,000 as April's beginning inventory in the purchases budget at cell D17, type a "formula" with the cell address for the beginning inventory from the preceding table, =D4 (the cell address preceded by an "=" sign—a spreadsheet rule to identify a formula; some spreadsheets use "+" to indicate a formula). Likewise, all the cells of the purchases budget will be composed of formulas containing cell addresses instead of numbers. The total needed in April (D16) is =D13 + D14, and purchases in April (D19) are budgeted to be =D16 − D17. The figures for May, June, and July are computed similarly within the respective columns. This approach gives the spreadsheet the most flexibility, because you could change any number in the budget data in Exhibit 7-7 (for example, a sales forecast), and the software automatically recalculates the numbers in the entire purchases budget. Exhibit 7-8 shows the formulas used for the purchases budget. Exhibit 7-9 is the purchases budget displaying the numbers generated by the formulas in Exhibit 7-8 using the input data in Exhibit 7-7.

Exhibit 7-9

The Cooking Hut Company

Purchases Budget

	A	B	C	D	E	F	G
11	Schedule c						
12	Purchases budget			April	May	June	July
13	Desired ending inventory			$64,800	$ 53,600	$48,000	$42,400
14	Plus cost of goods sold			35,000	56,000	42,000	35,000
15							
16	Total needed			99,800	109,600	90,000	77,400
17	Less beginning inventory			48,000	64,800	53,600	48,000
18							
19	Purchases			$51,800	$ 44,800	$36,400	$29,400
20							

Now, what if sales could be 10% higher than initially forecasted during April through August? What effect will this alternative forecast have on budgeted purchases? Even to revise this simple purchases budget would require a considerable number of manual recalculations. Merely changing the sales forecasts in spreadsheet Exhibit 7-7, however, results in a nearly instantaneous revision of the purchases budget. Exhibit 7-10 shows the alternative sales forecasts (in colored type) and other unchanged data along with the revised purchases budget. We could alter every piece of budget data in the table, and easily view or print out the effects on purchases. This sort of analysis, assessing the effects of varying one of the budget inputs, up or down, is called sensitivity analysis. **Sensitivity analysis** for budgeting is the systematic varying of budget data input to determine the effects of each change on the budget. This type of "what if" analysis is one of the most powerful uses of spreadsheets for financial planning models. Note, though, that it is not generally a good idea to vary more than one of the types of budget inputs at a time, unless they are obviously related, because doing so makes it difficult to isolate the effects of each change.

Every schedule, operating budget, and financial budget of the master budget can be prepared on the spreadsheet. Each schedule would be linked by the appropriate cell addresses just as the budget input data (Exhibit 7-7) are linked to the purchases budget (Exhibits 7-8 and 7-9). As in the purchases budget, ideally all cells in the master budget are formulas, not numbers. That way, every budget input can be the subject of sensitivity analysis, if desired, by simply changing the budget data in Exhibit 7-7.

sensitivity analysis
In budgeting, the systematic varying of budget data input to determine the effects of each change on the budget.

Exhibit 7-10

The Cooking Hut Company
Purchases Budget

	A	B	C	D	E	F	G
1	Budgeted data						
2	Sales forecasts		Other information				
3							
4	March (actual)	$40,000	Beginning inventory	$ 48,000			
5	April	55,000	Desired ending inventory: Base amount	$ 20,000			
6	May	88,000	Plus percent of next				
7	June	66,000	month's cost of				
8	July	55,000	goods sold	80%			
9	August	44,000	Cost of goods sold				
10			as percent of sales	70%			
11	Schedule c						
12	Purchases budget			April	May	June	July
13	Desired ending inventory			$ 69,280	$ 56,960	$50,800	$44,640
14	Plus cost of goods sold			38,500	61,600	46,200	38,500
15							
16	Total needed			107,780	118,560	97,000	83,140
17	Beginning inventory			48,000	69,280	56,960	50,800
18							
19	Purchases			$ 59,780	$ 49,280	$40,040	$32,340
20							

Preparing the master budget on a spreadsheet is time-consuming—the first time. After that, the time savings and planning capabilities through sensitivity analysis are enormous compared with a manual approach. A problem can occur, however, if the master budget model is not well documented and a person other than the author attempts to modify the spreadsheet model. Any assumptions that are made should be described either within the spreadsheet or in a separate budget preparation document.

Accounting Vocabulary

capital budget, p. 272
cash budget, p. 280
continuous budget, p. 272
financial budget, p. 273
financial planning model, p. 285

long-range planning, p. 272
master budget, p. 272
operating budget, p. 273
participative budgeting, p. 285
profit plan, p. 273

rolling budget, p. 272
sales budget, p. 283
sales forecast, p. 283
sensitivity analysis, p. 293
strategic plan, p. 272

Fundamental Assignment Material

Special note: Problems 7-A1 and 7-B1 provide single-problem reviews of most of the chapter topics. Those readers who prefer to concentrate on the fundamentals in smaller chunks should consider any of the other problems.

7-A1   Prepare Master Budget

Video Hut, Inc., has a strong belief in using highly decentralized management. You are the new manager of the company's store in the Mall of America. You know much about how to buy, how to display, how to sell, and how to reduce shoplifting. You know little about accounting and finance, however.

Top management is convinced that training for higher management should include the active participation of store managers in the budgeting process. You have been asked to prepare a complete master budget for your store for June, July, and August. You are responsible for its actual full preparation. All accounting is done centrally, so you have no expert help on the premises. In addition, tomorrow the branch manager and the assistant controller will be here to examine your work; at that time they will assist you in formulating the final budget document. The idea is to have you prepare the budget a few times so that you gain more confidence about accounting matters. You want to make a favorable impression on your superiors, so you gather the following data as of May 31, 2001.

			Recent and Projected Sales	
Cash	$ 29,000			
Inventory	420,000		April	$300,000
Accounts receivable	369,000		May	350,000
Net furniture and fixtures	168,000		June	700,000
Total assets	$986,000		July	400,000
Accounts payable	$475,000		August	400,000
Owners' equity	511,000		September	300,000
Total liabilities and				
owners' equities	$986,000			

Credit sales are 90% of total sales. Credit accounts are collected 80% in the month following the sale and 20% in the following month. Assume that bad debts are negligible and can be ignored. The accounts receivable on May 31 are the result of the credit sales for April and May: $(.20 \times .90 \times \$300,000 = \$54,000) + (1.0 \times .90 \times \$350,000 = \$315,000) = \$369,000$. The average gross profit on sales is 40%.

The policy is to acquire enough inventory each month to equal the following month's projected sales. All purchases are paid for in the month following purchase.

Salaries, wages, and commissions average 20% of sales; all other variable expenses are 4% of sales. Fixed expenses for rent, property taxes, and miscellaneous payroll and other items are $55,000 monthly. Assume that these variable and fixed expenses require cash disbursements each month. Depreciation is $3,000 monthly.

In June, $55,000 is going to be disbursed for fixtures acquired in May. The May 31 balance of accounts payable includes this amount.

Assume that a minimum cash balance of $25,000 is to be maintained. Also assume that all borrowings are effective at the beginning of the month and all repayments are made at the end of the month of repayment. Interest is paid only at the time of repaying principal. The interest rate is 10% per annum; round interest computations to the nearest ten dollars. All loans and repayments of principal must be made in multiples of a thousand dollars.

Required

1. Prepare a budgeted income statement for the coming quarter, a budgeted statement of monthly cash receipts and disbursements (for the next three months), and a budgeted balance sheet for August 31, 2001. All operations are evaluated on a before-income-tax basis, so income taxes may be ignored here.

2. Explain why there is a need for a bank loan and what operating sources supply cash for repaying the bank loan.

7-B1 Prepare Master Budget

Auckland Tent Company, a small New Zealand firm that sells tents on the Web at www.campout.co.nz, wants a master budget for the next three months, beginning January 1, 20X1. It desires an ending minimum cash balance of $NZ 5,000 each month. Sales are forecasted at an average wholesale selling price of $NZ 80 per tent. In January, Auckland Tent is beginning just-in-time (JIT) deliveries from suppliers, which means that purchases equal expected sales. On January 1, purchases will cease until inventory reaches $NZ 6,000, after which time purchases will equal sales. Merchandise costs average $NZ 40 per tent. Purchases during any given month are paid in full during the following month. All sales are on credit, payable within 30 days, but experience has shown that 60% of current sales are collected in the current month, 30% in the next month, and 10% in the month thereafter. Bad debts are negligible.

Monthly operating expenses are as follows:

Wages and salaries	$NZ 15,000
Insurance expired	125
Depreciation	400
Miscellaneous	2,500
Rent	$NZ 250/month + 10% of quarterly sales over $NZ 10,000

Cash dividends of $NZ 1,500 are to be paid quarterly, beginning January 15, and are declared on the 15th of the previous month. All operating expenses are paidas incurred, except insurance, depreciation, and rent. Rent of $NZ 250 is paid at the beginning of each month, and the additional 10% of sales is paid quarterly on the 10th of the month following the end of the quarter. The next settlement is due January 10.

The company plans to buy some new fixtures for $NZ 4,000 cash in March.

Money can be borrowed and repaid in multiples of $NZ 500 at an interest rate of 10% per annum. Management wants to minimize borrowing and repay rapidly. Interest is computed and paid when the principal is repaid. Assume that borrowing occurs at the beginning, and repayments at the end, of the months in question. Money is never borrowed at the beginning and repaid at the end of the same month. Compute interest to the nearest dollar.

Assets as of December 31, 20X0		Liabilities as of December 31, 20X0	
Cash	$NZ 5,000	Accounts payable	
Accounts receivable	12,500	(merchandise)	$NZ 35,550
Inventory*	39,050	Dividends payable	1,500
Unexpired insurance	1,500	Rent payable	7,800
Fixed assets, net	12,500		$NZ 44,850
	$NZ 70,550		

* November 30 inventory balance = $NZ 16,000.

Recent and forecasted sales:

October	$NZ 38,000	December	$NZ 25,000	February	$NZ 75,000	April	$NZ 45,000
November	25,000	January	62,000	March	38,000		

Required

1. Prepare a master budget including a budgeted income statement, balance sheet, statement of cash receipts and disbursements, and supporting schedules for the months January through March 20X1.

2. Explain why there is a need for a bank loan and what operating sources provide the cash for the repayment of the bank loan.

Additional Assignment Material

QUESTIONS

7-1. Is budgeting used primarily for scorekeeping, attention directing, or problem solving?

7-2. How do strategic planning, long-range planning, and budgeting differ?

7-3. "Capital budgets are plans for managing long-term debt and common stock." Do you agree? Explain.

7-4. "I oppose continuous budgets because they provide a moving target. Managers never know what to aim at." Discuss.

7-5. "Pro forma statements are those statements prepared in conjunction with continuous budgets." Do you agree? Explain.

7-6. Why is budgeted performance better than past performance as a basis for judging actual results?

7-7. "Budgets are okay in relatively certain environments. But everything changes so quickly in the electronics industry that budgeting is a waste of time." Comment on this statement.

7-8. What are the major benefits of budgeting?

7-9. "Budgeting is an unnecessary burden on many managers. It takes time away from important day-to-day problems." Do you agree? Explain.

7-10. Differentiate between an operating budget and a financial budget.

7-11. Why is the sales forecast the starting point for budgeting?

7-12. Distinguish between operating expenses and disbursements for operating expenses.

7-13. What is the principal objective of a cash budget?

7-14. Differentiate between a sales forecast and a sales budget.

7-15. What factors influence the sales forecast?

7-16. "Education and salesmanship are key features of budgeting." Explain.

7-17. What are financial planning models?

7-18. "Financial planning models guide managers through the budget process so that managers do not really need to understand budgeting." Do you agree? Explain.

7-19. "I cannot be bothered with setting up my monthly budget on a spreadsheet. It just takes too long to be worth the effort." Comment.

7-20. How do spreadsheets aid the application of sensitivity analysis?

COGNITIVE EXERCISES

7-21 Budgets as Limitations on Spending
Many nonprofit organizations use budgets primarily to limit spending. Why does this limit the effectiveness of budgets?

7-22 Sales Personnel and Budgeting
The sales budget is the foundation of the entire master budget. How do sales personnel help formulate the budget? Compare the role of sales personnel to that of a central staff function such as market research.

7-23 Master Budgets for Research and Development
The text focuses on budgets for organizations that have revenues and expenses. Suppose you were the manager of a research and development division of a biotech company. How would budgets be helpful to you?

7-24 Production Budgets and Performance Evaluation
The Akron plant of American Tire Company prepares an annual master budget each November for the following year. At the end of each year it compares the actual costs incurred to the budgeted costs. How can American Tire get employees to accept the budget and strive to meet or beat the budgeted costs?

EXERCISES

7-25 Fill In the Blanks
Enter the word or phrase that best completes the following:

1. The financial budget process includes the following budgets.

   a. _____

   b. _____

   c. _____

   d. _____

2. The master budget process usually begins with the _____ budget.
3. The production budget process usually begins with the _____ budget.
4. A _____ budget is a plan that is revised monthly or quarterly, dropping one period and adding another.
5. Strategic planning sets the _____.

7-26   Cash Budgeting

Brenda Peterson and Molly Chan are preparing a plan to submit to venture capitalists seeking funding for their business, Adventure.Com. The company plans to spend $300,000 on equipment in the first quarter of 2002. Salaries and other operating expenses (paid as incurred) will be $30,000 per month beginning in January 2002 and will continue at that level thereafter. The company will receive its first revenues in January 2003, with cash collections averaging $25,000 per month for all of 2003. In January 2004 cash collections are expected to increase to $100,000 per month and continue at that level thereafter.

How much venture capital funding should Adventure.Com seek? Assume that the company needs enough funding to cover all of its cash needs until cash receipts start exceeding cash disbursements.

Required

7-27   Purchases and Cost of Goods Sold

The Bridgeford Co., a wholesaler of auto parts, budgeted the following sales for the indicated months:

	June 20X2	July 20X2	August 20X2
Sales on account	$1,800,000	$1,920,000	$2,040,000
Cash sales	240,000	250,000	260,000
Total sales	$2,040,000	$2,170,000	$2,300,000

All merchandise is marked up to sell at its invoice cost plus 25%. Merchandise inventories at the beginning of each month are at 30% of that month's projected cost of goods sold.

1. Compute the budgeted cost of goods sold for the month of June 20X2.
2. Compute the budgeted merchandise purchases for July 20X2.

Required

7-28   Purchases and Sales Budgets

All sales of Acme Building Supplies (ABS) are made on credit. Sales are billed twice monthly, on the 10th of the month for the last half of the prior month's sales and on the 20th of the month for the first half of the current month's sales. The terms of all sales are 2/10, net 30. Based on past experience, the collection experience of accounts receivable is as follows:

Within the discount period	80%
On the 30th day	18%
Uncollectible	2%

The sales value of shipments for May 20X1 was $750,000. The forecast sales for the next 4 months are

June	$800,000
July	900,000
August	900,000
September	750,000

ABS's average markup on its products is 20% of the sales price.

ABS purchases merchandise for resale to meet the current month's sales demand and to maintain a desired monthly ending inventory of 25% of the next month's sales. All purchases are on credit with terms of net 30. ABS pays for one-half of a month's purchases in the month of purchase and the other half in the month following the purchase.

All sales and purchases occur uniformly throughout the month.

Required

1. How much cash can ABS plan to collect from accounts receivable collections during July 20X1?
2. How much can ABS plan to collect in September from sales made in August 20X1?
3. Compute the budgeted dollar value of ABS inventory on August 31, 20X1.
4. How much merchandise should ABS plan to purchase during June 20X1?
5. How much should ABS budget in August 20X1 for the payment for merchandise purchased?

7-29 Sales Budget

Suppose a Gap store has the following data:

- Accounts receivable, May 31: (.3 × May sales of $450,000) = $135,000
- Monthly forecasted sales: June, $400,000; July, $440,000; August, $500,000; September, $530,000

Sales consist of 70% cash and 30% credit. All credit accounts are collected in the month following the sales. Uncollectible accounts are negligible and may be ignored.

Required

Prepare a sales budget schedule and a cash collections budget schedule for June, July, and August.

7-30 Sales Budget

A Japanese clothing wholesaler was preparing its sales budget for the first quarter of 20X2. Forecast sales are (in thousands of yen)

January	¥180,000
February	¥210,000
March	¥240,000

Sales are 20% cash and 80% on credit. Fifty percent of the credit accounts are collected in the month of sale, 40% in the month following the sale, and 10% in the following month. No uncollectible accounts are anticipated. Accounts receivable at the beginning of 20X2 are ¥94 million (10% of November credit sales of ¥160 million and 50% of December credit sales of ¥156 million).

Required

Prepare a schedule showing sales and cash collections for January, February, and March, 20X2.

7-31 Cash Collection Budget

Mideast Carpet Specialties has found that cash collections from customers tend to occur in the following pattern:

Collected within cash discount period in month of sale	50%
Collected within cash discount period in first month after month of sale	10
Collected after cash discount period in first month after month of sale	25
Collected after cash discount period in second month after month of sale	12
Never collected	3
Total sales in any month (before cash discounts)	100%
Cash discount allowable as a percentage of invoice price	1%

Compute the total cash budgeted to be collected in March if sales are predicted as $350,000 for January, $400,000 for February, and $450,000 for March.

7-32 Purchase Budget

Quantrill Furniture Mart plans inventory levels (at cost) at the end of each month as follows: May, $250,000; June, $220,000; July, $270,000; August, $240,000.

Sales are expected to be: June, $440,000; July, $350,000; August, $400,000. Cost of goods sold is 60% of sales.

Purchases in April were $250,000; in May, $180,000. A given month's purchases are paid as follows: 10% during that month; 80% the next month; and the final 10% the next month.

Required

Prepare budget schedules for June, July, and August for purchases and for disbursements for purchases.

7-33 Purchase Budget

The inventory of the Dublin Appliance Company was £210,000 on May 31. The manager was upset because the inventory was too high. She has adopted the following policies regarding merchandise purchases and inventory. At the end of any month, the inventory should be £15,000 plus 90% of the cost of goods to be sold during the following month. The cost of merchandise sold averages 60% of sales. Purchase terms are generally net 30 days. A given month's purchases are paid as follows: 20% during that month and 80% during the following month.

Purchases in May had been £150,000. Sales are expected to be June, £300,000; July, £280,000; August, £340,000; and September, £400,000.

Required

1. Compute the amount by which the inventory on May 31 exceeded the manager's policies.
2. Prepare budget schedules for June, July, and August for purchases and for disbursements for purchases.

7-34 Cash Budget

Consider the income statement in Exhibit 7-11.

The cash balance, May 31, 20X1, is $18,000. Sales proceeds are collected as follows: 80% month of sale, 10% second month, 10% third month.

Accounts receivable are $40,000 on May 31, 20X1, consisting of $16,000 from April sales and $24,000 from May sales.

Accounts payable on May 31, 20X1, are $145,000. Durham Company pays 25% of purchases during the month of purchase and the remainder during the following month. All operating expenses requiring cash are paid during the month of recognition. Insurance and property taxes are paid annually in December, however.

Required

Prepare a cash budget for June. Confine your analysis to the given data. Ignore income taxes and other possible items that might affect cash.

Exhibit 7-11

Durham Company
Budgeted Income Statement
For the Month Ended June 30, 20X1 (in thousands)

Sales		$290
Inventory, May 31	$ 50	
Purchases	192	
Available for sale	242	
Inventory, June 30	40	
Cost of goods sold		202
Gross margin		$ 88
Operating expenses		
Wages	$ 36	
Utilities	5	
Advertising	10	
Depreciation	2	
Office expenses	4	
Insurance and property taxes	3	60
Operating income		$ 28

PROBLEMS

7-35 Cash Budget

Jean Kim is the manager of an airport gift shop, Kim News and Gifts. From the following data, Ms. Kim wants a cash budget showing expected cash receipts and disbursements for the month of April, and the cash balance expected as of April 30, 20X2.

- Bank note due April 10: $90,000 plus $4,500 interest
- Depreciation for April: $2,100
- Two-year insurance policy due April 14 for renewal: $1,500, to be paid in cash
- Planned cash balance, March 31, 20X2: $80,000
- Merchandise purchases for April: $450,000, 40% paid in month of purchase, 60% paid in next month
- Customer receivables as of March 31: $60,000 from February sales, $450,000 from March sales
- Payrolls due in April: $90,000
- Other expenses for April, payable in April: $45,000
- Accrued taxes for April, payable in June: $7,500
- Sales for April: $1,000,000, half collected in month of sale, 40% in next month, 10% in third month
- Accounts payable, March 31, 20X2: $460,000

Required Prepare the cash budget.

7-36 Cash Budget

Prepare a statement of estimated cash receipts and disbursements for October 20X1 for the Bouquet Company, which sells one product, herbal soap, by the case. On October 1, 20X1, part of the trial balance showed

Cash	$ 4,800	
Accounts receivable	15,600	
Allowance for bad debts		$1,900
Merchandise inventory	9,000	
Accounts payable, merchandise		6,600

The company pays for its purchases within 10 days. Assume that one-third of the purchases of any month are due and paid for in the following month.

The cost of the merchandise purchased is $12 per case. At the end of each month it is desired to have an inventory equal in units to 50% of the following month's sales in units.

Sales terms include a 1% discount if payment is made by the end of the calendar month. Past experience indicates that 60% of the billings will be collected during the month of the sale, 30% in the following calendar month, 6% in the next following calendar month. Four percent will be uncollectible. The company's fiscal year begins August 1.

Unit selling price	$ 20
August actual sales	$ 12,000
September actual sales	36,000
October estimated sales	30,000
November estimated sales	22,000
Total sales expected in the fiscal year	360,000

Exclusive of bad debts, total budgeted selling and general administrative expenses for the fiscal year are estimated at $61,500, of which $24,000 is fixed expense (which includes a $13,200 annual depreciation charge). The Bouquet Company incurs these fixed expenses uniformly throughout the year. The balance of the selling and general administrative expenses varies with sales. Expenses are paid as incurred.

7-41 Spreadsheets and Sensitivity Analysis of Operating Expenses

Study Appendix 7. The CD-ROM Division (CDRD) of Micro Storage, Inc., produces highest quality CD-ROM drives for personal computers. The drives are assembled from purchased components. The costs (value) added by CDRD are indirect costs (which include assembly labor), packaging, and shipping. CDRD produces two speeds of drives: 5X and 10X. Cost behavior of CDRD is as follows.

	Fixed	Variable
Purchased components		
10X Drives		$100 per component
5X Drives		40 per component
Indirect costs	$40,000	16 per component
Packaging	8,000	4 per drive
Shipping	8,000	2 per drive

Both CD-ROM drives require five components. Therefore, the total cost of components for 10X drives is $500 and for 5X drives is $200. CDRD uses a six-month continuous budget that is revised monthly. Sales forecasts for the next eight months are as follows:

	10X Drives	5X Drives
October	3,200 units	4,000 units
November	2,400	3,000
December	5,600	7,000
January	3,200	4,000
February	3,200	4,000
March	2,400	3,000
April	2,400	3,000
May	2,800	3,500

Treat each event in succession.

Required

1. Use spreadsheet software to prepare a table of budgeting information and an operating expense budget for the CD-ROM Division for October through March. Incorporate the expectation that sales of 5X drives will be 125% of 10X drives. Prepare a spreadsheet that can be revised easily for succeeding months.

2. October's actual sales were 2,800 10X drives and 3,600 5X drives. This outcome has caused CDRD to revise its sales forecasts downward by 10%. Revise the operating expense budget for November through April.

3. At the end of November, CDRD decides that the proportion of 10X to 5X is changing. Sales of 5X drives are expected to be 150% of 10X drive sales. Expected sales of 10X drives are unchanged from requirement 2. Revise the operating expense budget for December through May.

CASES

7-42 Comprehensive Cash Budgeting

Wilma Brown, treasurer of Columbia Civic Theater (CCT), was preparing a loan request to the Northeast National Bank in December 2001. The loan was necessary to meet the cash needs of the theater for year 2002. In a few short years, the CCT had established itself as a premier theater. In addition to its regular subscription series, it started a series for new playwrights and offered a very popular holiday production. In fact, the holiday production was the most financially successful of the theater's activities, providing a base to support innovative productions that were artistically important to the theater but did not usually succeed financially.

In total, the theater had done well financially, as shown in Exhibits 7-12 and 7-13. Its profitable operations had enabled it to build its own building and generally acquire a large number of assets. It had at least broken even every year since its incorporation, and management anticipates continued profitable operations. The Corporate Community for the Arts in Columbia and several private foundations had made many grants to the theater, and such grants are expected to continue. Most recently, the largest bank in town had agreed to sponsor the production of a new play by a local playwright. The theater's director of development, Richard Talman, expected such corporate sponsorships to increase in the future.

To provide facilities for the theater's anticipated growth, CCT began work on an addition to its building two years ago. The new facilities are intended primarily to support the experimental theater offerings that were becoming more numerous. The capital expansion was to be completed in 2002; all that remained was acquisition and installation of lighting, sound equipment, and other new equipment to be purchased in 2002.

Columbia Civic Theater had borrowed working capital from Northeast National Bank for the past several years. To qualify for the loans, the theater had to agree to

1. Completely pay off the loan for one month during the course of the year.
2. Maintain cash and accounts receivable balances equal to (or greater than) 120% of the loan.
3. Maintain a compensating cash balance of $200,000 at all times.

In the past, the theater has had no problem meeting these requirements. However, in 2001 the theater had been unable to reduce the loan to zero for an entire month. Although Northeast continued to extend the needed credit, the loan manager expressed concern over the situation. She asked for a quarterly cash budget to justify the financing needed for 2002. Ms. Brown began to assemble the data needed to prepare such a budget.

CCT received revenue from three main sources: ticket sales, contributions, and grants. Ms. Brown formed Exhibit 7-14 to calculate the accounts receivable balance for each of these sources for 2002. She assumed that CCT would continue its normal practices for collecting pledges and grant revenues.

Most expenses were constant from month to month. An exception was supplies, which were purchased twice a year in December and June. In 2002, CCT expects to purchase $200,000 of supplies in June and $700,000 in December on terms of net 30 days. The supplies inventory at the end

Required

Exhibit 7-12

Columbia Civic Theater

Balance Sheets as of December 31 (in thousands of dollars)

	1999	2000	2001
Assets			
Cash	$2,688	$ 229	$ 208
Accounts receivable	2,942	3,372	4,440
Supplies inventory	700	700	500
Total current assets	$6,330	$4,301	$ 5,148
Plant and equipment	2,643	4,838	5,809
Total assets	$8,973	$9,139	$10,957
Liabilities and Equities			
Bank loan	$ 0	$ 0	$ 1,620*
Accounts payable	420	720	780
Accrued payroll expenses	472	583	646
Mortgage, current	250	250	250
Total current liabilities	$1,142	$1,553	$ 3,296
Other payables	270		
Mortgage payable, long-term	3,750	3,500	3,250
Net assets**	3,811	4,086	4,411
Total liabilities and equities	$8,973	$9,139	$10,957

*Includes $32 thousand of accrued interest.

**The "Net assets" account for a nonprofit organization is similar to "Stockholders' equity" for a corporation.

Exhibit 7-13

Columbia Civic Theater

Income Statements for the Year Ended December 31 (in thousands of dollars)

	1999	2000	2001
Ticket sales	$3,303	$4,060	$5,263
Contributions	1,041	1,412	1,702
Grants and other revenues	1,202	1,361	1,874
Total revenues	$5,546	$6,833	$8,839
Expenses*			
Production	$4,071	$4,805	$6,307
Operations	271	332	473
Public relations and			
community development	1,082	1,421	1,734
Total expenses	$5,424	$6,558	$8,514
Excess of revenues over expenses	$ 122	$ 275	$ 325

*Expenses include depreciation of $355, $370, and $470 and general and administrative expenses of $1,549, $1,688, and $2,142 in the years 1999, 2000, and 2001, respectively.

of December was expected to be $600,000. Depreciation expense of $500,000 was planned for 2002, and other expenses were expected to run at a steady rate of $710,000 a month throughout the year, of which $700,000 was payroll costs. Salaries and wages were paid on the Monday of the first week following the end of the month. The other $10,000 of other expenses were paid as incurred.

The major portion of the new equipment to be installed in 2002 was to be delivered in September; payments totaling $400,000 would be made in four equal monthly installments beginning in September. In addition, small equipment purchases are expected to run $20,000 per month throughout the year. They will be paid for on delivery.

In late 1999 CCT had borrowed $4 million (classified as a mortgage payable) from Farmers' Life Insurance Company. The theater is repaying the loan over 16 years, in equal principal payments in June and December of each year. Interest at 5% annually is also paid on the unpaid balance on each of these dates. Total interest payments for 2002, according to Ms. Brown's calculations, would be $172,000.

Interest on the working capital loan from Northeast was at an annual rate of 8%; payment for 2001's interest would be made on January 10, 2002, and that for 2002's interest would be made on January 10, 2003. Working capital loans are taken out on the first day of the quarter that funds are needed and they are repaid on the last day of the quarter when extra funds are generated. CCT has tried to keep a minimum cash balance of $200,000 at all times, even if loan requirements do not require it.

Exhibit 7-14

Columbia Civic Theater

Estimated Quarterly Revenues and End of Quarter Receivables For the Year Ended December 31, 2002 (in thousands of dollars)

	Ticket Sales		Contributions		Grants	
	Revenues	End of Quarter Receivables	Revenues	End of Quarter Receivables	Revenues	End of Quarter Receivables
First Quarter	$ 852	$2,795	$ 75	$ 794	$ 132	$1,027
Second Quarter	1,584	3,100	363	888	448	1,130
Third Quarter	2,617	3,407	1,203	1,083	1,296	1,240
Fourth Quarter	1,519	3,683	442	1,170	528	1,342

1. Compute the cash inflows and outflows for each quarter of 2002. What are CCT's loan requirements each quarter?
2. Prepare a projected Income Statement and Balance Sheet for CCT for 2002.
3. Prepare the projected Statement of Cash Flows for 2002.
4. What financing strategy would you recommend for CCT?

7-43 Cash Budgeting for a Hospital

St. John Hospital provides a wide range of health services in its community. St. John's board of directors has authorized the following capital expenditures:

Intra-aortic balloon pump	$1,400,000
Computed tomographic scanner	850,000
X-ray equipment	550,000
Laboratory equipment	1,200,000
Total	$4,000,000

The expenditures are planned for October 1, 20X2, and the board wishes to know the amount of borrowing, if any, necessary on that date. Jill Todd, hospital controller, has gathered the following information to be used in preparing an analysis of future cash flows.

- Billings, made in the month of service, for the first 6 months of 20X2 are

Month	Actual Amount
January	$5,300,000
February	5,300,000
March	5,400,000
April	5,400,000
May	6,000,000
June	6,000,000

Ninety percent of St. John's billings are made to third parties such as Blue Cross, federal or state governments, and private insurance companies. The remaining 10% of the billings are made directly to patients. Historical patterns of billing collections are

	Third-Party Billings	Direct Patient Billings
Month of service		
20%	10%	
Month following service	50	40
Second month following service	20	40
Uncollectible	10	10

Estimated billings for the last six months of 20X2 are listed next. Todd expects the same billing and collection patterns that have been experienced during the first six months of 20X2 to continue during the last six months of the year.

Month	Estimated Amount
July	$5,400,000
August	6,000,000
September	6,600,000
October	6,800,000
November	7,000,000
December	6,600,000

- The following schedule presents the purchases that have been made during the past three months and the planned purchases for the last six months of 20X2.

Month	Amount
April	$1,300,000
May	1,450,000
June	1,450,000
July	1,500,000
August	1,800,000
September	2,200,000
October	2,350,000
November	2,700,000
December	2,100,000

All purchases are made on account, and accounts payable are remitted in the month following the purchase.

- Salaries for each month during the remainder of 20X2 are expected to be $1,800,000 per month plus 20% of that month's billings. Salaries are paid in the month of service.
- St. John's monthly depreciation charges are $150,000.
- St. John incurs interest expenses of $180,000 per month and makes interest payments of $540,000 on the last day of each calendar quarter.
- Endowment fund income is expected to continue to total $210,000 per month.
- St. John has a cash balance of $350,000 on July 1, 20X2, and has a policy of maintaining a minimum end-of-month cash balance of 10% of the current month's purchases.
- St. John Hospital employs a calendar-year reporting period.

Required

1. Prepare a schedule of budgeted cash receipts by month for the third quarter of 20X2.
2. Prepare a schedule of budgeted cash disbursements by month for the third quarter of 20X2.
3. Determine the amount of borrowing, if any, necessary on October 1, 20X2, to acquire the capital items totaling $4,000,000.

7-44 Comprehensive Budgeting for a University

Suppose you are the controller of Western Idaho State University. The university president, Willa Redcloud, is preparing for her annual fund-raising campaign for 2001–2002. To set an appropriate target, she has asked you to prepare a budget for the academic year. You have collected the following data for the current year (2000–2001):

	Undergraduate Division	Graduate Division
Average salary of faculty member	$46,000	$46,000
Average faculty teaching load in semester credit-hours per year (eight undergraduate or six graduate courses)	24	18
Average number of students per class	30	20
Total enrollment (full-time and part-time students)	3,600	1,800
Average number of semester credit-hours carried each year per student	25	20
Full-time load, semester hours per year	30	24

For 2001–2002, all faculty and staff will receive a 6% salary increase. Undergraduate enrollment is expected to decline by 2%, but graduate enrollment is expected to increase by 5%.

- The 2001–2002 budget for operation and maintenance of facilities is $500,000, which includes $240,000 for salaries and wages. Experience so far this year indicates that the budget is accurate. Salaries and wages will increase by 6% and other operating costs will increase by $12,000 in 2001–2002.

- The 2000–2001 and 2001–2002 budgets for the remaining expenditures are

	2000–2001	2001–2002
General administrative	$500,000	$525,000
Library		
Acquisitions	150,000	155,000
Operations	190,000	200,000
Health services	48,000	50,000
Intramural athletics	56,000	60,000
Intercollegiate athletics	240,000	245,000
Insurance and retirement	520,000	560,000
Interest	75,000	75,000

- Tuition is $70 per credit hour. In addition, the state legislature provides $780 per full-time-equivalent student. (A full-time equivalent is 30 undergraduate hours or 24 graduate hours.) Tuition scholarships are given to 30 full-time undergraduates and 50 full-time graduate students.

- Revenues other than tuition and the legislative apportionment are

	2000–2001	2001–2002
Endowment income	$200,000	$210,000
Net income from auxiliary		
services	325,000	335,000
Intercollegiate athletic receipts	290,000	300,000

- The chemistry/physics classroom building needs remodeling during the 2001–2002 period. Projected cost is $575,000.

Required

1. Prepare a schedule for 2001–2002 that shows, by division, (a) expected enrollment, (b) total credit hours, (c) full-time-equivalent enrollment, and (d) number of faculty members needed.
2. Calculate the budget for faculty salaries for 2001–2002 by division.
3. Calculate the budget for tuition revenue and legislative apportionment for 2001–2002 by division.
4. Prepare a schedule for President Redcloud showing the amount that must be raised by the annual fund-raising campaign.

COLLABORATIVE LEARNING EXERCISE

7-45 Personal Budgeting

Budgeting is useful to many different types of entities. One is the individual. Consider the entity that you know best, the college or university student. Form a group of two to six students, and pool the information that you have about what it costs to spend a year as a full-time student.

Prepare a revenue and expense budget for an average prospective full-time student at your college or university. Identify possible sources of revenue and the amount to be received from each. Identify the costs a student is likely to incur during the year. You can assume that cash disbursements are made immediately for all expenses, so the budgeted income statement and cash budget are identical.

When all groups have completed their budgets, compare those budgets. What are the differences? What assumptions led to the differences?

Internet Exercises

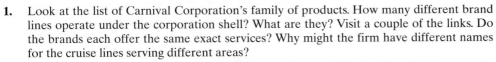

7-46 Carnival Corporation

The budgeting process helps firms to identify sources of revenues and expenses as well as the timing of cash flows. While many parts of the budgeting process are confidential, there are some things that may be identifiable by someone outside the firm who would like to make some potential budget projections for the following year. Consider Carnival Corporation, the cruise ship firm. Go to the Carnival Web site at http://www.carnivalcorp.com.

www.prenhall.com/horngren

1. Look at the list of Carnival Corporation's family of products. How many different brand lines operate under the corporation shell? What are they? Visit a couple of the links. Do the brands each offer the same exact services? Why might the firm have different names for the cruise lines serving different areas?

2. The sales figure is one of the most important pieces of information the firm uses in beginning the planning process. Carnival's sales figure is made up primarily of two parts—the number of passenger cruise days and the price charged for each passenger cruise day. Open Carnival's annual report for the most recent year using Adobe Acrobat Reader. Notice the total revenues for the year and then turn to the section on Management's Discussion and Analysis of Financial Condition and Results of Operations, which follows the financial statements and footnotes. Notice the information about the number of cruise days and the occupancy percentage. When the firm does the budget for next year for passenger cruise days, if they add no new cruises or any new ships, and if they expect 100% occupancy, what number of days should they use? Read the information provided by management with respect to growth for the next year. Does the company expect any increase in passenger capacity during the next year?

3. Using the estimated increase in cruise capacity for the next year, what would be the expected cruise days available? Should the firm expect an increase in costs associated with the increase in capacity? When budgeting for these costs, would the costs be proportional to the increase in revenues? Why or why not?

4. The other component in revenue is how much the passenger pays for the cruise. Select one of the cruise line links from the main page. Find the sub-link that takes you to information about cruise prices. Are all of the prices for the same length of cruise the same? Look at the fine print with respect to the cruise pricing—what does it tell about how the price is determined? Why might the capacity level of the cruise determine the price that is charged for the cruise?

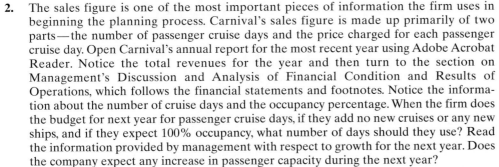

FLEXIBLE BUDGETS AND VARIANCE ANALYSIS

The golden arches can even be found
in Moscow. McDonald's restaurants
are located in more than 120
countries.

www.prenhall.com/horngren

Learning Objectives

When you have finished studying this chapter, you should be able to

1. Distinguish between flexible budgets and master (static) budgets.

2. Use flexible-budget formulas to construct a flexible budget based on the volume of sales.

3. Prepare an activity-based flexible budget.

4. Understand the performance evaluation relationship between master (static) budgets and flexible budgets.

5. Compute flexible-budget variances and sales-activity variances.

6. Compute and interpret price and usage variances for inputs based on cost-driver activity.

7. Compute variable overhead spending and efficiency variances.

8. **Understand how management uses flexible budgets to evaluate the company's financial performance.**

A recent survey ranked McDonald's as the world's greatest brand. More than 1,600 new McDonald's restaurants were opened in 2000, most of them outside the United States. You can eat a Big Mac under the Golden Arches in more than 120 countries.

With revenues exceeding $14 billion and more than 28,000 restaurants, the challenge is to ensure that the taste of each Big Mac is the same. How does McDonald's maintain cost and quality control? How does it ensure that each of the 35 million customers it serves daily receives the same value? It uses standards, budgets, and variance analysis. For example, the standards for material are the same for hamburgers wherever they are sold—1 bun, 1 hamburger patty, 1 pickle slice, 1/8 tablespoon of dehydrated onion, 1/4 tablespoon mustard, and 1/2 ounce of ketchup. Material variances are figured for each of these ingredients by computing the amount actually used compared to what should have been used, given the number and types of sandwiches sold.

McDonald's managers budget sales for each hour during the day. Based on the sales budgeted, labor is scheduled. If sales are lower than budgeted, managers can control labor cost by sending some employees home early.

McDonald's also uses nonfinancial standards to help achieve its quality and service goals. For example, the standard time for a drive-through customer is 310 seconds, from pulling up to the menu board to driving away. Cooked meat that is not used in a sandwich within 30 minutes is destroyed. Once a sandwich is made and placed in the transfer bin, it must be sold within 10 minutes or it will be thrown away.

As is the case at McDonald's, managers and employees of any organization want to know how they are doing in meeting their goals. Upper-level managers also want to know how the organization is meeting its financial objectives. Knowing what went wrong and what went right should help managers plan and manage more effectively in future periods.

This chapter introduces flexible budgets, which are budgets designed to direct management to areas of actual financial performance that deserve attention. Managers can apply this same basic process to control other important areas of performance such as quality and service.

FLEXIBLE BUDGETS: BRIDGE BETWEEN STATIC BUDGETS AND ACTUAL RESULTS

STATIC BUDGETS

static budget Another name for a master budget.

Static budget is really just another name for master budget. All the master budgets discussed in Chapter 7 are static or inflexible, because even though they may be easily revised, these budgets assume fixed levels of activity. In other words, a master budget is prepared for only one level of a given type of activity. For example, consider a company using a traditional costing system with only one cost driver. The Dominion Company is a one-department firm in Toronto that manufactures and sells a wheeled, collapsible suitcase carrier that is popular with airline flight crews. Manufacture of this suitcase carrier requires several manual and machine operations. The product has some variations, but may be viewed for our purposes essentially as a single product bearing one selling price. Assume that the cost driver is sales volume (that is, units sold), and the projected level of activity (sales volume) is 9,000 units. All of the budget figures are then based on projected sales of 9,000 units.

All actual results could be compared with the original budgeted amounts, even though, for example, sales volume turned out to be only 7,000 units instead of the originally planned 9,000 units. The master (static) budget for June 20X1 included the condensed income statement shown in Exhibit 8-1, column 2. The actual results for June 20X1 are in column 1. Differences or variances between actual results and the master budget are in column 3. The master budget called for production and sales of 9,000 units, but only 7,000 units were actually produced and sold. There were no beginning or ending inventories, so the units made in June were sold in June.

master budget variance (static budget variance) The variance of actual results from the master (static) budget.

The performance report in Exhibit 8-1 compares the actual results with the master budget. Performance report is a generic term that usually means a comparison of actual results with some budget. A helpful performance report will include variances that direct management's attention to significant deviations from expected results, allowing management by exception. Recall that a variance is a deviation of an actual amount from the expected or budgeted amount. Exhibit 8-1 shows variances of actual results from the master budget; these are called **master (static) budget variances.** Actual revenues that exceed expected revenues result in favorable revenue variances. When actual revenues are below expected revenues, variances are unfavorable. Similarly, actual expenses that exceed budgeted expenses result in **unfavorable expense variances,** and actual expenses that are less than budgeted expenses, result in **favorable expense variances.** Each significant variance should cause a manager to ask, "Why?" By explaining why a variance occurs, managers

unfavorable expense variance A variance that occurs when actual expenses are more than budgeted expenses.

favorable expense variance A variance that occurs when actual expenses are less than budgeted expenses.

Exhibit 8-1

Dominion Company

Performance Report Using Master Budget for the Month Ended June 30, 20X1

	Actual (1)	Master Budget (2)	Master Budget Variances (3)
Units	7,000	9,000	2,000
Sales	$217,000	$279,000	$62,000 U
Variable expenses			
Variable manufacturing expenses	$151,270	$189,000	$37,730 F
Shipping expenses (selling)	5,000	5,400	400 F
Administrative expenses	2,000	1,800	200 U
Total variable expenses	$158,270	$196,200	$37,930 F
Contribution margin	$ 58,730	$ 82,800	$24,070 U
Fixed expenses			
Fixed manufacturing expenses	$ 37,300	$ 37,000	$ 300 U
Fixed selling and administrative expenses	33,000	33,000	—
Total fixed expenses	$ 70,300	$ 70,000	$ 300 U
Operating income (loss)	$(11,570)	$ 12,800	$24,370 U

U = Unfavorable expense variances occur when actual expenses are more than budgeted expenses.

F = Favorable expense variances occur when actual expenses are less than budgeted expenses.

are forced to recognize changes that have affected revenues or costs and that might affect future decisions.

Suppose the president of Dominion Company asks you to explain why there was an operating loss of $11,570 when a profit of $12,800 was budgeted. Clearly, sales were $62,000 below expectations, but the favorable variances for the variable costs are misleading. Considering the lower-than-projected level of sales activity, was cost control really satisfactory? Would you really expect to pay $196,200 for variable expenses when only 7,000 units are produced? Of course not! Therefore, the comparison of actual results with a master budget is not very useful for management by exception.

FLEXIBLE BUDGETS

A more helpful benchmark for analysis is the flexible budget. A **flexible budget** (sometimes called variable budget) is a budget that adjusts for changes in sales volume and other cost-driver activities. The flexible budget is identical to the master budget in format, but managers may prepare it for any level of activity. So, when sales turn out to be 7,000 units instead of 9,000, managers can use the flexible budget to prepare a new budget based on this new cost-driver level. We can then see what the total variable expenses should be based on a sales level of 7,000 and compare this amount to the actual result. For performance evaluation, the flexible budget would be prepared at the actual levels of activity achieved. In contrast, the master budget is kept fixed or static to serve as the original benchmark for evaluating performance. It shows revenues and costs at only the originally planned levels of activity.

The flexible-budget approach says, "Give me any activity level you choose, and I'll provide a budget tailored to that particular level." Many companies routinely "flex" their budgets to help evaluate recent financial performance. For example, Ritz-Carlton managers evaluate monthly financial performance of all the company's hotels by comparing actual results to new, flexible budgets that are prepared for actual levels of activity.

flexible budget (variable budget) A budget that adjusts for changes in sales volume and other cost-driver activities.

Objective 1
Distinguish between flexible budgets and master (static) budgets.

Exhibit 8-2

Dominion Company
Flexible Budgets

	Flexible Budget Formula	Flexible Budgets for Various Levels of Sales/Production Activity		
Budget formula per unit				
Units		7,000	8,000	9,000
Sales	$ 31.00	$217,000	$248,000	$279,000
Variable costs/expense				
Variable manufacturing costs	$ 21.00	$147,000	$168,000	$189,000
Shipping expenses (selling)	.60	4,200	4,800	5,400
Administrative	.20	1,400	1,600	1,800
Total variable costs/expenses	$ 21.80	$152,600	$174,400	$196,200
Contribution margin	$ 9.20	$ 64,400	$ 73,600	$ 82,800
Budget formula per month				
Fixed costs				
Fixed manufacturing costs	$37,000	$ 37,000	$ 37,000	$ 37,000
Fixed selling and administrative costs	33,000	33,000	33,000	33,000
Total fixed costs	$70,000	$ 70,000	$ 70,000	$ 70,000
Operating income (loss)		$ (5,600)	$ 3,600	$ 12,800

FLEXIBLE-BUDGET FORMULAS

Objective 2
Use flexible-budget formulas to construct a flexible budget based on the volume of sales.

The flexible budget is based on assumptions of revenue and cost behavior (within the relevant range) with respect to appropriate cost drivers. The cost functions that you used in Chapter 2 and estimated in Chapter 3 can be used as flexible-budget formulas. The flexible budget incorporates effects on each cost and revenue caused by changes in activity. Exhibits 8-2 and 8-3 show Dominion Company's simple flexible budget, which has a single cost driver, units of output. Dominion Company's cost functions or flexible budget formulas are believed to be valid within the relevant range of 7,000 to 9,000 units. Be sure that you understand that each column of Exhibit 8-2 (7,000, 8,000, and 9,000 units, respectively) is prepared using the same flexible-budget formulas—and any activity level within

Exhibit 8-3

Dominion Company
Graph of Flexible Budget of Costs

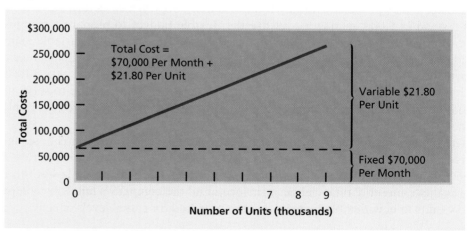

this range could be used, as shown in the graph in Exhibit 8-3. Note that fixed costs are expected to be constant across this range of activity.

ACTIVITY-BASED FLEXIBLE BUDGETS

The flexible budget for Dominion Company shown in Exhibit 8-2 is based on a single cost driver—units of product. For companies that use a traditional, volume-based costing system, this is an appropriate approach to flexible budgeting.

Companies that have an activity-based costing system use a more detailed approach. An **activity-based flexible budget** is based on budgeted costs for each activity and related cost driver. Exhibit 8-4 shows an activity-based flexible budget for the Dominion Company. There are four activities: processing, setup, marketing, and administration. Within each activity, costs depend on an appropriate cost driver. Compare the traditional flexible budget (Exhibit 8-2) and the activity-based flexible budget (Exhibit 8-4). Note that the 8,000-unit columns in Exhibits 8-4 and 8-2 are the same, but at other volumes the costs diverge. The key difference is that some manufacturing costs that are fixed with respect to units are variable with respect to the cost-driver "setups." That is, the fixed manufacturing costs ($37,000) in Exhibit 8-2 include setup costs that are largely fixed with respect to "units produced" but that vary with respect to the "number of setups." An example is the cost of supplies used to set up the production run. Each time a setup is done, supplies are used. Therefore, the cost of supplies varies directly with the number of setups. However, no setup supplies are used during production, so there is little change in the cost of supplies over wide ranges of units produced. This basic difference is why the total budgeted costs differ using the two approaches—activity-based flexible budgets provide more accurate measures of cost behavior.

When should a company use activity-based flexible budgets? When a significant portion of its costs vary with cost drivers other than units of production. In our Dominion example, the $500 per setup is the only such cost. For the rest of this chapter we will ignore the fact that this cost varies with number of setups, and go back to assuming that Dominion's operations are simple enough that a traditional flexible budget with a single cost driver is appropriate.

EVALUATION OF FINANCIAL PERFORMANCE USING FLEXIBLE BUDGETS

Comparing the flexible budget to actual results accomplishes an important performance evaluation purpose. There are two reasons why actual results might differ from the master budget. One is that sales and other cost-driver activities were not the same as originally forecasted. The second is that revenues or variable costs per unit of activity and fixed costs per period were not as expected. Though these reasons may not be completely independent (for example, higher unit sales prices may have caused lower unit sales levels), it is useful to separate these effects because different people may be responsible for each and because different management actions may be indicated.

The intent of using the flexible budget for performance evaluation is to isolate unexpected effects on actual results that can be corrected if adverse or enhanced if beneficial. Because the flexible budget is prepared at the actual level of activity (in our example, sales volume), any variances between the flexible budget and actual results cannot be due to activity levels. They must be due to departures of actual costs or revenues from flexible-budget formula amounts—because of pricing or cost control. These variances between the flexible budget and actual results are called **flexible-budget variance.**

In contrast, any differences or variances between the master budget and the flexible budget are due to activity levels, not cost control. These latter differences between the master budget amounts and the amounts in the flexible budget are called **activity-level variances.** In other words, the original difference we saw between actual results and the original master budget, which we earlier could not fully explain, actually has two components: the sales-activity variance and the flexible-budget variance.

Objective 3
Prepare an activity-based flexible budget.

activity-based flexible budget A budget based on budgeted costs for each activity and related cost driver.

Objective 4
Understand the performance evaluation relationship between master (static) budgets and flexible budgets.

flexible-budget variances The variances between the flexible budget and the actual results.

activity-level variances The differences between the master budget amounts and the amounts in the flexible budget.

Exhibit 8-4

Dominion Company

Activity-Based Flexible Budget for the Month Ended June 30, 20X1

	BUDGET FORMULA	Units		
		7,000	8,000	9,000
Sales	$31.00	$217,000	$248,000	$279,000
ACTIVITY				
Processing		*Cost Driver: Number of Machine Hours*		
Cost-driver level		14,000	16,000	18,000
Variable costs	$10.50	$147,000	$168,000	$189,000
Fixed costs	$13,000	13,000	13,000	13,000
Total costs of processing activity		$160,000	$181,000	$202,000
Setup		*Cost Driver: Number of Setups*		
Cost-driver level		21	24	27
Variable costs	$500	$ 10,500	$ 12,000	$ 13,500
Fixed costs	$12,000	12,000	12,000	12,000
Total costs of setup activity		$ 22,500	$ 24,000	$ 25,500
Marketing		*Cost Driver: Number of Orders*		
Cost-driver level		350	400	450
Variable costs	$12.00	$ 4,200	$ 4,800	$ 5,400
Fixed costs	$15,000	15,000	15,000	15,000
Total costs of marketing activity		$ 19,200	$ 19,800	$ 20,400
Administration		*Cost Driver: Number of Units*		
Cost-driver level		7,000	8,000	9,000
Variable costs	$.20	$ 1,400	$ 1,600	$ 1,800
Fixed costs	$18,000	18,000	18,000	18,000
Total costs of administration activity		$ 19,400	$ 19,600	$ 19,800
Total costs		$221,100	$244,400	$267,700
Operating income (loss)		$ (4,100)	$ 3,600	$ 11,300

Consider Exhibit 8-5. The flexible budget (column 3) taken from Exhibit 8-2 (and simplified) provides an explanatory bridge between the master budget (column 5) and the actual results (column 1). The variances for operating income are summarized at the bottom of Exhibit 8-5. Note that the sum of the activity-level variances (here sales-activity variances, because sales is the only activity used as a cost driver) and the flexible-budget variances equals the total of the master budget variances.

Exhibit 8-5

Dominion Company

Summary of Performance for the Month Ended June 30, 20X1

	Actual Results at Actual Activity Level* (1)	Flexible-Budget Variances† (2) = (1) − (3)	Flexible Budget for Actual Sales Activity‡ (3)	Sales-Activity Variances (4) = (3) − (5)	Master Budget (5)
Units	7,000	—	7,000	2,000 U	9,000
Sales	$217,000	—	$217,000	$62,000 U	$279,000
Variable costs	158,270	5,670 U	152,600	43,600 F	196,200
Contribution margin	$ 58,730	$5,670 U	$ 64,400	$18,400 U	$ 82,800
Fixed costs	70,300	300 U	70,000	—	70,000
Operating income	$(11,570)	$5,970 U	$ (5,600)	$18,400 U	$ 12,800

Total flexible-budget variances, $5,970 U

Total sales-activity variances, $18,400 U

Total master budget variances, $24,370 U

U = Unfavorable. F = Favorable.
* Figures are from Exhibit 8-1.
† Figures are shown in more detail in Exhibit 8-6.
‡ Figures are from the 7,000-unit column in Exhibit 8-2.

Consider a simple example of a company that plans to sell 1,000 units of a product for $2 per unit. Budgeted variable costs are $1 per unit, and budgeted operating income is $400. Suppose the company actually sells 800 units and makes an operating income of $200. Compute and interpret the master-budget variance, the sales-activity variance, and the flexible-budget variance.

ANSWER

The master budget variance is $400 − $200 = $200 U. The sales activity variance is the lost contribution margin on the 200 units of lost sales: $1.00 × 200 = $200. Therefore, the flexible budget variance is $0. The entire shortfall in operating income was caused by failing to meet the unit sales target of 1,000 units. The operation was efficient but not effective.

ISOLATING THE CAUSES OF VARIANCES

Managers use comparisons between actual results, master budgets, and flexible budgets to evaluate organizational performance. When evaluating performance, it is useful to distinguish between **effectiveness**—the degree to which a goal, objective, or target is met—and **efficiency**—the degree to which inputs are used in relation to a given level of outputs.

Performance may be effective, efficient, both, or neither. For example, Dominion Company set a master budget objective of manufacturing and selling 9,000 units. Only 7,000 units were actually made and sold, however. Performance, as measured by sales-activity variances, was ineffective because the sales objective was not met.

Was Dominion's performance efficient? Managers judge the degree of efficiency by comparing actual outputs achieved (7,000 units) with actual inputs (such as the costs of direct materials and direct labor). The less input used to produce a given output, the more efficient the operation. As indicated by the flexible-budget variances, Dominion was

effectiveness The degree to which a goal, objective, or target is met.

efficiency The degree to which inputs are used in relation to a given level of outputs.

inefficient because the actual cost of its inputs exceeded the cost expected for the actual level of output.

FLEXIBLE-BUDGET VARIANCES

Objective 5
Compute flexible-budget variances and sales-activity variances.

Recall that flexible-budget variances measure the *efficiency* of operations at the *actual* level of activity. The first three columns of Exhibit 8-5 compare the actual results with the flexible-budget amounts. The flexible-budget variances are the differences between columns 1 and 3, which total $5,970 unfavorable:

$$\text{total flexible-budget variance} = \text{total actual results} - \text{total flexible budget, planned results}$$
$$= (-\$11,570) - (-\$5,600)$$
$$= -\$5,970, \text{ or } \$5,970 \text{ unfavorable}$$

The total flexible-budget variance arises from sales prices received and the variable and fixed costs incurred. Dominion Company had no difference between actual sales price and the flexible-budgeted sales price, so we must focus on the differences between actual costs and flexible-budgeted costs at the actual 7,000-unit level of activity. Without the flexible budget in column 3, we cannot separate the effects of differences in cost behavior from the effects of changes in sales activity. The flexible-budget variances indicate whether operations were efficient or not, and may form the basis for periodic performance evaluation. Operations managers are in the best position to explain flexible-budget variances.

Companies that use variances primarily to fix blame often find that managers resort to cheating and subversion to beat the system. Managers of operations usually have more information about those operations than higher-level managers. If that information is used against them, lower-level managers can be expected to withhold or misstate valuable information for their own self-protection. For example, one manufacturing firm actually reduced the next period's departmental budget by the amount of the department's unfavorable variances in the current period. If a division had a $50,000 expense budget and experienced a $2,000 unfavorable variance, the following period's budget would be set at $48,000. This system led managers to cheat and to falsify reports to avoid unfavorable variances. We can criticize departmental managers' ethics, but the system was as much at fault as the managers.

Exhibit 8-6 gives an expanded, line-by-line computation of variances for all master budget items at Dominion. Note how most of the costs that had seemingly favorable variances when a master budget was used as a basis for comparison (see Exhibit 8-1) have, in reality, unfavorable variances. Do not conclude automatically that favorable flexible-budget variances are good and unfavorable flexible-budget variances are bad. Instead, interpret all variances as signals that actual operations have not occurred exactly as anticipated when the flexible-budget formulas were set. Any cost that differs significantly from the flexible budget deserves an explanation. The last column of Exhibit 8-6 gives possible explanations for Dominion Company's variances.

sales-activity variances
Variances that measure how effective managers have been in meeting the planned sales objective, calculated as actual unit sales less master budget unit sales times the budgeted unit contribution margin.

SALES-ACTIVITY VARIANCES

Sales-activity variances measure how effective managers have been in meeting the planned sales objective. In Dominion Company, sales activity fell 2,000 units short of the planned level. The final three columns of Exhibit 8-5 clearly show how the sales-activity variances (totaling $18,400 U) are unaffected by any changes in unit prices or variable costs. Why? Because the same budgeted unit prices and variable costs are used in constructing both the flexible and master budgets. Therefore, all unit prices and variable costs are held constant in columns 3 through 5.

Exhibit 8-6
Dominion Company
Cost-Control Performance Report for the Month Ended June 30, 20X1

	Actual Costs Incurred	Flexible Budget*	Flexible-Budget Variances[†]	Explanation
Units	7,000	7,000	—	
Variable costs				
Direct material	$ 69,920	$ 70,000	$ 80 F	Lower prices but higher usage
Direct labor	61,500	56,000	5,500 U	Higher wage rates and higher usage
Indirect labor	9,100	11,900	2,800 F	Decreased setup time
Idle time	3,550	2,800	750 U	Excessive machine breakdowns
Cleanup time	2,500	2,100	400 U	Cleanup of spilled solvent
Supplies	4,700	4,200	500 U	Higher prices and higher usage
Variable manufacturing costs	$151,270	$147,000	$4,270 U	
Shipping	5,000	4,200	800 U	Use of air freight to meet delivery
Administration	2,000	1,400	600 U	Excessive copying and long-distance calls
Total variable costs	$158,270	$152,600	$5,670 U	
Fixed costs				
Factory supervision	$ 14,700	$ 14,400	$ 300 U	Salary increase
Factory rent	5,000	5,000	—	
Equipment depreciation	15,000	15,000	—	
Other fixed factory costs	2,600	2,600	—	
Fixed manufacturing costs	$ 37,300	$ 37,000	$ 300 U	
Fixed selling and administrative costs	33,000	33,000	—	
Total fixed costs	$ 70,300	$ 70,000	$ 300 U	
Total variable and fixed costs	$228,570	$222,600	$5,970 U	

* From 7,000-unit column of Exhibit 8-2.

[†] This is a line-by-line breakout of the variances in column 2 of Exhibit 8-5.

The total of the sales-activity variances informs the manager that falling short of the sales target by 2,000 units caused operating income to be $18,400 lower than initially budgeted (a $5,600 loss instead of a $12,800 profit). In summary, the shortfall of sales by 2,000 units caused Dominion Company to incur a total sales activity variance of 2,000 units at a contribution margin of $9.20 per unit (from the first column of Exhibit 8-2):

$$\text{total sales-activity variance} = (\text{actual sales units} - \text{master budgeted sales units})$$
$$\times \text{budgeted contribution margin per unit}$$
$$= (9,000 - 7,000) \times \$9.20$$
$$= \$18,400 \text{ unfavorable}$$

Who has responsibility for the sales-activity variance? Marketing managers usually have the primary responsibility for reaching the sales level specified in the static budget. Of course variations in sales may be attributable to many factors.[1] Nevertheless, marketing managers are typically in the best position to explain why sales activities attained differed from plans.

---

[1] *For example, sales-activity variances can be subdivided into sales quantity, sales mix, market size, and market share variances. This more advanced treatment of sales-activity variances is covered in Charles T. Horngren, George Foster, and Srikant M. Datar,* Cost Accounting: A Managerial Emphasis *(Upper Saddle River, N.J.: Prentice Hall, 2000), pp. 573–580. These sales-activity variances might result from changes in the product, changes in customer demand, effective advertising, and so on.*

SETTING STANDARDS

expected cost The cost most likely to be attained.

standard cost A carefully determined cost per unit that should be attained.

Expected costs or standard costs are the building blocks of a planning and control system. An **expected cost** is the cost that is most likely to be attained. A **standard cost** is a carefully developed cost per unit that should be attained. It is often synonymous with the expected cost, but some companies intentionally set standards above or below expected costs to create desired incentives.

What standard of expected performance should be used in flexible budgets? Should it be so strict that it is rarely, if ever, attained? Should it be attainable 50% of the time? 90%? 20%? Individuals who have worked a lifetime setting and evaluating standards for performance disagree, so there are no universal answers to this question.

perfection standards (ideal standards) Expressions of the most efficient performance possible under the best conceivable conditions, using existing specifications and equipment.

Perfection standards (also called ideal standards) are expressions of the most efficient performance possible under the best conceivable conditions, using existing specifications and equipment. No provision is made for waste, spoilage, machine breakdowns, and the like. Those who favor using perfection standards maintain that the resulting unfavorable variances will constantly remind personnel of the continuous need for improvement in all phases of operations. Though concern for continuous improvement is widespread, these standards are not widely used because they have an adverse effect on employee motivation. Employees tend to ignore unreasonable goals, especially if they would not share the gains from meeting imposed perfection standards. Organizations that apply the JIT philosophy (discussed in Chapter 1, p. 23) attempt to achieve continuous improvement from "the bottom up," not by prescribing what should be achieved via perfection standards.

currently attainable standards Levels of performance that can be achieved by realistic levels of effort.

Currently attainable standards are levels of performance that can be achieved by realistic levels of effort. Allowances are made for normal defectives, spoilage, waste, and nonproductive time. There are at least two popular interpretations of the meaning of currently attainable standards. The first interpretation has standards set just tightly enough that employees regard their attainment as highly probable if normal effort and diligence are exercised. That is, variances should be random and negligible. Hence, the standards are predictions of what will likely occur, anticipating some inefficiencies. Managers accept the standards as being reasonable goals. The major reasons for "reasonable" standards, then, are

1. The resulting standards serve multiple purposes. For example, the same cost can be used for financial budgeting, inventory valuation, and budgeting departmental performance. In contrast, perfection standards cannot be used for inventory valuation or financial budgeting, because the costs are known to be inaccurate.

2. Reasonable standards have a desirable motivational impact on employees, especially when combined with incentives for continuous improvement. The standard represents reasonable future performance, not fanciful goals. Therefore, unfavorable variances direct attention to performance that is not meeting reasonable expectations.

A second interpretation of currently attainable standards is that standards are set tightly. That is, employees regard their fulfillment as possible, though unlikely. Standards can be achieved only by very efficient operations. Variances tend to be unfavorable; nevertheless, employees accept the standards as being tough but not unreasonable goals. Is it possible to achieve continuous improvement using currently attainable standards? Yes, but expectations must reflect improved productivity and must be tied to incentive systems that reward continuous improvement.

TRADE-OFFS AMONG VARIANCES

Because the operations of organizations are linked, the level of performance in one area of operations will affect performance in other areas. Nearly any combination of effects is

The use of standard costs and variance analysis came under attack during the last two decades of the twentieth century. Critics maintained that comparing actual costs to predetermined standards is a static approach that does not work well in today's dynamic, fast-paced, just-in-time environment. However, companies continue to use standards and to measure performance against them. Surveys in five different countries have shown that between 65% and 86% of manufacturing companies use standard costs, with the high level of 86% being applied in the United States. Companies have apparently adapted the approach to fit their modern environments.

To apply standards in a dynamic environment, how should managers measure and report variances? First, standards should be regularly evaluated. If a company is in a state of continuous improvement, standards must be constantly revised. Second, standards and variances should measure key strategic variables. The concept of setting a benchmark, comparing actual results to the benchmark, and identifying causes for any differences is universal. It can be applied to many types of measures, such as production quantity or quality, as well as to costs. Finally, variances should not lead to affixing blame. Standards are plans, and things do not always go according to plan—often with no one being at fault.

One company that has adapted standard costs to meets its particular needs is the Brass Products Division (BPD) at Parker Hannifin Corporation. The BPD uses standard costs and variances to pinpoint problem areas that need attention if the division is to meet its goal of continuous improvement. Among the changes that have

increased the value of the standard cost information are more timely product cost information, variances computed at more detailed levels, and regular meetings held to help employees understand their impact on the variances.

The BPD also created three new variances: (1) standard run quantity variance—examines the effect of actual compared to optimal batch size for production runs; (2) material substitution variance—compares material costs to the costs of alternative materials; and (3) method variance—measures costs using actual machines compared to costs using alternative machines. All three variances use the concept of setting a standard and comparing actual results to the standard, but they do not apply the traditional standard cost variance formulas.

It was premature to declare standard costs dead. They are alive and well in many companies. However, there are fewer and fewer environments where traditional variance analysis is useful, and more and more environments where managers and accountants must adapt the standard cost concept to fit the particular needs of a company.

Sources: Adapted from D. Johnsen and P. Sopariwala, "Standard Costing Is Alive and Well at Parker Brass," *Management Accounting Quarterly*, Winter 2000, pp. 12–20; C. B. Cheatham and L. R. Cheatham, "Redesigning Cost Systems: Is Standard Costing Obsolete?", *Accounting Horizons*, December 1996, pp. 23–31; and C. Horngren, G. Foster, and S. Datar, *Cost Accounting: A Managerial Emphasis* (Upper Saddle River, N.J.: Prentice Hall, 2000), p. 226.

possible: Improvements in one area could lead to improvements in others and vice versa. Likewise, substandard performance in one area may be balanced by superior performance in others. For example, a service organization may generate favorable labor variances by hiring less-skilled and thus lower-paid customer representatives, but this favorable variance may lead to unfavorable customer satisfaction and future unfavorable sales-activity variances. In another situation, a manufacturer may experience unfavorable materials variances by purchasing higher-quality materials at a higher than planned price, but this variance may be more than offset by the favorable variances caused by less waste, fewer inspections, and higher-quality products.

Because of the many interdependencies among activities, an "unfavorable" or "favorable" label should not lead the manager to jump to conclusions. By themselves, such labels merely raise questions and provide clues to the causes of performance. They are attention directors, not problem solvers. Furthermore, the cause of variances might be faulty expectations rather than the execution of plans by managers. One of the first questions a manager should consider when explaining a large variance is whether expectations were valid.

When to Investigate Variances

When should variances be investigated? Managers recognize that, even if everything operates as planned, variances are unlikely to be exactly zero. They predict a range of "normal" variances. This range is usually based on economic analysis of how big a variance must be before investigation could be worth the effort. For some critical items, any deviation may prompt a follow-up. For most items, a minimum dollar or percentage deviation from budget may be necessary before managers expect investigations to be worthwhile. For example, a 4% variance in a $1 million material cost may deserve more attention than a 20% variance in a $10,000 repair cost. Because knowing exactly when to investigate is difficult, many organizations have developed such rules of thumb as "Investigate all variances exceeding $5,000 or 25% of expected cost, whichever is lower."

Comparisons with Prior Period's Results

Some organizations compare the most recent budget period's actual results with last year's results for the same period rather than use flexible budget benchmarks. For example, an organization might compare June 20X2's actual results to June 20X1's actual results. In general these comparisons are not as useful for evaluating the performance of an organization as comparisons of actual outcomes with planned results for the same period. Why? Because many changes probably have occurred in the environment and in the organization. Such changes make a comparison across years invalid. Very few organizations and environments are so stable that the only difference between now and a year ago is merely the passage of time. Even comparisons with last month's actual results may not be as useful as comparisons with flexible budgets. Comparisons over time may be useful for analyzing trends in such key variables as sales volume, market share, and product mix, but they do not help answer questions such as "Why did we have a loss of $11,570 in June, when we expected a profit of $12,800?"

SUMMARY PROBLEM FOR YOUR REVIEW

Problem

Refer to the data contained in Exhibits 8-1 and 8-2. Suppose actual production and sales were 8,500 units instead of 7,000 units; actual variable costs were $188,800; and actual fixed costs were $71,200. The selling price remained at $31 per unit.

Required
1. Compute the master budget variance. What does this tell you about the efficiency of operations? The effectiveness of operations?
2. Compute the sales-activity variance. Is the performance of the marketing function the sole explanation for this variance? Why?
3. Using a flexible budget at the actual activity level, compute the budgeted contribution margin, budgeted operating income, and flexible-budget variance. What do you learn from this variance?

Solution

1.

$$\text{actual operating income} = (8,500 \times \$31) - \$188,800 - \$71,200 = \$3,500$$
$$\text{master budget operating income} = \$12,800 \text{ (from Exhibit 8-1)}$$
$$\text{master budget variance} = \$12,800 - \$3,500 = \$9,300 \text{ U}$$

Three factors affect the master budget variance: sales activity, efficiency, and price changes. There is no way to tell from the master budget variance alone how much of the $9,300 U was caused by each of these factors.

2.

sales-activity variance = budgeted unit contribution margin × difference between the master budget unit sales and the actual unit sales

$$= \$9.20 \text{ per unit CM} \times (9,000 - 8,500)$$

$$= \$4,600 \text{ U}$$

This variance is labeled as a sales-activity variance because it quantifies the impact on operating income of the deviation from an original sales target while holding price and efficiency factors constant. This is a measure of the effectiveness of the operations—Dominion was ineffective in meeting its sales objective. Of course, the failure to reach target sales may be traceable to several causes beyond the control of marketing personnel, including material shortages, factory breakdowns, and so on.

3. The budget formulas in Exhibit 8-2 are the basis for the following answers.

flexible-budget contribution margin = $9.20 × 8,500 = $78,200

flexible-budget operating income = $78,200 − $70,000 fixed costs = $8,200

actual operating income = $3,500 (from requirement 1)

flexible-budget variance = $8,200 − $3,500 = $4,700 U

The flexible-budget variance shows that the company spent $4,700 more to produce and sell the 8,500 units than it should have if operations had been efficient and unit sales prices had not changed. Note that this variance plus the $4,600 U sales-activity variance total to the $9,300 U master budget variance.

FLEXIBLE-BUDGET VARIANCES IN DETAIL

The rest of this chapter probes the flexible budget variance in detail. The emphasis is on subdividing labor, material, and overhead cost variances into their component parts. Note that in companies where direct-labor costs are small in relation to total costs (that is, in highly automated companies) direct-labor costs may be treated as an overhead-cost item. Such companies do not compute separate labor standards, budgets, or variances.

VARIANCES FROM MATERIAL AND LABOR STANDARDS

Consider Dominion Company's $10 standard cost of direct materials and $8 standard cost of direct labor. These standards per unit are derived from two components: a standard quantity of an input and a standard price for the input.

	Standards		
	Standard Inputs Expected per Unit of Output	*Standard Price Expected per Unit of Input*	*Standard Cost Expected per Unit of Output*
Direct material	5 pounds	$2/pound	$10
Direct labor	1/2 hour	16/hour	8

Once standards are set and actual results are observed, we can measure variances from the flexible budget. To show how the analysis of variances can be pursued more fully, we will reconsider Dominion's direct-material and direct-labor costs, as shown in Exhibit 8-6, and assume that the following actually occurred for the production of 7,000 units of output:

- Direct material: Dominion purchased and used 36,800 pounds of material at an actual unit price of $1.90 for a total actual cost of $69,920.
- Direct labor: Dominion used 3,750 hours of labor at an actual hourly price (rate) of $16.40, for a total cost of $61,500.

Flexible budget variances for direct material and direct labor are $80 F and $5,500 U, respectively:

	(1) Actual Costs	(2) Flexible Budget	(3) Flexible- Budget Variance
Direct material	$69,920	$70,000	$ 80 F
Direct labor	61,500	56,000	5,500 U

The flexible-budget totals [column (2)] for direct materials and direct labor are the amounts that would have been spent with expected efficiency. They are often labeled total standard costs allowed, computed as follows:

$$
\begin{array}{l}
\text{flexible} \\
\text{budget or} \\
\text{total standard} \\
\text{cost allowed}
\end{array}
=
\begin{array}{l}
\text{units of good} \\
\text{output} \\
\text{achieved}
\end{array}
\times
\begin{array}{l}
\text{input allowed} \\
\text{per unit of} \\
\text{output}
\end{array}
\times
\begin{array}{l}
\text{standard unit} \\
\text{price of input}
\end{array}
$$

$$
\begin{array}{l}
\text{standard direct-materials} \\
\text{cost allowed}
\end{array}
= 7{,}000 \text{ units} \times 5 \text{ pounds} \times \$2.00 \text{ per pound} = \$70{,}000
$$

$$
\begin{array}{l}
\text{standard direct-labor cost} \\
\text{allowed}
\end{array}
= 7{,}000 \text{ units} \times 1/2 \text{ hour} \times \$16.00 \text{ per hour} = \$56{,}000
$$

Objective 6
Compute and interpret price and usage variances for inputs based on cost-driver activity.

price variance The difference between actual input prices and expected input prices multiplied by the actual quantity of inputs used.

usage variance (quantity variance, efficiency variance) The difference between the quantity of inputs actually used and the quantity of inputs that should have been used to achieve the actual quantity of output multiplied by the expected price of the input.

Before reading on, note particularly that the flexible-budget amounts (that is, the standard costs allowed) are tied to an initial question: What was the output achieved? Always ask yourself: What was the good output? Then proceed with your computations of the total standard cost allowed for the good output achieved.

PRICE AND USAGE VARIANCES

Flexible-budget variances [column (3) in the table above] measure the relative efficiency with which Dominion produced its 7,000 units. We can examine this efficiency by analyzing whether Dominion (1) used more or less of the resource than planned for the actual level of output achieved and (2) paid more or less than planned for each unit of the resources used. We measure these two components by computing price and usage variances, which subdivide each flexible-budget variance into the following two parts:

1. **Price variance**—difference between actual input prices and standard input prices multiplied by the actual quantity of inputs used.
2. **Usage variance**—difference between the quantity of inputs actually used and the quantity of inputs that should have been used to achieve the actual quantity of output multiplied by the expected price of the input (also called a **quantity variance** or **efficiency variance**).

The objective of these variance calculations is to hold either price or usage constant so that the effect of the other can be isolated. When calculating the price variance, you hold use of inputs constant at the actual level of usage. When calculating the usage variance, you hold price constant at the standard price. For Dominion Company the price variances are

Direct-material price variance = (actual price − standard price) × actual quantity
= ($1.90 − $2.00) per pound × 36,800 pounds
= $3,680 favorable

Direct-labor price variance = (actual price − standard price) × actual quantity
= ($16.40 − $16.00) per hour × 3,750 hours
= $1,500 unfavorable

The usage variances are

Direct-material usage variance = (actual quantity used − standard quantity allowed)
× standard price
= [36,800 − (7,000 × 5)] pounds × $2.00 per pound
= (36,800 − 35,000) × $2
= $3,600 unfavorable

Direct-labor usage variance = (actual quantity used − standard quantity allowed)
× standard price
= [3,750 − (7,000 × 1/2)] hours × $16 per hour
= (3,750 − 3,500) × $16
= $4,000 unfavorable

To determine whether a variance is favorable or unfavorable, use logic rather than memorizing a formula. A price variance is favorable if the actual price is less than the standard. A usage variance is favorable if the actual quantity used is less than the standard quantity allowed. The opposite relationships imply unfavorable variances.

Note that the sum of the direct-labor price and usage variances equals the direct-labor flexible-budget variance. Furthermore, the sum of the direct-material price and usage variances equals the total direct-material flexible-budget variance.

Direct-materials flexible-budget variance = $3,680 favorable + $3,600 unfavorable
= $80 favorable

Direct-labor flexible-budget variance = $1,500 unfavorable + $4,000 unfavorable
= $5,500 unfavorable

INTERPRETATION OF PRICE AND USAGE VARIANCES

When feasible, managers try to separate the variances that are subject to their direct influence from those that are not. The usual approach is to separate price factors from usage factors. Price factors often are less subject to immediate control than are usage factors, principally because of external forces, such as general economic conditions, that can influence prices. Even when price factors are regarded as being outside management control, isolating them helps to focus on the efficient usage of inputs. For example, the commodity prices of wheat, oats, corn, and rice may be outside the control of General Mills.

By separating price variances from usage variances, the breakfast-cereal maker can focus on whether grain was used efficiently.

Price and usage variances are helpful because they provide feedback to those responsible for inputs. These variances should not be the only information used for decision making, control, or evaluation, however. Exclusive focus on material price variances by purchasing agents or buyers, for example, can work against an organization's JIT and total quality management goals. A buyer may be motivated to earn favorable material price variances by buying in large quantities and by buying low-quality material. The result could then be excessive inventory-handling and opportunity costs and increased manufacturing defects owing to faulty material. Similarly, exclusive focus on labor price and usage variances could motivate supervisors to use lower-skilled workers or to rush workers through critical tasks, both of which could impair quality of products and services.

Variances themselves do not show why the budgeted operating income was or was not achieved. They raise questions, provide clues, and direct attention, however. For instance, one possible explanation for Dominion's set of variances is that a manager might have made a trade-off—the manager might have purchased at a favorable price some materials that were substandard quality, saving $3,680 (the materials price variance). Excessive waste might have nearly offset this savings, as indicated by the $3,600 unfavorable material usage variance and net flexible-budget variance of $80 favorable. The material waste also might have caused at least part of the excess use of direct labor. Suppose more than $80 of the $4,000 unfavorable direct-labor usage variance was caused by reworking units with defective materials. Then the manager's trade-off was not successful. The cost inefficiencies caused by using substandard materials exceeded the savings from the favorable price.

Exhibit 8-7 shows the price and usage variance computations for labor graphically. The standard cost (or flexible budget) is the standard quantity multiplied by the standard price—the rectangle shaded light blue. The price variance is the difference between the unit prices, actual and standard, multiplied by actual quantity used—the rectangle shaded dark blue. The usage variance is the standard price multiplied by the difference between the actual quantity used and the standard quantity allowed for the good output achieved—the rectangle shaded gray. (Note that for clarity the graph portrays only unfavorable variances.)

Exhibit 8-7

Graphical Representation of Price and Usage Variances for Labor

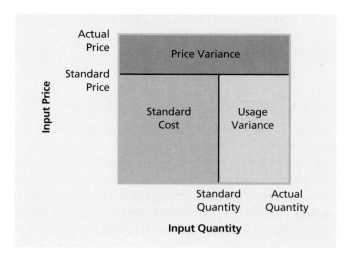

Consider a production plant that is supposed to produce 50 units per hour and work 8 hours each day. On March 23 the plant produced 325 units. Because of machine breakdowns, the plant operated for only 7.5 hours that day. Using the same conceptual framework as used for separating usage and price variances, determine how much of the 75 unit shortfall in production was caused by working only 7.5 hours and how much was caused by inefficiencies during the hours of actual operation.

ANSWER

Normal production would be $8 \times 50 = 400$ units per day. If the only difference from plan was the loss of 1/2 hour of productive time, production would have been $7.5 \times 50 = 375$ units. Therefore, 25 units of shortfall were caused by the machine breakdowns. The other $375 - 325 = 50$ units were caused by producing fewer than 50 units per hour. The actual rate of production was $325 \div 7.5 = 43.3$ units per hour, 6.7 units fewer than budgeted.

EFFECTS OF INVENTORIES

Analysis of Dominion Company was simplified because (1) there were no finished goods inventories—any units produced were sold in the same period—and (2) there was no direct-material inventory—the materials were purchased and used in the same period.

What if there are finished goods inventories and production does not equal sales? The sales-activity variance then is the difference between the static budget and the flexible budget for the number of units sold. In contrast, the flexible-budget cost variances compare actual costs with flexible-budgeted costs for the number of units produced.

What if there are direct materials inventories? Generally managers want quick feedback and want variances to be identified as early as is practical. In the case of the price of direct materials, that time is when the materials are purchased rather than when they are used, which may be much later. Therefore, the material price variance is usually based on the quantity purchased, measured at the time of purchase. The material usage variance remains based on the quantity used. Suppose Dominion Company purchased 40,000 pounds of material (rather than the 36,800 pounds used) at $1.90 per pound. The material price variance would be (actual price − standard price) × material purchased = ($1.90 − $2.00) per pound × 40,000 pounds = $4,000 favorable. The mateial usage variance would remain at $3,600 unfavorable because it is based on the material used.

OVERHEAD VARIANCES

We have just seen that direct-material and direct-labor variances are often subdivided into price and usage components. In contrast, many organizations believe that it is not worthwhile to monitor individual overhead items to the same extent. Therefore, overhead variances often are not subdivided beyond the flexible-budget variances—the complexity of the analysis may not be worth the effort.

Nevertheless, in some cases it may be worthwhile to subdivide the flexible-budget overhead variances, especially those for variable overhead. Part of the variable-overhead flexible-budget variance is related to control of the cost driver and part to the control of overhead spending itself. When actual cost-driver activity differs from the standard amount allowed for the actual output achieved, a **variable-overhead efficiency variance** will occur. Suppose that Dominion Company's cost of supplies, a variable-overhead cost, is driven by direct-labor hours. A variable-overhead cost rate of $.60 per unit at Dominion would be equivalent to $1.20 per direct-labor hour (because 1/2 hour is allowed per unit of

Objective 7
Compute variable overhead spending and efficiency variables.

variable-overhead efficiency variance An overhead variance caused by actual cost-driver activity differing from the standard amount allowed for the actual output achieved.

output). Of the $500 unfavorable variance, $300 unfavorable is due to using 3,750 direct-labor hours rather than the 3,500 allowed by the flexible budget, as calculated below:

$$\begin{array}{l} \text{variable-overhead} \\ \text{efficiency variance} \\ \text{for supplies} \end{array} = \left(\begin{array}{c} \text{actual direct} \\ \text{labor hours} \end{array} - \begin{array}{c} \text{standard direct-labor} \\ \text{hours allowed} \end{array} \right) \times \begin{array}{c} \text{standard} \\ \text{variable-overhead} \\ \text{rate per hour} \end{array}$$

$$= \left(\begin{array}{c} 3,750 \text{ actual} \\ \text{hours} \end{array} - \begin{array}{c} 3,500 \text{ standard} \\ \text{hours allowed} \end{array} \right) \times \$1.20 \text{ per hour}$$

$$= \$300 \text{ unfavorable}$$

This $300 excess usage of supplies is attributable to inefficient use of cost-driver activity, direct-labor hours. Whenever actual cost-driver activity exceeds that allowed for the actual output achieved, overhead efficiency variances will be unfavorable and vice versa. In essence this efficiency variance tells management the cost of not controlling the use of cost-driver activity. The remainder of the flexible-budget variance measures control of overhead spending itself, given actual cost-driver activity.

$$\begin{array}{l} \text{variable-overhead spending} \\ \text{variance for supplies} \end{array} = \begin{array}{c} \text{actual variable} \\ \text{overhead} \end{array} - \left(\begin{array}{c} \text{standard variable-} \\ \text{overhead rate} \end{array} \times \begin{array}{c} \text{actual direct-} \\ \text{labor hours used} \end{array} \right)$$

$$= \$4,700 - (\$1.20 \times 3,750 \text{ hours})$$

$$= \$4,700 - \$4,500$$

$$= \$200 \text{ unfavorable}$$

variable-overhead spending variance The difference between the actual variable overhead and the amount of variable overhead budgeted for the actual level of cost-driver activity.

That is, the **variable-overhead spending variance** is the difference between the actual variable overhead and the amount of variable overhead budgeted for the actual level of cost-driver activity.

As with other variances, the overhead variances by themselves cannot identify causes for results that differ from the static and flexible budgets. The only way for management to discover why overhead performance did not agree with the budget is to investigate possible causes. The distinction between spending and usage variances provides a springboard for more investigation, however.

GENERAL APPROACH

Exhibit 8-8 presents the analysis of direct material and direct labor in a format that deserves close study. The general approach is at the top of the exhibit. The specific applications then follow. Even though the exhibit may seem unnecessarily complex at first, its repeated use will solidify your understanding of variance analysis. Of course, the other flexible-budget variances in Exhibit 8-6 could be further analyzed in the same manner in which direct labor and direct material are analyzed in Exhibit 8-8. Such a detailed investigation depends on the manager's perception of whether the extra benefits will exceed the extra costs of the analysis.

Column A of Exhibit 8-8 contains the actual costs incurred for the inputs during the budget period being evaluated. Column B is the flexible-budgeted costs for the inputs given the actual inputs used, using expected prices but actual usage. Column C is the flexible-budget amount using both expected prices and expected usage for the outputs actually achieved. (This is the flexible-budget amount from Exhibit 8-6 for 7,000 units.) Column B is inserted between A and C by using expected prices and actual usage. The difference between columns A and B is attributed to changing prices because usage is held constant between A and B at actual levels. The difference between columns B and C is

Exhibit 8-8

**General Approach to Analysis of Direct-Labor
and Direct-Material Variances**

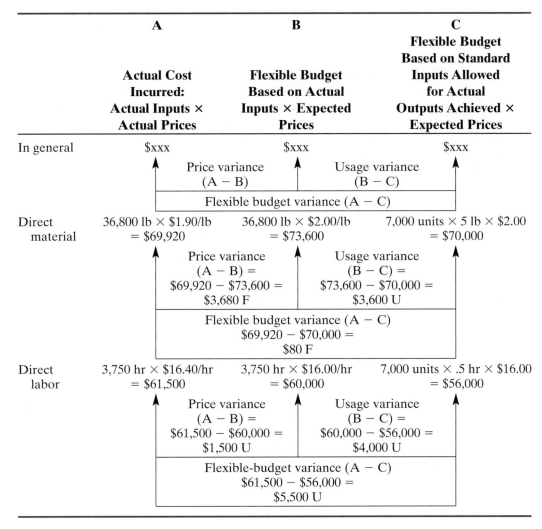

	A	**B**	**C**
			Flexible Budget Based on Standard Inputs Allowed for Actual
	Actual Cost Incurred: Actual Inputs × Actual Prices	**Flexible Budget Based on Actual Inputs × Expected Prices**	**Outputs Achieved × Expected Prices**
In general	$xxx	$xxx	$xxx

Price variance
(A − B)

Usage variance
(B − C)

Flexible budget variance (A − C)

| Direct material | 36,800 lb × $1.90/lb = $69,920 | 36,800 lb × $2.00/lb = $73,600 | 7,000 units × 5 lb × $2.00 = $70,000 |

Price variance
(A − B) =
$69,920 − $73,600 =
$3,680 F

Usage variance
(B − C) =
$73,600 − $70,000 =
$3,600 U

Flexible budget variance (A − C)
$69,920 − $70,000 =
$80 F

| Direct labor | 3,750 hr × $16.40/hr = $61,500 | 3,750 hr × $16.00/hr = $60,000 | 7,000 units × .5 hr × $16.00 = $56,000 |

Price variance
(A − B) =
$61,500 − $60,000 =
$1,500 U

Usage variance
(B − C) =
$60,000 − $56,000 =
$4,000 U

Flexible-budget variance (A − C)
$61,500 − $56,000 =
$5,500 U

attributed to changing usage because price is held constant between B and C at expected levels.

Actual output achieved in column C is measured in units of product. However, most organizations manufacture a variety of products. When the varieties of units are added together, the sum is frequently a nonsensical number (it is like adding apples and oranges). Therefore, all units of output are often expressed in terms of the standard inputs allowed for their production, such as pounds of fruit. Labor hours may also become the common denominator for measuring total output volume. Thus production, instead of being expressed as 12,000 chairs and 3,000 sofas, could be expressed as 20,000 standard hours allowed (or more accurately as standard hours of input allowed for outputs achieved). *Remember that standard hours allowed is a measure of actual output achieved.*

A key idea illustrated in Exhibit 8-8 is the versatility of the flexible budget. A flexible budget is geared to activity volume, and Exhibit 8-8 shows that activity volume can be measured in terms of either actual inputs used (columns A and B) or standard inputs allowed for actual outputs achieved (column C).

Exhibit 8-9

General Approach to Analysis of Overhead Variances

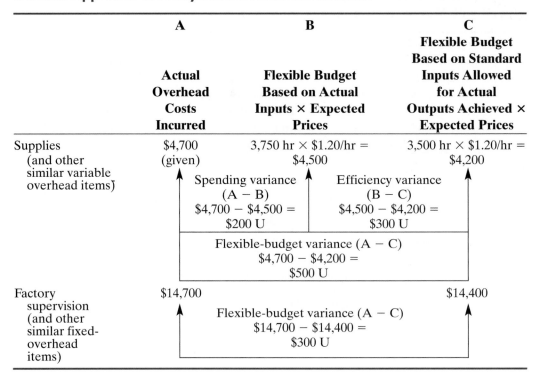

	A	B	C
	Actual Overhead Costs Incurred	**Flexible Budget Based on Actual Inputs × Expected Prices**	**Flexible Budget Based on Standard Inputs Allowed for Actual Outputs Achieved × Expected Prices**
Supplies (and other similar variable overhead items)	$4,700 (given)	3,750 hr × $1.20/hr = $4,500	3,500 hr × $1.20/hr = $4,200

Spending variance (A − B) $4,700 − $4,500 = $200 U

Efficiency variance (B − C) $4,500 − $4,200 = $300 U

Flexible-budget variance (A − C) $4,700 − $4,200 = $500 U

| Factory supervision (and other similar fixed-overhead items) | $14,700 | | $14,400 |

Flexible-budget variance (A − C) $14,700 − $14,400 = $300 U

Exhibit 8-9 summarizes the general approach to overhead variances. The flexible-budget variances for fixed-overhead items are not subdivided here. Fixed-overhead flexible-budget variances are discussed in more detail in Chapter 15. Note that the sales activity variance for fixed overhead is zero, because as long as activities remain within relevant ranges, the fixed-overhead budget is the same at both planned and actual levels of activity.

SUMMARY PROBLEM FOR YOUR REVIEW

PROBLEM

The following questions are based on the data contained in the Dominion Company illustration used in this chapter.

- Direct materials: standard, 5 pounds per unit @ $2 per pound
- Direct labor: standard, 1/2 hour @ $16 per hour

Suppose the following were the actual results for production of 8,500 units:

- Direct material: Dominion purchased and used 46,000 pounds at an actual unit price of $1.85 per pound, for an actual total cost of $85,100
- Direct labor: Dominion used 4,125 hours of labor at an actual hourly rate of $16.80, for a total actual cost of $69,300

1. Compute the flexible-budget variance and the price and usage variances for direct labor and direct material. **Required**

2. Suppose the company is organized so that the purchasing manager bears the primary responsibility for purchasing materials, and the production manager is responsible for the use of materials. Assume the same facts as in requirement 1 except that the purchasing manager bought 60,000 pounds of material. This means that there is an ending inventory of 14,000 pounds of material. Recompute the materials variances.

SOLUTION

1. The variances are

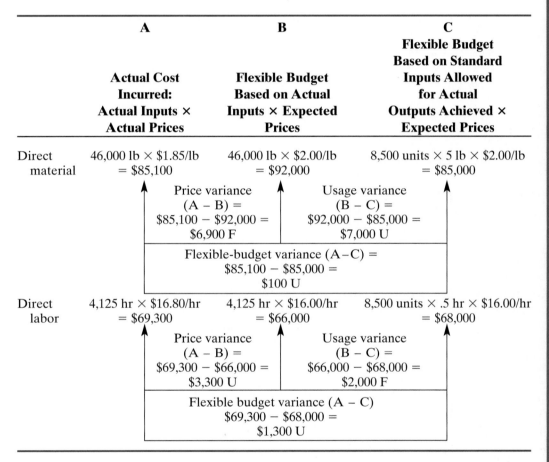

	A	B	C
	Actual Cost Incurred: Actual Inputs × Actual Prices	**Flexible Budget Based on Actual Inputs × Expected Prices**	**Flexible Budget Based on Standard Inputs Allowed for Actual Outputs Achieved × Expected Prices**
Direct material	46,000 lb × $1.85/lb = $85,100	46,000 lb × $2.00/lb = $92,000	8,500 units × 5 lb × $2.00/lb = $85,000

Price variance
(A − B) =
$85,100 − $92,000 =
$6,900 F

Usage variance
(B − C) =
$92,000 − $85,000 =
$7,000 U

Flexible-budget variance (A − C) =
$85,100 − $85,000 =
$100 U

| Direct labor | 4,125 hr × $16.80/hr = $69,300 | 4,125 hr × $16.00/hr = $66,000 | 8,500 units × .5 hr × $16.00/hr = $68,000 |

Price variance
(A − B) =
$69,300 − $66,000 =
$3,300 U

Usage variance
(B − C) =
$66,000 − $68,000 =
$2,000 F

Flexible budget variance (A − C)
$69,300 − $68,000 =
$1,300 U

2. Price variances are isolated at the most logical control point—time of purchase rather than time of use. In turn, the operating departments that later use the materials are generally charged at some predetermined budget, expected or standard price rather than at actual prices. This represents a slight modification of the approach in requirement 1 as shown at the top of the next page.

Note that this favorable price variance on balance may not be a good outcome—Dominion Company may not desire the extra inventory in excess of its immediate needs, and the favorable price variance may reflect that quality of the material is lower than planned. Note also that the usage variance is the same in requirements 1 and 2. Typically, the price and usage variances for materials now would be reported separately and not added together because they are based on different measures of volume. The price variance is based on inputs purchased, but the usage variance is based on inputs used.

Control point for direct materials	A Actual Cost Incurred: Actual Inputs × Actual Price	B Flexible Budget Based on Actual Inputs × Expected Price	C Flexible Budget Based on Standard Inputs Allowed for Actual Outputs Achieved × Expected Price
Purchasing	60,000 lb × $1.85/lb = $111,000	60,000 lb × $2.00/lb = $120,000	
		Price variance (A − B) = $111,000 − $120,000 = $9,000 F	
Using		46,000 lb × $2.00/lb = $92,000	8,500 units × 5 lb × $2.00/lb = $85,000
		Usage variance (B − C) = $92,000 − $85,000 = $7,000 U	

Highlights to Remember

Distinguish between flexible budgets and master (static) budgets.   Flexible budgets are geared to changing levels of cost-driver activity rather than to the single static level of the master (static) budget. Flexible budgets may be tailored to particular levels of sales or cost-driver activity—before or after the fact. They tell how much revenue and cost to expect for any level of activity.

Use flexible-budget formulas to construct a flexible budget based on the volume of sales. Cost functions, or flexible-budget formulas, reflect fixed- and variable-cost behavior and allow managers to compute budgets for any desired output or cost-driver activity level. The flexible-budget amounts are computed by multiplying the variable cost per cost-driver unit times the level of activity, as measured in cost-driver units.

Prepare an activity-based flexible budget.   When a significant portion of operating costs varies with cost drivers other than units of production, a company benefits from using activity-based flexible budgets. These budgets are based on budgeted costs for each activity and related cost driver.

Understand the performance evaluation relationship between master (static) budgets and flexible budgets.   The differences or variances between the master budget and the flexible budget are due to activity levels, not cost control. These variances are called activity-level variances.

Compute flexible-budget variances and sales-activity variances.   The flexible-budget variance is the difference between the total actual results and the total flexible-budget amounts for the actual unit volume. Sales-activity variances are calculated as actual unit sales less master budget unit sales times the budgeted unit contribution margin.

Compute and interpret price and usage variances for inputs based on cost-driver activity. Flexible-budget variances for variable inputs can be further broken down into price (or spending) and usage (or efficiency) variances. Price variances reflect the effects of changing input prices, holding usage of inputs constant at actual input use. Usage variances reflect the effects of different levels of input usage, holding prices constant at expected prices.

Compute variable overhead spending and efficiency variances.   The variable-overhead spending variance is the difference between the actual variable overhead and the amount of variable overhead budgeted for the actual level of cost-driver activity. The variable-overhead efficiency variance is the difference between the actual cost-driver activity and the amount allowed for the actual output achieved, costed at the standard variable-overhead rate.

Understand how management uses flexible budgets to evaluate the company's financial performance. The evaluation of performance is aided by feedback that compares actual results with budgeted expectations. The flexible-budget helps managers explain why the master budget was not achieved. Master budget variances are divided into (sales) activity and flexible-budget variances. Activity variances reflect the organization's effectiveness in meeting financial plans. Flexible-budget variances reflect the organization's efficiency at actual levels of activity.

Accounting Vocabulary

activity-based flexible budget, p. 315
activity-level variances, p. 315
currently attainable standards, p. 320
effectiveness, p. 317
efficiency, p. 317
efficiency variance, p. 324
expected cost, p. 320
favorable expense variance, p. 312

flexible budget, p. 313
flexible-budget variances, p. 315
ideal standards, p. 320
master budget variances, p. 312
perfection standards, p. 320
price variance, p. 324
quantity variance, p. 324
sales-activity variances, p. 318
standard cost, p. 320
static budget, p. 312

static budget variance, p. 312
unfavorable expense variance, p. 312
usage variance, p. 324
variable budget, p. 313
variable-overhead spending variance, p. 328
variable-overhead efficiency variance, p. 327

Fundamental Assignment Material

8-A1 Flexible and Static Budgets

Magellen Shipping Company's general manager reports quarterly to the company president on the firm's operating performance. The company uses a budget based on detailed expectations for the forthcoming quarter. The general manager has just received the condensed quarterly performance report shown in Exhibit 8-10.

Although the general manager was upset about not obtaining enough revenue, she was happy that her cost performance was favorable; otherwise, her net operating income would be even worse.

The president was totally unhappy and remarked, "I can see some merit in comparing actual performance with budgeted performance because we can see whether actual revenue coincided with our best guess for budget purposes. But I can't see how this performance report helps me evaluate cost control performance."

> **Required**

1. Prepare a columnar flexible budget for Magellen Shipping at revenue levels of $7,000,000, $8,000,000, and $9,000,000. Use the format of the last three columns of Exhibit 8-2, page 314. Assume that the prices and mix of products sold are equal to the budgeted prices and mix.
2. Express the flexible budget for costs in formula form.
3. Prepare a condensed table showing the master (static) budget variance, the sales activity variance, and the flexible-budget variance. Use the format of Exhibit 8-5, page 317

8-A2 Activity Level Variances

The systems consulting department of North Carolina Textiles designs data collecting, encoding, and reporting systems to fit the needs of other departments within the company. An overall cost driver is the number of requests made to the systems consulting department. The expected variable cost of handling a request was $500, and the number of requests expected for June 20X1 was 75. Monthly fixed costs for the department (salaries, equipment depreciation, space costs) were budgeted at $65,000.

The actual number of requests serviced by systems consulting in June 20X1 was 90, and the total costs incurred by the department was $114,000. Of that amount, $78,000 was for fixed costs.

Exhibit 8-10

Magellen Shipping Operating Performance Report
Second Quarter, 20X1

	Budget	Actual	Variance
Net revenue	$8,000,000	$7,600,000	$400,000 U
Fuel	$ 160,000	$ 157,000	$ 3,000 F
Repairs and maintenance	80,000	78,000	2,000 F
Supplies and miscellaneous	800,000	788,000	12,000 F
Variable payroll	5,360,000	5,200,000	160,000 F
Total variable costs*	$6,400,000	$6,223,000	$177,000 F
Supervision	$ 180,000	$ 184,000	$ 4,000 U
Rent	160,000	160,000	—
Depreciation	480,000	480,000	—
Other fixed costs	160,000	158,000	2,000 F
Total fixed costs	$ 980,000	$ 982,000	$ 2,000 U
Total costs charged against revenue	$7,380,000	$7,205,000	$175,000 F
Operating income	$ 620,000	$ 395,000	$225,000 U

U = Unfavorable. F = Favorable.

*For purposes of this analysis, assume that all these costs are totally variable with respect to sales revenue. In practice, many are mixed and have to be subdivided into variable and fixed components before a meaningful analysis can be made. Also assume that the prices and mix of services sold remain unchanged.

Required

Compute the master (static) budget variances and the flexible-budget variances for variable and fixed costs for the systems consulting department for June 20X1.

8-A3 Direct-Material and Direct-Labor Variances

Modern Outdoor Lighting, Inc., manufactures sculpted metal railings, lamp posts, and other ornaments. The following standards were developed for a line of lampposts.

	Standard Inputs Expected for Each Unit of Output Achieved	Standard Price per Unit of Input
Direct materials	5 pounds	$10 per pound
Direct labor	5 hours	$25 per hour

During April, 550 lampposts were scheduled for production. However, only 525 were actually produced.

Direct materials purchased and used amounted to 2,750 pounds at a unit price of $8.50 per pound. Direct labor actually paid was $26.00 per hour, and 2,850 hours were used.

Required

1. Compute the standard cost per lamppost for direct materials and direct labor.
2. Compute the price variances and usage variances for direct materials and direct labor.
3. Based on these sketchy data, what clues for investigation are provided by the variances?

8-B1 Summary Performance Reports

Consider the following data for Tax Preparation Services, Inc.:

- Master budget data: sales, 2,500 clients at $350 each; variable costs, $250 per client; fixed costs, $150,000.

- Actual results at actual prices: sales, 3,000 clients at $360 per client; variable costs, $800,000; fixed costs, $160,500.

Required

1. Prepare a summary performance report similar to Exhibit 8-5, page 317.
2. Fill in the blanks:

Master budget operating income	$—
Variances	
Sales-activity variances	$—
Flexible-budget variances	= =
Actual operating income	$

8-B2 Material and Labor Variances

Consider the following data:

	Direct Material	Direct Labor
Actual price per unit of input (lb and hr)	$8	$12
Standard price per unit of input	$7	$13
Standard inputs allowed per unit of output	10	2
Actual units of input	112,000	30,000
Actual units of output (product)	14,400	14,400

Required

1. Compute the price, usage, and flexible-budget variances for direct material and direct labor. Use U or F to indicate whether the variances are unfavorable or favorable.
2. Prepare a plausible explanation for the performance.

8-B3 Variable-Overhead Variances

You have been asked to prepare an analysis of the overhead costs in the order processing department of a mail-order clothing company like Lands' End. As an initial step, you prepare a summary of some events that bear on overhead for the most recent period. The variable-overhead flexible-budget variance was $6,000 unfavorable. The standard variable-overhead price per order was $.06. The rate of 10 orders per hour is regarded as standard productivity per clerk. The total overhead incurred was $203,200, of which $134,500 was fixed. There were no variances for fixed overhead. The variable-overhead spending variance was $1,500 favorable.

Find the following:

Required

1. Variable-overhead efficiency variance
2. Actual hours of input
3. Standard hours allowed for output achieved

Additional Assignment Material

QUESTIONS

8-1. Distinguish between favorable and unfavorable variances.

8-2. "The flex in the flexible budget relates solely to variable costs." Do you agree? Explain.

8-3. "We want a flexible budget because costs are difficult to predict. We need the flexibility to change budgeted costs as input prices change." Does a flexible budget serve this purpose? Explain.

8-4. Explain the role of understanding cost behavior and cost-driver activities for flexible budgeting.

8-5. "An activity-based flexible budget has a 'flex' for every activity." Do you agree? Explain.

8-6. "Effectiveness and efficiency go hand in hand. You can't have one without the other." Do you agree? Explain.

8-7. Differentiate between a master-budget variance and a flexible-budget variance.

8-8. "Managers should be rewarded for favorable variances and punished for unfavorable variances." Do you agree? Explain.

8-9. "A good control system places the blame for every unfavorable variance on someone in the organization. Without affixing blame, no one will take responsibility for cost control." Do you agree? Explain.

8-10. Who is usually responsible for sales-activity variances? Why?

8-11. Differentiate between perfection standards and currently attainable standards.

8-12. What are two possible interpretations of "currently attainable standards"?

8-13. "A standard is one point in a band or range of acceptable outcomes." Evaluate this statement.

8-14. "Price variances should be computed even if prices are regarded as being outside of company control." Do you agree? Explain.

8-15. What are some common causes of usage variances?

8-16. "Failure to meet price standards is the responsibility of the purchasing officer." Do you agree? Explain.

8-17. Are direct-material price variances generally recognized when the materials are purchased or when they are used? Why?

8-18. Why do the techniques for controlling overhead differ from those for controlling direct materials?

8-19. How does the variable-overhead spending variance differ from the direct-labor price variance?

COGNITIVE EXERCISES

8-20 Marketing Responsibility for Sales-Activity Variances
Suppose a company budgeted an operating profit of $100 on sales of $1,000. Actual sales were $900. The marketing department claimed that because sales were down 10%, it was responsible for a $10 drop in profit. Any further shortfall must be someone else's responsibility. Comment on this claim.

8-21 Production Responsibility for Flexible-Budget Variances
Suppose a plant manager planned to produce 100 units of product for $1,000. Instead, actual production was 110 units. When costs came in under $1,100, the plant manager claimed that she should get credit for a favorable variance equal to the amount by which the actual costs fell short of $1,100. Comment on this claim.

8-22 Responsibility of Purchasing Manager
A company's purchasing manager bought 5,000 pounds of material for $5.50 per pound instead of the budgeted $6.00 per pound, resulting in a favorable variance of $2,500. The company has a policy of rewarding employees with 20% of any cost savings they generate. Before awarding a $500 bonus to the purchasing manager, what other variances would you look at to determine the total effect of the purchasing decision? Explain.

8-23 Variable Overhead Efficiency Variance
Helton Company had a $1,000 U variable-overhead efficiency variance. Neither the plant manager, who was responsible primarily for labor scheduling, nor the administrative manager, who was responsible for most support services, felt responsible for the variance. Who should be held responsible? Why?

EXERCISES

8-24 Flexible Budget
Skadsberg Sports Equipment Company made 24,000 basketballs in a given year. Its manufacturing costs were $204,000 variable and $84,000 fixed. Assume that no price changes will occur in the following year and that no changes in production methods are applicable. Compute the budgeted cost for producing 30,000 basketballs in the following year.

8-25 Basic Flexible Budget
The superintendent of police of the city of Jacksonville is attempting to predict the costs of operating a fleet of police cars. Among the items of concern are fuel, $.15 per mile, and depreciation, $5,000 per car per year.

The manager is preparing a flexible budget for the coming year. Prepare the flexible-budget amounts for fuel and depreciation for each car at a level of 30,000, 40,000, and 50,000 miles.

8-26 Flexible Budget
Western Woolens has a department that makes wool scarves. Consider the following data for a recent month.

	Budget Formula per Unit	Various Levels of Output		
		6,000	7,000	8,000
Units	—	6,000	7,000	8,000
Sales	$18	$?	$?	$?
Variable costs				
Direct material	?	48,000	?	?
Fuel	2	?	?	?
Fixed costs				
Depreciation		?	16,000	?
Salaries		?	?	42,000

Fill in the unknowns.

Required

8-27 Basic Flexible Budget

The budgeted prices for materials and direct labor per unit of finished product are $13 and $5, respectively. The production manager is delighted about the following data.

	Master (Static) Budget	Actual Costs	Variance
Direct materials	$104,000	$98,000	$6,000 F
Direct labor	40,000	37,600	2,400 F

Is the manager's happiness justified? Prepare a report that might provide a more detailed explanation of why the static (master) budget was not achieved. Good output was 6,800 units.

Required

8-28 Activity-Level Variances

Materials support costs for the Pennsylvania Steel Company (PSC) are variable costs that depend on the weight of material (plate steel, castings, etc.) moved. For the current budget period and based on scheduled production, PSC expected to move 750,000 pounds of material at a cost of $.25 per pound. Several orders were canceled by customers, and PSC moved only 650,000 pounds of material. Total materials support costs for the period were $169,000.

Compare actual support costs to the master-budget support costs by computing master budget, activity-level, and flexible-budget variances for materials support costs.

Required

8-29 Direct-Material Variances

Custom Shirt Company uses a special fabric in the production of dress shirts. During August, Custom Shirt purchased 10,000 square yards of the fabric at $6.95 per yard and used 7,900 square yards in the production of 3,800 shirts. The standard allows 2 yards at $7.10 per yard for each shirt.

Calculate the material price variance and the material usage variance.

Required

8-30 Labor Variances

The city of Las Vegas has a sign shop where street signs of all kinds are manufactured and repaired. The manager of the shop uses standards to judge performance. Because a clerk mistakenly discarded some labor records, however, the manager has only partial data for April. She knows that the total direct-labor variance was $1,855 favorable, and that the standard labor price was $14 per hour. Moreover, a recent pay raise produced an unfavorable labor price variance for April of $980. The actual hours of input were 1,750.

1. Find the actual labor price per hour.
2. Determine the standard hours allowed for the output achieved.

Required

8-31 Usage Variances

Hong Kong Toy Company produced 9,000 stuffed bears. The standard direct-material allowance is two pounds per bear, at a cost per pound of $3. Actually, 16,500 pounds of materials (input) were used to produce the 9,000 bears (output).

Similarly, it is supposed to take 5 direct-labor hours to produce one bear, and the standard hourly labor cost is $3. But 46,500 hours (input) were used to produce the 9,000 bears.

Required Compute the usage variances for direct material and direct labor.

8-32 Labor and Material Variances

Standard direct-labor rate	$14.00
Actual direct-labor rate	$12.20
Standard direct-labor hours	12,000
Direct-labor usage variance—unfavorable	$14,000

Standard unit price of materials	$4.50
Actual quantity purchased	1,800
Standard quantity allowed for actual production	1,650
Materials purchase price variance—favorable	$288

Required
1. Compute the actual hours worked, rounded to the nearest hour.
2. Compute the actual purchase price per unit of materials, rounded to the nearest penny.

8-33 Material and Labor Variances

Consider the following data:

	Direct Material	Direct Labor
Costs incurred: actual inputs × actual prices incurred	$152,000	$79,000
Actual inputs × expected prices	165,000	74,000
Standard inputs allowed for actual outputs achieved × expected prices	172,500	71,300

Required Compute the price, usage, and flexible-budget variances for direct material and direct labor. Use U or F to indicate whether the variances are unfavorable or favorable.

PROBLEMS

8-34 National Park Service

The National Park Service prepared the following budget for one of its national parks for 20X1:

Revenue from fees	$5,000,000
Variable costs (miscellaneous)	500,000
Contribution margin	$4,500,000
Fixed costs (miscellaneous)	4,500,000
Operating income	$ 0

The fees were based on an average of 25,000 vehicle-admission days (vehicles multiplied by number of days in parks) per week for the 20-week season, multiplied by average entry and other fees of $10 per vehicle-admission day.

The season was booming for the first four weeks. There were major forest fires during the fifth week, however. A large percentage of the park was scarred by the fires. As a result, the number of visitors to the park dropped sharply during the remainder of the season.

Total revenues fell $1 million short of the original budget. Variable costs fell as expected, and fixed costs were unaffected except for hiring extra firefighters at a cost of $350,000.

Required

Prepare a columnar summary of performance, showing the original (static) budget, sales-activity variances, flexible budget, flexible-budget variances, and actual results.

8-35 Flexible and Static Budgets

Beta Alpha Psi, the accounting fraternity, recently held a dinner dance. The original (static) budget and actual results were as follows.

	Budget	Actual	Variance
Attendees	75	90	
Revenue	$2,625	$3,255	$630 F
Chicken dinners @ $17.60	1,320	1,668	348 U
Beverages, $6 per person	450	466	16 U
Club rental, $75 plus 8% tax	81	81	0
Music, 3 hours @ $250 per hour	750	875	125 U
Profit	$ 24	$ 165	$141 F

Required

1. Subdivide each variance into a sales activity variance portion and a flexible-budget variance portion. Use the format of Exhibit 8-5, page 317.
2. Provide possible explanations for the variances.

8-36 Summary Explanation

Capeletti Company produced 80,000 units, 8,000 more than budgeted. Production data are as follows. Except for physical units, all quantities are in dollars.

	Actual Results at Actual Prices	Flexible-Budget Variances	Flexible Budget	Sales-Activity Variances	Static (Master) Budget
Physical units	80,000	—	?	?	72,000
Sales	?	6,400 F	?	?	720,000
Variable costs	492,000	?	480,000	?	?
Contribution margin	?	?	?	?	?
Fixed costs	?	8,000 U	?	?	200,000
Operating income	?	?	?	?	?

Required

1. Fill in the unknowns.
2. Give a brief summary explanation of why the original target operating income was not attained.

8-37 Explanation of Variance in Income

Dominguez Credit Services produces reports for consumers about their credit ratings. The company's standard contribution margins average 70% of dollar sales, and average selling prices are $50 per report. Average productivity is four reports per hour. Some preparers work for sales commissions and others for an hourly rate. The master budget for 20X1 had predicted processing 800,000 reports, but only 700,000 reports were processed.

Fixed costs of rent, supervision, advertising, and other items were budgeted at $21 million, but the budget was exceeded by $700,000 because of extra advertising in an attempt to boost revenue.

There were no variances from the average selling prices, but the actual commissions paid to preparers and the actual productivity per hour resulted in flexible-budget variances (i.e., total price and efficiency variances) for variable costs of $900,000 unfavorable.

The president of Dominguez was unhappy because the budgeted operating income of $7 million was not achieved. He said, "Sure, we had unfavorable variable-cost variances, but our operating income was down far more than that. Please explain why."

Explain why the budgeted operating income was not attained. Use a presentation similar to Exhibit 8-5, page 317. Enough data have been given to permit you to construct the complete exhibit by filling in the known items and then computing the unknown. Complete your explanation by summarizing what happened, using no more than three sentences.

8-38 Activity and Flexible-Budget Variances at Burger King

Suppose a Burger King franchise in Bangkok had budgeted sales for 2000 of B 7.3 million (where B stands for baht, the Thai unit of currency). Cost of goods sold and other variable costs were expected to be 70% of sales. Budgeted annual fixed costs were B 1.8 million. A recovering Thai economy caused actual 2000 sales to soar to B 9.2 million and actual profits to increase to B 570,000. Fixed costs in 2000 were as budgeted. The franchise was pleased with the increase in profit.

1. Compute the sales activity variance and the flexible budget variance for 2000. What can the franchisee learn from these variances?

2. Suppose that in 2001 the Thai economy weakened, and the franchise's sales fell back to the B 7.3 million level. Given what happened in 2000, what do you expect to happen to profits in 2001?

8-39 Summary of Airline Performance

Consider the performance (in thousands of dollars) of Rocky Mountain Airlines for a given year in the following table.

	Actual Results at Actual Prices	Master Budget	Variance
Revenue	$?	$300,000	$?
Variable expenses	200,000	195,000*	5,000 U
Contribution margin	?	105,000	?
Fixed expenses	82,000	80,000	2,000 U
Operating income	$?	25,000	$?

* Includes jet fuel of $90,000.

The master budget had been based on a budget of $.20 per revenue passenger mile. A revenue passenger mile is one paying passenger flown one mile. An average airfare decrease of 8% had helped generate an increase in passenger miles flown that was 10% in excess of the static budget for the year.

The price per gallon of jet fuel rose above the price used to formulate the static budget. The average jet fuel price increase for the year was 10%.

1. As an explanation for the president, prepare a summary performance report that is similar to Exhibit 8-5, page 317.

2. Assume that jet fuel costs are purely variable and the use of fuel was at the same level of efficiency as predicted in the static budget. What part of the flexible-budget variance for variable expenses is attributable to jet fuel expenses? Explain.

8-40 University Flexible Budgeting

Inverness University offers an extensive continuing education program in many cities throughout Scotland. For the convenience of its faculty and administrative staff and also to save costs, the university operates a motor pool. The motor pool operated with 25 vehicles until February of this year, when an additional automobile was acquired. The motor pool furnishes gasoline, oil, and other supplies for the cars and hires one mechanic who does routine maintenance and minor repairs. Major repairs are done at a nearby commercial garage. A supervisor manages the operations.

Each year the supervisor prepares an operating budget, informing university management of the funds needed to operate the pool. Depreciation on the automobiles is recorded in the budget in order to determine the cost per kilometer.

The schedule below presents the annual budget approved by the university. The actual costs for March are compared with one-twelfth of the annual budget.

University Motor Pool

Budget Report for March 20X1

	Annual Budget	One-Month Budget	March Actual	Over (Under)
Gasoline	£ 82,500	£ 6,875	£ 8,200	£1,325
Oil, minor repairs, parts, and supplies	15,000	1,250	1,300	50
Outside repairs	2,700	225	50	(175)
Insurance	4,800	400	416	16
Salaries and benefits	21,600	1,800	1,800	—
Depreciation	22,800	1,900	1,976	76
	£ 149,400	£ 12,450	£ 13,742	£1,292
Total kilometres	1,500,000	125,000	140,000	
Cost per kilometer	£ .0996	£ .0996	£ 0.982	
Number of automobiles	25	25	26	

The annual budget was constructed based on the following assumptions.

1. 25 automobiles in the pool
2. 60,000 kilometres per year per automobile
3. 8 kilometres per liter for each automobile
4. £0.44 per liter of gas
5. £.01 per kilometre for oil, minor repairs, parts, and supplies
6. £108 per automobile in outside repairs

The supervisor is unhappy with the monthly report comparing budget and actual costs for March; she claims it presents her performance unfairly. Her previous employer used flexible budgeting to compare actual costs with budgeted amounts.

Required

1. Employing flexible-budgeting techniques, prepare a report that shows budgeted amounts, actual costs, and monthly variation for March.
2. Explain briefly the basis of your budget figure for outside repairs.

8-41 Activity-Based Flexible Budget

Cost behavior analysis for the four activity centers in the Billing Department of Portland Power Company is given below.

	Traceable Costs		
Activity Center	Variable	Fixed	Cost-Driver Activity
Account inquiry	$ 79,910	$155,270	3,300 labor hours
Correspondence	$ 9,800	$ 25,584	2,800 letters
Account billing	$154,377	$ 81,400	2,440,000 lines
Bill verification	$ 10,797	$ 78,050	20,000 accounts

The Billing Department constructs a flexible budget for each activity center based on the following ranges of cost-driver activity.

Activity Center	Cost Driver	Relevant Range	
Account inquiry	Labor hours	3,000	5,000
Correspondence	Letters	2,500	3,500
Account billing	Lines	2,000,000	3,000,000
Bill verification	Accounts	15,000	25,000

Required

1. Develop flexible-budget formulas for each of the four activity centers.
2. Compute the budgeted total cost in each activity center for each of these levels of cost driver activity: (a) the smallest activity in the relevant range, (b) the midpoint of the relevant range, and (c) the highest activity in the relevant range.
3. Determine the total cost function for the Billing Department.
4. The following table gives the actual results for the Billing Department. Prepare a cost-control performance report comparing the flexible budget to actual results for each activity center. Compute flexible budget variances.

Activity Center	Cost-Driver Level (Actual)	Actual Cost
Account inquiry	4,400 labor hours	$235,400
Correspondence	3,250 letters	$ 38,020
Account billing	2,900,000 lines	$285,000
Bill verification	22,500 accounts	$105,320

8-42 Straightforward Variance Analysis

Mesabi Iron Works, Inc., uses a standard cost system. The month's data regarding its iron castings follow:

- Material purchased and used, 3,300 pounds
- Direct-labor costs incurred, 5,500 hours, $20,900
- Variable-overhead costs incurred, $4,785
- Finished units produced, 1,000
- Actual material cost, $.95 per pound
- Variable-overhead rate, $.80 per hour
- Standard direct-labor cost, $4 per hour
- Standard material cost, $1 per pound
- Standard pounds of material in a finished unit, 3
- Standard direct-labor hours per finished unit, 5

Required

Prepare schedules of all variances, using the formats of Exhibits 8-8 and 8-9 on pages 329 and 330.

8-43 Variance Analysis

The Zurich Chocolate Company uses standard costs and a flexible budget to control its manufacture of fine chocolates. The purchasing agent is responsible for material price variances, and the production manager is responsible for all other variances. Operating data for the past week are summarized as follows:

1. Finished units produced: 4,000 boxes of chocolates.
2. Direct material: Purchases, 6,400 pounds of chocolate @ 15.5 Swiss francs (SF) per pound; standard price is 16 SF per pound. Used, 4,300 pounds. Standard allowed per box produced, 1 pound.
3. Direct labor: Actual costs, 6,300 hours @ 30.5 SF, or 192,150 SF. Standard allowed per box produced, 1-1/2 hours. Standard price per direct-labor hour, 30 SF.
4. Variable manufacturing overhead: Actual costs, 69,500 SF. Budget formula is 10 SF per standard direct-labor hour.

Required

Compute the following:

1.
   a. Material purchase-price variance
   b. Material usage variance
   c. Direct-labor price variance
   d. Direct-labor usage variance

e. Variable manufacturing-overhead spending variance
f. Variable manufacturing-overhead efficiency variance

(*Hint:* For format, see the solution to the Summary Problem for Your Review, pages 330–332.)
2.
a. What is the budget allowance for direct labor?
b. Would it be any different if production were 5,000 boxes?

8-44 Similarity of Direct-Labor and Variable-Overhead Variances

The C. Chan Company has had great difficulty controlling costs in Singapore during the past three years. Last month a standard cost and flexible-budget system was installed. A condensation of results for a department follows.

	Expected Cost per Standard Direct-Labor-Hour	Flexible-Budget Variance
Lubricants	$ .60	$330 F
Other supplies	.30	225 U
Rework	.60	450 U
Other indirect labor	1.50	450 U
Total variable overhead	$3.00	$795 U

F = Favorable. U = Unfavorable.

The department had initially planned to manufacture 9,000 audio speaker assemblies in 6,000 standard direct-labor hours allowed. Material shortages and a heat wave resulted in the production of 8,100 units in 5,700 actual direct-labor hours. The standard wage rate is $5.25 per hour, which was $.20 higher than the actual average hourly rate.

Required

1. Prepare a detailed performance report with two major sections: direct labor and variable overhead.
2. Prepare a summary analysis of price and usage variances for direct labor and spending and efficiency variances for variable overhead.
3. Explain the similarities and differences between the direct-labor and variable-overhead variances. What are some of the likely causes of the overhead variances?

8-45 Material, Labor, and Overhead Variances

Belfair Kayak Company makes molded plastic kayaks. Standard costs for an entry-level whitewater kayak are

Direct materials, 60 lb @ $5.50 per pound	$330
Direct labor, 1.5 hr @ $16 per hour	24
Overhead, @ $12 per kayak	12
Total	$366

The overhead rate assumes production of 450 kayaks per month. The overhead cost function is $2,808 + $5.76 × number of kayaks.
During March, Belfair produced 430 kayaks and had the following actual results.

Direct materials purchased:	28,000 pounds @ $5.30/lb
Direct materials used	27,000 pounds
Direct labor	660 hours @ $15.90/hr
Actual overhead	$5,320

Required

1. Compute material, labor, and overhead variances.
2. Interpret the variances.

3. Suppose variable overhead was $3.84 per labor hour instead of $5.76 per kayak. Compute the variable-overhead efficiency variance and the total overhead spending variance. Would these variances lead you to a different interpretation of the overhead variances from the interpretation in requirement 2? Explain.

8-46 Automation and Direct Labor as Overhead

Birmingham Precision Machining has a highly automated manufacturing process for producing a variety of auto parts. Through the use of computer-aided manufacturing and robotics, the company has reduced its labor costs to only 5% of total manufacturing costs. Consequently, labor is not accounted for as a separate item but is considered part of overhead.

Consider a part used in antilock braking systems. The static budget for producing 750 units in March 20X1 is

Direct materials	$18,000*
Overhead	
Supplies	1,875
Power	1,310
Rent and other building services	2,815
Factory labor	1,500
Depreciation	4,500
Total manufacturing costs	$30,000

*3 pounds per unit × $8 per pound × 750 units

Supplies and power are considered to be variable overhead. The other overhead items are fixed costs.

Actual costs in March 20X1 for producing 900 units of the brake part were

Direct materials	$21,645*
Overhead	
Supplies	2,125
Power	1,612
Rent and other building services	2,775
Factory labor	1,625
Depreciation	4,500
Total manufacturing costs	$34,282

*2,775 pounds purchased and used @ $7.80 per pound

1. Compute (a) the direct-materials price and usage variances and (b) the flexible-budget variance for each overhead item.

2. Comment on the way Birmingham Precision Machining accounts for and controls factory labor.

8-47 Standard Material Allowances

New Jersey Chemical Company supplies primarily industrial users. You have been asked to develop a standard product cost for a new solution the company plans to introduce.

The new chemical solution is made by combining altium and bollium, boiling the mixture, adding credix, and bottling the resulting solution in 20-liter containers. The initial mix, which is 20 liters in volume, consists of 24 kilograms of altium and 19.2 liters of bollium. A 20% reduction in volume occurs during the boiling process. The solution is then cooled slightly before 10 kilograms of credix are added; the addition of credix does not affect the total liquid volume.

The purchase prices of the raw materials used in the manufacture of this new chemical solution are as follows.

Altium	$2.10 per kilogram
Bollium	1.90 per liter
Credix	2.80 per kilogram

Determine the standard quantity for each of the raw materials needed to produce 20 liters of New Jersey Chemical Company's new chemical solution and the standard materials cost of 20 liters of the new product.

Required

8-48 Role of Defective Units and Nonproductive Time in Setting Standards

Tong Kim owns and operates KimTee Machining, a subcontractor to several aerospace industry contractors. When Mr. Kim wins a bid to produce a piece of equipment, he sets standard costs for the production of the item. He then compares actual manufacturing costs with the standards to judge the efficiency of production.

In April 20X1, KimTee won a bid to produce 15,000 units of a shielded component used in a navigation device. Specifications for the components were very tight, and Mr. Kim expected that 20% of the components would fail his final inspection, even if every care was exercised in production. There was no way to identify defective items before production was complete. Therefore 18,750 units had to be produced to get 15,000 good components. Standards were set to include an allowance for the expected number of defective items.

Each final component contained 3.2 pounds of direct materials, and normal scrap from production was expected to average an additional .4 pounds per unit. The direct material was expected to cost $11.25 per pound plus $.75 per pound for shipping and handling.

Machining of the components required close attention by skilled machinists. Each component required four hours of machining time. The machinists were paid $22 per hour and worked 40-hour weeks. Of the 40 hours, an average of 32 hours was spent directly on production. The other eight hours consisted of time for breaks and waiting time when machines were broken down or there was no work to be done. Nevertheless, all payments to machinists were considered direct labor, whether or not they were for time spent directly on production. In addition to the basic wage rate, KimTee paid fringe benefits averaging $6 per hour and payroll taxes of 10% of the basic wages.

Determine the standard cost of direct materials and direct labor for each good unit of output.

Required

8-49 Review of Major Points in This Chapter

The following questions are based on the Dominion Company data contained in Exhibit 8-1 (p. 313) and in the table on p. 323.

Required

1. Suppose actual production and sales were 8,000 units instead of 7,000 units. (a) Compute the sales-activity variance. Is the performance of the marketing function the sole explanation for this variance? Why? (b) Using a flexible budget, compute the budgeted contribution margin, the budgeted operating income, budgeted direct material, and budgeted direct labor.

2. Suppose the following were the actual results for the production of 8,000 units.

   Direct material: 42,000 pounds were used at an actual unit price of $1.85, for a total actual cost of $77,700.

   Direct labor: 4,140 hours were used at an actual hourly rate of $16.40, for a total actual cost of $67,896.

   Compute the flexible-budget variance and the price and usage variances for direct materials and direct labor. Present your answers in the form shown in Exhibit 8-8, p. 329.

3. Suppose the company is organized so that the purchasing manager bears the primary responsibility for the acquisition prices of materials, and the production manager bears the primary responsibility for usage but not responsibility for unit prices. Assume the same facts as in requirement 2 except that the purchasing manager acquired 60,000 pounds of materials at $1.85 per pound. This means that there is an ending inventory of 18,000 pounds. Would your variance analysis of materials in requirement 2 change? Why? Show computations.

8-50 Review Problem on Standards and Flexible Budgets; Answers Are Provided

The Aspen Leather Company makes a variety of leather goods. It uses standard costs and a flexible budget to aid planning and control. Budgeted variable overhead at a 45,000-direct-labor-hour level is $27,000.

During April the company had an unfavorable variable-overhead efficiency variance of $1,150. Material purchases were $241,900. Actual direct-labor costs incurred were $140,700. The direct-labor usage variance was $5,100 unfavorable. The actual average wage rate was $.20 lower than the average standard wage rate.

The company uses a variable-overhead rate of 20% of standard direct-labor cost for flexible-budgeting purposes. Actual variable overhead for the month was $30,750.

Required

Compute the following amounts; use U or F to indicate whether variances are unfavorable or favorable.

1. Standard direct-labor cost per hour
2. Actual direct-labor hours worked
3. Total direct-labor price variance
4. Total flexible budget for direct-labor costs
5. Total direct-labor variance
6. Variable-overhead spending variance in total

Answers to Problem 8-50

1. $3. The variable-overhead rate is $.60, obtained by dividing $27,000 by 45,000 hours. Therefore the direct-labor rate must be $.60 ÷ .20 = $3.
2. 50,250 hours. Actual costs, $140,700 ÷ ($3 − $.20) = 50,250 hours.
3. $10,050 F. 50,250 actual hours × $.20 = $10,050.
4. $145,650. Usage variance was $5,100 U. Therefore, excess hours must have been $5,100 ÷ $3 = 1,700. Consequently, standard hours allowed must be 50,250 − 1,700 = 48,550. Flexible budget = 48,550 × $3 = $145,650.
5. $4,950 F. $145,650 − $140,700 = $4,950 F; or $10,050 F − $5,100 U = $4,950 F.
6. $470 U. Flexible budget = 48,550 × .60 = $29,130. Total variance = $30,750 − $29,130 = $1,620 U. Price variance = $1,620 − $1,150. Efficiency variance = $470 U.

CASES

8-51   Hospital Costs and Explanation of Variances

The emergency room at St. Joseph's Hospital uses a flexible budget based on patients seen as a measure of activity. An adequate staff of attending and on-call physicians must be maintained at all times, so patient activity does not affect physician scheduling. Nurse scheduling varies as volume changes, however. A standard of .5 nurse-hours per patient visit was set. Average hourly pay for nurses is $15, ranging from $9 to $18 per hour. All materials are considered to be supplies, a part of overhead; there are no direct materials. A statistical study showed that the cost of supplies and other variable overhead is more closely associated with nurse-hours than with patient visits. The standard for supplies and other variable overhead is $10 per nurse-hour.

The head physician of the emergency room unit, Beverly Mossman, is responsible for control of costs. During October the emergency room unit treated 4,000 patients. The budget and actual costs were as follows:

	Budget	Actual	Variance
Patient visits	3,800	4,000	200
Nurse-hours	1,900	2,075	175
Nursing cost	$ 28,500	$ 33,125	$4,625
Supplies and other variable overhead	19,000	20,320	1,320
Fixed costs	92,600	92,600	0
Total cost	$140,100	$146,045	$5,945

Required

1. Calculate price and usage variances for nursing costs.
2. Calculate spending and efficiency variances for supplies and other variable overhead.
3. Dr. Mossman has been asked to explain the variances to the chief of staff. Provide possible explanations.

8-52 Activity-Based Costing and Flexible Budgeting

The new printing department provides printing services to the other departments of Connecticut Federal Insurance Company. Before the establishment of the in-house printing department, the departments contracted with external printers for their printing work. The Connecticut Federal printing policy is to charge using departments for the variable printing costs on the basis of number of pages printed. Fixed costs are recovered in pricing of external jobs.

The first year's budget for the printing department was based on the department's expected total costs divided by the planned number of pages to be printed.

The projected annual number of pages to be printed was 420,000, and total variable costs were budgeted to be $420,000. Most government accounts and all internal jobs were expected to use only single-color printing. Commercial accounts were primarily four-color printing. Variable costs were estimated based on the average variable cost of printing a four-color page that is one-fourth graphics and three-fourths text. The expected annual costs for each division were as follows.

Department	Planned Pages Printed	Variable Cost per Page	Budgeted Charges
Government accounts	120,000	$1	$ 90,000
Commercial accounts	250,000	1	300,000
Central administration	50,000	1	30,000
Total	420,000		$420,000

After the first month of using the internal printing department, the printing department announced that its variable cost estimate of $1 per page was too low. The first month's actual costs were $50,000 to print 40,000 pages.

Government accounts	9,000 pages
Commercial accounts	27,500
Central administration	3,500

Three reasons were cited for higher-than-expected costs: All departments were using more printing services than planned, and government and internal jobs were using more four-color printing and more graphics than expected. The printing department also argued that additional four-color printing equipment would have to be purchased if demand for four-color printing continued to grow.

Required

1. Compare the printing department actual results, static budget, and flexible budget for the month just completed.
2. Discuss possible reasons why the printing department static budget was inaccurate.
3. An activity-based costing (ABC) study completed by a consultant indicated that printing costs are driven by number of pages (@ $.30 per page), and use of colors (@ $1 extra per page for color).

   a. Discuss the likely effects of using the ABC results for budgeting and control of printing department use.
   b. Discuss the assumptions regarding cost behavior implied in the ABC study results.
   c. Commercial accounts during the first month (27,500 pages) used four colors per page. Compare the cost of commercial accounts under the old and the proposed ABC system.

8-53 Analyzing Performance

Springfield Community Hospital operates an outpatient clinic in a town several miles from the main hospital. For several years the clinic has struggled just to break even. The clinic's financial budget for 2001 is as follows:

Outpatient Clinic

2001 Budget

	Total	Per Patient
Revenues (4,000 patients @ $180 each)	$ 720,000	$180
Cost of services		
Physicians $240,000		
Nurses and technicians 180,000		
Supplies 60,000		
Overhead 252,000	732,000	183
Net loss	$(12,000)	$ (3)

On the average, billings for each patient-visit are expected to be $180. Costs in 2001 are expected to average $183 per patient-visit, as follows.

Physician time	$ 60
Nurse and technician time	45
Supplies	15
Overhead	63
Total	$183

The clinic is generally staffed by one physician, who must be present whether or not there is a patient to see. Currently about 10% of the physician's time is idle. The clinic employs nurses and technicians to meet the actual workload necessitated by patient appointments. Their cost averages $30 per hour, and usage varies proportionately with the number of patient-visits. Supplies cost is also variable with respect to patient-visits. Fixed overhead in 2001 was $180,000; the remaining $72,000 of overhead was variable with respect to patient visits. Included in the fixed overhead was $30,000 of hospitalwide administrative costs that the hospital allocates to the clinic and $37,500 of depreciation on the clinic's property and equipment.

Jeri McCullough, controller of Springfield Community Hospital, has reported that the loss in 2001 represented the fifth straight year of losses. She explained that she did not feel it was right for patients in the main hospital to subsidize those using the clinic. Therefore, she suggested that unless the situation could be changed, the clinic should be closed. Emilio Martinez, Administrative Vice President of the hospital, who was charged with oversight of the clinic, disagreed. "We provide a valuable service to the community with the clinic. Even if we are losing money, it is worthwhile to keep it open."

At the end of 2001, the clinic's actual results for the year were

	Total
Revenues (3,800 patients @ $180)	$684,000
Cost of services	
Physicians $231,000	
Nurses and technicians (5,800 hours) 182,700	
Supplies 58,500	
Overhead 232,000	704,200
Net loss	$(20,200)

Required

1. Would Springfield Community Hospital save money if the outpatient clinic was closed? Explain.

2. Explain the difference between the budgeted loss of $12,000 and the actual loss of $20,200 (that is, the master budget variance of $8,200) in as much detail as possible. From the analysis of the 2001 results, what actions would you suggest to avoid a loss in 2002?

COLLABORATIVE LEARNING EXERCISE

8-54 Setting Standards

Form groups of two to six persons each. The groups should each select a simple product or service. Be creative, but do not pick a product or service that is too complex. For those having difficulty choosing a product or service, some possibilities are

- One dozen chocolate-chip cookies
- A 10-mile taxi ride
- One copy of a 100-page course syllabus
- A machine-knit wool sweater
- A hand-knit wool sweater
- One hour of lawn mowing and fertilizing
- A hammer

Required

1. Each student should individually estimate the direct materials and direct labor inputs needed to produce the product or service. For each type of direct material and direct labor, determine the standard quantity and standard price. Also, identify the overhead support needed, and determine the standard overhead cost of the product or service. The result should be a total standard cost for the product or service.

2. Each group should compare the estimates of its members. Where estimates differ, determine why there were differences. Did assumptions differ? Did some members have more knowledge about the product or service than others? Form a group estimate of the standard cost of the product or service.

3. After the group has agreed on a standard cost, discuss the process used to arrive at the cost. What assumptions did the group make? Is the standard cost an "ideal" standard or a "currently attainable" standard? Note how widely standard costs can vary depending on assumptions and knowledge of the production process.

INTERNET EXERCISE

8.5 Flexible Budgets at Hershey Food Corporation

This chapter focused on flexible budgets and variance analysis. While the information used to determine both of these is generally for internal purposes only and not available to an outsider, it is possible to look at what information a firm reports and, based on that information, to make some judgments about what occurred.

www.prenhall.com/horngren

1. Look at the Hershey Food Web site found at http://www.Hersheys.com. Hershey has a varied choice of activities linking off the home page. Are there any new products listed by the firm? What are they? What is the firm doing to assist in promoting this product(s)? What do new products indicate about the need for a flexible budget?

2. Hershey Foods has a variety of products. Is the company's product line limited to only the United States? How many products does Hershey produce for distribution in the United States? Are there any products produced that aren't available in the United States? With the large number of products offered, would a static or flexible budget be more useful for planning purposes? Why?

3. Examine Hershey's most recent income statement. Suppose that in the following year net sales were expected to increase by 5%, but there was no expected increase in selling prices. Also assume that cost of sales is the only variable cost. Prepare a master budget income statement for the following year. Now suppose that selling prices were exactly as budgeted, but sales actually increased by 8% and net income increased by 10%. Determine the master budget variance, the sales-activity variance, and the flexible-budget variance.

4. Now let's see if Hershey has used good planning for production and sales in 2000. Click on Hershey's 1999 annual report. Look at the letter to investors written by the CEO. What explanations does he provide for possibly not meeting the planned sales for 2000? What actions did Hershey take during 2000 that caused sales in the last half of the year to be better than those in the first half? Given the information from Mr. Wolfe's letter, what type of variances do you suppose the firm experienced in the first half of 2000? Why?

Go to the "Flexible Budgeting and Variances" episode on the *Mastering Accounting* CD-ROM for an interactive, video-enhanced exercise that illustrates the problems that arise when different managers analyze reports and capture data differently.

MANAGEMENT CONTROL SYSTEMS AND RESPONSIBILITY ACCOUNTING

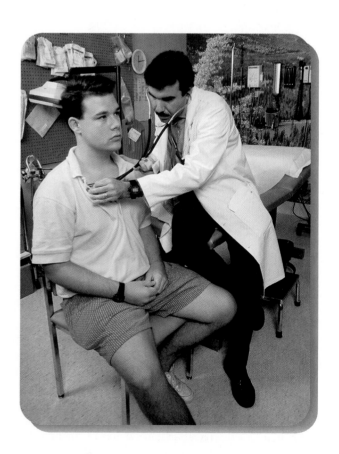

Doctors and patients at Foundation Health Systems benefit from the latest, state-of-the-art medical management system, offering the highest quality health care at an affordable price.

www.prenhall.com/horngren

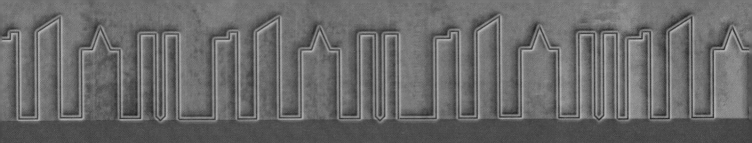

Learning Objectives

When you have finished studying this chapter, you should be able to

1. Describe the relationship of management control systems to organizational goals.

2. Use responsibility accounting to define an organizational subunit as a cost center, a profit center, or an investment center.

3. Compare financial and nonfinancial performance, and explain why the balanced scorecard is becoming an important management control tool.

4. Explain the importance of evaluating performance and how it impacts motivation, goal congruence, and employee effort.

5. Prepare segment income statements for evaluating profit and investment centers using the contribution margin and controllable-cost concepts.

6. Measure performance against quality, cycle time, and productivity objectives.

7. Describe the difficulties of management control in service and nonprofit organizations.

8. **Understand how a management control system uses accounting information.**

It's 2:30 A.M. You don't feel well. Should you call your doctor? Go to the emergency room? Is what you're feeling really something to worry about? What you need is good quality health care and you need it now, not tomorrow morning, and you do not want to worry about its cost. Sound familiar? This is a dilemma that we have all faced at some time. One health care organization that has a solution to this common problem is Foundation Health Systems, Inc. (FHS).

Foundation Health Systems, Inc., is one of the largest managed health care organizations in the United States. With more than 12,000 employees and 2000 revenues of more than $8.7 billion, FHS provides coverage to more than four million members.

Health care organizations must compete just as any other business, offering high quality health care at an affordable cost, and when it is needed. In order to maintain its competitive advantage, FHS started a major information systems development program called "fourth generation medical management." According to Dr. Malik Hasan, former chairman and chief executive officer of FHS, this new management control system was created "because the greatest opportunity for increasing overall quality and decreasing the cost of health care lies in managing patient care by seamlessly linking the entire health care delivery system electronically." The system "gives physicians and health care providers instant, user-friendly electronic access to comprehensive information about a patient's medical history and the best clinical treatments recommended."

The result? A fast and pre-approved referral to the best clinical resource, whether it be a specialist, the emergency room or urgent care center, your regular physician, or safe self-care. In other words, a satisfied customer! And as a bonus, costs are reduced. As Medical Director John Danaher, M.D., explains, "Paper charting and duplicative lab and radiology test are eliminated."

The previous chapters have presented many important cost-management tools used by management accountants. Tools such as activity-based costing, relevant costing, budgeting, and variance analysis are each useful by themselves. They are most useful, however, when they are parts of an integrated system—an orderly, logical plan to coordinate and evaluate all the activities of the organization's value chain. Just as in the case of FHS, managers of most organizations today realize that long-run success depends on focusing on cost, quality, and service—the three components of the competitive edge. This chapter considers how the management control system helps managers focus resources and talents of the individuals in an organization on such goals as cost, quality, and service. As you will see, no single management control system is inherently superior to another. The "best" system is the one that consistently leads to actions that meet the organization's goals and objectives.

This chapter builds on previous ones to present how the individual tools of management accounting are blended systematically to help achieve organizational goals.

MANAGEMENT CONTROL SYSTEMS

management control system A logical integration of techniques to gather and use information to make planning and control decisions, to motivate employee behavior, and to evaluate performance.

A **management control system** is a logical integration of techniques to gather and use information to make planning and control decisions, to motivate employee behavior, and to evaluate performance. The purposes of a management control system are

- to clearly communicate the organization's goals;
- to ensure that managers and employees understand the specific actions required of them to achieve organizational goals;
- to communicate results of actions across the organization; and
- to ensure that managers can adjust to changes in the environment.

Exhibit 9-1 shows the components of a management control system. We will refer to Exhibit 9-1 often in this chapter as we consider the design and operation of management control systems.

MANAGEMENT CONTROL SYSTEMS AND ORGANIZATIONAL GOALS

Objective 1
Describe the relationship of management control systems to organizational goals.

A well-designed management control system aids and coordinates the process of making decisions and motivates individuals throughout the organization to act in concert. It also facilitates forecasting revenue- and cost-driver levels, budgeting, and measuring and evaluating performance.

The first and most basic component in a management control system is the organization's goals. Why? Because the focus of the management control system is on internal management decision making and motivating (and then evaluating) performance consistent with the organization's goals. As shown in Exhibit 9-2, setting goals, choosing actions, and developing performance measures involves managers at all levels.

Exhibit 9-1

The Management Control System

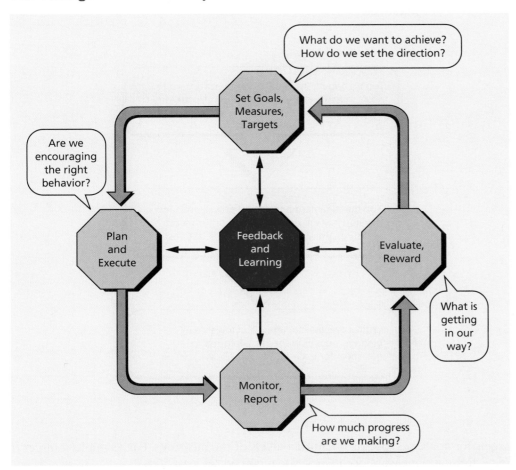

Exhibit 9-2 shows that top managers set organization-wide (overall company) goals, performance measures, and targets. Managers review these goals on a periodic basis, usually once a year. These goals provide a long-term framework around which an organization will form its comprehensive plan for positioning itself in the market. As Exhibit 9-1 shows, goals answer the question, "What do we want to achieve?" However, goals without performance measures do not motivate managers.

The purpose of performance measures is to set direction and to motivate managers. In their book, *Cracking the Value Code,* Boulton, Libert, and Samek state that we tend to "value what we measure but we do not always measure what we value." Measurements provide incentives, so it is important that performance measures be tied to valuable goals. Otherwise, managers who achieve high performance measures may not create value for the company and its owners. For example, a major luxury hotel chain, Luxury Suites, has the following goals and related performance measures:

Organizational Goals	Performance Measures
Exceed guest expectations	• Satisfaction index
	• Number of repeat stays
Maximize revenue yield	• Occupancy rate
	• Room rate
	• Income before fixed costs
Focus on innovation	• New products/services implemented per year
	• Number of employee suggestions

Exhibit 9-2

Setting Goals, Objectives, and Performance Measures

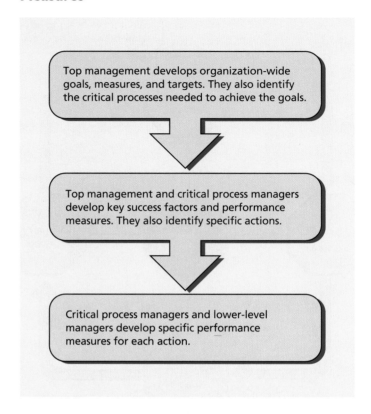

Top management develops organization-wide goals, measures, and targets. They also identify the critical processes needed to achieve the goals.

Top management and critical process managers develop key success factors and performance measures. They also identify specific actions.

Critical process managers and lower-level managers develop specific performance measures for each action.

Targets for goals are specific quantified levels of the measures. For example, a target for the performance measure occupancy rate might be "at least 70%."

As you can see, goals and their related performance measures are very broad. In fact, they are often too vague to guide managers and employees. As a result, top managers also identify key success factors. **Key success factors** are characteristics or attributes that managers must achieve in order to drive the organization toward its goals. Consider Luxury Suites. An example of a key success factor for the goal to exceed guest expectations is timeliness. That is, in order for Luxury Suites to achieve its goal of exceeding guest expectations it must provide timely service. Performance measures for timeliness would include check-in time, check-out time, and response time to guest requests (for example, number of rings before someone at the front desk answers the telephone).

Although key success factors and related performance measures give managers more focus than do overall, organization-wide goals, they still do not give lower-level managers and employees the direction they need to guide their daily actions. As shown in Exhibit 9-2, to set this direction, top managers work with lower-level managers within the appropriate business unit to select specific tangible actions (or activities) that can be carried out and observed on a short-term basis. Examples of specific actions related to timeliness are implementing an express check-in system and training staff to use the new check-in system.

Balancing the various goals is an important part of management control. Managers often face trade-off decisions. For example, a sales manager can increase the "employee satisfaction" measure (a survey of employees) by setting lower standards for responding to customer inquiries. This action may improve the employee satisfaction measure of the manager but result in unsatisfied customers.

To design a management control system that meets the organization's needs, managers need to identify responsibility centers, develop performance measures, establish a monitoring and reporting structure, weigh costs and benefits, and provide motivation to achieve goal congruence and managerial effort.

IDENTIFYING RESPONSIBILITY CENTERS

Designers of management control systems must consider the desired responsibility centers in an organization. A **responsibility center** is a set of activities and resources assigned to a manager, a group of managers, or other employees. A set of machines and machining activities, for example, may be a responsibility center for a production supervisor. The full production department may be a responsibility center for the department head. Finally, the entire organization may be a responsibility center for the president. In some organizations, management responsibility is shared by groups of employees to create wide "ownership" of management decisions, allow creative decision making, and prevent one person's concern (or lack of concern) for risks of failure to dominate decisions.

An effective management control system gives each manager responsibility for a group of activities and actions and then, as shown in Exhibit 9-1, monitors and reports on (1) the results of the activities, and (2) the manager's influence on those results. Such a system has innate appeal for most top managers because it helps them delegate decision making and frees them to plan and control. Lower-level managers appreciate the autonomy of decision making they inherit. Thus, system designers apply **responsibility accounting** to identify what parts of the organization have primary responsibility for each action, develop performance measures and targets, and design reports of these measures by responsibility center. Responsibility centers usually have multiple goals and actions that the management control system monitors. Responsibility centers usually are classified according to their financial responsibility as cost centers, profit centers, or investment centers.

Cost, Profit, and Investment Centers. A **cost center** is a responsibility center in which a manager is accountable for costs only. Its financial responsibilities are to control and report costs. An entire department may be considered a single cost center, or a department may contain several cost centers. For example, although an assembly department may be supervised by one manager, it may contain several assembly lines and regard each assembly line as a separate cost center. Likewise, within each line, separate machines or test equipment may be regarded as separate cost centers. The determination of the number of cost centers depends on cost-benefit considerations—do the benefits of smaller cost centers (for planning, control, and evaluation) exceed the higher costs of reporting?

Unlike cost centers, **profit centers** have responsibility for controlling revenues as well as costs (or expenses)—that is, profitability. Despite the name, a profit center can exist in nonprofit organizations (though it might not be referred to as such) when a responsibility center receives revenues for its services. For example, the Western Area Power Authority (WAPA) is charged with recovering its costs of operations through sales of power to electric utilities in the western United States. WAPA essentially is a profit center with the objective of breaking even. All profit center managers are responsible for both revenues and costs, but they may not be expected to maximize profits.

An **investment center** goes a step further than a profit center does. Its success is measured not only by its income but also by relating that income to its invested capital, as in a ratio of income to the value of the capital employed. In practice, the term *investment center* is not widely used. Instead, the term *profit center* is used indiscriminately to describe

---

responsibility center A set of activities and resources assigned to a manager, a group of managers, or other employees.

Objective 2
Use responsibility accounting to define an organizational subunit as a cost center, a profit center, or an investment center.

responsibility accounting Identifying what parts of the organization have primary responsibility for each action, developing measures and targets to achieve, and creating reports of these measures by organization subunit or responsibility center.

cost center A responsibility center in which a manager is accountable for costs only.

profit center A responsibility center for controlling revenues as well as costs (or expenses) —that is, profitability.

investment center A responsibility center whose success is measured not only by its income but also by relating that income to its invested capital, as in a ratio of income to the value of the capital employed.

centers that are always assigned responsibility for revenues and expenses, but may or may not be assigned responsibility for the capital investment.

DEVELOPING PERFORMANCE MEASURES

Business managers are increasingly recognizing the importance of effective performance measures. A typical attitude of managers is "You simply can't manage anything you can't measure." Because most responsibility centers have multiple goals and actions, only some of these goals and actions are expressed in financial terms, such as operations budgets, profit targets, or required return on investment, depending on the financial classification of the center. Other goals and actions, which are to be achieved concurrently, are nonfinancial in nature. For example, many companies list environmental stewardship, social responsibility, and organizational learning as key goals. The well-designed management control system develops and reports both financial and nonfinancial measures of performance. Good performance measures will

1. Relate to the goals of the organization
2. Balance long-term and short-term concerns
3. Reflect the management of key actions and activities
4. Be affected by actions of managers and employees
5. Be readily understood by employees
6. Be used in evaluating and rewarding managers and employees
7. Be reasonably objective and easily measured
8. Be used consistently and regularly

Both financial and nonfinancial performance measures are important. Sometimes accountants and managers focus too much on financial measures, such as profit or cost variances, because they are readily available from the accounting system. Managers, however, can improve operational control by also considering nonfinancial measures of performance. Such measures may be more timely and more closely affected by employees at lower levels of the organization, where the product is made or the service is rendered.

Nonfinancial measures are often easier to quantify and understand. Hence, employees can be easily motivated toward achieving performance goals. For example, AT&T Universal Card Services, which was awarded the prestigious Baldrige National Quality Award (presented by the U.S. Department of Commerce), uses 18 performance measures for its customer inquiries process. These measures include average speed of answer, abandon rate, and application processing time (three days compared to the industry average of 34 days).

Often the effects of poor nonfinancial performance (for example, lack of organizational learning and process improvement and low customer satisfaction) do not show up in the financial measures until considerable ground has been lost. Financial measures often are lagging indicators that arrive too late to help prevent problems and ensure the organization's health. What is needed are leading indicators. As a result, many companies now stress management of the activities that drive revenues and costs rather than waiting to explain the revenues or costs themselves after the activities have occurred. Superior financial performance usually follows from superior nonfinancial performance.

MONITORING AND REPORTING RESULTS
AND THE BALANCED SCORECARD

Notice that Exhibit 9-1 has feedback and learning at the center of the management control system. At all points in the planning and control process, it is vital that effective communications exist among all levels of management and employees. In fact, organization-wide learning is a foundation for gaining and maintaining financial strength. Rich Teerlink, former CEO of Harley-Davidson, said, "If you empower dummies, they make dumb decisions faster." Harley-Davidson spends $1,000 per year per employee on training. Harley had 2000 sales of nearly $2.9 billion, one-year sales growth of 18%, and one-year earnings growth of 30%. It has also been said that the only sustainable competitive advantage is the rate at which a company's managers learn. However, even this powerful competitive edge can be overcome by competitors who develop or hire intellectual capital faster.

Once a company has superior intellectual capital, how can it best maintain its leadership? Exhibit 9-3 shows how organizational learning leads to financial strength. Organizational learning is monitored by measures such as training time, employee turnover, and staff satisfaction scores on employee surveys. The result of learning is continuous process improvement that is monitored by measures such as cycle time, number of defects (quality), and activity cost. Customers will value improved response time (lower cycle time), higher quality, and lower prices, and thus increase their demand for products and services. Increased demand, combined with lower costs to make and deliver products and services, results in financial strength as monitored by such measures as product profitability and earnings. It is important to note that the successful organization does not stop with one cycle of learning → process improvement → increased customer satisfaction → improved financial strength. The benefits of improved financial strength, excess financial resources, must be reinvested within the organization by supporting both continuous learning and continuous process improvement. The message from Exhibit 9-3 is that a key driver of enterprise performance is the culture within the company that

Exhibit 9-3

The Components of a Successful Organization and Measures of Achievement

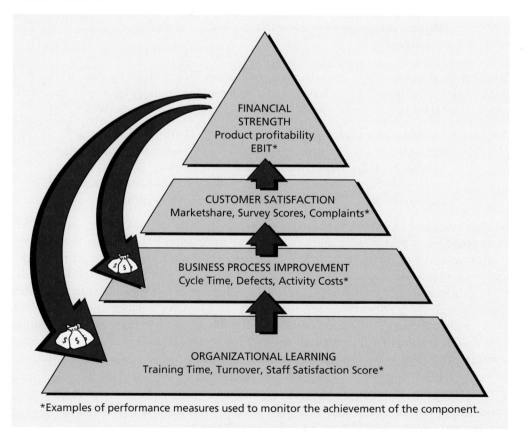

*Examples of performance measures used to monitor the achievement of the component.

fosters continual learning and growth at all levels of management. It is not adequate to use money to train managers if the resulting learning does not translate into improved processes, products, and services. This requires a culture of learning so that managers are motivated to translate learning into growth.

There are no guarantees that each of the components "automatically" follows from success at the previous component. If there is no improvement in one or more core business processes, the cause-effect chain can be broken. For example, a lack of improvement in marketing and distribution techniques can lead to failure due to the inability to place the "new and improved" products or services at the location desired by the customer. E-commerce is a good example of this. The point is that improvement in business processes must take place across all parts of the value chain.

One organization that provides a good example of the application of the enterprise learning culture is General Electric Company (GE). With sales of more than $100 billion, GE has demonstrated a remarkable ability to generate formidable profits in a wide range of industries, including broadcasting (NBC), transportation equipment, aircraft engines, appliances, lighting, electric distribution and control equipment, generators and turbines, nuclear reactors, medical imaging equipment, plastics, and financial services. In 1999, GE was named *Fortune* magazine's "Most Admired Company in America."

CEO John Welch claims GE's success is due to

> . . . *a General Electric culture that values the contributions of every individual, thrives on learning, thirsts for the better idea, and has the flexibility and speed to put the better idea into action every day. We are a learning company, a company that studies its own successes and failures and those of others—a company that has the self-confidence and the resources to take big swings and pursue numerous opportunities based on winning ideas and insights, regardless of their source. That appetite for learning, and the ability to act quickly on that learning, will provide GE with what we believe is an insurmountable and sustainable competitive advantage.*[1]

Removal of Boundaries. Exactly what does John Welch mean by the *"ability to act quickly on that learning"*? He refers to a management leadership philosophy that ignores organizational boundaries when implementing learning. According to Welch,

> *These new leaders are changing the very DNA of GE culture. Work-Out, in the '80s, opened our culture up to ideas from everyone, everywhere, killed NIH (Not Invented Here) thinking, decimated the bureaucracy, and made boundaryless behavior a reflexive and natural part of our culture, thereby creating the learning culture. . . .*[2]

As shown in Exhibit 9-1, monitoring and reporting the results of business activities is a key component of a management control system. Exhibit 9-2 indicates that managers identify actions and related performance measures that are linked to the achievement of goals and objectives. Once these performance measures and actions are identified, an organization must obtain information on the achievement of desired outcomes. This is done through the performance-reporting system. Effective performance reports align results with managers' goals and objectives, provide guidance to managers, communicate goals and their level of attainment throughout the organization, and enable organizations to anticipate and respond to change in a timely manner.

---

[1] *Source: General Electric's 1998 Annual Report.*
[2] *The term* Work-Out *refers to a process at GE where groups of employees meet at regular intervals to think of ways to improve GE. Then leadership comes in and listens to their ideas.*

The Balanced Scorecard.   There are several approaches to performance reporting. Each approach attempts to link organizational strategy to actions of managers and employees. One popular approach to performance reporting is the balanced scorecard. A **balanced scorecard** is a performance measurement and reporting system that strikes a balance between financial and operating measures, links performance to rewards, and gives explicit recognition to the diversity of organizational goals. Companies such as Champion International, AT&T, Allstate, and Apple Computer use the balanced scorecard to focus management's attention on items subject to action on a month-by-month and day-to-day basis.

One advantage of the balanced scorecard approach is that line managers can see the relationship between nonfinancial measures, which they often can relate more easily to their own actions, and the financial measures that relate to organizational goals. Another advantage of the balanced scorecard is its focus on performance measures from each of the four components of the successful organization shown in Exhibit 9-3. This enhances the learning process because managers learn the results of their actions and how these actions are linked to the organizational goals.

What does a balanced scorecard look like? Exhibit 9-4 shows a balanced scorecard for the Luxury Suites hotel chain. This scorecard is for the organization as a whole. It has performance measures for all four components of organizational success. There are many scorecards for an organization. In fact, each area of responsibility will have its own score-card. Scorecards for some lower-level responsibility centers that are centered strictly on day-to-day operations may be totally focused on only one of the four components. We should also note that not all performance measures appear on scorecards. Managers of responsibility centers include only those measures that are **key performance indicators**— measures that drive the organization to achieve its goals. For example, top management at Luxury Suites set "exceed guest expectations" as one organizational goal. The balanced scorecard should have at least one key performance indicator that is linked to this goal. The customer satisfaction index, brand loyalty index, number of improvements, and average cycle time for check-in and check-out measures all are linked to this goal.

balanced scorecard   A performance measurement and reporting system that strikes a balance between financial and operating measures, links performance to rewards, and gives explicit recognition to the diversity of organizational goals.

key performance indicators   Measures that drive the organization to achieve its goals.

When top managers set organizational goals, they should attempt to provide a balance between financial and nonfinancial goals. Using the four components of a successful organization shown in Exhibit 9-3, indicate the component associated with the following goals of Whirlpool:

People commitment
Total quality
Customer satisfaction
Financial performance
Growth and innovation

ANSWER

The components listed in Exhibit 9-3 are linked in a causal fashion from bottom to top. Using the five goals set by top managers at Whirlpool, we can make the following cause-effect statement:

If Whirlpool makes a solid commitment to its people, then growth and innovation will occur as part of the company's organizational learning. This will lead to business process improvements that increase the total quality of its products, which will then lead to increased customer satisfaction. The ultimate result of satisfied customers is improved financial performance. Sustainable financial strength should result in reinvestment in both Whirlpool's people and its internal processes.

Exhibit 9-4
Balanced Scorecard for Luxury Suites Hotels

Component and Measures	Target	Result
Financial Strength		
Revenue (millions of dollars) per new service	$50	$58
Revenue per arrival	$75	$81
Customer Satisfaction		
Customer satisfaction index	95	88
Brand loyalty index	60	40
Business Process Improvement		
Number of improvements	8	8
Average cycle time (minutes) for check-in and check-out	15	12
Organizational Learning		
Percent of staff retrained	80	85
Training hours per employee	30	25

SUMMARY PROBLEM FOR YOUR REVIEW

PROBLEM

Consider our example, the Luxury Suites hotel chain. As we have noted, top management established "exceed guest expectations" as one organization-wide goal. Among the key success factors are timeliness of customer service and quality of personalized service. Susan Pierce, Vice President of Sales, is the manager responsible for the actions required to meet the goal of exceeding guest expectations. She has already identified one action (objective) for the coming year—upgrade customer service department capabilities.

1. Identify several possible performance measures for the quality of personalized service key success factor.

2. Recommend several specific actions or activities associated with upgrading customer service department capabilities that would drive Luxury Suites to its goal of exceeding customer expectations.

SOLUTION

1. Performance measures for the quality of personalized service key success factor include number of changes to registration, rating on the "friendly, knowledgeable staff" question on the guest survey, number of complaints, percentage of return guests, and percentage of customers with completed customer profile (profiles special needs of customers).

2. Specific actions or activities include training employees, implementing a call checklist (list of services and options available to guest) and monitoring compliance with the list, developing a customer satisfaction survey, and reengineering the guest registration and reservation processes.

WEIGHING COSTS AND BENEFITS

The designer of the management control system must also weigh the costs and benefits of various alternatives, given the organization's needs. No system is perfect, but one system may be better than another if it can improve operating decisions at a reasonable cost.

Both benefits and costs of management control systems are often difficult to measure, and both may become apparent only after experimentation or use. For example, the director of accounting policy of Citicorp has stated that, after several years of experience with a very detailed management control system, the system has proved to be too costly to administer relative to the perceived benefits. Accordingly, Citicorp planned to return to a simpler, less costly—though less precise—management control system.

MOTIVATING EMPLOYEES TO ACHIEVE GOAL CONGRUENCE AND EXERT MANAGERIAL EFFORT THROUGH REWARDS

To achieve maximum benefits at minimum cost, a management control system must foster goal congruence and managerial effort. Goal congruence exists when individuals and groups aim at the same organizational goals. **Goal congruence** is achieved when employees, working in their own perceived best interests, make decisions that help meet the overall goals of the organization. **Managerial effort** is defined as exertion toward a goal or objective. Effort here means not merely working faster but also working better. As a result, effort includes all conscious actions (such as supervising, planning, and thinking) that result in more efficiency and effectiveness. Effort is a matter of degree—it is optimized when individuals and groups strive for their objectives.

Goal congruence can exist with little accompanying effort, and vice versa, but rewards are necessary for both to be achieved. As shown in Exhibit 9-1, the challenge of management control system design is to specify goals and actions and a performance evaluation and reward system that induce (or at least do not discourage) employee decisions that would achieve organizational goals. For example, an organization may specify one of its goals to be continuous improvement in employee efficiency and effectiveness. Employees, however, might perceive that continuous improvements will result in tighter standards, faster pace of work, and loss of jobs. Even though they may agree with management that continuous improvements are competitively necessary, they should not be expected to exert effort for continuous improvements unless rewards are in place to make this effort in their own best interests.

As another example, students may enroll in a college course because their goal is to learn about management accounting. The faculty and the students share the same goal, but goal congruence is not enough. Faculty also introduce rewards in the form of a grading system to spur student effort. Grading is a form of performance evaluation, as is use of management control reports for raises, promotions, and other forms of rewards in other settings. Performance evaluation is a widely used means of improving congruence and effort, because most individuals tend to perform better when they receive feedback that is tied to their own self-interest. Thus Allen-Bradley Co., Corning, and other manufacturers who set quality improvements as critical goals put quality targets into the bonus plans of top managers. Corning has quality incentives for factory workers as well.

To achieve goal congruence and managerial effort, designers of management control systems focus on motivating employees. **Motivation** has been defined as a drive toward some selected goal that creates effort and action toward that goal. Yet employees differ widely in their motivations. The system designer's task is more complex, ill structured, and more affected by human behavior than many people believe at first. The system designer must align individuals' self-interest with the goals of the organization. Thus, the designer must focus on the different motivational impact—how each system will cause people to respond—of one management control system versus another.

Responsibility accounting, budgets, variances, and the entire inventory of management control tools should constructively influence behavior. They may, however, be misused as negative weapons to punish, place blame, or find fault. Viewed positively, they assist employees to improve decisions. Used negatively, they pose a threat to employees, who will resist and undermine the use of such techniques.

To see how failure to anticipate motivational impact can cause problems, consider that some years ago in Russia, managers of the Moscow Cable Company decided to

goal congruence A condition where employees, working in their own personal interests, make decisions that help meet the overall goals of the organization.

managerial effort Exertion toward a goal or objective including all conscious actions (such as supervising, planning, and thinking) that result in more efficiency and effectiveness.

Objective 4
Explain the importance of evaluating performance and how it impacts motivation, goal congruence, and employee effort.

motivation The drive for some selected goal that creates effort and action toward that goal.

reduce copper wastage and actually slashed it by 60% that year. As a result they had only $40,000 worth of scrap instead of the $100,000 originally budgeted. Top management in the central government then fined the plant $45,000 for not meeting its scrap budget. What do you think this did to the cable company managers' motivation to control waste?

CONTROLLABILITY AND MEASUREMENT OF FINANCIAL PERFORMANCE

Management control systems often distinguish between controllable and uncontrollable events and between controllable and uncontrollable costs. Usually, responsibility center managers are in the best position to explain their center's results even if the managers had little influence over them. For example, an importer of grapes from Chile to the United States suffered a sudden loss of sales several years ago after a few of the grapes were found to contain poisonous cyanide. The tampering was beyond the importer's control, so the importer's management control system compared actual profits to flexible-budgeted profits (see Chapter 8), given that actual sales were unusually low. This comparison separated effects of activity volume—sales levels—from effects of efficiency, and reported the importer's profitability given the uncontrollable drop in sales.

uncontrollable cost Any cost that cannot be affected by the management of a responsibility center within a given time span.

An **uncontrollable cost** is any cost that cannot be affected by the management of a responsibility center within a given time span. For example, a mail-order supervisor may be responsible only for costs of labor, shipping costs, ordering errors and adjustments, and customer satisfaction. The supervisor would not be responsible for costs of the supporting information system because the supervisor cannot control that cost.

controllable cost Any cost that is influenced by a manager's decisions and actions.

Controllable costs include all costs that are influenced by a manager's decision and actions. For example, the costs of the mail-order information system, though uncontrollable by the mail-order supervisor, are controllable by the manager in charge of information systems.

In a sense, the term *controllable* is a misnomer because no cost is completely under the control of a manager. The term is widely used, however, to refer to any cost that is affected by a manager's decisions, even if not totally "controlled." Thus, the cost of operating the mail-order information system may be affected by equipment or software failures that are not completely—but are partially—under the control of the manager of information systems, who would be held responsible for all of the costs of the information system, even the costs of downtime.

The distinction between controllable and uncontrollable costs serves an information purpose. Costs that are completely uncontrollable tell nothing about a manager's decisions and actions because, by definition, nothing the manager does will affect the costs. Such costs should be ignored in evaluating the responsibility center manager's performance. In contrast, reporting controllable costs provides evidence about a manager's performance.

Because responsibility for costs may be widespread, systems designers must depend on understanding cost behavior to help identify controllable costs. This understanding is increasingly gained through activity-based costing (see Chapter 4). Both Procter & Gamble and Upjohn, Inc., for example, are experimenting with activity-based costing systems in some divisions. Procter & Gamble credits its experimental activity-based management control system for identifying controllable costs in one of its detergent divisions, which led to major strategic changes.

Objective 5
Prepare segment income statements for evaluating profit and investment centers using the contribution margin and controllable-cost concepts.

CONTRIBUTION MARGIN

Many organizations combine the contribution approach to measuring income with responsibility accounting—that is, they report by cost behavior as well as by degrees of controllability.

Exhibit 9-5 displays the contribution approach to measuring the financial performance of the various organizational units (or segments) of Barleycorn, Inc., a retail grocery company. **Segments** are responsibility centers for which a separate measure of revenues and costs is obtained. Study this exhibit carefully. It provides perspective on how a management control system can be designed to stress cost behavior, controllability, manager performance, and responsibility center performance simultaneously.

segments Responsibility centers for which a separate measure of revenues and costs is obtained.

Line a in Exhibit 9-5 shows the contribution margin, sales revenues less all variable expenses. The contribution margin is especially helpful for predicting the impact on income of short-run changes in activity volume. Managers may quickly calculate any expected changes in income by multiplying increases in dollar sales by the contribution margin ratio. The contribution margin ratio for meats in the West Division is $180 ÷ $900 = .20. Thus, a $1,000 increase in sales of meats in the West Division should produce a $200 increase in income (.20 × $1,000 = $200) if there are no changes in selling prices, per unit operating expenses, or mix of sales between stores 1 and 2.

CONTRIBUTION CONTROLLABLE BY SEGMENT MANAGERS

Lines b and c in Exhibit 9-5 separate the contribution that is controllable by segment managers (b) from the overall segment contribution (c). Designers of management control systems distinguish between the segment as an economic investment and the manager as a professional decision maker. For instance, an extended period of drought coupled with an aging population may adversely affect the desirability of continued economic investment in a ski resort, but the resort manager may be doing an excellent job under the circumstances.

The manager of store 1 may have influence over some local advertising but not other advertising, some fixed salaries but not other salaries, and so forth. Moreover, the meat manager at both the division and store levels may have zero influence over store depreciation or the president's salary. Therefore, Exhibit 9-5 separates costs by controllability. Managers on all levels are asked to explain the total segment contribution but are held responsible only for the controllable contribution.

Note that fixed costs controllable by the segment managers are deducted from the contribution margin to obtain the contribution controllable by segment managers. These controllable costs are usually discretionary fixed costs such as local advertising and some salaries, but not the manager's own salary. Other, noncontrollable, fixed costs (shown between lines a and b) are not allocated in the breakdown because they are not considered controllable this far down in the organization. That is, of the $160,000 fixed cost that is controllable by the manager of the West Division, $140,000 is also controllable by subordinates (grocery, produce, and meat managers), but $20,000 is not. The latter is controllable by the West Division manager but not by lower managers. Similarly, the $30,000 in that same line are costs that are attributable to the meat department of the West Division but not to individual stores.

In many organizations, managers have latitude to trade off some variable costs for fixed costs. To save variable material and labor costs, managers might make heavier outlays for automation, quality management and employee training programs, and so on. Moreover, decisions on advertising, research, and sales promotion have effects on sales activity and hence on contribution margins. The controllable contribution includes these expenses and attempts to capture the results of these trade-offs.

The distinctions in Exhibit 9-5 among which items belong in what cost classification are inevitably not clear-cut. For example, determining controllability is always a problem when service department costs are allocated to other departments. Should the store manager bear a part of the division headquarter's costs? If so, how much and on what basis? How much, if any, store depreciation or lease rentals should be deducted in computing the controllable contribution? There are no easy answers to these questions. Each organization picks ways that benefit it most with the lowest relative cost

Exhibit 9-5
Barleycorn, Inc.
Contribution Approach: Model Income Statement, by Segments* (thousands of dollars)

	Company as a Whole	Company Breakdown into Two Divisions		Breakdown of West Division Only				Breakdown of West Division, Meats Only		
		East Division	West Division	Not Allocated[†]	Groceries	Produce	Meats	Not Allocated[†]	Store 1	Store 2
Net sales	$4,000	$1,500	$2,500	—	$1,300	$300	$900	—	$600	$300
Variable costs										
Cost of merchandise sold	$3,000	$1,100	$1,900	—	$1,000	$230	$670	—	$450	$220
Variable operating expenses[‡]	260	100	160	—	100	10	50	—	35	15
Total variable costs	$3,260	$1,200	$2,060	—	$1,100	$240	$720	—	$485	$235
(a) Contribution margin	$ 740	$ 300	$ 440	—	$ 200	$ 60	$180	—	$115	$ 65
Less: fixed costs controllable by segment managers[§]	260	100	160	$ 20	40	10	90	$ 30	35	25
(b) Contribution controllable by segment managers	$ 480	$ 200	$ 280	$(20)	$ 160	$ 50	$ 90	$(30)	$ 80	$ 40
Less: fixed costs controllable by others[¶]	200	90	110	20	40	10	40	10	22	8
(c) Contribution by segments	$ 280	$ 110	$ 170	$(40)	$ 120	$ 40	$ 50	$(40)	$ 58	$ 32
Less: unallocated costs‖	100									
(d) Income before income taxes	$ 180									

* Three different types of segments are illustrated here: divisions, product lines, and stores. As you read across, note that the focus becomes narrower; from East and West divisions to West Division only, to meats in West Division only.

[†] Only those costs clearly identifiable to a product line should be allocated.

[‡] Principally wages and payroll-related costs.

[§] Examples are certain advertising, sales promotions, salespersons' salaries, management consulting, training and supervision costs.

[¶] Examples are depreciation, property taxes, insurance, and perhaps the segment manager's salary.

‖ These costs are not clearly or practically allocable to any segment except by some highly questionable allocation base.

(unlike the situation in external financial accounting systems, which must follow strict regulations).

CONTRIBUTION BY SEGMENTS

The contribution by segments, line c in Exhibit 9-5, is an attempt to approximate the financial performance of the segment, as distinguished from the financial performance of its manager, which is measured in line b. The "fixed costs controllable by others" typically include committed costs (such as depreciation and property taxes) and discretionary costs (such as the segment manager's salary). These costs are attributable to the segment but primarily are controllable only at higher levels of management.

UNALLOCATED COSTS

Exhibit 9-5 shows "unallocated costs" immediately before line d. They might include central corporate costs such as the costs of top management and some corporate-level services (for example, legal and taxation). When a persuasive cause-and-effect or activity-based justification for allocating such costs cannot be found, many organizations favor not allocating them to segments.

The contribution approach highlights the relative objectivity of various means of measuring financial performance. The contribution margin itself tends to be the most objective. As you read downward in the report, the allocations become more subjective, and the resulting measures of contributions or income become more subject to dispute. Though such disputes may be unproductive uses of management time, the allocations do direct managers' attention to the costs of the entire organization and lead to organizational cost control.

Managers should try to distinguish between controllable and uncontrollable events and costs when designing segment financial reports. For each of the following costs of a merchandising business (for example, a department store), indicate whether it is a variable cost, fixed cost controllable by segment managers, fixed cost controllable by someone other than the segment manager, or a cost that is normally unallocated.

Property taxes
Supervision of sales force
Depreciation of store
Cost of goods sold
Local store advertising
Corporate-level advertising
Corporate-level public relations
Temporary sales labor

ANSWERS

Variable costs are generally controllable by the store manager. Cost of goods sold and temporary sales labor are examples.

Fixed costs controllable by the segment (store) manager include local store advertising and supervision of the local sales force. The store manager usually decides the appropriate level for these costs.

Fixed costs controllable by those other than the store manager include property taxes and depreciation of the store. These costs relate directly to the store, but the store manager cannot change them.

Unallocated costs include corporate-level advertising and public relations. These costs have a tenuous link to the store.

NONFINANCIAL MEASURES OF PERFORMANCE

For many years organizations have monitored their nonfinancial performance. For example, sales organizations have followed up on customers to ensure their satisfaction and manufacturers have tracked manufacturing defects and product performance. In recent years, most organizations have developed a new awareness of the importance of controlling nonfinancial performance areas such as quality, cycle time, and productivity.

CONTROL OF QUALITY

quality control The effort to ensure that products and services perform to customer requirements.

Quality control is the effort to ensure that products and services perform to customer requirements. In essence, customers or clients define quality by comparing their needs to the attributes of the product or service. For example, buyers judge the quality of an automobile based on reliability, performance, styling, safety, and image relative to their needs, budget, and the alternatives. Defining quality in terms of customer requirements is only half the battle. There remains the problem of reaching and maintaining the desired level of quality. There are many approaches to controlling quality. The traditional approach in the United States was to inspect products after they were completed, and reject or rework those that failed the inspections. Because testing is expensive, often only a sample of products was inspected. The process was judged to be in control as long as the number of defective products did not exceed an acceptable quality level. This meant that some defective products could still make their way to customers.

In recent years, however, U.S. companies, confronted with the success of Japanese products, have learned that this is a very costly way to control quality. All the resources consumed to make a defective product and to detect it are wasted, or considerable rework may be necessary to correct the defects. In addition, it is very costly to repair products in use by a customer or to win back a dissatisfied customer. IBM's former Chief Executive Officer John Akers was quoted in the Wall Street Journal as saying, "I am sick and tired of visiting plants to hear nothing but great things about quality and cycle time—and then to visit customers who tell me of problems."[3] The high costs of achieving quality by "inspecting it in" are evident in a **cost of quality report,** which displays the financial impact of quality. The quality cost report shown in Exhibit 9-6 measures four categories of quality costs.

cost of quality report A report that displays the financial impact of quality.

1. Prevention—costs incurred to prevent the production of defective products or delivery of substandard services including engineering analyses to improve product design for better manufacturing, improvements in production processes, increased quality of material inputs, and programs to train personnel
2. Appraisal—costs incurred to identify defective products or services including inspection and testing
3. Internal failure—costs of defective components and final products or services that are scrapped or reworked; also costs of delays caused by defective products or services
4. External failure—costs caused by delivery of defective products or services to customers, such as field repairs, returns, and warranty expenses

This report shows that most of the costs incurred by Eastside Manufacturing Company are due to internal or external failures. These costs almost certainly are understated, however. Poor quality can result in large opportunity costs because of internal delays and lost sales. For example, quality problems in American-built automobiles in the

---

[3] *Quoted in Graham Sharman, "When Quality Control Gets in the Way of Quality,"* Wall Street Journal, *February 24, 1992, p. A14.*

Exhibit 9-6

Eastside Manufacturing Company

Quality Cost Report* (thousands of dollars)

Month			Quality Cost Area	Year to Date		
Actual	*Plan*	*Variance*		*Actual*	*Plan*	*Variance*
			1. Prevention Cost			
3	2	1	A. Quality—administration	5	4	1
16	18	(2)	B. Quality—engineering	37	38	(1)
7	6	1	C. Quality—planning by others	14	12	2
5	7	(2)	D. Supplier assurance	13	14	(1)
31	33	(2)	Total prevention cost	69	68	1
5.5%	6.1%		% of Total quality cost	6.2%	6.3%	
			2. Appraisal cost			
31	26	5	A. Inspection	55	52	3
12	14	(2)	B. Test	24	28	(4)
7	6	1	C. Insp. & test of purchased mat.	15	12	3
11	11	0	D. Product quality audits	23	22	1
3	2	1	E. Maint. of insp. & test equip.	4	4	0
2	2	0	F. Mat. consumed in insp. & test	5	4	1
66	61	5	Total appraisal cost	126	122	4
11.8%	11.3%		% of Total quality cost	11.4%	11.3%	
			3. Internal failure cost			
144	140	4	A. Scrap & rework—manuf.	295	280	15
55	53	2	B. Scrap & rework—engineering	103	106	(3)
28	30	(2)	C. Scrap & rework—supplier	55	60	(5)
21	22	(1)	D. Failure investigation	44	44	0
248	245	3	Total internal failure cost	497	490	7
44.3%	45.4%		% of Total quality cost	44.9%	45.3%	
345	339	6	Total internal quality cost (1 + 2 + 3)	692	680	12
61.6%	62.8%		% of Total quality cost	62.6%	62.8%	
			4. External failure quality cost			
75	66	9	A. Warranty exp.—manuf.	141	132	9
41	40	1	B. Warranty exp.—engineering	84	80	4
35	35	0	C. Warranty exp.—sales	69	70	(1)
46	40	6	D. Field warranty cost	83	80	3
18	20	(2)	E. Failure investigation	37	40	(3)
215	201	14	Total external failure cost	414	402	12
38.4%	37.2%		% of Total quality cost	37.4%	37.2%	
560	540	20	Total quality cost	1,106	1,082	24
9,872	9,800		Total product cost	20,170	19,600	
5.7%	5.5%		% Tot. qual. cost to tot. prod. cost	5.5%	5.5%	

* Adapted from Allen H. Seed III, *Adapting Management Accounting Practice to an Advanced Manufacturing Environment* (National Association of Accountants, 1988), Table 5-2, p. 76.

1970s and 1980s probably caused forgone sales that were significantly more costly than the tangible costs measured in any quality cost report.

In recent years, more and more U.S. companies have been rethinking this approach to quality control. Instead, they have adopted an approach first espoused by an American, W. Edwards Deming, and embraced by Japanese companies decades ago: **total quality management (TQM)**. Following the old adage "an ounce of prevention is worth a pound of cure," it focuses on prevention of defects and on customer satisfaction. The TQM approach is based on the assumption that the cost of quality is minimized when a firm achieves high quality levels. Total quality management is the application of quality principles to all of the organization's endeavors to satisfy customers. The U.S. Department of Commerce presents the Baldrige Award to companies that excel in quality, based on their customer-oriented

total quality management (TQM) The application of quality principles to all of the organization's endeavors to satisfy customers.

Penril DataComm, a Maryland designer and maker of data communications equipment, was on the brink of financial disaster resulting from the cost of poor quality. Penril was performing 100% inspection in many of its manufacturing processes and reworking or scrapping one-third of everything it produced. Penril turned its financial fortunes around based on a total quality effort. The results of a customized quality program included

1. 1,266% increase in profits per employee
2. 95% increase in revenues
3. 81% decrease in defects per unit
4. 83% decrease in out-of-box failures (failures during the first three months in the field)
5. 73% decrease in first-year warranty service repairs
6. reduced response time to customer's orders from 10 weeks to 3 days

Penril's new mission is "to build an environment where internal and external customer expectations are met in every transaction." Penril supports this mission by following six principles:

1. Quality is the number-one priority. This requires a shift from short-term to long-term thinking. Resources are allocated for quality efforts, and quality teams are rewarded for improvements.
2. Customer focus. Customers and suppliers serve on concurrent engineering teams to "build the voice of the customer into all aspects of the business."
3. Emphasize prevention and continuous improvement. "Inspection only maintains the status quo." Total quality means reforming designs, modifying policies and procedures, and training people in correct practices.
4. Management using data. Statistical analysis is used for control of processes.
5. Total employee involvement. According to Penril, the most important measure in the race for quality leadership is the rate of improvement, and this rate is maximized by involving everyone on a team. The team concept at Penril unleashes employee energy that improves morale, communication, respect, and trust. Training includes job skills, total quality management concepts, statistics, statistical process control, problem-solving skills, presentation skills, and communication skills.
6. Cross-functional management. Processes cross departments so each cross-functional team includes members from all areas involved in the process. Communication is enhanced by frequent meetings and newsletters. Employees present quality reports that document improvement efforts.

Perhaps the best measure of the success of Penril's new quality focus is in customer reaction—business has doubled in the three years since the program began. "We know of no greater testimony to a company's quality than to have another company ask it to design a product for them, build it for them, and put the customer's name on it."

Source: Adapted from "Poor Quality Nearly Short-Circuits Electronics Company," in Chet Marchwinski, ed., *Productivity*, February 1993, pp. 1–3.

quality achievements. TQM has significant implications for organization goals, structure, and management control systems. For TQM to work, though, employees must be very well trained in the process, the product or service, and the use of quality-control information.

To implement TQM, employees are trained to prepare, interpret, and act on quality-control charts, such as that shown in Exhibit 9-7. The **quality-control chart** is a statistical plot of measures of various product dimensions or attributes. This plot helps detect process deviations before the process generates defects. These plots also identify excessive variation in product dimensions or attributes that should be addressed by process or design engineers. The chart in Exhibit 9-7 shows that the Eastside Manufactur-

quality-control chart The statistical plot of measures of various product dimensions or attributes.

Exhibit 9-7

Eastside Manufacturing Company
Quality-Control Chart

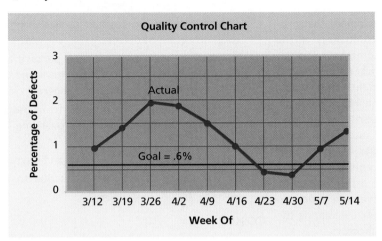

ing Company generally is not meeting its defects objective of .6% defects (which is a relatively high defect rate). A manager looking at this chart would know that corrective action must be taken.

CONTROL OF CYCLE TIME

One key to improving quality is to reduce cycle time. **Cycle time,** or throughput time, is the time taken to complete a product or service, or any of the components of a product or service. It is a summary measure of manufacturing or service efficiency and effectiveness, and an important cost driver. The longer a product or service is in process, the more costs are consumed. Low cycle time means quick completion of a product or service (without defects). Lowering cycle time requires smooth-running processes and high quality, and also creates increased flexibility and quicker reactions to customer needs. As cycle time is decreased, quality problems become apparent throughout the process and must be solved if quality is to be improved. Decreasing cycle time also results in bringing products or services more quickly to customers, a product or service characteristic customers value.

Firms measure cycle time for the important stages of a process and for the process as a whole. An effective means of measuring cycle time is to use bar coding, where a bar code (similar to symbols on most grocery products) is attached to each component or product, and read at the end of each stage of completion. Cycle time is measured for each stage as the time between readings of bar codes. Bar coding also permits effective tracking of materials and products for inventories, scheduling, and delivery.

Exhibit 9-8 shows a sample cycle-time report. (Cycle time can also be displayed on a control chart.) This report shows that Eastside Manufacturing Company is meeting its cycle-time objectives at two of its five production process stages. This report is similar to the flexible budget reports of Chapter 8. Explanations of the variances indicate that poor-quality materials and poor design led to extensive rework and retesting.

CONTROL OF PRODUCTIVITY

More than half the companies in the United States manage productivity as part of the effort to improve their competitiveness. **Productivity** is a measure of outputs divided by inputs. The fewer inputs needed to produce a given output, the more productive the

cycle time The time taken to complete a product or service, or any of the components of a product or service.

productivity A measure of outputs divided by inputs.

Often, companies do not invest in equipment that promotes quality because it is difficult to quantify all the benefits and costs of using such equipment. One company has developed a software program that enables a better measurement of these benefits and costs. Perceptron, Inc., based in Farmington Hills, Michigan, produces industrial measurement systems such as laser-based, optical, noncontact systems for automotive, appliance, aerospace, and furniture companies. These systems are used to measure product assembly accuracy. Assembly-line technicians can use the data provided by Perceptron's equipment to take preventive action to correct problems immediately, virtually eliminating the need for highly paid quality control inspectors.

Perceptron developed a computer software program that helps plant personnel to identify and quantify the hidden benefits and costs of acquiring and using quality equipment. Some of the major benefits and costs of the investment in in-line measurement systems and associated preventive activities are

QUANTIFIABLE BENEFITS

- quicker response to variation problems, leading to reduced average cost of manufacturing process problems

- reduced production costs of scrap and repair from early detection of defects
- reduced work-in-process and parts inventories lower the carrying costs of inventory and the costs of obsolescence because of engineering changes
- higher uptime and throughput from more stable processes reduces the costs of overtime and outsourcing
- reduced downstream production and warranty costs
- higher quality of supplier parts due to early in-process detection of defects

COSTS

- acquisition cost of equipment including transportation and installation
- training
- initial programming labor
- maintenance
- measurement labor
- process inspection

Source: Adapted from Alahassane Diallon Zafar, U. Khan, and Curtis F. Vail, "Measuring the Cost of Investment in Quality Equipment," *Management Accounting,* August 1994, pp. 32–35.

Exhibit 9-8

Eastside Manufacturing Company
Cycle Time Report for the Second Week of May

Process Stage	Actual Cycle Time*	Standard Cycle Time	Variance	Explanation
Materials processing	2.1	2.5	0.4 F	
Circuit board assembly	44.7	28.8	15.9 U	Poor quality materials caused rework
Power unit assembly	59.6	36.2	23.4 U	Engineering change required rebuilding all power units
Product assembly	14.6	14.7	0.1 F	
Functional and environmental test	53.3	32.0	21.3 U	Software failure in test procedures required retesting

F = Favorable. U = Unfavorable.
* Average time per stage over the week.

Exhibit 9-9

Measures of Productivity

Resource	Possible Outputs (Numerator)		Possible Inputs (Denominator)
Labor	Standard direct labor hours allowed for good output	÷	Actual direct labor hours used
	Sales revenue	÷	Number of employees
	Sales revenue	÷	Direct labor costs
	Bank deposit/loan activity (by a bank)	÷	Number of employees
	Service calls	÷	Number of employees
	Customer orders	÷	Number of employees
Materials	Weight of output	÷	Weight of input
	Number of good units	÷	Total number of units
Equipment, capital, physical capacity	Time (e.g., hours) used	÷	Time available for use
	Time available for use	÷	Time (e.g., 24 hours per day)
	Expected machine hours for good output	÷	Actual machine hours
	Sales revenue	÷	Direct labor cost

organization. This simple definition, however, raises difficult measurement questions. How should outputs and inputs be measured? Specific management control issues usually determine the most appropriate measures of inputs and outputs. Labor-intensive (especially service) organizations are concerned with increasing the productivity of labor, so labor-based measures are appropriate. Highly automated companies are concerned with machine use and productivity of capital investments, so capacity-based measures, such as the percentage of time machines are available, may be most important to them. Manufacturing companies in general are concerned with the efficient use of materials, and so for them measures of material yield (a ratio of material outputs over material inputs) may be useful indicators of productivity. In all cases of productivity ratios, a measure of the resource that management wishes to control is in the denominator (the input) and some measure of the objective of using the resource is in the numerator (the output).

Exhibit 9-9 shows 12 possible productivity measures. As you can see, they vary widely according to the type of resource with which management is concerned.

CHOICE OF PRODUCTIVITY MEASURES

Which productivity measures should a company choose to manage? The choice depends on the behaviors desired. Managers generally concentrate on achieving the performance levels desired by their superiors. Thus, if top management evaluates subordinates' performance based on direct-labor productivity, lower-level managers will focus on improving that specific measure.

The challenge in choosing productivity measures is that a manager may be able to improve a single measure but hurt performance elsewhere in the organization. For example, long production runs may improve machine productivity but result in excessive inventories. Alternatively, improved labor productivity in the short run may be accompanied by a high rate of product defects.

Use of a single measure of productivity is unlikely to result in overall improvements in performance. The choice of management controls requires balancing trade-offs that employees can be expected to make to improve their performance evaluations. Many

For the fourth year in a row, Nissan's plant in Smyrna, Tennessee, has been rated as the most productive assembly plant in North America. The measure used was the number of workers per vehicle. Nissan used 2.23 workers per vehicle compared to Ford's 3.09, Chrysler's 3.29, and GM's 3.47.

How did they do it? The key is a "highly motivated workforce," according to Barry Watson, Nissan's Smyrna plant department manager. A number of "simple but effective" efforts are at the heart of the plant's success. These efforts include

- Social events such as family day and picnics
- Continuous training
- Manager and employee involvement through

group meetings at the start of every shift. These open, two-way discussions focus on ideas for improving productivity and reducing costs.

- Impact teams of managers and employees for evaluation and implementation of ideas

For example, an idea was submitted to build a special table that would significantly reduce the time it takes to change equipment between production runs. The idea was implemented and resulted in a 15% increase in the number of units assembled on each production run.

Source: Harbour and Associates, Inc., *Auto Manufacturing Productivity Report*, June, 1997.

organizations focus management control on more fundamental activities, such as control of quality and service, and use productivity measures to monitor the actual benefits of improvements in these activities.

PRODUCTIVITY MEASURES OVER TIME

Be careful with comparing productivity measures over time. Changes in the process or in the rate of inflation can prove misleading. For example, consider labor productivity at SBC Communications, Inc. (the global U.S. telecommunications company). One measure of productivity tracked by SBC is sales revenue per employee.

	1999	1995	Percent Change
Total revenue (millions)	$ 49,489	$ 37,134	+33.3%
Employees	204,530	182,610	+12.0%
Revenue per employee (unadjusted for inflation)	$241,695	$203,351	+18.9%

By this measure, SBC appears to have achieved an 18.9% increase in the productivity of labor. Total revenue has not been adjusted for the effects of inflation, however. Because of inflation, each 1995 dollar was equivalent to 1.0909 1999 dollars. Therefore, SBC's 1995 sales revenue, expressed in 1999 dollars (to be equivalent with 1999 sales revenue), is $37,134 × 1.0909 = $40,509. The adjusted 1995 sales revenue per employee is as follows:

	1999	1995 (Adjusted)	Percent Change
Total revenue (millions)	$ 49,489	$ 40,509	22.2%
Employees	204,530	182,610	12.0%
Revenue per employee (adjusted for inflation)	$241,695	$221,833	9.1%

Adjusting for the effects of inflation reveals that SBC's labor productivity has increased only 9.1%, not 18.9%.

MANAGEMENT CONTROL SYSTEMS IN SERVICE, GOVERNMENT, AND NONPROFIT ORGANIZATIONS

Most service, government, and nonprofit organizations have more difficulty implementing management control systems than do manufacturing firms. Why? The main problem is that the outputs of service and nonprofit organizations are more difficult to measure than are the cars or computers that are produced by manufacturers. As a result, it may be more difficult to know whether the service provided is, for example, of top quality until long after the service has already been delivered.

Objective 7
Describe the difficulties of management control in service and nonprofit organizations.

The key to successful management control in any organization is proper training and motivation of employees to achieve goal congruence and effort, followed by consistent monitoring of objectives set in accordance with critical processes and success factors, but it is even more important in service-oriented organizations. For example, MBNA America, a large issuer of bank credit cards, identifies customer retention as its primary key success factor. MBNA trains its customer representatives carefully. Each day it measures and reports performance on 14 objectives consistent with customer retention and rewards every employee based on those 14 objectives. Measures include answering every call by the second ring, keeping the computer up 100% of the time, and processing credit-line requests within 1 hour. Employees have earned bonuses as high as 20% of their annual salaries by meeting those objectives.

Nonprofit and government organizations also have additional problems designing and implementing an objective that is similar to the financial "bottom line" that often serves as a powerful incentive in private industry. Furthermore, many people seek positions in nonprofit organizations primarily for other than monetary rewards. For example, volunteers in the Peace Corps receive very little pay but derive much satisfaction from helping to improve conditions in underdeveloped countries. Thus, monetary incentives are generally less effective in nonprofit organizations. Control systems in nonprofit organizations probably will never be as highly developed as are those in profit-seeking firms because

1. Organizational goals and objectives are less clear. Moreover, they are often multiple, requiring difficult trade-offs.

2. Professionals (for example, teachers, attorneys, physicians, scientists, economists) tend to dominate nonprofit organizations. Because of their perceived professional status, they have been less receptive to the installation or improvement of formal control systems.

3. Measurements are more difficult because

   a. There is no profit measure.

   b. There are heavy amounts of discretionary fixed costs, which make the relationships of inputs to outputs difficult to specify and measure.

4. There is less competitive pressure from other organizations or "owners" to improve management control systems. As a result, for example, many cities in the United States are "privatizing" some essential services such as sanitation by contracting with private firms.

5. The role of budgeting is often more a matter of playing bargaining games with sources of funding to get the largest possible authorization than it is rigorous planning.

6. Motivations and incentives of individuals may differ from those in for-profit organizations.

FUTURE OF MANAGEMENT CONTROL SYSTEMS

As organizations mature and as environments change, managers must expand and refine their management control tools. The management control techniques that were quite satisfactory 10 or 20 years ago may not be adequate for many organizations today.

A changing environment often means that organizations must set different goals or key success factors. Different goals create different actions and related targets as well as different benchmarks for evaluating performance. Obviously, the management control system must evolve, too, or the organization may not manage its resources effectively or efficiently. Certain management control principles that will always be important and that can guide the redesign of systems to meet new management needs follow.

1. Always expect that individuals will be pulled in the direction of their own self-interest. You may be pleasantly surprised that some individuals will act selflessly, but management control systems should be designed to take advantage of more typical human behavior. Be aware that self-interest may be perceived differently in different cultures.

2. Design incentives so that individuals who pursue their own self-interest are also achieving the organization's objectives. If there are multiple objectives (as is usually the case), then multiple incentives are appropriate. Do not underestimate the difficulty of balancing these incentives—some experimentation may be necessary to achieve multiple objectives.

3. Evaluate actual performance based on expected or planned performance, revised, if possible, for actual output achieved. The concept of flexible budgeting can be applied to most goals and actions, both financial and nonfinancial.

4. Consider nonfinancial performance to be just as important as financial performance. In the short run, a manager may be able to generate good financial performance while neglecting nonfinancial performance, but it is not likely over a longer haul.

5. Array performance measures across the entire value chain of the company. This ensures that all activities that are critical to the long-run success of the company are integrated into the management control system.

6. Periodically review the success of the management control system. Are goals being met? Does success in accomplishing an action mean that goals are being met, too? Do individuals have, understand, and use the management control information effectively?

7. Learn from the management control successes (and failures) of competitors around the world. Despite cultural differences, human behavior is remarkably similar. Successful applications of new technology and management controls may be observed in the performance of others.

SUMMARY PROBLEM FOR YOUR REVIEW

PROBLEM

The Book & Game Company has two bookstores: Auntie's and Merlin's. Each store has managers who have a great deal of decision authority over their store. Advertising, market research, acquisition of books, legal services, and other staff functions, however, are handled by a central office. The Book & Game Company's current accounting system allocates all costs to the stores. Results for 20X1 were

Item	Total Company	Auntie's	Merlin's
Sales revenue	$700,000	$350,000	$350,000
Cost of merchandise sold	450,000	225,000	225,000
Gross margin	250,000	125,000	125,000
Operating expenses			
Salaries and wages	63,000	30,000	33,000
Supplies	45,000	22,500	22,500
Rent and utilities	60,000	40,000	20,000
Depreciation	15,000	7,000	8,000
Allocated staff costs	60,000	30,000	30,000
Total operating expenses	243,000	129,500	113,500
Operating income (loss)	$ 7,000	$ (4,500)	$ 11,500

Each bookstore manager makes decisions that affect salaries and wages, supplies, and depreciation. In contrast, rent and utilities are beyond the managers' control because the managers did not choose the location or the size of the store.

Supplies are variable costs. Variable salaries and wages are equal to 8% of the cost of merchandise sold; the remainder of salaries and wages is a fixed cost. Rent, utilities, and depreciation also are fixed costs. Allocated staff costs are unaffected by any events at the bookstores, but they are allocated as a proportion of sales revenue.

Required

1. Using the contribution approach, prepare a performance report that distinguishes the performance of each bookstore from that of the bookstore manager.
2. Evaluate the financial performance of each bookstore.
3. Evaluate the financial performance of each manager.

SOLUTION

1. See Exhibit 9-10.
2. The financial performances of the bookstores (that is, segments of the company) are best evaluated by the line "contribution by bookstore." Merlin's has a substantially higher contribution, despite equal levels of sales revenues in the two stores. The major reason for this advantage is the lower rent and utilities paid by Merlin's.
3. The financial performance by managers is best judged by the line "contribution controllable by managers." By this measure, the performance of Auntie's manager is better than that of Merlin's. The contribution margin is the same for each store, but Merlin's manager paid $4,000 more in controllable fixed costs than did Auntie's manager. Of course, this decision could be beneficial in the long run. What is missing from each of these segment reports is the year's master budget and a flexible budget, which would be the best benchmark for evaluating both bookstore and bookstore manager.

Highlights to Remember

Describe the relationship of management control systems to organizational goals. The starting point for designing and evaluating a management control system is the identification of organizational goals as specified by top management.

Use responsibility accounting to define an organizational subunit as a cost center, a profit center, or an investment center. Responsibility accounting assigns particular revenue or cost objectives to the management of the subunit that has the greatest influence over them. Cost centers focus on costs only, profit centers on both revenues and costs, and investment centers on profits relative to the amount invested.

Exhibit 9-10

The Book & Game Company
Performance Report

Item	Total Company	Auntie's	Merlin's
Sales revenue	$700,000	$350,000	$350,000
Variable costs			
Cost of merchandise sold	450,000	225,000	225,000
Salaries and wages	36,000	18,000	18,000
Supplies	45,000	22,500	22,500
Total variable costs	531,000	265,500	265,500
Contribution margin by bookstore	169,000	84,500	84,500
Less: fixed costs controllable by bookstore managers			
Salaries and wages	27,000	12,000	15,000
Depreciation	15,000	7,000	8,000
Total controllable fixed costs	42,000	19,000	23,000
Contribution controllable by managers	127,000	65,500	61,500
Less: fixed costs controllable by others			
Rent and utilities	60,000	40,000	20,000
Contribution by bookstore	67,000	$ 25,500	$ 41,500
Unallocated costs	60,000		
Operating income	$ 7,000		

Compare financial and nonfinancial performance, and explain why the balanced scorecard is becoming an important management control tool. Nonfinancial performance is as important as financial performance. In fact, nonfinancial performance usually leads to financial performance in time. The balanced scorecard helps managers monitor actions that are designed to meet the various goals of the organization.

Explain the importance of evaluating performance and how it impacts motivation, goal congruence, and employee effort. The way performance is measured and evaluated affects individuals' behavior. The more that rewards are tied to performance measures, the more incentive there is to improve the measures. Poorly designed or balanced measures may actually work against the organization's goals.

Prepare segment income statements for evaluating profit and investment centers using the contribution margin and controllable-cost concepts. The contribution approach to measuring a segment's income aids performance evaluation by separating a segment's costs into those controllable by the segment management and those beyond management's control.

Measure performance against quality, cycle time, and productivity objectives. Measuring performance in areas such as quality, cycle time, and productivity causes employees to direct attention to those areas.

Describe the difficulties of management control in service and nonprofit organizations. Management control in service and nonprofit organizations is difficult because of a number of factors, chief of which is a relative lack of clearly observable outcomes.

Understand how a management control system uses accounting information. A management control system uses management accounting tools such as budgets and performance reports to focus resources and talents of the individuals in an organization on such goals as quality, cost, and service.

Accounting Vocabulary

Fundamental Assignment Material

9-A1 Responsibility of Purchasing Agent

Acme Electronics Company, a privately held enterprise, has a subcontract from a large aerospace company on the East Coast. Although Acme was a low bidder, the aerospace company was reluctant to award the business to Acme, a newcomer to this kind of activity. Consequently, Acme assured the aerospace company of its financial strength by submitting its audited financial statements. Moreover, Acme agreed to a penalty clause of $2,000 per day to be paid by Acme for each day of late delivery for whatever cause.

Jean Lou, the Acme purchasing agent, is responsible for acquiring materials and parts in time to meet production schedules. She placed an order with an Acme supplier for a critical manufactured component. The supplier, who had a reliable record for meeting schedules, gave Lou an acceptable delivery date. Lou checked up several times and was assured that the component would arrive at Acme on schedule.

On the date specified by the supplier for shipment to Acme, Lou was informed that the component had been damaged during final inspection. It was delivered 10 days late. Lou had allowed four extra days for possible delays, but Acme was six days late in delivering to the aerospace company and so had to pay a penalty of $12,000.

What department should bear the penalty? Why?

Required

9-A2 Contribution Approach to Responsibility Accounting

George McBee owns and operates a small chain of convenience stores in Denver and Colorado Springs. The company's organization chart follows:

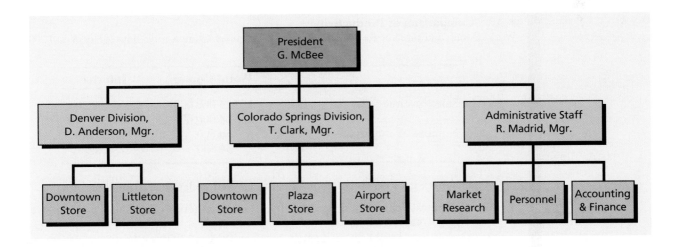

Mile High had the following financial results for 20X1 (in thousands):

Sales revenue	$8,000
Cost of merchandise sold	5,000
Gross margin	3,000
Operating expenses	2,200
Income before income taxes	$ 800

The following data about 20X1 operations were also available:

1. All five stores used the same pricing formula; therefore, all had the same gross margin percentage.

2. Sales were largest in the two Downtown stores, with 30% of the total sales volume in each. The Plaza and Airport stores each provided 15% of total sales volume, and the Littleton store provided 10%.

3. Variable operating costs at the stores were 10% of revenue for the Downtown stores. The other stores had lower variable and higher fixed costs. Their variable operating costs were only 5% of sales revenue.

4. The fixed costs over which the store managers had control were $125,000 in each of the Downtown stores, $160,000 at Plaza and Airport, and $80,000 at Littleton.

5. The remaining $910,000 of operating costs consisted of
   a. $180,000 controllable by the Colorado Springs division manager, but not by individual stores
   b. $130,000 controllable by the Denver division manager, but not by individual stores
   c. $600,000 controllable by the administrative staff

6. Of the $600,000 spent by the administrative staff, $350,000 directly supported the Colorado Springs division, with 20% for the Downtown store, 30% for each of the Plaza and Airport stores, and 20% for Colorado Springs operations in general. Another $150,000 supported the Denver division, 50% for the Downtown store, 25% for the Littleton store, and 25% supporting Denver operations in general. The other $100,000 was for general corporate expenses.

Required

Prepare an income statement by segments using the contribution approach to responsibility accounting. Use the format of Exhibit 9-5, page 364. Column headings should be

Company as a Whole	Breakdown into Two Divisions		Breakdown of Denver Division			Breakdown of Colorado Springs Division			
	Denver	Colorado Springs	Not allocated	Downtown	Littleton	Not allocated	Downtown	Plaza	Airport

9-A3 Comparison of Productivity

World Comm and Intertel are communications companies. Comparative data for 1995 and 2001 are

		World Comm	**Intertel**
Sales revenue	1995	$5,824,000,000	$7,658,000,000
	2001	$6,764,000,000	$9,667,000,000
Number of employees	1995	56,600	75,900
	2001	54,800	76,200

Assume that each 1995 dollar is equivalent to 1.2 2001 dollars, due to inflation.

Required

1. Compute 1995 and 2001 productivity measures in terms of revenues per employee for World Comm and Intertel.

2. Compare the change in productivity between 1995 and 2001 for World Comm with that for Intertel.

9-B1 Responsibility Accounting

The Filler Company produces precision machine parts. Filler uses a standard cost system, calculates standard cost variances for each department, and reports them to department managers. Managers use the information to improve their operations. Superiors use the same information to evaluate managers' performance.

Sharon Keller was recently appointed manager of the assembly department of the company. She has complained that the system as designed is disadvantageous to her department. Included among the variances charged to the departments is one for rejected units. The inspection occurs at the end of the assembly department. The inspectors attempt to identify the cause of the rejection so that the department where the error occurred can be charged with it. Not all errors can be easily identified with a department, however. The nonidentified units are totaled and apportioned to the departments according to the number of identified errors. The variance for rejected units in each department is a combination of the errors caused by the department plus a portion of the unidentified causes of rejects.

Required

1. Is Keller's complaint valid? Explain the reason(s) for your answer.
2. What would you recommend that the company do to solve its problem with Keller and her complaint?

9-B2 Divisional Contribution, Performance, and Segment Margins

The president of Northwest Railroad wants to obtain an overview of the company's operations, particularly with respect to comparing freight and passenger business. He has heard about "contribution" approaches to cost allocations that emphasize cost behavior patterns and contribution margins, contributions controllable by segment managers, and contributions by segments. The president has hired you as a consultant to help him. He has given you the following information.

Total revenue in 20X0 was $80 million, of which $72 million was freight traffic and $8 million was passenger traffic. Fifty percent of the latter was generated by Division 1; 40% by Division 2; and 10% by Division 3.

Total variable costs were $45 million, of which $36 million was caused by freight traffic. Of the $9 million allocable to passenger traffic, $3.3, $2.8, and $2.9 million could be allocated to Divisions 1, 2, and 3, respectively.

Total separable discretionary fixed costs were $8 million, of which $7.6 million applied to freight traffic. Of the remainder, $80,000 could not be allocated to specific divisions, although it was clearly traceable to passenger traffic in general. Divisions 1, 2, and 3 should be allocated $240,000, $60,000, and $20,000, respectively.

Total separable committed costs, which were not regarded as being controllable by segment managers, were $25 million, of which 90% was allocable to freight traffic. Of the 10% traceable to passenger traffic, Divisions 1, 2, and 3 should be allocated $1.5 million, $350,000, and $150,000, respectively; the balance was unallocable to a specific division.

The common fixed costs not clearly allocable to any part of the company amounted to $800,000.

Required

1. The president asks you to prepare statements, dividing the data for the company as a whole between the freight and passenger traffic and then subdividing the passenger traffic into three divisions.
2. Some competing railroads actively promote a series of one-day sightseeing tours on summer weekends. Most often, these tours are timed so that the cars with the tourists are hitched on with regularly scheduled passenger trains. What costs are relevant for making decisions to run such tours? Other railroads, facing the same general cost picture, refuse to conduct such sightseeing tours. Why?
3. For purposes of this analysis, even though the numbers may be unrealistic, suppose that Division 2's figures represented a specific run for a train instead of a division. Suppose further that the railroad has petitioned government authorities for permission to drop Division 2. What would be the effect on overall company net income for 20X1, assuming that the figures are accurate and that 20X1 operations are in all other respects a duplication of 20X0 operations?

9-B3 Quality Cost Report

The manufacturing division of Green River, Inc., makes a variety of home furnishings. The company prepares monthly reports on quality costs. In early 2001, Green River's president asked you, the controller, to compare quality costs in 2000 to those in 1998. He wanted to see only total annual numbers for 2000 compared with 1998. You have prepared the report shown in Exhibit 9-11.

Required

1. For each of the four quality cost areas, explain what types of costs are included and how those costs have changed between 1998 and 2000.
2. Assess overall quality performance in 2000 compared with 1998. What do you suppose has caused the changes observed in quality costs?

Exhibit 9-11

Green River, Inc.

Quality Cost Report (thousands of dollars)

Quality Cost Area	1998 Cost	2000 Cost
1. Prevention cost	45	107
% of Total quality cost	3.3%	12.4%
2. Appraisal cost	124	132
% of Total quality cost	9.1%	15.2%
3. Internal failure cost	503	368
% of Total quality cost	36.9%	42.5%
Total internal quality cost (1 + 2 + 3)	672	607
% of Total quality cost	49.3%	70.1%
4. External failure cost	691	259
% of Total quality cost	50.7%	29.9%
Total quality cost	1,363	866
Total product cost	22,168	23,462

Additional Assignment Material

QUESTIONS

9-1. What is a management control system?

9-2. What are the major components of a management control system?

9-3. What is a key success factor?

9-4. What are the purposes of a management control system?

9-5. "Goals are useless without performance measures." Do you agree? Explain.

9-6. "There are corporate goals other than improve profit." Name three.

9-7. How does management determine its key success factors?

9-8. Give three examples of how managers may improve short-run performance to the detriment of long-run results.

9-9. Name three kinds of responsibility centers.

9-10. How do profit centers and investment centers differ?

9-11. "Performance evaluation seeks to achieve goal congruence and managerial effort." Describe what is meant by this statement.

9-12. List five characteristics of a good performance measure.

9-13. "Managers of profit centers should be held responsible for the center's entire profit. They are responsible for profit even if they cannot control all factors affecting it." Discuss.

9-14. What is a balanced scorecard and why are more and more companies using one?

9-15. What are key performance indicators?

9-16. What are four nonfinancial measures of performance that managers find useful?

9-17. "Variable costs are controllable and fixed costs are uncontrollable." Do you agree? Explain.

9-18. "The contribution margin is the best measure of short-run performance." Do you agree? Explain.

9-19. Give four examples of segments.

9-20. "Always try to distinguish between the performance of a segment and its manager." Why?

9-21. "The contribution margin approach to performance evaluation is flawed because focusing on only the contribution margin ignores important aspects of performance." Do you agree? Explain.

9-22. There are four categories of cost in the quality cost report; explain them.

9-23. Why are companies increasing their quality control emphasis on the prevention of defects?

9-24. "Nonfinancial measures of performance can be controlled just like financial measures." Do you agree? Explain.

9-25. Identify three measures of labor productivity, one using all physical measures, one using all financial measures, and one that mixes physical and financial measures.

9-26. Discuss the difficulties of comparing productivity measures over time.

9-27. "Control systems in nonprofit organizations will never be as highly developed as in profit-seeking organizations." Do you agree? Explain.

COGNITIVE EXERCISES

9-28 Management Control Systems and Innovation

The president of a fast-growing high-technology firm remarked, "Developing budgets and comparing performance with the budgets may be fine for some firms. But we want to encourage innovations and entrepreneurship. Budgets go with bureaucracy, not innovation." Do you agree? How can a management control system encourage innovation and entrepreneurship?

9-29　Municipal Responsibility Accounting

In 1975 New York City barely avoided bankruptcy. By the 1990s it had one of the most sophisticated budgeting and reporting systems of any municipality, and its budgetary problems had nearly disappeared. The Integrated Financial Management System (IFMS) "clearly identifies managers in line agencies, and correlates allocations and expenditures with organizational structure. . . . In addition, managers have more time to take corrective measures when variances between budgeted and actual expenditures start to develop." (*FE — The Magazine for Financial Executives,* 1, no. 8, p. 26.)

Required

Discuss how a responsibility accounting system such as IFMS can help manage a municipality such as New York City.

9-30　Control Systems and Organizational Behavior

Why do accountants need to consider behavioral factors when designing a management control system?

9-31　Control Systems and the Production Function of the Value Chain

In recent years, many organizations have focused on the value of controlling nonfinancial performance as a key to improved productivity. In particular, to gain and maintain a competitive edge, companies focus on quality and cycle time. Discuss how quality, cycle time, and productivity are related.

EXERCISES

9-32　Key Performance Indicators

Research on performance management suggests that organizations can compete most effectively by identifying and monitoring those elements that are most closely linked to organizational success. A key performance indicator can be thought of as a measure that drives organizational success. For each of the following industries, identify two key performance indicators.

1. Airline industry
2. Retail merchandising industry
3. Technology
4. Public sector

9-33　Responsibility for Stable Employment Policy

The Sargent Metal Fabricating Company has been manufacturing machine tools for a number of years and has had an industrywide reputation for doing high-quality work. The company has been faced with irregularity of output over the years. It has been company policy to lay off welders as soon as there was insufficient work to keep them busy and to rehire them when demand warranted. The company, however, now has poor labor relations and finds it very difficult to hire good welders because of its lay-off policy. Consequently, the quality of the work has been declining steadily.

　　The plant manager has proposed that the welders, who earn $18 per hour, be retained during slow periods to do menial plant maintenance work that is normally performed by workers earning $14 per hour in the plant maintenance department.

　　You, as controller, must decide the most appropriate accounting procedure to handle the wages of the welders doing plant maintenance work. What department(s) should be charged with this work, and at what rate? Discuss the implications of your plan.

9-34　Salesclerk's Compensation Plan

You are manager of a department store in Kyoto. Sales are subject to month-to-month variations, depending on the individual salesclerk's efforts. A new salary-plus-bonus plan has been in effect for four months, and you are reviewing a sales performance report. The plan provides for a base salary of ¥45,000 per month, a ¥68,000 bonus each month if the monthly sales quota is met, and an additional commission of 5% of all sales over the monthly quota. The quota is set approximately 3% above the previous month's sales to motivate clerks toward increasing sales (in thousands).

		Salesclerk A	Salesclerk B	Salesclerk C
January	Quota	¥4,500	¥1,500	¥7,500
	Actual	1,500	1,500	9,000
February	Quota	¥1,545	¥1,545	¥9,270
	Actual	3,000	1,545	3,000
March	Quota	¥3,090	¥1,590	¥3,090
	Actual	5,250	750	9,000
April	Quota	¥5,400	¥ 775	¥9,270
	Actual	1,500	780	4,050

Required

1. Compute the compensation for each salesclerk for each month.
2. Evaluate the compensation plan. Be specific. What changes would you recommend?

9-35 Common Measures on a Balanced Scorecard
Listed below are common performance measures appearing on balanced scorecards. Indicate whether the listed measure is primarily associated with the financial, customer, internal processes, or learning and growth perspective.

- Product development cycle time
- Retention of target customers
- Net cash flow
- Training hours
- Employee turnover rate
- Material handling cost per unit
- Market share
- Return on sales
- Revenue growth in segments
- Occupational injuries and illness
- Days sales in inventory
- Average cost per invoice

9-36 Goals and Objectives at Foundation Health Systems
Foundation Health Systems, Inc., (FHS) provides health care to more than four million members. As a managed health care organization, the company strives to provide high-quality health care at a reasonable cost. Many stakeholders have an interest in FHS's operations, including doctors and other medical personnel, patients, insurance companies, government regulators, and the general public.

Required

Prepare a goal and one measure for assessing achievement of that goal for each of the following key areas:

Customer satisfaction
Efficient use of lab tests
Usage of physician time
Maintain state-of-the-art facilities
Overall financial performance

9-37 Performance Evaluation
Matthew Kennedy is a stock brokerage firm that evaluates its employees on sales activity generated. Recently, the firm also began evaluating its stockbrokers on the number of new accounts generated.

Required

Discuss how these two performance measures are consistent and how they may conflict. Do you believe that these measures are appropriate for the long-term goal of profitability?

9-38 Quality Theories Compared

Examine the two graphs below. Compare the total quality management approach to the traditional theory of quality. Which theory do you believe represents the current realities of today's global competitive environment? Explain.

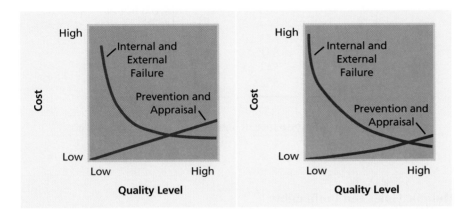

9-39 Quality Control Chart

Baffin Manufacturing Company was concerned about a growing number of defective units being produced. At one time the company had the percentage of defective units down to less than 50 per thousand, but recently rates of defects have been near, or even above, 1%. The company decided to graph its defects for the last eight weeks (40 working days), beginning Monday, September 1 through Friday, October 24. The graph is shown in Exhibit 9-12.

1. Identify two important trends evident in the quality control chart.
2. What might management of Baffin do to deal with each trend?

Required

9-40 Cycle-Time Reporting

MainFrame Computers monitors its cycle time closely to prevent schedule delays and excessive costs. The standard cycle time for the manufacture of printed circuit boards for one of its computers

Exhibit 9-12

Baffin Manufacturing Company

Quality Control Chart for September 1 through October 24

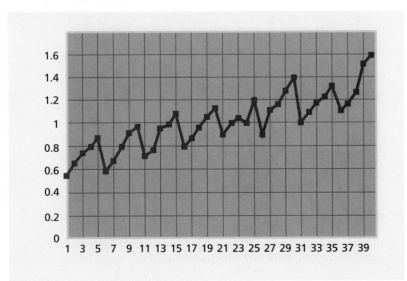

is 25.5 hours. Consider the following cycle-time data from the past six weeks of circuit board production:

Week	Units Completed	Total Cycle Time
1	564	14,108 hours
2	544	14,592
3	553	15,152
4	571	16,598
5	547	17,104
6	552	16,673

Required

Analyze circuit board cycle time performance in light of the 25.5-hour objective.

PROBLEMS

9-41 Multiple Goals and Profitability

The following multiple goals were identified by General Electric:

Profitability	Employee attitudes
Market position	Public responsibility
Productivity	Balance between short-range and long-range goals
Product leadership	
Personnel development	

General Electric is a huge, highly decentralized corporation. At the time it developed these goals, GE had approximately 170 responsibility centers called "departments," but that is a deceptive term. In most other companies, these departments would be called divisions. For example, some GE departments had sales of more than $500 million.

Each department manager's performance was evaluated annually in relation to the specified multiple goals. A special measurements group was set up to devise ways of quantifying accomplishments in each of the areas. In this way, the evaluation of performance would become more objective as the various measures were developed and improved.

Required

1. How would you measure performance in each of these areas? Be specific.
2. Can the other goals be encompassed as ingredients of a formal measure of profitability? In other words, can profitability per se be defined to include the other goals?

9-42 Responsibility Accounting, Profit Centers, and Contribution Approach

Consider the following data for the year's operations of an automobile dealer:

Sales of vehicles	$2,400,000
Sales of parts and service	600,000
Cost of vehicle sales	1,920,000
Parts and service materials	180,000
Parts and service labor	240,000
Parts and service overhead	60,000
General dealership overhead	120,000
Advertising of vehicles	120,000
Sales commissions, vehicles	48,000
Sales salaries, vehicles	60,000

The president of the dealership has long regarded the markup on material and labor for the parts and service activity as the amount that is supposed to cover all parts and service overhead plus all general overhead of the dealership. In other words, the parts and service department is viewed as a cost-recovery operation, and the sales of vehicles as the income-producing activity.

Required

1. Prepare a departmentalized operating statement that harmonizes with the views of the president.

2. Prepare an alternative operating statement that would reflect a different view of the dealership operations. Assume that $12,000 and $60,000 of the $120,000 general overhead can be allocated with confidence to the parts and service department and to sales of vehicles, respectively. The remaining $48,000 cannot be allocated except in some highly arbitrary manner.

3. Comment on the relative merits of requirements 1 and 2.

9-43 Incentives in the Former Soviet Union

Before the country's breakup, officials in what had been the Soviet Union had been rewarding managers for exceeding a five-year-plan target for production quantities. A problem arose, however, because managers naturally tended to predict low volumes so that the targets would be set low. This hindered planning; good information about production possibilities was lacking.

The Soviets then devised a new performance evaluation measure. Suppose F is the forecast of production, A is actual production, and X, Y, and Z are positive constants set by top officials, with $X, Y, Z > 0$. The following performance measure was designed to motivate both high production and accurate forecasts.

$$\text{performance} = (Y \times F) + [X \times (A - F)] \text{ if } F \leq A$$
$$(Y \times F) - [Z \times (F - A)] \text{ if } F > A$$

Consider the Moscow Automotive Factory. During 19X6 the factory manager, Nicolai Konstantin, had to predict the number of automobiles that could be produced during the next year. He was confident that at least 700,000 autos could be produced in 19X7, and most likely they could produce 800,000 autos. With good luck, they might even produce 900,000. Government officials told him that the new performance evaluation measure would be used, and that $X = .50$, $Y = .80$, and $Z = 1.00$ for 19X7 and 19X8.

Required

1. Suppose Konstantin predicted production of 800,000 autos and 800,000 were produced. Calculate the performance measure.

2. Suppose again that 800,000 autos were produced. Calculate the performance measure if Konstantin had been conservative and predicted only 700,000 autos. Also calculate the performance measure if he had predicted 900,000 autos.

3. Now suppose it is November 19X7 and it is clear that the 800,000 target cannot be achieved. Does the performance measure motivate continued efforts to increase production? Suppose it is clear that the 800,000 target will be met easily. Will the system motivate continued effort to increase production?

9-44 Balanced Scorecard

Zenon Medical Instruments Company (ZMIC) recently revised its performance evaluation system. The company identified four major goals and several objectives required to meet each goal. Ruth Sanchez, controller of ZMIC, suggested that a balanced scorecard be used to report on progress toward meeting the objectives. At a recent meeting, she told the managers of ZMIC that listing the objectives was only the first step in installing a new performance measurement system. Each objective has to be accompanied by one or more measures to monitor progress toward achieving the objectives. She asked the help of the managers in identifying appropriate measures.

The goals and objectives determined by the top management of ZMIC are

1. Maintain strong financial health
   a. Keep sufficient cash balances to assure financial survival
   b. Achieve consistent growth in sales and income
   c. Provide excellent returns to shareholders
2. Provide excellent service to customers
   a. Provide products that meet the needs of customers
   b. Meet customer needs on a timely basis
   c. Meet customer quality requirements
   d. Be the preferred supplier to customers
3. Be among the industry leaders in product and process innovations
   a. Bring new products to market before competition
   b. Lead competition in production process innovation
4. Develop and maintain efficient, state-of-the-art productions processes
   a. Excel in manufacturing efficiency
   b. Design products efficiently and quickly
   c. Meet or beat product introduction schedules

Propose at least one measure of performance for each of the objectives of ZMIC.

9-45 Productivity

In early 20X1, NorthernComm, a U.S.-based international telephone communications company, purchased the controlling interest in Telecom Corporation in an Eastern European country. A key productivity measure monitored by NorthernComm is the number of customer telephone lines per employee. Consider the following data:

	20X1 without Telecom	20X1 with Telecom	20X0
Customer lines	15,054,000	19,994,000	14,615,000
Employees	74,520	114,590	72,350
Lines per employee	202	174	202

1. What are NorthernComm's 20X0 productivity and its 20X1 productivity without Telecom?
2. What are NorthernComm's 20X1 productivity with Telecom and Telecom's productivity?
3. What difficulties do you foresee if NorthernComm brings Telecom's productivity in line?

9-46 Productivity Measurement

Grace Laundry had the following results in 20X1 and 20X3.

	20X1	20X3
Pounds of laundry processed	1,360,000 pounds	1,525,000 pounds
Sales revenue	$720,000	$1,394,000
Direct-labor hours worked	45,100 hours	46,650 hours
Direct-labor cost	$316,000	$498,000

Grace used the same facilities in 20X3 as in 20X1. During the past three years, however, the company put more effort into training its employees. The manager of Grace was curious about whether the training had increased labor productivity.

1. Compute a measure of labor productivity for 20X3 based entirely on physical measures. Do the same for 20X1. That is, from the data given, choose measures of physical output and physical input, and use them to compare the physical productivity of labor in 20X3 with that in 20X1.
2. Compute a measure of labor productivity for 20X3 based entirely on financial measures. Do the same for 20X1. That is, from the data given, choose measures of financial output and financial input, and use them to compare the financial productivity of labor in 20X3 with that in 20X1.
3. Suppose the following productivity measure was used:

$$\text{productivity} = \frac{\text{sales revenue}}{\text{direct labor hours worked}}$$

Because of inflation, each 20X1 dollar is equivalent to 1.4 20X3 dollars. Compute appropriate productivity numbers for comparing 20X3 productivity with 20X1 productivity.

CASES

9-47 Trade-Offs among Objectives

Computer Data Services (CDS) performs routine and custom information systems services for many companies in a large midwestern metropolitan area. CDS has built a reputation for high-quality customer service and job security for its employees. Quality service and customer satisfaction have been CDS's primary subgoals—retaining a skilled and motivated workforce has been an important factor in achieving those goals. In the past, temporary downturns in business did not mean layoffs of employees, though some employees were required to perform other than their usual tasks. In anticipation of growth in business, CDS leased new equipment that, beginning in August, added $10,000 per month in operating costs. Three months ago, however, a new competitor began offering the same services to CDS customers at prices averaging 20% lower than those of CDS. Rico Estrada, the company founder and president, believes that a significant price reduction is necessary to maintain the company's market share and avoid financial ruin, but he is puzzled about how to achieve it without compromising quality, service, and the goodwill of his workforce.

CDS has a productivity objective of 20 accounts per employee. Estrada does not think that he can increase this productivity and still maintain both quality and flexibility to customer needs. CDS also monitors average cost per account and the number of customer satisfaction adjustments (resolutions of complaints). The average billing markup rate is 25% of cost. Consider the following data from the past six months:

	June	July	August	September	October	November
Number of accounts	797	803	869	784	723	680
Number of employees	40	41	44	43	43	41
Average cost per account	$ 153	$ 153	$ 158	$ 173	$ 187	$ 191
Average salary per employee	$3,000	$3,000	$3,000	$3,000	$3,000	$3,000

Required

1. Discuss the trade-offs facing Rico Estrada.
2. Can you suggest solutions to his trade-off dilemma?

9-48 Relationship between Strategy and Key Success Factors, Goodyear

As is the case with any business, when competition increases, margins shrink and a key to sustained competitiveness is cost control. Often cost control translates into cost cutting via employee layoffs. In 1999, Goodyear laid off between 2,500 to 2,800 employees in North America, Asia, and Latin America in an effort to save up to $150 million a year. Targets for layoffs were old and inefficient plants such as the Gadsden, Alabama, plant that employed about 1,300 people.

How does the painful action of closing plants link to the overall corporate strategy? According to Goodyear, one of their four strategic goals is to "be the lowest cost producer of the 'Big Three' global companies." Key success factors for this goal include "continuous productivity improvements in the complete value chain" and "control of selling, administrative, and general expenses." One of the surest ways to rapidly improve overall production efficiency is to close an older, inefficient plant, especially when there exists an over-capacity situation. The link between action, critical success factors, and strategic objectives is made.

Required

Visit Goodyear's Web site and prepare a one-page report that updates the strategic plans of Goodyear. List Goodyear's overall goals, critical success factors and strategic actions.

9-49 The Learning Culture at General Electric

General Electric has been a leader in its commitment to a learning culture. Based on information from GE's Web site, prepare a one-page report that describes GE's programs that support a learning culture.

9-50 Quality Programs, Strategic Initiatives, General Electric

One of three major strategic initiatives of General Electric in 1998 was Six Sigma quality. The following comments were made by John Welch Jr., CEO of GE, in the 1998 *Annual Report.*

> *Six Sigma quality, our third growth initiative, is, in itself, a product of learning. After observing the transformational effects this science, this way of life and work, had on the few companies that pursued it, we plunged into Six Sigma with a Company-consuming vengeance just over three years ago. We have invested more than a billion dollars in the effort, and the financial returns have now entered the exponential phase—more than three quarters of a billion dollars in savings beyond our investment in 1998, with a billion and a half in sight for 1999.*

The Six Sigma–driven savings are impressive, but it is the radical change in the overall measures of operating efficiency that excite us most. For years—decades—we have been straining to improve operating margin and working capital turns. Our progress was typically measured in basis points for margins and decimal points in working capital turns. Six Sigma came along in 1995 when our margins were in the 13.6% range and turns at 5.8. At the end of 1998, margins hit 16.7% and turns hit 9.2. These numbers are an indicator of the progress and momentum in our Six Sigma journey.

The ratio of plant and equipment expenditures to depreciation is another measure of asset efficiency. This number in 1998 dropped to 1.2 and will be in the .7–.8 range in the future, as "hidden factory" after "hidden factory"—literally "free capacity"—is uncovered by Six Sigma process improvements.

Yes, we've had some early product successes, and those customers who have been touched by them understand what this Six Sigma they've heard so much about really means. But, as we celebrate our progress and count our financial gain, we need to focus on the most powerful piece of learning we have been given in 1998, summarized perfectly in the form of what most of our customers must be thinking, which is: "When do I get the benefits of Six Sigma?" "When does my company get to experience the GE I read about in the GE Annual Report?"

Questions like these are being asked because, up to now, our Six Sigma process improvements have concentrated primarily on our own internal processes and on internal measurements such as "order-to-delivery" or "shop turnaround time." And in focusing that way—inwardly on our processes—we have tended to use all our energy and Six Sigma science to "move the mean" to, for example, reduce order-to-delivery times from an average of, say, 18 days to 14 days, as reflected in the example below. We've repeated this type of improvement over and over again in thousands of GE processes and have been rewarded for it with less "rework" and greater cash flow.

Consider an example of the time it takes GE to deliver an order. Suppose a sample of 10 orders is taken before and after implementing Six Sigma, with the following results:

Order Deliver Times (Days)

Before Six Sigma	After Six Sigma
30	22
12	20
11	5
13	8
26	19
14	8
16	7
20	12
24	18
14	21

Required

Compute the mean and standard deviation of order delivery time before and after implementation of Six Sigma. From a customer's perspective, how would you view the results of Six Sigma as depicted in the example given by CEO Welch?

9-51 Review of Chapters 1–9

Ben Gleneagle, general manager of the Boulder Division of Colorado Enterprises, Inc., was preparing for a management meeting. His divisional controller gave him the following information.

1. The master budget for the fiscal year just ended on June 30, 20X1:

Sales (50,000 units of A and 70,000 units of B)	$850,000
Manufacturing cost of goods sold	670,000
Manufacturing margin	$180,000
Selling and administrative expenses	120,000
Operating income	$ 60,000

2. The standard variable manufacturing cost per unit:

	Product A		Product B	
Direct material	10 pieces @ $.25	$2.50	5 pounds @ $.10	$ .50
Direct labor	1 hour @ $3.00	3.00	.3 hours @ $2.50	.75
Variable overhead	1 hour @ $2.00	2.00	.3 hours @ $2.50	.75
Total		$7.50		$2.00

3. All budgeted selling and administrative expenses are common, fixed expenses; 60% are discretionary expenses.

4. The actual income statement for the fiscal year ended June 30, 20X1:

Sales (53,000 units of A and 64,000 units of B)	$850,000
Manufacturing cost of goods sold	685,200
Manufacturing margin	$164,800
Selling and administrative expenses	116,000
Operating income	$ 48,800

5. The budgeted sales prices for products A and B were $10 and $5, respectively. Actual sales prices equaled budgeted sales prices.

6. The schedule of the actual variable manufacturing cost of goods sold by product (actual quantities in parentheses):

Product A:	Material	$134,500	(538,000 pieces)
	Labor	156,350	(53,000 hours)
	Overhead	108,650	(53,000 hours)
Product B:	Material	38,400	(320,000 pounds)
	Labor	50,000	(20,000 hours)
	Overhead	50,000	(20,000 hours)
Total		$537,900	

7. Products A and B are manufactured in separate facilities. Of the budgeted fixed manufacturing cost, $130,000 is separable as follows: $45,000 to product A and $85,000 to product B. Ten percent of these separate costs are discretionary. All other budgeted fixed manufacturing expenses, separable and common, are committed.

8. There are no beginning or ending inventories.

During the upcoming management meeting it is quite likely that some of the information from your controller will be discussed. In anticipation you set out to prepare answers to possible questions.

Required

1. Determine the firm's budgeted break-even point in dollars, overall contribution-margin ratio, and contribution margins per unit by product.
2. Considering products A and B as segments of the firm, find the budgeted "contribution by segments" for each.

3. It is decided to allocate the budgeted selling and administrative expenses to the segments (in requirement 2) as follows: committed costs on the basis of budgeted unit sales mix and discretionary costs on the basis of actual unit sales mix. What are the final expense allocations? Briefly appraise the allocation method.

4. How would you respond to a proposal to base commissions to salespersons on the sales (revenue) value of orders received? Assume all salespersons have the opportunity to sell both products.

5. Determine the firm's actual "contribution margin" and "contribution controllable by segment managers" for the fiscal year ended June 30, 20X1. Assume no variances in committed fixed costs.

6. Determine the "sales-activity variance" for each product for the fiscal year ended June 30, 20X1.

7. Determine and identify all variances in variable manufacturing costs by product for the fiscal year ended June 30, 20X1.

COLLABORATIVE LEARNING EXERCISE

9-52 Goals, Objectives, and Performance Measures

There is increasing pressure on colleges and universities to develop measures of accountability. The objective is to specify goals and objectives and to develop measures to assess the achievement of those goals and objectives.

Form a group of four to six students to be a consulting team to the accounting department at your college or university. (If you are not using this book as part of a course in an accounting department, select any department at a local college or university.) Based on your collective knowledge of the department, its mission, and its activities, formulate a statement of goals for the department. From that statement, develop several specific objectives, each of which can be measured. Then develop one or more measures of performance for each objective.

An optional second step in this exercise is to meet with a faculty member from the department, and ask him or her to critique your objectives and measures. To the department member do the objectives make sense? Are the proposed measures feasible, and will they correctly measure attainment of the objectives? Will they provide proper incentives to the faculty? If the department has created objectives and performance measures, compare them to those your group developed.

INTERNET EXERCISE

www.prenhall.com/horngren

9-53 Management Control System at Procter and Gamble

Setting up management control systems and determining measurement methods and who should be responsible for particular revenues, costs, and information can be a large task. The structure of the organization plays a part in how well a particular measure is likely to work. Insuring that the goals of the organization are in concert with the management control system is also an important factor. It is not possible to evaluate a company's management control system from an Internet site. What we can do, however, is to use a site as an example and apply some of the concepts of the chapter to measures and tools that would be possibilities for a firm.

1. A well-known and well-established company with worldwide acceptance is Procter and Gamble. Log on to the company's Web site at http://www.pg.com. Let's determine the goals of the company. The goals of the company are listed in the "Action Plan" section of the 2000 annual report. Locate the 2000 annual report. Click on the "Annual Report Map" and then on the "Action Plan." What are the goals of the firm? Give an example for each of the goals.

2. The company has numerous products and the Web site divides them into different care lines. What are the major care lines the Web site utilizes? Visit the main page of the household care line. What types of items are contained in this line? How could a system be set up to help measure the success of the firm's first goal to build established brands in the household care line? What would be three possible financial measures? What about three nonfinancial measures?

3. Look at the notes to the financial statements. Does the firm recognize any business segments? How many have they identified? Which of these segments appears to be the fastest growing?

4. To achieve maximum benefits at minimum cost, a management control system must foster goal congruence and managerial effort. Managerial effort is defined as exertion toward a goal or objective. Effort here means not merely working faster but also working better. As a result, effort includes all conscious actions (such as supervising, planning, and thinking) that result in more efficiency and effectiveness. Effort is a matter of degree—it is optimized when individuals and groups strive for their objectives. Return to the PG home page and click on the "Jobs" section and then on the "Succeeding at P & G" section. Which of the skill areas that they list as being necessary do you believe would be most important? Why?

Go to the "Employee Performance Evaluation and Responsibility" episode on the *Mastering Accounting* CD-ROM for an interactive, video-enhanced exercise focused on how CanGo managers use income statements showing revenues for the whole organization and for individual subunits to assess the performance of individual product divisions.

MANAGEMENT CONTROL IN DECENTRALIZED ORGANIZATIONS

The Niketown store in New York City is a well-known landmark. Just say "Niketown" to a cab driver—it is just like saying "airport."

www.prenhall.com/horngren

Learning Objectives

When you have finished studying this chapter, you should be able to

1. Define decentralization and identify its expected benefits and costs.

2. Distinguish between profit centers and decentralization.

3. Define transfer prices and identify their purpose.

4. Identify the relative advantages and disadvantages of basing transfer prices on total costs, variable costs, and market prices.

5. Identify the factors affecting multinational transfer prices.

6. Explain how the linking of rewards to responsibility center results affects incentives and risk.

7. Compute ROI, residual income, and economic value added (EVA) and contrast them as criteria for judging the performance of organization segments.

8. Compare the advantages and disadvantages of various bases for measuring the invested capital used by organization segments.

9. **Understand the role of management control systems in decentralized organizations.**

Philip Knight, chief executive officer of Nike, tells a story. Recently, one of Nike's officers was in New York City and managed to get a cab with a driver who did not speak English. He made several attempts at making his directions understood, all without success. Then he asked, "Where's NIKETOWN?" Clearly, as if he had just graduated from speech class, the driver said, "NIKETOWN! Fifty-seventh and Fifth!"

From 1986 to 2000, Nike's revenues increased from $1 billion to more than $8 billion. During this same period, the percentage of revenues from outside the United States increased from 25% to 40%. Global apparel sales account for more than one-third of Nike's revenue. A sampling of endorsements (promotional contracts with famous sports teams, individuals, and organizations) gives another perspective of the company's global presence: Michael Jordan, the Italian National Soccer team, German tennis star Michael Stich, golf star Tiger Woods. In fact, watch almost any sports event on television and you are likely to see the Nike "Swoosh" logo.

Nike made a conscious decision to go global—a 10-year process that is now generating substantial financial rewards. What are some of the keys to success when a company such as Nike decides to significantly expand its operations abroad? One critical element is understanding the relevance of the brand to local markets. Nike has gained this understanding by delegating management decision making to the local market level.

For example, local Nike managers in Germany made the decision to sign an endorsement contract with world champion racecar driver Michael Schumacher. According to Philip Knight, "Five years ago it would have taken a move from within the company headquarters to strike such a deal. . . . But this time it was a decision made in country." The local German manager knew that Schumacher was extremely relevant to the German market and that this would be a "profit driven, culturally significant, and brand enhancing move." Knight credits this move toward decentralization for Nike's 36% increase in international sales. "It is a great example of what we are trying to do: Make decisions on the ground in faraway places."

As organizations like Nike grow and undertake more diverse and complex activities, many elect to delegate decision-making authority to managers throughout the organization. This delegation of the freedom to make decisions is called **decentralization.** The lower in the organization that this freedom exists, the greater the decentralization. Decentralization is a matter of degree along a continuum.

decentralization The delegation of freedom to make decisions. The lower in the organization that this freedom exists, the greater the decentralization.

This chapter focuses on the role of management control systems in decentralized organizations. After providing an overview of decentralization, the chapter addresses the special problems created when one segment of an organization charges another for providing goods or services. Then it discusses how performance measures can be used to motivate managers. Finally, measures used to assess the profitability of decentralized units are introduced and compared.

Increasing sophistication of telecommunications—especially e-mail and fax machines—aids decentralization. Geographical separation no longer must mean lack of access to information. Both sales and production divisions are being relocated far from headquarters without top management losing knowledge of what is happening in the units.

CENTRALIZATION VERSUS DECENTRALIZATION

Decentralization is not right for every firm. Consider the international airline industry in the mid-1990s. Most airlines, such as South China Airlines, Iberia Airlines, and Air France, were decentralizing. In contrast, at the same time, Sabena, Belgium's state-owned airline, was reorganizing to reverse its trend toward decentralization. In the insurance industry, Aetna was decentralizing at the same time Equitable was centralizing. Let's take a look at some of the reasons why companies choose to (or not to) decentralize.

Costs and Benefits

There are many benefits of at least some decentralization for most organizations. First, lower-level managers have the best information concerning local conditions and therefore may be able to make better decisions than their superiors. Second, decentralization gives managers decision-making ability and other management skills that help them move upward in the organization, ensuring continuity of leadership. In addition, managers enjoy higher status by being independent and thus are better motivated.

Of course, decentralization has its costs. Managers may make decisions that are not in the organization's best interests, either because they act to improve their own segment's performance at the expense of the organization or because they are not aware of relevant facts from other segments. Managers in decentralized organizations also tend to duplicate services that might be less expensive if centralized (e.g., accounting, advertising, and personnel). Furthermore, under decentralization, costs of accumulating and processing information frequently rise because responsibility accounting reports are needed for top management to learn about and evaluate decentralized units and their managers. Finally, managers in decentralized units may waste time negotiating with other units about goods or services one unit provides to the other.

Decentralization is more popular in profit-seeking organizations—where outputs and inputs can be measured—than it is in nonprofit organizations. Managers can be given more freedom when the results of their decisions are measurable so that they can be held accountable for them. Poor decisions in a profit-seeking firm become apparent from the inadequate profit generated. Most nonprofit organizations lack such a reliable performance measure, so granting their managers freedom is more risky.

Objective 1
Define decentralization and identify its expected benefits and costs.

Middle Ground

Philosophies of decentralization differ considerably. Cost-benefit considerations usually require that some management decisions be highly decentralized and others centralized. To illustrate, much of the controller's problem-solving and attention-directing functions may be decentralized and handled at lower levels, whereas income tax planning and mass scorekeeping such as payroll may be highly centralized.

Decentralization is most successful when an organization's segments are relatively independent of one another—that is, the decisions of a manager in one segment will not affect the fortunes of another segment. If segments do much internal buying or selling, much buying from the same outside suppliers, or much selling to the same outside markets, they are candidates for heavier centralization.

In Chapter 9, we stressed that cost-benefit tests, goal congruence, and managerial effort must all be considered when designing a control system. If management has decided in favor of heavy decentralization, **segment autonomy,** the delegation of decision-making power to managers of segments of an organization, is also crucial. For decentralization to work, however, this autonomy must be real, not just lip service. In most circumstances, top managers must be willing to abide by decisions made by segment managers.

segment autonomy The delegation of decision-making power to managers of segments of an organization.

Profit Centers and Decentralization

Do not confuse profit centers (accountability for revenue and expenses) with decentralization (freedom to make decisions). They are entirely separate concepts. Although profit centers can aid decentralization, one can exist without the other. Some profit center managers possess vast freedom to make decisions concerning labor contracts, supplier choices, equipment purchases, personnel decisions, and so on. In contrast, other profit center managers may need top-management approval for almost all the decisions just mentioned. Indeed, cost centers may be more heavily decentralized than profit centers if cost center managers have more freedom to make decisions.

Objective 2
Distinguish between profit centers and decentralization.

Many companies moved to decentralize their operations in one way or another during the last decade. Among these companies are PepsiCo, DuPont, and Procter & Gamble. But one company that stood out in its efforts to decentralize was Johnson & Johnson. Johnson & Johnson (2000 sales of $29 billion, 98,000 employees, and operations in 51 countries), maker of Tylenol, Band-Aids, Johnson's Baby Powder, PEPCID AC, and many other products, has a long history of decentralization, beginning in the 1930s. As stated in its 1999 *Annual Report,* the company considers it a primary competitive advantage that each of its 190 business units are empowered to act independently—"Our individual managements are responsible for their businesses. . . . Through decentralization we combine the advantages of being big with the agility and focus of smaller firms."

Although ultimately accountable to executives at J&J headquarters in New Brunswick, New Jersey, some segment presidents see their bosses as few as four times a year. An article in *Business Week* called J&J "a model of how to make decentralization work." CEO Ralph Larson says that decentralization "provides a sense of ownership and responsibility for a business that you simply cannot get any other way."

Larson sees his role as providing direction but giving managers creative freedom. J&J spent the early 1990s fine-tuning its decentralized system to erase costly mistakes that could have been avoided with more guidance from top management. Also, J&J had incurred high overhead costs as independent units duplicated many functions. Larson introduced methods of coordinating the independent units while still preserving the basics of decentralization. Although perhaps toning down the degree of decentralization, Larson vows that J&J "will never give up the principle of decentralization, which is to give our operating executives ownership of a business. They are ultimately responsible."

Sources: Adapted from "A Big Company That Works," *Business Week,* May 4, 1992, pp. 124–130; Johnson & Johnson 2000 *Annual Report.*

The literature contains many criticisms of profit centers on the grounds that managers are given profit responsibility without commensurate authority. Therefore, the criticism continues, the profit center is "artificial" because the manager is not free to make a sufficient number of the decisions that affect profit.

Such criticisms confuse profit centers and decentralization. The fundamental question in deciding between using a cost center or a profit center for a given segment is not whether heavy decentralization exists. Instead, the fundamental question is, "Will a profit center better solve the problems of goal congruence and management effort than a cost center?" In other words, "Do I predict that a profit center will induce the managers to make a better collective set of decisions from the viewpoint of the organization as a whole?"

All control systems are imperfect. Judgments about their merits should concentrate on which alternative system will bring more of the actions top management seeks. For example, a plant may seem to be a "natural" cost center because the plant manager has no influence over decisions concerning the marketing of its products. Still, some companies evaluate a plant manager by the plant's profitability. Why? Because this broader evaluation base will affect the plant manager's behavior. Instead of being concerned solely with running an efficient cost center, the plant manager now "naturally" considers quality control more carefully and reacts to customers' special requests more sympathetically. A profit center may thus obtain the desired plant-manager behavior that a cost center cannot. In designing accounting control systems, top managers must consider the system's impact on behavior desired by the organization.

TRANSFER PRICING

Very few problems arise in decentralized organizations when all the segments are independent of one another. Segment managers can then focus only on their own segments without hurting the organization as a whole. In contrast, when segments interact greatly, there is an increased possibility that what is best for one segment hurts another segment badly enough to have a negative effect on the entire organization. Such a situation may occur when one segment provides products or services to another segment and charges that segment a transfer price. **Transfer prices** are the amounts charged by one segment of an organization for a product or service that it supplies to another segment of the same organization. Most often, the term is associated with materials, parts, or finished goods. The transfer price is revenue to the segment producing the product or service, and it is a cost to the acquiring segment.

Objective 3
Define transfer prices and identify their purpose.

transfer price The amount charged by one segment of an organization for a product or service that it supplies to another segment of the same organization.

Purposes of Transfer Pricing

Why do transfer-pricing systems exist? The principal reason is to communicate data that will lead to goal-congruent decisions. For example, transfer prices should guide managers to make the best possible decisions regarding whether to buy or sell products and services inside or outside the total organization. Another important reason is to evaluate segment performance and thus motivate both the selling manager and the buying manager toward goal-congruent decisions. Finally, multinational companies use transfer pricing to minimize their worldwide taxes, duties, and tariffs. These are easy goals to describe, but they are difficult goals to achieve.

Organizations solve their problems by using cost-based prices for some transfers, market-based prices for other transfers, and negotiated prices for others. Therefore, do not expect to obtain a single, universally applicable answer in the area of transfer pricing. It is a subject of continuous concern to top management. Whenever there is a lull in a conversation with a manager, try asking, "Do you have any transfer-pricing problems?" The response is usually, "Let me tell you about the peculiar transfer-pricing difficulties in my organization." A manager in a large wood products firm called transfer pricing his firm's most troublesome management control issue.

Transfers at Cost

About half of the major companies in the world transfer items at cost. However, there are many possible definitions of cost. Some companies use only variable cost, others use full cost, and still others use full cost plus a profit markup. Some use standard costs and some use actual costs.

Objective 4
Identify the relative advantages and disadvantages of basing transfer prices on total costs, variable costs, and market prices.

When the transfer price is some version of cost, transfer pricing is nearly identical to cost allocation (see Chapters 4 and 12). Costs are accumulated in one segment and then assigned to (or transferred to) another segment. Details of this process are covered in Chapter 12, but two important points deserve mention here.

First, transferring or allocating costs can disguise a cost's behavior pattern. Consider a computer manufacturer, such as Apple, that makes keyboards in one division and transfers them to another division for assembly into personal computers. The manager of the Keyboard Division may have good knowledge of the cost drivers affecting the costs of keyboards. But if a single transfer price per unit is charged when transferring the keyboards to the Assembly Division, the only cost driver affecting the cost to the Assembly Division is "units of keyboards." Cost drivers other than units produced are ignored, and distinctions between fixed and variable costs are blurred. The Assembly Division manager sees the entire cost of keyboards as a variable cost, regardless of what the true cost behavior is.

Other problems arise if actual cost is used as a transfer price. Because actual cost cannot be known in advance, the buying segment will not be able to plan its costs. More important, because a transfer price based on actual costs merely passes cost inefficiencies along to the buying division, the supplying division lacks incentive to control its costs. Thus, using budgeted or standard costs instead of actual costs is recommended for both cost allocation and cost-based transfer pricing.

Teva Pharmaceutical Industries Ltd. is a worldwide manufacturer of proprietary drugs. It is headquartered in Israel and had 2000 sales of $1.75 billion. Teva entered the lucrative generic drug market in the mid-1980s. As part of its strategy, the company decentralized its pharmaceutical business into cost and profit centers as outlined here.

Each of the marketing divisions purchases generic drugs from the manufacturing division. Prior to decentralization, each marketing division was a revenue center. With the new organizational structure, management had to decide how to measure marketing division costs because profits were now the key financial performance measure.

A key cost to the marketing divisions is the transfer price paid for drugs purchased from the manufacturing division. Management considered several alternative bases for the company's transfer prices. Market price was rejected because there was not a ready market. Negotiated price was rejected because management believed that the resulting debates over the proper price would be lengthy and disruptive. Variable cost (raw material and packaging costs) was adopted for a short time. Eventually, however, it was rejected because it did not lead to congruent decisions—products using many scarce resources were not differentiated from those using few. Further, when a local source for the drug did exist, the market price was always above the variable-cost transfer price. Thus, managers in Teva's manufacturing division had little incentive to keep costs low.

Full cost was rejected because the traditional costing system did not capture the actual cost structure of the manufacturing division. Specifically, the system under-costed the low volume products and overcosted the large volume products. The system traced only raw materials directly to products. The remaining manufacturing costs were divided into two cost pools and allocated based on labor hours and machine hours. One problem with the traditional system was its inability to capture and correctly allocate the non-value-added cost of setup activity. The size of the errors in product cost was not known, but the lack of confidence in the traditional cost system led to full cost being rejected as the transfer-price base.

Teva's management adopted an activity-based-costing (ABC) system to improve the accuracy of its product costs. The ABC system has five activity centers and related cost pools: receiving, manufacturing, packaging, quality assurance, and shipping. Because of the dramatic increase in costing accuracy, management was able to adopt full activity-based cost as the transfer price.

Teva's managers are pleased with their transfer pricing system. The benefits include increased confidence that the costs being transferred are closely aligned with the actual short- and long-run costs being incurred, increased communication between divisions, and an increased awareness of the costs of low-volume products and the costs of capacity required to support these products.

Sources: Adapted from Robert Kaplan, Dan Weiss, and Eyal Desheh, "Transfer Pricing with ABC," *Management Accounting*, May, 1997, pp. 20–28; Teva Pharmaceutical Industries, LTD, 2000 *Annual Report*.

MARKET-BASED TRANSFER PRICES

If there is a competitive market for the product or service being transferred internally, using the market price as a transfer price will generally lead to the desired goal congruence and managerial effort. The market price may come from published price lists for similar products or services, or it may be the price charged by the producing division to its external customers. If the latter, the internal transfer price may be the external market price less the selling and delivery expenses that are not incurred on internal business. The major drawback to market-based prices is that market prices are not always available for items transferred internally.

Consider Outdoor Equipment Company, Inc. (OEC), a major outdoor equipment manufacturer that makes clothing and gear for all kinds of outdoor activities. One division of OEC makes fabrics that are used in many final products as well as being sold directly to external customers, and another division makes tents. A particular tent requires five square yards of a special waterproof fabric. Should the Tent Division obtain the fabric from the Fabric Division of the company or purchase it from an external supplier?

Suppose the market price of the fabric is $10 per square yard, or $50 per tent, and assume for the moment that the Fabric Division can sell its entire production to external customers without incurring any marketing or shipping costs. The Tent Division manager will refuse to pay a transfer price greater than $50 for the fabric for each tent. Why? Because if the transfer price is greater than $50, she will purchase the fabric from the external supplier in order to maximize her division's profit.

Furthermore, the manager of the Fabric Division will not sell five square yards of fabric for less than $50. Why? Because he can sell it on the market for $50, so any lower price will reduce his division's profit. The only transfer price that allows both managers to maximize their division's profit is $50, the market price. If the managers had autonomy to make decisions, one of them would decline the internal production of fabric at any transfer price other than $50.

Now suppose the Fabric Division incurs a $1 per square yard marketing and shipping cost that can be avoided by transferring the fabric to the Tent Division instead of marketing it to outside customers. Most companies would then use a transfer price of $9 per square yard, or $45 per tent, often called a "market-price-minus" transfer price. The Fabric Division would get the same net amount from the transfer ($45 with no marketing or shipping costs) as from an external sale ($50 less $5 marketing and shipping costs), whereas the Tent Division saves $5 per tent. Thus, OEC overall benefits.

VARIABLE-COST PRICING

Market prices have innate appeal in a profit-center context, but they are not cure-all answers to transfer-pricing problems. Sometimes market prices do not exist, are inapplicable, or are impossible to determine. For example, no intermediate markets may exist for specialized parts, or markets may be too thin or scattered to permit the determination of a credible price. When market prices cannot be used, versions of "cost-plus-a-profit" are often used as a fair substitute. To illustrate, consider Outdoor Equipment Company again. Exhibit 10-1 shows its selling prices and variable costs per unit. In this example, the Fabric Division's variable costs of $8 per yard are the only costs affected by producing the additional fabric for transfer to the Tent Division. On receiving five yards of fabric, the Tent Division spends an additional $53 to process and sell each tent. Whether the fabric should be manufactured and transferred to the Tent Division depends on the existence of idle capacity in the Fabric Division (insufficient demand from outside customers).

Exhibit 10-1
Data for Analysis of Transfer Prices

Sell Fabric Outside		Use Fabric to Make Tent			
Market price per yard of fabric to outsiders	$ 10	Sales price of finished tent			$ 100
		Variable costs:			
Variable costs per yard of fabric	8	Fabric Division			
Contribution margin per yard	$ 2	(5 yards @ $8)		$40	
Total company contribution		Tent Division			
for 50,000 yards	$100,000	Processing	$41		
		Selling	12	53	93
		Contribution margin			$ 7
		Total company contribution			
		for 10,000 tents			$70,000

As Exhibit 10-1 shows, if there were no idle capacity in the Fabric Division, the optimum action for the company as a whole would be for the Fabric Division to sell outside at $50. Why? Because the Tent Division would incur $53 of additional variable costs but add only $50 of additional revenue ($100 − $50). Using market price would provide the correct motivation for such a decision because, if the fabric were transferred, the Tent Division's cost would be $50 + $53 or $103, which would be $3 higher than its prospective revenue of $100 per unit. So the Tent Division would choose not to buy from the Fabric Division at the $50 market price. Of course, the Tent Division also would not buy from outside suppliers at a price of $50. If fabric is not available at less than $50 per tent, this particular tent will not be produced.

What if the Fabric Division has idle capacity sufficient to meet all the Tent Division's requirements? The optimum action would be to produce the fabric and transfer it to the Tent Division. Idle capacity implies that the Fabric Division could not sell the fabric to external customers and therefore would have zero contribution. If there were no production and transfer, the Tent Division and the company as a whole would forgo a total contribution of $70,000. In this situation, variable cost would be the better basis for transfer pricing and would lead to the optimal decision for the firm as a whole. To be more precise, the transfer price would be all additional costs that will be incurred by the production of the fabric to be transferred. For example, if a lump-sum set-up cost is required to produce the 50,000 square yards of fabric required, the set-up cost should be added to the variable cost in calculating the appropriate transfer price. (In the example there is no such cost.)

NEGOTIATED TRANSFER PRICES

Companies heavily committed to segment autonomy often allow managers to negotiate transfer prices. The managers may consider both costs and market prices in their negotiations, but no policy requires them to do so. Supporters of negotiated transfer prices maintain that the managers involved have the best knowledge of what the company will gain or lose by producing and transferring the product or service, so open negotiation allows the managers to make optimal decisions. Critics of negotiated prices focus on the time and effort spent negotiating, an activity that adds nothing directly to the profits of the company.

DYSFUNCTIONAL BEHAVIOR

dysfunctional behavior
Any action taken in conflict with organizational goals.

Virtually any type of transfer pricing policy can lead to **dysfunctional behavior**—actions taken in conflict with organizational goals. Gulf Oil provides a clear example. Segments tried to make their results look good at each other's expense. One widespread result: inflated transfer payments among the Gulf segments as each one vied to boost its own bottom line. A top manager, recognizing the problem, was quoted in *Business Week*: "Gulf doesn't ring the cash register until we've made an outside sale."

What prompts such behavior? Reconsider the situation shown in Exhibit 10-1. Suppose the Fabric Division has idle capacity. As we saw earlier, when there is idle capacity, the optimal transfer price is the variable cost of $40 (i.e., $8 per yard). As long as the fabric is worth at least $40 to the Tent Division, the company as a whole is better off with the transfer. Nevertheless, in a decentralized company the Fabric Division manager, working in the division's best interests, may argue that the transfer price should be based on the market price instead of variable cost. If the division is a profit center, its objective is to obtain as high a price as possible because such a price maximizes the contribution to the division's profit. (This strategy assumes that the number of units transferred will be unaffected by the transfer price—an assumption that is often shaky.)

If the company uses a market-based transfer-pricing policy when the Fabric Division has idle capacity, dysfunctional behavior can occur. At a $50 transfer price, the Tent

Division manager will not purchase the fabric and make the tent. Why? Because at a transfer price of $50 and with additional processing costs of $53, the division's cost of $103 will exceed the tent's $100 selling price. Because the true additional cost of the fabric to the company is $40, the company forgoes a contribution of $100 − ($40 + $53) = $7 per tent.

Now suppose the Fabric Division has no idle capacity. A variable-cost transfer-pricing policy can lead to dysfunctional decisions. The Tent Division manager might argue for a variable-cost-based transfer price. After all, the lowest possible transfer price will maximize the Tent Division's profit. But such a policy will not motivate the Fabric Division to produce fabric for the Tent Division. As long as output can be sold on the outside market for any price above the variable cost, the Fabric Division will use its capacity to produce for the market, regardless of how valuable the fabric might be to the Tent Division.

How are such dilemmas resolved? One possibility is for top management to impose a "fair" transfer price and insist that a transfer be made. But managers in a decentralized company often regard such orders as undermining their autonomy.

Alternatively, managers might be given the freedom to negotiate transfer prices on their own. The Tent Division manager might look at the selling price of the tent, $100, less the additional cost the division incurs in making it, $53, and decide to purchase fabric at any transfer price less than $100 − $53 = $47. The Tent Division will add to its profit by making the tent if the transfer price is below $47.

Similarly, the Fabric Division manager will look at what it costs to produce and transfer the fabric. If there is idle capacity, any transfer price above $40 will increase the Fabric Division's profit. However, if there is no idle capacity, so that transferring a unit causes the division to give up an external sale at $50, the minimum transfer price acceptable to the Fabric Division is $50.

Negotiation will result in a transfer if the maximum transfer price the Tent Division is willing to pay is greater than the minimum transfer price the Fabric Division is willing to accept. When the Fabric Division has idle capacity, a transfer at a price between $40 and $47 will occur. The exact transfer price may depend on the negotiating ability of the two division managers. However, if the Fabric Division has no idle capacity, a transfer will not occur. Therefore, the manager's decisions are congruent with the company's best interests.

What should top management of a decentralized organization do if it sees segment managers making dysfunctional decisions? As usual, the answer is, "It depends." Top management can step in and force transfers, but doing so undermines segment managers' autonomy and the overall notion of decentralization. Frequent intervention results in recentralization. Indeed, if more centralization is desired, the organization could be redesigned by combining segments.

Top managers who wish to encourage decentralization will often make sure that both producing and purchasing division managers understand all the facts and then allow the managers to negotiate a transfer price. Even when top managers suspect that a dysfunctional decision might be made, they may swallow hard and accept the segment manager's judgment as a cost of decentralization. (Of course, repeated dysfunctional decision making may be a reason to change the organizational design or to change managers.)

Well-trained and informed segment managers who understand opportunity costs and fixed and variable costs will often make better decisions than will top managers. The producing division manager knows best the various uses of its capacity, and the purchasing division manager knows best what profit can be made on the items to be transferred. In addition, negotiation allows segments to respond flexibly to changing market conditions when setting transfer prices. One transfer price may be appropriate in a time of idle capacity, and another when demand increases and operations approach full capacity.

To increase segment managers' willingness to accommodate one another's needs and benefit the organization as a whole, top managers rely on both formal and informal communications. They may informally ask segment managers to be "good company citizens" and to sacrifice results for the good of the organization. They may also formalize this communication by basing performance evaluation and rewards on companywide as well as segment results. In the case of our outdoor equipment maker, the contribution to the company as a whole, $70,000 in the idle capacity case, could be split between the Fabric and Tent Divisions, perhaps equally, perhaps in proportion to the variable costs of each, or perhaps via negotiation.

THE NEED FOR MANY TRANSFER PRICES

As you can see, there is seldom a single transfer price that will ensure the desired decisions. The "correct" transfer price depends on the economic and legal circumstances and the decision at hand. Organizations may have to make trade-offs between pricing for congruence and pricing to spur managerial effort. Furthermore, the optimal price for either may differ from that employed for tax reporting or for other external needs.

Income taxes, property taxes, and tariffs often influence the setting of transfer prices so that the firm as a whole will benefit, even though the performance of a segment may suffer. For example, to maximize tax deductions for percentage depletion allowances, which are based on revenue, a petroleum company may want to transfer crude oil to other segments at as high a price as legally possible.

Transfer pricing is also influenced in some situations by state fair-trade laws and national antitrust acts. Because of the differences in national tax structures around the world, or because of the differences in the incomes of various divisions and subsidiaries, the firm may wish to shift profits and "dump" goods, if legally possible. These considerations further illustrate the limits of decentralization where heavy interdependencies exist and explain why the same company may use different transfer prices for different purposes.

MULTINATIONAL TRANSFER PRICING

Objective 5
Identify the factors affecting multinational transfer prices.

Transfer-pricing policies of domestic companies focus on goal congruence and motivation. In multinational companies, other factors may dominate. For example, multinational companies use transfer prices to minimize worldwide income taxes, import duties, and tariffs.

Suppose a division in a high-income-tax-rate country produces a subcomponent for another division in a low-income-tax-rate country. By setting a low transfer price, most of the profit from the production can be recognized in the low-income-tax-rate country, thereby minimizing taxes. Likewise, items produced by divisions in a low-income-tax-rate country and transferred to a division in a high-income-tax-rate country should have a high transfer price to minimize taxes.

Sometimes income tax effects are offset by import duties. Usually import duties are based on the price paid for an item, whether bought from an outside company or transferred from another division. Therefore low transfer prices generally lead to low import duties.

Of course, tax authorities recognize the incentive to set transfer prices to minimize taxes and import duties. Therefore most countries have restrictions on allowable transfer prices. U.S. multinationals must follow an Internal Revenue Code rule specifying that transfers be priced at "arm's-length" market values, or at the values that would be used if the divisions were independent companies. Even with this rule, companies have some latitude in deciding an appropriate "arm's-length" price.

Consider an item produced by Division A in a country with a 25% income tax rate and transferred to Division B in a country with a 50% income tax rate. In addition, an import duty equal to 20% of the price of the item is assessed. Suppose the full unit cost of the item is $100, and the variable cost is $60. If tax authorities allow either variable- or full-cost transfer prices, which should be chosen? By transferring at $100 rather than $60, the company gains $2 per unit. Assume that import duties are not deductible for tax purposes.

Effect of Transferring at $100 Instead of at $60	
Income of A is $40 higher; therefore A pays 25% × $40 more income taxes	$(10)
Income of B is $40 lower; therefore B pays 50% × $40 less income taxes	20
Import duty is paid by B on an additional $100 − $60 = $40; therefore B pays 20% × $40 more duty	(8)
Net savings from transferring at $100 instead of $60	$ 2

Companies may also use transfer prices to avoid financial restrictions imposed by some governments. For example, a country might restrict the amount of dividends paid to foreign owners. It may be easier for a company to get cash from a foreign division as payment for items transferred than as cash dividends.

In summary, transfer pricing is more complex in a multinational company than it is in a domestic company. Multinational companies have more objectives to be achieved through transfer-pricing policies, and some of the objectives often conflict with one another.

An appropriate transfer price between two divisions of a company can be determined from the following data.

Fabricating Division
Market price of subassembly	$50
Variable cost of subassembly	$20
Excess capacity (in units)	1,000

Assembly Division
Number of units needed	900

What is the natural bargaining range for the two divisions?

ANSWER

The natural bargaining range for the two divisions is between $20 and $50. If the subassemblies are available for $50 each in the market, the assembly division will not be willing to pay more than $50 to the fabricating division. Because there is excess capacity in the fabricating division, any price above the variable cost of $20 will result in a positive contribution margin. No price below $20 would be acceptable to the fabricating division.

PERFORMANCE MEASURES AND MANAGEMENT CONTROL

Transfer pricing affects segment profit, thereby affecting the performance measures of profit centers. This section looks more generally at how performance measures affect managers' incentives.

Objective 6
Explain how the linking of rewards to responsibility center results affects incentives and risk.

MOTIVATION, PERFORMANCE, AND REWARDS

Exhibit 10-2 shows the criteria and choices faced by top management when designing a management control system. Using the criterion of cost-benefit and the motivational criteria of congruence and effort, top management chooses responsibility centers (for

Exhibit 10-2

Criteria and Choices When Designing a Management Control System

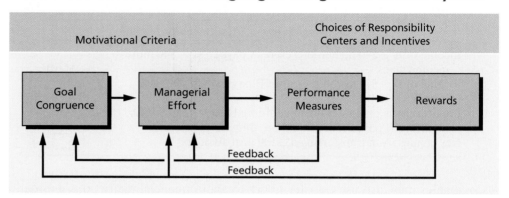

example, cost center versus profit center), performance measures, and rewards. **Incentives** are defined as those informal and formal performance-based rewards that enhance managerial effort toward organizational goals. For example, how the $70,000 contribution in Exhibit 10-1 is split between the Fabric and Tent Divisions affects the measures of their performance. In turn, the performance measures may affect the managers' rewards.

incentives Those informal and formal performance-based rewards that enhance managerial effort toward organizational goals.

Numerous performance measurement choices have been described in this book, such as whether to use tight or loose standards, whether to measure divisional performance by contribution margins or operating incomes, and whether to use both financial and nonfinancial measures of performance. Research on rewards has yielded a basic principle that is simple and important: Managers tend to focus their efforts in areas where performance is measured and where performance affects rewards. Research shows that the more objective the measures of performance, the more likely the manager will exert effort. Thus accounting measures, which provide relatively objective evaluations of performance, are important. Moreover, if individuals believe there is no connection between their behavior and their measure of performance, they will not see how to alter their performance to affect their rewards.

The choice of rewards clearly belongs with an overall system of management control. Rewards may be both monetary and nonmonetary. Examples include pay raises, bonuses, promotion, praise, self-satisfaction, elaborate offices, and private dining rooms. However, the design of a reward system is mainly the concern of top managers, who frequently listen to advice from many sources besides accountants.

AGENCY THEORY, PERFORMANCE, REWARDS, AND RISK

Linking rewards to performance is desirable. But often a manager's performance cannot be measured directly. For example, responsibility center results may be measured easily, but a manager's effect on those results (that is, managerial performance) may not. Ideally, rewards should be based on managerial performance, but in practice the rewards usually depend on the financial results in the manager's responsibility center. Managerial performance and responsibility center results are certainly related, but factors beyond a manager's control also affect results. The greater the influence of noncontrollable factors on responsibility center results, the more problems there are in using the results to represent a manager's performance. For example, the profits of a regional distribution center of Airborne Express increased dramatically in 1997. Which of the following factors that contributed to the increase in profit were controllable by the regional manager?

- A lengthy strike by workers of a competitor (UPS) resulted in many former UPS customers switching to Airborne.
- The regional center implemented a new cost management system resulting in a significant reduction in the costs of handling packages.
- Overall population growth in the region has been much higher than has been the average for the entire Airborne system.
- Fuel costs in the region have not increased as much as in the system overall.
- Employee turnover is lower than is the system average. Employees cite their excellent relationship with fellow employees and management as the reason for their high level of job satisfaction.

Should the regional manager's performance be measured by profit results compared to the overall Airborne system? What other measures could be used? From the factors listed, it is likely that a significant portion of the regional center profit was due to factors not controllable by the regional manager (the UPS strike, population growth, and fuel costs). But, it is likely that the manager did a good job of refining the cost management system and creating a productive working environment for all employees.

Economists describe the formal choices of performance measures and rewards as **agency theory.** When top management hires a manager, both should agree to an employment contract that details performance measures and how they will affect rewards.[1] For example, a manager might receive a bonus of 15% of her salary if her responsibility center achieves its budgeted profit. According to agency theory, employment contracts will trade off three factors:

> **agency theory** A theory used to describe the formal choices of performance measures and rewards.

1. Incentive: The more a manager's reward depends on a performance measure, the more incentive the manager has to take actions that maximize that measure. Top management should define the performance measure to promote goal congruence and base enough reward on it to achieve managerial effort.

2. Risk: The greater the influence of uncontrollable factors on a manager's reward, the more risk the manager bears. People generally avoid risk, so managers must be paid more if they are expected to bear more risk. Creating incentive by linking rewards to responsibility center results, which is generally desirable, has the undesirable side effect of imposing risk on managers.

3. Cost of measuring performance: The incentive versus risk trade-off is not necessary if a manager's performance is perfectly measured. Why? Because then a manager could be paid a fixed amount if he or she performs as expected, and nothing if not. Whether to perform or not is completely controllable by the manager, and observation of the level of performance is all that is necessary to determine the compensation earned. But directly measuring a manager's performance is usually expensive and sometimes infeasible. Responsibility center results are more readily available. The cost-benefit criterion usually indicates that perfect measurement of a manager's performance is not worth its cost.

Consider a concert promoter hired by a group of investors to promote and administer an outdoor rock performance. If the investors cannot directly measure the promoter's effort and judgment, they would probably pay a bonus based on the economic success of the concert. The bonus would motivate the promoter to put his effort toward generating a profit but the promoter is taking a big risk. For example, what happens if it rains? Through no fault of the promoter, the weather might keep fans away and ruin the concert. Factors such as bad weather also could affect the concert's economic success. The promoter might

---

[1] *Often performance measures and rewards are implicit. For example, promotion is a reward, but usually the requirements for promotion are not explicit.*

do an outstanding job and still not receive a bonus. Suppose the investors offer a contract with part guaranteed pay and part bonus. A larger bonus portion compared with the guaranteed portion creates more incentive, but it also means a larger expected total payment to compensate the promoter for the added risk.

SUMMARY PROBLEM FOR YOUR REVIEW

PROBLEM

Examine Exhibit 10-1 on page 399. In addition to the data there, suppose the Fabric Division has annual fixed manufacturing costs of $800,000 and expected annual production of 500,000 square yards. The "fully allocated cost" per square yard was computed as follows:

Variable costs per square yard	$8.00
Fixed costs, $800,000 ÷ 500,000 square yards	1.60
Fully allocated cost per square yard	$9.60

Therefore, the "fully allocated cost" of the five square yards required for one tent is $5 \times \$9.60 = \$48$.

Assume that the Fabric Division has idle capacity. The Tent Division is considering whether to buy enough fabric for 10,000 tents. Each tent will be sold for $100. The additional costs shown in Exhibit 10-1 for the Tent Division would prevail. If transfers were based on fully allocated cost, would the Tent Division manager buy? Explain. Would the company as a whole benefit if the Tent Division manager decided to buy? Explain.

SOLUTION

The Tent Division manager would not buy. The resulting transfer price of $48 would make the acquisition of the fabric unattractive to the Tent Division:

Tent Division		
Sales price of final product		$100
Deduct costs		
Transfer price paid to the Fabric Division (fully allocated cost)		$48
Additional costs (from Exhibit 10-1)		
Processing	$41	
Selling	12	53
Total costs to the Tent Division		1.60
Contribution to profit of the Tent Division		$ (1)
Contribution to company as a whole (from Exhibit 10-1)		$ 7

As Exhibit 10-1 shows, the company as a whole would benefit by $70,000 (10,000 tents × $7) if the fabric were transferred.

The major lesson here is that, when idle capacity exists in the supplier division, transfer prices based on fully allocated costs may induce the wrong decisions. Working in her own best interests, the Tent Division manager has no incentive to buy from the Fabric Division.

A favorite objective of top management is to maximize profitability. Segment managers in decentralized organizations are often evaluated based on their segment's profitability. The trouble is that profitability does not mean the same thing to all people. Is it net income? Income before taxes? Net income percentage based on revenue? Is it an absolute amount? A percentage? In this section we consider the strengths and weaknesses of several commonly used measures.

Objective 7
Compute ROI, residual income, and economic value added (EVA) and contrast them as criteria for judging the performance of organization segments.

RETURN ON INVESTMENT

Too often, managers stress net operating income or income percentages without tying the measure into the investment associated with generating the income. To say that project A has an operating income of $200,000 and project B has an operating income of $150,000 is an insufficient statement about profitability. A better test of profitability is the rate of **return on investment (ROI),** which is income (or profit) divided by the investment required to obtain that income or profit. Given the same risks, for any given amount of resources required, the investor wants the maximum income. If project A requires an investment of $500,000 and project B requires only $250,000, all other things being equal, where would you put your money?

return on investment (ROI) A measure of income or profit divided by the investment required to obtain that income or profit.

$$\text{ROI} = \frac{\text{income}}{\text{investment}}$$

$$\text{ROI project A} = \frac{\$200,000}{\$500,000} = 40\%$$

$$\text{ROI project B} = \frac{\$150,000}{\$250,000} = 60\%$$

ROI is a useful common denominator. It can be compared with rates inside and outside the organization, and with opportunities in other projects and industries. It is affected by two major items, **income percentage of revenue** (also called **return on sales**)—income divided by revenue—and **capital turnover**—revenue divided by invested capital.

income percentage of revenue (return on sales) Income divided by revenue.

$$\text{return on investment} = \frac{\text{income}}{\text{invested capital}}$$

$$= \frac{\text{income}}{\text{revenue}} \times \frac{\text{revenue}}{\text{invested capital}}$$

$$= \text{income percentage of revenue} \times \text{capital turnover}$$

capital turnover Revenue divided by invested capital.

An improvement in either of these rates without changing the other will improve the rate of return on invested capital. Consider an example of these relationships:

	Rate of Return on Invested Capital (%)	=	Income / Revenue	×	Revenue / Invested Capital
Present outlook	20	=	$\frac{16}{100}$	×	$\frac{100}{80}$
Alternatives					
1. Increase income percentage by reducing expenses	25	=	$\frac{20}{100}$	×	$\frac{100}{80}$
2. Increase turnover by decreasing investment	25	=	$\frac{16}{100}$	×	$\frac{100}{64}$

Alternative 1 is a popular way to improve performance. Alert managers try to decrease expenses without reducing sales or to boost sales without increasing related expenses. Alternative 2 is less obvious, but it may be a quicker way to improve performance. Increasing the turnover of invested capital means generating higher revenue for each dollar invested in such assets as cash, receivables, inventories, or equipment. There is an optimal level of investment in these assets. Having too much is wasteful, but having too little may hurt credit standing and the ability to compete for sales. Increasing turnover is one of the advantages of implementing the just-in-time (JIT) philosophy (see Chapter 1). Many companies implementing JIT purchasing and production systems have realized dramatic improvements in their ROI.

RESIDUAL INCOME (RI) AND ECONOMIC VALUE ADDED (EVA)

residual income (RI)
After-tax operating income less "imputed" interest.

cost of capital What a firm must pay to acquire more capital, whether or not it actually has to acquire more capital to take on a project.

Most managers agree that measuring return in relation to investment provides the ultimate test of profitability. ROI is one such comparison. However, some managers favor emphasizing an absolute amount of income rather than a percentage rate of return. They use **residual income (RI)**, defined as after-tax operating income less "imputed" interest. "Imputed" interest refers to the **cost of capital,** what the firm must pay to acquire more capital—whether or not it actually has to acquire more capital to take on a project. In short, RI tells you how much your company's after-tax operating income exceeds what it is paying for capital. For example, suppose a division's after-tax operating income was $900,000, the average invested capital (total assets) in the division for the year was $10 million, and the corporate headquarters assessed an imputed interest charge of 8%:

Divisional after-tax operating income	$900,000
Minus imputed interest on average invested capital (.08 × $10,000,000)	800,000
Equals residual income	$100,000

economic value added (EVA) Equals adjusted after-tax operating income minus the cost of invested capital multiplied by the adjusted average invested capital.

There are several different ways to calculate residual income depending on how a company chooses to define the terms used. One popular variant coined and marketed by Stern Stewart & Co. is called **economic value added** or **EVA.** In formula form, Stern Stewart defines EVA as

EVA = Adjusted after-tax operating income − Cost of invested capital (%)
× Adjusted average invested capital

The cost of invested capital (%) is the cost of long-term liabilities and stockholders' equity weighted by their relative size for the company or division. Stern Stewart makes specific adjustments to financial-reporting measures of after-tax operating income and invested capital. These adjustments convert after-tax operating income into a closer approximation of cash income and invested capital into a closer approximation of the cash invested in the economic resources the company uses to create value. Examples of these adjustments include:

- Use taxes paid rather than tax expense,
- Capitalize research and development expenses,
- Use FIFO for inventory valuation (thus companies using LIFO must add back the LIFO reserve to invested capital and the change in the reserve to after-tax operating income),

- Add unrecorded goodwill and accumulated goodwill amortization to capital and add back goodwill amortization to after-tax operating income, and
- If a company deducts any interest expense in computing operating income, it must add this (after-tax) interest expense to its after-tax operating income.

To illustrate, suppose a company invests $4 million on January 2, 20X0, on research and development on a product that proves to be a success with a product life cycle of 4 years (20X0 to 20X3). Before accounting for R & D, operating income each year is $12 million and capital is $50 million. The company's cost of capital is 10%. For simplicity, we will ignore income taxes, although EVA usually uses after-tax numbers.

Normally, financial reporting requires the company to expense the entire $4 million as incurred with no asset reported on the balance sheet. In short, generally accepted accounting principles assume that there is no future value to be realized from these expenditures. In contrast, EVA companies look upon R & D as a capital investment. For purposes of calculating EVA, this company would capitalize these expenditures and expense them over the product's life cycle. In addition, the company would deduct from the operating income a capital charge of 10% of the average capital balance outstanding during the year. A comparison of the income and capital effects between accounting for financial reporting and measuring EVA follows (in millions):

Year	Accounting Operating Income	Adjusted Operating Income	Accounting Capital	Adjusted Average Capital**	EVA Capital Charge @ 10%
20X0	$ 8	8 + 4 − 1 = $11*	$50	$53.5	$5.35
20X1	12	12 − 1 = 11	50	52.5	5.25
20X2	12	12 − 1 = 11	50	51.5	5.15
20X3	12	12 − 1 = 11	50	50.5	5.05

* Accounting operating income + R & D expense − R & D amortization = $8 + $4 − $1 = $11.

** Adjusted average capital: 20X0, ½ × ($54 + $53); 20X1, ½ × ($53 + $52); etc.

In essence, the EVA calculation says that the company needs to generate revenues less operating costs from this project exceeding $4.8 million before any economic value is added or created for the owners. The first $4 million covers the cost of the R & D itself, and the additional $.8 million pays for the capital needed. Note that the 4-year capital charge without the R & D investment would have been 4 × $50,000 × 10% = $20 million, compared to the $20.8 million capital charge with the R & D investment. In contrast, under conventional accounting, the company would report a positive "life cycle income" as soon as cumulative revenues less operating costs exceeded $4 million.

Stern Stewart has identified more than 100 different adjustments such as the one for R & D. However, most often it recommends only a few for a specific client. Many companies make their own adjustments, as well. Nevertheless, all EVA companies use the basic concept of after-tax operating income less a capital charge.

RI and EVA have received much attention recently as scores of companies are adopting them as financial performance measures. AT&T, Coca-Cola, CSX, FMC, and Quaker Oats claim that using EVA motivated managers to make decisions that increased shareholder value. All these companies are successful. Why? Because they do a better job than their competitors at allocating, managing, and redeploying scarce capital resources (fixed assets such as heavy equipment, computers, real estate, and working capital).

One company that has improved its EVA performance dramatically over the past decade is IBM. Compute the EVA for IBM for 2000 using the following data (millions of dollars):

	2000
After-tax operating income	$ 8,153
Average stockholders' equity	20,568
Average long-term liabilities	29,363
Cost of capital (assumed)	12%

ANSWER

EVA = After-tax operating income − cost-of-capital percentage × capital invested

$$= \$8,153 - .12 \times (\$20,568 + \$29,363)$$

$$= \$8,153 - .12 \times \$49,931$$

$$= \$8,153 - \$5,992$$

$$= \$2,161$$

Note that in 1993, IBM had a negative EVA of about $13 billion. This dramatic improvement in created value has resulted in IBM's position in *Fortune*'s market-value-added ranking rising from 1,000 to 11. We have used data reported in IBM's financial statements without adjustments such as advocated by Stern Stewart or others.

ROI OR RESIDUAL INCOME?

Why do some companies prefer residual income (or EVA) to ROI? For a division with net operating income of $900,000 and average invested capital of $10,000,000, the ROI approach shows

Divisional net operating income after taxes	$ 900,000
Average invested capital	$10,000,000
Return on investment	9%

Under ROI, the basic message is: Go forth and maximize your rate of return, a percentage. Thus, if performance is measured by ROI, managers of divisions currently earning 20% may be reluctant to invest in projects that earn only 15% because doing so would reduce their average ROI.

However, from the viewpoint of the company as a whole, top management may want this division manager to accept projects that earn 15%. Why? Suppose the company's cost of capital is 8%. Investing in projects earning 15% will increase the company's profitability. When performance is measured by residual income, managers tend to invest in any project earning more than the imputed interest rate and thus raise the firm's profits. That is, the residual income approach fosters goal congruence and managerial effort. Its basic message is: Go forth and maximize residual income, an absolute dollar amount.

General Electric (GE) was one of the first companies to adopt a residual income approach. Consider two divisions of GE as an example. Division A has net operating income of $200,000; Division B has operating income of $50,000. Both have average invested capital of $1 million. Suppose a project is proposed that can be undertaken by either A or B. The project will earn 15% annually on a $500,000 investment, or $75,000 a year. The cost of capital for the project is 8%. ROI and residual income with and without the project are as follows:

	Without Project		With Project	
	Division A	Division B	Division A	Division B
Net operating income	$ 200,000	$ 50,000	$ 275,000	$ 125,000
Invested capital	$1,000,000	$1,000,000	$1,500,000	$1,500,000
ROI (net operating income ÷ invested capital)	20%	5%	18.3%	8.3%
Capital charge (8% × invested capital)	$ 80,000	$ 80,000	$ 120,000	$ 120,000
Residual income (net operating income − capital charge)	$ 120,000	$ (30,000)	$ 155,000	$ 5,000

Suppose you are the manager of Division A. If your evaluation is based on ROI, would you invest in the project? No. It would decrease your ROI from 20 to 18.3%. But suppose you are in Division B. Would you invest? Yes, because ROI increases from 5 to 8.3%. In general, in companies using ROI, the least-profitable divisions have more incentive to invest in new projects than do the most profitable divisions.

Now suppose you are evaluated using residual income. The project would be equally attractive to either division. Residual income increases by $35,000 for each division, $155,000 − $120,000 for A and $5,000 − (−$30,000) for B. Both divisions have the same incentive to invest in the project, and the incentive depends on the profitability of the project compared with the cost of the capital used by the project.

In general, use of residual income or EVA will promote goal congruence and lead to better decisions than using ROI. Consider the following statements taken from recent annual reports.

By focusing on EVA, employees throughout Alltrista are making strategic and operating decisions that will increase EVA and in turn, shareholder value. EVA is our primary performance measure because . . . it aligns our internal processes, business strategies and employee behavior in the pursuit of realizing value creation potential.

—Alltrista Corporation

Siemens focuses on EVA as the yardstick by which we measure the success of our efforts. The EVA performance standard encourages our people to be efficient, productive and proactive in thinking about our customers and their customers. These attributes translate into profitable growth and higher returns.

—Siemens Corporation

Alltrista Corporation makes metal and plastic products. Examples of actions taken by Alltrista that helped improve the company's EVA include the sale of its Metal Services Company because the company was not earning enough return to cover the costs of invested capital. The acquisition of Kerr brand home canning products improved EVA because Kerr earned a return in excess of the capital used. Finally, Alltrista improved operating efficiencies at the Plastic Packaging division without using more capital.

Siemens Corporation, with 2000 sales of 78 billion euros (about $69 billion), designs, develops, and makes electrical and electronic systems. Products include generators for utilities, telecommunications equipment, wireless phones, and medical electronic equipment including cancer detection and therapy devices. Examples of actions taken by Siemens to improve EVA include the sale of Siecor, the fiberoptic cable business, to Corning, and the sale of its retail and banking business. As stated by Siemens, "Divesting selected businesses has generated funds for more strategic investments."

Still, most companies use ROI. Why? Probably because it is easier for managers to understand, and it facilitates comparison across divisions. Furthermore, combining ROI with appropriate growth and profit targets can minimize ROI's dysfunctional motivations.

A CLOSER LOOK AT INVESTED CAPITAL

Objective 8
Compare the advantages and disadvantages of various bases for measuring the invested capital used by organization segments.

To apply either ROI or residual income, both income and invested capital must be measured. However, there are many different interpretations of these concepts. To understand what ROI or residual income figures really mean, you must first determine how invested capital and income are being defined and measured. We discussed various definitions of income in Chapter 9, pages 362–385, we will not repeat them here. We will, however, explore various definitions of invested capital.

DEFINITION OF INVESTED CAPITAL

Consider the following balance sheet classifications:

Current assets	$ 400,000	Current liabilities	$ 200,000
Property, plant, and		Long-term liabilities	400,000
equipment, net	800,000	Stockholders' equity	700,000
Construction in		Total liabilities and stockholders' equity	$1,300,000
progress	100,000		
Total assets	$1,300,000		

Possible definitions of invested capital and their values on the preceding balance sheet include

1. *Total assets:* All assets are included, $1,300,000.

2. *Total assets employed:* All assets except agreed-on exclusion of construction in progress, $1,300,000 − $100,000 = $1,200,000.

3. *Total assets less current liabilities:* All assets except that portion supplied by short-term creditors, $1,300,000 − $200,000 = $1,100,000. This is sometimes expressed as long-term invested capital; note that it can also be computed by adding the long-term liabilities and the stockholders' equity, $400,000 + $700,000 = $1,100,000, which is the definition used for EVA.

4. *Stockholders' equity:* Focuses on the investment of the owners of the business, $700,000.

All the preceding should be computed as averages for the period under review. These averages may be based on simply the beginning and ending balances or on more complicated averages that weigh changes in investments through the months.

For measuring the performance of division managers, any of the three asset definitions is recommended rather than stockholders' equity. If the division manager's mission is to put all assets to their best use without regard to their financing, then total assets is best. If top management directs the manager to carry extra assets that are not currently productive, then total assets employed is best. If the manager has direct control over obtaining short-term credit and bank loans, then total assets less current liabilities is best. A key behavioral factor in choosing an investment definition is that managers will focus attention on reducing those assets and increasing those liabilities that are included in the definition. In practice, most companies using ROI or residual income include all assets in invested capital, and about half (primarily companies using EVA) deduct some portion of current liabilities.

A few companies allocate long-term debt to their divisions and thus have an approximation of the stockholders' equity in each division. However, this practice has doubtful merit. Division managers typically have little responsibility for the long-term financial management of their divisions, as distinguished from operating management. The investment bases of division managers from two companies could differ radically if one company has heavy long-term debt and the other is debt-free.

ASSET ALLOCATION TO DIVISIONS

Just as cost allocations affect income, asset allocations affect the invested capital of particular divisions. The aim is to allocate this capital in a manner that will be goal congruent, will spur managerial effort, and will recognize segment autonomy insofar as possible. (As long as the managers feel that they are being treated uniformly, though, they tend to be more tolerant of the imperfections of the allocation.)

A frequent criterion for asset allocation is avoidability. That is, the amount allocable to any given segment for the purpose of evaluating the division's performance is the amount that the corporation as a whole could avoid by not having that segment. Commonly used bases for allocation, when assets are not directly identifiable with a specific division, include

Asset Class	Possible Allocation Base
Corporate cash	Budgeted cash needs
Receivables	Sales weighted by payment terms
Inventories	Budgeted sales or usage
Plant and equipment	Usage of services in terms of long-run forecasts of demand or area occupied

The allocation base should be the output measure or cost driver of the activity that caused the asset to be acquired. When the allocation of an asset would indeed be arbitrary (i.e., no causal activity can be identified), many managers think that it is better not to allocate.

Should cash be included in a division's investment if corporate headquarters strictly controls the cash balances? Arguments can be made for both sides, but the manager is usually regarded as being responsible for the volume of business generated by the division. In turn, this volume is likely to have a direct effect on the overall cash needs of the corporation.

A popular allocation base for cash is sales dollars. However, the allocation of cash on the basis of sales dollars seldom gets at the economic rationale of cash holdings. As Chapter 7 explains, cash needs are influenced by a host of factors including payment terms of customers and creditors.

Central control of cash is usually undertaken to reduce the holdings from what would be used if each division had a separate account. Fluctuations in cash needs of each division might offset one another. For example, Division A might have a cash deficiency of $1 million in February, but Division B might have an offsetting cash excess of $1 million. Taken together for the year, Divisions A, B, C, D, and E might require a combined investment in cash of, say, $16 million if all were independent entities, but only $8 million if cash were controlled centrally. Hence, if Division C would ordinarily require a $4 million investment in cash as a separate entity, it would be allocated an investment of only $2 million as a segment of a company in which cash was controlled centrally.

VALUATION OF ASSETS

gross book value The original cost of an asset before deducting accumulated depreciation.

net book value The original cost of an asset less any accumulated depreciation.

Whatever assets are included in a division's invested capital must be measured in some way. Should the assets contained in the investment base be valued at gross book value or net book value? **Gross book value** is the original cost of an asset before deducting accumulated depreciation. **Net book value** is the original cost of an asset less any accumulated depreciation. Should values be based on historical cost or some version of current value? Practice is overwhelmingly in favor of using net book value based on historical cost. Very few companies use replacement cost or any other type of current value. Historical cost has been widely criticized for many years as providing a faulty basis for decision making and performance evaluation. As Chapters 5 and 6 point out, historical costs per se are irrelevant for making economic decisions. Despite these criticisms, managers have been slow to depart from historical cost.

Why is historical cost so widely used? Some critics would say that sheer ignorance is the explanation. But a more persuasive answer comes from cost-benefit analysis. Accounting systems are costly. Historical records must be kept for many legal purposes, so they are already in place. No additional money must be spent to evaluate performance based on historical costs. Furthermore, many top managers believe that such a system provides the desired goal congruence and managerial effort and that a more sophisticated system will not radically improve collective operating decisions. Some believe, in fact, that using current values would cause confusion unless huge sums were spent educating personnel.

Historical costs may even improve some decisions because they are more objective than current costs. Moreover, managers can better predict the historical-cost effects of their decisions, so their decisions may be more influenced by the control system. Furthermore, the uncertainty involved with current-cost measures may impose undesirable risks on the managers. In short, the historical-cost system may be superior for the routine evaluation of performance. In nonroutine instances, such as replacing equipment or deleting a product line, managers should conduct special studies to gather any current valuations that seem relevant.

Finally, although historical-cost systems are common, most well-managed organizations do not use historical-cost systems alone. The alternatives available to managers are not

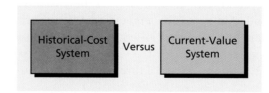

More accurately stated, the alternatives are

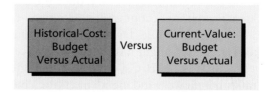

A budget system, whether based on historical cost or current value, causes managers to plan and control their operations. Most managers seem to prefer to concentrate on improving their existing historical-cost budget system.

In sum, our cost-benefit approach provides no universal answers with respect to such controversial issues as historical values versus current values or return on investment versus residual income. Instead, using a cost-benefit test, each organization must judge for itself whether an alternative control system or accounting technique will improve collective decision making. The latter is the primary criterion.

Too often, the literature engages in pro-and-con discussions about which alternative is more nearly perfect or truer than another in some logical sense. The cost-benefit approach is not concerned with "truth" or "perfection" by itself. Instead it asks, Do you think your perceived "truer" or "more logical" system is worth its added cost? Or will our existing imperfect system provide about the same set of decisions if it is skillfully administered?

PLANT AND EQUIPMENT: GROSS OR NET?

In valuing assets, it is important to distinguish between net and gross book values. Most companies use net book value in calculating their investment base. However, according to a recent survey, a significant minority uses gross book value. The proponents of gross book value maintain that it facilitates comparisons between years and between plants or divisions.

Consider an example of a $600,000 piece of equipment with a three-year life and no residual value.

| | Operating Income Before | | Operating | Average Investment | | | |
| | | | | Net Book | Rate of | Gross Book | Rate of |
Year	Depreciation	Depreciation	Income	Value*	Return	Value	Return
1	$260,000	$200,000	$60,000	$500,000	12%	$600,000	10%
2	260,000	200,000	60,000	300,000	20	600,000	10
3	260,000	200,000	60,000	100,000	60	600,000	10

* ($600,000 + $400,000) ÷ 2; ($400,000 + $200,000) ÷ 2; and so on.

The rate of return on net book value goes up as the equipment ages. It could increase even if operating income gradually declined through the years. In contrast, the rate of return on gross book value is unchanged if operating income does not change. The rate would decrease if operating income gradually declined through the years.

Advocates of using net book value maintain that

1. It is less confusing because it is consistent with the assets shown on the conventional balance sheet and with the net income computations.

2. The major criticism of net book value is not peculiar to its use for ROI purposes. It is really a criticism of using historical cost as a basis for evaluation.

The effect on motivation should be considered when choosing between net and gross book value. Managers evaluated using gross book value will tend to replace assets sooner than will those managers in firms using net book value. Consider a four-year-old machine with an original cost of $1,000 and net book value of $200. It can be replaced by a new machine that also costs $1,000. The choice of net or gross book value does not affect net income. However, the investment base increases from $200 to $1,000 in a net-book-value firm, but it remains at $1,000 in a gross-book-value firm. To maximize ROI or residual income, managers want a low-investment base. Managers in firms using net book value will tend to keep old assets with their low book value. Those in firms using gross book value will have less incentive to keep old assets. Therefore, to motivate managers to use state-of-the-art production technology, gross book value is preferred. Net asset value promotes a more conservative approach to asset replacement.

KEYS TO SUCCESSFUL MANAGEMENT CONTROL SYSTEMS

Successful management control systems have several key factors in addition to appropriate measures of profitability. We next explore some of these factors.

FOCUS ON CONTROLLABILITY

As Chapter 9 explained (see Exhibit 9-5, page 364), top management should distinguish between the performance of the division manager and the performance of the division as an investment by the corporation. They should evaluate managers on the basis of their controllable performance (in many cases, some controllable contribution in relation to controllable investment). However, they should base decisions such as increasing or decreasing investment in a division on the economic viability of the division, not the performance of its managers.

This distinction helps to clarify some vexing difficulties. For example, top management may want to use an investment base to gauge the economic performance of a retail store, but the manager may be best judged by focusing on income and forgetting about any investment allocations. If investment is assigned to the manager, the aim should be to assign only that investment that the manager can control. Controllability depends on what decisions managers can make regarding the size of the investment base. In a highly decentralized company, for instance, managers can influence the size of these assets and can exercise judgment regarding the appropriate amount of short-term credit and perhaps some long-term credit.

MANAGEMENT BY OBJECTIVES

management by objectives (MBO) The joint formulation by a manager and his or her superior of a set of goals and plans for achieving the goals for a forthcoming period.

Management by objectives (MBO) describes the joint formulation by a manager and his or her superior of a set of goals and plans for achieving the goals for a forthcoming period. For our purposes here, the terms goals and objectives are synonyms. The plans often take the form of a responsibility accounting budget (together with supplementary goals such as levels of management training and safety that may not be incorporated into the accounting budget). The manager's performance is then evaluated in relation to these agreed-on budgeted objectives.

Regardless of whether it is so labeled, an MBO approach lessens the complaints about lack of controllability because of its stress on budgeted results. That is, a budget is negotiated between a particular manager and his or her superior for a particular period and a particular set of expected outside and inside influences. In this way, a manager may more readily accept an assignment to a less successful segment. This is preferable to a system that emphasizes absolute profitability for its own sake. Unless focus is placed on currently attainable results, able managers will be reluctant to accept responsibility for segments that are in economic trouble.

Thus, skillful budgeting and intelligent performance evaluation will go a long way toward overcoming the common lament: "I'm being held responsible for items beyond my control."

TAILORING BUDGETS FOR MANAGERS

Many of the troublesome motivational effects of performance evaluation systems can be minimized by the astute use of budgets. The desirability of tailoring a budget to particular managers cannot be overemphasized. For example, either an ROI or a residual income system can promote goal congruence and managerial effort if top management gets everybody to focus on what is currently attainable in the forthcoming budget period. Typically, divisional managers do not have complete freedom to make major investment decisions without checking with senior management.

SUMMARY PROBLEM FOR YOUR REVIEW

PROBLEM

A division has assets of $200,000, current liabilities of $20,000, and net operating income of $60,000.

1. What is the division's ROI?
2. If the weighted-average cost of capital is 14%, what is the EVA?
3. What effects on management behavior can be expected if ROI is used to gauge performance?
4. What effects on management behavior can be expected if EVA is used to gauge performance?

SOLUTION

1. ROI = $60,000 ÷ $200,000 = 30%. An alternative is $60,000 ÷ $180,000 = 33%.
2. EVA = $60,000 − .14 ($180,000) = $60,000 − $25,200 = $34,800.
3. If ROI is used, the manager is prone to reject projects that do not earn an ROI of at least 30%. From the viewpoint of the organization as a whole, this may be undesirable because its best investment opportunities may lie in that division and have a rate of, say, 22%. If a division is enjoying a high ROI, it is less likely to expand if it is judged via ROI than if it is judged via EVA.
4. If EVA is used, the manager is inclined to accept all projects whose expected rate of return exceeds the weighted-average cost of capital. The manager's division is more likely to expand because his or her goal is to maximize a dollar amount rather than a rate.

Highlights to Remember

Define decentralization and identify its expected benefits and costs. As companies grow, the ability of managers to effectively plan and control becomes more and more difficult because top managers are further removed from day-to-day operations. One approach to effective planning and control in large companies is to decentralize decision making. This means that top management gives mid- and lower-level managers the freedom to make decisions that impact the subunit's performance. The more that decision making is delegated, the greater the decentralization. Often, the subunit manager is most knowledgeable of the factors that should be considered in the decision-making process.

Distinguish between profit centers and decentralization. Top management must design the management control system so that managers are motivated to act in the best interests of the company. This is done through the choice of responsibility centers and the appropriate performance measures and rewards. The degree of decentralization does not depend upon the type of responsibility center chosen. For example, a cost-center manager in one company may have more decision-making authority than does a profit-center manager in a highly centralized company.

Define transfer prices and identify their purpose. In large companies with many different segments, one segment often provide products or services to another segment. Deciding on the amount to be charged for these transfers (transfer price) is difficult. Companies use various types of transfer-pricing policies. The overall purpose of transfer prices is to motivate managers to act in the best interests of the company, not just the segment.

Identify the relative advantages and disadvantages of basing transfer prices on total costs, variable costs, and market prices. While there are no general rules that dictate what type of transfer price to use in a particular decision situation, each type of price has its own advantages and disadvantages. Cost-based prices are readily available but if actual costs are used, the receiving segment manager does not know the cost in advance, which makes cost planning difficult. When a competitive market exists for the product or service, using market-based transfer prices usually leads to goal congruence and optimal decisions. When idle capacity exists in the segment providing the product or service, the use of variable cost as the transfer price leads to goal congruence.

Identify the factors affecting multinational transfer prices. Multinational organizations often use transfer prices as a means of minimizing worldwide income taxes, import duties, and tariffs.

Explain how the linking of rewards to responsibility center results affects incentives and risk. It is generally a good idea to link manager's rewards to responsibility center results. Top management should use performance measures for the responsibility center that promote goal congruence. However, linking rewards to results creates risk for the manager. The greater the influence of uncontrollable factors on a manager's reward, the more risk the manager bears.

Compute ROI, residual income, and economic value added (EVA), and contrast them as criteria for judging the performance of organization segments. It is typical to measure the results of investment centers using a set of performance measures that include financial measures such as return on investment (ROI), residual income (RI), or economic value added (EVA). ROI is any income measure divided by the dollar amount invested and is expressed as a percentage. Residual income, or economic value added, is after-tax operating income less imputed interest on the capital invested (cost of capital) and is an absolute dollar amount.

Compare the advantages and disadvantages of various bases for measuring the invested capital used by organization segments. EVA and RI are similar, with the measure of capital investment being the sum of long-term liabilities and stockholders' equity (or total assets less current liabilities). Other definitions of invested capital used include total assets and stockholders' equity. Many managers prefer RI and EVA because they usually promote goal congruence better than ROI.

Understand the role of management control systems in decentralized organizations. Large, decentralized organizations use management control systems to help plan and control operations. A management control system consists of responsibility centers and incentive systems. When properly designed, a management control system promotes goal congruence and motivates managers to work diligently in the best interest of the company.

Accounting Vocabulary

agency theory, p. 405

capital turnover, p. 407

cost of capital, p. 408

decentralization, p. 394

dysfunctional behavior, p. 400

economic value added (EVA), p. 408

gross book value, p. 414

incentives, p. 404

income percentage of revenue, p. 407

management by objectives (MBO), p. 416

net book value, p. 414

residual income (RI), p. 408

return on investment (ROI), p. 407

return on sales, p. 407

segment autonomy, p. 395

transfer price, p. 397

Fundamental Assignment Material

10-A1 Rate of Return and Transfer Pricing

Consider the following data regarding budgeted operations of the Atlanta Division of Machine Products Inc.

Average available assets	
Receivables	$150,000
Inventories	300,000
Plant and equipment, net	450,000
Total	$900,000
Fixed overhead	$300,000
Variable costs	$1 per unit
Desired rate of return on average	
available assets	25%
Expected volume	150,000 units

Required

1. **a.** What average unit sales price is needed to obtain the desired rate of return on average available assets?

   b. What would be the expected asset turnover?

   c. What would be the operating income percentage on dollar sales?

2. **a.** If the selling price is as computed above, what rate of return will be earned on available assets if sales volume is 180,000 units?

   b. If sales volume is 120,000 units?

3. Assume that 45,000 units are to be sold to another division of the same company and that only 105,000 units can be sold to outside customers. The other division manager has balked at a tentative selling price of $4. She has offered $2.25, claiming that she can manufacture the units herself for that price. The manager of the selling division has examined his own data. He had decided that he could eliminate $60,000 of inventories, $90,000 of plant and equipment, and $22,500 of fixed overhead if he did not sell to the other division and sold only 105,000 units to outside customers. Should he sell for $2.25? Show computations to support your answer.

10-A2 Transfer-Pricing Dispute

Mason Corporation, a transportation equipment manufacturer, is heavily decentralized. Each division head has full authority on all decisions regarding sales to internal or external customers. The Pacific Division has always acquired a certain equipment component from the Southern Division. However, when informed that the Southern Division was increasing its unit price to $330, the Pacific Division's management decided to purchase the component from outside suppliers at a price of $300.

The Southern Division had recently acquired some specialized equipment that was used primarily to make this component. The manager cited the resulting high depreciation charges as the justification for the price boost. He asked the president of the company to instruct the Pacific Division to buy from Southern at the $330 price. He supplied the following data to back his request:

Pacific's annual purchases of component	2,000 units
Southern's variable costs per unit	$ 285
Southern's fixed costs per unit	$ 30

Required

1. Suppose there are no alternative uses of the Southern facilities. Will the company as a whole benefit if the Pacific Division buys from the outside suppliers for $300 per unit? Show computations to support your answer.

2. Suppose internal facilities of Southern would not otherwise be idle. The equipment and other facilities would be assigned to other production operations that would otherwise require an additional annual outlay of $40,500. Should the Pacific Division purchase from outsiders at $300 per unit?

3. Suppose that there are no alternative uses for Southern's internal facilities and that the outsiders' selling price drops by $30. Should the Pacific Division purchase from outsiders?

4. As the president, how would you respond to the Southern Division manager's request? Would your response differ, depending on the specific situations described in requirements 1 through 3 above? Why?

10-A3 Transfer Pricing

Refer to Problem 10-A2, requirement 1 only. Suppose the Southern Division could modify the component at an additional variable cost of $12 per unit and sell the 2,000 units to other customers for $330. Then would the entire company benefit if the Pacific Division purchased the 2,000 components from outsiders at $300 per unit?

10-A4 Simple ROI and Residual Income Calculations

Consider the following data (in thousands):

	Division		
	A	B	C
Average invested capital	$1,000	$ 600	$ 800
Revenue	3,600	1,800	8,000
Income	180	126	80

Required

1. For each division, compute the income percentage of revenue (or return on sales), the capital turnover, and the return on investment (ROI).

2. Which division is the best performer? Explain.

3. Suppose each division is assessed an imputed interest rate of 10% on invested capital. Compute the residual income for each division. Which division is the best performer based on residual income? Explain.

10-B1 Transfer Pricing

Burger-Rama Enterprises runs a chain of drive-in hamburger stands on Cape Cod during the 10-week summer season. Managers of all stands are told to act as if they owned the stand and are judged on their profit performance. Burger-Rama Enterprises has rented an ice-cream machine for the summer to supply its stands with ice cream. Rent for the machine is $1,800. Burger-Rama is not allowed to sell ice cream to other dealers because it cannot obtain a dairy license. The manager of the ice-cream machine charges the stands $4 per gallon. Operating figures for the machine for the summer are as follows:

Sales to the stands (8,000 gallons at $4)		$32,000
Variable costs, @ $2.10 per gallon	$16,800	
Fixed costs		
Rental of machine	1,800	
Other fixed costs	5,000	23,600
Operating margin		$ 8,400

The manager of the Cape Drive-In, one of the Burger-Rama drive-ins, is seeking permission to sign a contract to buy ice cream from an outside supplier at $3.30 a gallon. The Cape Drive-In uses 1,500 gallons of ice cream during the summer. Jane Garton, controller of Burger-Rama, refers this request to you. You determine that the other fixed costs of operating the machine will decrease by $480 if the Cape Drive-In purchases from an outside supplier. Garton wants an analysis of the request in terms of overall company objectives and an explanation of your conclusion. What is the appropriate transfer price?

10-B2 Rate of Return and Transfer Pricing

The Tokyo division of Toy King manufactures units of the game "Go" and sells them in the Japanese market for ¥6,000 each. The following data are from the Tokyo Division's 20X2 budget:

Variable cost	¥ 3,800 per unit
Fixed overhead	¥ 6,080,000
Total assets	¥12,500,000

Toy King has instructed the Tokyo Division to budget a rate of return on total assets (before taxes) of 20%.

Required

1. Suppose the Tokyo Division expects to sell 3,400 games during 20X2.
   a. What rate of return will be earned on total assets?
   b. What would be the expected capital turnover?
   c. What would be the operating income percentage of sales?
2. The Tokyo Division is considering adjustments in the budget to reach the desired 20% rate of return on total assets.
   a. How many units must be sold to obtain the desired return if no other part of the budget is changed?
   b. Suppose sales cannot be increased beyond 3,400 units. How much must total assets be reduced to obtain the desired return? Assume that for every ¥1,000 decrease in total assets, fixed costs decrease by ¥100.
3. Assume that only 2,400 units can be sold in the Japanese market. However, another 1,400 units can be sold to the American Marketing Division of Toy King. The Tokyo manager has offered to sell the 1,400 units for ¥5,500 each. The American Marketing Division manager has countered with an offer to pay ¥5,000 per unit, claiming that she can subcontract production to an American producer at a cost equivalent to ¥5,000. The Tokyo manager knows that if his production falls to 2,400 units, he could eliminate some assets, reducing total assets to ¥10 million and annual fixed overhead to ¥4.9 million. Should the Tokyo manager sell for ¥5,000 per unit? Support your answer with the relevant computations. Ignore the effects of income taxes and import duties.

10-B3 ROI or Residual Income

T. A. Lincoln Co. is a large integrated conglomerate with shipping, metals, and mining operations throughout the world. The general manager of the Heavy Metals Division plans to submit a proposed capital budget for 20X2 for inclusion in the companywide budget.

The division manager has for consideration the following projects, all of which require an outlay of capital. All projects have equal risk.

Project	Investment Required	Return
1	$4,800,000	$1,200,000
2	1,900,000	627,000
3	1,400,000	182,000
4	950,000	152,000
5	650,000	136,500
6	300,000	90,000

The division manager must decide which of the projects to take. The company has a cost of capital of 15%. An amount of $12 million is available to the division for investment purposes.

Required

1. What will be the total investment, total return, return on capital invested, and residual income of the rational division manager if
   a. The company has a rule that all projects promising at least 20% or more should be taken.
   b. The division manager is evaluated on his ability to maximize his return on capital invested (assume that this is a new division with no invested capital).
   c. The division manager is expected to maximize residual income as computed by using the 15% cost of capital.
2. Which of the three approaches will induce the most effective investment policy for the company as a whole? Explain.

Additional Assignment Material

QUESTIONS

10-1. "Decentralization has benefits and costs." Name three of each.

10-2. Sophisticated accounting and communications systems aid decentralization. Explain how they accomplish this.

10-3. "The essence of decentralization is the use of profit centers." Do you agree? Explain.

10-4. Why is decentralization more popular in profit-seeking organizations than in nonprofit organizations?

10-5. What kinds of organizations find decentralization to be preferable to centralization?

10-6. Why are transfer-pricing systems needed?

10-7. Describe two problems that can arise when using actual full cost as a transfer price.

10-8. How does the presence or absence of idle capacity affect the optimal transfer-pricing policy?

10-9. "We use variable-cost transfer prices to ensure that no dysfunctional decisions are made." Discuss.

10-10. What is the major advantage of negotiated transfer prices? What is the major disadvantage?

10-11. Discuss two factors that affect multinational transfer prices but have little effect on purely domestic transfers.

10-12. What is the major benefit of the ROI technique for measuring performance?

10-13. What two major items affect ROI?

10-14. Define economic value added (EVA) and describe three ways a company can improve its EVA.

10-15. Division A's ROI is 20%, and B's is 10%. Each division manager is paid a bonus based on his or her division's ROI. Discuss whether each division manager would accept or reject a proposed project with a rate of return of 15%. Would either of them make a different decision if managers were evaluated using residual income with an imputed interest rate of 11%? Explain.

10-16. Give four possible definitions of invested capital that can be used in measuring ROI or residual income.

10-17. "Managers who use a historical-cost accounting system look backward at what something cost yesterday, instead of forward to what it will cost tomorrow." Do you agree? Why?

10-18. Ross Company uses net book value as a measure of invested capital when computing ROI. A division manager has suggested that the company change to using gross book value instead. What difference in motivation of division managers might result from such a change? Do you suppose most of the assets in the division of the manager proposing the change are relatively new or old? Why?

10-19. Describe management by objectives (MBO).

COGNITIVE EXERCISES

10-20 Performance Measures and Economic Theory
Economists describe the formal choices of performance measures and rewards as agency theory. According to agency theory, employment contracts trade off three factors. Name and briefly describe the three.

10-21 Comparing Financial Measures of Performance
"Both ROI and residual income use profit and invested capital to measure performance. Therefore it really doesn't matter which we use." Do you agree? Explain.

10-22 Transfer Pricing and Organizational Behavior
The principle reason for transfer-pricing systems is to communicate data that will lead to goal-congruent decisions by managers of different business units. When managers take actions that conflict with organizational goals, dysfunctional behavior exists. Why does top management sometimes accept a division manager's judgments, even if the division manager appears to behave in a dysfunctional manner?

EXERCISES

10-23 Variable Cost as a Transfer Price
A desk calendar's variable cost is $5 and its market value is $6.25 at a transfer point from the Printing Division to the Binding Division. The Binding Division's variable cost of adding a simulated leather cover is $2.80, and the selling price of the final calendar is $8.50.

Required

1. Prepare a tabulation of the contribution margin per unit for the Binding Division's performance and overall company performance under the two alternatives of (a) selling to outsiders at the transfer point and (b) adding the cover and then selling to outsiders.

2. As Binding Division manager, which alternative would you choose? Explain.

10-24 Maximum and Minimum Transfer Price

Benson Company makes bicycles. Components are made in various divisions and transferred to the Omaha Division for assembly into final products. The Omaha Division can also buy components from external suppliers. The wheels are made in the Lincoln Division, which also sells wheels to external customers. All divisions are profit centers, and managers are free to negotiate transfer prices. Prices and costs for the Lincoln and Omaha divisions are

Lincoln Division	
Sales price to external customers	$12
Internal transfer price	?
Costs	
Variable costs per wheel	$8
Total fixed costs	$320,000
Budgeted production	64,000 wheels*

* Includes production for transfer to Omaha

Omaha Division	
Sales price to external customers	$160
Costs	
Wheels, per bicycle	?
Other components, per bicycle	$80
Other variable costs, per bicycle	$40
Total fixed costs	$640,000
Budgeted production	16,000 bicycles

Fixed costs in both divisions will be unaffected by the transfer of wheels from Lincoln to Omaha.

Required

1. Compute the maximum transfer price per wheel the Omaha Division would be willing to pay to buy wheels from the Lincoln Division.
2. Compute the minimum transfer price per wheel at which the Lincoln Division would be willing to produce and sell wheels to the Omaha Division. Assume that Lincoln has excess capacity.

10-25 Multinational Transfer Prices

Global Enterprises, Inc., has production and marketing divisions throughout the world. One particular product is produced in Japan, where the income tax rate is 30%, and transferred to a marketing division in Sweden, where the income tax rate is 60%. Assume that Sweden places an import tax of 10% on the product and that import duties are not tax deductible for income tax purposes.

The variable cost of the product is $200 and the full cost is $400. Suppose the company can legally select a transfer price anywhere between the variable and full cost.

Required

1. What transfer price should Global Enterprises use to minimize taxes? Explain why this is the tax-minimizing transfer price.
2. Compute the amount of taxes saved by using the transfer price in requirement 1 instead of the transfer price that would result in the highest taxes.

10-26 Simple ROI Calculations

You are given the following data:

Sales	$130,000,000
Invested capital	$ 50,000,000
Return on investment	12%

Compute the following:

Required

1. Turnover of capital
2. Net income
3. Net income as a percentage of sales

10-27 Simple ROI Calculation
Fill in the blanks:

	Division		
	A	B	C
Income percentage of revenue	7%	3%	__%
Capital turnover	4	____	4
Rate of return on invested capital	__%	24%	20%

10-28 Simple ROI and Residual Income Calculations
Consider the following data:

	Division		
	X	Y	Z
Invested capital	$2,000,000	$ _____	$1,250,000
Income	$ _____	$ 182,000	$ 150,000
Revenue	$4,000,000	$3,640,000	$ _____
Income percentage of revenue	2.5%	__%	__%
Capital turnover	____	____	3
Rate of return on invested capital	__%	14%	__%

Required

1. Prepare a similar tabular presentation, filling in all blanks.
2. Which division is the best performer? Explain.
3. Suppose each division is assessed an imputed interest rate of 12% on invested capital. Compute the residual income for each division.

10-29 EVA at Briggs & Stratton
Briggs & Stratton Corporation is the world's largest maker of air-cooled gasoline engines for outdoor power equipment. The company's engines are used by the lawn and garden equipment industry. According to the company's 1999 *Annual Report*, "management subscribes to the premise that the value of Briggs & Stratton is enhanced if the capital invested in the company's operations yields a cash return that is greater than that expected by the provider of capital."

The following data are from Briggs & Stratton's 1999 *Annual Report* (thousands of dollars):

	1999	1998
Adjusted before tax operating profit	$187,994	$131,546
Cash taxes	65,255	41,102
Adjusted average invested capital	697,887	716,112
Cost of capital	10.3%	10.0%

Required

1. Compute the economic value added for Briggs & Stratton for 1998 and 1999.
2. Did Briggs & Stratton's overall performance improve from 1998 to 1999? Explain.

10-30 Comparison of Asset and Equity Bases
Alamo Footware has assets of $2 million and a long-term, 10% debt of $800,000. Shirley Shoes has assets of $2 million and no long-term debt. The annual operating income (before interest) of both companies is $500,000.

Required

1. Compute the rate of return on
   a. Assets available
   b. Stockholders' equity
2. Evaluate the relative merits of each base for appraising operating management.

10-31 Finding Unknowns
Consider the following data:

	Division		
	J	K	L
Income	$140,000	$_____	$_____
Revenue	$_____	$_____	$_____
Invested capital	$_____	$3,000,000	$16,000,000
Income percentage of revenue	7%	4%	_____%
Capital turnover	4	_____	3
Rate of return on invested capital	_____%	20%	15%
Imputed interest rate on invested capital	20%	12%	_____%
Residual income	$_____	$_____	$ 480,000

Required

1. Prepare a similar tabular presentation, filling in all blanks.
2. Which division is the best performer? Explain.

PROBLEMS

10-32 Profit Centers and Transfer Pricing in an Automobile Dealership
A large automobile dealership is installing a responsibility accounting system and three profit centers: parts and service, new vehicles, and used vehicles. The three department managers have been told to run their shops as if they were in business for themselves. However, there are interdepartmental dealings. For example:

a. The parts and service department prepares new cars for final delivery and repairs used cars prior to resale.

b. The used-car department's major source of inventory has been cars traded in as partial payment for new cars.

The owner of the dealership has asked you to draft a company policy statement on transfer pricing, together with specific rules to be applied to the examples cited. He has told you that clarity is of paramount importance because your statement will be relied on for settling transfer-pricing disputes.

10-33 Transfer Pricing
The Riply Pump Division of Dependable Motors Company produces water pumps for automobiles. It has been the sole supplier of water pumps to the Automotive Division and charges $30 per unit, the current market price for very large wholesale lots. The Riply Pump division also sells to outside retail outlets, at $38 per unit. Normally, outside sales amount to 25% of a total sales volume of 1 million water pumps per year. Typical combined annual data for the division follows:

Sales	$32,000,000
Variable costs, @ $24 per water pump	$24,000,000
Fixed costs	$ 3,000,000
Total costs	$27,000,000
Gross margin	$ 5,000,000

Farmington Pump Company, an entirely separate entity, has offered the Automotive Division comparable water pumps at a firm price of $28 per unit. The Riply Pump Division claims that it cannot possibly match this price because it could not earn any margin at $28.

Required

1. Assume that you are the manager of the Automotive Division. Comment on the Riply Pump Division's claim. Assume that normal outside volume cannot be increased.

2. The Riply Pump Division feels that it can increase outside sales by 750,000 water pumps per year by increasing fixed costs by $2 million and variable costs by $3 per unit while reducing the selling price to $36. Assume that maximum capacity is 1 million pumps per year. Should the division reject intracompany business and concentrate on outside sales?

10-34 Transfer Pricing Concession

You are the divisional controller of the Nashville Division of General Electronics, Inc. Your division is operating at capacity. The Memphis Division has asked Nashville to supply Part #A45K, which it will use in a new model boom box that it is introducing. Nashville currently sells Part #A45K to outside customers at $10.00 each.

The Memphis Division has offered to pay $6.90 for each part. The total cost of the boom box is

Purchased parts from outside vendors	$28.10
Nashville Part #A45K	6.90
Other variable costs	17.50
Fixed overhead	10.00
Total	$62.50

Memphis is operating at 50% of capacity, and this boom box is an important new product introduction to increase its use of capacity. Based on a target-costing approach, the Memphis Division management has decided that paying more than $6.90 for the part would make production of the boom box infeasible because the predicted selling price for the boom box is only $62.50.

General Electronics evaluates divisional managers on the basis of pretax return on investment and dollar profits compared to the budget.

Required

1. As divisional controller of the Nashville Division, would you recommend supplying Part #A45K to the Memphis Division for $6.90 each? Why or why not?

2. Would it be to the short-run economic advantage of General Electronics for the Nashville Division to supply the part to the Memphis Division? Explain your answer.

3. Discuss the organizational and behavioral difficulties, if any, inherent in this situation. As the Nashville controller, what would you advise the General Electronics president to do in this situation?

10-35 Transfer Prices and Idle Capacity

The Grand Rapids Division of National Woodcraft purchases lumber, which it uses to fabricate tables, chairs, and other wood furniture. Most of the lumber is purchased from Northwoods Mill, also a division of National Woodcraft. Both the Grand Rapids Division and Northwoods Mill are profit centers.

The Grand Rapids Division proposes to produce a new Shaker-style chair that will sell for $92. The manager is exploring the possibility of purchasing the required lumber from Northwoods Mill. Production of 800 chairs is planned, using capacity in the Grand Rapids Division that is currently idle.

The Grand Rapids Division can purchase the lumber from an outside supplier for $72. National Woodcraft has a policy that internal transfers are priced at fully allocated cost.

Assume the following costs for the production of one chair and the lumber required for the chair:

Northwoods Mill		Grand Rapids Division		
Variable cost	$48	Variable costs		
Allocated fixed cost	22	Lumber from Northwoods Mill		$70
Fully allocated cost	$70	Grand Rapids Division variable costs		
		Manufacturing	$21	
		Selling	6	27
		Total variable cost		$97

Required

1. Assume that the Northwoods Mill has idle capacity and therefore would incur no additional fixed costs to produce the required lumber. Would the Grand Rapids division manager buy the lumber for the chair from the Northwoods Mill, given the existing transfer-pricing

policy? Why or why not? Would the company as a whole benefit if the manager decides to buy from the Northwoods Mill? Explain.

2. Assume that there is no idle capacity at the Northwoods Mill and the lumber required for one chair can be sold to outside customers for $72. Would the company as a whole benefit if the manager decides to buy? Explain.

10-36 Transfer-Pricing Principles

A consulting firm, Galaxy, Inc., is decentralized with 25 offices around the country. The headquarters is based in San Francisco. Another operating division is located in San Jose, 50 miles away. A subsidiary printing operation, Kwik Print, is located in the headquarters building. Top management has indicated the desirability of the San Jose office using Kwik Print for printing reports. All charges are eventually billed to the client, but Galaxy was concerned about keeping such charges competitive.

Kwik Print charges San Jose the following:

Photographing page for offset printing (a set-up cost)	$.25
Printing cost per page	.014

At this rate, Kwik Print sales have a 60% contribution margin to fixed overhead.

Outside bids for 100 copies of a 120-page report needed immediately have been

Print 4U	$204.00
Jiffy Press	180.25
Kustom Print	186.00

These three printers are located within a five-mile radius of Galaxy–San Jose and can have the reports ready in two days. A messenger would have to be sent to drop off the original and pick up the copies. The messenger usually goes to headquarters, but in the past, special trips have been required to deliver the original or pick up the copies. It takes three to four days to get the copies from Kwik Print (because of the extra scheduling difficulties in delivery and pickup).

Quality control at Kwik Print is poor. Reports received in the past have contained wrinkled pages, have occasionally been miscollated, or have had pages deleted altogether. (In one circumstance an intracompany memorandum indicating Galaxy's economic straits was inserted in a report. Fortunately, the San Jose office detected the error before the report was distributed to the clients.) The degree of quality control in the three outside print shops is unknown.

(Although the differences in costs may seem immaterial in this case, regard the numbers as significant for purposes of focusing on the key issues.)

Required

1. If you were the decision maker at Galaxy–San Jose, to which print shop would you give the business? Is this an optimal economic decision from the entire corporation's viewpoint?
2. What would be the ideal transfer price in this case, if based only on economic considerations?
3. Time is an important factor in maintaining client goodwill. There is potential return business from this client. Given this perspective, what might be the optimal decision for the company?
4. Comment on the wisdom of top management in indicating that Kwik Print should be used.

10-37 Negotiated Transfer Prices

The Assembly Division of Chicago Office Furniture, Inc., needs 1,200 units of a subassembly from the Fabricating Division. The company has a policy of negotiated transfer prices. The Fabricating Division has enough excess capacity to produce 2,000 units of the subassembly. Its variable cost of production is $22. The market price of the subassembly is $50.

Required

What is the natural bargaining range for a transfer price between the two divisions? Explain why no price below your range would be acceptable. Also explain why no price above your range would be acceptable.

10-38 Multinational Transfer Prices

Malone's Medical Instruments, Inc., produces a variety of medical products at its plant in Seattle. The company has sales divisions worldwide. One of these sales divisions is located in Oslo, Norway.

Assume that the U.S. income tax rate is 34%, the Norwegian rate is 60%, and a 15% import duty is imposed on medical supplies brought into Norway.

One product produced in Seattle and shipped to Norway is a heart monitor. The variable cost of production is $300 per unit, and the fully allocated cost is $550 per unit.

Required

1. Suppose the Norwegian and U.S. governments allow either the variable or fully allocated cost to be used as a transfer price. Which price should Malone's Medical Instruments choose to minimize the total of income taxes and import duties? Compute the amount the company saves if it uses your suggested transfer price instead of the alternative. Assume import duties are not deductible for tax purposes.

2. Suppose the Norwegian parliament passed a law decreasing the income tax rate to 50% and increasing the duty on heart monitors to 20%. Repeat requirement 1, using these new facts.

10-39 Agency Theory

The Lambo Company plans to hire a manager for its division in Kenya. Lambo's president and vice president of personnel are trying to decide on an appropriate incentive employment contract. The manager will operate far from the London corporate headquarters, so evaluation by personal observation will be limited. The president insists that a large incentive to produce profits is necessary; he favors a salary of £14,000 and a bonus of 10% of the profits above £120,000. If operations proceed as expected, profits will be £460,000, and the manager will receive £48,000. But both profits and compensation might be more or less than planned.

The vice president of personnel responds that £48,000 is more than most of Lambo's division managers make. She is sure that a competent manager can be hired for a guaranteed salary of £36,000. "Why pay £48,000 when we can probably hire the same person for £36,000?" she argued.

Required

1. What factors would affect Lambo's choice of employment contract? Include a discussion of the pros and cons of each proposed contract.

2. Why is the expected compensation more with the bonus plan than with the straight salary?

10-40 Margins and Turnover

Return on investment is often expressed as the product of two components—capital turnover and return on sales. You are considering investing in one of three companies, all in the same industry, and are given the following information.

	Company		
	X	Y	Z
Sales	$6,000,000	$ 2,500,000	$37,500,000
Income	900,000	375,000	375,000
Capital	3,000,000	12,500,000	12,500,000

Required

1. Why would you desire the breakdown of return on investment into return on sales and turnover on capital?

2. Compute the return on sales, turnover on capital, and return on investment for the three companies, and comment on the relative performance of the companies as thoroughly as the data permit.

10-41 EVA versus Residual Income, Briggs & Stratton

This is an expansion of exercise 10-29. The primary difference between the economic value added and residual income measures is the increased focus on cash flow by EVA. EVA companies make several adjustments to both operating income from the income statement and invested capital from the balance sheet. Common examples of these adjustments include capitalizing research and development costs and reporting warrantee costs on a cash basis. Most EVA companies make only a few such adjustments (from 5 to 15).

The following data were taken from the 1999 *Annual Report* of Briggs & Stratton (thousands of dollars).

Income from operations	$180,136
Provision for income taxes	63,670
Net adjustments added to income from operations for EVA	7,858
Weighted average capital employed for EVA	697,887
Total shareholders' equity, June 27, 1999	365,910
Cash taxes	65,255
Total current liabilities, June 27, 1999	282,502
Total assets, June 27, 1999	875,885
Total shareholders' equity, June 28, 1998	316,488
Total current liabilities, June 28, 1998	222,945
Total assets, June 28, 1998	793,409
Management's estimate of the cost-of-capital	10.3%

Required

Prepare a schedule that calculates and compares economic value added to residual income for Briggs & Stratton.

10-42 ROI by Business Segment

Weston Services Inc. does business in three different business segments: (1) Entertainment, (2) Publishing/Information, and (3) Consumer/Commercial Finance. Results for a recent year were (in millions)

	Revenues	Operating Income	Total Assets
Entertainment	$1,272.2	$223.0	$1,120.1
Publishing/Information	705.5	121.4	1,308.7
Consumer/Commercial Finance	1,235.0	244.6	924.4

Required

1. Compute the following for each business segment.
   a. Income percentage of revenue
   b. Capital turnover
   c. ROI
2. Comment on the differences in return on investment among the business segments. Include reasons for the differences.

10-43 Economic Value Added at Nike

Nike, Inc., is the largest seller of athletic footwear and athletic apparel in the world. Its financial results for the 1999 and 2000 fiscal years include (in millions)

	2000	1999
Revenues	$8,995	$8,777
Operating expenses	8,010	7,920
Interest expense	45	44
Income taxes	340	295
Average invested capital (total assets less current liabilities)	3,759	3,748

Required

1. Suppose that Nike's cost of a capital is 12.5%. Compute the company's economic value added (EVA) for 1999 and 2000. Assume definitions of after-tax operating income and invested capital as reported in Nike's annual reports without adjustments advocated by Stern Stewart or others.
2. Discuss the change in EVA between 1999 and 2000.

10-44 Evaluation of Divisional Performance

As the chief executive officer of Tiger Shoe Company, you examined the following measures of the performance of three divisions (in thousands of dollars):

	Net Assets Based on		Operating Income Based on*	
Division	*Historical Cost*	*Replacement Cost*	*Historical Cost*	*Replacement Cost*
Shoes	$15,000	$15,000	$2,700	$2,700
Clothing	45,000	55,000	6,750	6,150
Accessories	30,000	48,000	4,800	3,900

* The differences in operating income between historical and replacement cost are attributable to the differences in depreciation revenues.

Required

1. Calculate for each division the rate of return on net assets and the residual income based on historical cost and on replacement cost. For purposes of calculating residual income, use 10% as the minimum desired rate of return.

2. Rank the performance of each division under each of the four different measures computed in requirement 1.

3. What do these measures indicate about the performance of the divisions? Of the division managers? Which measure do you prefer? Why?

10-45 Economic Value Added

The Coca-Cola Company uses economic value added (EVA) to evaluate top management performance. In 2000, Coca-Cola had net operating income of $3,691 million, income taxes of $1,222 million, and average noncurrent liabilities plus stockholders' equity of $11,640 million. The company's capital is about 30% long-term debt and 70% equity. Assume that the after-tax cost of debt is 5% and the cost of equity is 12%.

Required

1. Compute Coca-Cola's economic value added (EVA). Assume definitions of after-tax operating income and invested capital as reported in Coca-Cola's annual reports without adjustments advocated by Stern Stewart or others.

2. Explain what EVA tells you about the performance of the top management of Coca-Cola in 1999.

10-46 Use of Gross or Net Book Value of Fixed Assets

Assume that a particular plant acquires $800,000 of fixed assets with a useful life of four years and no residual value. Straight-line depreciation will be used. The plant manager is judged on income in relation to these fixed assets. Annual net income, after deducting depreciation, is $80,000.

Assume that sales, and all expenses except depreciation, are on a cash basis. Dividends equal net income. Thus, cash in the amount of the depreciation charge will accumulate each year. The plant manager's performance is judged in relation to fixed assets because all current assets, including cash, are considered under central-company control. Assume (unrealistically) that any cash accumulated remains idle. Ignore taxes.

Required

1. Prepare a comparative tabulation of the plant's rate of return and the company's overall rate of return based on
   a. Gross (i.e., original cost) assets.
   b. Net book value of assets.

2. Evaluate the relative merits of gross assets and net book value of assets as investment bases.

10-47 Role of Economic Value and Replacement Value

(This problem requires understanding of the concept of present values. See Appendix B.)

"To me, economic value is the only justifiable basis for measuring plant assets for purposes of evaluating performance. By economic value, I mean the present value of expected future services. Still, we do not even do this on acquisition of new assets—that is, we may compute a positive net present value, using discounted cash flow; but we record the asset at no more than its cost. In this way, the excess present value is not shown in the initial balance sheet. Moreover, the use of replacement costs in subsequent years is also unlikely to result in showing economic values. The replacement cost will probably be less than the economic value at any given instant of an asset's life.

"Market values are totally unappealing to me because they represent a second-best alternative value—that is, they ordinarily represent the maximum amount obtainable from an alternative that has been rejected. Obviously, if the market value exceeds the economic value of the assets in use, they should be sold. However, in most instances, the opposite is true; market values of individual assets are far below their economic value in use.

"The obtaining and recording of total present values of individual assets based on discounted-cash-flow techniques is an infeasible alternative. I, therefore, conclude that replacement cost (less accumulated depreciation) of similar assets producing similar services is the best practical approximation of the economic value of the assets in use. Of course, it is more appropriate for the evaluation of the division's performance than the division manager's performance."

Critically evaluate these comments. Please do not wander; concentrate on the issues described by the quotation.

Required

10-48 Review of Major Points in This Chapter

The Indiana Instruments Company uses the decentralized form of organizational structure and considers each of its divisions as an investment center. The Fort Wayne Division is currently selling 15,000 air filters annually, although it has sufficient productive capacity to produce 21,000 units per year. Variable manufacturing costs amount to $17 per unit, while the total fixed costs amount to $90,000. These 15,000 air filters are sold to outside customers at $37 per unit.

The Indianapolis Division, also a part of Indiana Instruments, has indicated that it would like to buy 1,500 air filters from the Fort Wayne Division, but at a price of $36 per unit. This is the price the Indianapolis Division is currently paying an outside supplier.

Required

1. Compute the effect on the operating income of the company as a whole if the Indianapolis Division purchases the 1,500 air filters from the Fort Wayne Division.

2. What is the minimum price that the Fort Wayne Division should be willing to accept for these 1,500 air filters?

3. What is the maximum price that the Indianapolis Division should be willing to pay for these 1,500 air filters?

4. Suppose instead that the Fort Wayne Division is currently producing and selling 21,000 air filters annually to outside customers. What is the effect on the overall Indiana Instruments Company operating income if the Fort Wayne Division is required by top management to sell 1,500 air filters to the Indianapolis Division at (a) $17 per unit and (b) $36 per unit?

5. For this question only, assume that the Fort Wayne Division is currently earning an annual operating income of $36,000, and the division's average invested capital is $300,000. The division manager has an opportunity to invest in a proposal that will require an additional investment of $20,000 and will increase annual operating income by $2,200. (a) Should the division manager accept this proposal if the Indiana Instruments Company uses ROI in evaluating the performance of its divisional managers? (b) If the company uses economic value added? (Assume a cost of capital of 9%.)

CASES

10-49 Management by Objectives

Roger Brandt is the chief executive officer of Langston Company. Brandt has a financial management background and is known throughout the organization as a "no-nonsense" executive. When Brandt became chief executive officer, he emphasized cost reduction and savings and introduced a comprehensive cost control and budget system. The company goals and budget plans were established by Brandt and given to his subordinates for implementation. Some of the company's key executives were dismissed or demoted for failing to meet projected budget plans. Under the leadership of Roger Brandt, Langston has once again become financially stable and profitable after several years of poor performance.

Recently Brandt has become concerned with the human side of the organization and has become interested in the management technique referred to as "management by objectives" (MBO). If there are enough positive benefits of MBO, he plans to implement the system throughout the company. However, he realizes that he does not fully understand MBO because he does not understand how it differs from the current system of establishing firm objectives and budget plans.

1. Briefly explain what MBO entails and identify its advantages and disadvantages.

2. Does Roger Brandt's management style incorporate the human value premises and goals of MBO? Explain your answer.

10-50   Profit Centers and Central Services

Sun Manufacturing, Inc., manufacturer of Sunlite brand small appliances, has an Engineering Consulting Department (ECD). The department's major task has been to help the production departments improve their operating methods and processes.

For several years, Sun has charged the cost of consulting services to the production departments based on a signed agreement between the managers involved. The agreement specifies the scope of the project, the predicted savings, and the number of consulting hours required. The charge to the production departments is based on the costs to the Engineering Department of the services rendered. For example, senior engineer hours cost more per hour than junior engineer hours. An overhead cost is included. The agreement is really a "fixed-price" contract. That is, the production manager knows the total cost of the project in advance. A recent survey revealed that production managers have a high level of confidence in the engineers.

The ECD department manager oversees the work of about 40 engineers and 10 technicians. She reports to the engineering manager, who reports to the vice president of manufacturing. The ECD manager has the freedom to increase or decrease the number of engineers under her supervision. The ECD manager's performance evaluation is based on many factors including the annual incremental savings to the company in excess of the costs of operating the ECD department.

The production departments are profit centers. Their goods are transferred to subsequent departments, such as a sales department or sales division, at prices that approximate market prices for similar products.

Top management is seriously considering a "no-charge" plan. That is, production departments would receive engineering services at absolutely no cost. Proponents of the new plan maintain that it would motivate the production managers to take better advantage of engineering talent. In all other respects, the new system would be unchanged from the present system.

1. Compare the present and proposed plans. What are their strong and weak points? In particular, will the ECD manager tend to hire the "optimal" amount of engineering talent?

2. Which plan do you favor? Why?

COLLABORATIVE LEARNING EXERCISE

10-51   Return on Investment

Form groups of three to six students. Each student should select a company. Coordinate the selection of companies so that each group has companies from a wide variety of industries. For example, a good mix of industries for a group of five students would be a retail company, a basic manufacturing company, a computer software company, a bank, and an electric utility.

1. Each student should find the latest annual report for his or her company. (The Internet is a good source. If you cannot find the company's home page, try http://sec.gov, and search the Security and Exchange Commission's Edgar files for the company's 10-K report, which will contain its financial statements.) Compute

   a. Income percentage of revenue (return on sales)
   b. Capital turnover
   c. Return on investment (ROI)

2. As a group, compare these performance measures for the chosen companies. Why do they differ across companies? What characteristic of the company and its industry might explain the differences in the measures?

INTERNET EXERCISE

10-52   Decentralization at Marriott International

Decentralization of an organization can occur for many reasons. It may be that the organization is involved in multiple activities that are not closely related to each other, such as construction and auto sales. In other cases the decision may be due to the structure of the firm's ownership and how it chooses to manage its image. Let's look at a firm that falls under this category—Marriott International.

www.prenhall.com/horngren

1. Log on to the Web site for Marriott International at http://www.marriott.com. What does the home page emphasize about Marriott's operations? What is the corporation's current focus according to the *spotlight*?

2. Look at the information bar provided on the left-hand side of the home page. What different types of links does it show? Do you believe that any of these links are likely to be treated as a decentralized operation? Why?

3. Can you identify any potential cost centers that the corporation might have? What might be classified as profit centers? Do you believe that any investment centers exist in the firm? Would decentralization be a positive or negative in managing these centers? Why?

4. Go to the most recent annual report by clicking on "Corporate Information" on the home page. Locate the information on business segments in the footnotes. How many segments does Marriott identify? What are these segments? What information does the firm report with respect to each of the different segments?

5. Both income and assets are provided for each of the segments. Calculate the ROI (return on investment) for the past 2 years for each of the segments.

6. What was the ROI for the corporation as a whole for each of the past two years? Given the different nature of the company's business segments, do you think that ROI would be a good measure for evaluating the individual segment? What factors might influence your answer?

11 CAPITAL BUDGETING

Skiers do not often realize the planning and investment that goes into preparing the slopes. Managers at Deer Valley Lodge, a ski resort in Utah's Wasatch Mountains and one of the hosts of the 2002 Winter Olympics, understand this fully. Much effort goes into their capital budgeting decisions—decisions that affect the fun, comfort, and safety of their guests.

www.prenhall.com/horngren

Learning Objectives

When you have finished studying this chapter, you should be able to

1. Describe capital budgeting decisions and use the net-present-value (NPV) method to make such decisions.

2. Evaluate projects using sensitivity analysis.

3. Calculate the NPV difference between two projects using both the total project and differential approaches.

4. Identify relevant cash flows for NPV analyses.

5. Compute the after-tax net present values of projects.

6. Explain the after-tax effect on cash of disposing of assets.

7. Compute the impact of inflation on a capital-budgeting project.

8. Use the payback model and the accounting rate-of-return model and compare them with the NPV model.

9. Reconcile the conflict between using an NPV model for making a decision and using accounting income for evaluating the related performance.

10. **Understand how companies make long-term capital investment decisions and how such decisions can affect the companies' financial results for years to come.**

Capital investment is probably the last thing you would think of while schussing down the snow-covered slopes of the Rockies—unless you happen to be the manager of a ski resort. A resort guest might see slopes, chairlifts, and a nice warm lodge, while a resort manager will see millions of dollars worth of investments.

Consider Deer Valley Lodge, a posh ski resort in the Wasatch Mountains of Utah. Deer Valley has a strong customer orientation—what Director of Finance Jim Madsen calls "the Deer Valley difference." From valets who help with skis to gourmet meals in the lodges, Deer Valley is a first-class resort. When facilities become too crowded, the resort limits sales of lift tickets to keep lift lines from getting too long. After crowding forced Deer Valley officials to close ticket sales offices early several times in 1994–1995, managers started thinking it was time to expand.

Deer Valley keeps a 10-year plan for capital expansion. Recent plans included five new lifts that will expand operations into neighboring Empire Canyon, a day lodge, and a new parking facility. By continually measuring crowding, using measures such as waiting time for lifts and length of lines at restaurants and cafeterias, Deer Valley managers decide when the next capital expansion phase is needed.

One capital expansion phase will be needed just before Deer Valley hosts the Olympic Winter Games in 2002. Deer Valley will feature slalom and freestyle skiing, with slalom competition on a ski run called Know You Don't, moguls on Champion, and aerial events on White Owl. Just as athletes hone their skills to compete in these events, Deer Valley managers must improve their facilities through additional capital investments.

CAPITAL BUDGETING FOR PROGRAMS OR PROJECTS

capital budgeting The long-term planning for making and financing investments that affect financial results over more than just the next year.

Ski resorts such as Deer Valley are not the only companies that face decisions about capital investment and expansion. At some time, every company needs to decide where and how to spend its money on major projects that will affect company financial results for years to come. This chapter concentrates on the planning and controlling decisions for programs or projects that affect financial results over more than just the next year. Such decisions require investments of large amounts of resources (capital) that are often called capital outlays. The term **capital budgeting** describes the long-term planning for making and financing such outlays.

Capital budgeting has three phases: (1) identifying potential investments, (2) choosing which investments to make (which includes gathering data to aid the decision), and (3) follow-up monitoring, or "postaudit," of the investments. Accountants usually are not involved in the first phase, but they play important roles in phases 2 and 3.

Why are accountants involved in capital budgeting decisions? They function primarily as information specialists. As you know, one of the purposes of a cost management system is to provide cost measurements for strategic decisions such as major capital-budgeting decisions.

Accountants will gather and interpret as much information as possible to help managers make such decisions. To help organize what could be pages and pages worth of information, accountants rely on capital-budgeting models. Let's take a look at how some of these models work.

DISCOUNTED-CASH-FLOW MODELS

discounted-cash-flow (DCF) models A type of capital-budgeting model that focuses on cash inflows and outflows while taking into account the time value of money.

The most widely used capital-budgeting models are **discounted-cash-flow (DCF) models.** These models focus on a project's cash inflows and outflows while taking into account time value of money. They are based on the old adage that a bird in the hand is worth two in the bush—that a dollar in the hand today is worth more than a dollar to be received (or spent) five years from today. This adage applies because the use of money has a cost (interest), just as the use of a building or an automobile may have a cost (rent). More than 85% of the large industrial firms in the United States use a DCF model.

MAJOR ASPECTS OF DCF

As the name suggests, DCF models focus on expected cash inflows and outflows rather than on net income. Companies invest cash today in order to receive cash in future periods. DCF models compare the value of today's *cash outflows* with the value of the future *cash inflows.*

DCF methods are based on the theory of compound interest which you should be familiar with from your course in financial accounting. For those of you whose knowledge of compound interest and time value of money is a little rusty, be sure to read Appendix B, pages B1–B8. Do not try to learn about the DCF methods until you are able to use Tables 1 (p. B7) and 2 (p. B8) in Appendix B.

To illustrate how DCF models work, we will use the following example throughout the rest of this section: A buildings and grounds manager at the University of Minnesota is contemplating the purchase of some lawn maintenance equipment that is expected to increase efficiency and produce cash-operating savings of $2,000 per year. The useful life of the equipment is four years, after which it will have a net disposal value of zero. The equipment will cost $6,075 now, and the minimum desired rate of return is 10% per year.

NET PRESENT VALUE (NPV)

We will focus on the most popular version of DCF, the **net-present-value (NPV) method.** The NPV method computes the present value of all expected future cash flows using a minimum desired rate of return. The minimum desired rate of return depends on the risk of a proposed project—the higher the risk, the higher the rate. Based on the cost of capital—what the firm pays to acquire more capital—this minimum rate is also called the **required rate of return, hurdle rate,** or **discount rate.** Using this required rate, managers determine the sum of the present values of all expected cash flows from the project. If this sum is positive, the project is desirable. If the sum is negative, the project is undesirable. Why? A positive NPV means that accepting the project will increase the value of the firm because the present value of the project's cash inflows exceeds the present value of its cash outflows. (An NPV of zero means that the present value of the inflows equals the present value of the outflows, and the project will exactly break even.) When choosing among several investments, managers should pick the one with the greatest net present value.

net-present-value (NPV) method A discounted-cash-flow approach to capital budgeting that computes the present value of all expected future cash flows using a minimum desired rate of return.

required rate of return (hurdle rate, discount rate) The minimum desired rate of return, based on the firm's cost of capital.

APPLYING THE NPV METHOD

To apply the NPV method, you can use the following three steps, which are shown in Exhibit 11-1.

1. *Prepare a diagram of relevant expected cash inflows and outflows:* The right-hand side of Exhibit 11-1 shows how these cash flows are sketched. Outflows are in parentheses. Be sure to include the outflow at time zero, the date of acquisition. You do not have to use a sketch, but sketches do help you to see costs and cost relationships.

2. *Find the present value of each expected cash inflow or outflow:* Examine Table 1 in Appendix B on page B7. Find the present-value (PV) factor for each year's cash flow from the correct row and column of the table. Multiply each expected cash inflow or outflow by the appropriate present-value factor. For example, the $2,000 cash savings that will occur two years hence is worth $2,000 × .8264 = $1,653 today.

3. *Sum the individual present values:* The sum is the project's NPV. Accept a project whose NPV is positive, and reject a project whose NPV is negative.

The value today (at time zero) of the four $2,000 cash inflows is $6,340. The manager pays only $6,075 to obtain these cash inflows. Thus, the net present value is $6,340 − $6,075 = $265, so the investment is desirable.

Exhibit 11-1

Net-Present-Value Method

Original investment, $6,075. Useful life, four years. Annual cash inflow from operations, $2,000. Minimum desired rate of return, 10%. Cash outflows are in parentheses; cash inflows are not. Total present values are rounded to the nearest dollar.

	Present Value of $1, Discounted at 10%	Total Present Value	Sketch of Cash Flows at End of Year				
			0	1	2	3	4

Approach 1: Discounting Each Year's Cash Inflow Separately*

Cash flows							
Annual savings	.9091	$1,818		$2,000			
	.8264	1,653			$2,000		
	.7513	1,503				$2,000	
	.6830	1,366					$2,000
Present value of future inflows		$6,340					
Initial outlay	1.0000	(6,075)	$(6,075)				
Net present value		$ 265					

Approach 2: Using Annuity Table†

Annual savings	3.1699	$6,340		$2,000	$2,000	$2,000	$2,000
Initial outlay	1.0000	(6,075)	$(6,075)				
Net present value		$ 265					

*Present values from Table 1, Appendix B, page B7.
†Present values of annuity from Table 2, Appendix B, page B8. (Incidentally, calculators or computers may give slightly different answers than tables because of rounding differences.)

438

CHOICE OF THE CORRECT TABLE

Exhibit 11-1 also shows another way to calculate the NPV, shown here as approach 2. The basic steps are the same as for approach 1. The only difference is that approach 2 uses Table 2 in Appendix B (see page B8) instead of Table 1. Table 2 is an annuity table that provides a shortcut to reduce hand calculations. It gives discount factors for computing the present value of a *series* of equal cash flows at equal intervals. Because the four cash flows in our example are all equal, you can use Table 2 to make one present-value computation instead of using Table 1 to make four individual computations. Table 2 merely sums up the pertinent present-value factors of Table 1. Therefore the annuity factor for four years at 10% is[1]

$$.9091 + .8264 + .7513 + .6830 = 3.1698$$

Beware of using the wrong table. You should use Table 1 for discounting individual amounts, Table 2 for a series of equal amounts. Of course, Table 1 is the basis for Table 2, and it can be used for all present-value calculations.

You can avoid Tables 1 and 2 entirely by using the present-value function on a hand-held calculator or the present-value function on a computer spreadsheet program. However, we encourage you to use the tables when learning the NPV method. Using the tables will let you better understand the process of present-value computation. Once you are comfortable with the method, you can take advantage of the speed and convenience of calculators and computers.

To confirm your understanding of Tables 1 and 2, compute the following using a discount rate of 8%.

1. Present value of $1,000 to be received in 5 years.
2. Present value of $1,000 to be received at the end of each year for 5 years.
3. Present value of $1,000 to be received at the end of years 3, 4, and 5.

ANSWERS
The solution to 1 requires the factor from row 5, 8% column of Table 1:
$1,000 × .6806 = $680.60.
The solution to 2 requires the factor from row 5, 8% column of Table 2:
$1,000 × 3.9927 = $3,9927.00.
The solution to 3 can be done in several ways. Two of them are
Use only Table 2: $1,000 × (3.9927 − 1.7833) = $2,209.40
Use Tables 1 and 2: $1,000 × 2.5771 × .8573 = $2,209.35
These two solutions differ by a $.05 rounding error.

EFFECT OF MINIMUM RATE

The minimum desired rate of return can have a large effect on NPVs. The higher the minimum desired rate of return, the lower the present value of each future cash inflow. Why? Because the higher the rate of return, the more it costs you to wait for the cash rather than having it available to invest today. Thus, higher required rates lead to lower project NPVs. For example, at a rate of 16%, the NPV of the project in Exhibit 11-1 would be −$479 (that is, $2,000 × 2.7982 = $5,596, which is $479 less than the required investment

---

[1] *Rounding error causes a .0001 difference between the Table 2 factor and the summation of Table 1 factors.*

of $6,075), instead of the +$265 computed with a 10% rate. (Present-value factor 2.7982 is taken from Table 2 in Appendix B on page B8.) When the desired rate of return is 16% rather than 10%, the project is undesirable at a price of $6,075.

ASSUMPTIONS OF THE NPV MODEL

We have to make two major assumptions to use the NPV model. First, we assume a world of certainty. That is, we act as if the predicted cash inflows and outflows are certain to occur at the times specified. Second, we assume perfect capital markets. That is, if we need to have extra cash at any time, we can borrow or lend money at the same interest rate. This rate is our minimum desired rate of return. If these assumptions are met, no model could possibly be better than the NPV model.

Unfortunately, the real world has neither certainty nor perfect capital markets. Nevertheless, the NPV model is usually preferred to other models because the assumptions of most other models are even less realistic. The NPV model is not perfect, but it generally meets our cost-benefit criterion. That is, the benefit of better decisions based on NPV is greater than the cost of applying it. More sophisticated models often do not improve decisions enough to be worth their cost.

DEPRECIATION AND NPV

NPV calculations do not include deductions for depreciation. Why not? Because NPV is based on inflows and outflows of cash and not on the accounting concepts of revenues and expenses.[2] Depreciation is not a cash flow. It is a way of allocating the cost of a long-lived asset (which was usually paid for in cash upon purchase) to different periods. Because the cash outflow for the cost of the asset has already been recorded and accounted for, deducting depreciation from future cash flows would be like counting this cost twice—once at purchase and again over the asset's life.

REVIEW OF DECISION RULES

Be sure that you understand why the NPV method works, not just how to apply it. The decision maker in our example cannot directly compare an immediate outflow of $6,075 with a series of future inflows of $2,000 each because of the time value of money. The NPV model aids comparison by expressing all amounts in today's monetary units (such as dollars, francs, marks, or yen) at time zero. The required rate of return measures the cost of using money. At a rate of 12%, the comparison would be

Outflow in today's dollars	$(6,075)
Inflow equivalent in today's dollars @ 12%	6,075
Net present value	$ 0

Therefore, at a required rate of return of 12%, the decision maker is indifferent between having $6,075 now or having a stream of four annual inflows of $2,000 each. If

[2] *Throughout this chapter, our examples often assume that cash inflows are equivalent to revenues and that cash outflows are equivalent to expenses (except for depreciation). Of course, if the revenues and expenses are accounted for on the accrual basis of accounting, there will be leads and lags of cash inflows and cash outflows that a precise DCF model must recognize. For example, a $10,000 sale on credit may be recorded as revenue in one period, but the related cash inflow would not be recognized in a DCF model until collected, which may be in a second period. Such refinements are not made in this chapter.*

the interest rate were 16%, the decision maker would find the project unattractive because the net present value would be a negative $479, as shown in the following graph.

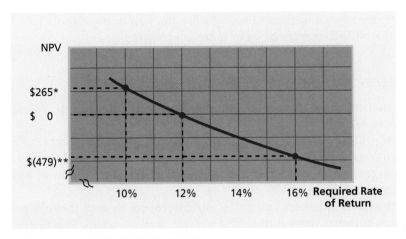

*($2,000 × 3.1699) − $6,075 = $265
**($2,000 × 2.7982) − $6,075 = $(479)

At 10%, the NPV is a positive $265, so the project is desirable. At all rates below 12%, the NPV is positive. At all rates above 12%, the NPV is negative.

SENSITIVITY ANALYSIS AND RISK ASSESSMENT IN DCF MODELS

Because the future is uncertain, actual cash inflows may differ from what was expected or predicted. To examine this uncertainty, managers often use sensitivity analysis, which shows the financial consequences that would occur if actual cash inflows and outflows differ from those expected. It can answer such what-if? questions as: What will happen to my NPV if my predictions of useful life or cash flows change? The best way to understand sensitivity analysis is to see it in action, so let's take a look at an example.

Suppose that a manager knows that the actual cash inflows in Exhibit 11-1 could fall below the predicted level of $2,000. How far below $2,000 must the annual cash inflow drop before the NPV becomes negative? The cash inflow at the point where NPV = 0 is the "break-even" cash flow:

$$NPV = 0$$
$$(3.1699 \times \text{cash flow}) - \$6,075 = 0$$
$$\text{cash flow} = \$6,075 \div 3.1699$$
$$= \$1,916$$

If the annual cash inflow is less than $1,916, the NPV is negative, and the project should be rejected. Therefore annual cash inflows can drop only $2,000 − $1,916 = $84, or 4.2%, before the manager would change the decision.

Managers like sensitivity analysis because it can give them immediate answers about possible future events. It also shows managers how risky a given project might be by showing how sensitive the decision is to changes in predictions. The more sensitive to change a project is (the more NPV changes as cash flows change), the riskier it is. Of course, sensitivity analysis can become complicated very quickly, and doing all of the calculations by hand can be tricky and tedious. Fortunately, there is a good deal of sensitivity analysis software available that lets managers and accountants sit back while computers do all the work.

THE NPV COMPARISON OF TWO PROJECTS

So far we have seen how to use the NPV method to evaluate a single given project. In practice, managers very rarely look at one project or option at a time. Instead, managers need to compare several options to see which is the best or most profitable. We will now see how to use NPV to compare two or more alternatives.

TOTAL PROJECT VERSUS DIFFERENTIAL APPROACH

total project approach A method for comparing alternatives that computes the total impact on cash flows for each alternative and then converts these total cash flows to their present values.

differential approach A method for comparing alternatives that computes the differences in cash flows between alternatives and then converts these differences in cash flows to their present values.

Two common methods for comparing alternatives are (1) the total project approach and (2) the differential approach.

The **total project approach** computes the total impact on cash flows for each alternative and then converts these total cash flows to their present values. It is the most popular approach and can be used for any number of alternatives. The alternative with the largest NPV of total cash flows is best.

The **differential approach** computes the differences in cash flows between alternatives and then converts these differences to their present values. This method cannot be used to compare more than two alternatives. Often the two alternatives being compared are (1) take on a project and (2) do nothing.

Let's compare the differential and total project approaches. Suppose a company owns a packaging machine that it purchased three years ago for $56,000. The machine has a remaining useful life of five years but will require a major overhaul at the end of two more years at a cost of $10,000. Its disposal value now is $20,000. Its predicted disposal value in five years is $8,000, assuming that the $10,000 major overhaul will be done on schedule. The predicted cash-operating costs of this machine are $40,000 annually. A sales representative has offered a substitute machine for $51,000, or for $31,000 plus the old machine. The new machine will reduce annual cash-operating costs by $10,000, will not require any overhauls, will have a useful life of five years, and will have a disposal value of $3,000. If the minimum desired rate of return is 14%, what should the company do to minimize long-run costs? (Try to solve this problem yourself before examining the solution that follows.)

Regardless of the approach used, perhaps the hardest part of making capital-budgeting decisions is predicting the relevant cash flows. Seeing which events will cause money to flow either in or out can be very tricky, especially when there are many sources of cash flows. However, you cannot compare alternatives if you do not know their costs, so the first step for either the total project or differential approach is to arrange the relevant cash flows by project. Exhibit 11-2 shows how the cash flows for each alternative are sketched. The next step depends on the approach used.

Total Project Approach: Determine the net present value of the cash flows for each individual project. Choose the project with the largest positive net present value (i.e., the largest benefit) or smallest negative net present value (i.e., the smallest cost).

Differential Approach: Compute the differential cash flows. In other words, subtract the cash flows for project B from the cash flows for project A for each year. Remember that cash inflows are positive numbers, while cash outflows are negative. Next, calculate the present value of the differential cash flows. If this present value is positive, choose project A; if it is negative, choose project B.

Exhibit 11-2 illustrates both the total project approach and the differential approach. Note that both methods produce the same answer. As a result, these methods can be used interchangeably, as long as there are only two alternatives under consideration. Because our example had only two alternatives, we could use either method. If our example had more than two alternatives, our only choice would be to use the total project approach.

Exhibit 11-2
Total Project versus Differential Approach to Net Present Value

	Present Value Discount Factor, at 14%	Total Present Value	Sketch of After-Tax Cash Flows at End of Year 0	1	2	3	4	5
I. Total Project Approach								
A. Replace								
Recurring cash operating costs, using an annuity table*	3.4331	$ (102,993)		($30,000)	($30,000)	($30,000)	($30,000)	($30,000)
Disposal value, end of year 5	.5194	1,558						$3,000
Initial required investment	1.0000	(31,000)	($31,000)					
Present value of net cash outflows		$ (132,435)						
B. Keep								
Recurring cash operating costs, using an annuity table*	3.4331	$ (137,324)		($40,000)	($40,000)	($40,000)	($40,000)	($40,000)
Overhaul, end of year 2	.7695	(7,695)			$(10,000)			
Disposal value, end of year 5	.5194	4,155						$8,000
Present value of net cash outflows		$ (140,864)						
Difference in favor of replacement		$ 8,429						
II. Differential Approach								
A – B. Analysis confined to differences								
Recurring cash operating savings, using an annuity table*	3.4331	$ 34,331		$10,000	$10,000	$10,000	$10,000	$10,000
Overhaul avoided, end of year 2	.7695	7,695			$10,000			
Difference in disposal values, end of year 5	.5194	(2,597)						$(5,000)
Incremental initial investment	1.0000	(31,000)	($31,000)					
Net present value of replacement		$ 8,429						

*Table 2, Appendix B.

RELEVANT CASH FLOWS FOR NPV

Objective 4
Identify relevant cash flows for NPV analyses.

As we said earlier, predicting cash flows is the hardest part of capital budgeting. When you array the relevant cash flows, be sure to consider four types of inflows and outflows: (1) initial cash inflows and outflows at time zero, (2) investments in receivables and inventories, (3) future disposal values, and (4) operating cash flows.

Initial Cash Inflows and Outflows at Time Zero. These cash flows include both outflows for the purchases and installation of equipment and other items required by the new project, and either inflows or outflows from disposal of any items that are replaced. In Exhibit 11-2 the $20,000 received from selling the old machine was offset against the $51,000 purchase price of the new machine, resulting in a net cash outflow of $31,000. If the old machine could not be sold, any cost incurred to dismantle and discard it would have been added to the purchase price of the new machine.

Investments in Receivables and Inventories. Investments in receivables and inventories are initial cash outflows just like investments in plant and equipment. In the NPV model, the initial outlays are entered in the sketch of cash flows at time zero. However, receivables and inventories usually differ from plant and equipment at the end of the useful life of the project. Investment in plant and equipment is usually used up during the life of the project, leaving little, if any, salvage value. In contrast, the entire original investments in receivables and inventories are usually recouped when the project ends. Therefore all initial investments are typically regarded as outflows at time zero, and their terminal disposal values, if any, are regarded as inflows at the end of the project's useful life.

The example in Exhibit 11-2 required no additional investment in inventory or receivables. However, the expansion of a retail store, for example, entails an additional investment in a building and fixtures plus inventories. Such investments would be shown in the format of Exhibit 11-2 as follows:

	Sketch of Cash Flows			
End of year	0	1	2 . . . 19	20
Investment in building and fixtures	(10)			1
Investment in working capital (inventories)	(6)			6

As the table shows, the residual value of the building and fixtures might be small. However, the entire investment in inventories would ordinarily be recouped when the company terminates the venture.

The difference between the initial outlay for working capital (mostly receivables and inventories) and the present value of its recovery is the present value of the cost of using working capital in the project.

Future Disposal Values. Assets other than receivables and inventories may have relevant disposal values. The disposal value at the end of a project is an increase in the cash inflow in the year of disposal. Errors in forecasting terminal disposal values are usually not crucial because the present value is usually small.

Operating Cash Flows. The major purpose of most investments is to affect operating cash inflows and outflows. Many of these effects are difficult to measure, and three points deserve special mention.

First, using relevant-cost analysis, the only relevant cash flows are those that will differ among alternatives. Often fixed overhead will be the same under all the available alternatives. If so, it can be safely ignored. In practice, it is not easy to identify exactly which costs will differ among alternatives.

Recent surveys have shown that nearly all large companies use discounted-cash-flow (DCF) methods for their capital-budgeting decisions. This is true in most of the developed countries in the world, not just the United States. But even as DCF is becoming dominant, it is being criticized by some for leading to overly cautious investment decisions in information technology (IT). The critics maintain that the benefits of IT investments are difficult to quantify and such investments lead to unforeseen opportunities. By ignoring some of the potential benefits and opportunities, companies pass up desirable IT investments.

Recently, two ways to rectify this situation have been suggested. Both use the basic tenets of DCF analysis but add degrees of sophistication to help identify and value all the benefits of IT investments: (1) use of activity-based costing (ABC) to better define and quantify the benefits of IT investments and (2) use of options pricing models to recognize the value of future options that result from IT investments.

Using ABC to better assess the benefits of an IT investment is simply a refinement in how to measure the cash flows for a DCF model. Scott Gamster of Grant Thornton's Performance Management Practice suggests that capital budgeting analyses of IT investments often look primarily at the direct costs and benefits and ignore many of the savings in indirect costs. Because an ABC system focuses on indirect costs, it can help identify other cost impacts of new IT systems. The attention to activities lets managers better assess the various impacts on a new IT system. For example, an enterprise resource planning (ERP) system will transform much of the work in many of a company's activities. Examining each activity in light of the potential implementation of an ERP will help managers assess the full impact of the new system.

The other suggestion is to use options pricing theory for valuing IT investments. This is a refinement of DCF, not an alternative to it. It was applied to the decision on timing of the deployment of point-of-sale-debit services by the Yankee 24 shared electronic banking network in New England. It explicitly recognizes the future opportunities created by a current investment decision, and it uses the complete range of possible outcomes to determine a potential investment's value. It is not our purpose to describe options pricing models; we leave that to the finance textbooks. However, the essence of the models is the impact of the possible future options on the value of a current investment decision. For example, investment today may eliminate the option of making a similar investment in six months when more information is available. Or investment today may create an infrastructure that will allow additional investments in the future that would not be otherwise possible. Limiting or expanding future options by today's investment decision can certainly affect the desirability of the investment.

Criticisms of DCF models for IT investments should lead to refinements of DCF, not rejection of it. Of course, if refinements are not used, managers must use judgment regarding subjective impacts of the investment that are not measured in the DCF analysis.

Sources: Adapted from S. Gamster, "Using Activity Based Management to Justify ERP Implementations," *Journal of Cost Management,* September/October 1999, pp. 24–33; M. Benaroch and R. J. Kauffman, "A Case for Using Real Options Pricing Analysis to Evaluate Information Technology Project Investments," *Information Systems Research,* March 1999, pp. 70–76; and G. C. Arnold and P. D. Aatzopoulos, "The Theory-Practice Gap in Capital Budgeting: Evidence from the United Kingdom," *Journal of Business Finance and Accounting,* June/July 2000, pp. 603–626.

Second, as mentioned earlier, depreciation and book values should be ignored. The cost of assets is recognized by the initial outlay, not by depreciation as computed under accrual accounting.

Third, a reduction in a cash outflow is treated the same as a cash inflow. Both signify increases in value.

CASH FLOWS FOR INVESTMENTS IN TECHNOLOGY

Many capital-budgeting decisions compare undertaking a possible investment with doing nothing. One such decision is investment in a highly automated production system to replace a traditional system. Cash flows predicted for the automated system should be compared with those predicted for continuation of the present system into the future. The latter are not necessarily the cash flows currently being experienced. Why? Because the competitive environment is changing. If others invest in automated systems, failure to invest may cause a decline in sales and an uncompetitive cost structure. The future without an automated system might be a continual decline in cash flows.

Suppose a company has a $10,000 net cash inflow this year using a traditional system. Investing in an automated system will increase the net cash inflow to $12,000. Failure to invest will cause net cash inflows to fall to $8,000. The benefit from the investment is a cash inflow of $12,000 − $8,000 = $4,000, not $12,000 − $10,000 = $2,000.

SUMMARY PROBLEM FOR YOUR REVIEW

PROBLEM

Review the problem and solution shown in Exhibit 11-2, page 443. Conduct a sensitivity analysis as indicated below. Consider each requirement as independent of other requirements.

1. Compute the NPV if the minimum desired rate of return were 20%.
2. Compute the NPV if predicted cash operating costs were $35,000 instead of $30,000, using the 14% discount rate.
3. By how much may the cash operating savings fall short of the $30,000 predicted before the NPV of the project reaches zero, using the original discount rate of 14%?

SOLUTION

1. Either the total project approach or the differential approach could be used. The differential approach would show:

	Total Present Value
Recurring cash operating savings, using an annuity table (Table 2, p. B8): 2.9906 × $10,000 =	$29,906
Overhaul avoided: .6944 × $10,000 =	6,944
Difference in disposal values: .4019 × $5,000 =	(2,010)
Incremental initial investment	(31,000)
NPV of replacement	$ 3,840

2.

NPV value in Exhibit 11-2	$ 8,429
Present value of additional $5,000 annual operating costs 3.4331 × $5,000	(17,166)
New NPV	$(8,737)

With $5,000 less in annual savings, the new machine has a negative NPV and therefore is not desirable.

3. Le X = annual cash operating savings and find the value of X that NPV = 0. Then

$$0 = 3.4331(X) + \$7,695 - \$2,597 - \$31,000$$
$$3.4331X = \$25,902$$
$$X = \$7,545$$

(Note that the $7,695, $2,597, and $31,000 are at the bottom of Exhibit 11-2.)

If the annual savings fall from $10,000 to $7,545, a decrease of $2,455 or almost 25%, the NPV will hit zero.

An alternative way to obtain the same answer would be to divide the NPV of $8,429 (see bottom of Exhibit 11-2) by 3.4331, obtaining $2,455, the amount of the annual difference in savings that will eliminate the $8,429 of NPV.

INCOME TAXES AND CAPITAL BUDGETING

We must consider another type of cash flow when making capital-budgeting decisions: income taxes. Income taxes paid by companies are cash outflows. Their basic role in capital budgeting does not differ from that of any other cash outflow. However taxes tend to narrow the cash differences between projects. For example, if the cash savings from operations of one project over another were $1 million, a 40% tax rate would shrink the savings to $600,000. Why? Because $400,000 (40% × $1 million) of the savings would have to be paid in taxes.

Corporations in the United States must pay both federal income taxes and state income taxes. Federal taxes are based on income, with tax rates rising as income rises. The current federal tax rate on ordinary corporate taxable income below $50,000 is 15%. Rates then increase until companies with taxable income over $335,000 pay between 34% and 38% on additional income. State tax rates vary widely from state to state. Therefore, the total tax rate a company has to pay, federal rates plus state rates, also varies widely.

In capital budgeting, the relevant tax rate is the **marginal income tax rate,** that is, the tax rate paid on additional amounts of pretax income. Suppose a corporation pays income taxes of 15% on the first $50,000 of pretax income and 30% on pretax income over $50,000. What is the company's *marginal income tax rate* when it has $75,000 of pretax income? The marginal rate is 30%, because the company will pay 30% of any additional income in taxes. In contrast, the company's *average income tax rate* is only 20% (i.e., 15% × $50,000 + 30% × $25,000 = $15,000 of taxes on $75,000 of pretax income). When we assess tax effects of capital-budgeting decisions, we will always use the marginal tax rate because that is the rate applied to the additional cash flows generated by a proposed project.

EFFECTS OF DEPRECIATION DEDUCTIONS

Organizations that pay income taxes generally keep two sets of books—one for reporting to the public and one for reporting to the tax authorities. In the United States, this practice is not illegal or immoral—in fact, it is necessary. Tax reporting must follow detailed rules designed to achieve certain social goals. These rules do not usually lead to financial statements that best measure an organization's financial results and position, so it is more informative to financial statement users if a separate set of rules is used for financial reporting. In this chapter, we are concerned with measuring cash payments for taxes. Therefore we focus on the tax reporting rules, not those for public financial reporting.

One item that often differs between tax reporting and public reporting is depreciation. Recall that depreciation spreads the cost of an asset over its useful life. Income tax laws and regulations generally permit the cost to be spread over depreciable lives that are shorter than the assets' useful lives. In addition, U.S. tax authorities allow **accelerated depreciation,** which charges a larger proportion of an asset's cost to the earlier years and less to later years. In contrast, an asset's depreciation for public reporting purposes is usually the same each year, called straight-line depreciation. For example, a $10,000 asset depreciated over a 5-year useful life would result in *straight-line depreciation* of $10,000 ÷ 5 = $2,000 each year but *accelerated depreciation* of more than $2,000 per year in the early years and less than $2,000 in the later years.

Exhibit 11-3 shows the interrelationship of income before taxes, income taxes, and depreciation for Martin's Printing. Assume that the company has a single fixed asset, a

Objective 5
Compute the after-tax net present values of projects.

marginal income tax rate
The tax rate paid on additional amounts of pretax income.

accelerated depreciation
A pattern of depreciation that charges a larger proportion of an asset's cost to the earlier years and less to later years.

Exhibit 11-3

Martin's Printing

Basic Analysis of Income Statement, Income Taxes, and Cash Flows

	Traditional Annual Income Statement	
(S)	Sales	$130,000
(E)	Less: Expenses, excluding depreciation	$ 70,000
(D)	Depreciation (straight-line)	25,000
	Total expenses	$ 95,000
	Income before taxes	$ 35,000
(T)	Income taxes @ 40%	14,000
(I)	Net income	$ 21,000
	Total after-tax effect on cash is	
	either S − E − T = $130,000 − $70,000 − $14,000 = $46,000	
	or I + D = $21,000 + $25,000 = $46,000	

	Analysis of the Same Facts for Capital Budgeting	
	Cash effects of operations:	
(S − E)	Cash inflow from operations: $130,000 − $70,000	$ 60,000
	Income tax outflow @ 40%	24,000
	After-tax inflow from operations	
	(excluding depreciation)	$ 36,000
	Cash effects of depreciation:	
(D)	Straight-line depreciation:	
	$125,000 ÷ 5 = $25,000	
	Income tax savings @ 40%	10,000
	Total after-tax effect on cash	$ 46,000

recovery period The number of years over which an asset is depreciated for tax purposes.

printing press, that it purchased for $125,000 cash. The press has a 5-year **recovery period,** which is the number of years over which an asset is depreciated for tax purposes. Using the press produces annual sales revenue of $130,000 and expenses (excluding depreciation) of $70,000. The purchase cost of the press is tax deductible in the form of yearly depreciation.

Depreciating a fixed asset such as the press creates future tax deductions. In this case, these deductions will total the full purchase price of $125,000. The present value of this deduction depends directly on its specific yearly effects on future income tax payments. Therefore the recovery period, the depreciation method selected, the tax rates, and the discount rate all affect the present value.

Exhibit 11-4 analyzes the Martin's Printing data for capital budgeting, assuming that the company uses straight-line depreciation for tax purposes. The net present value is $40,821 for the investment in this asset.

The $125,000 investment really buys two streams of cash: (1) net inflows from operations plus (2) savings of income tax outflows (which have the same effect in capital budgeting as do additions to cash inflows) because the company can deduct depreciation in computing taxable income. The choice of depreciation method will not affect the cash inflows from operations. But different depreciation methods will affect the cash outflows for income taxes. That is, a straight-line method will produce one present value of tax savings, and an accelerated method will produce a different present value.

Tax Deductions, Cash Effects, and Timing

Note that the net cash effects of operations in Exhibit 11-4 are computed by multiplying the pretax amounts by one minus the tax rate, or 1 − .40 = .60. The total effect is the cash

Exhibit 11-4

Impact of Income Taxes on Capital-Budgeting Analysis

Assume: original cost of equipment, $125,000; 5-year life; zero terminal disposal value; pretax annual cash inflow from operations, $60,000; income tax rate, 40%; required after-tax rate of return, 12%. All items are in dollars except discount factors. The after-tax cash flows are from Exhibit 11-3.

	12% Discount Factors, from Appropriate Tables	Total Present Value at 12%	Sketch of After-Tax Cash Flows at End of Year					
			0	1	2	3	4	5
Cash effects of operations, excluding depreciation, $60,000 × (1 − .4)	3.6048	$129,773		36,000	36,000	36,000	36,000	36,000
Cash effects of straight-line depreciation: savings of income taxes, $25,000 × .4	3.6048	36,048		10,000	10,000	10,000	10,000	10,000
Total after-tax effect on cash		165,821						
Investment	1.0000	(125,000)	(125,000)					
Net present value of the investment		$ 40,821						

449

flow itself less the tax effect. Each additional $1 of sales also adds $.40 of taxes, leaving a net cash inflow of $.60. Each additional $1 of cash expense reduces taxes by $.40, leaving a net cash outflow of $.60. Thus, the after-tax effect of the $130,000 − $70,000 = $60,000 net cash inflow from operations is $130,000 × .6 − $70,000 × .6 = ($130,000 − $70,000) × .6 = $60,000 × .6 = $36,000.

In contrast, the after-tax effects of the *noncash* expenses (depreciation) are computed by multiplying the tax deduction of $25,000 by the tax rate itself, or $25,000 × .40 = $10,000. Note that this is a cash inflow because it is a decrease in the tax payment. The total cash effect of a noncash expense is only the tax-savings effect.

Throughout the illustrations in this chapter, we assume that all income tax flows occur at the same time as the related pretax cash flows. For example, we assume that both the net $60,000 pretax cash inflow and the related $24,000 tax payment occurred in year 1 and that no part of the tax payment was delayed until year 2. We also assume that the companies in question are profitable. That is, the companies will have enough taxable income from all sources to use all income tax benefits in the situations described.

ACCELERATED DEPRECIATION

Governments frequently allow accelerated depreciation to encourage investments in long-lived assets. To see why accelerated depreciation is attractive to investors, reconsider the facts in Exhibit 11-4. Suppose, as is the case in some countries, that the entire initial investment can be written off immediately for income tax reporting. We see that net present value will rise from $40,821 to $54,773.

	Present Values	
	As in Exhibit 11-4	*Complete Write-Off Immediately*
Cash effects of operations	$129,773	$ 129,773
Cash effects of depreciation	36,048	50,000*
Total after-tax effect on cash	165,821	179,773
Investment	(125,000)	(125,000)
Net present value	$ 40,821	$ 54,773

*Assumes that the tax effect occurs simultaneously with the investment at time zero: $125,000 × .40 = $50,000.

In summary, the earlier you can take the depreciation, the greater the present value of the income tax savings. The total tax savings will be the same regardless of the depreciation method. In the example, the tax savings from the depreciation deduction is either .40 × $125,000 = $50,000 immediately or .40 × $25,000 = $10,000 per year for five years, a total of $50,000. However, the time value of money makes the immediate savings worth more than future savings. The mottoes in income tax planning are "When there is a legal choice, take the deduction sooner rather than later," and "Recognize taxable income later rather than sooner."

Managers have an obligation to stockholders to minimize and delay taxes to the extent permitted by law. For example, astute managers use accelerated depreciation instead of straight-line depreciation whenever the law permits its use. This is called tax avoidance. Careful tax planning can have large financial payoffs. In contrast, managers must not engage in tax evasion, which is illegally reducing taxes by recording fictitious deductions or failing to report income. Managers who *avoid* taxes get bonuses; those who *evade* taxes often land in jail.

Exhibit 11-5

Examples of Assets in Modified Accelerated Cost Recovery System (MACRS) Classes

3-year	Special tools for several specific industries; tractor units for over-the-road.
5-year	Automobiles; trucks; research equipment; computers; machinery and equipment in selected industries.
7-year	Office furniture; railroad tracks; machinery and equipment in a majority of industries.
10-year	Water transportation equipment; machinery and equipment in selected industries.
15-year	Most land improvements; machinery and equipment in selected industries.
20-year	Farm buildings; electricity generation and distribution equipment.
27.5-year	Residential rental property.
31.5-year	Nonresidential real property.

Modified Accelerated Cost Recovery System (MACRS)

Under U.S. income tax laws, companies depreciate most assets using the Modified Accelerated Cost Recovery System (MACRS). This system specifies a recovery period and an accelerated depreciation schedule for all types of assets. Each asset is placed in one of the eight classes shown in Exhibit 11-5.

Exhibit 11-6 presents MACRS depreciation schedules for recovery periods of 3, 5, 7, and 10 years. Note that each schedule extends one year beyond the recovery period because MACRS assumes one half-year of depreciation in the first year and one half-year in the final year. Thus, a 3-year MACRS depreciation schedule has one half-year of depreciation in years 1 and 4 and a full year of depreciation in years 2 and 3. We can apply MACRS depreciation to the example in Exhibit 11-4 as follows, assuming that the printing press that was purchased is a 5-year MACRS asset.

Year	Tax Rate (1)	PV Factor @12% (2)	Depreciation (3)	Present Value of Tax Savings (1) × (2) × (3)
1	.40	0.8929	$125,000 × .2000 = $25,000	$ 8,929
2	.40	0.7972	125,000 × .3200 = 40,000	12,755
3	.40	0.7118	125,000 × .1920 = 24,000	6,833
4	.40	0.6355	125,000 × .1152 = 14,400	3,660
5	.40	0.5674	125,000 × .1152 = 14,400	3,268
6	.40	0.5066	125,000 × .0576 = 7,200	1,459
				$36,904

How much did Martin's Printing gain by using MACRS instead of straight-line depreciation? The $36,904 present value of tax savings is $856 higher with MACRS than the $36,048 achieved with straight-line depreciation (see Exhibit 11-4 on p. 449).

Present Value of MACRS Depreciation

In capital-budgeting decisions managers often want to know the present value of the tax savings from depreciation. Exhibit 11-7 provides present values for $1 to be depreciated over MACRS schedules for 3-, 5-, 7-, and 10-year recovery periods for a variety of interest

Exhibit 11-6
Selected MACRS Depreciation Schedules

Tax Year	3-Year Property	5-Year Property	7-Year Property	10-Year Property
1	33.33%	20.00%	14.29%	10.00%
2	44.45	32.00	24.49	18.00
3	14.81	19.20	17.49	14.40
4	7.41	11.52	12.49	11.52
5		11.52	8.93	9.22
6		5.76	8.92	7.37
7			8.93	6.55
8			4.46	6.55
9				6.56
10				6.55
11				3.28

rates. For example, consider a company with a 3-year asset and 10% minimum desired rate of return. The present value of $1 of MACRS depreciation is:

Year	Depreciation* (1)	PV Factor @10% (2)	PV of Depreciation (1) × (2)
1	$0.3333	0.9091	$0.3030
2	0.4445	0.8264	0.3673
3	0.1481	0.7513	0.1113
4	0.0741	0.6830	0.0506
Total Depreciation	1.0000		
Present Value of $1 depreciation, shown in Exhibit 11-7			$0.8322

*From the 3-Year Property column of Exhibit 11-6.

Exhibit 11-7
Present Value of $1 of MACRS Depreciation

Discount Rate	3-year	5-year	7-year	10-year
3%	0.9439	0.9215	0.9002	0.8698
4%	0.9264	0.8975	0.8704	0.8324
5%	0.9095	0.8746	0.8422	0.7975
6%	0.8931	0.8526	0.8155	0.7649
7%	0.8772	0.8315	0.7902	0.7344
8%	0.8617	0.8113	0.7661	0.7059
9%	0.8468	0.7919	0.7432	0.6792
10%	0.8322	0.7733	0.7214	0.6541
12%	0.8044	0.7381	0.6810	0.6084
14%	0.7782	0.7055	0.6441	0.5678
15%	0.7657	0.6902	0.6270	0.5492
16%	0.7535	0.6753	0.6106	0.5317
18%	0.7300	0.6473	0.5798	0.4993
20%	0.7079	0.6211	0.5517	0.4702
22%	0.6868	0.5968	0.5257	0.4439
24%	0.6669	0.5740	0.5019	0.4201
25%	0.6573	0.5631	0.4906	0.4090
26%	0.6479	0.5526	0.4798	0.3985
28%	0.6299	0.5327	0.4594	0.3787
30%	0.6128	0.5139	0.4404	0.3606
40%	0.5381	0.4352	0.3632	0.2896

You can find the present value of tax savings in three steps:

1. Find the factor from Exhibit 11-7 for the appropriate recovery period and required rate of return.
2. Multiply the factor by the tax rate to find the tax savings per dollar of investment.
3. Multiply the result by the amount of the investment to find the total tax savings.

Consider our investment of $125,000 in equipment with a 5-year MACRS recovery period. A 12% after-tax required rate of return and a 40% tax rate produce a tax savings with a present value of .7381 × .40 × $125,000 = $36,905. This differs from the $36,904 calculated earlier by a $1 rounding error.

Why do managers like accelerated depreciation for tax purposes? Consider an investment of $100,000 in an asset with a 10-year economic life and a 10-year MACRS recovery period. The asset has no salvage value at the end of ten years. The tax rate is 40%, and the required rate of return is 10%. What is the present value of the depreciation tax savings using straight-line depreciation? What is the present value of the depreciation tax savings using MACRS depreciation? Which depreciation method is most beneficial to the company?

ANSWERS

Straight-line depreciation = $10,000 per year, so tax savings is .40 × $10,000 = $4,000 per year. Thus, the present value of the tax savings is $4,000 × 6.1446 = $24,578.40.

The present value of MACRS depreciation is .6541 × .40 × $100,000 = $26,164.00. Although the total tax savings is $40,000 regardless of the depreciation method, the MACRS accelerated depreciation schedule creates a greater present value by $26,164.00 − $24,578.40 = $1,585.60.

GAINS OR LOSSES ON DISPOSAL

The disposal of equipment for cash can also affect income taxes. Suppose Martin's Printing sells its $125,000 press at the end of year 3 after taking three years of straight-line depreciation. If Martin's Printing sells it for its book value, $125,000 − (3 × $25,000) = $50,000, there is no tax effect. If Martin's Printing receives more than $50,000, there is a gain and an additional tax payment. If the company receives less than $50,000 there is a loss and a tax savings. The following table shows the effects on cash flow for sales prices of $70,000 and $20,000:

Objective 6
Explain the after-tax effect on cash of disposing of assets.

(a)	Cash proceeds of sale	$70,000	$ 20,000
	Book value: [$125,000 − 3 ($25,000)]	50,000	50,000
	Gain (loss)	$20,000	$(30,000)
	Effect on income taxes at 40%:		
(b)	Tax saving, an inflow effect: .40 × loss		$ 12,000
(c)	Tax paid, an outflow: .40 × gain	$(8,000)	
	Net cash inflow from sale:		
	(a) plus (b)		$ 32,000
	(a) minus (c)	$62,000	

SUMMARY PROBLEM FOR YOUR REVIEW

PROBLEM

Consider the investment opportunity in Exhibit 11-4, page 449: original cost of equipment, $125,000; 5-year economic life; zero terminal salvage value; pretax annual cash inflow from operations, $60,000; income tax rate, 40%; required after-tax rate of return,

12%. Assume the equipment is a 5-year MACRS asset for tax purposes. The net present value (NPV) is

	Present Values (PV)
Cash effects of operations,*	
$60,000 × (1 − .40) × 3.6048	$129,773
Cash effects of depreciation on income	
tax savings using MACRS,	
$125,000 × .40 × .7381†	36,905
Total after-tax effect on cash	$166,678
Investment	125,000
Net present value	$ 41,678

*See Exhibit 11-4, page 449, for details.
†Factor .7381 is from Exhibit 11-7, page 452.

Consider each requirement independently. Compute the NPV of the investment for each.

Required

1. Suppose the equipment was expected to be sold for $20,000 cash immediately after the end of year 5.

2. Ignore the assumption in requirement 1. Return to the original data. Suppose the economic life of the equipment was 8 years, not 5 years. But, MACRS cost recovery over 5 years is still allowed for tax purposes.

SOLUTION

1. Net present value as given		$41,678
Cash proceeds of sale	$ 20,000	
Book value	0	
Gain	$ 20,000	
Income taxes at 40%	8,000	
Total after-tax effect on cash	$ 12,000	
PV of $12,000 to be received in		
5 years at 12%, $12,000 × .5674		6,809
NPV of investment		$48,487
2. Net present value as given		$41,678
Add the present value of $36,000 per year for 8 years		
Discount factor of 4.9676 × $36,000 =	$178,834	
Deduct the present value of $36,000 per year for 5 years	129,773	
Increase in present value		49,061
Net present value		$90,739

The investment would be very attractive. Note especially that the recovery period for tax purposes and the economic useful life of the asset need not be equal. The tax law specifies lives (or recovery periods) for various types of depreciable assets. The economic useful life of the asset does not affect the tax life. Thus, a longer useful life for an asset increases operating cash flows without decreasing the present value of the tax savings.

CONFUSION ABOUT DEPRECIATION

The meanings of *depreciation* and *book value* are widely misunderstood. Let's review their role in decisions. Suppose a bank is considering the replacement of some old copying equipment with a book value of $30,000, an expected terminal disposal value of zero, a current disposal value of $12,000, and a remaining useful life of three years. For

Exhibit 11-8
Perspective on Book Value and Depreciation

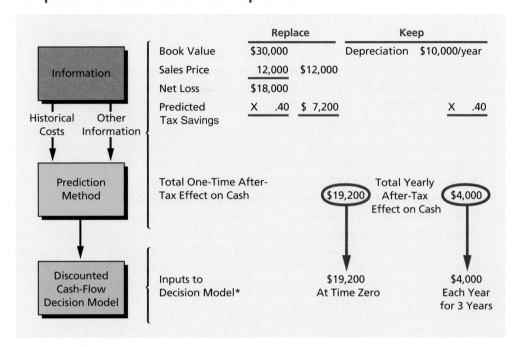

		Replace		Keep	
Book Value		$30,000		Depreciation	$10,000/year
Sales Price		12,000	$12,000		
Net Loss		$18,000			
Predicted Tax Savings		X .40	$ 7,200		X .40
Total One-Time After-Tax Effect on Cash			$19,200	Total Yearly After-Tax Effect on Cash	$4,000
Inputs to Decision Model*			$19,200 At Time Zero		$4,000 Each Year for 3 Years

Information — Historical Costs — Other Information

Prediction Method

Discounted Cash-Flow Decision Model

*There will, of course, be other related inputs to this decision model—for example, the cost of the new equipment and the differences in future annual cash flows from operations.

simplicity, assume that the bank will take straight-line depreciation of $10,000 yearly. The tax rate is 40%.

These data should be examined in perspective, as Exhibit 11-8 indicates. In particular, note that the inputs to the decision model are the predicted income tax effects on cash. Book values and depreciation may be necessary for making predictions. By themselves, however, they are not inputs to DCF decision models.

CAPITAL BUDGETING AND INFLATION

In addition to taxes, capital-budgeting decision makers should consider the effects of inflation on their cash-flow predictions. **Inflation** is the decline in the general purchasing power of the monetary unit. For example, a dollar today will buy only half as much as it did in the early 1980s. At a 5% annual inflation rate, average prices rise more than 60% over 10 years. In countries such as Brazil and Argentina, triple-digit annual inflation rates (that is, average prices more than doubling each year) have been commonplace and have significantly affected business decisions. If significant inflation is expected over the life of a project, it should be specifically and consistently analyzed in a capital-budgeting model.

inflation The decline in the general purchasing power of the monetary unit.

Objective 7
Compute the impact of inflation on a capital-budgeting project.

WATCH FOR CONSISTENCY

The key to appropriate consideration of inflation in capital budgeting is consistent treatment of the minimum desired rate of return and the predicted cash inflows and outflows. We can achieve such consistency by including an element for inflation in both the minimum desired rate of return and in the cash-flow predictions.

Many firms base their minimum desired rate of return on market interest rates, also called **nominal rates,** that include an inflation element. For example, consider three possible components of a 12% nominal rate.

nominal rate Quoted market interest rate that includes an inflation element.

(a)	Risk-free element—the "pure" rate of interest	3%
(b)	Business-risk element—the "risk" premium that is demanded for taking larger risks	5
(a) + (b)	Often called the "real rate"	8%
(c)	Inflation element—the premium demanded because of expected deterioration of the general purchasing power of the monetary unit	4
(a) + (b) + (c)	Often called the "nominal rate"	12%

Four percentage points out of the 12% return compensate an investor for receiving future payments in inflated dollars, that is, in dollars with less purchasing power than those invested. Therefore, basing the minimum desired rate of return on quoted market rates automatically includes an inflation element in the rate. Companies that base their minimum desired rate of return on market rates should also adjust their cash-flow predictions for anticipated inflation. For example, suppose a company expects to sell 1,000 units of a product in each of the next two years. Assume this year's price is $50, and inflation causes next year's price to be $52.50. This year's predicted cash inflow is 1,000 × $50 = $50,000 and next year's inflation-adjusted cash inflow is 1,000 × $52.50 = $52,500. Inflation-adjusted cash flows are the inflows and outflows expected after adjusting prices to reflect anticipated inflation.

Consider another illustration: purchase cost of equipment, $200,000; useful life, 5 years; zero terminal salvage value; pretax operating cash savings per year, $83,333 (in 20X0 dollars); income tax rate, 40%. For simplicity, we assume ordinary straight-line depreciation of $200,000 ÷ 5 = $40,000 per year. The after-tax minimum desired rate, based on quoted market rates, is 25%. It includes an inflation factor of 10%.

Exhibit 11-9 displays correct and incorrect ways to analyze the effects of inflation. The key words are *internal consistency*. The correct analysis (1) uses a minimum desired rate that includes an element attributable to inflation and (2) explicitly adjusts the predicted operating cash flows for the effects of inflation. Note that the correct analysis favors the purchase of the equipment, but the incorrect analysis does not.

The incorrect analysis in Exhibit 11-9 is inherently inconsistent. The predicted cash inflows exclude adjustments for inflation. Instead, they are stated in 20X0 dollars. However, the discount rate includes an element attributable to inflation. Such an analytical flaw may induce an unwise refusal to purchase.

ROLE OF DEPRECIATION

The correct analysis in Exhibit 11-9 shows that the tax effects of depreciation are not adjusted for inflation. Why? Because U.S. income tax laws permit a depreciation deduction based on the original dollars invested, nothing more.

Critics of income tax laws emphasize that capital investment is discouraged by not allowing the adjusting of depreciation deductions for inflationary effects. For instance, the net present value in Exhibit 11-9 would be larger if depreciation were not confined to the $40,000 amount per year. The latter generates a $16,000 saving in 20X1 dollars, then $16,000 in 20X2 dollars, and so forth. Defenders of existing U.S. tax laws assert that capital investment is encouraged in many other ways. The most prominent example is provision for accelerated depreciation over lives that are much shorter than the economic lives of the assets.

IMPROVEMENT OF PREDICTIONS WITH FEEDBACK

The ability to forecast and cope with changing prices is a valuable management skill, especially when inflation is significant. Auditing and feedback should help evaluate management's predictive skills.

Exhibit 11-9
Inflation and Capital Budgeting

Description	At 25% PV Factor	At 25% Present Value	Sketch of Relevant Cash Flows (at End of Year) 0	1	2	3	4	5
Correct Analysis (Be sure the discount rate includes an element attributable to inflation and adjust the predicted cash flows for inflationary effects.)								
Cash operating inflows:								
Pretax inflow in 20X0 dollars $83,333								
Income tax effect at 40% 33,333								
After-tax effect on cash $50,000				$55,000*	$60,500	$66,550	$73,205	$80,526
	.8000	$ 44,000						
	.6400	38,720						
	.5120	34,074						
	.4096	29,985						
	.3277	26,388						
Subtotal		$173,167						
Annual depreciation $200,000 ÷ 5 = $40,000								
Cash effect of depreciation Savings in income taxes @ 40% = $40,000 × .40 = $16,000				$16,000†	$16,000	$16,000	$16,000	$16,000
	2.6893	43,029						
Investment in equipment	1.0000	(200,000)	($200,000)					
Net present value		$ 16,196						
Incorrect Analysis (A common error is to include an inflation element in the discount rate as above, but not adjust the predicted cash inflows.)								
Cash operating inflows after taxes	2.6893	$134,465		$50,000	$50,000	$50,000	$50,000	$50,000
Tax effect of depreciation	2.6893	43,029		16,000	16,000	16,000	16,000	16,000
Investment in equipment	1.0000	(200,000)	($200,000)					
Net present value		$ 22,506						

*Each year is adjusted for anticipated inflation: $50,000 × 1.10, $50,000 × 1.10², $50,000 × 1.10³, and so on.

†Inflation will not affect the annual savings in income taxes from depreciation. Why? Because the income tax deduction must be based on original cost of the asset in 20X0 dollars.

457

The adjustment of the operating cash flows in Exhibit 11-9 uses a *general-price-level* rate of 10%. However, where feasible, managers should use *specific* rates or tailor-made predictions for price changes in materials, labor, and other items. These predictions may have different percentage changes from year to year.

SUMMARY PROBLEMS FOR YOUR REVIEW

PROBLEM

Examine the correct analysis in Exhibit 11-9, page 457. Suppose the cash-operating inflows persisted for an extra year. Compute the present value of the inflow for the sixth year. Ignore depreciation.

SOLUTION

The cash operating inflow would be $50,000 × 1.10^6, or $80,526 × 1.10, or $88,579. Its present value would be $88,579 × .2621, the factor from Table 1 of Appendix B (period 6 row, 25% column), or $23,217.

PROBLEM

Examine the MACRS depreciation schedule near the middle of page 452. Assume an anticipated inflation rate of 7%. How would you change the present values of depreciation to accommodate the inflation rate?

SOLUTION

The computations on page 452 would not change. Inflation does not affect the tax effects of depreciation. U.S. income tax laws permit a deduction based on the original dollars invested, nothing more.

OTHER MODELS FOR ANALYZING LONG-RANGE DECISIONS

Objective 8
Use the payback model and the accounting rate-of-return model and compare them with the NPV model.

Although more and more companies are using DCF models to make their capital-budgeting decisions, there are still other models in use. All of these models are simpler than NPV, but they are also less useful. However, many companies still use these lesser models, which can provide some interesting supplemental information to DCF models. We will examine the payback and accounting-rate-of-return models.

PAYBACK MODEL

payback time (payback period)
The time it will take to recoup, in the form of cash inflows from operations, the initial dollars invested in a project.

Payback time or **payback period** is the time it will take to recoup, in the form of cash inflows from operations, the initial dollars invested in a project. Assume that $12,000 is spent for a machine with an estimated useful life of 8 years. Annual savings of $4,000 in cash outflows are expected from operations. Depreciation is ignored. The payback period is three years, calculated as follows.

$$\text{payback time} = \frac{\text{initial incremental amount invested}}{\text{equal annual incremental cash inflow from operations}}$$

$$P = \frac{I}{O} = \frac{\$12,000}{\$4,000} = 3 \text{ years}$$

This formula for payback time can be used only when there are equal annual cash inflows from operations. When annual cash inflows are not equal, we must add up each year's net cash flows until the initial investment is recouped. Assume the following cash flow pattern:

End of Year	0	1	2	3
Investment	($31,000)			
Cash inflows		$10,000	$20,000	$10,000

The calculation of the payback period is

	Initial	Net Cash Inflows	
Year	Investment	Each Year	Accumulated
0	$31,000	—	—
1	—	$10,000	$10,000
2	—	20,000	30,000
2.1	—	1,000	31,000

In this case, the payback time is slightly beyond the second year. Interpolation within the third year reveals that an additional .1 years is needed to recoup the final $1,000, making the payback period 2.1 years:

$$2 \text{ years} + \left(\frac{\$1,000}{\$10,000} \times 1 \text{ year} \right) = 2.1 \text{ years}$$

A major weakness of the payback model is that it does not measure profitability, which is a primary goal of businesses. The payback model merely measures how quickly investment dollars may be recouped. However, a project with a shorter payback time is not necessarily preferable to one with a longer payback time. After all, a company can recoup its entire investment immediately by not investing.

Sometimes managers use the payback period as a rough estimate of the riskiness of a project. Suppose a company faces rapid technological changes. Cash flows beyond the first few years may be extremely uncertain. In such a situation, projects that recoup their investment quickly may be less risky than those that require a longer wait until the cash starts flowing in.

ACCOUNTING RATE-OF-RETURN MODEL

The **accounting rate-of-return (ARR) model** expresses a project's return as the increase in expected average annual operating income divided by the initial required investment.

$$\text{accounting rate-of-return (ARR)} = \frac{\substack{\text{increase in expected average} \\ \text{annual operating income}}}{\substack{\text{initial required} \\ \text{investment}}}$$

$$= \frac{O - D}{I} = \frac{\substack{\text{average annual incremental cash inflow from operations} \\ - \text{ incremental average annual depreciation}}}{\text{initial required investment}}$$

Its computations dovetail most closely with conventional accounting models of calculating income and required investment, and they show the effect of an investment on an organization's financial statements.

accounting rate-of-return (ARR) model A non-DCF capital-budgeting model expressed as the increase in expected average annual operating income divided by the initial required investment.

To see how ARR works, assume the same facts as in Exhibit 11-1: Investment is $6,075, useful life is four years, estimated disposal value is zero, and expected annual cash inflow from operations is $2,000. Annual depreciation would be $6,075 ÷ 4 = $1,518.75, rounded to $1,519. Substitute these values in the accounting rate-of-return equation:

$$ARR = \frac{\$2,000 - \$1,519}{\$6,075} = 7.9\%$$

Some companies use the "average" investment (often assumed for equipment as being the average book value over the useful life) instead of original investment in the denominator. Therefore, the denominator[3] becomes $6,075 ÷ 2 = $3,037.50:

$$ARR = \frac{\$2,000 - \$1,519}{\$3,037.50} = 15.8\%$$

The accounting rate-of-return model is based on the familiar financial statements prepared under accrual accounting. Unlike the payback model, the accounting model at least has profitability as an objective. Nevertheless, it has a major drawback. The accounting model ignores the time value of money. Expected future dollars are erroneously regarded as equal to present dollars. DCF models explicitly allow for the force of interest and the timing of cash flows. In contrast, the accounting model is based on annual averages. It uses concepts of investment and income that were originally designed for the quite different purpose of accounting for periodic income and financial position.

PERFORMANCE EVALUATION

POTENTIAL CONFLICT

Objective 9
Reconcile the conflict between using an NPV model for making a decision and using accounting income for evaluating the related performance.

Many managers are reluctant to accept DCF models as the best way to make capital-budgeting decisions. Their reluctance stems from the wide usage of accounting income for evaluating performance. That is, managers become frustrated if they are instructed to use a DCF model for making decisions but are evaluated later using a non-DCF model, such as the typical accounting rate-of-return model.

To illustrate, consider the potential conflict that might arise in the example of Exhibit 11-1. Recall that the NPV was $265 based on a 10% required rate of return and an outlay of $6,075 that would generate cash savings of $2,000 for each of 4 years and have no terminal disposal value. Using accounting income computed with straight-line depreciation, the evaluation of performance for years one through four would be

	Year 1	Year 2	Year 3	Year 4
Cash-operating savings	$2,000	$2,000	$2,000	$2,000
Straight-line depreciation, $6,075 ÷ 4	1,519	1,519	1,519	1,519*
Effect on operating income	481	481	481	481
Book value at beginning of year	6,075	4,556	3,037	1,518
Accounting rate of return	7.9%	10.6%	15.8%	31.7%

*Total depreciation of 4 × $1,519 = $6,076 differs from $6,075 because of rounding error.

Many managers would be reluctant to replace equipment, despite the positive NPV, if their performance were evaluated by accounting income. They might be especially

---

[3] *The average investment committed to the project would decline at a rate of $1,519 per year from $6,075 to zero; hence the average investment would be the beginning balance plus the ending balance ($6,075 + 0) divided by 2, or $3,037.50.*

reluctant if they are likely to be transferred to new positions every year or two. Why? This accrual accounting system understates the return in early years, especially in year 1 when the return is below the required rate, and a manager might not be around to reap the benefits of the later overstatement of returns.

As Chapter 6 indicated, managerial reluctance to replace is reinforced if a heavy book loss on old equipment would appear in year 1's income statement—even though such a loss would be irrelevant in a properly constructed decision model. Thus, performance evaluation based on typical accounting measures can cause the rejection of major, long-term projects such as investments in technologically advanced production systems. This pattern may help explain why many U.S. firms seem to be excessively short-term oriented.

RECONCILIATION OF CONFLICT

The best way to reconcile any potential conflict between capital budgeting and performance evaluation is to use DCF for both capital-budgeting decisions and performance evaluation. Companies that use Economic Value Added (EVA) for performance evaluation, as described in Chapter 10, p. 408, avoid some of the conflict. Although EVA uses accrual accounting measures of profit and investment rather than cash flows, it is conceptually very similar to the NPV method of capital budgeting. Both EVA and NPV recognize that value is created only after a project covers its cost of capital.

Another way to reconcile conflict is to conduct a follow-up evaluation of capital-budgeting decisions, often called a **postaudit.** Most large companies (76% in a recent survey) postaudit at least some capital-budgeting decisions. The purposes of a postaudit include

postaudit A follow-up evaluation of capital-budgeting decisions.

1. Seeing that investment expenditures are proceeding on time and within budget.
2. Comparing actual cash flows with those originally predicted, in order to motivate careful and honest predictions.
3. Providing information for improving future predictions of cash flows.
4. Evaluating the continuation of the project.

By focusing the postaudit on actual versus predicted cash flows, the evaluation is consistent with the decision process.

However, postauditing of all capital-budgeting decisions is costly. Most accounting systems are designed to evaluate operating performances of products, departments, divisions, territories, and so on, year by year. In contrast, capital-budgeting decisions frequently deal with individual projects, not the collection of projects that are usually being managed at the same time by divisional or department managers. Therefore, usually only selected capital-budgeting decisions are audited.

The conflicts between the longstanding, pervasive accrual accounting model and various formal decision models represent one of the most serious unsolved problems in the design of management control systems. Top management cannot expect goal congruence if it favors the use of one type of model for decisions and the use of another type for performance evaluation.

Highlights to Remember

Describe capital-budgeting decisions and use the net-present-value (NPV) method to make such decisions. Capital budgeting is long-term planning for proposed capital outlays and their financing. The net-present-value (NPV) model aids this process by computing the present value of all expected future cash flows using a minimum desired rate of return. Projects with an NPV greater than zero should be accepted.

Evaluate projects using sensitivity analysis. Managers use sensitivity analysis to aid risk assessment by examining the effects if actual cash flows differ from those expected.

Calculate the NPV difference between two projects using both the total project and differential approaches. The total project approach compares the NPVs of the cash flows from each project, while the differential approach computes the NPV of the difference in cash flows between two projects. Both produce the same results if there are two alternatives. The total project approach must be used with more than two alternatives.

Identify relevant cash flows for NPV analyses. Predicting cash flows is the hardest part of capital budgeting. Managers should consider four categories of cash flows: initial cash inflows and outflows at time zero, investments in receivables and inventories, future disposal values, and operating cash flows.

Compute the after-tax net present values of projects. Income taxes can have a significant effect on the desirability of an investment. Additional taxes are cash outflows, and tax savings are cash inflows. Accelerated depreciation speeds up a company's tax savings. Generally, companies should take depreciation deductions as early as legally permitted.

Explain the after-tax effect on cash of disposing of assets. When companies sell assets for more than their book value, the gain generates additional taxes. When they sell assets for less than their book value, the loss generates tax savings.

Compute the impact of inflation on a capital-budgeting project. Consistency is the key in adjusting capital-budgeting analyses for inflation. The required rate of return should include an element attributable to anticipated inflation, and cash-flow predictions should be adjusted for the effects of anticipated inflation.

Use the payback model and the accounting rate-of-return model and compare them with the NPV model. The payback model is simple to apply, but it does not measure profitability. The accounting rate-of-return model uses accounting measures of income and investment, but it ignores the time value of money. Both models are inferior to the NPV model.

Reconcile the conflict between using an NPV model for making a decision and using accounting income for evaluating the related performance. NPV is a summary measure of all the cash flows from a project. Accounting income is a one-period measure. A positive NPV project can have low (or even negative) accounting income in the first year. Managers may be reluctant to invest in such a project, despite its positive value to the company, especially if they expect to be transferred to a new position before the positive returns are recognized.

Understand how companies make long-term capital investment decisions and how such decisions can affect the companies' financial results for years to come. Long-term capital investments are critical to a company's financial success. Using a discounted cash-flow method, such as NPV, helps managers make optimal capital budgeting decisions. Predicting cash flows, including the effects of taxes and inflation, is an important part of capital-budgeting decisions.

Accounting Vocabulary

accelerated depreciation, p. 447

accounting rate-of-return (ARR) model, p. 459

capital budgeting, p. 436

differential approach, p. 442

discount rate, p. 437

discounted-cash-flow (DCF) models, p. 436

hurdle rate, p. 437

inflation, p. 455

marginal income tax rate, p. 447

net-present-value (NPV) method, p. 437

nominal rate, p. 455

payback period, p. 458

payback time, p. 458

postaudit, p. 461

recovery period, p. 448

required rate of return, p. 437

total project approach, p. 442

Fundamental Assignment Material

Special note: In all assignment material where taxes are considered, assume, unless directed otherwise, that (1) all income tax cash flows occur simultaneously with the pretax cash flows, and (2) the companies in question will have enough taxable income from other sources to use all income tax benefits from the situations described.

11-A1 Exercises in Compound Interest: Answers Supplied

Use the appropriate interest table from Appendix B (see pp. B7 or B8) to complete the following exercises. The answers appear at the end of the assignment material for this chapter, page 480.

1. It is your 55th birthday. You plan to work five more years before retiring. Then you and your spouse want to take $20,000 for a round-the-world tour. What lump sum do you have to invest now to accumulate the $20,000? Assume that your minimum desired rate of return is

   a. 5%, compounded annually
   b. 10%, compounded annually
   c. 20%, compounded annually

2. You want to spend $2,000 on a vacation at the end of each of the next five years. What lump sum do you have to invest now to take the five vacations? Assume that your minimum desired rate of return is

   a. 5%, compounded annually
   b. 10%, compounded annually
   c. 20%, compounded annually

3. At age 60, you find that your employer is moving to another location. You receive termination pay of $100,000. You have some savings and wonder whether to retire now.

   a. If you invest the $100,000 now at 5%, compounded annually, how much money can you withdraw from your account each year so that at the end of five years there will be a zero balance?
   b. Answer part a assuming that you invest it at 10%.

4. Two NBA basketball players, Johnson and Jackson, signed five-year, $30 million contracts. At 16%, compounded annually, which of the following contracts is more desirable in terms of present values? Show computations to support your answer.

Annual Cash Inflows (000)		
Year	*Johnson*	*Jackson*
1	$10,000	$ 2,000
2	8,000	4,000
3	6,000	6,000
4	4,000	8,000
5	2,000	10,000
	$30,000	$30,000

11-A2 NPV for Investment Decisions

A manager of the Administrative Computer Center of Western State University is contemplating acquiring 60 computers. The computers will cost $330,000 cash, have zero terminal salvage value and a useful life of three years. Annual cash savings from operations will be $150,000. The required rate of return is 14%. There are no taxes.

Required

1. Compute the net present value.
2. Should the Computer Center acquire the computers? Explain.

11-A3 Taxes, Straight-Line Depreciation, and Present Values

A manager of BankSoft.com is contemplating acquiring 60 computers used for designing software. The computers will cost $330,000 cash and will have zero terminal salvage value. The recovery period and useful life are both three years. Annual pretax cash savings from operations will be $150,000. The income tax rate is 40%, and the required after-tax rate of return is 12%.

1. Compute the net present value, assuming straight-line depreciation of $110,000 yearly for tax purposes. Should BankSoft.com acquire the computers? Explain.

2. Suppose the computers will be fully depreciated at the end of year 3 but can be sold for $45,000 cash. Compute the net present value. Should BankSoft.com acquire the computers? Explain.

3. Ignore requirement 2. Suppose the required after-tax rate of return is 8% instead of 12%. Should the computers be acquired? Show computations.

11-A4   MACRS and Present Values

The president of Tristate Power Company is considering whether to buy some equipment for its South Plains plant. The equipment will cost $1.5 million cash and will have a 10-year useful life and zero terminal salvage value. Annual pretax cash savings from operations will be $350,000. The income tax rate is 40%, and the required after-tax rate of return is 16%.

1. Compute the net present value, using a 7-year recovery period and MACRS depreciation for tax purposes. Should the equipment be acquired?

2. Suppose the economic life of the equipment is 15 years, which means that there will be $350,000 additional annual cash savings from operations in each of years 11 to 15. Assume that a 7-year recovery period is used. Should the equipment be acquired? Show computations.

11-A5   Gains or Losses on Disposal

An asset with a book value of $50,000 was sold for cash on January 1, 20X1.

Assume two selling prices: $60,000 and $30,000. For each selling price, prepare a tabulation of the gain or loss, the effect on income taxes, and the total after-tax effect on cash. The applicable income tax rate is 30%.

11-B1   Exercises in Compound Interest

Use the appropriate table to compute the following:

1. You have always dreamed of taking a trip to the Great Barrier Reef. What lump sum do you have to invest today to have the $12,000 needed for the trip in three years? Assume that you can invest the money at

   a. 4%, compounded annually
   b. 10%, compounded annually
   c. 18%, compounded annually

2. You are considering partial retirement. To do so you need to use part of your savings to supplement your income for the next five years. Suppose you need an extra $15,000 per year. What lump sum do you have to invest now to supplement your income for five years? Assume that your minimum desired rate of return is

   a. 4%, compounded annually
   b. 10%, compounded annually
   c. 18%, compounded annually

3. You just won a lump sum of $400,000 in a local lottery. You have decided to invest the winnings and withdraw an equal amount each year for 10 years. How much can you withdraw each year and have a zero balance left at the end of 10 years if you invest at

   a. 5%, compounded annually
   b. 10%, compounded annually

4. A professional athlete is offered the choice of two 4-year salary contracts, contract A for $1.4 million and contract B for $1.3 million:

	Contract A	**Contract B**
End of year 1	$ 200,000	$ 450,000
End of year 2	300,000	350,000
End of year 3	400,000	300,000
End of year 4	500,000	200,000
Total	$1,400,000	$1,300,000

Which contract has the higher present value at 14% compounded annually? Show computations to support your answer.

11-B2 NPV for Investment Decisions

The head of the Oncology Department of St. Vincent's Hospital is considering the purchase of some equipment used for cancer research. The cost is $400,000, the economic life is five years, and there is no terminal disposal value. Annual cash inflows from operations would increase by $140,000 and the required rate of return is 16%. There are no taxes.

Required

1. Compute the net present value.
2. Should the equipment be acquired? Explain.

11-B3 Taxes, Straight-Line Depreciation, and NPV

The president of Biogen, Inc., a biotechnology company, is considering the purchase of some equipment used for research and development. The cost is $400,000, the economic life and the recovery period are both five years, and there is no terminal disposal value. Annual pretax cash inflows from operations would increase by $140,000, the income tax rate is 40%, and the required after-tax rate of return is 14%.

Required

1. Compute the net present value, assuming straight-line depreciation of $80,000 yearly for tax purposes. Should Biogen acquire the equipment?
2. Suppose the asset will be fully depreciated at the end of year 5 but is sold for $30,000 cash. Should Biogen acquire the equipment? Show computations.
3. Ignore requirement 2. Suppose the required after-tax rate of return is 10% instead of 14%. Should Biogen acquire the equipment? Show computations.

11-B4 MACRS and Present Values

The general manager of an Alaskan mining company has a chance to purchase a new drill at a total cost of $250,000. The recovery period is five years. Additional annual pretax cash inflow from operations is $82,000, the economic life of the equipment is five years, there is no salvage value, the income tax rate is 35%, and the after-tax required rate of return is 16%.

Required

1. Compute the net present value, assuming MACRS depreciation for tax purposes. Should the company acquire the equipment?
2. Suppose the economic life of the equipment is six years, which means that there will be an $82,000 cash inflow from operations in the sixth year. The recovery period is still five years. Should the company acquire the equipment? Show computations.

11-B5 Income Taxes and Disposal of Assets

Assume that income tax rates for Ibanez Company are 30%.

1. The book value of an old machine is $20,000. Ibanez sold the machine for $9,000 cash. What is the effect of this decision on cash flows, after taxes?
2. The book value of an old machine is $20,000. Ibanez sold the machine for $35,000 cash. What is the effect on cash flows, after taxes, of this decision?

Additional Assignment Material

QUESTIONS

11-1. Capital budgeting has three phases: (1) identification of potential investments, (2) selection of investments, and (3) postaudit of investments. What is the accountant's role in each phase?

11-2. Why is discounted cash flow a superior method for capital budgeting?

11-3. "The higher the minimum desired rate of return, he higher the price that a company will be willing to pay for cost-saving equipment." Do you agree? Explain.

11-4. "The DCF model assumes certainty and perfect capital markets. Thus, it is impractical to use it in most real-world situations." Do you agree? Explain.

11-5. "Double-counting of costs occurs if depreciation is separately considered in DCF analysis." Do you agree? Explain.

11-6. "We can't use sensitivity analysis because our cash-flow predictions are too inaccurate." Comment.

11-7. Why should the differential approach to alternatives always lead to the same decision as the total project approach?

11-8. "The NPV model should not be used for investment decisions about advanced technology such as computer-integrated manufacturing systems." Do you agree? Explain.

11-9. Distinguish between average and marginal tax rates.

11-10. "Congress should pass a law forbidding corporations to keep two sets of books." Do you agree? Explain.

11-11. Distinguish between tax avoidance and tax evasion.

11-12. Explain why accelerated depreciation methods are superior to straight-line methods for income tax purposes.

11-13. "An investment in equipment really buys two streams of cash." Do you agree? Explain.

11-14. Why should tax deductions be taken sooner rather than later?

11-15. "The MACRS half-year convention causes assets to be depreciated beyond the lives specified in the MACRS recovery schedules." Do you agree? Explain.

11-16. "When there are income taxes, depreciation is a cash outlay." Do you agree? Explain.

11-17. What are the three components of market (nominal) interest rates?

11-18. Describe how internal consistency is achieved when considering inflation in a capital-budgeting model.

11-19. "Capital investments are always more profitable in inflationary times because the cash inflows from operations generally increase with inflation." Comment on this statement.

11-20. "If DCF approaches are superior to the payback and the accounting rate-of-return methods, why should we bother to learn the others? All it does is confuse things." Answer this contention.

11-21. What is the basic flaw in the payback model?

11-22. Explain how a conflict can arise between capital-budgeting decision models and performance evaluation methods.

COGNITIVE EXERCISES

11-23 Investment in Research and Development

"It is impossible to use DCF methods for evaluating investments in research and development. There are no cost savings to measure, and we don't even know what products might come out of our R&D activities." This is a quote from an R&D manager who was asked to justify investment in a major research project based on its expected net present value. Do you agree with her statement? Explain.

11-24 Business Valuation and Net Present Value

When a company elects to invest in a project with a positive net present value, what will generally happen to the value of the company? What will happen to this value when the company invests in a negative net present value project?

11-25 Replacement of Production Facilities

A manufacturing company recently considered replacing one of its forming machines with a newer, faster, more accurate model. What cash flows would this decision be likely to affect? List both cash flows that would be easy to quantify and those for which measurement would be difficult.

EXERCISES

11-26 Exercise in Compound Interest

Rose Francisco wishes to purchase a $300,000 house. She has accumulated a $100,000 downpayment, but she wishes to borrow $200,000 on a 30-year mortgage. For simplicity, assume annual mortgage payments at the end of each year and no loan fees.

Required

1. What are Francisco's annual payments if her interest rate is (a) 8%, (b) 10%, and (c) 12%, compounded annually?

2. Repeat requirement 1 for a 15-year mortgage.

3. Suppose Francisco had to choose between a 30-year and a 15-year mortgage, either one at a 10% interest rate. Compute the total payments and total interest paid on (a) a 30-year mortgage and (b) a 15-year mortgage.

11-27 Exercise in Compound Interest

Suppose General Electric (GE) wishes to borrow money from Chase Manhattan Bank. They agree on an annual rate of 12%.

1. Suppose GE agrees to repay $500 million at the end of 4 years. How much will Chase Manhattan lend GE?

2. Suppose GE agrees to repay a total of $500 million at a rate of $125 million at the end of each of the next 4 years. How much will Chase Manhattan lend GE?

11-28 Exercise in Compound Interest

A building contractor has asked you for a loan. You are pondering various proposals for repayment:

1. Lump sum of $800,000 four years hence. How much will you lend if your desired rate of return is (a) 12%, compounded annually, and (b) 20%, compounded annually?

2. Repeat requirement 1, but assume that the interest rates are compounded semi-annually.

3. Suppose the loan is to be paid in full by equal payments of $200,000 at the end of each of the next four years. How much will you lend if your desired rate of return is (a) 12%, compounded annually, and (b) 20%, compounded annually?

11-29 Basic Relationships in Interest Tables

1. Suppose you borrow $100,000 now at 14% interest, compounded annually. The borrowed amount plus interest will be repaid in a lump sum at the end of 8 years. How much must be repaid? Use Table 1 (p. B7) and the basic equation PV = future amount × conversion factor.

2. Assume the same facts as previously except that the loan will be repaid in equal installments at the end of each of eight years. How much must be repaid each year? Use Table 2 (p. B8) and the basic equation: PV = future annual amounts × conversion factor.

11-30 Present Value and Sports Salaries

Because of a salary cap, National Basketball Association teams are not allowed to exceed a certain annual limit in total player salaries. Suppose the Los Angeles Lakers had scheduled salaries exactly equal to their cap of $30 million for 20X1. Kobe O'Neal, a star player, was scheduled to receive $6 million in 20X1. To free up money to pay a prize rookie, O'Neal agreed to defer $2 million of his salary for two years, by which time the salary cap will have been increased. His contract called for salary payments of $6 million in 20X1, $7 million in 20X2, and $8 million in 20X3. Now he will receive $4 million in 20X1, still $7 million in 20X2, and $10 million in 20X3. For simplicity, assume that all salaries are paid on July 1 of the year they are scheduled. O'Neal's minimum desired rate of return is 12%.

Did the deferral of salary cost O'Neal anything? If so, how much? Compute the present value of the sacrifice on July 1, 20X1. Explain.

11-31 Simple NPV

Fill in the blanks.

	Number of Years			
	8	18	20	28
Amount of annual cash inflow*	$10,000	$____	$ 9,000	$ 7,000
Required initial investment	$____	$80,000	$65,000	$29,099
Minimum desired rate of return	14%	20%	$____	25%
NPV	$ 5,613	($13,835)	$ 2,225	$____

*To be received at the end of each year.

11-32 New Equipment

The Lippert Office Equipment Company has offered to sell some new packaging equipment to the Diaz Company. The list price is $42,000, but Lippert has agreed to allow a trade-in allowance of

$15,000 on some old equipment. The old equipment was carried at a book value of $7,700 and could be sold outright for $10,000 cash. Cash-operating savings are expected to be $5,000 annually for the next 12 years. The minimum desired rate of return is 12%. The old equipment has a remaining useful life of 12 years. Both the old and the new equipment will have zero disposal values 12 years from now.

Required Should Diaz buy the new equipment? Show your computations, using the NPV method. Ignore income taxes.

11-33 Present Values of Cash Inflows
Lighting.com Company has just been established. Operating plans indicate the following expected cash flows:

	Outflows	Inflows
Initial investment now	$220,000	$ —
End of year: 1	150,000	200,000
2	200,000	250,000
3	250,000	300,000
4	300,000	400,000
5	350,000	450,000

Required
1. Compute the NPV for all of these cash flows. This should be a single amount. Use a discount rate of 14%.
2. Suppose the minimum desired rate was 12%. Without further calculations, determine whether the NPV is positive or negative. Explain.

11-34 Sensitivity Analysis
Pennsylvania Optical Group is considering the replacement of an old billing system with new software that should save $5,000 per year in net cash operating costs. The old system has zero disposal value, but it could be used for the next 12 years. The estimated useful life of the new software is 12 years, and it will cost $25,000. The minimum desired rate of return is 10%.

Required
1. What is the payback period?
2. Compute the net present value (NPV).
3. Management is unsure about the useful life. What would be the NPV if the useful life were (a) 5 years instead of 12 or (b) 20 years instead of 12?
4. Suppose the life will be 12 years, but the savings will be $3,000 per year instead of $5,000. What would be the NPV?
5. Suppose the annual savings will be $4,000 for eight years. What would be the NPV?

11-35 NPV and Sensitivity Analysis
Skykomish County Jail currently has its laundry done by a local cleaners at an annual cost of $46,000. It is considering a purchase of washers, dryers, and presses at a total installed cost of $50,000 so that inmates can do the laundry. The county expects savings of $15,000 per year, and the machines are expected to last five years. The desired rate of return is 10%.

Answer each part separately.

Required
1. Compute the NPV of the investment in laundry facilities.
2. a. Suppose the machines last only four years. Compute the NPV.
   b. Suppose the machines last seven years. Compute the NPV.
3. a. Suppose the annual savings are only $12,000. Compute the NPV.
   b. Suppose the annual savings are $18,000. Compute the NPV.

4. a. Compute the most optimistic estimate of NPV, combining the best outcomes in requirements 2 and 3.

   b. Compute the most pessimistic estimate of NPV, combining the worst outcomes in requirements 2 and 3.

5. Accept the expected life estimate of five years. What is the minimum annual savings that would justify the investment in the laundry facilities?

11-36 Depreciation, Income Taxes, Cash Flows

Fill in the unknowns (in thousands of dollars):

(S)	Sales	540
(E)	Expenses excluding depreciation	350
(D)	Depreciation	100
	Total expenses	450
	Income before income taxes	?
(T)	Income taxes at 40%	?
(I)	Net income	?
	Cash effects of operations	
	Cash inflow from operations	?
	Income tax outflow at 40%	?
	After-tax inflow from operations	?
	Effect of depreciation	
	Depreciation, ?	
	Income tax savings	?
	Total after-tax effect on cash	?

11-37 After-Tax Effect on Cash

The 20X0 income statement of CableNet Company included the following:

Sales	$1,200,000
Less: Expenses, excluding depreciation	$ 600,000
Depreciation	400,000
Total expenses	$1,000,000
Income before taxes	$ 200,000
Income taxes (40%)	80,000
Net income	$ 120,000

Required

Compute the total after-tax effect on cash. Use the format of the second part of Exhibit 11-3, page 448, "Analysis of the Same Facts for Capital Budgeting."

11-38 MACRS Depreciation

In 2001, Elston Shoe Company acquired the following assets and immediately placed them into service.

1. Special tools (a 3-year-MACRS asset) that cost $40,000 on February 1.

2. A desktop computer that cost $7,000 on December 15.

3. Special calibration equipment that was used in research and development and cost $5,000 on July 7.

4. A set of file cabinets that cost $4,000, purchased on March 1.

Compute the depreciation for tax purposes, under the prescribed MACRS method, in 2001 and 2002.

11-39 Present Value of MACRS Depreciation

Compute the present value of the MACRS tax savings for each of the following five assets:

	Asset Cost	Recovery Period	Discount Rate	Tax Rate
(a)	$220,000	3-year	12%	35%
(b)	$560,000	5-year	10%	40%
(c)	$ 55,000	7-year	16%	50%
(d)	$910,000	10-year	8%	35%
(e)	$390,000	10-year	15%	25%

11-40 Inflation and Capital Budgeting

The head of the small business division of a major consulting firm has proposed investing $300,000 in personal computers for the staff. The useful life and recovery period for the computers are both five years. MACRS depreciation is used. There is no terminal salvage value. Labor savings of $125,000 per year (in year-zero dollars) are expected from the purchase. The income tax rate is 45%, the after-tax required rate of return is 20%, which includes a 4% element attributable to inflation.

1. Compute the net present value of the computers. Use the nominal required rate of return and adjust the cash flows for inflation. (For example, year 1 cash flow = 1.04 × year 0 cash flow.)

2. Compute the net present value of the computers using the nominal required rate of return without adjusting the cash flows for inflation.

3. Compare your answers in requirements 1 and 2. Which is correct? Would using the incorrect analysis generally lead to overinvestment or underinvestment? Explain.

11-41 Sensitivity of Capital Budgeting to Inflation

Raul Montoya, the president of a Mexican wholesale company, is considering whether to invest 425,000 pesos in new semiautomatic loading equipment that will last five years, have zero scrap value, and generate cash operating savings in labor usage of 160,000 pesos annually, using 20X0 prices and wage rates. It is December 31, 20X0.

The minimum desired rate of return is 18% per year after taxes.

1. Compute the net present value of the project. Use 160,000 pesos as the savings for each of the five years. Assume a 40% tax rate and, for simplicity, assume ordinary straight-line depreciation of 425,000 pesos ÷ 5 = 85,000 pesos annually for tax purposes.

2. Montoya is wondering if the model in requirement 1 provides a correct analysis of the effects of inflation. He maintains that the 18% rate embodies an element attributable to anticipated inflation. For purposes of this analysis, he assumes that the existing rate of inflation, 10% annually, will persist over the next five years. Repeat requirement 1, adjusting the cash operating savings upward by using the 10% inflation rate.

3. Which analysis, the one in requirement 1 or 2, is correct? Why?

11-42 NPV, ARR, and Payback

Long Lake Dairy King is considering a proposal to invest in a speaker system that would allow its employees to service drive-through customers. The cost of the system (including installation of special windows and driveway modifications) is $60,000. Jenna Holding, Manager of Long Lake Dairy King, expects the drive-through operations to increase annual sales by $50,000, with a 40% contribution margin ratio. Assume that the system has an economic life of six years, at which time it will have no disposal value. The required rate of return is 12%. Ignore taxes.

1. Compute the payback period. Is this a good measure of profitability?
2. Compute the NPV. Should Holding accept the proposal? Why or why not?
3. Using the accounting rate of return model, compute the rate of return on the initial investment.

11-43 Comparison of Capital-Budgeting Techniques

Sunnyside Swim Club is considering the purchase of a new pool heater at a cost of $16,000. It should save $4,000 in cash operating costs per year. Its estimated useful life is 8 years, and it will have zero disposal value. Ignore taxes.

Required

1. What is the payback time?
2. Compute the net present value if the minimum rate of return desired is 8%. Should the company buy? Why?
3. Using the accounting rate-of-return model, compute the rate of return on the initial investment.

PROBLEMS

11-44 Replacement of Office Equipment

Northern Illinois University is considering replacing some Canon copiers with faster copiers purchased from Kodak. The administration is very concerned about the rising costs of operations during the last decade.

To convert to Kodak, two operators would have to be retrained. Required training and remodeling would cost $4,000.

Northern Illinois's three Canon machines were purchased for $10,000 each, five years ago. Their expected life was 10 years. Their resale value now is $1,000 each and will be zero in five more years. The total cost of the new Kodak equipment will be $49,000; it will have zero disposal value in five years.

The three Canon operators are paid $8 an hour each. They usually work a 40-hour week. Machine breakdowns occur monthly on each machine, resulting in repair costs of $50 per month and overtime of four hours, at time-and-one-half, per machine per month, to complete the normal monthly workload. Toner, supplies, and so on, cost $100 a month for each Canon copier.

The Kodak system will require only two regular operators, on a regular work week of 40 hours each, to do the same work. Rates are $10 an hour, and no overtime is expected. Toner, supplies, and so on, will cost a total of $3,300 annually. Maintenance and repairs are fully serviced by Kodak for $1,050 annually. (Assume a 52-week year.)

Required

1. Using DCF techniques, compute the present value of all relevant cash flows, under both alternatives, for the five-year period discounted at 12%. As a nonprofit university, Northern Illinois does not pay income taxes.
2. Should Northern Illinois keep the Canon copiers or replace them if the decision is based solely on the given data?
3. What other considerations might affect the decision?

11-45 Replacement Decision for Railway Equipment

The Sante Fe Railroad is considering replacement of a power jack tamper, used for maintenance of track, with a new automatic raising device that can be attached to a production tamper.

The present power jack tamper cost $24,000 five years ago and had an estimated life of 12 years. A year from now, the machine will require a major overhaul estimated to cost $6,000. It can be disposed of now via an outright cash sale for $4,000. There will be no value at the end of another seven years.

The automatic raising attachment has a delivered selling price of $72,000 and an estimated life of 12 years. Because of anticipated future developments in combined maintenance machines, it is felt that the machine would be disposed of at the end of the seventh year to take advantage of newly developed machines. Estimated sales value at the end of seven years is $5,000.

Tests have shown that the automatic raising machine will produce a more uniform surface on the track than the power jack tamper now in use. The new equipment will eliminate one laborer whose annual compensation, including fringe benefits, is $30,000.

Track maintenance work is seasonal, and the equipment normally works from May 1 to October 31 each year. Machine operators and laborers are transferred to other work after October 31, at the same rate of pay.

The salesman claims that the annual normal maintenance of the new machine will run about $1,000 per year. Because the automatic raising machine is more complicated than the manually operated machine, it will probably require a thorough overhaul at the end of the fourth year at an estimated cost of $7,000.

Records show the annual normal maintenance of the power jack tamper to be $1,200. Fuel consumption of the two machines is equal.

Required

Should Santa Fe keep or replace the power jack tamper? A 10% rate of return is desired. Compute present values. Ignore income taxes.

11-46 Discounted Cash Flow, Uneven Revenue Stream, Relevant Costs

T. Green, the owner of a nine-hole golf course on the outskirts of a large city, is considering a proposal that the course be illuminated and operated at night. Ms. Green purchased the course early last year for $450,000. Her receipts from operations during the 28-week season were $125,000. Total disbursements for the year, for all purposes, were $78,000.

The required investment in lighting this course is estimated at $100,000. The system will require 300 lamps of 1,000 watts each. Electricity costs $.08 per kilowatt-hour. The expected average hours of operation per night is five. Because of occasional bad weather and the probable curtailment of night operation at the beginning and end of the season, it is estimated that there will be only 130 nights of operation per year. Labor for keeping the course open at night will cost $75 per night. Lightbulb cost is estimated at $1,500 per year; other maintenance and repairs, per year, will amount to 4% of the initial cost of the lighting system. Property taxes on this equipment will be about 1.7% of its initial cost. It is estimated that the average revenue, per night of operation, will be $450 for the first two years.

Considering the probability of competition from the illumination of other golf courses, Ms. Green decides that she will not make the investment unless she can make at least 10% per annum on her investment. Because of anticipated competition, revenue is expected to drop to $300 per night for years 3 through 5. It is estimated that the lighting equipment will have a salvage value of $35,000 at the end of the five-year period.

Required

Using DCF techniques, determine whether Ms. Green should install the lighting system.

11-47 Investment in Machine and Working Capital

The Edinburgh Company has an old brewing machine with a net disposal value of £15,000 now and £4,000 five years from now. A new brewing machine is offered for £62,000 cash or £47,000 with a trade-in. The new machine will result in an annual operating cash outflow of £40,000 as compared with the old machine's annual outflow of £52,000. The disposal value of the new machine five years hence will be £4,000.

Because the new machine will produce output more rapidly, the average investment in inventories by using the new machine will be £160,000 instead of £200,000.

The minimum desired rate of return is 20%. The company uses DCF techniques to guide these decisions.

Required

Should the new brewing machine be acquired? Show your calculations. Company procedures require the computing of the present value of each alternative. The most desirable alternative is the one with the least cost. Assume that the PV of £1 at 20% for five years is £.40; the present value of an annuity of £1 at 20% for five years is £3.

11-48 Replacement Decision

Metropolitan Commuter Rail, Inc., has included a cafeteria car on the passenger train it operates. Yearly operations of the cafeteria car have shown a consistent loss, which is expected to persist, as follows:

Revenue (in cash)		$200,000
Expenses for food, supplies, etc. (in cash)	$100,000	
Salaries	110,000	210,000
Net loss (ignore depreciation on the dining car itself)		$(10,000)

The Auto-vend Company has offered to sell automatic vending machines to Metropolitan for $22,000, less a $3,000 trade-in allowance on old equipment (which is carried at $3,000 book value, and which can be sold outright for $3,000 cash) now used in the cafeteria car operation. The useful life of the vending equipment is estimated at 10 years, with zero scrap value. Experience elsewhere has led executives to predict that the equipment will serve 50% more food than the dining car, but prices will be 50% less, so the new revenue will probably be $150,000. The variety and mix of food sold are expected to be the same as for the cafeteria car. A catering company will completely service and supply food and beverages for the machines, paying 10% of revenue to Metropolitan and bearing all costs of food, repairs, etc. All dining car employees will be discharged immediately. Their termination pay will total $30,000. However, an attendant who has some general knowledge of vending machines will be needed for one shift per day. The annual cost to Metropolitan for the attendant will be $13,000.

For political and other reasons, the railroad will definitely not abandon its food service. The old equipment will have zero scrap value at the end of 10 years.

Using the preceding data, compute the following. Label computations. Ignore income taxes.

Required

1. Use the NPV method to analyze the incremental investment. Assume a minimum desired rate of return of 10%. For this problem, assume that the PV of $1 at 10% to be received at the end of ten years is $.400 and that the PV of an annuity of $1 at 10% for 10 years is $6.000.

2. What would be the minimum amount of annual revenue that Metropolitan would have to receive from the catering company to justify making the investment? Show computations.

11-49 Minimization of Transportation Costs without Income Taxes

The Lumens Company produces industrial and residential lighting fixtures at its manufacturing facility located in Phoenix. Shipment of company products to an eastern warehouse is handled by common carriers at a rate of $.26 per pound of fixtures. The warehouse is located in Cleveland, 2,500 miles from Phoenix.

Audrey Harris, the treasurer of Lumens, is considering whether to purchase a truck for transporting products to the eastern warehouse. The following data on the truck are available:

Purchase price	$35,000
Useful life	5 years
Salvage value after 5 years	0
Capacity of truck	10,000 lb
Cash costs of operating truck	$.90 per mile

Harris feels that an investment in this truck is particularly attractive because of her successful negotiation with Retro, Inc., to back-haul Retro's products from Cleveland to Phoenix on every return trip from the warehouse. Retro has agreed to pay Lumens $2,400 per load of Retro's products hauled from Cleveland to Phoenix up to and including 100 loads per year.

Lumens' marketing manager has estimated that 500,000 pounds of fixtures will have to be shipped to the eastern warehouse each year for the next five years. The truck will be fully loaded on each round trip.

Ignore income taxes.

Required

1. Assume that Lumens requires a minimum rate of return of 20%. Should the truck be purchased? Show computations to support your answer.

2. What is the minimum number of trips that must be guaranteed by Retro, Inc., to make the deal acceptable to Lumens, based on the foregoing numbers alone?

3. What qualitative factors might influence your decision? Be specific.

11-50 Straight-Line Depreciation, MACRS Depreciation, and Immediate Write-Off

Mr. Wong bought a new $30,000 freezer for his grocery store on January 2, 2001. The freezer has a five-year economic life and recovery period, Mr. Wong's minimum desired rate of return is 12%, and his tax rate is 40%.

Required

1. Suppose Mr. Wong uses straight-line depreciation for tax purposes. Compute the present value of the tax savings from depreciation. Assume that a full year of depreciation is taken at the end of 2001.

2. Suppose Mr. Wong uses MACRS depreciation for tax purposes. Compute the present value of the tax savings from depreciation.

3. Suppose Mr. Wong was allowed to immediately deduct the entire cost of the freezer for tax purposes. Compute the present value of the tax savings from depreciation.

4. Which of the three methods of deducting the cost of the freezer would Mr. Wong prefer if all three were allowable for tax purposes? Why?

11-51 MACRS, Residual Value

The Maddox Company estimates that it can save $10,000 per year in annual operating cash costs for the next five years if it buys a special-purpose machine at a cost of $33,000. Residual value is expected to be $4,000, although no residual value is being provided for in using MACRS depreciation (five-year recovery period) for tax purposes. The equipment will be sold at the beginning of the sixth year; for purposes of this analysis assume that the proceeds are received at the end of the fifth year. The minimum desired rate of return, after taxes, is 12%. Assume the income tax rate is 45%.

Required

1. Using the net-present-value method, show whether the investment is desirable.
2. Suppose the equipment will produce savings for seven years instead of five. Residual value is expected to be zero at the end of the seventh year. Using the net-present-value method, show whether the investment is desirable.

11-52 Purchase of Equipment

The Kansas City Clinic, a for-profit medical facility, is planning to spend $45,000 for modernized x-ray equipment. It will replace equipment that has zero book value and no salvage value, although the old equipment would last another seven years.

The new equipment will save $13,500 in cash operating costs for each of the next seven years, at which time it will be sold for $6,000. A major overhaul costing $5,000 will occur at the end of the fourth year; the old equipment would require no such overhaul. The entire cost of the overhaul is deductible for tax purposes in the fourth year. The equipment has a five-year recovery period. MACRS depreciation is used for tax purposes.

The minimum desired rate of return after taxes is 12%. The applicable income tax rate is 40%.

Required

Compute the after-tax net present value. Is the new equipment a desirable investment?

11-53 Minimization of Transportation Costs After Taxes, Inflation

(This problem is a version of 11-49 that includes taxes and inflation elements.) The Lumens Company produces industrial and residential lighting fixtures at its manufacturing facility in Phoenix. Shipment of company products to an eastern warehouse is handled by common carriers at a rate of 26¢ per pound of fixtures (expressed in year-zero dollars). The warehouse is located in Cleveland, 2,500 miles from Phoenix. The rate will increase with inflation.

Audrey Harris, the treasurer of Lumens, is presently considering whether to purchase a truck for transporting products to the eastern warehouse. The following data on the truck are available:

Purchase price	$35,000
Useful life	5 years
Terminal residual value	0
Capacity of truck	10,000 lb
Cash costs of operating truck (expressed in year-1 dollars)	$.90 per mile

Harris feels that an investment in this truck is particularly attractive because of her successful negotiation with Retro, Inc., to back-haul Retro's products from Cleveland to Phoenix on every return trip from the warehouse. Retro has agreed to pay Lumens $2,400 per load of Retro's products hauled from Cleveland to Phoenix for as many loads as Lumens can accommodate, up to and including 100 loads per year over the next five years.

Lumens' marketing manager has estimated that 500,000 pounds of fixtures will have to be shipped to the eastern warehouse each year for the next five years. The truck will be fully loaded on each round trip.

Make the following assumptions:

a. Lumens requires a minimum 20% after-tax rate of return, which includes a 10% element attributable to inflation.
b. A 40% tax rate.
c. MACRS depreciation based on five-year cost recovery period.
d. An inflation rate of 10%.

Required

1. Should the truck be purchased? Show computations to support your answer.
2. What qualitative factors might influence your decision? Be specific.

11-54 Inflation and Nonprofit Institution

The city of Mobile is considering the purchase of a photocopying machine for $7,100 on December 31, 20X0. The machine will have a useful life of five years and no residual value. The cash operating savings are expected to be $2,000 annually, measured in 20X0 dollars.

The minimum desired rate is 14%, which includes an element attributable to anticipated inflation of 6%. (Remember that the city pays no income taxes.)

Required

Use the 14% minimum desired rate for requirements 1 and 2:

1. Compute the net present value of the project without adjusting the cash operating savings for inflation.
2. Repeat requirement 1, adjusting the cash operating savings upward in accordance with the 6% inflation rate.
3. Compare your results in requirements 1 and 2. What generalization seems applicable about the analysis of inflation in capital budgeting?

11-55 MACRS and Low-Income Housing

Hector Ramirez is a real estate developer who specializes in residential apartments. A complex of 20 run-down apartments has recently come on the market for $310,000. Ramirez predicts that after remodeling, the 12 one-bedroom units will rent for $380 per month and the 8 two-bedroom apartments for $440. He budgets 15% of the rental fees for repairs and maintenance. The apartments should last for 30 years if the remodeling is done well. Remodeling costs are $12,000 per apartment. Both purchase price and remodeling costs qualify as 27.5-year MACRS property.

Assume that the MACRS schedule assigns an equal amount of depreciation to each of the first 27 years and one-half year to the 28th year. The present value at 10% of $1 of cost recovery spread over the 28 years in this way is $.3372.

Ramirez does not believe he will keep the apartment complex for its entire 30-year life. Most likely he will sell it just after the end of the tenth year. His predicted sales price is $900,000.

Ramirez's after-tax required rate of return is 10%, and his tax rate is 38%.

Required

Should Ramirez buy the apartment complex? What is the after-tax net present value? Ignore the investment tax credit and other tax complications such as capital gains.

11-56 Present Value of After-Tax Cash Flows, Payback, and ARR

Yokahama Chemicals Company, located in Yokahama, Japan, is planning to buy new equipment to expand their production of a popular solvent. Estimated data are (monetary amounts are in thousands of Japanese yen):

Cash cost of new equipment now	¥400,000
Estimated life in years	10
Terminal salvage value	¥ 60,000
Incremental revenues per year	¥320,000
Incremental expenses per year other than depreciation	¥165,000

Assume a 60% flat rate for income taxes. All revenues and expenses other than depreciation will be received or paid in cash. Use a 14% discount rate. Assume that ordinary straight-line depreciation based on a 10-year recovery period is used for tax purposes. Also assume that the terminal salvage value will affect the depreciation per year.

Required

Compute

1. Depreciation expenses per year
2. Anticipated net income per year
3. Annual net cash flow
4. Payback period
5. Accounting rate of return on initial investment
6. Net present value

11-57 Fixed and Current Assets; Evaluation of Performance

Bedford Clinic has been under pressure to keep costs down. Indeed, the clinic administrator has been managing various revenue-producing centers to maximize contributions to the recovery of the operating costs of the clinic as a whole. The administrator has been considering whether to buy a special-purpose x-ray machine for $193,000. Its unique characteristics would generate additional cash operating income of $50,000 per year for the clinic as a whole.

The machine is expected to have a useful life of six years and a terminal salvage value of $22,000. The machine is delicate. It requires a constant inventory of various supplies and spare parts. When these items can no longer be used, they are instantly replaced, so an investment of $16,000 must be maintained at all times. However, this investment is fully recoverable at the end of the useful life of the machine.

Required

1. Compute NPV if the required rate of return is 14%.
2. Compute the accounting rate of return on (a) the initial investment and (b) the "average" investment.
3. Why might the administrator be reluctant to base her decision on the DCF model?

11-58 Deer Valley Lodge

Deer Valley Lodge, a ski resort in the Wasatch Mountains of Utah, has plans to eventually add five new chairlifts. Suppose that one of the lifts costs $2 million, and preparing the slope and installing the lift costs another $1.3 million. The lift will allow 300 additional skiers on the slopes, but there are only 40 days a year when the extra capacity will be needed. (Assume that Deer park will sell all 300 lift tickets on those 40 days.) Running the new lift will cost $500 a day for the entire 200 days the lodge is open. Assume that lift tickets at Deer Valley cost $55 a day, and added cash expenses for each skier-day are $5. The new lift has an economic life of 20 years.

Required

1. Assume that the before-tax required rate of return for Deer Valley is 14%. Compute the before-tax NPV of the new lift and advise the managers of Deer Valley about whether adding the lift will be a profitable investment.
2. Assume that the after-tax required rate of return for Deer Valley is 8%, the income tax rate is 40%, and the MACRS recovery period is 10 years. Compute the after-tax NPV of the new lift and advise the managers of Deer Valley about whether adding the lift will be a profitable investment.
3. What subjective factors would affect the investment decision?

CASES

11-59 Investment in CAD/CAM

The Gustav Borg Manufacturing Company is considering the installation of a computer-aided design/computer-aided manufacturing (CAD/CAM) system. The current proposal calls for implementation of only the CAD portion of the system. Bergit Olsson, the manager in charge of production design and planning, has estimated that the CAD portion of CAD/CAM could do the work of five designers, who are each paid SKr 260,000 per year (52 weeks × 40 hours × SKr 125 per hour), where SKr is the symbol for Swedish Kroner.

The CAD/CAM system can be purchased for SKr 1.6 million. (The CAD portion cannot be purchased separately.) The annual out-of-pocket costs of running the CAD portion of the system are SKr 900,000. The system is expected to be used for eight years. Gustov Borg's minimum desired rate of return is 12%.

Required

1. Compute the NPV of the investment in the CAD/CAM system. Should the system be purchased? Explain.
2. Suppose Olsson was not certain about her predictions of savings and economic life. Possibly only four designers will be replaced, but if everything works out well, as many as six might be replaced. If better systems become available, the CAD/CAM system might be used only five years, but it might last as long as 10 years. Prepare pessimistic, most likely, and optimistic predictions of NPV. Would this analysis make you more confident or less confident in your decision in requirement 1? Explain.
3. What subjective factors might influence your decision?

11-60 Investment in Technology

Kentucky Auto Parts Company is considering installation of a computer-integrated manufacturing (CIM) system as part of its implementation of a JIT philosophy. Benjamin Goldworthy, company president, is convinced that the new system is necessary, but he needs the numbers to convince the Board of Directors. This is a major move for the company, and approval at board level is required.

Leah Goldworthy, Benjamin's daughter, has been assigned the task of justifying the investment. She is a business school graduate and understands the use of NPV for capital budgeting decisions. To identify relevant costs, she developed the following information.

Kentucky Auto Parts Company produces a variety of small automobile components and sells them to auto manufacturers. It has a 40% market share, with the following condensed results expected for 2001:

Sales		$12,000,000
Cost of goods sold		
Variable	$4,000,000	
Fixed	4,300,000	8,300,000
Selling and administrative expenses		
Variable	$2,000,000	
Fixed	400,000	2,400,000
Operating income		$ 1,300,000

Installation of the CIM system will cost $6 million, and the system is expected to have a useful life of six years with no salvage value. In 2002, the training costs for personnel will exceed any cost savings by $400,000. In years 2003 through 2007, variable cost of goods sold will decrease by 40%, an annual savings of $1.6 million. There will be no savings in fixed cost of goods sold—in fact, it will increase by the amount of the straight-line depreciation on the new system. Selling and administrative expenses will not be affected. The required rate of return is 12%. Assume that all cash flows occur at the end of the year, except the initial investment, which occurs at the beginning of 2002.

Required

1. Suppose that Leah Goldworthy assumes that production and sales would continue for the next six years as they were in 2001 in the absence of investment in the CIM. Compute the NPV of investing in the CIM.

2. Now suppose Leah predicts that it will be difficult to compete if the CIM is not installed. In fact, she has undertaken market research that estimates a drop in market share of 3 percentage points a year starting in 2002 in the absence of investment in the CIM (i.e., market share will be 37% in 2002, 34% in 2003, 31% in 2004, etc.). Her study also showed that the total market sales level will stay the same, and market prices are not expected to change. Compute the NPV of investing in the CIM.

3. Prepare a memo from Leah Goldworthy to the Board of Directors of Kentucky Auto Parts Company. In the memo, explain why the analysis in requirement 2 is appropriate and why analyses such as that in requirement 1 cause companies to underinvest in high-technology projects. Include an explanation of qualitative factors that are not included in the NPV calculation.

11-61 Investment in Quality

The Brisbane Manufacturing Company produces a single model of a CD player that is sold to Australian manufacturers of sound systems. Each CD player is sold for $210, resulting in a contribution margin of $70 before considering any costs of inspection, correction of product defects, or refunds to customers.

In 20X1, top management at Brisbane is contemplating a change in its quality control system. Currently, $40,000 is spent annually on quality control inspections. Brisbane produces and ships 50,000 CD players a year. In producing those CD players, an average of 2,000 defective units are produced. Of these, 1,500 are identified by the inspection process, and an average of $85 is spent on each to correct the defects. The other 500 players are shipped to customers. When a customer discovers a defective CD player, Brisbane refunds the $210 purchase price.

As more and more customers change to JIT inventory systems and automated production processes, the receipt of defective goods poses greater and greater problems for them. Sometimes a defective CD player causes them to delay their whole production line while the CD player is being replaced. Companies competing with Brisbane recognize this situation, and most have already begun extensive quality control programs. If Brisbane does not improve quality, sales volume is expected to fall by 5,000 CD players a year, beginning after 20X2:

	Predicted Sales Volume in Units without Quality Control Program	Predicted Sales Volume in Units with Quality Control Program
20X2	50,000	50,000
20X3	45,000	50,000
20X4	40,000	50,000
20X5	35,000	50,000

The proposed quality control program has two elements. First, Brisbane would spend $900,000 immediately to train workers to recognize and correct defects at the time they occur. This is expected to cut the number of defective CD players produced from 2,000 to 500 without incurring additional manufacturing costs. Second, an earlier inspection point would replace the current inspection. This would require purchase of an x-ray machine at a cost of $200,000 plus additional annual operating costs of $50,000 more than the current inspection costs. Early detection of defects would reduce the average amount spent to correct defects from $85 to $50, and only 50 defective CD players would be shipped to customers. To compete, Brisbane would refund one-and-one-half times the purchase price ($315) for defective CD players delivered to customers.

Top management at Brisbane has decided that a four-year planning period is sufficient for analyzing this decision. The minimum required rate of return is 20%. For simplicity, assume that under the current quality control system, if the volume of production decreases, the number of defective CD players produced remains at 2,000. Also assume that all annual cash flows occur at the end of the relevant year.

Required

Should Brisbane Manufacturing Company undertake the new quality control program? Explain, using the NPV model. Ignore income taxes.

11-62 Make or Buy and Replacement of Equipment

Ships Ahoy Company is one of the largest producers of miniature ships in a bottle. An especially complex part of one of the ships needs special tools that are not useful for other products. These tools were purchased on July 1, 1997, for $200,000.

It is now July 1, 2001. The manager of the Model Ships Division, Ramona Ruiz, is contemplating three alternatives. First, she could continue to produce the ship using the current tools; they will last another five years, at which time they would have zero terminal value. Second, she could sell the tools for $30,000 and purchase the parts from an outside supplier for $11 each. Third, she could replace the tools with new, more efficient tools costing $180,000.

Ruiz expects to produce 8,000 units of the ship each of the next five years. Manufacturing costs for the ship have been as follows, and no change in costs is expected:

Direct material	$ 3.80
Direct labor	3.70
Variable overhead	1.70
Fixed overhead*	4.50
Total unit cost	$13.70

*Depreciation accounts for two-thirds of the fixed overhead. The balance is for other fixed overhead costs of the factory that require cash outlays, 60% of which would be saved if production of the parts were eliminated.

The outside supplier offered the $11 price as a once-only offer. It is unlikely such a low price would be available later. Ships Ahoy would also have to guarantee to purchase at least 7,000 parts for each of the next five years.

The new tools that are available would last for five years with a disposal value of $40,000 at the end of five years. The old tools are a five-year MACRS property, the new tools are a three-year MACRS property, and both use the current MACRS schedules. Straight-line depreciation is used for book purposes and MACRS for tax purposes. The sales representative selling the new tools stated, "The new tools will allow direct labor and variable overhead to be reduced by $2.10 per unit." Ruiz thinks this estimate is accurate. However, she also knows that a higher quality of materials would be necessary with the new tools. She predicts the following costs with the new tools:

Direct material	$ 4.00
Direct labor	2.50
Variable overhead	.80
Fixed overhead	6.00*
Total unit cost	$13.30

*The increase in fixed overhead is caused by depreciation on the new tools.

The company has a 40% marginal tax rate and requires a 12% after-tax rate of return.

Required

1. Calculate the net present value of each of the three alternatives. Recognize the tax implications. Which alternative should Ruiz select?
2. What are some factors besides the net present value that should influence Ruiz's selection?

COLLABORATIVE LEARNING EXERCISE

11-63 Capital Budgeting, Sensitivity Analysis, and Ethics

James LaGrande had recently been appointed Controller of the Breakfast Cereals Division of a major food company. The Division Manager, Renee Osterland, was known as a hard-driving, intelligent, noncompromising manager. She had been very successful, and was rumored to be on the fast track to corporate top management, maybe even in line for the company presidency. One of Jim's first assignments was to prepare the financial analysis for a new cold cereal, Krispie Krinkles. This product was especially important to Ms. Osterland because she was convinced that it would be a success and thereby a springboard for her ascent to top management.

Mr. LaGrande discussed the product with the food lab that had designed it, with the market research department that had tested it, and with the finance people who would have to fund its introduction. After putting together all the information, he developed the following optimistic and pessimistic sales projections:

	Optimistic	Pessimistic
Year 1	$ 1,600,000	$ 800,000
Year 2	3,600,000	1,200,000
Year 3	5,000,000	1,000,000
Year 4	8,000,000	800,000
Year 5	10,000,000	400,000

The optimistic predictions assume a successful introduction of a popular product. The pessimistic predictions assume that the product is introduced but does not gain wide acceptance and is terminated after 5 years. LaGrande thinks the most likely results are halfway between the optimistic and pessimistic predictions.

LaGrande learned from finance that this type of product introduction requires a predicted rate of return of 16% before top management will authorize funds for its introduction. He also determined that the contribution margin should be about 50% on the product, but could be as low as 42% or as high as 58%. Initial investment would include $3 million for production facilities, $2.5 million for advertising and other product introduction expenses, and $500,000 for working capital (inventory, etc.). The production facilities would have a value of $800,000 after five years.

Based on his preliminary analysis, LaGrande recommended to Osterland that the product not be launched. Osterland was not pleased with the recommendation. She claimed that LaGrande was much too pessimistic and asked him to redo his numbers so that she could justify the product to top management.

LaGrande carried out further analysis, but his predictions came out no differently. In fact, he became even more convinced that his projections were accurate. Yet, he was certain that if he returned to Osterland with numbers that did not support introduction of the product, he would incur her wrath. And, in fact, she could be right—that is, there is so much uncertainty in the forecasts that he could easily come up with believable numbers that would support going forward with the product. He would not believe them, but he thinks he could convince top management that they are accurate.

Required

This role-play could be done as an entire class or in teams of three to six persons. It will be explained here as if being done by a team.

Choose one member of the team to be James LaGrande and one to be Renee Osterland.

1. With the help of the entire team except the person chosen to be Osterland, LaGrande should prepare the capital-budgeting analysis used for his first meeting with Osterland.

2. Next, LaGrande should meet again with Osterland. They should try to agree on the analysis to take forward to top management. As they discuss the issues and try to come to an agreement, the remaining team members should record all the ethical judgments each discussant makes.

3. After LaGrande and Osterland have completed their role-play assignment, the entire team should assess the ethical judgments made by each and recommend an appropriate position for LaGrande to take in this situation.

INTERNET EXERCISE

www.prenhall.com/horngren

11-64 Capital Budgeting at Carnival Corporation

Many companies have a goal of continuing to grow and develop. Some companies grow through expansion of existing operations and increased utilization of existing assets. Other firms will grow through the acquisition of other firms that may be in the same industry the firm currently operates within, or by purchasing a firm that covers new territory for the firm. No matter which method the firm selects, capital budgeting is an important part of a systematic expansion plan. Consider the expansion activities of Carnival Corporation, a firm that has expanded through acquisition, new assets and also consider asset replacement.

1. Go to the home page for Carnival Corporation at http://www.carnivalcorp.com. Select the link to the investor overview. What cruise lines does Carnival own or have an interest in? How many current ships does Carnival operate? What type of plans does the firm list for future expansion? What does this information indicate about the intent of the firm?

2. As we can see, the firm has looked ahead to buying new ships. To get additional information click on the link to the annual reports, and then select the most recent annual report and open it using Adobe Acrobat Reader. Go to the section on Management's Discussion and Analysis of Financial Condition and Results of Operations near the end of the report. Looking at the operating results summary, use the passenger cruise days and occupancy percentage to compute Carnival's capacity in passenger cruise days. How has this capacity changed over the past three years?

3. Now backtrack to the beginning of the annual report and read the CEO's letter. What does the letter tell the investor about new investment during the current year? What form did the investment/expansion take? What are the investment plans for the future?

4. While acquiring contracts for new ships and increasing ownership of other lines is noteworthy, the firm must in some manner plan to pay for this expansion. Let's look at the Statement of Cash Flows to see if we can determine where the firm got the cash to pay for the new ships. Based on your review of the cash flow statement, how much money did the firm invest in new assets? Where did Carnival generate these funds?

5. Another example of Carnival's plan for expansion is found in the footnote on Commitments and Contingencies (footnote 8 in 1999). What information does this footnote provide? How does this information indicate that Carnival has considered a capital budget of some sort?

Solutions to Exercises in Compound Interest, Problem 11-A1

The general approach to these exercises centers on one fundamental question: Which of the two basic tables am I dealing with? No calculations should be made until after this question is answered with assurance. If you made any errors, it is possible that you used the wrong table.

1. From Table 1, Appendix B, page B7:
   a. $15,670
   b. $12,418
   c. $8,038

   The $20,000 is an amount of future worth. You want the present value of that amount:

   $$PV = \$20,000 \times \left[\frac{1}{(1 + i)^n}\right]$$

   The conversion factor, $1/(1 + i)^n$, is on line 5 of Table 1. Substituting,

   $$PV = \$20,000(.7835) = \$15,670$$
   $$PV = \$20,000(.6209) = \$12,418$$
   $$PV = \$20,000(.4019) = \$8,038$$

   Note that the higher the interest rate, the lower the present value.

2. From Table 2, Appendix B, page B8:
   a. $8,659.00
   b. $7,581.60
   c. $5,981.20

   The $2,000 withdrawal is a uniform annual amount, an annuity. You need to find the present value of an annuity for five years:

   $$PV_A = \text{annual withdrawal} \times F, \text{ where F is the conversion factor.}$$
   Substituting:
   $$PV_A = \$2,000(4.3295) = \$8,659.00$$
   $$PV_A = \$2,000(3.7908) = \$7,581.60$$
   $$PV_A = \$2,000(2.9906) = \$5,981.20$$

3. From Table 2:
   a. $23,097.36
   b. $26,379.66

   You have $100,000, the present value of your contemplated annuity. You must find the annuity that will just exhaust the invested principal in five years:

   $$PVA = \text{annual withdrawal} \times F$$
   $$\$100,000 = \text{annual withdrawal} \times 4.3295$$
   $$\text{annual withdrawal} = \$100,000 \div 4.3295$$
   $$= \$23,097.36$$
   $$\$100,000 = \text{annual withdrawal} \times 3.7908$$
   $$\text{annual withdrawal} = \$100,000 \div 3.7908$$
   $$= \$26,379.66$$

4. Amounts are in thousands. From Table 1: Johnson's contract is preferable; its present value exceeds that of Jackson's contract by $21,572 − $17,720 = $3,852. Note that the nearer dollars are more valuable than the distant dollars.

Year	Present Value @ 16% from Table 1	Present Value of Johnson's Contract	Present Value of Jackson's Contract
1	.8621	$ 8,621	$ 1,724
2	.7432	5,946	2,973
3	.6407	3,844	3,844
4	.5523	2,209	4,418
5	.4761	952	4,761
		$21,572	$17,720

12

COST ALLOCATION

Kevin Rollins, President and Chief Operating Officer at Dell Computer Corporation, with a Dell Workstation. The workstation is used by engineers, financial traders, and others to run complex applications such as three-dimensional computer-aided design, software development, and financial/economic modeling.

www.prenhall.com/horngren

Learning Objectives

When you have finished studying this chapter, you should be able to

1. Explain the major reasons for allocating costs.

2. Allocate the variable and fixed costs of service departments to other organizational units.

3. Allocate the central costs of an organization.

4. Use the direct and step-down methods to allocate service department costs to user departments.

5. Use activity-based costing to allocate costs in a modern manufacturing environment to products or services.

6. Use the physical-units and relative-sales-value methods to allocate joint costs to products.

7. **Understand how cost allocation is used in cost planning and control.**

With annual revenues of more than $31 billion, Dell Computer Corporation is the leading producer of computer systems (desktops, notebooks, and network servers for large businesses) in the United States and number 1 worldwide. With manufacturing facilities in Tennessee, Texas, Brazil, China, Ireland, and Malaysia, Dell has earned a reputation for high-quality computer products and personalized service. The company earned the Readers Choice Award for Personal Service and Reliability from *Fortune* magazine and was ranked number 3 on *Fortune*'s list of most-admired U.S. companies. Many organizations, including the U.S. Census Bureau, Toyota Motor Sales, U.S.A., and Boeing, have selected Dell's computers because of their quality and Dell's commitment to service.

Like any business, Dell's managers know that some of their products are more profitable than others. They also know that some distribution methods are more costly than others. Unfortunately, until Dell's accountants redesigned its costing system, managers did not have a solid understanding of which products or channels of distribution were more or less profitable.

Why? Because Dell's old cost allocation system was not accurate enough. A simple cost accumulation system was used to collect costs into direct labor, direct materials, and indirect cost categories. The system did not allocate the indirect costs of most value-chain functions to the products. Instead, Dell added an overall markup to production costs for the costs of value-chain functions such as research and development, design, marketing, distribution, and customer service. When Dell's profitability and growth plateaued in the 1990s, managers determined that a key to the company's long-run success was to design a costing system that accurately allocated all value-chain costs to products and distribution channels and thus would enable managers to determine product and channel profitability.

Dell's new cost-allocation system—an activity-based-costing system (ABC)—has been in place for several years and is still evolving. The initial development process took a significant commitment from managers at all levels but was wholeheartedly embraced by the management team. The benefits have been clear. In fact, the results of an ABC analysis led Dell to discontinue distribution to the consumer market through retail channels. According to John Jonez, vice president and controller for Dell Americas Operations, "ABC has really allowed Dell to go to the next level of understanding of its profitability for each of the products it sells."

Just as is the case for Dell, cost allocation is of strategic importance to most businesses. For example, a university's computer is used for teaching and for performing government-funded research. How much of its cost should be assigned to the research projects? A city creates a special police unit to investigate a series of related assaults. What is the total cost of the effort? A company uses a machine to make two different product lines. How much of the cost of the machine belongs to each product line? These are all problems of cost allocation, the subject of this chapter.

cost accounting systems The techniques used to determine the cost of a product, service, or other cost objective by collecting and classifying costs and assigning them to cost objects.

Chapters 12 through 14 describe **cost accounting systems**—the techniques used to determine the cost of a product, service, customer, or other cost objective. A cost accounting system collects and classifies costs and assigns them to cost objects. The goal of a cost accounting system is to measure the cost of designing, developing, producing (or purchasing), selling, distributing, and servicing particular products or services. Cost allocation is at the heart of most cost accounting systems.

COST ALLOCATION IN GENERAL

As Chapter 4 pointed out, cost allocation is fundamentally a problem of linking some cost or group of costs with one or more cost objectives, such as products, departments, customer classes, activities, and divisions. Ideally, cost allocation should assign each cost to the cost objective that caused it.

cost-allocation base A cost driver that is used for allocating costs.

We link costs with cost objectives by selecting appropriate cost drivers. A cost driver that is used for allocating costs is often called a **cost-allocation base.** Companies often allocate major costs such as newsprint for a newspaper and direct professional labor for a law firm to departments, jobs, and projects on an item-by-item basis, using obvious cost drivers such as tons of newsprint consumed or direct-labor-hours used. Other costs that are not important enough to justify being allocated individually are pooled and then allocated together. Recall that a cost pool is a group of individual costs that is allocated to cost objectives using a single cost driver. For example, building rent, utilities cost, and janitorial services may be in the same cost pool because a company allocated all of them on the basis of square footage of space occupied. Or a university could pool all the operating costs of its registrar's office and allocate them to its colleges on the basis of the number of students in each college. In summary, all costs in a given cost pool should be caused by the same factor. That factor is the cost driver.

Many different terms are used to describe cost allocation in practice. You may encounter terms such as allocate, apply, absorb, attribute, reallocate, trace, assign, distribute, redistribute, load, burden, apportion, and reapportion being used interchangeably to describe the allocation of costs to cost objectives.

ALLOCATION AND COST MANAGEMENT SYSTEMS

What logic should we use for allocating costs? This question bothers many internal users and suppliers of services in all organizations. The answer depends on the principal purpose(s) of the cost allocation.

Objective 1
Explain the major reasons for allocating costs.

Costs are allocated for various reasons, each of which has its roots in the major purposes of any cost management system (CMS). As discussed in Chapter 4, a cost accounting system is a primary tool used to implement a cost management system, and cost allocation is a key element of the cost accounting system. Recall that the three major purposes of a cost management system are to provide cost measurements for external reporting, strategic decision making, and operational control. Let's see how the following four reasons for allocation support the major purposes of a CMS.

1. *To predict the economic effects of planning and control decisions and to provide feedback for performance evaluation*: Managers within an organizational unit should be aware of all the consequences of their decisions, even consequences outside of their unit. Examples are the addition of a new course in a university that causes additional work in the registrar's office, the addition of a new flight or an additional passenger on an airline that requires reservation and booking services, and the addition of a new specialty in a medical clinic that produces more work for the medical records department. This reason supports the strategic decision-making and operational control purposes of a CMS.

2. *To obtain desired motivation*: Cost allocations often influence management behavior and thus promote goal congruence and managerial effort. Consequently, in some organizations, the costs of legal or internal auditing services or internal management consulting services are not allocated because top management wants to encourage their use. In other organizations, the costs of such items to spur managers to make sure the benefits of the specified services exceed the costs. This reason supports the operational control purpose of a CMS.

3. *To compute income and asset valuations*: Companies allocate costs to products and projects to measure inventory costs and cost of goods sold. This reason supports the external reporting purpose of a CMS.

4. *To justify costs or obtain reimbursement*: Sometimes prices are based directly on costs. For example, government contracts often specify a price that includes reimbursement for costs plus some profit margin. In these instances, cost allocations become substitutes for the usual working of the marketplace in setting prices. This reason supports the external reporting and strategic purposes of a CMS.

Ideally, a single cost allocation serves all purposes simultaneously. But thousands of managers and accountants will testify that for most costs this ideal is rarely achieved. Instead, cost allocations are often a major source of discontent and confusion to the affected parties. Allocating fixed costs usually causes the greatest problems. When all purposes cannot be attained simultaneously, the manager and the accountant should start attacking a cost-allocation problem by trying to identify which of the purposes should dominate in the particular situation at hand.

Often inventory-costing for external reporting purposes dominate by default because they are externally imposed. When managers use allocations in decision making and performance evaluation, they should consider adjusting the allocations used to satisfy inventory-costing purposes. Often the added benefit of using separate allocations for planning and control and inventory-costing purposes is much greater than the added cost.

Exhibit 12-1

Three Types of Cost Allocations

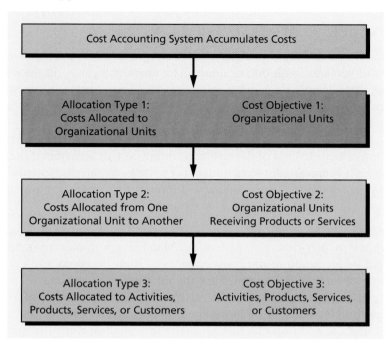

THREE TYPES OF ALLOCATIONS

As Exhibit 12-1 shows, there are three basic types of cost allocations.

1. Allocation of costs to the appropriate organizational unit: Direct costs are physically traced to the unit, but costs of resources that are used jointly by more than one unit are allocated based on cost-driver activity in the unit. Examples are allocating rent to departments based on floor space occupied, allocating depreciation of heating and air conditioning equipment based on cubic feet, and allocating general administrative expense based on total direct cost.

2. Reallocation of costs from one organizational unit to another: When one unit provides products or services to another, the costs are transferred along with the products or services. Some units, called **service departments,** exist only to support other departments, and their costs are totally reallocated. Examples include personnel departments, laundry departments in hospitals, and legal departments in industrial firms.

3. Allocation of costs of a particular organizational unit to activities, products, services, or customers: The pediatrics department of a medical clinic allocates its costs to patients, the assembly activity of a manufacturing firm to units assembled, and the tax department of a CPA firm to clients. The costs allocated to activities, products, services, or customers include those costs allocated to the organizational unit in allocation types 1 and 2.

All three types of allocations are fundamentally similar. Let us look first at how service department costs are allocated to production departments.

service departments
Units that exist only to support other departments.

GENERAL GUIDELINES

The preferred guidelines for allocating service department costs are

1. Establish part or all of the details regarding cost allocation in advance of rendering the service rather than after the fact. This approach establishes the "rules of the game" so that all departments can plan appropriately.

2. Allocate variable- and fixed-cost pools separately. Note that one service department (such as a computer department) can contain multiple cost pools if more than one cost driver causes the department's costs. At a minimum, there should be a variable-cost pool and a fixed-cost pool.

3. Evaluate performance using budgets for each service (staff) department, just as for each production or operating (line) department. The performance of a service department is evaluated by comparing actual costs with a budget, regardless of how the costs are allocated. From the budget, variable-cost pools and fixed-cost pools can be identified for use in allocation.

Consider an example of a computer department of a university that serves two major users, the School of Business and the School of Engineering. Exhibit 12-2 shows the allocation system. We show all three types of allocation in Exhibit 12-2. Type 1 allocations include costs such as energy and building costs. These costs are first accumulated by the cost accounting system and then allocated to organizational units including the computer department. Type 2 allocations include the allocation of the variable-cost and fixed-cost resources from the computer department to the business and engineering schools. Finally, the allocation of business and engineering school costs to programs are type 3 allocations. Let's focus on the type 2 allocation from the computer department to the business and engineering schools.

Suppose there are two major reasons for the allocation: (1) predicting economic effects of the use of the computer, and (2) motivating the two schools and individuals to use its capabilities more fully. How should the university allocate the costs of the computer department (salaries, depreciation, energy, materials, and so on) to the two schools?

We begin by analyzing the costs of the computer department in detail. The primary activity performed is computer processing. The computer mainframe was acquired on a five-year lease that is not cancelable unless high cost penalties are paid. Resources consumed include processing time, operator time, energy, materials, and building space. Suppose the university performed cost behavior analysis and the budget formula for the forthcoming year is $100,000 monthly fixed cost plus $200 variable cost per hour of computer time used. Refer to Exhibit 12-2 as we show how to apply guideline 2—the topic of the next two sections.

VARIABLE-COST POOL

Costs in the variable-cost pool include energy and materials. The cost driver for the variable-cost pool is actual hours of computer time used. Therefore, the university should allocate variable costs as follows:

$$\text{budgeted unit rate} \times \text{actual hours of computer time used}$$

The cause-and-effect relationship is clear: The heavier the usage, the higher the total costs. In this example, the rate used would be the budgeted rate of $200 per hour. The rate would be determined by dividing the total budgeted costs of energy and materials by the total budgeted hours of computer time.

Exhibit 12-2

Allocations of Variable- and Fixed-Cost Pools

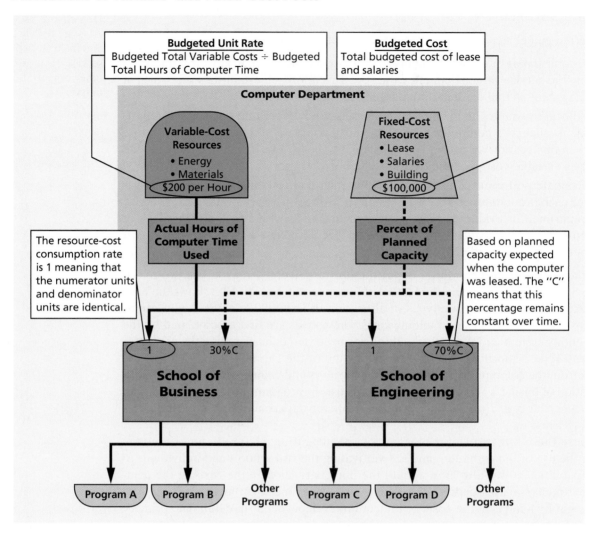

The use of budgeted cost rates rather than actual cost rates for allocating variable costs of service departments protects the using departments from intervening price fluctuations and also often protects them from inefficiencies in the service departments. When an organization allocates actual total service department cost, it holds user department managers responsible for costs beyond their control and provides less incentive for service departments to be efficient. Both effects are undesirable.

Consider the allocation of variable costs to a department that uses 600 hours of computer time. Suppose inefficiencies in the computer department caused the variable costs to be $140,000 instead of the 600 hours × $200 = $120,000 budgeted. A good cost-allocation scheme would allocate only the $120,000 to the consuming departments and would let the $20,000 remain as an unallocated unfavorable budget variance of the computer department. This scheme holds computer department managers responsible for the $20,000 variance and reduces the resentment of user managers. User department managers sometimes complain more vigorously about uncertainty over allocations and the poor management of a service department than about the choice of a cost driver (such as direct-labor dollars or number of employees).

Such complaints are less likely if the service department managers have budget responsibility and the user departments are protected from short-run price fluctuations and inefficiencies.

Consider an automobile repair and maintenance department for a state government. Agencies who use the department's service should receive firm prices for various services. Imagine the feelings of an agency head who had an agency automobile repaired and was told, "Normally your repair would have taken five hours. However, we had a new employee work on it, and the job took him 10 hours. Therefore, we must charge you for 10 hours of labor time."

FIXED-COST POOL

Consider again our example of the university computer department. Costs in the fixed-cost pool include the lease payment, salaries of operators and occupancy costs of the building (depreciation, insurance, and so on). The cost driver for the fixed-cost pool is the amount of capacity the two schools estimated they required when the university acquired the computer facilities. Therefore, fixed costs should be allocated as follows:

budgeted percent of capacity available for use × total budgeted fixed costs

Suppose the deans had originally predicted the long-run average monthly usage by Business at 210 hours, and by Engineering at 490 hours, a total of 700 hours. These estimates by the deans resulted in a set of committed fixed costs that remain largely uncontrollable over many years. The fixed-cost pool would be allocated as follows:

	Business	Engineering
Fixed costs per month		
210/700, or 30% of $100,000	$30,000	
490/700, or 70% of $100,000		$70,000

This predetermined lump-sum approach is based on the long-run capacity available to the user, regardless of actual usage from month to month. The reasoning is that long-range planning regarding the overall level of service and the relative expected usage affect the level of fixed costs, not short-run fluctuations in service levels and relative actual usage. Notice the allocation of these six costs in Exhibit 12-2.

A major strength of using capacity available rather than capacity used when allocating budgeted fixed costs is that short-run allocations to user departments are not affected by the actual usage of other user departments. Such a budgeted lump-sum approach is more likely to have the desired motivational effects with respect to the ordering of services in both the short run and the long run.

In practice, fixed-cost pools often are inappropriately allocated on the basis of capacity used, not capacity available. Suppose the computer department allocated the total actual costs after the fact. At the end of the month, total actual costs would be allocated in proportion to the actual hours used by the consuming departments. Compare the costs borne by the two schools when Business uses 200 hours and Engineering 400 hours.

Total costs incurred, $100,000 + (600 × $200) = $220,000	
Business: 200/600 × $220,000 =	$ 73,333
Engineering: 400/600 × $220,000 =	146,667
Total cost allocated	$220,000

What happens if Business uses only 100 hours during the following month, and Engineering still uses 400 hours?

Total costs incurred, $100,000 + (500 × $200) = $200,000	
Business: 100/500 × $200,000 =	$ 40,000
Engineering: 400/500 × $200,000 =	160,000
Total cost allocated	$200,000

Engineering has done nothing differently, but it must bear an additional cost of $13,333, an increase of 9%. Its short-run costs depend on what other consumers have used, not solely on its own actions. This phenomenon is caused by a faulty allocation method for the fixed portion of total costs, a method whereby the allocations are highly sensitive to fluctuations in the actual volumes used by the various consuming departments. This weakness is avoided by using a predetermined lump-sum allocation of fixed costs, based on budgeted usage.

Consider the preceding automobile repair shop example. You would not be happy if you came to get your car and were told, "Our daily fixed overhead is $1,000. Yours was the only car in our shop today, so we are charging you the full $1,000. If we had processed 100 cars today, your charge would have been only $10."

TROUBLES WITH USING LUMP SUMS

Using lump-sum allocations can cause problems, however. If a company allocates fixed costs on the basis of long-range plans, there is a natural tendency on the part of managers to underestimate their planned usage and thus obtain a smaller fraction of the cost allocation. Top management can counteract these tendencies by monitoring predictions and by following up and using feedback to keep future predictions more honest.

In some organizations, there are even definite rewards in the form of salary increases for managers who make accurate predictions. Moreover, some cost-allocation methods provide for penalties for underpredictions. For example, suppose a manager predicts usage of 210 hours and then demands 300 hours. The manager either doesn't get the hours or pays a dear price for every hour beyond 210 in such systems.

ALLOCATION OF CENTRAL COSTS

The seeming need to allocate central costs is a manifestation of a widespread, deep-seated belief that all costs must somehow be fully allocated to the revenue-producing (operating) parts of the organization. Such allocations are neither necessary from an accounting viewpoint nor useful as management information. For this reason, central costs are not considered part of the value chain in this text. However, most managers accept them as a fact of life—as long as all managers seem to be treated alike and thus "fairly."

Whenever possible, the preferred cost driver for central services is usage, either actual or estimated. But the costs of such services as public relations, top corporate management overhead, a real estate department, and a corporate-planning department are the least likely to be allocated on the basis of usage. Data processing, advertising, and operations research are the most likely to choose usage as a cost driver.

Companies that allocate central costs by usage tend to generate less resentment. Consider the experience of JCPenney Co. as reported in *Business Week*:

> *The controller's office wanted subsidiaries such as Thrift Drug Co. and the insurance operations to base their share of corporate personnel, legal, and auditing costs on their revenues. The subsidiaries contended that they maintained their own personnel and legal departments, and should be assessed far less. . . . The subcommittee addressed the issue by asking the corporate departments to approximate the time and costs involved in servicing the subsidiaries. The final allocation plan, based on these studies, cost the divisions less than they were initially assessed but more than they had wanted to pay. Nonetheless, the plan was implemented easily.*

Usage is not always an economically viable way to allocate central costs, however. Also, many central costs, such as the president's salary and related expenses, public relations, legal services, income tax planning, companywide advertising, and basic research, are difficult to allocate on the basis of cause and effect. As a result, some companies use cost drivers such as the revenue of each division, the cost of goods sold by each division, the total assets of each division, or the total costs of each division (before allocation of the central costs) to allocate central costs.

The use of the foregoing cost drivers might provide a rough indication of cause-and-effect relationship. Basically, however, they represent an "ability to bear" philosophy of cost allocation. For example, the costs of companywide advertising, such as the goodwill sponsorship of a program on a noncommercial television station, might be allocated to all products and divisions on the basis of the dollar sales in each. But such costs precede sales. They are discretionary costs as determined by management policies, not by sales results. Although 60% of the companies in a large survey use sales revenue as a cost driver for cost allocation purposes, it is seldom truly a cost driver in the sense of being an activity that causes the costs.

USE OF BUDGETED SALES FOR ALLOCATION

If a company feels it must allocate the costs of central services based on sales, even though the costs do not vary in proportion to sales, the use of budgeted sales is preferable to the use of actual sales. At least this method means that the fortunes of other departments will not affect the short-run costs of a given department.

Objective 3
Allocate the central costs of an organization.

For example, suppose a company allocates $100 of fixed central advertising costs on the basis of potential sales in two territories.

| | Territories | | Total | Percent |
	A	B		
Budgeted sales	$500	$500	$1,000	100
Central advertising allocated	$ 50	$ 50	$ 100	10

Consider the possible differences in allocations when actual sales become known.

| | Territories | |
	A	B
Actual sales	$300	$600
Central advertising		
1. Allocated on basis of budgeted sales	$ 50	$ 50
or		
2. Allocated on basis of actual sales	$ 33	$ 67

Compare allocation 1 with 2. Allocation 1 is preferable. It indicates a low ratio of sales to advertising in territory A. It directs attention where it is deserved. In contrast, allocation 2 soaks territory B with more advertising cost because of the achieved results and relieves territory A despite its lower success. This is another example of the confusion that can arise when cost allocations to one consuming department depend on the activity of other consuming departments.

RECIPROCAL SERVICES

Objective 4
Use the direct and step-down methods to allocate service department costs to user departments.

In our computer department example, we assumed that computer services were provided only to two other units. What if the computer department also provided computer services to other service units such as the administration and library? Service departments often support other service departments in addition to producing departments. These services are called reciprocal or interdepartmental services.

Consider a manufacturing company with two producing departments, molding and finishing, and two service departments, facilities management (rent, heat, light, janitorial services, and so on) and personnel. All costs in a given service department are assumed to be caused by, and therefore vary in proportion to, a single cost driver. The company has decided that the best cost driver for facilities management costs is square footage occupied and the best cost driver for personnel is the number of employees. Exhibit 12-3 shows the direct costs, square footage occupied, and number of employees for each department. Note that facilities management provides services for the personnel department in addition to providing services for the producing departments, and that personnel aids employees in facilities management as well as those in production departments.

There are two popular methods for allocating service department costs in such cases: the direct method and the step-down method.

direct method A method for allocating service department costs that ignores other service departments when any given service department's costs are allocated to the revenue-producing (operating) departments.

Direct Method. As its name implies, the **direct method** ignores other service departments when allocating any given service department's costs to the revenue-producing (operating) departments. In other words, the direct method ignores the services that facilities management provides for personnel and the services that personnel provides to facilities management. Facilities management costs are allocated based on the relative square footage occupied by the production departments only.

Exhibit 12-3

Cost Drivers

	Service Departments		Production Departments	
	Facilities Management	*Personnel*	*Molding*	*Finishing*
Direct department costs	$126,000	$24,000	$100,000	$160,000
Square feet	3,000	9,000	15,000	3,000
Number of employees	20	30	80	320
Direct-labor hours			2,100	10,000
Machine-hours			30,000	5,400

- Total square footage in production departments = 15,000 + 3,000 = 18,000
- Facilities management cost allocated to molding = (15,000 ÷ 18,000) × $126,000 = $105,000
- Facilities management cost allocated to finishing = (3,000 ÷ 18,000) × $126,000 = $21,000

Likewise, personnel department costs are allocated only to the production departments on the basis of the relative number of employees in the production departments.

- Total employees in production departments = 80 + 320 = 400
- Personnel costs allocated to molding = (80 ÷ 400) × $24,000 = $4,800
- Personnel costs allocated to finishing = (320 ÷ 400) × $24,000 = $19,200

Step-down Method. The **step-down method** recognizes that some service departments support the activities in other service departments as well as those in operating departments. A sequence of allocations is chosen, usually by starting with the service department that renders the greatest service (as measured by costs) to the greatest number of other service departments. The last service department in the sequence is the one that renders the least service to the least number of other service departments. Once a department's costs are allocated to other departments, no subsequent service department costs are allocated back to it.

In our example, we allocate facilities management costs first. Why? Because facilities management renders more support to personnel than personnel provides for facilities management.[1] Examine Exhibit 12-4. After allocating facilities management costs, we do not allocate any costs back to facilities management, even though personnel does provide some services for facilities management. The personnel costs to be allocated to the production departments include the amount allocated to personnel from facilities management ($42,000) in addition to the direct personnel department costs of $24,000.

Examine the last column of Exhibit 12-4. Before allocation, the four departments incurred costs of $410,000. In step 1, we deducted $126,000 from facilities management and added it to the other three departments. There was no net effect on the total cost. In step 2, we deducted $66,000 from personnel and added it to the remaining two departments. Again, total cost was unaffected. After allocation, all $410,000 remains, but it is all in molding and finishing. None was left in facilities management or personnel.

> **step-down method** A method for allocating service department costs that recognizes that some service departments support the activities in other service departments as well as those in operating departments.

---

[1] *How should we determine which of the two service departments provides more service to the other? One way is to carry out step 1 of the step-down method with facilities management allocated first, and then repeat it assuming personnel is allocated first. With facilities management allocated first, $42,000 is allocated to personnel, as shown in Exhibit 12-4. If personnel had been allocated first, (20 ÷ 420) × $24,000 = $1,143 would have been allocated to facilities management. Because $1,143 is smaller than $42,000, facilities management is allocated first.*

Exhibit 12-4

Step-Down Allocation

	Facilities Management	Personnel	Molding	Finishing	Total
Direct department costs before allocation	$ 126,000	$ 24,000	$100,000	$160,000	$410,000
Step 1					
Facilities management	$ (126,000)	(9 ÷ 27) × $126,000 = $ 42,000	(15 ÷ 27) × $126,000 = $ 70,000	(3 ÷ 27) × $126,000 = $ 14,000	
Step 2					
Personnel		$(66,000)	(80 ÷ 400) × $66,000 = $ 13,200	(320 ÷ 400) × $66,000 = $ 52,800	
Total cost after allocation	$ 0	$ 0	$183,200	$226,800	$410,000

Comparison of the Methods. Compare the costs of the production departments under direct and step-down methods, as shown in Exhibit 12-5. Note that the method of allocation can greatly affect the costs. Molding appears to be a much more expensive operation to a manager using the direct method than it does to one using the step-down method. Conversely, finishing seems more expensive to a manager using the step-down method.

Which method is better? Generally, the step-down method.[2] Why? Because it recognizes the effects of the most significant support provided by service departments to other service departments. In our example, the direct method ignores the following possible cause-effect link: If the cost of facilities management is caused by the space used, then the space used by personnel causes $42,000 of facilities management cost. If the space used in personnel is caused by the number of production department employees supported, then the number of production department employees, not the square footage, causes $42,000 of the facilities management cost. The producing department with the most employees, not the one with the most square footage, should bear this cost.

The greatest virtue of the direct method is its simplicity. If the two methods do not produce significantly different results, many companies elect to use the direct method because it is easier for managers to understand.

Exhibit 12-5

Direct Versus Step-Down Method

	Molding		Finishing	
	*Direct**	*Step-down***	*Direct**	*Step-down***
Direct department costs	$100,000	$100,000	$160,000	$160,000
Allocated from facilities management	105,000	70,000	21,000	14,000
Allocated from personnel	4,800	13,200	19,200	52,800
Total costs	$209,800	$183,200	$200,200	$226,800

*From Exhibit 12-3.
** From Exhibit 12-4.

[2] *The most defensible theoretical accuracy is generated by the reciprocal cost method, which is rarely used in practice because it is more difficult to understand. Simultaneous equations and linear algebra are used to solve for the impact of mutually interacting services.*

Costs Not Related to Cost Drivers

Our example illustrating direct and step-down allocation methods assumed that a single cost driver could be used to allocate all costs in a given service department. For example, we assumed that square footage occupied could be used to allocate all facilities management costs. Additional square footage would result in additional facilities management cost. But what if some of the costs in facilities management are independent of square footage?

Three alternative methods of allocation should be considered:

1. **Identify additional cost drivers.** Divide facilities management costs into two or more different cost pools and use a different cost driver to allocate the costs in each pool. Some companies may even adopt ABC systems to improve the allocation system. Key activities performed in the facilities management department are identified along with plausible and reliable cost drivers. These cost drivers become the allocation bases to be used to allocate facilities management activity costs to using departments.

2. Divide facilities management costs into two cost pools, one with costs that vary in proportion to the square footage (variable costs) and one with costs not affected by square footage (fixed costs). Allocate the former using the direct or step-down method, but do not allocate the latter. Costs not allocated are period costs for the organization but are not regarded as a cost of a particular operating department.

3. Allocate all costs by the direct or step-down method using square footage as the cost driver. This alternative implicitly assumes that, in the long run, square footage causes all facilities management costs—even if a short-term causal relationship is not easily identifiable. In other words, using more square footage may not cause an immediate increase in all facilities management costs, but eventually such costs will creep up in proportion to increases in square footage.

Suppose that a single cost driver causes most costs in a service department. Then alternatives 2 and 3 have much appeal. Only a small portion of costs would be unallocated (in alternative 2) or arbitrarily allocated (in alternative 3). But if large amounts of cost are not related to the single cost driver, alternative 1 should be seriously considered.

Suppose you are on a cross-functional team that is discussing how to allocate the costs of a purchasing department. It has been suggested that "number of purchase orders issued" is the best cost driver. However, a scatter graph of total costs versus number of purchase orders issued shows the following:

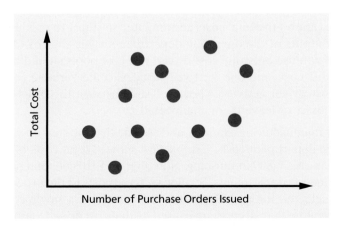

Because the data clearly indicate (too much scatter in the data) that the single cost driver "number of purchase orders issued" is not a reliable measure of the work done in the department, the team investigated. It discovered that the work of the purchasing department involved certifying new vendors in addition to issuing purchase orders. What alternative method of allocation would you recommend?

ANSWER

Because a large percentage of the costs of the purchasing department are not related to the single cost driver "number of purchase orders," a second cost pool should be used with another cost driver such as "number of new vendors."

ALLOCATION OF COSTS TO FINAL COST OBJECTS

Up to this point, we have concentrated on cost allocation to divisions, departments, and similar segments of a company. Cost allocation is almost always carried one step further—to the final cost objects. Examples are products, such as automobiles, furniture, and newspapers, services, such as banking, health care, and education, and customers. Sometimes the allocation of total departmental costs to the revenue-producing products or services is called **cost application** or cost attribution. Costs are allocated to products for inventory valuation purposes (external reporting) and for decision purposes such as pricing, and adding or deleting products (strategic decisions). Cost allocation is also performed for cost reimbursement purposes. As noted earlier, many defense contractors are reimbursed for the "cost" of producing products for the government. We will focus on the two major approaches to cost allocation to final cost objects—the traditional approach and activity-based-costing approach. Keep in mind the primary objective of allocation is achieving an accuracy level that supports management's purposes of allocation.

cost application The allocation of total departmental costs to the revenue-producing products or services.

TRADITIONAL APPROACH

The traditional approach uses the following steps for allocating costs to products, services, or customers is the following:

1. Allocate production-related costs to the operating (line) or production or revenue-producing departments. This includes allocating service department costs to the production departments following the preceding guidelines. The production departments then contain all the costs: their direct department costs and the service department costs.

2. Select one or more cost drivers in each production department. For example, you might allocate a portion of the departmental costs on the basis of direct-labor hours, another portion on the basis of machine hours, and the remainder on the basis of number of machine setups.

3. Allocate (apply) the total costs accumulated in step 1 to products or services that are the outputs of the operating departments using the cost drivers specified in step 2. If you use only one cost driver, two cost pools should be maintained, one for variable costs and one for fixed costs. Allocate variable costs on the basis of actual cost-driver activity. Allocate fixed costs on the basis of budgeted cost-driver activity or leave them unallocated.

Consider our manufacturing example, and assume that the step-down method was used to allocate service department costs. Exhibit 12-4 showed total costs of $183,200 accumulated in molding and $226,800 in finishing. Note that all $410,000 total manufacturing costs reside in the production departments. To allocate these costs to the products produced, cost drivers must be selected for each department. We will use a single cost driver for each department and assume that all costs are caused by that cost driver. Suppose machine hours is the best measure of what causes costs in the molding department, and direct-labor hours drive costs in finishing. Exhibit 12-3 showed 30,000 total machine hours used in molding and 10,000 direct-labor hours in finishing. Therefore costs are allocated to products as follows:

Molding: $183,200 ÷ 30,000 machine hours = $6.11 per machine hour

Finishing: $226,800 ÷ 10,000 direct-labor hours = $22.68 per direct-labor hour

A product that takes four machine hours in molding and two direct-labor hours in finishing would have a cost of

$$(4 \times \$6.11) + (2 \times \$22.68) = \$24.44 + \$45.36 = \$69.80$$

The traditional approach to allocation of costs to the final cost objects focuses on accumulating costs within departments and then allocating departmental costs to operating departments, and finally to products, services, or customers. Poorly designed traditional costing systems can result in incentives for managers to use resources (and services) incorrectly when there is a lack of a good cause-effect relationship between costs allocated and actual resources (and services) consumed. Because of the potential for misleading cost information, many companies seek to improve strategic and operational decision making by increasing the accuracy of product, service, or customer costs. They have adopted a different approach to the design of their cost allocation systems activity-based costing (ABC).

ACTIVITY-BASED-COSTING (ABC) APPROACH

The basic difference between traditional cost allocation systems and ABC systems is that ABC systems focus on accumulating costs into key activities, whereas traditional cost allocation focuses on accumulating costs into organizational units such as departments. The accuracy of allocation in ABC systems is greater than traditional costing systems because of the emphasis on choosing cost drivers having a cause-effect relationship with activities and resources consumed. ABC systems also are more complex due to the necessary detail in accumulating costs by activities. In ABC, we focus first on the activities required to produce the product or service. Then we accumulate all resource costs based on their use in performing the activities.

Many managers in modern manufacturing firms (and automated service companies) believe it is inappropriate to allocate all costs based on measures of volume. Using direct-labor hours or cost—or even machine hours—as the only cost driver seldom meets the cause-effect criterion desired in cost allocation. If many costs are caused by non-volume-based cost drivers, activity-based costing (ABC) should be considered. Recall from Chapter 4 that when we design an activity-based-costing system, accountants identify significant overhead activities (machine processing, assembly, quality inspection, and so on). Then they allocate the costs of overhead resources used to perform these activities to the activities using cost drivers. Finally, they allocate the pooled costs of each activity to products using cost drivers (sometimes called activity drivers). In effect, the ABC system has taken one large overhead cost pool and broken it down into several pools, each associated with a key activity.

ILLUSTRATION OF THE ACTIVITY-BASED-COSTING
APPROACH IN MANUFACTURING

Chapter 4 introduced a four-step procedure for the design and implementation of activity-based-costing systems. We consider this same four-step procedure for the Molding Department of a manufacturing company that produces plastic parts using injection molding machines. The molding process produces three product lines with diverse demands on various activities and resources. Product line A consists of simple products that are produced in high volume (tape holders). Line B products are of medium volume and complexity (flashlight casings). Product line C consists of complex products that are

> **Objective 5**
> Use activity-based costing to allocate costs in a modern manufacturing environment to products or services.

Exhibit 12-6

Product Cost Based on Traditional Costing System

	Product Line A	Product Line B	Product Line C
Direct material	$1,050,000	$ 575,000	$240,000
Direct labor (operators)	344,000	303,000	123,000
Factory overhead @ $27 per DLH			
Product line A (18,000 DLH)	486,000		
Product line B (16,000 DLH)		432,000	
Product line C (6,000 DLH)			162,000
Total cost	$1,880,000	$1,310,000	$525,000
Units produced	1,000,000	500,000	150,000
Unit cost	$1.88	$2.62	$3.50

produced in small lots (small camera casings). The former, traditional, costing system allocated factory overhead costs based on the amount of direct-labor hours used to produce each product. The rate used to allocate factory overhead was $27 per direct-labor hour. This rate was calculated by dividing the total expected factory overhead ($1,080,000) by the total expected direct-labor hours (40,000). The company allocated $6 \div 40 = 15\%$ of total overhead resource costs to product line C because 6,000 of the 40,000 total direct-labor hours were required to produce the 150,000 units of C. The use of this volume-based driver to allocate factory overhead (indirect) cost resulted in the unit cost for the three product lines shown in the last row of Exhibit 12-6.

Management implemented activity-based costing in this manufacturing department using the four-step procedure outlined in Chapter 4. Product line C is typical of complex products that require relatively more indirect resources from setup and machining activity. Management believed that the former costing system may have undercosted such products.

Step 1: Determine the cost objective, key activity centers, resources, and related cost drivers. The costing objective is to determine the costs of product lines A, B, and C. Direct material and direct labor (machine operators) are traced directly to each product.

Exhibit 12-7

Activity Centers, Cost Drivers, and Resources
Molding Department

Activity Center	Cost Driver	Resources Consumed
Setup	Number of setups	Maintenance mechanic time Power (machines had to remain on during setup activity) Occupancy space Molding machine time
Molding process	Machine hours	Supplies Power Molding machine time Occupancy space Maintenance mechanic time

Exhibit 12-7 lists the remaining indirect resources together with the two activity centers and chosen cost drivers.

Step 2: Develop a process-based map representing the flow of activities, resources, and their interrelationships. The interrelationships between activities and resources were determined based on interviews with key personnel. Exhibit 12-8 depicts the flow of

Exhibit 12-8
Process-Based Map of the Molding Department's Operations

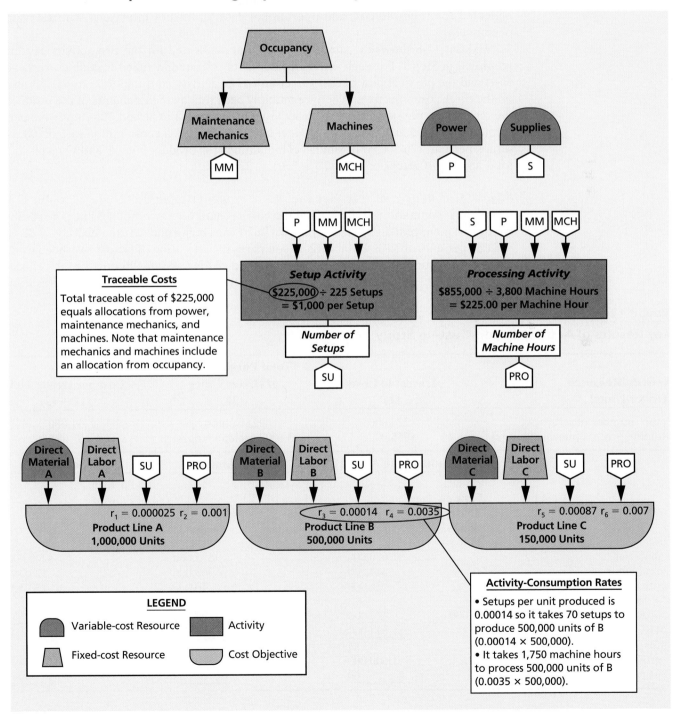

activities and resources. Note that the cost behavior for each resource is also shown. Understanding the cost behavior of resources is vital during the planning process. For example, if the volume of product line A is expected to increase (within the relevant range of activity), machine hours and the number of setups would increase. However, the only costs that would be expected to increase are direct materials, supplies, and power because they are variable-cost resources. Because the remaining resources are fixed-cost resources, their costs would not increase in response to increased setups or machine hours.

Step 3: Collect relevant data concerning costs and the physical flow of cost-driver units among resources and activities. Using the process map as a guide, accountants collected the required cost and operational data by further interviews with relevant personnel.

Exhibit 12-8 shows the summary of the data collected for the two activity centers identified in Step 1. For each activity center, data collected included traceable overhead costs and the physical flow of cost-driver units. The activity-consumption rates are shown on the three cost objectives. When we multiply each rate by the total units of the product, the result is the physical flow of each activity. For example, last period, 70 setups were performed to make 500,000 units of product line B. That gives a consumption rate of .00014 setups per unit (70/500,000). Similar computations for product lines A and C result in a total number of setups of (25 + 70 + 130) = 225.

Step 4: Calculate and interpret the new activity-based information. Exhibit 12-9 shows the computations to determine the cost per unit for each product line. The results confirmed management's belief—product line C was being undercosted by $4.86 − $3.50 = $1.36 per unit, or 39%. Exhibit 12-10 compares the allocation of factory overhead using the former costing system with the activity-based-costing system. Product line A's allocation of overhead decreased from 45% to 23.1%, while product line C's allocation

Exhibit 12-9

Key Results of Activity-Based-Costing Study

Activity/Resource [Driver Units]	Traceable Costs (1)	Total Physical Flow of Driver Units (2)	Cost per Driver Unit (1) ÷ (2)
Setup [number of setups]	$225,000	225 Setups	$1,000
Molding process [machine hours]	$855,000	3,800 Machine Hours	$ 225

	Cost per Driver Unit	Product Line A Physical Flow of Driver Units	Cost	Product Line B Physical Flow of Driver Units	Cost	Product Line C Physical Flow of Driver Units	Cost
Direct material			$1,050,000		$ 575,000		$240,000
Direct labor			344,000		303,000		123,000
Setup costs	$1,000	25	25,000	70	70,000	130	130,000
Molding process	$ 225	1,000	225,000	1,750	393,750	1,050	236,250
Total			$1,644,000		$1,341,750		$729,250
Units produced			1,000,000		500,000		150,000
Cost per unit			$ 1.64		$ 2.68		$ 4.86

increased from 15% to 33.9%. Notice that the use of just two additional cost drivers (machine hours and setups) can make a significant difference in product costing. Many companies use more than 20 different cost drivers to improve the accuracy of their production costing system, but the costs associated with using many activity centers can be high. The benefit-cost criteria must be applied in each case.

Confirm your understanding of traditional and ABC allocation systems by computing the allocation of overhead costs to the deluxe-type speaker for the Louder is Better Company. The company makes two types of speakers, a standard (S) and a deluxe (D) model. The diagrams below show how allocation would be done under ABC versus traditional allocation systems. The production department has overhead costs of $36,000. How would ABC versus traditional allocation differ?

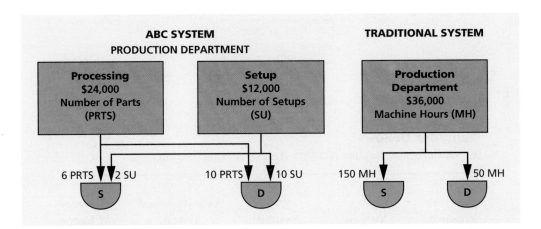

ABC Allocation to Deluxe, D	Traditional Allocation to Deluxe, D

$$\$24{,}000 \times (10/16) + \$12{,}000 \times (10/12) =$$

$$\$36{,}000 \times (50/200) = \$9{,}000$$

$$\$15{,}000 + \$10{,}000 = \$25{,}000$$

ANSWER

In the traditional system the deluxe product receives only 25% of the overhead costs because it uses only 25% of the machine hours. But in the ABC system it receives 72% of the overhead because it uses 63% of the parts and 83% of the setups.

Effect of Activity-Based Costing.   Many companies have adopted activity-based costing in recent years. For example, consider Schrader Bellows, which increased the number of cost drivers used to allocate costs to products. The cost driver having the largest effect on unit costs was number of machine setups. The resulting changes in unit costs for the company's seven products were dramatic, as shown in Exhibit 12-11. Except for product 7, the products with low volume and a high number of setups per unit had large increases in unit costs. The products with high volume and fewer setups per unit had decreases in unit costs. Although product 7 had low volume, its unit cost dropped because it was assembled from components used in large volumes in other products. The unit cost of the components decreased because of their high volume and relatively few setups.

Exhibit 12-10
Comparison of Costing Systems

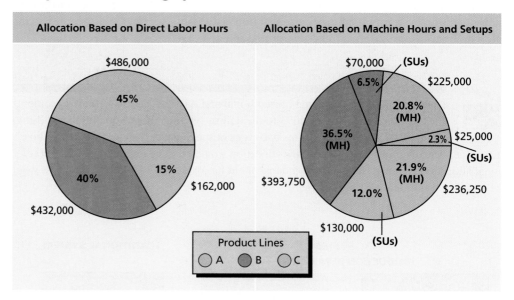

Exhibit 12-11
Schrader Bellows*
Costs Before and After Activity-Based-Costing System

Product	Unit Cost Sales Volume	Old System	Activity-based System	Percent Change
1	43,562 units	$7.85	$7.17	(8.7)
2	500	8.74	15.45	76.8
3	53	12.15	82.49	578.9
4	2,079	13.63	24.51	79.8
5	5,670	12.40	19.99	61.2
6	11,169	8.04	7.96	(1.0)
7	423	8.47	6.93	(18.2)

* This example is from "How Cost Accounting Systematically Distorts Product Costs" by R. Cooper and R. Kaplan, in *Accounting and Management: Field Study Perspectives* by W. Bruns Jr., and R. Kaplan (Boston, Mass.: Harvard Business School Press, 1987), pp. 204–228.

ALLOCATION OF JOINT COSTS AND BY-PRODUCT COSTS

Joint costs and by-product costs create especially difficult cost-allocation problems. By definition, such costs relate to more than one product and cannot be separately identified with an individual product. Let's now examine these special cases, starting with joint costs.

JOINT COSTS

Objective 6
Use the physical-units and relative-sales-value methods to allocate joint costs to products.

So far, we have assumed that cost drivers could be identified with an individual product. For example, if we are allocating activity costs to products or services on the basis of machine hours, we have assumed that the amount of machine time consumed in making each product can be measured. However, sometimes inputs are added to the production process before individual products are separately identifiable (i.e., before the split-off point). Recall from Chapter 6 (page 236) that we call such costs *joint costs*. Joint costs include all inputs of material, labor, and overhead costs that are incurred before the split-off point.

Suppose a department has more than one product and some costs are joint costs. How should such joint costs be allocated to the products? As noted in Chapter 6, allocation of joint costs should not affect decisions about the individual products. Nevertheless, joint product costs are routinely allocated to products for purposes of inventory valuation and income determination.

Consider the example of joint product costs that we used in Chapter 6. A department in Dow Chemical Company produces two chemicals, X and Y. The joint cost is $100,000, and production is 1,000,000 liters of X and 500,000 liters of Y. X sells for $.09 per liter and Y for $.06 per liter. Ordinarily, some part of the $100,000 joint cost will be allocated to the inventory of X and the rest to the inventory of Y. Such allocations are useful for inventory purposes only. As explained in Chapter 6, joint cost allocations should be ignored for decisions such as selling a joint product or processing it further.

Two conventional ways of allocating joint costs to products are widely used: physical units and relative sales values. If a company uses physical units, it would allocate the joint costs as follows.

	Liters	Weighting	Allocation of Joint Costs	Sales Value at Split-Off
X	1,000,000	10/15 × $100,000	$ 66,667	$ 90,000
Y	500,000	5/15 × $100,000	33,333	30,000
	1,500,000		$100,000	$120,000

This approach shows that the $33,333 joint cost of producing Y exceeds its $30,000 sales value at split-off, seemingly indicating that Y should not be produced. However, such an allocation is not helpful in making production decisions. Neither of the two products could be produced separately.

A decision to produce Y must be a decision to produce X and Y. Because total revenue of $120,000 exceeds the total joint cost of $100,000, both will be produced. The allocation was not useful for this decision.

The physical-units method requires a common physical unit for measuring the output of each product. For example, board feet is a common unit for a variety of products in the lumber industry. However, sometimes such a common denominator is lacking. Consider the production of meat and hides from butchering a steer. You might use pounds as a common denominator, but pounds is not a good measure of the output of hides. As an alternative, many companies use the relative-sales-value method for allocating joint costs. The following allocation results from applying the relative-sales-value method to the Dow Chemical department:

	Relative Sales Value at Split-Off	Weighting	Allocation of Joint Costs
X	$ 90,000	90/120 × $100,000	$ 75,000
Y	30,000	30/120 × $100,000	25,000
	$120,000		$100,000

The weighting is based on the sales values of the individual products. Because the sales value of X at split-off is $90,000 and total sales value at split-off is $120,000, X is allocated 90/120 of the joint cost.

Now each product would be assigned a joint cost portion that is less than its sales value at split-off. Note how the allocation of a cost to a particular product such as Y depends not only on the sales value of Y but also on the sales value of X. For example, suppose you were the product manager for Y. You planned to sell your 500,000 liters for $30,000, achieving a profit of $30,000 − $25,000 = $5,000. Everything went as expected except that the price of X fell to $.07 per liter for revenue of $70,000 rather than $90,000. Instead of 30/120 of the joint cost, Y received 30/100 × $100,000 = $30,000 and had a profit of $0. Despite the fact that Y operations were exactly as planned, the cost-allocation method caused the profit on Y to be $5,000 below plan.

The relative-sales-value method can also be used when one or more of the joint products cannot be sold at the split-off point. To apply the method, we approximate the sales value at split-off as follows:

$$\text{Sales value at split-off} = \text{Final sales value} - \text{Separable costs}$$

For example, suppose the 500,000 liters of Y requires $20,000 of processing beyond the split-off point, after which it can be sold for $.10 per liter. The sales value at split-off would be ($.10 × 500,000) − $20,000 = $50,000 − $20,000 = $30,000.

BY-PRODUCT COSTS

by-product A product that, like a joint product, is not individually identifiable until manufacturing reaches a split-off point, but has relatively insignificant total sales value.

By-products are similar to joint products. A **by-product** is a product that, like a joint product, is not individually identifiable until manufacturing reaches a split-off point. By-products differ from joint products because they have relatively insignificant total sales values in comparison with the other products emerging at split-off. In contrast, joint products have relatively significant total sales values at split-off in comparison with the other jointly produced items. Examples of by-products are glycerine from soap making and mill ends of cloth and carpets.

If we account for an item as a by-product, we allocate only separable costs to it. We allocate all joint costs to the main products. Any revenues from by-products, less their separable costs, are deducted from the cost of the main products.

Consider a lumber company that sells sawdust generated in the production of lumber to companies making particle board. Suppose the company regards the sawdust as a by-product. In 20X1, sales of sawdust totaled $30,000, and the cost of loading and shipping the sawdust (i.e., costs incurred beyond the split-off point) was $20,000. The inventory cost of the sawdust would consist of only the $20,000 separable cost. The company would allocate none of the joint cost of producing lumber and sawdust to the sawdust. It would deduct the difference between the revenue and separable cost, $30,000 − $20,000 = $10,000, from the cost of the lumber produced.

SUMMARY PROBLEM FOR YOUR REVIEW

PROBLEM

Nonmanufacturing organizations often find it useful to allocate costs to final products or services. Consider a hospital. The output of a hospital is not as easy to define as the output of a factory. Assume the following measures of output in three revenue-producing departments:

Department	Measures of Output*
Radiology	X-ray films processed
Laboratory	Tests administered
Daily Patient Services[†]	Patient-days of care (i.e., the number of patients multiplied by the number of days of each patient's stay)

* These become the "product" cost objectives, the various revenue-producing activities of a hospital.
[†] There would be many of these departments, such as obstetrics, pediatrics, and orthopedics. Moreover, there may be both inpatient and outpatient care.

Budgeted output for 20X1 is 60,000 x-ray films processed in Radiology, 50,000 tests administered in the Laboratory, and 30,000 patient-days in Daily Patient Services.

In addition to the revenue-producing departments, the hospital has three service departments: Administrative and Fiscal Services, Plant Operations and Maintenance, and Laundry. (Of course, real hospitals have more than three revenue-producing departments and more than three service departments. This problem is simplified to keep the data manageable.)

The hospital has decided that the cost driver for Administrative and Fiscal Services costs is the direct department costs of the other departments. The cost driver for Plant Operations and Maintenance is square feet occupied, and for Laundry is pounds of laundry. The pertinent budget data for 20X1 are

	Direct Department Costs	Square Feet Occupied	Pounds of Laundry
Administrative and Fiscal Services	$1,000,000	1,000	—
Plant Operations and Maintenance	800,000	2,000	—
Laundry	200,000	5,000	—
Radiology	1,000,000	12,000	80,000
Laboratory	400,000	3,000	20,000
Daily Patient Services	1,600,000	80,000	300,000
Total	$5,000,000	103,000	400,000

Required

1. Allocate service department costs using the direct method.
2. Allocate service department costs using the step-down method. Allocate Administrative and Fiscal Services first, Plant Operations and Maintenance second, and Laundry third.
3. Compute the cost per unit of output in each of the revenue-producing departments using (a) the costs determined using the direct method for allocating service department costs (requirement 1) and (b) the costs determined using the step-down method for allocating service department costs (requirement 2).

SOLUTION

1. Exhibit 12-12 shows the solutions to all three requirements. The direct method is presented first. Note that no service department costs are allocated to another service department. Therefore, allocations are based on the relative amounts of the cost driver in the revenue-producing department only. For example, in allocating Plant Operations and Maintenance, square footage occupied by the service departments is ignored. The cost driver is the 95,000 square feet occupied by the revenue-producing departments.

Exhibit 12-12
Allocation of Service Department Costs: Direct and Step-Down Methods

	Administrative and Fiscal Services	Plant Operations and Maintenance	Laundry	Radiology	Laboratory	Daily Patient Services
Accumulated Base	*Accumulated Costs*	*Sq. Footage*	*Pounds*			
1. Direct Method						
Direct departmental costs before allocation	$1,000,000	$ 800,000	$200,000	$1,000,000	$400,000	$1,600,000
Administrative and Fiscal Services	(1,000,000)	—	—	333,333*	133,333	533,334
Plant Operations and Maintenance		(800,000)	—	101,053†	25,263	673,684
Laundry			(200,000)	40,000‡	10,000	150,000
Total costs after allocation				$1,474,386	$568,596	$2,957,018
Product output in films, tests, and patient-days, respectively				60,000	50,000	30,000
3a. Cost per unit of output				$24.573	$11.372	$98.567
2. Step-Down Method						
Direct departmental costs before allocation	$1,000,000	$ 800,000	$200,000	$1,000,000	$400,000	$1,600,000
Administrative and Fiscal Services	(1,000,000)	200,000§	50,000	250,000	100,000	400,000
Plant Operations and Maintenance		(1,000,000)	50,000¶	120,000	30,000	800,000
Laundry			(300,000)	60,000#	15,000	225,000
Total costs after allocation				$1,430,000	$545,000	$3,025,000
Product output in films, tests, and patient-days, respectively				60,000	50,000	30,000
3b. Cost per unit of output				$23.833	$10.900	$100.833

* $1,000,000 ÷ (1,000,000 + 400,000 + 1,600,000) = $.33 1/3; × 1,000,000 = $333,333; and so on.
† $800,000 ÷ (12,000 + 3,000 + 80,000) = $8.4210526; $8.4210526 × 12,000 sq. ft. = $101,053; and so on.
‡ $200,000 ÷ (80,000 + 20,000 + 300,000) = $.50; $.50 × 80,000 = $40,000; and so on.
§ $1,000,000 ÷ (800,000 + 200,000 + 1,000,000 + 400,000 + 1,600,000) = $.25; .25 × 800,000 = $200,000; and so on.
¶ $1,000,000 ÷ (5,000 + 12,000 + 3,000 + 80,000) = $10.00; $10.00 × 5,000 sq. ft. = $50,000; and so on.
# $300,000 ÷ (80,000 + 20,000 + 300,000) = $.75; $.75 × 80,000 = $60,000; and so on.

Note that the total cost of the revenue-producing departments after allocation, $1,474,386 + $568,596 + $2,957,018 = $5,000,000, is equal to the total of the direct department costs in all six departments before allocation.

2. The lower half of Exhibit 12-12 shows the step-down method. The costs of Administrative and Fiscal Services are allocated to all five other departments. Because a department's own costs are not allocated to itself, the cost driver consists of the $4,000,000 direct department costs in the five departments excluding Administrative and Fiscal Services.

   Plant Operations and Maintenance is allocated second on the basis of square feet occupied. No cost will be allocated to itself or back to Administrative and Fiscal Services. Therefore, the square footage used for allocation is the 100,000 square feet occupied by the other four departments.

   Laundry is allocated third. No cost would be allocated back to the first two departments, even if they had used laundry services.

   As in the direct method, note that the total costs of the revenue-producing departments after allocation, $1,430,000 + $545,000 + $3,025,000 = $5,000,000, equals the total of the direct department costs before allocation.

3. The solutions are labeled 3a and 3b in Exhibit 12-12. Compare the unit costs derived from the direct method with those of the step-down method. In many instances, the final product costs may not differ enough to warrant investing in a cost-allocation method that is any fancier than the direct method. But sometimes even small differences may be significant to a government agency or anybody paying for a large volume of services based on costs. For example, in Exhibit 12-12 the "cost" of an "average" laboratory test is either $11.37 or $10.90. This may be significant for the fiscal committee of the hospital's board of trustees, who must decide on hospital prices. Thus cost allocation often is a technique that helps answer the vital question, "Who should pay for what, and how much?"

Highlights to Remember

Explain the major reasons for allocating costs. The four main purposes of cost allocation are to predict the economic effects of planning and control decisions, to motivate managers and employees, to measure the costs of inventory and cost of goods sold, and to justify costs for pricing or reimbursement.

Allocate the variable and fixed costs of service departments to other organizational units. The dual method of allocation is used for service department costs. Variable costs should be allocated using budgeted cost rates times the actual cost driver level. Fixed costs should be allocated using budgeted percent of capacity available for use times the total budgeted fixed costs.

Allocate the central costs of an organization. Central costs include public relations, top corporate management overhead, legal, data processing, controller's department, and companywide planning. Often, it is best to allocate only those central costs of an organization for which measures of usage by departments are available.

Use the direct and step-down methods to allocate service department costs to user departments. When service departments support other service departments in addition to producing departments, there are two methods for allocation. The direct method ignores other service departments when allocating costs. The step-down method recognizes other service departments use of services.

Use activity-based costing to allocate costs in a modern manufacturing environment to products or services. In activity-based costing, the focus shifts from accumulating costs by department to accumulating costs by key activities performed. For each activity, supporting resources are identified. Cost drivers are used to allocate resource costs to activities and then from activities to products or services.

Use the physical-units and relative-sales-value methods to allocate joint costs to products.
Joint costs are often allocated to products for inventory valuation and income determination using the physical-units or relative-sales-value method. However, such allocations should not affect decisions.

Understand how cost allocation is used in cost planning and control. Across the entire value chain, managers need accurate cost information in order to effectively plan and control operations. The proportion of total costs that are indirect has increased in most companies due to increased business complexity. As a result, the need for accurate and timely cost allocation has also increased.

Accounting Vocabulary

by-product, p. 504	cost application, p. 496	service departments, p. 486
cost accounting systems, p. 484	direct method, p. 492	step-down method, p. 493
cost-allocation base, p. 484		

Fundamental Assignment Material

12-A1 Allocation of Central Costs

The Central Railroad allocates all central corporate overhead costs to its divisions. Some costs, such as specified internal auditing and legal costs, are identified on the basis of time spent. However, other costs are harder to allocate, so the revenue achieved by each division is used as an allocation base. Examples of such costs were executive salaries, travel, secre-tarial, utilities, rent, depreciation, donations, corporate planning, and general marketing costs.

Allocations on the basis of revenue for 20X1 were (in millions):

Division	Revenue	Allocated Costs
Northern	$120	$ 6
Mesa	240	12
Plains	240	12
Total	$600	$30

In 20X2, Northern's revenue remained unchanged. However, Plains' revenue soared to $280 million because of unusually large imports. The latter are troublesome to forecast because of variations in world markets. Mesa had expected a sharp rise in revenue, but severe competitive conditions resulted in a decline to $200 million. The total cost allocated on the basis of revenue was again $30 million, despite rises in other costs. The president was pleased that central costs did not rise for the year.

Required

1. Compute the allocations of costs to each division for 20X2.
2. How would each division manager probably feel about the cost allocation in 20X2 as compared with 20X1? What are the weaknesses of using revenue as a basis for cost allocation?
3. Suppose the budgeted revenues for 20X2 were $120, $240, and $280, respectively, and the budgeted revenues were used as a cost driver for allocation. Compute the allocations of costs to each division for 20X2. Do you prefer this method to the one used in requirement 1? Why?
4. Many accountants and managers oppose allocating any central costs. Why?

12-A2 Direct and Step-Down Methods of Allocation

Pinney Tool and Die has three service departments:

	Budgeted Department Costs
Cafeteria, revenue of $100,000	
less expenses of $250,000	$ 150,000
Engineering	2,500,000
General factory administration	950,000

Cost drivers are budgeted as follows:

Production Departments	Employees	Engineering Hours Worked for Production Departments	Total Labor Hours
Machining	100	50,000	250,000
Assembly	450	20,000	600,000
Finishing and painting	50	10,000	100,000

Required

1. Pinney allocates all service department costs directly to the production departments without allocation to other service departments. Show how much of the budgeted costs of each service department are allocated to each production department. To plan your work, examine requirement 2 before undertaking this question.

2. The company has decided to use the step-down method of cost allocation. General factory administration would be allocated first, then cafeteria, then engineering. Cafeteria employees worked 30,000 labor hours per year. There were 50 engineering employees with 100,000 total labor hours. Recompute the results in requirement 1, using the step-down method. Show your computations. Compare the results in requirements 1 and 2. Which method of allocation do you favor? Why?

12-A3 Two-Stage Activity-Based Costing

Yamaguchi Company makes printed circuit boards in a suburb of Kyoto. The production process is automated with computer-controlled robotic machines assembling each circuit board from a supply of parts and then soldering the parts to the board. Material-handling and quality-assurance activities use a combination of labor and equipment. Although a few resources that are used are variable with respect to changes in the demand of boards, these costs are not material compared to the fixed-cost resources that are used.

Yamaguchi makes three types of circuit boards, models 1, 2, and 3. Steps 1 to 3 of the design process for an ABC system have been completed. Exhibit 12-13 on page 510 shows the process-based map of Yamaguchi's operations.

Required

1. Compute the cost of production of the three types of circuit boards and the cost per circuit board for each type.

2. Suppose the design of model 1 could be simplified so that it required only 10 distinct parts (instead of 20) and took only 3 minutes of testing time (instead of 5). Compute the cost of model 1 circuit boards and the cost per circuit board. Will the costs per circuit board for models 2 and 3 change? Explain.

12-A4 Joint Products

Benjamin Metals, Inc., buys raw ore on the open market and processes it into two final products, A and B. The ore costs $12 per pound, and the process separating it into A and B has a cost of $4 per pound. During 20X1, Benjamin plans to produce 200,000 pounds of A and 600,000 pounds of B from 800,000 pounds of ore. A sells for $30 a pound and B for $15 a pound. The company allocated joint costs to the individual products for inventory valuation purposes.

Required

1. Allocate all the joint costs to A and B using the physical-units method.
2. Allocate all the joint costs to A and B using the relative-sales-value method.

Exhibit 12-13

Yamaguchi Company's Two-Stage ABC System

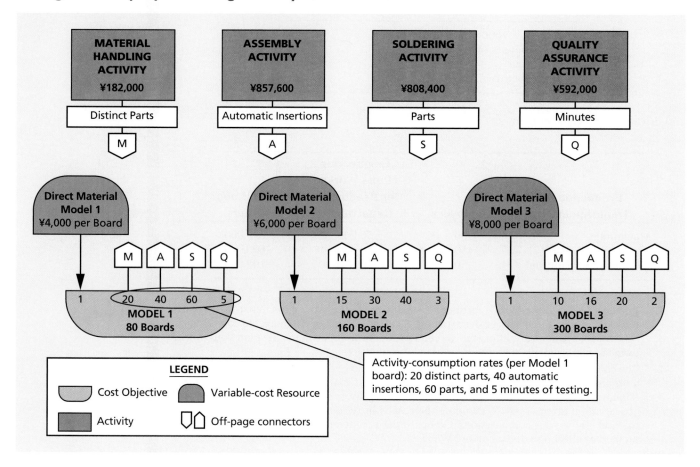

3. Suppose B cannot be sold in the form in which it emerges from the joint process. Instead, it must be processed further at a fixed cost of $300,000 plus a variable cost of $1 per pound. Then it can be sold for $21.50 a pound. Allocate all the joint costs to A and B using the relative-sales-value method.

12-B1 Allocation of Computer Costs

Review the section "Allocation of Service Department Costs," pages 487–496, especially the example of the use of the computer by the university. Recall that the budget formula was $100,000 fixed cost monthly plus $200 per hour of computer time used. Based on long-run predicted usage, the fixed costs were allocated on a lump-sum basis, 30% to Business and 70% to Engineering.

Required

1. Show the total allocation if Business used 210 hours and Engineering used 390 hours in a given month. Assume that the actual costs coincided exactly with the budgeted amount for total usage of 600 hours.

2. Assume the same facts as in requirement 1 except that the fixed costs were allocated on the basis of actual hours of usage. Show the total allocation of costs to each school. As the dean of Business, would you prefer this method or the method in requirement 1? Explain.

12-B2 Allocation of Service Department Costs

Chief Cleaning, Inc., provides cleaning services for a variety of clients. The company has two producing divisions, Residential and Commercial, and two service departments, Personnel and Administrative. The company has decided to allocate all service department costs to the producing departments—Personnel on the basis of number of employees, and Administrative on the basis of direct department costs. The budget for 20X2 shows

	Personnel	Administrative	Residential	Commercial
Direct department costs	$70,000	$90,000	$240,000	$400,000
Number of employees	6	10	36	24
Direct-labor hours			30,000	45,000
Square feet cleaned			4,500,000	9,970,000

Required

1. Allocate service department costs using the direct method.
2. Allocate service department costs using the step-down method. The Personnel Department costs should be allocated first.
3. Suppose the company prices by the hour in the Residential Department and by the square foot cleaned in Commercial. Using the results of the step-down allocations in requirement 2,
   a. Compute the cost of providing one direct-labor hour of service in the Residential Department.
   b. Compute the cost of cleaning one square foot of space in the Commercial Department.

12-B3 Activity-Based Costing

The Cunningham Novelty Company makes a variety of souvenirs for visitors to New Zealand. The Beebee Division manufactures stuffed kiwi birds using a highly automated operation. A recently installed activity-based-costing system has four activity centers.

Activity Center	Cost Driver	Cost per Driver Unit
Materials receiving and handling	Kilograms of materials	$1.20 per kg
Production setup	Number of setups	$50 per setup
Cutting, sewing, and assembly	Number of units	$.40 per unit
Packing and shipping	Number of orders	$10 per order

Two products are called "standard kiwi" and "giant kiwi." They require .20 and .40 kg of materials, respectively, at a materials cost of $1.30 for standard kiwis and $2.20 for giant kiwis. One computer-controlled assembly line makes all products. When a production run of a different product is started, a set-up procedure is required to reprogram the computers and make other changes in the process. Normally, 500 standard kiwis are produced per setup, but only 200 giant kiwis. Products are packed and shipped separately, so a request from a customer for, say, three different products is considered three different orders.

The Ausiland Waterfront Market just placed an order for 100 standard kiwis and 50 giant kiwis.

Required

1. Compute the cost of the products shipped to the Ausiland Waterfront Market.
2. Suppose the products made for the Ausiland Waterfront Market required "AWM" to be printed on each kiwi. Because of the automated process, printing the initials takes no extra time or materials, but it requires a special production setup for each product. Compute the cost of the products shipped to the Ausiland Waterfront Market.
3. Explain how the activity-based-costing system helps Cunningham Novelty to measure costs of individual products or orders better than a traditional system that allocates all nonmaterials costs based on direct labor.

12-B4 Joint Products

Manhattan Milling buys oats at $.50 per pound and produces MM Oat Flour, MM Oat Flakes, and MM Oat Bran. The process of separating the oats into oat flour and oat bran costs $.30 per pound. The oat flour can be sold for $1.50 per pound, the oat bran for $2.00 per pound. Each pound of oats has .2 pounds of oat bran and .8 pounds of oat flour. A pound of oat flour can be made into oat flakes for a fixed cost of $240,000 plus a variable cost of $.50 per pound. Manhattan Milling plans to process 1 million pounds of oats in 20X2, at a purchase price of $500,000.

Required

1. Allocate all the joint costs to oat flour and oat bran using the physical-units method.
2. Allocate all the joint costs to oat flour and oat bran using the relative-sales-value method.
3. Suppose there were no market for oat flour. Instead, it must be made into oat flakes to be sold. Oat flakes sell for $2.80 per pound. Allocate the joint cost to oat bran and oat flakes using the relative-sales-value method.

Additional Assignment Material

QUESTIONS

12-1. What is the purpose of a cost accounting system?

12-2. "A cost pool is a group of costs that is physically traced to the appropriate cost objective." Do you agree? Explain.

12-3. List five terms that are sometimes used as substitutes for the term *allocate*.

12-4. What are four purposes for cost allocation?

12-5. What are the three types of allocations?

12-6. List three guidelines for the allocation of service department costs.

12-7. Why should budgeted cost rates, rather than actual cost rates, be used for allocating the variable costs of service departments?

12-8. "We used a lump-sum allocation method for fixed costs a few years ago, but we gave it up because managers always predicted usage below what they actually used." Is this a common problem? How might it be prevented?

12-9. Briefly describe the two popular methods for allocating service department costs.

12-10. "The step-down method allocates more costs to the producing departments than does the direct method." Do you agree? Explain.

12-11. How does the term *cost application* differ from *cost allocation*?

12-12. What is a non-volume-related cost driver? Give two examples.

12-13. How are costs of various overhead resources allocated to products, services, or customers in an ABC system?

12-14. "A cost pool for a particular resource is either a variable cost pool or a fixed cost pool. There should be no mixed-cost pools." Do you agree? Explain.

12-15. Give four examples of activities and related cost drivers that can be used in an ABC system to allocate costs to products, services, or customers.

12-16. Chapter 6 explained that joint costs should not be allocated to individual products for decision purposes. For what purposes are such costs allocated to products?

12-17. Briefly explain each of the two conventional ways of allocating joint costs of products.

12-18. What are by-products and how do we account for them?

COGNITIVE EXERCISES

12-19 Allocation and Cost Behavior

There are three general guidelines to use when allocating service department (support) costs. One of these guidelines deals with the cost behavior of support costs. Why do many companies allocate fixed support costs separately from variable support costs?

12-20 Allocation and the Sales Function

Confusion can arise when cost allocations to one consuming department depend on the activity of another consuming department. "A commonly misused basis for allocation of central support costs is *actual* dollar sales." Explain.

12-21 Allocation and Marketing

Many companies are allocating more non-production costs because of the increasing magnitude of these value-chain costs. One value-chain function that is receiving more attention is marketing. How should national advertising costs be allocated to territories?

12-22 Cost Management Systems and Activity-Based Allocation

Many managers are confused regarding the value of activity-based allocation. A typical comment is, "Activity-based allocation is useful for product costing, but not for operational control." Do you agree? Explain.

EXERCISES

12-23 Fixed- and Variable-Cost Pools

The city of Cedarwood signed a lease for a photocopy machine at $2,000 per month and $.02 per copy. Operating costs for toner, paper, operator salary, and so on are all variable at $.03 per copy. Departments had projected a need for 50,000 copies a month. The Public Works Department predicted its usage at 18,000 copies a month. It made 21,000 copies in August.

Required

1. Suppose one predetermined rate per copy was used to allocate all photocopy costs. What rate would be used and how much cost would be allocated to the Public Works Department in August?

2. Suppose fixed- and variable-cost pools were allocated separately. Specify how each pool should be allocated. Compute the cost allocated to the Public Works Department in August.

3. Which method, the one in requirement 1 or the one in requirement 2, do you prefer? Explain.

12-24 Sales-Based Allocations

Pionier's Markets has three grocery stores in the metropolitan Topeka area. Central costs are allocated using sales as the cost driver. Following are budgeted and actual sales during November:

	Sunnyville	Wedgewood	Capital
Budgeted sales	$600,000	$1,000,000	$400,000
Actual sales	600,000	700,000	500,000

Central costs of $180,000 are to be allocated in November.

Required

1. Compute the central costs allocated to each store with budgeted sales as the cost driver.
2. Compute the central costs allocated to each store with actual sales as the cost driver.
3. What advantages are there to using budgeted rather than actual sales for allocating the central costs?

12-25 Direct and Step-Down Allocations, Activity-Based Allocation and Process Map

Dallas Building Maintenance, Inc., provides cleaning services for a variety of clients. The company has two producing divisions, Residential and Commercial, and two service departments, Personnel and Administrative. The company uses an activity-based allocation system in each of its producing divisions. Previously, the costs of service support departments has been unallocated. However, the company has decided to allocate all service department costs to the producing departments— Personnel on the basis of number of employees, and Administrative on the basis of the direct costs of the activities in each division. Dallas uses a process map as part of their activity-based allocation system. The map based on the budget for 20X2 is shown in Exhibit 12-14 on page 514.

Required

1. Determine the costs allocated to the Residential and Commercial divisions using the direct method.
2. Determine the costs allocated to the Residential and Commercial divisions using the step-down method. The Personnel Department costs should be allocated first.
3. Explain how costs would be allocated to each customer in both the Residential and Commercial divisions.

12-26 Direct and Step-Down Allocations

Butler Home Products has two producing departments, Machining and Assembly, and two service departments, Personnel and Custodial. The company's budget for April 20X2 is

	Service Departments		Production Departments	
	Personnel	*Custodial*	*Machining*	*Assembly*
Direct department costs	$32,000	$70,000	$600,000	$800,000
Square feet	2,000	1,000	10,000	25,000
Number of employees	15	30	200	250

Butler allocates personnel costs on the basis of number of employees. Butler allocates custodial costs on the basis of square feet.

Required

1. Allocate personnel and custodial costs to the producing departments using the direct method.
2. Allocate personnel and custodial costs to the producing departments using the step-down method. Allocate personnel costs first.

12-27 Joint Costs

Robinson Chemical Company's production process for two of its solvents can be diagrammed as follows:

Exhibit 12-14

Dallas Building Maintenance, Inc. Allocation System

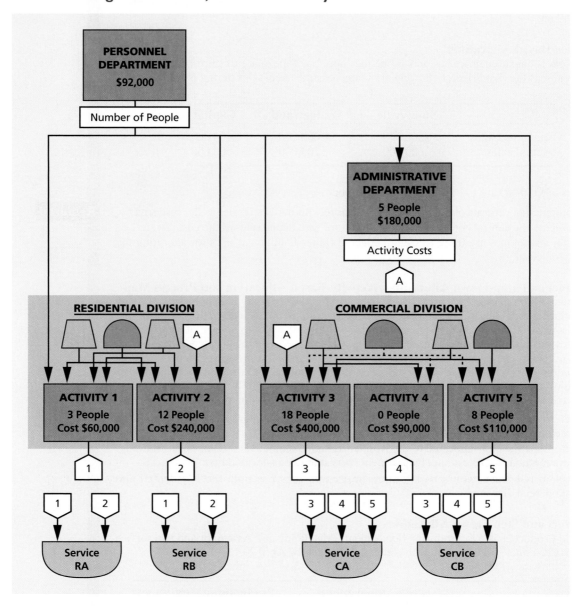

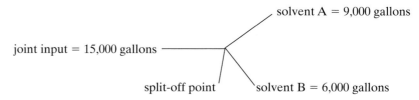

The cost of the joint input, including processing costs before the split-off point, is $300,000. Solvent A can be sold at split-off for $30 per gallon and solvent B for $45 per gallon.

Required

1. Allocate the $300,000 joint cost to solvents A and B by the physical-units method.
2. Allocate the $300,000 joint cost to solvents A and B by the relative-sales-value method.

12-28 Joint Costs and Process Map

Hernandez Chemical Company's production process for two of its solvents can be diagrammed using a process map as shown in Exhibit 12-15.

Exhibit 12-15
Hernandez Chemical Company's Joint Process

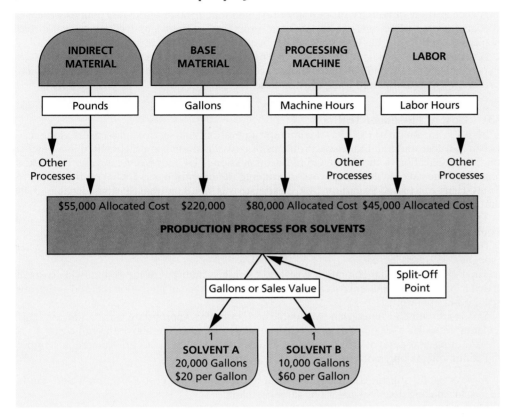

The cost of the joint input, including processing costs before the split-off point, is $400,000. Solvent A can be sold at split-off for $20 per gallon and solvent B for $60 per gallon.

Required

1. Allocate the $400,000 joint cost to solvents A and B by the physical-units method.
2. Allocate the $400,000 joint cost to solvents A and B by the relative-sales-value method.

12-29 By-Product Costing
The Jones Press Company buys apples from local orchards and presses them to produce apple juice. The pulp that remains after pressing is sold to farmers as livestock food. This livestock food is accounted for as a by-product.

During the 20X2 fiscal year, the company paid $800,000 to purchase 8 million pounds of apples. After processing, 1 million pounds of pulp remained. Jones spent $30,000 to package and ship the pulp, which was sold for $50,000.

Required

1. How much of the joint cost of the apples is allocated to the pulp?
2. Compute the total inventory cost (and therefore the cost of goods sold) for the pulp.
3. Assume that $130,000 was spent to press the apples and $150,000 was spent to filter, pasteurize, and pack the apple juice. Compute the total inventory cost of the apple juice produced.

PROBLEMS

12-30 Hospital Allocation Base
Jose Ortiz, the administrator of Saint Jude Hospital, has become interested in obtaining more accurate cost allocations on the basis of cause and effect. The $150,000 of laundry costs had been allocated on the basis of 600,000 pounds processed for all departments, or $.25 per pound.

Ortiz is concerned that government health care officials will require weighted statistics to be used for cost allocation. He asks you, "Please develop a revised base for allocating laundry costs. It should be better than our present base, but not be overly complex either."

You study the situation and find that the laundry processes a large volume of uniforms for student nurses and physicians and for dietary, housekeeping, and other personnel. In particular, the coats or jackets worn by personnel in the radiology department take an unusual amount of handwork.

A special study of laundry for radiology revealed that 7,500 of the 15,000 pounds were jackets and coats that were five times as expensive to process as regular laundry items. Several reasons explained the difference, but it was principally because of handwork involved.

Assume that no special requirements were needed in departments other than radiology. Revise the cost-allocation base and compute the new cost-allocation rate. Compute the total cost charged to radiology using pounds and using the new base.

12-31 Cost of Passenger Traffic

Southern Pacific Railroad (SP) has a commuter operation that services passengers along a route between San Jose and San Francisco. Problems of cost allocation were highlighted in a news story about SP's application to the Public Utilities Commission (PUC) for a rate increase. The PUC staff claimed that the "avoidable annual cost" of running the operation was $700,000, in contrast to SP officials' claim of a loss of $9 million. PUC's estimate was based on what SP would be able to save if it shut down the commuter operation.

The SP loss estimate was based on a "full-allocation-of-costs" method, which allocates a share of common maintenance and overhead costs to the passenger service.

If the PUC accepted its own estimate, a 25% fare increase would have been justified, whereas SP sought a 96% fare increase.

The PUC stressed that commuter costs represent less than 1% of the system-wide costs of SP and that 57% of the commuter costs are derived from some type of allocation method—sharing the costs of other operations.

SP's representative stated that "avoidable cost" is not an appropriate way to allocate costs for calculating rates. He said that "it is not fair to include just so-called above-the-rail costs" because there are other real costs associated with commuter service. Examples are maintaining smoother connections and making more frequent track inspections.

Required

1. As public utilities commissioner, what approach toward cost allocation would you favor for making decisions regarding fares? Explain.
2. How would fluctuations in freight traffic affect commuter costs under the SP method?

12-32 Allocation of Automobile Costs

The motor pool of a major city provides automobiles for the use of various city departments. Currently, the motor pool has 50 autos. A recent study showed that it costs $2,400 of annual fixed cost per automobile plus $.10 per mile variable cost to own, operate, and maintain autos such as those provided by the motor pool.

Each month, the costs of the motor pool are allocated to the user departments on the basis of miles driven. On average, each auto is driven 24,000 miles annually, although wide month-to-month variations occur. In April 20X1, the 50 autos were driven a total of 50,000 miles. The motor pool's total costs for April were $19,000.

The chief planner for the city always seemed concerned about her auto costs. She was especially upset in April when she was charged $5,700 for the 15,000 miles driven in the department's five autos. This is the normal monthly mileage in the department. Her memo to the head of the motor pool stated, "I can certainly get autos at less than the $.38 per mile you charged in April." The response was, "I am under instructions to allocate the motor pool costs to the user departments. Your department was responsible for 30% of the April usage (15,000 miles ÷ 50,000 miles), so I allocated 30% of the motor pool's April costs to you (.30 × $19,000). That just seems fair."

Required

1. Calculate the city's average annual cost per mile for owning, maintaining, and operating an auto.
2. Explain why the allocated cost in April ($.38 per mile) exceeds the average in requirement 1.
3. Describe any undesirable behavioral effects of the cost-allocation method used.
4. How would you improve the cost-allocation method?

12-33 Allocation of Costs

The Vigil Trucking Company has one service department and two regional operating departments. The budgeted cost behavior pattern of the service department is $750,000 monthly in fixed costs plus $.75 per 1,000 ton-miles operated in the North and South regions. (Ton-miles are the number of tons carried times the number of miles traveled.) The actual monthly costs of the service department are allocated using ton-miles operated as the cost driver.

1. Vigil processed 500 million ton-miles of traffic in April, half in each operating region. The actual costs of the service department were exactly equal to those predicted by the budget for 500 million ton-miles. Compute the costs that would be allocated to each operating region on an actual ton-miles basis.

2. Suppose the North region was plagued by strikes, so that the freight handled was much lower than originally anticipated. North moved only 150 million ton-miles of traffic. The South region handled 250 million ton-miles. The actual costs were exactly as budgeted for this lower level of activity. Compute the costs that would be allocated to North and South on an actual ton-mile basis. Note that the total costs will be lower.

3. Refer to the facts in requirement 1. Various inefficiencies caused the service department to incur total costs of $1,250,000. Compute the costs to be allocated to North and South. Are the allocations justified? If not, what improvement do you suggest?

4. Refer to the facts in requirement 2. Assume that assorted investment outlays for equipment and space in the service department were made to provide a basic maximum capacity to serve the North region at a level of 360 million ton-miles and the South region at a level of 240 million ton-miles. Suppose fixed costs are allocated on the basis of this capacity to serve. Variable costs are allocated by using a predetermined standard rate per 1,000 ton-miles. Compute the costs to be allocated to each department. What are the advantages of this method over other methods?

12-34 Hospital Equipment

Many states have a hospital commission that must approve the acquisition of specified medical equipment before the hospitals in the state can qualify for cost-based reimbursement related to that equipment. That is, hospitals cannot bill government agencies for the use of the equipment unless the commission originally authorized the acquisition.

Two hospitals in one such state proposed the acquisition and sharing of some expensive x-ray equipment to be used for unusual cases. The depreciation and related fixed costs of operating the equipment were predicted at $15,000 per month. The variable costs were predicted at $30 per patient procedure.

The commission asked each hospital to predict its usage of the equipment over its expected useful life of 5 years. Premier Hospital predicted an average usage of 75 x rays per month; St. Mary's Hospital of 50 x rays. The commission regarded this information as critical to the size and degree of sophistication that would be justified. That is, if the number of x rays exceeded a certain quantity per month, a different configuration of space, equipment, and personnel would be required that would mean higher fixed costs per month.

1. Suppose fixed costs are allocated on the basis of the hospitals' predicted average use per month. Variable costs are allocated on the basis of $30 per x ray, the budgeted variable-cost rate for the current fiscal year. In October, Premier Hospital had 50 x rays and St. Mary's Hospital had 50 x rays. Compute the total costs allocated to Premier Hospital and to St. Mary's Hospital.

2. Suppose the manager of the equipment had various operating inefficiencies so that the total October costs were $19,500. Would you change your answers in requirement 1? Why?

3. A traditional method of cost allocation does not use the method in requirement 1. Instead, an allocation rate depends on the actual costs and actual volume encountered. The actual costs are totaled for the month and divided by the actual number of x rays during the month. Suppose the actual costs agreed exactly with the budget for a total of 100 actual x rays. Compute the total costs allocated to Premier Hospital and to St. Mary's Hospital. Compare the results with those in requirement 1. What is the major weakness in this traditional method? What are some of its possible behavioral effects?

4. Describe any undesirable behavioral effects of the method described in requirement 1. How would you counteract any tendencies toward deliberate false predictions of long-run usage?

12-35 Direct Method for Service Department Allocation

Sanders Instruments Company has two producing departments, Mechanical Instruments and Electronic Instruments. In addition, there are two service departments, Building Services and Materials Receiving and Handling. The company purchases a variety of component parts from which the departments assemble instruments for sale in domestic and international markets.

The Electronic Instruments division is highly automated. The manufacturing costs depend primarily on the number of subcomponents in each instrument. In contrast, the Mechanical Instruments division relies primarily on a large labor force to hand-assemble instruments. Its costs depend on direct-labor hours.

The costs of Building Services depend primarily on the square footage occupied. The costs of Materials Receiving and Handling depend primarily on the total number of components handled.

Instruments M1 and M2 are produced in the Mechanical Instruments department, and E1 and E2 are produced in the Electronic Instruments department. Data about these products follow:

	Direct-Material Cost	Number of Components	Direct-Labor Hours
M1	$74	25	4.0
M2	86	21	8.0
E1	63	10	1.5
E2	91	15	1.0

Budget figures for 20X2 include:

	Building Service	Materials Receiving and Handling	Mechanical Instruments	Electronic Instruments
Direct department costs (excluding direct materials cost)	$180,000	$120,000	$680,000	$548,000
Square footage occupied		5,000	50,000	25,000
Number of final instruments produced			8,000	10,000
Average number of components per instrument			10	16
Direct-labor hours			30,000	8,000

Required

1. Allocate the costs of the service departments using the direct method.
2. Using the results of requirement 1, compute the cost per direct-labor hour in the Mechanical Instruments Department and the cost per component in the Electronic Instruments Department.
3. Using the results of requirement 2, compute the cost per unit of product for instruments M1, M2, E1, and E2.

12-36 Step-Down Method for Service Department Allocation

Refer to the data in Problem 12-35.

Required

1. Allocate the costs of the service departments using the step-down method.
2. Using the results of requirement 1, compute the cost per direct-labor hour in the Mechanical Instruments Department and the cost per component in the Electronic Instruments Department.
3. Using the results of requirement 2, compute the cost per unit of product for instruments M1, M2, E1, and E2.

12-37 Direct and Step-Down Methods of Allocation

The Maton Company has prepared departmental overhead budgets for normal activity levels before allocations as follows:

Building and grounds	$ 20,000
Personnel	1,200
General factory administration*	28,020
Cafeteria operating loss	1,430
Storeroom	2,750
Machining	35,100
Assembly	56,500
Total	$145,000

* To be allocated before cafeteria.

Management has decided that the most sensible product costs are achieved by using departmental overhead rates. These rates are developed after allocating appropriate service department costs to production departments.

Cost drivers for allocation are to be selected from the following data:

Department	Direct-Labor Hours	Number of Employees	Square Feet of Floor Space Occupied	Total Labor Hours	Number of Requisitions
Building and grounds	—	—	—	—	—
Personnel*	—	—	2,000	—	—
General factory administration	—	35	7,000	—	—
Cafeteria operating loss	—	10	4,000	1,000	—
Storeroom	—	5	7,000	1,000	—
Machining	5,000	50	30,000	8,000	3,000
Assembly	15,000	100	50,000	17,000	1,500
	20,000	200	100,000	27,000	4,500

* Basis used is number of employees.

Required

1. Allocate service department costs by the step-down method. Develop overhead rates per direct-labor hour for machining and assembly.
2. Same as in requirement 1, using the direct method.
3. What would be the plantwide factory-overhead application rate, assuming that direct-labor hours are used as a cost driver?
4. Using the following information about two jobs, prepare three different total overhead costs for each job, using rates developed in requirements 1, 2, and 3.

	Direct-Labor Hours	
	Machining	Assembly
Job K10	19	2
Job K12	3	18

12-38 Activity-Based Allocations

St. Louis Wholesale Distributors uses an activity-based-costing system to determine the cost of handling its products. One important activity is receiving of shipments in the warehouse. Three resources support that activity: (1) recording and record keeping, (2) labor, and (3) inspection.

Recording and record keeping is a variable cost driven by number of shipments received. The cost per shipment is $16.50.

Labor is driven by pounds of merchandise received. Because labor is hired in shifts, it is fixed for large ranges of volume. Currently labor costs are running $23,000 per month for handling 460,000 pounds. This same cost would apply to all volumes between 300,000 pounds and 550,000 pounds.

Finally, inspection is a variable cost driven by the number of boxes received. Inspection costs are $2.75 per box.

One product distributed by St. Louis Wholesale Distributors is candy. There is a wide variety of candy, so many different shipments are handled in the warehouse. In July, the warehouse received 550 shipments, consisting of 4,000 boxes weighing a total of 80,000 pounds.

Required

1. Compute the cost of receiving candy shipments during July.
2. Management is considering elimination of brands of candy that have small sales levels. This would reduce the warehouse volume to 220 shipments, consisting of 2,500 boxes weighing a total of 60,000 pounds. Compute the amount of savings from eliminating the small-sales-level brands.
3. Suppose receiving costs were estimated on a per pound basis. What was the total receiving cost per pound of candy received in July? If management had used this cost to estimate the effect of eliminating the 20,000 pounds of candy, what mistake might be made?

12-39 Activity-Based Allocations at Dell Computer

Dell Computer Corporation installed an activity-based-costing system to help determine its product and customer profitability. The system is quite complex and took several years to fully implement. Consider a simplified hypothetical example of one component of such a system.

Dell offers three lines of notebook computers that use Pentium processors. Consider the Inspiron 7500 line. Suppose that there are only three activities necessary to produce one of these notebook computers: (1) receiving subcomponents, (2) assembling computers, and (3) inspecting computers. Computers are made to order, so each order has a potentially different cost. Therefore, to assess either product or customer profitability, it is important that Dell managers know how much each order costs. Assume that the cost of an order of computers is simply the cost of the subcomponents used plus the cost of the three activities needed to convert the subcomponents into final products.

Suppose that an activity analysis has revealed that the full cost of receiving subcomponents is 4% of the value of those subcomponents, the full cost of assembly is $24 per subcomponent, and the full cost of inspection is $56 per computer. The inspection cost is almost entirely variable, but only about one-half of the receiving and assembly costs is variable at current levels of operations.

Suppose Dell received an order from a CPA firm for 15 computers for its audit staff. The computers are identical, and each requires 12 subcomponents that cost Dell $1,100. The list price of the computers in the configuration required was $1,990.

Required

1. Compute the cost per computer for the 15 computers ordered by the CPA firm.
2. Suppose the customer was negotiating for a 10% discount from list price. What would be Dell's profit on the order for 15 computers if it allows the discount?
3. What role should cost play in the pricing of Dell's computers?

12-40 Joint Costs and Decisions

A chemical company has a batch process that takes 1,000 gallons of a raw material and transforms it into 80 pounds of X1 and 400 pounds of X2. Although the joint costs of their production are $1,200, both products are worthless at their split-off point. Additional separable costs of $350 are necessary to give X1 a sales value of $1,000 as product A. Similarly, additional separable costs of $200 are necessary to give X2 a sales value of $1,000 as product B.

Required

You are in charge of the batch process and the marketing of both products. (Show your computations for each answer.)

1. a. Assuming that you believe in assigning joint costs on a physical basis, allocate the total profit of $250 per batch to products A and B.

   b. Would you stop processing one of the products? Why?

2. a. Assuming that you believe in assigning joint costs on a net-realizable-value (relative-sales-value) basis, allocate the total operating profit of $250 per batch to products A and B. If there is no market for X1 and X2 at their split-off point, a net realizable value is usually imputed by taking the ultimate sales values at the point of sale and working backward to obtain approximated "synthetic" relative sales values at the split-off point. These synthetic values are then used as weights for allocating the joint costs to the products.

   b. You have internal product-profitability reports in which joint costs are assigned on a net-realizable-value basis. Your chief engineer says that, after seeing these reports, he has developed a method of obtaining more of product B and correspondingly less of product A from each batch, without changing the per-pound cost factors. Would you approve this new method? Why? What would the overall operating profit be if 40 pounds more of B were produced and 40 pounds less of A?

CASES

12-41 Allocation, Department Rates, and Direct-Labor Hours versus Machine Hours

The Tolbert Manufacturing Company has two producing departments, machining and assembly. Mr. Tolbert recently automated the machining department. The installation of a CAM system, together with robotic workstations, drastically reduced the amount of direct labor required. Meanwhile, the assembly department remained labor intensive.

The company had always used one firmwide rate based on direct-labor hours as the cost driver for applying all costs (except direct materials) to the final products. Mr. Tolbert was considering two alternatives: (1) continue using direct-labor hours as the only cost driver, but use different rates in machining and assembly, and (2) using machine hours as the cost driver in the machining department while continuing with direct-labor hours in assembly.

Budgeted data for 20X2 are

	Machining	Assembly	Total
Total cost (except direct materials), after allocating service department costs	$525,000	$420,000	$945,000
Machine hours	105,000	*	105,000
Direct-labor hours	15,000	30,000	45,000

*Not applicable.

Required

1. Suppose Tolbert continued to use one firmwide rate based on direct-labor hours to apply all manufacturing costs (except direct materials) to the final products. Compute the cost-application rate that would be used.

2. Suppose Tolbert continued to use direct-labor hours as the only cost driver but used different rates in machining and assembly.

   a. Compute the cost-application rate for machining.

   b. Compute the cost-application rate for assembly.

3. Suppose Tolbert changed the cost accounting system to use machine hours as the cost driver in machining and direct-labor hours in assembly.

   a. Compute the cost-application rate for machining.

   b. Compute the cost-application rate for assembly.

4. Three products use the following machine hours and direct-labor hours.

	Machine Hours in Machining	Direct-Labor Hours in Machining	Direct-Labor Hours in Assembly
Product A	10.0	1.0	14.0
Product B	17.0	1.5	3.0
Product C	14.0	1.3	8.0

   a. Compute the manufacturing cost of each product (excluding direct materials) using one firmwide rate based on direct-labor hours.

   b. Compute the manufacturing cost of each product (excluding direct materials) using direct-labor hours as the cost driver, but with different cost-application rates in machining and assembly.

   c. Compute the manufacturing cost of each product (excluding direct materials) using a cost-application rate based on direct-labor hours in assembly and machine hours in machining.

   d. Compare and explain the results in requirements 4a, 4b, and 4c.

12-42 Multiple Allocation Bases

The Glasgow Electronics Company produces three types of circuit boards; call them L, M, and N. The cost accounting system used by Glasgow until 2000 applied all costs except direct materials to the products using direct-labor hours as the only cost driver. In 2000, the company undertook a cost study. The study determined that there were six main factors causing costs to be incurred. A new system was designed with a separate cost pool for each of the six factors. The factors and the costs associated with each are as follows:

1. Direct-labor hours—direct-labor cost and related fringe benefits and payroll taxes

2. Machine hours—depreciation and repairs and maintenance costs

3. Pounds of materials—materials receiving, handling, and storage costs

4. Number of production setups—labor used to change machinery and computer configurations for a new production batch

5. Number of production orders—costs of production scheduling and order processing
6. Number of orders shipped—all packaging and shipping expenses

The company is now preparing a budget for 2002. The budget includes the following predictions:

	Board L	Board M	Board N
Units to be produced	10,000	800	5,000
Direct-material cost	£66/unit	£88/unit	£45/unit
Direct-labor hours	4/unit	18/unit	9/unit
Machine hours	7/unit	15/unit	7/unit
Pounds of materials	3/unit	4/unit	2/unit
Number of production setups	100	50	50
Number of production orders	300	200	70
Number of orders shipped	1,000	800	2,000

The total budgeted cost for 2002 is £3,712,250, of which £955,400 was direct-materials cost, and the amount in each of the six cost pools defined above is

Cost Pool*	Cost
1	£1,391,600
2	936,000
3	129,600
4	160,000
5	25,650
6	114,000
Total	£2,756,850

*Identified by the cost driver used.

Required

1. Prepare a budget that shows the total budgeted cost and the unit cost for each circuit board. Use the new system with six cost pools (plus a separate direct application of direct-materials cost).
2. Compute the budgeted total and unit costs of each circuit board if the old direct-labor-hour-based system had been used.
3. How would you judge whether the new system is better than the old one?

12-43 Allocation of Data Processing Costs

The Gibralter Insurance Co. (GIC) established a Systems Department to implement and operate its own data processing systems. GIC believed that its own system would be more cost-effective than the service bureau it had been using.

GIC's three departments—Claims, Records, and Finance—have different requirements with respect to hardware and other capacity-related resources and operating resources. The system was designed to recognize these differing needs. In addition, the system was designed to meet GIC's long-term capacity needs. The excess capacity designed into the system would be sold to outside users until needed by GIC. The estimated resource requirements used to design and implement the system are shown in the following schedule:

	Hardware and Other Capacity-Related Resources	Operating Resources
Records	25%	60%
Claims	50	15
Finance	20	20
Expansion (outside use)	5	5
Total	100%	100%

GIC currently sells the equivalent of its expansion capacity to a few outside clients.

At the time the system became operational, management decided to redistribute total expenses of the Systems Department to the user departments based on actual computer time used. The actual costs for the first quarter of the current fiscal year were distributed to the user departments as follows:

Department	Percentage Utilization	Amount
Records	60%	$330,000
Claims	15	82,500
Finance	20	110,000
Outside	5	27,500
Total	100%	$550,000

The three user departments have complained about the cost distribution method since the Systems Department was established. The Records Department's monthly costs have been as much as three times the costs experienced with the service bureau. The Finance Department is concerned about the costs distributed to the outside user category because these allocated costs form the basis for the fees billed to the outside clients.

Mostafa Al Rashed, GIC's controller, decided to review the cost-allocation method. The additional information he gathered for his review is reported in Tables 1, 2, and 3.

Table 1
Systems Department Costs and Activity Levels

	Annual Budget		First Quarter Budget		Actual	
	Hours	*Dollars*	*Hours*	*Dollars*	*Hours*	*Dollars*
Hardware and other capacity-related costs	—	$ 600,000	—	$150,000	—	$155,000
Software development	18,750	562,500	4,725	141,750	4,250	130,000
Operations						
Computer related	3,750	750,000	945	189,000	920	187,000
Input/output related	30,000	300,000	7,560	75,600	7,900	78,000
Total		$2,212,500		$556,350		$550,000

Table 2
Historical Usage

	Hardware and Other Capacity Needs	Software Development		Operations Computer		Operations Input/Output	
		Range	*Average*	*Range*	*Average*	*Range*	*Average*
Records	25%	0–30%	15%	55–65%	60%	10–30%	15%
Claims	50	15–60	40	10–25	15	60–80	75
Finance	20	25–75	40	10–25	20	3–10	5
Outside	5	0–25	5	3–8	5	3–10	5
	100%		100%		100%		100%

Table 3

Usage of Systems Department's Services
First Quarter (in hours)

	Software Development	Operations Computer Related	Input/Output
Records	450	540	1,540
Claims	1,800	194	5,540
Finance	1,600	126	410
Outside	400	60	410
Total	4,250	920	7,900

Al Rashed has concluded that the method of cost allocation should be changed. He believes that the hardware and capacity-related costs should be allocated to the user departments in proportion to the planned long-term needs. Any difference between actual and budgeted hardware costs would not be allocated to the departments but remain with the Systems Department.

The costs for software development and operations would be charged to the user departments based on actual hours used. A predetermined hourly rate based on the annual budget data would be used. The hourly rates that would be used for the current fiscal year are as follows:

Function	Hourly Rate
Software development	$ 30
Operations	
Computer related	200
Input/output related	10

Al Rashed plans to use first-quarter activity and cost data to illustrate his recommendations. The recommendations will be presented to the Systems Department and the user departments for their comments and reactions. He then expects to present his recommendations to management for approval.

Required

1. Calculate the amount of data processing costs that would be included in the Claims Department's first-quarter budget according to the method Mostafa Al Rashed has recommended.

2. Prepare a schedule to show how the actual first-quarter costs of the Systems Department would be charged to the users if GIC adopts Al Rashed's recommended method.

3. Explain whether Al Rashed's recommended system for charging costs to the user departments will:
   a. Improve cost control in the Systems Department
   b. Improve planning and cost control in the user departments

COLLABORATIVE LEARNING EXERCISE

12-44 Library Research on ABC

Form groups of three to six students. Each student should choose a different article about activity-based costing (ABC) or activity-based management (ABM) from the current literature. The article should include information about at least one company's application of ABC. Such articles are available in a variety of sources. You might try bibliographic searches for "activity-based costing" or "activity-based management." Journals that will have articles on ABC and ABM include

Strategic Finance (formerly *Management Accounting*) (USA)
Management Accounting (United Kingdom)
Journal of Cost Management
CMA Magazine (Canada)
Management Accounting Quarterly

1. After reading the article, note the following (if given in the article) for one company:
   a. The benefits of ABC or ABM
   b. The problems encountered in implementing ABC or ABM
   c. Suggestions by the author(s) about employing ABC or ABM
2. As a group, using the collective wisdom garnered from the articles, respond to the following:
   a. What kinds of companies can benefit from ABC or ABM?
   b. What kinds of companies have little to gain from ABC or ABM?
   c. What steps should be taken to ensure successful implementation of ABC or ABM?
   d. What potential pitfalls are there to avoid in implementing ABC or ABM?

INTERNET EXERCISES

12-45 Cost Allocation at Target Corporation

Allocating indirect costs can be a challenging task. Almost all firms have some type of cost centers (departments)—whether it is the administration overseeing the corporation as a whole, or the accounting department processing billing and invoicing of customers. What to do with the costs generated by these cost centers can be a tricky task. Let's take a look at Target Corporation, a firm that has multiple divisions.

www.prenhall.com/horngren

1. Go to the home page for Target, Inc. at http://www.target.com. Click on the "Company" icon. Go to the Target Corporation site. How many companies are listed under the umbrella of "Target Corporation"? What are these companies? How many of them are located in the area where you are located? If one or more is not located in your area, have you heard of it before?
2. Go to the information on Marshall Field's. What type of a focus does this company have? Does the company have a separate Web site? Do you think that some of the cost of the Target Web site should be allocated to Marshall Field's? Why or why not? If the firm was going to allocate costs, what measurement tool would you recommend that the firm consider.
3. Locate Target Corporation's most recent annual report by clicking on "Investor Information" at the home page for Target Corporation. Click on "annual reports" and then on the most recent annual report. Look at the financial review section. Did the firm provide any information on segment revenues? Sum the pre-tax segment profit of the segments for the current year. What is this figure? Now look at the income statement for the current year. What is the income before taxes and extraordinary items for the year? Why is it different than the sum of the segment pre-tax profit?
4. Assume that the difference in the pre-tax segment profit and the corporation's pre-tax profit is due to service department costs. If Target wants to allocate these costs to the major segments based on segment pre-tax income using the direct method, how much would be allocated to each segment? What would be the allocation if the corporation used the number of stores as the allocation basis.

Go to the "Job-Order Product Costing" episode on the *Mastering Accounting* CD-ROM for an interactive, video-enhanced exercise on CanGo managers' use of continually updated accounting reports to pinpoint problems related to a new product offering.

JOB-COSTING SYSTEMS

Dell Computer Corporation's
workers assemble computers based
on individual customer specifications.
The assembly activity is a key part of
the production process.

www.prenhall.com/horngren

Learning Objectives

When you have finished studying this chapter, you should be able to

1. Distinguish between job-order costing and process costing.

2. Prepare summary journal entries for the typical transactions of a job-costing system.

3. Compute budgeted factory-overhead rates and factory overhead applied to production.

4. Use appropriate cost drivers for overhead application.

5. Identify the meaning and purpose of normalized overhead rates.

6. Use an activity-based-costing system in a job-order environment.

7. Show how job costing is used in service organizations.

8. **Understand how a job-order-costing system tracks the flow of costs to products.**

Dell Computer Corporation is the world's leading direct marketer of made-to-order computer systems. Dell does not manufacture computer components (e.g., circuit boards, hard drives), but instead assembles them into computers on a made-to-order basis.

Dell pioneered the "direct business model"—selling directly to end users instead of using a network of dealers, which avoids the dealer markup and gives Dell a competitive price advantage. Customers can design their own computer systems to specifications they desire, choosing from among a full complement of options. Before ordering, customers can receive advice and price quotes for a wide variety of computer configurations.

Once an order is taken, it is assembled in a manufacturing work cell called a mod. There is a separate mod for each of Dell's "lines of business" (Dimension Desktop PCs, OptiPlex Desktops for networked environments, Latitude and Inspiron Notebooks, PowerEdge and PowerApp network servers, and Precision workstation products). Management considers rapid response to customer orders a key to gaining and maintaining a competitive edge.

Orders at Dell can be taken over the phone or placed over the Internet. In fact, about 50% of Dell's revenues are derived from the company's Internet site, www.dell.com, with daily revenues in excess of $40 million and weekly "hits" of over 3,000,000. Customers may review, configure, and price systems within Dell's entire product line. Web sites also offer personalized system-support pages and technical services. "The Internet was tailor-made for Dell," said Michael Dell, chairman and chief executive officer. "Customers of all kinds prefer direct. They like the immediacy, convenience, savings and personal touches the Internet-direct customer experience provides." Because each computer is built to customer specifications, each order is considered a separate job for costing purposes.

Why would managers at Dell and other companies need to know product cost? Accountants compute product costs for both decision-making and financial-reporting purposes. They supply product costs to managers for evaluating pricing policy and product lines. For example, Chrysler managers need to know the cost of each kind of auto being produced to set prices, to determine marketing and production strategies for various models, and to evaluate production operations. At the same time, product costs appear as cost of goods sold in income statements and as finished-goods inventory values in balance sheets. Although it would be possible to have two product-costing systems, one for management decision making and one for financial reporting, seldom do the benefits of using two completely separate systems exceed the costs. Therefore, both decision-making and financial-reporting needs influence the design of product-costing systems.

In this chapter, we focus on one type of product-costing system—the job-order-costing system. We look at the elements of such systems and how they track the flow of costs. This system focuses on costs involved in the production of goods and services (i.e., on the production phase of the value chain). Costs of activities in the other phases of the value chain (R&D, design, distribution, marketing, and customer service) are period costs, not product costs, and they are expensed immediately and excluded from the costs of product for inventory valuation and other external reporting purposes. Because this chapter draws heavily on terminology and concepts explained in Chapters 4 and 12, you might want to review those chapters before reading further.

DISTINCTION BETWEEN JOB COSTING AND PROCESS COSTING

Objective 1
Distinguish between job-order costing and process costing.

job-order costing (job costing) The method of allocating costs to products that are readily identified by individual units or batches, each of which requires varying degrees of attention and skill.

process costing The method of allocating costs to products by averaging costs over large numbers of nearly identical products.

The two most common systems of product costing are job-order costing and process costing. **Job-order costing** (or simply **job costing**) allocates costs to products that are readily identified by individual units or batches, each of which requires varying degrees of attention and skill. Industries that commonly use job-order methods include construction, printing, aircraft, furniture, special-purpose machinery, and any manufacture of tailor-made or unique goods.

Process costing averages costs over large numbers of nearly identical products. It is most often found in such industries as chemicals, oil, plastics, rubber, lumber, food processing, glass, mining, cement, and meatpacking. These industries involve mass production of like units, that usually pass in continuous fashion through a series of uniform production steps called operations or processes.

The distinction between the job-cost and the process-cost methods centers largely on how product costing is accomplished. Job costing applies costs to specific jobs, which may consist of either a single physical unit (such as a custom sofa) or a few like units (such as a dozen tables) in a distinct batch or job lot. In contrast, process costing deals with great masses of like units and broad averages of unit costs.

The most important point is that product costing is an averaging process. The unit cost used for inventory purposes is the result of taking some accumulated cost (e.g., the sum of production-related activity costs) of production and dividing it by some measure of production. The basic distinction between job-order costing and process costing is the breadth of the denominator: In job-order costing, the denominator is small (e.g., one painting, 100 advertising circulars, or one special packaging machine);

however, in process costing, the denominator is large (e.g., thousands of pounds, gallons, or board feet).

Job costing and process costing are extremes along a continuum of potential costing systems. Each company designs its own accounting system to fit its underlying production activities. Some companies use hybrid costing systems, which are blends of ideas from both job costing and process costing. Chapter 14 describes process costing.

ILLUSTRATION OF JOB COSTING

Job costing is best learned by example. But first we examine the basic records used in a job-cost system. The centerpiece of a job-costing system is the **job-cost record** (also called a **job-cost sheet** or **job order**), shown in Exhibit 13-1. All costs for a particular product,

job-cost record (job-cost sheet, job order) A document that shows all costs for a particular product, service, or batch of products.

Exhibit 13-1
Completed Job-Cost Record and Sample Source Documents

Job Cost Record: _____ Machining _____ **Department**

| Date Started | 1/7/20X2 | Job No. | 963 |
| Date Completed | 1/14/20X2 | Units Completed | 12 |

Cost	Date	Ref.	Quantity	Amount	Summary
Direct Materials:					
6" Bars	1/7/20X2	N41	24	120.00	
Casings	1/9/20X2	K56	12	340.00	460.00
Direct Labor:					
Drill	1/8/20X2	7Z4	7.0	105.00*	
	1/9/20X2	7Z5	5.5	82.50	
Grind	1/13/20X2	9Z2	4.0	80.00	267.50
Factory Overhead:					
Applied	1/14/20X2		9.0 Mach. Hrs.	180.00	180.00
Total Cost					907.50
Unit Cost					75.625

Direct Materials Requisition: No. N41
Job No. _____ **Date** 1/7/20X2
Department Machining

Descript	Quantity	Unit Cost	Amount
6" Bars	24	5.00	120.00

Authorization J. Hays

Time Ticket: No. 7Z4
Employee No. 464-89-7265
Department Machining
Date 1/8/20X2

Start	End	Hours	Rate	Amount	Job
8:00	11:30	3.5	15.00	52.50	963
12:30	4:00	3.5	15.00	52.50	963
4:00	5:00	1.0	15.00	15.00	571
Totals		8.0		120.00	

Supervisor M. Butler

* Note that 7 of the 8 hours and $105 of the $120 in time ticket 7Z4 belong to job no. 963.

service, or batch of products are recorded on the job-cost record. A file of job-cost records for partially completed jobs provides supporting details for the Work-in-Process Inventory account, often simply called Work in Process (WIP). A file of completed job-cost records comprises the Finished-Goods Inventory account.

As Exhibit 13-1 shows, the job-cost record summarizes information contained on source documents such as materials requisitions and labor time tickets. **Materials requisitions** are records of materials used in particular jobs. **Labor time tickets** (or **time cards**) record the time a particular direct laborer spends on each job.

Today job-cost records and source documents are likely to be computer files, not paper records. In fact, with on-line data entry, bar coding, and optical scanning, much of the information needed for such records enters the computer without ever being written on paper. Nevertheless, whether records are on paper or in computer files, the accounting system must collect and maintain the same basic information.

As each job begins, its own job-cost record is created. As units are worked on, entries are made on the job-cost record. Three classes of costs are accumulated on the job-cost record as units pass through the departments: Materials requisitions are the source of direct-material costs, time tickets provide direct-labor costs, and budgeted overhead rates (a separate rate for each overhead cost pool) are used to apply factory overhead to products. (The computation of these budgeted rates will be described later in this chapter.)

materials requisitions Records of materials issued to particular jobs.

labor time tickets (time cards) The record of the time a particular direct laborer spends on each job.

BASIC RECORDS OF ENRIQUEZ MACHINE PARTS COMPANY

To illustrate the functioning of a job-order-costing system, we will use the records and journal entries of the Enriquez Machine Parts Company. On December 31, 20X1, the firm had the following inventories.

Direct materials (12 types)	$110,000
Work in process	—
Finished goods (unsold units from two jobs)	12,000

The following is a summary of pertinent transactions for the year 20X2:

	Machining	**Assembly**	**Total**
1. Direct materials purchased on account	—	—	$1,900,000
2. Direct materials requisitioned for manufacturing	$1,000,000	$890,000	1,890,000
3. Direct-labor costs incurred	200,000	190,000	390,000
4a. Factory overhead incurred	290,000	102,000	392,000
4b. Factory overhead applied	280,000*	95,000	375,000
5. Cost of goods completed and transferred to finished-good inventory	—	—	2,500,000
6a. Sales on account	—	—	4,000,000
6b. Cost of goods sold	—	—	2,480,000

* We explain the nature of factory overhead applied later in this chapter.

Exhibit 13-2
Job-Order Costing, General Flow of Costs (Thousands)

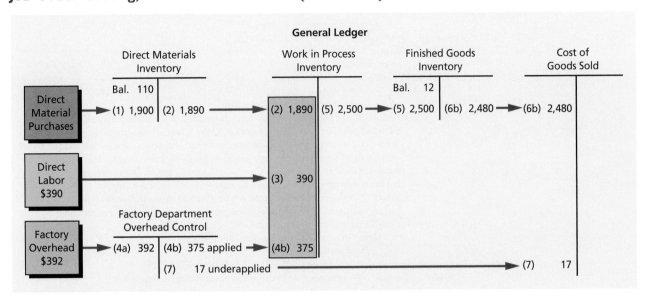

Exhibit 13-2 is an overview of the general flow of costs through the Enriquez Machine Parts Company's job-order-costing system.[1] The exhibit summarizes the effects of transactions on the key manufacturing accounts in the firm's books. As you proceed through the detailed explanation of transactions, keep checking each explanation against the overview in Exhibit 13-2.

EXPLANATION OF TRANSACTIONS

The following transaction-by-transaction summary analysis will explain how product costing is achieved. Entries are usually made as transactions occur. However, to obtain a sweeping overview, our illustration uses a summary for the entire year 20X2.

Objective 2
Prepare summary journal entries for the typical transactions of a job-costing system.

1. Transaction: Direct materials purchased, $1,900,000.
    Analysis: The asset Direct-Materials Inventory is increased. The liability Accounts Payable is increased.
    Journal Entry: Direct-Materials Inventory 1,900,000
                Accounts Payable 1,900,000

---

[1] *Exhibit 13-2 and the following explanation of transactions assume knowledge of basic accounting procedures. We will use the T-account format for a company's accounts. Entries on the left of the "T" are debits and those on the right are credits. Asset T-accounts, such as the inventory accounts, show increases on the left (debit) side and decreases on the right (credit) side of the "T":*

	Inventory	
Beginning Balance		Decreases
Increases		
Ending Balance		

Transactions affecting the accounts are recorded as journal entries. Debit (left side) entries are shown flush with the left margin, and credit (right side) entries are indented, and often an explanation is included. For example, a $10,000 transfer from Direct Materials Inventory to WIP (Work in Process) Inventory would be shown as follows:

WIP Inventory 10,000
     Direct Materials Inventory 10,000
   To increase WIP Inventory and decrease Direct
     Materials Inventory by $10,000.

2. Transaction: Direct materials requisitioned, $1,890,000.
    Analysis: The asset Work in Process (WIP) Inventory is increased. The asset
    Direct-Materials Inventory is decreased.
    Journal Entry: WIP Inventory 1,890,000
                        Direct-Materials Inventory 1,890,000

3. Transaction: Direct-labor cost incurred, $390,000.
    Analysis: The asset WIP Inventory is increased. The liability Accrued Payroll
    is increased.
    Journal Entry: WIP Inventory 390,000
                        Accrued Payroll 390,000

4a. Transaction: Factory overhead incurred, $392,000.
    Analysis: These actual costs are first charged to departmental overhead accounts, which may be
    regarded as assets until their amounts are later "cleared" or transferred to other
    accounts. Each department has detailed overhead accounts such as indirect labor,
    utilities, repairs, depreciation, insurance, and property taxes. These details support a
    summary Factory Department Overhead Control account. The managers are responsi-
    ble for regulating these costs, item by item. As these costs are charged to the depart-
    ments, the other accounts affected will be assorted assets and liabilities. Examples
    include cash, accounts payable, accrued payables, and accumulated depreciation.
    Journal Entry: Factory Department Overhead Control 392,000
                        Cash, Accounts Payable, and various other balance
                        sheet accounts 392,000

4b. Transaction: Factory overhead applied, $95,000 + $280,000 = $375,000.
    Analysis: The asset WIP Inventory is increased. The asset Factory Department
    Overhead Control is decreased. (A fuller explanation occurs
    later in this chapter.)
    Journal Entry: WIP Inventory 375,000
                        Factory Department Overhead
                        Control 375,000

5. Transaction: Cost of goods completed, $2,500,000.
    Analysis: The asset Finished Goods Inventory is increased. The asset
    WIP Inventory is decreased.
    Journal Entry: Finished Goods Inventory 2,500,000
                        WIP Inventory 2,500,000

6a. Transaction: Sales on account, $4,000,000.
    Analysis: The asset Accounts Receivable is increased. The
    revenue account Sales is increased.
    Journal Entry: Accounts Receivable 4,000,000
                        Sales 4,000,00

6b. Transaction: Cost of goods sold, $2,480,000.
    Analysis: The expense Cost of Goods Sold is increased. The asset
    Finished Goods Inventory is decreased.
    Journal Entry: Cost of Goods Sold 2,480,000
                        Finished Goods Inventory 2,480,000

Confirm your understanding of product costing in a job-order environment by indicating the transactions that occurred for each of the following journal entries. Which
of these transactions records actual costs versus cost estimates?

1. WIP Inventory XXX
        Accrued Payroll XXX
2. WIP Inventory XXX
        Factory Department Overhead Control XXX
3. Cost of Goods Sold XXX
        Finished Goods XXX

ANSWER

The first entry records the actual cost of direct labor that is traced to the specific order being
costed. The second entry is made when the order is completed to record the application of factory overhead. This is an estimate of the costs of indirect resources used to complete the order.
The last entry records the cost of goods sold when the order is shipped. This cost is a mix of
actual costs (direct material and direct labor) and estimated costs (applied factory overhead).

SUMMARY OF TRANSACTIONS

Review Exhibit 13-2. It summarizes the Enriquez transactions for the year, focusing on the inventory accounts. WIP Inventory receives central attention. The costs of direct material used, direct labor, and factory overhead applied to product are brought into WIP. In turn, the costs of completed goods are transferred from WIP to Finished Goods. As goods are sold, their costs become expense in the form of Cost of Goods Sold. The year-end accounting for the $17,000 of underapplied overhead is explained later.

ACCOUNTING FOR FACTORY OVERHEAD

In the Enriquez Machine Parts Company example, factory overhead of $375,000 was applied to the WIP account. This section describes how to determine the amount of applied factory overhead.

HOW FACTORY OVERHEAD IS APPLIED TO PRODUCTS

Managers need to know product costs in order to make ongoing decisions such as which products to emphasize and which to deemphasize and product pricing. Ideally, all costs, including overhead, are known when these decisions must be made. Unfortunately, actual overhead costs are not available when managers need them. For this reason, budgeted (predetermined) overhead rates are used to apply overhead to jobs as they are completed.

The size of overhead costs in many manufacturing companies is large enough to motivate companies to search for ways to convert them into direct costs. Dell Computer Corporation has increased the accuracy of its product cost information by converting some of its factory-overhead costs from indirect to direct costs. How was this done? By dedicating assembly labor and factory equipment to specific product lines. Work cells (mods) do the assembly and software loading for specific product lines. This makes it easier to trace equipment costs to products. Nevertheless, significant overhead costs remain to be allocated.

BUDGETED OVERHEAD APPLICATION RATES

The following steps summarize how to account for factory overhead:

1. Select one or more cost drivers to serve as a base for applying overhead costs. Examples include direct-labor hours, direct-labor costs, machine hours, and production setups. The cost driver should be an activity that is the common denominator for systematically relating a cost or a group of costs, such as machinery cost, set-up costs, or energy cost, with products. The cost driver(s) should be the best available measure of the cause-and-effect relationships between overhead costs and production volume.

2. Prepare a factory-overhead budget for the planning period, ordinarily a year. The two key items are (1) budgeted overhead and (2) budgeted volume of the cost driver. There will be a set of budgeted overhead costs and an associated budgeted cost-driver level for each overhead cost pool. In businesses with simple production systems, there may be just one set.

3. Compute the **budgeted factory-overhead rate**(s) by dividing the budgeted total overhead for each cost pool by the budgeted cost-driver level.

budgeted factory-overhead rate The budgeted total overhead for each cost pool divided by the budgeted cost-driver level.

4. Obtain actual cost-driver data (such as machine hours) as jobs are produced.

5. Apply the budgeted overhead to the jobs by multiplying the budgeted rate(s) times the actual cost-driver data.

6. At the end of the year, account for any differences between the amount of overhead actually incurred and overhead applied to products.

ILLUSTRATION OF OVERHEAD APPLICATION

Objective 3
Compute budgeted factory-overhead rates and factory overhead applied to production.

Now that you know the steps in accounting for factory overhead in a job-costing system, we can examine how they work in a real example. Consider the Enriquez illustration again.

This manufacturing-overhead budget has been prepared for the coming year, 20X3:

	Machining	**Assembly**
Indirect labor	$ 75,600	$ 36,800
Supplies	8,400	2,400
Utilities	20,000	7,000
Repairs	10,000	3,000
Factory rent	10,000	6,800
Supervision	42,600	35,400
Depreciation on equipment	104,000	9,400
Insurance, property taxes, etc.	7,200	2,400
Total	$277,800	$103,200

As products are worked on, Enriquez applies the factory overhead to the jobs. A budgeted overhead rate is used, computed as follows:

$$\text{budgeted overhead application rate} = \frac{\text{total budgeted factory overhead}}{\text{total budgeted amount of cost driver}}$$
$$\text{(such as direct-labor costs or machine hours)}$$

Suppose machine hours are chosen as the only cost driver in the Machining Department, and direct-labor cost is chosen in the Assembly Department. The overhead rates are as follows.

	Year 20X3	
	Machining	*Assembly*
Budgeted manufacturing overhead	$277,800	$103,200
Budgeted machine hours	69,450	
Budgeted direct-labor cost		$206,400
Budgeted overhead rate, per machine hour: $277,800 ÷ 69,450 =	$4	
Budgeted overhead rate, per direct-labor dollar: $103,200 ÷ $206,400 =		50%

Note that the overhead rates are budgeted; they are estimates. These rates are then used to apply overhead based on actual events. That is, the total overhead applied in our illustration is the result of multiplying actual machine hours or labor cost by the budgeted overhead rates:

Machining: actual machine hours of 70,000 × $4 = $280,000
Assembly: actual direct-labor cost of $190,000 × .50 = 95,000
Total factory overhead applied $ 375,200

The summary journal entry for the application (entry 4b) is

4b. WIP Inventory 375,000
      Factory Department Overhead Control 375,000

In 1999, Milwaukee-based Harley-Davidson, the motorcycle manufacturer, captured the number one market position from Honda for the first time in three decades. Harley-Davidson (2000 sales of $2.9 billion) is the only major U.S.–based motorcycle producer. One of the keys to the company's return to competitiveness was the adoption of a just-in-time (JIT) philosophy. It is not unusual for a company to discover that a change in an important component of operations requires a corresponding change in the company's accounting system. The main focus of the accounting system was direct labor, which not only made up a part of product cost itself, but also functioned as an all-purpose base for allocating overhead. However, direct labor was only 10% of total product cost. It certainly did not generate a majority of overhead costs. As Harley-Davidson's production process had changed, the accounting system had remained static.

The first point that became apparent with the JIT system was that detailed information on direct-labor costs was not useful to managers. It was costly to have each direct laborer record the time spent on each product or part and then enter the information from these time cards into the accounting system. For example, if each of 500 direct laborers works on 20 products per day, the system must record 10,000 entries per day, which is 200,000 entries per month. The time spent by direct laborers to record the time, by clerks to enter the data into the system, and by accountants to check the data's accuracy is enormous—and all to produce product cost information that was used for financial reporting but was useless to managers.

The JIT system forced manufacturing managers to focus on satisfying customers and minimizing non-value-added activities. Gradually, accountants began to focus on the same objectives. Accounting's customers were the managers who used the accounting information, and effort put into activities that did not help managers was deemed counterproductive (non-value-added). Therefore, eliminating the costly, time-consuming recording of detailed labor costs became a priority. Direct labor was eliminated as a direct cost, and consequently it could not be used for overhead allocation. After considering process hours, flow-through time, material value, and individual cost per unit as possible cost drivers for allocating overhead, the company selected process hours. Direct labor and overhead were combined to form conversion costs, which were applied to products on the basis of total process hours. This did not result in costs significantly different from the old system, but the new system was much simpler and less costly. Only direct material was traced directly to the product. Conversion costs were applied at completion of production based on a simple measure of process time.

Accounting systems should generate benefits greater than their costs. More sophisticated systems are not necessarily better systems. Harley-Davidson's main objective in changing its accounting system was simplification—eliminating unnecessary tasks and streamlining others. These changes resulted in a revitalized accounting system.

Sources: Adapted from W. T. Turk, "Management Accounting Revitalized: The Harley-Davidson Experience," in B. J., Brinker, ed., *Emerging Practices in Cost Management* (Boston: Warren, Gorham & Lamont, 1990), pp.155–166; K. Barron, "Hog Wild," *Forbes*, May 15, 2000.

CHOICE OF COST DRIVERS

As we have noted several times in this text, no one cost driver is right for all situations. The accountant's goal is to find the driver that best links cause and effect. In the Enriquez Machining Department, use of machines causes most overhead cost, for example, depreciation and repairs. Therefore, machine hours is the cost driver and the appropriate base for applying overhead costs. Thus, Enriquez must keep track of the machine hours used for each job, creating an added data collection cost. That is, direct-materials costs, direct-labor costs, and machine hours must be accumulated for each job.

In contrast, direct labor is the principal cost driver in the Enriquez Assembly Department because parts are assembled by hand. The workers are paid equal hourly rates. Therefore, all that is needed is to apply the 50% overhead rate to the cost of direct

Objective 4
Use appropriate cost drivers for overhead application.

labor already entered on the job-cost records. No separate job records of the labor hours have to be kept. If the hourly labor rates differ greatly for individuals performing identical tasks, the hours of labor, rather than the dollars spent for labor, might be used as a base. Otherwise, a $9-per-hour worker would cause more overhead applied than an $8-per-hour worker, even though the same time would probably be taken and the same facilities used by each employee for the same work.

Sometimes direct-labor cost is the best overhead cost driver even if wage rates vary within a department. For example, higher-skilled labor may use more costly equipment and have more indirect labor support. Moreover, many factory-overhead costs include costly labor fringe benefits such as pensions and payroll taxes. The latter are often more closely driven by direct-labor cost than by direct-labor hours.

If a department identifies more than one cost driver for overhead costs, these costs ideally should be put into as many cost pools as there are cost drivers. In practice, such a system is too costly for many organizations. Instead, these organizations select a few cost drivers (often only one) to serve as a basis for allocating overhead costs. The 80-20 rule can be used in these situations. In many cases, 80% of total overhead cost can be accounted for with just a few drivers (20% of all the drivers identified). For example, a company may identify 10 separate overhead pools with 10 different drivers. Often, approximately 80% of the total cost can be applied with only two drivers.

The selected cost drivers should be the ones that cause most of the overhead costs. For example, suppose machine hours cause 70% of the overhead costs in a particular department, number of component parts causes 20%, and five assorted cost drivers cause the other 10%. Instead of using seven cost pools allocated on the basis of the seven cost drivers, most managers would use one cost driver—machine hours—to allocate all overhead costs. Others would assign all cost to two cost pools, one allocated on the basis of machine hours and one on the basis of number of component parts.

No matter which cost drivers are chosen, the overhead rates are applied day after day throughout the year to cost the various jobs worked on by each department. All overhead is applied to all jobs worked on during the year on the appropriate basis of machine hours or direct-labor costs of each job. Suppose management predictions coincide exactly with actual amounts (an extremely unlikely situation). Then the total overhead applied to the year's jobs via these budgeted rates would be equal to the total overhead costs actually incurred.

Consider Dell Computer Corporation. As we said earlier, Dell has converted many of its overhead costs into direct costs. However, two important costs that cannot be directly traced (i.e., indirect costs) are facilities and engineering. Facilities cost includes occupancy costs such as depreciation on the factory, insurance, and taxes. These costs are allocated using the cost driver "square footage used by each line of business (assembly line)." Product and process engineering activities are part of the design phase of the company's value chain and the associated costs incurred are significant. These costs are allocated to lines of business using a "complexity" cost driver (e.g., number of distinct parts in the mother board). Server computer products, for example, require much more engineering time and effort due to the complexity of the product compared to laptops or PCs, so this would be reflected in a greater number of distinct parts in the mother board. Thus, server products receive a much greater allocation of engineering costs than laptops or PCs.

PROBLEMS OF OVERHEAD APPLICATION

Objective 5
Identify the meaning and purpose of normalized overhead rates.

NORMALIZED OVERHEAD RATES

Basically, our illustration has demonstrated the normal costing approach. Why the term *normal*? Because an annual average overhead rate is used consistently throughout the year for product costing, without altering it from day to day and from month to month.

The resultant "normal" product costs include an average or normalized chunk of overhead. As actual overhead costs are incurred by departments from month to month, they are charged to the departments. Hence, we shall label the system a **normal costing system.** The cost of the manufactured product is composed of actual direct material, actual direct labor, and normal applied overhead.

normal costing system
The cost system in which overhead is applied on an average or normalized basis, in order to get representative or normal inventory valuations.

During the year and at year-end, the actual overhead amount incurred will rarely equal the amount applied. This variance between incurred and applied cost can be analyzed. The most common—and important—contributor to these variances is operating at a different level of volume than the level used as a denominator in calculating the budgeted overhead rate (for instance, using 100,000 budgeted direct-labor-hours as the denominator and then actually working only 80,000 hours). Other frequent contributory causes include poor forecasting, inefficient use of overhead items, price changes in individual overhead items, erratic behavior of individual overhead items (e.g., repairs made only during slack time), and calendar variations (e.g., 20 workdays in one month, 22 in the next).

All these peculiarities of overhead are mingled in an annual overhead pool. Thus, an annual rate is budgeted and used regardless of the month-to-month peculiarities of specific overhead costs. Such an approach is more defensible than, say, applying the actual overhead for each month. Why? Because a normal product cost is more useful for decisions, and more representative for inventory-costing purposes, than an "actual" product cost that is distorted by month-to-month fluctuations in production volume and by the erratic behavior of many overhead costs. For example, the employees of a gypsum plant using an "actual" product cost system had the privilege of buying company-made items "at cost." Employees joked about the benefits of buying "at cost" during high-volume months, when unit costs were lower because volume was higher, as shown in the following table.

	Actual Overhead			Direct-Labor Hours	Actual Overhead Application Rate* per Direct-Labor Hour
	Variable	Fixed	Total		
Peak-volume month	$60,000	$40,000	$100,000	100,000	$1.00
Low-volume month	30,000	40,000	70,000	50,000	1.40

* Divide total overhead by direct-labor hours. Note that the presence of fixed overhead causes the fluctuation in unit overhead costs from $1.00 to $1.40. The variable component is $.60 an hour in both months, but the fixed component is $.40 in the peak-volume month ($40,000 ÷ 100,000) and $.80 in the low-volume month ($40,000 ÷ 50,000).

The overall system we have just described is sometimes called an actual costing system because every effort is made to trace the actual costs, as incurred, to the physical units benefited.

DISPOSITION OF UNDERAPPLIED OR OVERAPPLIED OVERHEAD

Our Enriquez illustration contained the following data:

	Transaction	
4a.	Factory overhead incurred	$392,000
4b.	Factory overhead applied	375,000
	Underapplied factory overhead	$ 17,000

Total costs of $392,000 must eventually be charged to expense in some way. The $375,000 will become part of the Cost of Goods Sold expense when the products to which it is applied are sold. The remaining $17,000 must also become expense by some method.

When budgeted rates are used, the difference between incurred and applied overhead is typically allowed to accumulate during the year. When the amount applied to product exceeds the amount incurred by the departments, the difference is called **overapplied overhead.** When the amount applied is less than incurred, the difference is called **underapplied overhead.** At year-end, the difference ($17,000 underapplied in our illustration) is disposed of through either a write-off or through proration.

overapplied overhead
The excess of overhead applied to products over actual overhead incurred.

underapplied overhead
The excess of actual overhead over the overhead applied to products.

IMMEDIATE WRITE-OFF

Under the immediate write-off method, the $17,000 is regarded as a reduction in current income by adding the underapplied overhead to the cost of goods sold. The same logic is followed for overapplied overhead except that the result would be a decrease in cost of goods sold.

The theory underlying the direct write-off is that most of the goods worked on have been sold, and a more elaborate method of disposition is not worth the extra trouble. Another justification is that the extra overhead costs represented by underapplied overhead do not qualify as part of ending inventory costs because they do not represent assets. They should be written off because they largely represent inefficiency or the underutilization of available facilities in the current period.

The immediate write-off eliminates the $17,000 difference with a simple journal entry, labeled as transaction 7 in Exhibit 13-2.

```
7. Cost of Goods Sold (or a separate
      charge against revenue) .........................  17,000
         Factory Department Overhead Control  ...........           17,000
      To close ending underapplied overhead directly to Cost of
      Goods Sold.
```

Because of its simplicity, the immediate write-off method is most commonly used.

PRORATION AMONG INVENTORIES

prorate To assign underapplied overhead or overapplied overhead in proportion to the sizes of the ending account balances.

Another method prorates over- or underapplied overhead among WIP, Finished Goods, and Cost of Goods Sold. To **prorate** underapplied overhead means to assign it in proportion to the sizes of the ending account balances. Theoretically, if the objective is to obtain as accurate a cost allocation as possible, all the overhead costs of the individual jobs worked on should be recomputed, using the actual, rather than the budgeted, rates. This approach is rarely feasible, so a practical attack is to prorate on the basis of the ending balances in each of three accounts (WIP, $155,000; Finished Goods, $32,000; and Cost of Goods Sold, $2,480,000).

	(1) Unadjusted Balance, End of 20X2*	(2) Proration of Underapplied Overhead	(3) Adjusted Balance, End of 20X2
WIP	$ 155,000	155/2,667 × 17,000 = $ 988	$ 155,988
Finished Goods	32,000	32/2,667 × 17,000 = 204	32,204
Cost of Goods Sold	2,480,000	2,480/2,667 × 17,000 = 15,808	2,495,808
Total	$2,667,000	$17,000	$2,684,000

* See Exhibit 13-2 for details.

The journal entry for the proration follows:

WIP	988	
Finished Goods	204	
Cost of Goods Sold	15,808	
Factory Department Overhead Control		17,000
To prorate ending underapplied overhead among three accounts.		

The amounts prorated to inventories here are not significant. In actual practice, pro-rating is done only when inventory valuations would be materially affected.

THE USE OF VARIABLE AND FIXED APPLICATION RATES

As we have seen, overhead application is the most troublesome aspect of product costing. The presence of fixed costs is a major reason for the costing difficulties. Most companies have made no distinction between variable- and fixed-cost behavior in the design of their accounting systems. For instance, the Machining Department at Enriquez Machine Parts Company developed the following rate:

$$\text{budgeted overhead application rate} = \frac{\text{budgeted total overhead}}{\text{budgeted machine hours}}$$

$$= \frac{\$277,800}{69,450} = \$4 \text{ per machine hour}$$

Some companies, though, do distinguish between variable overhead and fixed over-head for product costing as well as for control purposes. If the Machining Department at Enriquez had made this distinction, then rent, supervision, depreciation, and insurance would have been considered the fixed portion of the total manufacturing overhead, and two rates would have been developed:

$$\text{budgeted variable-overhead application rate} = \frac{\text{budgeted total variable overhead}}{\text{budgeted machine hours}}$$

$$= \frac{\$114,000}{69,450}$$

$$= \$1.64 \text{ per machine hour}$$

$$\text{budgeted fixed-overhead application rate} = \frac{\text{budgeted total fixed overhead}}{\text{budgeted machine hours}}$$

$$= \frac{\$163,800}{69,450}$$

$$= \$2.36 \text{ per machine hour}$$

Such rates can be used for product costing. Distinctions between variable- and fixed-overhead incurrence can also be made for control purposes.

ACTIVITY-BASED COSTING/MANAGEMENT IN A JOB-COSTING ENVIRONMENT

Regardless of the nature of the company's production system, there will always be resources that are shared among different products. The costs of these resources are part of overhead and must be accounted for in the company's cost accounting system. In many cases, the magnitude of overhead is large enough to justify investing in a costing system that provides accurate cost information. Whether this cost information is being used for inventory reporting, to cost jobs, or for cost planning and control, most often the benefits of more accurate costs exceed the costs of installing and maintaining the cost system. As we have seen, activity-based costing usually increases costing accuracy because it focuses on the cause-and-effect relationships between work performed (activities) and the consumption of resources (costs).

ILLUSTRATION OF ACTIVITY-BASED COSTING IN A JOB-ORDER ENVIRONMENT

Objective 6
Use an activity-based-costing system in a job-order environment.

We illustrate an activity-based-costing (ABC) system in a job-order environment by again considering Dell Computer Corporation. What motivated Dell to adopt activity-based costing? Company managers cite two reasons: (1) the aggressive cost reduction targets set by top management and (2) the need to understand product-line profitability. As is the case with any business, understanding profitability means understanding the cost structure of the entire business. One of the key advantages of an ABC system is its focus on understanding how work (activity) is related to the consumption of resources (costs). So, an ABC system was a logical choice for Dell. And, of course, once Dell's managers improved their understanding of the company's cost structure, cost reduction through activity-based management was much easier.

Like most companies that implement ABC, Dell began developing its ABC system by focusing on the most critical (core) processes across the value chain. These were the design and production processes. After the initial system was in place, the remaining phases of the value chain were added. Exhibit 13-3 shows the functions (or core

Exhibit 13-3
Dell Computer Corporation's Value Chain and ABC System

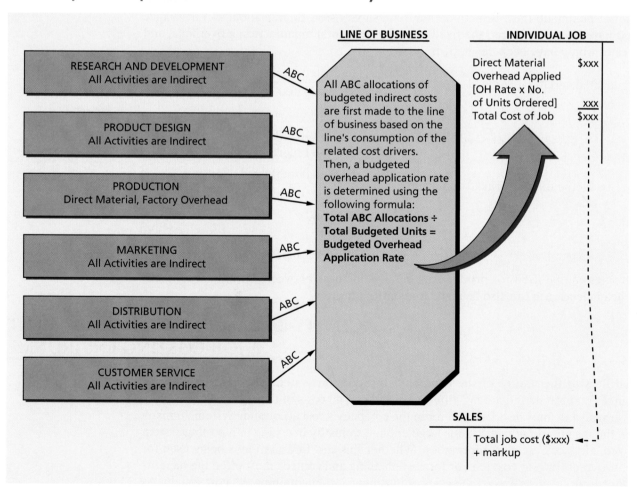

processes) that add value to the company's products and how the costs of these functions are assigned to an individual job under the current ABC system.

To understand product-line profitability, Dell managers identified key activities for the research and development, product design, production, distribution, marketing, and customer service phases. Then, they used appropriate cost drivers to allocate activity costs to the produced product lines. While each of the phases shown in Exhibit 13-3 is important, we will focus on the product design and production phases. Product design is one of Dell's most important value-adding functions. The role of design is providing a defect-free computer product that is easy to manufacture and reliable to the customer. Engineering costs (primarily salaries and CAD equipment depreciation) account for most of the design costs. These costs are indirect and thus must be allocated to product lines using a cost driver.

The production costs include direct materials and factory overhead. Factory overhead consists of six activity centers and related cost pools: receiving, preparation, assembly, testing, packaging, and shipping. Facility costs (plant depreciation, insurance, taxes) are considered part of the production function and are allocated to each activity center based on the square feet occupied by the center.

At Dell the total annual budgeted indirect cost allocated to a product line is divided by the total budgeted units produced to find a budgeted overhead rate. This rate, which is adjusted periodically to reflect changes in the budget, is used to cost individual jobs.

Dell is now breaking down the costs in each activity center into value added and non-value added. Non-value-added costs are targeted for cost reduction programs. An example of a non-value-added activity is the preparation activity in the production function.

Refer to Exhibit 13-3. One of the primary purposes of an ABC system is to increase the accuracy of product costs so that managers have a high level of confidence in cost-based decisions. Assume that Dell's managers determine prices for computers by adding a markup to the cost computed in Exhibit 13-3. For example, if the computed total job cost is $1,200, a markup sufficient to "cover" all unallocated costs and provide a reasonable profit is added. Using the table below, determine whether the percentage markup under the ABC system is higher or lower than under the 1993 system. Which system produces a higher confidence level that the price for a computer is adequate to cover all costs and provide a reasonable profit? Why?

	ABC or Unallocated	
Value Chain Function	*1993 Costing System*	*ABC Costing System*
Research and Development	Unallocated	ABC
Design	Unallocated	ABC
Production	Traditional Allocation	ABC
Marketing	Unallocated	ABC
Distribution	Unallocated	ABC
Customer Service	Unallocated	ABC

ANSWER

In 1993, the markup on cost was based on only the cost of production. Thus, the markup was high so that all the unallocated costs would be covered and a reasonable profit would result. Managers had a low level of confidence in this cost system. The ABC system provided improved estimates of all value chain costs. The size of the markup was low, and the confidence level in the costs provided was high.

PRODUCT COSTING IN SERVICE AND NONPROFIT ORGANIZATIONS

Objective 7
Show how job costing is used in service organizations.

This chapter has concentrated on how to apply costs to manufactured products. However, the job-costing approach is used in nonmanufacturing situations too. For example, universities have research "projects," airlines have repair and overhaul "jobs," and public accountants have audit "engagements." In such situations, the focus shifts from the costs of products to the costs of services.

In nonprofit organizations, the "product" is usually not called a "job order." Instead, it may be called a program or a class of service. A "program" is an identifiable group of activities that frequently produces outputs in the form of services rather than goods. Examples include a safety program, an education program, and a family counseling program. Costs or revenues may be traced to individual hospital patients, individual social welfare cases, and individual university research projects. However, departments often work simultaneously on many programs, so the "job-order" costing challenge is to "apply" the various department costs to the various programs. Only then can managers make wiser decisions regarding the allocation of limited resources among competing programs.

In service industries—such as repairing, consulting, legal, and accounting services—each customer order is a different job with a special account or order number. Sometimes only costs are traced directly to the job, sometimes only revenue is traced, and sometimes both. For example, automobile repair shops typically have a repair order for each car worked on, with space for allocating materials and labor costs. Customers are permitted to see only a copy showing the retail prices of the materials, parts, and labor billed to their orders. If the repair manager wants cost data, a system may be designed so that the "actual" parts and labor costs of each order are traced to a duplicate copy of the repair order. That is why you often see auto mechanics "punching in" and "punching out" their starting and stopping times on "time tickets" as each new order is worked on.

BUDGETS AND CONTROL OF ENGAGEMENTS

In many service organizations and some manufacturing operations, job orders are used not only for product costing, but also for planning and control purposes. For example, a public accounting firm might have a condensed budget for 20X2 as follows:

Revenue	$10,000,000	100%
Direct labor (for professional hours charged to engagements)	2,500,000	25%
Contribution to overhead and operating income	$ 7,500,000	75%
Overhead (all other costs)	6,500,000	65%
Operating income	$ 1,000,000	10%

In this illustration:

$$\text{budgeted overhead rate} = \frac{\text{budgeted overhead}}{\text{budgeted direct labor}}$$

$$= \frac{\$6,500,000}{\$2,500,000} = 260\%$$

As each engagement is budgeted, the partner in charge of the audit predicts the expected number of necessary direct-professional hours. Direct-professional hours are those worked by partners, managers, and subordinate auditors to complete the engagement. The budgeted direct-labor cost is the pertinent hourly labor costs multiplied by the budgeted hours. Partners' time is charged to the engagement at much higher rates than subordinates' time.

How is overhead applied? Accounting firms usually use either direct-labor cost or direct-labor hours as the cost driver for overhead application. In our example, the firm uses direct-labor cost. Such a practice implies that partners require proportionately more overhead support for each of their hours charged.

The budgeted total cost of an engagement is the direct-labor cost plus applied overhead (260% of direct-labor cost in this illustration) plus any other direct costs.

The engagement partner uses a budget for a specific audit that includes detailed scope and steps. For instance, the budget for auditing cash or receivables would specify the exact work to be done, the number of hours, and the necessary hours of partner time, manager time, and subordinate time. The partner monitors progress by comparing the hours logged to date with the original budget and with the estimated hours remaining on the engagement. Obviously, if a fixed audit fee has been quoted, the profitability of an engagement depends on whether the audit can be accomplished within the budgeted time limits.

ACCURACY OF COSTS OF ENGAGEMENTS

Suppose the accounting firm has costs on an auditing engagement as follows:

Direct-professional labor	$ 50,000
Applied overhead, 260% of $50,000	130,000
Total costs excluding travel costs	$180,000
Travel costs	14,000
Total costs of engagement	$194,000

Two direct costs, professional labor and travel costs, are traced to the jobs. But only direct-professional labor is a cost driver for overhead. (Note that costs reimbursed by the client—such as travel costs—do not add to overhead costs and should not be subject to any markups in the setting of fees.)

Managers of service firms, such as auditing and consulting firms, frequently use either the budgeted or "actual" costs of engagements as guides to pricing and to allocating effort among particular services or customers. Hence, the accuracy of costs of various engagements may affect decisions.

ACTIVITY-BASED COSTING IN SERVICE AND NONPROFIT ENVIRONMENTS

Our accounting firm example described a widely used, relatively simple job-costing system. Only two direct-cost items (direct-professional labor and travel costs) are used, and only a single overhead application rate is used.

In recent years, to obtain more accurate costs, many professional service firms have refined their data processing systems and adopted activity-based costing. Computers help accumulate information that is far more detailed than was feasible a few years ago. As noted in earlier chapters, firms that use activity-based costing generally shift cost classifications from overhead to direct costs. Using our previously assumed numbers for direct labor ($50,000) and travel ($14,000), we recast the costs of our audit engagement as follows:

Direct-professional labor	$ 50,000
Direct-support labor, such as secretarial costs	10,000
Fringe benefits for all direct labor*	24,000
Telephone calls	1,000
Photocopying	2,000
Computer time	7,000
Total direct costs	94,000
Applied overhead†	103,400
Total costs excluding travel costs	197,400
Travel costs	14,000
Total costs of engagement	$211,400

* 40% assumed rate multiplied by ($50,000 + $10,000) = $24,000.
† 110% assumed rate multiplied by total direct costs of $94,000 = $103,400.

In an ABC system, costs such as direct-support labor, telephone calls, photocopying, and computer time are applied by directly measuring their usage on each engagement. The remaining costs to be allocated are assigned to cost pools based on their cause. The cost driver for other overhead is total direct costs.

The more detailed approach of activity-based costing will nearly always produce total costs that differ from the total costs in the general approach shown earlier: $211,400 compared with $194,000. Of course, any positive or negative difference is attributable to having more types of costs traced directly to the engagement.

EFFECTS OF CLASSIFICATIONS ON OVERHEAD RATES

The activity-based-costing approach also has a lower overhead application rate, assumed at 110% of total direct costs instead of the 260% of direct labor used in the first example, for two reasons. First, there are fewer overhead costs because more costs are traced directly. Second, the application base is broader including all direct costs rather than only direct labor.

Even with activity-based costing, some firms may prefer to continue to apply their overhead based on direct-labor costs rather than total direct costs. Why? Because the partners believe that overhead is dominantly affected by the amount of direct-labor costs rather than other direct costs such as telephone calls. But at least the activity-based-costing firm has made an explicit decision that direct-labor costs is the best cost driver.

Whether the overhead cost driver should be total direct costs, direct-professional labor costs or hours, or some other cost driver is a knotty problem for many firms, including most professional service firms. Ideally, activity analysis should uncover the principal cost drivers, and those cost drivers should all be used for overhead application. In practice, only one or two cost drivers are usually used.

SUMMARY PROBLEM FOR YOUR REVIEW

PROBLEM

Review the Enriquez illustration, especially Exhibit 13-2, page 531. Prepare an income statement for 20X2 through the gross profit line. Use the immediate write-off method for overapplied or underapplied overhead.

SOLUTION

Exhibit 13-4 recapitulates the final impact of the Enriquez illustration on the financial statements. Note how the immediate write-off means that the $17,000 is added to the cost of goods sold. As you study Exhibit 13-4, trace the three major elements of cost (direct material, direct labor, and factory overhead) through the accounts.

Exhibit 13-4
Relation of Costs to Financial Statements

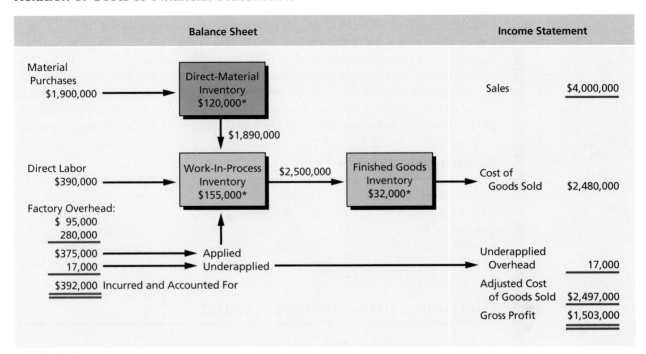

* Ending balance.

Highlights to Remember

Distinguish between job-order costing and process costing.   Product costing is an averaging process. Process costing deals with broad averages and great masses of like units. Job costing deals with narrow averages and unique units or a small batch of like units.

Prepare summary journal entries for the typical transactions of a job-costing system.
The focus of journal entries in a job-order-costing system is on inventory accounts. The WIP Inventory account receives central attention. Direct material used, direct labor, and factory overhead applied are accumulated in WIP. In turn, the cost of completed goods is transferred from WIP to Finished Goods.

Compute budgeted factory-overhead rates and factory overhead applied to production.
Indirect manufacturing costs (factory overhead) are often applied to products using budgeted overhead rates. The rates are computed by dividing total budgeted overhead by a measure of cost-driver activity such as expected machine hours.

Use appropriate cost drivers for overhead application.   There should be a strong cause-and-effect relationship between cost drivers and the overhead costs that are allocated using these drivers.

Identify the meaning and purpose of normalized overhead rates.   Budgeted overhead rates are usually annual averages. The resulting product costs are normal costs, consisting of actual direct material plus actual direct labor plus applied overhead using the budgeted rates. Normal product costs are more useful for decision-making and inventory-costing purposes.

Use an activity-based-costing system in a job-order environment.   Activity-based costing can be used for any type of business that has significant levels of shared resources. In a job-order system, ABC helps managers understand the cost structure of the business on a job-by-job basis. Overhead costs are assigned to activity centers and then to jobs based on appropriate cost drivers. Activity-based management uses ABC information and the increased understanding of the organization's cost structure to control and reduce overhead costs.

Show how job costing is used in service organizations. The job-costing approach is used in nonmanufacturing as well as in manufacturing. Examples include costs of services such as auto repair, consulting, and auditing. For example, the job order is a key device for planning and controlling an audit engagement by a public accounting firm.

Understand how a job-order-costing system tracks the flow of costs to products. The basic records (source documents) used to accumulate and track costs in a job-order-costing system are materials requisitions, labor time tickets, and job-cost records. The job-cost record summarizes information on the direct materials and direct labor used as well as the factory overhead applied. Journal entries that record the basic transactions center on the three inventory accounts, with particular focus on the WIP Inventory account.

Accounting Vocabulary

budgeted factory-overhead rate, p. 533	job order, p. 529	overapplied overhead, p. 538
job costing, p. 528	job-order costing, p. 528	process costing, p. 528
job-cost record, p. 529	labor time tickets, p. 530	prorate, p. 538
job-cost sheet, p. 529	materials requisitions, p. 530	time cards, p. 530
	normal costing system, p. 537	underapplied overhead, p. 538

Fundamental Assignment Material

13-A1 Basic Journal Entries

The following data (in thousands) summarize the factory operations of the Lewis Manufacturing Co. for the year 20X1, its first year in business:

a. Direct materials purchased for cash	$360
b. Direct materials issued and used	330
c. Labor used directly on production	125
d1. Indirect labor	80
d2. Depreciation of plant and equipment	55
d3. Miscellaneous factory overhead (ordinarily would be detailed)	40
e. Overhead applied: 180% of direct labor	?
f. Cost of production completed	625
g. Cost of goods sold	400

Required | 1. Prepare summary journal entries. Omit explanations. For purposes of this problem, combine the items in d as "overhead incurred."

2. Show the T-accounts for all inventories, Cost of Goods Sold, and Factory Department Overhead Control. Compute the ending balances of the inventories. Do not adjust for underapplied or overapplied factory overhead.

13-A2 Accounting for Overhead, Budgeted Rates

McFarland Aeronautics Company uses a budgeted overhead rate in applying overhead to individual job orders on a machine-hour basis for Department A and on a direct-labor-hour basis for Department B. At the beginning of 20X1, the company's management made the following budget predictions:

	Department A	Department B
Direct-labor cost	$1,500,000	$1,200,000
Factory overhead	$1,820,000	$1,000,000
Direct-labor hours	90,000	125,000
Machine hours	350,000	20,000

Cost records of recent months show the following accumulations for Job Order No. 455:

	Department A	Department B
Material placed in production	$12,000	$32,000
Direct-labor cost	$10,800	$10,000
Direct-labor hours	900	1,250
Machine hours	3,500	150

Required

1. What is the budgeted overhead rate that should be applied in Department A? in Department B?
2. What is the total overhead cost of Job Order No. 455?
3. If Job Order No. 455 consists of 120 units of product, what is the unit cost of this job?
4. At the end of 20X1, actual results for the year's operations were as follows:

	Department A	Department B
Actual overhead costs incurred	$1,300,000	$1,200,000
Actual direct-labor hours	80,000	120,000
Actual machine hours	300,000	25,000

Find the underapplied or overapplied overhead for each department and for the factory as a whole.

13-A3 Disposition of Overhead

Shoreline Marine Manufacturing applies factory overhead using machine hours and number of component parts as cost drivers. In 20X1, actual factory overhead incurred was $134,000 and applied factory overhead was $126,000. Before disposition of underapplied or overapplied factory overhead, the cost of goods sold was $525,000, gross profit was $60,000, and ending inventories were

Direct materials	$ 25,000
WIP	75,000
Finished goods	150,000
Total inventories	$250,000

Required

1. Was factory overhead overapplied or underapplied? By how much?
2. Assume that Shoreline writes off overapplied or underapplied factory overhead as an adjustment to cost of goods sold. Prepare the journal entry, and compute adjusted gross profit.
3. Assume that Shoreline prorates overapplied or underapplied factory overhead based on end-of-the-year unadjusted balances. Prepare the journal entry, and compute adjusted gross profit.
4. Assume that actual factory overhead was $124,000 instead of $134,000, and that Shoreline writes off overapplied or underapplied factory overhead as an adjustment to cost of goods sold. Prepare the journal entry, and compute adjusted gross profit.

13-B1 Basic Journal Entries

Consider the following data for London Printing Company (in thousands):

Inventories, December 31, 20X1	
Direct materials	£ 18
Work in process	25
Finished goods	100

Summarized transactions for 20X2 are

a.	Purchases of direct materials	£109
b.	Direct materials used	95
c.	Direct labor	105
d.	Factory overhead incurred	90
e.	Factory overhead applied, 80% of direct labor	?
f.	Cost of goods completed and transferred to finished goods	280
g.	Cost of goods sold	350
h.	Sales on account	600

Required

1. Prepare summary journal entries for 20X2 transactions. Omit explanations.
2. Show the T-accounts for all inventories, Cost of Goods Sold, and Factory Department Overhead Control. Compute the ending balances of the inventories. Do not adjust for underapplied or overapplied factory overhead.

13-B2 Disposition of Overhead
MacLachlan Mfg. Co. had overapplied overhead of $20,000 in 20X1. Before adjusting for overapplied or underapplied overhead, the ending inventories for Direct Materials, WIP, and Finished Goods were $75,000, $100,000, and $150,000, respectively. Unadjusted cost of goods sold was $250,000.

Required

1. Assume that the $20,000 was written off solely as an adjustment to cost of goods sold. Prepare the journal entry.
2. Management has decided to prorate the $20,000 to the appropriate accounts (using the unadjusted ending balances) instead of writing it off solely as an adjustment of cost of goods sold. Prepare the journal entry. Would gross profit be higher or lower than in requirement 1? By how much?

13-B3 Application of Overhead Using Budgeted Rates
The Bellevue Clinic computes a cost of treating each patient. It allocates costs to departments and then applies departmental overhead costs to individual patients using a different budgeted overhead rate in each department. Consider the following predicted 20X2 data for two of Bellevue's departments:

	Pharmacy	**Medical Records**
Department overhead cost	$225,000	$300,000
Number of prescriptions filled	90,000	
Number of patient visits		60,000

The cost driver for overhead in Pharmacy is number of prescriptions filled; in Medical Records it is number of patient visits.

In June 20X1, David Li paid two visits to the clinic and had four prescriptions filled at the pharmacy.

Required

1. Compute departmental overhead rates for the two departments.
2. Compute the overhead costs applied to the patient David Li in June 20X1.
3. At the end of 20X1, actual overhead costs were

Pharmacy	$217,000
Medical records	$325,000

The pharmacy filled 85,000 prescriptions, and the clinic had 63,000 patient visits during 20X1. Compute the overapplied or underapplied overhead in each department.

Additional Assignment Material

QUESTIONS

13-1. "There are different product costs for different purposes." Name at least two purposes.

13-2. Distinguish between job costing and process costing.

13-3. How does hybrid costing relate to job costing and process costing?

13-4. Describe the supporting details for work in process in a job-cost system.

13-5. What types of source documents provide information for job-cost record?

13-6. Suppose a company uses machine hours as a cost driver for factory overhead. How does the company compute a budgeted overhead application rate? How does it compute the amounts of factory overhead applied to a particular job?

13-7. Explain the role of the factory department overhead control account in a job-cost system.

13-8. "Each department must choose one cost driver to be used for cost application." Do you agree? Explain.

13-9. "Sometimes direct-labor cost is the best cost driver for overhead allocation even if wage rates vary within a department." Do you agree? Explain.

13-10. Identify four cost drivers that a manufacturing company might use to apply factory overhead costs to jobs.

13-11. Is the comparison of actual overhead costs to budgeted overhead costs part of the product-costing process or part of the control process? Explain.

13-12. What are some reasons for differences between the amounts of incurred and applied overhead?

13-13. "Under actual overhead application, unit costs soar as volume increases and vice versa." Do you agree? Explain.

13-14. Define normal costing.

13-15. What is the best theoretical method of allocating underapplied or overapplied overhead, assuming that the objective is to obtain as accurate a cost application as possible?

13-16. State three examples of service industries that use the job-costing approach.

13-17. "As data processing becomes more economical, more costs than just direct material and direct labor will be classified as direct costs wherever feasible." Give three examples of such costs.

COGNITIVE EXERCISES

13-18 Purposes of Accumulating Job Costs
"Job costs are accumulated for purposes of inventory valuation and income determination." State two other purposes.

13-19 Job-Order Compared to Process Costing
"The basic distinction between job-order costing and process costing is the breadth of the denominator." Explain.

13-20 Relationship Between Cost Drivers and Factory Overhead
"There should be a strong relationship between the factory overhead incurred and the cost driver chosen for its application." Why?

13-21 Cost Allocation in Service Firms
"Service firms trace only direct-labor costs to jobs. All other costs are applied as a percentage of direct-labor cost." Do you agree? Explain.

EXERCISES

13-22 Direct Materials
For each of the following independent cases, fill in the blanks (in millions of dollars):

	1	2	3	4
Direct-materials inventory, Dec. 31, 20X1	8	8	5	—
Purchased	5	9	—	8
Used	7	—	7	3
Direct-materials inventory, Dec. 31, 20X2	—	6	9	7

13-23 Direct Materials

Genesis Athletic Shoes had an ending inventory of direct materials of $8 million. During the year the company had acquired $15 million of additional direct materials and had used $12 million. Compute the beginning inventory.

13-24 Use of WIP Inventory Account

September production resulted in the following activity in a key account of Colebury Casting Company (in thousands):

WIP Inventory	
September 1 balance	12
Direct material usedz	50
Direct labor charged to jobs	25
Factory overhead applied to jobs	55

Job Orders 13N and 37Q, with total costs of $70,000 and $54,000, respectively, were completed in September.

Required

1. Journalize the completed production for Setember.
2. Compute the balance in WIP Inventory, September 30, after recording the completed production.
3. Journalize the credit sale of Job 13N for $98,000.

13-25 Job-Cost Record

Western State University uses job-cost records for various research projects. A major reason for such records is to justify requests for reimbursement of costs on projects sponsored by the federal government.

Consider the following summarized data regarding a cancer research project in the Medical School:

- Jan. 5   Direct materials, various medical supplies, $925
- Jan. 7   Direct materials, various chemicals, $780
- Jan. 5–12   Direct labor, research associates, 120 hours
- Jan. 7–12   Direct labor, research assistants, 180 hours

Research associates receive $32 per hour; assistants, $19. The overhead rate is 70% of direct-labor cost.

Required

Sketch a job-cost record. Post all the data to the project-cost record. Compute the total cost of the project through January 12.

13-26 Analysis of Job-Cost Data

Job-cost records for Naomi's Remodeling, Inc., contained the following data:

Job No.	Dates			Total Cost of Job at May 31
	Started	*Finished*	*Sold*	
1	April 19	May 14	May 15	$2,800
2	April 26	May 22	May 25	8,800
3	May 2	June 6	June 8	7,200
4	May 9	May 29	June 5	8,100
5	May 14	June 14	June 16	3,900

Compute Naomi's (1) WIP Inventory at May 31, (2) Finished-Goods Inventory at May 31, and (3) Cost of Goods Sold for May.

13-27 Analysis of Job-Cost Data

The Cabrillo Construction Company constructs houses on speculation. That is, the houses are begun before any buyer is known. Even if the buyer agrees to purchase a house under construction, no sales are recorded until the house is completed and accepted for delivery. The job-cost records contained the following (in thousands):

		Dates		Total Cost of Job at Sept. 30	Total Construction Cost Added in Oct.
Job No.	Started	Finished	Sold		
43	4/26	9/7	9/8	$180	
51	5/17	9/14	9/17	170	
52	5/20	9/30	10/4	150	
53	5/28	10/14	10/18	200	$50
61	6/3	10/20	11/24	115	20
62	6/9	10/21	10/27	180	25
71	7/7	11/6	11/22	118	36
81	8/7	11/24	12/24	106	48

Required

1. Compute Cabrillo's cost of (a) construction-in-process inventory at September 30 and October 31, (b) finished-houses inventory at September 30 and October 31, and (c) cost of houses sold for September and October.
2. Prepare summary journal entries for the transfer of completed houses from construction in process to finished houses for September and October.
3. Record the cash sale (price = $345,000) and cost of house sold for Job 53.

13-28 Discovery of Unknowns

DeMond Chemicals has the following balances (in millions) on December 31, 20X1:

Factory overhead applied	$200
Cost of goods sold	500
Factory overhead incurred	215
Direct-materials inventory	30
Finished-goods inventory	160
WIP inventory	120

The cost of goods completed was $420. The cost of direct materials requisitioned for production during 20X1 was $210. The cost of direct materials purchased was $225. Factory overhead was applied to production at a rate of 160% of direct-labor cost.

Required

Compute the beginning inventory balances of direct materials, WIP, and finished goods. Make these computations before considering any possible adjustments for overapplied or underapplied overhead.

13-29 Discovery of Unknowns

The Chickadee Manufacturing Company has the following balances (in millions) as of December 31, 20X1:

WIP inventory	$ 14
Finished-goods inventory	175
Direct-materials inventory	65
Factory overhead incurred	180
Factory overhead applied at 150% of direct-labor cost	150
Cost of goods sold	350

The cost of direct materials purchased during 20X1 was $275. The cost of direct materials requisitioned for production during 20X1 was $235. The cost of goods completed was $493, all in millions.

Required

Before considering any year-end adjustments for overapplied or underapplied overhead, compute the beginning inventory balances of direct materials, WIP, and finished goods.

13-30 Journal Entries for Overhead
Consider the following summarized data regarding 20X1:

	Budget	Actual
Indirect labor	$ 310,000	$ 325,000
Supplies	35,000	30,000
Repairs	80,000	75,000
Utilities	110,000	103,000
Factory rent	125,000	125,000
Supervision	60,000	70,000
Depreciation, equipment	220,000	220,000
Insurance, property taxes, etc.	40,000	42,000
a. Total factory overhead	$ 980,000	$ 990,000
b. Direct materials used	$1,650,000	$1,570,000
c. Direct labor	$1,225,000	$1,200,000

Omit explanations for journal entries.

Required

1. Prepare a summary journal entry for the actual overhead incurred for 20X1.
2. Prepare summary journal entries for direct materials used and direct labor.
3. Factory overhead was applied by using a budgeted rate based on budgeted direct-labor costs. Compute the rate. Prepare a summary journal entry for the application of overhead to products.
4. Post the journal entries to the T-accounts for WIP and Factory Department Overhead Control.
5. Suppose overapplied or underapplied factory overhead is written off as an adjustment to cost of goods sold. Prepare the journal entry. Post the overhead to the overhead T-account.

13-31 Relationships among Overhead Items
Fill in the unknowns:

	Case A	Case B	Case C
Budgeted factory overhead	$3,600,000	$?	$1,500,000
Budgeted cost drivers			
Direct-labor cost	$2,000,000		
Direct-labor hours		450,000	
Machine hours			250,000
Overhead application rate	?	$5	?

13-32 Relationship among Overhead Items
Fill in the unknowns:

	Case 1	Case 2
a. Budgeted factory overhead	$600,000	$420,000
b. Cost driver, budgeted direct-labor cost	400,000	?
c. Budgeted factory-overhead rate	?	120%
d. Direct-labor cost incurred	570,000	?
e. Factory overhead incurred	830,000	425,000
f. Factory overhead applied	?	?
g. Underapplied (overapplied) factory overhead	?	35,000

13-33 Underapplied and Overapplied Overhead

Starr Welding Company applies factory overhead at a rate of $8.50 per direct-labor hour. Selected data for 20X1 operations are (in thousands):

	Case 1	Case 2
Direct-labor hours	30	36
Direct-labor cost	$220	$245
Indirect-labor cost	32	40
Sales commissions	20	15
Depreciation, manufacturing equipment	22	32
Direct-material cost	230	250
Factory fuel costs	35	47
Depreciation, finished-goods warehouse	5	17
Cost of goods sold	420	510
All other factory costs	138	204

Required

Compute for both cases

1. Factory overhead applied.
2. Total factory overhead incurred.
3. Amount of underapplied or overapplied factory overhead.

13-34 Disposition of Overhead

Assume the following at the end of 20X1 (in thousands):

Cost of goods sold	$250
Direct-materials inventory	80
WIP	100
Finished goods	150
Factory department overhead control (credit balance)	50

Required

1. Assume that the underapplied or overapplied overhead is regarded as an adjustment to cost of goods sold. Prepare the journal entry.
2. Assume that the underapplied or overapplied overhead is prorated among the appropriate accounts in proportion to their ending unadjusted balances. Show computations and prepare the journal entry.

3. Which adjustment, the one in requirement 1 or 2, would result in the higher gross profit? Explain, indicating the amount of the difference.

13-35 Disposition of Overhead

A Paris manufacturer uses a job-order system. At the end of 20X1, the following balances existed (in millions of euros):

Cost of goods sold	€150
Finished goods	120
WIP	30
Factory overhead (actual)	70
Factory overhead (applied)	50

Required

1. Prepare journal entries for two different ways to dispose of the underapplied overhead.
2. Gross profit, before considering the effects in requirement 1, was €43 million. What is the adjusted gross profit under the two methods demonstrated?

13-36 Disposition of Year-End Underapplied Overhead

Gloria Cosmetics uses a normal cost system and has the following balances at the end of its first year's operations.

WIP inventory	$200,000
Finished-goods inventory	200,000
Cost of goods sold	400,000
Actual factory overhead	409,000
Factory overhead applied	453,000

Required

Prepare journal entries for two different ways to dispose of the year-end overhead balances. By how much would gross profit differ?

PROBLEMS

13-37 Job Costing at Dell Computer

Dell Computer Corporation's manufacturing process at its Austin, Texas, facility consists of assembly, functional testing, and quality control of the company's computer systems. The company's build-to-order manufacturing process is designed to allow the company to quickly produce customized computer systems. For example, the company contracts with various suppliers to manufacture unconfigured base Latitude notebook computers and then Dell customizes these systems for shipment to customers. Quality control is maintained through the testing of components, parts, and subassemblies at various stages in the manufacturing process.

Required

Describe how Dell might set up a job-costing system to determine the costs of its computers. What is a "job" to Dell? How might the costs of components, assembly, testing, and quality control be allocated to each "job"?

13-38 Relationships of Manufacturing Costs

Selected data concerning the past fiscal year's operations of the Wallis Manufacturing Company are (in thousands)

	Inventories	
	Beginning	*Ending*
Raw materials	$ 70	$ 90
WIP	75	35
Finished goods	100	120
Other data:		
Raw materials used		$ 468
Total manufacturing costs charged to production during the year (includes raw materials, direct labor, and factory overhead applied at a rate of 80% of direct-labor cost)		864
Cost of goods available for sale		1,026
Selling and general expenses		50

Required

Answer for each of the following items:

1. Compute the cost of raw materials purchased during the year.
2. Compute the direct-labor costs charged to production during the year.
3. Compute the cost of goods manufactured during the year.
4. Compute the cost of goods sold during the year.

13-39 Relationship of Subsidiary and General Ledgers, Journal Entries

The following summarized data are available on three job-cost records of Red Lake Manufacturing Company, a producer of packaging equipment.

	Job 412		Job 413		Job 414
	April	*May*	*April*	*May*	*May*
Direct materials	$9,000	$2,500	$12,000	—	$13,000
Direct labor	4,000	1,500	5,000	2,500	2,000
Factory overhead applied	8,000	?	10,000	?	?

The company's fiscal year ends on May 31. Factory overhead is applied as a percentage of direct-labor costs. The balances in selected accounts on April 30 were direct-materials inventory, $19,000; finished-goods inventory, $18,000.

Job 412 was completed during May and transferred to finished goods. Job 413 was still in process at the end of May, as was Job 414, which had begun on May 24. These were the only jobs worked on during April and May.

Job 412 was sold, along with other finished goods, by May 30. The total cost of goods sold during May was $33,000. The balance in Cost of Goods Sold on April 30 was $450,000.

Required

1. Prepare a schedule showing the balance of the WIP Inventory, April 30. This schedule should show the total costs of each job record. Taken together, the job-cost records are the subsidiary ledger supporting the general ledger balance of work in process.
2. What is the overhead application rate?
3. Prepare summary general journal entries for all costs added to WIP during May. Also prepare entries for all costs transferred from WIP to Finished Goods and from Finished Goods to Cost of Goods Sold. Post to the appropriate T-accounts.
4. Prepare a schedule showing the balance of the WIP Inventory, May 31.

13-40 Straightforward Job Costing

The Metalcase Office Furniture Company has two departments. Data for 20X1 include the following:

Direct materials (30 types)	$65,000
WIP (in assembly)	50,000
Finished goods	40,000

Manufacturing overhead budget for 20X1

	Machining	Assembly
Indirect labor	$250,000	$ 410,000
Supplies	45,000	40,000
Utilities	110,000	75,000
Repairs	140,000	110,000
Supervision	130,000	215,000
Factory rent	95,000	75,000
Depreciation on equipment	160,000	105,000
Insurance, property taxes, etc.	60,000	70,000
Total	$990,000	$1,100,000

Budgeted machine hours were 90,000; budgeted direct-labor cost in Assembly was $2,200,000. Manufacturing overhead was applied using budgeted rates on the basis of machine hours in Machining and on the basis of direct-labor cost in Assembly.

Following is a summary of actual events for the year:

	Machining	Assembly	Total
a. Direct materials purchased			$ 1,900,000
b. Direct materials requisitioned	$1,100,000	$ 750,000	1,850,000
c. Direct-labor costs incurred	900,000	2,800,000	3,700,000
d1. Factory overhead incurred	1,100,000	1,100,000	2,200,000
d2. Factory overhead applied	880,000	?	?
e. Cost of goods completed	—	—	7,820,000
f1. Sales	—	—	13,000,000
f2. Cost of goods sold	—	—	7,800,000

The ending work in process (all in Assembly) was $60,000.

Required

1. Compute the budgeted overhead rates.
2. Compute the amount of the machine hours actually worked.
3. Compute the amount of factory overhead applied in the Assembly Department.
4. Prepare general journal entries for transactions a through f. Work solely with the total amounts, not the details for Machining and Assembly. Explanations are not required. Show data in thousands of dollars. Present T-accounts, including ending inventory balances, for direct materials, WIP, and finished goods.
5. Prepare a partial income statement similar to the one illustrated in Exhibit 13-4, page 545. Overapplied or underapplied overhead is written off as an adjustment of current cost of goods sold.

13-41 Nonprofit Job Costing

Job-order costing is usually identified with manufacturing companies. However, service industries and nonprofit organizations also use the method. Suppose a social service agency has a cost accounting system that tracks cost by department (e.g., family counseling, general welfare, and foster children) and by case. In this way, Hillary Pratt, the manager of the agency, is better able to determine how its limited resources (mostly professional social workers) should be allocated.

Furthermore, the manager's interactions with superiors and various politicians are more fruitful when she can cite the costs of various types of cases.

The condensed line-item budget for the general welfare department of the agency for 20X1 showed:

Professional salaries		
Level 12	5 @ $35,000 = $175,000	
Level 10	21 @ $26,000 = 546,000	
Level 8	34 @ $18,000 = 612,000	$1,333,000
Other costs		479,880
Total costs		$1,812,880

For costing various cases, the manager favored using a single overhead application rate based on the ratio of total overhead to direct labor. The latter was defined as those professional salaries assigned to specific cases.

The professional workers filled out a weekly "case time" report, which approximated the hours spent for each case.

The instructions on the report were as follows: "Indicate how much time (in hours) you spent on each case. Unassigned time should be listed separately." About 20% of available time was unassigned to specific cases. It was used for professional development (e.g., continuing education programs). "Unassigned time" became a part of "overhead," as distinguished from the direct labor.

Required

1. Compute the "overhead rate" as a percentage of direct labor (i.e., the assignable professional salaries).

2. Suppose that last week a welfare case, Client No. 537, required two hours of Level 12 time, four hours of Level 10 time, and nine hours of Level 8 time. How much job cost should be allocated to Client No. 537 for the week? Assume that all professional employees work a 1,800-hour year.

13-42 Job Costing in a Consulting Firm

Lubbock Engineering Consultants is a firm of professional civil engineers. It mostly does surveying jobs for the heavy construction industry throughout Texas. The firm obtains its jobs by giving fixed-price quotations, so profitability depends on the ability to predict the time required for the various subtasks on the job. (This situation is similar to that in the auditing profession, where times are budgeted for such audit steps as reconciling cash and confirming accounts receivable.)

A client may be served by various professional staff, who hold positions in the hierarchy from partners to managers to senior engineers to assistants. In addition, there are secretaries and other employees.

Lubbock Engineering has the following budget for 20X2:

Compensation of professional staff	$3,600,000
Other costs	1,449,000
Total budgeted costs	$5,049,000

Each professional staff member must submit a weekly time report, which is used for charging hours to a client job-order record. The time report has seven columns, one for each day of the week. Its rows are as follows:

- Chargeable hours
    Client 156
    Client 183
    Etc.

- Nonchargeable hours
    Attending seminar on new equipment
    Unassigned time
    Etc.

In turn, these time reports are used for charging hours and costs to the client job-order records. The managing partner regards these job records as absolutely essential for measuring the profitability of various jobs and for providing an "experience base for improving predictions on future jobs."

Required

1. This firm applies overhead to jobs at a budgeted percentage of the professional compensation charged directly to the job ("direct labor"). For all categories of professional personnel, chargeable hours average 85% of available hours. Nonchargeable hours are regarded as additional overhead. What is the overhead rate as a percentage of "direct labor," the chargeable professional compensation cost?

2. A senior engineer works 48 weeks per year, 40 hours per week. His compensation is $60,000. He has worked on two jobs during the past week, devoting 10 hours to Job 156 and 30 hours to Job 183. How much cost should be charged to Job 156 because of his work there?

13-43 Choice of Cost Drivers in Accounting Firm

Brenda McCoy, the managing partner of McCoy, Brennan, and Cable, a public accounting firm, is considering the desirability of tracing more costs to jobs than just direct labor. In this way, the firm will be able to justify billings to clients.

Last year's costs were

Direct-professional labor	$ 5,000,000
Overhead	10,000,000
Total costs	$15,000,000

The following costs were included in overhead:

Computer time	$ 750,000
Secretarial cost	700,000
Photocopying	250,000
Fringe benefits to direct labor	800,000
Phone call time with clients (estimated but not tabulated)	500,000
Total	$3,000,000

The firm's data processing techniques now make it feasible to document and trace these costs to individual jobs.

As an experiment, in December Brenda McCoy arranged to trace these costs to six audit engagements. Two job records showed the following:

	Engagement	
	Eagledale Company	*First Valley Bank*
Direct-professional labor	$15,000	$15,000
Fringe benefits to direct labor	3,000	3,000
Phone call time with clients	1,500	500
Computer time	3,000	700
Secretarial costs	2,000	1,500
Photocopying	500	300
Total direct costs	$25,000	$21,000

1. Compute the overhead application rate based on last year's costs.

2. Suppose last year's costs were reclassified so that $3 million would be regarded as direct costs instead of overhead. Compute the overhead application rate as a percentage of direct labor and as a percentage of total direct costs.

3. Using the three rates computed in requirements 1 and 2, compute the total costs of engagements for Eagledale Company and First Valley Bank.

4. Suppose that client billing was based on a 30% markup of total job costs. Compute the billings that would be forthcoming in requirement 3.

5. Which method of job costing and overhead application do you favor? Explain.

13-44 Allocated Costs and Public Services

The Napa County (California) Grand Jury charged the city of St. Helena with overbilling customers for water and sewer services. The city allocated "administrative overhead" to the water and sewer department's budget. These costs were then added to the "jobs," that is, to the accounts of the customers of the water and sewer department. The Grand Jury called the $76,581.20 allocated to the department in 1996–1997 "merely a ruse" to generate funds to cover city expenses that are unrelated to water and sewer services, resulting in "bloated water bills" for local customers.

The city finance director explained that the overhead allocation was the way in which the city bills the water and sewer department for time that other departments spend on water and sewer issues. Mayor John Brown concluded that "it was very clear to me that they [the Grand Jury] didn't know what they were talking about."

1. Was the overhead charge to the water and sewer department a legitimate cost to be covered by water and sewer bills? Explain your reasoning to the citizens of St. Helena.

2. Assume that at least part of the overhead charge is a legitimate cost of the water and sewer department. Suggest possible changes in the accounting system that would provide a more accurate measure of the cost of services provided to the water and sewer department by other departments.

13-45 Reconstruction of Transactions

(This problem is more challenging than the others in this chapter.)

You are asked to bring the following incomplete accounts of a printing plant acquired in a merger up to date through January 31, 20X2. Also consider the data that appear after the T-accounts.

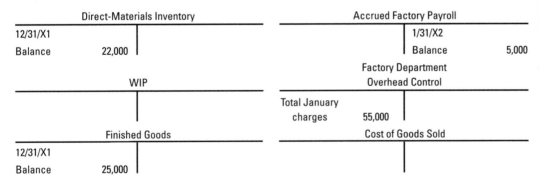

Additional information:

1. The overhead is applied using a budgeted rate that is set every December by forecasting the following year's overhead and relating it to forecasted direct-labor costs. The budget for 20X2 called for $640,000 of direct labor and $800,000 of factory overhead.

2. The only job unfinished on January 31, 20X2, was No. 419, on which total labor charges were $3,000 (200 direct-labor hours), and total direct-materials charges were $21,000.

3. Total materials placed into production during January totaled $140,000.

4. Cost of goods completed during January was $260,000.

5. January 31 balances of direct materials totaled $25,000.
6. Finished-goods inventory as of January 31 was $35,000.
7. All factory workers earn the same rate of pay. Direct-labor hours for January totaled 3,000. Indirect labor and supervision totaled $12,000.
8. The gross factory payroll paid on January paydays totaled $55,000. Ignore withholdings.
9. All "actual" factory overhead incurred during January has already been posted.

Required

Compute the following:

a. Direct materials purchased during January
b. Cost of goods sold during January
c. Direct-labor costs incurred during January
d. Overhead applied during January
e. Balance, Accrued Factory Payroll, December 31, 20X1
f. Balance, WIP, December 31, 20X1
g. Balance, WIP, January 31, 20X2
h. Overapplied or underapplied overhead for January

13-46 Overhead Accounting for Control and for Product Costing

The pickle department of a major food manufacturer has an overhead rate of $5 per direct-labor hour, based on expected variable overhead of $150,000 per year, expected fixed overhead of $350,000 per year, and expected direct-labor hours of 100,000 per year.

Data for the year's operations follow:

	Direct-Labor Hours Used	Overhead Costs Incurred*
First six months	55,000	$262,000
Last six months	41,000	236,500

* Fixed costs incurred were exactly equal to budgeted amounts throughout the year.

Required

1. What is the underapplied or overapplied overhead for each six-month period? Label your answer as underapplied or overapplied.
2. Explain briefly (not more than 50 words for each part) the probable causes for the underapplied or overapplied overhead. Focus on variable and fixed costs separately. Give the exact figures attributable to the causes you cite.

CASES

13-47 Multiple Overhead Rates and Activity-Based Costing

A division of Hewlett-Packard assembles and tests printed circuit (PC) boards. The division has many different products. Some are high volume; others are low volume. For years, manufacturing overhead was applied to products using a single overhead rate based on direct-labor dollars. However, direct labor has shrunk to 6% of total manufacturing costs.

Managers decided to refine the division's product-costing system. Abolishing the direct-labor category, they included all manufacturing labor as a part of factory overhead. They also identified several activities and the appropriate cost driver for each. The cost driver for the first activity, the start station, was the number of raw PC boards. The application rate was computed as follows:

$$\text{application rate for start station activity} = \frac{\text{budgeted total factory overhead at the activity}}{\text{budgeted raw PC boards for the year}}$$

$$= \frac{\$150,000}{125,000} = \$1.20$$

Each time a raw PC board passes through the start station activity, $1.20 is added to the cost of the board. The product cost is the sum of costs directly traced to the board plus the indirect costs (factory overhead) accumulated at each of the manufacturing activities undergone.

Using assumed numbers, consider the following data regarding PC Board 37:

Direct materials	$55.00
Factory overhead applied	?
Total manufacturing product cost	?

The activities involved in the production of PC Board 37 and the related cost drivers were

Activity	Cost Driver	Factory-Overhead Costs Applied for Each Activity
1. Start station	No. of raw PC boards	$1 \times \$1.20 = \$1.20$
2. Axial insertion	No. of axial insertions	$39 \times .07 = ?$
3. Dip insertion	No. of dip insertions	$? \times .20 = 5.60$
4. Manual insertion	No. of manual insertions	$15 \times ? = 6.00$
5. Wave solder	No. of boards soldered	$1 \times 3.20 = 3.20$
6. Backload	No. of backload insertions	$8 \times .60 = 4.80$
7. Test	Standard time board is in test activity	$.15 \times 80.00 = ?$
8. Defect analysis	Standard time for defect analysis and repair	$.05 \times ? = 4.50$
Total		$\$ \ ?$

Required

1. Fill in the blanks.
2. How is direct labor identified with products under this product-costing system?
3. Why would managers favor this multiple-overhead rate, activity-based-costing system instead of the older system?

13-48 One or Two Cost Drivers
The Matterhorn Instruments Co. in Geneva, Switzerland, has the following 20X1 budget for its two departments in Swiss francs (SF):

	Machining	Finishing	Total
Direct labor	SF 300,000	SF 800,000	SF 1,100,000
Factory overhead	SF 960,000	SF 800,000	SF 1,760,000
Machine hours	60,000	20,000	80,000

In the past, the company has used a single plantwide overhead application rate based on direct-labor cost. However, as its product line has expanded and as competition has intensified, Hans Volkert, the company president, has questioned the accuracy of the profits or losses shown on various products.

Matterhorn makes custom tools on special orders from customers. To be competitive and still make a reasonable profit, it is essential that the firm measure the cost of each customer order. Mr. Volkert has focused on overhead allocation as a potential problem. He knows that changes in costs are more heavily affected by machine hours in the machining department and by direct-labor costs in the finishing department. As company controller, you have gathered the following data regarding two typical customer orders:

	Order Number	
	K102	*K156*
Machining		
Direct materials	SF 4,000	SF 4,000
Direct labor	SF 3,000	SF 1,500
Machine hours	1,200	100
Finishing		
Direct labor	SF 1,500	SF 3,000
Machine hours	120	120

Required

1. Compute six factory overhead application rates, three based on direct-labor cost and three based on machine hours for machining, finishing, and for the plant as a whole.
2. Use the application rates to compute the total costs of orders K102 and K156 as follows: (a) plantwide rate based on direct-labor cost and (b) machining based on machine hours and finishing based on direct-labor cost.
3. Evaluate your answers in requirement 2. Which set of job costs do you prefer? Why?

COLLABORATIVE LEARNING EXERCISE

13-49 Accounting for Overhead

Form groups of four to six persons. Each group should identify a cost accountant at a local company to interview. The interviewee could be the top financial officer of a small company, but a division controller or cost analyst might be more appropriate for a large company. The essential factor is that the person chosen understands how overhead costs are allocated to products or services in the company.

Set up an interview with the cost accountant, and explore the following issues. Be prepared with follow-up questions if your question receives a superficial answer. Your goal should be to get as much operational detail as possible about the procedures used for allocating overhead costs at the company. If the company is large, you may want to focus on one department, one product line, or some other subdivision of the company.

The issues to explore are

1. What types of costs are included in overhead? How large is overhead compared with direct material and labor costs?
2. What types of overhead cost pools exist? Are there different pools by department? by activity? by cost driver? by fixed or variable cost? Be prepared to explain what you mean by these terms, because terminology varies widely.
3. How is overhead applied to final products or services? What cost drivers are used?

After the interview, draw a diagram of the cost allocation system in as much detail as possible. Be prepared to share this with the entire class, using it to explain the overhead cost allocation system at the company your group studied.

INTERNET EXERCISE

www.prenhall.com/horngren

13-50 Costing at Ethan Allen

Manufacturing companies design costing systems for external reporting and internal decision-making purposes. Job costing and process costing are extremes along a continuum of potential costing systems. Each company designs its own costing system to fit its underlying production activities. Some companies use hybrid costing systems, which are blends of ideas from both job costing and process costing. Furniture manufacturing can involve high levels of activity and/or high dollars of cost. For this exercise we'll look at Ethan Allen, Inc., a furniture manufacturer.

1. Log on to the Ethan Allen Web site at http://www.ethanallen.com. Click on the "products" icon. Then click on "sofas & more." What does it tell you about the sofas? Click on the "sofa" sub-icon on the panel bar. How many different sofas does Ethan Allen display in this area?
2. Find the Jacobson Sofa-88″. What are the measurements of this sofa? What are the fabric choices for this sofa? Where can this sofa be purchased?

3. Click on the information about pricing the Jacobson Sofa-88″. What is the listed price for the sofa? Is there currently a sale price available? What is the pricing policy of the firm? Why do you think that the firm has this policy?

4. What type of costing system do you think would work best for Ethan Allen in manufacturing Jacobson sofas and why?

5. Do you think that an activity-based costing system could be used for the Jacobson sofas? Why or why not?

6. Go to the section on "quality and care" and then to the sub-section on "sofas and more." Look at "what to look for." Assume that Ethan Allen has an activity-based costing system for its upholstery manufacturing business. Identify four activities and one resource that would be consumed by each activity.

PROCESS-COSTING SYSTEMS

In this mine, owned and operated by Nally and Gibson Georgetown, Inc., limestone rock is mined from a quarry, shipped to this processing facility, processed, and stored. The company uses a process-costing system to determine the costs of these activities.

www.prenhall.com/horngren

Learning Objectives

When you have finished studying this chapter, you should be able to

1. Explain the basic ideas underlying process costing and how they differ from job costing.

2. Compute output in terms of equivalent units.

3. Compute costs and prepare journal entries for the principal transactions in a process-costing system.

4. Demonstrate how the presence of beginning inventories affects the computation of unit costs under the weighted-average method.

5. Demonstrate how the presence of beginning inventories affects the computation of unit costs under the first-in, first-out method.

6. Use backflush costing with a JIT production system.

7. **Understand how a process-costing system tracks costs to products.**

Don't look now, but you are most likely surrounded by the product produced by Nally and Gibson Georgetown, Inc. In fact, if you are in a typical residence or dormitory room, there are probably about 400 tons of this product close by—in the street and driveway, the sidewalk, the walls, and maybe even your toothpaste. What is it? Limestone. Nally and Gibson is a leading producer of limestone products used for industrial and commercial purposes. Limestone is used in highways, high school track beds, concrete sidewalks, buildings, soil enhancement products, residential homes, and about a million other places (yes, even in some toothpastes).

The making of limestone products is an excellent example of a process production system. A single output—limestone rock—is subjected to several processes that result in finished limestone products. The basic production processes that convert limestone rock into usable limestone are easy to understand and are reasonably simple. Basically, the limestone rock is mined from Nally and Gibson's quarry and mine in Georgetown, Kentucky, and shipped to the processing facility. There it passes through several stages of crushing and grinding, depending on how fine the finished product needs to be. The ease and homogeneous nature of these processes might make you think that the cost accounting system used to track product costs should also be fairly simple and perhaps even unimportant to the success of the company. However, accurate and timely cost information is critical to both product costing and decision making at Nally and Gibson.

For example, the accurate allocation of the costs of mining and transporting limestone and then crushing the limestone to form the various products is essential to the success of the company. The company's cost accounting system accumulates the costs of these processes and then calculates an average cost per ton of product. According to company president Frank Hamilton Jr., "If Nally and Gibson did not keep a handle on costs, we would not be here."

How does a company like Nally and Gibson assign costs to its products? After all, it is rather difficult to assign costs to individual pieces of crushed limestone. Companies that produce large quantities of a generic or homogeneous product, such as staples or sliced potato strips for french frying, in a continual process do not use the job-costing techniques we have already seen. Why? First, because there are no discreet jobs. The company does not wait for a specific customer order before producing the product. The company makes a forecast of the demand for the product and produces to meet this expected demand. Second, it is amazingly difficult (and costly) to trace cost to a specific french fry or even a single truckload of limestone. And there would be no benefit in doing so in terms of increased accuracy. So the cost-benefit criterion clearly dictates that the company determine unit costs using much larger quantities—say, a whole month's production.

Process costing assigns costs by measuring overall production costs and averaging them based on total production in units over a period of time—usually a month. The resulting average unit costs are then used to determine inventory cost and the cost of goods sold. This chapter will explain process costing.

PROCESS COSTING BASICS

As we noted in Chapter 13, all product costing uses averaging to determine costs per unit of production. Sometimes those averages apply to a relatively small number of units such as a particular printing job produced in a job-order production system. Other times the averages might have to be extremely broad, based on generic products from a continual-process production system, such as limestone road fill. Process-costing systems apply costs to like products that are usually mass produced in continuous fashion through a series of production processes. These processes usually occur in separate departments, although a single department sometimes contains more than one process.

PROCESS COSTING COMPARED WITH JOB COSTING

Objective 1
Explain the basic ideas underlying process costing and how they differ from job costing.

It is probably easiest to understand process costing if you compare it with something you already know: job costing. Job costing and process costing are used for different types of products. Firms in industries such as printing, construction, and furniture manufacturing, in which each unit or batch (job) of product is unique and easily identifiable, use job-order costing. Process costing is used when there is mass production through a sequence of several processes, such as mixing and cooking. Examples include chemicals, flour, glass, toothpaste, and limestone.

Exhibit 14-1 shows the major differences between job-order costing and process costing. Process costing requires several work-in-process accounts, one for each process (or department). As goods move from process to process, their costs are transferred accordingly.

Consider Nally and Gibson's process-costing system. The company's production system has four core processes as shown in Exhibit 14-2. Limestone rock is first obtained from surface quarries or from mines. The rock is then transported to the plant by rail or truck. At the plant, the rock is crushed and screened to various sizes demanded by customers. The crushed limestone is then stocked in large piles of inventory for shipment. Each process requires resources. The direct-materials resource is the limestone rock that is quarried or mined. Direct-labor and overhead resources are used in all four processes.

The process-costing approach does not distinguish among individual units of product. Instead, it accumulates costs for a period and divides them by quantities produced during

Exhibit 14-1

Comparison of Job-Order and Process Costing

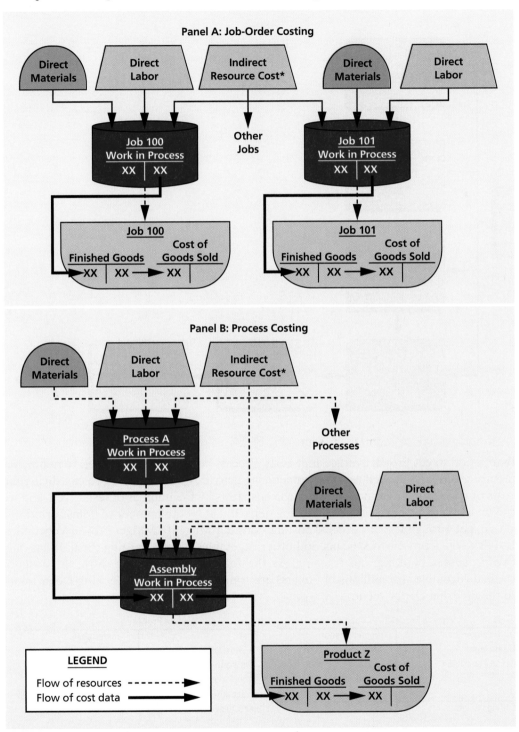

*For simplicity, we show only one indirect-resource cost pool that has fixed-cost behavior. In reality, there would be several cost pools with fixed- and variable-cost behavior. Each of these indirect-resource-cost pools would be allocated using an appropriate cost driver.

Exhibit 14-2

Process Costing at Nally and Gibson

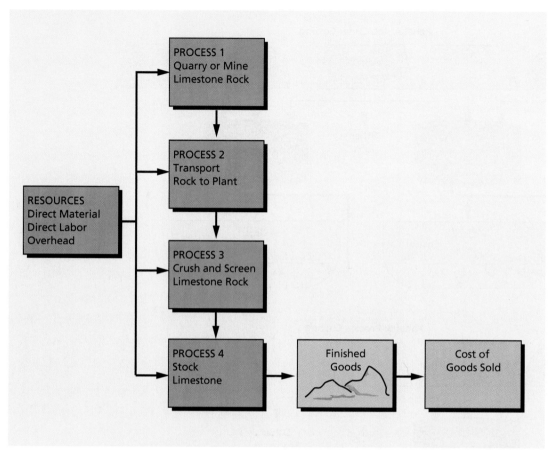

that period to get broad, average unit costs. Process costing can be applied to nonmanufacturing activities as well as to manufacturing activities. For example, we can divide the costs of giving state automobile driver's license tests by the number of tests given, and we can divide the cost of a post office sorting department by the number of items sorted.

To get a rough feel for process costing, consider Magenta Midget Frozen Vegetables. It quick-cooks tiny carrots, beans, and other vegetables before freezing them. It has only two processes, cooking and freezing. As the following T-accounts show, the costs of cooked vegetables (in millions of dollars) are transferred from the Cooking Department to the Freezing Department:

Work in Process — Cooking			
Direct materials	14	Transfer cost of	
Direct labor	4	goods completed	
Factory overhead	8	to next	
	26	department	24
Ending inventory	2		

Work in Process — Freezing			
Cost		Transfer cost	
transferred		of goods	
in from		completed	
cooking	24	to finished	
Direct labor	1	goods	25
Factory overhead	2		
	27		
Ending inventory	2		

The amount of cost to be transferred is determined by dividing the accumulated costs in the Cooking Department by the pounds of vegetables processed. The resulting cost per pound is then multiplied by the pounds of vegetables physically transferred to the Freezing Department.

The journal entries for process-costing systems are similar to those for the job-order-costing system. That is, direct materials, direct labor, and factory overhead are accounted for as before. However, now there is more than a single work-in-process account for all units being manufactured. There is one work-in-process account for each processing department, Work in Process—Cooking and Work in Process—Freezing, in our example. The Magenta Midget data would be recorded as follows:

1. Work in Process—Cooking	14	
Direct-materials inventory		14
To record direct materials used		
2. Work in Process—Cooking	4	
Accrued payroll		4
To record direct labor		
3. Work in Process—Cooking	8	
Factory overhead		8
To record factory overhead applied to product		
4. Work in Process—Freezing	24	
Work in Process—Cooking		24
To transfer goods from the cooking process		
5. Work in Process—Freezing	1	
Accrued payroll		1
To record direct labor		
6. Work in Process—Freezing	2	
Factory overhead		2
To record factory overhead applied to product		
7. Finished goods	25	
Work in Process—Freezing		25
To transfer goods from the freezing process		

The central product-costing problem is how each department should compute the cost of goods transferred out and the cost of goods remaining in the department. If the same amount of work was done on each unit transferred and on each unit in ending inventory, the solution is easy. Total costs are simply divided by total units. Then, this unit cost is used to calculate the total cost of units transferred out and the remaining cost of unfinished units. However, if the units in the inventory are each partially completed, the product-costing system must distinguish between the costs of fully completed units transferred out and the costs of partially completed units not yet transferred.

Process manufacturing systems vary in design. The design shown in panel B of Exhibit 14-1 (as well as Exhibit 14-2) is sequential—units pass from process A to process B and so on until the product is finished. Many other designs are found in practice—each tailored to meet specific production requirements. For example, processes can be operated in parallel until final assembly. In this case, process A and process B might occur at the same time to produce different parts of the finished product. Whatever the specific layout, the basic principles of process costing are the same.

APPLICATION OF PROCESS COSTING

To help you better understand our discussion of process costing, we will use the example of Oakville Wooden Toys, Inc. The company buys wood as a direct material for its Forming Department. The department processes only one type of toy, marionettes. The marionettes are transferred to the Finishing Department, where they are hand-shaped and strings, paint, and clothing are added.

The Forming Department manufactured 25,000 identical units during April, and its costs that month were

Direct materials		$ 70,000
Conversion costs		
Direct labor	$10,625	
Factory overhead	31,875	42,500
Costs to account for		$112,500

CHAPTER 14   PROCESS-COSTING SYSTEMS   **569**

The unit cost of goods completed would simply be $112,500 ÷ 25,000 = $4.50. An itemization would show

Direct materials, $70,000 ÷ 25,000	$2.80
Conversion costs, $42,500 ÷ 25,000	1.70
Unit cost of a whole completed marionette	$4.50

But what if not all 25,000 marionettes were completed during April? For example, assume that 5,000 were still in process at the end of April—only 20,000 were started and fully completed. All units—both those transferred out and those still in inventory—have received all of the necessary direct materials. However, only the transferred units have received the full amount of conversion resources. The 5,000 marionettes that remain in process have received only 25% of conversion resources. How should the Forming Department calculate the cost of goods transferred and the cost of goods remaining in the ending work-in-process inventory? The answer lies in the following five key steps.

- Step 1: Summarize the flow of physical units.
- Step 2: Calculate output in terms of equivalent units.
- Step 3: Summarize the total costs to account for, which are the costs applied to work in process.
- Step 4: Calculate unit costs.
- Step 5: Apply costs to units completed and to units in the ending work in process.

PHYSICAL UNITS AND EQUIVALENT UNITS (STEPS 1 AND 2)

Objective 2
Compute output in terms of equivalent units.

Step 1, as the first column in Exhibit 14-3 shows, tracks the physical units of production. How should the output—the results of the department's work—be measured? This tracking tells us we have a total of 25,000 physical units to account for, but not all of these units count the same in the Forming Department's output. Why not? Because only 20,000 units were fully completed and transferred out. The remaining 5,000 units are only partially complete, and partially complete units cannot be given the same weight as the completed output. As a result, we have to state output not in terms of physical units but in terms of equivalent units.

equivalent units The number of completed units that could have been produced from the inputs applied.

Equivalent units are the number of completed units that could have been produced from the inputs applied. For example, four units that are each one-half completed represent two equivalent units. If each unit had been one-fourth completed, the four together

Exhibit 14-3

Forming Department Output in Equivalent Units
Month Ended April 30, 20X1

	(Step 1) Physical Units	(Step 2) Equivalent Units	
Flow of Production		Direct Materials	Conversion
Started and completed	20,000	20,000	20,000
Work in process, ending inventory	5,000	5,000	1,250*
Units accounted for	25,000		
Work done to date		25,000	21,250*

* 5,000 physical units × .25 degree of completion of conversion costs.

would have represented one equivalent unit. So, equivalent units are determined by multiplying physical units by the percent of completion.

In our example, as step 2 in Exhibit 14-3 shows, the output would be measured as 25,000 equivalent units of direct-materials cost but only 21,250 equivalent units of conversion costs. Why do we have only 21,250 equivalent units of conversion costs but 25,000 of direct-materials cost? Because direct materials had been fully added to all 25,000 units. In contrast, only 25% of the conversion costs were applied to the 5,000 partially completed units, which would have been sufficient to complete only 1,250 units in addition to the 20,000 units that were actually completed.

Of course, to compute equivalent units, you need to estimate how much of a given resource was applied to units in process, which is not always an easy task. Some estimates are easier to make than others. For example, estimating the amount of direct materials used is fairly easy. However, how do you measure how much energy, maintenance labor, or supervision was used on a given unit? Conversion costs can involve a number of these hard-to-measure resources, which leaves you estimating both how much total effort it takes to complete a unit and how much of that effort has already been put into the units in process. Coming up with accurate estimates is further complicated in industries such as textiles, where there is a great deal of work in process at all times. To simplify estimation, some companies have decided that all work in process must be deemed either one-third, one-half, or two-thirds complete. In cases where continuous processing leaves roughly the same amount in process at the end of every month, accountants ignore work in process altogether and assign all monthly production costs to units completed and transferred out.

Measures in equivalent units are not confined to manufacturing situations. Such measures are a popular way of expressing workloads in terms of a common denominator. For example, radiology departments measure their output in terms of weighted units. Various x-ray procedures are ranked in terms of the time, supplies, and related costs devoted to each. A simple chest x ray may receive a weight of one. But a skull x ray may receive a weight of three because it uses three times the resources (for example, technicians' time) as does a procedure with a weight of one.

Confirm your understanding of the equivalent units concept by computing the equivalent units for material, direct labor, and overhead for the following hypothetical case at Nally and Gibson (refer to Exhibit 14-2).

In process 3—crush and screen limestone rock—400 tons of limestone rock were transported to the plant during March. There was no beginning inventory of rock. During March, 320 tons were crushed, screened, and stocked. At the end of March, 80 tons of rock were 40% crushed and screened. Direct labor and overhead are incurred evenly during the crushing and screening process.

ANSWER

The direct material is the limestone rock that is delivered to the plant. Because crushing and screening the rock can begin immediately, we assume that direct material is always 100% completed. Thus, the equivalent units of direct material is the entire 400 tons. The 320 tons of rock that have been stocked are 100% complete with respect to both direct labor and overhead. The 80 tons of rock that are in process at the end of March are 40% complete. This is 32 equivalent tons (80 tons × .40). Thus, the total work done during March is 400 tons of direct material and 352 (that is, 320 + 32) equivalent tons of direct labor and overhead.

CALCULATION OF PRODUCT COSTS (STEPS 3 TO 5)

Exhibit 14-4 is a production-cost report. It shows steps 3 to 5 of process costing. Step 3 summarizes the total costs to account for (that is, the total costs in, or debits to, Work in Process—Forming). Step 4 obtains unit costs by dividing the two categories of total costs by

Exhibit 14-4

Forming Department Production Cost Report
Month Ended April 30, 20X1

		Total Costs	Direct Materials	Conversion Costs
			Details	
(Step 3)	Costs to account for	$112,500	$70,000	$42,500
(Step 4)	Divide by equivalent units		÷25,000	÷21,250
	Unit costs	$ 4.80	$ 2.80	$ 2.00
(Step 5)	Application of costs			
	To units completed and transferred to the Finishing Department, 20,000 units @ $4.80	$ 96,000		
	To units not completed and still in process, April 30, 5,000 units			
	Direct materials	$ 14,000	5,000 ($2.80)	
	Conversion costs	2,500		1,250 ($2.00)
	Work in process, April 30	$ 16,500		
	Total costs accounted for	$112,500		

Objective 3
Compute costs and prepare journal entries for the principal transactions in a process-costing system.

the appropriate measures of equivalent units. The unit cost of a completed unit—materials cost plus conversion costs—is $2.80 + $2.00 = $4.80.[1] Step 5 then uses these unit costs to apply costs to products. The 20,000 finished units are complete in terms of both direct materials and conversion costs. Thus, we can multiply the full unit cost times the number of completed units to determine their costs. The 5,000 physical units in process are fully completed in terms of direct materials. Therefore, the direct materials applied to work in process are 5,000 equivalent units times $2.80, or $14,000. In contrast, the 5,000 physical units are 25% completed in terms of conversion costs. Therefore, the conversion costs applied to work in process are 1,250 equivalent units (25% of 5,000 physical units) times $2.00, or $2,500.

Journal entries for the data in our illustration would appear as

```
1. Work in Process—Forming .........................   70,000
       Direct-materials inventory  .......................              70,000
   Materials added to production in April
2. Work in Process—Forming.........................   10,625
       Accrued payroll.................................              10,625
   Direct labor in April
3. Work in Process—Forming .........................   31,875
       Factory overhead ..............................              31,875
   Factory overhead applied in April
4. Work in Process—Finishing  ........................   96,000
       Work in Process—Forming ......................              96,000
   Cost of goods completed and transferred in April from Forming to Assembly
```

The $112,500 added to the Work in Process—Forming account less the $96,000 transferred out leaves an ending balance of $16,500:

Work in Process—Forming			
1. Direct materials	$ 70,000	4. Transferred out to finishing	$96,000
2. Direct labor	10,625		
3. Factory overhead	31,875		
Costs to account for	112,500		
Bal. April 30	$ 16,500		

[1] *Why is the unit cost $4.80 instead of the $4.50 calculated on page 570. Because the $42,500 conversion cost is spread over 21,250 units instead of 25,000 units.*

SUMMARY PROBLEM FOR YOUR REVIEW

PROBLEM

Taylor Plastics makes a variety of plastic products. Its Extruding Department had the following output and costs:

Units
   Started and completed: 30,000 units
   Started and still in process: 10,000 units; 100% completed for direct
     materials, but 60% completed for conversion costs
Costs applied
   Total: $81,600; direct materials, $60,000; conversion, $21,600

Compute the cost of work completed and the cost of the ending inventory of work in process for Taylor's Extruding Department.

SOLUTION

		(Step 2) Equivalent Units	
Flow of Production	(Step 1) Physical Units	Direct Materials	Conversion
Started and completed	30,000	30,000	30,000
Ending work in process	10,000	10,000*	6,000*
Units accounted for	40,000		
Work done to date		40,000	36,000

* 10,000 × 100% = 10,000; 10,000 × 60% = 6,000.

		Total Costs	Details	
			Direct Materials	Conversion Costs
(Step 3)	Costs to account for	$81,600	$60,000	$21,600
(Step 4)	Divide by equivalent units		÷40,000	÷36,000
	Unit costs	$ 2.10*	$ 1.50	$ .60
(Step 5)	Application of costs			
	To units completed and transferred, 30,000 units @ $2.10	$63,000		
	To ending work in process, 10,000 units			
	Direct materials	$15,000	10,000 ($1.50)	
	Conversion costs	3,600		6,000 ($.60)
	Work in process, ending inventory	$18,600		
	Total costs accounted for	$81,600		

* Unit cost ($2.10) = direct materials costs ($1.50) + conversion costs ($.60).

EFFECTS OF BEGINNING INVENTORIES

So far, our example has been very straightforward because all units were started during the period. In other words, there were no units in beginning inventory. The presence of units in beginning inventory actually complicate matters a great deal.

So how do we account for product costs now that there are units in beginning inventory? Well, we still use the same five steps as we did before, but now our results depend on which inventory system we use. The two most popular inventory systems are the weighted-average method and the first-in, first-out method. In the next two sections, we will explore each of these methods using the following data from our Oakville example for the month of May. Recall that the ending work-in-process inventory for April in the Forming Department was 5,000 units. These units will be the beginning inventory for May.

Units
    Work in process, April 30: 5,000 units; 100% completed for materials, but only 25% completed for conversion costs
    Units started in May: 26,000
    Units completed in May: 24,000
    Work in process, May 31: 7,000 units; 100% completed for materials, but only 60% completed for conversion costs
Costs
    Work in process, April 30

Direct materials	$14,000	
Conversion costs	2,500	$ 16,500
Direct materials added during May		82,100
Conversion costs added during		
May ($14,560 + $42,160)		56,720
Total costs to account for		$155,320*

* Note that the $155,320 total costs to account for include the $16,500 of beginning inventory in addition to the $138,820 added during May.

WEIGHTED-AVERAGE METHOD

weighted-average (WA) process-costing method
A process-costing method that adds the cost of (1) all work done in the current period to (2) the work done in the preceding period on the current period's beginning inventory of work in process, and divides the total by the equivalent units of work done to date.

The **weighted-average (WA) process-costing method** determines total costs by adding the cost of (1) all work done in the current period to (2) the work done in the preceding period on the current period's beginning inventory of work in process. This total is divided by the equivalent units of work done to date, whether that work was done in the current period or previously.

Why is the term *weighted-average* used to describe this method? Primarily because the unit costs used for applying costs to products are affected by the total cost incurred to date, regardless of whether those costs were incurred during or before the current period.

Exhibit 14-5 shows the first two steps in this method, computation of physical units and equivalent units. The computation of equivalent units ignores whether all 31,000 units to account for came from beginning work in process, or all were started in May, or some combination thereof. Exhibit 14-6 presents a production-cost report, summarizing steps 3 to 5 regarding computations of product costs.

FIRST-IN, FIRST-OUT METHOD

first-in, first-out (FIFO) process-costing method
A process-costing method that sharply distinguishes the current work done from the previous work done on the beginning inventory of work in process.

The **first-in, first-out (FIFO) process-costing method** sharply distinguishes the current work done from the previous work done on the beginning inventory of work in process. The calculation of equivalent units is confined to the work done in the current period (May in this illustration).

Exhibit 14-7 presents steps 1 and 2. The easiest way to compute equivalent units under the FIFO method is, first, compute the costs associated with work done to date, as shown in Exhibit 14-7. Second, deduct the work done before the current period. The remaining costs represent the work done during the current period, which is the key to computing the unit costs by the FIFO method.

Exhibit 14-5

Forming Department Output in Equivalent Units
Weighted-Average Method
Month Ended May 31, 20X1

	(Step 1) Physical Units	(Step 2) Equivalent Units	
Flow of Production		Direct Materials	Conversion
Work in process, April 30	5,000 (25%)*		
Started in May	26,000		
To account for	31,000		
Completed and transferred out during current period	24,000	24,000	24,000
Work in process, May 31	7,000 (60%)*	7,000	4,200†
Units accounted for	31,000		
Work done to date		31,000	28,200

* Degrees of completion for conversion costs at the dates of inventories.
† .60 × 7,000 = 4,200.

Exhibit 14-8 is the production-cost report. It presents steps 3 to 5. The $16,500 beginning inventory balance is kept separate from current costs because the calculations of equivalent unit costs are confined to costs added in May only.

The bottom half of Exhibit 14-8 shows two ways to compute the costs of goods completed and transferred out. The first and faster way is to compute the $30,943 ending work in process and then deduct it from the $155,320 total costs to account for,

Exhibit 14-6

Forming Department Production-Cost Report
Weighted-Average Method
Month Ended May 31, 20X1

		Totals	Details Direct Materials	Conversion Costs
(Step 3)	Work in process, April 30	$ 16,500	$14,000	$ 2,500
	Costs added currently	138,820	82,100	56,720
	Total costs to account for	$155,320	$96,100	$59,220
(Step 4)	Divisor, equivalent units for work done to date*		31,000	28,200
	Unit costs (weighted averages)	$ 5.20	$ 3.10	$ 2.10
(Step 5)	Application of costs			
	Completed and transferred, 24,000 units ($5.20)	$124,800		
	Work in process, May 31, 7,000 units			
	Direct materials	$ 21,700	7,000 ($3.10)	
	Conversion costs	8,820		4,200* ($2.10)
	Total work in process	$ 30,520		
	Total costs accounted for	$155,320		

* Equivalent units of work done. For more details, see Exhibit 14-5.

Exhibit 14-7

Forming Department Output in Equivalent Units, FIFO Method

Month Ended May 31, 20X1

		(Step 1)	(Step 2) Equivalent Units	
Same as Exhibit 14-5		Physical	Direct	
Flow of Production		**Units**	*Materials*	*Conversion*
Work in process, April 30		5,000 (25%)*		
Started in May		26,000		
To account for		31,000		
Completed and transferred out				
during current period		24,000	24,000	24,000
Work in process, May 31		7,000 (60%)*	7,000	4,200[†]
Units accounted for		31,000		
Work done to date			31,000	28,200
Less: equivalent units of work				
from previous periods included				
in beginning inventory			5,000[‡]	1,250[§]
Work done in current period only			26,000	26,950

* Degrees of completion for conversion costs at the dates of inventories.

[†] $7,000 \times .60 = 4,200$ equivalent units; [‡] $5,000 \times 1.00 = 5,000$ equivalent units; [§] $5,000 \times .25 = 1,250$ equivalent units.

Exhibit 14-8

Forming Department Production-Cost Report, FIFO Method

Month Ended May 31, 20X1

			Details	
			Direct	Conversion
		Totals	*Materials*	*Costs*
(Step 3) Work in process, April 30		$ 16,500	(work done before May)	
Costs added currently		138,820	$82,100	$56,720
Total costs to account for		$155,320		
(Step 4) Divisor, equivalent units of				
work done in May only			26,000*	26,950*
Unit costs (for FIFO basis)		$ 5.2623	$3.1577	$2.1046
(Step 5) Application of costs				
Work in process, May 31				
Direct materials		$ 22,104	7,000 ($3.1577)	
Conversion costs		8,839		4,200* ($2.1046)
Total work in process				
(7,000 units)		30,943		
Completed and trans-				
ferred out (24,000 units),				
$155,320 − $30,943		124,377[†]		
Total costs accounted for		$155,320		

*Equivalent units of work done. See Exhibit 14-7 for more details.

[†]Check Work in process, April 30 ..... $ 16,500

Additional costs to complete, conversion costs of
75% of 5,000 × $2.1046 = ... 7,892

Started and completed, 26,000 − 7,000 = 19,000;
19,000 × $5.2623 = ... 99,984

Total cost transferred ..... $124,376 ($1 rounding error)

Unit cost transferred, $124,376 ÷ 24,000 = $5.1823

obtaining $124,377. As a check on accuracy, it is advisable to use a second way: Compute the cost of goods transferred in the detailed manner displayed in the footnote in Exhibit 14-8.

Differences between FIFO and Weighted-Average Methods

The key difference between the FIFO and weighted-average methods is the calculation of equivalent units:

- FIFO—Equivalent units are based on the work done in the current period only.
- Weighted-average—Equivalent units are based on the work done in the current period as well as the earlier work done on the current period's beginning inventory of work in process.

These differences in equivalent units lead to differences in unit costs, as well as differences in costs applied to goods completed and still in process. In our example, the FIFO method results in a larger work-in-process inventory on May 31 and a smaller May cost of goods transferred out:

	Weighted Average*	FIFO†
Cost of goods transferred out	$124,800	$124,377
Ending work in process	30,520	30,943
Total costs accounted for	$155,320	$155,320

* From Exhibit 14-6.
† From Exhibit 14-8.

Differences in unit costs between FIFO and weighted-average methods are ordinarily insignificant because (1) changes in material prices, labor wage rates, and other manufacturing costs from month to month tend to be small, and (2) changes in the volume of production and inventory levels also tend to be small.

You have no doubt noticed that the FIFO method involves more detailed computations than does the weighted-average method. That is why FIFO is almost never used in practice for product-costing purposes. However, the FIFO equivalent units for current work done are essential for planning and control purposes. Why? Because they isolate the output for one particular period. Consider our example. The FIFO computations of equivalent units help managers to measure the efficiency of May's performance independent of April's performance. Thus, budgets or standards for each month's departmental costs can be compared against actual results in light of the actual work done during any given month.

Transferred-In Costs

Many companies that use process costing have sequential production processes. For example, Oakville Wooden Toys transfers the items completed in its Forming Department to the Finishing Department. The Finishing Department would call the costs of the items it receives **transferred-in costs**—costs incurred in a previous department for items that have been received by a subsequent department. They are similar to, but not identical to, additional direct-materials costs. Because transferred-in costs are a combination of all types of costs (direct-materials and conversion costs) incurred

transferred-in costs In process costing, costs incurred in a previous department for items that have been received by a subsequent department.

in previous departments, they should not be called a direct-materials cost in a subsequent department.

We account for transferred-in costs just as we account for direct materials, with one exception: Transferred-in costs are kept separate from the direct materials added in the department. Therefore, reports such as Exhibits 14-6 and 14-8 will include three columns of costs instead of two: transferred-in costs, direct-material costs, and conversion costs. The total unit cost will be the sum of all three types of unit costs.

Refer to Exhibit 14-1, Panel B, on page 567. Identify an example of (1) a transferred-in cost, (2) a variable-cost resource, (3) a fixed-cost resource, and (4) an indirect resource cost for the process-costing system.

ANSWER

An example of a transferred-in cost is the total cost accumulated and recorded in the Process A work-in-process account. This cost is transferred to the Assembly process as a "transferred-in cost." The direct materials added in Process A and the Assembly process are variable costs. Direct labor costs in Process A and Assembly are fixed costs. An example of an indirect resource cost is the indirect material and indirect labor used for Process A and the Assembly process. Note that, although we show the indirect resource costs as a fixed, these costs can be both fixed, variable, or mixed.

BUSINESS FIRST
Activity-Based Costing at a Snack Peanut Company

Americans consume more than 300 million pounds of snack peanuts each year. The leading producer of snack peanuts is Planters Specialty Products Company, an operating unit of Nabisco, Inc. Planters markets regular-roast, dry-roast, salted, and unsalted peanuts in the United States. Processing a peanut snack food involves several activities. Most snack peanuts are blanched (removing the skins) before roasting. Peanuts can be oil-roasted or dry-roasted before being packaged and shipped.

What would an activity-based-costing system look like at a snack peanut company? First, let's look at the big picture. The major activities in the processing of peanuts are shown below. Note that in an ABC system, attention is focused on the operating relationships between major activities without regard to "departmental boundaries." In a traditional system, we typically would have a few operating departments such as the "blanching and frying department" and the "packing and shipping department." The receiving, moving, and storing activities would be part of the support (services) function or department in a traditional system. While these departments still exist in a company using an ABC system, the focus is on understanding the interrelationships between activities without regard to departments.

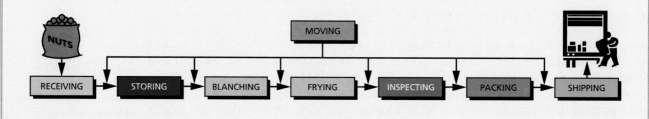

Activity-Based Costing at a Snack Peanut Company (Continued)

Now, let's take a closer look at the blanching and frying activities and the related resources and the support activity, moving. To keep our presentation [illegible] such as indirect materials and supervision have been omitted.

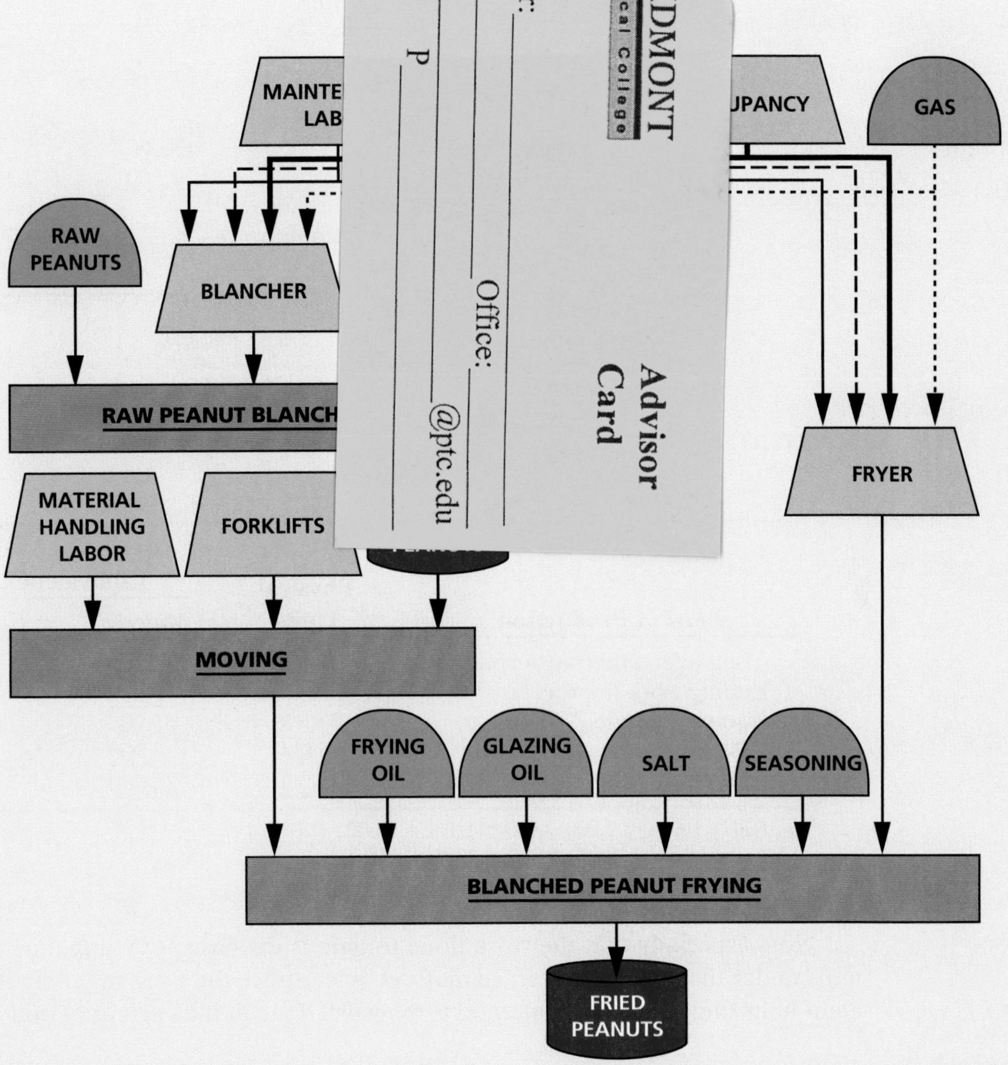

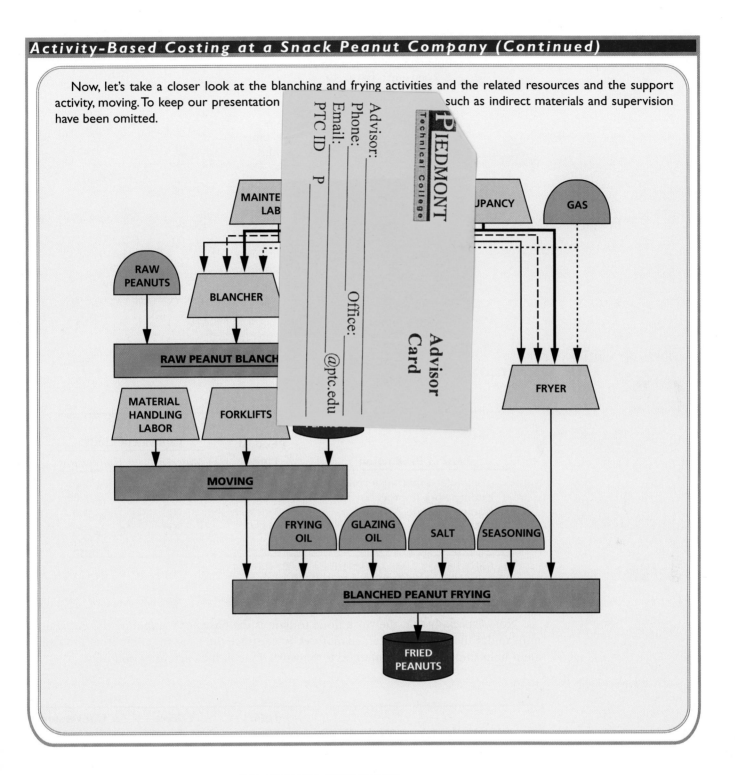

SUMMARY PROBLEM FOR YOUR REVIEW

PROBLEM

Consider the Cooking Department of Middleton Foods, a British food-processing company. Compute the cost of work completed and the cost of the ending inventory of work in process, using both the (1) weighted-average (WA) method and (2) FIFO method.

Units
    Beginning work in process:
        5,000 units; 100% completed
        for materials, 40% completed
        for conversion costs
    Started during month: 28,000 units
    Completed during month: 31,000 units
    Ending work in process: 2,000 units;
        100% completed for materials,
        50% for conversion costs
Costs
    Beginning work in process
        Direct materials   £8,060
        Conversion costs   1,300   £ 9,360
    Direct materials added in current month   41,440
    Conversion costs added in current month   14,700
    Total costs to account for   £65,500

SOLUTION

Flow of Production	(Step 1) Physical Units	(Step 2) Equivalent Units	
		Material	*Conversion*
Completed and transferred out	31,000	31,000	31,000
Ending work in process	2,000	2,000*	1,000*
1. Equivalent units, WA	33,000	33,000	32,000
Less: beginning work in process	5,000	5,000†	2,000†
2. Equivalent units, FIFO	28,000	28,000	30,000

* $2,000 \times 100\% = 2,000; 2,000 \times 50\% = 1,000.$
† $5,000 \times 100\% = 5,000; 5,000 \times 40\% = 2,000.$

Note especially that the work done to date is the basis for computing the equivalent units under the weighted-average method. In contrast, the basis for computing the equivalent units under the FIFO method is the work done in the current period only.

1.

Weighted-Average Method	Total Cost	Direct Materials	Conversion Costs
Beginning work in process	£ 9,360	£ 8,060	£ 1,300
Costs added currently	56,140	41,440	14,700
Total costs to account for	£65,500	£49,500	£16,000
Equivalent units, weighted-average		÷33,000	÷32,000
Unit costs, weighted-average	£ 2.00	£ 1.50	£ 0.50
Transferred out, 31,000 × £2.00	£62,000		
Ending work in process			
Direct materials	£ 3,000	2,000 (£1.50)	
Conversion cost	500		1,000 (£.50)
Total work in process	£ 3,500		
Total costs accounted for	£65,500		

2.

FIFO Method	Total Cost	Direct Materials	Conversion Costs
Beginning work in process	£ 9,360	(work done before month)	
Costs added currently	56,140	£41,440	£14,700
Total costs to account for	£65,500		
Equivalent units, FIFO		÷28,000	÷30,000
Unit costs, FIFO	£ 1.97	£ 1.48	£ 0.49
Ending work in process			
Direct materials	£ 2,960	2,000 (£1.48)	
Conversion cost	490		1,000 (£.49)
Total work in process	£ 3,450		
Transferred out,			
£65,500 − £3,450	£62,050*		
Total costs accounted for	£65,500		

* Check		
Beginning work in process		£ 9,360
Costs to complete, 60% × 5,000 × £.49		1,470
Started and completed,		
(31,000 − 5,000) (£1.48 + £.49)		51,220
Total cost transferred		£62,050
Unit cost transferred, £62,050 ÷ 31,000 = £2.00161		

PROCESS COSTING IN A JIT SYSTEM: BACKFLUSH COSTING

Objective 6
Use backflush costing with a JIT production system.

Tracking costs through various stages of inventory—raw material, work-in-process, inventory for each process (or department), and finished goods inventory—makes accounting systems complex. If there were no inventories, all costs would be charged directly to cost of goods sold, and accounting systems would be much simpler. Organizations using just-in-time (JIT) production systems usually have very small inventories or no inventories at all. As a result, a traditional accounting system that traces costs through several different types of inventories may be inappropriate or even useless for them. One such company is Eagle-Gypsum Products Company. The company operates in the Colorado Rockies and manufactures gypsum wallboard for commercial and residential use. Like many companies that use the JIT production system, Eagle-Gypsum has very low inventory levels and uses **backflush costing,** an accounting system that applies costs to products only when the production is complete. How does backflush costing work? As we shall see, it is a fairly simple costing system.

backflush costing An accounting system that applies costs to products only when the production is complete.

PRINCIPLES OF BACKFLUSH COSTING

Backflush costing has only two categories of costs: materials and conversion costs. Its unique feature is an absence of a work-in-process account. Actual material costs are entered into a materials inventory account, and actual labor and overhead costs are entered into a conversion costs account. Costs are transferred from these two temporary accounts directly into finished-goods inventories. Some backflush systems even eliminate the finished-goods inventory accounts and transfer costs directly to cost of goods sold, especially if goods are not kept in inventory but are shipped immediately on completion. Backflush systems assume that production is completed so soon after the application of conversion activities that balances in the conversion costs accounts always should remain near zero. Costs are transferred out almost immediately after being initially recorded.

EXAMPLE OF BACKFLUSH COSTING

Speaker Technology Inc. (STI) produces speakers for automobile stereo systems. STI recently introduced a JIT production system and backflush costing. Consider the July production for speaker model AX27. The standard material cost per unit of AX27 is $14, and the standard unit conversion cost is $21. During July, STI purchased materials for $5,600, incurred conversion costs of $8,400 (which included all labor costs and manufacturing overhead), and completed and sold 400 units of AX27.

Backflush costing is accomplished in three steps:

1. *Record actual materials and conversion costs.* For simplicity, we assume for now that actual materials and conversion costs were identical to the standard costs. As materials are purchased, backflush systems add their cost to the materials inventory account:

Materials inventory	5,600	
Accounts payable (or cash)		5,600
To record material purchases		

   Similarly, as direct labor and manufacturing overhead costs are incurred, they are added to the conversion-costs account:

Conversion costs	8,400	
Accrued wages and other accounts		8,400
To record conversion costs incurred		

2. *Apply costs to completed units.* When production is complete, costs from materials inventory and conversion-costs accounts are transferred directly to finished goods, based on the number of units completed and a standard cost of each unit:

Finished goods inventory (400 × $35)	14,000	
Materials inventory		5,600
Conversion costs		8,400
To record costs of completed production		

   Because of short production cycle times, there is little lag between additions to the conversion-costs account and transfers to finished goods. The conversion-costs account, therefore, remains near zero.

3. *Record cost of goods sold during the period.* The standard cost of the items sold is transferred from finished goods inventory to cost of goods sold:

Cost of goods sold	14,000	
Finished goods inventory		14,000
To record cost of 400 units sold @$35 per unit		

   Suppose completed units are delivered immediately to customers, so that finished goods inventories are negligible. Steps 2 and 3 can then be combined and the finished goods inventory account eliminated:

Cost of goods sold	14,000	
Material inventory		5,600
Conversion costs		8,400

What if actual costs added to the conversion-costs account do not equal the standard amounts that are transferred to finished-goods inventory? Variances are treated like over-applied or underapplied overhead. Backflush systems assume that conversion-costs account balances should be approximately zero at all times. Any remaining balance in the account at the end of an accounting period is charged to cost of goods sold. Suppose actual conversion costs for July had been $8,600 and the amount transferred to finished goods (i.e., applied to the product) was $8,400. The $200 balance in the conversion-costs account at the end of the month would be written off to cost of goods sold:

```
Cost of goods sold  .......................  200
       Conversion costs  ...................       200
   To recognize underapplied conversion costs
```

SUMMARY PROBLEM FOR YOUR REVIEW

PROBLEM

The most extreme (and simplest) version of backflush costing makes product costing entries at only one point. Suppose Speaker Technology Inc. (STI) had no materials inventory account (in addition to no work-in-process inventory account). Materials are not "purchased" until they are needed for production. Therefore, STI enters both material and conversion costs directly into its finished goods inventory account.

Required

Prepare journal entries (without explanations) and T-accounts for July's production of 400 units. As given earlier, materials purchases totaled $5,600, and conversion costs were $8,400. Why might a company use this extreme type of backflush costing?

SOLUTION

In one step, material and conversion costs are applied to finished goods inventories:

```
Finished goods inventories  ...................  14,000
       Accounts payable  ...................          5,600
       Wages payable and other accounts  ......       8,400
```

	Finished Goods Inventories		Accounts Payable, Wages Payable, and Other Accounts	
Materials	5,600			5,600
Conversion costs	8,400			8,400

This example shows that backflush costing is simple and inexpensive. Backflush costing provides reasonably accurate product costs if (1) materials inventories are low (most likely because of JIT delivery schedules), and (2) production cycle times are short, so that at any time only inconsequential amounts of material costs or conversion costs have been incurred for products that are not yet complete.

Highlights To Remember

Explain the basic ideas underlying process costing and how they differ from job costing. Process costing is used for inventory costing when there is continuous mass production of like units. Process-cost systems accumulate costs by department (or process); each department has its own work-in-process account. Job-order cost systems differ because costs are accumulated and tracked by the individual job order.

Compute output in terms of equivalent units. The key concept in process costing is that of equivalent units, the number of fully completed units that could have been produced from the inputs applied.

Compute costs and prepare journal entries for the principal transactions in a process-costing system. There are five basic steps to process costing:

1. Summarize the flow of physical units.
2. Calculate output in terms of equivalent units.
3. Summarize the total costs to account for.
4. Calculate unit costs (Step 3 ÷ Step 2).
5. Apply costs to units completed and to units in the ending work in process.

Steps 3 and 5 provide the data for journal entries. These entries all involve the work-in-process accounts for the various departments (processes) producing products. **Demonstrate how the presence of beginning inventories affects the computation of unit costs under the weighted-average method.** Process costing is complicated by the presence of beginning inventories. The weighted-average method includes the work done in previous periods on the current period's beginning inventory with work done in the current period to compute unit costs.

Demonstrate how the presence of beginning inventories affects the computation of unit costs under the first-in, first-out method. The FIFO method focuses on the work done only in the current period.

Use backflush costing with a JIT production system. Many companies with JIT production systems use backflush costing. Such systems have no work-in-process inventory account and apply costs to products only after the production process is complete.

Understand how a process-costing system tracks costs to products. A process-costing system tracks costs to products using broad averages. These averages represent equivalent unit costs incurred in each of several departments or processes. Unit costs from one department or process becomes the transferred-in material for downstream departments or processes until the product is finished.

Appendix 14: Hybrid Systems — Operation Costing

Job costing and process costing are actually extremes along a continuum of potential costing systems. Each company designs its own accounting system to fit its underlying production activities. Many companies use **hybrid-costing systems,** which are blends of ideas from both job costing and process costing. This appendix discusses one of many possible hybrid-costing systems, operation costing.

Nature of Operation Costing

hybrid-costing system
An accounting system that is a blend of ideas from both job costing and process costing.

operation costing A hybrid-costing system often used in the batch or group manufacturing of goods that have some common characteristics plus some individual characteristics.

Operation costing is a hybrid-costing system often used in the batch or group manufacturing of goods that are similar but have enough individual characteristics to be distinct from one another. Such products—for example, personal computers, clothing, and semiconductors—are specifically identified by work orders and are often variations of a single design but require different operations to be completed. For instance, suits of clothes may differ, requiring various materials and hand operations. Similarly, a textile manufacturer may apply special chemical treatments (such as waterproofing) to some fabrics but not to others.

Operation costing may entail mass production, but there is sufficient product variety to have products scheduled in different batches or groups, each requiring a particular sequence of operations.

An operation is a standardized method or technique that is repetitively performed, regardless of the distinguishing features of the finished product. Examples include cutting, planing, sanding, painting, and chemical treating. Products proceed through the various operations in groups as specified by work orders or production orders. These work orders list the necessary direct materials and the step-by-step operations required to make the finished product.

Suppose a clothing manufacturer produces two lines of blazers. The wool blazers use better materials and undergo more operations than do the polyester blazers, as follows:

	Wool Blazers	Polyester Blazers
Direct materials	Wool Satin lining Bone buttons	Polyester Rayon lining Plastic buttons

Operations	1. Cutting cloth
	2. Checking edges
	3. Sewing body
	4. Checking seams
	5. —
	
	6. Sewing collars and
	   lapels by hand
		1. Cutting cloth
		—
		3. Sewing body
		—
		5. Sewing collars and
		   lapels by machine
		—

The costs of the blazers are compiled by work order. As in job costing, the direct materials—different for each work order—are specifically identified with the appropriate order. Conversion costs—direct labor plus factory overhead—are initially compiled for each operation. A cost driver, such as the number of units processed or minutes or seconds used, is identified for each operation, and a conversion cost per unit of cost driver activity is computed. Then conversion costs are applied to products in a manner similar to the application of factory overhead in a job-cost system.

EXAMPLE OF OPERATION-COSTING ENTRIES

Suppose our manufacturer has two work orders, one for 100 wool blazers and the other for 200 polyester blazers, as follows:

	Wool Blazers	Polyester Blazers
Number of blazers	100	200
Direct materials	$2,500	$3,100
Conversion costs		
1. Cutting cloth	600	1,200
2. Checking edges	300	—
3. Sewing body	500	1,000
4. Checking seams	600	—
5. Sewing collars and lapels by machine	—	800
6. Sewing collars and lapels by hand	700	—
Total manufacturing costs	$5,200	$6,100

Direct labor and factory overhead vanish as separate classifications in an operation-costing system. The sum of these costs is most frequently called conversion cost. The conversion cost is applied to products based on the company's budgeted rate for performing each operation. For example, suppose the conversion costs of operation 1, cutting cloth, are driven by machine hours and are budgeted for the year as follows:

$$\begin{array}{l}\text{budgeted rate for applying} \\ \text{conversion costs for} \\ \text{cutting cloth to product}\end{array} = \dfrac{\begin{array}{l}\text{budgeted conversion cost for cutting cloth} \\ \text{for the year (direct labor, power, repairs,} \\ \text{supplies, other factory overhead of this operation)}\end{array}}{\begin{array}{l}\text{budgeted machine hours for the year for} \\ \text{cutting cloth}\end{array}}$$

$$\text{rate per machine hours} = \frac{\$150{,}000 + \$450{,}000}{20{,}000 \text{ machine hours}} = \$30 \text{ per machine hour}$$

As goods are manufactured, conversion costs are applied to the work orders by multiplying the $30 hourly rate times the number of machine hours used for cutting cloth.

If 20 machine hours are needed to cut the cloth for the 100 wool blazers, then the conversion cost involved is $600 (20 hours × $30 per hour). For the 200 polyester blazers, the conversion cost for cutting cloth is twice as much, $1,200 (40 hours × $30), because each blazer takes the same cutting time, and there are twice as many polyester blazers.

Summary journal entries for applying costs to the polyester blazers follow. (Entries for the wool blazers would be similar.)

The journal entry for the requisition of direct materials for the 200 polyester blazers is

Work-in-process inventory (polyester blazers)	3,100	
Direct-materials inventory		3,100

Direct labor and factory overhead are subparts of a conversion-costs account in an operation-costing system. Suppose actual conversion costs of $3,150 were entered into the conversion-costs account:

Conversion costs	3,150	
Accrued payroll, accumulated depreciation,		
accounts payable, etc.		3,150

The application of conversion costs to products in operation costing is similar to the application of factory overhead in job-ordering costing. A budgeted rate per unit of cost-driver activity is used. To apply conversion costs to the 200 polyester blazers, the following summary entry is made for operations 1, 3, and 5 (cutting cloth, sewing body, and sewing collars and lapels by machine):

Work-in-process inventory (polyester blazers)	3,000	
Conversion costs, cutting cloth		1,200
Conversion costs, sewing body		1,000
Conversion costs, sewing collars		
and lapels by machine		800

After posting, work-in-process inventory has the following debit balance

Work-in-Process Inventory (polyester blazers)		
Direct materials	3,100	
Conversion costs applied	3,000	
Balance	6,100	

As the blazers are completed, their cost is transferred to finished-goods inventory in the usual manner.

Any overapplication or underapplication of conversion costs is disposed of at the end of the year in the same manner as overapplied or underapplied overhead in a job-order costing system. In this case, conversion costs have been debited for actual cost of $3,150 and credited for costs applied of $3,000. The debit balance of $150 indicates that conversion costs are underapplied.

Accounting Vocabulary

backflush costing, p. 581

equivalent units, p. 570

first-in, first-out (FIFO)
process-costing method,
p. 574

hybrid-costing system, p. 584

operation costing, p. 584

transferred-in costs, p. 577

weighted-average (WA)
process-costing method,
p. 574

Fundamental Assignment Material

14-A1 Basic Process Costing

Rockmania, Inc., produces portable compact disk (CD) players in large quantities. For simplicity, assume that the company has two departments, assembly and testing. The manufacturing costs in the Assembly Department during February were

Direct materials added		$ 60,800
Conversion costs		
Direct labor	$50,000	
Factory overhead	40,000	90,000
Assembly costs to account for		$150,800

There was no beginning inventory of work in process. Suppose work on 19,000 CD players was begun in the assembly department during February, but only 17,000 CD players were fully completed. All the parts had been made or placed in process, but only half the labor had been completed for each of the CD players still in process.

Required

1. Compute the equivalent units and unit costs for February.
2. Compute the costs of units completed and transferred to the Testing Department. Also compute the cost of the ending work in process. (For journal entries, see Problem 14-21.)

14-A2 Weighted-Average Process-Costing Method

The Lucero Company manufactures electric drills. Material is introduced at the beginning of the process in the Assembly Department. Conversion costs are applied uniformly throughout the process. As the process is completed, goods are immediately transferred to the Finishing Department.

Data for the Assembly Department for the month of July 20X1 follow:

Work in process, June 30: $175,500 (consisting of $138,000 materials and $37,500 conversion costs); 100% completed for direct materials, but only 25% completed for conversion costs	10,000 units
Units started during July	80,000 units
Units completed during July	70,000 units
Work in process, July 31: 100% completed for direct materials, but only 50% completed for conversion costs	20,000 units
Direct materials added during July	$852,000
Conversion costs added during July	$634,500

Required

1. Compute the total cost of goods transferred out of the Assembly Department during July.
2. Compute the total costs of the ending work in process. Prepare a production-cost report or a similar orderly tabulation of your work. Assume weighted-average product costing. (For the FIFO method and journal entries, see Problems 14-31 and 14-38.)

14-A3 Backflush Costing

Thermo Controls, Inc., makes electronic thermostats for homes and offices. The Westplains Division makes one product, Autotherm, which has a standard cost of $37, consisting of $22 of materials and

$15 of conversion costs. In January, actual purchases of materials totaled $45,000, labor payroll costs were $11,000, and manufacturing overhead was $19,000. Completed output was 2,000 units.

The Westplains Division uses a backflush-costing system that records costs in materials inventory and conversion costs accounts and applies costs to products at the time production is completed. There were no finished goods inventories on January 1 and 20 units on January 31.

Required

1. Prepare journal entries (without explanations) to record January's costs for the Westplains Division. Include the purchase of materials, incurrence of labor and manufacturing overhead costs, application of product costs, and recognition of cost of goods sold.

2. Suppose January's actual manufacturing overhead costs had been $22,000 instead of $19,000. Prepare the journal entry to recognize underapplied conversion costs at the end of January.

14-B1 Basic Process Costing

McClure Company produces digital watches in large quantities. The manufacturing costs of the Assembly Department were

Direct materials added		$1,620,000
Conversion costs		
Direct labor	$415,000	
Factory overhead	260,000	675,000
Assembly costs to account for		$2,295,000

For simplicity, assume that this is a two-department company, assembly and finishing. There was no beginning work in process.

Suppose 900,000 units were begun in the Assembly Department. There were 600,000 units completed and transferred to the Finishing Department. The 300,000 units in ending work in process were fully completed regarding direct materials but half-completed regarding conversion costs.

Required

1. Compute the equivalent units and unit costs in the Assembly Department.

2. Compute the costs of units completed and transferred to the Finishing Department. Also compute the cost of the ending work in process in the Assembly Department.

14-B2 Weighted-Average Process-Costing Method

The Rainbow Paint Co. uses a process-costing system. Materials are added at the beginning of a particular process, and conversion costs are incurred uniformly. Work in process at the beginning of the month is 40% complete; at the end, 20%. One gallon of material makes one gallon of product. Data follow.

Beginning inventory	550 gal
Direct materials added	7,150 gal
Ending inventory	400 gal
Conversion costs incurred	$35,724
Cost of direct materials added	$65,340
Conversion costs, beginning inventory	$ 1,914
Cost of direct materials, beginning inventory	$ 3,190

Required

Use the weighted-average method. Prepare a schedule of output in equivalent units and a schedule of application of costs to products. Show the cost of goods completed and cost of ending work in process. (For journal entries, see Problem 14-30. For the FIFO method, see Problem 14-37.)

14-B3 Backflush Costing

Acme Auto Parts, Inc., recently installed a backflush-costing system in its Audio Components Department. One department makes 4-inch speakers with a standard cost as follows:

Materials	$ 9.80
Conversion costs	4.20
Total	$14.00

Speakers are scheduled for production only after orders are received, and products are shipped to customers immediately on completion. Therefore, no finished goods inventories are kept, and product costs are applied directly to cost of goods sold.

In October, 1,500 speakers were produced and shipped to customers. Materials were purchased at a cost of $15,500, and actual conversion costs (labor plus manufacturing overhead) of $6,300 were recorded.

Required

1. Prepare journal entries to record October's costs for the production of 4-inch speakers.
2. Suppose October's actual conversion costs had been $6,000 instead of $6,300. Prepare a journal entry to recognize overapplied conversion costs.

Additional Assignment Material

QUESTIONS

14-1. Give three examples of industries where process-costing systems are probably used.

14-2. Give three examples of nonprofit organizations where process-costing systems are probably used.

14-3. "There are five key steps in process-cost accounting." What are they?

14-4. Identify the major distinction between the first two and the final three steps of the five major steps in accounting for process costs.

14-5. Suppose a university has 10,000 full-time students and 5,000 half-time students. Using the concept of equivalent units, compute the number of "full-time equivalent" students.

14-6. "Equivalent units are the work done to date." What method of process costing is being described?

14-7. Present an equation that describes the physical flow in process costing when there are beginning inventories in work in process.

14-8. "The beginning inventory is regarded as if it were a batch of goods separate and distinct from the goods started and completed by a process during the current period." What method of process costing is being described?

14-9. Why is "work done in the current period only" a key measurement of equivalent units?

14-10. "The total conversion costs are divided by the equivalent units for the work done to date." Does this quotation describe the weighted-average method or does it describe FIFO?

14-11. "FIFO process costing is helpful for planning and control even if it is not used for product costing." Do you agree? Explain.

14-12. How are transferred-in costs similar to direct materials costs? How are they different?

14-13. Explain what happens in a backflush-costing system when the amount of actual conversion cost in a period exceeds the amount applied to the products completed during that period.

14-14. Give three examples of industries that probably use operation costing.

14-15. "In operation costing, average conversion costs are applied to products in a manner similar to the application of factory overhead in a job-cost system." Do you agree? Explain.

COGNITIVE EXERCISES

14-16   Purpose of Product Costing in a Process Production Environment
All product costing uses averages to determine costs per unit of product produced. In job-order production systems, the averages are based on a relatively small number of units. In a process production environment the number of units is much larger. Once the average unit cost is determined, what is the central product-costing problem in process costing?

14-17   Weighted Average and FIFO Methods
"Ordinarily, the differences in unit costs under FIFO and weighted-average methods are insignificant." Do you agree? Explain.

14-18   Process Costing in a JIT Environment
Companies using JIT production systems usually have very small inventories or no inventories at all. As a result, a traditional accounting system may be inappropriate. Many of these companies have adopted backflush-costing systems. Do backflush-costing systems work only for companies using a JIT production system? Explain.

EXERCISES

14-19   Basic Process Costing
A department of Mayberry Textiles produces cotton fabric. All direct materials are introduced at the start of the process. Conversion costs are incurred uniformly throughout the process.

In May, there was no beginning inventory. Units started, completed, and transferred: 650,000. Units in process, May 31: 220,000. Each unit in ending work in process was 60% converted. Costs incurred during May: direct materials, $3,654,000; conversion costs, $860,200.

Required

1. Compute the total work done in equivalent units and the unit cost for April.
2. Compute the cost of units completed and transferred. Also compute the cost of units in ending work in process.

14-20 Uneven Flow

One department of Wamago Technology Company manufactures basic handheld calculators. Several materials are added at various stages of the process. The outer front shell and the carrying case, which represent 10% of the total material cost, are added at the final step of the assembly process. All other materials are considered to be "in process" by the time the calculator reaches a 50% stage of completion.

Seventy-four thousand calculators were started in production during 20X1. At year-end, 6,000 calculators were in various stages of completion, but all of them were beyond the 50% stage and, on the average, they were regarded as being 70% completed.

The following costs were incurred during the year: direct materials, $205,520; conversion costs, $397,100. There were no work-in-process inventories.

Required

1. Prepare a schedule of physical units and equivalent units.
2. Tabulate the unit costs, cost of goods completed, and cost of ending work in process.

14-21 Journal Entries

Refer to the data in Problem 14-A1. Prepare summary journal entries for the use of direct materials, direct labor, and factory overhead applied. Also prepare a journal entry for the transfer of goods completed and transferred. Show the postings to the Work-in-Process account.

14-22 Journal Entries

Refer to the data in Problem 14-B1. Prepare summary journal entries for the use of direct materials, direct labor, and factory overhead applied. Also prepare a journal entry for the transfer of goods completed and transferred. Show the posting to the Work-in-Process—Assembly Department account.

14-23 Physical Units

Fill in the unknowns in physical units:

	Case	
Flow of Production	*A*	*B*
Work in process, beginning inventory	1,500	4,000
Started	6,000	?
Completed and transferred	?	8,000
Work in process, ending inventory	2,000	3,000

14-24 Flow of Production, FIFO

Fill in the unknowns in physical or equivalent units:

	Physical	Equivalent Units	
Flow of Production	**Units**	*Direct Materials*	*Conversion Costs*
Beginning work in process	1,000 (50%)*		
Started	?		
To account for	36,000		
Completed and transferred out	33,000	33,000	33,000
Ending work in process	? (30%)*	?	?
Units accounted for	?		
Work done to date		?	?
Equivalent units in beginning inventory		?	?
Work done in current period only		?	?

* Degree of completion of conversion costs at dates of inventory. Assume that all materials are added at the beginning of the process.

14-25 Equivalent Units

The Preparation Department of Blackburn Paints, Inc., had the following flow of latex paint production (in gallons) for the month of April:

Gallons completed	
From work in process on April 1	5,000
From April production	25,000
	30,000

Direct materials are added at the beginning of the process. Gallons of work in process at April 30 were 10,000. The work in process at April 1 was 30% complete as to conversion costs, and the work in process at April 30 was 50% complete as to conversion costs.

What are the equivalent units (gallons) of production for (a) direct materials and (b) conversion costs for the month of April using the FIFO method?

14-26 Equivalent Units, FIFO

Fill in the unknowns.

Flow of Production in Units	(Step 1) Physical Units	(Step 2) Equivalent Units Direct Materials	Conversion Costs
Work in process, beginning inventory	30,000*		
Started	45,000		
To account for	75,000		
Completed and transferred out	?	?	?
Work in process, ending inventory	2,000†	?	?
Units accounted for	75,000		
Work done to date		?	?
Less: Equivalent units of work from previous periods included in beginning inventory		?	?
Work done in current period only (FIFO method)		?	?

* Degree of completion: direct materials, 80%; conversion costs, 40%.
† Degree of completion: direct materials, 40%; conversion costs, 10%.

14-27 Compute Equivalent Units

Consider the following data for 20X1:

	Physical Units
Started in 20X1	80,000
Completed in 20X1	90,000
Ending inventory, work in process	10,000
Beginning inventory, work in process	20,000

The beginning inventory was 80% complete regarding direct materials and 40% complete regarding conversion costs. The ending inventory was 20% complete regarding direct materials and 10% complete regarding conversion costs.

Prepare a schedule of equivalent units for the work done to date and the work done during 20X1 only.

14-28 FIFO and Unit Direct-Materials Costs

The Lindberg Company uses the FIFO process-cost method. Consider the following for July:

- Beginning inventory, 15,000 units, 70% completed regarding direct materials, which cost $89,250
- Units completed, 80,000
- Cost of materials placed in process during July, $580,000
- Ending inventory, 5,000 units, 60% completed regarding materials

Compute the direct-materials cost per equivalent unit for the work done in July only.

14-29 FIFO Method, Conversion Cost

Given the following information, compute the unit conversion cost for the month of June for the Abraham Company, using the FIFO process-costing method. Show details of your calculation.

- Units completed, 45,000
- Conversion cost in beginning inventory, $30,000
- Beginning inventory, 10,000 units with 75% of conversion cost
- Ending inventory, 15,000 units with 30% of conversion cost
- Conversion costs put into production in June, $180,600

14-30 Journal Entries

Refer to the data in Problem 14-B2. Prepare summary journal entries for the use of direct materials and conversion costs. Also prepare a journal entry for the transfer of goods completed, assuming that the goods are transferred to another department.

14-31 Journal Entries

Refer to the data in Problem 14-A2. Prepare summary journal entries for the use of direct materials and conversion costs. Also prepare a journal entry for the transfer of the goods completed and transferred from the Assembly Department to the Finishing Department.

PROBLEMS

14-32 Process Costing at Nally and Gibson

Nally and Gibson produces crushed limestone among other products, used in highway construction. To produce the crushed limestone, the company starts with limestone rocks from its quarry in Georgetown, Kentucky, and puts the rocks through a crushing process. Suppose that on May 1, Nally and Gibson has 24 tons of rock (75% complete) in the crushing process. The cost of that beginning work-in-process inventory was $6,000. During May, the company added 288 tons of rock from its quarry, and at the end of the month 15 tons remained in process, on average one-third complete. The cost of rocks from the quarry for the last five months has been $120 per ton. Labor and overhead cost during May in the rock crushing process were $40,670. Nally and Gibson uses weighted-average process costing.

1. Compute the cost per ton of crushed rock for production in May.
2. Compute the cost of the work in process inventory at the end of May.
3. Suppose the flexible budget for labor and overhead was $16,000 plus $80 per ton. Evaluate the control of overhead and labor costs during May.

14-33 Process and Activity-Based Costing

Consider the potato chip production process at a company such as Frito-Lay. Frito-Lay uses a continuous flow technology that is suited for high volumes of product. At the Plano, Texas, facility, between 6,000 and 7,000 pounds of potato chips are produced each hour. The plant operates 24 hours a day. It takes 30 minutes to completely produce a bag of potato chips from the raw potato to the packed end-product.

1. What product and process characteristics of potato chips dictate the cost accounting system used? Describe the costing system best suited to Frito-Lay.
2. What product and process characteristics dictate the use of an activity-based-costing system? What implications does this have for Frito-Lay?
3. When beginning inventories are present, product costing becomes more complicated. Estimate the relative magnitude of beginning inventories at Frito-Lay compared to total production. What implication does this have for the costing system?

14-34 Nonprofit Process Costing

The IRS must process millions of income tax returns yearly. When the taxpayer sends in a return, documents such as withholding statements and checks are matched against the data submitted. Then various other inspections of the data are conducted. Of course, some returns are more complicated than others, so the expected time allowed to process a return is geared to an "average" return.

Some work-measurement experts have been closely monitoring the processing at a particular branch. They are seeking ways to improve productivity.

Suppose 3 million returns were received on April 15. On April 22, the work-measurement teams discovered that all supplies (punched cards, inspection check-sheets, and so on) had been affixed to the returns, but 40% of the returns still had to undergo a final inspection. The other returns were fully completed.

1. Suppose the final inspection represents 20% of the overall processing time in this process. Compute the total work done in terms of equivalent units.
2. The materials and supplies consumed were $600,000. For these calculations, materials and supplies are regarded just like direct materials. The conversion costs were $4,830,000. Compute the unit costs of materials and supplies and of conversion.
3. Compute the cost of the tax returns not yet completely processed.

14-35 Two Materials

The following data pertain to the Mixing Department at Foster Chemicals for April:

Units	
Work in process, March 31	0
Units started	60,000
Completed and transferred	
to finishing department	40,000
Costs	
Materials	
Plastic compound	$300,000
Softening compound	$ 80,000
Conversion costs	$192,000

The plastic compound is introduced at the start of the process, while the softening compound is added when the product reaches an 80% stage of completion. Conversion costs are incurred uniformly throughout the process.

The ending work in process is 40% completed for conversion costs. None of the units in process reached the 80% stage of completion.

1. Compute the equivalent units and unit costs for April.
2. Compute the total cost of units completed and transferred to finished goods. Also compute the cost of the ending work in process.

14-36 Materials and Cartons

A Manchester, England, company manufactures and sells small portable tape recorders. Business is booming. Several materials are added at various stages in the assembly department. Costs are accounted for on a process-cost basis. The end of the process involves conducting a final inspection and adding a cardboard carton.

The final inspection requires 5% of the total processing time. All materials, besides the carton, are added by the time the recorders reach an 80% stage of completion of conversion.

There were no beginning inventories. One hundred fifty thousand recorders were started in production during 20X1. At the end of the year, which was not a busy time, 5,000 recorders were in various stages of completion. All the ending units in work in process were at the 95% stage. They awaited final inspection and being placed in cartons.

Total direct materials consumed in production, except for cartons, cost £2,250,000. Cartons used cost £319,000. Total conversion costs were £1,198,000.

1. Present a schedule of physical units, equivalent units, and unit costs of direct materials, cartons, and conversion costs.
2. Present a summary of the cost of goods completed and the cost of ending work in process.

14-37 FIFO Computations

Refer to Problem 14-B2. Using FIFO, answer the same questions.

14-38 FIFO Methods

Refer to Problem 14-A2. Using FIFO costing, answer the same questions.

14-39 Backflush Costing

Everest Controls manufactures a variety of measuring instruments. One product is an altimeter used by hikers and mountain climbers. Everest adopted a JIT philosophy with an automated, computer-controlled, robotic production system. The company schedules production only after an order is received, materials and parts arrive just as they are needed, the production cycle time for altimeters is less than one day, and completed units are packaged and shipped as part of the production cycle.

Everest's backflush-costing system has only three accounts related to production of altimeters: materials and parts inventory, conversion costs, and finished goods inventory. At the beginning of

April (as at the beginning of every month), each of the three accounts had a balance of zero. Following are the April transactions related to the production of altimeters.

Materials and parts purchased	$287,000
Conversion costs incurred	$ 92,000
Altimeters produced	11,500 units

The budgeted (or standard) cost for one altimeter is $24 for materials and parts and $8 for conversion costs.

Required

1. Prepare summary journal entries for the production of altimeters in April.
2. Compute the cost of goods sold for April. Explain any assumptions you make.
3. Suppose the actual conversion costs incurred during April were $95,000 instead of $92,000, and all other facts were as given. Prepare the additional journal entry that would be required at the end of April. Explain why the entry was necessary.

14-40 Basic Operation Costing

Study Appendix 14. Oak Furniture, Inc., manufactures a variety of wooden chairs. The company's manufacturing operations and costs applied to products for June were

	Cutting	Assembly	Finishing
Direct labor	$ 60,000	$30,000	$ 96,000
Factory overhead	115,500	37,500	156,000

Three styles of chairs were produced in June. The quantities and direct-materials costs were

Style	Quantities	Direct-Materials Costs
Standard	6,000	$108,000
Deluxe	4,500	171,000
Unfinished	3,000	66,000

Each unit, regardless of style, required the same cutting and assembly operations. The unfinished chairs, as the name implies, had no finishing operations whatsoever. Standard and deluxe styles required the same finishing operations.

Required

1. Tabulate the total conversion costs of each operation, the total units produced, and the conversion cost per unit.
2. Tabulate the total costs, the units produced, and the cost per unit.

14-41 Operation Costing with Ending Work in Process

Study Appendix 14. Sonar Instruments, Inc., uses three operations in sequence to make two models of its depth finders for sport fishing. Production information for March follows:

	Production Orders	
	For 1,000 Standard Depth Finders	For 1,000 Deluxe Depth Finders
Direct materials (actual costs applied)	$57,000	$100,000
Conversion costs (predetermined costs applied on the basis of machine hours used)		
Operation 1	19,000	19,000
Operation 2	?	?
Operation 3	—	15,000
Total manufacturing costs applied	$?	$?

1. Operation 2 was highly automated. Product costs depended on a budgeted application rate for conversion costs, based on machine hours. The budgeted costs for 20X1 were $220,000 direct labor and $580,000 factory overhead. Budgeted machine hours were 20,000. Each depth finder required six minutes of time in operation 2. Compute the costs of processing 1,000 depth finders in operation 2.

2. Compute the total manufacturing costs of 1,000 depth finders and the cost per standard depth finder and deluxe depth finder.

3. Suppose that at the end of the year 500 standard depth finders were in process through operation 1 only and 600 deluxe depth finders were in process through operation 2 only. Compute the cost of the ending work-in-process inventory. Assume that no direct materials are applied in operation 2, but that $10,000 of the $100,000 direct-materials cost of the deluxe depth finders are applied to each 1,000 depth finders processed in operation 3.

COLLABORATIVE LEARNING EXERCISE

14-42 Job, Process, and Hybrid Costing

Form groups of three to six students. For each of the following production processes, assess whether a job-cost, process-cost, or hybrid-cost system is most likely to be used to determine the cost of the product or service. Also, explain why you think that system is most logical. (This can be done by individuals, but it is a much richer experience when done as a group, because the knowledge and judgment of several students interact to produce a much better analysis than a single student can produce.)

a. Producing Cheerios by General Mills.
b. Producing a 4-Runner sport utility vehicle by Toyota.
c. Processing an application for life insurance by Prudential.
d. Producing a couch by Ethan Allen.
e. Building a bridge by Kiewit Construction Co.
f. Producing gasoline by Chevron.
g. Producing 200 copies of a 140-page course packet by Kinkos.
h. Producing a superferry by Todd Shipyards.

INTERNET EXERCISE

14-43 Processing Costing at a Variety of Companies

Process costing assigns costs by measuring overall production costs and averaging them based on total production in units over a period of time—usually a month. The resulting average unit costs are then used to determine inventory cost and the cost of goods sold. Let's look at some companies and see if any of them might be candidates for using a process-costing system.

www.prenhall.com/horngren

1. Log on to Land's End's Web site at http://www.landsend.com. Click on "General Information" on the left panel. What type of a firm is Land's End? What is the main activity of the firm? Do you think that the firm would be a good candidate for using a process-costing system? Why or why not?

2. Log on to La-Z-Boy's Web site at http://www.lazboy.com. Click on "about LA-Z-BOY." What type of a firm is La-Z-Boy? What is the main activity of the firm? Do you think that the firm would be a good candidate for using a process-costing system? Why or why not?

3. Log on to Tasty Baking Company's Web site at http://www.tastykake.com. What type of a firm is Tasty Baking Company? What is the main activity of the firm? Do you think that the firm would be a good candidate for using a process-costing system? Why or why not?

4. Take the Tastykake factory tour by strolling through the Tasty Bakery. Look into the oven window for a peek at how the Tastykakes are made. Assume that Tastykake uses a process-costing system. After watching the tour, do you believe that they would have more than one processing department? If you said yes, identify the departments you would expect. If you responded no, explain why one department would be sufficient for the processing.

5. Refer to Tasty Baking Company's most recent annual report. What type of inventory accounts do you find? Where did you locate the information on inventory? Can you tell from the information provided what type of costing system that Tasty Baking Company uses?

15

OVERHEAD APPLICATION: VARIABLE AND ABSORPTION COSTING

L.A. Darling Company designs, makes, and installs displays, such as this one at Best Buy Computers.

www.prenhall.com/horngren

Learning Objectives

When you have finished studying this chapter, you should be able to

1. Construct an income statement using the variable-costing approach.

2. Construct an income statement using the absorption-costing approach.

3. Compute the production-volume variance and show how it should appear in the income statement.

4. Differentiate among the three alternative cost bases of an absorption-costing system: actual, normal, and standard.

5. Explain why a company might prefer to use a variable-costing approach.

6. Identify the two methods for disposing of the standard cost variances at the end of a year and give the rationale for each.

7. **Understand how product-costing systems affect operating income.**

Recall the last time you shopped in one of the following stores—Wal-Mart, JCPenney, Kmart, Dillards, Best Buy, T.J. Maxx. Do you remember anything about the store fixtures? Chances are, the answer is "no." Store fixtures such as shelving, counters, garment racks, and displays are an important part of the merchandising programs of all leading discount, specialty, and department stores, but not many people are aware of them when shopping. One company that is an industry leader in store fixtures is L.A. Darling Company.

L.A. Darling Company works in partnership with major retailers such as Wal-Mart to design, manufacture, and install store fixtures. Darling traces its roots back to 1897, and today it employs about 2,500 people. It is a member of the Marmon Group, an international association of more than 100 manufacturing and service companies. Marmon's annual sales exceed $6.5 billion.

Recently, when a major retailer undertook an aggressive growth program, it selected Darling to meet its fixturing needs. According to Ray Watson, Controller, "One of the advantages Darling offers companies is its large production capacity." But while this gives the company a competitive advantage, accounting for capacity costs, most of which are fixed manufacturing overhead, is a real challenge. How should Darling account for these fixed overhead costs for product costing and income determination purposes? Should Darling consider these costs when evaluating a manager's performance? Watson explains that the absorption approach is required for external reporting but provides little value for measuring customer profitability. As a result, Darling uses the contribution approach, combined with activity-based costing, for decision making and performance evaluation purposes.

Many companies base the evaluation of managers at least partly on the income of the organizational segment they manage. Therefore, managers strive to make their performance look good by making decisions that increase income. But how should we measure income? Accountants make many judgments when measuring income, and one of the most important is choosing the appropriate method for calculating product costs. Some managers think product costing is a subject of interest only to accountants. However, when they realize that product costs affect their evaluations, they quickly begin to pay attention to the determination of product costs. Only by knowing what influences product costs will they be able to predict how their decisions will affect income and hence their evaluations.

In the preceding three chapters, we concentrated on how an accounting system accumulates costs by departments or activities and applies costs to the products or services that are produced by those departments or activities. This chapter focuses on two major variations of product costing: variable costing and absorption costing. Note that although we use a standard product-costing system here for illustrative purposes, these variations can be used in nonstandard product-costing systems too.

VARIABLE VERSUS ABSORPTION COSTING

ACCOUNTING FOR FIXED MANUFACTURING OVERHEAD

We compare two major methods of product costing in this chapter: variable costing (the contribution approach) and absorption costing (the functional, full-costing, or financial-reporting approach). These methods differ in only one respect: Fixed manufacturing overhead is excluded from the cost of products under variable costing but is included in the cost of products under absorption costing.

As Exhibit 15-1 shows, a variable-costing system treats fixed manufacturing overhead (fixed factory overhead) as a period cost to be immediately charged against sales—not as a product cost to be counted as inventory and charged against sales as cost of goods sold when the inventory is sold. Note that the only difference between variable and absorption costing is the accounting for fixed manufacturing overhead.[1]

Absorption costing is more widely used than variable costing. Why? Because neither the public accounting profession nor the U.S. IRS approves of variable costing for external-reporting or tax purposes. Therefore, all U.S. firms use absorption costing for their reports to shareholders and tax authorities.

However, the growing use of the contribution approach in performance measurement and cost analysis has led to increasing use of variable costing for internal-reporting purposes. Over half the major firms in the United States use variable costing for some internal reporting, and nearly a quarter use it as the primary internal format. For example, the Muncie, Indiana, plant of BorgWarner Corporation recently changed its product-line performance reporting from an absorption-costing approach to variable costing. Why? Because variable costing "links manufacturing performance more closely with measures of that performance by removing the impact of changing inventory levels from financial results."

Until the last decade or two, use of variable costing for internal reporting was expensive. It requires information to be processed two ways, one for external reporting and one

---

[1] *Variable costing is sometimes called direct costing. However, variable costing is a more descriptive term, so we will use it exclusively in this text.*

Exhibit 15-1

Comparison of Flow of Costs

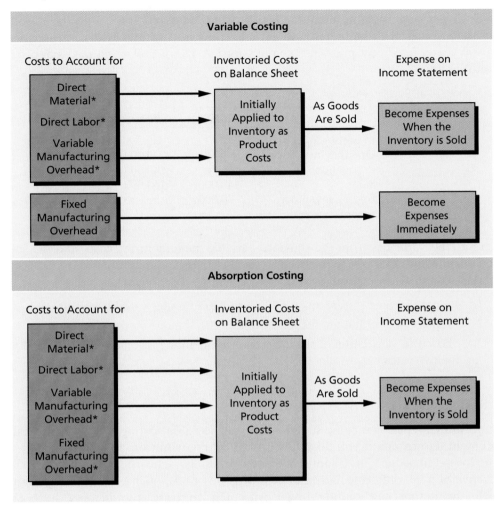

*As goods are manufactured, the costs are "applied" to inventory, usually via the use of unit costs.

for internal reporting. The increasing use and decreasing cost of computers has reduced the added cost of a variable-costing system. Most managers no longer face the question of whether to invest in a separate variable-costing system. Rather, they simply choose a variable-costing or absorption-costing format for reports. Many well-designed accounting systems used today can produce either format.

FACTS FOR ILLUSTRATION

To see exactly how these two product costing systems work, we will use the Greenberg Company as an illustration. The Greenberg Company makes a replacement part (a plastic ring) for large plastic injection molding machines. Each machine requires four new rings a year. In 20X0 and 20X1, the company had the following standard costs for production of rings.

Basic Production Data at Standard Cost	
Direct material	$1.30
Direct labor	1.50
Variable manufacturing overhead	.20
Standard variable costs per ring	$3.00

The annual budget for fixed manufacturing overhead (fixed factory overhead) is $150,000. Expected (or budgeted) production is 150,000 rings per year, and the sales price is $5 per ring. For simplicity, we will assume that the single cost driver for the $.20 per-ring variable-manufacturing overhead is rings produced.[2] Also, we will assume that both budgeted and actual selling and administrative expenses are $65,000 yearly fixed cost plus sales commissions at 5% of dollar sales. Actual product quantities are

	20X0	20X1
In units (rings)		
Opening inventory	—	30,000
Production	170,000	140,000
Sales	140,000	160,000
Ending inventory	30,000	10,000

There are no variances from the standard variable manufacturing costs, and the actual fixed manufacturing overhead incurred is exactly $150,000 each year.

Based on this information, we can

1. Prepare income statements for 20X0 and 20X1 under variable costing.
2. Prepare income statements for 20X0 and 20X1 under absorption costing.
3. Show a reconciliation of the difference in operating income for 20X0, 20X1, and the two years as a whole.

VARIABLE-COSTING METHOD

Objective 1
Construct an income statement using the variable-costing approach.

We begin by preparing income statements under variable costing. The variable-costing statement shown in Exhibit 15-2 has a familiar contribution-approach format, the same format introduced in Chapter 6. The only new characteristic of Exhibit 15-2 is the presence of a detailed calculation of cost of goods sold, which is affected by changes in the beginning and ending inventories. (In contrast, the income statements in earlier chapters assumed that there were no changes in the beginning and ending inventories.)

We account for the costs of the product by applying all variable manufacturing costs to the goods produced, at a rate of $3 per ring; thus we value inventories at standard variable costs. In contrast, we do not apply any fixed manufacturing costs to products but we regard them as expenses in the period they are incurred.

Before reading on, be sure to trace the facts from our Greenberg example to the presentation in Exhibit 15-2, step by step. Note that we deduct both variable cost of goods sold and variable selling and administrative expenses in computing the contribution margin. However, variable selling and administrative expenses are not inventoriable. They are affected only by the level of sales, not by changes in inventory.

Objective 2
Construct an income statement using the absorption-costing approach.

ABSORPTION-COSTING METHOD

Exhibit 15-3 shows the standard absorption-costing framework. As you can see, it differs from the variable-costing format in three ways.

---

[2] *Increasingly, companies are using activity analysis to identify relevant cost drivers for manufacturing overhead. The use of cost drivers other than units of production does not affect the basic principles illustrated in the examples that follow.*

Exhibit 15-2

Greenberg Company: Comparative Income Statements
Using Variable Costing
Years 20X0 and 20X1 (thousands of dollars)

		20X0		20X1	
Sales, 140,000 and 160,000 rings, respectively	(1)		$700		$800
Variable expenses:					
Variable manufacturing cost of goods sold					
Opening inventory, at standard variable					
costs of $3		$ —		$ 90	
Add: variable cost of goods manufactured					
at standard, 170,000 and 140,000 rings,					
respectively		510		420	
Available for sale, 170,000 rings					
in each year		$510		$510	
Deduct: ending inventory, at standard					
variable cost of $3		90*		30†	
Variable manufacturing cost of goods sold		$420		$480	
Variable selling expenses, at 5% of dollar sales		35		40	
Total variable expenses	(2)		455		520
Contribution margin	(3) = (1) − (2)		$245		$280
Fixed expenses:					
Fixed factory overhead		$150		$150	
Fixed selling and administrative expenses		65		65	
Total fixed expenses	(4)		215		215
Operating income, variable costing	(3) − (4)		$ 30		$ 65

* 30,000 rings × $3 = $90,000.
† 10,000 rings × $3 = $30,000.

First, the unit product cost used for computing cost of goods sold is $4, not $3. Why? Because fixed manufacturing overhead of $1 is added to the $3 variable manufacturing cost. The $1 of fixed manufacturing overhead applied to each unit is the **fixed-overhead rate.** We determine this rate by dividing the budgeted fixed overhead by the expected cost-driver activity, in this case expected volume of production, for the budget period:

$$\text{fixed-overhead rate} = \frac{\text{budgeted fixed manufacturing overhead}}{\text{expected volume of production}} = \frac{\$150,000}{150,000 \text{ units}} = \$1$$

Second, fixed factory overhead does not appear as a separate line in an absorption-costing income statement. Instead, the fixed factory overhead appears in two places: as part of the cost of goods sold and as a production-volume variance.[3] A **production-volume variance** (which we explain further in the next section of this chapter) appears whenever actual production deviates from the expected volume of production used in computing the fixed overhead rate:

$$\text{production-volume variance} = (\text{actual volume} - \text{expected volume}) \times \text{fixed-overhead rate}$$

fixed-overhead rate
The amount of fixed manufacturing overhead applied to each unit of production. It is determined by dividing the budgeted fixed overhead by the expected volume of production for the budget period.

production-volume variance A variance that appears whenever actual production deviates from the expected volume of production used in computing the fixed overhead rate. It is calculated as (actual volume − expected volume) × fixed-overhead rate.

---

[3] *In general, this will be a cost-driver activity variance. In our example, production volume is the only cost driver, so it can be called a production-volume variance.*

Exhibit 15-3

Greenberg Company: Comparative Income Statements Using Absorption Costing

Years 20X0 and 20X1 (thousands of dollars)

	20X0		20X1	
Sales		$700		$800
Cost of goods sold:				
Opening inventory, at standard absorption cost of $4*	$ —		$120	
Cost of goods manufactured at standard of $4	680		560	
Available for sale	680		680	
Deduct: ending inventory at standard absorption cost of $4	120		40	
Cost of goods sold, at standard		560		640
Gross profit at standard		140		160
Production-volume variance†		20 F		10 U
Gross margin or gross profit, at "actual"		160		150
Selling and administrative expenses		100		105
Operating income		$ 60		$ 45

* Variable cost	$3
Fixed cost ($150,000 ÷ 150,000)	1
Standard absorption cost	$4

† Computation of production-volume variance based on expected volume of production of 150,000 rings:

	20X0	$20,000 F	(170,000 − 150,000) × $1
	20X1	10,000 U	(140,000 − 150,000) × $1
Two years together		$10,000 F	(310,000 − 300,000) × $1

U = Unfavorable. F = Favorable.

Finally, the format for an absorption-costing income statement separates costs into the major categories of manufacturing and nonmanufacturing. In contrast, a variable-costing income statement separates costs into the major categories of fixed and variable. In an absorption-costing statement, revenue less manufacturing cost (both fixed and variable) is gross profit or gross margin. In a variable-costing statement, revenue less all variable costs (both manufacturing and nonmanufacturing) is the contribution margin. This difference is illustrated by a condensed comparison of 20X1 income statements (in thousands of dollars):

Variable Costing		**Absorption Costing**	
Revenue	$800	Revenue	$800
All variable costs	520	All manufacturing costs*	650
Contribution margin	280	Gross margin	150
All fixed costs	215	All nonmanufacturing costs	105
Operating income	$ 65	Operating income	$ 45

* Standard absorption cost of goods sold plus production-volume variance.

Despite the importance of such differences in most industries, more and more firms are not concerned with the choice between variable and absorption costing.

Why? Because they have implemented just-in-time (JIT) production methods (see Chapter 1) and sharply reduced inventory levels. There is no difference between variable-costing and absorption-costing income if the inventory level does not change, and companies with little inventory generally experience only insignificant *changes* in inventory.

BUSINESS FIRST
Variable Costing at Nortel Networks

Nortel Networks is a $21-billion Canada-based "global leader in telephone, data, wireless, and wireline solutions for the Internet." In the 1990s, while still known as Northern Telecom, Nortel gradually came to understand that its standard absorption costing income statement did not provide the information that managers needed. The company also realized that the problem was one of format more than of substance. The information needed for a more meaningful income statement was in the accounting system, but the traditional reported income statement did not present the information in the most useful way. Therefore, Nortel's accountants adopted a "variable costing" approach to the income statement.

Statutory and regulatory reporting requirements did not allow Northern Telecom to completely abandon absorption costing. The company's solution left the top line—revenue—and the bottom line—earnings before tax—unchanged. But everything in between was reported differently, in the following format:

Revenue
  Product cost
Product margin
  Manufacturing/operational costs
  Inventory provisions
  New product introduction
  Selling and marketing
Direct margin
  Administrative cost
  Other operating (income) expense
Operating profit
  Corporate assessments
  Other nonoperating (income) expense
Earnings before balance sheet adjustments
  Balance sheet adjustment
Earnings before tax

This format represents an extreme application of variable costing. Only direct-materials costs are considered product costs. All other costs, including direct labor and variable overhead, are period costs that are charged to expense when incurred, not added to inventory. For example, direct labor is part of manufacturing costs. The amount charged in any period is the amount actually incurred that period, regardless of whether the labor is related to goods sold or those still in inventory. Four measures of "profit" are used by managers: product margin (to measure the value added), direct margin (to measure results of product production and sales), operating profit (to measure total results of operations), and earnings before balance sheet adjustments (to measure effect on companywide profits).

The main difference between the old absorption-costing system and the new system is that the new system expenses all costs except material costs, while the old system capitalized a portion of them. Reconciling the two systems was an accounting problem, unrelated to operating the business. Therefore, a final line was added to the income statement to provide a reconciliation—balance sheet adjustment. This represents the difference between the absorption and variable costing statements, as needed for statutory and regulatory reporting, but it can be ignored by managers.

Nortel's efforts illustrate two important points. First, it is possible to adapt accounting methods to meet the specific needs of managers. Second, companies often do not have to choose between absorption and variable costing—either format can be produced by the same basic accounting system.

Source: From P. Sharman, "Time to Re-examine the P&L," *CMA Magazine*, September 1991, pp. 22–25, and Nortel Networks 1999 *Annual Report* (http://www.nortelnetworks.com/corporate/investor/reports/index.html).

Don't confuse *gross margin* and *contribution margin*. List the ways in which these two margins differ.
ANSWER

Among the differences are the following:

- Gross margin appears in an absorption-costing income statement; contribution margin is in a variable-costing income statement.

- Gross margin is revenue less manufacturing cost; contribution margin is revenue less all variable costs.

- Gross margin is based on a categorization of costs by function; contribution margin divides costs by cost behavior.

- Gross margin is required for financial reporting; contribution margin is most useful for short-term management decisions.

FIXED OVERHEAD AND ABSORPTION COSTS OF PRODUCT

All three differences between variable- and absorption-costing formats arise solely because the two formats treat fixed manufacturing overhead differently. In this and subsequent sections, we explore how to account for factory overhead in an absorption-costing system.

VARIABLE AND FIXED UNIT COSTS

Continuing our example of the Greenberg Company, we begin by comparing (1) the manufacturing overhead costs in the flexible budget used for departmental budgeting and control purposes with (2) the manufacturing overhead costs applied to products under an absorption-costing system. To stress the basic assumptions behind absorption costing, we will also split manufacturing overhead into variable and fixed components. (Most real absorption-costing systems do not make such a split.)

Consider the following graphs of variable-overhead costs:

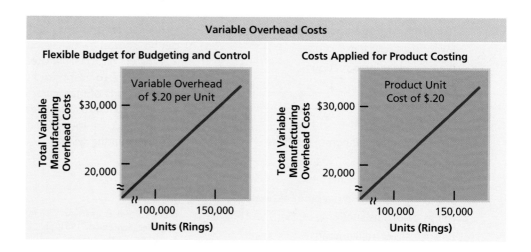

Note that the two graphs are identical. The expected variable-overhead costs from the flexible budget are the same as the variable-overhead costs applied to the products. Both budgeted and applied variable overhead are $.20 per ring. Each time we produce

1,000 additional rings, we expect to incur an additional $200 of variable overhead, and we add $200 of variable-overhead cost to the inventory account for rings. The variable costs used for budgeting and control are the same as those used for product costing.

In contrast, the graph for applied fixed-overhead costs differs from that for the flexible budget:

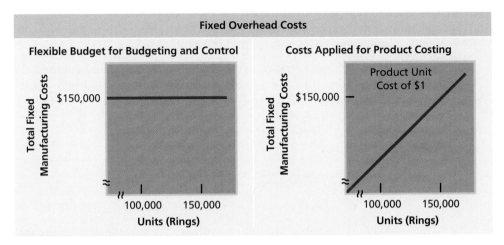

Note: These graphs are not to the same scale as the preceding graphs.

The flexible budget for fixed overhead is a lump-sum budgeted amount of $150,000. It is unaffected by volume. In contrast, the applied fixed cost depends on actual volume.

$$\text{Fixed cost applied} = \text{actual volume} \times \text{fixed-overhead rate}$$

$$= \text{units produced} \times \$1$$

Suppose actual volume equals the expected volume of 150,000 rings. Applied fixed overhead would be 150,000 rings × $1 per ring = $150,000, the same as the flexible-budget amount. However, whenever actual volume differs from expected volume, the costs used for budgeting and control differ from those used for product costing. For budgeting and control purposes, managers use the actual cost behavior pattern for fixed costs. In contrast, as the graphs indicate, the absorption product-costing approach treats these fixed costs as though they had a variable-cost behavior pattern. The difference between applied and budgeted fixed overhead is the production-volume variance.

NATURE OF PRODUCTION-VOLUME VARIANCE

We calculate the production-volume variance as follows:

$$\text{production-volume variance} = \text{applied fixed overhead} - \text{budgeted fixed overhead}$$

$$= (\text{actual volume} \times \text{fixed-overhead rate})$$
$$- (\text{expected volume} \times \text{fixed-overhead rate})$$

or

$$\text{production-volume variance} = (\text{actual volume} - \text{expected volume})$$
$$\times \text{fixed-overhead rate}$$

In practice, the production-volume variance is usually called simply the **volume variance.** We use the term *production-volume variance* because it is a more precise description of the fundamental nature of the variance.

Objective 3
Compute the production-volume variance and show how it should appear in the income statement.

volume variance A common name for production-volume variance.

A production-volume variance arises when the actual production volume achieved does not coincide with the expected volume of production used as a denominator for computing the fixed-overhead rate for product-costing purposes:

1. When expected production volume and actual production volume are identical, there is no production-volume variance.

2. When actual volume is less than expected volume, the production-volume variance is unfavorable because usage of facilities is less than expected and fixed overhead is underapplied. It is measured in Exhibit 15-3 for 20X1 as follows:

$$\text{production volume variance} = (\text{actual volume} - \text{expected volume}) \times \text{budgeted fixed-overhead rate}$$

$$= (140{,}000 \text{ units} - 150{,}000 \text{ units}) \times \$1$$

$$= -\$10{,}000 \text{ or } \$10{,}000 \text{ U}$$

or

$$\text{production-volume variance} = \text{budget minus applied}$$

$$= \$150{,}000 - \$140{,}000 = \$10{,}000 \text{ U}$$

The $10,000 unfavorable production-volume variance increases the manufacturing costs shown on the income statement. Why? Recall that $150,000 of fixed manufacturing cost was incurred, but only $140,000 was applied to inventory. Therefore only $140,000 will be charged as expense when the inventory is sold. But the actual cost of $150,000 must be charged to expense sometime, so the extra $10,000 is an added expense in the current income statement.

3. When actual volume exceeds expected volume, as was the case in 20X0, the production-volume variance is favorable because use of facilities is better than expected, and fixed overhead is overapplied.

$$\text{production-volume variance} = (170{,}000 \text{ units} - 150{,}000 \text{ units}) \times \$1 = \$20{,}000 \text{ F}$$

In this case, $170,000 will be charged through inventory. Because Greenberg incurs actual costs of only $150,000, future expenses will be overstated by $20,000. Therefore, we reduce current period expenses by the $20,000 favorable variance.

The production-volume variance is the conventional measure of the cost of departing from the level of activity originally used to set the fixed-overhead rate.[4] Most companies consider production-volume variances to be beyond immediate control, although sometimes a manager responsible for volume has to do some explaining or investigating. Sometimes, failure to reach the expected volume is caused by idleness because of disappointing total sales, poor production scheduling, unusual machine breakdowns, shortages of skilled workers, strikes, storms, and the like.

There is no production-volume variance for variable overhead. The concept of production-volume variance arises for fixed overhead because of the conflict between accounting for control (by flexible budgets) and accounting for product costing (by application rates). Note again that the fixed-overhead budget serves the control purpose, whereas the development of a product-costing rate results in the treatment of fixed overhead as if it were a variable cost.

Above all, remember that fixed costs are simply not divisible as variable costs are. Rather, they come in big chunks and are related to the provision of big chunks of production or sales capability, not to the production or sale of a single unit of product.

---

[4] *Do not confuse the production-volume variance described here with the sales-volume variance described in Chapter 8. Despite similar nomenclature, they are completely different concepts.*

Some accountants claim that the production-volume variance is a good measure of how well a company uses its capacity: Favorable (unfavorable) variances imply effective (ineffective) use of capacity. Do not fall into that trap. Why?

ANSWER

The production volume variance tells you one thing and only one thing—whether actual production was above or below the predicted volume used in setting the fixed overhead rate. If a manager can avoid an unfavorable production-volume variance by lowering the price enough to use up the idle capacity but the result is a decline in contribution margin (i.e., the new price is less than the variable cost), this would not be an effective use of the capacity. If a favorable production-volume variance occurs because excess production is being forced through despite quality declines or other inefficiencies caused by overburdened production facilities, the "favorable" variance is certainly not desirable.

SELECTION OF EXPECTED ACTIVITY LEVEL FOR COMPUTING THE FIXED-OVERHEAD RATE

The fixed-overhead rate in an absorption-costing framework depends on the expected activity level chosen as the denominator in the computation. The higher the level of activity, the lower the rate.

The selection of an appropriate activity level for the denominator is a matter of judgment. Management usually wants to apply a single representative standard fixed cost for a unit of product over a period of at least one year, despite month-to-month changes in activity level. Therefore, the predicted total fixed cost and the expected activity level used in calculating the fixed-overhead rate should cover at least a one-year period. Most managers favor using the budgeted annual activity level as the expected activity level in the denominator. Others favor using some longer-run (three- to five-years) approximation of "normal" activity. Still others favor using maximum or full capacity (often called **practical capacity**).

Although fixed-overhead rates are often important for product costing and long-run pricing, such rates have limited significance for control purposes. At the lower levels of management activity, almost no fixed costs are under direct control. Even at higher levels of management activity, many fixed costs are uncontrollable in the short run, within wide ranges of anticipated activity.

ACTUAL, NORMAL, AND STANDARD COSTING

Overhead variances are not restricted to standard-costing systems. Many companies trace actual direct materials and actual direct-labor costs to products or services but use budgeted rates for applying overhead. We call such a procedure **normal costing.** The following chart compares normal costing with two other basic ways for applying costs by the absorption-costing method.

practical capacity
Maximum or full capacity.

Objective 4
Differentiate among the three alternative cost bases of an absorption-costing system: actual, normal, and standard.

normal costing A costing system that traces actual direct materials and actual direct-labor costs to products or services but uses budgeted rates for applying overhead.

	Actual Costing	Normal Costing	Standard Costing
Direct materials	Actual costs	Actual costs	Standard prices or rates × standard inputs allowed for actual output achieved
Direct labor	Actual costs	Actual costs	
Variable factory overhead	Actual costs	Budgeted rates × actual inputs	
Fixed factory overhead			

Dropping fixed factory overhead from this chart produces a comparison of the same three basic ways of applying costs by the variable-costing method.

Both normal absorption costing and standard absorption costing generate production-volume variances. In addition, normal- and standard-costing systems produce all other overhead variances under both variable and absorption formats.

RECONCILIATION OF VARIABLE COSTING AND ABSORPTION COSTING

We can easily reconcile the operating incomes shown in Exhibits 15-2 and 15-3. The difference in income equals the difference in the total amount of fixed manufacturing overhead charged as an expense during a given year. (See Exhibit 15-4.) The $150,000 fixed manufacturing overhead incurred in 20X1 is automatically the amount recognized as an expense on a variable-costing income statement. Under absorption costing, fixed manufacturing overhead appears in two places: cost of goods sold and production-volume variance.

Exhibit 15-4

Flow of Fixed Manufacturing Overhead Costs during 20X1

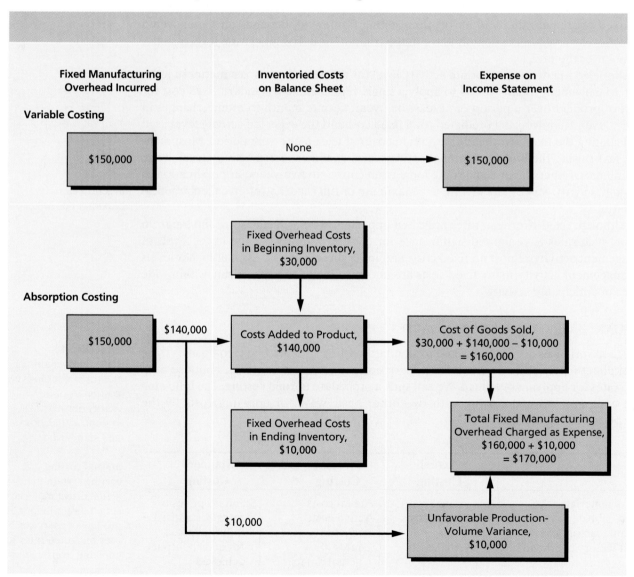

Under absorption costing, $30,000 of the fixed costs were incurred before 20X1 and held over in the beginning inventory. During 20X1, $140,000 of fixed manufacturing overhead was added to inventory, and $10,000 was still lodged in the ending inventory of 20X1. Thus, the fixed manufacturing overhead included in cost of goods sold for 20X1 was $30,000 + $140,000 − $10,000 = $160,000. In addition, the production-volume variance is $10,000, unfavorable. The total fixed manufacturing overhead charged as 20X1 expenses under absorption costing is $170,000, or $20,000 more than the $150,000 charged under variable costing. Therefore, 20X1 variable-costing income is higher by $20,000.

We can quickly explain the difference in variable-costing and absorption-costing operating income by multiplying the fixed-overhead product-costing rate by the change in the total units in the beginning and ending inventories. Consider 20X1: The change in inventory was 20,000 units, so the difference in net income would be 20,000 units × $1.00 = $20,000.

Remember that it is the relationship between sales and production that determines the difference between variable-costing and absorption-costing income. Whenever sales exceed production, that is, when inventory decreases, variable-costing income is greater than absorption-costing income.

In a just-in-time inventory and production system, the inventories are minimal so sales and production are almost equal. This means that the difference between variable and absorption income in JIT systems is not significant.

WHY USE VARIABLE COSTING?

Why do many companies use variable costing for internal statements? One reason is that production volume affects absorption-costing income but has no effect on variable-costing income. Consider the 20X1 absorption-costing statement in Exhibit 15-3, which shows operating income of $45,000. Suppose a manager decides to produce 10,000 additional units in December 20X1 even though they will remain unsold. Will this affect operating income? First, note that the gross profit will not change. Why? Because it is based on sales, not production. However, the production-volume variance will change:

Objective 5
Explain why a company might prefer to use a variable-costing approach.

If production = 140,000 units

Production-volume variance = (150,000 − 140,000) × $1 = $10,000 U

If production = 150,000 units

Production-volume variance = (150,000 − 150,000) × $1 = 0

Because there is no production-volume variance when 150,000 units are produced, the new operating income equals gross profit less selling and administrative expenses, $160,000 − $105,000 = $55,000. Therefore, increasing production by 10,000 units without any increase in sales increases absorption-costing operating income by $10,000, from $45,000 to $55,000.

How will such an increase in production affect the variable-costing statement in Exhibit 15-2? Nothing will change. Production does not affect operating income under variable costing.

Suppose the evaluation of a manager's performance is heavily based on operating income. If the company uses the absorption-costing approach, a manager might be tempted to produce unneeded units just to increase reported operating income. No such temptation exists with variable costing.

Companies also choose variable or absorption costing based on which system they believe gives a better signal about performance. A sales-oriented company may prefer variable costing because its income is affected primarily by the level of sales. In contrast, a production-oriented company, for example, a company that can easily sell all the units it produces, might prefer absorption costing. Why? Because additional production increases the operating income with absorption costing but not with variable costing.

EFFECT OF OTHER VARIANCES

So far, our example has deliberately ignored the possibility of any variance except the production-volume variance, which appears only on an absorption-costing statement. All other variances appear on both variable- and absorption-costing income statements. In this section, we will consider other variances that were explained in Chapter 8.

FLEXIBLE-BUDGET VARIANCES

Returning again to the Greenberg Company, we will assume some additional facts for 20X1 (the second of the two years covered by our example):

Flexible-budget variances	
Direct material	None
Direct labor	$ 34,000 U
Variable factory overhead	$ 3,000 U
Fixed factory overhead	$ 7,000 U
Supporting data (used to compute the above variances as shown in Appendix 15):	
Standard direct-labor-hours allowed for 140,000 units of output produced	35,000
Standard direct-labor rate per hour	$6.00
Actual direct-labor-hours of inputs	40,000
Actual direct-labor rate per hour	$6.10
Variable manufacturing overhead actually incurred	$ 31,000
Fixed manufacturing overhead actually incurred	$157,000

As Chapter 8 explained, flexible-budget variances may arise for both variable overhead and fixed overhead. Consider the following:

	Actual Amounts	Flexible-Budget Amounts @ 140,000 Units	Flexible-Budget Variances
Variable factory overhead	$ 31,000	$ 28,000	$3,000 U
Fixed factory overhead	157,000	150,000	7,000 U

Exhibit 15-5 shows the relationship between the fixed-overhead flexible-budget variance and the production-volume variance. The difference between the actual fixed overhead and that applied to products is the underapplied (or overapplied) overhead. Because the actual fixed overhead of $157,000 exceeds the $140,000 applied, fixed overhead is underapplied by $17,000, which means that the variance is unfavorable. The $17,000 underapplied fixed overhead has two components: (1) a production-volume variance of $10,000 U and (2) a fixed-overhead flexible-budget variance (also called the fixed-overhead spending variance or simply the fixed-overhead budget variance) of $7,000 U.

All variances other than the production-volume variance are essentially flexible-budget variances. They measure components of the differences between actual amounts and the flexible-budget amounts for the output achieved. Flexible budgets are primarily designed to assist planning and control rather than product costing. The production-volume variance is not a flexible-budget variance. It is designed to aid product costing.

Exhibit 15-6 contains the income statement under absorption costing that incorporates these new facts. These new variances hurt income by $44,000 because, like the production-volume variance, they are all unfavorable variances that are charged against income in 20X1. When cost variances are favorable, they increase operating income.

Exhibit 15-5

Fixed-Overhead Variances for 20X1 (data are from Exhibit 15-3)

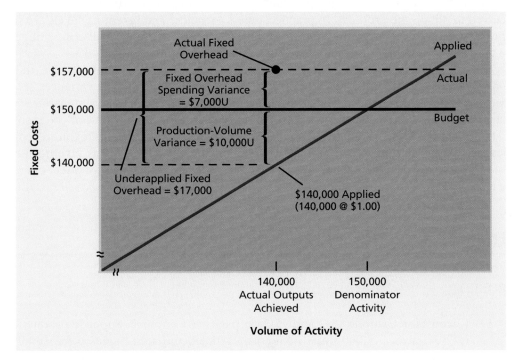

DISPOSITION OF STANDARD-COST VARIANCES

Advocates of standard costing contend that variances are generally subject to current control, especially when the standards are viewed as being currently attainable. Therefore, they believe that variances are not inventoriable and should be considered as adjustments to the income of the period instead of being added to inventories. In this way, inventory valuations will be more representative of desirable and attainable costs.

Objective 6
Identify the two methods for disposing of the standard cost variances at the end of a year and give the rationale for each.

Exhibit 15-6

Absorption Costing Modification of Exhibit 15-3 for 20X1
(additional facts are in text)

		(in thousands)
Sales, 160,000 at $5		$800
Opening inventory at standard, 30,000 at $4	$120	
Cost of goods manufactured at standard, 140,000 at $4	560	
Available for sale, 170,000 at $4	$680	
Deduct ending inventory at standard, 10,000 at $4	40	
Cost of goods sold at standard, 160,000 at $4		640
Gross profit at standard		$160
Flexible-budget variances, both unfavorable		
Variable manufacturing costs ($34,000 + $3,000)	$37	
Fixed factory overhead	7	
Production-volume variance (arises only because of		
fixed overhead), unfavorable	10	
Total variances		54
Gross profit at "actual"		$106
Selling and administrative expenses		105
Operating income		$ 1

prorating the variances
Assigning the variances to the inventories and cost of goods sold related to the production during the period the variances arose.

Others favor assigning the variances to the inventories and cost of goods sold related to the production during the period the variances arose. This is often called **prorating the variances.** Prorating makes inventory valuations more representative of the "actual" costs incurred to obtain the products. In practice, unless variances and inventory levels are significant, the variances are usually not prorated. Therefore, in practice, all cost variances are typically regarded as adjustments to current income.

Where variances appear on the income statement is generally unimportant. Exhibit 15-6 shows variances as a component of gross profit at "actual." But the variances could appear instead as a completely separate section elsewhere in the income statement. Such placement would help to distinguish between product costing (i.e., the cost of goods sold, at standard) and loss recognition (unfavorable variances are "lost" or "expired" costs because they represent waste and inefficiency thereby not qualifying as inventoriable costs; that is, waste is not an asset). The placement of the variance does not affect operating income.

SUMMARY PROBLEM FOR YOUR REVIEW

PROBLEM

1. Reconsider Exhibits 15-2 and 15-3 on pages 601 and 602. Suppose production in 20X1 was 145,000 units instead of 140,000 units, but sales were 160,000 units. Assume that the net variances for all variable manufacturing costs were $37,000, unfavorable. Regard these variances as adjustments to the standard cost of goods sold. Also assume that actual fixed costs were $157,000. Prepare income statements for 20X1 under variable costing and under absorption costing.

2. Explain why operating income was different under variable costing from what it was under absorption costing. Show your calculations.

3. Without regard to requirement 1, would variable costing or absorption costing give a manager more leeway in influencing short-run operating income through production-scheduling decisions? Why?

SOLUTION

1. See Exhibits 15-7 and 15-8. Note that the ending inventory will be 15,000 units instead of 10,000 units.

2. Decline in inventory levels is 30,000 − 15,000, or 15,000 units. The fixed-overhead rate per unit in absorption costing is $1. Therefore $15,000 more fixed overhead was charged against operations under absorption costing than under variable costing. The variable-costing statement shows fixed factory overhead of $157,000, whereas the absorption-costing statement includes fixed factory overhead in three places: $160,000 in cost of goods sold, $7,000 U in fixed factory overhead flexible-budget variance, and $5,000 U as a production-volume variance, for a total of $172,000. Generally, when inventories decline, absorption costing will show less income than will variable costing; when inventories rise, absorption costing will show more income than variable costing.

3. Absorption costing will give a manager more leeway in influencing operating income via production scheduling. Operating income will fluctuate in harmony with changes in net sales under variable costing, but it is influenced by both production and sales under absorption costing. For example, compare the

Exhibit 15-7

Greenberg Company

Income Statement (variable costing), Year 20X1 (thousands of dollars)

Sales			$800
Opening inventory, at variable standard cost of $3	$ 90		
Add: variable cost of goods manufactured	435		
Available for sale	$525		
Deduct: ending inventory, at variable standard cost of $3	45		
Variable cost of goods sold, at standard		$480	
Net flexible-budget variances for all variable costs, unfavorable		37	
Variable cost of goods sold, at actual		$517	
Variable selling expenses, at 5% of dollar sales		40	
Total variable costs charged against sales			557
Contribution margin			$243
Fixed factory overhead		$157*	
Fixed selling and administrative expenses		65	
Total fixed expenses			222
Operating income			$ 21†

* This could be shown in two lines, $150,000 budget plus $7,000 variance.
† The difference between this and the $65,000 operating income in Exhibit 15-2 occurs because of the $37,000 unfavorable variable-cost variances and the $7,000 unfavorable fixed-cost flexible-budget variance.

Exhibit 15-8

Greenberg Company

Income Statement (absorption costing), Year 20X1 (thousands of dollars)

Sales			$800
Opening inventory, at standard cost of $4		$120	
Cost of goods manufactured, at standard		580	
Available for sale		$700	
Deduct: ending inventory, at standard		60	
Cost of goods sold, at standard		$640	
Net flexible-budget variances for all variable manufacturing costs, unfavorable	$37		
Fixed factory overhead flexible-budget variance, unfavorable	7		
Production-volume variance, unfavorable	5*		
Total variances		49	
Cost of goods sold, at actual			689†
Gross profit, at "actual"			$111
Selling and administrative expenses			
Variable		40	
Fixed		65	105
Operating income			$ 6‡

* Production-volume variance is $1 × (150,000 expected volume − 145,000 actual production).
† This format differs slightly from Exhibit 15-6. The difference is deliberate; it illustrates that the formats of income statements are not rigid.
‡ Compare this result with the $1,000 operating income in Exhibit 15-6. The only difference is traceable to the production of 145,000 units instead of 140,000 units, resulting in an unfavorable production-volume variance of $5,000 instead of $10,000.

variable costing in Exhibits 15-2 and 15-7. As the second note to Exhibit 15-7 indicates, the operating income may be affected by assorted variances (but not the production-volume variance) under variable costing, but production scheduling per se will have no effect on operating income.

On the other hand, compare the operating income of Exhibits 15-6 and 15-8. As the third note to Exhibit 15-8 explains, production scheduling as well as sales influence operating income. Production was 145,000 rather than 140,000 units. So $5,000 of fixed overhead became a part of ending inventory (an asset) instead of part of the production-volume variance (an expense)—that is, the production-volume variance is $5,000 lower and the ending inventory contains $5,000 more fixed overhead in Exhibit 15-8 than in Exhibit 15-6. The manager adds $1 to 20X1 operating income with each unit of production under absorption costing, even if the unit is not sold.

Highlights to Remember

Construct an income statement using the variable-costing approach. Two major methods of product costing are variable (contribution approach) and absorption costing. The variable-costing method emphasizes the effects of cost behavior on income. This method excludes fixed manufacturing overhead from the cost of products and expenses it immediately.

Construct an income statement using the absorption-costing approach. The absorption or traditional approach ignores cost behavior distinctions. As a result, all costs incurred in the production of goods are inventoried. Thus, we add fixed manufacturing overhead to inventory and it appears on the income statement only when the goods are sold.

Compute the production-volume variance and show how it should appear in the income statement. Whenever the absorption method is used and the actual production volume does not equal the expected (budgeted) volume that is used for computing the fixed-overhead rate, a production volume variance arises. When the actual volume is less than budgeted, the variance is unfavorable and the amount is equal to the fixed-overhead rate times the difference between the budgeted and actual volume. The opposite is true when actual production volume exceeds budgeted production volume; that is, a favorable volume variance arises. Both types of variances are usually adjustments to the current period income. Favorable variances increase current-period income and unfavorable variances reduce current-period income.

Differentiate among the three alternative cost bases of an absorption-costing system: actual, normal, and standard. Absorption costing accumulates product costs using a variety of systems. Actual costing is based on actual costs for direct materials, direct labor, and factory overhead. Normal costing is based on actual costs for direct materials and direct labor but budgeted rates for applying factory overhead. Standard costing uses budgeted prices or rates times standard inputs for actual output of production. Both normal- and standard-costing systems will generate production-volume variances.

Explain why a company might prefer to use a variable-costing approach. Companies that use operating income to measure results usually prefer variable costing. This is because changes in production volume affect absorption-costing income but not variable-costing income. A company that wants to focus managers' energies on sales would prefer to use variable costing, since the level of sales is the primary driver of variable-costing income.

Identify the two methods for disposing of the standard cost variances at the end of a year and give the rationale for each. There are two main ways to account for variances arising in a standard costing system. They may be prorated to cost of goods sold and ending

Exhibit 15-9

Comparative Income Effects

	Variable Costing	Absorption Costing	Comments
1. Fixed factory overhead inventoried?	No	Yes	Basic theoretical question of when a cost should become an expense.
2. Production-volume variance?	No	Yes	Choice of expected volume of production affects measurement of operating income under absorption costing.
3. Treatment of other variances?	Same	Same	Underscores the fact that the basic difference is the accounting for fixed factory overhead, not the accounting for variable factory overhead.
4. Classifications between variable and fixed costs are routinely made?	Yes	No	However, absorption cost can be modified to obtain subclassifications of variable and fixed costs, if desired.
5. Usual effects of changes in inventory levels on operating income			Differences are attributable to timing of the transformation of fixed factory overhead into expense.
Production = sales	Equal	Equal	
Production > sales	Lower*	Higher†	
Production < sales	Higher	Lower	
6. Cost-volume-profit relationships	Tied to sales	Tied to production and sales	Management control benefit: Effects of changes in volume on operating income are easier to understand under variable costing.

* That is, lower than absorption costing.

† That is, higher than variable costing.

inventories. This adjusts inventories and cost of goods sold to actual costs. Usually, however, companies do not prorate variances. Instead, they treat variances as an adjustment to current income.

Understand how product-costing systems affect operating income.　Managers' performance measures and rewards are most often based on operating income. As a result, managers are motivated to take actions that improve current operating income. Each of the topics covered in this chapter has an effect on income. Absorption- and variable-costing systems report different operating incomes because of their treatment of fixed factory overhead. Absorption-costing systems, both normal and standard, generate production-volume variances that also affect income. Exhibit 15-9 compares variable- and absorption-costing effects.

Appendix 15: Comparisons of Production-Volume Variance with Other Variances

The only new variance introduced in this chapter is the production-volume variance, which arises because fixed-overhead accounting must serve two masters: the control-budget purpose and the product-costing purpose. Let's examine this variance in perspective by using the approach originally demonstrated in Exhibit 8-9. The results of the approach appear in Exhibit 15-10, which deserves your careful study, particularly the two footnotes. Please ponder the exhibit before reading on.

Exhibit 15-10

Analysis of Variances
(Data Are from Text for 20X1)

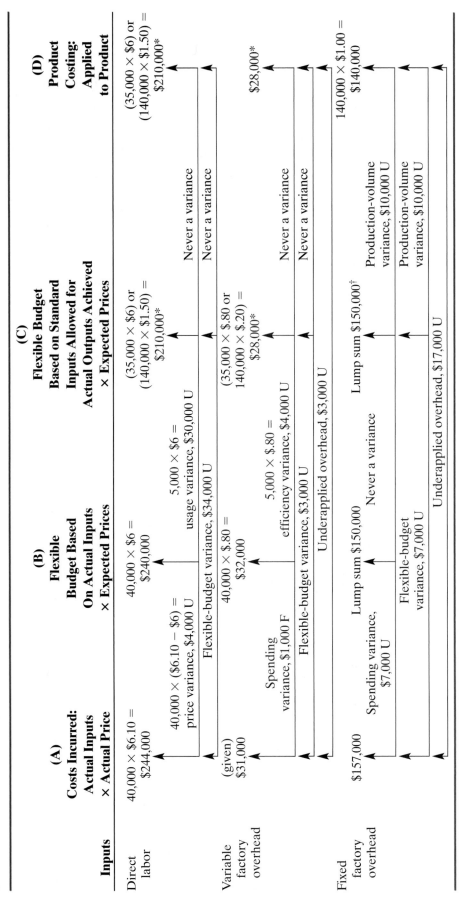

Inputs	(A) Costs Incurred: Actual Inputs × Actual Price	(B) Flexible Budget Based On Actual Inputs × Expected Prices	(C) Flexible Budget Based on Standard Inputs Allowed for Actual Outputs Achieved × Expected Prices	(D) Product Costing: Applied to Product
Direct labor	40,000 × $6.10 = $244,000	40,000 × $6 = $240,000	(35,000 × $6) or (140,000 × $1.50) = $210,000*	(35,000 × $6) or (140,000 × $1.50) = $210,000*
		40,000 × ($6.10 − $6) = price variance, $4,000 U	5,000 × $6 = usage variance, $30,000 U	Never a variance
		Flexible-budget variance, $34,000 U		Never a variance
Variable factory overhead	(given) $31,000	40,000 × $.80 = $32,000	(35,000 × $.80 or 140,000 × $.20) = $28,000*	$28,000*
		Spending variance, $1,000 F	5,000 × $.80 = efficiency variance, $4,000 U	Never a variance
		Flexible-budget variance, $3,000 U		Never a variance
		Underapplied overhead, $3,000 U		
Fixed factory overhead	$157,000	Lump sum $150,000	Lump sum $150,000†	140,000 × $1.00 = $140,000
		Spending variance, $7,000 U	Never a variance	Production-volume variance, $10,000 U
		Flexible-budget variance, $7,000 U		Production-volume variance, $10,000 U
		Underapplied overhead, $17,000 U		

U = Unfavorable. F = Favorable.

* Note especially that the flexible budget for variable costs rises and falls in direct proportion to production. Note also that the control-budget purpose and the product-costing purpose harmonize completely. The total costs in the flexible budget will always agree with the standard variable costs applied to the product because they are based on standard costs per unit multiplied by units produced.

† In contrast with variable costs, the flexible-budget total for fixed costs will always be the same regardless of the units produced. However, the control-budget purpose and the product-costing purpose conflict; whenever actual production differs from expected production, the standard costs applied to the product will differ from the flexible budget. This difference is the production-volume variance. In this case, the production-volume variance may be computed by multiplying the $1 rate times the difference between the 150,000 expected volume and the 140,000 units of output achieved.

Exhibit 15-11

Comparison of Control and Product-Costing Purposes, Variable Overhead, and Fixed Overhead (not to scale)

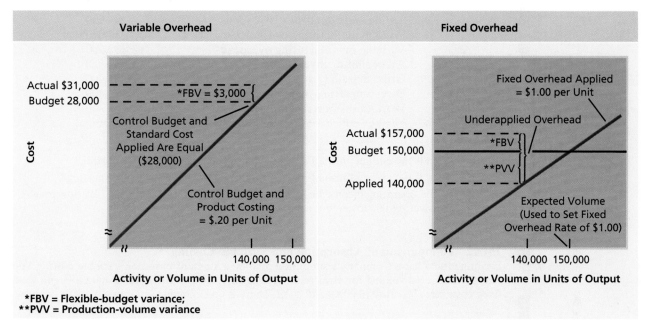

*FBV = Flexible-budget variance;
**PVV = Production-volume variance

Exhibit 15-11 graphically compares the variable- and fixed-overhead costs analyzed in Exhibit 15-10. Note how the control-budget line and the product-costing line (the applied line) are superimposed in the graph for variable overhead but differ in the graph for fixed overhead.

Underapplied or overapplied overhead is always the difference between the actual overhead incurred and the overhead applied. An analysis may then be made:

$$\text{underapplied overhead} = \begin{pmatrix} \text{flexible-budget} \\ \text{variance} \end{pmatrix} + \begin{pmatrix} \text{production-volume} \\ \text{variance} \end{pmatrix}$$

$$\text{for variable overhead} = \$3{,}000 + 0 = \$3{,}000$$

$$\text{for fixed overhead} = \$7{,}000 + \$10{,}000 = \$17{,}000$$

Accounting Vocabulary

fixed-overhead rate, p. 601
normal costing, p. 607
practical capacity, p. 607

production-volume variance,
p. 601

prorating the variance, p. 612
volume variance, p. 605

Fundamental Assignment Material

15-A1   Comparison of Variable Costing and Absorption Costing
Consider the following information pertaining to a year's operation of Conigliaro Company:

Units produced	3,000
Units sold	2,250
Direct labor	$4,500
Direct material used	$3,000
Selling and administrative expenses (all fixed)	$ 900
Fixed manufacturing overhead	$4,000
Variable manufacturing overhead	$2,500
All beginning inventories	$ 0
Gross margin (gross profit)	$2,400
Direct-materials inventory, end	$ 400
Work-in-process inventory, end	$ 0

Required

1. What is the ending finished-goods inventory cost under variable costing?
2. What is the ending finished-goods inventory cost under absorption costing?
3. Would operating income be higher or lower under variable costing? By how much? Why? (Answer: $1,000 lower, but explain why.)

15-A2   Comparison of Absorption and Variable Costing

Examine the Zhang Company's simplified income statement based on variable costing. Assume that the budgeted volume for absorption costing in 20X0 and 20X1 was 1,400 units and that total fixed costs were identical in 20X0 and 20X1. There is no beginning or ending work in process.

Income Statement
Year Ended December 31, 20X1

Sales, 1,280 units @ $12		$15,360
Deduct variable costs		
Beginning inventory, 110 units @ $7	$ 770	
Variable manufacturing cost of goods manufactured, 1,200 units @ $7	8,400	
Variable manufacturing cost of goods available for sale	$9,170	
Ending inventory, 30 units @ $7	210	
Variable manufacturing cost of goods sold	$8,960	
Variable selling and administrative expenses	600	
Total variable costs		9,560
Contribution margin		$ 5,800
Deduct fixed costs		
Fixed factory overhead at budget	$4,200	
Fixed selling and administrative expenses	350	
Total fixed costs		4,550
Operating income		$ 1,250

Required

1. Prepare an income statement based on absorption costing. Assume that actual fixed costs were equal to budgeted fixed costs.
2. Explain the difference in operating income between absorption costing and variable costing. Be specific.

15-B1   Comparison of Variable Costing and Absorption Costing

Consider the following information pertaining to a year's operations of Lake Erie Manufacturing, Inc.:

Units sold	1,400
Units produced	1,600
Direct labor	$4,200
Direct material used	$3,500
Fixed manufacturing overhead	$2,200
Variable manufacturing overhead	$ 300
Selling and administrative expenses (all fixed)	$ 700
Beginning inventories	$ 0
Contribution margin	$5,600
Direct-material inventory, end	$ 800

There are no work-in-process inventories.

Required

1. What is the ending finished-goods inventory cost under absorption costing?
2. What is the ending finished-goods inventory cost under variable costing?

15-B2 Extension of Chapter Illustration

Reconsider Exhibits 15-2 and 15-3, pages 601 and 602. Suppose that in 20X1 production was 155,000 rings instead of 140,000 rings, and sales were 150,000 rings. Also assume that the net variances for all variable manufacturing costs were $15,000, unfavorable. Also assume that actual fixed manufacturing costs were $156,000.

Required

1. Prepare income statements for 20X1 under variable costing and under absorption costing. Use a format similar to Exhibits 15-7 and 15-8, page 613.
2. Explain why operating income was different under variable costing and absorption costing. Show your calculations.

Additional Assignment Material

QUESTIONS

15-1. "With variable costing, only direct material and direct labor are inventoried." Do you agree? Why?

15-2. "Absorption costing regards more categories of costs as product costs." Explain. Be specific.

15-3. "An increasing number of companies are using variable costing in their corporate annual reports." Do you agree? Explain.

15-4. Why is variable costing used only for internal reporting and not for external financial reporting or tax purposes?

15-5. Compare the contribution margin with the gross margin.

15-6. How is fixed overhead applied to products?

15-7. Name the three ways that an absorption-costing format differs from a variable-costing format.

15-8. "The flexible budget for budgeting and control differs from the costs applied for product costing." What type of cost is being described? Explain.

15-9. "Variable costing is consistent with cost-volume-profit analysis." Explain.

15-10. "In a standard absorption-costing system, the amount of fixed manufacturing overhead applied to the products rarely equals the budgeted fixed manufacturing overhead." Do you agree? Explain.

15-11. "The dollar amount of the production-volume variance depends on what expected volume of production was chosen to determine the fixed-overhead rate." Explain.

15-12. Why is there no production-volume variance for direct labor?

15-13. "An unfavorable production-volume variance means that fixed manufacturing costs have not been well controlled." Do you agree? Explain.

15-14. "The fixed cost per unit is directly affected by the expected volume selected as the denominator." Do you agree? Explain.

15-15. "Production-volume variances arise with normal-absorption and standard-absorption costing, but not with actual costing." Explain.

15-16. "Absorption-costing income exceeds variable-costing income when the number of units sold exceeds the number of units produced." Do you agree? Explain.

15-17. Suppose a manager is paid a bonus only if standard absorption-costing operating income exceeds the budget. If operating income through November is slightly below budget, what might the manager do in December to increase his or her chance of getting the bonus?

15-18. Why are companies with small levels of inventory generally unconcerned with the choice of variable or absorption costing?

15-19. "Overhead variances arise only with absorption-costing systems." Do you agree? Explain.

COGNITIVE EXERCISES

15-20 Accounting for Fixed Costs

Applying fixed costs to products seems to cause all kinds of problems. Why do companies continue to use accounting systems that assign fixed costs to products on a per unit basis?

15-21 Marketing Decisions and Absorption Costing

Product pricing and promotion decisions should usually be based on their effect on contribution margin, not on gross margin. Explain how using an absorption costing format for the income statement can provide misleading information on the effect of pricing and promotion decisions.

15-22 Evaluating Production Using the Production-Volume Variance

The sales-volume variance (see Chapter 8) highlights the effect on income of sales exceeding or falling short of sales targets. Does the production-volume variance provide parallel information for evaluating the effect of exceeding or falling short of production targets? Explain.

15-23 Absorption Costing and the Value Chain

Many costs on a product's value chain, such as research and development and product design costs, are considered period costs and are not assigned to units of product. An absorption-costing system could be expanded to apply such costs to the products. What would be the advantages and disadvantages of doing so? Would this help managers make better decisions?

EXERCISES

15-24 Simple Comparison of Variable and Absorption Costing

Hassan Company began business on January 1, 20X0, with assets of $150,000 cash and equities of $150,000 capital stock. In 20X0, it manufactured some inventory at a cost of $60,000, including $16,000 for factory rent and other fixed factory overhead. In 20X1, it manufactured nothing and sold half of its inventory for $43,000 cash. In 20X2, it manufactured nothing and sold the remaining half for another $43,000 cash. It had no fixed expenses in 20X1 or 20X2.

There are no other transactions of any kind. Ignore income taxes.

Required

Prepare an ending balance sheet plus an income statement for 20X0, 20X1, and 20X2 under (1) absorption costing and (2) variable costing (direct costing).

15-25 Comparisons over Four Years

The Ramanathan Corporation began business on January 1, 20X0, to produce and sell a single product. Reported operating income figures under both absorption and variable costing for the first four years of operation are

Year	Absorption Costing	Variable Costing
20X0	$80,000	$60,000
20X1	70,000	60,000
20X2	50,000	50,000
20X3	40,000	70,000

Standard production costs per unit, sales prices, application (absorption) rates, and expected volume levels were the same in each year. There were no flexible-budget variances for any type of cost. All nonmanufacturing expenses were fixed, and there were no nonmanufacturing cost variances in any year.

Required

1. In what year(s) did "units produced" equal "units sold"?
2. In what year(s) did "units produced" exceed "units sold"?
3. What is the dollar amount of the December 31, 20X3 finished-goods inventory? (Give absorption-costing value.)
4. What is the difference between "units produced" and "units sold" in 20X3, if you know that the absorption-costing fixed-manufacturing-overhead application rate is $3·per unit? (Give answer in units.)

15-26 Variable and Absorption Costing

Des Moines Manufacturing Company data for 20X1 follow:

Sales: 12,000 units at $17 each	
Actual production	15,000 units
Expected volume of production	18,000 units
Manufacturing costs incurred	
Variable	$120,000
Fixed	63,000
Nonmanufacturing costs incurred	
Variable	$ 24,000
Fixed	18,000

Required

1. Determine operating income for 20X1, assuming the firm uses the variable-costing approach to product costing. (Do not prepare a statement.)

2. Assume that there is no January 1, 20X1 inventory; no variances are allocated to inventory; and the firm uses a "full absorption" approach to product costing. Compute (a) the cost assigned to December 31, 20X1, inventory; and (b) operating income for the year ended December 31, 20X1. (Do not prepare a statement.)

15-27 Computation of Production-Volume Variance

Hiramatsu Manufacturing Company budgeted its 20X0 variable overhead at ¥14,100,000 and its fixed overhead at ¥26,230,000. Expected 20X0 volume was 6,100 units. Actual costs for production of 5,800 units during 20X0 were

Variable overhead	¥14,160,000
Fixed overhead	26,340,000
Total overhead	¥40,500,000

Required

Compute the production-volume variance. Be sure to label it favorable or unfavorable.

15-28 Reconciliation of Variable-Costing and Absorption-Costing Operating Income

Decker Tools, Inc., produced 12,000 electric drills during 20X1. Expected production was only 10,500 drills. The company's fixed-overhead rate is $8 per drill. Absorption-costing operating income for the year is $18,000, based on sales of 11,000 drills.

1. Compute
   a. Budgeted fixed overhead
   b. Production-volume variance
   c. Variable-costing operating income

2. Reconcile absorption-costing operating income and variable-costing operating income. Include the amount of the difference between the two and an explanation for the difference.

15-29 Overhead Variances

Study Appendix 15. Consider the following data for the Gonzalez Company:

	Factory Overhead	
	Fixed	*Variable*
Actual incurred	$14,300	$13,300
Budget for standard hours allowed		
for output achieved	12,500	11,000
Applied	11,600	11,000
Budget for actual hours of input	12,500	11,400

From the above information, fill in the blanks below. Be sure to mark your variances *F* for favorable and *U* for unfavorable.

a.	Flexible-budget variance	\$_____	Fixed \$_____
			Variable \$_____
b.	Production-volume variance	\$_____	Fixed \$_____
			Variable \$_____
c.	Spending variance	\$_____	Fixed \$_____
			Variable \$_____
d.	Efficiency variance	\$_____	Fixed \$_____
			Variable \$_____

15-30 Variances

Study Appendix 15. Consider the following data regarding factory overhead:

	Variable	Fixed
Budget for actual hours of input	\$45,000	\$70,000
Applied	41,000	64,800
Budget for standard hours allowed for actual output achieved	?	?
Actual incurred	48,500	69,500

Required

Using the above data, fill in the following blanks with the variance amounts. Use *F* for favorable or *U* for unfavorable for each variance.

	Total Overhead	Variable	Fixed
1. Spending variance	_____	_____	_____
2. Efficiency variance	_____	_____	_____
3. Production-volume variance	_____	_____	_____
4. Flexible-budget variance	_____	_____	_____
5. Underapplied overhead	_____	_____	_____

PROBLEMS

15-31 Comparison of Variable Costing and Absorption Costing

Simple numbers are used in this problem to highlight the concepts covered in the chapter.

Assume that the Perth Woolen Company produces a rug that sells for \$20. Perth uses a standard cost system. Total standard variable costs of production are \$8 per rug, fixed manufacturing costs are \$150,000 per year, and selling and administrative expenses are \$30,000 per year, all fixed. Expected production volume is 25,000 rugs per year.

Required

1. For each of the following nine combinations of actual sales and production (in thousands of units) for 20X1, prepare condensed income statements under variable costing and under absorption costing.

	(1)	(2)	(3)	(4)	(5)	(6)	(7)	(8)	(9)
Sales units	15	20	25	20	25	30	25	30	35
Production units	20	20	20	25	25	25	30	30	30

Use the following formats:

Variable Costing		Absorption Costing	
Revenue	$ aa	Revenue	$ aa
Cost of goods sold	(bb)	Cost of goods sold	(uu)
Contribution margin	$ cc	Gross profit at standard	$ vv
Fixed manufacturing costs	(dd)	Favorable (unfavorable)	
Fixed selling and		production-volume	
administrative expenses	(ee)	variance	ww
		Gross profit at "actual"	$ xx
		Selling and administrative	
		expenses	(yy)
Operating income	$ ff	Operating income	$ zz

2. **a.** In which of the nine combinations is variable-costing income greater than absorption-costing income? In which is it lower? The same?

   b. In which of the nine combinations is the production-volume variance unfavorable? Favorable?

   c. How much profit is added by selling one more unit under variable costing? Under absorption costing?

   d. How much profit is added by producing one more unit under variable costing? Under absorption costing?

   e. Suppose sales, rather than production, is the critical factor in determining the success of Perth Woolen Company. Which format, variable costing or absorption costing, provides the better measure of performance?

15-32 All-Fixed Costs

The Gibralter Company has built a massive water-desalting factory next to an ocean. The factory is completely automated. It has its own source of power, light, heat, and so on. The salt water costs nothing. All producing and other operating costs are fixed; they do not vary with output because the volume is governed by adjusting a few dials on a control panel. The employees have flat annual salaries.

The desalted water is not sold to household consumers. It has a special taste that appeals to local breweries, distilleries, and soft-drink manufacturers. The price, $.60 per gallon, is expected to remain unchanged for quite some time.

The following are data regarding the first two years of operations:

	In Gallons		Costs (All Fixed)	
	Sales	*Production*	*Manufacturing*	*Other*
20X0	1,500,000	3,000,000	$600,000	$200,000
20X1	1,500,000	0	600,000	200,000

Orders can be processed in four hours, so management decided, in early 20X1, to gear production strictly to sales.

Required

1. Prepare three-column income statements for 20X0, for 20X1, and for the two years together using (a) variable costing and (b) absorption costing.
2. What is the break-even point under (a) variable costing and (b) absorption costing?
3. What inventory costs would be carried on the balance sheets on December 31, 20X0 and 20X1, under each method?
4. Comment on your answers in requirements 1 and 2. Which costing method appears more useful?

15-33 Semifixed Costs

The Plymouth Company differs from the Gibralter Company (described in Problem 15-32) in only one respect: It has both variable and fixed manufacturing costs. Its variable costs are $.14 per gallon, and its fixed manufacturing costs are $390,000 per year.

1. Using the same data as in the preceding problem, except for the change in production-cost behavior, prepare three-column income statements for 20X0, for 20X1, and for the two years together using (a) variable costing and (b) absorption costing.
2. What inventory costs would be carried on the balance sheets on December 31, 20X0 and 20X1, under each method?

15-34 Absorption and Variable Costing
The Bohren Company had the following actual data for 20X0 and 20X1:

	20X0	20X1
Units of finished goods		
Opening inventory	—	2,000
Production	15,000	13,000
Sales	13,000	14,000
Ending inventory	2,000	1,000

The basic production data at standard unit costs for the 2 years were

Direct materials	$22
Direct labor	18
Variable factory overhead	4
Standard variable costs per unit	$44

Fixed factory overhead was budgeted at $98,000 per year. The expected volume of production was 14,000 units, so the fixed overhead rate was $98,000 ÷ 14,000 = $7 per unit.

Budgeted sales price was $75 per unit. Selling and administrative expenses were budgeted at variable, $9 per unit sold, and fixed, $85,000 per month.

Assume that there were absolutely no variances from any standard variable costs or budgeted selling prices or budgeted fixed costs in 20X0.

There were no beginning or ending inventories of work in process.

Required

1. For 20X0, prepare income statements based on standard variable (direct) costing and standard absorption costing. (The next problem deals with 20X1.)
2. Explain why operating income differs between variable costing and absorption costing. Be specific.

15-35 Absorption and Variable Costing
Assume the same facts as in the preceding problem. In addition, consider the following actual data for 20X1:

Direct materials	$ 285,000
Direct labor	174,200
Variable factory overhead	36,000
Fixed factory overhead	95,000
Selling and administrative costs	
Variable	118,400
Fixed	85,000
Sales	1,068,000

Required

1. For 20X1, prepare income statements based on standard variable (direct) costing and standard absorption costing.
2. Explain why operating income differs between variable costing and absorption costing. Be specific.

15-36 Fundamentals of Overhead Variances

The Durant Company is installing an absorption standard-cost system and a flexible-overhead budget. Standard costs have recently been developed for its only product and are as follows:

Direct material, 3 pounds @ $20	$60
Direct labor, 2 hours @ $14	28
Variable overhead, 2 hours @ $5	10
Fixed overhead	?
Standard cost per unit of finished product	$?

Expected production activity is expressed as 7,500 standard direct-labor hours per month. Fixed overhead is expected to be $60,000 per month. The predetermined fixed-overhead rate for product costing is not changed from month to month.

Required

1. Calculate the proper fixed-overhead rate per standard direct-labor hour and per unit.
2. Graph the following for activity from zero to 10,000 hours.
   a. Budgeted variable overhead
   b. Variable overhead applied to product
3. Graph the following for activity from zero to 10,000 hours.
   a. Budgeted fixed overhead
   b. Fixed overhead applied to product
4. Assume that 6,000 standard direct-labor hours are allowed for the output achieved during a given month. Actual variable overhead of $31,000 was incurred; actual fixed overhead amounted to $62,000. Calculate the
   a. Fixed-overhead flexible-budget variance
   b. Fixed-overhead production-volume variance
   c. Variable-overhead flexible-budget variance
5. Assume that 7,800 standard direct-labor hours are allowed for the output achieved during a given month. Actual overhead incurred amounted to $99,700, $62,000 of which was fixed. Calculate the
   a. Fixed-overhead flexible-budget variance
   b. Fixed-overhead production-volume variance
   c. Variable-overhead flexible-budget variance

15-37 Production-Volume Variance at L.A. Darling Company

L.A. Darling Company receives $6.5 billion of revenue each year from designing, manufacturing, and installing store fixtures in retail stores. Accounting for fixed manufacturing overhead is a challenge for the company. Suppose a manufacturing division of the company has the following budgeted costs for production of 700,000 shelving units in 2000:

Direct materials	$140,000,000
Direct labor	20,000,000
Other variable manufacturing costs	15,000,000
Fixed manufacturing costs	105,000,000
Total manufacturing cost	$280,000,000

During 2000, this division of L.A. Darling produced 750,000 of the shelving units and sold 720,000 of them for $360 million. Assume that L.A. Darling does not allocate selling or administrative costs to the individual products.

Required

1. Compute the following budgeted unit costs for 2000:

Variable manufacturing costs per unit	?
Fixed manufacturing costs per unit	?
Total manufacturing costs per unit	?

2. Compute the production-volume variance for 2000. Be sure to label it favorable or unfavorable.

3. Compute the 2000 profit from the production and sales of the shelving using absorption costing. Ignore selling and administrative costs.

4. Compute the 2000 profit from the production and sales of the shelving using variable costing. Ignore selling and administrative costs.

5. Which measure of profit, absorption-costing profit or variable-costing profit, is a better measure of performance during 2000? Explain.

15-38 Fixed Overhead and Practical Capacity

The expected activity of the paper-making plant of Goldberg Paper Company was 45,000 machine hours per month. Practical capacity was 60,000 machine hours per month. The standard machine hours allowed for the actual output achieved in January were 54,000. The budgeted fixed-factory-overhead items were

Depreciation, equipment	$340,000
Depreciation, factory building	64,000
Supervision	47,000
Indirect labor	234,000
Insurance	18,000
Property taxes	17,000
Total	$720,000

Because of unanticipated scheduling difficulties and the need for more indirect labor, the actual fixed factory overhead was $747,000.

Required

1. Using practical capacity as the base for applying fixed factory overhead, prepare a summary analysis of fixed-overhead variances for January.

2. Using expected activity as the base for applying fixed factory overhead, prepare a summary analysis of fixed-overhead variances for January.

3. Explain why some of your variances in requirements 1 and 2 are the same and why some differ.

15-39 Selection of Expected Volume

Rosanne McIntire is a consultant to Georgia Paper Products Company. She is helping one of the company's divisions to install a standard cost system for 20X2. For product-costing purposes, the system must apply fixed factory costs to products manufactured. She has decided that the fixed-overhead rate should be based on machine hours, but she is uncertain about the appropriate volume to use in the denominator. Georgia Paper has grown rapidly; the division has added production capacity approximately every 4 years. The last addition was completed in early 20X2, and the total capacity is now 2,800,000 machine hours per year. McIntire predicts the following operating levels (in machine hours) through 20X6:

Year	Capacity Used
20X2	2,250,000 hours
20X3	2,450,000 hours
20X4	2,700,000 hours
20X5	2,800,000 hours
20X6	2,900,000 hours

The current plan is to add another 500,000 machine hours of capacity in 20X6.

McIntire has identified three alternatives for the allocation base:

a. Predicted volume for the year in question

b. Average volume over the four years of the current production setup

c. Practical (or full) capacity

1. Suppose annual fixed factory overhead is expected to be $36,400,000 through 20X5. For simplicity, assume no inflation. Calculate the fixed-overhead rates (to the nearest cent) for 20X3, 20X4, and 20X5, using each of the three alternative allocation bases.

2. Provide a brief description of the effect of using each method of computing the allocation base.

3. Which method do you prefer? Why?

Required

15-40 Extension of Appendix 15 Illustration

Study the format of the analysis of variances in Exhibit 15-10, page 616. Suppose production is 156,000 units. Also assume

Standard direct-labor hours allowed per unit produced	.25
Standard direct-labor rate per hour	$6.00
Actual direct-labor hours of input	42,000
Actual direct-labor rate per hour	$6.15
Variable manufacturing overhead actually incurred	$ 36,000
Fixed manufacturing overhead actually incurred	$152,000

Other data are as shown in Exhibit 15-10.

Prepare an analysis of variances similar to that shown in Exhibit 15-10.

Required

15-41 Analysis of Operating Results

Leeds Tool Company produces and sells a variety of machine-tooled products. The company employs a standard cost accounting system for record-keeping purposes.

At the beginning of 20X1, the president of Leeds Tool presented the budget to the company's board of directors. The board accepted a target 20X1 profit of £16,800 and agreed to pay the president a bonus if profits exceeded the target. The president has been confident that the year's profit would exceed the budget target, since the monthly sales reports that he has been receiving have shown that sales for the year will exceed budget by 10%. The president is both disturbed and confused when the controller presents an adjusted forecast as of November 30, 20X1, indicating that profit will be 14% under budget:

Leeds Tool Company
Forecasts of Operating Results

	Forecasts as of	
	1/1/X1	11/30/X1
Sales	£156,000	£171,600
Cost of sales at standard	108,000*	118,800
Gross margin at standard	£ 48,000	£ 52,800
Over- (under-) absorbed fixed manufacturing overhead	0	(6,000)
Actual gross margin	£ 48,000	£ 46,800
Selling expenses	£ 11,200	£ 12,320
Administrative expenses	20,000	20,000
Total operating expenses	£ 31,200	£ 32,320
Earnings before tax	£ 16,800	£ 14,480

* Includes fixed manufacturing overhead of £30,000.

There have been no sales price changes or product-mix shifts since the January 1, 20X1, forecast. The only cost variance on the income statement is the underabsorbed manufacturing overhead. This arose because the company produced only 16,000 standard machine hours (budgeted machine hours were 20,000) during 20X1, as a result of a shortage of raw materials while its principal supplier was closed by a strike. Fortunately, Leeds Tool's finished-goods inventory was large enough to fill all sales orders received.

1. Analyze and explain why the profit has declined despite increased sales and good control over costs. Show computations.
2. What plan, if any, could Leeds Tool Company adopt during December to improve its reported profit at year-end? Explain your answer.
3. Illustrate and explain how Leeds Tool Company could adopt an alternative internal cost-reporting procedure that would avoid the confusing effect of the present procedure. Show the revised forecasts under your alternative.
4. Would the alternative procedure described in requirement 3 be acceptable to the board of directors for financial-reporting purposes? Explain.

15-42 Standard Absorption and Standard Variable Costing

Schlosser Company has the following results for a certain year. All variances are written off as additions to (or deductions from) the standard cost of goods sold. Find the unknowns, designated by letters.

Sales: 150,000 units, @ $20	$3,000,000
Net variance for standard variable manufacturing costs	$33,000, unfavorable
Variable standard cost of goods manufactured	$11 per unit
Variable selling and administrative expenses	$3 per unit
Fixed selling and administrative expenses	$650,000
Fixed manufacturing overhead	$165,000
Maximum capacity per year	190,000 units
Expected production volume for year	150,000 units
Beginning inventory of finished goods	15,000 units
Ending inventory of finished goods	10,000 units
Beginning inventory: variable-costing basis	a
Contribution margin	b
Operating income: variable-costing basis	c
Beginning inventory: absorption-costing basis	d
Gross margin	e
Operating income: absorption-costing basis	f

15-43 Disposition of Variances

In January 20X1, Louisiana Garden Equipment Company started a division for making grass clippers. Management hoped that these grass clippers were significantly better than most competitors in the market. During 20X1, it produced 100,000 grass clippers. Financial results were as follows:

- Sales: 75,000 units @ $18
- Direct labor at standard: $100,000 \times \$8 = \$800,000$
- Direct-labor variances: $34,000 U
- Direct materials at standard: $100,000 \times \$5 = \$500,000$
- Direct-material variances: $9,500 U
- Overhead incurred at standard: $100,000 \times \$4 = \$400,000$
- Overhead variances: $3,500 F

Louisiana uses an absorption-costing system and allows divisions to choose one of two methods of accounting for variances:

a. Direct charge to income.
b. Proration to the production of the period. Method b requires variances to be spread equally over the units produced during the period.

1. Calculate the division's operating income (a) using method a and (b) using method b. Assume no selling and administrative expenses.

2. Calculate ending inventory value (a) using method a and (b) using method b. Note that there was no beginning inventory.

3. What is the major argument in support of each method?

15-44 Comparison of Performance of Two Plants

On your first day as assistant controller of FBN Electronics, your in-box contains the following memo:

> To: Assistant Controller
> From: The President
> Subject: PDA Situation
>
> This note is to bring you up to date on one of our acquisition problem areas. Market research detected the current growth in the personal digital assistant (PDA) market and concluded that FBN should acquire a position in this market. Research data showed that FBN PDAs could become profitable ($50 contribution margin on a $130 sales price) at a volume of 4,000 units per plant if they competed successfully against Palm Pilot and other PDAs. Consequently, we acquired facilities in Minneapolis and San Diego, staffed them, and asked them to keep us posted on operations.
>
> Friday, I got preliminary information from accounting that is unclear. I want you to find out why their costs of goods sold are far apart and how we should have them report in the future to avoid confusion. This is particularly important in the PDA case, as market projections look bad and we may have to close one plant. I guess we'll close the San Diego plant unless you can show otherwise.

Preliminary Accounting Report

	Minneapolis	San Diego
Sales	$520,000	$520,000
Cost of goods sold	320,000	490,000
Gross margin	$200,000	$ 30,000
Administration costs (fixed)	30,000	30,000
Net income	$170,000	$ 0
Production	8,000 units	4,000 units
Variances (included in cost of goods sold)	$170,000, F	$ 85,000, U

U = Unfavorable. F = Favorable.

Required

Reconstruct the given income statements in as much detail as possible. Then explain in detail why the income statements differ, and clarify this situation confronting the president. Assume that there are no price, efficiency, or spending variances.

15-45 Straightforward Problem on Standard Cost System

Study Appendix 15. The Winnipeg Chemical Company uses flexible budgets and a standard cost system.

- Direct-labor costs incurred, 12,000 hours, $150,000
- Variable-overhead costs incurred, $37,000
- Fixed-overhead flexible-budget variance, $1,600, favorable
- Finished units produced, 1,800
- Fixed-overhead costs incurred, $38,000
- Variable overhead applied at $3 per hour

- Standard direct-labor cost, $13 per hour

- Denominator production per month, 2,000 units

- Standard direct-labor hours per finished unit, 6

Prepare an analysis of all variances (similar to Exhibit 15-10, p. 616).

15-46 Straightforward Problem on Standard Cost System

Study Appendix 15. The München Company uses a standard cost system. The month's data regarding its single product follow (where EUR stands for the euro, the European currency):

- Fixed-overhead costs incurred, EUR 6,300

- Variable overhead applied at EUR 11 per hour

- Standard direct-labor cost, EUR 44 per hour

- Denominator production per month, 220 units

- Standard direct-labor hours per finished unit, 5

- Direct-labor costs incurred, 1,000 hours, EUR 42,500

- Variable-overhead costs incurred, EUR 10,400

- Fixed-overhead budget variance, EUR 300, favorable

- Finished units produced, 180

Required   Prepare an analysis of all variances (similar to Exhibit 15-10, p. 616).

CASES

15-47 Absorption Costing and Incentive to Produce

Charlene Wolcott is manager of the Boulder Division of Colorado Metals, Inc. Her division makes a single product that is sold to industrial customers. Demand is seasonal but is readily predictable. The division's budget for 20X1 called for production and sales of 120,000 units, with production of 10,000 units each month and sales varying between 8,000 and 13,000 units a month. The division's budget for 20X1 had operating income of $660,000:

Sales (120,000 × $55)	$6,600,000
Cost of goods sold (120,000 × $45)	5,400,000
Gross margin	$1,200,000
Selling and administrative expenses (all fixed)	540,000
Operating income	$ 660,000

By the end of November, sales had lagged projections, with only 105,000 units sold. Sales of 9,000 units were originally budgeted and are still expected in December. Production through November had remained stable at 10,000 units per month, and the cost of production had been exactly as budgeted:

Direct materials, 110,000 × $14	$1,540,000
Direct labor, 110,000 × $10	1,100,000
Variable overhead, 110,000 × $8	880,000
Fixed overhead	1,430,000
Total production cost	$4,950,000

The division's operating income for the first eleven months of 20X1 was:

Sales (105,000 × $55)	$5,775,000
Cost of goods sold (105,000 × $45)	4,725,000
Gross margin	$1,050,000
Selling and administrative expenses (all fixed)	495,000
Operating income	$ 555,000

Wolcott receives an annual bonus only if her division's operating income exceeds the budget. She sees no way to increase sales beyond 9,000 units in December.

Required

1. From the budgeted and actual income statements shown, determine whether Colorado Metals uses direct or absorption costing.
2. Suppose Colorado Metals uses a standard absorption-costing system. (a) Compute the 20X1 operating income if 10,000 units are produced and 9,000 units are sold in December. (b) How could Wolcott achieve her budgeted operating income for 20X1?
3. Suppose Colorado Metals uses a standard variable-costing system. (a) Compute the 20X1 operating income if 10,000 units are produced and 9,000 units are sold in December. (b) How could Wolcott achieve her budgeted operating income for 20X1?
4. Which system motivates Wolcott to make the decision that is in the best interests of Colorado Metals? Explain.

15-48 Inventory Measures, Production Scheduling, and Evaluating Divisional Performance

The Calais Company stresses competition between the heads of its various divisions, and it rewards stellar performance with year-end bonuses that vary between 5 and 10% of division net operating income (before considering the bonus or income taxes). The divisional managers have great discretion in setting production schedules.

The Brittany Division produces and sells a product for which there is a long-standing demand but which can have marked seasonal and year-to-year fluctuations. On November 30, 20X0, Veronique Giraud, the Brittany Division Manager, is preparing a production schedule for December. The following data are available for January 1 through November 30 (EUR means euro, the European unit of currency).

Beginning inventory, January 1, in units	10,000
Sales price, per unit	EUR 400
Total fixed costs incurred for manufacturing	EUR 9,350,000
Total fixed costs: other (not inventoriable)	EUR 9,350,000
Total variable costs for manufacturing	EUR 18,150,000
Total other variable costs (fluctuate with units sold)	EUR 4,000,000
Units produced	110,000
Units sold	100,000
Variances	None

Production in October and November was 10,000 units each month. Practical capacity is 12,000 units per month. Maximum available storage space for inventory is 25,000 units. The sales outlook for December through February is 6,000 units monthly. To retain a core of key employees, monthly production cannot be scheduled at less than 4,000 units without special permission from the president. Inventory is never to be less than 10,000 units.

The denominator used for applying fixed factory overhead is regarded as 120,000 units annually. The company uses a standard absorption-costing system. All variances are disposed of at year-end as an adjustment to standard cost of goods sold.

Required

1. Given the restrictions as stated, and assuming that Giraud wants to maximize the company's net income for 20X0,
   a. How many units should be scheduled for production in December?

b. What net operating income will be reported in 20X0 as a whole, assuming that the implied cost behavior patterns will continue in December as they did throughout the year to date? Show your computations.

c. If December production is scheduled at 4,000 units, what would reported net income be?

2. Assume that standard variable costing is used rather than standard absorption costing.

a. What would net income for 20X0 be, assuming that the December production schedule is the one in requirement 1a?

b. Assuming that December production was 4,000 units?

c. Reconcile the net incomes in this requirement with those in requirement 1.

3. From the viewpoint of the long-run interests of the company as a whole, what production schedule should the division manager set? Explain fully. Include in your explanation a comparison of the motivating influence of absorption and variable costing in this situation.

4. Assume standard absorption costing. Giraud wants to maximize her after-income-tax performance over the long run. Given the data at the beginning of the problem, assume that income tax rates will be halved in 20X1. Assume also that year-end write-offs of variances are acceptable for income tax purposes. How many units should be scheduled for production in December? Why?

15-49 Performance Evaluation

A division of Iowa/Illinois Corn Company produces seed corn for farmers throughout the Midwest. Jens Jensen became president in 20X0. He is concerned with the ability of his division manager to control costs. To aid his evaluation, Jensen set up a standard cost system.

Standard costs were based on 20X0 costs in several categories. Each 20X0 cost was divided by 1,520,000 cwt, the volume of 20X0 production, to determine a standard for 20X1 (cwt means hundredweight, or 100 pounds):

	20X0 Cost (thousands)	20X1 Standard (per hundredweight)
Direct materials	$1,824	$1.20
Direct labor	836	.55
Variable overhead	1,596	1.05
Fixed overhead	2,432	1.60
Total	$6,688	$4.40

At the end of 20X1, Jensen compared actual results with the standards he established. Production was 1,360,000 cwt, and variances were as follows:

	Actual	Standard	Variance
Direct materials	$1,802	$1,632	$170 U
Direct labor	735	748	13 F
Variable overhead	1,422	1,428	6 F
Fixed overhead	2,412	2,176	236 U
Total	$6,371	$5,984	$387 U

Jensen was not surprised by the unfavorable variance in direct materials. After all, corn prices in 20X1 averaged 10% above those in 20X0. But he was disturbed by the lack of control of fixed overhead. He called in the production manager and demanded an explanation.

1. Prepare an explanation for the large unfavorable fixed-overhead variance.
2. Discuss the appropriateness of using one year's costs as the next year's standards.

COLLABORATIVE LEARNING EXERCISE

15-50 Variable and Absorption Costing

Form groups of four persons each. Each person should select one of the following four roles (if groups have between four and eight persons, two persons can play any of the roles in the exercise):

Bernard Schwartz, President
Ramona Sanchez, Controller
Leonard Swanson, Marketing Manager
Kate Cheung, Treasurer

Each of the four should prepare a justification for the type of financial statements, variable or absorption costing, that he or she favors. The setting is explained in the case, "Boylston Company," that follows.

BOYLSTON COMPANY

Bernard Schwartz took over as president of Boylston Company in mid-May, 2001. The company's operating income for May was $4,000, and Schwartz was determined that June would be a better month. But he was shocked when he received the following income statements for May and June:

	May	June
Sales	$280,000	$340,000
Standard cost of sales	150,000	180,000
Gross margin	130,000	160,000
Variances:		
Labor	6,000 F	4,000 F
Material	5,000 U	3,000 U
Overhead:		
Volume	1,000 F	27,000 U
Spending	2,000 U	1,000 U
Selling & administrative	126,000	136,000
Operating income (loss)	$ 4,000	$ (3,000)

He called Ramona Sanchez, the company's controller, and said, "Sales were up by $60,000 in June. How could operating income possibly have decreased by $7,000? There must be something wrong with your numbers."

Sanchez replied, "The numbers are right. I agree with you that they don't make sense, but since our production was down in June, operating income suffered." Schwartz wasn't satisfied with that explanation. "If your accounting numbers don't give a good signal about performance, what good are they?"

Sanchez had anticipated this reaction. She suggested charging the fixed manufacturing costs as a period cost instead of including them in the product cost. Her reworked income statement was as follows:

	May	June
Sales	$280,000	$340,000
Standard cost of sales	102,000	125,000
Gross margin	178,000	215,000
Fixed overhead	66,000	67,000
Variances:		
Labor	6,000 F	4,000 F
Material	5,000 U	3,000 U
Overhead spending	2,000 U	1,000 U
Selling & administrative	126,000	136,000
Operating income (loss)	$(15,000)	$ 12,000

Sanchez also called on Leonard Swanson, Marketing Manager, to support her new statements. He pointed out that the current accounting system did not provide the right incentives to his sales force. For example, he pointed to two products, A and B, with the following price and costs:

Product	Price	Standard Cost	Margin	% of Sales
A	$1.90	$1.10	$ .80	42.1
B	2.30	1.30	1.00	43.5

The sales force would be inclined to focus on Product B because of its higher margin as a percent of sales. However, he believed the following figures, based on the controller's new product costs, were a better measure of the relative profitability of the products.

Product	Price	Standard Cost	Margin	% of Sales
A	$1.90	$ .50	$1.40	73.7
B	$2.30	1.00	1.30	56.5

After some discussion, Schwartz brought in Kate Cheung, Corporate Treasurer, who was skeptical about the new system. She maintained that "the salesforce will start cutting prices if we leave fixed costs out of our product costs. They will try for the same margin over the reduced costs, and we will not be able to cover our fixed costs. Further, it's lack of control of long-run costs, not short-run variable costs, that can destroy a company. In the short-run, things constantly change and we don't make much of a commitment. But if long-run costs get out of control, there isn't much we can do about it."

Cheung was not finished. "And what about taxes? The government won't let us use your new system. And what about the balance sheet? Inventories that we now show at about $520,000 would have to be shown at about $365,000 if the fixed costs are not considered product costs. That sure doesn't make us look better to investors."

Although Schwartz liked the June profit shown by the revised statements, he thought there was some truth in all of the comments made. He wasn't sure how to proceed.

INTERNET EXERCISE

www.prenhall.com/horngren

15-51   Harley-Davidson Company

Published income statements use the absorption costing basis—after all, that is the method that is acceptable for use under United States generally accepted accounting principles. But the absorption costing statement might not really provide the information that management needs to make future decisions because it does not separate fixed from variable costs. This exercises focuses on extracting contribution information from published absorption-costing financial statements of Harley-Davidson Company. As a manufacturer of motorcycles, Harley-Davidson has become a well-known household name. In the past it was impossible to just walk into the showroom and buy a new motorcycle—instead, customers placed an order and waited for delivery! Now, through increased production levels, the wait time has been reduced and in some cases, if no customization is desired, a bike may be available today!

1.   Go to the home page for Harley-Davidson at http://www.harley-davidson.com. Take a look at one of the new models being offered. Click on the Products drop down menu and select the most recent model year. Once you've clicked in to that, choose a bike that you'd like to see. Once you've arrived at the product page, what type of information do you find about the bike? What information is available about prices? Is it possible that the model could have more than one price? Why or why not?

2.   Now go to the Investor Relations section of the site and choose Financial Information from the pull-down menu. Click on the Production and Marketing information section of the report. Now look at the information for the most recent year with respect to shipments. What can you see in the shipping report? Did the number of units shipped increase or decrease over the prior year? Record the total number of bikes shipped for the most recent full year of information.

3. Look at the most recent annual report for Harley-Davidson. Go to the section on Management's Discussion and Analysis of Financial Condition and Results of Operations. What was the total revenue for the Harley-Davidson motorcycle units? What is the average selling price for a Harley-Davidson motorcycle? How does this price compare to the suggested price for the bike you looked at? Why do you think that the prices differ? Which sell for a higher price, Harley-Davidson motorcycles or Buell Motorcycles? By how much?

4. Look at the most recent Consolidated Statement of Operations. What were the cost of goods sold and the selling, administrative, and engineering expenses for the current year? Refer to the cash flow statement for the current year. How much was the depreciation and amortization for the current year? Assume that 80% of these expenses are related to motorcycles (since 80% of Harley-Davidson's revenue comes from motorcycle sales) and that depreciation and amortization is the only fixed expense that Harley-Davidson had during the year. Compute the average variable cost of goods sold per unit for a motorcycle. Compute the average contribution margin per motorcycle. What would be the breakeven number of motorcycles to produce and sell under this scenario? Does this seem reasonable given the current income reported by the firm?

16

BASIC ACCOUNTING: CONCEPTS, TECHNIQUES, & CONVENTIONS

Lands' End is a mail-order retailer of clothing and other items. The company's accounting system gives financial results for each product line. For example, managers can determine the profitability of Polartec Pullovers, shown here.

www.prenhall.com/horngren

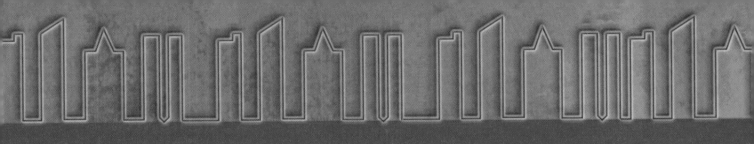

Learning Objectives

When you have finished studying this chapter, you should be able to

1. Read and interpret the basic financial statements.

2. Analyze typical business transactions using the balance sheet equation.

3. Distinguish between the accrual basis of accounting and the cash basis of accounting.

4. Relate the measurement of expenses to the expiration of assets.

5. Explain the nature of dividends and retained income.

6. Select relevant items from a set of data and assemble them into a balance sheet, an income statement, and a statement of retained income.

7. Distinguish between the reporting of corporate owner's equity and the reporting of owner's equity for partnerships and sole proprietorships.

8. Identify how the measurement conventions of recognition, matching and cost recovery, and stable monetary unit affect financial reporting.

9. **Understand how managers and investors can learn about the financial position and prospects of an organization from its financial statements.**

Chances are you or someone you know is one of the 8 million customers of Lands' End, the Wisconsin-based mail-order company. Most people who order from Lands' End are concerned about the company's prices, quality, and customer service. Lands' End managers are also concerned about these factors, and they take pride in their high ratings for customer satisfaction. Just as important to Lands' End's managers is whether the company is making a profit. How can the company's managers see how much profit Lands' End is making? The same way you can—by reading the company's financial statements.

Financial statements are generated by a company's financial accounting system. Lands' End has a financial accounting system that not only generates financial statements but also provides additional information about the company's financial success. And most important to managers, it also provides detailed information about the financial results of each product. As Don Hughes, Lands' End's Vice President of Finance, says, "We record all the activities [of Lands' End] in the financial statements. We make decisions primarily from the financial information about individual products."

Suppose you want to buy Lands' End stock instead of its clothes. Then you, too, would be interested in the company's financial statements. You would want to know the company's financial position and prospects to judge whether it is wise to invest in Lands' End stock. The company's financial statements can be a great help in making this judgment, but only if you know a bit about accounting.

Accounting is the language of business. Its special vocabulary conveys the financial story of organizations. To understand corporate annual reports, you must learn this language—the words and ideas used by accountants and other managers when discussing financial matters.[1]

This chapter explores the essence of profit-making activities and how accountants portray them in financial statements. The more technical topics are left for the chapter appendices. As you examine what accountants do, you will also learn many of the relevant concepts and conventions of accounting. Although the focus will be on profit-seeking organizations, the main ideas also apply to nonprofit organizations.

THE NEED FOR ACCOUNTING

Most people think of accountants as scorekeepers who determine how much money a business is making. In fact, all kinds of organizations—government agencies, nonprofit organizations, and others—rely on accounting to gauge their progress.

Managers, investors, and other interest groups often want the answers to two important questions about an organization: How well did the organization perform for a given period? Where does the organization stand at a given point? Accountants answer these questions with three major financial statements: an income statement, a statement of cash flows, and a balance sheet. This chapter discusses the income statement and balance sheet. The next chapter introduces the statement of cash flows.

transaction Any event that affects the financial position of an organization and requires recording.

To prepare data for the financial statements, accountants record an organization's transactions. A **transaction** is any event that affects the financial position of an organization and requires recording. Many concepts, conventions, and rules determine what events are to be recorded as accounting transactions and how their financial impact is measured. As you learn about those transactions, you will also learn about financial statements, which are summarized reports of accounting transactions.

FINANCIAL STATEMENTS

Objective 1
Read and interpret the basic financial statements.

An efficient way to learn about accounting is to study a specific illustration. Suppose King Hardware Company began business as a **corporation**—a business organized as a separate legal entity and owned by its stockholders—on March 1. An opening balance sheet follows:

corporation A business organized as a separate legal entity and owned by its stockholders.

King Hardware
Balance Sheet (Statement of Financial Position)
As of March 1, 20X1

Assets		Equities	
Cash	$100,000	Paid-in capital	$100,000

[1] *The aim of this section of the book (Chapters 16–19) is to provide a brief overview of financial accounting. For expanded coverage, see* Introduction to Financial Accounting, *Charles T. Horngren, Gary L. Sundem, and John A. Elliott (Upper Saddle River, N.J.: Prentice Hall, 2002).*

The **balance sheet** (also called **statement of financial position** or **statement of financial condition**) is a snapshot of the financial status of an organization at an instant of time. It has two sections—assets and equities. **Assets** are economic resources that are expected to benefit future activities. **Equities** are the claims against, or interests in, the assets.

You can think of the balance sheet as an equation:

$$\text{assets} = \text{equities}$$

The equities side of this equation is often divided into two parts:

$$\text{assets} = \text{liabilities} + \text{owners' equity}$$

Liabilities are the entity's economic obligations to nonowners. **Owners' equity** is the excess of the assets over the liabilities. Because the owners of a corporation are its stockholders, the owners' equity of a corporation is called **stockholders' equity.** In turn, the stockholders' equity is composed of the ownership claim arising from funds paid-in by the owners **(paid-in capital),** plus the ownership claim arising from reinvestment of previous profits **(retained income** or **retained earnings):**

$$\text{assets} = \text{liabilities} + \text{stockholders' equity}$$
$$= \text{liabilities} + (\text{paid-in capital} + \text{retained earnings})$$

Consider a summary of King Hardware's transactions in March:

1. Initial investment by owners, $100,000 cash.
2. Acquisition of inventory for $75,000 cash.
3. Acquisition of inventory for $35,000 on open account. A purchase on open account allows the buyer to pay cash some time after the date of sale, often in 30 days. Amounts owed to vendors for purchases on open accounts are usually called **accounts payable,** liabilities of the purchasing entity.
4. Merchandise carried in inventory at a cost of $100,000 was sold on open account for $120,000. The amounts due from customers for sales on open accounts are called **accounts receivable,** assets of the selling entity.
5. Cash collections of accounts receivable, $30,000.
6. Cash payments of accounts payable, $10,000.
7. On March 1, King Hardware paid $3,000 cash for store rent for March, April, and May. Rent is $1,000 per month, payable quarterly in advance, beginning March 1.

We can analyze the foregoing transactions using the balance sheet equation, as shown in Exhibit 16-1. Note that most of these are summarized transactions. For example, all the sales did not occur at once, nor did all purchases of inventory, collections from customers, or disbursements to suppliers. Many repetitive transactions occur in practice, and accountants use specialized data collection techniques to measure the effects of the transactions on the organization.

Transaction 1, the initial investment by owners, increases assets and increases equities. That is, cash increases and so does paid-in capital—the claim arising from the owners' total initial investment in the corporation.

Transactions 2 and 3, the purchases of inventory, are exchanges of one asset for another. Neither total assets nor claims on those assets changes.

Transaction 4 is the sale of $100,000 of inventory for $120,000. Two things happened simultaneously: A new asset, Accounts Receivable, is acquired (4a) in exchange for the giving up of Inventory (4b), and the retained earnings portion of Stockholders' Equity is increased by the amount of the asset received ($120,000) and decreased by the amount of the asset given up ($100,000). The $20,000 net increase in retained earnings represents stockholders' claims arising from the profitable sale.

balance sheet (statement of financial position, statement of financial condition) A snapshot of the financial status of an organization at an instant of time.

assets Economic resources that are expected to benefit future activities.

equities The claims against, or interests in, an organization's assets.

liabilities The entity's economic obligations to nonowners.

owners' equity The excess of the assets over the liabilities.

stockholders' equity The owners' equity of a corporation.

paid-in capital The ownership claim arising from funds paid-in by the owners.

retained income (retained earnings) The ownership claim arising from the reinvestment of previous profits.

accounts payable Amounts owed to vendors for purchases on open accounts.

accounts receivable Amounts due from customers for sales on open account.

Objective 2
Analyze typical business transactions using the balance sheet equation.

Exhibit 16-1

King Hardware Co.

Analysis of Transactions (in Dollars) for March 20X1

	Assets					=	Liabilities	+	Stockholders' Equity	
									Equities	
	Cash	+	Accounts Receivable	+	Inventory	+	Prepaid Rent	=	Accounts Payable	+	Paid-in Capital	+	Retained Income

Transactions	Cash	Accounts Receivable	Inventory	Prepaid Rent	Accounts Payable	Paid-in Capital	Retained Income
1. Initial investment	+100,000					+100,000	
2. Acquire inventory for cash	− 75,000		+ 75,000				
3. Acquire inventory for credit			+ 35,000		+35,000		
4a. Sales on credit		+120,000					+120,000 (revenue)
4b. Cost of inventory sold			−100,000				−100,000 (expense)
5. Collect from customers	+ 30,000	− 30,000					
6. Pay accounts of suppliers	− 10,000				−10,000		
7a. Pay rent in advance	− 3,000			+3,000			
7b. Recognize expiration of rental services				−1,000			− 1,000 (expense)
Balance, 3/31/X1	+ 42,000	+ 90,000	+ 10,000	+2,000	+25,000	+100,000	+ 19,000
	144,000				144,000		

Transaction 5, cash collection of accounts receivable, is another example of an event that has no impact on stockholders' equity. Collections are merely the transformation of one asset (Accounts Receivable) into another (Cash).

Transaction 6, cash payment of accounts payable, also does not affect stockholders' equity—it affects assets and liabilities only. In general, collections from customers and payments to suppliers have no direct impact on stockholders' equity.

Transaction 7, the cash disbursement for rent, is made to acquire the right to use store facilities for the next three months. On March 1, the $3,000 measured the future benefit from these services, so the asset Prepaid Rent was created (7a). Prepaid rent is an asset even though you cannot see or touch it as you can such assets as cash or inventory. Assets also include legal rights to future services such as the use of facilities.

Transaction 7b recognizes that one-third of the rental services has expired during March, so the asset is reduced and stockholders' equity is also reduced by $1,000. This means that $1,000 of the asset Prepaid Rent has been "used up" (or has flowed out of the entity) in the conduct of operations during March, so stockholders no longer have a claim on this $1,000.

The balance sheet for King Hardware at the end of March follows.

King Hardware Co.
Balance Sheet as of March 31, 20X1

Assets		Liabilities and Stockholders' Equity		
Cash	$ 42,000	Liabilities: accounts payable		$ 25,000
Accounts receivable	90,000	Stockholders' equity		
Inventory	10,000	Paid-in capital	$100,000	
Prepaid rent	2,000	Retained income	19,000	119,000
Total	$144,000	Total		$144,000

REVENUES AND EXPENSES

Let's review transaction 4 in more detail. Recall that this transaction has two phases, (a) and (b). Transaction 4a illustrates the recognition of revenue. **Revenues** are increases in ownership claims arising from the delivery of goods or services. To be recognized (i.e., formally recorded in the accounting records as revenue during the current period), revenue must ordinarily meet two tests. First, revenues must be *earned*. That is, the goods must be delivered or services must be fully rendered to customers. Second, revenues must be *realized*. That is, the seller must be reasonably sure of receiving the resources promised in exchange for the goods or services. For example, if the seller does not receive cash directly, the collectibility of the account receivable must be reasonably assured.

Transaction 4b illustrates the incurrence of an expense. **Expenses** are decreases in ownership claims arising from delivering goods or services or using up assets.

Transactions 4a and 4b also illustrate the fundamental meaning of **profits** or **earnings** or **income,** which is the excess of revenues over expenses. As the Retained Income column in Exhibit 16-1 shows, increases in revenues also increase stockholders' equity. In contrast, increases in expenses decrease stockholders' equity.

RELATIONSHIP OF BALANCE SHEET AND INCOME STATEMENT

A company's **income statement** summarizes its revenues and expenses. It measures the performance of an organization by matching its accomplishments (revenue from customers, which is usually called *sales*)[2] and its efforts (*cost of goods sold* and other

revenue Increases in ownership claims arising from the delivery of goods or services.

expenses Decreases in ownership claims arising from delivering goods or services or using up assets.

profits (earnings, income) The excess of revenues over expenses.

income statement A statement that summarizes a company's revenues and expenses. It measures the performance of an organization by matching its accomplishments (revenue from customers, which is usually called sales) and its efforts (cost of goods sold and other expenses).

---

[2] *Income statements for British companies use "turnover" instead of "sales." Other countries' financial statements use the same basic approach as U.S. statements, but terminology and specific measurement rules may differ.*

expenses). Recall that the balance sheet shows the organization's financial position at an instant of time. In contrast, the income statement measures performance for a *span of time,* whether it be a month, a quarter, or longer.

The King Hardware income statement for the month of March follows:

King Hardware Co.
Income Statement for the
Month Ended March 31, 20X1

Sales (revenue)		$120,000
Expenses		
Cost of goods sold	$100,000	
Rent	1,000	
Total expenses		101,000
Net income		$ 19,000

The income statement is the major link between balance sheets:

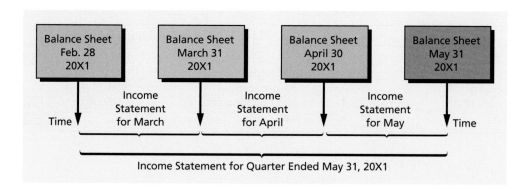

Examine the changes in retained income in Exhibit 16-1. The revenues and expenses during March explain why retained earnings changed from $0 at the beginning of the month to $19,000 at the end of the month. The income statement measures financial performance during the month, while the balance sheet measures financial position at the end of the month.

account Each item in a financial statement.

Each item in a financial statement is an **account.** Expense accounts are basically negative elements of the stockholders' equity account. Similarly, the sales (revenue) account is a positive element of stockholders' equity.

Real income statements and balance sheets use the same formats as those for King Hardware, though they usually contain more details. Consider Microsoft, the world's largest software company. A simplified version of its balance sheet follows (in millions):

Microsoft Corporation
Balance Sheet June 30, 2000

Assets:		Liabilities and Stockholders' Equity	
Cash	$23,798	Liabilities	$ 9,753
Accounts receivable	3,250	Stockholders' equity:	
Other assets	23,394	Paid-in capital	22,516
		Retained earnings	18,173
Total assets	$50,442	Total liabilities & stockholders' equity	$50,442

Microsoft's condensed income statement shows that retained earnings increased by $9,421 million because of profitable operations in 2000 (in millions):

Microsoft Corporation
Income Statement for the
Year Ended June 30, 2000

Sales	$22,956
Expenses	13,535
Net income	$ 9,421

THE ANALYTICAL POWER OF THE BALANCE SHEET EQUATION

The balance sheet equation can highlight the link between the income statement and balance sheet. Indeed, the entire accounting system is based on the simple balance sheet equation

$$\text{assets (A)} = \text{liabilities (L)} + \text{stockholders' equity (SE)} \tag{1}$$

SE equals the original ownership claim plus the increase in ownership claim because of profitable operations. That is, SE equals the claim arising from paid-in capital plus the claim arising from retained income. Therefore,

$$A = L + \text{paid-in capital} + \text{retained income} \tag{2}$$

Then, because retained income equals revenue minus expenses (see Exhibit 16-1)

$$A = L + \text{paid-in capital} + \text{revenue} - \text{expenses} \tag{3}$$

Revenue and expense accounts are nothing more than subdivisions of stockholders' equity—temporary stockholders' equity accounts. They summarize the sales and expenses, so that management can easily see the reasons for the increases and decreases in stockholders' equity in the course of ordinary operations. In this way, managers can make comparisons, set standards or goals, and exercise better control.

Notice in Exhibit 16-1 that, for each transaction, the equation is *always* in balance. If the items affected are confined to one side of the equation, you will find that the total amount added is equal to the total amount subtracted on that side. If the items affected are on both sides, then equal amounts are simultaneously added or subtracted on each side.

Consider the relationship between the balance sheet and the income statement. Suppose a company has no transactions with its owners during 20X1. That is, paid-in capital remains unchanged and retained earnings increases by the entire amount of the net income. During 20X1 the company's net income is $100,000. At the beginning of the year, the company's balance sheet equation was:

Assets = Liabilities + Stockholders' Equity
$500,000 = $200,000 + $300,000

What do you know about the balance sheet equation at the end of 20X1?
    ANSWER
The one thing that we know for sure is that Stockholders' Equity at the end of 20X1 must be $300,000 + $100,000 = $400,000 because retained income increased by $100,000 and paid-in capital was unchanged. Also, assets minus liabilities must also be $400,000, compared with $300,000 at the beginning of the year. We don't know whether assets increased by $100,000, or liabilities decreased by $100,000, or there is some combination of increase in assets and decrease in liabilities equaling $100,000, but we know that the difference must increase by $100,000 to keep the balance sheet equation in balance.

The striking feature of the balance sheet equation is its universal applicability. No transaction has ever been conceived, no matter how simple or complex, that cannot be analyzed via the equation. The top technical partners in the world's largest professional accounting firms, when confronted with the most intricate transactions of multinational companies, will inevitably discuss and think about their analyses in terms of the balance sheet equation.

ACCRUAL BASIS AND CASH BASIS

Objective 3
Distinguish between the accrual basis of accounting and the cash basis of accounting.

accrual basis A process of accounting that recognizes the impact of transactions on the financial statements in the time periods when revenues and expenses occur instead of when cash is received or disbursed.

cash basis A process of accounting where revenue and expense recognition would occur when cash is received and disbursed.

Measurements of income and financial position use the accrual basis of accounting. The **accrual basis** recognizes the impact of transactions on the financial statements in the periods when revenues and expenses occur instead of when the company receives or pays cash. That is, we record revenue as it is earned, and we record expenses as they are incurred—not necessarily when cash changes hands.

Transaction 4a in Exhibit 16-1, page 640, shows an example of the accrual basis. King Hardware recognizes revenue when it makes sales on credit, not when it receives cash. Similarly, transactions 4b and 7b (for cost of goods sold and rent) show that King Hardware records expenses as it expends efforts or uses services to obtain the revenue (regardless of when it disburses cash). Therefore, measurements of noncash resources and obligations directly affect income. The accrual basis is the principal conceptual framework for relating accomplishments (revenues) with efforts (expenses).

More than 95% of all business is conducted on a credit basis; cash receipts and disbursements are not the critical transactions for the recognition of revenue and expense. Thus, the accrual basis evolved in response to a desire for a more complete, and therefore more accurate, report of the financial impact of various events.

If King Hardware used the **cash basis** of accounting instead of the accrual basis, revenue and expense recognition would occur when the company received and disbursed cash. In March, King Hardware would show $30,000 of revenue, the amount of cash collected from customers. Similarly, cost of goods sold would be the $10,000 cash payment for the purchase of inventory, and rent expense would be $3,000 (the cash disbursed for rent) rather than the $1,000 rent applicable to March. A cash measurement of net income or net loss is obviously ridiculous in this case, and it could mislead those unacquainted with the fundamentals of accounting.

Ponder the rent example. Under the cash basis, March must bear expenses for the entire quarter's rent of $3,000, merely because cash outflows occurred then. In contrast, the accrual basis measures performance more sharply by allocating the rental expenses to the operations of each of the three months that benefited from the use of the facilities. In this way, the economic performance of each month will be comparable. Most accountants maintain that it is nonsense to say that March's rent expense was $3,000 and April's and May's was zero.

The major deficiency of the cash basis of accounting is that it is incomplete. It fails to match efforts and accomplishments (expenses and revenues) in a manner that properly measures economic performance and financial position. Moreover, it omits key assets (such as accounts receivable and prepaid rent) and key liabilities (such as accounts payable) from balance sheets.

NONPROFIT ORGANIZATIONS

The examples in this chapter focus on profit-seeking organizations, but nonprofit organizations also use balance sheets and income statements. For example, hospitals and universities have income statements, although they are called "statements of revenue and expense." The "bottom line" is frequently called "excess of revenue over expense" rather than "net income."

The basic concepts of assets, liabilities, revenues, and expenses apply to all organizations, whether they be utilities, symphony orchestras, private, public, American, Asian, and so forth. However, some nonprofit organizations have been slow to adopt several ideas that are widespread in progressive companies. For example, many government organizations still use the cash basis of accounting. The lack of accrual-based financial statements has hampered the evaluation of the performance of such organizations.

ADJUSTMENTS TO THE ACCOUNTS

To measure income under the accrual basis, accountants use adjustments at the end of each reporting period. **Adjustments** record *implicit transactions,* in contrast to the *explicit transactions* that trigger nearly all day-to-day routine entries.

adjustments Recording of implicit transactions, in contrast to the explicit transactions that trigger nearly all day-to-day routine entries.

Earlier, we defined a *transaction* as any economic event that should be recorded by the accountant. Note that this definition is not confined to market transactions, which are actual exchanges of goods and services between the entity and another party. For instance, the losses of assets from fire or theft are also transactions even though no market exchange occurs.

Entries for explicit transactions such as credit sales, credit purchases, cash received on account, and cash disbursed on account are supported by explicit evidence, usually in the form of **source documents** (e.g., sales slips, purchase invoices, and employee time records). In contrast, companies prepare adjustments for implicit transactions, such as unpaid wages, prepaid rent, interest owed, and the like, from special schedules or memorandums that recognize events (such as the passage of time) that are temporarily ignored in day-to-day recording procedures. Adjustments refine the accountant's accuracy and provide a more complete measure of efforts, accomplishments, and financial position. They are an essential part of accrual accounting. Companies generally make adjustments when the financial statements are about to be prepared.

source documents Explicit evidence of any transactions that occur in the entity's operation, for example, sales slips and purchase invoices.

We classify the principal adjustments into four types:

I. Expiration of Unexpired Costs
II. Recognition (Earning) of Unearned Revenues
III. Accrual of Unrecorded Expenses
IV. Accrual of Unrecorded Revenues

ADJUSTMENT TYPE I: EXPIRATION OF UNEXPIRED COSTS

Assets frequently expire because of the passage of time. We illustrated this first type of adjustment in Exhibit 16-1 by recognizing the rent expense in transaction 7b.

Objective 4
Relate the measurement of expenses to the expiration of assets.

Assets may be viewed as bundles of economic services awaiting future use. You can think of assets, other than cash and receivables, as prepaid or stored costs that are carried forward to future periods rather than immediately charged as expenses:

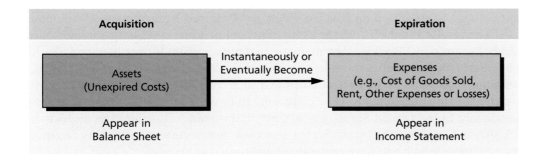

unexpired cost Any asset that ordinarily becomes an expense in future periods, for example, inventory and prepaid rent.

Expenses are used-up assets. An **unexpired cost** is any asset that ordinarily becomes an expense in future periods. Examples in our King Hardware Co. illustration are inventory and prepaid rent. Other examples are equipment and various prepaid expenses such as prepaid insurance and prepaid property taxes. When costs expire, accountants often say they are *written off* to expenses.

The analysis of the inventory and rent transactions in Exhibit 16-1 maintains this distinction of acquisition and expiration. The unexpired costs of inventory and prepaid rent are assets until they are used up, at which time they become expenses.

TIMING OF ASSET EXPIRATION

Sometimes companies acquire and use services almost instantaneously. Examples are advertising services, interest services (the cost of money, which is a service), miscellaneous supplies, and sales salaries and commissions. Conceptually, these costs should, at least momentarily, be viewed as assets on acquisition before being written off as expenses. For example, suppose an eighth transaction in Exhibit 16-1 was newspaper advertising acquired for $1,000 cash. The transaction might be analyzed in two phases:

		Assets		=	Liabilities	+	Stockholders' Equity	
Transaction	Cash	+ Other Assets	+ Unexpired Advertising	=			Paid-in Capital	+ Retained Income
8a. Acquire advertising services	−1,000		+1,000	=				
8b. Use advertising services			−1,000	=				−1,000 (expense)

However, companies often use services so quickly after acquiring them that accountants do not bother recording an asset such as Unexpired Advertising for them. Instead, they take a shortcut:

Transaction	Cash + Other Assets = Liabilities + Paid-in Capital + Retained Income
8	−1,000 = −1,000 (expense)

Making the entry in two steps instead of one is cumbersome from a practical bookkeeping viewpoint. But our purpose is not to teach you to be efficient bookkeepers. We want you to develop an orderly way of thinking about what managers do. Managers acquire goods and services, not expenses per se. These goods and services become expenses as managers use them to obtain revenue.

When does an asset expire and become an expense? Sometimes this question is hard to answer. For example, some accountants prefer to record research and development costs as assets (listed on balance sheets as "Deferred Research and Development Costs") and write them off (charge as an expense) in some systematic manner over a period of years. Why? Because they maintain that money spent for research and development creates future benefits and thus qualifies as an asset. But the regulators of financial accounting in the United States have ruled that such costs have vague future benefits that are difficult to measure reliably. Thus, companies must write off research costs as expenses immediately. In the United States, you will not find research costs listed as assets in balance sheets. Outside the United States, however, many countries, such as Japan and France, allow research and development to be recorded as an asset.

DEPRECIATION

To keep the expense-adjustment illustration simple, until now we have deliberately ignored the accounting for long-lived assets such as equipment. Equipment is really a bundle of future services that will have a limited useful life. Accountants usually (1) predict the length of the useful life, (2) predict the ultimate **residual value** (the predicted sales value of a long-lived asset at the end of its useful life), and (3) allocate the cost of the equipment to the years of its useful life in some systematic way. This process, called the recording of depreciation expense, applies to physical assets such as buildings, equipment, furniture, and fixtures owned by the entity. (Land is not subject to depreciation.)

residual value The predicted sales value of a long-lived asset at the end of its useful life.

The most popular depreciation method for financial reporting is the *straight-line method,* which depreciates an asset by the same amount each year. Suppose King Hardware Co. had acquired some store equipment for $14,000 on March 1. The predicted life of the equipment is 10 years, and the estimated residual value is $2,000:

$$\text{straight-line depreciation per year} = \frac{\text{original cost} - \text{estimated residual value}}{\text{years of useful life}}$$

$$= \frac{\$14,000 - \$2,000}{10}$$

$$= \$1,200 \text{ per year, or } \$100 \text{ per month}$$

We discuss depreciation in more detail in subsequent chapters. But the essence of the general concept of expense should be clear by now. The purchase and use of a good or service (e.g., inventories, rent, or equipment) ordinarily consists of two basic steps: (1) the acquisition of the asset (transactions 2, 3, and 7a) and (2) the expiration of the asset as an expense (transactions 4b and 7b). When an asset expires, both the value of the asset and owners' equity are decreased.

SUMMARY PROBLEM FOR YOUR REVIEW

PROBLEM

The King Hardware Co. transactions for March were analyzed in Exhibit 16-1, page 640. The balance sheet showed the following balances as of March 31, 20X1:

	Assets	Equities
Cash	$ 42,000	
Accounts receivable	90,000	
Inventory	10,000	
Prepaid rent	2,000	
Accounts payable		$ 25,000
Paid-in capital		100,000
Retained income		19,000
	$144,000	$144,000

The following is a summary of the transactions that occurred during the next month, April:

1. Cash collections of accounts receivable, $88,000.
2. Cash payments of accounts payable, $24,000.

3. Acquisitions of inventory on open account, $80,000.

4. Merchandise carried in inventory at a cost of $70,000 was sold on open account for $85,000.

5. Adjustment for recognition of rent expense for April.

Required Using the accrual basis of accounting, prepare an analysis of transactions, employing the equation approach demonstrated in Exhibit 16-1.

SOLUTION

The answer is in the top half of Exhibit 16-2. We will explain the bottom half of the exhibit in the following sections.

ADJUSTMENT TYPE II: RECOGNITION (EARNING) OF UNEARNED REVENUES

Consider the following transaction for King Hardware:

6. Some customers paid $3,000 in advance for merchandise that they ordered but that King did not expect to deliver until mid-May.

unearned revenue (deferred revenue)
Collections from customers received and recorded before they are earned.

See transaction 6 in Exhibit 16-2. We call this $3,000 collected from customers and recorded before it was earned **unearned revenue** or **deferred revenue.** It is a liability because the retailer is obligated to deliver the goods ordered or to refund the money if the goods are not delivered. Some companies call this account *advances from customers* or *customer deposits,* but it is an unearned revenue account no matter what its label. That is, it is revenue collected in advance that has not yet been earned. Advance collections of rent and magazine subscriptions are other examples.

Sometimes it is easier to see how accountants analyze transactions by visualizing the financial positions of both parties to a contract. For instance, consider the rent transaction of March 1. Compare the financial impact on King Hardware Co. with the impact on the landlord who received the rental payment:

	Owner of Property (Landlord, Lessor)				King Hardware Co. (Tenant, Lessee)			
	A	=	L	+	SE	A		=	L + SE
	Cash		Unearned Rent Revenue		Rent Revenue	Cash	Prepaid Rent		Rent Expense
(a) Explicit transaction (advance payment of three months' rent)	+3,000	=	+3,000			−3,000	+3,000	=	
(b) March adjustment (for one month's rent)		=	−1,000		+1,000		−1,000	=	−1,000
(c) April adjustment (for one month's rent)		=	−1,000		+1,000		−1,000	=	−1,000
(d) May adjustment (for one month's rent)		=	−1,000		+1,000		−1,000	=	−1,000

You are already familiar with the King Hardware analysis. The $1,000 monthly entries for King Hardware are examples of the first type of adjustments, the expiration of unexpired costs.

Now study the transactions from the viewpoint of the owner of the rental property. The first transaction recognizes unearned revenue, which is a liability because the lessor is

Exhibit 16-2

King Hardware Co.

Analysis of Transactions (in Dollars) for April 20X1

	Assets				=	Liabilities			+	Stockholders' Equity	
Transaction	Cash +	Accounts Receivable +	Inventory +	Prepaid Rent	=	Accounts Payable +	Accrued Wages Payable +	Unearned Sales Revenue* +		Paid-in Capital +	Retained Income
Bal. 3/31/X1	+42,000	+90,000	+10,000	+2,000	=	+25,000				+100,000	+19,000
1.	+88,000	−88,000			=						
2.	−24,000				=	−24,000					
3.			+80,000		=	+80,000					
4a.		+85,000			=						+85,000 (revenue)
4b.			−70,000		=						−70,000 (expense)
5.				−1,000	=						−1,000 (expense)
6.	+3,000				=			+3,000*			
7.	−6,000				=						−6,000 (expense)
8.					=		+600				−600 (expense)
9.	−18,000				=						−18,000 (dividend)
4/30/X1	+85,000	+87,000	+20,000	+1,000	=	+81,000	+600	+3,000		+100,000	+8,400
	193,000				=	193,000					

* Some accountants would call this account "Customer Deposits," "Advances from Customers," "Deferred Sales Revenue," or "Unrealized Sales Revenue."

obligated to deliver the rental services (or to refund the money if the services are not delivered).

As you can see from the table on p. 648, adjustments for the expiration of unexpired costs (Type I) and for the realization of unearned revenues (Type II) are really mirror images of each other. If one party to a contract has a prepaid expense, the other has unearned revenue. A similar analysis could be conducted for, say, a three-year fire insurance policy or a three-year magazine subscription. The buyer recognizes a prepaid expense (asset) and uses adjustments to spread the initial cost to expense over the life of the services. In turn, the seller, such as a magazine publisher, must initially recognize its liability, unearned subscription revenue. The *unearned* revenue is then recognized as *earned* revenue when the company delivers magazines throughout the life of the subscription.

You have now seen how two types of adjustments might occur: (1) expiration of unexpired costs and (2) recognition (earning) of unearned revenues. Next we consider the third type of adjustment: accrual of unrecorded expenses.

ADJUSTMENT TYPE III: ACCRUAL OF UNRECORDED EXPENSES

accrue To accumulate a receivable or payable during a given period even though no explicit transaction occurs.

Accrue means to accumulate a receivable or payable during a given period even though no explicit transaction occurs. Examples of accruals are the wages of employees for partial payroll periods and the interest on borrowed money before the interest payment date. The receivables or payables grow as the clock ticks or as some services are continuously acquired and used, so they are said to accrue (accumulate).

Computerized accounting systems can make weekly, daily, or even "real-time" recordings in the accounts for many accruals. However, such frequent entries are often costly and unnecessary. Usually, adjustments are made to bring each expense (and corresponding liability) account up to date just before the formal financial statements are prepared.

ACCOUNTING FOR PAYMENT OF WAGES

Consider the following two transactions relating to wages paid by King Hardware to its employees:

7. Total wages of $6,000 (which were ignored for simplicity in March) were paid on four Fridays in April. King Hardware recognizes these payments for employee services by increasing Wages Expense and decreasing Cash.

8. King Hardware incurred wages of $600 near the end of April, but it did not pay the employees until after April 30. Accordingly, the accountant increased Wages Expense and increased a liability, Accrued Wages Payable.

Most companies pay their employees at predetermined times. Here is a sample calendar for April:

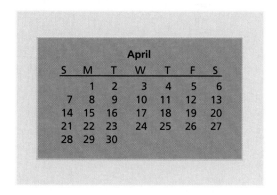

April						
S	M	T	W	T	F	S
	1	2	3	4	5	6
7	8	9	10	11	12	13
14	15	16	17	18	19	20
21	22	23	24	25	26	27
28	29	30				

King Hardware pays its employees each Friday for services rendered during that week. For example, wages paid on April 26 are compensation for the week ended April 26. The cumulative total wages paid on the Fridays during April were $6,000. King Hardware accounts for wages expense using the shortcut procedure described earlier for goods and services that are routinely consumed in the period of their purchase. Transaction 7 in Exhibit 16-2 (and summarized below) shows King Hardware's entry for April's wages through April 26:

	Assets (A) = Liabilities (L) + Stockholders' Equity (SE)		
	Cash		Wages Expense
7. Routine entry for explicit transactions	−6,000 =		−6,000

ACCOUNTING FOR ACCRUAL OF WAGES

King Hardware's wages are $300 per day. At the end of April, in addition to the $6,000 already paid, King Hardware owes $600 for employee services rendered during the last two days of April. King Hardware will not pay the employees for these services until the next regular weekly payday, May 3, so an accrual is necessary. Periodic adjustments ensure that the financial statements adhere to accrual accounting. King Hardware accomplishes this with entry 8:

	A	=	L	+	SE
			Accrued Wages Payable		Wages Expense
8. Adjustment for implicit transaction, the accrual of unrecorded wages		=	+600		−600

Conceptually, we could divide entries 7 and 8 into the asset acquisition-asset expiration sequence, but companies seldom use this two-step sequence in practice for expenses that represent services that are purchased and used in the same accounting period.

Accrued expenses arise when payment *follows* the rendering of services; prepaid expenses arise when payment *precedes* the services. Other examples of accrued expenses include sales commissions, property taxes, income taxes, and interest on borrowed money. Interest is rent paid for the use of money, just as rent is paid for the use of buildings or automobiles. The interest accumulates (accrues) as time unfolds, regardless of when the actual cash for interest is paid.

ADJUSTMENT TYPE IV: ACCRUAL OF UNRECORDED REVENUES

The final type of adjustment, the realization of revenues that have been earned but not yet recorded as such in the accounts, is not illustrated in Exhibit 16-2. It is the mirror image of the accrual of unrecorded expenses. Suppose Security State Bank lends cash to King Hardware Co. on a 3-month promissory note for $50,000 with interest at 1% per month payable at maturity. The following tabulation shows the mirror-image effect of the adjustment for interest at the end of the first month (.01 × $50,000 = $500):

	Security State Bank (Lender)				King Hardware Co. (Borrower)			
A	=	L	+	SE	A	=	L	+	SE
Accrued Interest Receivable				*Interest Revenue*			*Accrued Interest Payable*	*Interest Expense*
+500	=			+500		=	+500	−500

Consider the four types of accrual adjustments. Prepare a 2 × 2 matrix with the first column labeled Expense and the second column labeled Revenue. Label the first row "Payment precedes recognition of expense or revenue" and the second row "Recognition of expense or revenue precedes payment." Fill in each of the four cells of the matrix with the type of accrual adjustment represented in that cell and give one example of that type of adjustment.

ANSWER

See Exhibit 16-3.

DIVIDENDS AND RETAINED INCOME

Objective 5
Explain the nature of dividends and retained income.

Exhibit 16-2 shows how revenues increase and expenses decrease the retained income portion of stockholders' equity. Transaction 9 shows another type of transaction that affects retained income—payment of dividends:

9. Cash dividends declared by the board of directors and disbursed to stockholders on April 29 equaled $18,000.

DIVIDENDS ARE NOT EXPENSES

dividends Distributions of assets to stockholders that reduce retained income.

Dividends are distributions of assets to stockholders that reduce retained income. (Cash dividends are distributions of cash rather than some other asset.) Dividends are not expenses like rent and wages. Companies do not deduct them from revenues when measuring income because dividends do not relate directly to the generation of sales or the conduct of operations.

Exhibit 16-3

Four Major Types of Accounting Adjustments Before Preparation of Financial Statements

		Expense		Revenue
Payment Precedes Recognition of Expense or Revenue	I	Expiration of unexpired costs. *Illustration:* The write-off of prepaid rent as rent expense (Exhibit 16-2, entry 5)	II	Recognition (earning) of unearned revenues. *Illustration:* The mirror image of Type I, whereby the landlord recognizes rent revenue and decreases unearned rent revenue (rent collected in advance)
Recognition of Expense or Revenue Precedes Payment	III	Accrual of unrecorded expenses. *Illustration:* Wage expense for wages earned by employees but not yet paid (Exhibit 16-2, entry 8)	IV	Accrual of unrecorded revenues. *Illustration:* Interest revenue earned but not yet collected by a financial institution

Profitable operations create the ability to pay dividends. Retained income increases as profits accumulate and decreases as dividends occur.

You can think of the entire right-hand side of the balance sheet equation as claims against the total assets. The liabilities are the claims of creditors. The stockholders' equity represents the claims of owners arising out of their initial investment (paid-in capital) and subsequent profitable operations (retained income). As a company grows, the retained income account can soar enormously if the company does not pay dividends. Retained income is frequently the largest stockholders' equity account. For example, General Electric had retained income of $57,749 million in 2000 compared to paid-in capital of only $669 million.

RETAINED INCOME IS NOT CASH

Although retained income is a result of profitable operations, it is not a pot of cash awaiting distribution to stockholders. Consider the following illustration:

Step 1. Assume an opening balance sheet of

Cash	$100	Paid-in capital	$100

Step 2. Purchase inventory for $50 cash. The balance sheet now reads

Cash	$ 50	Paid-in capital	$100
Inventory	50		
	$100		

Steps 1 and 2 demonstrate a fundamental point. Ownership equity (paid-in capital, here) is an undivided claim against the total assets (in the aggregate). For example, half the shareholders do not have a specific claim on cash, and the other half do not have a specific claim on inventory. Instead, all the shareholders have an undivided claim against (or, if you prefer, an undivided interest in) all the assets.

Step 3. Now sell the inventory for $80, which produces a retained income of $80 − $50 = $30:

Cash	$130	Paid-in capital	$100
		Retained income	30
		Total equities	$130

At this stage, the retained income might be related to a $30 increase in cash. But the $30 in retained income connotes only a general claim against total assets. This may be clarified by the transaction that follows.

Step 4. Purchase equipment and inventory, in the amounts of $70 and $50, respectively. Now cash is $130 − $70 − $50 = $10:

Cash	$ 10	Paid-in capital	$100
Inventory	50	Retained income	30
Equipment	70		
Total assets	$130	Total equities	$130

To what assets is the $30 in retained income related? Is it linked to Cash, to Inventory, or to Equipment? The answer is, to all three. This example helps to explain the nature of the Retained Income account. It is a claim, not a pot of gold. You cannot buy a loaf of bread with retained income. Retained income (and also paid-in capital) is a general claim against, or undivided interest in, total assets, not a specific claim against cash or against any other particular asset. Do not confuse the assets themselves with the claims against the assets.

NATURE OF DIVIDENDS

As stated earlier, dividends are distributions of assets that reduce ownership claims. The cash assets that companies disburse typically arise from profitable operations. Thus, dividends or withdrawals are often spoken of as "distributions of profits" or "distributions of retained income." Dividends are often erroneously described as being "paid out of retained income." In reality, cash dividends are distributions of assets that liquidate a portion of the ownership claim. The distribution is made possible by profitable operations.

The amount of cash dividends declared by the board of directors of a company depends on many factors, the least important of which is usually the balance in retained income. Although profitable operations are generally essential, the company's cash position and future needs for cash to pay debts or to purchase additional assets also influences its dividend policy. In addition, many companies are committed to a stable dividend policy or to a policy that ties dividends to fluctuations in net income. Under a stable policy, a company may pay dividends consistently even if it encounters a few years of little or no net income.

PREPARING FINANCIAL STATEMENTS

Objective 6
Select relevant items from a set of data and assemble them into a balance sheet, an income statement, and a statement of retained income.

You can use the balance sheet equation to prepare a company's financial statement. King Hardware's April financial statements are based on the information in Exhibit 16-2. The income statement and balance sheet, shown in Exhibits 16-4 and 16-5, are similar to those illustrated earlier. A third financial statement, the Statement of Retained Earnings, is shown in Exhibit 16-6. It is a formal presentation of the items affecting retained earnings during April. It starts with the beginning balance, adds net income for the period, and deducts cash dividends, to arrive at the ending balance. Frequently, this statement is tacked on to the bottom of an income statement. If so, the result is a combined statement of income and statement of retained income.

Exhibit 16-4

King Hardware Company
Balance Sheet as of April 30, 20X1

Assets		Liabilities and Stockholders' Equity		
Cash	$ 85,000	Liabilities		
Accounts receivable	87,000	Accounts payable	$ 81,000	
Inventory	20,000	Accrued wages payable	600	
Prepaid rent	1,000	Unearned sales revenue	3,000	$ 84,600
		Stockholders' equity		
		Paid-in capital	$100,000	
		Retained income	8,400	108,400
Total assets	$193,000	Total equities		$193,000

Exhibit 16-5

King Hardware Company

Income Statement for the Month Ended
April 30, 20X1

Sales		$85,000
Cost of goods sold		70,000
Gross profit		$15,000
Operating expenses		
Rent	$1,000	
Wages	6,600	7,600
Net income		$ 7,400

Exhibit 16-6

King Hardware Company

Statement of Retained Income for the
Month Ended April 30, 20X1

Retained income, March 31, 20X1	$19,000
Net income for April	7,400
Total	$26,400
Dividends	18,000
Retained income, April 30, 20X1	$ 8,400

Accountants call the income statement in Exhibit 16-5 a "multiple-step" statement because it includes a subtotal for gross profit. *Gross profit* (sometimes called *gross margin*) is the excess of sales over the cost of the inventory that was sold. A "single step" statement would merely list all the expenses, including cost of goods sold, and deduct the total from sales.

SOLE PROPRIETORSHIPS AND PARTNERSHIPS

This chapter has focused on the accounting for a corporation, King Hardware Co. However, the basic accounting concepts that underlie the owners' equity are unchanged regardless of whether ownership takes the form of a corporation, a **sole proprietorship**—a business entity with a single owner, or a **partnership**—an organization that joins two or more individuals together as co-owners. However, in proprietorships and partnerships, distinctions between paid-in capital (i.e., the investments by owners) and retained income are rarely made. Compare the possibilities for King Hardware Co. as of April 30:

sole proprietorship A business entity with a single owner.

partnership An organization that joins two or more individuals together as co-owners.

Objective 7
Distinguish between the reporting of corporate owners' equity and the reporting of owners' equity for partnerships and sole proprietorships.

Owners' Equity for a Corporation		
Stockholders' equity		
Capital stock (paid-in capital)	$100,000	
Retained income	8,400	
Total stockholders' equity		$108,400

Owner's Equity for a Sole Proprietorship	
Alice Walsh, capital	$108,400

Owners' Equity for a Partnership	
Susan Zingler, capital	$ 54,200
John Martin, capital	54,200
Total partners' equity	$108,400

In contrast to corporations, sole proprietorships and partnerships are not legally required to account separately for paid-in capital (i.e., proceeds from issuances of capital stock) and for retained income. Instead, they typically accumulate a single amount for each owner's original investments, subsequent investments, share of net income, and withdrawals. In the case of a sole proprietorship, then, the owner's equity will consist of a lone capital account.

net worth A synonym for owner's equity.

Note that, although owners' equity is sometimes called **net worth,** owners' equity is not a measure of the "current value" of the business to an outside buyer. The selling price of a business depends on future profit projections that may have little relationship to the existing assets or equities of the entity as measured by its accounting records. For example, Dell Computer's shareholders' equity (or net worth) in 2000 was about $6 billion, while its market value was more than $90 billion. Even more extreme was Amazon.com with a negative net worth of nearly $1 billion and a market value of $15 billion.

GENERALLY ACCEPTED ACCOUNTING PRINCIPLES

Accounting is more an art than a science. It is based on a set of principles on which there is general agreement, not on rules that can be "proved."

AUDITOR'S INDEPENDENT OPINION

The financial statements of publicly held corporations and many other corporations are subject to an independent audit that forms the basis for a professional accounting firm's opinion, typically including the following key phrasing:

> *In our opinion, such financial statements present fairly, in all material respects, the financial position of Microsoft Corporation and subsidiaries as of June 30, 1999 and 2000, and the results of their operations and their cash flows for each of the three years in the period ended June 30, 2000, in conformity with generally accepted accounting principles.*

audit An examination or in-depth inspection of financial statements and companies' records that is made in accordance with generally accepted auditing standards. It culminates with the accountant's testimony that management's financial statements are in conformity with generally accepted accounting principles.

An accounting firm must conduct an audit before it can render an opinion. An **audit** is an "examination" or in-depth inspection of financial statements and companies' records made in accordance with generally accepted auditing standards, which have been developed primarily by the American Institute of Certified Public Accountants (AICPA), the leading organization of auditors. After auditing a company, an accountant issues an independent opinion—the accountant's assurance that management's financial statements are in conformity with generally accepted accounting principles.

The auditor's opinion usually appears at the end of annual reports prepared for the stockholders and other external users. Investors often mistakenly rely on the opinion as an infallible guarantee of financial truth. Somehow, accounting is thought to be an exact science, perhaps because of the aura of precision that financial statements possess. But, as noted earlier, accounting is more art than science. The financial reports may appear accurate because of their neatly integrated numbers, but they are the result of a complex measurement process that rests on a huge bundle of assumptions and conventions.

The conventions, rules, and procedures that together make up accepted accounting practice at any given time are called generally accepted accounting principles (GAAP). Accounting principles become "generally accepted" by agreement. Such agreement is not influenced solely by formal logical analysis. Experience, custom, usage, and practical necessity contribute to the set of principles. Accordingly, it might be better to call them conventions, because principles suggest that they are the product of airtight logic.

FASB AND SEC

American GAAP is largely the work of the **Financial Accounting Standards Board (FASB).** The FASB, consisting of seven full-time members, is an independent creation of the private sector. It is financially supported by various companies and professional accounting associations. International GAAP is set by the **International Accounting Standards Board (IASB).**

By federal law, the **Securities and Exchange Commission (SEC),** a government agency, has the ultimate responsibility for specifying GAAP for U.S. companies whose stock is held by the general investing public. However, the SEC has informally delegated much rule-making power to the FASB. This public-sector–private-sector relationship may be sketched as follows:

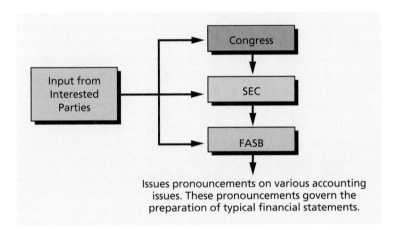

Issues pronouncements on various accounting issues. These pronouncements govern the preparation of typical financial statements.

Financial Accounting Standards Board (FASB) The primary regulatory body over accounting principles and practices in the United States. Consisting of seven full-time members, it is an independent creation of the private sector.

International Accounting Standards Board (IASB) The group that establishes international GAAP.

Securities and Exchange Commission (SEC) By federal law, the agency with the ultimate responsibility for specifying the generally accepted accounting principles for U.S. companies whose stock is held by the general investing public.

The FASB issues pronouncements on various accounting issues. These pronouncements govern the preparation of typical financial statements.

Consider this three-tiered structure. Note that Congress can overrule both the SEC and FASB, and the SEC can overrule the FASB. Such undermining of the FASB occurs rarely, but corporations and other interested parties exert pressure on all three tiers if they think an impending pronouncement is "wrong." Hence, the setting of accounting principles is a complex process involving heavy interactions among the affected parties: public regulators (Congress and SEC), private regulators (FASB), companies, the public accounting profession, representatives of investors, and other interested groups.

THREE MEASUREMENT CONVENTIONS

Three broad measurement or valuation conventions (principles) underlie accrual accounting: *recognition* (when to record revenue), *matching* and *cost recovery* (when to record expense), and the *stable monetary unit* (what unit of measure to use).

Objective 8
Identify how the
measurement
conventions of
recognition, matching
and cost recovery, and
stable monetary unit
affect financial
reporting.

matching The linking of
revenues (as measured by
the selling prices of goods
and services delivered) and
efforts or expenses (as
measured by the cost of
goods and services used)
with a particular period for
which a measurement of
income is desired.

cost recovery A concept
in which assets such as
inventories, prepayments,
and equipment are carried
forward as assets because
their costs are expected to
be recovered in the form of
cash inflows (or reduced
cash outflows) in future
periods.

RECOGNITION

We discussed the first convention, *recognition,* earlier in this chapter in the section "Revenues and Expenses." In general, companies recognize revenue when they deliver the goods or services to customers.

MATCHING AND COST RECOVERY

You may often encounter a favorite buzzword in accounting: *matching.* **Matching** is the linking of revenues (as measured by the selling prices of goods and services delivered) with the expenses (as measured by the cost of goods and services used) incurred to generate the revenues. Matching is a fundamental principle of the accrual basis for measuring income.

Accountants apply matching as follows:

1. Identify the revenue recognized during the period.
2. Link the expenses to the recognized revenue directly (e.g., sales commissions or costs of inventories sold to customers) or indirectly (e.g., wages of janitors and supplies used). The latter expenses are costs of operations during a specific time period that have no measurable benefit for a future period and are thus linked to the current period's revenues.

The heart of recognizing expense is the **cost recovery** concept. That is, companies carry forward as assets such items as inventories, prepayments, and equipment. Why? Because companies expect to recover their costs in the form of cash inflows (or reduced cash outflows) in future periods. At the end of each period, the accountant examines the evidence to be assured that these assets—these unexpired costs—should not be written off as an expense of the current period. For instance, in our chapter example, King Hardware carried forward the asset prepaid rent of $2,000 on March 31 because the accountant is virtually certain that it represents a future benefit. Why? Because without the prepayment, King Hardware would have to pay $2,000 in April and May. So the presence of the prepayment is a benefit in the sense that future cash outflows will be reduced by $2,000. Furthermore, future revenue (sales) will be high enough to ensure the recovery of the $2,000.

STABLE MONETARY UNIT

The monetary unit (e.g., the dollar) is the principal means for measuring assets and equities. It is the common denominator for quantifying the effects of a wide variety of transactions. While companies in the United States, Canada, Australia, and New Zealand use the dollar as the monetary unit, in other countries they use the franc, pound, mark, yen, ruble, or some other monetary unit.

Such measurement assumes that the monetary unit—the dollar, for example—is an unchanging yardstick. Yet, we all know that a 2002 dollar does not have the same purchasing power as a 1992 or 1982 dollar. Therefore, users of accounting statements that include dollars from different years must recognize the limitations of the basic measurement unit.

Accountants have been criticized for not making explicit and formal adjustments to remedy the defects of their measuring unit. In the face of this, some accountants maintain that price-level adjustments would lessen objectivity and would add to the general confusion. They claim that the price-level problem has been exaggerated, and that the adjustments would not significantly affect the vast bulk of corporate statements because most accounts are in current or nearly current dollars.

On the other hand, inflation has been steady and its effects are sometimes surprisingly pervasive. Several countries, including Brazil and Argentina, routinely adjust their accounting numbers for the effects of inflation. The most troublesome aspect, however, is how to interpret the results after they are measured. Investors and managers in the United States are accustomed to the conventional statements. The intelligent interpretation of statements adjusted for changes in the price level will require extensive changes in the habits of users.

The body of generally accepted accounting principles contains more than the measurement conventions just discussed. Other major concepts include going concern, objectivity, materiality, and cost benefit. We discuss these in Appendix 16A.

SUMMARY PROBLEM FOR YOUR REVIEW

PROBLEM

The following interpretations and remarks are sometimes encountered regarding financial statements. Do you agree or disagree? Explain fully.

1. "If I purchase 100 shares of the outstanding common stock of General Motors Corporation, I invest my money directly in that corporation. General Motors must record that transaction."

2. "Sales show the cash coming in from customers and the various expenses show the cash going out for goods and services. The difference is net income."

3. Consider the following recent accounts of Walgreen, the largest U.S. drugstore chain:

Paid-in capital	$ 337,300,000
Retained earnings	3,147,000,000
Total stockholders' equity	$3,484,300,000

A shareholder commented, "Why can't that big drugstore pay higher wages and dividends? It can use its hundreds of millions of dollars of retained earnings to do so."

4. "The total Walgreens stockholders' equity measures the amount that the shareholders would get today if the corporation were liquidated."

SOLUTION

1. Money is invested directly in a corporation only upon original issuance of the stock by the corporation. For example, 100,000 shares of stock may be issued at $80 per share, bringing in $8 million to the corporation. This is a transaction between the corporation and the stockholders. It affects the corporate financial position:

Cash	$8,000,000	Stockholders' equity	$8,000,000

In turn, an original stockholder (A) may sell 100 shares of that stock to another individual (B) for $92 per share. This is a private transaction; no cash comes to the corporation. Of course, the corporation records the fact that 100 shares originally owned by A are now owned by B, but the corporate financial position is unchanged. Accounting focuses on the business entity; the private dealings of the owners have no direct effect on the financial position of the entity and hence are unrecorded except for detailed records of the owners' identities.

2. Cash receipts and disbursements are not the fundamental basis for the accounting recognition of revenues and expenses. Credit, not cash, lubricates the economy. Therefore, if a company renders services or goods to a customer, a collectible claim to cash in the form of a receivable is sufficient justification for recognizing revenue; similarly, if a company uses up services or goods, an obligation in the form of a payable is justification for recognizing expense.

   This approach to the measurement of net income is the accrual basis. Revenue is recognized as it is earned and realized. Expenses or losses are recognized when goods or services are used up in the obtaining of revenue (or when such goods or services cannot justifiably be carried forward as an asset because they have no potential future benefit). Companies deduct the expenses and losses from the revenue, and the result of this matching process is net income, the net increase in stockholders' equity from the conduct of operations.

3. As the chapter indicated, retained earnings is not cash. It is a stockholders' equity account that represents the accumulated increase in ownership claims because of profitable operations. A company may partially liquidate this claim or interest by the payment of cash dividends, but a growing company will reinvest cash to increase the investments in receivables, inventories, plant, equipment, and other assets so necessary for expansion. As a result, the ownership claims reflected by retained earnings may become "permanent" in the sense that, as a practical matter, the company will never liquidate them as long as the company remains in business.

   This linking of retained earnings and cash is only one example of erroneous interpretation. As a general rule, there is no direct relationship between the individual items on the two sides of the balance sheet. For example, Walgreens had cash of less than $142 million on the given balance sheet date when its retained earnings were nearly $3.5 billion.

4. Stockholders' equity is a difference, the excess of assets over liabilities. If the assets were carried in the accounting records at their liquidating value today, and the liabilities were carried at the exact amounts needed for their extinguishment, the remark would be true. But such valuations would be coincidental because companies customarily carry assets at historical cost expressed in an unchanging monetary unit. Intervening changes in markets and general price levels in inflationary times may mean that the assets are woefully understated. Investors may make a critical error if they think that balance sheets indicate current values.

   Furthermore, the "market values" for publicly owned shares are usually determined by daily trading conducted in the financial marketplaces such as the New York Stock Exchange. Numerous factors affect these values, including the expectations of (a) price appreciation and (b) cash flows in the form of dividends. The focus is on the future; the present and the past are examined only as clues to what may be forthcoming. Therefore, the present stockholders' equity is usually of only incidental concern. For example, stockholders' equity for Walgreens was $3,484,300,000 ÷ 1,004,022,258 shares, or $3.47 per share, while the company's market price per common share fluctuated between about $25 and $30.

Highlights to Remember

Read and interpret the basic financial statements.   An underlying structure of concepts, techniques, and conventions provides a basis for accounting practice. We present two basic financial statements, the balance sheet (or statement of financial position) and income statement, in this chapter. Their main elements are assets, liabilities, owners' equity, revenues, and expenses. Income statements and balance sheets are linked because the revenues and expenses appearing on income statements are components of stockholders' equity. Revenues increase stockholders' equity; expenses decrease stockholders' equity.

Analyze typical business transactions using the balance sheet equation. The balance sheet equation provides a framework for recording accounting transactions: Assets = Liabilities + Owners' Equity.

Distinguish between the accrual basis of accounting and the cash basis of accounting. The accrual basis is the heart of accounting. Under accrual accounting, companies recognize revenues as they are earned, and they record expenses as resources are used, rather than as related cash is received or disbursed. Do not confuse expense with the term *cash disbursement*, or revenue with the term *cash receipt*.

Relate the measurement of expenses to the expiration of assets. At the end of each accounting period, companies must make adjustments so that financial statements may be presented on a full-fledged accrual basis. The major adjustments are for (1) expiration of unexpired costs, (2) recognition (earning) of unearned revenues, (3) accrual of unrecorded expenses, and (4) accrual of unrecorded revenues.

Explain the nature of dividends and retained income. Dividends are not expenses; they are distributions of assets that reduce ownership claims. Similarly, retained income is not cash; it is a claim against total assets.

Select relevant items from a set of data and assemble them into a balance sheet, an income statement, and a statement of retained income. After a company records transactions and makes adjustments, it can compile the data into financial statements. The changes in the retained income account form the basis for the income statement and the statement of retained income.

Distinguish between the reporting of corporate owners' equity and the reporting of owners' equity for partnerships and sole proprietorships. Entities can be organized as corporations, partnerships, or sole proprietorships. The type of organization does not affect most accounting entries. Only the owners' equity section will differ among organizational types.

Identify how the measurement conventions of recognition, matching and cost recovery, and stable monetary unit affect financial reporting. Three major conventions that affect accounting are recognition, matching and cost recovery, and stable monetary unit. Recognition affects when companies record revenues in the income statement, matching and cost recovery specify when to record expenses, and stable monetary units justify use of a unit of currency (the dollar in the United States) to measure accounting transactions.

Understand how managers and investors can learn about the financial position and prospects of an organization from its financial statements. The financial statements in this chapter form the basis of many financial judgments of managers and investors. They describe the financial results of an organization in a consistent way that allows comparison to historical results of the organization and to the results of other organizations.

Appendix 16A: Additional Accounting Concepts

This appendix describes several concepts that are prominent parts of the body of generally accepted accounting principles: continuity or going concern, objectivity or verifiability, materiality, conservatism, and cost-benefit.

THE CONTINUITY OR GOING CONCERN CONVENTION

The **continuity** or **going concern convention** is the assumption that an organization will continue to exist and operate. This notion implies that a company will use existing resources, such as plant assets, to fulfill the general purposes of a continuing entity rather than sell them in tomorrow's real estate or equipment markets. It also implies that the company will pay existing liabilities at maturity in an orderly manner.

continuity convention (going concern convention) The assumption that an organization will continue to exist and operate.

Suppose some old specialized equipment has a depreciated cost (i.e., original cost less accumulated depreciation) of $10,000, a replacement cost of $12,000, and a realizable value of $7,000 on the used-equipment market. The continuity convention is often cited as the justification for adhering to acquisition cost less depreciation, $10,000 in this example, as the primary basis for valuing assets such as inventories, land, buildings, and equipment. Some critics of these accounting practices believe that such valuations are not as informative as their replacement cost ($12,000) or their realizable values on sale ($7,000). Defenders of using $10,000 as an appropriate asset valuation argue that a going concern will generally use the asset as originally intended. Therefore, the recorded cost (the acquisition cost less depreciation) is the preferable basis for accountability and evaluation of performance. Hence, other values are not germane because replacement or disposal will not occur en masse as of the balance sheet date.

The opposite view to this going concern or continuity convention is an immediate-liquidation assumption, whereby a company values all items on a balance sheet at the amounts appropriate if its assets were to be sold and its liabilities paid in piecemeal fashion within a few days or months. A company would use this liquidation approach to valuation only when it is in severe, near-bankrupt straits.

OBJECTIVITY OR VERIFIABILITY

objectivity (verifiability) Accuracy supported by a high extent of consensus among independent measures of an item.

Users want assurance that management or accountants have not fabricated the numbers in the financial statements to mislead or falsify the firm's financial position and performance. Consequently, accountants seek and prize **objectivity** (or **verifiability**) as an essential characteristic of measurement. A financial statement item is objective or verifiable if there would be a high extent of consensus among independent measures of the item. For example, the amount paid for assets is usually highly verifiable, but the predicted cost to replace assets often is not.

Many critics of existing accounting practices want to trade objectivity for what they conceive as more relevant or valid information. For example, the accounting literature is peppered with suggestions that accounting should attempt to measure "economic income," even though it may reduce objectivity. This particular suggestion often involves introducing asset valuations at replacement costs when these are higher than historical costs. The accounting profession has generally rejected these suggestions, even when reliable replacement price quotations are available, because many accountants believe that only a bona fide sale is sufficient to justify income recognition.

MATERIALITY

materiality The accounting convention that justifies the omission of insignificant information when its omission or misstatement would not mislead a user of the financial statements.

Because accounting is a practical art, the practitioner often tempers accounting reports by applying judgments about **materiality.** A financial statement item is not *material* if it is sufficiently small that its omission or misstatement would not mislead a user of the financial statements. Many outlays that should theoretically be recorded as assets are immediately written off as expenses because of their lack of significance. For example, many corporations have a rule that requires the immediate write-off to expense of all outlays under a specified minimum of, say, $100, regardless of the useful life of the asset acquired. In such a case, coat hangers may be acquired that may last indefinitely but may never appear in the balance sheet as assets. The resulting $100 understatement of assets and stockholders' equity would be too trivial to worry about.

When is an item material? There will probably never be a definitive answer. What is trivial to IBM may be material to a two-person e-business start-up. A working rule is that an item is material if its proper accounting would probably affect the decision of a knowledgeable user. In sum, although materiality is an important convention, it is difficult to use anything other than prudent judgment to tell whether an item is material.

The Conservatism Convention

Conservatism has been a hallmark of accounting. In a technical sense, the **conservatism convention** means selecting the method of measurement that yields the gloomiest immediate results. This attitude is reflected in such working rules as "Anticipate no gains, but provide for all possible losses," and "If in doubt, write it off."

Accountants have traditionally regarded the historical costs of acquiring an asset as the ceiling for its valuation. Assets may be written up only upon an exchange, but they may be written down without an exchange. For example, inventories are written down (and a loss is recognized) when replacement costs decline, but they are never written up when replacement costs increase.

Conservatism has been criticized as being inherently inconsistent. If replacement market prices are sufficiently objective and verifiable to justify write-downs, why aren't they just as valid for write-ups? Furthermore, the critics maintain, conservatism is not a fundamental concept. Accounting reports should try to present the most accurate picture feasible—neither too high nor too low. Accountants defend their attitude by saying that erring in the direction of conservatism would usually have less severe economic consequences than erring in the direction of overstating assets and net income.

Conservatism that leads to understating net income in one period also creates an overstatement of net income in a future period. For example, if a $100 inventory is written down to $80, operating income is reduced by $20 in the period of the write-down but increased by $20 in the period the inventory is sold.

conservatism convention
Selecting the method of measurement that yields the gloomiest immediate results.

Cost-Benefit

Accounting systems vary in complexity from the minimum crude records kept to satisfy government authorities to the sophisticated budgeting and feedback schemes that are at the heart of management planning and controlling. As companies change their accounting systems, the potential benefits should exceed the additional costs. Often, the benefits are difficult to measure but this **cost-benefit criterion** at least implicitly underlies the decisions about the design of accounting systems. Sometimes, the reluctance to adopt suggestions for new ways of measuring financial position and performance is because of inertia. More often, it is because the apparent benefits do not exceed the obvious costs of gathering and interpreting the information.

cost-benefit criterion
An approach that implicitly underlies the decisions about the design of accounting systems. As a system is changed, its potential benefits should exceed its additional costs.

Room for Judgment

Accounting is commonly misunderstood as being a precise discipline that produces exact measurements of a company's financial position and performance. As a result, many individuals regard accountants as little more than mechanical tabulators who grind out financial reports after processing an imposing amount of detail in accordance with stringent predetermined rules. Although accountants take methodical steps with masses of data, their rules of measurement allow much room for judgment. Managers and accountants who exercise this judgment have more influence on financial reporting than is commonly believed. These judgments are guided by the basic concepts, techniques, and conventions called GAAP. Examples of the latter include the basic concepts just discussed. Their meaning will become clearer as these concepts are applied in future chapters.

Appendix 16B: Using Ledger Accounts

Chapter 16 focused on the balance sheet equation, the general framework used by accountants to record economic transactions. This appendix focuses on some of the main techniques that accountants use to record the transactions illustrated in the chapter.

THE ACCOUNT

To begin, consider how the accountant would record the King Hardware Co. transactions that were introduced in the chapter. Exhibit 16-1 (p. 640) showed their effects on the elements of the balance sheet equation:

	A		=	L	+	SE
	Cash	Inventory		Accounts Payable		Paid-in Capital
1. Initial investment by owners	+100,000		=			+100,000
2. Acquire inventory for cash	− 75,000	+75,000	=			
3. Acquire inventory on credit		+35,000	=	+35,000		

This balance sheet equation approach emphasizes the concepts, but it can become unwieldy if many transactions occur. Changes in the balance sheet equation can occur many times daily. In large businesses, such as in a department store, hundreds or thousands of repetitive transactions occur hourly. In practice, accountants use **ledger accounts** to keep track of how these multitudes of transactions affect each particular asset, liability, revenue, expense, and so forth. We use simplified versions of ledger accounts called T-accounts because they take the form of the capital letter T. The following T-accounts illustrate the preceding transactions:

ledger accounts A method of keeping track of how multitudes of transactions affect each particular asset, liability, revenue, and expense.

Assets = Liabilities + Stockholders' Equity

Cash			
Increases		Decreases	
(1)	100,000	(2)	75,000
Bal.	25,000		

Accounts Payable			
Decreases		Increases	
		(3)	35,000

Inventory			
Increases		Decreases	
(2)	75,000		
(3)	35,000		
Bal.	110,000		

Paid-in Capital			
Decreases		Increases	
		(1)	100,000

double-entry system A method of record keeping in which each transaction affects at least two accounts.

We made the T-account entries using a **double-entry system,** whereby each transaction affects at least two accounts. Asset accounts have balances on the left side of the T-account. Entries on the left side increase the accounts and entries on the right side decrease them.

Liabilities and stockholders' equity accounts have right-side balances. They are increased by entries on the right side and decreased by entries on the left side.

Each T-account is similar to a column in the balance sheet equation. However, the format of the T-account eliminates the use of negative numbers. Any entry that reduces an account balance is added to the side of the account that decreases the account balance.

Each T-account summarizes the changes in a particular asset or equity. Each transaction is keyed in some way, such as by the numbering used in this illustration or by date or both. This keying facilitates the rechecking (auditing) process by aiding the tracing of transactions to original sources. You can compute the balance of any account by totaling each side of the account and deducting the smaller total amount from the larger. Accounts exist to keep an up-to-date summary of the changes in specific assets and equities.

Accountants can prepare a balance sheet at any time if the accounts are up to date. The accounts contain all the necessary information. For example, the balance sheet for King Hardware after the first three transactions is

Assets		Liabilities and Stockholders' Equity	
Cash	$ 25,000	Liabilities	
Inventory	110,000	Accounts payable	$ 35,000
		Stockholders' equity	
		Paid-in capital	100,000
Total assets	$135,000	Total equities	$135,000

GENERAL LEDGER

King Hardware's **general ledger,** shown in Exhibit 16-7, is defined as a collection of the group of accounts that supports the items shown in the major financial statements.[3] Exhibit 16-7 is merely a recasting of the facts that were analyzed in Exhibit 16-1. Study Exhibit 16-7 by comparing its analysis of each transaction against its corresponding analysis in Exhibit 16-1, page 640.

general ledger A collection of the group of accounts that supports the items shown in the major financial statements.

DEBITS AND CREDITS

When placing transaction amounts in the appropriate accounts, accountants often use the technical terms *debit* and *credit*. **Debit** means one thing and one thing only—"left side of an account" (not "bad," "something coming," etc.). **Credit** means one thing and one thing only—"right side of an account" (not "good," "something owed," etc.).

For example, if you asked an accountant what entry to make for transaction 4b, the answer would be "I would debit (or *charge*) Cost of Goods Sold for $100,000; and I would credit Inventory for $100,000." This is an abbreviated way of saying, "Place $100,000 on the left (debit) side of the Cost of Goods Sold T-account and place $100,000 on the right (credit) side of the Inventory T-account." Note that the total dollar amounts of the debits (entries on the left side of the account[s] affected) will *always* equal the total dollar amount of credits (entries on the right side of the account[s] affected) because the whole accounting system is based on an equation.

Debit and credit are used as verbs, adjectives, or nouns. The instruction "debit $1,000 to cash" uses *debit* as a verb, meaning that $1,000 should be placed on the left side of the cash account. When "a debit is made to cash," *debit* is a noun. In the statement "cash has a debit balance of $12,000," *debit* is an adjective that describes the status of a particular account.

In our everyday conversation, we sometimes use the words *debits* and *credits* in a general sense that may completely diverge from their technical accounting uses. For instance, we may give praise by saying, "She deserves plenty of credit for her good deed" or "That misplay is a debit on his ledger." When you study accounting, forget these general uses and misuses of the words. Merely think right side or left side entries to T-accounts.

Assets generally have left-side (debit) balances. Why do expenses also carry debit balances? Expense accounts are places to temporarily record reductions in stockholders' equity. To reduce stockholders' equity we place entries on the left side of the accounts. Why?

debit An entry on the left side of an account.

credit An entry on the right side of an account.

---

[3] *The general ledger is usually supported by various subsidiary ledgers that provide details for accounts in the general ledger. For instance, an accounts receivable subsidiary ledger would contain a separate account for each credit customer. The accounts receivable balance that appears in the Sears balance sheet is in a single account in the Sears general ledger. However, that single balance is the sum of the detailed individual accounts receivable balances of millions of credit customers.*

Exhibit 16-7
General Ledger of King Hardware Co.

Assets
(Increases on Left, Decreases on Right)

Cash

(1)	100,000	(2)	75,000
(5)	30,000	(6)	10,000
		(7a)	3,000
3/31 Bal.	42,000		

Accounts Receivable

(4a)	120,000	(5)	30,000
3/31 Bal.	90,000		

Inventory

(2)	75,000	(4b)	100,000
(3)	35,000		
3/31 Bal.	10,000		

Prepaid Rent

(7a)	3,000	(7b)	1,000
3/31 Bal.	2,000		

Liabilities and Stockholders' Equity
(Decreases on Left, Increases on Right)

Accounts Payable

(6)	10,000	(3)	35,000
		3/31 Bal.	25,000

Paid-In Capital

	(1)	100,000
	3/31 Bal.	100,000

Retained Income

	3/31 Bal.	19,000*

Expense and Revenue Accounts

Sales

	(4a)	120,000

Cost of Goods Sold

(4b)	100,000

Rent Expense

(7b)	1,000

Because they offset the normal (i.e., right-side) stockholders' equity balances. Because expenses decrease stockholders' equity, they are carried as left-side (debit) balances.

To recapitulate:

Assets		=	Liabilities		+	Stockholders' Equity	
Increase	Decrease		Decrease	Increase		Decrease	Increase
+	−		−	+		−	+
debit	credit		debit	credit		debit	credit
left	right		left	right		left	right

Because revenues increase stockholders' equity, we record them as credits. Because expenses decrease stockholders' equity, we record them as debits.

Accounting Vocabulary

More new terms were introduced in this chapter (and its appendices) than in any other, so be sure that you understand the following:

account, p. 642
accounts payable, p. 639
accounts receivable, p. 639
accrual basis, p. 644
accrue, p. 650
adjustments, p. 645
assets, p. 639
audit, p. 656
balance sheet, p. 639
cash basis, p. 644
conservatism convention, p. 663
continuity convention, p. 661
corporation, p. 638
cost-benefit criterion, p. 663
cost recovery, p. 658
credit, p. 665
debit, p. 665
deferred revenue, p. 648
dividends, p. 652
double-entry system, p. 664
earnings, p. 641

equities, p. 639
expenses, p. 641
Financial Accounting
   Standards Board (FASB),
   p. 657
general ledger, p. 665
going concern convention,
   p. 661
income, p. 641
income statement, p. 641
International Accounting
   Standards Board (IASB),
   p. 657
ledger accounts, p. 664
liabilities, p. 639
matching, p. 658
materiality, p. 662
net worth, p. 656
objectivity, p. 662
owners' equity, p. 639

paid-in capital, p. 639
partnership, p. 655
profits, p. 641
residual value, p. 647
retained earnings, p. 639
retained income, p. 639
revenue, p. 641
Securities and Exchange
   Commission (SEC), p. 657
sole proprietorship, p. 655
source documents, p. 645
statement of financial condition, p. 639
statement of financial position,
   p. 639
stockholders' equity, p. 639
transaction, p. 638
unearned revenue, p. 648
unexpired cost, p. 646
verifiability, p. 662

Assignment Material

The assignment material for each remaining chapter is divided as follows:

- Fundamental Assignment Material
     General Exercises and Problems
     Understanding Published Financial Reports
- Additional Assignment Material
     Questions
     General Exercises and Problems
     Understanding Published Financial Reports
- Collaborative Learning Exercise
- Internet Exercise

The "General Exercises and Problems" subgroups focus on concepts and procedures that are applicable to a wide variety of specific settings. Many instructors believe that these "traditional" types of exercises and problems have proved their educational value over many years of use in introductory textbooks.

The "Understanding Published Financial Reports" subgroups focus on real-life situations. They have the same basic aims as the "General Exercises and Problems" subgroups. Indeed, some instructors may confine their assignments to the "Understanding Published Financial Reports" subgroups. The distinctive characteristic of the latter subgroups is the use of actual companies and news events to enhance the student's interest in accounting. Many students and instructors get more satisfaction out of a course that frequently uses actual situations as a means of learning accounting methods and concepts.

Fundamental Assignment Material

GENERAL EXERCISES AND PROBLEMS

16-A1   Balance Sheet Equation

For each of the following independent cases, compute the amounts (in thousands) for the items indicated by letters, and show your supporting computations:

	Case		
	1	2	3
Revenues	$145	$ K	$300
Expenses	120	170	270
Dividends declared	–0–	5	Q
Additional investment by stockholders	–0–	30	35
Net income	E	20	P
Retained income			
Beginning of year	40	50	100
End of year	D	J	110
Paid-in capital			
Beginning of year	15	10	N
End of year	C	H	85
Total assets			
Beginning of year	85	F	L
End of year	90	275	M
Total liabilities			
Beginning of year	A	100	105
End of year	B	G	95

16-A2   Analysis of Transactions, Preparation of Statements

The Nagarajan Company was incorporated on April 1, 20X1. Nagarajan had 10 holders of common stock. Ramesh Nagarajan, who was the president and chief executive officer, held 51% of the shares. The company rented space in chain discount stores and specialized in selling ladies' shoes. Nagarajan's first location was a store in Import Market Centers, Inc.

The following events occurred during April:

1. The company was incorporated. Common stockholders invested $100,000 cash.
2. Purchased merchandise inventory for cash, $35,000.
3. Purchased merchandise inventory on open account, $25,000.
4. Merchandise carried in inventory at a cost of $37,000 was sold for cash for $25,000 and on open account for $65,000, a grand total of $90,000. Nagarajan carries and collects these accounts receivable.
5. Collection of the above accounts receivable, $15,000.

6. Payments of accounts payable, $18,000. See transaction 3.

7. Special display equipment and fixtures were acquired on April 1 for $36,000. Their expected useful life was 36 months with no terminal scrap value. Straight-line depreciation was adopted. This equipment was removable. Nagarajan paid $12,000 as a down payment and signed a promissory note for $24,000.

8. On April 1, Nagarajan signed a rental agreement with Import Market Centers. The agreement called for a flat $2,000 per month, payable quarterly in advance. Therefore, Nagarajan paid $6,000 cash on April 1.

9. The rental agreement also called for a payment of 10% of all sales. This payment was in addition to the flat $2,000 per month. In this way, Import Market Centers would share in any success of the venture and be compensated for general services such as cleaning and utilities. This payment was to be made in cash on the last day of each month as soon as the sales for the month were tabulated. Therefore, Nagarajan made the payment on April 30.

10. Wages, salaries, and sales commissions were all paid in cash for all earnings by employees. The amount was $40,000.

11. Depreciation expense was recognized. See transaction 7.

12. The expiration of an appropriate amount of prepaid rental services was recognized. See transaction 8.

Required

1. Prepare an analysis of Nagarajan Company's transactions, employing the equation approach demonstrated in Exhibit 16-1. Two additional columns will be needed: Equipment and Fixtures and Note Payable. Show all amounts in thousands.

2. Prepare a balance sheet as of April 30, 20X1, and an income statement for the month of April. Ignore income taxes.

3. Given these sparse facts, analyze Nagarajan's performance for April and its financial position as of April 30, 20X1.

16-A3   Cash Basis Versus Accrual Basis

Refer to the preceding problem. If Nagarajan Company measured income on the cash basis, what revenue would be reported for April? Which basis (accrual or cash) provides a better measure of revenue? Why?

UNDERSTANDING PUBLISHED FINANCIAL REPORTS

16-B1   Balance Sheet Equation

Micron Technology is one of the leading producers of semiconductor components. Its revenue grew from $506 million in 1992 to more than $7.3 billion in 2000. The company's actual data (in millions of dollars) follow for its fiscal year ended September 2, 1999:

Assets, beginning of period	$4,551.4
Assets, end of period	E
Liabilities, beginning of period	A
Liabilities, end of period	2,832.8
Paid-in capital, beginning of period	587.0
Paid-in capital, end of period	D
Retained earnings, beginning of period	2,114.3
Retained earnings, end of period	C
Revenues	3,764.0
Costs and expenses	B
Net income (loss)	(68.9)
Dividends	0.0
Additional investments by stockholders	1,331.7

Required

Find the unknowns (in millions), showing computations to support your answers.

16-B2   Analysis of Transactions, Preparation of Statements

PACCAR produces Kenworth and Peterbilt trucks. The company's actual condensed balance sheet data for January 1, 2000 follows (in millions):

Assets		Equities	
Cash	$ 528	Accounts payable	$1,734
Accounts receivable	5,337	Other liabilities	4,088
Inventories	385		
Prepaid expenses and other assets	716	Stockholders' equity	2,111
Property, plant, and equipment	967		
Total	$7,933	Total	$7,933

Suppose the following summarizes some major transactions during January (in millions):

1. Trucks carried in inventory at a cost of $400 were sold for cash of $150 and on open account of $500, a grand total of $650.
2. Acquired inventory on account, $500.
3. Collected receivables, $300.
4. On April 2, used $250 cash to prepay some rent and insurance for 2000.
5. Payments on accounts payable (for inventories), $450.
6. Paid selling and administrative expenses in cash, $100.
7. A total of $90 of prepaid expenses for rent and insurance expired in January 2000.
8. Depreciation expense of $20 was recognized for January.

Required

1. Prepare an analysis of the PACCAR transactions, employing the equation approach demonstrated in Exhibit 16-1, p. 640. Show all amounts in millions of dollars. (For simplicity, only a few major transactions are illustrated here.)
2. Prepare an income statement for the month ended January 31 and a balance sheet as of January 31. Ignore income taxes.

16-B3   Cash Basis Versus Accrual Basis

Refer to the preceding problem. If PACCAR measured income on the cash basis, what revenue would be reported for January? Which basis (accrual or cash) provides a better measure of revenue? Why?

Additional Assignment Material

QUESTIONS

16-1. What types of questions are answered by the income statement and balance sheet?

16-2. Criticize: "Assets are things of value owned by an organization."

16-3. How are the income statement and balance sheet related?

16-4. Criticize: "Net income is the difference in the ownership capital account balances at two points in time."

16-5. Distinguish between the accrual basis and the cash basis of accounting.

16-6. How do adjusting entries differ from routine entries?

16-7. Explain why advertising should be viewed as an asset on acquisition.

16-8. Why is it better to refer to the costs, rather than values, of assets such as plant or inventories?

16-9. "Depreciation is cost allocation, not valuation." Do you agree? Explain.

16-10. Criticize: "As a stockholder, I have a right to more dividends. You have millions stashed away in retained earnings. It's about time that you let the true owners get their hands on that pot of gold."

16-11. Criticize: "Dividends are distributions of profits."

16-12. Explain the relationship between the FASB and the SEC.

16-13. What is the major criticism of the dollar as the principal accounting measure?

16-14. What does the accountant mean by going concern?

16-15. What does the accountant mean by objectivity?

16-16. What is the role of cost-benefit (economic feasibility) in the development of accounting principles?

COGNITIVE EXERCISES

16-17 Accounting Valuation of Fixed Assets
Consider two types of assets held by Weyerhaeuser Company: timber-growing land purchased in 1910 when the company was known as Weyerhaeuser Timber Company and machinery purchased and installed at its paper processing plant in Saskatchewan, Canada, in 1998. How close do you suppose the December 31, 2001, balance sheet value of each asset is to the market value of the asset at that date?

16-18 Marketing, the Income Statement, and the Balance Sheet
The marketing manager of a major consumer products company said, "The balance sheet isn't of much use to me. It is so static. But the income statement is a primary tool for managing my dynamic business." Why would a marketing manager find the income statement more useful than the balance sheet?

16-19 Revenue Recognition and Evaluation of Sales Staff
Revenue on an accrual-accounting basis must be both earned and realized before it is recognized in the income statement. Revenue in cash-basis accounting must be received in cash. Is an accrual-basis or cash-basis recognition of revenue more relevant for evaluating the performance of a sales staff? Why?

GENERAL EXERCISES AND PROBLEMS

16-20 True or False
Use *T* or *F* to indicate whether each of the following statements is true or false. Change each false statement into one that is true.

1. Inventories should be classified as a stockholders' equity item.
2. Retained earnings should be accounted for as an asset item.
3. Machinery used in the business should be recorded at replacement cost.
4. The large cash balance is the best evidence of previous profitable operations.
5. It is not possible to determine changes in the condition of a business from a single balance sheet.
6. From a single balance sheet, you can find stockholders' equity for a period but not for a specific day.

16-21 Nature of Retained Income
This is an exercise on the relationships among assets, liabilities, and ownership equities. The numbers are small, but the underlying concepts are large.

1. Prepare an opening balance sheet of

Cash	$1,500	Paid-in capital	$1,500

2. Purchase inventory for $600 cash. Prepare a balance sheet. A heading is unnecessary in this and subsequent requirements.
3. Sell the entire inventory for $850 cash. Prepare a balance sheet. Where is the retained income in terms of relationships within the balance sheet? That is, what is the meaning of the retained income? Explain in your own words.
4. Buy inventory for $400 cash and equipment for $750 cash. Prepare a balance sheet. Where is the retained income in terms of relationships within the balance sheet? That is, what is the meaning of the retained income? Explain in your own words.
5. Buy inventory for $450 on open account. Prepare a balance sheet. Where is the retained income and account payable in terms of the relationships within the balance sheet? That is, what is the meaning of the account payable and the retained income? Explain in your own words.

16-22   Income Statement
Here is a proposed income statement of an antiques dealer:

South Street Antiques
Statement of Profit and Loss, December 31, 20X1

Revenues		
Sales	$1,500,000	
Increase in market value of land and building	200,000	$1,700,000
Deduct expenses		
Advertising	$ 100,000	
Sales commissions	60,000	
Utilities	20,000	
Wages	150,000	
Dividends	200,000	
Cost of antiques purchased	800,000	1,330,000
Net profit		$ 370,000

Required

List and describe any shortcomings of this statement.

16-23   Customer and Airline
Suppose Amazon.com decided to hold a managers' meeting in Cancun in February. To take advantage of special fares, Amazon purchased airline tickets in advance from United Airlines at a total cost of $70,000. These were acquired on December 1 for cash.

Required

Using the balance sheet equation format, analyze the impact of the December payment and the February travel on the financial position of both Amazon and United.

16-24   Tenant and Landlord
Blaine Hardware, a franchise of Ace Hardware Corporation, pays quarterly rent on its store at the beginning of each quarter. The rent per quarter is $9,000. The owner of the building in which the store is located is the Klastorin Corporation.

Required

Using the balance sheet equation format, analyze the effects of the following on the tenant's and the landlord's financial position:

1. Blaine Hardware pays $9,000 rent on July 1.
2. Adjustment for July.
3. Adjustment for August.
4. Adjustment for September.

16-25   Find Unknowns
The following data pertain to Andaman Cruises, a company in Thailand where the currency is the baht (B). Total assets at January 1, 20X1, were B 100,000; at December 31, 20X1, B 120,000. During 20X1, sales were B 260,000, cash dividends were B 16,000, and operating expenses (exclusive of costs of goods sold) were B 50,000. Total liabilities at December 31, 20X1, were B 55,000; at January 1, 20X1, B 40,000. There was no additional capital paid in during 20X1.

Required

Calculate the following items.

(These need not be computed in any particular order.)

1. Stockholders' equity, for January 1, 20X1
2. Net income for 20X1
3. Cost of goods sold for 20X1

16-26   Balance Sheet Equation; Solving for Unknowns
Compute the unknowns (X, Y, Z, A, and B) in each of the individual cases, Columns 1 through 7, in Exhibit 16–8.

16-27   Fundamental Transaction Analysis and Preparation of Statements
Three former college classmates have decided to pool a variety of work experiences by opening a store near campus to sell wireless equipment to students. The first products were Palm Pilots and

Exhibit 16–8
Data for Exercise 16–26

Given	1	2	3	4	5	6	7
Assets at beginning of period		$ 9,000				B	$ 8,200
Assets at end of period		11,000					9,600
Liabilities at beginning of period		6,000				$12,000	4,000
Liabilities at end of period		Y					6,000
Stockholders' equity at beginning of period	$8,000	X				A	X
Stockholders' equity at end of period	X	5,000				10,000	Y
Sales			$15,000		X	14,000	20,000
Inventory at beginning of period			6,000	$ 8,000		Z	
Inventory at end of period			7,000	7,000		7,000	
Purchase of inventory			10,000	12,000		6,000	
Gross profit			Y		$3,000	6,000	A
Cost of goods sold*			X	X	4,500	X	B
Other expenses			4,000			4,000	5,000
Net profit	3,000	Z	Z			Y	Z
Dividends	2,000	–0–				1,500	400
Additional investments by stockholders						5,000	–0–

*Note that cost of goods sold = beginning inventory + purchases − ending inventory.

Nokia cell phones. The business has been incorporated as University Wireless. The following transactions occurred during March.

1. On March 1, 20X1, each of the three invested $10,000 in cash in exchange for 1,000 shares of stock each.
2. The corporation quickly acquired $40,000 in inventory, half of which had to be paid for in cash. The other half was acquired on open accounts that were payable after 30 days.
3. A store was rented for $500 monthly. A lease was signed for 1 year on March 1. The first 2 months' rent were paid in advance. Other payments were to be made on the second of each month.
4. Advertising during March was purchased on open account for $3,000 from a newspaper owned by one of the stockholders. Additional advertising services of $6,000 were acquired for cash.
5. Sales were $60,000. Merchandise was sold for twice its purchase cost. Seventy-five percent of the sales were on open account.
6. Wages and salaries incurred in March amounted to $11,000, of which $5,000 was paid.
7. Miscellaneous services paid for in cash were $1,510.

8. On March 1, fixtures and equipment were purchased for $6,000 with a downpayment of $1,000 plus a $5,000 note payable in one year.

9. See transaction 8 and make the March 31 adjustment for interest expense accrued at 9.6%. (The interest is not due until the note matures.)

10. See transaction 8 and make the March 31 adjustment for depreciation expense on a straight-line basis. The estimated life of the fixtures and equipment is 10 years with no expected terminal scrap value. Straight-line depreciation here would be $6,000 ÷ 10 years = $600 per year, or $50 per month.

11. Cash dividends of $4,000 were declared and disbursed to stockholders on March 30.

Required

1. Using the accrual basis of accounting, prepare an analysis of transactions, employing the equation approach demonstrated in Exhibit 16-1, page 640. Use the following headings: Cash, Accounts Receivable, Inventory, Prepaid Rent, Fixtures and Equipment, Accounts Payable, Notes Payable, Accrued Wages Payable, Accrued Interest Payable, Paid-in Capital, and Retained Income.

2. Prepare a balance sheet and a multiple-step income statement. Also prepare a statement of retained income.

3. What advice would you give the owners based on the information compiled in the financial statements?

16-28   Debits and Credits

Study Appendix 16B. Determine for the following transactions whether the account named in parentheses is to be debited or credited.

1. Borrowed money from a bank (Notes Payable), $12,000.
2. Bought merchandise on open account (Accounts Payable), $5,000.
3. Sold merchandise (Merchandise Inventory), $1,000.
4. Paid Johnson Associates $3,000 owed them (Accounts Payable).
5. Paid dividends (Cash), $500.
6. Delivered merchandise to customers (Merchandise Inventory), $3,000.
7. Received cash from customers on accounts due (Accounts Receivable), $2,000.

16-29   True or False

Study Appendix 16B. Use *T* or *F* to indicate whether each of the following statements is true or false. For each false statement, explain why it is false.

1. Debit entries must always be recorded on the left. Credit entries can be either on the right or on the left.
2. Money borrowed from the bank should be credited to Cash and debited to Notes Payable.
3. Decreases in accounts must be shown on the debit side.
4. Both increases in liabilities and decreases in assets should be entered on the right.
5. Equipment purchases for cash should be debited to Equipment and credited to Cash.
6. Asset credits should be on the right and liability credits on the left.
7. Payments on mortgages should be debited to Cash and credited to Mortgages Payable. Mortgages are long-term debts.
8. Increases in asset accounts must always be entered on the left.
9. Increases in stockholders' equity always should be entered as credits.
10. Purchase of inventory on account should be credited to Inventory and debited to Accounts Payable.
11. Decreases in liability accounts should be recorded on the right.

16-30   Use of T-Accounts

The Junior League of Adams County had the following transactions during June:

a. Collected $300 of dues that had been billed in May.
b. Sold an old computer for $150 cash and a promise to pay $200 in one month. The book value of the computer was $350.
c. Bought a postage meter on credit for $130.
d. Received the $200 promised in transaction b.

1. Set up T-accounts for the following accounts:

> Cash
> Dues receivable
> Accounts receivable
> Equipment
> Accounts payable

2. Make entries for each of the four transactions into the T-accounts. Label each entry with a, b, c, or d.

16-31 Use of T-Accounts
Study Appendix 16B. Refer to Problem 16-A2. Make entries for April in T-accounts. Key your entries and check to see that the ending balances agree with the financial statements.

16-32 Use of T-Accounts
Study Appendix 16B. Refer to Problem 16-27. Use T-accounts to present an analysis of March transactions. Key your entries and check to see that the ending balances agree with the financial statements.

16-33 Measurement of Income for Tax and Other Purposes
The following are the summarized transactions of Dr. JoAnne Pullem, a dentist, for 20X1, her first year in practice.

1. Acquired equipment and furniture for $69,000. Its expected useful life is six years. Straight-line depreciation will be used, assuming zero terminal disposal value.
2. Fees collected, $81,000. These fees included $2,000 paid in advance by some patients on December 31, 20X1.
3. Rent is paid at the rate of $500 monthly, payable quarterly on the 25th of March, June, September, and December for the following quarter. Total disbursements during 20X1 for rent were $7,500 including an initial payment on January 1.
4. Fees billed but uncollected, December 31, 20X1, $20,000.
5. Utilities expense paid in cash, $600. Additional utility bills unpaid at December 31, 20X1, $100.
6. Salaries expense of dental assistant and secretary, $16,000 paid in cash. In addition, $1,000 was earned but unpaid on December 31, 20X1.

Dr. Pullem may elect either the cash basis or the accrual basis of measuring income for income tax purposes, provided that she uses it consistently in subsequent years. Under either alternative, the original cost of the equipment and furniture must be written off over its six-year useful life rather than being regarded as a lump-sum expense in the first year.

Required

1. Prepare income statements on both the cash and accrual bases, using one column for each basis.
2. Which basis do you prefer as a measure of Dr. Pullem's performance? Why? What do you think is the justification for the government's allowing the use of the cash basis for income tax purposes?

UNDERSTANDING PUBLISHED FINANCIAL REPORTS

16-34 Balance Sheet Effects
Washington Mutual, Inc., the largest savings institution and ninth largest bank in the United States, showed the following items (among others) on its balance sheet at January 1, 2000:

Cash (an asset)	$ 3,040,167,000
Total deposits (a liability)	$81,129,768,000

Required

1. Suppose you made a deposit of $1,000 in the bank. How would each of the bank's assets and equities be affected? How much would each of your personal assets and equities be affected? Be specific.
2. Suppose Washington Mutual makes a $800,000 loan to a local hospital for remodeling. What would be the effect on each of the bank's assets and equities immediately after the loan is made? Be specific.
3. Suppose you borrowed $10,000 from Washington Mutual on a personal loan. How would such a transaction affect each of your personal assets and equities?

16-35 Preparation of Balance Sheet for Lands' End

Lands' End is a mail-order clothing store based in Dodgeville, Wisconsin. Its annual report included the following balance sheet items at January 28, 2000 (in thousands of dollars):

Accrued liabilities	$ 43,754
Cash	76,413
Total stockholders' equity	?
Total liabilities	?
Long-term liabilities	9,117
Receivables	17,753
Common stock	402
Inventory	?
Accounts payable	74,510
Property, plant, and equipment	165,822
Other stockholders' equity	295,805
Other assets	34,015
Other liabilities	32,608
Total assets	456,196

Required

Prepare a condensed balance sheet including amounts for

a. Inventory. What do you think of its relative size?
b. Total stockholders' equity.
c. Total liabilities.

16-36 Net Income and Retained Income

Walt Disney Company is a well-known entertainment company. The following data are from its 2000 annual report (in millions):

Walt Disney Company

Retained earnings,		Dividends paid	$	?
end of year	$12,767	Retained earnings,		
Revenues	25,402	beginning of year	12,281	
Net interest		Operating costs and expenses	22,158	
expense	558			
Income taxes	1,606			
Other expenses, net	160			

Required

1. Prepare the following for the year:
   a. Income statement. The final three lines of the income statement were labeled as income before taxes, income taxes, and net income.
   b. Statement of retained income. Compute the amount of dividends paid.
2. Comment briefly on the relative size of the cash dividend.

16-37 Earnings Statement, Retained Earnings

The Procter & Gamble Company has many well-known products, including Tide, Crest, Jif, and Prell. The following is a reproduction of the terms and amounts in the financial statements contained in a recent annual report regarding the fiscal year ended June 30, 2000 (in millions):

Net sales	$39,951	Retained earnings at	
Cash	1,415	beginning of year	$10,778
Interest and other expense	418	Cost of products sold	21,514
Income taxes	1,994	Dividends to shareholders	1,796
Accounts payable	2,209	Marketing, research, and	
Other decreases in		administrative expenses	12,483
retained earnings	1,814		

Choose the relevant data and prepare (1) the income statement for the fiscal year and (2) the statement of retained income for the fiscal year. The final three lines of the income statement were labeled as earnings before income taxes, income taxes, and net earnings.

COLLABORATIVE LEARNING EXERCISE

16-38 Implicit Transactions

Form groups of from three to six "players." Each group should have a die and paper (or board) with four columns labeled

1. Expiration of unexpired costs
2. Realization of unearned revenues
3. Accrual of unrecorded expenses
4. Accrual of unrecorded revenues

The players should select an order in which they wish to play. Then, the first player rolls the die. If he or she rolls a 5 or 6, the die passes to the next player. If he or she rolls a 1, 2, 3, or 4, he or she must, within 20 seconds, name an example of a transaction that fits in the corresponding category; for example, if a 2 is rolled, the player must give an example of realization of unearned revenues.

Each time a correct example is given, the player receives one point. If someone doubts the correctness of a given example, he or she can challenge it. If the remaining players unanimously agree that the example is incorrect, the challenger gets a point and the player giving the example does not get a point for the example and is out of the game. If the remaining players do not unanimously agree that the answer is incorrect, the challenger loses a point and the player giving the example gets a point for a correct example.

If a player fails to give an example within the time limit or gives an incorrect example, he or she is out of the game (except for voting when an example is challenged), and the remaining players continue until everyone has failed to give a correct example within the time limit. Each correct answer should be listed under the appropriate column. The player with the most points is the group winner.

When all groups have finished a round of play, a second level of play can begin. All the groups should get together and list all the examples for each of the four categories by group. Discussion can establish the correctness of each entry; the faculty member or an appointed discussion leader will be the final arbitrator of the correctness of each entry. Each group gets one point for each correct example and loses one point for each incorrect entry. The group with the most points is the overall winner.

INTERNET EXERCISE

16-39 Land's End's Financial Statements

Go to http://www.landsend.com to find Lands' End's home page. Select "About Lands' End" from the menu, and click on the most recent annual report.

Answer the following questions:

1. Name two items on Lands' End's balance sheet that most likely represent unexpired (prepaid) costs. Name two items that most likely represent accruals of unrecorded expenses.

www.prenhall.com/horngren

2. Does Lands' End prepare a single- or multi-step income statement? How can you tell?
3. Determine Lands' End's gross profit divided by sales for the past two years. Is the change favorable or not? What does Lands' End management have to say about the change? (Hint: look in Management's Discussion and Analysis.) If nothing was said, why do you think management chose not to comment? How do you think management determines the reason that gross profit changed, given the condensed nature of the income statement?
4. Which financial statements provide evidence that Lands' End is a corporation, not a sole proprietorship or partnership?
5. Where can you find evidence in Lands' End's annual report that the financial statements were prepared using GAAP?
6. Explain how Lands' End's financial statements illustrate one of the basic concepts or principles found in this chapter of the text.

Go to the "Deferrals (Unearned Revenues and Prepaid Expenses)" and "Generally Accepted Accounting Principles and Audited Financial Statements" episodes on the *Mastering Accounting* CD-ROM for interactive, video-enhanced exercises.

17

UNDERSTANDING CORPORATE ANNUAL REPORTS: BASIC FINANCIAL STATEMENTS

Lawrence J. Ellison, Chairman and CEO of Oracle, expounds on the "software that powers the Internet." In 2000 Oracle used its own application software, Oracle E-Business Suite, to put every aspect of its business on the Internet.

www.prenhall.com/horngren

Learning Objectives

When you have finished studying this chapter, you should be able to

1. Identify and explain the main types of assets in the balance sheet of a corporation.

2. Identify and explain the main types of liabilities in the balance sheet of a corporation.

3. Identify and explain the main elements of the stockholders' equity section of the balance sheet of a corporation.

4. Identify and explain the principal elements in the income statement of a corporation.

5. Identify and explain the elements in the statement of retained earnings.

6. Identify activities that affect cash, and classify them as operating, investing, or financing activities.

7. Interpret a statement of cash flows that uses the direct method.

8. Understand the reconciliation of net income to net cash provided by operations.

9. Explain the role of depreciation in the statement of cash flows.

10. **Understand how investors and managers use balance sheets, income statements, and cash flow statements to aid their decision making.**

Not many companies seek the permission of the CIA when naming products. Yet that's precisely what System Development Laboratories did back in 1977 when it created a new type of database. Called the "Oracle," this new relational database structure would soon prove to be the world's most popular form. For the company, now called Oracle Corporation, it was a huge financial success. Revenues for its most recent fiscal year-end topped $10 billion for software sales worldwide.

Of course, sales revenue is important to Oracle's management team. But for every sale generated, the company must either collect cash or record an accounts receivable from the customer. It must then collect the receivable so that the company has adequate cash to continue its operations. Managing accounts receivable and collecting cash is a key activity for Oracle. The faster it can collect the cash, the more use of it the company will have. But good accounts receivable management also plays other vital roles for the company. For example, at quarter-end and year-end, Oracle must report its financial results to the investment community. Recording sales revenue in the right time period is essential if the matching principle is to be followed for sales and expenses on the income statement. There is a balance sheet effect, too. The cash and receivables associated with sales revenue show up as current assets, and if not properly recorded, will distort Oracle's financial position.

Of course, sales revenue, cash, and receivables aren't the only items of interest for Oracle. The company reports information about assets such as investments and software development costs. It reports liabilities related to debt and unearned revenues on its financial statements. It lists stockholders' equity positions with their changes, and it shows the cash flows surrounding operating, investing, and financing activities.

Investors use all this information to make stock purchase decisions. Thus, Oracle's financial reports affect the price of its stock. As Oracle grew in the late 1990s, most of the reports were good, and stock purchased for $10 per share in 1996 could be sold for more than $150 in 2000. For Oracle, whose very company name means "source of wisdom," issuing timely and accurate financial statements is smart business.

This chapter focuses on what investors and other decision makers can learn from financial statements such as those of Oracle. It extends the discussion of balance sheets and income statements from the preceding chapter and introduces another major financial statement, the statement of cash flows.

Accounting is commonly misunderstood as being a precise discipline that produces exact measurements of a company's financial position and performance. As a result, many individuals regard accountants as little more than mechanical tabulators who grind out financial reports after processing an imposing amount of detail in accordance with stringent predetermined rules. Although accountants do take methodical steps with masses of data, their rules of measurement allow room for judgment. Managers and accountants who exercise this judgment have more influence on financial reporting than is commonly believed. To understand financial statements fully, you must recognize the judgments that go into their construction.

CLASSIFIED BALANCE SHEET

Objective 1
Identify and explain the main types of assets in the balance sheet of a corporation.

Exhibit 17-1 shows the 1999 and 2000 classified balance sheets for Nike, Inc., maker of athletic footwear and other leisure wear. They classify assets and equities into five main sections: current assets, noncurrent assets, current liabilities, noncurrent liabilities, and shareholders' equity. Be sure to locate each of these items in the exhibit when you read the description of the item in the following pages.

CURRENT ASSETS

current assets Cash and all other assets that are reasonably expected to be converted to cash or sold or consumed within one year or during the normal operating cycle, if longer than a year.

Current assets include cash and all other assets that are reasonably expected to be converted to cash or sold or consumed within one year or during the normal operating cycle, if longer than a year. An **operating cycle** is the time span during which a company spends cash to acquire goods and services that it uses to produce the organization's output, which in turn it sells to customers, who in turn pay for their purchases with cash. Consider a retail business. The following diagram illustrates its operating cycle (figures are hypothetical):

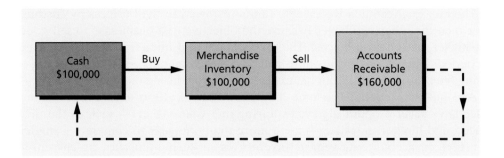

Exhibit 17-1

Nike, Inc.

Balance Sheet (in millions)

	May 31	
	1999	*2000*
ASSETS		
Current assets		
Cash and equivalents	$ 198.1	$ 254.3
Accounts receivable, less allowance for doubtful accounts of 73.2 and 65.4	1,540.1	1,567.2
Inventories	1,170.6	1,446.0
Prepaid expenses	219.6	215.2
Other current assets	136.5	113.7
Total current assets	3,264.9	3,596.4
Noncurrent assets		
Property, plant, and equipment		
At cost	2,001.3	2,393.8
Less: accumulated depreciation	735.5	810.4
Net property, plant, and equipment	1,265.8	1,583.4
Intangible assets and goodwill	426.6	410.9
Other assets	290.4	266.2
Total noncurrent assets	1,982.8	2,260.5
Total assets	$5,247.7	$5,856.9
LIABILITIES AND SHAREHOLDERS' EQUITY		
Current liabilities		
Notes payable	$ 419.1	$ 924.2
Accounts payable	473.6	543.8
Accrued liabilities	553.2	621.9
Current portion of long-term debt	1.0	50.1
Total current liabilities	1,446.9	2,140.0
Noncurrent liabilities		
Long-term debt	386.1	470.3
Deferred income taxes and other liabilities	79.8	110.3
Total noncurrent liabilities	465.9	580.6
Total liabilities	1,912.8	2,720.6
Shareholders' equity		
Redeemable preferred stock	0.3	0.3
Common stock at stated value	2.9	2.8
Capital in excess of stated value	334.1	369.0
Retained earnings	3,066.5	2,887.0
Other	(68.9)	(122.8)
Total shareholders' equity	3,334.9	3,136.3
Total liabilities and shareholders' equity	$5,247.7	$5,856.9

The box for Accounts Receivable (amounts owed to the business by customers) is larger than the other two boxes because the objective of a business is to sell goods at a price higher than acquisition cost. The total amount of profit a firm earns during a particular period depends on how much its selling prices exceed its costs of producing or purchasing the products and additional expenses incurred during the period.

Accountants sometimes assume that an operating cycle is one year. But some businesses have several operating cycles during one year. Others—such as the distillery, tobacco, and lumber industries—need more than one year to complete a single cycle. Nevertheless, accountants regard inventories in such industries as current assets. Similarly, they classify installment accounts and notes receivable as current assets, even though they may not be fully collected within one year.

As Exhibit 17-1 shows, current assets fall into several broad categories, such as cash and cash equivalents, accounts receivable, inventories, prepaid expenses, and other current assets. Cash consists of bank deposits in checking accounts plus money on hand. **Cash equivalents** are short-term investments that a company can easily convert into cash with little delay. Examples include money market funds and Treasury bills. They represent an investment of excess cash not needed immediately. The balance sheet usually shows these securities at cost or market price, whichever is lower. The market price is disclosed parenthetically if it is above cost. In 2000, Nike had $254.3 million in cash and cash equivalents.

Accounts receivable is the total amount owed to the company by its customers. Because some customers ultimately will not pay their bill, the total is reduced by an allowance or provision for doubtful accounts (i.e., possible "bad debts"). The difference represents the net amount that the company will probably collect. At the end of the 2000 fiscal year,[1] Nike had gross accounts receivable of $1,632.6 million, but after deducting $65.4 million for doubtful accounts, the company expects to collect $1,567.2 million from its accounts receivable.

Inventories consist of merchandise, finished products of manufacturers, goods in the process of being manufactured, and raw materials. Accountants state inventories at their cost or market price (defined as replacement cost), whichever is lower. Cost of manufactured products normally includes raw material cost plus the costs of converting it into a finished product (direct labor and manufacturing overhead). Nike's 2000 inventories stood at $1,446.0 million.

Prepaid expenses are advance payments to suppliers. They are usually unimportant in relation to other assets. Examples are prepayment of rent and insurance premiums for coverage over the coming operating cycle. They belong in current assets because, if they were not present, more cash would be needed to conduct current operations. In 2000, Nike shows $215.2 million of prepaid expenses, which is less than 6% of total current assets.

Other current assets are miscellaneous current assets that do not fit into the listed categories. They might include notes receivable and short-term investments that are not cash equivalents. For Nike, such assets amounted to $113.7 million in 2000.

NONCURRENT ASSETS: PROPERTY, PLANT, AND EQUIPMENT

Property, plant, and equipment are examples of **fixed assets** or **tangible assets**—physical items that a person can see and touch. Companies usually provide details about property, plant, and equipment in a footnote to the financial statements, such as the one for Nike shown in Exhibit 17-2. Footnotes are an integral part of financial statements. They contain explanations for the summary figures that appear in the statements.

Companies typically show *land* as a separate item and carry it indefinitely at its original cost.

cash equivalents Short-term investments that a company can easily convert into cash with little delay.

fixed assets (tangible assets) Physical items that a person can see and touch, such as property, plant, and equipment.

---

[1] *A fiscal year is defined as the year established for accounting purposes for the preparation of annual reports. Nike's fiscal year is June 1 through May 31.*

Exhibit 17-2

Nike, Inc.

Footnote 3 to the 2000 Financial Statements

	Note 3. Property, Plant, and Equipment (millions)	
	---	---
	1999	*2000*
Land	$ 99.6	$ 180.6
Buildings	374.2	503.4
Machinery and equipment	923.3	981.9
Leasehold improvements	273.4	279.6
Construction-in-progress	330.8	448.3
	2,001.3	2,393.8
Less: accumulated depreciation	735.5	810.4
Net property, plant, and equipment	$1,265.8	$1,583.4

They also initially record *buildings* and *machinery and equipment* at cost: the invoice amount, plus freight and installation, less cash discounts. However, buildings, machinery, and equipment gradually decline in value through depreciation (see Chapter 16, page 647). The major difficulties of measurement center on the choice of depreciation method—that is, the allocation of the original cost to the particular periods or products that benefit from the use of the assets. Remember that depreciation only means allocating the original cost of plant and equipment, not valuing them in the ordinary sense of the term. Balance sheets typically do not show replacement cost, resale value, or the price changes since acquisition. The balance sheet amount is simply the original cost less the *accumulated depreciation,* which is the sum of all depreciation taken to date on the asset.

The amount of depreciation charged as expense each year depends on three factors:

1. The depreciable amount (the difference between the total acquisition cost and the estimated residual value). The residual value is the amount a company expects to receive when selling the asset at the end of its economic life.

2. The estimate of the asset's useful life. This estimate is influenced by estimates of physical wear and tear, technological change, and economic obsolescence. Thus, the useful life is usually less than the physical life.

3. The depreciation method. There are three general methods of depreciation: straight line, accelerated, and units of production. The straight-line method allocates the same cost to each year of an asset's useful life. Accelerated methods allocate more of the cost to the early years and less to the later years.[2] The units-of-production method allocates cost based on the amount of production rather than the passage of time.

Which method is best? It depends on the firm's goals, the asset involved, and the type of financial statement being prepared. The straight-line method is most popular. More than 90% of all firms use it for at least some assets when preparing financial statements for reporting to the public. In contrast, most U.S. firms use accelerated depreciation when preparing financial statements for tax reporting to the IRS.

Suppose a business spends $42,000 to buy equipment with an estimated useful life of four years and an estimated residual value of $2,000. Using the straight-line method of depreciation, the annual depreciation expense in each of the four years would be

---

[2] *Methods of accelerated depreciation are described in Chapter 11. However, knowledge of accelerated depreciation methods is not necessary for understanding this chapter.*

Exhibit 17-3

Straight-line Depreciation
(figures assumed)

	Balances at End of Year			
	1	*2*	*3*	*4*
Plant and equipment (at original acquisition cost)	$42,000	$42,000	$42,000	$42,000
Less: accumulated depreciation (the portion of original cost that has already been charged to operations as depreciation expense)	10,000	20,000	30,000	40,000
Net book value (the portion of original cost not yet charged as expense)	$32,000	$22,000	$12,000	$ 2,000

$$\frac{\text{original cost} - \text{estimated residual value}}{\text{years of useful life}}$$

$$= \frac{(\$42,000 - \$2,000)}{4}$$

$$= \$10,000 \text{ per year}$$

Exhibit 17-3 shows how the asset would be displayed in the balance sheet. In Exhibits 17-1 and 17-2, the original cost of fixed assets on Nike's 2000 balance sheet is $2,393.8 million. There is accumulated depreciation of $810.4 million, the portion of the original cost of the asset that was previously charged as depreciation expense, so the net property, plant, and equipment at May 31, 2000 is $2,393.8 million − $810.4 million = $1,583.4 million.

Depreciation is the part of an asset that has been used up. It is gone. It is not a pool of cash set aside to replace the asset. If a company decides to accumulate specific cash to replace assets, such cash should be specifically labeled as a cash fund for replacement and expansion. Holiday Inns, Inc., has used such a fund, calling it a capital construction fund. Such funds are quite rare because most companies can earn better returns by investing any available cash in ordinary operations rather than in special funds. Typically, companies use or acquire cash for the replacement and expansion of plant assets only as specific needs arise.

Leasehold improvements are investments made by a lessee (tenant) in items such as painting, decorating, fixtures, and air-conditioning equipment that cannot be removed from the premises when a lease expires. The costs of leasehold improvements are written off in the same manner as depreciation, but their periodic write-off is called amortization.

Construction in progress is shown separately from other assets because the assets are not yet ready for use. It represents assets that will be part of buildings or machinery and equipment when completed.

We do not illustrate natural resources, such as mineral deposits, but they are typically grouped with plant assets. Companies write off their original cost in the form of depletion as they use the resources. For example, a coal mine may cost $10 million and originally contain an estimated 5 million tons. The depletion rate would be $2 per ton. If 500,000 tons were mined during the first year, depletion would be $1 million for that year. If 300,000 tons were mined the second year, depletion would be $600,000. Such depletion charges would continue until the entire $10 million has been charged as depletion expense.

Long-term investments are also noncurrent assets. They include long-term holdings of securities of other firms. We discuss the accounting for such investments in Chapter 18. Nike does not have any long-term investments, unless they are combined with other small, miscellaneous noncurrent assets in the $113.7 million of other assets shown in Exhibit 17-1.

INTANGIBLE ASSETS

Tangible assets such as cash or equipment can be physically observed. In contrast, **intangible assets** are a class of long-lived assets that are not physical in nature. They are rights to expected future benefits deriving from their acquisition and continued possession. Examples are goodwill, franchises, patents, trademarks, and copyrights. In Exhibit 17-1, Nike shows intangible assets and goodwill of $410.9 million at May 31, 2000.

Goodwill, which we will discuss in more detail in the next chapter, is the excess of the cost of an acquired company over the sum of the fair market values of its identifiable individual assets less its liabilities. For example, Nike acquired Cole Haan for $95 million. It could assign only $13 million to various identifiable assets such as receivables, plant, and patents less liabilities assumed by Nike; it recorded the remainder, $82 million, as goodwill.

The accounting for goodwill illustrates how an exchange transaction is a basic concept of accounting. After all, many owners could obtain a premium price if they sold their companies. But such goodwill is never recorded. Only the goodwill arising from an actual acquisition should be shown as an asset on the purchaser's records.

For shareholder-reporting purposes, between 1970 and 2001 companies had to amortize (depreciate) goodwill, generally in a straight-line manner, over the periods benefited. In the United States, the longest allowed amortization period was 40 years. Nike is amortizing its $82 million of goodwill from the Cole Haan purchase at the rate of $82,000,000 ÷ 40 = $2,050,000 per year.

Based on a ruling in 2001, goodwill is no longer amortized. Instead, it remains on a company's books until it is determined that its value is impaired. The 2001 decision reversed a position that had stood for more than 30 years. Before 1970, the amortization of goodwill was not mandatory in the United States. But in 1970, the regulators ruled that the values of all intangible assets eventually disappear, thus making amortization mandatory. Now we have come full circle. However, even though amortization is not mandatory, an impairment test must be applied annually to assure that the goodwill has kept its value.

Companies in many countries also regard research and development costs as assets. They assume that companies incur research costs to purchase an asset that would benefit future operations and thus amortize research costs over the years of expected benefit, usually three to six years. In the United States, however, the FASB has banned deferral and required write-off of these costs as incurred. The FASB admits that research and development costs may generate many long-term benefits, but the general high degree of uncertainty about the extent and measurement of future benefits has led to conservative accounting in the form of immediate write-off.

LIABILITIES

Assets are, of course, only part of the picture of any organization's financial health. Its liabilities, both current and noncurrent, are equally important.

Current liabilities are an organization's debts that fall due within the coming year or within the normal operating cycle if longer than a year. Turn again to Exhibit 17-1 on page 681. Notes payable are short-term debts backed by formal promissory notes held by a bank or business creditors. Accounts payable are amounts owed to suppliers who extended credit for purchases on open account. Accrued liabilities or accrued expenses payable are recognized for wages, salaries, interest, and similar items. The accountant recognizes expenses as they occur—regardless of when they are paid for in cash. Income taxes payable is a special accrued expense of enough magnitude to warrant a separate classification. The current portion of long-term debt shows the payments due within the next year on bonds and other long-term debt.

Some companies also list unearned revenue, also called deferred revenue. Such revenue occurs when a company receives cash before delivering the related goods or

intangible assets Long-lived assets that are not physical in nature. Examples are goodwill, franchises, patents, trademarks, and copyrights.

goodwill The excess of the cost of an acquired company over the sum of the fair market values of its identifiable individual assets less its liabilities.

current liabilities An organization's debts that fall due within the coming year or within the normal operating cycle if longer than a year.

Objective 2
Identify and explain the main types of liabilities in the balance sheet of a corporation.

services. For example, *Newsweek* magazine has such an account because it is obligated to send magazines to subscribers with prepaid subscriptions. Nike had no unearned revenue in 2000, but it did have current liabilities totaling $2,140.0 million.

noncurrent liabilities (long-term liabilities) An organization's debts that fall due beyond one year.

Noncurrent liabilities, also called **long-term liabilities,** are an organization's debts that fall due beyond one year. Exhibit 17-1 shows Nike's noncurrent liabilities for 2000 as $580.6 million, making its total liabilities $2,720.6 million. Nike has two noncurrent liabilities, long-term debt (which we will discuss in more depth in a moment) and deferred income taxes. The latter rather technical and controversial item arises because the financial statements used for reporting to shareholders differ legitimately from those used for reporting to the income tax authorities. Appendix 17 provides more details about deferred taxes.

Exhibit 17-4 is a footnote from the financial statements that provides details about Nike's long-term debts. Note especially the next to last line in this exhibit, "Less: current maturities." This item refers to payments due in the next year. Nike subtracts the $50.1 million noted on this line from long-term debt because the company has already included it in current liabilities. Nike shows the remaining $470.3 million as "Long-term debt" in Exhibit 17-1. Long-term debt may be secured or unsecured. Secured debt provides debtholders with first claim on specified assets. Mortgage bonds are an example of secured debt. If the company is unable to meet its regular obligations on the bonds, it may sell the specified assets and use the proceeds to pay off the firm's obligations to its bondholders, in which case secured debt holders have first claim.

debentures Formal certificates of indebtedness that are accompanied by a promise to pay interest at a specified annual rate.

Unsecured debt consists of **debentures** (i.e., bonds, notes, or loans), which are formal certificates of indebtedness that are accompanied by a promise to pay interest at a specified annual rate. Unsecured debt holders are general creditors who have a general claim against total assets rather than a specific claim against particular assets. Most of Nike's long-term debt is unsecured. Holders of **subordinated** bonds or debentures are junior to the other creditors in exercising claims against assets.

subordinated A creditor claim that is junior to the other creditors in exercising claims against assets.

Consider the following simplified example. Suppose a corporation is liquidated. **Liquidation** means converting assets to cash and using the cash to pay off outside claims. The company had a single asset, a building, that it sold for $120,000 cash:

liquidation Converting assets to cash and using the cash to pay off outside claims.

Assets		Liabilities and Stockholders' Equity	
Cash	$120,000	Accounts payable	$ 60,000
		First-mortgage bonds payable	80,000
		Subordinated debentures payable	40,000
		Total liabilities	$180,000
		Stockholders' equity (negative)	(60,000)
Total assets	$120,000	Total liabilities and stockholders' equity	$120,000

The company would pay the mortgage (secured) bondholders in full ($80,000). It would pay trade creditors, such as suppliers, the remaining $40,000 for their $60,000 claim ($.67 on the dollar). Other claimants would get nothing. If the debentures were unsubordinated, the $40,000 of cash remaining after paying $80,000 to the mortgage holders would be used to settle the $100,000 claims of the unsecured creditors as follows:

To trade creditors	6/10 × $40,000 =	$24,000
To debenture holders	4/10 × $40,000 =	16,000
Total cash distributed		$40,000

Exhibit 17-4

Nike, Inc.

Footnote 5 to the 2000 Financial Statements

	May 31	
Note 5. Long-Term Debt (millions)	*1999*	*2000*
6.375% Medium term notes, payable December 1, 2003	$199.5	$199.6
4.3% Japanese yen notes, payable June 26, 2011	84.6	98.2
2.6% Japanese yen loans, payable November 20, 2020	—	84.2
2.0% Japanese yen loans, payable November 20, 2020	—	37.4
6.51% Medium term notes, payable June 16, 2000	50.0	50.0
6.69% Medium term notes, payable June 17, 2002	50.0	50.0
Other	3.0	1.0
	387.1	520.4
Less: Current maturities	1.0	50.1
Total	$386.0	$ 470.3

To increase the appeal of their bonds, many companies issue debt that is convertible into common stock. Convertibility allows bondholders to participate in a company's success without the risk of holding common stock. Suppose a company issues convertible bonds for $1,000 when the stock price is $22, with a provision that each bond can be converted into 40 common shares. If the stock price increases by 50% to $33 a share, the bondholder could exchange the $1,000 bond for 40 shares worth 40 × $33 = $1,320. If the stock price falls (or does not increase beyond $25 a share), the bondholder can keep the bond and receive $1,000 at maturity.

STOCKHOLDERS' EQUITY

Objective 3
Identify and explain the main elements of the stockholders' equity section of the balance sheet of a corporation.

The final element of a balance sheet is stockholders' equity (also called shareholders' equity or owners' equity or capital or net worth), the total residual interest in the business. As noted in Chapter 16, it is the excess of total assets over total liabilities. The main elements of stockholders' equity arise from two sources: (1) contributed or paid-in capital, and (2) retained income.

Paid-in capital typically comes from owners who invest in the business in exchange for stock certificates, which are issued as evidence of stockholder rights. There are two major classes of capital stock: common stock and preferred stock. Some companies have several categories of each, all with a variety of different attributes.

All corporations have **common stock.** Such stock has no predetermined rate of dividends and is the last to obtain a share in the assets when the corporation is dissolved. Common shares usually have voting power to elect the board of directors of the corporation. Common stock is usually the riskiest investment in a corporation, being unattractive in dire times but attractive in prosperous times because, unlike other stocks, there is no limit to the stockholder's potential participation in earnings.

Exhibit 17-1 shows that Nike has a small amount of preferred stock, in addition to common stock. About 40% of the major companies in the United States issue **preferred stock.** It typically has some priority over other shares regarding dividends or the distribution of assets on liquidation. For example, Nike pays an annual preferred stock dividend of $.10 per share, or $30,000 in total. Nike must pay these dividends in full before it pays dividends to any other classes of stock. Preferred shareholders in Nike, as in most companies with preferred stock, do not have voting privileges regarding the management of the corporation.

Stock frequently has a designated **par** or **legal** or **stated value** that is printed on the face of the certificate. For preferred stock (and bonds), par is a basis for designating the amount

common stock Stock that has no predetermined rate of dividends and is the last to obtain a share in the assets when the corporation is dissolved. It usually has voting power to elect the board of directors of the corporation.

preferred stock Stock that typically has some priority over other shares regarding dividends or the distribution of assets upon liquidation.

par value (legal value, stated value) The value that is printed on the face of the certificate.

of dividends or interest. Many preferred stocks have $100 par values. That is, a 9%, $100-par preferred stock would carry a $9 annual dividend. Most bonds have par values of $1,000. Thus, an 8% bond usually means that the investor is entitled to annual interest of $80.

In contrast, par value has no practical importance for common stock. Historically, the par amount of common stock specified the maximum legal liability of the stockholder in case the corporation could not pay its debts. (Shareholders typically have **limited liability,** which means that a company's creditors cannot seek payment from stockholders as individuals if the corporation itself cannot pay its debts.) Currently, companies set par at a nominal amount (e.g., $1) in relation to the market value of the stock on issuance (e.g., $70). It is generally illegal for a corporation to sell an original issue of its common stock below par.

limited liability Creditors cannot seek payment from shareholders as individuals if the corporation itself cannot pay its debts.

Capital in excess of stated value is the excess received over the stated, par, or legal value of the shares issued. Common shares are almost always issued at a price substantially greater than par. Suppose all outstanding common shares of Nike had been issued for cash. The cumulative balance sheet effect at May 31, 2000, would be

Cash	$371,800,000	Common stock, at stated value	$ 2,800,000
		Capital in excess of stated value	369,000,000
		Total paid-in capital	$371,800,000

Retained earnings, also called retained income, is the increase in stockholders' equity caused by profitable operations (see Chapter 16). Retained earnings is the dominant item of stockholders' equity for most companies. For instance, as of May 31, 2000, Nike had common stockholders' equity of $3,136.3 million of which $2,887.0 million was retained earnings.

treasury stock A corporation's own stock that has been issued and subsequently repurchased by the company and is being held for a specific purpose.

Many companies have **treasury stock,** which is a corporation's own stock that the company issued and subsequently repurchased and is holding for a specific purpose. Such repurchase is a decrease in ownership claims. It should therefore appear on a balance sheet as a deduction from total stockholders' equity. The stock is not retired; it is only held temporarily "in the treasury" to be distributed later, possibly as a part of an employee stock purchase plan or as an executive bonus or for use in acquiring another company. A company does not pay cash dividends on shares held in the treasury. Companies distribute dividends only to the outstanding shares (those in the hands of stockholders). Nike had no treasury stock in 2000. In contrast, McDonald's Corporation had more than $8 billion of treasury stock:

Shareholders' equity before deducting treasury stock	$17,315,500,000
Treasury stock	(8,111,100,000)
Total shareholders' equity	$ 9,204,400,000

SUMMARY PROBLEMS FOR YOUR REVIEW

PROBLEM

"The book value of plant assets is the amount that would be spent today for their replacement." Do you agree? Explain.

SOLUTION

Net book value of the plant assets is the result of deducting accumulated depreciation from original cost. This process does not attempt to capture all the technological and economic events that may affect replacement value. Consequently, there is little likelihood that net book value will approximate replacement cost.

PROBLEM

On December 31, 20X1, a magazine publishing company receives $150,000 in cash for three-year subscriptions. It regards this sum as unearned revenue. Show the balances in that account at December 31, 20X2, 20X3, and 20X4. How much revenue would be earned in each of those three years?

SOLUTION

The balance in unearned revenue would decline at the rate of $50,000 yearly. The company would recognize $50,000 as earned revenue in each of the three years.

	December 31			
	20X1	*20X2*	*20X3*	*20X4*
Unearned revenue	$150,000	$100,000	$50,000	$0

INCOME STATEMENT

Most investors are vitally concerned about a company's ability to produce long-run earnings and dividends. In this regard, income statements are more important than balance sheets. Income statements show revenue first; this represents the total sales value of products delivered and services rendered to customers. Then they list expenses, which are deducted to get net income.

Objective 4
Identify and explain the principal elements in the income statement of a corporation.

USE OF SUBTOTALS

An income statement can take one of two major forms: single step or multiple step. A single-step statement merely lists all expenses without drawing subtotals, whereas a multiple-step statement contains one or more subtotals. Subtotals highlight significant relationships.

Exhibit 17-5 illustrates the two most common subtotals: gross profit and income from operations (also called operating income or operating profit). Gross profit or gross margin is sales less cost of goods sold. It measures the size of the margin above merchandise costs and is an important statistic for many managers and analysts. Operating income (or loss) summarizes the results of the basic operating activities of the company. Income statements often group depreciation expense, selling expenses, and administrative expenses as "operating expenses" and deduct them from the gross profit to obtain operating income. (Of course, cost of goods sold is also an operating expense. Why? Because it is also deducted from sales revenue to obtain "operating income.") In 2000, Nike had a gross profit of $3,591.3 million and operating income of $984.9 million.

To interpret a company's financial statements, it is important to identify whether a particular account is an asset, liability, stockholders' equity, revenue, or expense account.

Identify the type of account for each of the following accounts: accounts receivable, accounts payable, investments in marketable securities, depreciation, paid-in capital, cost of goods sold, income taxes, income taxes payable, bank loans, common stock, and inventories.

ANSWER

Asset accounts are accounts receivable, investments in marketable securities, and inventories. Liability accounts are accounts payable and bank loans. Stockholders' equity accounts are paid-in capital and common stock. No revenue accounts are listed. Expense accounts are depreciation, cost of goods sold, and income taxes.

Exhibit 17-5

Nike, Inc.

Statement of Income (millions except per share data)

	Year Ended May 31	
	1999	*2000*
Revenues	$8,776.9	$8,995.1
Cost of sales	5,493.5	5,403.8
Gross profit	$3,283.4	$3,591.3
Selling and administrative expenses	2,426.6	2,606.4
Income from operations	$ 856.8	$ 984.9
Other expense (income)		
Interest expense	$ 44.1	$ 45.0
Other income/expense, net	66.6	20.7
Total other expense	$ 110.7	$65.7
Income before income taxes	$ 746.1	$ 919.2
Income taxes	294.7	340.1
Net income	$ 451.4	$ 579.1
Earnings per share*	$1.59	$2.10

*Computation of earnings per share:

	1999	**2000**
Net income	$451,400,000	$579,100,000
Divided by average common shares outstanding	283,300,000	275,700,000
Earnings per share	$1.59	$2.10

OPERATING AND FINANCIAL MANAGEMENT

Operating income is a popular subtotal because of the often made distinction between operating management and financial management. Operating management focuses on the major day-to-day activities that generate sales revenue. In contrast, financial management focuses on where to get cash and how to use cash for the benefit of the organization. That is, financial management attempts to answer such questions as: How much cash should be held in checking accounts? Should we pay a dividend? Should we borrow or issue common stock? The best managers are superb at both operating management and financial management. However, many managers are better operating managers than financial managers, or vice versa.

Because financial rather than operating decisions affect interest income and expense, they often appear as separate items after operating income. This approach facilitates comparisons of operating income between years and between companies. Some companies make heavy use of debt, which causes high interest expense, whereas other companies incur little debt and interest expense. Other nonoperating items might include gains or losses from foreign exchange transactions or from disposals of fixed assets.

INCOME, EARNINGS, AND PROFITS

Although this book tends to use the term *income* most often, you will also see the terms *earnings* and *profits* used as synonyms. Other names for the income statement include *statement of earnings, statement of profit and loss,* and *P&L statement*. Most companies still use net income on their income statements, but the term *earnings* is becoming increasingly popular because it has a preferable image. Nike's 2000 net income was $579.1 million.

Exhibit 17-6

Nike, Inc.
Statement of Retained Earnings for the Year
Ended May 31, 2000 (millions of dollars)

Retained earnings, May 31, 1999	$3,066.5
Net income (Exhibit 17-5)	579.1
Total	3,645.6
Deduct: dividends on common stock	131.5
Repurchase of common stock	627.1
Retained earnings, May 31, 2000	$2,887.0

The term **net income** is the popular "bottom line"—the residual after deducting all expenses including income taxes. The term *net* is seldom used for any subtotals that precede the calculation of net income. Instead, the subtotals are called *income*. Thus, the appropriate term is *operating income* or *income from operations,* not *net operating income.*

Income taxes are often a prominent expense and are not merely listed with operating expenses. Instead, income statements usually deduct income taxes as a separate item immediately before net income, as in Exhibit 17-5.

Income statements conclude with disclosure of **earnings per share.** Exhibit 17-5 illustrates this as the net income divided by the average number of common shares outstanding during the year. Nike earned $2.10 per share in 2000.

net income The popular "bottom line"—the residual after deducting from revenues all expenses, including income taxes.

earnings per share Net income divided by the average number of common shares outstanding during the year.

STATEMENT OF RETAINED EARNINGS

To explain the changes in retained earnings, companies frequently include a separate financial statement, the **statement of retained earnings** (also called **statement of retained income**). This may also be one part of a larger statement, the statement of changes in stockholders' equity. As Exhibit 17-6 demonstrates, the major reasons for changes in retained earnings are dividends and net income. Net income increases retained earnings, and losses and dividends reduce retained earnings. Note especially that dividends are not expenses; they are not deductions in computing net income, as explained in Chapter 16 on page 652.

Objective 5
Identify and explain elements in the statement of retained earnings.

statement of retained earnings (statement of retained income) A financial statement that analyzes changes in the retained earnings or retained income account for a given period.

SUMMARY PROBLEM FOR YOUR REVIEW

PROBLEM

Companies sometimes combine the income statement and statement of retained earnings into a single statement. Prepare a combined income statement and statement of retained earnings from the following data. Use a multiple-step format for the income statement.

Cost of goods sold	$420,000
Net sales	750,000
Income taxes	80,000
Beginning retained earnings	440,000
Dividends	30,000
Interest expense	20,000
Selling and administrative expenses	110,000

SOLUTION

Statement of Income and Retained Earnings

Net sales	$750,000
Cost of goods sold	420,000
Gross margin	330,000
Selling and administrative expenses	110,000
Operating income	220,000
Interest expense	20,000
Income before income taxes	200,000
Income taxes	80,000
Net income	120,000
Beginning retained earnings	440,000
Dividends	(30,000)
Ending retained earnings	$530,000

STATEMENT OF CASH FLOWS

statement of cash flows A statement that reports the cash receipts and cash payments of an organization during a particular period.

Until recently, many decision makers focused primarily on the income statement and the balance sheet. However, an increasing number of decision makers are now carefully examining another important statement, the statement of cash flows. A **statement of cash flows** reports the cash receipts and cash payments of an organization during a particular period. The statement has the following purposes:

1. It shows the relationship of net income to changes in cash balances. Cash balances can decline despite positive net income and vice versa.

2. It reports past cash flows as an aid to
   a. Predicting future cash flows
   b. Evaluating management's generation and use of cash
   c. Determining a company's ability to pay interest and dividends, and to pay debts when they are due

3. It reveals commitments to assets that may restrict or expand future courses of action.

BASIC CONCEPTS

Recall that balance sheets show the status of an entity at a day in time. In contrast, statements of cash flows, income statements, and statements of retained income cover periods. They provide the explanations of why the balance sheet items have changed. The accompanying diagram depicts this linkage:

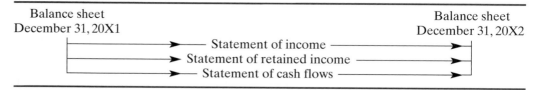

In particular, the statement of cash flows explains where cash came from during a period and where it was spent.

The statement of cash flows explains changes in cash and cash equivalents, both of which can quickly be used to meet obligations. Cash equivalents, as noted earlier in this chapter, are highly liquid short-term investments that a company can easily convert into cash with little delay. Hereafter, when we refer to cash, we mean both cash and cash equivalents.

TYPICAL ACTIVITIES AFFECTING CASH

The fundamental approach to the statement of cash flows is simple: (1) List the activities that increased cash (i.e., cash inflows) and those that decreased cash (cash outflows), and (2) place each cash inflow and outflow into one of three categories according to the type of activity that caused it: operating activities, investing activities, and financing activities.

The following activities are those found most often in statements of cash flows:

Operating Activities

Cash Inflows	*Cash Outflows*
Collections from customers	Cash payments to suppliers
Interest and dividends collected	Cash payments to employees
Other operating receipts	Interest paid
	Taxes paid
	Other operating cash payments

Investing Activities

Cash Inflows	*Cash Outflows*
Sale of property, plant, and equipment	Purchase of property, plant, and equipment
Sale of securities that are not cash equivalents	Purchase of securities that are not cash equivalents
Receipt of loan repayments	Making loans

Financing Activities

Cash Inflows	*Cash Outflows*
Borrowing cash from creditors	Repayment of amounts borrowed
Issuing equity securities	Repurchase of equity shares (including the purchase of treasury stock)
	Payment of dividends

As the lists of activities indicate, **cash flows from operating activities** are generally the effects of transactions that affect the income statement (e.g., sales and wages). Investing activities include (1) lending and collecting on loans and (2) acquiring and selling long-term assets. Financing activities include obtaining resources from creditors and owners and providing them with returns of their investments and owners with returns on their investments in the form of cash dividends.

cash flows from operating activities The section in the statement of cash flows that lists the cash-flow effects of transactions that affect the income statement.

Perhaps the most troublesome classifications are the receipts and payments of interest and the receipts of dividends. After all, these items are associated with investment and financing activities. After much debate, the FASB decided to include these items with cash flows from operating activities. Why? Mainly because they affect the computation of income. In contrast, payments of cash dividends are financing activities because they do not affect income.

FOCUS OF A STATEMENT OF CASH FLOWS

To see the basic ideas underlying the statement of cash flows, consider the Balmer Company. Exhibit 17-7 shows the company's condensed balance sheets and income statement.

Because the statement of cash flows explains the causes for the change in cash, the first step is to compute the amount of the change (which represents the net effect to be explained):

Cash, December 31, 20X1	$25,000
Cash, December 31, 20X2	16,000
Net decrease in cash	$ 9,000

Exhibit 17-7

Balmer Company

Statement of Income for the Year Ended
December 31, 20X2 (in thousands)

Sales		$200
Costs and expenses		
Cost of goods sold	$100	
Wages and salaries	36	
Depreciation	17	
Interest	4	
Total costs and expenses		157
Income before income taxes		43
Income taxes		20
Net income		$ 23

Balmer Company

Balance Sheet as of December 31 (in thousands)

Assets	20X2	20X1	Increase (Decrease)	Liabilities and Stockholders' Equity	20X2	20X1	Increase (Decrease)
Current assets				Current liabilities			
Cash	$ 16	$ 25	$ (9)	Accounts payable	$ 74	$ 6	$ 68
Accounts receivable	45	25	20	Wages and salaries			
Inventory	100	60	40	payable	25	4	21
Total current assets	161	110	51	Total current liabilities	99	10	89
Fixed assets, gross	581	330	251	Long-term debt	125	5	120
Less accum. depreciation	(101)	(110)	9	Stockholders' equity	417	315	102
Net fixed assets	480	220	260	Total liabilities and			
Total assets	$641	$330	$311	stockholders' equity	$641	$330	$311

Exhibit 17-8 illustrates a statement of cash flows with this information shown at the bottom. The statement adds the beginning cash balance to the net change to compute the ending cash balance. Another common practice is to place the beginning cash balance at the top of the statement and the ending cash balance at the bottom. However, there is no requirement that the statement of cash flows explicitly show the beginning and ending cash balances. Showing only the net change is sufficient.

When business expansion occurs, as in this case, and where there is a strong cash position at the outset, cash often declines. Why? Because growing companies usually need cash for investment in various business assets required for expansion, including investment in accounts receivable and inventories.

The statement in Exhibit 17-8 gives a direct picture of where cash came from and where it went. In this instance, the excess of cash outflows over cash inflows reduced cash by $9,000. Without the statement of cash flows, the readers of the annual report would have to conduct their own analyses of the beginning and ending balance sheets, the income statement, and the statement of retained income to get a grasp of the impact of financial management decisions.

Most important, this illustration demonstrates how a firm may simultaneously (1) have a significant amount of net income, as computed by accountants on the accrual basis, and yet (2) have a decline in cash that could become severe. Indeed, many growing businesses are desperate for cash even though reported net income zooms upward.

Exhibit 17-8

Balmer Company

Statement of Cash Flows for the Year Ended December 31, 20X2 (in thousands)

Cash Flows from Operating Activities		
Cash collections from customers		$180
Cash payments		
To suppliers	$72	
To employees	15	
For interest	4	
For taxes	20	
Total cash payments		(111)
Net cash provided by operating activities		$ 69

Cash Flows from Investing Activities		
Purchases of fixed assets	$(287)	
Proceeds from sale of fixed assets	10	
Net cash used in investing activities		(277)

Cash Flows from Financing Activities		
Proceeds from issue of long-term debt	$120	
Proceeds from issue of common stock	98	
Dividends paid	(19)	
Net cash provided by financing activities		199
Net decrease in cash		$ (9)
Cash, December 31, 20X1		25
Cash, December 31, 20X2		$ 16

INTERPRETATION OF A STATEMENT OF CASH FLOWS: THE DIRECT METHOD

Objective 7
Interpret a statement of cash flows that uses the direct method.

Now that you know why statements of cash flows are important, we can consider the interpretation of such statements. The first major section in the statement of cash flows in Exhibit 17-8 is cash flows from operating activities. The section might also be called cash flow from operations, cash provided by operations, or, if operating activities decrease cash, cash used for operations.

Collections from sales to customers are almost always the major operating activity that increases cash. Correspondingly, payments for purchases of goods to be sold and operating expenses are almost always the major operating cash outflows. The excess of collections over payments is the net cash provided by operating activities. There are two ways to display this amount: the direct method and the indirect method.

We will consider the direct method first. The FASB favors the direct method because it is easier to understand. Exhibit 17-8 uses the direct method: Collections minus operating payments equals net cash provided by operating activities—$180,000 − $111,000 = $69,000.

WORKING FROM INCOME STATEMENT AMOUNTS TO CASH AMOUNTS

To interpret items on a statement of cash flows, it helps to understand how they relate to the balance sheet and income statement amounts. For instance, consider the $180,000 of cash collections from Balmer Company customers for 20X2. This cash flow represents the sales in the income statement (an amount calculated using the accrual basis) plus (or minus) the decrease (or increase) in the accounts receivable balance. A detailed analysis of collections and other operating items follows.

a. Balmer Company recognized $200,000 of revenue in 20X2, but because accounts receivable increased by $20,000, Balmer collected only $180,000 from customers:

Sales	$200,000
+ Beginning accounts receivable	25,000
Potential collections	$225,000
− Ending accounts receivable	45,000
Cash collections from customers	$180,000

Instead of adding the beginning accounts receivable balance and then deducting the ending accounts receivable, we could add the decrease in accounts receivable (or deduct the increase):

Sales	$200,000
Decrease (increase) in accounts receivable	(20,000)
Cash collections from customers	$180,000

b. Changes in inventory and accounts payable explain the difference between the $100,000 cost of goods sold and the $72,000 cash payment to suppliers. The $40,000 increase in inventory indicates that purchases exceeded the cost of goods sold by $40,000:

Ending inventory	$100,000
+ Cost of goods sold	100,000
Inventory to account for	$200,000
− Beginning inventory	(60,000)
Purchases of inventory	$140,000

Although purchases were $140,000, payments to suppliers were only $72,000. Why? Because trade accounts payable increased by $68,000, from $6,000 to $74,000:

Beginning trade accounts payable	$ 6,000
+ Purchases	140,000
Total amount to be paid	$146,000
− Ending trade accounts payable	(74,000)
Accounts paid in cash	$ 72,000

We can combine the effects of inventory and trade accounts payable as follows:

Cost of goods sold	$100,000
Increase (decrease) in inventory	40,000
Decrease (increase) in trade accounts payable	(68,000)
Payments to suppliers	$ 72,000

c. Cash payments to employees were only $15,000 because the wages and salaries expense of $36,000 was offset by a $21,000 increase in wages and salaries payable:

Beginning wages and salaries payable	$ 4,000
+ Wages and salaries expense	36,000
Total to be paid	$40,000
− Ending wages and salaries payable	(25,000)
Cash payments to employees	$15,000

or

Wages and salaries expense	$36,000
Decrease (increase) in wages and salaries payable	(21,000)
Cash payments to employees	$15,000

d. Note that both interest payable and income taxes payable were zero at the beginning and at the end of 20X2. Therefore the entire $4,000 interest expense and the $20,000 income tax expense were paid in cash in 20X2.

Exhibit 17-9 summarizes the differences between Balmer Company's net income of $23,000 and net cash provided by operating activities of $69,000 in 20X2. Examine Exhibit 17-8 and confirm that the first section of the statement of cash flows shows the $69,000 cash inflow from operating activities.

INVESTING AND FINANCING CASH FLOWS

The second and third major sections of the statement present examples of cash flows from investing activities ($277,000 outflow) and financing activities ($199,000 inflow), respectively. Balmer Company's investing and financing cash flows relate to changes in all balance sheet items except current assets and current liabilities. (Changes in most noncash current assets and current liabilities relate to operating cash flows.) The following rules pertain:

- Increases in cash (cash inflows) are from

    Increases in liabilities or stockholders' equity

    Decreases in noncash assets

- Decreases in cash (cash outflows) are from

    Decreases in liabilities or stockholders' equity

    Increases in noncash assets

Consider Balmer Company's balance sheet (Exhibit 17-7, page 694). All noncash current assets and current liabilities of Balmer Company are linked only to operating activities, which we just discussed. Now let's look at three noncurrent accounts: fixed assets, long-term debt, and stockholders' equity.

a. Fixed assets increased by $260,000 in 20X2. To understand why fixed assets increased by $260,000, we must look at two cash-flow items (asset acquisitions and asset disposals) and one income statement item (depreciation):

increase in net plant assets = acquisitions − disposals − depreciation expense

$260,000 = $287,000 − $10,000 − $17,000

This shows that investments exceeded the disposals and depreciation by $260,000. Balmer Company received exactly the book value for the assets sold. (We discuss disposals for other than book value later in this chapter.) Both asset acquisitions and asset disposals are investing activities that affect cash.

Exhibit 17-9

Comparison of Net Income and Net Cash Provided by Operating Activities

	Income Statement	Adjustments	Cash Flows Statement
Sales	$200,000		
Increase in accounts receivable		$(20,000)	
Cash collections from customers			$180,000
Cost of goods sold	(100,000)		
Increase in inventory		(40,000)	
Increase in accounts payable		68,000	
Cash payments to suppliers			(72,000)
Wages and salaries expense	(36,000)		
Increase in wages and salaries payable		21,000	
Cash paid to employees			(15,000)
Interest: expense equals cash flow	(4,000)		(4,000)
Income taxes: expense equals cash flow	(20,000)		(20,000)
Depreciation: deducted in computing net income but not a cash outflow	(17,000)	17,000	—
Net income	$ 23,000		
Total additions (deductions)		$ 46,000	
Net cash provided by operating activities			$ 69,000

b. Long-term debt increased by $125,000 − $5,000 = $120,000. Balmer issued long-term debt, which is a financing activity that increased cash, and it retired no debt.

c. The $102,000 increase in stockholders' equity can be explained by three factors: (1) issuance (or repurchase) of capital stock, (2) net income (or loss), and (3) dividends. Therefore,

increase in stockholders' equity = new issuance + net income = dividends

$$\$102,000 = \text{new issuance} + \$23,000 - \$19,000$$

Both the issuance of new shares and the payment of cash dividends are financing activities that affect cash.

Reexamine Exhibit 17-8, page 695. The statement lists the asset acquisitions and disposals from paragraph **a** with cash flows from investing activities, and shows the effects of debt and equity issues and dividend payments from paragraphs **b** and **c** with cash flows from financing activities.

NONCASH INVESTING AND FINANCING ACTIVITIES

In a schedule that accompanies the statement of cash flows, companies must report major investment and financing activities that do not affect cash. For example, consider the acquisition of a $120,000 warehouse in exchange for the issuance of capital stock. The transaction would not be included in the body of the statement of cash flows. Why? Because cash was unaffected. But the transaction is almost identical to one in which a company issues capital stock for cash of $120,000, which is immediately used to purchase the warehouse. Therefore, companies should disclose such a transaction to readers of a statement of cash flows. A schedule that follows directly after the statement contains such disclosures. Balmer Company did not have such a transaction in 20X2.

CASH FLOW AND EARNINGS

cash flow Usually refers to the net cash flow from operating activities.

A focal point of the statement of cash flows is the net cash flow from operating activities. Frequently this is called simply **cash flow.** Some accountants debate which is most important, net income or cash flow. Fortunately, we do not have to make a choice. Cash flow and income both convey useful information about an entity. As Professor Loyd Heath said, "Asking which one is better, cash flow or earnings, is like asking which shoe is more useful, your right or your left."

INTERPRETATION OF A STATEMENT OF CASH FLOWS: THE INDIRECT METHOD

Instead of using the direct method as the format for statements of cash flows, most companies use the indirect method. The **indirect method** directly reconciles net income to the net cash provided by operating activities, showing the link between the income statement and the statement of cash flows.

indirect method In a statement of cash flows, the method that reconciles net income to the net cash provided by operating activities.

RECONCILIATION OF NET INCOME TO NET CASH
PROVIDED BY OPERATIONS

The reconciliation begins with net income. Accountants then make additions or deductions for items that affect net income and net cash flow differently. Recall that Exhibit 17-9 shows such items. Exhibit 17-10 shows how the reconciliation appears in the statement of cash flows. Consider the logic applied in the reconciliation in Exhibit 17-10:

Objective 8
Understand the reconciliation of net income to net cash provided by operations.

1. Depreciation is an expense but not a cash flow. Accountants deduct it in computing net income. However, if the purpose is to show cash provided by operations rather than net income, the depreciation of $17,000 should not be subtracted. Why? Because it is not a cash flow this period. Since it was subtracted in computing net income, we must now add it back to income to get cash from operations. The add back simply cancels the earlier deduction.

2. Increases in noncash current assets such as receivables and inventory result in less cash flow from operations. For instance, suppose the $20,000 increase in receivables resulted from credit sales made near the end of the year. Net income would include the $20,000 sales figure, but the $20,000 would not have increased cash flow from operations. Therefore the reconciliation deducts the $20,000 from the net income to help pinpoint the effects on cash. Similarly, the $40,000 increase in inventory represents cash outflows that do not affect income.

3. Increases in current liabilities such as accounts payable and wages payable result in more cash flow from operations. For instance, suppose the $21,000 increase in wages payable resulted from wages earned near the end of the year, but not yet paid in cash. The $21,000 wages expense would be deducted in computing net income, but the $21,000 would not have decreased cash flow from operations.

Exhibit 17-10

Reconciliation of Net Income to Net Cash Provided by Operating Activities (in thousands)

Net income		$23
Adjustments to reconcile net income		
to net cash provided by operating activities		
Depreciation	$17	
Net increase in accounts receivable	(20)	
Net increase in inventory	(40)	
Net increase in accounts payable	68	
Net increase in wages and salaries payable	21	
Total additions and deductions		46
Net cash provided by operating activities		$69

Therefore, the reconciliation adds the $21,000 to net income to offset the deduction and thereby shows the effect on cash.

The reconciliation's most common additions or deductions from net income are

- Add decreases (or deduct increases) in accounts receivable
- Add decreases (or deduct increases) in inventories
- Add increases (or deduct decreases) in accounts payable
- Add increases (or deduct decreases) in wages and salaries payable
- Add increases (or deduct decreases) in unearned revenue

The general rules for reconciling for these items are

- Deduct increases in noncash current assets
- Add decreases in noncash current assets
- Add increases in current liabilities
- Deduct decreases in current liabilities

A final step is to reconcile for amounts that are included in net income but represent investing or financing activities (in contrast to operating activities). Examples include

- Add loss (or deduct gain) from sale of fixed assets
- Add loss (or deduct gain) on extinguishment of debt

In our earlier example, Balmer Company had no losses or gains that were a result of investing or financing activities. However, suppose Balmer Company sold another asset for $12,000 cash. The asset had a book value of $8,000, so a gain of $4,000 would be part of pretax income:

Proceeds from sale of fixed asset	$12,000
Book value of asset sold	8,000
Gain on sale of asset	$ 4,000

For simplicity, assume that this sale did not affect income taxes. Therefore Balmer Company's net income would be $23,000 (from Exhibit 17-7, p. 694) plus the gain of $4,000, or a total of $27,000.

The sale of the asset is an investing activity, so the entire cash inflow would be listed under investing activities in the statement of cash flows:

Proceeds from sale of fixed asset	$12,000

This sale should not affect the section "cash flows from operating activities." But net income includes the $4,000 gain. In a reconciliation schedule that begins with net income (as in Exhibit 17-10), the gain must be subtracted:

Net income ($23,000 from Exhibit 17-7 plus $4,000 gain)	$27,000
Plus adjustments in Exhibit 17-9	46,000
Less gain on disposal of fixed assets	(4,000)
Net cash provided by operating activities	$69,000

Note that the sale of the asset affected net income because of the gain, but it did not affect net cash provided by operating activities.

RECONCILIATION SCHEDULE UNDER DIRECT AND INDIRECT METHODS

The FASB requires all statements of cash flows to use either the direct or the indirect format. Furthermore, the statements must include a reconciliation schedule in some fashion under either the direct or the indirect method:

- Direct Method (favored by FASB)

  Exhibit 17-8 as the body. Include Exhibit 17-10 as a supporting schedule.

- Indirect Method (permitted by FASB)

  Alternative Format 1:

  Exhibit 17-8 as the body. However, replace the first section with a one-line item, net cash provided by operating activities. Include Exhibit 17-10 as a supporting schedule.

  Alternative Format 2:

  Exhibit 17-8, except use Exhibit 17-10 in the body as the first section, cash flows from operating activities. Exhibit 17-11, Nike's statement of cash flows, illustrates this widely used method.

ROLE OF DEPRECIATION

Readers of statements of cash flows sometimes misunderstand the reason for adding depreciation to net income when computing cash flows from operating activities. Depreciation is an allocation of historical cost to expense. Therefore, depreciation expense does not entail a current outflow of cash. Consider again the comparison of Balmer Company's net income and cash flows in Exhibit 17-9 on page 698. Why is the $17,000 of depreciation added to net income to compute cash flow? Simply to cancel its deduction in calculating net income. Unfortunately, use of the indirect method may at first glance create an erroneous impression that depreciation is added because it, by itself, is a source of cash. If that were really true, a corporation could merely double or triple its bookkeeping entry for depreciation expense when it needs cash! What would happen? Income would decline, but cash provided by operations would be unaffected. Suppose depreciation for Balmer Company were doubled:

Objective 9
Explain the role of depreciation in the statement of cash flows.

	With Depreciation of $17,000	With Depreciation of $34,000
Sales	$200,000	$200,000
All expenses except depreciation (including income taxes)*	(160,000)	(160,000)
Depreciation	(17,000)	(34,000)
Net income	$ 23,000	$ 6,000
Nondepreciation adjustments†	29,000	29,000
Add depreciation	17,000	34,000
Net cash provided by operating activities	$ 69,000	$ 69,000

* $100,000 + $36,000 + $4,000 + $20,000 = $160,000
† $(20,000) + $(40,000) + $68,000 + $21,000 = $29,000

The doubling would affect depreciation and net income, but it would have no direct influence on cash provided by operations, which would still amount to $69,000.

Exhibit 17-11

Nike, Inc.

Statement of Cash Flows for the Year Ended May 31, 2000 (millions)

Cash provided (used) by operations:	
Net income	$579.1
Income charges (credits) not affecting cash	
Depreciation	188.0
Deferred income taxes	36.8
Amortization and other	35.6
Changes in certain working capital components:	
Increase in inventories	(275.4)
Increase in accounts receivable	(27.1)
Decrease in other current assets	65.6
Increase in accounts payable, accrued	
liabilities, and income taxes payable	157.3
Cash provided by operations	759.9
Cash provided (used) by investing activities:	
Additions to property, plant, and equipment	(419.9)
Disposals of property, plant, and equipment	25.3
Increase in other assets	(51.3)
Increase in other liabilities	5.9
Cash used by investing activities	(440.0)
Cash provided (used) by financing activities:	
Additions to long-term debt	0.1
Reductions in long-term debt including current portion	(1.8)
Increase in notes payable	505.1
Proceeds from exercise of options	23.9
Repurchase of stock	(646.3)
Dividends–common and preferred	(133.1)
Cash used by financing activities	(252.1)
Other	(11.6)
Net increase in cash and equivalents	56.2
Cash and equivalents, beginning of year	198.1
Cash and equivalents, end of year	$254.3
Noncash investing and financing activity:	
Assumption of long-term debt to acquire property, plant, and equipment	$108.9

STATEMENT OF CASH FLOWS FOR NIKE, INC.

Exhibit 17-11 contains the 2000 statement of cash flows for Nike, Inc. Most publicly held corporations use this general format for their statement of cash flows. Like Nike, they use the indirect method in the body of the statement of cash flows to report the cash flows from operating activities.

Most of the items in Exhibit 17-11 have been discussed earlier in the chapter, but three deserve mention here. First, deferred income taxes are added back to net income. These taxes are charged as expense but are not currently payable. Therefore they are a noncash expense, similar to depreciation. Second, proceeds from the exercise of options are cash received from issuance of shares to executives as part of a stock option compensation plan. Finally, Nike shows a noncash investing and financing activity. Instead of paying $108.9 million in cash to acquire some property, plant, and equipment, Nike assumed the seller's debt of $108.9 million.

You might also notice that changes in account balances cannot be computed directly from the balance sheets in Exhibit 17-1. This is a result of factors beyond the scope of this text, primarily the incorporation of the accounts of companies acquired by Nike during fiscal 2000.

SUMMARY PROBLEM FOR YOUR REVIEW

PROBLEM

The Buretta Company has prepared the data in Exhibit 17-12. In December 20X1, Buretta paid $54 million cash for a new building acquired to accommodate an expansion of operations. This was financed partly by a new issue of long-term debt for $40 million cash. During 20X1, the company also sold fixed assets for $5 million cash, which was equal to their book value. All sales and purchases of merchandise were on credit.

Because the net income of $4 million was the highest in the company's history, Mr. Buretta, the Chairman of the Board, was perplexed by the company's extremely low cash balance.

Exhibit 17-12

Buretta Co.

Income Statement and Statement of Retained Earnings for the Year Ended December 31, 20X1 (millions)

Sales		$100
Less cost of goods sold		
Inventory, December 31, 20X0	$ 15	
Purchases	104	
Cost of goods available for sale	$119	
Inventory, December 31, 20X1	46	73
Gross profit		$ 27
Less other expenses		
General expenses	$ 8	
Depreciation	8	
Property taxes	4	
Interest expense	3	23
Net income		$ 4
Retained earnings, December 31, 20X0		7
Total		$ 11
Dividends		1
Retained earnings, December 31, 20X1		$ 10

Balance Sheets as of December 31 (millions)

Assets	20X1	20X0	Increase (Decrease)
Cash	$ 1	$20	$(19)
Accounts receivable	20	5	15
Inventory	46	15	31
Prepaid general expenses	4	2	2
Fixed assets, net	91	50	41
	$162	$92	$ 70

Equities	20X1	20X0	Increase (Decrease)
Accounts payable for merchandise	$ 39	$14	$ 25
Accrued property tax payable	3	1	2
Long-term debt	40	—	40
Capital stock	70	70	—
Retained earnings	10	7	3
	$162	$92	$ 70

1. Prepare a statement of cash flows. Ignore income taxes. You may wish to use Exhibit 17-8, page 695, as a guide. Use the direct method for reporting cash flows from operating activities.

2. Prepare a supporting schedule that reconciles net income to net cash provided by operating activities.

3. What is revealed by the statement of cash flows? Does it help you reduce Mr. Buretta's puzzlement? Why?

SOLUTION

1. See Exhibit 17-13. We can explain cash flows from operating activities as follows (in millions):

Sales	$100
Less increase in accounts receivable	(15)
Cash collections from customers	$ 85
Cost of goods sold	$ 73
Plus increase in inventory	31
Purchases	$104
Less increase in accounts payable	(25)
Cash paid to suppliers	$ 79
General expenses	$ 8
Plus increase in prepaid general expenses	2
Cash payment for general expenses	$ 10
Property taxes	$ 4
Less increase in accrued property tax payable	(2)
Cash paid for property taxes	$ 2
Cash paid for interest	$ 3

Exhibit 17-13

Buretta Company

Statement of Cash Flows for the Year Ended December 31, 20X1 (in millions)

Cash Flows from Operating Activities		
Cash collections from customers		$ 85
Cash payments		
Cash paid to suppliers	$(79)	
General expenses	(10)	
Interest paid	(3)	
Property taxes	(2)	(94)
Net cash used by operating activities		$ (9)

Cash Flows from Investing Activities		
Purchase of fixed assets (building)	$(54)	
Proceeds from sale of fixed assets	5	
Net cash used by investing activities		(49)

Cash Flows from Financing Activities		
Long-term debt issued	$40	
Dividends paid	(1)	
Net cash provided by financing activities		39
Net decrease in cash		$(19)
Cash balance, December 31, 20X1		20
Cash balance, December 31, 20X2		$ 1

Exhibit 17-14

Buretta Company

Reconciliation of Net Income to Net Cash Provided by Operating
Activities for the Year Ended December 31, 20X1 (millions)

Supporting Schedule to Statement of Cash Flows	
Net income (from income statement)	$ 4
Adjustments to reconcile net income to net cash provided by operating activities	
Add: depreciation, which was deducted in the computation of net income but does not decrease cash	8
Deduct: increase in accounts receivable	(15)
Deduct: increase in inventory	(31)
Deduct: increase in prepaid general expenses	(2)
Add: increase in accounts payable	25
Add: increase in accrued property tax payable	2
Net cash provided by operating activities	$ (9)

2. Exhibit 17-14 reconciles net income to net cash provided by operating activities.

3. The statement of cash flows shows where cash has come from and where it has gone. Operations used $9 million of cash. Why? Exhibit 17-14 shows that large increases in accounts receivable ($15 million) and inventory ($31 million), plus a $2 million increase in prepaid expenses, used $48 million of cash. In contrast, only $39 million (i.e., $4 + $8 + $25 + $2 million) was generated. Exhibit 17-13 explains the $9 million use of cash slightly differently. It shows directly the $85 million of cash receipts and $94 million in disbursements. Investing activities also consumed cash because Buretta invested $54 million in a building, and it received only $5 million from sales of fixed assets. Financing activities generated $39 million cash, which was $19 million less than the $58 million used by operating and investing activities.

Mr. Buretta should no longer be puzzled. The statement of cash flows shows clearly that cash payments exceeded receipts by $19 million. However, he may still be concerned about the depletion of cash. Either Buretta must change operations so that they do not require so much cash, or it must curtail investment, or it must raise more long-term debt or ownership equity. Otherwise, Buretta Company will soon run out of cash.

Highlights to Remember

Identify and explain the main types of assets in the balance sheet of a corporation. Assets are divided into current and noncurrent categories. Common current assets are cash, accounts receivable, inventories, and prepaid expenses. The largest noncurrent (or fixed) asset is generally property, plant, and equipment, which is shown at acquisition cost less accumulated depreciation.

Identify and explain the main types of liabilities in the balance sheet of a corporation. Liabilities are divided into current liabilities and long-term liabilities. Current liabilities include notes payable and accounts payable. Long-term debt in the form of debentures or mortgages is the most common noncurrent liability.

Identify and explain the main elements of the stockholders' equity section of the balance sheet of a corporation. Stockholders' equity contains paid-in capital and retained earnings. Paid-in capital is often divided into a par value amount and an amount in excess of par value.

Identify and explain the principal elements in the income statement of a corporation. Income statements contain revenues and expenses. Multistep income statements have some of the following subtotals: gross profit (gross margin), operating income, and income before income taxes.

Identify and explain the elements in the statement of retained earnings. Net income increases retained earnings and losses and dividends decrease them. For large profitable companies, retained earnings may be by far the largest component of stockholders' equity.

Identify activities that affect cash, and classify them as operating, investing, or financing activities. The statement of cash flows lists cash inflows and cash outflows in one of three categories. Operating cash flows include collections from customers and payments to suppliers. Investing cash flows include purchases and sales of fixed assets. Financing cash flows include borrowings and repayment of borrowings, sales of shares of stock, and payment of dividends.

Interpret a statement of cash flows that uses the direct method. In the direct method, cash flows from operating activities include all cash receipts from customers and all cash payments to suppliers, employees, the government, and others for activities supporting basic operations.

Understand the reconciliation of net income to net cash provided by operations. A reconciliation of net income and cash flow from operations begins with net income, adds depreciation and other noncash expenses, adds (subtracts) decreases (increases) in operating current assets, and adds (subtracts) increases (decreases) in operating current liabilities.

Explain the role of depreciation in the statement of cash flows. Depreciation is not a cash inflow. A reconciliation statement adds it to net income to get cash flow from operating activities only to offset the fact that it was deducted in computing net income.

Understand how investors and managers use balance sheets, income statements, and cash-flow statements to aid their decision making. Managers and investors use balance sheets to assess a company's financial position at a point in time. They use income statements and statements of cash flows to assess performance over a period of time.

Appendix 17A: Shareholder Reporting, Income Tax Reporting, and Deferred Taxes

In the United States, reports to stockholders must abide by "generally accepted accounting principles (GAAP)." In contrast, reports to income tax authorities must abide by the income tax rules and regulations. These rules comply with GAAP in many respects, but in others they diverge. Therefore, there is nothing immoral or unethical about "keeping two sets of books." In fact, it is necessary.

Keep in mind that the income tax laws are patchworks that often are designed to give taxpayers special incentives for making investments. For example, tax authorities in some countries have permitted taxpayers to write off the full cost of new equipment as expense in the year acquired. Although tax authorities may permit (or even require) such a total write-off, GAAP does not permit it for shareholder reporting purposes.

Major differences between U.S. GAAP and the U.S. tax laws exist in accounting for amortization and depreciation. For example, consider how the GAAP and tax accounting practices for perpetual franchises and trademarks differ. Companies must amortize their acquisition costs for shareholder reporting. However, the IRS will not allow amortization, because it believes such assets have indefinite useful lives. Tax reporting and shareholder reporting are required to differ.

Depreciation causes the largest differences between tax and shareholder reporting in the United States. Most companies use straight-line depreciation for reporting to shareholders. Why? Managers believe that it best matches expenses with revenues. But companies use accelerated depreciation for tax reporting because it postpones (or defers) tax payments. Congress provided this deferral opportunity to motivate companies to increase their investment.

For reporting to shareholders, accountants must match income tax expense with the revenues and expenses that cause the taxes. When revenues and expenses on the statement to tax authorities differ from the revenues and expenses on the shareholders' report, deferred taxes can arise. Most often, deferred taxes arise when tax expenses exceed book expenses. The result is a deferred tax liability.

Consider a simple example. The total depreciation on a company's only asset over a two-year period, 20X0–20X1, was $20,000. Revenue was $100,000 each year, expenses (other than depreciation) were $80,000, and the combined federal and state income tax rate was 40%. For tax purposes, the company charged the entire $20,000 of depreciation as an expense in 20X0; for shareholder reporting, it charged $10,000 each year. Such differences in timing of expenses are completely legitimate.

Exhibit 17-15 illustrates tax deferral. Total operating income over the two years was $20,000, and total taxes were $8,000. According to U.S. tax law, all $20,000 of operating income and $8,000 of taxes applied to 20X1. In contrast, for financial reporting, the company recognized half of the operating income each year, so half of the taxes should be recognized each year. Although $4,000 of taxes was related to 20X0 revenues and expenses, the payment was postponed (deferred) to 20X1. The 20X0 financial reporting income statement included a $4,000 expense for deferred taxes, and the obligation for future payment of the tax became a liability on the balance sheet. In 20X1, $4,000 of tax expense was again related to the revenues and expenses of the period. However, the tax payment was $8,000. The payment covers the $4,000 expense for 20X1 and pays off the $4,000 of taxes deferred from 20X0.

Exhibit 17-15

Illustration of Deferred Taxes

	20X0	20X1	Total
Income statement for tax purposes			
Revenue	$100,000	$100,000	$200,000
Expenses, except depreciation	80,000	80,000	160,000
Depreciation	20,000	0	20,000
Operating income			
(or taxable income)	$ 0	$ 20,000	$ 20,000
Taxes payable @ 40%	0	8,000	8,000
Net income	$ 0	$ 12,000	$ 12,000
Income statement for			
shareholder reporting			
Revenue	$100,000	$100,000	$200,000
Expenses, except depreciation	80,000	80,000	160,000
Depreciation	10,000	10,000	20,000
Operating income	$ 10,000	$ 10,000	$ 20,000
Less income taxes			
Paid or payable almost			
immediately	0	8,000	8,000
Deferred	4,000	(4,000)	0
Net income	$ 6,000	$ 6,000	$ 12,000

	December 31	
	20X0	*20X1*
Balance sheet effect		
Liability: Deferred income taxes	$4,000	$0

Accounting Vocabulary

cash equivalents, p. 682

cash flow, p. 698

cash flows from operating activities, p. 693

common stock, p. 687

current assets, p. 680

current liabilities, p. 685

debentures, p. 686

earnings per share, p. 691

fixed assets, p. 682

goodwill, p. 685

indirect method, p. 699

intangible assets, p. 685

legal value, p. 687

limited liability, p. 688

liquidation, p. 686

long-term liabilities, p. 686

net income, p. 691

noncurrent liabilities, p. 686

operating cycle, p. 681

par value, p. 687

preferred stock, p. 687

stated value, p. 687

statement of cash flows, p. 692

statement of retained earnings, p. 691

statement of retained income, p. 691

subordinated, p. 686

tangible assets, p. 682

treasury stock, p. 688

Fundamental Assignment Material

GENERAL EXERCISES AND PROBLEMS

17-A1 Balance Sheet and Income Statement

The Risoen Company had the following items on its December 31, 20X0, balance sheet and 20X0 income statement (in dollars except for number of shares outstanding):

Cash and equivalents	$ 53,000
Revenues	800,000
Notes payable	40,000
Long-term debt, excluding current portion	210,000
Accounts receivable, net	49,000
Provision for income taxes	55,000
Other long-term assets	110,000
Interest expense	55,000
Deferred income tax liability	44,000
Retained earnings	?
Income taxes payable	37,000
Cost of sales	460,000
Inventories	31,000
Prepaid expenses	15,000
Common stock (50,000 shares outstanding)	25,000
Property, plant, and equipment, at cost	580,000
Accounts payable	48,000
Interest income	20,000
Goodwill, patents, and trademarks	75,000
Current portion of long-term debt	16,000
Less: accumulated depreciation	170,000
Selling and administrative expenses	150,000
Additional paid-in capital	121,000

Required

Prepare in proper form the December 31, 20X0, balance sheet and the 20X0 income statement for Risoen Company. Include the proper amount for additional paid-in capital.

17-A2 Statement of Cash Flows, Direct Method

ZZZ Auto Parts had a cash balance on December 31, 20X0, of $48 thousand. Its net income for 20X1 was $464 thousand. Its 20X1 transactions affecting income or cash were (in thousands):

1. Sales of $1,600, all on credit. Cash collections from customers, $1,450.
2. The cost of items sold, $850. Purchases of inventory totaled $900; inventory and accounts payable were affected accordingly.

3. Cash payments on trade accounts payable, $775.
4. Salaries and wages: accrued, $190; paid in cash, $200.
5. Depreciation, $45.
6. Interest expense, all paid in cash, $11.
7. Other expenses, all paid in cash, $100.
8. Income taxes accrued, $40; income taxes paid in cash, $30.
9. Bought plant and facilities for $435 cash.
10. Issued debt for $110 cash.
11. Paid cash dividends of $39.

Prepare a statement of cash flows using the direct method for reporting cash flows from operating activities. Omit supporting schedules. **Required**

17-A3 Reconciliation of Net Income and Net Cash Provided by Operating Activities
Refer to Problem 17-A2. Prepare a supporting schedule that reconciles net income to net cash provided by operating activities.

17-A4 Depreciation and Cash Flows
O'Brien Company had sales of $700,000, all received in cash. Total operating expenses were $600,000. All except depreciation were paid in cash. Depreciation of $90,000 was included in the $600,000 of operating expenses. Ignore income taxes.

1. Compute net income and net cash provided by operating activities. **Required**
2. Assume that depreciation is tripled. Compute net income and net cash provided by operating activities.

UNDERSTANDING PUBLISHED FINANCIAL REPORTS

17-B1 Classified Balance Sheet
Intel, the world's largest microprocessor chip company, lists the following balance sheet items for December 30, 1999 (in millions):

Property, plant, and equipment, at cost	$23,557
Short-term investments	7,705
Common stock and capital in excess of par value	7,316
Cash and cash equivalents	3,695
Other accrued liabilities	1,741
Accounts receivable	3,700
Other current assets	1,241
Accumulated depreciation	(11,842)
Accounts payable	1,370
Other long-term liabilities	130
Inventories	1,478
Deferred income on shipments to distributors	609
Income taxes payable	?
Other assets	1,470
Goodwill and other intangibles	4,934
Accrued compensation and benefits	1,454
Long-term investments	7,911
Other stockholders' equity	3,791
Deferred tax liability	3,130
Short-term debt	230
Long-term debt	955
Retained earnings	21,428

Prepare a balance sheet in proper form for Intel. Include the proper amount for income taxes payable. **Required**

17-B2   Preparation of Statement of Cash Flows

Walgreens Co., the largest drugstore chain in the United States, had the following items in its financial statements for the fiscal year ended August 31, 2000 (in millions):

Net sales	$21,207
Net earnings	777
Additions to property and equipment	(1,119)
Depreciation and amortization	230
Cash dividends paid	(134)
Other non-cash expenses	52
Proceeds from the surrender of corporate-owned life insurance	47
Increases in inventories	(368)
Net borrowing from corporate-owned life insurance	11
Increases in trade accounts payable	234
Increases in other current assets	32
Other cash from financing activities	(8)
Net proceeds from employee stock plans	79
Increases in accrued expenses and other liabilities	101
Increases in accounts receivable	(136)
Retained earnings	3,788
Deferred income taxes	21
Increases in income taxes payable	29
Disposition of property and equipment	23
Total assets	7,104
Cash and cash equivalents at end of year	13
Net decrease in cash and cash equivalents	(129)

Required

Select the items from this list that would appear in Walgreens' statement of cash flows and prepare the statement in proper form. Use the indirect method for reporting cash flows from operating activities. (*Note:* Deferred income taxes is a noncash expense, borrowing on corporate-owned life insurance and proceeds from the surrender of corporate-owned life insurance are investing activities, and net proceeds from employee stock plans is a financing activity.)

17-B3   Cash Provided by Operations

Target Corporation, operator of retail stores such as Target, Mervyn's, Dayton's, Marshall Field's, and Hudson's, had net income of $1,185 million in the fiscal year ending January 29, 2000. Additional information follows (in millions):

	Year Ended January 29, 2000	
Depreciation and amortization	$854	
Other noncash charges	$238	
Interest expense	$393	
Provision for income taxes	$751	
Changes in noncash working capital accounts		
Receivables	$181	Increase
Inventories	$323	Increase
Other assets	$122	Increase
Accrued liabilities	$100	Increase
Accounts payable	$364	Increase
Income taxes payable	$137	Increase

Compute the net cash provided by operating activities. Explain why the net cash provided by operating activities is so much greater than the net income.

Additional Assignment Material

QUESTIONS

17-1. "The operating cycle for a company is one year." Do you agree? Why?

17-2. Why should short-term prepaid expenses be classified as current assets?

17-3. Enumerate the items most commonly classified as current assets.

17-4. "Sometimes an investment of 100 shares of stock should be classified as current assets and sometimes not." Explain.

17-5. "Accumulated depreciation is the cumulative amount charged as expense." Explain.

17-6. "Accumulated depreciation is a sum of cash being accumulated for the replacement of fixed assets." Do you agree? Explain.

17-7. "Most companies use straight-line depreciation, but they should use accelerated depreciation." Criticize this quote.

17-8. Criticize: "Depreciation is the loss in value of a fixed asset over a given span of time."

17-9. What factors influence the estimate of useful life in depreciation accounting?

17-10. "Accountants sometimes are too concerned with physical objects or contractual rights." Explain.

17-11. "Goodwill may have nothing to do with the personality of the manager or employees." Do you agree? Explain.

17-12. What is a subordinated debenture?

17-13. What is the role of the par value of stocks or bonds?

17-14. "Common shareholders have limited liability." Explain.

17-15. "Treasury stock is negative stockholders' equity." Do you agree? Explain.

17-16. "The statement of cash flows is an optional statement included by most companies in their annual reports." Do you agree? Explain.

17-17. What are the purposes of a statement of cash flows?

17-18. What three types of activities are summarized in the statement of cash flows?

17-19. Name four major operating activities included in a statement of cash flows.

17-20. Name three major investing activities included in a statement of cash flows.

17-21. Name three major financing activities included in a statement of cash flows.

17-22. Where does interest received or paid appear on the statement of cash flows? Explain.

17-23. Why is there usually a difference between the cash collections from customers and sales revenue in a period's financial statements?

17-24. What are the two major ways of computing net cash provided by operating activities? How do they differ?

17-25. The indirect method for reporting cash flows from operating activities can create an erroneous impression about noncash expenses (such as depreciation). What is the impression and why is it erroneous?

17-26. An investor's newsletter had the following item: "The company expects increased cash flow in 2002 because depreciation charges will be substantially greater than they were in 2001." Comment.

17-27. "Net losses mean drains on cash." Do you agree? Explain.

17-28. "Depreciation is an integral part of a statement of cash flows." Do you agree? Explain.

17-29. XYZ Company's only transaction in 20X1 was the sale of a fixed asset for cash of $20,000. The income statement included only "Gain on sale of fixed asset, $4,000." Correct the following statement of cash flows:

Cash flows from operating activities	
Gain on sale of fixed asset	$ 4,000
Cash flows from investing activities	
Proceeds from sale of fixed asset	20,000
Total increase in cash	$24,000

17-30. Why are noncash investing and financing activities listed on a separate schedule accompanying the statement of cash flows?

17-31. The Lawrence Company sold fixed assets with a book value of $5,000 and recorded a $3,000 gain. How should this be reported on a statement of cash flows?

17-32. Study Appendix 17. "The presence of a deferred tax liability on the balance sheet means that cumulative tax payments have exceeded the cumulative tax expense charged on financial reports to shareholders." Do you agree? Explain.

COGNITIVE EXERCISES

17-33 Production Facilities and Depreciation

A manager complained about the amount of depreciation charged on the plant for which she was responsible: "The market value of my plant just continues to increase, yet I am hit with large depreciation charges on my income statement and the value of my plant and equipment on the balance sheet goes down each year. This doesn't seem fair." Comment on this statement, focusing on the relation of asset values on the balance sheet to market values of the assets.

17-34 Research and Development and the Recognition of Intangible Assets

In the United States expenditures for research and development are charged directly to expense. In other countries such costs can be recognized as assets. Suppose you were a manager of a research and development department. Which method of accounting for research and development would be most consistent with the information you use for decision making? Explain.

17-35 Using the Income Statement to Evaluate Sales Success

The net income of a company is the result of many factors. Sometimes managers want to measure the performance of one part of the organization separate from the effects of other parts. How might a company evaluate the success of its sales efforts using a classified income statement? Assume that the sales department is responsible for pricing and thus influences both the total amount sold and the margin on the items sold.

17-36 Capital Investment and the Statement of Cash Flows

Growing companies often need capital to purchase or build additional facilities. There are many potential sources of such capital. Describe how an investor might use the statement of cash flows to learn how a company financed its capital expansion.

Exercises

17-37 Meaning of Book Value

Schultz Properties purchased an office building near Bonn, 25 years ago, for 1 million euros (EUR), EUR 200,000 of which was attributable to land. The mortgage has been fully paid. The current balance sheet follows:

Cash		EUR 400,000	Stockholders'	
Land		200,000	equity	EUR 760,000
Building at cost	EUR 800,000			
Accumulated depreciation	640,000			
Book value		160,000		
Total assets		EUR 760,000		

The company is about to borrow EUR 1.8 million on a first mortgage to modernize and expand the building. This amounts to 60% of the combined appraised value of the land and building before the modernization and expansion.

Required

Prepare a balance sheet after the loan is made and the building is expanded and modernized, but before any further depreciation is charged. Comment on its significance.

17-38 Balance Sheet and Income Statement

The fiscal year for Sapporo Company ends on May 31. Results for the year ended May 31, 20X1, included (in millions of Japanese yen except for number of shares outstanding):

Cash and cash equivalents	¥ 29,000
Cost of goods sold	170,000
Inventories	31,000
Other current assets	6,000
Fixed assets, net	217,000
Net sales	390,000
Receivables	22,000
Debentures	77,000
Research and development expenses	42,000
Administrative and general expenses	65,000
Other income (expenses), net	(12,000)
Capital construction fund	28,000
Selling and distribution expenses	41,000
Other current liabilities	9,000
Less: treasury stock	(13,000)
Long-term investments	?
Retained income, appropriated for self-insurance	16,000
Accounts payable	19,000
Mortgage bonds	84,000
Deferred income tax liability	12,000
Redeemable preferred stock	15,000
Common stock, at par (50,000 shares outstanding)	5,000
Paid-in capital in excess of par	102,000
Income tax expense	51,000
Accrued expenses payable	16,000
Retained income, unrestricted	27,000
Intangible assets	21,000

Required

Prepare in proper form the balance sheet as of May 31, 20X1, and the income statement for the year ended May 31, 20X1. Include the proper amount for long-term investments.

17-39 Cash Received from Customers

Sales for Reno Construction Company during 20X1 were $650,000, 80% of them on credit and 20% for cash. During the year, accounts receivable increased from $66,000 to $72,000, an increase of $6,000. What amount of cash did Reno receive from customers during 20X1?

17-40 Cash Paid to Suppliers

Cost of goods sold for Reno Construction Company during 20X1 was $360,000. Beginning inventory was $95,000 and ending inventory was $120,000. Beginning trade accounts payable were $24,000, and ending trade accounts payable were $47,000. What amount of cash did Reno pay to suppliers?

17-41 Cash Paid to Employees

Reno Construction Company reported wage and salary expenses of $195,000 on its 20X1 income statement. It reported cash paid to employees of $165,000 on its statement of cash flows. The beginning balance of accrued wages and salaries payable was $20,000. What was the ending balance in accrued wages and salaries payable? Ignore payroll taxes.

17-42 Simple Cash Flows from Operating Activities

Kinserdal and Associates provides consulting services in Oslo. In 20X0, net income was Nkr 200,000 on revenues of Nkr 480,000 and expenses of Nkr 280,000 (Nkr stands for Norwegian kroner). The only noncash expense was depreciation of Nkr 50,000. The company has no inventory. Accounts receivable increased by Nkr 11,000 during 20X0, and accounts payable and salaries payable were unchanged.

Required

Prepare a statement of cash flows from operating activities. Use the direct method. Omit supporting schedules.

17-43 Net Income and Cash Flow
Refer to Problem 17-42. Prepare a schedule that reconciles net income to net cash provided by operating activities.

17-44 Net Loss and Cash Flows from Operating Activities
The Visquel Company had a net loss of $42,000 in 20X2. The following information is available:

Depreciation	$22,000
Decrease in accounts receivable	4,000
Increase in inventory	2,000
Increase in accounts payable	17,000
Increase in salaries and wages payable	5,000

Required Present a schedule that reconciles net income (loss) to net cash provided by operating activities.

17-45 Preparation of a Statement of Cash Flows
Polanski Bottlers is a microbrewery in Milwaukee. By the end of 20X1, the company's cash balance had dropped to $10 thousand, despite net income of $240 thousand in 20X1. Its transactions affecting income or cash in 20X1 were (in thousands):

1. Sales were $3,003, all on credit. Cash collections from customers were $2,901.
2. The cost of items sold was $2,096.
3. Inventory increased by $56.
4. Cash payments on trade accounts payable were $2,140.
5. Payments to employees were $305; accrued wages payable decreased by $24.
6. Other operating expenses, all paid in cash, were $104.
7. Interest expense, all paid in cash, was $26.
8. Income tax expense was $105; cash payments for income taxes were $108.
9. Depreciation was $151.
10. A warehouse was acquired for $540 cash.
11. Equipment was sold for $37 cash; original cost was $196, accumulated depreciation was $159.
12. Received $28 for issue of common stock.
13. Retired long-term debt for $25 cash.
14. Paid cash dividends of $88.

Required Prepare a statement of cash flows using the direct method for reporting cash flows from operating activities. Omit supporting schedules.

17-46 Reconciliation of Net Income and Net Cash Provided by Operating Activities
Refer to Problem 17-45. Prepare a supporting schedule to the statement of cash flows that reconciles net income to net cash provided by operating activities.

17-47 Depreciation and Cash Flows
The following condensed income statement and reconciliation schedule are from the annual report of Chippewa Company (in millions):

Sales	$210
Expenses	188
Net income	$ 22

Reconciliation Schedule of Net Income to Net Cash Provided by Operating Activities	
Net income	$22
Add noncash expenses	
Depreciation	17
Deduct net increase in noncash	
operating working capital	(15)
Net cash provided by operating activities	$24

A shareholder has suggested that the company switch from straight-line to accelerated depreciation on its annual report to shareholders. He maintains that this will increase the cash flow provided by operating activities. According to his calculations, using accelerated methods would increase depreciation to $27 million, an increase of $10 million; net cash flow from operating activities would then be $34 million.

1. Suppose Chippewa Company adopts the accelerated depreciation method proposed. Compute net income and net cash flow from operating activities. Ignore income taxes.

2. Use your answer to requirement 1 to prepare a response to the shareholder.

17-48 Cash Flows, Indirect Method
The Anchorage Company has the following balance sheet data (in millions):

| | December 31 | | | | December 31 | | |
	20X2	20X1	Change		20X2	20X1	Change
Current assets				Current liabilities			
Cash	$ 13	$ 20	$ (7)	(detailed)	$105	$ 30	$ 75
Receivables, net	66	30	36	Long-term debt	120	—	120
Inventories	100	50	50	Stockholders' equity	224	170	54
Total current assets	$179	$100	$ 79				
Plant assets (net of accumulated depreciation)	270	100	170				
				Total liabilities and			
Total assets	$449	$200	$249	stockholders' equity	$449	$200	$249

Net income for 20X2 was $60 million. Net cash inflow from operating activities was $69 million. Cash dividends paid were $6 million. Depreciation was $20 million. Fixed assets were purchased for $190 million, $120 million of which was financed via the issuance of long-term debt outright for cash.

Colleen Eaglefeather, the president and majority stockholder of Anchorage, was a superb operating executive. She was imaginative and aggressive in marketing and ingenious and creative in production. But she had little patience with financial matters. After examining the most recent balance sheet and income statement, she muttered, "We've enjoyed 10 years of steady growth; 20X2 was our most profitable ever. Despite such profitability, we're in the worst cash position in our history. Just look at those current liabilities in relation to our available cash! This whole picture of the more you make, the poorer you get, just does not make sense. These statements must be cockeyed."

1. Prepare a statement of cash flows using the indirect method. Include a schedule reconciling net income to net cash provided by operating activities in the body of the statement.

2. Using the statement of cash flows and other information, write a short memorandum to Eaglefeather, explaining why there is such a squeeze on cash.

17-49 Preparation of Statement of Cash Flows
The Huang Company has assembled the (a) balance sheet and (b) income statement and statement of retained earnings for 20X1 shown in Exhibit 17-16 on page 716. On December 30, 20X1, Huang paid $102 million in cash to acquire a new plant to expand operations. This was partly financed by an issue of long-term debt for $50 million. Plant assets were sold for their book value of $6 million during 20X1. Because net income was $19 million, the highest in the company's history, James Li, the chief executive officer, was distressed by the company's extremely low cash balance.

1. Prepare a statement of cash flows using the direct method for reporting cash flows from operating activities. You may wish to use Exhibit 17-8, page 695, as a guide.

2. Prepare a schedule that reconciles net income to net cash provided by operating activities.

3. What is revealed by the statement of cash flows? Does it help you reduce Mr. Li's distress? Why? Briefly explain to Mr. Li why cash has decreased even though net income was $19 million.

Exhibit 17-16

Huang Co.

Balance Sheet December 31, 20X1 (in millions)

	20X1	20X0	Change
Assets			
Cash	$ 6	$ 25	$(19)
Accounts receivable	50	28	22
Inventory	70	50	20
Prepaid general expenses	4	3	1
Plant assets, net	206	150	56
	$336	$256	$ 80
Liabilities and shareholders' equity			
Accounts payable for merchandise	$ 74	$ 60	$ 14
Accrued tax payable	3	2	1
Long-term debt	50	—	50
Capital stock	100	100	—
Retained earnings	109	94	15
	$336	$256	$ 80

Huang Co.

Income Statement and Statement of Retained Earnings for the Year Ended
December 31, 20X1 (in millions)

Sales		$260
Less cost of goods sold		
Inventory, December 31, 20X0	$ 50	
Purchases	160	
Cost of goods available for sale	$210	
Inventory, December 31, 20X1	70	140
Gross profit		$120
Less other expenses		
General expense	$ 51	
Depreciation	40	
Taxes	10	101
Net income		$ 19
Dividends		4
Net income of the period retained		$ 15
Retained earnings, December 31, 20X0		94
Retained earnings, December 31, 20X1		$109

17-50 Gain on Disposal of Equipment

Gouda Life Insurance Company (GLIC) sold a computer. It had purchased the computer four years ago for 660 euros, and accumulated depreciation at the time of sale was 490 euros.

Required

1. Suppose GLIC received 170 euros cash for the computer. How would the sale be shown on the statement of cash flows?

2. Suppose GLIC received 195 euros for the computer. How would the sale be shown on the statement of cash flows (including the schedule reconciling net income and net cash provided by operating activities)?

UNDERSTANDING PUBLISHED FINANCIAL REPORTS

17-51 Various Intangible Assets

Consider the following:

1. a. Dow Chemical Company's annual report indicated that research and development expenditures were $845 million during 1999. How did this amount affect operating income, which was $2,476 million?

b. Suppose the entire $845 million arose from outlays for patents acquired from various outside parties on December 30, 1999. What would be the operating income for 1999?

c. How would the Dow balance sheet, December 31, 1999, be affected by a?

2. Suppose that on December 30, 2001, Verizon Wireless acquired new patents on some communications equipment for $40 million. Technology changes quickly. The equipment's useful life is expected to be four years rather than the 17-year life of the patent. What will be the amortization for 2002?

3. Hilton Hotels has an account classified under assets in its balance sheet called pre-opening costs. A footnote said that these costs "are deferred and charged to income over a three-year period after the opening date." Suppose expenditures for pre-opening costs in 2001 were $2,000,000 and the pre-opening costs account balance on December 31, 2001, was $1,840,000 and on December 31, 2000, it was $2,390,000. What amount was amortized for 2001?

4. Philip Morris purchased Kraft for approximately $13 billion. Of the $13 billion purchase price, only about $2 billion could be assigned to identifiable individual assets. Assume that the acquisition occurred on January 2. What was the total amount of goodwill from the purchase recorded on the Philip Morris balance sheet? Under today's accounting rules, what would happen to the goodwill in the years after the acquisition?

17-52 Various Liabilities

For each of the following items, indicate how the financial statements will be affected. Identify the affected accounts specifically.

1. Maytag Corporation sells electric appliances, including automatic washing machines. Suppose that experience in recent years has indicated that warranty costs average 3.2% of sales. Sales of washing machines for October were $3 million. Cash disbursements and obligations for warranty service on washing machines during October totaled $84,000.

2. Pepsi-Cola Company of New York gets cash deposits for its returnable bottles. In August, it received $100,000 cash and disbursed $93,000 for bottles returned.

3. Bank of America received a $1,200 savings deposit on April 1. On June 30, it recognized interest thereon at an annual rate of 5%. On July 1, the depositor closed her account with the bank.

4. The Seattle Repertory Theater sold for $100,000 cash a "season's series" of tickets in advance of December 31 for four plays, each to be held in successive months beginning in January. (a) What is the effect on the balance sheet, December 31? (b) What is the effect on the balance sheet, January 31?

17-53 Exercises in Assets, Liabilities, and Stockholders' Equity

Gateway Inc., is a leading direct marketer of computers. The company's 1999 net income was more than $425 million on sales of nearly $9 billion.

Required

1. At the end of 1998, Gateway had accounts receivable totaling $573,799,000 on its books, and after subtracting estimated uncollectible accounts of $14,948,000 the company reported net accounts receivable of $558,851,000 on its balance sheet. In 1999, accounts receivable before subtracting estimated uncollectibles increased by $89,012,000 and estimated uncollectible accounts increased by $1,524,000. What amount was reported for net accounts receivable on Gateway's 1999 balance sheet?

2. Gateway began the 1999 fiscal year with approximately $14,775,000 in long-term debt. The company repaid $6,287,000 during the year and did not borrow any additional funds. How much long-term debt was shown on Gateway's 1999 balance sheet?

3. Retained earnings at the end of the 1998 fiscal year were shown at $980,908,000 on Gateway's balance sheet. During 1999, net income was $427,944,000 and Gateway paid no dividends. What was the balance in retained earnings in Gateway's 1999 balance sheet?

17-54 Classified Balance Sheet — Germany

Siemens, the giant German electrical engineering and electronics company, has annual net income (measured in U.S. dollars at the exchange rate on September 30, 2000) of more than $9 billion on sales of nearly $90 billion. The company's presented its classified balance sheet for September 30, 2000, as follows:

Siemens AG Balance Sheet
September 30, 2000 (in millions of euros)

Assets	
Intangible assets	6,367
Property, plant and equipment, net	15,250
Investments	11,796
Noncurrent assets	**33,413**
Inventories	20,785
Less advances received from customers	(14,113)
	6,672
Accounts receivable and miscellaneous assets	31,002
Liquid assets	7,872
Current assets	**45,546**
Prepaid expenses	**296**
Total assets	**79,255**
Shareholders' equity and liabilities	
Shareholders' equity	**25,640**
Pension plans and similar commitments	12,449
Other accrued liabilities	14,019
Accrued liabilities	**26,468**
Debt	**9,134**
Other liabilities	**17,159**
Deferred income	**854**
Total shareholders' equity and liabilities	**79,255**

Required

Suppose Siemens used the format adopted by most U.S. companies for its balance sheet. How would the format of Siemens' balance sheet differ from that shown?

17-55 Gain on Airplane Crash

Several years ago, a Delta Airlines 727 crashed in Dallas. The crash resulted in a gain of $.11 per share of Delta. How could this happen? Consider the accounting for airplanes. Airlines insure their craft at market value, $6.5 million for Delta's 727. However, the planes' book values are often much less because of large accumulated depreciation amounts. The book value of Delta's 727 was only $962,000.

Required

1. Suppose Delta received the insurance payment and immediately purchased another 727 for $6.5 million. Compute the effect of the crash on pretax income. Also compute the effect on Delta's total assets.

2. Do you think a casualty loss should generate a reported gain? Why?

17-56 Identification of Operating, Investing, and Financing Activities

The items listed below were found on the statement of cash flows of Level 3 Communications, Inc., a broadband infrastructure provider to Internet service providers, applications service providers, Web-hosting companies, streaming media companies, and many other Web-centric companies. For each item, indicate which section of the statement should contain the item — the operating, investing, or financing section.

a. Capital expenditures
b. Depreciation and amortization
c. Change in working capital items
d. Repurchases of common stock
e. Long-term debt borrowings
f. Net earnings (loss)
g. Dividends paid
h. Issuances of common shares
i. Proceeds from sale of property, plant and equipment

17-57 Interest Expense

In 2000, Hewlett-Packard reported interest expense of $257 million on its income statement. Its supplemental cash flow information showed a cash payment for interest of $198 million. Suppose that accrued interest, a current liability on the balance sheet, was $55 million on January 1, 1999.

Required

1. Describe how the transactions relating to interest would be shown in the body of the statement of cash flows. Assume that Hewlett-Packard uses the direct method for reporting cash flows from operating activities.
2. Describe how the transactions relating to interest would be shown on a supplementary schedule that reconciles net income and net cash provided by operating activities.

17-58 Indirect and Direct Cash Flows from Operations

Cutter & Buck sells upscale sportswear primarily through golf pro shops, resorts, and other specialty retailers. Sales increased from $70 million in 1998 to more than $152 million in 2000. The following items were in the company's statement of cash flows for the fiscal year ending April 30, 2000 (in millions):

Increase in inventories	$ 758,482
Net income	5,660,068
Depreciation and amortization	1,385,616
Increase in income taxes payable	1,009,573
Increase in accounts payable and accrued liabilities	1,495,273
Increase in receivables	5,797,613
Other decreases in cash	686,810

The company's income statement showed (in millions):

Net sales	$ 70,104,015
Cost of goods sold	(40,642,031)
Other operating expenses	(20,958,986)
Operating income	48,502,998
Other income	77,070
Income before income taxes	8,580,068
Income tax	(2,920,000)
Net income	$ 5,660,068

Required

1. Prepare a statement of cash flows from operating activities using the indirect method.
2. Prepare a statement of cash flows from operating activities using the direct method. Assume that all other income was received in cash, and that all depreciation and other decreases in cash are included in other operating expenses.

17-59 Statement of Cash Flows, Direct and Indirect Methods

Nordstrom, Inc., the Seattle-based department store, had the following income statement for the year ended January 31, 2000 (in millions):

Net sales		$5,124
Costs and expenses		
Cost of sales	$3,360	
Selling, general, and administrative	1,491	
Interest	50	
Less: Other income	(109)	
Total costs and expenses		4,792
Earnings before income taxes		$ 332
Income taxes		129
Net earnings		$ 203

The company's net cash provided by operating activities, prepared using the indirect method, was

Net earnings	$203
Adjustments to reconcile net earnings to net cash provided by operating activities	
Depreciation and amortization	194
Other noncash expenses (revenues)	(3)
Changes in	
Accounts receivable	(30)
Merchandise inventories	(48)
Prepaid expenses	(23)
Accounts payable	51
Accrued salaries and wages	15
Other liabilities	7
Income taxes payable	12
Net cash provided by operating activities	$378

Required

Prepare a statement showing the net cash provided by operating activities using the direct method. Assume that all "other income" was received in cash and that prepaid expenses, accrued salaries and wages, and other accrued expenses relate to selling, general, and administrative expenses.

17-60 Comprehensive Review: Reconstruct Transactions

Childrobics, Inc., was incorporated in the state of New York on May 7, 1993. The company owns and operates indoor recreation facilities for children and their families in the New York metropolitan area. The company prepared financial statements on February 28, 1994, for the period since incorporation. Slightly revised versions of the company's balance sheet and statement of cash flows follow. Footnotes pointed out that, in exchange for a note payable of $250,000, the creditors supplied $146,000 in cash and $104,000 in property and equipment.

Required

Compute amounts to replace each of the question marks in the Childrobics' balance sheet.

Childrobics, Inc., Balance Sheet
February 28, 1994

Assets		
Current assets		
Cash		$?
Property and equipment		
At cost	$?	
Accumulated depreciation	?	
Net		?
Other assets		25,300
Total assets		$?
Liabilities and Stockholders' Equity		
Current liabilities		
Accounts payable and accrued expenses	$?	
Deferred revenue	?	
Note payable	?	
Total current liabilities		$?
Stockholders' equity		
Common stock: $.01 par value, 25,000,000 shares authorized, 975,000 shares issued and outstanding	$?	
Additional paid-in capital	?	
Retained earnings	?	
Total stockholders' equity		?
Total liabilities and stockholders' equity		$?

Childrobics, Inc.
Statement of Cash Flows for the Period Ended February 28, 1994

Operating Activities		
Net income	$ 2,516	
Adjustment to reconcile net income to net cash provided by operating activities		
Depreciation	10,947	
Change in assets and liabilities		
Account payable and accrued expenses	59,871	
Deferred revenue—customer deposits	13,450	
Net cash—operating activities		$ 86,784
Investing Activities		
Purchases of property and equipment	$(192,583)	
Expenditures for other assets	(25,300)	
Net cash—investing activities		(217,883)
Financing Activities		
Loans	$ 146,000	
Common stock	25,000	
Net cash—financing activities		171,000
Net increase in cash		39,901
Cash, beginning of period		0
Cash, end of period		$ 39,901

COLLABORATIVE LEARNING EXERCISE

17-61 Income Statement and Balance Sheet Accounts

Form teams of two persons each. Each person should make a list of ten account names, with approximately half being income statement accounts and half being balance sheet accounts. Give the list to the other member of the team, who is to write beside each account name the financial statement (I for income statement or B for balance sheet) on which it belongs. If there are errors or disagreements in classification, discuss the account and come to an agreement about which financial statement it belongs to.

INTERNET EXERCISE

17-62 Oracle's Financial Statements

Go to www.oracle.com to locate Oracle's home page and financial information.

www.prenhall.com/horngren

Answer the following questions about the company:

Required

1. On Oracle's Consolidated Balance Sheet, the company lists "Computer Software Development Costs." Why isn't this an expense on the Consolidated Statements of Operations?

2. Examine Oracle's balance sheet. Which method of accounting for uncollectible accounts does the company use? How can you tell? Which accounting principle does this method support?

3. Turn to the Notes to Consolidated Financial Statements. What is Oracle's revenue recognition policy for license and sublicense fees?

4. What classes of stock are listed on Oracle's balance sheet? What is the par value of each, and how many shares have been authorized? How many shares are outstanding?

5. Which method does Oracle use for its Consolidated Statements of Cash Flows? Does the company report any noncash investing or financing activities? If so, what are they?

6. What supplemental information does Oracle provide to support its cash flow data?

Go to the "Alternative Income Statement Formats and Extraordinary Items," "Statement of Cash Flows," and "Dividends and Treasury Stock" episodes on the *Mastering Accounting* CD-ROM for interactive, video-enhanced exercises.

More on Understanding Corporate Annual Reports

If General Motors (GM) had to rely on customers to pay cash for an auto like this one, it would not sell many cars. So GM created a subsidiary company, General Motors Acceptance Corporation (GMAC), to help customers finance the purchase of GM cars. Because of GMAC, General Motors sells more automobiles and earns profits from the interest paid by borrowers. The financial results of GM and GMAC are consolidated into one set of financial statements.

www.prenhall.com/horngren

Learning Objectives

When you have finished studying this chapter, you should be able to

1. Contrast accounting for investments using the equity method and the market method.

2. Explain the basic ideas and methods used to prepare consolidated financial statements.

3. Describe how goodwill arises and how to account for it.

4. Explain and use a variety of popular financial ratios.

5. Identify the major implications that efficient stock markets have for accounting.

6. **Understand how financial analysts use ratios and other analysis techniques to interpret the consolidated financial statements of a company.**

Deciding how to buy and finance a new car is one of life's more important decisions. If you have gone through this process, you know that auto dealers sell financing (auto loans) as well as automobiles. If you buy a General Motors car, you can finance it on the spot at the dealership, through a fully owned subsidiary of GM, General Motors Acceptance Corporation (GMAC). Just what is the relationship between General Motors and GMAC? They are separate entities, each with its own financial records. However, they are so closely related that authorities require them to combine their financial records when preparing financial statements for the public.

GM is not the only company that has to combine the financial records of its subsidiaries. Pick up the annual report of almost any major company and you will find *consolidated financial statements*. This term means that the books of two or more separate legal entities have been combined into the statements presented. General Motors describes its statements as follows: "The consolidated financial statements include the accounts of General Motors Corporation and domestic and foreign subsidiaries that are more than 50% owned, principally General Motors Acceptance Corporation (GMAC) and Hughes Electronics Corporation."

The consolidated General Motors statements you see in the company's annual report combine the financial results of companies making millions of transactions in many different currencies throughout the world. And if you buy a GM car or finance one through GMAC, your transaction will be consolidated into the overall GM financial statements as well.

Part One of this chapter shows how to account for the investments one company makes in another, such as General Motors's investment in GMAC, with a focus on consolidated financial statements. Part Two covers the analysis of financial statements. Either part may be studied independently, depending on your specific interest.

PART ONE: INTERCORPORATE INVESTMENTS INCLUDING CONSOLIDATIONS

Firms often invest in the equity securities of another company. The investor may be simply investing excess cash, or it may be seeking some degree of control over the investee. How we account for these investments depends on why management makes the investment.

An investor that holds less than 20% of another company is assumed to be a passive investor—it cannot significantly influence the decisions of the investee—and it uses the *market method.* Investors with between 20% and 50% have the ability to exert significant influence on the investee. They use the *equity method.* For example, Ford uses the equity method to account for its 33% interest in Mazda Motor Corporation of Japan. Companies with an interest in excess of 50% must use the *consolidation approach.*

MARKET AND EQUITY METHODS

market method The method of accounting for investments in equity securities that shows the investment on the balance sheet at market value.

trading securities Investments that the investor company intends to sell shortly.

available-for-sale securities Investments that the investor company has no intention to sell in the near future.

equity method Accounts for the investment at the acquisition cost adjusted for dividends received and the investor's share of earnings or losses of the investee after the date of investment.

Consider first an investment in less than 20% of the common stock of another company, which requires use of the market method. An investor using the **market method** shows the investment on its balance sheet at market value (also called fair value). Such investments are often called *marketable securities* in the financial statements.

The effect of such securities on the income statement depends on whether management classifies them as *trading securities* or *available-for-sale securities.* **Trading securities** are investments that the investor company intends to sell shortly. **Available-for-sale securities** are investments that the investor company has no intention to sell in the near future. Trading securities and available-for-sale securities provide returns to the investor in two ways: (1) dividend revenue, and (2) changes in market value. The investor company records dividend revenue on its income statement when received for both types of investments. However, we account for changes in market value differently for trading securities than for available-for-sale securities.

As the market value of *trading securities* changes, companies report the gains from increases in price and losses from decreases in price in the income statement. In contrast, as market values of *available-for-sale securities* rise and fall, there is no income statement effect. Instead, we add such unrealized gains and losses to a separate valuation allowance account in the stockholders' equity section of the balance sheet. This account increases stockholders' equity for securities whose price has increased since purchase. It decreases stockholders' equity for securities that have experienced a drop in prices.

Now consider investors who hold 20% to 50% of the common shares of another company and thus must use the equity method. The **equity method** accounts for the investment at the acquisition cost adjusted for dividends received and the investor's share of earnings or losses of the investee after the date of investment. Investors increase both income and the carrying amount of the investment by their share of the investee's earnings and reduce both income and the carrying amount by dividends received from the investee and by their share in the investee's losses.

Compare the market and equity methods. Suppose IBM acquires 40% of the voting stock of Start-up Computer Corporation (SCC) for $80 million. In year 1, SCC has a net income of $30 million and pays cash dividends of $10 million. IBM's 40% shares of income and dividends would be $12 million and $4 million, respectively. At the end of the year the market value of IBM's investment is $90 million. For illustrative purposes, suppose that IBM could use either the market or equity method. (In reality, IBM must use the equity method.) The balance sheet equation would be affected as follows under each of the methods (in millions):

| | Equity Method | | | | | Market Method | | | | |
| | Assets | | = | Equities | | Assets | | = | Equities | |
	Cash	Investments		Liab.	Stk. Eq.	Cash	Investments		Liab.	Stk. Eq.
1. Acquisition	−80	+80	=			−80	+80	=		
2. Net income of SCC		+12	=		+12	No entry and no effect				
3. Dividends from SCC	+4	−4	=			+4		=		+4
4. Increase in SCC market value	No entry and no effect						+10			+10
Effects for year	−76	+88	=		+12	−76	+90	=		+14

The investment account will have a net increase of $8 million for the year. The dividend will increase the cash account by $4 million.

The investment account will increase by the $10 million increase in market value. The dividend will increase the cash account by $4 million.

Under the market method, the $10 million increase in stockholders' equity would be part of retained earnings if IBM classified the investment as a trading security. It would be in a separate stockholders' equity valuation allowance account if IBM classified the investment as an available-for-sale security.

Under the equity method, IBM would recognize income as SCC earns it rather than when SCC pays dividends or when market values change. Cash dividends do not affect net income; they increase cash and decrease the investment balance. In a sense, IBM's "claim" on SCC grows by its share of SCC's net income. The dividend is a partial liquidation of IBM's claim. The receipt of a dividend is similar to the collection of an account receivable, from an accounting standpoint. A company recognizes the revenue from a sale of merchandise on account when it creates the receivable, so to include the collection also as revenue would be double-counting. Similarly, it would be double-counting to include the $4 million of dividends as income because the $12 million of income is already recognized as it is earned.

Suppose IBM were allowed to account for this investment using the market method. IBM would receive cash and recognize income each time SCC pays a dividend. In addition, at the end of each accounting period, IBM would find the market price of the shares and increase income (if it is a trading security) or the valuation allowance (if it is an available-for-sale security) for increases in price and decrease the same accounts for decreases in price.

Objective 1
Contrast accounting for investments using the equity method and the market method.

Suppose a company is considering purchasing about 20% of the common stock of another company. This is a strategic purchase and the investor plans to hold the stock indefinitely. What difference would it make if the company purchases 19.5% of the stock rather than 20.5%?

ANSWER

The accounting for the investment would be different under these two options. If the company purchases 19.5%, it must treat this as an available-for-sale investment and use the market method. This means that the investor's balance sheet will include the market value of the investment, and its income statement will include only the dividends received. In contrast, if the company purchases 20.5% of the stock, it will use the equity method. The investment account on the balance sheet will grow with the net income of the investee less dividends received. It will not fluctuate with market values. In addition, the income statement will include the investor's share of the investee's net income, regardless of dividend payments or changes in market prices.

If the investor expects the investee to grow, it probably expects it to have increasing earnings but pay few dividends. In such a case, the investor would recognize more income from the investment under the equity method. Further, wide swings in the market value of the investee will not affect the investor's books under the equity method. However, because of this, the investor's books would get no immediate benefit from large increases in the market value of the investee for an equity-method investment. The choice of the amount of investment can have a major impact on the investor's future financial statements. Depending on what an investor company wants to accomplish, it might prefer either the market or the equity method. The only way to select one or the other is to invest the right amount in the investee.

CONSOLIDATED FINANCIAL STATEMENTS

parent company A company owning more than 50% of another business's stock.

subsidiary A company owned by a parent company that owns more than 50% of its stock.

consolidated financial statements Financial statements that combine the financial statements of the parent company with those of various subsidiaries, as if they were a single entity.

Objective 2
Explain the basic ideas and methods used to prepare consolidated financial statements.

Suppose one firm owns more than 50% of the stock in another business. The stockholding firm obviously has a great deal of influence over the other business. Because of this influence, the company owning more than 50% of the other business's stock is called the **parent company.** The company whose stock is owned by the other business is called the **subsidiary.** Although parent and subsidiary companies typically are separate legal entities, in many regards they function as one unit.

Why have subsidiaries? Why not have the corporation take the form of a single legal entity? The reasons include limiting the liabilities in a risky venture, saving income taxes, conforming with government regulations, doing business in a foreign country, and expanding in an orderly way. For example, there are often tax advantages in acquiring the capital stock of a going concern rather than its individual assets.

The parent-subsidiary relationship requires special accounting treatment. Under U.S. regulations, parent companies must issue **consolidated financial statements** that combine the financial statements of the parent company with those of its subsidiaries. That is, we account for the parent and subsidiary companies as if they were a single entity. Why? Because consolidated statements give investors a more accurate picture of the whole organization's health.

THE ACQUISITION

When consolidating parent and subsidiary financial statements, accountants must avoid double-counting of assets and equities. Suppose Company P (parent) acquired 100% of the common stock of S (subsidiary) for $210 million cash at the beginning of the year.[1]

---

[1] In this example, the purchase price equals the stockholders' equity of the acquired company. On pages 731–735 we discuss the preparation of consolidated statements in situations in which these two amounts differ.

The following table analyzes the balance sheet accounts of both companies. (Investment in S appears in the first column because it is a focal point in this chapter, not because it comes first in actual balance sheets.) Figures in this and subsequent tables are in millions of dollars:

| | Assets | | = | Liabilities | + | Stockholders' Equity |
	Investment in S	+	*Cash and Other Assets*	=	*Accounts Payable, Etc.*	+	*Stockholders' Equity*
P's accounts, January 1							
Before acquisition			650	=	200	+	450
Acquisition of S	+210		−210	=			
S's accounts, January 1			400	=	190	+	210
Intercompany elimina- tions for a consolidated balance sheet	−210			=			−210
Consolidated, January 1	0	+	840	=	390	+	450

Note that P pays the $210 million to the former owners of S as private investors. The $210 million is not an addition to the existing assets and stockholders' equity of S. That is, P's purchase of stock in S does not affect S's books. S does not disappear, but it lives on as a separate legal entity. Each legal entity has its individual set of books. The consolidated entity does not keep a separate set of books.

Let's prepare a consolidated balance sheet immediately after the acquisition. The consolidated statement shows the details of all assets and liabilities of both the parent and the subsidiary. The Investment in S account on P's books is the evidence of P's ownership interest in all the assets and liabilities of S. The consolidated statements cannot show both the evidence of interest plus the detailed underlying assets and liabilities. To avoid such double-counting, we eliminate the evidence of ownership present in two places: (1) the Investment in S on P's books and (2) the Stockholders' Equity on S's books.

In summary, if the $210 million elimination of the reciprocal accounts did not occur, there would be a double-counting in the consolidated statement:

Entity	Types Of Records
P	Parent books
+S	Subsidiary books
=Preliminary consolidated report	No separate books for the consolidated entity, but periodically P and S assets and liabilities are added together via work sheets
−E	"Eliminating entries" to remove double-counting
=Consolidated report to investors	

AFTER ACQUISITION

Investments in 50- to 100%-owned subsidiaries, such as this investment in S, are carried in the *investor's* balance sheet by the equity method, described earlier in this chapter. Suppose S has a net income of $50 million for the year. If P were reporting alone, it would account for the net income of its subsidiary by increasing its Investment in S account and its Stockholders' Equity account (in the form of Retained Earnings) by 100% of $50 million.

The income statements for the year would be (numbers in millions):

	P	S	Consolidated
Sales	$900	$300	$1,200
Expenses	800	250	1,050
Operating income	$100	$ 50	$ 150
Pro-rata share (100%) of subsidiary net income	50	—	
Net income	$150	$ 50	

P's parent-company-only income statement (the first column) shows its own sales and expenses plus its pro-rata share of S's net income (as the equity method requires). The consolidated statement (the last column) adds together all the revenues and expenses of the parent and the subsidiary.

Reflect on the changes in P's accounts, S's accounts, and the consolidated accounts (in millions of dollars):

	Assets			=	Liabilities	+	Stockholders' Equity
	Investment in S	+	Cash and Other Assets	=	Accounts Payable, Etc.	+	Stockholders' Equity
P's accounts							
Beginning of year	210	+	440	=	200	+	450
Operating income			+100	=			+100*
Share of S income	+50			=			+50*
End of year	260	+	540	=	200	+	600
S's accounts							
Beginning of year			400	=	190	+	210
Net income			+50	=			+50*
End of year			450	=	190	+	260
Intercompany eliminations	−260			=			−260
Consolidated, end of year	0	+	990	=	390	+	600

* Changes in the retained earnings portion of stockholders' equity.

Note that consolidated statements summarize the individual accounts of two or more separate legal entities, eliminating double-counting.[2] The income statement for P shows a $150 million net income; for S, a $50 million net income; for P and S consolidated, a $150 million net income.

MINORITY INTERESTS

When a parent holds less than 100% of the stock of a subsidiary, a consolidated balance sheet includes an account on the equities side called *Minority Interests in Subsidiaries,* or simply **Minority Interests.** The account shows the outside stockholders' interest, as

minority interests An account that shows the outside stockholders' interest, as opposed to the parent's interest, in a subsidiary corporation.

[2] *Another example of double-counting is sales by P to S (or by S to P), which do not exist in this example. A consolidated income statement should not include the sale when P sells the item to S and again when S sells it to an outsider. Suppose P bought an item for $1,000 and sold it to S for $1,200. P recognized revenue of $1,200, cost of goods sold of $1,000, and income of $200. S recorded an inventory item of $1,200. In consolidation, this transaction must be eliminated. After adding together the individual accounts of P and S, you must deduct $1,200 from revenue, $1,000 from cost of goods sold, and $200 from inventory. This eliminates the $200 of income that P recognized and reduces inventory to the original $1,000 that P paid for the item.*

opposed to the parent's interest, in a subsidiary corporation. It arises because the consolidated balance sheet includes *all* the assets and liabilities of a subsidiary. Suppose the parent owns 90% of the subsidiary stock, and outsiders to the consolidated group own the other 10%. The Minority Interests account is a measure of the outside stockholders' interest. The diagram that follows shows the area encompassed by the consolidated statements; it includes all the subsidiary's assets and liabilities, item by item. However, because of the outsiders' ownership interests, P does not have a claim on all the assets and liabilities listed. The creation of an account for minority interests, in effect, corrects this overstatement. The remainder after deducting minority interests is P's total ownership interest:

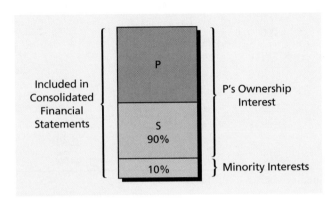

The next table, using the basic figures of the previous example, shows the overall approach to a consolidated balance sheet immediately after the acquisition. Suppose P bought 90% of the stock of S for a cost of 0.90 × $210, or $189 million. The minority interest would be 10%, or $21 million.

	Assets		=	Liabilities +		Stockholders' Equity		
	Investment in S	+ *Cash and Other Assets*	=	*Accounts Payable, Etc.*	+ *Minority Interest*	+	*Stockholders' Equity*	
P's accounts, January 1								
Before acquisition		650	=	200		+	450	
Acquisition of 90% of S	+189	−189	=					
S's accounts, January 1		400	=	190		+	210	
Intercompany eliminations	−189		=		+21		−210	
Consolidated, January 1	0 +	861	=	390	+ 21	+	450	

Again, suppose S has a net income of $50 million for the year. The same basic procedures are followed by P and by S regardless of whether S is 100% owned or 90% owned. However, the presence of a minority interest changes the consolidated income statement slightly, as follows:

	P	**S**	**Consolidated**
Sales	$900	$300	$1,200
Expenses	800	250	1,050
Operating income	$100	$ 50	$ 150
Pro-rata share (90%) of subsidiary net income	45	—	
Net income	$145	$ 50	
Minority interest (10%) in subsidiaries' net income			5
Net income to consolidated entity			$ 145

Consolidated balance sheets at the end of the year would also be affected, as follows:

	Assets		=	Liabilities	+	Stockholders' Equity		
	Investment in S	+ *Cash and Other Assets*	=	*Accounts Payable, Etc.*	+	*Minority Interest*	+	*Stockholders' Equity*
P's accounts								
Beginning of year, before acquisition		650	=	200		+		450
Acquisition	189	−189	=					
Operating income		+100	=					+100
Share of S income	+45		=					+45
End of year	234	+ 561	=	200		+		595
S's accounts								
Beginning of year		400	=	190		+		210
Net income		+50	=					+50
End of year		+ 450	=	190		+		260
Intercompany eliminations	−234		=			+26*		−260
Consolidated, end of year	0	+ 1,011	=	390	+	26	+	595

* Beginning minority interest plus minority interest in net income: $21 + (0.10 \times 50) = 21 + 5 = 26$.

As indicated in the table, the entry to consolidate the statements eliminates $260 million of stockholders' equity (on S's books) and $234 million of investment in S (on P's books). The $26 million difference is the minority interest (on consolidated statements). It identifies the interest of those shareholders who own the 10% of the subsidiary stockholders' equity that is not eliminated by consolidation.

PERSPECTIVE ON CONSOLIDATED STATEMENTS

To get a clear idea of the consolidation process and its effect on balance sheets and income statements, consider the following hypothetical relationships that exist for Goliath Corporation, which for more realism could be viewed as a simplified version of General Motors:

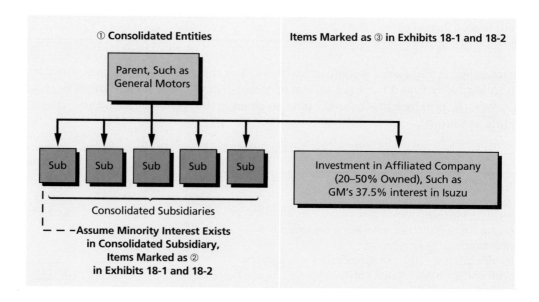

Exhibits 18-1 and 18-2 provide an overall look at how consolidated balance sheets and income statements for such a company appear in corporate annual reports. The circled items ①, ②, and ③ in the exhibits deserve special mention:

① The headings indicate that these are consolidated financial statements.

② On balance sheets, the minority interest typically appears just above the stockholders' equity section, as Exhibit 18-1 shows. On income statements, the minority interest in net income is deducted as if it were an expense of the consolidated entity, as Exhibit 18-2 demonstrates. It generally follows all other expenses. Sometimes you will find minority interest before income taxes and sometimes after. Note that minority interest is a claim of outside stockholders' interest in a consolidated subsidiary company. Note also that minority interests arise only in conjunction with consolidated financial statements.

③ As described earlier in the chapter, investments in equity securities that represent 20% to 50% ownership are accounted for under the equity method. These investments are frequently called **investments in affiliates** or **investments in associates.** General Motors would account for its 37.5% investment in Isuzu in this manner. Exhibit 18-1 shows how the Investment account in the balance sheet has risen by the pro-rata share of the current earnings of affiliates, the $1 million shown in the income statement in Exhibit 18-2.

investments in affiliates (investments in associates) Investments in equity securities that represent 20 to 50% ownership. They are accounted for under the equity method.

Some accountants argue against consolidating subsidiaries in businesses totally different from those of the parent. Such 50- to 100%-owned subsidiaries could be accounted for using the equity method, as if they were affiliated companies. Supporters of this approach maintain that a consolidated statement for such distinctly different businesses would produce a meaningless hodgepodge. For example, they believe that General Motors (GM) should not consolidate the accounts for General Motors Acceptance Corporation (GMAC), a finance company subsidiary, even though GM's interest is 100%.

Nevertheless, the FASB requires all subsidiaries to be consolidated. The major reason for forcing consolidation is to provide a more complete picture of the economic entity. The FASB believes that excluding some subsidiaries from consolidation results in the omission of significant amounts of assets, liabilities, revenues, and expenses from the consolidated statements of many companies.

There are exceptions to the general rule, but they are rare. A subsidiary is not consolidated if control is likely to be temporary or it does not rest with the majority owner. For example, a subsidiary could be in bankruptcy or operating under foreign exchange restrictions or other controls. In these cases, subsidiaries are carried on the equity basis until control by the parent is resumed.

Exhibit 18-3 summarizes all the relationships depicted in Exhibits 18-1 and 18-2. Take a few moments to review all three exhibits. In particular, note that minority interests arise only in conjunction with consolidated subsidiaries. Why? Because consolidated balance sheets and income statements aggregate 100% of the detailed assets, liabilities, sales, and expenses of the subsidiary companies. Thus, if we do not recognize a minority interest, the financial statements would overstate the stockholders' equity and net income of the consolidated enterprise.

In contrast, minority interests do not arise in connection with the accounting for investments in affiliated companies. Why? Because consolidated statements do not contain detailed assets, liabilities, revenues, and expenses of the affiliated companies. Investors record their interests in these companies on a pro-rata basis only.

ACCOUNTING FOR GOODWILL

In Chapter 17, we defined goodwill as the excess of cost over fair (market) value of net identifiable assets of businesses acquired. We will now see how goodwill arises when one company purchases another.

Objective 3
Describe how goodwill arises and how to account for it.

Exhibit 18-1

Goliath Corporation

① Consolidated Balance Sheets as of December 31 (millions of dollars)

Assets		20X1	20X0
Current assets			
Cash		$ 90	$ 56
Short-term investments in debt securities at cost (which approximates market value)		—	28
Accounts receivable (less allowance for doubtful accounts of $2,000,000 and $2,100,000 at their respective dates)		91	95
Inventories at average cost		120	130
Total current assets		301	309
③ Investments in affiliated companies		10	9
Property, plant, and equipment			
Land at original cost		50	39
Plant and equipment			
	20X1 / 20X0		
Original cost	$255 / $190		
Accumulated depreciation	126 / 112		
Net plant and equipment		129	78
Total property, plant, and equipment		179	117
Other assets			
Franchises and trademarks		15	16
Deferred charges and prepayments		3	4
Total other assets		18	20
Total assets		$508	$455

Liabilities and Stockholders' Equity	20X1	20X0
Current liabilities		
Accounts payable	$100	$ 84
Notes payable	10	—
Accrued expenses payable	32	22
Accrued income taxes payable	34	38
Total current liabilities	176	144
Long-term liabilities		
First mortgage bonds, 5% interest, due December 31, 20X4	25	25
Subordinated debentures, 6% interest, due December 31, 20X7	30	20
Total long-term liabilities	55	45
Deferred income*	12	9.3
② Minority interest in consolidated subsidiaries	6	5.7
Total liabilities	249	204
Stockholders' equity		
Preferred stock, 100,000 shares, $30 par†	3	3
Common stock, 1,000,000 shares, $1 par	1	1
Paid-in capital in excess of par	55	55
Retained earnings	200	192
Total stockholders' equity	259	251
Total liabilities and stockholders' equity	$508	$455

* Advances from customers on long-term contracts. Other examples are collections for rent and subscriptions, which often are classified as current liabilities.

† Dividend rate is $5 per share; each share is convertible into two shares of common stock. The shares were originally issued for $100. The excess over par is included in "paid-in capital in excess of par." Liquidating value is $100 per share.

Exhibit 18-2

Goliath Corporation

① Consolidated Income Statements for the Years Ended December 31
(in thousands)

	20X1	20X0
Net sales and other operating revenues	$507,000	$609,100
Cost of goods sold and operating expenses, exclusive of depreciation	468,750	554,550
Depreciation	14,000	11,000
Total operating expenses	482,750	565,550
Operating income	24,250	43,550
③ Equity in earnings of affiliates	1,000	900
Total income before interest expense and income taxes	25,250	44,450
Interest expense	2,450	2,450
Income before income taxes	22,800	42,000
Income taxes	12,000	21,900
Income before minority interests	10,800	20,100
② Minority interest in consolidated subsidiaries' net income	300	600
Net consolidated income to Goliath Corporation*	10,500	19,500
Preferred dividends	500	500
Net income to Goliath Corporation common stock	$ 10,000	$ 19,000
Earnings per share of common stock On shares outstanding (1,000,000 shares)	$10.00†	$19.00

* This is the total figure in dollars that the accountant traditionally labels net income. It is reported accordingly in the financial press.
† This is the figure most widely quoted by the investment community: $10,000,000 ÷ 1,000,000 = $10.00; $19,000,000 ÷ 1,000,000 = $19.00.

Exhibit 18-3

Summary of Equity Method and Consolidations

Items in Exhibits 18-1 and 18-2	Percentage of Ownership	Type of Accounting	Balance Sheet Effects	Income Statement Effects
①	100%	Consolidation	Individual assets, individual liabilities added together	Individual revenues, individual expenses added together
②	Greater than 50% and less than 100%	Consolidation	Same as ①, but recognition given to minority interest in liability section	Same as ①, but recognition given to minority interest near bottom of statement when consolidated net income is computed
③	20% to and including 50%	Equity method	Investment carried at cost plus pro-rata share of subsidiary earnings less dividends received	Equity in earnings of affiliated or associated companies shown on one line as addition to income

Our previous example of Companies P and S assumed that the acquisition cost of S by P was equal to the amount of the stockholders' equity, or the book value, of S. However, the total purchase price paid by P often exceeds the book values of the assets acquired. In fact, the purchase price also often exceeds the sum of the fair market values (current values) of the identifiable individual assets less the liabilities. For example, when Philip Morris paid $13 billion for Kraft, it assigned only $2 billion to identifiable individual assets. It assigned the remainder to goodwill.

To see the impact of goodwill on the consolidated statements, refer to our initial example on consolidations, where P acquired a 100% interest in S for $210 million. Suppose the price were $40 million higher, or a total of $250 million cash. For simplicity, assume that the fair values of the individual assets of S are equal to their book values. The balance sheets immediately after the acquisition are

	Assets				=	Liabilities	+	Stockholders' Equity
	Investment in S	+	Goodwill	+	Cash and Other Assets	=	Accounts Payable, Etc.	+	Stockholders' Equity
P's accounts									
Before acquisition					650	=	200	+	450
Acquisition	+250				−250	=			
S's accounts					400	=	190	+	210
Intercompany eliminations	−250	+	40			=			−210
Consolidated	0	+	40*	+	800	=	390	+	450

* The $40 million "goodwill" would appear in the consolidated balance sheet as a separate intangible asset account. It often is the final item in a listing of assets.

What if the book values of the individual assets of S are not equal to their fair values? The usual procedures are

1. S continues as a going concern and keeps its accounts on the same basis as before.
2. P records its investment at its acquisition cost (the agreed purchase price).
3. For consolidated reporting purposes, we first assign part of the excess of the acquisition cost over the book value of S to the individual assets, item by item, to increase each to its fair market value at the time of the acquisition. We label any remaining excess as purchased goodwill.

Suppose the fair value of the assets of S (e.g., machinery and equipment) exceeded their book value by $30 million in our example. The balance sheets immediately after acquisition would be the same as previously, with a single exception. The $40 million goodwill would now be only $10 million. The remaining $30 million would appear in the consolidated balance sheet as an integral part of the individual assets. That is, S's equipment would be shown at $30 million higher in the consolidated balance sheet than the carrying amount on S's books. Similarly, the depreciation expense on the consolidated income statement would be higher. For instance, if the equipment had five years of useful life remaining, the straight-line depreciation would be $30 million ÷ 5 = $6 million higher per year.

As in the preceding tabulation, the $10 million "goodwill" would appear in the consolidated balance sheet as a separate intangible asset account.

GOODWILL AND ABNORMAL EARNINGS

Goodwill is frequently misunderstood. The layperson often thinks of goodwill as being the friendly attitude of the neighborhood store manager. But goodwill can have many aspects. A purchaser may be willing to pay more than the current values of the individual assets received because the acquired company is able to generate abnormally high earnings. The causes of this excess earning power may be traceable to personalities, skills, locations, operating methods, and so forth. For example, a purchaser may be willing to pay extra because excess earnings can be forthcoming from

1. Saving in time and costs by purchasing a corporation having a share of the market in a type of business or in a geographical area where the acquiring corporation planned expansion
2. Excellent general management skills or a unique product line
3. Potential efficiency by combination, rearrangement, or elimination of duplicate facilities and administration

Of course, "goodwill" is originally generated internally. For example, a happy combination of advertising, research, management talent, and timing may give a particular company a dominant market position for which another company is willing to pay dearly. This ability to command a premium price for the total business creates goodwill. Nevertheless, the selling company never records such goodwill. Therefore the only goodwill generally recognized as an asset is that identified when one company purchases another. The consolidated company must then show the purchased goodwill in its financial statements.

SUMMARY PROBLEM FOR YOUR REVIEW

PROBLEM

1. Review the section on minority interests, pages 728–730. Suppose P purchases 60% of the stock of S for a cost of .60 × $210, or $126 million cash. The total assets of P consist of this $126 million plus $524 million of other assets, a total of $650 million. The assets, liabilities, and shareholders' equity of S are unchanged from the amounts given in the example on minority interests. Prepare an analysis showing what amounts would appear in a consolidated balance sheet immediately after the acquisition.
2. Suppose S has a net income of $50 million for the year, and P has an operating income of $100 million. Other details are described in the example on page 729. Prepare an analysis showing what amounts would appear in a consolidated income statement and year-end balance sheet.

SOLUTION

1.

	Assets			=	Liabilities	+	Stockholders' Equity		
	Investment in S	+	*Cash Other Assets*	=	*Accounts Payable, Etc.*	+	*Minority Interest*	+	*Stockholders' Equity*
P's accounts, January 1:									
Before acquisition			650	=	200			+	450
Acquisition of 60% of S	+126		−126	=					
S's accounts, January 1			400	=	190			+	210
Intercompany eliminations	−126			=			+84		−210
Consolidated, January 1	0	+	924	=	390	+	84	+	450

2.

	P	S	Consolidated
Sales	$900	$300	$1,200
Expenses	800	250	1,050
Operating income	$100	$ 50	$ 150
Pro-rata share (60%) of unconsolidated subsidiary net income	30	—	
Net income	$130	$ 50	
Minority interest (40%) in consolidated subsidiary net income			20
Net income to consolidated entity			$ 130

	Assets	=	Liabilities		+	Stockholders' Equity		
	Investment in S	+	Cash and Other Assets	=	Accounts Payable, Etc.	+	Minority Interest	+	Stockholders' Equity
P's accounts								
Beginning of year, before acquisition			650	=	200		+	450
Acquisition	126		−126	=				
Operating income			+100	=				+100
Share of S income	+30			=				+ 30
End of year	156	+	624	=	200		+	580
S's accounts								
Beginning of year			400	=	190		+	210
Net income			+ 50	=				+ 50
End of year			450	=	190		+	260
Intercompany eliminations	−156			=			+104*	−260
Consolidated, end of year	0	+	1,074	=	390	+	104	+	580

* 84 beginning of year + (0.40 × 50) = 84 + 20 = 104.

Highlights to Remember: Part One

Contrast accounting for investments using the equity method and the market method.
Companies often invest in the equity securities of another company. If they own less than 20% of a company, they use the market method to account for the investment. Under the market method, the balance sheet shows the market value of the securities. If a company expects to sell the securities shortly, it calls them trading securities, and changes in market value are part of income. If there is no intention to sell the securities in the near future, they are available-for-sale securities, and changes in market value are placed in a separate valuation allowance account in stockholders' equity.

Explain the basic ideas and methods used to prepare consolidated financial statements.
When a parent company owns more than 50% of a subsidiary company, the companies must prepare consolidated financial statements. Each company continues to keep its own books, but for reporting to the public they combine their assets and liabilities, eliminating double counting. If the parent owns less than 100% of a subsidiary, the statements will show a minority interest.

Describe how goodwill arises and how to account for it.   If a parent pays more than the fair market value of the net assets when acquiring a subsidiary, it must record the difference as goodwill. Goodwill is an intangible asset that remains on the company's books until its value is impaired.

Accounting Vocabulary

available-for-sale securities, p. 724

consolidated financial statements, p. 726

equity method, p. 724

investments in affiliates, p. 731

investments in associates, p. 731

market method, p. 724

minority interests, p. 728

parent company, p. 726

subsidiary, p. 726

trading securities, p. 724

PART TWO: ANALYSIS OF FINANCIAL STATEMENTS

For financial statements to be useful, managers and investors need to be able to analyze and interpret the statements. Careful analysis of financial statements can help decision makers evaluate an organization's past performance and predict its future performance. Such evaluations help managers, investors, and others make intelligent, informed financial decisions. We use the 1999 and 2000 financial statements of Microsoft Corporation in Exhibits 18-4 and 18-5 to focus on financial statement analysis.

Exhibit 18-4

Microsoft Corporation
Balance Sheet (millions)

	June 30			
	1999		*2000*	
Assets				
Current assets				
Cash and short-term investments	$17,236		$23,798	
Accounts receivable	2,245		3,250	
Other	752		1,552	
Total current assets		$20,233		$28,600
Long-term assets*				
Property, plant and equipment, net		1,611		1,903
Equity and other investments		14,372		17,726
Other assets		940		2,213
Total assets		$37,156		$50,442
Liabilities and Stockholders' Equity				
Current liabilities				
Accounts payable	$ 874		$ 1,083	
Income taxes payable	1,607		583	
Accrued compensation	396		557	
Unearned revenue	4,239		4,816	
Other	1,602		2,714	
Total current liabilities		$ 8,718		$ 9,753
Stockholders' equity				
Convertible preferred stock	$ 980		$ 0	
Paid-in capital	13,844		22,516	
Retained earnings	13,614		18,173	
Total shareholders' equity		28,438		40,689
Total liabilities and shareholders' equity		$37,156		$50,442

*This caption is frequently omitted. Instead, the long-term assets are merely listed as separate items following the current assets.

Decisions based on comparisons of financial statements span a wide range. For example, investors use them to decide whether to buy, sell, or hold common stock. Managers and the financial community (such as bank officers and stockholders) use them as clues to help evaluate the operating and financial outlook for an organization. Budgets or pro forma statements—carefully formulated expressions of predicted results, including a schedule of the amounts and timing of cash repayments—are helpful to extenders of credit, who want assurance of being paid in full and on time. For example, a set of budgeted financial statements is one of the first things a banker will request from an entrepreneur proposing a new business. Even well established companies usually need to provide pro forma statements to assure creditors that the company will pay back the amounts borrowed.

COMPONENT PERCENTAGES

component percentages
Analysis and presentation of financial statements in percentage form to aid comparability, frequently used when companies differ in size.

When comparing companies that differ in size, analysts often apply percentage relationships, called **component percentages,** to income statements and balance sheets (see Exhibit 18-6). We call the resulting statements **common-size statements.** For example, it is difficult to compare Microsoft's $28,600 billion of current assets with the $13.1 million of Interlinq, a smaller software company. It's much easier to compare Microsoft's 57% current asset percentage (shown in Exhibit 18-6) with Interlinq's $13.1 million ÷ $21.8 million = 60%.

common-size statements
Financial statements expressed in component percentages.

Income statement percentages are usually based on sales = 100%. Microsoft seems reasonably profitable, but such percentages would have more meaning when compared

Exhibit 18-5

Microsoft Corporation Statement of Income
(millions except earnings per share)

	For the Year Ended June 30			
	1999		2000	
Net revenues		$19,747		$22,956
Cost of revenues*		2,814		3,002
Gross profit		16,933		19,954
Operating expenses:				
General and administrative	$ 689		$1,009	
Research and development	2,970		3,775	
Sales and marketing	3,231		4,141	
Other expenses	115	7,005	92	9,017
Operating income		9,928		10,937
Other income (expense)†		1,963		3,338
Income before income taxes		11,891		14,275
Provision for income taxes		4,106		4,854
Net income		7,785		9,421
Preferred stock dividends		28		0
Net income available for common shareholders		$ 7,757		$9,421
Earnings per share‡		$ 1.54		$ 1.81

* Also called cost of goods sold.
† Primarily investment revenue.
‡ Microsoft pays no dividends. Publicly held companies must show earnings per share on the face of the income statement, but it is not necessary to show dividends per share. Average shares outstanding for computation of EPS are approximately 5,028 million in 1999 and 5,188 million in 2000.

Exhibit 18-6

Microsoft Corporation

Common-Size Statements (millions except percentages)

	For the Year Ended June 30			
Statement of Income	1999		2000	
Net revenues	$19,747*	100%	$22,956	100%
Cost of revenues	2,814	14	3,002	13
Gross profit (or gross margin)	$16,933	86%	$19,954	87%
General and administrative	$ 689	4%	$ 1,009	4%
Research and development	2,970	15	3,775	16
Sales and marketing	3,231	16	4,141	18
Other	115	1	92	1
Operating expenses	$ 7,005	36%	$ 9,017	39%
Operating income	$ 9,928	50%	$10,937	48%
Other income (expense)	1,963	10	3,338	14
Income before income taxes	$11,891	60%	$14,275	62%
Provision for income taxes	4,106	21	4,854	21
Net income	$ 7,785	39%	$ 9,421	41%
Balance Sheet				
Current assets	$20,233	55%	$28,600	57%
Plant, property, and equipment, net	1,611	4	1,903	4
Other assets	15,312	41	19,939	39
Total assets	$37,156	100%	$50,442	100%
Current liabilities	$ 8,716	23%	$ 9,753	19%
Long-term liabilities	0	0	0	0
Stockholders' equity	28,438	77	40,689	81
Total equities	$37,156	100%	$50,442	100%

* Note the use of dollar signs in columns of numbers. Frequently, they are used at the top and bottom only and not for every subtotal. Their use by companies depends on the preference of management.

with the budgeted performance for the current year (not shown here). Both the gross margin rate and net income percentage seem outstanding. However, averages for these items vary greatly by industry. Comparison with other similar firms or industry averages is necessary to interpret the rates fully. Changes between one year and the next can also reveal important information. Microsoft's net income rose from 39% to 41% of sales, primarily because of an increase in other income. Net income rose despite an increase in operating expenses (from 36% to 39% of sales).

Balance sheet percentages are usually based on total assets = 100%. Note in Exhibit 18-6 that Microsoft's current assets and stockholders' equity increased, while current liabilities decreased.

Corporate annual reports to the public must contain a section that is usually labeled *management's discussion and analysis.* This section concentrates on explaining the major changes in the income statement, changes in liquidity and capital resources, and the impact of inflation. The focus is on a comparison of one year with the next. For example, Microsoft's annual report had several pages of detailed discussions, including

> The Company's revenue growth rate was 28% in fiscal 1998, 29%
> in fiscal 1999, and 16% in fiscal 2000. Revenue growth in fiscal
> 2000 was driven by strong licensing of the Microsoft suite of prod-
> ucts including Microsoft Windows NT® Workstation, Windows
> 2000 Professional, Windows NT Server, Windows 2000 Server,

Microsoft Office 2000, and SQL Server 7.0. . . . Cost of revenue as a percent of revenue was 16.1% in 1998, 14.3% in 1999, and 13.1% in 2000. Cost of revenue in fiscal 2000 reflected lower costs associated with WebTV Networks' operations, partially offset by the growth in hardware peripherals costs. . . . Investment income increased primarily as a result of a larger investment portfolio generated by cash from operations in 1998, 1999, and 2000, coupled with realized gains from the sale of securities in 1999 and 2000. . . . The Company's cash and short-term investment portfolio totaled $23.80 billion at June 30, 2000. The portfolio consists primarily of fixed-income securities, diversified among industries and individual issuers. . . . Management believes existing cash and short-term investments together with funds generated from operations will be sufficient to meet operating requirements. . . . Microsoft has not paid cash dividends on its common stock.

USES OF RATIOS

Objective 4
Explain and use a variety of popular financial ratios.

In addition to or instead of budgets and common-size statements, investors and creditors often use ratios computed from published financial statements. Exhibit 18-7 shows how some typical ratios are computed. Many more ratios could be computed. For example, Standard & Poor's Corporation sells a COMPUSTAT service which, via computer, can provide financial and statistical information for more than 16,000 companies. The information includes 332 financial statement items on an annual basis and 128 items on a quarterly basis, plus limited footnote information. Exhibit 18-7 contains only the most popular ratios.

COMPARISONS

time-series comparisons
Comparison of a company's financial ratios with its own historical ratios.

benchmarks General rules of thumb specifying appropriate levels for financial ratios.

cross-sectional comparisons
Comparisons of a company's financial ratios with ratios of other companies or with industry averages for the same period.

Evaluation of a financial ratio requires a comparison. There are three main types of comparisons: (1) with a company's own historical ratios (called **time-series comparisons**), (2) with general rules of thumb or **benchmarks,** and (3) with ratios of other companies or with industry averages for the same period (called **cross-sectional comparisons**).

Consider first time-series comparisons. Much can be learned by examining the trend of a company's ratios. This is why annual reports typically contain a table of comparative statistics for 5 or 10 years. For example, consider the trends in three of Microsoft's profitability ratios.

	1996	**1997**	**1998**	**1999**	**2000**
Return on sales	24.3%	28.9%	29.4%	39.4%	41.0%
Return on stockholders' equity	35.6%	39.1%	32.8%	34.6%	27.3%
Earnings per share	$.46	$.72	$.92	$1.54	$1.81

Note that return on sales increased significantly in 1999 and return on stockholders' equity had increases in both 1997 and 1998 before a large decrease in 2000. Earnings per share has increased substantially each year.

The second type of comparison uses broad rules of thumb as benchmarks. For instance, the most quoted benchmark is a current ratio of 2 to 1. Others are described in *Key Business Ratios* by Dun & Bradstreet, a financial services firm. For example,

Total debt to equity. In general, total liabilities shouldn't exceed net worth [equity] (100%) since in such cases creditors have more at stake than owners.

Exhibit 18-7
Some Typical Financial Ratios

Typical Name of Ratio	Numerator	Denominator	Appropriate Microsoft Numbers Applied to June 30 of Year	
			1999	**2000**
Short-term ratios				
Current ratio	Current assets	Current liabilities	$20,233 \div 8,718 = 2.3$	$28,600 \div 9,753 = 2.9$
Average collection period in days	Average accounts receivable[†] × 365	Sales on account	$[1/2(2,245 + 1,460) \times 365]$ $\div 19,747 = 34$ days*	$[1/2(3,250 + 2,245) \times 365]$ $\div 22,956 = 44$ days
Debt-to-equity ratio				
Total debt to equity	Total liabilities	Stockholders' equity	$8,718 \div 28,438 = 30.7\%$	$9,753 \div 40,689 = 24.0\%$
Profitability ratios				
Gross profit rate or percentage	Gross profit or gross margin	Sales	$16,933 \div 19,747 = 85.7\%$	$19,954 \div 22,956 = 86.9\%$
Return on sales	Net income	Sales	$7,785 \div 19,747 = 39.4\%$	$9,421 \div 22,956 = 41.0\%$
Return on stockholders' equity	Net income	Average stockholders' equity[†]	$7,785 \div 1/2(28,438 + 16,627)$ $= 34.6\%$	$9,421 \div 1/2(40,689 + 28,438)$ $= 27.3\%$
Earnings per share	Net income less dividends on preferred stock, if any	Average common shares outstanding	$7,757 \div 5,028 = \$1.54$	$9,421 \div 5,188 = \$1.81$
Price earnings	Market price per share of common stock[‡]	Earnings per share	$77 \div 1.54 = 50.0$	$62 \div 1.81 = 34.3$
Dividend ratios				
Dividend yield	Dividends per common share	Market price per common share[‡]	$0 \div 77 = 0.0\%$	$0 \div 62 = 0.0\%$
Dividend payout	Dividends per common share	Earnings per share	$0 \div 1.54 = 0.0\%$	$0 \div 1.81 = 0.0\%$

* This may be easier to see as follows:
Average receivables = 1/2 (2,245 + 1,460) = 1,852.5
Average receivables as a percentage of annual sales = 1,852.5 ÷ 19,747 = 9.38%
Average collection period = 9.38% × 365 days = 34 days
[†] Relevant 1998 amounts: accounts receivable, $1,460 million; stockholders' equity, $16,627 million.
[‡] Market price: June 30, 1999, $77; June 30, 2000, $62.

Return on equity. *Generally, a relationship of at least 10 percent is regarded as a desirable objective.*

Obviously, such benchmarks are only general guides. More specific analyses come from the third type of comparisons, examining ratios of similar companies or industry averages. Dun & Bradstreet informs its subscribers of the creditworthiness of thousands of individual companies. In addition, the firm regularly compiles many ratios of the companies it monitors. Each ratio in Exhibit 18-7 can be compared with industry statistics. For example, some of the Dun & Bradstreet ratios for 411 prepackaged software companies showed:

	Current Ratio	Collection Period	Total Debt to Equity	Return on Sales	Return on Stockholders' Equity
	(Times)	*(Days)*	*(Percent)*	*(Percent)*	*(Percent)*
649 companies					
Upper quartile*	4.5	39	25.0	12.6	45.0
Median	2.4	72	51.5	6.1	16.9
Lower quartile	1.4	103	126.0	0.6	2.4
Microsoft†	2.9	44	24.0	41.0	27.3

* The individual ratios are ranked from best to worst. The middle figure is the median. The figure ranked halfway between the median and the best is the upper quartile. Similarly, the figure ranked halfway between the median and the worst is the lower quartile.
† Ratios are from Exhibit 18-7. Please consult that exhibit for an explanation of the components of each ratio.

Our illustration focuses on one company and one or two years. This is sufficient as a start, but analysts also examine other firms in the industry, industry averages, and a series of years to get a better perspective. Above all, recognize that a ratio by itself is of limited use. There must be a standard for comparison—a history, a similar entity, an industry average, a benchmark, or a budget.

DISCUSSION OF SPECIFIC RATIOS

Consider again the ratios in Exhibit 18-7. Shown first is the current ratio, a widely used statistic. Other things being equal, the higher the current ratio, the more assurance the creditor has about being paid in full and on time. Microsoft's current ratio of 2.9 has improved from 2.3 and is above the industry median of 2.4.

Microsoft's average collection period of 44 days places Microsoft just below the upper quartile of prepackaged software firms, according to Dun & Bradstreet industry data. A lengthening collection period might indicate increasing acceptance of poor credit risks or less energetic collection efforts.

Note how the average collection period depends on sales on account. The computation in Exhibit 18-7 assumes that all sales are credit sales. However, if we relax our assumption, the 44-day period would rise markedly. For example, if half the sales were for cash, the average collection period for accounts receivable would change from 44 to 87 days:

$$\frac{\frac{1}{2}\,(3{,}250\,+\,2{,}245)\,\times\,365}{\frac{1}{2}\,(22{,}956)} = 87 \text{ days}$$

The third column of the Dun & Bradstreet tabulation shows the total debt-to-equity ratio. Both creditors and shareholders watch this ratio to judge the degree of risk of insolvency and stability of profits. Typically, companies with heavy debt in relation to ownership capital are in greater danger of suffering net losses or even bankruptcy when business conditions sour. Why? Because revenues and many expenses decline, but interest expenses and maturity dates do not change. Microsoft's ratio of 24.0% is well below the median for the industry; it reflects low levels of risk or uncertainty concerning the company's ability to pay its debts on time.

Investors find profitability ratios especially helpful. Examine the gross profit rate and the return on sales. Microsoft's gross profit rate increased from 85.7% in 1999 to 86.9% in 2000, and its return on sales increased from 39.4% to 41.0%. These are both measures of *operating success*. Dun & Bradstreet does not report gross profit rates, but Microsoft's return on sales is high enough to rank high in the top quartile of prepackaged software companies.

More important to shareholders is the rate of return on their invested capital, a measure of overall accomplishment. Microsoft's 2000 rate of 27.3% is down from the 34.6% of 1999, but it is well above the industry median of 16.9%.

The final four ratios in Exhibit 18-7 are based on earnings and dividends. The first, earnings per share of common stock (EPS), is the most popular of all ratios. This is the only ratio that is required as part of the body of financial statements of publicly held companies in the United States. Companies must present the EPS on the face of the income statement. Most companies calculate it as in Exhibit 18-7: net income less dividends on preferred stock divided by average common shares outstanding. For companies holding securities that can be exchanged for or converted to common shares, EPS calculations are more complex. Such computations are beyond the scope of this discussion.

The computation of three other ratios is shown in Exhibit 18-7: price earnings, dividend yield, and dividend payout. These ratios are especially useful to investors in the common stock of the company. Because Microsoft pays no dividends, the last two ratios are both zero.

OPERATING PERFORMANCE RATIOS

In addition to the more focused ratios just cited, businesspeople often look at the rate of return on invested capital as an important measure of overall accomplishment:

$$\text{rate of return on investment} = \frac{\text{income}}{\text{invested capital}} \tag{1}$$

On the surface, this measure is straightforward, but its ingredients may differ according to the purpose it is to serve. What is invested capital, the denominator of the ratio? What income figure is appropriate?

The measurement of operating performance (how profitably assets are employed) should not be influenced by the management's financial decisions (i.e., how assets are obtained). The best measure of operating performance is pretax operating rate of return on average total assets:

$$\text{pretax operating rate of return on average total assets} = \frac{\text{operating income}}{\text{average total assets}} \tag{2}$$

For Microsoft, this ratio is $10,937 \div \$43,799 = 25.0\%$

The right-hand side of equation 2 consists, in turn, of two important ratios:

$$\frac{\text{operating income}}{\text{average total assets}} = \frac{\text{operating income}}{\text{sales}} \times \frac{\text{sales}}{\text{average total assets}} \tag{3}$$

The right-hand terms in equation 3 are often called the *operating income percentage on sales* and *total asset turnover,* respectively. Therefore, Microsoft's operating performance can be expressed as :

$$\begin{array}{c}\text{pretax operating rate} \\ \text{of return on average total assets}\end{array} = \begin{array}{c}\text{operating income} \\ \text{percentage on sales}\end{array} \times \begin{array}{c}\text{total asset} \\ \text{turnover}\end{array}$$

$$= \frac{10{,}937}{\$22{,}956} \times \frac{\$22{,}956}{\frac{1}{2}(\$50{,}442 + \$37{,}156)} \qquad (4)$$

$$= 47.64\% \times .5241 = 25.0\%$$

When analysts use ratios to evaluate operating performance, they usually exclude extraordinary items. Such items are not expected to recur, and therefore they should not be included in measures of normal performance.

A scrutiny of equation 4 shows that there are two basic factors in profit making: operating margin percentages and turnover. An improvement in either will, by itself, increase the rate of return on total assets.

 Which is better, an investment in Wal-Mart or one in Saks, Incorporated, operators of Saks Fifth Avenue? How might one use financial ratios to better understand the different ways that Wal-Mart and Saks create value for investors? Would you expect Wal-Mart and Saks to have different pretax operating rate of return on average total assets? Would you expect them to have different operating income percentage on sales and total asset turnover?

ANSWERS

Investors have many different alternative investments. If either Wal-Mart or Saks offered lower returns to investors, they would not find many people willing to invest. (This assumes that the riskiness of investing in the two companies is about the same.) However, even if the two companies seek the same total return on assets, they pursue this return quite differently. Wal-Mart has a high total asset turnover and a low operating income percentage on sales, while Saks has the opposite (dollar amounts are in millions):

Wal-Mart: Operating income percentage on sales = \$8,309 ÷ \$165,013 = 5.0%
    Total asset turnover = \$165,013 ÷ ½ (\$70,349 + \$49,996) = 2.74
    Return on assets = 5.0% × 2.74 = 13.7%
  Saks: Operating income percentage on sales = \$510.3 ÷ \$6,423.8 = 7.9%
    Total asset turnover = \$6,423.8 ÷ ½ (\$5,099 + \$5,189) = 1.75
    Return on assets = 7.9% × 1.75 = 9.8%

The year 2000 was better for Wal-Mart than for Saks as judged by their return on assets. Saks has the higher return or sales, but Wal-Mart had the higher total asset turnover.

EFFICIENT MARKETS AND INVESTOR DECISIONS

efficient capital market A market in which market prices fully reflect all information available to the public.

How investors use accounting information depends on whether they believe stock markets are "efficient." An **efficient capital market** is one in which market prices "fully reflect" all information available to the public. Therefore, searching for "underpriced" securities in such a market would be fruitless unless an investor has information that is not generally available. If the real-world markets are indeed efficient, a relatively inactive portfolio approach would be an appropriate investment strategy for most investors. The hallmarks of the approach are risk control, high diversification, and low turnover of securities. The role of accounting information would mainly be in identifying the different degrees of risk among various stocks so that investors can maintain desired levels of risk and diversification.

Research has shown that financial ratios and other data such as reported earnings help predict such economic phenomena as financial failure or earnings growth. Furthermore, analysts use many ratios simultaneously rather than one at a time for such predictions. Above all, the research shows that accounting reports are only one source of information and that in the aggregate the market is not fooled by companies that choose the least-conservative accounting policies. In sum, the market as a whole generally sees through any attempts by companies to gain favor through the choice of accounting policies that tend to boost immediate income. Thus, there is evidence that the stock markets may indeed be "efficient," at least in their reflection of most accounting data.[3]

Objective 5
Identify the major implications that efficient stock markets have for accounting.

Suppose you are the chief executive officer of a company with reported earnings of $4 per share and a stock price of $40. You are contemplating changing your method of depreciation for investor-reporting purposes from accelerated to straight-line. Your competitors use straight-line. You think your company's stock price unjustifiably suffers in comparison with other companies in the same industry.

If straight-line depreciation is adopted, your company's reported earnings will be $5 instead of $4 per share. Would the stock price rise accordingly from $40 to $50? No, the research on these issues indicates that the stock price would remain at $40 (all other things equal).

Many managers share the chief executive's beliefs illustrated in the preceding example. They essentially adhere to an extremely narrow view of the role of an income statement. Such a "bottom-line" mentality is slowly, surely, and sensibly falling into disrepute. At the risk of unfair exaggeration, the view is summarized as

1. The income statement is the sole (or at least the primary) source of information about a company.
2. Lenders and shareholders invest in a company because of its reported earnings. For instance, the higher the reported earnings per share, the higher the stock price, and the easier it is to raise capital.

Basically, these arguments assume that investors can be misled by how companies measure reported earnings. But there is considerable evidence that securities markets are not fooled with respect to accounting changes that are devoid of economic substance (i.e., have no effect on cash flows). Why? Because the change generally reveals no new information, so no significant change in stock price is likely.

Remember that the market is efficient only with respect to publicly available information. Therefore, accounting issues that deal with the disclosure of new information are more important than those that simply change the format for reporting already available data.

Be aware also that accounting statements are not the only source of financial information about companies. Some alternative sources are the following: company press releases (e.g., capital expenditure announcements); trade association publications (e.g., reports with industry statistics); brokerage house analyses (e.g., company or industry studies); and government economic reports (e.g., gross national product and unemployment figures). If accounting reports are to be useful, they must have some advantage over alternative sources in disclosing new information. Financial statement information may be more directly related to the item of interest, and it may be more reliable, less costly, or more timely than information from alternative sources.

The research described previously concentrates on the effects of accounting on investors in the aggregate. Individual investors vary in how they analyze financial

---

[3] *Several "anomalies" prevent unqualified endorsement of stock market efficiency. Recent research shows that accounting data may be combined to yield information that is not reflected in stock prices. Nevertheless, the evidence that stock prices efficiently reflect basic accounting data is quite strong.*

statements. One by one, individual users must either incur the costs of conducting careful analyses or delegate that chore to professional analysts. In any event, intelligent analysis cannot be accomplished without an understanding of the assumptions and limitations of financial statements including the presence of various alternative accounting methods.

SUMMARY PROBLEM FOR YOUR REVIEW

PROBLEM

Examine Exhibits 18-4 and 18-5, pages 737–738. Assume some new data in place of certain old data for the June 30, 2000, balance sheet (in millions):

	Old Data	New Data
Accounts receivable	$ 3,250	$ 3,500
Total current assets	28,600	31,200
Paid-in capital	22,516	27,000
Total stockholders' equity	40,689	45,000

Compute the following ratios applicable to June 30, 2000, or to the fiscal year 2000, as appropriate: current ratio, average collection period, and return on stockholders' equity. Compare this new set of ratios with the old set of ratios. Are the new ratios more desirable? Explain.

SOLUTION

All the ratios would be affected.

$$\text{current ratio} = \frac{\text{current assets}}{\text{current liabilities}}$$

$$= \frac{\$31,200}{\$ 9,753} = 3.2 \text{ instead of } 2.9$$

$$\text{average collection period} = \frac{\text{average accounts receivable}}{\text{sales on account}} \times 365$$

$$= \frac{\frac{1}{2}(\$3,500 + \$2,245) \times 365}{\$22,956}$$

$$= \frac{\$2,872.5 \times 365}{\$22,956} = 46 \text{ days instead of } 44 \text{ days}$$

$$\text{return on stockholders' equity} = \frac{\text{net income}}{\text{average stockholders' equity}}$$

$$= \frac{\$9,421}{\frac{1}{2}(\$45,000 + \$28,438)}$$

$$= 25.7\% \text{ instead of } 27.3\%$$

The new set of ratios has good news and bad news. The good news is that the company would appear to be slightly more liquid (a current ratio of 3.2 instead of 2.9). The bad news is that the average collection period and the rate of return on stockholders' equity are less attractive.

Highlights to Remember: Part Two

Explain and use a variety of popular financial ratios.   Financial ratios aid the intelligent analysis of financial statements. To compare companies that differ in size, analysts use component percentages. They also prepare a variety of ratios and compare them with the company's own historical ratios, with general benchmarks, and with ratios of other companies or industry averages. They use short-term ratios, debt-to-equity ratios, profitability ratios, and dividend ratios. An especially important ratio for assessing operating performance is the rate of return on invested capital.

Identify the major implications that efficient stock markets have for accounting. Financial statements are only one source of information used by investors. Evidence indicates that stock prices fully reflect most publicly available information, including accounting numbers. The format of the information apparently does not fool investors. Therefore, accounting regulators should focus on disclosure issues, not format.

Understand how financial analysts use ratios and other analysis techniques to interpret the consolidated financial statements of a company.   Financial analysts and other investment advisors use financial statements to assess the prospects for companies that they consider for investment. They use the various ratios and other techniques shown in this chapter, together with other information, for the investment decisions.

Accounting Vocabulary

For various financial ratios, see Exhibit 18-7, page 741. Also become familiar with

benchmarks, p. 740

common-size statements, p. 738

component percentages, p. 738

cross-sectional comparisons, p. 740

efficient capital market, p. 744

time-series comparisons, p. 740

Fundamental Assignment Material

Special Note: Problems relating to Part One of the chapter are presented first in each subgrouping of the assignment material.

GENERAL EXERCISES AND PROBLEMS

18-A1   Market or Equity Method
Suppose DaimlerChrysler AG acquired 25% of the voting stock of Goodstone Tire Co. for $70 million cash. In year 1, Goodstone Tire had a net income of $48 million and paid a cash dividend of $32 million. The investment had a market value of $76 million at the end of the year.

Required

1. Using the equity method, show the effects of the three transactions on the accounts of DaimlerChrysler. Use the balance sheet equation format.
2. Assume that DaimlerChrysler could use the market method for this investment and that DaimlerChrysler classified the investment as an available-for-sale security. Show the effects of the three transactions on the accounts of Daimler-Chrysler. Use the balance sheet equation format.

18-A2   Consolidated Financial Statements
Suppose Toronto Publishing Company acquired all the common shares of Lincoln Book Company for $50 million cash at the start of the year. Immediately before the business combination, each company had the following condensed balance sheet accounts (in millions):

	Toronto	Lincoln
Cash and other assets	$320	$70
Accounts payable, etc.	$100	$20
Stockholders' equity	220	50
Total equities	$320	$70

Required

1. Prepare a tabulation of the consolidated balance sheet accounts immediately after the acquisition. Use the balance sheet equation format.

2. Suppose Toronto and Lincoln have the following results for the year:

	Toronto	Lincoln
Sales	$330	$100
Expenses	245	90

Prepare income statements for the year for Toronto, Lincoln, and the consolidated entity. Assume that neither Toronto nor Lincoln sells items to the other.

3. Present the effects of the operations for the year on Toronto's accounts and on Lincoln's accounts, using the balance sheet equation. Also tabulate the consolidated balance sheet accounts at the end of the year. Assume that liabilities are unchanged.

4. Suppose Lincoln paid a cash dividend of $7 million. What accounts in requirement 3 would be affected and by how much?

18-A3 Minority Interests

This modifies and extends the preceding problem. However, this problem is self-contained because all the facts are reproduced below. Toronto Publishing Company acquired 80% of the common shares of Lincoln Book Company for $40 million cash at the start of the year. Immediately before the business combination, each company had the following condensed balance sheet accounts (in millions):

	Toronto	Lincoln
Cash and other assets	$320	$70
Accounts payable, etc.	$100	$20
Stockholders' equity	220	50
Total equities	$320	$70

Required

1. Prepare a tabulation of the consolidated balance sheet accounts immediately after the acquisition. Use the balance sheet equation format.

2. Suppose Toronto and Lincoln have the following results for the year:

	Toronto	Lincoln
Sales	$330	$100
Expenses	245	90

Prepare income statements for the year for Toronto, Lincoln, and the consolidated entity.

3. Using the balance sheet equation format, present the effects of the operations for the year on Toronto's accounts and Lincoln's accounts. Also tabulate consolidated balance sheet accounts at the end of the year. Assume that liabilities are unchanged.

4. Suppose Lincoln paid a cash dividend of $7 million. What accounts in requirement 3 would be affected and by how much?

18-A4 Goodwill and Consolidation

This modifies and extends Problem 18-A2. However, this problem is self-contained because all the facts are reproduced below. Toronto Publishing Company acquired all the common shares of

Lincoln Book Company for $80 million cash at the start of the year. Immediately before the business combination, each company had the following condensed balance sheet accounts (in millions):

	Toronto	Lincoln
Cash and other assets	$320	$70
Accounts payable, etc.	$100	$20
Stockholders' equity	220	50
Total equities	$320	$70

Assume that the fair values of Lincoln's individual assets were equal to their book values.

Required

1. Prepare a tabulation of the consolidated balance sheet accounts immediately after the acquisition. Use the balance sheet equation format.
2. Suppose the book values of Lincoln's individual assets are equal to their fair market values except for equipment. The net book value of equipment is $15 million and its fair market value is $30 million. The equipment has a remaining useful life of four years. Straight-line depreciation is used.
   a. Describe how the consolidated balance sheet accounts immediately after the acquisition would differ from those in requirement 1. Be specific as to accounts and amounts.
   b. By how much will consolidated income differ in comparison with the consolidated income that would be reported when the entire excess of purchase cost over book value of assets was assigned to goodwill? Assume no amortization of goodwill.

18-A5 Rate-of-Return Computations

1. Collins Chemical Company reported a 6% operating margin on sales, a 12% pretax operating return on total assets, and $500 million of total assets. Compute the (a) operating income, (b) total sales, and (c) total asset turnover.
2. Okamoto Electronics Corporation reported ¥300 million of sales, ¥12 million of operating income, and a total asset turnover of 5 times. (¥ is Japanese yen.) Compute the (a) total assets, (b) operating income percentage on sales, and (c) pretax operating return on total assets.

UNDERSTANDING PUBLISHED FINANCIAL REPORTS

18-B1 Equity and Market Methods
Suppose Oracle acquired one-third of the common shares of Tanlami Software Corporation for $50 million cash. In year 1, Tanlami had a net income of $60 million and paid cash dividends of $24 million. At the end of the year, the market value of the investment had fallen to $43 million.

Required

Prepare a tabulation that compares the equity method and the market method of accounting for Oracle's investment in Tanlami. Show the effects on the balance sheet equation under each method. (Assume that under the market method this investment is a trading security.) What is the year-end balance in the Investment in Tanlami account under the equity method? Under the market method? Which method should Oracle use for reporting its investment in Tanlami?

18-B2 Consolidated Financial Statements
Consider the actual purchase of boat maker Bayliner Inc., by Brunswick Corporation. The purchase price was $400 million for a 100% interest.

Assume that the book value and the fair market value of Bayliner's net assets was $400 million. The balance sheet accounts immediately after the transaction were approximately (in millions):

	Brunswick	Bayliner
Investment in Bayliner	$ 400	—
Cash and other assets	1,000	$600
Total assets	$1,400	$600
Liabilities	$ 800	$200
Stockholders' equity	600	400
Total equities	$1,400	$600

1. Using the balance sheet equation format, prepare a tabulation of the consolidated balance sheet accounts immediately after the acquisition.
2. Suppose Bayliner had sales of $600 million and expenses of $500 million for the year, and Brunswick had sales of $1,800 million and expenses of $1,300 million. Prepare income statements for Brunswick, for Bayliner, and for the consolidated company. Assume that neither Brunswick nor Bayliner sold items to the other.
3. Using the balance sheet equation, present the effects of the operations for the year on the accounts of Bayliner and Brunswick. Also tabulate the consolidated balance sheet accounts at the end of the year. Assume that liabilities are unchanged.
4. Suppose Bayliner paid a cash dividend of $15 million. What accounts in requirement 3 would be affected and by how much?

18-B3 Investment in Equity Securities

Ford owns 33% of the stock of Mazda Corporation. In 1999, Mazda reported a net income of approximately $320 million and declared cash dividends of $40 million. Ford accounted for its investment in Mazda by the equity method.

1. Compute the amount of income (loss) recognized by Ford in 1999 from its investment in Mazda.
2. Suppose Ford had a balance of $2.1 billion in its "Investment in Mazda" account at the beginning of 1999. Compute the balance in the account at the end of 1999.
3. Suppose Ford had used the market method to account for its investment in Mazda and had classified this investment as an available-for-sale security. Assume that the market value of Ford's Mazda securities was $2.5 billion at the end of 1999.
   a. Compute the amount of income (loss) recognized by Ford in 1999 from its investment in Mazda.
   b. Assume that Ford had a balance of $2.1 billion in its "Investment in Mazda" account at the beginning of 1999. Compute the balance in the account at the end of 1999.
   c. Explain how Ford would account for the $25 million increase in market value.
4. Indicate briefly how the following three classes of investments should be accounted for: (a) greater than 50% interest, (b) 20% through 50% interest, and (c) less than 20% interest.

18-B4 Income Ratios and Asset Turnover

A semiannual report to the stockholders of Texaco included the following comments on earnings:

> *On an annualized basis, net income represented an 8.9% return on average total assets of approximately $27.3 billion and an 18.9% return on average stockholders' equity. . . . Net income per gallon on all petroleum products sold worldwide averaged 3.6 cents. Net income was 4 cents on each dollar of revenue.*

Using only this information, compute the (1) total asset turnover, (2) net income, (3) total revenues, (4) average stockholders' equity, and (5) gallons of petroleum products sold.

18-B5 Financial Ratios

Albertson's has 2,492 stores in 37 states and is one of the largest retail food and drug chains in the United States. Excerpts from the company's 2000 annual report are in Exhibit 18-8. Albertson's paid cash dividends of $.72 per common share in fiscal 2000, and an average of 422 million shares were outstanding during the year. Assume that Albertson's has no stock options or convertible securities. The company's market price on February 3, 2000, was $30 per share.
Compute the following financial ratios for fiscal 2000:

1. Current ratio	6. Earnings per share
2. Total debt to equity	7. Price earnings
3. Gross profit rate	8. Dividend yield
4. Return on sales	9. Dividend payout
5. Return on stockholders' equity	

Exhibit 18-8

Albertson's, Inc.

Income Statement and Balance Sheet (in millions)

Income Statement for the Year Ended February 3, 2000

Sales	$37,478
Cost of sales	27,164
Gross profit	$10,314
Other expenses (summarized)	9,438
Earnings before income taxes	$ 876
Income taxes	472
Net earnings	$ 404

	February 3, 2000	January 28, 1999
Balance Sheet		
Assets		
Inventories	$ 3,481	$ 3,249
Other current assets (summarized)	1,101	959
Total current assets	$ 4,582	$ 4,208
Land, buildings, and equipment (net)	8,913	8,545
Other assets	2,206	2,378
Total assets	$15,701	$15,131
Liabilities and stockholders' equity		
Current liabilities (summarized)	$ 4,055	$ 3,351
Long-term liabilities (summarized)	5,944	6,258
Total liabilities	$ 9,999	$ 9,609
Stockholders' equity (summarized)	5,702	5,522
Total liabilities and stockholders' equity	$15,701	$15,131

Additional Assignment Material

QUESTIONS

18-1. Distinguish between trading securities and available-for-sale securities.

18-2. What is the equity method?

18-3. Contrast the market method and the equity method.

18-4. "The equity method is usually used for long-term investments." Do you think this is appropriate? Explain.

18-5. Distinguish between control of a company and a significant influence over a company.

18-6. What criterion is used to determine whether a parent-subsidiary relationship exists?

18-7. Why have subsidiaries? Why not have the corporation take the form of a single legal entity?

18-8. "A consolidated financial statement simply adds together the separate accounts of a parent company and its subsidiaries." Do you agree? Explain.

18-9. What is a minority interest?

18-10. "Goodwill is the excess of purchase price over the book values of the individual assets acquired." Do you agree? Explain.

18-11. "It is better to recognize goodwill than to write up assets to their fair market values." Do you agree? Why?

18-12. "Pro forma statements are the formal financial statements that companies file with the Securities and Exchange Commission." Do you agree? Explain.

18-13. Name the three types of comparisons made with ratios.

18-14. Why is it useful to analyze income statements and balance sheets by component percentages?

18-15. What two ratios are multiplied together to give the pre-tax operating rate of return on average total assets?

18-16. "Ratios are mechanical and incomplete." Explain.

18-17. "An efficient capital market is one where securities are traded through stockbrokers." Do you agree? Explain.

18-18. Give three sources of information for investors besides accounting information.

18-19. Evaluate the following quotation from *Forbes*: "If IBM had been forced to expense [the software development cost of] $785 million, its earnings would have been cut by 72 cents a share. With IBM selling at 14 times earnings, expensing the costs might have knocked over $10 off IBM's share price."

18-20. Is return on sales a good measure of a company's performance?

18-21. Suppose the president of your company wanted to switch depreciation methods to increase reported net income: "Our stock price is 10% below what I think it should be; changing depreciation method will increase income by 10%, thus getting our share price up to its proper level." How would you respond?

COGNITIVE EXERCISES

18-22 Depreciation in Consolidated Financial Statements

Suppose Company P buys 100% of the common stock of Company S for more than the book value of S. After one year the consolidated entity prepares financial statements. Two expense items appear on the consolidated income statement that are not on the individual statements of P and S:

1. Depreciation on equipment in excess of that in the individual statements
2. Write-off of goodwill

Explain why these two accounts exist. That is, what was there about the acquisition that generated the need for these two accounts?

18-23 Market Method, Equity Method, and Total Assets

Suppose America Online bought 20% of the common shares of a small software company that recently went public. The management of America Online believed that patents developed by the software company would make the company very valuable in a year or two. Near-term profits may not be high, but large increases in the share price are likely. No dividends are expected. How would the choice of accounting method, the market method or the equity method, affect America Online's total assets reported on its balance sheet in the next couple years if its expectations about the software firm come true? Explain.

18-24 Just-in-Time (JIT) Inventory and Current Ratio

Many companies have adopted JIT inventory methods to reduce the size of their inventories. What would you expect to happen to the current ratios of such companies? Would you interpret the current ratio differently for JIT companies compared to other companies? Explain.

EXERCISES

18-25 Equity Method

Company X acquired 25% of the voting stock of Company Y for $90 million cash. In year 1, Y had a net income of $40 million and paid cash dividends of $24 million. At the end of the year, the total market value of Company Y was $400 million.

Required

Prepare a tabulation that compares the equity method and the market method of accounting for X's investment in Y. Show the effects on the balance sheet equation under each method. What is the year-end balance in the Investment in Y account under the equity method? Under the market method? What difference in accounting would there be if the investment were a trading security instead of an available-for-sale security?

18-26 Consolidated Financial Statements

Nevada Development Company (the parent) owns 100% of the common stock of Elko Company (the subsidiary), which was acquired at the start of 20X1. Their financial statements follow:

	Nevada Development (Parent)	Elko (Subsidiary)
Income Statement for 20X1		
Revenue and "other income"	$5,400,000	$1,000,000
Expenses	5,100,000	900,000
Net income	$ 300,000	$ 100,000
Balance Sheets, December 31, 20X1		
Assets	$1,000,000	$ 400,000
Liabilities to creditors	$ 450,000	$ 100,000
Stockholders' equity	550,000	300,000
Total liabilities and stockholders' equity	$1,000,000	$ 400,000

Required

1. Elko had enjoyed a fantastically profitable year in 20X1. Nevada Development's income statement had been prepared by showing its claim to Elko's income as part of "other income." On the other hand, Nevada Development's balance sheet is really not

completed. The $1 million of assets of Nevada Development includes a $200,000 investment in Elko and does not include Nevada Development's claim to Elko's 20X1 net income.

Prepare a consolidated income statement and a consolidated balance sheet. Use the balance sheet equation format for the latter.

2. Suppose Nevada Development Company owned 60% of Elko Company. Liabilities to creditors are unchanged. The assets of Nevada Development include a $120,000 investment in Elko instead of $200,000. However, assume the total assets are $1 million. The balance sheet is really not completed because the investment account does not reflect the claim to Elko's 20X1 net income. Similarly, Nevada Development's revenue and other income is $5.36 million, not $5.4 million, but expenses remain at $5.1 million as in requirement 1.

Prepare a consolidated income statement and a consolidated balance sheet. Use the balance sheet equation format for the latter.

18-27 Determination of Goodwill
Refer to the preceding problem, requirement 1. Suppose the investment in Elko in requirement 1 was $280,000 instead of the $200,000 as stated. This would mean that the "other assets" would be $720,000 instead of $800,000. Would the consolidated income differ? How? Be as specific as possible. Would the consolidated balance sheet differ? How? Be as specific as possible.

18-28 Purchased Goodwill
Consider the following balance sheets (in millions):

	Lubbock Minerals Company	Cheney Oil Company
Cash	$ 690	$ 80
Inventories	360	70
Plant assets, net	390	60
Total assets	$1,440	$210
Common stock and paid-in capital	$ 470	$120
Retained income	970	90
Total liabilities and stockholders' equity	$1,440	$210

Lubbock paid $290 million to Cheney stockholders for all their stock. The "fair value" of the plant assets of Cheney is $140 million. The fair value of cash and inventories is equal to their carrying amounts. Lubbock and Cheney still keep separate books.

Required

1. Prepare a tabulation showing the balance sheets of Lubbock, of Cheney, Intercompany Eliminations, and Consolidated immediately after the acquisition.
2. Suppose only $100 million rather than $140 million of the total purchase price of $290 million could be logically assigned to the plant assets. How would the consolidated accounts be affected?
3. Refer to the facts in requirement 1. Suppose Lubbock had paid $350 million rather than $290 million. State how your tabulation in requirement 1 would change.

18-29 Amortization and Depreciation
Refer to the preceding problem, requirement 3. Suppose a year passes, and Lubbock and Cheney generate individual net incomes of $105 million and $35 million, respectively. The latter is after a deduction by Cheney of $12 million of straight-line depreciation. Compute the consolidated net income if (1) goodwill is not amortized and (2) half of the goodwill is written off at the end of the year. Ignore income taxes.

18-30 Allocating Total Purchase Price to Assets
Two Hollywood companies had the following balance sheet accounts as of December 31, 20X0 (in millions):

	Sonex Films	Bradley Productions		Sonex Films	Bradley Productions
Cash and receivables	$ 30	$ 22	Current liabilities	$ 50	$ 20
Inventories	120	3	Common stock	100	10
Plant assets, net	150	95	Retained income	150	90
Total assets	$300	$120	Total liab. and stk. eq.	$300	$120
Net income for 20X0	$ 19	$ 4			

On January 4, 20X1, these firms merged. Sonex issued $180 million of its shares (at market value) in exchange for all the shares of Bradley, a motion picture division of a large company. The inventory of films acquired through the combination had been fully amortized on Bradley's books.

During 20X1, Bradley received revenue of $21 million from the rental of films from its inventory. Sonex earned $20 million on its other operations (i.e., excluding Bradley) during 20X1. Bradley broke even on its other operations (i.e., excluding the film rental contracts) during 20X1.

Required

1. Prepare a consolidated balance sheet for the combined company immediately after the combination. Assume that $80 million of the purchase price was assigned to the inventory of films.

2. Prepare a comparison of Sonex's net income between 20X0 and 20X1 where the cost of the film inventories would be amortized on a straight-line basis over four years. What would be the net income for 20X1 if the $80 million were assigned to goodwill rather than to the inventory of films and the value of goodwill was maintained?

18-31 Preparation of Consolidated Financial Statements

The Balachandran Medical Instruments Company's fiscal year ends on December 31. The company had the following items on its 20X1 income statement and balance sheet (in millions):

Net sales and other operating revenue	$890
Investments in affiliated companies	100
Common stock, 10,000,000, $1 par	10
Depreciation and amortization	20
Accounts payable	210
Cash	30
Paid-in capital in excess of par	102
Interest expense	25
Retained income	198
Accrued income taxes payable	20
Cost of goods sold and operating expenses, exclusive of depreciation and amortization	640
Subordinated debentures, 11% interest, due December 31, 20X7	100
Minority interest in consolidated subsidiaries' net income	20
Goodwill	95
First-mortgage bonds, 10% interest, due December 31, 20X9	80
Property, plant, and equipment, net	125
Preferred stock, 2,000,000 shares, $50 par, dividend rate is $5 per share, each share is convertible into one share of common stock	100
Short-term investments at market value	45
Income tax expense	90
Accounts receivable, net	175
Minority interest in subsidiaries	90
Inventories at average cost	340
Dividends declared and paid on preferred stock	10
Equity in earnings of affiliated companies	20

Required

Prepare Balachandran's consolidated 20X1 income statement and its consolidated balance sheet for December 31, 20X1.

18-32 Financial Ratios

The annual reports of Tromso Fiske, a Norwegian fishing supply company, included the following selected data (in millions):

	20X2	20X1	20X0
Annual amounts:			
Net income	Nkr 95*	Nkr 60	Nkr 25
Gross margin on sales	520	380	200
Cost of goods sold	980	620	300
Operating expenses	380	295	165
Income tax expense	45	25	10
Dividends declared	30	15	5
End-of-year amounts:			
Long-term assets	Nkr 240	Nkr 220	Nkr 180
Long-term debt	80	65	40
Current liabilities	70	55	35
Cash	30	5	10
Accounts receivable	85	70	40
Merchandise inventory	120	85	60
Paid-in capital	205	205	205
Retained income	120	55	10

* Nkr is Norwegian kroner. In recent years, the exchange rate has varied between seven and ten Nkr per dollar.

During each of the three years, there were outstanding 10 million shares of capital stock, all common. Assume that all sales were on account and that the applicable market prices per share of stock were Nkr 30 for 20X1 and Nkr 40 for 20X2.

Required

1. Compute each of the following for each of the last two years, 20X1 and 20X2:
   a. Rate of return on sales
   b. Rate of return on stockholders' equity
   c. Current ratio
   d. Ratio of total debt to stockholders' equity
   e. Ratio of current debt to stockholders' equity
   f. Gross profit rate
   g. Average collection period for accounts receivable
   h. Price-earnings ratio
   i. Dividend-payout percentage
   j. Dividend yield
2. Answer yes or no to each of these questions and indicate which of the computations in requirement 1 support your answer:
   a. Is there a decrease in the effectiveness of collection efforts?
   b. Has gross profit rate improved?
   c. Has the rate of return on sales deteriorated?
   d. Has the rate of return on owners' investment increased?
   e. Are dividends relatively more generous?
   f. Have the risks of insolvency changed significantly?
   g. Has the market price of the stock become cheaper relative to earnings?
   h. Have business operations improved?
   i. Has there been a worsening of the company's ability to pay current debts on time?
   j. Has there been a decline in the cash return on the market value of the capital stock?
   k. Did the collectibility of the receivables improve?
3. Basing your observations on only the available data and the ratios you computed, prepare some brief comments on the company's operations and financial changes during the three years.

UNDERSTANDING PUBLISHED FINANCIAL REPORTS

18-33 Classification on Balance Sheet

The following accounts appeared in the annual report of the Mitsubishi Kasei Corporation, Japan's premier integrated chemical company:

1. Minority interests in consolidated subsidiaries
2. Current maturities of long-term debt
3. Investments in and advances to nonconsolidated subsidiaries and affiliates
4. Prepaid expenses
5. Accrued income taxes
6. Treasury stock at cost

Required

Indicate in detail in which section of the balance sheet each account should appear.

18-34 Meaning of Account Descriptions

The following account descriptions were found in an annual report of E.I. duPont de Nemours Company:

- Minority interests in earnings of consolidated subsidiaries
- Minority interest in consolidated subsidiaries
- Investments in affiliates
- Equity in earnings of affiliates

Required

In your own words, explain what each type of account represents. Indicate whether the item appears on the balance sheet or the income statement.

18-35 Effect of Transactions under the Equity Method

Enron Corporation, recently named by *Fortune* as the "Most Innovative Company in America," is a former utility and pipeline company that has introduced exciting new concepts to the marketplace, including cross-commodity trading, weather derivatives, energy outsourcing, and brokering of broadband services. Some of Enron's diversification has been accomplished by purchasing between 20% and 50% of companies they call "unconsolidated equity affiliates." Enron's December 31, 1999 balance sheet showed (in millions)

	December 31	
	1999	*1998*
Investments in unconsolidated equity affiliates	$5,036	$4,433

Enron's equity in the earnings of unconsolidated equity affiliates in 1999 was $309 million, and it received dividends of $482 from these affiliates. Enron had income before interest, minority interests, and income taxes of $1,995 million.

Required

1. How much did Enron's investments in unconsolidated equity affiliates add to its income before interest, minority interests and income taxes in 1999? What percentage of this income came from these investments?
2. Compute the additional investment that Enron made in its equity affiliates in 1999. *Hint*: Use a T-account to aid your analysis.
3. Suppose Enron received only $241 million rather than $482 million in dividends from its equity affiliates in 1999. What income would Enron recognize from its equity affiliates in 1999?

18-36 Consolidations in Japan

A few years ago, Japan's finance ministry issued a directive requiring the 600 largest Japanese companies to produce consolidated financial statements. The previous practice had been to use parent-company-only statements. A story in *Business Week* said, "Financial observers hope that the move will help end the tradition-honored Japanese practice of 'window dressing' the parent company financial results by shoving losses onto hapless subsidiaries, whose red ink was seldom revealed. . . . When companies needed to show a bigger profit, they would sell their product to subsidiaries at an inflated price. . . . Or the parent company charged a higher rent to a subsidiary company using its building."

Could a parent company follow the quoted practices and achieve window dressing in its parent-only financial statements if it used the equity method of accounting for its intercorporate investments? Explain.

Required

18-37 Minority Interests

The consolidated financial statements of Anchor Gaming, Inc., include the accounts of Colorado Grande Enterprises, Inc., an 80%-owned subsidiary. Anchor Gaming makes gambling machines and runs casinos. Colorado Grande Enterprises operates the Colorado Grande Casino in Cripple Creek, 45 miles from Colorado Springs. Colorado Grande Enterprises is Anchor Gaming's only consolidated subsidiary with minority interests. Anchor Gaming's 1999 income statement contained the following:

Income before minority interest and taxes	$87,599,000
Taxes	39,422,000
Minority interest in earnings of consolidated subsidiary	670,000
Net income	$47,507,000

Anchor Gaming's account "Minority Interest in Consolidated Subsidiary" listed $1,061,000 at the beginning of 1999. Colorado Grande Enterprises paid dividends of $2,380,000 in 1999. Anchor Gaming did not buy or sell any of its interest in Colorado Grande Enterprises during 1999.

Required

1. Compute the 1999 net income of Colorado Grande Enterprises.
2. What proportion of Anchor Gaming's $47,507,000 net income was contributed by Colorado Grande Enterprises?
3. Compute Anchor Gaming's balance in "Minority Interest in Consolidated Subsidiary" at the end of 1999.

18-38 General Motors and GMAC

The consolidated financial statements of General Motors include the results of GMAC, its financing subsidiary. Some investors think the business of a financing subsidiary is so different from that of its parent that the two should not be consolidated. For those investors, in 1997 General Motors also presented financial statements that treat GMAC as an equity-method affiliate. The income statements prepared both ways are presented as follows for the year ended December 31, 1997 (in millions):

	Consolidated Statement	Unconsolidated Statement
Net sales and revenues		
Manufactured products	$153,683	
Financial services	12,762	
Other income	11,729	
Total net sales and revenues	178,174	$153,781
Costs and expenses		
Cost of sales and other operating charges, exclusive of items listed below	130,028	130,042
Selling, general and administrative expenses	16,192	13,254
Depreciation and amortization expenses	16,616	11,803
Interest expense	6,113	971
Other deductions (income)	1,511	(7,836)
Total costs and expenses	170,460	148,234
Income from continuing operations before income taxes and minority interests	7,714	5,547
Income taxes	1,069	155
Income from continuing operations before minority interests and earnings of nonconsolidated affiliates	6,645	5,392
Minority interests	53	66
Earnings of nonconsolidated affiliates		1,240
Net Income	$ 6,698	$ 6,698

1. What would be the net income of General Motors if it did not own GMAC, but all other results were as reported?
2. Explain why the net income in both the consolidated statement and the unconsolidated statement are the same, $6,698 million.
3. What advantages does the consolidated statement have? What advantages does the unconsolidated statement have?

18-39 Goodwill

When Worldcom purchased MCI for $37 billion, there was only $4 million in identifiable net assets. Worldcom recorded $30 billion in goodwill and wrote off $3 billion for purchased research and development (R&D). (A special rule allows companies to immediately write off to expense that part of the purchase price that relates to the value of R&D that would have been expensed if it had been undertaken directly by the purchasing company.)

1. When the purchase was made, goodwill had to be amortized over a period of no more than 40 years. Compute the minimum amount of goodwill to be amortized in the year following the purchase.
2. Suppose the entire $30 billion of goodwill were assigned to assets with an average life of 10 years. Compute the amount of depreciation charged on those assets in the year following the purchase.
3. Why might a manager want this $30 million recorded as goodwill rather than as assets that have a life less than 40 years? Why might he or she prefer even more to recognize a part of the purchase price as "purchased R&D"?

18-40 Accounting for Goodwill

On December 7, 1999, Infinity Broadcasting Corporation, the largest owner of radio stations in the United States, bought 100% of Outdoor Systems, the largest "out-of-home" media company in North America, for a purchase price of $6.772 billion. The fair value of Outdoor Systems' assets and liabilities at acquisition were (in millions):

Assets	
Cash	$ 38
Receivables	192
Property and equipment	1,846
Other assets	228
Liabilities	
Debt	$1,865
Deferred income taxes	92
Other liabilities	106

1. Compute the amount of goodwill recognized at the time of purchase.
2. Infinity Broadcasting announced that it will amortize goodwill over a 30-year period. Compute the amount of goodwill to be amortized in the year 2000.
3. Infinity Broadcasting had net earnings of $377 million in 1999. (Assume that these are without any earnings or losses from Outdoor Systems.) Outdoor Systems had net earnings of approximately $60 million in 1999. Assume that these same results occurred in 2000, when the results of the two companies would be consolidated. What would be the consolidated net income?

18-41 Income Ratios and Asset Turnover

Briggs & Stratton is the world's largest producer of air-cooled gasoline engines for outdoor power equipment. Its 2000 annual report to stockholders included the following data (in millions):

Net income	$136.5
Total assets	
Beginning of year	875.9
End of year	930.2
Net income as a percent of	
Total revenue	8.58%
Average stockholders' equity	35.21%

Using only the data given, compute the (1) net income percent of average assets, (2) total revenues, (3) average stockholders' equity, and (4) asset turnover (using two different approaches).

Required

18-42   Financial Ratios

Honda Motor Company is a Japanese company with sales equivalent to $57 billion. The company's income statement and balance sheet for the year ended March 31, 2000, are shown in Exhibits 18-9 and 18-10. Monetary amounts are in Japanese yen (¥).

Required

1. Prepare a common-size income statement, that is, one showing component percentages.
2. Compute the following ratios:
   a. Current ratio
   b. Total debt to equity
   c. Gross profit rate
   d. Return on stockholders' equity (1999 stockholders' equity was ¥1,764 billion)
   e. Price-earnings ratio (assume that the market price was ¥4,000 per share)
   f. Dividend-payout ratio
3. What additional information would help you interpret the percentages and ratios you calculated?

18-43   Intercorporate Investments and Ethics

Hans Rasmussen and Alex Renalda were best friends at a small undergraduate college and they fought side-by-side in the jungles of Vietnam. Upon returning to the United States, they went their separate ways to pursue MBA degrees, Hans to a prestigious East Coast business school and Alex to an equally prestigious West Coast school. But 30 years later, their paths crossed again.

By 1998, Alex had become President and CEO of Medusa Electronics, after 21 years with the firm. Hans had started working for American Airlines, but had left after nine years to start his own firm, Rasmussen Transport. In April of 1998, Rasmussen Transport was near bankruptcy when Hans approached his old friend for help. Alex Renalda answered his friend's call, and Medusa Electronic bought 19% of Rasmussen Transport.

In 2001, Rasmussen was financially stable and Medusa was struggling. In fact, Alex Renalda thought his job as CEO might be in jeopardy if Medusa did not report income up to expectations. Late in 2001, Alex approached Hans with a request—quadruple Rasmussen's dividends so that Medusa could recognize $760,000 of investment income. Medusa had listed its investment in Rasmussen as an available-for-sale security, so changes in the market value of Rasmussen were

---

Exhibit 18-9

Honda Motor Company, Ltd.

Income Statement for the Year Ended March 31, 2000 (billions)

Net sales	¥6,099
Cost of sales	4,206
Gross profit	¥1,893
Selling and administrative	1,133
Research and development	334
Operating income	¥ 426
Other income (expenses)	
Interest income	¥ 11
Interest expense	(19)
Other	14
Total	6
Income before income taxes	¥ 432
Income taxes	170
Net income	¥ 262
Amounts per share	
Net income	¥ 269
Cash dividends	¥ 21

Exhibit 18-10

Honda Motor Company, Ltd.
Balance Sheet March 31, 2000 (billions)

Assets	
Current assets	
Cash and marketable securities	¥ 431
Receivables	1,122
Inventories	568
Other	335
Total current assets	¥2,456
Property, plant, and equipment, net	1,121
Investments	389
Other assets	932
Total assets	¥4,898
Liabilities and Stockholders' Equity	
Current liabilities	
Bank loans	¥ 496
Payables	697
Accrued expenses	484
Current portion of long-term debt	343
Other	182
Total current liabilities	¥2,202
Long-term liabilities	
Long-term debt	¥ 575
Other	191
Total long-term liabilities	¥ 766
Stockholders' equity	
Common stock (974,414,215 shares outstanding)	¥ 86
Additional paid-in capital	172
Retained earnings	2,219
Other	(547)
Total stockholders' equity	¥1,930
Total liabilities and stockholders' equity	¥4,898

recorded directly in stockholders' equity. However, dividends paid were recognized in Medusa's income statement.

Although Rasmussen had never paid dividends of more than 25% of net income, and it had plenty of uses for excess cash, Hans felt a deep obligation to Alex. Thus, he agreed to a $4 million dividend on net income of $4.17 million.

Required

1. Why does the dividend policy of Rasmussen Transport affect the income of Medusa Electronics? Is this consistent with the intent of the accounting principles relating to the market and equity methods for intercorporate investments? Explain.

2. Comment on the ethical issues in the arrangements between Hans Rasmussen and Alex Renalda.

COLLABORATIVE LEARNING EXERCISE

18-44   Financial Ratios
Form groups of four to six persons each. Each member of the group should pick a different company and find the most recent annual report for that company. (If you do not have printed annual reports, try searching the Internet for one.)

Required

1. Each member should compute the following ratios for his or her company:
   a. Earnings per share
   b. Price-earnings ratio

    c.   Dividend-yield ratio

    d.   Dividend-payout ratio

2. As a group, list two possible reasons that each ratio differs across the selected companies. Focus on comparing the companies with the highest and lowest values for each ratio, and explain how the nature of the company might be the reason for the differences in ratios.

18-45 INTERNET EXERCISE

www.prenhall.com/horngren

Go to http://mcdonalds.com to locate McDonald's home page. Select "Investor," then "Annual Reports."

    Answer the following questions about McDonald's:

1. Read McDonald's Summary of Significant Accounting Policies following the financial statements. What is McDonald's policy for advertising costs? Why do you think they handle costs this way? The policy is an example of which accounting principle?

2. McDonald's uses accrual-basis accounting to prepare its financial statements. What evidence do you see of this?

3. McDonald's must report results of operations for its company-owned restaurants as well as its subsidiaries. What method does the company use when accounting for investments in affiliates? What percentage investment range does this method imply?

4. What amount does McDonald's report for goodwill on its balance sheet? What can you conclude from your discovery?

5. In its section on current performance, what time-series comparisons does McDonald's provide?

6. Calculate McDonald's current ratio for the past two fiscal years. What does the trend tell you?

19 DIFFICULTIES IN MEASURING NET INCOME

Home Depot keeps a large stock of inventory to serve its customers better. Although holding all this inventory is expensive, it is worth it if it creates happy customers—especially customers who return again and again to shop at Home Depot.

www.prenhall.com/horngren

Learning Objectives

When you have finished studying this chapter, you should be able to

1. Describe the four major methods of accounting for inventories.

2. Compare FIFO and LIFO, and explain why most U.S. firms use LIFO.

3. Explain the lower-of-cost-or-market method.

4. Distinguish between financial capital maintenance and physical capital maintenance.

5. Explain and illustrate four methods of measuring income: historical cost/nominal dollars, current cost/nominal dollars, historical cost/constant dollars, and current cost/constant dollars.

6. **Understand why and how managers and investors adjust their financial statements to account for changes in prices paid for inventories.**

Have you ever gone to your local hardware store and been frustrated because they did not have what you wanted? A goal of Home Depot is to help you avoid this frustration. They do it by keeping a large inventory—40,000 to 50,000 different items, more than three times the number at a typical hardware store. As former CEO and Chairman Bernie Marcus says, one of the three main values at Home Depot is assortment—"Everything a do-it-yourselfer needs to complete a project."

Inventory requires a large investment by retail companies—$5.5 billion at Home Depot, about 32% of the company's total assets—and accounting for the inventory is important. Home Depot uses the FIFO method, which is described in this chapter. By carefully monitoring levels, Home Depot makes sure it does not lose sales by having too little inventory and does not lose money by investing in too much inventory.

A company's inventory method affects its income statement as well as its balance sheet. The largest cost on Home Depot's income statement is the cost of goods sold, that is, the cost of the items in inventory that it sells during the year. This chapter focuses on how choices in accounting for inventory can significantly affect a company's reported net income. Part One examines the principal inventory methods a company can choose, and Part Two presents some alternative ways to account for changing prices.

PART ONE: PRINCIPAL INVENTORY METHODS

Each period, accountants must divide the costs of merchandise acquired between cost of goods sold and cost of items remaining in ending inventory. Various inventory methods accomplish this division. If unit prices and costs did not fluctuate, all inventory methods would show identical results. But prices change, and these changes raise central issues regarding cost of goods sold (income measurement) and inventories (asset measurement).

Let's explore inventory accounting using a simple example. Consider a new vendor of a cola drink at the fairgrounds. He began the week with no inventory. He bought one can of cola on Monday for 30 cents; a second can on Tuesday for 40 cents; and a third can on Wednesday for 56 cents. He then sold one can on Thursday for 90 cents. What is his gross profit? What is his ending inventory?

Before reading through this chapter, consider how you would answer these questions. Then ask a classmate or two how they would respond. Chances are your answers will differ from those of your colleagues. Who is right and who is wrong? It is not easy to say. In fact, accountants would not all agree on the appropriate answers.

FOUR MAJOR INVENTORY METHODS

Objective 1
Describe the four major methods of accounting for inventories.

Four principal inventory methods are generally accepted in the United States: specific identification, weighted average, FIFO, and LIFO. Panel I of Exhibit 19-1 provides a quick glimpse of the nature of these four methods and applies them to our example of the cola vendor. (Panel II of Exhibit 19-1 is described later in the chapter.) As you can see, the choice of an inventory method often can significantly affect gross profit and hence net income (and also ending inventory valuation for balance sheet purposes).

SPECIFIC IDENTIFICATION

specific identification An inventory method that recognizes the actual cost paid for the specific item sold.

The **specific identification** method (column 1) recognizes the actual cost paid for the specific physical item sold. Gross profit depends on which can the vendor sells. As Panel I of Exhibit 19-1 shows, gross profit for operations of Monday through Thursday could be 60 cents, 50 cents, or 34 cents, depending on the particular can handed to the customer. By reaching for the "Monday" can instead of the "Wednesday" can, the vendor makes a gross profit of 60 cents instead of 34 cents.

Specific identification, which uses physical observation or the labeling of items in stock with individual numbers or codes, is easy and economically justifiable for relatively expensive merchandise such as custom artwork, diamond jewelry, and automobiles. However, many organizations have vast segments of inventories that are too numerous and insufficiently valuable per unit to warrant such individualized attention. In addition, because the specific item handed to the customer affects the cost of goods sold, this method permits managers to manipulate income and inventory values by filling a sales order by selecting a particular item from several physically equivalent items with different historical costs.

FIRST-IN, FIRST-OUT (FIFO) METHOD

first-in, first-out (FIFO) An inventory method that assumes that the stock acquired earliest is sold (used up) first.

The **first-in, first-out (FIFO)** method (column 2) assumes that the stock acquired earliest is sold (used up) first. Thus the "Monday" can is deemed to have been sold before the "Tuesday" can regardless of the actual can the vendor delivers to the customer.

By using the latest costs to measure the ending inventory, FIFO tends to provide inventory valuations that closely approximate the actual market value of the inventory at the balance sheet date. In addition, in periods of rising prices, FIFO leads to higher gross profit (60 cents in Panel I of Exhibit 19-1). Why? Because older, lower costs are charged as cost of goods sold.

Exhibit 19-1

Comparison of Inventory Methods for Cola Vendor
(all monetary amounts are in cents)

	(1A)	(1) Specific Identification (1B)	(1C)	(2) FIFO	(3) LIFO	(4) Weighted Average
Panel I						
Income Statement for the Period Monday through Thursday						
Sales (1 unit @ 90)	90	90	90	90	90	90
Deduct cost of goods sold*						
1 30-cent (Monday) unit	30			30		
1 40-cent (Tuesday) unit		40				
1 56-cent (Wednesday) unit			56		56	
1 weighted-average unit [(30 + 40 + 56) ÷ 3 = 42]						42
Gross profit for Monday through Thursday	60	50	34	60	34	48
Ending Inventory, Thursday, 2 units/ [(30 + 40 + 56) − cost of goods sold]	96	86	70	96	70	84
Panel II						
Income Statements for Friday Only and for Monday through Friday						
Sales, 2 units @ 90 on Friday	180	180	180	180	180	180
Cost of goods sold (Thursday ending inventory from above)	96	86	70	96	70	84
Gross profit, Friday only	84	94	110	84	110	96
Gross profit, Monday through Thursday (from above)	60	50	34	60	34	48
Gross profit, Monday through Friday (3 cans sold)	144	144	144	144	144	144

*The cost of goods sold can also be computed as follows, using FIFO cost of goods sold as an example:

Beginning inventory	0
+ Purchases	126
= Cost of goods available for sale	126
− Ending inventory	96
= Cost of goods sold	30

Higher reported incomes may favorably affect investor attitudes toward the company. Similarly, higher reported incomes may lead to higher salaries, higher bonuses, or higher status for the management of the company. Unlike specific identification, FIFO dictates the order in which acquisition costs will become cost of goods sold. Thus managers cannot affect income by choosing to sell one item rather than another identical one.

LAST-IN, FIRST-OUT (LIFO) METHOD

The **last-in, first-out (LIFO)** method (column 3) assumes that the stock acquired most recently is sold (used up) first. That is, FIFO associates the most recent costs with inventories, whereas LIFO treats the most recent costs as cost of goods sold. Thus the "Wednesday" can is deemed to have been sold regardless of the actual can delivered. Many accountants believe that LIFO provides a more realistic income number because net income measured using LIFO combines current sales prices and current acquisition costs.

In contrast, LIFO inventory values on the balance sheet are less realistic because they are older costs. In a period of rising prices and constant or growing inventories, LIFO yields lower net income than the other inventory methods (34 cents in Panel I of Exhibit

last-in, first-out (LIFO)
An inventory method that assumes that the stock acquired most recently is sold (used up) first.

19-1) because it charges recent higher costs as cost of goods sold. Why is lower net income such an important feature of LIFO? Because LIFO is an acceptable inventory accounting method for U.S. income tax purposes. When a company reports lower income to the tax authorities, it pays lower taxes. Because the Internal Revenue Code requires that LIFO be used for financial reporting purposes if it is used for tax purposes, it is not surprising that almost two-thirds of U.S. corporations use LIFO for at least some of their inventories.

Inflationary periods often cause firms to change from FIFO to LIFO. For example, the *Wall Street Journal* reported that Chicago Heights Steel Co. "boosted cash by 5 to 10% by lowering income taxes when it switched to LIFO." When Becton, Dickinson and Company changed to LIFO, its annual report stated that its "change to the LIFO method . . . for both financial reporting and income tax purposes resulted in improved cash flow due to lower income taxes paid." Indeed, some observers maintain that executives are guilty of mismanagement if they do not adopt LIFO when FIFO produces significantly higher taxable income.

A disadvantage of LIFO is that it permits management to influence income by the timing of purchases of inventory items. Consider our cola vendor. Suppose acquisition prices increase from 56 cents on Wednesday to 68 cents on Thursday, the day of the sale of the one unit. How does the acquisition of one more unit on Thursday affect net income? Under LIFO, cost of goods sold would change from 56 cents to 68 cents (the cost of the last unit purchased, the one bought on Thursday), and profit would fall by 12 cents. In contrast, a FIFO valuation of the cost of goods sold and gross profit would be unchanged:

	LIFO		FIFO	
	Without Thursday Purchase (cents)	*With Thursday Purchase (cents)*	*Without Thursday Purchase (cents)*	*With Thursday Purchase (cents)*
Sales	90	90	90	90
Cost of goods sold	56	68	30	30
Gross profit	34	22	60	60
Ending inventory (cents)				
(30 + 40)	70			
(30 + 40 + 56)		126		
(40 + 56)			96	
(40 + 56 + 68)				164

Another disadvantage of LIFO is that income can soar when a company reduces its inventories. Under LIFO, inventory consists of **LIFO layers** (or **LIFO increments**), which are separately identifiable additions to inventory. All units in a particular LIFO layer have the same cost. For example, on Wednesday our cola vendor had three LIFO layers:

- Layer 1: 30-cent unit purchased on Monday
- Layer 2: 40-cent unit purchased on Tuesday
- Layer 3: 56-cent unit purchased on Wednesday

As a company grows, the LIFO layers tend to pile on one another as the years go by. Thus, many LIFO companies show inventories that have ancient layers (going back to 1940 in some instances). The reported LIFO value may therefore be far below what FIFO values might otherwise show.

When a company reduces its inventory, old LIFO layers become the cost of goods sold. These old values may be much below current replacement values, leading to overstatement of income. In other words, the LIFO method usually gives lower net income because the most recent values are used for the cost of goods sold. But when a company reduces its inventories, LIFO can lead to just the opposite effect. Cost of goods sold includes old values, and net income is higher under LIFO than under other methods.

For example, suppose a new company bought 100 units of inventory in 1960 for $10 per unit. Each year since, the company purchased and sold exactly 200 units. In 2000, the purchase price was $40 per unit. In early 2001, the company installed a new inventory system, reducing the needed level of inventory to 50 units. Therefore, in 2001, the company purchased only 150 units at $40 per unit, even though sales remained at 200 units. The 2001 sales price is $50 per unit. Gross profit for 2001 under FIFO and LIFO would be

	FIFO	LIFO
Sales (200 units @ $50/unit)	$10,000	$10,000
Deduct cost of goods sold		
100 2000 units	(4,000)	
100 2001 units	(4,000)	
150 2001 units		(6,000)
50 1960 units		(500)
Gross profit	$ 2,000	$ 3,500

This disadvantage of LIFO is especially relevant in today's environment because many companies are increasingly concerned with reducing inventory levels.

Consider, for a moment, LIFO versus FIFO when prices are falling. Suppose Compaq Computer Corporation assembles a particular laptop for which the cost of the 1,000 units in inventory at the end of 2000 is $1,000 each. In 2001 Compaq produces 10,000 units at a cost of $700 each and sells 10,000 units. Compare the cost of goods sold using FIFO with that using LIFO.

ANSWER

Under LIFO, all 10,000 units sold have a cost of $700—the latest costs—for a total cost of goods sold of $7 million. Under FIFO, the first 1,000 units sold will have a cost of $1,000 each, and the last 9,000 sold will have a cost of $700, for a total cost of goods sold of $7.3 million. Thus, the cost of goods sold is $300,000 higher under FIFO, so operating income is $300,000 lower under FIFO than under LIFO. This is the opposite of what occurs when prices are rising.

WEIGHTED-AVERAGE COST

The **weighted-average cost** method assigns the same unit cost to each unit available for sale. The unit cost is the cost of all units available for sale divided by the number of units available, as shown in Exhibit 19-1. The weighted-average method usually produces a gross profit somewhere between that obtained under FIFO and LIFO (48 cents as compared with 60 cents and 34 cents in Panel I of Exhibit 19-1).

To understand better the term *weighted average,* assume that our cola vendor bought two cans rather than one on Monday at 30 cents each. To get the weighted average, we must consider not only the price paid, but also the number of units purchased:

weighted average = cost of goods available for sale
÷ units available for sale

weighted average = [(2 × 30 cents) + (1 × 40 cents) + (1 × 56 cents)] ÷ 4

= 156 cents ÷ 4 = 39 cents

weighted-average cost
The inventory method that assigns the same unit cost to each unit available for sale. The unit cost is computed by dividing the cost of all units available for sale by the number of units available.

The weighted-average method produces less extreme results than either LIFO or FIFO on both the income statement and the balance sheet, as the comparisons in Exhibit 19-1 show. Also, the weighted average is subject to minimal manipulation by managers.

CHOICE AND USE OF INVENTORY METHODS

Each of the four inventory methods has different strengths and weaknesses. Among the issues facing management when choosing a method are such questions as, Which method provides the highest reported net income? Which method provides management the most flexibility to affect reported earnings? How do the methods affect income tax obligations? Which method produces an inventory valuation that approximates the actual value of the inventory?

In choosing an inventory method, it is important to recognize the link between the cost of goods sold and the valuation of ending inventory. The cola vendor began his business, acquired three cans of cola during the week, and had a total cost of goods available for sale of $1.26. At the end of the period, this $1.26 must be allocated either to cans sold or to cans in ending inventory. The higher the cost of goods sold, the lower the ending inventory. Exhibit 19-2 illustrates this interdependence. At one extreme, FIFO treats the 30-cent cost of the first can acquired as the cost of goods sold and 96 cents as ending inventory. At the other extreme, LIFO treats the 56-cent cost of the last can acquired as the cost of goods sold and the 70 cents as ending inventory.

One thing to consider in choosing among inventory methods is how physical units flow. Consider four different ways that our cola vendor might physically store and sell his cola. One way—specific identification—would be to mark each can with its cost, and record that cost as a cost of goods sold when the can is handed to a customer. This method can be used only when the physical procedure allows the seller to track each item of inventory. Another way—LIFO—would be to put each new can acquired into the top of a cooler. As each customer arrives, the top can is the one sold. In contrast, if our vendor places each new can at the back of the cooler to chill, and sells the oldest, coldest can first, FIFO captures the physical flow. Finally, if the cans are just mixed together, the weighted-average method is a rough approximation of what is known about the cost of the can sold.

Although we can relate the four methods to the physical flow of the cola cans, the accounting profession has concluded that this is not important to the choice of the

Exhibit 19-2

Diagram of Inventory Methods
(data are from Exhibit 19-1; monetary amounts are in cents)

Beginning inventory	+	Merchandise purchases	=	Cost of goods available for sale	
0	+	126	=	126	
Cost of goods available for sale	−	Cost of goods sold	=	Ending inventory	
1 @ 30 1 @ 40 1 @ 56	−	30 or 40 or 56	=	96 or 86 or 70	Specific identification
126	−	30	=	96	FIFO
	−	56	=	70	LIFO
	−	42	=	84	Weighted average

inventory accounting method. Why? Many vendors have substantial choice over the physical flow of their products, but that choice often has little importance to the financial success of the business. Therefore, companies may choose any of the four methods to record the cost of goods sold, but they must apply the method consistently. That is, they cannot change the choice of method from period to period. Because the method is not linked to the physical flow of the merchandise, inventory methods are often referred to as *cost flow assumptions*. For example, when we decide that the cost of the first inventory item purchased will be matched with the sales revenue from the first item sold to calculate the gross profit from the sale, we are adopting the FIFO cost flow assumption.

Panel II of Exhibit 19-1 shows the results of selling the remaining two cans of inventory on Friday. Note that cumulative gross profit over the life of the vendor's business would be the same $1.44 under any of the inventory methods. These methods are important only because we must match particular costs to particular periods during the life of the business to prepare financial statements and evaluate performance. We must understand how the inventory cost flow assumption affects a company's financial statements for a particular period before we can use the statements to evaluate performance over that period.

As mentioned earlier, taxes have a major influence on the choice of inventory methods. LIFO is the most popular inventory method for large U.S. companies, but it is seldom used in countries that do not allow it for tax purposes. About two-thirds of large U.S. companies use LIFO for at least some of their inventories.

A recent study showed that fewer than 25% of the responding companies in the U.S. electronics and business equipment industries use LIFO. If tax benefits are so important, why doesn't everyone use LIFO? Recall that LIFO yields lower net income and lower taxes in a period of rising prices and constant or growing inventories. But some industries do not face rising prices. For such industries, FIFO yields lower net income and lower taxes. In electronics, for example, technology has been a consistent force driving prices down. Think back to 10 years of constant reductions in prices for computers, radios, stereo systems, and watches.

LOWER-OF-COST-OR-MARKET (LCM) METHOD

Regardless of the inventory method used, accountants must decrease the inventory value if the inventory's market price drops below its acquisition cost. As a general rule, the acquisition cost provides a ceiling for the valuation of all assets; their balance sheet values can be increased only upon an exchange. However, asset values can be decreased without an exchange.

Inventory accounting uses the **lower-of-cost-or-market (LCM)** method, whereby the current market price of inventory is compared with its cost (derived by specific identification, FIFO, LIFO, or weighted average), and the lower of the two is selected as the basis for the valuation of goods at a specific inventory date.

Market generally means the *current replacement cost* or its equivalent. It ordinarily does not mean the ultimate selling price to customers. Consider the following facts. A company has 100 units in its ending FIFO inventory on December 31, 20X0. Its gross profit for 20X0 has been tentatively computed as follows:

Sales	$2,180
Cost of goods available for sale	$1,980
Ending inventory, at cost of 100 units	790
Cost of goods sold	$1,190
Gross profit	$ 990

Objective 3
Explain the lower-of-cost-or-market method.

lower-of-cost-or-market (LCM) An inventory method in which the current market price of inventory is compared with its cost (derived by specific identification, FIFO, LIFO, or weighted average) and the lower of the two is selected as the basis for the valuation of goods at a specific inventory date.

However, market prices during the final week of December suddenly declined to $4 per unit. If the lower market price is indicative of lower ultimate sales prices, an inventory write-down of $790 − (100 × $4), or $390, is in order. Therefore reported income for 20X0 would be $390 lower:

	Before $390 Write-Down	After $390 Write-Down	Difference
Sales	$2,180	$2,180	
Cost of goods available	$1,980	$1,980	
Ending inventory	790	400	−$390
Cost of goods sold	$1,190	$1,580	+$390
Gross profit	$ 990	$ 600	−$390

The theory states that of the $790 cost, $390 expired during 20X0 because we cannot justify carrying the cost forward to the future as an asset.

Now suppose the replacement prices rise to $8 per unit in January 20X1. Authorities do not permit restoration of the December write-down. In short, the lower-of-cost-or-market method would regard the $4 cost as of December 31 as the "new cost" of the inventory. Original acquisition cost is the ceiling for valuation under generally accepted accounting principles.

SUMMARY PROBLEM FOR YOUR REVIEW

PROBLEM

Refer to Exhibit 19-1, page 765. Suppose the vendor sold two cans on Thursday for 90 cents each. All other data are unchanged.

Required

1. Compute (a) the gross profit for Monday through Wednesday, (b) the gross profit for Thursday, and (c) the ending inventory on Thursday, under FIFO and under LIFO.

2. Assume the same facts as in requirement 1 except that the vendor purchased one additional can of cola on Thursday for 65 cents. Compute Thursday's gross profit under FIFO and under LIFO.

SOLUTION

All amounts are in cents.

1. **a.** The vendor would recognize no gross profit on Monday through Wednesday because he had no sales.

   b.

	FIFO		LIFO	
Sales		180		180
Cost of goods sold				
Beginning inventory (from Exhibit 19-1)	126		126	
Purchases	0		0	
Cost of goods available for sale	126		126	
Ending inventory	56		30	
Cost of goods sold		70		96
Gross profit, Thursday		110		84

c. The ending inventory on Thursday was one Wednesday unit @ 56 cents under FIFO and one Monday unit @ 30 cents under LIFO.

2. Note how the late purchase affects LIFO gross profit but not FIFO gross profit:

	FIFO		LIFO	
Sales		180		180
Cost of goods sold				
Beginning inventory (from Exhibit 19-1)	126		126	
Purchases	65		65	
Cost of goods available for sale	191		191	
Ending inventory*	121		70	
Cost of goods sold		70		121
Gross profit, Thursday		110		59

*Wednesday and Thursday units for FIFO (56 cents + 65 cents) and Monday and Tuesday units for LIFO (30 cents + 40 cents).

Highlights to Remember: Part One

Describe the four major methods of accounting for inventories. Companies in the United States use four principal inventory methods: specific identification, weighted average, FIFO, and LIFO. These methods measure the cost of goods sold that is recognized when an item is delivered to a customer. Each of the methods represents a specific physical flow of inventory, but a method can be used even if it doesn't match the actual physical flow.

Compare FIFO and LIFO, and explain why most U.S. firms use LIFO. LIFO is the most popular inventory method in the United States because it offers income tax advantages that become most pronounced during times of steady or rising inventories combined with rising prices. Unfortunately, LIFO also allows management to influence income by the timing of purchases of inventory items, and income can soar if a company penetrates old, low-cost LIFO layers.

Explain the lower-of-cost-or-market method. Accountants apply the lower-of-cost-or-market method to inventories. Companies cannot write up inventories above cost, but they do write them down if replacement costs fall below acquisition costs.

Accounting Vocabulary: Part One

first-in, first-out (FIFO), p. 764
last-in, first-out (LIFO), p. 765
LIFO increments, p. 766

LIFO layers, p.766
lower-of-cost-or-market (LCM), p. 769

specific identification, p. 764
weighted-average cost, p. 767

PART TWO: CHANGING PRICES AND INCOME MEASUREMENT

The use of historical cost in measuring income is one of the most controversial subjects in accounting. The remainder of this chapter focuses on how inflation affects the income statement.

COMPLAINTS ABOUT HISTORICAL COST

Accountants have traditionally maintained that net income is a return on the capital invested by shareholders. Suppose shareholders receive cash dividends equal to the amount of net income of a period. In the absence of inflation, such a payment leaves the shareholders' invested capital at the end of the period equal to the beginning capital. However, when prices change, this relationship between income and capital is altered. In times of generally rising prices, paying dividends equal to net income, as conventionally measured, usually amounts to paying out some capital itself as well as the return on capital.

In particular, industries with huge investments in plant and equipment claim that their profits in times of inflation are badly misstated by generally accepted accounting principles. For instance, consider NYNEX, a company that emerged from the breakup of the Bell System and has since merged into Verizon Wireless. During a year of high inflation in the 1980s, NYNEX reported net income of $1,095 million, which would have been a net loss of $82 million if depreciation had been adjusted for inflation. Because inflation rates have been small in the last decade, such dramatic differences are rare. However, even an inflation rate of 4% results in a doubling of prices every 18 years, which is less than the economic life of many assets.

Because of the soaring inflation of the late 1970s in the United States, the Financial Accounting Standards Board (FASB) issued *Statement No. 33,* "Financial Reporting and Changing Prices." The statement required no changes in the primary financial statements. However, it required large companies to include supplementary inflation-adjusted schedules in their annual reports.

Statement No. 33 was experimental, and its requirements were in place for 8 years. By then, inflation had subsided, and the FASB decided not to continue requiring inflation-adjusted disclosures. Although U.S. companies do not need to report inflation-adjusted numbers, a basic knowledge about reporting the effects of changing prices is useful for at least three reasons: (1) High inflation is still present in many countries, and accounting reports in those countries must cope with the effects of inflation; (2) if history is any indication, higher inflation rates will return to the United States sooner or later, and when they do, users of financial statements will again become concerned with inflation-adjusted statements; and (3) understanding the limitations of traditional financial statements is enhanced by knowing how inflation affects (or does not affect) such financial statements.

INCOME OR CAPITAL

Objective 4
Distinguish between financial capital maintenance and physical capital maintenance.

financial capital maintenance The concept that income emerges after financial resources are recovered.

physical capital maintenance The concept that income emerges only after recovering an amount that allows physical operating capability to be maintained.

To understand inflation's effects on financial statements, you must understand the concepts of income and capital. Stockholders invest financial resources (capital) with the expectation of an eventual return *of* that capital together with additional amounts representing the return *on* that capital (income). Separating returns *of* capital from returns *on* capital is difficult in inflationary times.

Consider an example. A new company receives an investment (capital) from owners of $1,000 and uses it immediately to purchase inventory. It then sells the inventory a year later for $1,500. Meanwhile, the cost of replacing the inventory has risen to $1,200.

Most accountants and managers believe that income emerges after investors recover their financial resources, a concept called **financial capital maintenance.** Because investors have recovered the $1,000 capital, $500 is the measure of income. This is the concept underlying traditional historical-cost accounting.

On the other hand, some accountants believe that income emerges only after recovering an amount that allows a company to maintain physical operating capability, called **physical capital maintenance.** Because $1,200 is the current cost of inventory (cost of maintaining physical capability) at the date of sale, $300 is the measure of income.

	Financial Capital Maintenance	Physical Capital Maintenance
Sales	$1,500	$1,500
Cost of goods sold	1,000	1,200
Income	$ 500	$ 300

MEASUREMENT ALTERNATIVES UNDER INFLATION

Inflation, a general rise in prices causing a decline in the purchasing power of the monetary unit, has caused accountants to consider two types of changes in financial reporting:

1. Switch from measuring transactions in **nominal dollars,** which are dollar measurements that are not restated for fluctuations in the general purchasing power of the monetary unit, to **constant dollars,** which are nominal dollars that are restated in terms of current purchasing power.

2. Instead of reporting the **historical cost** of an asset, which is the amount originally paid to acquire it, use the **current cost,** which is generally the cost to replace it.

Traditional accounting uses *nominal* (rather than constant) dollars and *historical* (rather than current) costs. Using historical costs implies maintenance of *financial* capital; current costs imply physical capital maintenance. Historical cost/nominal dollar accounting has almost exclusively dominated financial reporting throughout this century. Yet, as noted earlier, criticism of this type of accounting abounds when inflation is present.

The two nontraditional alternatives, which can be applied separately or in combination, address separate but related problems caused by inflation: (1) Constant-dollar disclosures account for general changes in the purchasing power of the dollar, and (2) current-cost disclosures account for changes in prices of specific assets. The two approaches create the following four alternatives for measuring income:

nominal dollars Dollar measurements that are not restated for fluctuations in the general purchasing power of the monetary unit.

constant dollars Nominal dollars that are restated in terms of current purchasing power.

historical cost The amount originally paid to acquire an asset.

current cost The cost to replace an asset, as opposed to its historical cost.

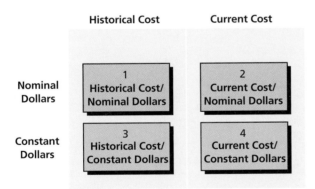

In the following discussion of these alternatives, we will consider the situation of the Marsalis Company. Marsalis has the following traditional balance sheets at December 31 (based on historical costs in nominal dollars):

	20X0	20X1
Cash	$ 0	$10,500
Inventory, 400 and 100 units, respectively	8,000	2,000
Total assets	$8,000	$12,500
Original paid-in capital	$8,000	$ 8,000
Retained income	—	4,500
Stockholders' equity	$8,000	$12,500

The company had acquired all 400 units of inventory at $20 per unit (total of $8,000) on December 31, 20X0, and had held the units until December 31, 20X1. The company sold 300 units for $35 per unit (total of $10,500 cash) on December 31, 20X1. The replacement cost of the inventory at that date was $30 per unit. The general-price-level index was 100 on December 31, 20X0, and 110 on December 31, 20X1. Assume that these are the only transactions. Ignore income taxes.

Objective 5
Explain and illustrate four methods of measuring income: historical cost/nominal dollars, current cost/nominal dollars, historical cost/constant dollars, and current cost/constant dollars.

HISTORICAL COST/NOMINAL DOLLARS

Exhibit 19-3 is the basis for the explanations that follow. The first two columns of Exhibit 19-3 show financial statements prepared using the time-honored historical cost/nominal dollars approach (method 1). This method measures invested capital in nominal dollars. It is the most popular approach to income measurement and is commonly called the historical-cost method. Operating income (equal to net income in this case) is the excess of revenue ($10,500 in 20X1) over the original acquisition costs of assets used in obtaining that revenue. As we have already seen, when using the conventional accrual basis of accounting,

Exhibit 19-3

Four Major Methods to Measure Income and Capital (dollars)

	Nominal Dollars*				Constant Dollars*			
	(Method 1)		(Method 2)		(Method 3)		(Method 4)	
	Historical Cost		Current Cost		Historical Cost		Current Cost	
Balance Sheets as of December 31	20X0	20X1	20X0	20X1	20X0	20X1	20X0	20X1
Cash	—	10,500	—	10,500	—	10,500	—	10,500
Inventory, 400 and 100 units, respectively	8,000	2,000[b]	8,000	3,000[c]	8,800[e]	2,200[e]	8,800[e]	3,000[c]
Total assets	8,000	12,500	8,000	13,500	8,800	12,700	8,800	13,500
Original paid-in capital	8,000	8,000	8,000	8,000	8,800[f]	8,800[f]	8,800[f]	8,800[f]
Retained income (confined to operating income)		4,500		1,500		3,900		1,500
Revaluation equity (accumulated holding gains)				4,000				3,200
Total liabilities and shareholders' equity	8,000	12,500	8,000	13,500	8,800	12,700	8,800	13,500
Income Statements for 20X1								
Sales, 300 units @ $35		10,500		10,500		10,500		10,500
Cost of goods sold, 300 units		6,000[b]		9,000[c]		6,600[e]		9,000[c]
Operating income (to retained income)		4,500		1,500		3,900		1,500
Holding gains[a]								
On 300 units sold				3,000[d]				2,400[g]
On 100 units unsold				1,000[d]				800[g]
Total holding gains[a] (to revaluation equity)				4,000				3,200

*Nominal dollars are not restated for a general price index, whereas constant dollars are restated.

[a]Many advocates of this current-cost method favor showing these gains in a completely separate statement of holding gains rather than as a part of the income statement. Others favor including some or all of these gains as a part of income for the year.

[b]100 × $20, [c]100 × $30, [d]300 × ($30 − 20), [e]110/100 × $8,000, [f]110/100 × $8,000.
  300 × $20,   300 × $30,   100 × ($30 − 20).   110/100 × $2,000,
                                                 110/100 × $6,000.

[g]$9,000 − [(110/100) × $6,000] = $2,400 $3,000 − [(110/100) × $2,000] = $800
or   or
300 × [$30 − (110/100) × $20] = $2,400.   100 × [$30 − (110/100) × $20] = $800.

an exchange transaction is ordinarily necessary before recording revenues (and resulting incomes). Thus, no income generally appears until the company sells the asset. We ignore the intervening price fluctuations.

CURRENT COST/NOMINAL DOLLARS

The second set of financial statements in Exhibit 19-3 illustrates a **current-cost method** that has especially strong advocates in the United Kingdom and Australia (method 2). This method uses current cost/nominal dollars. The focus is on operating income. This model emphasizes that operating income should be "distributable" income. That is, Marsalis Company could pay dividends of only $1,500 and still leave enough assets to allow for replacement of the inventory that has just been sold.

Critics of traditional accounting claim that the $4,500 historical-cost measure of operating income is misleading because it overstates the net increment in distributable assets. If Marsalis were to pay a $4,500 dividend, the company would not be able to continue operations at the same level as before. Accountants frequently call the $3,000 difference between the two operating incomes ($4,500 − $1,500 = $3,000) an "inventory profit" or an "inflated profit." Why? Because $9,000 instead of $6,000 is now necessary to replace the 300 units sold (300 × the increase in price from $20 to $30 equals the $3,000 difference).

The current-cost method stresses a separation between *operating income*—the excess of revenue over the current costs of the assets consumed in obtaining that revenue—and **holding gains (or losses)**—increases (or decreases) in the replacement costs of the assets held during the current period. Accountants differ sharply on how to account for holding gains or losses. The "correct" accounting depends on distinctions between capital and income. That is, income cannot occur until invested capital is "recovered" or "maintained." Exhibit 19-3 illustrates the issue of capital maintenance. Advocates of a physical concept of capital maintenance claim that companies should exclude from income all holding gains (both those gains related to the units sold and the gains related to the units unsold). Instead, they should become a part of stockholders' equity called **revaluation equity.** Why? Because holding gains represent the amount that a company must reinvest to maintain physical capital at its beginning-of-the-year level. Holding gains become part of capital, not a return on capital.

HISTORICAL COST/CONSTANT DOLLARS

Method 3 of Exhibit 19-3 shows the results of applying a general price index adjustment to historical costs. For our purpose, a **general price index** compares the average price of a group of goods and services at one date with the average price of a similar group at another date. To apply method 3, we restate the income measurements in each year from *nominal dollars* (possessing different general purchasing power of various years) to *constant dollars* (possessing the same general purchasing power of the current year). Because of inflation, dollars spent or received in 20X1 have a different value than dollars spent or received in 20X0. Adding 20X0 dollars to 20X1 dollars is like adding apples and oranges. Constant-dollar accounting measures all items on the 20X1 financial statements in 20X1 dollars.

Consider the objections to method 1. Deducting 6,000 20X0 dollars from 10,500 20X1 dollars to obtain $4,500 is akin to deducting 60 centimeters from 105 inches and calling the result 45. In either case, the result is nonsense.

Method 3, historical cost/constant dollars, attempts to remedy the foregoing objections. It uses *general price indexes* to restate the amounts of the historical cost/nominal dollar method. Examples of such indexes are the Gross National Product Implicit Price Deflator and the Consumer Price Index for All Urban Consumers (CPI). Anyone who has lived long enough to be able to read this book is aware that the purchasing power of the dollar is unstable. Index numbers gauge the relationship between current conditions and some norm or baseline condition (which is assigned the index number of 100).

A price index is an average. It does not measure the behavior of the individual component prices. Some individual prices may move in one direction and some in another. The general consumer price level may soar while the prices of eggs and chickens decline.

Do not confuse *general* indexes, which are used in constant-dollar accounting, with *specific* indexes. The two have entirely different purposes. Sometimes **specific price indexes** are used to approximate the current costs of particular assets or types of assets. That is, companies use specialized indexes to get approximations of current costs without having to pay professional appraisers. For example, Inland Steel used the *Engineering News Record Construction Cost Index* to value most of its property, plant, and equipment for purposes of using the current-cost method.

Note that the historical-cost/constant-dollar approach (method 3) is not a fundamental departure from historical costs. Instead, it maintains that all historical costs to be matched against revenue should be restated on some constant-dollar basis so that all revenues and all expenses can be expressed in dollars of the same (usually current) purchasing power. The restated figures are historical costs expressed in constant dollars via the use of a general price index. They are not current costs.

Constant-dollar financial statements generally measure all amounts using the most recent dollar because users tend to think in such terms instead of in terms of old dollars with significantly different purchasing power. The original units in inventory would be updated on each year's balance sheet along with their effect on stockholders' equity. For example, the December 31, 20X0, balance sheet would be stated for comparative purposes on December 31, 20X1:

	Unrestated Cost	Multiplier	Restated Cost
Inventory	$8,000	110/100	$8,800
Original paid-in capital	8,000	110/100	8,800

To extend the illustration, suppose Marsalis held all the inventory for 2 full years and that the general price index rose from 110 to 132 during 20X2. Marsalis would restate the December 31, 20X1, balance sheet items for comparative purposes on December 31, 20X2, using 20X2 dollars:

	Restated Cost 12/31/X2	Multiplier	Restated Cost 12/31/X3
Inventory	$8,800	132/110	$10,560*
Original paid-in capital	8,800	132/110	10,560*

* The same result could be tied to the year of acquisition:
Inventory $8,000 × 132/100 = $10,560
Original paid-in capital $8,000 × 132/100 = $10,560

The restated amount is just that—a restatement of original cost in terms of current (20X2) dollars. It is not a gain in any sense. Therefore, this approach differs from an application of "current-cost" accounting. Using this approach, if the specific current cost of the inventory goes up or down, the restated cost is unaffected.

The restated historical-cost approach harmonizes with the concept of maintaining the general purchasing power of the invested capital (a financial concept of capital maintenance) in total rather than maintaining "specific invested capital," item by item.

---

specific price index An index used to approximate the current costs of particular assets or types of assets.

CURRENT COST/CONSTANT DOLLARS

Method 4 of Exhibit 19-3 shows the results of applying general index numbers to current costs. As the footnotes of the exhibit explain in more detail, Marsalis adjusts the nominal gains reported under method 2 so that it reports only gains in constant dollars. For example, suppose you buy 100 units on December 31, 20X0, for $2,000 cash and hold it until December 31, 20X1, when its replacement cost is $3,000. Suppose also that the general price index has risen from 100 to 110. Your nominal gain is $1,000, but your "real" gain in constant dollars in 20X1 is only $800: the $3,000 current cost minus the restated historical cost of $2,000 × 1.10 = $2,200.

Suppose Marsalis holds the 100 units throughout 20X2. The general price index rises from 110 to 132. The replacement cost rises from $30 to $34, a nominal holding gain for 20X2 of $4 × 100 = $400. However, because the original cost adjusted for price increases is $2,200 × (132 ÷ 110) = $2,640 at the end of 20X1, an increase of $440 over the 20X0 amount, the current-cost/constant-dollar approach (method 4) would report a real holding loss:

	12/31/X0	12/31/X1	12/31/X2
Original cost restated for changes in the price level	$2,000	$2,200	$2,640
Current cost	2,000	3,000	3,400
Increase in current cost		1,000*	400*
Increase due to price level		200†	440†
Holding gain (loss)		$ 800	$ (40)

*3,000 − 2,000 = 1,000, and 3,400 − 3,000 = 400
†2,200 − 2,000 = 200, and 2,640 − 2,200 = 440

Many accountants disagree on the relative merits of historical-cost approaches versus miscellaneous versions of current-cost approaches to income measurement. But there is general agreement among most accountants that restatements in constant dollars would be an improvement regardless of whether historical or current costs are used (ignoring practical barriers), because otherwise income includes illusory gains caused by using an unstable measuring unit.

Consider the concept of a holding gain on inventory. Holding gains arise only when using current rather than historical costs. They measure the specific price increases of inventory held by a company compared to some benchmark. Under the current-cost/nominal-dollars method, the benchmark is the original cost of the inventory. Under the current-cost/constant-dollars method the benchmark is the price-level adjusted historical cost of the inventory. Suppose a company purchased $5,000 of inventory at the beginning of the year and held it until the end of the year, when its replacement cost was $6,000. The price-level index was 100 at the beginning of the year and 112 at the end of the year. Compute the holding gain under (1) the current-cost/nominal-dollars method and (2) the current-cost/constant-dollars method.

ANSWER

Under the current-cost/nominal-dollars method, the entire $1,000 price increase is a holding gain. It reflects the fact that inventory purchased for $5,000 is now worth $6,000. Under the current-cost/constant-dollar method, only $400 of the price increase is a holding gain. The original $5,000 of inventory is worth $5,000 × (112 ÷ 100) = $5,600 in end-of-year dollars. The only real gain is $6,000 − $5,600 = $400; the other $600 increase in value merely offsets the decline in the value of the dollar.

SUMMARY PROBLEM FOR YOUR REVIEW

PROBLEM

In 1980, a company purchased a parcel of land, call it parcel 1, for $1,200. The company purchased an identical parcel, 2, today for $3,600. The general-price-level index has risen from 100 in 1980 to 300 now. Fill in the blanks in the following table.

Parcel	(1) Historical Cost Measured in 1980 Purchasing Power	(2) Historical Cost Measured in Current Purchasing Power	(3) Historical Cost as Originally Measured
1	_____	_____	_____
2	_____	_____	_____
Total	_____	_____	_____

1. Compare the figures in the three columns. Which total presents a nonsense result? Why?
2. Does the write-up of parcel 1 in column 2 result in a gain? Why?
3. Assume that these parcels are the only assets of the business. There are no liabilities. Prepare a balance sheet for each of the three columns.

SOLUTION

Parcel	(1) Historical Cost Measured in 1980 Purchasing Power	(2) Historical Cost Measured in Current Purchasing Power	(3) Historical Cost as Originally Measured
1	$1,200	$3,600	$1,200
2	1,200	3,600	3,600
Total	$2,400	$7,200	$4,800

1. The addition in column 3 produces a nonsense result. In contrast, the other two sums are the results of applying a standard unit of measure. The computations in columns 1 and 2 are illustrations of a restatement of historical cost in terms of a common dollar, a standard unit of measure. Such computations have been frequently called adjustments for changes in the general price level. Whether the company makes the restatement using the 1980 dollar or the current dollar is a matter of personal preference; columns 1 and 2 yield equivalent results. Restatement in terms of the current dollar (column 2) is most popular because the current dollar has more meaning than the old dollar to readers of the financial statements.

2. The mere restatement of identical assets in terms of different but equivalent measuring units does not create a gain. Expressing parcel 1 as $1,200 in column 1 and $3,600 in column 2 is like expressing parcel 1 in terms of, say, either 1,200 square yards or $9 \times 1,200 = 10,800$ square feet. Surely the "write-up" from 1,200 square yards to 10,800 square feet is not a gain; it is merely another way

of measuring the same asset. That is basically what general-price-level account-ing is all about. It says you cannot measure one plot of land in square yards and another in square feet and add them together. You must first convert them to some common measure. Unfortunately, column 3 fails to perform such a con-version before adding the two parcels together; hence the total is internally inconsistent.

3. The balance sheets would be

	(1)	**(2)**	**(3)**
Land	$2,400	$7,200	$4,800
Paid-in capital	$2,400	$7,200	$4,800

Note that (1) is expressed in 1980 dollars, (2) is in current dollars, and (3) is a mixture of 1980 and current dollars.

Highlights to Remember: Part Two

Distinguish between financial capital maintenance and physical capital maintenance. The matching of historical costs with revenue is the generally accepted means of measuring net income. Such net income assumes a goal of financial capital mainte-nance. However, this method is often criticized in times of high inflation. Some critics suggest using a concept of physical capital maintenance instead of financial capital maintenance.

Explain and illustrate four methods of measuring income: historical cost/nominal dollars, current cost/nominal dollars, historical cost/constant dollars, and current cost/constant dollars. There are four alternatives for measuring income that can be summarized as follows:

	Financial Capital Maintenance	**Physical Capital Maintenance**
Mixed measuring unit	Historical cost/nominal dollars	Current cost/nominal dollars
Common measuring unit	Historical cost/constant dollars	Current cost/constant dollars

Historical cost/nominal dollars is the traditional method of measuring income. Historical cost/constant dollars uses a general price index to create a common measuring unit, dollars of the same purchasing power, but it is not a departure from historical cost. A more fundamental change is to use current costs instead of historical costs. Proponents claim that such a measure, based on physical capital maintenance, is a better gauge of the distinction between income (the return on capital) and capital maintenance (the return of capital).

Understand why and how managers and investors adjust their financial statements to account for changes in prices paid for inventories. Inflation is a fact of life. It affects investment decisions, and it affects operating decisions of companies. Financial state-ments that ignore inflation disregard an important economic factor affecting companies. This is not a serious omission when inflation rates are low, but it can be significant when rates soar or as inflation effects build up over time. If financial statements ignore the effects of inflation (as is the case in most of the world, including the United States), users should at least recognize the potential weaknesses in the statements.

Accounting Vocabulary: Part Two

constant dollars, p. 773

current cost, p. 773

current-cost method, p. 775

financial capital maintenance,
   p. 772

general price index, p. 775

historical cost, p. 773

holding gains (or losses), p. 775

nominal dollars, p. 773

physical capital maintenance,
   p. 772

revaluation equity, p. 775

specific price index, p. 776

Fundamental Assignment Material

Special Note: Problems relating to Part One of the chapter are presented first in each subgrouping of the assignment material. For coverage of the basic ideas of inflation accounting, Problem 19-A2 is especially recommended. For a closer but still fundamental look, Problem 19-35 is especially recommended.

GENERAL EXERCISES AND PROBLEMS

19-A1 LIFO, FIFO, Cash Effects

Duwamish Hardware Company had sales revenue of $360,000 in 20X1. Pertinent data for its only product in 20X1 included:

Inventory, December 31, 20X0	14,000 units @ $6	$ 84,000
February purchases	20,000 units @ $7	140,000
August purchases	32,000 units @ $8	256,000
Sales for the year	30,000 units	

Required

1. Prepare a statement of gross margin for 20X1. Use two columns, one assuming LIFO and one assuming FIFO.

2. Assume a 40% income tax rate. Suppose all transactions are for cash. Which inventory method results in more cash for Duwamish? By how much?

19-A2 Four Versions of Income and Capital

Kilpatrick Company has the following comparative balance sheets as of December 31 (based on historical costs in nominal dollars):

	20X0	20X1
Cash	$ —	$3,900
Inventory, 100 and 40 units, respectively	5,000	2,000
Total assets	$5,000	$5,900
Paid-in capital	$5,000	$5,000
Retained income	—	900
Stockholders' equity	$5,000	$5,900

The general-price-level index was 100 on December 31, 20X0, and 115 on December 31, 20X1. The company had acquired 100 units of inventory on December 31, 20X0, for $50 each and had held them throughout 20X1. The company sold 60 units on December 31, 20X1, for $65 cash each. The replacement cost of the inventory at that date was $60 per unit. Assume that these are the only transactions. Ignore income taxes.

Required

Use four columns to prepare comparative balance sheets as of December 31, 20X0 and 20X1, and income statements for 20X1 under (1) historical cost/nominal dollars, (2) current cost/nominal dollars, (3) historical cost/constant dollars, and (4) current cost/constant dollars.

UNDERSTANDING PUBLISHED FINANCIAL REPORTS

19-B1   Comparison of Inventory Methods

Unisys Corporation is a producer of computer-based information systems. The following actual data and descriptions are from the company's quarterly report for the second quarter of 2000 (in millions):

	December 31	June 30
	1999	*2000*
Inventories	$399.4	$372.9

A footnote states that "Inventories are valued at the lower of cost or market. Cost is determined principally on the first-in, first-out method."

The income statement for the six months ended June 30, 2000, included (in millions):

Total revenues	$3,265.8
Cost of revenue	2,245.7

Suppose a division of Unisys had the accompanying data regarding computer parts that it acquires and resells to customers for maintaining equipment (dollars are not in millions):

	Units	Total
Inventory (December 31, 1999)	100	$ 400
Purchase (February 20, 2000)	200	1,000
Sales (March 17)	150	1,200
Purchase (April 25, 2000)	140	840
Sales (June 27, 2000)	160	1,280

Required

1. For these computer parts only, prepare a tabulation of the cost-of-goods-sold section of the income statement for the six months ended June 30, 2000. Support your computations. Round totals to the nearest dollar. Show your tabulation for four different inventory methods: (a) FIFO, (b) LIFO, (c) weighted-average, and (d) specific identification.

    For requirement (d), assume that the purchase of February 20 was identified with the sale of March 17. Also assume that the purchase of April 25 was identified with the sale of June 27; the additional units sold were identified with the beginning inventory.

2. By how much would income taxes differ if Unisys used (a) LIFO instead of FIFO for this inventory item? (b) LIFO instead of weighted average? Assume a 40% tax rate.

19-B2   Effects of Late Purchases

Refer to the preceding problem. Suppose Unisys acquired 60 extra units at $7 each on June 29, 2000, a total of $420. How would gross margin and income taxes be affected under FIFO? That is, compare FIFO results before and after the purchase of 60 extra units. Under LIFO? That is, compare LIFO results before and after the purchase of 60 extra units. Show computations and explain.

19-B3   Accounting for Changing Prices

ConAgra, the food products company with brands such as Healthy Choice, Wesson, Hunt's, Armour, and Swiss Miss, had historical-cost inventory on May 28, 2000, of $3,787 million. Suppose ConAgra purchased the entire 2000 inventory on May 27 when the price index was 100. Half the inventory was sold for $2,000 million on May 27, 2001, when the price index was 110; the other half remained in inventory. An amount of inventory identical to the amount sold was immediately purchased for $2,000 million.

1. Compute the amount ConAgra would show in its annual report for the year ended May 28, 2001, for (a) inventory, May 28, 2000; (b) inventory, May 28, 2001; (c) cost of goods sold for the year ended May 28, 2001; and (d) holding gains (losses) for the year ended May 28, 2001, under each of the following four measurement methods: historical cost/nominal dollars, current cost/nominal dollars, historical cost/constant dollars, and current cost/constant dollars.

2. Suppose the sale of this inventory was ConAgra's only revenue in the year ended May 28, 2001. Compute ConAgra's gross margin under historical cost/nominal dollars, current cost/nominal dollars, historical cost/constant dollars, and current cost/constant dollars.

Additional Assignment Material

QUESTIONS

19-1. Name and briefly describe each of the four inventory methods that are generally accepted in the United States.

19-2. Suppose prices are rising and inventories are increasing. Which of the four generally accepted inventory methods will usually result in the highest net income? Explain.

19-3. Which inventory method, FIFO or LIFO, comes closer to describing what operating managers actually do? Explain.

19-4. "FIFO produces more net income than LIFO over the life of the business." Do you agree? Explain.

19-5. LIFO sometimes produces absurd inventory valuations. Why?

19-6. "Purchases of inventory at the end of a fiscal period can have a direct effect on income under LIFO." Do you agree? Explain.

19-7. "There is a single dominant reason why more and more U.S. companies have adopted LIFO." What is the reason?

19-8. "Switching from FIFO to LIFO will lower our profits. Therefore, the stockholders would be hurt by such a switch." Do you agree? Explain.

19-9. "LIFO is desirable only as long as inventories continue to increase." Explain.

19-10. "In applying the lower-of-cost-or-market method to inventories, inventory values are written down when replacement cost falls. If the replacement cost then increases, inventory values are written up, but not to an amount greater than the original cost." Do you agree? Explain.

19-11. Explain the difference between return on capital and return of capital.

19-12. "Because of pressure from the SEC, the FASB issued a revolutionary statement in 1979 abandoning the historical-cost method of income measurement and replacing it with a current-cost method." Do you agree? Explain.

19-13. Distinguish between the physical and the financial concepts of maintenance of invested capital.

19-14. What are the two major approaches to recognizing changing prices in measuring income?

19-15. "The choice among accounting measures of income is often expressed as either historical-cost accounting or general-price-level accounting or current-cost accounting." Do you agree? Explain.

19-16. "General-price-level accounting is a loose way of achieving replacement-cost accounting." Do you agree? Explain.

19-17. Explain what a general price index represents.

19-18. Explain how net income is measured under the current-cost approach.

19-19. What is the common meaning of current cost?

19-20. "All holding gains should be excluded from income." What is the major logic behind this statement?

COGNITIVE EXERCISES

19-21 Purchasing Operations and LIFO versus FIFO

Suppose that the evaluation of the purchasing officer for a refinery is based on the gross margin on the oil products produced and sold during the year. During the year the price of a barrel of oil has increased from $20 to $30. All the inventory of oil at the beginning of the year is valued at $20 or less. On the last day of the year, the purchasing agent is contemplating the purchase of additional oil at $30 per barrel. Is she more likely to purchase additional oil if the company uses the FIFO or the LIFO method for its inventories? Explain.

19-22 Sales Incentives and Lower of Cost or Market

Schilbred Company bought inventory for $50 per unit. The current replacement cost of the inventory is $45 per unit, and the company does not expect this cost to rise in the near future. How will a write-down of the inventory affect current and future profits? Under what circumstances might a sales manager oppose a write-down? Under what circumstances might she favor a write-down?

19-23   Inflation and Financing Decisions

Investors expect a return on their investments and an eventual return of their investments. Suppose that the treasurer of a company decides to pay dividends that will be a reasonable return on investment but not return any of the original investment. Since the original investment, there has been substantial inflation. How should the treasurer decide the amount of dividends to pay if he uses the concept of financial capital maintenance? How should he decide if he uses the concept of physical capital maintenance? If you were an investor in this company, which concept of capital maintenance would you prefer the treasurer to use?

GENERAL EXERCISES AND PROBLEMS

19-24   LIFO and FIFO

The inventory of the Paniagua Gravel Company on April 30 shows 500 tons at $7 per ton. A physical inventory on May 31 shows a total of 600 tons on hand. Revenue from sales of gravel for May totals $16,000. The following purchases were made during May:

May 5	1,000 tons @ $ 8 per ton
May 15	250 tons @ $ 9 per ton
May 25	300 tons @ $10 per ton

Required

1. Compute the inventory value as of May 31, using (a) FIFO and (b) LIFO.
2. Compute the gross profit using each method.

19-25   Comparison of Inventory Methods

The 110 In The Shade Co. is a wholesaler of air-conditioning equipment. The data concerning Hitachi model RAS-05 for the year 20X2 follow:

	Purchases		Sold*	Balance
December 31, 20X1				150 @ $80 = $12,000
January 20, 20X2	90 @ $100 =	$ 9,000		
February 5			80	
May 20	100 @ $120 =	$12,000		
June 17			110	
October 24	80 @ $140 =	$11,200		
November 29			60	
Total	270	$32,200	250	
December 31, 20X2				170 @ ?

* The sales during 20X2 were made at the following selling prices:

80 @ 140	=	$11,200
110 @ 160	=	$17,600
60 @ 180	=	$10,800
250		$39,600

Required

1. Prepare a comparative statement of gross profit for the year ended December 31, 20X2, using FIFO, LIFO, and weighted-average inventory methods.
2. By how much would income taxes differ if 110 In The Shade used LIFO instead of FIFO for Hitachi model RAS-05? Assume a 40% income tax rate.

19-26   Effects of Late Purchases

Refer to the preceding problem. Suppose 100 extra units were acquired on December 30 for $140 each, a total of $14,000. How would net income and income taxes be affected under FIFO? Under LIFO? Show a tabulated comparison.

19-27   LIFO, FIFO, Purchase Decisions, and Earnings per Share

Suppose the Sosa Company has 1 million shares of common stock outstanding and has had the following transactions during 20X1, its first year in business:

Sales	1,000,000 units @ $7
Purchases	800,000 units @ $3
	300,000 units @ $4

The current income tax rate is a flat 50%; the rate next year is expected to be 40%. Prices on inventory increased from $3 to $4 during the year.

It is December 20, and, as the president, you are trying to decide whether you should buy the 600,000 units you need for inventory now or early next year. The current price is $5 per unit. Prices on inventory are expected to remain stable; in any event, no decline in prices is anticipated.

You have not chosen an inventory method as yet, but you will pick either LIFO or FIFO. Other expenses for the year will be $2.4 million.

Required

1. Using LIFO, prepare a comparative income statement assuming the 600,000 units (a) are not purchased, (b) are purchased. The statement should end with reported earnings per share.

2. Repeat requirement 1, using FIFO.

3. Comment on the results obtained. What method would you choose? Why? Be specific.

4. Suppose that in year 2 the tax rate drops to 40%, prices remain stable, 1 million units are sold at $7, enough units are purchased at $5 so that the ending inventory will be 700,000 units, and other expenses are reduced to $1,800,000.

    a. Prepare a comparative income statement for the second year showing the impact of each of the four alternatives in requirements 1 and 2 on net income and earnings per share.

    b. Explain any difference in net income that you encounter among the four alternatives.

    c. Why is there a difference in ending inventory values under LIFO even though the same amount of physical inventory is in stock?

    d. What is the total cash outflow for income taxes for the two years together, under the four alternatives?

    e. Would you change your answer in requirement 3 now that you have completed requirement 4? Why?

19-28 LIFO, FIFO, Prices Rising and Falling

The Lopez Fertilizer Company had inventory on December 31, 20X0, of 20,000 bags at $10 = $200,000. Purchases during 20X1 were 30,000 bags. Sales were 28,000 bags for sales revenue of $20 per bag.

Required

Prepare a four-column comparative statement of gross margin for 20X1:

1. Assume that purchases were at $12 per unit. Assume FIFO and then LIFO (columns 1 and 2).

2. Assume that purchases were at $8 per unit. Assume FIFO and LIFO (columns 3 and 4).

3. Assume an income tax rate of 40%. Suppose all transactions are for cash.

    a. Which inventory method in requirement 1 results in more cash for Lopez Company? By how much?

    b. Which inventory method in requirement 2 results in more cash for Lopez Company? By how much?

19-29 FIFO and LIFO

Two divisions of Alberta Metals, Inc., are in the scrap metal warehousing business, the Calgary Division and the Edmonton Division. The manager of each division receives a bonus based on the division's pretax income. The divisions are about the same size and, in 20X1, coincidentally encountered seemingly identical operating situations. However, their accounting systems differ; Calgary uses FIFO and Edmonton uses LIFO.

Both divisions reported the following data for 20X1:

Beginning inventory, 10,000 tons @ $50 per ton	$ 500,000
Purchase, February 15, 20X1, 20,000 tons @ $70 per ton	1,400,000
Purchase, October 6, 20X1, 30,000 tons @ $90 per ton	2,700,000
Sales, 45,000 tons @ $110 per ton	4,950,000
Other expenses (in addition to cost of goods sold but excluding income taxes)	1,140,000

The income tax rate is 45%.

Required

1. Compute net income for the year for each division. Show your calculations.
2. Which division had the better performance for the year? Which accounting system would you prefer if you were manager of one of the divisions? Why? Explain fully. Include your estimate of the overall effect of these events on the cash balance of each division, assuming that all transactions during 20X1 were direct receipts or disbursements of cash.

19-30   Effects of LIFO and FIFO

The Bangalore Trading Company is starting in business on December 31, 20X0. In each half year, from 20X1 through 20X4, it expects to purchase 500 units and sell 250 units for the amounts listed below. In 20X5, it expects to purchase no units and sell 2,000 units for the amount indicated below. Monetary amounts are in thousands of rupees (R).

	20X1	20X2	20X3	20X4	20X5
Purchases					
First 6 months	R 2,000	R 4,000	R 6,000	R 6,000	R 0
Second 6 months	4,000	9,000	6,000	8,000	0
Total	R 6,000	R 13,000	R 12,000	R 14,000	R 0
Sales (at selling price)	R 10,000	R 10,000	R 10,000	R 10,000	R 40,000

Assume that there are no costs or expenses other than those shown. The income tax rate is 60%, and taxes for each year are payable on December 31 of that year. Bangalore Trading Company is trying to decide whether to use FIFO or LIFO throughout the five-year period.

Required

1. What was net income under FIFO for each of the five years? Under LIFO? Show calculations.
2. Explain briefly which method, LIFO or FIFO, seems more advantageous, and why.

19-31   Effects of LIFO on Purchase Decisions

The Sasaki Corporation is nearing the end of its first year in business. The following purchases of its single product have been made (monetary amounts in thousands of Japanese yen):

	Units	Unit Price	Total Cost
January	400	¥20	¥ 8,000
March	400	20	8,000
May	400	22	8,800
July	400	26	10,400
September	400	28	11,200
November	400	30	12,000
Total	2,400		¥58,400

Sales for the year will be 2,000 units for ¥96,000,000. Expenses other than cost of goods sold will be ¥16,000,000.

The president is undecided about whether to adopt FIFO or LIFO for income tax purposes. The company has ample storage space for up to 3,000 units of inventory. Inventory prices are expected to stay at ¥30,000 per unit for the next few months. Assume that Japanese tax authorities allow use of either LIFO or FIFO for accounting for inventories.

Required

1. If the president decided to purchase 1,600 units @ ¥30,000 in December, what would be the net income before taxes, the income taxes, and the net income after taxes for the year under (a) FIFO and (b) LIFO? Assume that income tax rates are 25% on the first ¥25,000,000 of net taxable income and 40% on the excess.
2. If the company sells its year-end inventory in year 2 @ ¥48,000 per unit and goes out of business, what would be the net income before taxes, the income taxes, and the net income after taxes under (a) FIFO and (b) LIFO? Assume that other expenses in year 2 are ¥16,000,000.

3. Repeat requirements 1 and 2, assuming that 1,600 units @ ¥30,000, were not purchased until January of the second year. Generalize on the effect on net income of the timing of purchases under FIFO and LIFO.

19-32 Lower of Cost or Market

Dilbert Toy Company uses cost or market, whichever is lower, for its inventories. There were no sales or purchases during the periods indicated, although selling prices generally fluctuated in the same directions as replacement costs. What amount for merchandise inventories would you show on the balance sheet on the dates listed below?

	Invoice Cost	Replacement Cost
December 31, 20X0	$100,000	$ 80,000
April 30, 20X1	100,000	90,000
August 31, 20X1	100,000	110,000
December 31, 20X1	100,000	70,000

19-33 Meaning of General Price Index Applications and Choice of Base Year

Paulsell Real Estate Company acquired land in mid-1981 for $3 million. In mid-2001, it acquired a substantially identical parcel of land for $8 million. Suppose the general price index annual averages were

2001 — 350.0	1991 — 175.0	1981 — 105.0

Required

1. In four columns, show the computations of the total cost of the two parcels of land expressed in (a) costs as traditionally recorded, (b) dollars of 2001 purchasing power, (c) 1991 purchasing power, and (d) 1981 purchasing power.
2. Explain the meaning of the figures that you computed in requirement 1.

19-34 Concepts of Income

Suppose you are in the business of investing in land and holding it for resale. On December 31, 20X0, a parcel of land has a historical cost of $200,000 and a current value of $800,000; the general price index had tripled since the land was acquired. Suppose that the land is sold on December 31, 20X1, for $920,000. The general price level rose by 5% during 20X1.

Required

1. Prepare a tabulation of income from continuing operations and holding gains for 20X1, using the four methods illustrated in Exhibit 19-3, page 774.
2. In your own words, explain the meaning of the results, giving special attention to what income represents.

19-35 Four Versions of Income and Capital

Reexamine Exhibit 19-3, page 774. Suppose the replacement cost at December 31, 20X1, had been $25 instead of $30. Suppose also that the general price index had been 115 instead of 110. All other facts are unchanged. Use four columns to prepare balance sheets as of December 31, 20X1 (only), and income statements for 20X1 under the four concepts shown in Exhibit 19-3. Explain the differences between your solution and the results shown in Exhibit 19-3.

UNDERSTANDING PUBLISHED FINANCIAL REPORTS

19-36 Switch from LIFO to FIFO

This is a classic problem. Effective January 1, 1970, Chrysler Corporation adopted the FIFO method for inventories previously valued by the LIFO method. The 1970 annual report stated, "This . . . makes the financial statements with respect to inventory valuation comparable with those of the other United States automobile manufacturers."

The Wall Street Journal reported

> *The change improved Chrysler's 1970 financial results several ways. Besides narrowing the 1970 loss by $20 million it improved Chrysler's working capital.*

*The change helped Chrysler's balance sheet by boosting inventories,
and thus current assets, by $150 million at the end of 1970 over what they
would have been under LIFO. As Chrysler's profit has collapsed over the
last two years and its financial position tightened, auto analysts have eyed
warily Chrysler's shrinking ratio of current assets to current liabilities.*

*Chrysler's short-term debt stood at $374 million at year-end, down
from $477 million a year earlier but up slightly from $370 million on
September 30. Chrysler's cash and marketable securities shrank during the
year to $156.4 million at year-end, down from $309.3 million a year earlier
and $220 million on Sept. 30.*

*To get the improvements in its balance sheet and results,
however, Chrysler paid a price. Roger Helder, vice president and comptroller, said Chrysler owed the government $53 million in tax savings it accu-
mulated by using the LIFO method since it switched from FIFO in 1957.
The major advantage of LIFO is that it holds down profit and thus tax liabilities. The other three major auto makers stayed on the FIFO method. Mr.
Helder said Chrysler now has to pay back that $53 million to the govern-
ment over 20 years, which will boost Chrysler's tax bills about $3 million a
year.*

Required

Given the content of this chapter, do you think the Chrysler decision to switch from LIFO to FIFO
was beneficial to its stockholders? Explain, being as specific and using as much data as you can.

19-37 LIFO and FIFO at Home Depot

Home Depot, the eighth largest retailer in the United States, uses the FIFO inventory method. On
January 30, 2000, the company reported merchandise inventory of $5.5 billion; at the beginning of
the year the inventory amount was only $4.3 billion. Cost of merchandise sold for the year ended
January 30, 2000 (fiscal 2000) was $27.0 billion, and operating income was $3.8 billion. During the
year, Home Depot purchased merchandise for $28.2 billion.

Suppose Home Depot had changed to LIFO on the first day of fiscal 2000, using the current
inventory amount ($4.3 billion) as the first LIFO layer. Assume that its LIFO inventory on January
30, 2000 was $5.3 billion instead of the FIFO value of $5.5 billion.

Required

1. Compute Home Depot's cost of merchandise sold and operating income for the year
   ended January 30, 2000, assuming that the switch to LIFO had been made at the beginning
   of fiscal 2000.

2. How would the switch to LIFO have affected Home Depot's fiscal 2000 income taxes,
   assuming a 40% tax rate?

3. Were the prices Home Depot paid for merchandise inventory rising or falling during fiscal
   2000? How do you know?

19-38 Effect of LIFO

General Mills, producer of Wheaties, Cheerios, Gold Medal Flour, and many other food products,
reported fiscal 2000 operating income of $947.0 million. Part of footnote 1 to the financial state-
ments stated

> *Certain domestic inventories are valued using the LIFO method, while other
> inventories are generally valued using the FIFO method.*

Inventories are valued at the lower of cost or market as follows (in millions):

	May 30, 1999	May 28, 2000
Inventories	$426.7	$510.5

If LIFO inventories were valued at the lower of FIFO cost or market, the inventories would have
been $32.4 million and $34.0 million higher than those reported for fiscal 2000 and 1999, respectively.

Required

Suppose the FIFO method had always been used for all inventories. Calculate General Mills's operating income for fiscal 2000. By how much would the cumulative operating income for all years through 2000 differ from that reported? Would it be more or less than that reported?

19-39 LIFO Liquidation

Tesoro Petroleum Corporation is the second-largest independent refiner and marketer in the western United States, with refineries in Washington State, Hawaii, and Alaska. In 1999 Tesoro had pretax operating income of $51.2 million. A footnote to the company's 1999 financial statements included the following:

> *During 1999, certain inventory quantities were reduced, resulting in a liquidation of applicable LIFO inventory quantities carried at lower costs prevailing in previous years. This LIFO liquidation resulted in a decrease in cost of sales of $8.4 million.*

Required

1. Compute the pretax operating income that Tesoro would have reported if there had been no LIFO liquidation. What percentage increase in net income was caused by the LIFO liquidation in 1999?

2. Suppose the income tax rate was 40%. What was the effect of the LIFO liquidations on Tesoro's income taxes for 1999?

3. How could Tesoro have avoided the extra taxes?

19-40 Lower of Cost or Market

Polaroid Corporation's 1999 annual report stated, "Inventories are valued on a first-in, first-out basis at the lower of cost or market value. Market value is determined by replacement cost or net realizable value." The total value of Polaroid's inventories at December 31, 1999, was $396 million.

Assume that severe price competition in 2000 necessitated a write-down on December 31 for a class of camera inventories bearing a standard cost of $10 million. The appropriate valuation at market was deemed to be $8 million.

Suppose the product line had been terminated in early 2001 and the remaining inventory had been sold for $8 million.

Required

1. Assume that sales of this line of camera for 2000 were $21 million and cost of goods sold was $16 million. Prepare a statement of gross margin for 2000 and 2001. Show the results under a strict FIFO cost method in the first two columns and under a lower-of-FIFO-cost-or-market method in the next two columns.

2. Assume that Polaroid did not discontinue the product line. Instead, a new marketing campaign spurred market demand. Replacement cost of the cameras in the December 31 inventory was $9 million on January 31, 2001. What inventory valuation would be appropriate if the inventory of December 31, 2000, was still held on January 31, 2001?

19-41 Effects of General versus Specific Price Changes

The following data are from the annual reports of Gannett Co. (owner of 125 newspapers), Zayre Corp. (operator of over 360 discount stores and over 700 specialty stores), and Goodyear Tire and Rubber Company, respectively (in millions):

	Gannett	Zayre	Goodyear
Increase in specific prices of assets held during the year	$45.8	$ 24.9	$ (4.7)
Less: effect of increase in general price level	37.5	55.5	252.0
Excess of increase in specific prices over increase in the general price level	$ 8.3	$(30.6)	$(256.7)

Required

Compare and contrast the relationship between changes in the general price level and changes in the price of specific assets of each of the three companies.

COLLABORATIVE LEARNING EXERCISE

19-42 Understanding Inventory Methods

Form groups of three students each. (If there are more than three students in a group, extras can be paired up.) Each student should select or be assigned one of the following inventory methods:

1. Specific identification
2. LIFO
3. FIFO

Consider the following information from the fiscal 2000 annual report of Levitz Corporation, one of the largest specialty retailers of furniture in the United States. Levitz uses the LIFO method to account for its inventories.

For the Year Ended March 31, 2000:	
Sales	$535,052
Cost of goods sold (using LIFO)	303,016
Other operating expenses	$254,656
Operating income (loss)	$ (22,620)
Purchases of inventory	$299,077
At March 31, 2000:	
Inventories @ LIFO	$ 80,293
Inventories @ FIFO	90,393
At March 31, 1999:	
Inventories @ LIFO	$ 84,232
Inventories @ FIFO	93,032

Assume that in fiscal 2001, Levitz had exactly the same physical sales as in fiscal 2000, but prices were 5% higher. Thus, 2001 sales were 1.05 × $535,052 = $561,805. Assume that other operating expenses in 2001 were exactly the same as in 2000. Further assume that the physical level of inventories at the end of fiscal 2001 was the same as at the end of fiscal 2000, but because of a 5% price increase on April 1, 2000, purchases of inventories in fiscal 2001 were $318,167. [Note that if there had been no price increase, the purchases of inventories in 2001 would have been $303,016.]

Required

1. Compute both fiscal 2000 and fiscal 2001 operating income (loss) for Levitz using the inventory method to which you were assigned. Those using the LIFO and FIFO methods have all the information needed for the calculations. Those using specific identification must make some assumptions, and their operating income (loss) number will depend on the assumptions made.
2. Explain to the other members of the group how you computed the operating income (loss), including an explanation of how you chose the assumptions you made.

INTERNET EXERCISE

19-43 Financial Reporting at Deckers Outdoor Corporation

Go to http://www.deckers.com/finance.html to locate the home page for Deckers Outdoor Corporation. Deckers Outdoor Corporation is the exclusive licensee for the manufacture of Teva footwear. Click on the latest 10K filing to find financial report data. The Deckers Website sends you to SEC's Edgar files, where you should use the name "Deckers Outdoor Corp." to find the 10K.

www.prenhall.com/horngren

Answer the following questions about Deckers:

Required

1. Under Part 1 "General," what percentage of revenues does Teva represent? Have revenues related to Teva products increased or decreased over the past few years?
2. Scroll through several pages to locate "Inventory Risk." What does Deckers say about its inventory policy?
3. Read the Summary of Significant Accounting Policies section of the Notes to Consolidated Financial Statements. How are inventories valued and accounted for? Why do you think the company uses this particular costing method?
5. Locate the Selected Financial Data. How much gross profit is reported for the most recent year? Has this amount increased or decreased compared to the previous year? What explanation does management give for the changes? (Hint: look in the Management's Discussion and Analysis section.)

Go to the "Depreciation Methods and Inventory Cost Flow Assumptions" episode on the *Mastering Accounting* CD-ROM for an interactive, video-enhanced exercise on the different methods for depreciation and inventory.

RECOMMENDED READINGS

The following readings will aid readers who want to pursue some topics in more depth than is possible in this book. There is a hazard in compiling a group of recommended readings. Inevitably, some worthwhile books or periodicals are omitted. Moreover, such a list cannot include books published subsequent to the compilation date. The list is not comprehensive, but it suggests many excellent readings.

PERIODICALS

PROFESSIONAL JOURNALS

The following professional journals are typically available in university libraries and include articles on the application of management accounting:

- *Accounting Horizons.* Published by the American Accounting Association; stresses current practice-oriented articles in all areas of accounting.

- *CMA Management.* Published by CMA Canada; includes much practice-oriented research in management accounting.

- *Financial Executive.* Published by the Financial Executives Institute; emphasizes general policy issues for accounting and finance executives.

- *GAO Journal.* Covers managerial accounting issues of interest to the General Accounting Office of the U.S. government.

- *Harvard Business Review.* Published by Harvard Business School; directed to general managers, but contains excellent articles on applications of management accounting.

- *Journal of Accountancy.* Published by the American Institute of CPAs; emphasizes financial accounting and is directed at the practicing CPA.

- *Journal of Strategic Performance Measurement.* Covers issues related to performance measurement.

- *Management Accounting Quarterly.* Published by the Institute of Management Accountants; practical articles with an academic bent.

- *Strategic Finance.* Published by the Institute of Management Accountants; many articles on actual applications by individual organizations.

- *Business Week, Forbes, Fortune, The Economist, The Wall Street Journal.* Popular publications that cover a variety of business and economics topics; often their articles relate to management accounting.

ACADEMIC JOURNALS

The academic journal that focuses most directly on current management and cost accounting research is the *Journal of Management Accounting Research,* published by the Management Accounting section of the American Accounting Association. *The Accounting Review,* the general research publication of the American Accounting Association, and *Journal of Accounting Research,* published at the University of Chicago, and *Contemporary Accounting Research,* published by the Canadian Academic Association, cover all accounting topics at a more theoretical level. *Accounting, Organizations and Society,* a British journal, publishes much research on behavioral aspects of management accounting. *The Journal of Accounting and Economics* covers economics-based accounting research.

Most of the topics in this text are covered in more detail in the many books entitled *Cost Accounting including Cost Accounting: A Managerial Emphasis* by C. T. Horngren, G. Foster, and Srikant Datar (Prentice Hall, 2000). You can find more advanced coverage in *Advanced Management Accounting,* 3rd ed. by R. S. Kaplan and Anthony A. Atkinson (Prentice Hall, 1998).

The Financial Executives Institute, 10 Madison Avenue, P.O. Box 1938, Morristown, NJ 07960, and the Institute of Management Accounting, 10 Paragon Drive, P.O. Box 433, Montvale, NJ 07645-0433, have long lists of accounting research publications.

HANDBOOKS, GENERAL TEXTS, AND CASE BOOKS

The books in this list have wide application to management accounting issues. The handbooks are basic references. The textbooks are designed for classroom use but may be useful for self-study. The case books present applications from real companies.

- Belkaoui, A., *Handbook of Cost Accounting.* Quorum Books, 1991.

- Bierman, H., Jr., C. Bonini, and W. Hausman, *Quantitative Analysis for Management,* 9th ed. Homewood, IL: Richard D. Irwin, 1997.

- Bierman, H., Jr., and S. Smidt, *The Capital Budgeting Decision,* 8th ed. New York: Macmillan, 1992. Expands the capital budgeting discussion in Chapter 11.

- Brinker, B. ed. *Guide to Cost Management.* New York: John Wiley & Sons, 2000.

- Lukka, K., and T. Groot (eds.), *Cases in Management Accounting: Practices in European Companies.* London: Financial Times Management, 2000.

- Manning, G., *Financial Investigation and Forensic Accounting.* Boca Raton, FL: CRC Press, 1999.

- Pryor, T., et al., *Activity Dictionary: A Comprehensive Reference Tool for ABM and ABC,* ICMS, Inc., 1992.

- Rotch, W., B. Allen, and R. Brownlee, *Cases in Management Accounting and Control Systems* 3rd ed., Upper Saddle River, NJ: Prentice Hall, 1995.

- Shank, J., *Cases in Cost Management: A Strategic Emphasis,* 2nd Ed. Cincinnati, South-Western, 2000.

STRATEGIC NATURE OF MANAGEMENT ACCOUNTING

Management accountants realize that cost and performance information is most useful to organizations when it helps define strategic alternatives and helps in the management of resources to achieve strategic objectives. The books in this list, though not necessarily accounting books, provide valuable foundation to the interaction of strategy and accounting information.

- Ansari, S., and J. Bell, *Target Costing: The Next Frontier in Strategic Cost Management,* Chicago: Irwin, 1997.

- Ehrbar, A., *EVA: The Real Key to Creating Wealth,* New York: Wiley, 1998.

- Hronec, S., *Vital Signs.* New York: Amacom, 1993.

- Porter, M., *The Michael Porter Trilogy.* New York: Free Press, 1998.

- Rappaport, A., *Creating Shareholder Value: A Guide for Manager's and Investors.* New York: Free Press, 1997.

- Small, P., *The Ultimate Game of Strategy: Establishing a Personal Niche in the World of e-Business*, Upper Saddle River, N.J.: Prentice Hall, 2001.
- Stewart, G., *The Quest for Value,* Harper Business, 1999.

MODERN MANUFACTURING

The following books provide background on the nature of modern manufacturing.

- Chase, R., and N. Aquilano, *Production and Operation Management.* Homewood, IL: Irwin, 1997.
- *Heizer, J. and B. Render, Principles of Operations Management and Interactive CD,* Fourth Edition, Upper Saddle River, N.J.: Prentice Hall, 2001.
- Schonberger, R., *World Class Manufacturing: The Next Decade.* New York, Free Press, 1996.
- Teece, D., *Competitive Challenge.* Harper Business, 1987.
- Zuboff, S., *In the Age of the Smart Machine.* New York: Basic Books, 1989.

MANAGEMENT ACCOUNTING IN MODERN MANUFACTURING SETTINGS

These books present responses of management accountants and others to changes in manufacturing methods and practices.

- Atkinson, A., R. Banker, R. Kaplan, and S. Young, *Management Accounting,* 2nd ed., Upper Saddle River, NJ: Prentice Hall, 1997.
- Bennett, R., J. Hendricks, D. Keys, and E. Rudnicki, *Cost Accounting for Factory Automation.* Montvale, NJ: National Association of Accountants, 1987.
- Cooper, R. and R. Kaplan, *Design of Cost Management Systems,* Second Edition, Upper Saddle River, N.J.: Prentice Hall, 1999.
- Goldratt, E., and J. Cox, *The Goal.* Croton-On-Hudson, NY: North River Press, Inc., 1992. A novel illustrating the new manufacturing environment.
- Goldratt, E., *Critical Chain.* Croton-On-Hudson, NY: North River Press, Inc., 1997.
- Kaplan R. and R. Cooper, *Cost & Effect,* Boston: Harvard Business School Press, 1998.
- Kaplan, R., ed., *Measures for Manufacturing Excellence,* Boston, MA: Harvard Business School Press, 1990.
- Player, S. and R. Lacerda, *Arthur Andersen's Global Lessons in Activity-Based Management,* New York, Wiley, 1999.

MANAGEMENT CONTROL SYSTEMS

The topics of Chapters 7 to 10 can be explored further in several books, including:

- Anthony, R. N., and V. Govindarajan, *Management Control Systems,* 10th Irwin/McGraw-Hill, 2001.
- Arrow, K. J., *The Limits of Organization.* New York: Norton, 1974. A readable classic by the Nobel laureate.
- Brimson, J. and J. Antos, *Driving Value Using Activity-Based Budgeting,* Wiley, 1999.

- Emmanuel, C., K. Merchant, and D. Otley, *Accounting for Management Control.* Chapman & Hall, 1990.

- Kaplan, R., and D. Norton, *The Balanced Scorecard.* Boston: Harvard Business School Press, 1996.

- Maciariello, J. A. and C. Kirby, *Management Control Systems: Using Adaptive Systems to Attain Control,* Upper Saddle River, NJ: Prentice Hall, 1994.

- Merchant, K., *Modern Management Control Systems:* Text and Cases, Upper Saddle River, N.J.: Prentice Hall, 1998.

- Simons, R., *Performance Measurement and Control Systems for Implementing Strategy,* Upper Saddle River, N.J.: Prentice Hall, 2000.

- Solomons, D., *Divisional Performance: Measurement and Control.* New York: Markus Wiener, 1983. A reprint of a 1965 classic that is still relevant.

MANAGEMENT ACCOUNTING IN NONPROFIT ORGANIZATIONS

Many books discuss management accounting in nonprofit organizations, especially in health care. Four examples are

- Anthony, R. N., and D. W. Young, *Management Control in Nonprofit Organizations,* 6th ed. Homewood, IL: Irwin, 1998.

- Brimson, J., and J. Antos, *Activity Based Management for Service Industries, Government Entities, and Non-Profit Organizations.* New York: Wiley, 1998.

- Herzlinger, R. and D. Nitterhouse, *Financial Accounting and Managerial Control for Nonprofit Organizations.* Cincinnati, OH: Southwestern Publishing Co., 1994.

- Neumann, B., and K. Boles, *Management Accounting for Healthcare Organizations,* 5th Ed. Precept Press, 1998.

BOOKS IN FINANCIAL ACCOUNTING

This book's companion volume, *Introduction to Financial Accounting,* provides an expansion of the financial accounting material (Chapters 16–19). A more detailed coverage of the topics can be found in books entitled *Intermediate Accounting* including that by D. Kieso, J. Weygandt, and T. Warfield (John Wiley, 2000).

Opinions of the Accounting Principles Board are available from the American Institute of CPAs, 1211 Avenue of the Americas, New York, NY 10036-8775. The institute also has a series of research studies on a variety of topics. The pronouncements of the Financial Accounting Standards Board are available from the board's offices, 401 Merritt 7, P.O. Box 5116, Norwalk, CT 06856-5116.

Financial accounting has such an extensive literature that it is impossible to provide a short list of books that adequately covers the field. However, we will mention a couple of books that cover a wide range of issues. For a perspective on the large firms practicing accounting, see two books by M. Stevens, *The Accounting Wars* (Macmillan, 1985) and *The Big Six* (Touchstone Books, 1992). The interaction of financial reporting and management's economic incentives is covered in text and readings in R. Ball and C. Smith, *The Economics of Accounting Policy Choice,* New York: McGraw-Hill, 1992. Application of this research to financial statement analysis is provided in C. Stickney, and P. Brown *Financial Statement Analysis,* 4th Ed. (Harcourt Brace, 1999).

ONLINE RESOURCES

The online resources are too extensive for a comprehensive list. The best way to access them may be to use a good search routine. However, we will list a few URLs that can help you get started:

- ABC Technologies: Information about activity-based costing at http://www.abctech.com/.

- AICPA's Center for Excellence in Financial Management: Information for CPAs in business and industry at http://www.aicpa.org/cefm/index.htm.

- BetterManagement.com: Includes materials on both activity-based costing and balanced scorecard at http://www.bettermanagement.com.

- CMA Canada: Many services including Strategic Management Accounting Practice Standards at http://www.cma-canada.org/cmabusiness.asp.

- Consortium for Advanced Manufacturing International (CAM-I): Online library at http://www.cam-i.org/Web_store/web_store.cgi?page=management.html.

- Economic Profit Frontiers: Additional information about economic value added at http://www.epfrontiers.com.

- Hyperion Solutions: Software for both activity-based management and the balanced scorecard at http://www.hyperion.com/.

- Institute of Management Accountants: A variety of services including index of research publications at http://www.imanet.org/.

- Metrus Group: A variation of the balance scorecard at http://www.metrus.com/spg.shtml.

- Stern Stewart: Information about economic value added by the firm that developed the technique at http://www.eva.com/.

B FUNDAMENTALS OF COMPOUND INTEREST AND THE USE OF PRESENT-VALUE TABLES

NATURE OF INTEREST

Interest is the cost of using money. It is the rental charge for cash, just as rental charges are often made for the use of automobiles or boats.

Interest does not always entail an outlay of cash. The concept of interest applies to ownership funds as well as to borrowed funds. The reason why interest must be considered on *all* funds in use, regardless of their source, is that the selection of one alternative necessarily commits funds that could otherwise be invested in some other opportunity. The measure of the interest in such cases is the return foregone by rejecting the alternative use. For instance, a wholly owned home or business asset is not cost free. The funds so invested could alternatively be invested in government bonds or in some other venture. The measure of this opportunity cost depends on what alternative incomes are available.

Newspapers often contain advertisements of financial institutions citing interest rates that are "compounded." This appendix explains compound interest, including the use of present-value tables.

Simple interest is calculated by multiplying an interest rate by an unchanging principal amount. In contrast, *compound interest* is calculated by multiplying an interest rate by a principal amount that is increased each interest period by the previously accumulated (unpaid) interest. The accumulated interest is added to the principal to become the principal for the new period. For example, suppose you deposited $10,000 in a financial institution that promised to pay 10% interest per annum. You then let the amount accumulate for three years before withdrawing the full balance of the deposit. The *simple-interest* deposit would accumulate to $13,000 at the end of three years:

	Principal	Simple Interest	Balance, End of Year
Year 1	$10,000	$10,000 × 0.10 = $1,000	$11,000
Year 2	10,000	10,000 × 0.10 = 1,000	12,000
Year 3	10,000	10,000 × 0.10 = 1,000	13,000

Compound interest provides interest on interest. That is, the principal changes from period to period. The deposit would accumulate to $10,000 \times (1.10)^3 = \$10,000 \times 1.331 = \$13,310$:

	Principal	Compound Interest	Balance, End of Year
Year 1	$10,000	$10,000 × 0.10 = $1,000	$11,000
Year 2	11,000	11,000 × 0.10 = 1,100	12,100
Year 3	12,100	12,100 × 0.10 = 1,210	13,310

The "force" of compound interest can be staggering. For example, the same deposit would accumulate as follows:

	At End of		
	10 Years	20 Years	40 Years
Simple interest			
$10,000 + 10 ($1,000) =	$20,000		
10,000 + 20 ($1,000) =		$30,000	
10,000 + 40 ($1,000) =			$ 50,000
Compound interest			
$10,000 × $(1.10)^{10}$ = $10,000 × 2.5937 =	$25,937		
$10,000 × $(1.10)^{20}$ = $10,000 × 6.7275 =		$67,275	
$10,000 × $(1.10)^{40}$ = $10,000 × 45.2593 =			$452,593

Hand calculations of compound interest quickly become burdensome. Therefore compound interest tables have been constructed to ease computations. (Indeed, many hand-held calculators contain programs that provide speedy answers.) Hundreds of tables are available, but we will use only the two most useful for capital budgeting.[1]

TABLE 1: PRESENT VALUE OF $1

How shall we express a future cash inflow or outflow in terms of its equivalent today (at time zero)? Table 1 provides factors that give the present value of a single, lump-sum cash flow to be received or paid at the end of a future period.[2]

Suppose you invest $1.00 today. It will grow to $1.06 in one year at six percent interest; that is, $1 × 1.06 = $1.06. At the end of the second year its value is ($1 × 1.06) × 1.06 = $1 × $(1.06)^2$ = $1.124, and at the end of the third year it is $1 × $(1.06)^3$ = 1.191. In general, $1.00 grows to $(1 + i)^n$ in n years at i percent interest.

To determine *the present value,* you reverse this accumulation process. If $1.00 is to be received in one year, it is worth $1 ÷ 1.06 = $0.9434 today at an interest rate of 6%. Suppose you invest $0.9434 today. In one year you will have $0.9434 × 1.06 = $1.00. Thus $0.9434 is the *present value* of $1.00 a year hence at 6%. If the dollar will be received in two years, its present value is $1.00 ÷ $(1.06)^2$ = $0.8900. The general formula for the present value (PV) of an amount S to be received or paid in n periods at an interest rate of i% per period is

$$PV = \frac{S}{(1 + i)^n}$$

Table 1 on page B7 gives factors for the present value of $1.00 at various interest rates over several different periods. Present values are also called *discounted* values, and the process of finding the present value is *discounting.* You can think of this as discounting

---

[1] *For additional tables, see R. Vichas,* Handbook of Financial Mathematics, Formulas and Tables *(Upper Saddle River, NJ: Prentice Hall, 1979).*

[2] *The factors are rounded to four decimal places. The examples in this text use these rounded factors. If you use tables with different rounding, or if you use a calculator or personal computer, your answers may differ from those given because of a small rounding error.*

(decreasing) the value of a future cash inflow or outflow. Why is the value discounted? Because the cash is to be received or paid in the future, not today.

Assume that a prominent city is issuing a 3-year non-interest-bearing note payable that promises to pay a lump sum of $1,000 exactly three years from now. You desire a rate of return of exactly 6%, compounded annually. How much would you be willing to pay now for the 3-year note? The situation is sketched as follows:

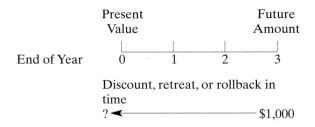

The factor in the period 3 row and 6% column of Table 1 is 0.8396. The present value of the $1,000 payment is $1,000 × 0.8396 = $839.60. You would be willing to pay $839.60 for the $1,000 to be received in three years.

Suppose interest is compounded semiannually rather than annually. How much would you be willing to pay? The three years become six interest payment periods. The rate per period is half the annual rate, or 6% ÷ 2 = 3%. The factor in the period 6 row and 3% column of Table 1 is 0.8375. You would be willing to pay $1,000 × 0.8375 or only $837.50 rather than $839.60.

As a further check on your understanding, review the earlier example of compound interest. Suppose the financial institution promised to pay $13,310 at the end of three years. How much would you be willing to deposit at time zero if you desired a 10% rate of return compounded annually? Using Table 1, the period 3 row and the 10% column show a factor of 0.7513. Multiply this factor by the future amount:

$$PV = 0.7513 \times \$13,310 = \$10,000$$

A diagram of this computation follows:

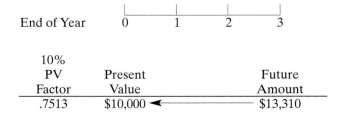

Pause for a moment. Use Table 1 to obtain the present values of

1. $1,700, at 20%, at the end of 20 years
2. $8,300, at 10%, at the end of 12 years
3. $8,000, at 4%, at the end of 4 years

Answers:

1. $1,700 (0.0261) = $44.37
2. $8,300 (0.3186) = $2,644.38
3. $8,000 (0.8548) = $6,838.40

An ordinary annuity is a series of equal cash flows to take place at the end of successive periods of equal length. Its present value is denoted PV_A. Assume that you buy a note from a municipality that promises to pay $1,000 at the end of *each* of three years. How much should you be willing to pay if you desire a rate of return of 6%, compounded annually?

You could solve this problem using Table 1. First, find the present value of each payment, and then add the present values as in Exhibit B-1. You would be willing to pay $943.40 for the first payment, $890.00 for the second, and $839.60 for the third, a total of $2,673.00.

Since each cash payment is $1,000 with equal 1-year periods between them, the note is an ordinary annuity. Table 2 provides a shortcut method. The present value in Exhibit B-1 can be expressed as

$$PV_A = \$1,000 \times \frac{1}{1.06} + \$1,000 \times \frac{1}{(1.06)^2} + \$1,000 \times \frac{1}{(1.06)^3}$$

$$= \$1,000 \left[\frac{1}{1.06} + \frac{1}{(1.06)^2} + \frac{1}{(1.06)^3} \right]$$

The three terms in brackets are the first three numbers from the 6% column of Table 1, and their sum is in the third row of the 6% column of Table 2: .9434 + .8900 + .8396 = 2.6730. Instead of calculating three present values and adding them, you can simply multiply the PV factor from Table 2 by the cash payment: 2.6730 × $1,000 = $2,673.

This shortcut is especially valuable if the cash payments or receipts extend over many periods. Consider an annual cash payment of $1,000 for 20 years at 6%. The present value, calculated from Table 2, is $1,000 × 11.4699 = $11,469.90. To use Table 1 for this calculation, you would perform 20 multiplications and then add the twenty products.

The factors in Table 2 can be calculated using the following general formula:

$$PV_A = \frac{1}{i} \left[1 - \frac{1}{(1 + i)^n} \right]$$

Applied to our illustration:

$$PV_A = \frac{1}{.06} \left[1 - \frac{1}{(1.06)^3} \right] = \frac{1}{.06} (1 - .8396) = \frac{.1604}{.06} = 2.6730$$

Use Table 2 to obtain the present values of the following ordinary annuities:

1. $1,600 at 20% for 20 years
2. $8,300 at 10% for 12 years
3. $8,000 at 4% for 4 years

Exhibt B-1

Payment	End of Year Table One Factor	0 Present Value	1	2	3
1	$\frac{1}{1.06} = .9434$	$ 943.40	$1,000		
2	$\frac{1}{(1.06)^2} = .8900$	890.00		1,000	
3	$\frac{1}{(1.06)^3} = .8396$	839.60			$1,000
Total		$2,673.00			

Answers:

1. $1,600 (4.8696) = $7,791.36
2. $8,300 (6.8137) = $56,553.71
3. $8,000 (3.6299) = $29,039.20

In particular, note that the higher interest rate, the lower the present value.

Table I
Present Value of $1

$$PV = \frac{1}{(1+i)^n}$$

Periods	3%	4%	5%	6%	7%	8%	10%	12%	14%	16%	18%	20%	22%	24%	25%	26%	28%	30%	40%
1	.9709	.9615	.9524	.9434	.9346	.9259	.9091	.8929	.8772	.8621	.8475	.8333	.8197	.8065	.8000	.7937	.7813	.7692	.7143
2	.9426	.9246	.9070	.8900	.8734	.8573	.8264	.7972	.7695	.7432	.7182	.6944	.6719	.6504	.6400	.6299	.6104	.5917	.5102
3	.9151	.8890	.8638	.8396	.8163	.7938	.7513	.7118	.6750	.6407	.6086	.5787	.5507	.5245	.5120	.4999	.4768	.4552	.3644
4	.8885	.8548	.8227	.7921	.7629	.7350	.6830	.6355	.5921	.5523	.5158	.4823	.4514	.4230	.4096	.3968	.3725	.3501	.2603
5	.8626	.8219	.7835	.7473	.7130	.6806	.6209	.5674	.5194	.4761	.4371	.4019	.3700	.3411	.3277	.3149	.2910	.2693	.1859
6	.8375	.7903	.7462	.7050	.6663	.6302	.5645	.5066	.4556	.4104	.3704	.3349	.3033	.2751	.2621	.2499	.2274	.2072	.1328
7	.8131	.7599	.7107	.6651	.6227	.5835	.5132	.4523	.3996	.3538	.3139	.2791	.2486	.2218	.2097	.1983	.1776	.1594	.0949
8	.7894	.7307	.6768	.6274	.5820	.5403	.4665	.4039	.3506	.3050	.2660	.2326	.2038	.1789	.1678	.1574	.1388	.1226	.0678
9	.7664	.7026	.6446	.5919	.5439	.5002	.4241	.3606	.3075	.2630	.2255	.1938	.1670	.1443	.1342	.1249	.1084	.0943	.0484
10	.7441	.6756	.6139	.5584	.5083	.4632	.3855	.3220	.2697	.2267	.1911	.1615	.1369	.1164	.1074	.0992	.0847	.0725	.0346
11	.7224	.6496	.5847	.5268	.4751	.4289	.3505	.2875	.2366	.1954	.1619	.1346	.1122	.0938	.0859	.0787	.0662	.0558	.0247
12	.7014	.6246	.5568	.4970	.4440	.3971	.3186	.2567	.2076	.1685	.1372	.1122	.0920	.0757	.0687	.0625	.0517	.0429	.0176
13	.6810	.6006	.5303	.4688	.4150	.3677	.2897	.2292	.1821	.1452	.1163	.0935	.0754	.0610	.0550	.0496	.0404	.0330	.0126
14	.6611	.5775	.5051	.4423	.3878	.3405	.2633	.2046	.1597	.1252	.0985	.0779	.0618	.0492	.0440	.0393	.0316	.0254	.0090
15	.6419	.5553	.4810	.4173	.3624	.3152	.2394	.1827	.1401	.1079	.0835	.0649	.0507	.0397	.0352	.0312	.0247	.0195	.0064
16	.6232	.5339	.4581	.3936	.3387	.2919	.2176	.1631	.1229	.0930	.0708	.0541	.0415	.0320	.0281	.0248	.0193	.0150	.0046
17	.6050	.5134	.4363	.3714	.3166	.2703	.1978	.1456	.1078	.0802	.0600	.0451	.0340	.0258	.0225	.0197	.0150	.0116	.0033
18	.5874	.4936	.4155	.3503	.2959	.2502	.1799	.1300	.0946	.0691	.0508	.0376	.0279	.0208	.0180	.0156	.0118	.0089	.0023
19	.5703	.4746	.3957	.3305	.2765	.2317	.1635	.1161	.0829	.0596	.0431	.0313	.0229	.0168	.0144	.0124	.0092	.0068	.0017
20	.5537	.4564	.3769	.3118	.2584	.2145	.1486	.1037	.0728	.0514	.0365	.0261	.0187	.0135	.0115	.0098	.0072	.0053	.0012
21	.5375	.4388	.3589	.2942	.2415	.1987	.1351	.0926	.0638	.0443	.0309	.0217	.0154	.0109	.0092	.0078	.0056	.0040	.0009
22	.5219	.4220	.3418	.2775	.2257	.1839	.1228	.0826	.0560	.0382	.0262	.0181	.0126	.0088	.0074	.0062	.0044	.0031	.0006
23	.5067	.4057	.3256	.2618	.2109	.1703	.1117	.0738	.0491	.0329	.0222	.0151	.0103	.0071	.0059	.0049	.0034	.0024	.0004
24	.4919	.3901	.3101	.2470	.1971	.1577	.1015	.0659	.0431	.0284	.0188	.0126	.0085	.0057	.0047	.0039	.0027	.0018	.0003
25	.4776	.3751	.2953	.2330	.1842	.1460	.0923	.0588	.0378	.0245	.0160	.0105	.0069	.0046	.0038	.0031	.0021	.0014	.0002
26	.4637	.3607	.2812	.2198	.1722	.1352	.0839	.0525	.0331	.0211	.0135	.0087	.0057	.0037	.0030	.0025	.0016	.0011	.0002
27	.4502	.3468	.2678	.2074	.1609	.1252	.0763	.0469	.0291	.0182	.0115	.0073	.0047	.0030	.0024	.0019	.0013	.0008	.0001
28	.4371	.3335	.2551	.1956	.1504	.1159	.0693	.0419	.0255	.0157	.0097	.0061	.0038	.0024	.0019	.0015	.0010	.0006	.0001
29	.4243	.3207	.2429	.1846	.1406	.1073	.0630	.0374	.0224	.0135	.0082	.0051	.0031	.0020	.0015	.0012	.0008	.0005	.0001
30	.4120	.3083	.2314	.1741	.1314	.0994	.0573	.0334	.0196	.0116	.0070	.0042	.0026	.0016	.0012	.0010	.0006	.0004	.0000
40	.3066	.2083	.1420	.0972	.0668	.0460	.0221	.0107	.0053	.0026	.0013	.0007	.0004	.0002	.0001	.0001	.0001	.0000	.0000

Table 2
Present Value of Ordinary Annuity of $1

$$PV_A = \frac{1}{i}\left[1 - \frac{1}{(1+i)^n}\right]$$

Periods	3%	4%	5%	6%	7%	8%	10%	12%	14%	16%	18%	20%	22%	24%	25%	26%	28%	30%	40%
1	.9709	.9615	.9524	.9434	.9346	.9259	.9091	.8929	.8772	.8621	.8475	.8333	.8197	.8065	.8000	.7937	.7813	.7692	.7143
2	1.9135	1.8861	1.8594	1.8334	1.8080	1.7833	1.7355	1.6901	1.6467	1.6052	1.5656	1.5278	1.4915	1.4568	1.4400	1.4235	1.3916	1.3609	1.2245
3	2.8286	2.7751	2.7232	2.6730	2.6243	2.5771	2.4869	2.4018	2.3216	2.2459	2.1743	2.1065	2.0422	1.9813	1.9520	1.9234	1.8684	1.8161	1.5889
4	3.7171	3.6299	3.5460	3.4651	3.3872	3.3121	3.1699	3.0373	2.9137	2.7982	2.6901	2.5887	2.4936	2.4043	2.3616	2.3202	2.2410	2.1662	1.8492
5	4.5797	4.4518	4.3295	4.2124	4.1002	3.9927	3.7908	3.6048	3.4331	3.2743	3.1272	2.9906	2.8636	2.7454	2.6893	2.6351	2.5320	2.4356	2.0352
6	5.4172	5.2421	5.0757	4.9173	4.7665	4.6229	4.3553	4.1114	3.8887	3.6847	3.4976	3.3255	3.1669	3.0205	2.9514	2.8850	2.7594	2.6427	2.1680
7	6.2303	6.0021	5.7864	5.5824	5.3893	5.2064	4.8684	4.5638	4.2883	4.0386	3.8115	3.6046	3.4155	3.2423	3.1611	3.0833	2.9370	2.8021	2.2628
8	7.0197	6.7327	6.4632	6.2098	5.9713	5.7466	5.3349	4.9676	4.6389	4.3436	4.0776	3.8372	3.6193	3.4212	3.3289	3.2407	3.0758	2.9247	2.3306
9	7.7861	7.4353	7.1078	6.8017	6.5152	6.2469	5.7590	5.3282	4.9464	4.6065	4.3030	4.0310	3.7863	3.5655	3.4631	3.3657	3.1842	3.0190	2.3790
10	8.5302	8.1109	7.7217	7.3601	7.0236	6.7101	6.1446	5.6502	5.2161	4.8332	4.4941	4.1925	3.9232	3.6819	3.5705	3.4648	3.2689	3.0915	2.4136
11	9.2526	8.7605	8.3064	7.8869	7.4987	7.1390	6.4951	5.9377	5.4527	5.0286	4.6560	4.3271	4.0354	3.7757	3.6564	3.5435	3.3351	3.1473	2.4383
12	9.9540	9.3851	8.8633	8.3838	7.9427	7.5361	6.8137	6.1944	5.6603	5.1971	4.7932	4.4392	4.1274	3.8514	3.7251	3.6059	3.3868	3.1903	2.4559
13	10.6350	9.9856	9.3936	8.8527	8.3577	7.9038	7.1034	6.4235	5.8424	5.3423	4.9095	4.5327	4.2028	3.9124	3.7801	3.6555	3.4272	3.2233	2.4685
14	11.2961	10.5631	9.8986	9.2950	8.7455	8.2442	7.3667	6.6282	6.0021	5.4675	5.0081	4.6106	4.2646	3.9616	3.8241	3.6949	3.4587	3.2487	2.4775
15	11.9379	11.1184	10.3797	9.7122	9.1079	8.5595	7.6061	6.8109	6.1422	5.5755	5.0916	4.6755	4.3152	4.0013	3.8593	3.7261	3.4834	3.2682	2.4839
16	12.5611	11.6523	10.8378	10.1059	9.4466	8.8514	7.8237	6.9740	6.2651	5.6685	5.1624	4.7296	4.3567	4.0333	3.8874	3.7509	3.5026	3.2832	2.4885
17	13.1661	12.1657	11.2741	10.4773	9.7632	9.1216	8.0216	7.1196	6.3729	5.7487	5.2223	4.7746	4.3908	4.0591	3.9099	3.7705	3.5177	3.2948	2.4918
18	13.7535	12.6593	11.6896	10.8276	10.0591	9.3719	8.2014	7.2497	6.4674	5.8178	5.2732	4.8122	4.4187	4.0799	3.9279	3.7861	3.5294	3.3037	2.4941
19	14.3238	13.1339	12.0853	11.1581	10.3356	9.6036	8.3649	7.3658	6.5504	5.8775	5.3162	4.8435	4.4415	4.0967	3.9424	3.7985	3.5386	3.3105	2.4958
20	14.8775	13.5903	12.4622	11.4699	10.5940	9.8181	8.5136	7.4694	6.6231	5.9288	5.3527	4.8696	4.4603	4.1103	3.9539	3.8083	3.5458	3.3158	2.4970
21	15.4150	14.0292	12.8212	11.7641	10.8355	10.0168	8.6487	7.5620	6.6870	5.9731	5.3837	4.8913	4.4756	4.1212	3.9631	3.8161	3.5514	3.3198	2.4979
22	15.9369	14.4511	13.1630	12.0416	11.0612	10.2007	8.7715	7.6446	6.7429	6.0113	5.4099	4.9094	4.4882	4.1300	3.9705	3.8223	3.5558	3.3230	2.4985
23	16.4436	14.8568	13.4886	12.3034	11.2722	10.3711	8.8832	7.7184	6.7921	6.0442	5.4321	4.9245	4.4985	4.1371	3.9764	3.8273	3.5592	3.3254	2.4989
24	16.9355	15.2470	13.7986	12.5504	11.4693	10.5288	8.9847	7.7843	6.8351	6.0726	5.4509	4.9371	4.5070	4.1428	3.9811	3.8312	3.5619	3.3272	2.4992
25	17.4131	15.6221	14.0939	12.7834	11.6536	10.6748	9.0770	7.8431	6.8729	6.0971	5.4669	4.9476	4.5139	4.1474	3.9849	3.8342	3.5640	3.3286	2.4994
26	17.8768	15.9828	14.3752	13.0032	11.8258	10.8100	9.1609	7.8957	6.9061	6.1182	5.4804	4.9563	4.5196	4.1511	3.9879	3.8367	3.5656	3.3297	2.4996
27	18.3270	16.3296	14.6430	13.2105	11.9867	10.9352	9.2372	7.9426	6.9352	6.1364	5.4919	4.9636	4.5243	4.1542	3.9903	3.8387	3.5669	3.3305	2.4997
28	18.7641	16.6631	14.8981	13.4062	12.1371	11.0511	9.3066	7.9844	6.9607	6.1520	5.5016	4.9697	4.5281	4.1566	3.9923	3.8402	3.5679	3.3312	2.4998
29	19.1885	16.9837	15.1411	13.5907	12.2777	11.1584	9.3696	8.0218	6.9830	6.1656	5.5098	4.9747	4.5312	4.1585	3.9938	3.8414	3.5687	3.3317	2.4999
30	19.6004	17.2920	15.3725	13.7648	12.4090	11.2578	9.4269	8.0552	7.0027	6.1772	5.5168	4.9789	4.5338	4.1601	3.9950	3.8424	3.5693	3.3321	2.4999
40	23.1148	19.7928	17.1591	15.0463	13.3317	11.9246	9.7791	8.2438	7.1050	6.2335	5.5482	4.9966	4.5439	4.1659	3.9995	3.8458	3.5712	3.3332	2.5000

GLOSSARY

absorption approach A costing approach that considers all factory overhead (both variable and fixed) to be product (inventoriable) costs that become an expense in the form of manufacturing cost of goods sold only as sales occur.

accelerated depreciation A pattern of depreciation that charges a larger proportion of an asset's cost to the earlier years and less to later years.

account analysis Selecting a plausible cost driver and classifying each account as a variable cost or as a fixed cost.

account Each item in a financial statement.

accounting rate-of-return (ARR) model A non-DCF capital-budgeting model expressed as the increase in expected average annual operating income divided by the initial required investment.

accounting system A formal mechanism for gathering, organizing, and communicating information about an organization's activities.

accounts payable Amounts owed to vendors for purchases on open accounts.

accounts receivable Amounts due from customers for sales on open account.

accrual basis A process of accounting that recognizes the impact of transactions on the financial statements in the time periods when revenues and expenses occur instead of when cash is received or disbursed.

accrue To accumulate a receivable or payable during a given period even though no explicit transaction occurs.

activity analysis The process of identifying appropriate cost drivers and their effects on the costs of making a product or providing a service.

activity-based costing (ABC) systems A system that first accumulates overhead costs for each of the activities of the area being costed, and then assigns the costs of activities to the products, services, or other cost objects that require that activity.

activity-based flexible budget A budget based on budgeted costs for each activity and related cost driver.

activity-based management (ABM) Using an activity-based costing system to improve the operations of an organization.

activity-level variances The differences between the master budget amounts and the amounts in the flexible budget.

adjustments Recording of implicit transactions, in contrast to the explicit transactions that trigger nearly all day-to-day routine entries.

agency theory A theory used to describe the formal choices of performance measures and rewards.

assets Economic resources that are expected to benefit future activities.

attention directing Reporting and interpreting information that helps managers to focus on operating problems, imperfections, inefficiencies, and opportunities.

audit An examination or in-depth inspection of financial statements and companies' records that is made in accordance with generally accepted auditing standards. It culminates with the accountant's testimony that management's financial statements are in conformity with generally accepted accounting principles.

available-for-sale securities Investments that the investor company has no intention to sell in the near future.

avoidable costs Costs that will not continue if an ongoing operation is changed or deleted.

B2B Electronic commerce from one business to another business.

B2C Electronic commerce from a business to a customer.

backflush costing An accounting system that applies costs to products only when the production is complete.

balance sheet (statement of financial position, statement of financial condition) A snapshot of the financial status of an organization at an instant of time.

balanced scorecard A performance measurement and reporting system that strikes a balance between financial and operating measures, links performance to rewards, and gives explicit recognition to the diversity of organizational goals.

behavioral implications The accounting system's effect on the behavior (decisions) of managers.

benchmarking The continuous process of measuring products, services, and activities against the best levels of performance.

benchmarks General rules of thumb specifying appropriate levels for financial ratios.

book value (net book value) The original cost of equipment less accumulated depreciation, which is the summation of depreciation charged to past periods.

break-even point The level of sales at which revenue equals expenses and net income is zero.

budget A quantitative expression of a plan of action, and an aid to coordinating and implementing the plan.

budgeted factory-overhead rate The budgeted total overhead for each cost pool divided by the budgeted cost-driver level.

by-product A product that, like a joint product, is not individually identifiable until manufacturing reaches a split-off point, but has relatively insignificant total sales value.

capacity costs The fixed costs of being able to achieve a desired level of production or to provide a desired level of service while maintaining product or service attributes, such as quality.

capital budget A budget that details the planned expenditures for facilities, equipment, new products, and other long-term investments.

capital budgeting The long-term planning for making and financing investments that affect financial results over more than just the next year.

capital turnover Revenue divided by invested capital.

cash basis A process of accounting where revenue and expense recognition would occur when cash is received and disbursed.

cash budget A statement of planned cash receipts and disbursements.

cash equivalents Short-term investments that can easily be converted into cash with little delay.

cash flow Usually refers to the net cash flow from operating activities.

cash flows from operating activities The first major section in the statement of cash flows.

cellular manufacturing A production system in which machines are organized in cells according to the specific requirements of a product family.

Certified Management Accountant (CMA) The management accountant's counterpart to the CPA.

Certified Public Accountant (CPA) In the United States, an accountant earns this designation by a combination of education, qualifying experience, and the passing of a two-day written national examination.

coefficient of determination (R^2) A measurement of how much of the fluctuation of a cost is explained by changes in the cost driver.

committed fixed costs Costs arising from the possession of facilities, equipment, and a basic organization: large, indivisible chunks of cost that the organization is obligated to incur or usually would not consider avoiding.

common costs Those costs of facilities and services that are shared by users.

common stock Stock that has no predetermined rate of dividends and is the last to obtain a share in the assets when the corporation is dissolved. It usually has voting power to elect the board of directors of the corporation.

common-size statements Financial statements expressed in component percentages.

component percentages Analysis and presentation of financial statements in percentage form to aid comparability, frequently used when companies differ in size.

computer-integrated manufacturing (CIM) systems Systems that use computer-aided design and computer-aided manufacturing, together with robots and computer-controlled machines.

conservatism convention Selecting the method of measurement that yields the gloomiest immediate results.

consolidated financial statements Financial statements that combine the financial statements of the parent company with those of various subsidiaries, as if they were a single entity.

constant dollars Nominal dollars that are restated in terms of current purchasing power.

continuity convention (going concern convention) The assumption that an organization will continue to exist and operate.

continuous budget (rolling budget) A common form of master budget that adds a month in the future as the month just ended is dropped.

contribution approach A method of internal (management accounting) reporting that emphasizes the distinction between variable and fixed costs for the purpose of better decision making.

contribution margin (marginal income) The sales price minus the variable cost per unit.

controllable cost Any cost that is influenced by a manager's decisions and actions.

controller (comptroller) The top accounting officer of an organization. The term *comptroller* is used primarily in government organizations.

conversion costs Direct labor costs plus factory overhead costs.

corporation A business organized as a separate legal entity and owned by its stockholders.

cost A sacrifice or giving up of resources for a particular purpose, frequently measured by the monetary units that must be paid for goods and services.

cost accounting systems The techniques used to determine the cost of a product, service, or other cost objective by collecting and classifying costs and assigning them to cost objects.

cost accounting That part of the accounting system that measures costs for the purposes of management decision making and financial reporting.

cost accumulation Collecting costs by some natural classification such as materials, or labor or activities performed.

cost allocation Tracing and reassigning costs to one or more cost objectives such as activities, departments, customers, or products.

cost-allocation base A cost driver when it is used for allocating costs.

cost application The allocation of total departmental costs to the revenue-producing products or services.

cost behavior How costs are related to and affected by the activities of an organization.

cost-benefit balance Weighing estimated costs against probable benefits, the primary consideration in choosing among accounting systems and methods.

cost-benefit criterion An approach that implicitly underlies the decisions about the design of accounting systems. As a system is changed, its potential benefits should exceed its additional costs.

cost center A responsibility center in which a manager is accountable for costs only.

cost driver Any output measure that causes costs (that is, causes the use of costly resources).

cost function An algebraic equation used by managers to describe the relationship between a cost and its cost driver(s).

cost-management system (CMS) Identifies how management's decisions affect costs, by first measuring the resources used in performing the organization's activities and then assessing the effects on costs of changes in those activities.

cost measurement Estimating or predicting costs as a function of appropriate cost drivers.

cost objective (cost object) Anything for which a separate measurement of costs is desired. Examples include departments, products, activities, and territories.

cost of capital What a firm must pay to acquire more capital, whether or not it actually has to acquire more capital to take on a project.

cost of goods sold The cost of the merchandise that is acquired or manufactured and resold.

cost of quality report A report that displays the financial impact of quality.

cost pool A group of individual costs that is allocated to cost objectives using a single cost driver.

cost prediction The application of cost measures to expected future activity levels to forecast future costs.

cost recovery A concept in which assets such as inventories, prepayments, and equipment are carried forward as assets because their costs are expected to be recovered in the form of cash inflows (or reduced cash outflows) in future periods.

cost-volume-profit (CVP) analysis The study of the effects of output volume on revenue (sales), expenses (costs), and net income (net profit).

credit An entry on the right side of an account.

critical process A series of related activities that directly affects the achievement of organizational goals.

cross-sectional comparisons Comparisons of a company's financial ratios with ratios of other companies or with industry averages for the same period.

current assets Cash and all other assets that are reasonably expected to be converted to cash or sold or consumed within one year or during the normal operating cycle, if longer than a year.

current cost The cost to replace an asset, as opposed to its historical cost.

current-cost method The measurement method that uses current costs and nominal dollars.

current liabilities An organization's debts that fall due within the coming year or within the normal operating cycle if longer than a year.

currently attainable standards Levels of performance that can be achieved by realistic levels of effort.

cycle time The time taken to complete a product or service, or any of the components of a product or service.

debentures Formal certificates of indebtedness that are accompanied by a promise to pay interest at a specified annual rate.

debit An entry on the left side of an account.

decentralization The delegation of freedom to make decisions. The lower in the organization that this freedom exists, the greater the decentralization.

decision making The purposeful choice from among a set of alternative courses of action designed to achieve some objective.

decision model Any method for making a choice, sometimes requiring elaborate quantitative procedures.

depreciation The periodic cost of equipment that is spread over (or charged to) the future periods in which the equipment is expected to be used.

differential approach A method for comparing alternatives that computes the differences in cash flows between alternatives and then converts these differences in cash flows to their present values.

differential cost (revenue) The difference in total cost (revenue) between two alternatives.

direct costs Costs that can be identified specifically and exclusively with a given cost objective in an economically feasible way.

direct-labor costs The wages of all labor that can be traced specifically and exclusively to the manufactured goods in an economically feasible way.

direct-material costs The acquisition costs of all materials that are physically identified as a part of the manufactured goods and that may be traced to the manufactured goods in an economically feasible way.

direct method A method for allocating service department costs that ignores other service departments when any given service department's costs are allocated to the revenue-producing (operating) departments.

discounted-cash-flow (DCF) models A type of capital-budgeting model that focuses on cash inflows and outflows while taking into account the time value of money.

discretionary fixed costs Costs determined by management as part of the periodic planning process in order to meet the organization's goals. They have no obvious relationship with levels of capacity or output activity.

discriminatory pricing Charging different prices to different customers for the same product or service.

dividends Distributions of assets to stockholders that reduce retained income.

double-entry system A method of record keeping in which each transaction affects at least two accounts.

dysfunctional behavior Any action taken in conflict with organizational goals.

e-procurement Buying manufacturing or operating inputs electronically.

earnings per share Net income divided by the average number of common shares outstanding during the year.

economic value added (EVA) Equals net operating income minus the after-tax weighted-average cost of capital multiplied times the sum of long-term liabilities and stockholders' equity.

effectiveness The degree to which a goal, objective, or target is met.

efficiency The degree to which inputs are used in relation to a given level of outputs.

efficient capital market A market in which market prices fully reflect all information available to the public.

electronic commerce (e-commerce) Net income divided by the average number of common shares outstanding during the year.

engineering analysis The systematic review of materials, supplies, labor, support services, and facilities needed for products and services; measuring cost behavior according to what costs should be, not by what costs have been.

equities The claims against, or interests in, an organization's assets.

equity method Accounts for the investment at the acquisition cost adjusted for dividends received and the investor's share of earnings or losses of the investee after the date of investment.

equivalent units The number of completed units that could have been produced from the inputs applied.

expected cost The cost most likely to be attained.

expenses Decreases in ownership claims arising from delivery goods or services or using up assets.

favorable expense variance A variance that occurs when actual expenses are less than budgeted expenses.

financial accounting The field of accounting that develops information for external decision makers such as stockholders, suppliers, banks, and government regulatory agencies.

Financial Accounting Standards Board (FASB) The primary regulatory body over accounting principles and practices in the U.S. Consisting of seven full-time members, it is an independent creation of the private sector.

financial budget The part of a master budget that focuses on the effects that the operating budget and other plans (such as capital budgets and repayments of debt) will have on cash.

financial capital maintenance The concept that income emerges after financial resources are recovered.

financial planning models Mathematical models of the master budget that can react to any set of assumptions about sales, costs, or product mix.

first-in, first-out (FIFO) An inventory method that assumes that the stock acquired earliest is sold (used up) first.

first-in, first-out (FIFO) process-costing method A process-costing method that sharply distinguishes the current work done from the previous work done on the beginning inventory of work in process.

fixed assets (tangible assets) Physical items that a person can see and touch, such as property, plant, and equipment.

fixed cost A cost that is not immediately affected by changes in the cost driver.

fixed-overhead rate The amount of fixed manufacturing overhead applied to each unit of production. It is determined by dividing the budgeted fixed overhead by the expected volume of production for the budget period.

flexible budget (variable budget) A budget that adjusts for changes in sales volume and other cost-driver activities.

flexible-budget variances The variances between the flexible budget and the actual results.

Foreign Corrupt Practices Act U.S. law forbidding bribery and other corrupt practices, and requiring that accounting records be maintained in reasonable detail and accuracy, and that an appropriate system of internal accounting controls be maintained.

full cost (fully allocated cost) The total of all manufacturing costs plus the total of all selling and administrative costs.

general ledger A collection of the group of accounts that supports the items shown in the major financial statements.

general price index A comparison of the average price of a group of goods and services at one date with the average price of a similar group at another date.

generally accepted accounting principles (GAAP) Broad concepts or guidelines and detailed practices, including all conventions, rules, and procedures that together make up accepted accounting practice at a given time.

goal congruence   A condition where employees, working in their own personal interests, make decisions that help meet the overall goals of the organization.

goodwill   The excess of the cost of an acquired company over the sum of the fair market values of its identifiable individual assets less its liabilities.

gross book value   The original cost of an asset before deducting accumulated depreciation.

gross margin (gross profit)   The excess of sales over the total cost of goods sold.

high-low method   A simple method for measuring a linear-cost function from past cost data, focusing on the highest-activity and lowest-activity points and fitting a line through these two points.

historical cost   The amount originally paid to acquire an asset.

holding gains (or losses)   Increases (or decreases) in the replacement costs of the assets held during the current period.

hybrid-costing system   An accounting system that is a blend of ideas from both job costing and process costing.

imperfect competition   A market in which the price a firm charges for a unit will influence the quantity of units it sells.

incentives   Those formal and informal performance-based rewards that enhance managerial effort toward organizational goals.

income percentage of revenue (return on sales)   Income divided by revenue.

income statement   A statement that measures the performance of an organization by matching its accomplishments (revenue from customers, which is usually called sales) and its efforts (cost of goods sold and other expenses).

incremental cost   Another term for differential costs when one alternative includes all the costs of the other plus some additional costs.

incremental effect   The change in total results (such as revenue, expenses, or income) under a new condition in comparison with some given or known condition.

indirect costs   Costs that cannot be identified specifically and exclusively with a given cost objective in an economically feasible way.

indirect manufacturing costs (factory burden, factory overhead, manufacturing overhead)   All costs other than direct material or direct labor that are associated with the manufacturing process.

indirect method   In a statement of cash flows, the method that reconciles net income to the net cash provided by operating activities.

inflation   The decline in the general purchasing power of the monetary unit.

Institute of Management Accountants (IMA)   The largest U.S. professional organization of accountants whose major interest is management accounting.

intangible assets   Long-lived assets that are not physical in nature. Examples are goodwill, franchises, patents, trademarks, and copyrights.

International Accounting Standards Committee (IASC)   The group that establishes international GAAP.

inventory turnover   The number of times the average inventory is sold per year.

investment center   A responsibility center whose success is measured not only by its income but also by relating that income to its invested capital, as in a ratio of income to the value of the capital employed.

investments in affiliates (investments in associates)   Investments in equity securities that represent 20% to 50% ownership. They are accounted for under the equity method.

job-cost record (job-cost sheet, job order)   A document that shows all costs for a particular product, service, or batch of products.

job-order costing (job costing)   The method of allocating costs to products that are readily identified by individual units or batches, each of which requires varying degrees of attention and skill.

joint costs   The costs of manufacturing joint products prior to the split-off point.

joint products   Two or more manufactured products that (1) have relatively significant sales values and (2) are not separately identifiable as individual products until their split-off point.

just-in-time (JIT) philosophy   A philosophy to eliminate waste by reducing the time products spend in the production process and eliminating the time products spend on activities that do not add value.

just-in-time (JIT) production system   A system in which an organization purchases materials and parts and produces components just when they are needed in the production process, the goal being to have zero inventory, because holding inventory is a non-value-added activity.

kaizen costing   The Japanese term for continuous improvement during manufacturing.

key performance indicators   Measures that drive the organization to achieve its goals.

key success factor   Actions that must be done well in order to drive the organization towards its goals.

labor time tickets (time cards)   The record of the time a particular direct laborer spends on each job.

last-in, first-out (LIFO)   An inventory method that assumes that the stock acquired most recently is sold (used up) first.

least-squares regression (regression analysis)   Measuring a cost function objectively by using statistics to fit a cost function to all the data.

ledger accounts A method of keeping track of how multitudes of transactions affect each particular asset, liability, revenue, and expense.

liabilities The entity's economic obligations to nonowners.

LIFO layers (LIFO increments) Separately identifiable additional layers of LIFO inventory.

limited liability Creditors cannot seek payment from shareholders as individuals if the corporation itself cannot pay its debts.

limiting factor (scarce resource) The item that restricts or constrains the production or sale of a product or service.

linear-cost behavior Activity that can be graphed with a straight line because costs are assumed to be either fixed or variable.

line authority Authority exerted downward over subordinates.

liquidation Converting assets to cash and using the cash to pay off outside claims.

long-range planning Producing forecasted financial statements for five- to ten-year periods.

lower-of-cost-or-market (LCM) An inventory method in which the current market price of inventory is compared with its cost (derived by specific identification, FIFO, LIFO, or weighted average) and the lower of the two is selected as the basis for the valuation of goods at a specific inventory date.

management accounting The process of identifying, measuring, accumulating, analyzing, preparing, interpreting, and communicating information that helps managers fulfill organizational objectives.

management audit A review to determine whether the policies and procedures specified by top management have been implemented.

management by exception Concentrating on areas that deviate from the plan and ignoring areas that are presumed to be running smoothly.

management by objectives (MBO) The joint formulation by a manager and his or her superior of a set of goals and plans for achieving the goals for a forthcoming period.

management control system A logical integration of techniques to gather and use information to make planning and control decisions, to motivate employee behavior, and to evaluate performance.

managerial effort Exertion toward a goal or objective including all conscious actions (such as supervising, planning, and thinking) that result in more efficiency and effectiveness.

margin of safety The planned unit sales less the break-even unit sales; it shows how far sales can fall below the planned level before losses occur.

marginal cost The additional cost resulting from producing and selling one additional unit.

marginal income tax rate The tax rate paid on additional amounts of pretax income.

marginal revenue The additional revenue resulting from the sale of an additional unit.

market method The method of accounting for investments in equity securities that shows the investment on the balance sheet at market value.

markup The amount by which price exceeds cost.

master budget A budget that summarizes the planned activities of all subunits of an organization.

master budget variance (static budget variance) The variance of actual results from the master budget.

matching The relating of accomplishments or revenues (as measured by the selling prices of goods and services delivered) and efforts or expenses (as measured by the cost of goods and services used) to a particular period for which a measurement of income is desired.

materiality The accounting convention that justifies the omission of insignificant information when its omission or misstatement would not mislead a user of the financial statements.

materials requisitions Records of materials issued to particular jobs.

measurement of cost behavior Understanding and quantifying how activities of an organization affect levels of costs.

minority interests An account that shows the outside stockholders' interest, as opposed to the parent's interest, in a subsidiary corporation.

mixed costs Costs that contain elements of both fixed- and variable-cost behavior.

motivation The drive for some selected goal that creates effort and action toward that goal.

multistage ABC systems Costing systems with more than two stages of allocations and cost drivers other than percentages.

net book value The original cost of an asset less an accumulated depreciation.

net income The popular "bottom line"—the residual after deducting from revenues all expenses, including income taxes.

net worth A synonym for owner's equity.

net-present-value (NPV) method A discounted-cash-flow approach to capital budgeting that computes the present value of all expected future cash flows using a minimum desired rate of return.

nominal dollars Dollar measurements that are not restated for fluctuations in the general purchasing power of the monetary unit.

nominal rate Quoted market interest rate that includes an inflation element.

non-value-added costs Costs that can be eliminated without affecting a product's value to the customer.

noncurrent liabilities (long-term liabilities) An organization's debts that fall due beyond one year.

normal costing system The cost system in which overhead is applied on an average or normalized basis, in order to get representative or normal inventory valuations.

normal costing A cost system that applies actual direct materials and actual direct-labor costs to products or services but uses budgeted rates for applying overhead.

objectivity (verifiability) Accuracy supported by a high extent of consensus among independent measures of an item.

operating budget (profit plan) A major part of a master budget that focuses on the income statement and its supporting schedules.

operating cycle The time span during which a company spends cash to acquire goods and services that it uses to produce the organization's output, which in turn it sells to customers, who in turn pay for their purchases with cash.

operating leverage A firm's ratio of fixed to variable costs.

operation costing A hybrid-costing system often used in the batch or group manufacturing of goods that have some common characteristics plus some individual characteristics.

opportunity cost The maximum available contribution to profit foregone (or passed up) by using limited resources for a particular purpose.

outlay cost A cost that requires a future cash disbursement.

overapplied overhead The excess of overhead applied to products over actual overhead incurred.

owners' equity The excess of the assets over the liabilities.

paid-in capital The ownership claim arising from funds paid-in by the owners.

par value (legal value, stated value) The value that is printed on the face of the certificate.

parent company A company owning more than 50 percent of another business's stock.

participative budgeting Budgets formulated with the active participation of all affected employees.

partnership An organization that joins two or more individuals together as co-owners.

payback time (payback period) The time it will take to recoup, in the form of cash inflows from operations, the initial dollars invested in a project.

perfect competition A market in which a firm can sell as much of a product as it can produce, all at a single market price.

perfection standards (ideal standards) Expressions of the most efficient performance possible under the best conceivable conditions, using existing specifications and equipment.

performance reports Feedback provided by comparing results with plans and by highlighting variances.

period costs Costs that are deducted as expenses during the current period without going through an inventory stage.

physical capital maintenance The concept that income emerges only after recovering an amount that allows physical operating capability to be maintained.

postaudit A follow-up evaluation of capital-budgeting decisions.

practical capacity Maximum or full capacity.

predatory pricing Establishing prices so low that competitors are driven out of the market. The predatory pricer then has no significant competition and can raise prices dramatically.

preferred stock Stock that typically has some priority over other shares regarding dividends or the distribution of assets upon liquidation.

price elasticity The effect of price changes on sales volume.

price variance The difference between actual input prices and expected input prices multiplied by the actual quantity of inputs used.

prime costs Direct labor costs plus direct materials costs.

problem solving The aspect of accounting that quantifies the likely results of possible courses of action and often recommends the best course of action to follow.

process costing The method of allocating costs to products by averaging costs over large numbers of nearly identical products.

product costs Costs identified with goods produced or purchased for resale.

production cycle time The time from initiating production to delivering the goods to the customer.

production-volume variance A variance that appears whenever actual production deviates from the expected volume of production used in computing the fixed overhead rate. It is calculated as (actual volume − expected volume) × fixed-overhead rate.

productivity A measure of outputs divided by inputs.

product life cycle The various stages through which a product passes, from conception and development through introduction into the market through maturation and, finally, withdrawal from the market.

profit center A responsibility center for controlling revenues as well as costs (or expenses)—that is, profitability.

profits (earnings, income) The excess of revenues over expenses.

prorate To assign underapplied overhead or overapplied overhead in proportion to the sizes of the ending account balances.

prorating the variances Assigning the variances to the inventories and cost of goods sold related to the production during the period the variances arose.

quality control The effort to ensure that products and services perform to customer requirements.

quality-control chart The statistical plot of measures of various product dimensions or attributes.

recovery period The number of years over which an asset is depreciated for tax purposes.

relevant information The predicted future costs and revenues that will differ among alternative courses of action.

relevant range The limit of cost-driver activity level within which a specific relationship between costs and the cost driver is valid.

required rate of return (hurdle rate, discount rate) The minimum desired rate of return, based on the firm's cost of capital.

residual income (RI) Net operating income less "imputed" interest.

residual value The predicted sales value of a long-lived asset at the end of its useful life.

responsibility accounting Identifying what parts of the organization have primary responsibility for each objective, developing measures and targets to achieve, and creating reports of these measures by organization subunit or responsibility center.

responsibility center A set of activities assigned to a manager, a group of managers, or other employees.

retained income (retained earnings) The ownership claim arising from the reinvestment of previous profits.

return on investment (ROI) A measure of income or profit divided by the investment required to obtain that income or profit.

revaluation equity A portion of stockholders' equity that shows all accumulated holding gains.

revenue Increases in ownership claims arising from the delivery of goods or services.

sales-activity variances Variances that measure how effective managers have been in meeting the planned sales objective, calculated as actual unit sales less master budget unit sales times the budgeted unit contribution margin.

sales budget The result of decisions to create conditions that will generate a desired level of sales.

sales forecast A prediction of sales under a given set of conditions.

sales mix The relative proportions or combinations of quantities of products that constitute total sales.

scorekeeping The accumulation and classification of data.

Securities and Exchange Commission (SEC) By federal law, the agency with the ultimate responsibility for specifying the generally accepted accounting principles for U.S. companies whose stock is held by the general investing public.

segment autonomy The delegation of decision-making power to managers of segments of an organization.

segments Responsibility centers for which a separate measure of revenues and costs is obtained.

sensitivity analysis The systematic varying of budget data input to determine the effects of each change on the budget.

separable costs Any cost beyond the split-off point.

service departments Units that exist only to support other departments.

sole proprietorship A business entity with a single owner.

source documents Explicit evidence of any transactions that occur in the entity's operation, for example, sales slips and purchase invoices.

specific identification An inventory method that recognizes the actual cost paid for the specific item sold.

specific price index An index used to approximate the current costs of particular assets or types of assets.

split-off point The juncture of manufacturing where the joint products become individually identifiable.

staff authority Authority to advise but not command. It may be exerted downward, laterally, or upward.

standard cost A carefully determined cost per unit that should be attained.

standard cost systems Accounting systems that value products according to standard costs only.

Standards of Ethical Conduct for Practitioners of Management Accounting and Financial Management Codes of conduct developed by the Institute of Management Accountants, which include competence, confidentiality, integrity, and objectivity.

statement of cash flows A statement that reports the cash receipts and cash payments of an organization during a particular period.

statement of retained earnings (statement of retained income) A financial statement that analyzes changes in the retained earnings or retained income account for a given period.

step costs Costs that change abruptly at intervals of activity because the resources and their costs come in indivisible chunks.

step-down method A method for allocating service department costs that recognizes that some service departments support the activities in other service departments as well as those in production departments.

stockholders' equity The owners' equity of a corporation.

strategic plan A plan that sets the overall goals and objectives of the organization.

subordinated A creditor claim that is junior to the other creditors in exercising claims against assets.

subsidiary A company owned by a parent company that owns more than 50 percent of its stock.

sunk cost A cost that has already been incurred and, therefore, is irrelevant to the decision making process.

target costing A cost management tool for making cost a key focus throughout the life of a product.

time-series comparisons Comparison of a company's financial ratios with its own historical ratios.

total project approach A method for comparing alternatives that computes the total impact on cash flows for each alternative and then converts these total cash flows to their present values.

total quality management (TQM) The application of quality principles to all of the organization's endeavors to satisfy customers.

trading securities Investments that the investor company buys only with intent to sell them shortly.

traditional costing systems One that does not accumulate or report costs of activities or processes.

transaction Any event that affects the financial position of an organization and requires recording.

transfer price The amount charged by one segment of an organization for a product or service that it supplies to another segment of the same organization.

transferred-in costs In process costing, costs incurred in a previous department for items that have been received by a subsequent department.

treasury stock A corporation's own stock that has been issued and subsequently repurchased by the company and is being held for a specific purpose.

two-stage ABC system A costing system with two stages of allocation to get from the original cost to the final product or service cost. The first stage allocates resource costs to activity-cost pools. The second stage allocates activity costs to products or services.

unallocated costs Costs for which we can identify no relationship to a cost objective.

unavoidable costs Costs that continue even if an operation is halted.

uncontrollable cost Any cost that cannot be affected by the management of a responsibility center within a given time span.

underapplied overhead The excess of actual overhead over the overhead applied to products.

unearned revenue (deferred revenue) Collections from customers received and recorded before they are earned.

unexpired cost Any asset that ordinarily becomes an expense in future periods, for example, inventory and prepaid rent.

unfavorable expense variance A variance that occurs when actual expenses are more than budgeted expenses.

usage variance (quantity variance, efficiency variance) The difference between the quantity of inputs actually used and the quantity of inputs that should have been used to achieve the actual quantity of output multiplied by the expected price of the input.

value-added cost The necessary cost of an activity that cannot be eliminated without affecting a product's value to the customer.

value chain The set of business functions that add value to the products or services of an organization.

value engineering A cost-reduction technique, used primarily during design, that uses information about all value-chain functions to satisfy customer needs while reducing costs.

variable cost A cost that changes in direct proportion to changes in the cost driver level.

variable-cost ratio (variable-cost percentage) All variable costs divided by sales.

variable-overhead efficiency variance An overhead variance caused by actual cost-driver activity differing from the standard amount allowed for the actual output achieved.

variable-overhead spending variance The difference between the actual variable overhead and the amount of variable overhead budgeted for the actual level of cost-driver activity.

variances Deviations from plans.

visual-fit method A method in which the cost analyst visually fits a straight line through a plot of all the available data.

volume variance A common name for production-volume variance.

weighted-average cost The inventory method that assigns the same unit cost to each unit available for sale. The unit cost is computed by dividing the cost of all units available for sale by the number of units available.

weighted-average (WA) process-costing method A process-costing method that adds the cost of (1) all work done in the current period to (2) the work done in the preceding period on the current period's beginning inventory of work in process, and divides the total by the equivalent units of work done to date.

INDEX

and activity-based costing, 540–541
product and service decisions, 89
Value chain functions, examples of costs and cost drivers, 43
Value engineering, 205
Variable application rates, 539
Variable budgets, 313. *See also* Flexible budgets
Variable-cost behavior, 44
Variable-costing method
about, 600
comparative income statements with, 601
real-life example, 603
reasons for using, 609
reconciliation of, 608–609
vs. absorption-costing method, 598–600, 602–603
Variable-cost percentage, 58
Variable-cost pools, 487–489
Variable-cost pricing, 399–400
Variable-cost ratio, 58
Variable costs
confusion of fixed costs and, 187–188
defined, 43
fixed costs compared to, 43–47
Variable-overhead efficiency variances, 327–328
Variable-overhead spending variances, 328
Variable unit costs, 604–605
Variances
activity-level variances, 315–317
analysis of, 616
defined, 10
favorable expense variance, 312
flexible-budget variances, 315–317, 318
interpretation of price and usage variances, 325–327
investigating, 322
isolating causes of, 317–322
master-budget variance, 312
from material and labor standards, 323–324, 328–330
other variances
comparison with production-volume variance, 615–617
effects of, 610–612
overhead variances, 327–328
price variances, 324–325
prorating, 612
sales-activity variances, 318–319
trade-offs among, 320–321
unfavorable expense variance, 312
usage variances, 324–325
Verifiability, 662. *See also* Objectivity
Vick, Ralph, 269
Visual-fit method, 102–103
Volume, change effects on operating income, 200
Volume variance, 605–607. *See also* Production-volume variance

Wages, accounting for payment of, 650–651
Watson, Barry, 372
Watson, Ray, 597
Weighted-average cost inventory method, 767–768
Weighted-average process-costing method
about, 574
first-in, first-out process-costing method compared to, 577
output in equivalent units, 575
production cost report, 575

Welch, John, 358
Wholesale companies, income statement presentation of costs, 138
Woods, Tiger, 393

Zampino, Peter, 206

INDEX OF COMPANIES

Real companies are in bold type.

ABC, Inc., 111
Abraham Company, 592
Acapulco Transformer Company, 112
Ace Hardware Corporation, 672
Ackerloff Signs, 111
Acme Auto Parts, Inc., 588–589
Acme Building Supplies, 297–298
Acme Electronics Company, 377
Advanced Medical Systems, 8–9
Adventure.Com, 297
Aetna, 394
Airborne Express, 404–405
Air France, 394
Alamo Footware, 424
Alaska Airlines, 260
Alberta Metals, Inc., 784–785
Albertson's, 750–751
Alcoa, 30
Algona Beach Jail, 118
Allen-Bradley Company, 361
All Seasons Hotel, 78
Allstate, 359
Alltrista Corporation, 411
Amazon.com, 32, 33, 656, 672
American Airlines, 41, 258
American Tire Company, 296
America Online, 752
America West, 84–85, 118
Amtrak, 190*n*
Anchorage Company, 715
Anchor Gaming, Inc., 757
Andaman Cruises, 672
Andre's Hair Styling, 73
Andy's Ale House, 74
A & P, 132
Apple Computer, 359, 397
Arizona Outdoor Equipment Company, 121
Arkansas Blue Cross Blue Shield, 154
Aspen Leather Company, 345–346
AT&T Corporation, 128–130, 142, 177–178, 359, 409
AT&T Universal Card Services, 356
Auckland Tent Company, 295–296
Austin Motors, 215–216
Auto-vend Company, 472–473
Avignon Company, 224, 266
Azteca Company, 257

Baffin Manufacturing Company, 383
Balachandran Medical Instruments Company, 754
Baldwin, 60
Balmer Company, 693–699, 700–701
Bangalore Trading Company, 785
Bank of America, 717
BankSoft.com, 463–464
Barleycorn, Inc., 363–365
Bayliner, Inc., 749–750
Becton, Dickinson and Company, 766

Bedford Clinic, 475–476
Belfair Kayak Company, 343–344
Bellevue Clinic, 548
Belltown Athletic Supply, 213–214
Benjamin Metals, Inc., 509–510
Benson Company, 423
Best Bank, 158–159
Best Buy, 596–597
Best Cost Corporation, 217
Beta Alpha Psi, 30, 339
Better Bank, 164–167, 174–177
Biogen, Inc., 465
Birmingham Collectibles, 255–256
Birmingham Precision Machining, 344
Blackburn Paints, Inc., 591
Blackmar Company, 216
Blaine Hardware, 672
Blockbuster Video, 72–73
Block Company, 234–236
Blue Cross and Blue Shield of Florida, 140
BMW, 251
Boeing Commercial Airplane Group, 213
Boeing Company, 4, 22, 32, 33, 35, 40–42, 77, 182, 207, 231, 483
Bohren Company, 624
Boise Technology, 112
Book & Game Company, 374–375, 376
Borders Books, 302
Borg-Warner Automotive, 286
Borg-Warner Company, 139, 598
Bose, 254–255
Boulder Systems Group, 71
Bouquet Company, 300
Boylston Company, 633–634
Bradley Productions, 753–754
Braxton Industries, 36
Bridgeford Company, 297
Briggs & Stratton Corporation, 424, 428–429, 758–759
Brisbane Manufacturing Company, 477–478
British Airways, 41
Brunswick Corporation, 749–750
Buretta Company, 703–705
Burger King, 340
Burger-Rama Enterprises, 420
Butler Home Products, 513

C. Chan Company, 343
CableNet Company, 469
Cabrillo Construction Company, 551
Calais Company, 631–632
Camden Foods, Inc., 264
Capeletti Company, 339
Carnival Corporation, 309, 480
Casaverde Company, 11–12
Caterpillar, 207
Central Railroad, 508
Champion Exposition Services, 22
Champion International Corporation, 21, 359
Chase Manhattan Bank, 466–467
Cheney Oil Company, 753
Chevron, 255, 595
Chez Bonaparte, 4
Chicago Heights Steel Company, 766
Chicago Office Furniture, 427
Chickadee Manufacturing Company, 551–552
Chief Cleaning, Inc., 510–511
Childrobics, Inc., 720–721
Chippewa Company, 714–715

Photo Credits